CONCISE OX

DICTIONA OF
OPERA

BY

HAROLD ROSENTHAL

AND

JOHN WARRACK

LONDON

OXFORD UNIVERSITY PRESS

Oxford University Press, Ely House, London W. 1

GLASGOW NEW YORK TORONTO MELBOURNE WELLINGTON
CAPE TOWN IBADAN NAIROBI DAR ES SALAAM LUSAKA ADDIS ABABA
DELHI BOMBAY CALCUTTA MADRAS KARACHI LAHORE DACCA
KUALA LUMPUR SINGAPORE HONG KONG TOKYO

LIMP BOUND EDITION ISBN 0 19 311312 0
HARD BOUND EDITION ISBN 0 19 311305 8

First published 1964
Reprinted with corrections 1964, 1966, 1972, and 1973

PRINTED IN GREAT BRITAIN

[illegible]ORD

MANY operatic refe[illegible]t. The first was made by the Chiot scholar L[illegible]who became librarian of the Vatican and in 1666 p[illegible] *Drammaturgia* (a catalogue of all dramatic works per[illegible] that date). His work has found a number of successors, [illegible]ly Dassori's *Opere e Operisti* (1903) and Loewenberg's cele[illegible]ated *Annals of Opera* (1943, rev. 1954). Other guides, companions, introductions, and collections of analyses and synopses abound, to say nothing of the mass of specialist literature on every aspect of operatic history, theory, and performance. Upon large numbers of these we have drawn, as well as upon original scores, upon copious correspondence with scholars, archivists, and artists all over the world, and upon our own records and research. What we have had in mind is to provide the ordinary opera-goer with a concise but comprehensive work of reference—and perhaps also of some entertainment.

We have, naturally, been obliged to lean heavily on our distinguished predecessors in their various fields; but wherever possible, every fact has been checked against several authorities. In a few instances we have been able to establish dates or other facts that have eluded them. We have thought it more useful to give brief summaries, critical as well as factual, of composers' work in opera rather than to chronicle the events of their lives yet again, since these are amply discussed in readily available general reference books. Obviously in a volume of this nature more space will be given to Menotti than to Beethoven; by this token we have not on the whole felt bound to use space as a criterion of worth but allowed subjects to find their own length.

But we may perhaps point out three categories of entry on which we have laid special weight. We have compiled entries under most countries in the world to show the spread and development of opera from Italy. Special emphasis has been laid on the growth of opera in Eastern Europe, since this is a little-known process; we have not retold the more familiar story of its growth in Italy or Germany in proportionately greater detail, though the reader will find under these and all countries cross-references to the most important operatic centres, where local history is given. Secondly, there will be found a large number of literary references. Completeness is unattainable here, as elsewhere, but we have listed as many operas as we can on the works of important writers and on famous subjects (e.g. Don Juan). Not only will the reader find the literary source of each opera given, where one exists, but under Shakespeare, for instance, he will find what we believe to be a complete list of Shakespeare operas to date. Thirdly, we have included rather a large proportion of singers, since most general works of reference tend, reasonably, to place the interpreter below the creator in importance. It goes without saying that this posed us our most difficult problem of selection. As far as the past is concerned, we have tried not to leave out anyone whose artistry influenced composers and fellow performers, thus contributing to operatic history. Contemporary artists presented more difficulty, but we have included a generous selection of those who have either already established themselves internationally, and about whom the opera-goer might wish to know, or who are likely to do so within the next few years. We have allowed ourselves to include a few who may not rank as international figures but are highly prized in their own country. Every reference book must face the challenge of why one subject is in, another out. We are well aware that different compilers would have chosen differently; our dictionary claims conciseness rather than completeness. It is no less obvious that every reference book becomes out of date as soon as it is published: we have had to make our closing date the autumn of 1963.

Though we have not made much use of abbreviations, except chiefly for the names of opera houses (see list on pp. xiii–xiv), there are a number of usages that require elucidation.

Dates of operas, unless otherwise explained, are of first production; we have normally added the composition date only when it antedates production by a significant number of years. We should have preferred to give composition dates in all cases, but they are so often undiscoverable that we have had to bow to consistency. Opera titles are normally in the original language (though there are exceptions here: we have not used Russian titles nor indeed the Cyrillic alphabet at all); the English translation in brackets is often literal rather than a suggestion for general use. When an opera is known in England only by an English title (e.g. the inaccurately translated *Bartered Bride*) we give the original in brackets. In the singer entries, the seasons and appearances are only the most notable ones. We have used the conventional, if misleading, term 'created . . .' to mean 'first singer of . . .'.

Place-names have presented the usual problem. We have, with very few exceptions, given the name currently used in the country concerned: that is, Ljubljana (not Laibach), Oslo (not Christiania). We have given alternative names in brackets, though without explanation, which would usually involve a short historical essay. There are two natural exceptions to this rule. We follow normal English usage in writing Munich, Warsaw, Florence, &c., though we give the originals in brackets in their main entries (Ger., München; Pol., Warszawa; It., Firenze). And when a town has changed its own name, we give it according to how it was known at the time: thus, as in *Grove*, it becomes possible for a stay-at-home composer to be born in St. Petersburg, study in Petrograd, and die in Leningrad, though never for another to be born in Pressburg, study in Pozsony, and die in Bratislava. Cross-references help to clear up these matters. In the case of the Alsatian capital, we take the liberty of settling for Strasbourg.

It goes without saying that we spell all personal names as the owner would himself, complete with accents even when it is unlikely that many English readers are familiar with the effect of Latvian apostrophes or Hungarian double-acutes. Transliteration from Cyrillic (and to a lesser extent Greek) has been as difficult as always. Though basically we follow that approved by the School of Slavonic Studies, we do make certain deviations, preferring clarity and familiarity to total consistency (Tchaikovsky, not Chaykovsky). The Italian 'long i' is discarded (Barbaia, not Barbaja) except in initials: no one will look up Iommelli.

A certain number of brief synopses will be found. While it is obvious that we are not competing with Kobbé, Lubbock, and similar books, we felt that a fairly full reminder might be useful in the case of repertory operas; rarer works are usually given a sentence or two indicating the plot or at least the subject. We have not generally taken up space with the plots of stories very familiar from other contexts: there is no synopsis of Britten's *A Midsummer Night's Dream*, since, despite the composer's special view of the work, the plot is Shakespeare's.

As regards dates, we follow Blom (*Everyman* and *Grove*) in retaining the old-style English dates before the adoption of the

Gregorian calendar in 1752. Russian dates are given in New Style only, even though Old Style persisted down to the 1917 revolution.

We owe so much to so many kind people that the problem of selection once again becomes troublesome. Firstly, we owe thanks to the late Eric Blom, whose encouragement in the initial stages was much needed. For advice, help, and information on specific subjects, we are particularly indebted to Senhor A. F. de Almeida, Miss Lies Askonas, Dr. L. Báty, Sgr Rodolfo Celletti, Mr. Christopher Cowley, Mr. Wilfrid Cowley, Mr. Eric Crozier, Sgr Dario Daris, Mr. Winton Dean, M. Alfred De'Cock, Mr. Norman Del Mar, Mr. Ian Docherty, the late Mr. Lionel Dunlop, Dr. Pavel Eckstein, Dr. Alfred Frankenstein, Mr. Frank Freudenthal, Sgr Giorgio Gualerzi, M. Jacques Gheusi, the Earl of Harewood, Mr. Michael Kennedy, the late Dr. Joseph Löwenbach, Mr. Mark Lubbock, Mr. Richard Macnutt, Mr. William Marshall, Mr. Julius Mattfeld, Mr. Manoug Parikian, Mr. Ralph Parker, Sra Pavolini, Mr. Georgi Polyanovsky, Mr. Leo Riemens, Sgr Claudio Sartori, Mr. Nicolas Slonimsky, Mr. Jani Strasser, Sgr Raffaele Vegeto, Mr. William Weaver, Mr. Joseph Wechsberg, and M. Stéphane Wolff. We are also grateful to the following for supplying invaluable information; the Director of the Genossenschaft Deutscher Bühnenangehörigen: Messrs. Ingpen and Williams: the Teatro Nacional de San Carlos, Lisbon; the Director of the Rumanian National Theatre; and the Director of the Armenian National Theatre. To the patient staffs of the London Library and the British Museum Reading Room we owe a debt for their tolerance of all our importunities and for their knowledge of many rare sources. We are particularly grateful to Mr. Frank Merkling, Mr. Andrew Porter, and Mr. Robert Tuggle, all of whom read the entire typescript and made large numbers of useful suggestions and corrections; they are not responsible for any of the book's shortcomings, but have certainly prevented there being many more. Lastly, a heroic labour of deciphering and typing was undertaken by Mrs. Doreen Robertson and Mrs. Doris Tomlin; Mrs. Elizabeth Warrack helped with this in the early stages.

H. D. R.

J. W.

London—Durweston
January 1964

NOTE ON THE 1966 REPRINT

For this reprint we have taken the opportunity of adding the more important débuts and also the deaths that took place after the book was first published. We have not altered the composer entries to include the newest operas, as this would often involve substantial new discussion, even revision, in an entry: that must wait for the second edition. But even at the expense of total consistency it seemed worth inserting what new information we could without disturbing the layout of the book. We have also corrected the mistakes which we have discovered in the course of subsequent research and which have been drawn to our attention by correspondents in all parts of the world. Many of the writers were previously unknown to us, and troubled to send sometimes a single new fact. We are deeply grateful.

H. D. R.
J. W.

NOTE ON THE 1972 REPRINT

As in 1966, we have added those extra details that could be conveniently inserted without disturbing the layout, and made further corrections to mistakes we have discovered or had drawn to our attention by correspondents. In a very few cases we have rewritten part or the whole of an important entry when this could be managed in the same space available. We have thought it worth making these small additions and alterations so as to bring at any rate some of the book up to date, while recognizing that it is now inevitably inconsistent in such matters. We hope that readers will nevertheless find it more useful in this form than if we had left the original unamended; a full revision is at present in hand for a Second Edition.

H. D. R.
J. W.

BIBLIOGRAPHY

This brief list is intended as a guide for those wishing to look a stage further than our concise dictionary.

We have already given, under individual singers, details of their memoirs and biographies; these often provide a vivid and entertaining picture of the contemporary scene. With composers, there is more of a problem. The 'Master Musicians' volumes are useful and reliable. The more detailed specialist literature is nowadays vast: we mention a few books of outstanding importance under Synopses, and good leads for further exploration are given in the bibliographies at the end of the 'Master Musicians' volumes and of the composer articles in *Grove's Dictionary of Music and Musicians* (5th edn., ed. Blom, 1954). *Grove* is the standard work of general musical reference, and should be in all reference libraries. A few (e.g. the London Library, the Westminster Central Library) also keep the superb Italian *Enciclopedia dello Spettacolo* (9 vols., 1954–62), which covers all forms of theatrical entertainment and is well illustrated. P. A. Scholes's *Oxford Companion to Music* (9th edn., 1955) and *Concise Oxford Dictionary of Music* (2nd edn., 1964) provide a great deal of information and are less expensive; and Eric Blom's *Everyman's Dictionary of Music* (rev. Westrup, 1962) packs an immense amount of information into a small space. *The International Cyclopedia of Music and Musicians* (ed. Oscar Thompson; rev. Slonimsky, 1956) includes a useful 150-page section on opera plots, including many not easily found elsewhere. George W. Martin's *The Opera Companion* (1962) is a sensible book for beginners, including synopses, sections on history, vocal technique, and opera-house histories, lists of operatic terms, opera-house repertories, and statistics.

SYNOPSES

Gustave Kobbé: *The Complete Opera Book* (rev. Harewood, 1954).
The standard work, including details of first performances, first casts, &c.

Rudolf Fellner: *Opera Themes and Plots* (1958).
Fewer operas than Kobbé, but more detailed plots and more music examples.

Henry W. Simon: *The Festival of Opera* (rev. 1963), abridged as paperback edition, *100 Great Operas and their Stories* (1960).

Mark Lubbock: *The Complete Book of Light Opera* (1962).
The Kobbé of operetta, opéra-comique, and musical.

For more exhaustive accounts of a select number of operas the best guides are Ernest Newman's *Opera Nights* (1943), *More Opera Nights* (1954), and *Wagner Nights* (1949). Mention should also be made of E. J. Dent's *Mozart's Operas* (rev. 1947), Francis Toye's *Verdi* (1931), and Mosco Carner's *Puccini* (1958): Dent has little to say about Mozart's early operas, but otherwise these classic books include synopses and thorough discussions of every opera by the composer concerned. George W. Marek's *Opera as Theatre* (1962) deals with the transformation of a literary original into a music drama.

ANNALS

Alfred Loewenberg: *Annals of Opera* (rev. Walker, 1953).
The standard work, giving details of performances in every country of several thousand operas.

Félix Clément and Pierre Larousse: *Dictionnaire des Opéras* (1864: regular supplements to 1904, the whole rev. Pougin).
Many obscure details, especially of 19th-century operas, but inaccurate.

Carlo Dassori: *Opere e Operisti* (1903).
Longer list than Loewenberg, but no details except original date; rather inaccurate.

William C. Smith: *The Italian Opera and Contemporary Ballet in London, 1789–1820* (1955).
Annotated and with contemporary comments; includes over 100 works not in Loewenberg.

Julius Mattfeld: *A Handbook of American Operatic Premières, 1731–1962* (1963).
Includes new information sometimes correcting Loewenberg.

Most opera houses keep their annals up to date and in more or less good order, and will welcome the serious researcher. Some maintain an archivist; others combine his function with that of Press Officer and general researcher (in Germany, the *Dramaturg*). The annual index to *Opera* gives references to most events during the year, covered in the magazine's monthly issues. *Opera Annual* (1956–62) includes statistics of premières during the year.

Spike Hughes's *Great Opera Houses* (1956) is a readable general account; below are a few of the principal works on leading opera houses.

LONDON
Desmond Shawe-Taylor: *Covent Garden* (1948).
A brief but attractive illustrated history.
Harold Rosenthal: *Two Centuries of Opera at Covent Garden* (1958).
A comprehensive season-by-season history, with Press reactions.
Dennis Arundell: *The Story of Sadler's Wells* (1965).

BERLIN
Hugo Fetting: *Die Geschichte der Deutschen Staatsoper* (1955).

BOSTON
Quaintance Eaton: *The Boston Opera Company* (1965).

MILAN
Pompeo Cambiasi: *La Scala e la Canobbiana, 1778–1906* (1906).
Guido Marangoni and Carlo Vanbianchi: *La Scala* (1922).
Continues Cambiasi to 1920 in same format.
Franco Armani: *La Scala, 1946–56* (1957).

MUNICH — Hermann Friess and Rudolf Goldschmidt: *Nationaltheater, München* (1963).

NEW YORK — W. H. Seltsam: *Metropolitan Opera Annals* (rev. 1949).
Quaintance Eaton: *Opera Caravan, 1883–1956* (1951). Details of the Met. tours, with cast-lists as in Seltsam.
Irving Kolodin: *The Story of the Metropolitan Opera, 1883–1950* (1951).

PARIS — J. G. Prod'homme: *L'Opéra, 1669–1925* (1925).
Stéphane Wolff: *L'Opéra au Palais Garnier, 1875–1962* (1962).
Stéphane Wolff: *Un Demi-Siècle d'Opéra-Comique, 1900–50* (1953).

SAN FRANCISCO — Arthur J. Bloomfield: *The San Francisco Opera: 1923–61* (1961).

VIENNA — Emil Pirchan, Alexander Witeschnik, and Otto Fritz: *300 Jahre Wiener Operntheater* (1953).
Heinrich Kralik: *The Vienna Opera* (1963).
Marcel Prawy: *The Vienna Opera* (1970).

HISTORIES

There is a good general history by Wallace Brockway and Herbert Weinstock, *The World of Opera: the Story of its Development and the Lore of its Performance, 1600–1941* (rev. 1963); another is Donald Jay Grout's *A Short History of Opera* (1947). E. J. Dent's *Opera* (1940) and Richard Capell's little essay *Opera* (1930) are excellent short histories. Philip Hope-Wallace's *A Picture History of Opera* (1959) is admirably compiled and captioned.

There are many books on the history of national opera available in the countries concerned. The two best histories of English opera are by E. J. Dent, *The Foundations of English Opera* (1928), and Eric Walter White, *The Rise of English Opera* (1951). We list below the standard English works of memoirs and criticism.

Charles Burney: *A General History of Music*, vol. iv (1789; new edn., 1935).
This volume gives a good summary of the operas produced in London down to the end of 1788.
Lord Mount-Edgcumbe: *Musical Reminiscences* (1827).
Henry Chorley: *Thirty Years' Musical Recollections* (1862; ed. Newman, 1926).
Covers the period 1830–59.
[Cox]: *Musical Recollections of the Last Half-Century* (1872).
G. B. Shaw: *London Music in 1888–9 as heard by Corno di Bassetto* (1937).
G. B. Shaw: *Music in London, 1890–4* (3 vols., 1932).

G. B. Shaw: *How to Become a Musical Critic* (1960).
The above three books collect Shaw's brilliant and vividly personal criticisms.
Herman Klein: *Thirty Years of Musical Life in London, 1870–1900* (1903).
Herman Klein: *The Golden Age of Opera* (1933).

The above are accounts by critics and amateurs of opera; the following three books of memoirs by theatre managers are also useful.

John Ebers: *Seven Years of the King's Theatre* (1828).
Covers the period 1821–7, including details of repertories, salaries, and working conditions.
Benjamin Lumley: *Reminiscences of the Opera* (1864).
Covers the 1840's and 1850's from Lumley's viewpoint as manager of Her Majesty's Theatre.
Col. J. H. Mapleson: *The Mapleson Memoirs, 1848–88* (1888; ed. Rosenthal, 1966).
Covers Mapleson's varied and diverting activities from 1861.

OPERETTA

Mark Lubbock's *Complete Book of Light Opera* has already been mentioned under Synopses. The French scene is admirably described by Martin Cooper in *Opéra Comique* (1949). There is an excellent critical examination of all important operetta composers by Gervase Hughes, *Composers of Operetta* (1962). Cecil Smith's *Musical Comedy in America* (1950) is also useful.

MISCELLANEOUS

Practical details of the forces required in operas, with brief synopses, are given in Quaintance Eaton's *Opera Production* (1961). *The Opera Directory* (1961) also carries much practical and professional information about singers. Harold Barlow and Sam Morgenstern provide, in *A Dictionary of Vocal Themes* (1956), an ingenious method of identifying tunes; the book is also useful in that it contains incipits of nearly all famous arias.

Librettos, once thought indispensable to the opera-goer, are less used now; yet they provide an excellent cheap way of approaching an opera. They are generally on sale in opera houses, or can be obtained from the composer's publishers in the original language and sometimes in translation (as can the vocal and sometimes the miniature or full scores). Record companies now normally provide a libretto, including a parallel translation, with their albums of complete operas.

ABBREVIATIONS

OPERA HOUSES AND CONSERVATORIES

BERLIN	K.O.	Komische Oper
	S.O.	Staatsoper
	Sch.	Schauspielhaus
BRUSSELS	La M.	Théâtre de la Monnaie
GENOA	C.F.	Teatro Carlo Felice
LONDON	C.G.	Covent Garden
	D.L.	Drury Lane
	G.S.M.	Guildhall School of Music
	Hm.	Haymarket
	H.M.'s	His (Her) Majesty's Theatre
	Ly.	Lyceum Theatre (English Opera House)
	R.A.H.	Royal Albert Hall
	R.A.M.	Royal Academy of Music
	R.C.M.	Royal College of Music
	R.F.H.	Royal Festival Hall
	St. J's.	St. James's Theatre
	S.W.	Sadler's Wells Theatre
	T.C.L.	Trinity College, London
MANCHESTER	R.M.C.M.	Royal Manchester College of Music
MILAN	Sc.	Teatro alla Scala (La Scala)
	T.d.V.	Teatro dal Verme
	T.L.	Teatro Lirico
	T.R.D.	Teatro Regio Ducal
MOSCOW	B.	Bolshoy Teatr
MUNICH	N.	Hof- und Nationaltheater
	P.	Prinzregententheater
NAPLES	S.B.	Teatro San Bartolomeo
	S.C.	Teatro San Carlo
NEW YORK	Ac. of M.	Academy of Music
	C.C.	City Center
	Met.	Metropolitan Opera House
	P.O.H.	Palmo's Opera House
PARIS	B.-P.	Bouffes-Parisiens
	Ch.-É.	Théâtre des Champs-Élysées
	C.-I.	Comédie-Italienne
	F.-P.	Fantaisies-Parisiennes
	O.	Opéra (Académie Royale de Musique, etc.)
	O.C.	Opéra-Comique
	T.-I.	Théâtre-Italien
	Th. S.B.	Théâtre Sarah Bernhardt
	T.-L.	Théâtre-Lyrique

PHILADELPHIA	Ac. of M.	Academy of Music
PRAGUE	N.	Narodni Divadlo (National Theatre)
	Cz.	Czech Theatre
ROME	Ap.	Teatro Apollo
	Arg.	Teatro Argentina
	C.	Teatro Costanzi
	T.R.	Teatro Reale
TURIN	T.R.	Teatro Regio
	V.E.	Teatro Vittorio Emanuele
VENICE	F.	Teatro La Fenice
	S.G.Cr.	Teatro San Giovanni Crisostomo
	S.G.P.	Teatro Santi Giovanni e Paolo
	S. Sam.	Teatro San Samuele
VIENNA	B.	Burgtheater
	Kä.	Kärntnerthor-Theater
	S.O.	Staatsoper
	V.O.	Volksoper
	W.	Theater auf der Wieden (later Theater an der Wien)

NATIONALITIES AND LANGUAGES

Cz.	Czechoslovak	It.	Italian
Dan.	Danish	Lat.	Latin
Flem.	Flemish	Pol.	Polish
Fr.	French	Port.	Portuguese
Ger.	German	Rum.	Rumanian
Gr.	Greek	Yug.	Yugoslav

MISCELLANEOUS

B.B.C.	British Broadcasting Corporation
B.N.O.C.	British National Opera Company
cap.	capacity
Carn.	Carnival (usually beginning 26 Dec. of previous year and lasting until Feb. or Mar.)
C.B.S.	Columbia Broadcasting System
C.R.	Carl Rosa Opera Company
cond.	conductor, conducted
E.O.G.	English Opera Group
O.H.	Opera House
prod.	producer, produced
(R)	has recorded in opera
T.	Theatre
T.H.	Town Hall
TV	Television

KEY TO VOCAL COMPASSES

CONCISE DICTIONARY OF OPERA

Aachen (Fr. Aix-la-Chapelle). Town in NW. Germany. Present theatre (cap. 944) opened 23 Dec. 1951. Though a small house, it has a high reputation as the 'cradle' of many distinguished artists.

Abbey, Henry Eugene (b. Akron, Ohio, 27 June 1846; d. New York, 17 Oct. 1896). American impresario. First manager of the Metropolitan Opera (1883); lost nearly $500,000. Shared management with Grau and Schoeffel, 1891–6.

Abbott, Emma (b. Chicago, 9 Dec. 1850; d. Salt Lake City, 5 Jan. 1891). American soprano. Studied New York with Achille Errani and in Europe with Mathilde Marchesi, Sangiovanni, and Delle Sedie. Début London, C.G., 1876, Marie (*La Fille du Régiment*) and N.Y., same role, 1877. Married Eugene Wetherell 1875; together promoted Emma Abbott English Grand Opera Company. Introduced 'specialities', such as popular ballads, into operas in which she appeared.

Abencérages, Les; ou L'Étendard de Grenade. Opera in 3 acts by Cherubini; text by V. J. Étienne de Jouy after J. P. Florian's novel *Gonzalve de Cordove* (1791). Prod. Paris, O., 6 Apr. 1813, in the presence of Napoleon. First revival since 1828, Florence Festival 1957 under Giulini. The confused plot tells of the disputed triumphs of Almansor, the last of the Moorish Abenceragi warriors.

Abigaille. Nabucco's daughter (sop.) in Verdi's *Nabucco*.

Abonnement (Fr. = subscription). The term used in German and French opera houses for the various subscription series. These are the financial mainstay of the season. The subscribers are known in Germany as Abonnenten, in France, as Abonnés.

Ábrányi, Emil (b. Budapest, 22 Sept. 1882). Hungarian composer and conductor. The list of his ten operas includes the first ever written on the life of Bach, *A Tamás templon karnagya*. He has held opera-conducting posts at Cologne and Budapest.

Abreise, Die (The Departure). Opera in 1 act by D'Albert; text by Ferdinand von Sporck after August von Steigentesch's drama. Prod. Frankfurt 20 Oct. 1898; London, King's, Hammersmith, 3 Sept. 1925. His most successful comic opera.

Abscheulicher! Leonore's aria in Act 1 of Beethoven's *Fidelio*, in which she first rages against her husband's imprisoner Don Pizarro, and then prays for a rescue.

Abu Hassan. Operetta in 1 act by Weber; text by Franz Karl Hiemer after a tale in *The Arabian Nights*. Prod. Munich 4 June 1811; London, D.L., trans. W. Dimond with music adapted by T. S. Cooke, 4 Apr. 1825; N.Y. (London version) 5 Nov. 1827. Abu Hassan and his wife Fatima attempt to pay their creditors by obtaining money as benefit for each other's faked death. The Caliph's concern for them exposes the plot, but they are forgiven.

Académie de Musique, Paris. The official name of the Paris Opéra. First theatre built after Louis XIV granted letters patent to Abbé Pierre Perrin, Cambert, and the Marquis de Sourceaux to establish an *académie* which would present operas in French. Opened 3 Mar. 1671 with Cambert's *Pomone*. Lully controlled the Académie 1672–87, producing 20 grand operas. Twenty-four of Rameau's operas were produced between 1737 and 1760. Theatre destroyed by fire 1763, as was its successor 1781. Académie transferred to the rue de Richelieu 1794, as the Théâtre des Arts. Here it assumed a more democratic guise, with seats in the pit for the first time. Spontini and Cherubini were active 1804–14. Theatre moved to the rue Favart 1821, and to the rue Lepeletier 1822, where operas by Rossini, Donizetti, Weber, and Mozart entered the repertory.

There followed a glorious period in its history with Meyerbeer, Auber and Hérold as principal composers. Operas by Rossini (*Guillaume Tell*), Donizetti (*La Favorite*), and Verdi (*Les Vêpres Siciliennes* and *Don Carlos*) were commissioned, and the singers included Cinti-Damoreau, Falcon, Viardot, Nourrit, Duprez, Marie Sass, and Faure. A new luxurious theatre, planned in 1861, was delayed by the Franco-Prussian war. Charles Garnier's sumptuous theatre opened on 5 Jan. 1875 with an opera/ballet evening, followed three days later by *La Juive*. Directors of the Opéra have included Ritt and Pierre Gailhard (q.v.) 1885–91, Gailhard alone 1899–1906, Jacques Rouché 1915–45, Maurice Lehmann 1945–6 and 1951–5, Georges Hirsch 1946–51 and 1956–9, A. M. Julien 1959–62, Georges Auric 1962–8, and René Nicoly 1969–71. A complete reorganization, with Rolf Liebermann as general administrator and Georg Solti as musical adviser, was scheduled to become effective in the 1972–3 season. In 1939 the separate Opéra and Opéra-Comique were administratively merged as the Réunion des Théâtres Lyriques Nationaux. The present building seats 2,600; the stage, the largest in the world, is 100 ft. wide and 112 ft. deep.

Academy of Music, New York. Opera house that formerly stood at the NE. corner of Irving Place and 14th Street. Opened 2 Oct. 1854, with Grisi and Mario in *Norma*, succeeding the Astor Place Opera House. Home of all the New York Mapleson seasons and scene of the American débuts of Patti and Tietjens, and of the American premières of most Verdi operas, *Rienzi*, *Roméo et Juliette*, and *Mefistofele*. Succeeded by the Metropolitan, 1883, as the leading New York opera house, but still used for opera until the turn of the century, when it became a theatre and then a cinema. Demolished 1925.

Ach, ich fühl's. Pamina's (sop.) aria in Act 2 of Mozart's *Die Zauberflöte*, lamenting Tamino's apparent indifference.

Acis and Galatea. Masque, serenata, or pastoral opera in 3 acts by Handel; text by John Gay and others. Probably written and performed at Cannons between 1718 and 1720; London, Hm., 17 May 1732. The story originally occurs in Ovid, and tells of the nymph Galatea's love for Acis; the giant Polyphemus crushed him under a rock, and his blood was turned to a river. Other operas on the subject are by Lully (1686), Stolzel (1715), Haydn (1790), Bianchi (1792), Naumann (1801), Hatton (1844), and Zarbo (1892).

Ackermann, Otto (b. Bucharest, 18 Oct. 1909; d. Berne, 9 Mar. 1960). Swiss conductor. Studied Bucharest and Berlin. When 15 conducted Royal Rumanian Opera Company on tour. Düsseldorf 1927–32; Brno 1932–5; Berne 1935–46; guest conductor at leading Italian opera houses, Vienna, Paris, Brussels, Barcelona, 1946–53; Generalmusikdirektor, Cologne, 1953–8; Zürich 1958–60. (R)

Ackté, Aino (orig. Achté) (b. Helsinki, 23 Apr. 1876; d. Nummela, 8 Aug. 1944). Finnish soprano. Daughter of Lorenz Nikolai Achté, baritone and conductor, and Emmy Achté (Strömer), soprano. Studied with her mother and then Duvernoy in Paris. Début Paris, O., 1897, Marguerite; Paris until 1903; N.Y., Met., 1904–6; London, C.G., 1907. First British Salome 1910. Had a voice of purity and power, an excellent dramatic instinct and stage presence. Director of the Finnish National Opera, 1938. (R)

Action Musicale. The name used by D'Indy for his operas *Fervaal* and *L'Étranger*. The French equivalent of Wagner's *Handlung für Musik*.

Adalgisa. Norma's confidante and rival (sop.) in Bellini's *Norma*.

Adam, Adolphe (b. Paris, 24 July 1803; d. Paris, 3 May 1856). French composer. Overcoming strenuous parental opposition, he studied music first secretly and then at the Conservatoire. Boïeldieu exerted a cordial and beneficial influence on him, steering his talents into the medium for which they were best suited, *opéra comique*. His fluency worked against his success in more serious forms; but, as he said himself, 'my only aim is to write music which is transparent, easy to understand, and amusing to the public'. He wrote some 20 *opéras comiques* between 1829 and his death. The most enduringly successful of these has been *Le Postillon de Longjumeau* (1836), though others are occasionally to be seen, among them *Si j'étais roi* (1852).

Adamberger, Valentin (b. Munich, 6 July 1743; d. Vienna, 24 Aug. 1804). German tenor. Active in Vienna, also visiting Italy and London. According to his friend Mozart, a singer 'of whom Germany may well be proud'. For him Mozart wrote the part of Belmonte.

Adami, Giuseppe (b. Verona, 4 Feb. 1878; d. Milan, 12 Oct. 1946). Italian librettist. Furnished Puccini with librettos for *La Rondine*, *Il Tabarro*, and (with Simoni) *Turandot*. Also wrote texts for operas by Vittadini and Zandonai.

Adams, Suzanne (b. Cambridge, Mass., 28 Nov. 1872; d. London, 5 Feb. 1953). American soprano. Studied Paris with Bouhy. Début Paris, O., 1895, Juliette. London, C.G., 1898 in the same role, which, like that of Marguerite, she studied with Gounod. Created Hero in Stanford's *Much Ado About Nothing* in 1904. Married the cellist Leo Stein. His death in 1904 led to her retirement from the stage three years later. (R)

Added Numbers. In days when the singer was regarded with greater respect than the composer, separate songs were sometimes added purely as display items. Mozart wrote several arias for insertion into other composers' works, e.g. 'Mandina amabile' for Bianchi's *La Villanella Rapita*. A more familiar example is the Lesson Song often substituted for Rossini's 'Contro un cor' in Act 2 of *Il Barbiere di Siviglia*. For this a number of different pieces have been used, including arias prophetically produced from the future by various prima donnas, and ballads. Melba used to have a piano wheeled on to the stage and turn the Lesson Scene into a ballad concert, generally ending with 'Home, Sweet Home'.

Addio del passato. Violetta's (sop.) aria in the last act of Verdi's *La Traviata*. It follows her reading of Germont's letter and bids farewell to her happy past with Alfredo.

Addio fiorito asil. Pinkerton's (ten.) aria in the last act of Puccini's *Madama Butterfly*, bidding farewell to the home where he had lived with Butterfly.

Addio senza rancor. Mimì's (sop.) aria bidding farewell to Rodolfo in Act 3 of Puccini's *La Bohème*.

Adele. The maid (sop.) in J. Strauss's *Die Fledermaus*.

Adieu, notre petite table. Manon's (sop.) aria in Act 2 of Massenet's opera, bidding farewell to the little table in the room she has shared with Des Grieux.

Adina. The heroine (sop.) of Donizetti's *L'Elisir d'Amore*.

Adler, Kurt Herbert (b. Vienna, 2 Apr. 1905). Austrian, now American, conductor and manager. After conducting in Europe and assisting Toscanini at Salzburg, went to America 1938. Conducted Chicago Opera. Connected with San Francisco Opera since 1943; Director since 1953.

Adler, Peter Herman (b. Jablonec, 2 Dec. 1899). Czech, now American, conductor. Studied Prague Conservatoire. After holding various posts in Europe (Brno, Bremen, Kiev, Prague), went to America 1939, making his début (1940) in a concert in New York. Assisted Fritz Busch to launch the New Opera Company, N.Y., 1941, conducting *The Queen of Spades*. Director, Columbia Concerts Opera from 1944. Since 1949, Director, N.B.C. Television Opera; responsible for broadcasts of *Billy Budd*, *War and Peace*, *Der Rosenkavalier*, *The Carmelites*, and many others. Cond. première of Menotti's *Maria Golovin*, Brussels World Fair 1958.

Admeto, Re di Tessaglia. Opera in 3 acts by Handel; text an altered version by Haym or Rolli of an Italian libretto by Aurelio Aureli, *L'Antigone Delusa da Alceste*. Prod. London, Hm., 31 Jan. 1727, with Bordoni and Cuzzoni.

Adriana Lecouvreur. Opera in 4 acts by Cilea; text by Colautti from the drama by Scribe and Legouvé (1849).

Prod. Milan, T.L., 6 Nov. 1902, with Pandolfini, Caruso, De Luca; London, C.G., 8 Nov. 1904; N.Y., Met., 18 Nov. 1907. Concerns the famous 18th-century Parisian actress, rival of Princess Bouillon for the love of Maurice de Saxe. Still performed in Italy. Other operas on the subject are by Vera (1856), Benvenuto, and Perosio (1889).

Aennchen. Agathe's cousin and friend (sop.) in Weber's *Der Freischütz*.

Africaine, L'. Opera in 5 acts by Meyerbeer; text by Scribe. Prod. posth. Paris, O., 28 Apr. 1865, with Marie Sass, Marie Battu, Naudin, Faure; London, C.G., 22 July 1865; N.Y., Ac. of M., 1 Dec. 1865. Meyerbeer spent some 20 years on this, his last opera. It tells how Vasco da Gama (ten.) sailed to find a new land beyond Africa, and was wrecked on the African coast. He returned to Portugal with two captives, Nelusko (bar.) and Selika (sop.) ('l'Africaine' of the title), with whom he has fallen in love. She finally sacrifices her life so that Vasco can marry his former lover, Inez (sop.). The opera was enormously popular in the last century and received nearly 60 performances during its first four London seasons.

After Dinner Opera Company. Founded by Richard Stuart Flusser, New York 1949. Like England's Intimate Opera Company (q.v.) this is a Chamber Group which tours (in the United States, and more recently Europe under the auspices of Washington) with a repertory of chamber works including *Une Éducation Manquée* (Chabrier), *Apollo and Persephone* (Cockshott), *The Telephone* (Menotti), and *Three's Company* (Hopkins).

Agathe. The heroine (sop.) of Weber's *Der Freischütz*, betrothed to Max.

Agnesi, Luigi (orig. Louis Ferdinand Leopold Agniez) (b. Erpent, Namur, 17 July 1833; d. London, 2 Feb. 1875). Belgian bass. Studied Brussels Conservatoire and Paris with Duprez. Member of Morelli's Italian Company in Germany and Holland. Début Paris, Th. I., 1864, Assur (*Semiramide*); London, H.M.'s, 1865. Famous for his Rossini singing.

Agram. See *Zagreb*.

Agrippina. Opera in 3 acts by Handel; text by Vincenzo Grimani. Prod. Venice, S.G.Cr., 26 Dec. 1709. Probably Handel's only opera produced in Italy during his three-year stay.

Aguiari (or **Agujari), Lucrezia** (b. Ferrara, 1743; d. Parma, 18 May 1783). Italian soprano. Also known, from her illegitimacy, as La Bastardella or La Bastardina. Following a brilliant début in Florence in 1764, she embarked upon a highly successful career. Mozart says that she had 'a lovely voice, a flexible throat, and an incredibly high range', going on to quote a passage he heard her sing that ranges from $C^{\prime}$ to $C^{\prime\prime\prime\prime}$. She was engaged for the Panthéon, London, in 1775 and 1776 to sing two songs at £100 a night.

Ägyptische Helena, Die (The Egyptian Helen). Opera in 2 acts by Strauss; text by Hugo von Hofmannsthal, based on hints from Homer, Euripides, and Goethe. Prod. Dresden, 6 June 1928, with Elisabeth Rethberg, Maria Rajdl, Kurt Taucher, conductor Fritz Busch; N.Y., Met., 6 Nov. 1928. Originally conceived as an operetta. Revised for the 1933 Salzburg Festival, and again by Clemens Krauss and Rudolf Hartmann, Munich, 1940.

Ah! fors' è lui. The Andantino opening to Violetta's (sop.) aria 'Sempre libera' in Act 1 of Verdi's *La Traviata*, in which she asks herself whether she is really falling in love.

Ah, fuyez, douce image. Des Grieux's (ten.) outburst in Saint-Sulpice in Act 3 of Massenet's *Manon*, when he tries in vain to drive the vision of Manon from his mind.

Ah! non credea mirarti. Amina's (sop.) sleep-walking aria from the last act of Bellini's *La Sonnambula*, which leads to the final rondo:

Ah! non giunge! which she sings as she awakens and sees her beloved Elvino beside her.

Ah sì, ben mio. Manrico's (ten.) aria to his beloved Leonora, consoling her as they shelter in a fortress, in Act 3 of Verdi's *Il Trovatore*.

Aida. Opera in 4 acts by Verdi; text by Antonio Ghislanzoni from the French prose of Camille du Locle (1868), plot by Mariette Bey. Prod. Cairo 24 Dec. 1871, with Pozzoni, Grossi, Mongini, Stella; Milan, Sc., 8 Feb. 1872; N.Y., Ac. of M., 26 Nov. 1873; London, C.G., 22 June 1876, with Patti in the title role.

Aida was not, as generally supposed, written for the opening of the Suez Canal (1869), but was commissioned by the Khedive of Egypt to open the new Cairo Opera House the same year. Owing to the Franco-Prussian war the première had to be postponed from Jan. 1871, for scenery and costumes were then unable to leave besieged Paris.

The opera takes place in ancient Egypt.

Act 1. Radamès (ten.), captain of the guard, hopes he may be chosen to lead the Egyptian armies against the Ethiopians, and win the hand of Aida (sop.), the Ethiopian slave-girl of Amneris (mezzo), the King's daughter. Amneris herself loves Radamès. Radamès is appointed commander, and Aida is torn between her love for him and for her own people. In the Temple of Isis, Radamès is invested with consecrated armour by the High Priest, Ramfis (bass).

Act 2. Amneris longs for Radamès's return but fears he may love Aida. She questions Aida and declares her rivalry. They go with the rest of the court and the people to the Gates of Thebes to welcome the victorious Radamès. Among the Ethiopian prisoners is King Amonasro (bar.), Aida's father. He conceals his rank, but is retained as a hostage while the other prisoners are released. The King rewards Radamès with Amneris's hand in marriage.

Act 3. Amneris comes to the Temple of Isis by the banks of the Nile to spend the night before her wedding in prayer. Aida arrives to meet Radamès. Her father, who has followed her, draws so grim a picture of her country's plight that she tricks Radamès into betraying a military secret. Amneris overhears this treachery, and while Aida and her father escape, Radamès surrenders to Ramfis.

Act 4. Amneris pleads in vain for Radamès to save himself by renouncing Aida. Nor will he defend himself before the priests, who condemn him to be buried alive. Amneris calls down the curses of heaven upon them. As the last stone is placed above the tomb, Radamès discovers Aida hiding there. They die in each other's arms, Amneris, above, praying that the gods may grant Radamès eternal rest.

Aiglon, L' (The Eaglet). Opera in 5 acts by Honegger and Ibert; text by Henri Cain after Edmond Rostand's drama (1900). Prod. Monte Carlo 11 Mar. 1937, with Fanny Heldy and Vanni Marcoux. Announced for production at Naples in Feb. 1939 but cancelled on Mussolini's orders after the dress rehearsal. Revived Paris, O., 1953, with Geori Boué in the title role (a travesti part) of the Duke of Reichstadt who escapes from Schönbrunn. The first and last acts are by Ibert, the middle three by Honegger.

Ai nostri monti. The duet sung by Manrico (ten.) and Azucena (mezzo) in the last act of Verdi's *Il Trovatore*, in which they console one another with memories of the mountains of their homeland.

Aix-en-Provence. Town in Provence, France. At the annual summer festival, founded by Gabriel Dussurget and Roger Bigonnet in 1948, operas are mostly performed in the fine open-air theatre in the Archbishop's Palace designed by Cassandre, and occasionally elsewhere, e.g. Les Baux (*Mireille*, 1954) and the Parc du Tholonet (*Carmen*, 1957). The Festival has given performances of Mozart, Rossini, Cimarosa, Rameau, Grétry, Gluck, Monteverdi, and Haydn, and has introduced to a wider public Graziella Sciutti, Teresa Berganza, Teresa Stich-Randall, and Léopold Simoneau.

Aladdin. (1) Fairy opera by Bishop; text by G. Soane. Prod. London, D.L., 29 Apr. 1826, as a counter-attraction to Weber's *Oberon* at C.G. Possessing an even more ridiculous plot, it was a complete failure and had to be withdrawn. Weber was present at the first performance, and noted a charming hunting chorus; but the audience greeted it by whistling the *Freischütz* hunting chorus for him. Bishop's only opera without spoken dialogue.

(2) Opera by Atterberg. Prod. Stockholm, 18 Mar. 1941. Also opera by Horneman (1888).

Albanese, Licia (b. Bari, 22 July 1913). Italian, now American, soprano. Studied with Giuseppina Baldassarre-Tedeschi. Début Milan, T.L., 1934, Butterfly. Winner over 300 contestants in a nation-wide competition sponsored by the Italian government. Formal début Parma 1935, Butterfly; London, C.G., 1937; N.Y., Met., 1940–66. Chosen by Toscanini for his broadcasts (also recorded) of *La Bohème* and *Traviata*. (R)

Albani, Emma (Dame) (orig. Marie Louise Cécile Lajeunesse) (b. Chambly, nr. Montreal, 1 Nov. 1847; d. London, 3 Apr. 1930). Canadian soprano. Educated Montreal, then New York, where her singing in the choir of the Roman Catholic Cathedral so impressed the bishop that he advised her father to let her take up music. Studied Paris with Duprez and subsequently Milan with Lamperti. Début Messina, 1869, Amina, adopting the name of Albani for professional purposes; London, C.G., 1872–96; N.Y., Met., 1890. First C.G. Mignon, Elsa, Elisabeth, Senta, Desdemona. Married Ernest Gye, son of C.G.'s director, and later manager of the theatre himself. Continued to sing in concerts until 1911 and then devoted herself to teaching. Autobiography, *40 Years of Song* (1911). (R)

Alberich. A Nibelung (bass-bar.) in Wagner's *Ring* whose renunciation of love and theft of the Rhinegold precipitates the events of the whole cycle.

Albert, Eugen d' (b. Glasgow, 10 Apr. 1864; d. Riga, 3 Mar. 1932). German pianist and composer of French descent and British birth. Studied at National Training School in London, and had an early success as a pianist; later pupil of Liszt in Vienna. Very active as an opera composer in Germany from 1893, though of his 20 operas only *Die Abreise* and *Tiefland* have endured.

Albert Herring. Opera in 3 acts by Britten; text by Eric Crozier after Maupassant's story *Le Rosier de Madame Husson* (1888). Prod. Glyndebourne 20 June 1947 with Peter Pears, Joan Cross, cond. composer; Tanglewood, Mass., 1949. Britten's first comedy. It describes the election of the only virtuous young person in a village as King of the May and his subsequent disgrace but emancipation.

Alboni, Marietta (orig. Maria Anna Marzia)(b. Città di Castello, 6 Mar. 1823; d. Ville d'Avray, 23 June 1894). Italian contralto. Studied with Bertoletti. So impressed Rossini that he taught her the contralto roles in his operas. Début Bologna 1842, Pacini's *Saffo*. Engaged as leading contralto C.G. 1847, its first season as Royal Italian Opera, making début on opening night as Arsace (*Semiramide*). So enthusiastically received that she became the rival attraction to Jenny Lind at H.M.'s, and her salary was raised from £500 to £2,000. In 1848 at C.G. Meyerbeer wrote for her the Page's aria in *Les Huguenots*, and the same year she agreed to sing the baritone role of Carlos in the first Covent Garden *Ernani* after the part had been turned down by both Tamburini and Ronconi. Continued to appear in London intermittently until 1858. Toured U.S. 1853; retired 1863, following her marriage to Conte Pepoli. Sang at Rossini's funeral with Patti. Her voice, a true contralto, ranged from g to g''. One of the greatest contraltos in operatic history.

Alceste. Opera in 3 acts by Gluck; text by Calzabigi, after the drama by Euripides (438 B.C.). Prod. Vienna, B., 26 Dec. 1767, with Antonia Bernasconi; London 30 Apr. 1795; N.Y., Wellesley College, 11 Mar. 1938; French version revised by Gluck, with text by Du Roullet, prod. Paris, O., 23 Apr. 1776 with Levasseur. The preface to the score, one of the most important documents in the history of opera, embodies Gluck's view that opera should not be an elegant concert in costume but a step towards what was later known as music drama. The story tells how Alcestis offered to die in place of her beloved husband Admetus, but was brought back from Hades by Hercules. Other operas on the subject are by Lully (1674—saluted by Mme de Sévigné as 'un prodige de beauté'), Strungk (1682), Draghi (1699), Schürmann (1719), Handel (1734), Lampugnani (1745), Schweitzer (1773—intended as the first step towards a German national opera), Gresnick (1786), Portogallo (1793), Staffa (1852), Gambaro (1882), Boughton (1922), and Wellesz (1924).

Alcina. Opera in 3 acts by Handel; text by Antonio Marchi after Ariosto's *Orlando Furioso* (1516). Prod. London, C.G., 16 Apr. 1735, with Carestini. Revived London, Handel Opera Society, 1957, and subsequently by Zeffirelli in Italy, U.S.A., and London. The plot centres on the sorceress Alcina who wins Ruggiero's love, then falling in love with him in truth, so that she loses her magic powers. His lover Bradamante comes in man's disguise to rescue him, and eventually Alcina is overthrown.

Alda, Frances (orig. Davis) (b. Christchurch, New Zealand, 31 May 1883; d. Venice, 18 Sept. 1952). New Zealand soprano. Studied Paris, Mathilde Marchesi; début Paris, O.C., 1904, Manon. After appearances at Brussels, La M., London, C.G., and Milan, Sc.—where she met Toscanini, who became her life-long friend, and Gatti-Casazza, whom she later married—was engaged N.Y., Met., 1908, until 1930. Created Roxane in Damrosch's *Cyrano de Bergerac*, title role in Victor Herbert's *Madeleine*, and Cleopatra in Hadley's *Cleopatra's Night*. The first Louise at La Scala, under Toscanini. Famed for her volatile temperament, professional quarrels, and many law cases. Autobiography, *Men, Women and Tenors* (1937). (R)

Aldeburgh Festival. Founded in 1948 by Benjamin Britten, Eric Crozier, and Peter Pears, devoted to music and the other arts and held at Britten's home town of Aldeburgh, on the Suffolk coast. Britten's music and taste are the dominant features of the festival, which combines high quality with a pleasantly local, informal character. First performances have included *Let's Make an Opera* (1949), Berkeley's *A Dinner Engagement* (1954), *Noyes Fludde* (1958), *A Midsummer Night's Dream* (1960), Britten's 3 Church Parables, Williamson's *English Eccentrics* (1964), and Birtwistle's *Punch & Judy* (1968).

Alessandro. Opera in 3 acts by Handel; text by Paulo Antonio Rolli. Prod. London, Hm., 5 May 1726, with Faustina Bordoni making her début, as Rossane. Revived as *Roxana, or Alexander in India*, probably with additions by Lampugnani, King's, 15 Nov. 1743. The subject made one of Metastasio's most successful librettos, set by some 40 composers.

Alessandro Stradella. Opera in 3 acts by Flotow; text by 'W. Friedrich' (Friedrich Wilhelm Riese) after a French *comédie mêlée de chant* by P. A. A. Pittaud de Forges and P. Duport, originally produced, with new airs by Flotow, in 1837. Concerns Stradella's sensational life. Prod. Hamburg 30 Dec. 1844; London, D.L., in English with music arranged by Benedict, 6 Jun. 1846; N.Y. 29 Nov. 1853.

Alfano, Franco (b. Posillipo, nr. Naples, 8 Mar. 1876; d. San Remo, 26 Oct. 1954). Italian composer. Studied Naples Conservatory with De Nardis and Serrao, and then Leipzig with Kadassohn. First operas *Miranda* (1896) and *La Fonte di Enschir* (1898) soon forgotten. Established with *Risurrezione* (after Tolstoy, Turin 1904), a favourite of Mary Garden. Later works, including *L'Ombra di Don Giovanni*, *Sakuntala*, and *Cyrano de Bergerac*, still occasionally performed in Italy. Alfano broke away from the Italian verismo school; he retained a love of melody and wrote well for the voice. Best remembered for his completion of Puccini's *Turandot*.

Alfio. Husband (bar.) of Lola, rival and eventually killer of Turiddù in Mascagni's *Cavalleria Rusticana*.

Alfonso. (1) Alfonso XI, King of Castile (bar.), in Donizetti's *La Favorite*.

(2) Don Alfonso (bass), the cynical philosopher who proposes the wager that produces the plot of Mozart's *Così fan tutte*.

Alfred. Rosalinde's tenor lover in Johann Strauss's *Die Fledermaus*.

Alfredo. The younger Germont (ten.), lover of Violetta in Verdi's *La Traviata*.

Alice. Ford's wife (sop.) in Verdi's *Falstaff*.

Allegra, Salvatore (b. Palermo, 13 July 1898). Italian composer. Pupil of Cilea and Favara. His operas include *Ave Maria* (1934), *I Viandanti* (1936), *Il Medico suo malgrado* (1938), and *Romulus* (1952).

Allegranti, Maddalena (b. Florence, *c.* 1750; d. ? Ireland, ?). Italian soprano. Début Venice 1770; then studied Mannheim. Great success in Germany until 1778; London from 1781 to 1783. For some years then *prima donna buffa* at Dresden. Earlier in her career Burney had noted her 'pretty, unaffected manner'; while Mozart thought her far better than Ferraresi, though he added that this was not saying much.

Allestimento. The Italian term used for a stage production in the *cartellone* (q.v.) announcing the season's plans.

Allin, Norman (b. Ashton-under-Lyne, 19 Nov. 1884). English bass. Studied R.M.C.M. 1906–10, with John Acton and Francis Harford. Originally intended to teach, but after marriage in 1912 to the mezzo-soprano Edith Clegg concentrated on singing. Début with Beecham Company 1916, London, Aldwych, as Aged Hebrew (*Samson et Dalila*); graduated to King Mark, Dositheus, Méphistophélès, &c. C.G. début 1919, Konchak, later that year Gurnemanz. Leading bass and director of B.N.O.C. 1922–9. Bartolo in the opening performance, Glyndebourne 1934; Carl Rosa 1942–9. Professor, R.A.M. since 1935 and R.M.C.M. 1938–42. One of England's finest basses. (R)

Almaviva. The Count, who, as a tenor, woos and wins Rosina in Rossini's *Barbiere di Siviglia*; and, as a baritone, has to be taught a lesson for his infidelity to her in Mozart's *Nozze di Figaro*.

Almaviva, ossia L'Inutile Precauzione. See *Barbiere di Siviglia*.

Almira. Opera in 3 acts by Handel; text by Friedrich Feustking after an Italian libretto by Boniventi. Prod. Hamburg 8 Jan. 1705. Handel's first opera, containing 41 German and 15 Italian airs. Text also set by Boniventi (1691), Fedeli (1703), and Keiser (1706).

Althouse, Paul (b. Reading, Pa., 2 Dec. 1889; d. New York, 6 Feb. 1954). American tenor. Début Philadelphia, Hammerstein Opera; N.Y., Met., 1913, Dimitri. The first American to be engaged without previous European experience. Created roles in *Shanewis* (Cadman), *Madeleine* (Herbert), *Canterbury Pilgrims* (De Koven), *The Legend* (Breil). Studied in Europe for nine years, then re-engaged for Met., as Heldentenor 1934–40. Siegmund at Flagstad's Met. début as Sieglinde, first American Tristan there. After his retirement, pupils included Richard Tucker, Eleanor Steber, and Irene Dalis. (R)

Alto. (It. = high.) A term for certain voices. The female alto is usually known as contralto (q.v.). The male alto is often confused with counter-tenor (q.v.), from which it differs in that it is usually a bass voice singing falsetto. See also *Castrato*. The range is about from f to a''.

Alva, Luigi (b. Lima, 10 Apr. 1927). Peruvian tenor. Studied Lima and Milan. Début Lima 1949. Milan, Piccola Scala, 1955, Paolino; Edinburgh 1957; London, C.G., 1960, Almaviva. Has sung extensively in Europe including Holland and Aix Festivals, where he is especially admired in Mozart and Rossini. (R)

Alvarez, Albert (orig. Raymond Gourron) (b. Bordeaux, 1861; d. Nice, 26 Feb. 1933). French tenor. Studied in Paris with Martini. Début Ghent; appearances in French provinces. Paris, O., 1892, Faust; London, C.G., 1893, Leicester in De Lara's *Amy Robsart*. N.Y., Met., 1899–1903. Created Nicias (*Thaïs*), Helion (De Lara's *Messaline*), and Aragui (*La Navarraise*). Possessed a robust voice coupled with fine physique and stage presence. (R)

Alvarez, Marguerite d' (orig. Marguerite Alvarez de Rocafuarte) (b. Liverpool, 1886 (?); d. Alassio, 18 Oct. 1953). English contralto of Peruvian parentage. When 16 sang at a diplomatic reception in London. After three years' study in Brussels, début Rouen, Dalila. American début, N.Y., with Hammerstein Company, 1909, Fidès; London, London Opera House (Stoll), 1911, Queen (*Hérodiade*). Also sang at C.G., Chicago, and Boston. A highly emotional and dramatic artist who was hardly suited to the concert platform where she chose to spend the greater part of her career. Autobiography, *Forsaken Altars* (1954). (R)

Alvaro. The hero (ten.) of Verdi's *La Forza del Destino*, lover of Leonora.

Alvary, Max (orig. Maximilian Achenbach) (b. Düsseldorf, 3 May 1856; d. Gross-Tabarz, Thuringia, 7 Nov. 1898). German tenor. Son of painter Andreas Achenbach. Despite parental opposition studied with Stockhausen in Frankfurt and Lamperti in Milan. Début Weimar; N.Y., Met., 1885, Don José (opposite Lilli Lehmann, also making her American début), remaining with the company until 1889. First N.Y. Loge and young Siegfried. Sang Tristan and Tannhäuser, Bayreuth 1891, and in the first C.G. *Ring* under Mahler 1892, which was begun with *Siegfried* so that Alvary could make his début in his favourite role. Forced by illness to leave the stage 1897. First singer to play Wagner heroes without a beard.

Alzira. Opera in 2 acts by Verdi; text by Salvatore Cammarano after Voltaire's drama *Alzire* (1730). Prod. Naples, S.C., 12 Aug. 1845, with Tadolini in title role. One of Verdi's rare failures; he later called it 'really ugly'('tutto brutto').

Amadis. Opera in a prologue and 5 acts by Lully; text by Philippe Quinault. Prod. Paris, O., 18 Jan. 1684. Other operas on same subject by Handel (*Amadigi di Gaula*; London, Hm., 25 May 1715), Berton (1771), J. C. Bach (1779), Stengel (1798), and Massenet (*Amadis*: Monte Carlo, 1 Apr. 1922, though composed in 1902). A parody by Romagnesi and Riccobini was produced in Paris, Nouveau Théâtre-Italien, 19 Dec. 1740). A sequel, *Amadis de Grèce*, perhaps by Feliciano de Silva, was set by Destouches (1699).

Amahl and the Night Visitors. Opera in 1 act by Menotti; text by composer after Bosch's painting *The Adoration of the Magi*. Prod. N.B.C. Television 24 Dec. 1951. The first opera written for television, it has become a regular Christmas feature. First stage production, Indiana University, 21 Feb. 1952. It describes the reception of the Magi, on their way to Bethlehem, by a little crippled boy.

Amara, Lucine (orig. Armaganian) (b. Hartford, Conn., 1 Mar. 1925). American soprano of Armenian parentage. Studied with Stella Eisner-Eyn in San Francisco. Joined chorus of San Francisco Opera 1945–6. In a contest in 1948 won $2,000 and a contract to sing at the Hollywood Bowl. Scholarship at University of Southern California. Met. since 1950. Glyndebourne 1954, Ariadne; Vienna 1960, Aida. (R)

Amato, Pasquale (b. Naples, 21 Mar. 1878; d. Long Island, New York, 12 Aug. 1942). Italian baritone. Début Naples, Teatro Bellini, 1900, Germont. London, C.G., 1904, with San Carlo Company; but despite success never returned. N.Y., Met., 1908–21, where created Jack Rance in *La Fanciulla del West*, Cyrano de Bergerac in Damrosch's opera, and Napoleon in Giordano's *Madame Sans-Gêne*. Retired owing to ill health and went to live in Italy, but returned to America in 1933 and sang Germont at the N.Y. Hippodrome on the 25th anniversary of his American début. In 1935 appointed head of voice and opera at Louisiana University. (R)

Amelia. (1) Renato's wife (sop.) and Riccardo's lover in Verdi's *Un Ballo in Maschera*.

(2) Boccanegra's daughter Maria, brought up as Amelia Grimaldi (sop.) in Verdi's *Simone Boccanegra*.

Amelia al Ballo. Comic opera in 1 act by Menotti; text by composer, English trans. *Amelia Goes to the Ball* by George Meade. Prod. (in English) Philadelphia, Ac. of M., 1 Apr. 1937; (in Italian) San Remo 4 Apr. 1938; Liverpool 19 Nov. 1956. Menotti's first mature opera, and first success. The complicated buffo-type plot describes the effort of Amelia to be taken to a ball: having disposed of both husband and lover, she achieves this on the arm of the Chief of Police.

Amfiparnaso, L'. *Comedia harmonica* by Vecchi, the second of his four madrigal comedies. Probably first sung in Modena 1594. Though attempts at staging have been made, this succession of five-part songs is a predecessor of opera rather than an early example. Dramatic continuity is given to a number of 16th-century vocal forms. The work is the culmination of an Italian tradition of such works. Revived at the Florence Festivals of 1933 and 1939.

Amfortas. The Keeper of the Grail (bar.) in Wagner's *Parsifal*.

Amico Fritz, L' (Friend Fritz). Opera in 3 acts by Mascagni; text by P. Suardon (N. Daspuro) after Erckmann-Chatrian's novel (1864). Prod. Rome, C., 31 Oct. 1891, with Calvé, Synnemberg, De Lucia, Lhérie; London, C.G., 23 May 1892; Philadelphia 8 June 1892. A light pastoral comedy about the confirmed bachelor Fritz, a rich landowner; Rabbi David, the professional match-maker; and Suzel, the charming daughter of one of Fritz's tenants, with whom Fritz eventually falls in love.

Amneris. The King of Egypt's daughter (mezzo) and Aida's rival for Radamès in Verdi's *Aida*.

Amonasro. The King of Ethiopia (bar.), Aida's father, in Verdi's *Aida*.

Amore dei tre Re, L' (The Love of the Three Kings). Opera in 3 acts by Montemezzi; text by Benelli after his verse tragedy (1910). Prod. Milan, Sc., 10 Apr. 1913, with Villani, Ferrari-Fontana, Galeffi, De Angelis, cond. Serafin; N.Y., Met., 2 Jan. 1914, cond. Toscanini; London, C.G., 27 May 1914. Fiora (sop.) has been forced for political reasons to marry Manfredo (bar.) son of King Archibaldo (bass). While Manfredo is absent on a campaign, the old king murders his daughter-in-law for refusing to reveal the name of her lover, Avito (ten.). He poisons her lips hoping that Avito will come to see her body. Avito dies from kissing the poison, as does Manfredo, who cannot live without his wife. One of the more successful modern Italian operas, especially in U.S.A. where the role of Fiora has attracted Bori, Ponselle, Grace Moore; and that of Archibaldo, Didur, Lazzari, and Pinza.

Amour est un oiseau rebelle, L'. Carmen's (mezzo) Habanera in Act 1 of Bizet's *Carmen*.

Amsterdam. Capital of Holland. Amsterdam has traditionally shared with The Hague the many short-lived Dutch national opera companies, as well as the visiting foreign companies. The Italian company which appeared from 1897 to 1942 always enjoyed great popularity. Still more important was the Wagnervereeniging (founded by Henry Viotta) which gave seasons from 1893 to 1939, and again briefly after the war. These centred on Wagner performances with the best Wagner singers under Muck, Kleiber, Strauss, and Tietjen. In 1941 the Municipal Theatre Enterprise was founded by Johannes den Hertog, developing from the opera class at the Amsterdam Conservatory; this was succeeded by the Nederlandse Opera (orig. founded 1886). This gave 200 performances a year not only in Amsterdam and The Hague but in north Holland, Rotterdam, Utrecht, and Hilversum. It was reorganized as the Nieuwe Nederlandse Opera in 1965 (director Maurice Huismann) and worked in close collaboration with La Monnaie, Brussels. In 1971 Hans de Roo succeeded Huismann as administrator. The organization has been renamed De Nederlandse Operastichting. See also *Holland*.

Am stillen Herd. Walther's (ten.) aria in Act 1 of Wagner's *Die Meistersinger* telling the Masters where and from whom he learned to sing.

Ancona, Mario (b. Leghorn, 28 Feb. 1860; d. Florence, 22 Feb. 1931). Italian baritone. A lawyer and diplomat before studying singing with

G. Cima. Début Trieste 1889; brought to London by Lago for a scratch season at the Olympic Theatre. Engaged by Augustus Harris for C.G. 1893, singing Tonio in first London *Pagliacci*, and in Stanford's *The Veiled Prophet*. London regularly until 1901. N.Y., Met., 1893–7, and Manhattan Opera 1906–7. Retired shortly before the 1914–18 war and taught in Italy. (R)

Anders, Peter (b. Essen, 1 July 1908; d. Hamburg, 10 Sept. 1954). German tenor. Début Berlin 1931 in Max Reinhardt's production of *La Belle Hélène*. Berlin State Opera 1936–48 in the lighter lyric roles; especially successful as a Mozart singer. His voice then began to grow heavier, and in 1950 he sang Walther and Otello in Hamburg. British début 1950, Edinburgh Festival, Bacchus under Beecham, under whom he also sang Walther at C.G. 1951. One of the most intelligent and musical of German tenors. Died after a car accident. (R)

Andersen, Hans (b. Odense, 2 Apr. 1805; d. Copenhagen, 4 Aug. 1875). Danish writer, best known for his fairy-tales, the first volume of which appeared in 1835. As librettist he adapted Scott for Bredal's *Bride of Lammermoor* (1832) and Weyse's *Kenilworth*, and Manzoni's *I Promessi Sposi* for Gläser's *The Wedding on Lake Como* (1849). Operas based on his fairy-tales are Hartmann's *The Raven* (1832) and *Little Christina* (1846), Enna's *The Match Girl* (1897) and *The Princess on the Pea* (1900), Leoni's *Ib and Little Christina* (1901), Guzewski's *The Maiden of the Glaciers* (1907), Enna's *The Nightingale* (1912), Stravinsky's *Le Rossignol* (1914), Bruneau's *Le Jardin du Paradis* (1923), Stanford's *The Travelling Companion* (1925), Sekles's *Die zehn Küsse* (1926), Toch's *Die Prinzessin auf der Erbse* (1927), Hoffding's *The Emperor's New Clothes* (1928), Wagner-Régeny's *Der nackte König* (1928), Němeček's *The Garden of Eden* (1933), Reutter's *Die Prinzessin und der Schweinehirt* (1938), Irmler's *Die Nachtigall* (1939), Hamerik's *The Travelling Companion* (1946), Schanazara's *Die Nachtigall* (1947), Douglas Stuart Moore's *The Emperor's New Clothes* (1948), Fougstedt's *The Tinderbox* (1950), Margaret More's *The Mermaid* (1951), and Hollier's *The Mother* (1954).

Anderson, Marian (b. Philadelphia, 17 Feb. 1902). American contralto. Most of career a concert artist, but first Negro singer at Met. (Ulrica 1955). 'The voice that comes once in a hundred years' (Toscanini). (R)

Andrade, Francisco d' (b. Lisbon, 11 Jan. 1859; d. Berlin, 8 Feb. 1921). Portuguese baritone. Began as amateur, later studied with Miraglia and Ronconi. Début San Remo 1882, Amonasro; London, C.G., 1886, Rigoletto; returned there yearly until 1890. Hofoper, Berlin, 1906–21. Particularly remembered for his elegant portrayal of *Don Giovanni*. (R) His brother, Antonio d'Andrade, was a tenor (C.G. 1889–90). (R)

Andrea Chénier. Opera in 4 acts by Giordano; text by Luigi Illica. Prod. Milan, Sc., 28 Mar. 1896, with Carrera, Borgatti, Sammarco; N.Y., Ac. of M., 13 Nov. 1896; London, Camden Town Theatre (in English), 16 Apr. 1903.

Act 1. In the ballroom of the Château de Coigny, in June 1789, preparations are being made for a party. One of the servants, Carlo Gérard (bar.), who is secretly in love with Madeleine de Coigny (sop.), pours scorn on the aristocrats. The guests arrive, among them the poet Andrea Chénier (ten.) who improvises a poem contrasting the beauty of nature with the greed of the church and the aristocracy. To the further embarrassment of the guests Gérard admits a group of peasants who beg for alms, and then leaves with them.

Act 2. June 1793: the Revolution is over and the Terror established. At the Café Hottot, Chénier is urged by his friend Roucher to flee as he has enemies. But Chénier waits for a woman who has been sending him anonymous letters. When Madeleine comes, she and Chénier declare their love, but they are interrupted by Gérard, now an important revolutionary; the two men fight. Gérard is wounded but allows Chénier, whom he remembers, to escape.

Act 3. A year later. Chénier is to appear before the Revolutionary Tribunal. Gérard is persuaded to write out an indictment against Chénier. Madeleine comes to plead for Chénier; she offers herself to Gérard. He is touched, and promises to help her. The tribunal assembles and Chénier is allowed to defend himself, but neither his words nor those of Gérard are heeded, and he is condemned to death.

Act 4. In the courtyard of the St-Lazare Prison, Chénier awaits his execution. Gérard arrives with Madeleine, and bribes the jailer to let her die with her lover.

Andrésen, Ivar (b. Oslo, 27 July 1896; d. Stockholm, 26 Nov. 1940). Norwegian bass. Début Stockholm 1919, the King (*Aida*). Dresden State Opera 1920's; Berlin State Opera 1935–40; Bayreuth 1927–36; and was made a German Kammersänger. London, C.G., 1928–31, singing leading Wagner bass roles, as well as Sarastro, which he repeated at Glyndebourne in 1935, and Osmin. N.Y., Met., 1930–2. He possessed a beautiful voice, noble in sound, and was a fine artist. (R)

Anfossi, Pasquale (b. Taggia, nr. San Remo, 25 Apr. 1727; d. Rome, Feb. 1797). Italian composer. His 70-odd operas, among them *La Finta Giardiniera* (1774—a year before Mozart's setting), *L'Avaro* (1775), *La Vera Costanza* (1776), and *Il Curioso Indiscreto* (1777) won him wide fame and respect; but they have not lasted as well as the other works of the period.

Angeles, Victoria de los. See *Los Angeles, Victoria de.*

Angélique. Opera in 1 act by Ibert; text by Nino. Prod. Paris, Théâtre Bériza, 28 Jan. 1927; N.Y. 8 Nov. 1937; London, Fortune Theatre, 20 Feb. 1950. Ibert's first and most successful opera. Boniface, the owner of a Paris china shop, is persuaded by his friend Charlot that the only way to rid himself of his shrewish wife Angélique is to put her up for sale.

Anitúa, Fanny (b. Durango, 22 Jan. 1887). Mexican mezzo-soprano. Studied Rome. Début Rome, C., 1909, Orfeo. Milan, Sc., from 1910, where she sang in the première of *Fedra* (Pizzetti) 1915, and was chosen by Toscanini to sing Orfeo and Azucena 1923–6. Sang regularly in America, now teaches in Mexico City. (R)

Anna Bolena. Opera in 2 acts by Donizetti; text by Romani. Prod. Milan, T. Carcano, 26 Dec. 1830, with Pasta, Orlandi, Rubini, F. Galli; London, H.M.'s, 8 July 1831, with Pasta, Rubini, Lablache; New Orleans Nov. 1839. Frequently performed with Grisi and Tietjens, but then fell out of the repertory until the production by Visconti at Milan, Sc., in 1957 with Callas. Revived Glyndebourne, 1965.

Annibale, Domenico (b. Macerata, *c.* 1705; d. Rome (?), 1779). Italian male soprano. After successes at Rome and Venice, and at Dresden in Hasse's operas, he was engaged by Handel for C.G. 1736–7, where he made his début in the title role of *Poro*. After further Handel performances he returned to Dresden, and eventually to Italy.

Ansaldo, Pericle (b. Genoa, 1 Jan. 1884; d. Rome, 29 Sept. 1969). Italian stage technician. Collaborated with his father, Giovanni Ansaldo, until the end of 1927. Responsible for the mechanical improvements and technical installation when the Teatro Costanzi became the Teatro Reale dell'Opera, Rome, 1927, and helped to adapt the Terme di Caracalla for opera. Installed new stage mechanism at the Verona Arena, 1948. Has held appointments at La Scala (Milan) and the Colón (Buenos Aires).

Anselmi, Giuseppe (b. Catania, 16 Nov. 1876; d. Zoagli, nr. Genoa, 27 May 1929). Italian tenor. Studied violin and composition, then joined an operetta company touring Italy and the Near East. Heard by Giulio Ricordi who suggested that he study with Mancinelli. Début Athens 1896, Turiddu; Italian début 1898; London, C.G., same year. Reappeared C.G. intermittently until 1909. Greatly admired in Buenos Aires, and appeared regularly in Warsaw, St. Petersburg, and Madrid. Had a great affection for Madrid and left his heart to the theatrical museum there, where it is preserved. One of the foremost exponents of the art of *bel canto*, with a beautiful voice and a finished style. (R)

Ansseau, Fernand (b. Boussu-Bois, nr. Mons, 6 Nov. 1890). Belgian tenor. Studied Brussels with Demest. Trained as a baritone for two years, as a tenor for three. Début Dijon 1913, Jean (*Hérodiade*). Career interrupted by the war, but in 1918 sang at the reopening of La Monnaie, Brussels. London, C.G., 1919, and subsequently Paris, O.C., 1920 and 1921. Chicago 1923–8. Confined his career to Belgium and France from 1930, retiring at the height of his powers in Feb. 1939. Professor of Singing at the Brussels Conservatoire 1939. One of the finest tenors of the inter-war years. (R)

Antheil, George (b. Trenton, 8 June 1900; d. New York, 12 Feb. 1959). American composer. Studied with Sternberg and Bloch. His first opera, *Transatlantic* (1930), in which he employed jazz rhythms, aroused some interest. Other stage works include *Helen Retires* (1934), *Volpone* (1953), and two 1-act operas, *The Brothers* and *The Wish*.

Antigone. The daughter of Oedipus by his mother Jocasta. After Oedipus had put out his eyes, she accompanied him to Colonus, returning to Thebes in order to defy the tyrant Creon's ban on the burial of her brother. She was shut up in a cave, where she and her lover Haemon, Creon's son, killed themselves. Sophocles' drama (Athens 441 B.C.) has been the subject of some 30 operas, including works by Orlandini (1718), Zingarelli (1790), Honegger (1927), Pallantio (1942), and Orff (1949).

Antonia. The consumptive singer (sop.), one of Hoffmann's loves in Offenbach's *Les Contes d'Hoffmann*.

Antwerp (Flem. Antwerpen). Town in Belgium. The home of the Royal Flemish Opera, founded in 1893 by Hendrik Fontaine. Performances were originally given in the Royal Dutch Theatre, but since 1907 the Opera has had its own theatre. The company is subsidized by state, city, and province. All operas are sung in Flemish and over 300 artists are employed each season (end of Sept. to end of July). The large repertory includes works by Flemish composers, among them Jan Blockx and August de Boeck.

Anvil. A percussion instrument, imitating a real anvil, used in Wagner's *Ring* and other works. Real anvils appear on the stage in *Il Trovatore*, *Benvenuto Cellini*, and *Philémon et Baucis*; an anvil is split by Siegfried in Act 2 of *Siegfried* with the newly forged sword Nothung.

Apollo et Hyacinthus, seu Hyacinthi Metamorphosis. Latin comedy by Mozart; text by Rufinus Widl. Prod. Salzburg 13 May 1767; London, Fortune Theatre, 24 Jan. 1955. Not strictly an opera, but a set of nine musical intermezzi to Widl's *Clementia Croesi*.

Appia, Adolphe (b. Geneva, 1 Sept. 1862; d. Nyon, 29 Feb. 1928). Swiss scenic artist. After studying in Paris came under the influence of Bayreuth and Wagner. One of the first modern scenic reformers, relying on the minimum of scenery and on subtle lighting. Encouraged by the Countess de Béarn, who built a theatre in the grounds of her Paris house for him, and by Wolf Dohrn in Dresden. In 1923 invited to Milan, Sc., to design *Tristan*. His designs for *The Ring* (1899) and his analysis of *Tristan*, in which he differentiates between general brightness and what he termed 'formative light', greatly influenced modern designers. Among his writings, *La Mise-en-Scène du Drame Wagnérien* (Paris 1895) and *Die Musik und die Inszenierung* (Munich 1899) are the most important.

Arabella. Opera in 3 acts by Richard Strauss; text by Hugo von Hofmannsthal. Prod. Dresden 1 July 1933, with Ursuleac, Bokor, Jerger, cond. Krauss. London, C.G., 17 May 1934, same cast; N.Y., Met., 10 Feb. 1955, with Steber, Gueden, London, cond.

Kempe. Hofmannsthal's last Strauss libretto.

The story concerns the efforts of the impoverished Count Waldner (bass) to make a profitable marriage for his daughter Arabella (sop.). A wealth of Viennese complications intervenes before she is happily betrothed to Mandryka (bar.), and her younger sister Zdenka (sop.) to Arabella's former admirer Matteo (ten.).

Araia, Francesco (b. Naples, 25 June 1709; d. Bologna (?), before 1770 (?)). Italian composer. Notable as first of many Italian composers to serve the Russian court, and as the composer of the first opera in Russian, *Cephalus and Procris*, text by A. P. Sumarokov (St. Petersburg 10 Mar. 1755). The first opera composed for the Russian court was his *La Semiramide Riconosciuta* (St. Petersburg 1737). He returned to Italy after the death of Peter III in 1762.

Arangi-Lombardi, Giannina (b. Marigliano, Naples, 20 June 1891; d. Milan, 9 July 1951). Italian soprano. Studied Conservatorio San Pietro, Maiella, with Carelli. Début as mezzo, Rome, C., 1920, Lola. Soprano début Milan, Sc., 1923. Sang there 1923–30 under Toscanini; chosen by Melba to tour Australia with her, 1928; sang in leading opera houses of Europe (not Covent Garden) and South America. Noted for her Lucrezia Borgia, La Vestale, Gioconda, and Aida. Taught at the Conservatorio Giuseppe Verdi, Milan, 1938–47, and in Ankara from then until shortly before her death. (R)

Archibaldo. The blind King of Altura (bass) in Montemezzi's *L'Amore dei tre Re.*

Ardon gl'incensi. The opening words of Lucia's Mad Scene in Act 3 of Donizetti's *Lucia di Lammermoor*. Sung to flute obbligato.

Arditi, Luigi (b. Crescentino, nr. Vercelli, 22 July 1822; d. Hove, 1 May 1903). Italian conductor and composer. After appearances in America, he settled in London, where he conducted regularly at H.M.'s and C.G. Conducted many touring companies including those organized by Mapleson with Patti. Conducted first London performance of *Mefistofele*, *Cavalleria Rusticana*, and *Hänsel und Gretel*. Remembered as composer of the song 'Il Bacio'. Autobiography, *My Reminiscences* (1896).

Argentina (see *Buenos Aires*). Also the name of one of Rome's leading opera houses until the building of the Costanzi in 1880, and the scene of the premières of *Il Barbiere di Siviglia*, *I Due Foscari*, and *La Battaglia di Legnano*.

Aria (It. = air). The elaborated song-form of opera (and oratorio). Subdivisible into many detailed categories in the 18th century, but usually cast in three parts with the third a repeat of the first (**da capo aria**). An **arietta** is simpler, usually with no second, central part; an **ariette** is now the same, but once meant a short, light song inserted in a play or an opera with dialogue. An **arioso** stands roughly half-way between aria and recitative, the words being delivered in declamatory fashion over a more formal accompaniment.

Ariadne. Daughter of Minos and Pasiphae, who saved Theseus from the Minotaur's labyrinth by giving him a guide thread, and was later abandoned by him on Naxos, where she was married to Dionysos. The first Ariadne opera was Monteverdi's once famous *L'Arianna*, of which only the beautiful lament is extant. Another lost Ariadne opera is by Cambert or Grabu (1674). Among some 25 surviving are works by Kusser (1692), Porpora (1714), Handel (1734), Benda (1775—a melodrama which Mozart thought 'really excellent'), Edelmann (1782), Massenet (1906), Strauss (see below), Marcello (1727), and Milhaud's *L'Abandon d'Ariane* and *La Délivrance de Thésée* (1928).

Ariadne auf Naxos (Ariadne on Naxos). Opera in 1 act, later with a scenic prelude, by Strauss; text by Hugo von Hofmannsthal. Originally to be given after Molière's *comédie-ballet, Le Bourgeois Gentilhomme* (1670), for which Strauss had written incidental music; in this form prod. Stuttgart 25 Oct. 1912, with Jeritza,

Siems, Jadlowker; cond. Strauss. London, H.M.'s, 27 May 1913, with Von der Osten, Bosetti, Marak; cond. Beecham. Second version prod. Vienna 4 Oct. 1916, with Jeritza, Kurz, Környey, Lehmann; cond. Schalk. London, C.G., 27 May 1924; N.Y., Juilliard School, 5 Dec. 1934.

The work's first form was impracticable, requiring both a theatrical and an operatic company for the same evening. The second version substitutes for Molière's play a prelude in which word is sent from the *bourgeois gentilhomme*, who has engaged an opera company and a *commedia dell'arte* troupe, that their entertainments must take place simultaneously so as to be over in time for a firework display. The enraged, idealistic Composer (sop.) is soothed first by the old Music Master (bar.), then by Zerbinetta (sop.), leader of the rival group, and lastly by his faith in music.

On her island, Ariadne (sop.) is the subject of much comment from the comedians. She sings of her longing for the kingdom of death, to which Zerbinetta replies by trying to convert her to a more flirtatious philosophy. When Bacchus (ten.) arrives, Ariadne greets him as Death, and there follows a long love duet. They ascend into the sky together, which Zerbinetta considers acceptance of her advice.

Ariane et Barbe-Bleue (Ariadne and Bluebeard). Opera in 3 acts by Dukas; text adapted from Maeterlinck's drama (1901), written with Dukas in mind. Prod. Paris, O.C., 10 May 1907, with Georgette Leblanc, Vieuille; N.Y. 29 Mar. 1911, with Farrar, cond. Toscanini; London, C.G., 20 Apr. 1937, with Lubin. Dukas's only opera, initially successful. See also *Bluebeard*.

Arié, Raphael (b. Sofia, 22 Aug. 1920). Bulgarian bass. Began to study violin when 15, but three years later his voice was discovered by Cristo Brambaroff, leading baritone of the Sofia Opera, who suggested he study for opera. Concert début 1939, but career interrupted by war. After the liberation, Sofia Opera in *Eugene Onegin*, *Boris Godunov*, and *Prince Igor*. First prize Geneva 1946, which led to Scala début as the King in *The Love of the Three Oranges*, 1947. Appears regularly at the leading Italian Opera houses; Trulove in the world première of *The Rake's Progress* (Venice 1951). (R)

Arioso. See *Aria*.

Arkel. The blind, aged King of Allemonde (bass) in Debussy's *Pelléas et Mélisande*.

Arkor, André d' (b. Liège, 23 Feb. 1901). Belgian tenor. Studied Liège with Malherbe and Seguin. Début Liège, appearances at Ghent and Lyons. Leading tenor, Brussels, La M., for 17 years. Guest appearances at the Paris O.C. A distinguished Mozart singer. After the war director of the Théâtre Royal, Liège. (R)

Arlecchino. Theatrical capriccio in 1 act by Busoni; text by composer. Prod. in the same bill as his *Turandot*, Zürich 11 May 1917; London (B.B.C.) 1939; Glyndebourne 25 June 1954.

Arlesiana, L'. Opera in 3 acts (originally 4) by Cilea; text by Leopoldo Marenco, based on Alphonse Daudet's drama (1872). Prod. Milan, T.L., 27 Nov. 1897, with Caruso. Three-act version 1898. Revived occasionally in Italy, and best known for its tenor aria 'È la solita storia'.

Arline. The daughter (sop.) of Count Arnheim in Balfe's *The Bohemian Girl*.

Arme Heinrich, Der (Poor Henry). Opera in 3 acts by Pfitzner; text by James Grun after a medieval legend. Prod. Mainz, 2 Apr. 1895. Pfitzner's first opera.

Armenia. See *Yerevan*.

Armide. Opera in 5 acts by Gluck; text by Philippe Quinault, after Tasso's poem *Gerusalemme Liberata* (1575). Prod. Paris, O., 23 Sept. 1777, with Levasseur in the title role; London, C.G., 6 July 1906, with Bréval; N.Y., Met., 14 Nov. 1910, with Fremstad. Armida, a beautiful queen with supernatural powers, tries to win Rinaldo, but grows cooler by the time he begins to love her. When he is summoned away she sets her palace on fire and disappears. Among some 40 operas based on Tasso's story are works by Benedetto Ferrari (1639), Lully (1686), Handel (*Rinaldo*, 1711), Traetta (1761), Jommelli (1770), Salieri (1773), Mysliveček (1779), Haydn (1784), Häffner (*Renaud*, 1801), Righini (2-act operas, *Gerusalemme Liberata* and *La Selva Incantata*, 1803), Rossini (1817), and Dvořák (1904).

Arne, Thomas Augustine (b. London, 12 Mar. 1710; d. London, 5 Mar. 1778). English composer. By practising secretly he became successful enough to overcome parental opposition to a musical career. His first opera *Rosamond*, a resetting of a text by Addison, was well received in 1733. Other operas followed, and in 1738 his reputation was fully established with his music for Milton's *Comus*. He visited Ireland several times, producing operas there, and also became composer at Drury Lane and the Vauxhall Gardens. In 1760 he moved to Covent Garden, producing there his *Thomas and Sally*. In 1762 he successfully produced *Artaxerxes*, which he translated from Metastasio and set in Italian style with recitative replacing dialogue. There followed *Love in a Village* (1762) and *Olimpiade* (1764), in which Metastasio was now set in Italian. Arne was the finest English composer of his age, an age overshadowed by Handel and the Italians, but one to which he was able to make a distinctive contribution.

Arne, Michael (b. London, 1740 or 1741; d. London, 14 Jan. 1786). English composer, son of Thomas Arne. In the course of a chequered career that included periods devoted to alchemy, he wrote a number of operas and other stage pieces.

Arnold. A Swiss patriot (ten.) in love with the tyrant Gessler's daughter Mathilde in Rossini's *Guillaume Tell*.

Arnold, Samuel (b. London, 10 Aug. 1740; d. London, 22 Oct. 1802). English composer, organist, conductor, and editor. Best known in the operatic field for his numerous popular operas and other stage works written for London theatres.

Arnoldson, Sigrid (b. Stockholm, 20 Mar. 1861; d. Stockholm, 7 Feb. 1943). Swedish soprano. Daughter of the tenor Oscar Arnoldson, with whom she studied. Later studied with Maurice Strakosch, who taught her several of his sister-in-law Patti's roles; then Berlin with Désirée Artôt-Padilla. Début Moscow 1886, Rosina. Engaged by Augustus Harris for his trial season of Italian opera, London, D.L., 1887; C.G. 1888 and 1892–4; N.Y., Met., 1893. Charlotte in first London *Werther*. Retired in the early 1900's. (R)

Aroldo. See *Stiffelio*.

Artaxerxes. Opera in 3 acts by Arne; text by Metastasio in composer's translation. Prod. London, C.G., 2 Feb. 1762, when riots ensued because of the increased seat prices; N.Y. 31 Jan. 1828. Metastasio's famous libretto was first set by Leonardo Vinci in 1730; among some 45 other operas on the story are works by Hasse (also 1730), Gluck (his first opera—1741), Graun (1743), Terradellas (1744), Jommelli (1749), Galuppi (1751), Paisiello (1765), Piccinni (1766), Sacchini (1768), Cimarosa (1781), Anfossi (1788), and Isouard (1795).

Artists in Opera. Benvenuto Cellini (1500–71) has attracted many composers. Berlioz's *Benvenuto Cellini*, in which one scene depicts the casting of his Perseus, is by far the most famous; but he is also the subject of operas by Rossi (1845), Schlosser (1847), Lachner (1849), and Diaz. Albrecht Dürer appears in Baussnern's *Dürer in Venice* (1901); Mathias Grünewald is the subject of Hindemith's *Mathis der Maler* (1938); Michelangelo gave his name to operas by Isouard (1802) and Buongiorno (1903). Leonardo da Vinci's *Mona Lisa* is the title of Schillings's opera (1915); Rembrandt van Rijn was the subject of operas by Badings and Paul von Klenau; Granados's *Goyescas* was inspired by Goya; Stravinsky's *The Rake's Progress* by Hogarth; Gardner's *The Moon and Sixpence* by Gauguin; Menotti's *Amahl and the Night Visitors* by Hieronymus Bosch; and Strauss's *Friedenstag* by Velasquez.

Artôt, Désirée (b. Paris, 21 July 1835; d. Berlin, 3 Apr. 1907). Belgian mezzo-soprano, later soprano. Daughter of Jean Artôt, horn-player at Brussels, La M. Studied with M. Audran and Pauline Viardot. Engaged for Paris, O., on Meyerbeer's suggestion. After appearances in Italy and Germany in mezzo roles, emerged as a soprano, and sang as such in London concerts 1859–60; H.M.'s 1863 as Marie (*Fille du Régiment*), Violetta, and Adalgisa (then sung invariably by sopranos); C.G. 1864–6. On her visit to Russia in 1868 Tchaikovsky proposed marriage, but next year she married the Spanish baritone Mariano Padilla y Ramos, with whom she often sang thereafter. Their daughter **Lola Artôt de Padilla** (b. Sèvres, 5 Oct. 1880; d. Berlin, 12 Apr. 1933) was a pupil of her mother. Début 1904 Paris, O.C. After appearances at Berlin, K.O., joined Berlin Hofoper 1909. The first Berlin Octavian. (R)

Arts Council of Great Britain. An independent body, working without any interference from the Government. Its primary responsibility, as laid down in its Royal Charter (9 Aug. 1946), is 'to preserve and improve standards of performance in the various arts'. The council makes grants to C.G., S.W., and other operatic organizations, professional and amateur.

Arundell, Dennis (b. London, 22 July 1898). English actor, producer, author, and composer. Began to study the piano at the age of 6; educated Tonbridge and Cambridge (Cyril Rootham and Stanford). Prod. Rootham's *The Two Sisters*, Cambridge 1922, and first stage performance of *Semele*, Cambridge 1925. Other important Cambridge productions included *The Soldier's Tale* (1928), Honegger's *King David* (his own translation, 1929), and *The Fairy Queen* (1931). Since the war has been responsible for a number of productions at Sadler's Wells, including *The School for Fathers* (*I Quattro Rusteghi*) (1946), *Schwanda* (own translation, 1948), *Faust* (1949), *Tosca* (1949), *Kat'a Kabanova* (1951), *Werther* (1952), *The Consul* (1954), and *The Flying Dutchman* (1958). Collaborated with Sir Thomas Beecham in his 1951 production of *The Bohemian Girl* at Covent Garden, and has produced several radio operas, including *A Tale of Two Cities* and *The Rake's Progress*. Abroad has worked at Helsinki and with the Elizabethan Opera Trust in Australia. Has composed two operas, *Ghost of Abel* and *A Midsummer Night's Dream*, and written three books, one on Purcell (1927), *The Critic at the Opera* (1957), and *The Story of Sadler's Wells* (1965).

Ascanio in Alba. *Serenata teatrale* in 2 acts by Mozart; text by Giuseppe Parini, perhaps after Count Claudio Nicolo Stampa. Prod. Milan, T.R.D., 17 Oct. 1771, a day after Hasse's last opera *Ruggiero*. It was then that Hasse may have made his legendary remark, 'This boy will make us all be forgotten.'

Astuzie Femminili, Le (Feminine Wiles). Opera in 2 acts by Cimarosa; text by Giovanni Palomba. Prod. Naples, Fondo, 16 Aug. 1794; London 21 Feb. 1804; occasionally revived in Italy.

Atanasov, Georgi (b. Plovdiv, 6 May 1881; d. Lago di Garda, 18 Nov. 1931). Bulgarian composer. Known as The Maestro and regarded as the founder of Bulgarian opera. Studied locally, at Bucharest Conservatory, and under Mascagni. Conducted military bands, symphony concerts, and from 1919 to 1923 Sofia Opera. Composed six operas—*Borislav* (1911), *Gergana* (1917), *Zapustyalata Vodenica* (1923), *Tsveta* (1929), *Kosara* (1929), *Altsek* (1930)—together with many operettas. He employed Bulgarian national themes and rhythms.

Athanael. The coenobite monk (bar.) who tries to save and then falls in love with Thaïs in Massenet's opera.

Athens (Gr. Athenai). Capital of Greece. Opera in Greece was for long given mostly by visiting companies (the first Italian opera was *Barbiere* in 1837), but the National Hellenic Opera was opened in 1898 by Denis Lavranga (q.v.). In 1940 the National Lyric Theatre was established in Athens. In 1944 this became the National Opera, and its first production was Samara's *Rhea*. Greek artists who have established themselves internationally since the war include Maria Callas, Arda Mandikian, Eleanor Nikolaidi, and Nicola Zaccaria. In 1955 the International Festival of Music and Drama was held in Athens, and performances of *Orfeo*, *Idomeneo*, and other works, with several international guest artists in leading roles, were given at the open-air theatre of Herodes Atticus. Special performances of *Norma* and *Medea*, with Callas, have been given in the ancient theatre at Epidauros.

Atlantide, L'. Opera in 4 acts by Tomasi; text by Francis Didelot, after Pierre Benoit's novel. Prod. Mulhouse 26 Feb. 1954. Also title of a cantata by Falla, prod. Milan, Sc., 14 June 1962.

Attaque du Moulin, L' (The Attack on the Mill). Opera in 4 acts by Bruneau; text by Louis Gallet after the story in Zola's *Soirées de Médan* (1880). Prod. Paris, O.C., 23 Nov. 1893; London, C.G., 4 July 1894; N.Y., New Theatre, 8 Feb. 1910.

Atterberg, Kurt (b. Göteborg, 12 Dec. 1887). Swedish composer. His works, well regarded in Sweden, include five operas—*Härvard Harpoklekare* (1919), *Bäckahästen* (1925), *Fanal* (1934), *Aladdin* (1941), and *Stormen* (1948).

At the Boar's Head. Opera in 1 act by Holst; text by composer after Shakespeare's dramas *Henry IV*, Parts 1 and 2 (1597–8). Prod. Manchester, by B.N.O.C., 3 Apr. 1925, with Allin, T. Davies, Constance Willis, cond. Sargent; N.Y., MacDowell Club, 16 Feb. 1935.

Attila. Opera in prologue and 3 acts by Verdi; text by Temistocle Solera. Prod. Venice, F., 17 Mar. 1846, with Sophie Lowe, Guasco, Marini, and Costantini; London, H.M.'s, 14 Mar. 1848; N.Y. 15 Apr. 1850. Revived in concert form, Venice 1951; revived on stage, Florence 1962. One of Verdi's patriotic operas, concerning the invasion of Italy by the Huns and Attila's murder by his intended bride Odabella. Its trio for soprano, tenor, and bass has frequently been sung in church with adapted sacred words.

Auber, Daniel François Esprit (b. Caen, 29 Jan. 1782; d. Paris, 12 May 1871). French composer. His early career was hampered by his extreme shyness, but he had won some recognition before turning to opera. *L'Erreur d'un Moment* (1805), his first opera, was a relative failure; his first success came with *La Bergère Châtelaine* (1820). From then on he joined forces with Scribe; together they produced a long series of comic and serious operas, the most famous being *Le Maçon* (1825), *La Muette de Portici* (1828), *Fra Diavolo* (1830), *Le Cheval de Bronze* (1835), *Le Domino Noir* (1837), and *Les Diamants de la Couronne* (1841). Auber's gifts exactly coincided with a fashion in taste. Scribe, the most adept theatrical craftsman of the day, provided neat, effective plots. The charm, sparkle, and verve of Auber's music delighted a public with no wish beyond the lightest entertainment—though thinner than Hérold's, less well constructed than Boïeldieu's, its brilliance was all-compensating. Auber's grand opera *La Muette de Portici*, also known from its hero as *Masaniello*, is another matter; greater depth of feeling pervades the music, as well as an originality much admired by Wagner. It is also the first opera in which the people and their aspirations are treated heroically: a performance in Brussels in 1830 was the spark that touched off the revolution against the Dutch.

Auden, W. H. (b. York, 21 Feb. 1907). English poet. He has written libretti for several operas—Britten's *Paul Bunyan* (New York, Columbia University, 1941—unpublished and withdrawn) and, with Chester Kallman, Stravinsky's *The Rake's Progress* (Venice 1951), Henze's *Elegy for Young Lovers* (1960) and *The Bassarids* (1966), and Nabokov's *Love's Labour's Lost*. Also with Kallman, has translated *Don Giovanni* and *Die Zauberflöte*.

Audience. The audience is an integral part of an operatic performance, and its reaction to artists and to the work can make or mar a performance. Audience reaction can even colour a work's career, as with the disastrous premières of *Il Barbiere di Siviglia*, *Norma*, *La Traviata*, *Tannhäuser* (Paris version), and more recently Nono's *Intolleranza*. Demonstrations by claques (q.v.) or cliques against the composer, individual artists, and conductors may be cited as instances of professional or semi-professional audience intervention. In days when opera was principally the pastime of the nobility, the audience regarded itself as no less important than events on the stage. The house lights were left on, so that ladies could quiz each other through their opera glasses, commenting upon their rivals' appearance and demeanour.

Audience participation in Italy is a source of great enjoyment, if not always to the performers, and Italians resent attempts by uninstructed visitors at obtaining silence during the music. The audience at La Scala (except for the noisy members of the first and second galleries) has a reputation among singers for 'sitting on its hands'. In Naples, however, the audience behaves as a large family outing, arriving late, chatting during tedious parts of the work, and purring with pleasure when a favourite singer neatly turns a phrase or produces a fine top note. Notoriously the hardest audience to please is at Parma, a town which is therefore much feared by singers. It is said that a tenor leaving by train the morning after a poor performance asked for his bags to be carried by a porter, who declined on artistic grounds.

German and Austrian audiences are far more serious, their demeanour sometimes approaching that of a church congregation. This is especially so at Bayreuth, where the slightest creak from the uncomfortable wooden seats is regarded as want of seriousness. English audiences continually surprise visiting singers by their warmth and discrimination. Americans are generally regarded as much more prodigal with their enthusiasm.

The largest opera audiences are to be found in the great open-air performances in Italy during the summer, e.g. at the Verona Arena. The smallest audience in operatic history was King Ludwig of Bavaria, who commanded private performances of Wagner in the National Theatre in Munich.

Audran, Edmond (b. Lyons, 12 Apr. 1840; d. Tierceville, 17 Aug. 1901). French composer, principally of operettas. The most popular was *La Mascotte* (1880), a success he never equalled despite considerable subsequent development and expansion of his style. *La Poupée* (1896) represents the culmination of this, and has been claimed as his masterpiece.

Aufstieg und Fall der Stadt Mahagonny (Rise and Fall of the City of Mahagonny). Opera in 3 acts by Weill; text by Brecht. Prod. Leipzig 9 Mar. 1930 (orig. prod. as a *Songspiel* [*sic*], Baden-Baden, 1927); London, S.W., 16 Jan. 1963. Revivals in Germany and Italy since 1945.

Mahagonny is the city of material pleasure. Jenny and her colleagues move in, followed by Jimmy and his lumberjack friends on the spend; there develops a love affair between the two, based upon hard cash as well as affection. A hurricane threatens the city, but is miraculously deflected. Act 2 illustrates Gluttony, Love, Fighting, and Drinking, all carried on to excess and without restraint. Jimmy cannot pay for his drinks: tried according to Mahagonny's scale of values, he is sentenced to two days for indirect murder, four years for 'seduction, by means of money', and, for not paying his whisky bill, death.

Au fond du temple saint. The tenor-baritone duet for Nadir and Zurga in Scene 1 of Bizet's *Les Pêcheurs de Perles*, in which they recall the beautiful Leïla they both once loved.

Auftrittslied (Ger. = Entry Song). The aria in which a character introduces himself to the audience either directly or by addressing another character, e.g. Papageno's 'Der Vogelfänger' in Mozart's *Die Zauberflöte*.

Augsburg. Town in Bavaria, Germany. The present Stadttheater (cap. 1,010) was opened in Nov. 1956 with *Figaro*. In the summer, open-air performances are given at the Roten Tor, and since the war there have been revivals of *Rienzi* and *Nabucco*.

Austin, Frederick (b. London, 30 Mar. 1872; d. London, 10 Apr. 1952). English baritone. Studied under Charles Lunn. Début London, C.G.,

1908, Gunther in the English *Ring* under Richter; then principal baritone, Beecham Company. Peachum in his new version of *The Beggar's Opera* (Lyric, Hammersmith, 1920). Artistic Director of the B.N.O.C. 1924. General administrator of Beecham's Imperial League of Opera in the 1920's. Taught on retirement—pupils include Constance Shacklock. (R) His son **Richard** (b. 26 Dec. 1903) has conducted with the Carl Rosa and at Sadler's Wells. Head of the opera department, R.C.M., from 1953. (R)

Austin, Sumner (b. London, 24 Sept. 1888). English baritone. Carl Rosa 1919, then sang with the O'Mara Opera Company. Valuable member of Old Vic Opera Company in the 1920's; Sadler's Wells until 1940, being particularly distinguished in Mozart. Produced several operas at Sadler's Wells, including *The Travelling Companion*, *The Bartered Bride*, *Falstaff*, *Walküre*, *Don Carlos*, and *The Wreckers*. After the war taught at the G.S.M., and produced *Wozzeck* (1951) and *Tannhäuser* (1955) at C.G.

Austral (orig. Wilson), **Florence** (b. Melbourne, 26 Apr. 1894; d. Newcastle, N.S.W., 15 May 1968). As a child was known by her stepfather's name, Favaz. Scholarship, Melbourne Conservatory, 1914. Went to New York, 1918, for further study with Sibella and offered Met. contract, which she refused. Engaged by C.G. for the Grand Season of 1921 which was abandoned. Début 1922, Brünnhilde, B.N.O.C. Also Aida and Isolde with company, and Brünnhilde during international seasons 1924, 1929, and 1933. Guest artist, S.W., 1937–9; appearances in Berlin, America, and Australia. (R)

Australia. Until after the Second World War, opera in Australia was mostly based on visiting companies. The first opera performance was of Bishop's *Clari* in 1834, followed ten years later by *Cenerentola*. In 1845 Carandini, a political refugee, founded an opera company, with his wife as prima donna, and gave performances of *Freischütz* and *Fra Diavolo*. From 1850 to 1860 the Anna Bishop Opera Company gave seasons in New South Wales and Victoria, and then various touring companies visited the country until the turn of the century. One of the most enterprising of these was the Martin Simonson Italian Grand Opera Company in 1886–7 which gave performances of such rarities as *Belisario* and *Roberto Devereux*. From 1901 until the First World War the J. C. Williamson and Quinlan companies gave seasons and the artists included John MacCormack, Eleanora de Cisneros, and Scandiani. In 1924 Melba organized a company for her farewell tour and the artists included Toti dal Monte, Lina Scavizzi, Dino Borgioli, and Apollo Granforte; the company returned in 1928 strengthened by Arangi-Lombardi, Merli, Autori, De Muro Lomanto, and the conductor Bavagnoli. In 1932 the Imperial Grand Opera Company, with Lina Pagliughi, Primo Montanari, Pedro Mirassou, and Granforte, visited Australia.

After the Second World War further Italian seasons were organized by Nevin Tait under the musical direction of Franco Ghione and Manno Wolf-Ferrari. The two leading native groups, the National Theatre Opera Company of Melbourne and the New South Wales National Opera of Sydney, pooled their resources in 1952 as the first step towards a national opera, each receiving grants of £A5,000 from their states. Singers in these two companies included Elizabeth Fretwell, Marie Collier, and Ronald Dowd, who later came to London. A rivalry developed between the two organizations, and both carried on their separate existences until the establishment of the Elizabethan Theatre Trust in 1954 which suggested a merger of the two companies. In 1955 another Italian company visited Australia, and that year Warwick Braithwaite (q.v.) assumed the artistic directorship of the Sydney company, resigning half-way through the season because of managerial interference. With the arrival of Hugh Hunt, director of the Elizabethan Trust, it was announced that the Trust would not take over the N.O.C., but that a new company, under the Trust, would tour the Commonwealth. In 1955 the

N.S.W. State government launched an international competition for the design of a new Sydney opera house, won by the Dane Joern Utzon. In July 1956 the Trust launched its first season at Adelaide with a four-week season of Mozart operas, produced by Dennis Arundell and conducted by Joseph Post, followed by a tour of the main cities lasting until February 1957. The 1957–8 season saw the return of Joan Hammond, Elsie Morison, and Ronald Dowd. In December 1957 Karl Rankl (q.v.) was appointed musical director of the Trust. He launched his first season in July 1958. Several singers who had sung under him at Covent Garden were invited, including Sylvia Fisher, Rosina Raisbeck, Constance Shacklock, and Raymond Nilsson. He resigned in 1961. In 1965, Joan Sutherland toured the country with her own opera company; her husband, Richard Bonynge, was music director.

In 1969 the Trust was renamed the Australian Opera Company, with Carlo Felice Cillario as music director. Cillario resigned in 1971, and Edward Downes was appointed music director from 1 January 1972. Stephen Hall is artistic director and Lord Harewood European adviser. The new opera house is scheduled to open in the spring of 1973.

Austria. See *Bregenz*, *Graz*, *Salzburg*, *Vienna*.

Autori, Fernando (b. Calatafime, 1884; d. Florence, 4 Oct. 1937). Italian bass. Studied medicine, then singing with M. Cantelli. Début Palermo, 1913. Milan, Sc., 1923–36; London, C.G., 1924–34. Noted for his Leporello, Don Basilio, Geronimo, and other buffo roles, as well as Archibaldo in *L'Amore dei tre Re*. Was a member for a short time of the Covent Garden touring company and sang in English. An attempt to sing the title role in *Casanova* at the London Coliseum was a failure. His clever caricatures of himself and his colleagues were often exhibited at Covent Garden. (R)

Avant de quitter ces lieux. Valentine's (bar.) aria in Act 2 of Gounod's *Faust*. Composed for the English production with Santley.

Ayrton, William (b. London, 24 Feb. 1777; d. London, 8 Mar. 1858). English writer on music and theatrical manager. As music director of the King's Theatre gave English premières of *Così fan tutte* (1811), *Zauberflöte* (1811), and *Don Giovanni* (1817).

Azerbaijan. See *Baku*.

Azione sacra (It. = sacred action). Italian term occasionally used for an opera on a religious subject, e.g. Refice's *Cecilia*.

Azione teatrale (It. = theatrical action). Italian 17th-century term for an opera or musical festival play.

Azucena. The gipsy (con.), Manrico's mother, in Verdi's *Il Trovatore*.

B

Baccaloni, Salvatore (b. Rome, 14 Apr. 1900; d. N.Y., 31 Dec. 1969). Italian bass. Boy sopr. Sistine Chapel. Studied with Kaschmann. Début Rome, Ap., 1922, Bartolo (*Barbiere*). Engaged 1926 by Toscanini for La Scala, where after three seasons in normal bass repertory he specialized in buffo roles. London, C.G., 1928–9; Glyndebourne 1936–9, Leporello, Bartolo, Osmin, Alfonso, and Pasquale (his greatest role); N.Y., Met., since 1940. Appeared in every major opera house and considered by many the greatest buffo since Lablache. (R)

Bacchus. The god (ten.) who finally appears and carries off Ariadne in Strauss's *Ariadne auf Naxos*.

Bach, John Christian (b. Leipzig, 5 Sept. 1735; d. London, 1 Jan. 1782). German composer. The youngest son of Johann Sebastian and Anna Magdalena Bach. Visited Italy in 1756, where his first opera *Artaserse* was produced in 1761. Quickly established himself in London from 1762, initially with *Orione*, in which he introduced clarinets into an English opera orchestra for the first time. Appointed music-master to the queen. Seven of his 13 operas were first produced in London.

Bada, Angelo (b. Novara, 1875; d. Novara, 24 Mar. 1941). Italian tenor. Sang small roles at Milan, Sc., London, C.G., &c., and was leading comprimario tenor at N.Y., Met., 1908–38, singing in many American premières. Considered one of the best interpreters of Shuisky, Spoletta, Flaminio (*L'Amore dei tre Re*), and Valzacchi. (R)

Badini, Ernesto (b. Milan, 14 Sept. 1876; d. Milan, 6 July 1937). Italian baritone. Studied Milan Conservatory. Début Pavia 1900, Figaro (*Barbiere*). Studied buffo roles with Cesari from 1906; second début Milan, T. d. V., 1908, Beckmesser. Sang Ford at the Verdi celebrations, Parma 1913, under Toscanini, who brought him to La Scala in 1921 where he remained until his death. C.G.'s first Schicchi, and sang regularly there until 1931. Also Salzburg and Florence Festivals. (R)

Bahr-Mildenburg, Anna (b. Vienna, 29 Nov. 1872; d. Vienna, 27 Jan. 1947). Austrian soprano. Studied Vienna with Papier, Hamburg with Pollini. Début Hamburg 1895. Soon became leading Wagnerian soprano. Bayreuth 1897 Kundry, and later Ortrud. London, C.G., 1906, Isolde and Elisabeth, and first London Klytemnestra 1910; Vienna 1908–17. After retirement taught in Munich, and 1921–6 stage director at Nationaltheater. 1938 taught in Berlin. Married writer Hermann Bahr 1909, with whom she wrote *Bayreuth und das Wagner-Theater* (1910). (R)

Baklanov, George (b. St. Petersburg, 18 Jan. 1882; d. Basle, 6 Dec. 1938). Russian baritone. Studied St. Petersburg with Prianishnikov, and Milan. Début Kiev 1903; London, C.G., 1910; Boston 1916; Chicago 1917–26. Much admired as Scarpia, Rigoletto, and Manfredo (*L'Amore dei tre Re*). (R)

Baku. Town in the U.S.S.R., capital of Azerbaijan. Baku has had a primitive form of opera known as *mugam* (still performed) since the 14th or 15th century. The opera house, one of the first in the Near and Middle East, was founded in 1908, and has occupied an important place in the city's life. The first Azerbaijani opera was Hadjibekov's *Leila and Medjnun* (1907); this and the same composer's *Kerogly* (1937) and *Arshin Mal Alan* (*The Commercial Traveller*) are in the repertory alongside Russian and European classics.

Bâle. *See* Basel.

Balfe, Michael (b. Dublin, 15 May 1808; d. Rowney Abbey, Herts., 20 Oct. 1870). Irish composer and singer. Studied in Ireland and did various odd musical jobs in London before leaving for Italy, where he continued his studies, some under Filippo Galli. Paris 1827, Figaro, with Rossini's approval. Principal baritone Palermo, 1829–30, where his first complete opera, *I Rivali di Se Stesso*, was produced. He returned to London in 1835, and began his career as a composer of English operas with *The Siege of Rochelle* (Drury Lane). He also sang Papageno in the first performance in English of *The Magic Flute*. Back in Paris by 1841, he continued his career there, returning to England for the greatest success of his 29 operas, *The Bohemian Girl* (1843). After *Bianca* (1860) he was closely associated with the Pyne–Harrison project for an English national opera. He continued to travel, making two successful visits to Russia, before turning gentleman farmer and retiring to an estate in Hertfordshire. His highest aspiration as a composer would have been to be considered an English Bellini: his easy melodies, grateful alike to singer and listener, won him wide popularity, especially in his ballads. However, Sir Thomas Beecham's revival of *The Bohemian Girl* at C.G. in 1951 was coolly received.

Ballet in Opera. Just as ballet had been an integral part of the masque and other entertainments from which opera derived, so it was often retained in one form or another in opera until almost the end of the 19th century. Although ballets were included in some of the works of Rossini, Donizetti, and Verdi (there is even ballet music for *Otello*), they were rarely an integral part of Italian opera. In France, however, where ballet became established in the French court in the 16th century, it assumed considerable importance in the works of Lully and Rameau, and even Gluck, who strove to reform opera, had to include formal ballets in his French operas as well as in his Paris version of *Orfeo*. Rousseau, in his *Dictionary of Music*, deplored the irrelevance of the opera ballets of his time. Meyerbeer naturally provided for spectacular ballets in his French grand operas, and so popular did the opera ballet become in Paris that Wagner had to rewrite and develop the opening scene of *Tannhäuser* (the Venusberg scene) to meet the demands of the Parisians—he refused to write a ballet for the second act, however. Berlioz, another reformer, was asked to orchestrate Weber's *Invitation to the Dance* for the 1841 Paris production of *Der Freischütz*, and dances from *L'Arlésienne* have been utilized as a ballet in the last act of *Carmen*.

Russian opera composers have made much use of ballet, especially in scenes of pageantry and spectacle (*Eugene Onegin*, *Prince Igor*, *May Night*, &c.); and operas by composers of other nationalities often include dances in their works (e.g. Smetana in *The Bartered Bride*, Dvořák in *Rusalka*, Vaughan Williams in *Hugh the Drover*, Britten in *Gloriana*). See also *Opera-ballet*.

Balling, Michael (b. Heidingsfeld am M., 29 Aug. 1866; d. Darmstadt, 1 Sept. 1925). German conductor. Educated Würzburg. Viola player at Bayreuth, where he became assistant conductor 1896; conducted *Parsifal*, *Tristan*, and *Ring* between 1904 and 1924. Conducted *Ring* in English for the Denhof Company in Edinburgh 1910, and *Orfeo* with Brema in London, Savoy. Succeeded Richter as conductor of Hallé 1912. From 1919 music director at Darmstadt. From 1912 editor of Breitkopf and Härtel's edition of Wagner.

Ballo in Maschera, Un (A Masked Ball). Opera in 3 acts by Verdi; text by Somma based on Scribe's libretto for Auber's *Gustave III ou Le Bal Masqué*, in turn based on fact. Prod. Rome, Ap., 17 Feb. 1859; N.Y., Ac. of M., 11 Feb. 1861; London, Ly., 15 June 1861, with Tietjens, Giuglini, Delle Sedie.

When Verdi first submitted his libretto to the San Carlo Theatre, Naples, the Neapolitan censor protested that the assassination of a king could not be shown on the opera stage and demanded that Verdi adapt his music to a new libretto; Verdi refused and left Naples. A Rome impresario offered to produce an altered version of the work; and so the locale was changed from 18th-century Stockholm to 17th-century Boston, King Gustavus of Sweden becoming Count Riccardo,

Governor of Boston. In this form it has generally remained until the present. Another version used at the Paris première sets the story in Naples, making Gustavus the Duke of Olivarez. At C.G. in 1952 (Dent's translation) the action was placed again in Sweden and the characters given their original names; this version was adopted in one or two German theatres, and at Paris in 1958. The Stockholm Opera's 1958 production is particularly accurate in details of the original events.

Act 1. Sam and Tom (Counts Ribbing and Horn) (basses), leaders of a conspiracy to murder Riccardo (King Gustavus III), await him with friends and courtiers. Oscar (sop.), the page, hands Riccardo (ten.) a list of guests for the Masked Ball, including Amelia, wife of Riccardo's friend and secretary Renato (Count Anckerstroem) (bar.). Riccardo is secretly in love with her. The Minister of Justice asks Riccardo to banish Ulrica (Mam'zelle Arvidson) (mezzo), a fortune-teller in whose hut political plots are hatched. Riccardo proposes that all the court should visit her disguised.

Amelia (sop.) has come to Ulrica for help in combating her love for Riccardo. The latter overhears Ulrica tell Amelia to seek a magic herb that grows beneath the gallows outside the city walls. Riccardo now asks for his fortune to be told, and learns that he will be killed by the first person to shake his hand. No one will take his hand; then Renato, anxious for Riccardo's safety, arrives. Riccardo seizes the hand of his best friend, and treats the whole thing as a joke.

Act 2. Amelia comes to pick the herb. She is joined by Riccardo, and they declare their love. Riccardo's departure from the city has been noticed and the conspirators are on their way to murder him, but Renato arrives with a warning. Amelia veils her face, Renato and Riccardo exchange cloaks, and the latter asks his friend to escort Amelia home without attempting to recognize her. But Renato is prevented from leaving by the arrival of Sam and Tom and the conspirators. To save her husband's life, Amelia reveals her identity; the jealous Renato asks Sam and Tom to meet him at his home and drags Amelia away.

Renato tells Amelia she must die. Sam and Tom arrive, and Renato reveals that he knows their plot, but asks to join them. They decide to draw lots for the privilege of killing Riccardo, and when Amelia appears Renato makes her draw a name from an urn. It is his own.

Act 3. Riccardo has decided to end the affair by sending Amelia and her husband abroad. Oscar arrives with a note from an unknown lady warning him that his life is in danger.

The Masked Ball is in progress. Renato tricks Oscar into divulging Riccardo's costume, and just as he is bidding a last farewell to Amelia, Renato stabs him (shoots him, in the Stockholm setting). Riccardo declares that Amelia is innocent, and dies forgiving his enemies.

Bampton, Rose (b. Cleveland, 28 Nov. 1908). American soprano, orig. contralto. Studied Curtis Institute, Philadelphia, with Connell and Queena Mario. Début Chautauqua 1929, Siebel. N.Y., Met., 1932, as Laura (*Gioconda*). Sop. début N.Y., Met., May 1937, Leonora (*Trovatore*), but two months later sang Amneris, C.G. Won warm praise as Donna Anna and Alceste, and in the 1940's undertook several Wagner roles including Kundry and Sieglinde. (R)

Banti, Brigida Giorgi (b. nr. Piacenza, *c.* 1756; d. Bologna, 18 Feb. 1806). Italian soprano. She began life as a street singer, and made her way to Paris singing at inns and cafés. The Director of the Opéra heard her and engaged her after a brilliant audition. Difficulties followed a spectacular début owing to her carelessness and lack of training, though she later had considerable successes in other countries, especially England (1779–1802). Her voice was said to have been pure, rich, and even throughout a wide range, with a beautiful cantabile; while her acting ability and high spirits made her unfailingly popular. After Mrs. Billington's return to London she went back to Italy; she bequeathed her larynx, which was of great size, to the municipality of Bologna, who preserved it in spirits. Her life by her son appeared in 1869.

Bantock, Granville (b. London, 7 Aug. 1868; d. London, 16 Oct. 1946). English composer. He developed late, though already as a student he had written a 1-act opera *Caedmar* (Crystal Palace, 18 Oct. 1893). He took on various conducting jobs while gradually emerging as a composer. In 1900 he became principal of the Birmingham and Midland Institute School of Music; from this period his own mature works date. He was attracted by oriental subjects and Hebridean folklore. In 1924 produced, with Marjorie Kennedy-Fraser as librettist, *The Seal-Woman* (Birmingham). Though unfashionable now, his music has geniality and enterprise. (R)

Baranović, Krešimir (b. Šibenik, 25 July 1894). Yugoslav conductor and composer. Has held appointments in Zagreb, Belgrade, and Bratislava, and toured with Pavlova's company in 1927 and 1928. Professor at the Belgrade Academy and a director and conductor of the Serbian State Symphony Orchestra. Has written two operas, *Striženo-Košeno* and *The Turks are Coming*. (R)

Barbaia, Domenico (b. Milan, *c.* 1775; d. Posilippo, 16 Oct. 1841). Italian impresario. Starting as a waiter (inventing *Schlagobers*) and a circus manager, he became director of the Teatro San Carlo in Naples (1809–24) and of the Kärntnertor Theatre and the Theater an der Wien in Vienna (1821–8). Here he introduced Rossini's operas and commissioned *Euryanthe*. He was manager of the Scala, Milan (1826–32), and again of the San Carlo. He commissioned Bellini's first successes, and works from Rossini and Donizetti. Emil Lucka's novel, *Der Impresario* (Vienna 1937), deals with his life.

Barber, Samuel (b. Westchester, Pa., 9 Mar. 1910). American composer. He did not attempt an opera until 1958, when *Vanessa*, libretto by Menotti, was produced at the Met., and at Salzburg that summer. His *Antony and Cleopatra* opened the new Met. in 1966.

Barbier, Jules (b. Paris, 8 Mar. 1822; d. Paris, 16 Jan. 1901). French librettist. He collaborated with Michel Carré on many French librettos, principally those for Gounod's *Faust*, *Polyeucte*, *Philémon et Baucis*, and *Roméo et Juliette*, Meyerbeer's *Dinorah*, Thomas's *Mignon*, *Francesca da Rimini*, and *Hamlet*, and Offenbach's *Contes d'Hoffmann*.

Barbier von Bagdad, Der (The Barber of Bagdad). Opera in 2 acts by Cornelius; text by composer, based on the *Thousand and One Nights*. Prod. Weimar (under Liszt) 15 Dec. 1858; N.Y. 3 Jan. 1890; London, Savoy, 9 Dec. 1891. Owing to local intrigues, at first a failure; since Mottl's revision and revival (Karlsruhe 1884) it has become popular.

The plot is highly complicated, turning on the efforts of Nureddin, abetted by the barber Abul Hassan, at contriving a meeting with Margiana, the Caliph's daughter, whom he loves. Despite Nureddin's imprisonment and near-suffocation in a chest, all is eventually resolved and the Caliph's blessing obtained.

Barbiere di Siviglia, Il (orig. Almaviva, ossia L'Inutile Precauzione) (The Barber of Seville). Opera in 2 acts by Rossini; text by Sterbini, after Beaumarchais's comedy (1778). Prod. Rome, Arg., 20 Feb. 1816, with Giorgi-Righetti (coloratura-mezzo, though the role is now usually taken by a soprano), M. Garcia, Zamboni, cond. Rossini; London, Hm., 10 Mar. 1818, with Fodor, Garcia, Naldi; N.Y., Park Theatre, 3 May 1819. The first performance in Rome was one of the greatest fiascos in opera, as is related by Stendahl and Giorgi-Righetti among others. As Paisiello's opera enjoyed great popularity, the opera was originally called *Almaviva, ossia L'Inutile Precauzione*; the title *Il Barbiere di Siviglia* was first used at Bologna in 1816. The overture to the opera had already been used by Rossini for *Aureliano in Palmira* and *Elisabetta, Regina d'Inghilterra*.

Act 1. Count Almaviva (ten.), pretending to be Lindoro, a poor student, is serenading Rosina (sop.), ward of the old Doctor Bartolo, who wants to marry her himself. Aided by Figaro (bar.), barber and general factotum, he plans to gain entrance to Bartolo's house disguised as a drunken soldier.

Rosina writes a note to Almaviva. Bartolo (bass) becomes highly suspicious when he hears that Almaviva has been seen in town. Don Basilio (bass), the rascally music master, suggests that a little slander will sully Almaviva's reputation. When they go to draw up a bill of marriage for Bartolo and Rosina, she gives Figaro her note. Almaviva now appears in his disguise as a soldier and demands lodgings. A brawl ensues, and soldiers enter to arrest him. Almaviva discloses his identity to the officer and the soldiers all salute him, much to Bartolo's amazement.

Act 2. Almaviva now returns disguised as Don Alonso, a singing teacher, and tells Bartolo that he is Basilio's deputy. Rosina sings a piece to show off her voice (generally 'Contro un cor', though it is customary for the piece to be chosen by the soprano—see *Added Numbers*). Basilio arrives, but is bribed by Almaviva. While Figaro is shaving Bartolo, the latter overhears Rosina and Almaviva making plans to elope that night. Bartolo tells Rosina that Lindoro is not true to her and is planning to hand her over to his master Almaviva. Rosina is distraught and agrees to marry Bartolo, who sends for a notary. A storm breaks out, and up a ladder climb Figaro and Almaviva. Rosina accuses him of treachery, but he reveals his true identity to her. The notary arrives and is forced by Figaro to marry the couple, with Basilio as a witness. When Bartolo learns that Almaviva does not require the dowry set aside for Rosina, he accepts his fate philosophically.

Other operas on the play are by Elsperger (1783), Benda (1785), Schulz (1786), Isouard (1796), Morlacchi (1816), Dallargine (1868), and Graffigna (1879). See also below.

Barbiere di Siviglia, Il, ossia La Precauzione Inutile. Opera in 4 acts by Paisiello; text by Petrosellini after Beaumarchais's comedy (1778). Prod. St. Petersburg 26 Sept. 1782; London, Hm., 11 June 1789, with Storace, Kelly, Benucci; Philadelphia 1794(?). Various revivals in modern times.

Barbieri, Fedora (b. Trieste, 4 June 1920). Italian mezzo. Début Florence 1940, Fidalma. After appearances at all leading Italian opera houses, sang at Buenos Aires, Colón, 1947; C.G. 1950, with Scala Company as Quickly, and again 1957–8 as Azucena, Amneris, and Eboli; N.Y., Met., 1950–4 and 1956–7, making début on opening night of Bing's régime as Eboli. In Italy much admired as Orfeo and Carmen. (R)

Barbieri-Nini, Marianna (b. Florence, *c.* 1820; d. Florence, 27 Nov. 1887). Italian soprano. Teachers included Romani, Vaccai, and Pasta. Début Florence 1840, Lucrezia Borgia, appearing masked throughout first act and completely conquering the public by her voice alone. Considered one of the finest dramatic sopranos of her day and chosen by Verdi to create the leading soprano role in his *Due Foscari*, *Il Corsaro*, and *Macbeth*.

Barbirolli, (Sir) John (b. London, 2 Dec. 1899; d. London, 29 July 1970). English conductor of Italian parentage. Studied London, T.C.L. and R.A.M. Began career as cellist. Formed string orchestra in 1924; invited to join B.N.O.C. 1926. London, C.G., 1928, conducting *Butterfly* and *Bohème*. Music director C.G. English Company 1930. Conducted at C.G. until 1933 and again 1937 (*Tosca* and *Turandot*). Guest conductor S.W. Vienna State Opera 1946–7. Returned to C.G., Oct. 1951; guest conductor until 1954. In charge of new production of *Orfeo* with Ferrier, 1953, and *Tristan* when Fisher sang her first Isolde. (R)

Barcarolle. The generally accepted French for the Italian *barcaruola*, a boat-song. The rhythm, ostensibly imitating the motion of a gondola or other boat, is a gentle 6/8 with alternating strong and weak main beats. It has been used in opera by Hérold in *Zampa*, by Auber in *La Muette de Portici*, by Donizetti in *Marino Faliero*, by Verdi in *Un Ballo in Maschera*, and, most famously, by Offenbach in *Les Contes d'Hoffmann*.

Barcelona. Town in Cataluña, Spain. Opera was first given there at the Teatro de Santa Cruz, opened in 1708 with Caldara's *Il Più Bel Nome.* The first opera by a Catalan composer for the theatre was Durán's *Antigono* (1760). In 1838 a rival theatre was opened, Teatro Montesion, and the Santa Cruz changed its name to the Teatro Municipal. In 1843 opera was given at the Teatro Nuovo, and four years later the Teatro Liceo (cap. 4,000) opened; this was built with money raised by the Liceo Filarmonico and designed by Miguel Garriga Rocca. In 1861 it was destroyed by fire; 1,000 shares were issued to raise funds to rebuild the theatre, and the descendants of the shareholders still own the Liceo with the permanent right to the individual ownership of a seat. The present house (cap. 3,000) was designed by José Oriol Mistress and opened on 20 Apr. 1862; by its charter it must give at least one Spanish opera a year. The first opera in Catalan, Goula's *A la Voreta del Mar* (*On the Seashore*) was given there in 1881. Opera seasons are given yearly from Nov. until Mar. when French, German, Italian, and even Russian companies appear. Most great singers and conductors have appeared there.

Bardi, Giovanni, Count of Verino. See *Camerata.*

Bari. Town in Puglia, Italy. Opera seasons are regularly given at the Teatro Petruzzelli (cap. 4,000) opened on 11 Apr. 1903 with La Rotella's *Dea.* Its predecessor was the Teatro Piccinni (still in use), opened in 1853 with Donizetti's *Poliuto.*

Baritone (Gr. βαρύτονος = heavy-tone). The middle category of natural male voice. Several subdivisions exist within opera houses: the commonest in general use (though seldom by composers in scores) are given below, with examples of roles and their approximate *tessitura.* These divisions often overlap, and do not correspond from country to country. In general, distinction is more by character than by *tessitura,* especially in France: thus the examples of the roles give a more useful indication of the different voices' quality than any attempted technical definition.

German: Spielbariton (Don Giovanni: A♭–g'); Heldenbariton (Orestes in *Iphigénie en Tauride*: c–a♭'); hoher Bariton (Hans Heiling: c–a♭'); Kavalierbariton (the Count in *Capriccio*: c–a♭'). There is also the Bass-bariton (Wotan, Sachs: A♭–f).

The Italian baritono (Dandini: c–a♭') is not generally subdivided, though professionals may speak of *baritono brillante* and *baritono cantante.*

French: bariton (Toreador: c–a♭'); bariton-Martin (Pelléas: c–a').

Barnaba. The Inquisition spy (bar.) in Ponchielli's *La Gioconda.*

Barraud, Henry (b. Bordeaux, 23 Apr. 1900). French composer. His two operas, *La Farce de Maître Pathelin* (after a medieval play) (1938) and *Numance* (Salvador de Madariaga, after Cervantes) (1950), show his taste for medieval subjects.

Barrientos, Maria (b. Barcelona, 10 Mar. 1883; d. Ciboure, 8 Aug. 1946). Spanish soprano. Studied violin and piano Barcelona Conservatory, and then after only six months' vocal study made début at Barcelona as Inez when 15. London, C.G., 1903; N.Y., Met., 1916–20, where she was the first Queen of Shemakhan in 1918. *Puritani, Lakmé,* and *Sonnambula* were specially produced in N.Y. for her. (R)

Barsova, Valerija (b. Astrakhan, 13 June 1892; d. Sochi, 1967). Russian soprano. Studied Moscow. Début Moscow. Leading soprano at Bolshoy Theatre 1920–48, singing in 22 operas. Roles include Ludmilla, Antonida, Rosina, Violetta, Gilda. Later Professor of Singing at Moscow Conservatory.

Bartered Bride, The (Cz. Prodaná Nevěsta). Opera in 3 acts by Smetana; text by Sabina. Prod. Prague 30 May 1866; Chicago, Haymarket, 20 Aug. 1893; London, D.L., 26 June 1895. After the first few performances in Prague, where it was given in two acts with spoken dialogue, Smetana made several alterations to the score. A second version was heard in Prague in 1869 and a third and definitive version

—in which sung recitatives replaced the spoken dialogue and the two acts became three—in Sept. 1870.

The opera takes place during spring festival time in a village in Bohemia in the middle of the last century.

Act 1. The Village Square. Mařenka (sop.) is sad while the village rejoices. She loves Jeník (ten.), a handsome young stranger, but her parents have decided she must marry a man she has never seen, the son of Tobias Mícha. Kecal (bass), the marriage broker, has arranged this and paints a glowing picture of the prospective bridegroom, but Mařenka refuses to think of anyone but Jeník. The act ends with a spirited polka.

Act 2. The Village Inn. After a chorus in praise of beer and a gay dance, the inn empties and Vašek (ten.), Mícha's son, enters. He is slow-witted and stammers. Mařenka enters and realizes that this is the man she must marry. Vašek does not know who she is, so she draws a very unflattering picture of herself and makes Vašek promise not to have anything to do with Mařenka. Kecal now arrives and tries to interest Jeník in another girl whose name he has on his books. He offers him 300 crowns to renounce Mařenka. Jeník agrees, if Mařenka will marry the son of Mícha. Kecal agrees and calls in the villagers to witness the document.

Act 3. The Village Square. A travelling circus arrives, and Vašek falls for the dancer Esmeralda, who suggests to the circus-master that he should replace the drunkard who plays the performing bear. She teaches Vašek to dance. His parents want him to meet Mařenka but he refuses. Mařenka now appears, heart-broken by the news that Jeník has sold her. She agrees to consider marrying Vašek, and laments her sad lot. When the cheerful Jeník arrives he so annoys Mařenka that she resolves to marry Vašek. Kecal, the villagers, the parents of both Mařenka and Vašek return, and all urge Mařenka to sign the contract. Then Jeník is recognized by Mícha as his lost son—Kecal has been outwitted. The opera ends with a scene of general merry-making and reconciliation.

Bartoletti, Bruno (b. Sesto Fiorentino, 1926). Italian conductor. Début Florence 1953. Chicago since 1957. Conducts regularly Florence and Rome. One of the most gifted Italian opera conductors.

Bartók, Béla (b. Nagyszentmiklós, 25 Mar. 1881; d. New York, 26 Sept. 1945). Hungarian composer. His large and magnificent output included only one opera, and that an early 1-act work, *Duke Bluebeard's Castle* (1911, prod. Budapest 1918). Nevertheless, its extraordinary dramatic power, its rich and original score, above all the striking handling of the Bluebeard legend as a drama of questing man, make this short work one of the most interesting in all his output. (R)

Basel (Fr. Bâle). Town in Switzerland. Opera was performed at the Theater auf dem Blömlein, built 1834. The present Stadttheater (cap. 1,150) was opened on 20 Sept. 1909 with *Tannhäuser*. Honegger's *Jeanne d'Arc au Bûcher* received its première there in 1938, and Menotti's *The Consul* its first European perf. 1951.

Bass (It. basso = low). The lowest category of male voice. Many subdivisions exist within opera houses: the commonest in general use (though seldom by composers in scores) are given below, with examples of roles and their approximate *tessitura*. These divisions often overlap, and do not correspond exactly from country to country. In general, distinction is more by character than by *tessitura*, especially in France: thus, the examples of the roles give a more useful indication of the different voices' quality than any attempted technical definition.

German: tiefer Bass (Sarastro: E–e); Bass-buffo or Komischer Bass (Osmin: F–f); hoher Bass (Kaspar: G–f).

Italian: basso profondo (Ramfis: D–e); basso comico or bass-buffo (Bartolo, Basilio: F–f); basso cantante (Padre Guardiano: F–f).

French: basse-bouffe (Jupiter: F–f); basse de caractère (Méphistophélès: G–e); basse chantante or basse noble (Brogni: F–f).

Slavonic basses are able to achieve great depth, sometimes reaching G^1.

Bass-baritone. The male voice which combines, as in the part of Wotan, the qualities of *basso profondo* and *basso cantante*.

Bassi, Amedeo (b. Florence, 20 July 1874; d. Florence, 14 Jan. 1949). Italian tenor. Studied Florence with Pavosi. Début Castelfiorentino 1897, *Ruy Blas* (Marchetti). Chosen to sing Radamès at opening of Colón, Buenos Aires, 1908. N.Y., Manhattan Opera, 1906–8; London, C.G., 1907, first London Walther (*Loreley*), Frederico (*Germania*) (1907), and Dick Johnson (1911). Created Frederico (Milan 1902), Lionello in Mascagni's *Amica* (Monte Carlo 1905), and Angel Clare in D'Erlanger's *Tess* (Naples 1906). During Toscanini's régime at La Scala 1921–6 sang Loge, Parsifal, and Siegfried. (R)

Bassi, Carolina (b. Naples, 10 Jan. 1781; d. Cremona, 12 Dec. 1862). Italian contralto. One of the outstanding singers of her day, she created leading roles in Meyerbeer's *La Semiramide Riconosciuta*, *Margherita d'Anjou*, and *L'Esule di Granata*, Rossini's *Bianca e Faliero*, and in works by Pacini and Mercadante. Retired 1828. Her brother **Nicola** (1767–1825), considered by Stendhal to be the best buffo bass of the day, sang in Paris and Milan. Another brother, **Adolfo**, was a composer and for some years director of the Teatro Nuovo, Trieste, where his five operas were produced.

Bassi, Luigi (b. Pesaro, 5 Sept. 1766; d. Dresden, 13 Sept. 1825). Italian baritone for whom Mozart wrote *Don Giovanni*. Sang in Prague 1784–1806; director of the Italian opera at Dresden from 1815.

Bastianini, Ettore (b. Siena, 24 Sept. 1922; d. Sirmione, 25 Jan. 1967). Ital. baritone. Début (bass) Ravenna 1945, Colline. While preparing Guardiano in *Forza del Destino* sang some of the tenor music of that opera, and decided to raise his voice to baritone. Second début Dec. 1951, Germont. N.Y., Met., 1953–9. London, C.G., 1962; Milan, Sc.; Salzburg, &c. Created role of Prince Andrei in first stage performance of Prokofiev's *War and Peace* (Florence 1953). Greatly admired as a Verdi baritone. (R)

Bastien und Bastienne. *Singspiel* in 1 act by Mozart; text by Friedrich Wilhelm Weiskern, after Charles Simon Favart's parody of Jean-Jacques Rousseau's *Le Devin du Village* (1752). Prod. Vienna, in Anton Mesmer's garden theatre, Sept. 1768—the only production for 122 years; London, Daly's, 26 Dec. 1894; N.Y. 26 Oct. 1916.

Battaglia di Legnano, La (The Battle of Legnano). Opera in 3 acts by Verdi; text by Salvatore Cammarano. Prod. Rome, Arg., 27 Jan. 1849. It celebrates the defeat of the Emperor Frederick Barbarossa by the armies of the Lombard League at Legnano (1176); as later with *Un Ballo in Maschera*, the touchy censor insisted on a change of names and place, but the public was not deceived. Revived Parma, Verdi Celebrations, 1951, Florence Festival 1959. First perf. Gt. Britain, Cardiff, 31 Oct. 1960 as *The Battle*, with action transferred to Italy during the Nazi occupation.

Batti, batti, O bel Masetto. Zerlina's (sop.) aria in Act 1 of Mozart's *Don Giovanni*, in which she invites her lover's wrath but regains his heart.

Battistini, Mattia (b. Rome, 27 Feb. 1856; d. Rieti, 7 Nov. 1928). Italian baritone. Studied law until 20, then turned to singing. Studied with Eugenio Terziani and Persichini in Rome. Début Rome, Arg., 1878, Alfonso (*Favorite*). London, C.G., 1883, Riccardo (*Puritani*), with little success; D.L. 1887, and not again in London until 1905, by which time he had established himself as the greatest living Italian baritone. Possessed a high baritone of exceptional range (Massenet rewrote Werther for him), reaching a', and could sing florid music with great agility. Had a repertory of more than 80 operas, and continued to sing until he was over 70. Visited S. America, 1881 and 1889, with Tamagno, but never sang in U.S.A. Was highly esteemed in Russia and Poland. (R)

Bauermeister, Mathilde (b. Hamburg, 1849; d. Herne Bay, 15 Oct. 1926). German, later British, soprano. First appearance when 13, taken up by Tietjens who took charge of her musical education and sent her to the R.A.M., where she studied under Schira. Début London, C.G., 1868, Siebel; sang there intermittently until 1885 and then every year from 1887 to 1905, when she made her farewell in a special matinée organized by Melba. Made 16 trips to America, first as a member of Mapleson's Company and then at the Met. Sang more than 100 roles, most of them at C.G., including Aennchen (*Freischütz*), Magdalena, Mamma Lucia. In 1892 she saved a *Don Giovanni* performance by singing Elvira at a few hours' notice in place of Sofia Ravogli, who was ill.

Baylis, Lilian (b. London, 9 May 1874; d. London, 25 Nov. 1937). English musician and theatre manager. Daughter of Newton Baylis, a singer, and Liebe Cons, singer and pianist. Her aunt, Emma Cons, became lessee of the Royal Victorian Coffee Music-hall, known as the Old Vic, and invited her to manage it, which she did from 1898 to her death. She laid the foundations of a national English opera company, and, with Ninette de Valois, of a ballet company. In 1931 she re-opened Sadler's Wells Theatre as the north London equivalent of the Old Vic, but after two seasons it became exclusively the home of the opera and ballet companies, the Old Vic being used for drama.

Bayreuth. Town in Bavaria, Germany. It was once ruled over by the sister of Frederick the Great, and has been the home of the Richard Wagner Festivals since 1876. Wagner had originally hoped to build his festival theatre in Munich under the patronage of King Ludwig II, and plans were drawn up by Gottfried Semper; but these had to be abandoned owing to various intrigues against Wagner and Ludwig in the Bavarian capital. In 1871 Wagner succeeded in persuading the Bayreuth authorities to provide the necessary land on which to build a theatre and a home ('Wahnfried'). The foundation-stone of the theatre was laid on 22 May 1872, when Wagner conducted Beethoven's 9th symphony in the local theatre with an orchestra consisting of many of Germany's leading musicians, among them Richter as timpanist.

The theatre (cap. 1,800), originally planned as a temporary structure, is mostly made of wood and brick, with an auditorium resembling a classical amphitheatre. It has superb acoustics, largely due to the innovation of a covered orchestral pit. The theatre opened on 13 Aug. 1876 with *Rheingold*, which launched the first complete *Ring* cycle ever to be given. Richter conducted and the singers included Materna, Unger, Niemann, Betz; Lilli and Marie Lehmann were two of the Rhinemaidens and Valkyries. The audience included Liszt, Grieg, Bruckner, Mahler, Tchaikovsky, Saint-Saëns, Nietzsche, Kaiser Wilhelm I, and Ludwig II. The first season lost more than £12,000 and there were no further performances until 1882 when *Parsifal* was given its première. From 1883 until 1908 Cosima Wagner was the director of the festivals; from 1908 to 1930 Siegfried Wagner; from 1931 to 1944 Winifred Wagner; from 1951 to 1966, Wieland and Wolfgang Wagner; from 1966, Wolfgang Wagner. The conductors have included, up to 1914, Richter, Levi, Mottl, Strauss, Siegfried Wagner, Seidl, Muck, Balling; up to 1944 Busch, von Hoesslin, Elmendorff, Toscanini, Furtwängler, Strauss, Tietjen, De Sabata, Abendroth; and since 1951 Knappertsbusch, Karajan, Keilberth, Krauss, Jochum, Cluytens, Sawallisch, Kempe, Maazel, Stein, Varviso, and Böhm.

The greatest revolution in staging took place after the Second World War when Wagner's grandsons simplified the production, costumes, and settings, and purged the works of most of their naturalistic appurtenances and their Germanism, emphasizing instead their symbolism and universality.

Beard, John (b. London (?), *c.* 1717; d. Hampton, 5 Feb. 1791). English tenor. One of the most famous English singers of his day, which was still dominated by the castratos. Début in Galliard's *Royal Chase*; also sang in a number of Handel performances at C.G., dividing his appearances between there and Drury Lane. A famous Macheath in various revivals of *The Beggar's Opera*. Succeeded Rich as manager of C.G. in 1761, resigning in 1767 chiefly on account of deafness. His voice was described as being powerful rather than sweet, but flexible and wide in range, a manly sound in comparison with the rival castratos; for him Handel wrote the tenor parts in *Samson*, *Judas Maccabaeus*, *Jephtha*, *Israel in Egypt*, *Hercules*, and *Belshazzar*.

Béatrice et Bénédict. Opera in 2 acts by Berlioz; text by the composer after Shakespeare's comedy *Much Ado About Nothing* (1598–9). Prod. Baden-Baden 9 Aug. 1862; Glasgow 24 Mar. 1936; N.Y., Carnegie Hall, 21 Mar. 1960.

Beaumarchais, Pierre Augustin Caron de (b. Paris, 24 Jan. 1732; d. Paris, 19 May 1799). French playwright and amateur musician. His fame rests upon the first two plays of the *Figaro* trilogy, *Le Barbier de Séville* (Comédie-Française 1775) and *La Folle Journée, ou Le Mariage de Figaro* (Comédie-Française 1784). For the former he wrote some songs, possibly adapted from Spanish airs. The third play of the *Figaro* trilogy, *La Mère Coupable* (Théâtre du Marais 1792), represents a return to the *larmoyant* style of his early plays, and tells how the Countess has a child by Cherubino and how Figaro saves his master from the grip of a swindling Irish infantry officer. As a librettist Beaumarchais is known chiefly for *Tarare*, a 5-act opera with music by Salieri (Paris, O., 1787). The second edition of the libretto contains an interesting preface addressed 'Aux abonnés de l'Opéra, qui voudraient aimer l'opéra': it claims a greater importance for words (coupled with the comment that operatic music is apt to be too dense in weight for them), touches on the legitimate subjects for librettos, and concludes by saying something about the collaboration with Salieri in *Tarare* itself. Beaumarchais's colourful and versatile personality is sketched in his own Figaro.

Bechi, Gino (b. Florence, 16 Oct. 1913). Italian baritone. Began studies at 17 with Raoul Frazzi and then with De Giorgi. Début Empoli 1936, Germont. Speedily became Italy's leading baritone and sang with great success at the Scala, Rome, Lisbon, South America, &c. His interpretations of Iago, Nabucco, Amonasro, Gérard, Hamlet, and other dramatic roles gained him a reputation which was not upheld when he sang Iago and Falstaff in London, C.G., with the Scala Company in 1950. He returned to London (D.L.) to sing William Tell in 1958. Retired 1965 (R)

Beckmans, José (b. Liège, 4 Jan. 1897). French baritone. Studied Liège. Début Liège 1919, Escamillo. Paris, O.C., 1925–35, O. since 1935; London, C.G., 1935, Escamillo. Has produced many works at the Opéra, where he is *Directeur de la mise-en-scène*, including *L'Étranger*, *L'Atlantide*, *Fliegende Holländer*, and *Lohengrin*. (R)

Beckmesser. The pedantic town-clerk (bass), unsuccessful aspirant to Eva's hand in Wagner's *Die Meistersinger von Nürnberg*.

Beecham, (Sir) Thomas (b. St. Helens, 29 Apr. 1879; d. London, 8 Mar. 1961). English conductor. Son of Joseph Beecham, a wealthy industrialist and musical amateur. No formal musical education, but after Oxford travelled extensively abroad. Conductor of a small touring opera company 1902–4. Greatly interested in opera and influenced by Maurel (q.v.) who had settled in London and had set up a private school there. In 1910, backed by his father, launched his first opera season at C.G., which opened with the first English *Elektra*, and included works by two other composers with whom Beecham became closely identified, Ethel Smyth's *The Wreckers* and Delius's *A Village Romeo and Juliet*. An autumn season that year lasted three months and introduced *Salome* to London. Beecham also introduced *Feuersnot*, *Ariadne auf Naxos*, and *Rosenkavalier* to London before the First World War. Responsible for the Russian opera seasons at D.L. in 1913 and 1914. During the First World War he financed and established the Beecham Opera Company (q.v.). In 1919 he found himself lessee of C.G. and in 1920, owing to financial difficulties, his company went into liquidation and he himself withdrew from operatic activity for nearly 12 years. Was able to return to C.G. in 1932, and from then until 1939 was its chief conductor, artistic director, and financier.

Appeared as guest conductor at the Cologne, Munich, and Berlin operas during the inter-war years, and at the Met. and other American theatres 1941–4. After the war he conducted little opera in England, notable exceptions being *Ariadne auf Naxos* at Edinburgh 1950; *Meistersinger* and *The Bohemian Girl*, C.G. 1951; Delius's *Irmelin*, Oxford 1953; *Zémire et Azor*, Bath 1955; and a number of works for the B.B.C. In 1958 he conducted a series of Italian, French, and German operas at the Teatro Colón, Buenos Aires. Beecham's contribution to opera in England cannot be overestimated. The tragedy is that he was never able to settle and build a permanently based organization after the demise of his war-time company. (R)

Beecham Opera Company. Although Sir Thomas Beecham organized an English Opéra Comique Company at Her Majesty's Theatre in 1910, and took over the Denhof Company in 1913, it was not until October 1915 that the permanent Beecham Company came into being with a short season at the Shaftesbury Theatre, London, which included the production of Stanford's *The Critic* and Ethel Smyth's *The Boatswain's Mate*. In the spring of 1916 the company gave a season at the Aldwych Theatre followed by an enormously successful season at the New Queen's Theatre in Manchester, when, according to Sir Thomas, the company 'evolved overnight from the chrysalis state of a smallish troupe of Opéra Comique dimensions into the full growth of a Grand Opera organization, with an enlarged quota of principals and an augmented chorus and orchestra'. Beecham had inherited the scenery used by the Diaghilev Company at Drury Lane in 1914 and left in England at the outbreak of war, and was so able to give performances of *Boris*, *Ivan the Terrible*, *Prince Igor*, &c.

The repertory further included a number of works by Wagner, the inclusion of which was attacked by the more reactionary press at that time; Playfair's classic productions of *Figaro*, *Così fan tutte*, and *Die Zauberflöte*; the stock Verdi works, including *Otello*, which had one of its greatest interpreters in Frank Mullings, and *Falstaff*. Beecham's singers included the best of an outstanding generation of British artists—Agnes Nicholls, Rosina Buckmann, Jeanne Brola, Edith Clegg, Désirée Ellinger, Edna Thornton, Miriam Licette, Mignon Nevada; Frederick Austin, Norman Allin, Maurice D'Oisly, Walter Hyde, Frank Mullings, Robert Parker, Robert Radford, Frederick Ranalow; and the conductors besides Beecham were Buesst, Coates, Harrison, Goossens (II and III), and Pitt.

The company continued to function until December 1920, when it was forced into liquidation after the débâcle of Beecham's International season at C.G. It was not allowed to die, however, and was organized into the B.N.O.C.

Beethoven, Ludwig van (b. Bonn, 15 or 16 Dec. 1770; d. Vienna, 26 Mar. 1827). German composer. Beethoven's only completed opera, *Fidelio* (q.v.), was the result of a commission from the Theater an der Wien; and even after the revisions urged upon him by friends, the form of the work remains unbalanced. Beginning as a simple setting of a popular escape story, this conventional *Singspiel* is convulsed by the electric current of Beethoven's humane passion from comedy thriller into an uneven but magnificent expression of faith in liberty and loathing of tyranny. Not only do the individual characters transcend themselves and become universal symbols: the opera itself has become a symbol of liberty, and has frequently been chosen to reopen opera houses after destruction or enforced closure by war. Beethoven also made sketches for *Vestas Feuer*, to a libretto by Schikaneder, and wrote some of a Witches' Chorus for *Macbeth.* He contemplated many other subjects, including *Faust.*

Beggar's Opera, The. Ballad opera in 3 acts arranged, adapted, and partly composed by Pepusch; text by John Gay. Prod. London, Lincoln's Inn Fields, 29 Jan. 1728; New York 3 Dec. 1750. The first and most famous and popular of ballad operas, it may have been suggested to Gay by a remark of Swift that an opera set in a prison 'would make an odd pretty sort of thing'. The purpose is doubly satirical, lampooning politicians of the day (Walpole in Macheath) as well as famous singers (the notorious Cuzzoni–Bordoni battle during an opera performance in the Polly–Lucy rivalry), and mocking the operatic conventions of the period—the prologue and the artificial happy ending among others. The tunes derive mostly from popular ballads of the day. The work was popular up to 1886, when Sims Reeves sang Macheath. Its modern vogue dates from Frederick Austin's version given at the Lyric, Hammersmith, from 5 June 1920 for 1,463 nights—the longest run of any opera. Later versions have been made by Dent (Birmingham, in a circus tent on a bombsite, 22 May 1944); by Arthur Bliss for a film (with Laurence Olivier making his first singing appearance, 1953); and in a recomposition so thorough as to amount to an original work by Benjamin Britten (Cambridge, Arts, 1948). Weill's *Die Dreigroschenoper*, to a text by Bertolt Brecht, is only marginally related to the original both in subject and music. There have been other versions in different countries at different times.

Begnis, Giuseppe de, and **Giuseppe Ronzi de.** See *De Begnis.*

Bei Männern. Duet in Act 1 of Mozart's *Die Zauberflöte* in which Pamina (sop.) and Papageno (bar.) sing of the joys and power of love.

Bel canto. (It. = beautiful singing, beautiful song.) The traditional Italian art of singing in which beautiful tone, fine legato phrasing, and impeccable technique are stressed, even if at the expense of the more dramatic style favoured in Germany. *Bel canto* flourished between the 17th and 19th centuries, and is now in decline.

Belcore. The sergeant of the garrison (bar.) in Donizetti's *L'Elisir d'Amore.*

Belgium. See *Antwerp, Brussels, Ghent, Liège.*

Belgrade (Yug. Beograd). Capital of Yugoslavia. In 1829 King Miloš invited Josef Šezinger, the conductor at the Novi Sad Theatre (then Ujvidék, in Hungary) to organize musical life in Belgrade, recently freed from Turkish occupation. At first *Singspiele* were popular and when the Belgrade National Theatre opened in 1882 they formed the backbone of the musical performances. The first Serbian opera to be performed was at the National Theatre 1903, Binički's *Na Uranku* (*At Dawn*). In 1909 a private opera company was formed by a bass named Savić, but after two years the company moved to Novi Sad. In 1920 the Belgrade Opera became an independent body and gave regular performances until the war. It was re-formed in 1944. A second company performs operetta at the Belgrade Komedija Theatre. Since the war the Opera has toured abroad and recorded several Russian operas.

Bella figlia dell'amore. Quartet in Act 3 of Verdi's *Rigoletto* for Gilda (sop.), Maddalena (mezzo), the Duke (ten.), and Rigoletto (bar.).

Belle Hélène, La (Fair Helen). Operetta in 3 acts by Offenbach; text by Meilhac and Halévy. Prod. Paris, Variétés, 17 Dec. 1864; London, Adelphi, 30 June 1866; Chicago, 14 Sept. 1867. A highly spectacular and successful revival was staged in Paris 1960, with Geori Boué in the title role.

Belle nuit, O nuit d'amour. Barcarolle (q.v.) for Giulietta (sop.) and Niklausse (mezzo) in Offenbach's *Les Contes d'Hoffmann.*

Belletti, Giovanni Battista (b. Sarzana, 17 Feb. 1813; d. Sarzana, 27 Dec. 1890). Italian baritone. Début Stockholm 1837; here and later in London he had great successes with Jenny Lind. Toured U.S.A. under Barnum. One of the great baritones of the 19th century, especially admired in his Meyerbeer roles.

Bellezza, Vincenzo (b. Bitonto, Bari, 17 Feb. 1888 d. Rome, 8 Feb. 1964). Italian conductor. Trained Naples Conservatory. Début Naples, S.C., 1908, *Aida*. Conducted widely in Italy, and then was engaged at Buenos Aires, Colón, 1920. N.Y., Met., 1926–35; London, C.G., 1926–30 and 1935–6. Conducted Melba's Farewell (1926), first English *Turandot* (1927), and London débuts of Ponselle, Gigli, and other artists. Rome Opera and other Italian theatres since 1935. Returned London 1957, Stoll, and 1958, D.L. (R)

Bellincioni, Gemma (b. Monza, 17 Aug. 1864; d. Naples, 23 Apr. 1950). Italian soprano. Daughter of Cesare Bellincioni, a bass-buffo. Studied Milan. Début Naples 1881, *Tutti in Maschera*. When only 18 sang Gilda opposite Tamberlik (q.v.), then 68. Sang widely in Europe and America. The first Santuzza (1890), Fedora (1898), and Italian Salome. London, H.M.'s, 1889, and C.G. 1895. Married the tenor **Robert Stagno** who was also her teacher and the original Turiddu. Their daughter **Bianca** (b. Budapest, 23 Jan. 1888) was also a singer. Bellincioni's autobiography, *Io e il Palcoscenico*, was published in Milan 1920, and a joint biography of herself and Stagno by their daughter was published in Florence in 1943. (R)

Bellini, Vincenzo (b. Catania, 3 Nov. 1801; d. Puteaux, 23 Sept. 1835). Italian composer. Studied under Zingarelli at the San Sebastiano Conservatory, Naples. His student works, including an operetta and his first opera, *Adelson e Salvina* (1825), displayed gifts for lyricism and flowing melodies which were to characterize all his compositions. *Adelson*, performed in the theatre attached to the conservatory, was heard by Barbaia, the impresario of both La Scala and the San Carlo, who immediately commissioned an opera from Bellini for the latter theatre; this was *Bianca e Fernando* (1826), first performed before King Francis I. Barbaia immediately gave a second commission, this time for La Scala, which resulted in *Il Pirata* (1827); its success was helped by Rubini's singing of the tenor role, specially composed for him, which broke away from the florid Rossini style then in vogue. *La Straniera* (1829) and *Zaira* (1829) met with rather less success; but *I Capuletti ed i Montecchi* (1830), as its recent revivals in Italy have shown, contains some of the composer's most beautiful music. With *La Sonnambula* and *Norma* (both 1831), Bellini's gifts reached maturity. The first work is a tenderly elegiac rustic idyll; the latter a great lyric drama reaching tragic grandeur in its last act. It was much admired by Wagner, not least for Romani's libretto: 'Bellini is one of my predilections because his music is strongly felt and intimately bound up with the words.' *Norma* was followed by *Il fù ed il sarà* (1832, privately performed) and *Beatrice di Tenda* (1833) which was not a success, though its revival at Palermo (1959), in a revised form by Gui, revealed many hidden treasures in a work that looked forward to Verdi. Bellini's last opera, *I Puritani* (1835), despite a poor libretto by Pepoli, triumphed because of its ravishing melodies. Overworked and weak in health, he fell ill while visiting a friend at Puteaux and died there of dysentery. He was buried at Paris, but his remains were removed to Catania in 1871.

Bellini's melodic form exercised a strong influence on a whole generation of musicians, including Chopin and Berlioz. For a time his works were under a cloud, being considered weak in dramatic force, no more than display pieces for singers. But revivals in recent years with singers of the stature of Callas, Sutherland, and Simionato, have resulted in their winning new appreciation.

Belloc, Teresa Giorgi (orig. Trombetta)(b. San Benigno, nr. Turin, 2 July 1784; d. San Giorgio, 13 May 1855). Italian mezzo-soprano of French parentage. Début Turin 1801. Rossini wrote roles for her in his *L'Inganno*

Felice, *Tancredi*, and *La Gazza Ladra*. She appeared in London as Bellochi and was particularly successful as Tancredi. According to Stendhal, however, she had an 'ugly and coarse-grained voice'.

Bell Song. The name usually given to the soprano aria 'Où va la jeune Hindoue?' sung by Lakmé in Act 2 of Délibes's *Lakmé*.

Belmonte. A Spanish nobleman, the hero (ten.) of Mozart's *Entführung aus dem Serail*.

Benda, Jiří Antonín (b. Stáre Benátky, 30 June 1722; d. Köstritz, 6 Nov. 1795). Czech composer. Moved from his native country to Prussia, where he became Kapellmeister at Gotha. At the age of 52 he suddenly appeared as the master of a new form of music with his spoken 'duodramas' *Ariadne auf Naxos* and *Medea*, which influenced the course of German opera and impressed a large number of contemporaries, among them Mozart, who carried them about with him. He wrote some 16 stage works in all.

Bender, Paul (b. Driedorf, 28 July 1875; d. Munich, 25 Nov. 1947). German bass. Studied with Luise Ress and Baptist Hoffmann. Début Breslau 1900; Munich 1903; London, C.G., 1914 (first Amfortas in England) and 1924; N.Y., Met., 1922–7. Distinguished in Wagner and as Osmin, Sarastro, and Baron Ochs. Bavarian Kämmersänger, and teacher at Munich Music School till his death. (R)

Benedict, (Sir) Julius (b. Stuttgart, 27 Nov. 1804; d. London, 5 June 1885). German composer, conductor, and teacher, later naturalized Englishman. Studied at Stuttgart and Weimar, where he met Weber, whose protégé he became. Weber took him to Vienna in 1823, where he was appointed conductor of the Kärntnertor-Theater. In 1825 went to Naples and conducted at the San Carlo, from thence to Paris (1834) where he met Malibran who suggested he visit London, which he did in 1835, remaining there until his death. He held appointments at Drury Lane, the Lyceum, and Her Majesty's and was active in the heyday of English opera, composing several himself of which the best known is *The Lily of Killarney*. He was intensely active in the concert hall, conducting Jenny Lind's first oratorio appearance (*Elijah*, 1848) and directing most of her concerts in the U.S.A. Knighted in 1871.

Benefit. In the 18th and 19th centuries, these were special performances, generally at the end of the season, the proceeds of which went to a certain composer, singer, or impresario. In our day, benefit or charity performances of opera are given in aid of an organization or institution. These are very common in New York, where during the course of the season the Metropolitan gives several benefits, generally at increased prices.

Benjamin, Arthur (b. Sydney, 18 Sept. 1893; d. London, 10 Apr. 1960). Australian composer. Studied R.C.M. Professor of pianoforte, Sydney, 1919–21, then returned to England. His four operas are the farcical *The Devil Take Her* (1931); the sparkling *opera buffa*, *Prima Donna* (1933, prod. 1949); the full-scale *A Tale of Two Cities* (1949–50) which was awarded a prize in the Festival of Britain Competition, but had to wait for its first professional performance until 1957; and *Tartuffe* posth. prod., (S.W.) 1964)

Benois, Nicola (Nikolai Alexandrovich) (b. St. Petersburg, 2 May 1901). Russian scenic designer, son of Alexandre Benois. Worked with his father in Russia, France, and England, mostly on ballet; then summoned to La Scala by Toscanini in 1924 to design *Boris Godunov* and *Khovanshchina*. Has remained in Italy ever since, and is the Scala's chief designer. Has been responsible not only for Russian operas in the repertory but has designed the *Ring* and other German and Italian works. Has also worked at the Rome Opera and the Colón, Buenos Aires.

Benucci, Francesco (b. *c*. 1745; d. Florence, 5 Apr. 1824). Italian bass. The original Figaro (1786) and Guglielmo in *Così fan tutte* (1790). He was less admired in London in his season as principal bass at the King's in 1788 than his high reputation warranted.

Benvenuto Cellini. Opera in 2 acts by Berlioz; text by Léon de Wailly and Auguste Barbier after *The Autobiography of Benvenuto Cellini* (begun 1558). Prod. Paris, O., 10 Sept. 1838; London, C.G., 25 June 1853 N.Y., concert perf. Philharmonic) Hall, 22 Mar. 1965. Berlioz's first opera, it was initially a failure, though later championed by Liszt in performances at Weimar (from 20 Mar. 1852 in a revised 3-act version); the London première, in Queen Victoria's presence, also failed through engineered opposition, and Berlioz immediately withdrew the work. The plot tells of the love of Cellini for Teresa, and how he successfully confounded his rival Fieramosca and cast the famous Perseus statue. Other operas on Cellini are by Schlösser (1845), Lachner (1849), Bozzano (1871), Orsini (1875), and Diaz (1890).

Berenice. Opera in 3 acts by Handel; text by Antonio Salvi (first composed by Perti in 1709). Prod. London, C.G., 18 May 1737. Unsuccessful. There are some 20 other operas on the subject.

Berg, Alban (b. Vienna, 9 Feb. 1885; d. Vienna, 24 Dec. 1935). Austrian composer. Studied with Schoenberg, 1904–10, who exercised a deep influence on him and to whom *Lulu* is dedicated. *Wozzeck* (1925) and *Lulu* (unfinished, prod. 1937) are among the most powerful and original music dramas of this century, each expressing in its way Berg's profound compassion for the lowest in humanity. In *Wozzeck* this is for the materially underprivileged. Though the opera is fascinatingly constructed out of instrumental forms such as suite, sonata, and rondo, Berg stressed that tenderness for the dregs of humanity, transcending the fate of the individual Wozzeck, should fill the listener's mind and not curiosity about formal means. Unlike *Wozzeck*, *Lulu* is a dodecaphonic opera, with a musical form now attached to each of the characters. These are entirely creatures of instinct, and it is for the tragic direction in which this takes them that Berg invites compassion. Lulu herself represents raw female sexuality and its destructive effect upon the others. Musically *Lulu* rises to greater heights than *Wozzeck*, though the latter's more easily shared compassion has helped to make it one of the most successful modern operas.

Berg, Natanaël (b. Stockholm, 9 Feb. 1879; d. Stockholm, 14 Oct. 1957). Swedish composer. He has had five operas produced in Stockholm, all with librettos by himself: *Leila*, after Byron's *Giaour* (29 Feb. 1912); *Engelbrekt* (21 Sept. 1929); *Judith*, after Hebbel's play (22 Feb. 1936); *Birgitta* (10 Jan. 1942); and *Genoveva*, after Hebbel's play (25 Oct. 1947).

Bergamo. Town in Lombardy, Italy. Opera was first given there in 1786 (*Didone*) at the Teatro T. Riccardi. In 1897 the Teatro Donizetti (cap. 2,000) was built. In 1937 it was rechristened the Teatro della Novità, and since then has given the premières of more than 50 new works, including Ghedini's *Maria d'Alessandria* (1937), Barilli's *Medusa* (1938), Napoli's *Un Curioso accidente* (1950), Tosatti's *Il Sistema della Dolcezza* (1951), Malipiero's *Il Festino* and *Donna Urraca* (1954), Viozzi's *Allamistakeo* (1954), Hazon's *Requiem per Elisa* (1957), and Ferrari's *Cappuccia o della Libertà* (1958). It has also revived Donizetti's *Rita*, *Anna Bolena*, *Maria di Rohan*, and *Maria Stuarda*. The Bergamo audience is considered, after that of Parma, the most difficult to please in Italy.

Berganza, Teresa (b. Madrid, 16 Mar. 1934). Spanish mezzo-soprano. Studied with Lola Rodrigues Aragon. Début Aix-en-Provence 1957, Dorabella. Milan, Sc., 1957–8; Glyndebourne 1958, Cherubino, 1959, Cenerentola; London, C.G., 1960, Rosina, 1963, Cherubino. A typically rich-voiced Spanish mezzo-soprano, and an excellent singer of florid music. (R)

Berger, Erna (b. Dresden, 19 Oct. 1900). German soprano. Studied at Dresden with Heta Boeckel and Melita Hitzl. Début Dresden 1926, First Boy

(*Zauberflöte*); Bayreuth 1929–31; Salzburg 1934, Blondchen; Berlin, Städtische Oper, 1930–2, Staatsoper from 1934; London, C.G., 1934, 1935, 1938, and after the war (Queen of Night, Sophie, Gilda). Also appeared N.Y., Met., and continued to sing in opera in Germany and Austria until 1955, when she devoted herself to teaching. Her most successful pupil is Rita Streich (q.v.). Berger's voice retained its youthful freshness and girlish quality throughout her long career. (R)

Berglund, Joel (Ingemar) (b. Torsåker, 4 June 1903). Swedish bass-baritone. Studied Stockholm Conservatory 1922–8. Début Stockholm 1929, Monterone (*Rigoletto*). Soon established himself as leading Wagnerian singer and sang in Buenos Aires, Zürich, Vienna, and Chicago before the war as Sachs, Wotan, and Dutchman. Bayreuth 1942, Dutchman. N.Y., Met., 1945–9. Director of Stockholm Royal Opera 1949–52; still makes occasional appearances in opera. (R)

Bergonzi, Carlo (b. Parma, 13 July 1924). Italian tenor, formerly baritone. Studied Parma. Début Lecce 1948, Figaro (Rossini). Sang baritone roles for three years; then, after further period of study, second début Bari 1951, Chénier. London, Stoll, 1953, Alvaro; Chicago 1955; N.Y., Met., since 1956. (R)

Berkeley, Lennox (b. Oxford, 12 May 1903). English composer. He took up music seriously after leaving Oxford in 1926, and studied with Nadia Boulanger for six years. He did not write an opera until 1953, when he produced a full-scale 3-act setting of a libretto by Alan Pryce-Jones, *Nelson* (S.W.), a comparative failure, due in part to a lengthy plot with contrived situations. Berkeley next turned to Paul Dehn for a libretto to a 1-act comic opera, *A Dinner Engagement* (Aldeburgh, Jubilee Hall, 1954). His third opera, *Ruth* (1 act), with libretto by Eric Crozier based on the Book of Ruth in the Bible, was again produced by the English Opera Group (London, Scala, 1956). His fourth, *The Castaway*, was produced by the Group at Aldeburgh in 1967.

Berkshire Festival. An annual summer festival given at Tanglewood, Mass., and instituted by Serge Koussevitzky in 1937. The operatic contribution to the festival is generally provided by the opera department of the Berkshire Music Center under the direction of Boris Goldovsky. The American premières of *Peter Grimes*, *Albert Herring*, *Zaïde*, *Idomeneo*; revivals of *Il Turco in Italia*, *Queen of Spades*; and the first performances of works by American composers—Mennini's *The Rope*, Bucci's *Tale for a Deaf Ear*, and Lukas Foss's *Griffelkin*—have been features of the festivals since 1947. Singers who were heard at Tanglewood in the early days of their careers include Mario Lanza, James Pease, Mack Harrell, Frances Yeend, and Irene Jordan.

Berlin. Town in Germany, former capital of united Germany. Opera in Berlin is given in three theatres: the Deutsche Staatsoper Unter den Linden, the Deutsche Oper, and the Komische Oper. The first and last are in the eastern sector, the second in the western sector of the city. Opera in Berlin dates from 1688 when performances of Italian works and French ballet were given in the court theatre during the reign of Frederick III and his wife Charlotte. It was not until the reign of Frederick the Great that Berlin had its own opera house, the Hofoper, opened in 1742. Spontini was the theatre's Music Director 1819–42; he was succeeded by Meyerbeer, with Nicolai as one of the conductors; the latter's *Die Lustigen Weiber von Windsor* had its première there in 1849. Under Weingartner (1891–8), Muck (1908–12), and Strauss (1898–1918), and with an ensemble that included Destinn, Hempel, Baptist Hoffmann, Knüpfer, and Kirchhoff, a high musical and vocal standard was reached. In 1896 Kaiser Wilhelm II planned a new opera house in Berlin, and the Krolls Theater in the Königplatz was bought for this purpose. After many delays building was planned to begin in 1914, but the war intervened. In 1924 the new theatre was opened, and from 1927 to 1931 under

Klemperer (q.v.) it became the leading experimental opera theatre in Europe. In 1933 the Oper am Königplatz became the home of the Reichstag.

The Staatsoper's Intendants from 1918 until 1943, when the house in the Unter den Linden was bombed, were Richard Strauss (1918), Max von Schillings (1919–25), and Heinz Tietjen (1927–43). The theatre's Music Directors were Blech (1918–23, 1926–37) who shared the position with Kleiber (1924–34). Then came Furtwängler (1933–4), Krauss (1934–5), and from 1936 until 1943 Heger, Schüler, Egk, Karajan, and Elmendorff. During the years 1927–31, when the Kroll Oper was also open, Klemperer was its Music Director and his productions included *Cardillac*, *Neues vom Tage*, *Erwartung*, *Die glückliche Hand*, *Oedipus Rex*; while under Kleiber the Staatsoper Unter den Linden saw the premières of *Wozzeck* and *Christopher Columbus* (Milhaud). Kleiber returned to Berlin for a short period after the Second World War. The Staatsoper's singers during 1918–43 included Ivogün, Leider, Lemnitz, Ljungberg, Branzell, Klose, Cebotari, Müller, Ursuleac; Anders, Bockelmann, Domgraf-Fassbaender, Lorenz, Schlusnus, Soot, Roswaenge, Völker, and Wittrisch.

In 1945 the Staatsoper resumed activities in the Admiralspalast, with Ernst Legal as Intendant, and on 4 Sept. 1955 it returned home to the Unter den Linden, where the house had been rebuilt at the cost of £3 m. on the old plans of Knobelsdorff, the original architect. The house holds 1,500 and the first musical director was Franz Konwitschny, 1955–62. Otmar Suitner was music director from 1964 to 1971.

The Städtische Oper (originally the Deutsches Opernhaus on the Bismarckstrasse, and sometimes known as the Charlottenburg Opera) was opened in Nov. 1912. It seated 2,300 and its Intendant was Georg Hartmann. From 1925 to 1934 it reached a high artistic level, with Walter, Denzler, and Stiedry as its conductors, and Tietjen, Singer, and Ebert as Intendants. During the Nazi régime Wilhelm Rode, the baritone, was its Intendant, and Göbbels its guiding spirit, just as Göring was that of the Staatsoper. Rother, Schmitt-Isserstedt, and Ludwig were its chief conductors. It was destroyed by bombs in 1944. After the war it reopened in the Theater des Westens, former home of the Volksoper (cap. 1,529) with Bohnen as its Intendant; he was succeeded by Tietjen in 1948; and by Carl Ebert in 1955. Leo Blech returned from exile to conduct, 1949–54. Fricsay was for a short time music director but resigned after a number of disagreements. Since then the conducting has been shared between Richard Kraus, Arthur Rother, and guests; and the singers have included Elisabeth Grümmer, Lisa Otto, Helene Werth, Fischer-Dieskau, Beirer, Greindl, Haefliger, Konya, Neralic, and Suthaus. The rebuilt house on the Bismarckstrasse opened in 1961 with Gustav Sellner as Intendant and reverted to the name Deutsche Oper. Lorin Maazel was music director from 1965 to 1971.

The Komische Oper, formerly the Scala Theatre, opened in 1947 (cap. 1,338) and under Walter Felsenstein (q.v.) has become one of the most discussed opera houses in Europe. The brilliant productions of *The Cunning Little Vixen*, *Figaro*, *Zauberflöte*, *Falstaff*, *Hoffmann*, and *Otello* have attracted opera-goers from all countries.

Berlioz, Hector (b. La Côte-Saint-André, Isère, 11 Dec. 1803; d. Paris, 8 Mar. 1869). French composer. Almost all Berlioz's music was dramatic in conception, whether ostensibly a symphony (*Symphonie Fantastique*), a concerto (*Harold en Italie*), or one of his hybrids—the 'symphony' *Roméo et Juliette*, the monodrama *Lélio* (significantly a sequel to the *Symphonie Fantastique*), and the *légende dramatique*, *La Damnation de Faust*. Faced with public neglect in the field of opera after the failure of *Benvenuto Cellini* (q.v.), he was cut off from the medium into which his talents should naturally have flowed. Thus when he set himself the congenial if enormous task of making an opera out of his beloved Virgil, he took less account of practical considerations of performance. *Les Troyens* (q.v.) triumphs over its unwieldy structure and vast length by reason of the genius that flares through it; it is an epic that embraces the spectacular and the lyrical, that combines the most shattering originalities with a classical grandeur not found in opera since Gluck; that must stand as one of the greatest monuments of operatic imagination in the history of the art. The comic *Béatrice et Bénédict* (q.v.) was written, so Berlioz said, as a rest after the exertions of *Les Troyens*, as well as being a tribute to his abiding love for Shakespeare; and its German successes, before the production of the greater work, gave Berlioz false hopes of *Les Troyens*'s success.

In 1847 he was invited by Jullien to become music director at Drury Lane as part of an ill-fated attempt to found an English national opera.

Bern (Fr. Berne). Town in Switzerland. Opera is performed at the Stadttheater (cap. 1,000), opened 25 Sept. 1903 with *Tannhäuser*.

Bernacchi, Antonio (b. Bologna, 23 June 1685(?); d. Bologna, Mar. 1756). Italian male contralto. Studied with Pistocchi and Ricieri. After appearances in Venice and Bologna went to London in 1716. In 1717 he sang *Goffredo*, in a revival of Handel's *Rinaldo*, a role previously sung by women contraltos and sopranos. Engaged in 1729 by Handel to replace Senesino, he created the title role in Handel's *Lotario*, and Arsace in *Partenope*. His compass was narrower than Senesino's (a-e'', with a single f'' in *Partenope*). After 1730 he taught in Italy.

Bernauerin, Die. Opera by Orff; text by the composer in Bavarian dialect after an old Bavarian play. Prod. Stuttgart 15 June 1947.

Bernstein, Leonard (b. Lawrence, Mass., 25 Aug. 1918). American composer and conductor. Educated Boston and Harvard. Studied composition with Edward Hill and Walter Piston; then conducting at Curtis Institute under Reiner. Koussevitzky's assistant Tanglewood 1942, where he directed the American première of *Peter Grimes* (1946); Rodzinski's in N.Y. 1943. Conducted his own *Trouble in Tahiti* at Brandeis University 1952 and N.Y. City Center 1958, and the Visconti–Callas *Medea* and *Sonnambula* at La Scala, Milan, 1954 and 1955; N.Y., Met., 1964; Vienna, 1966. (R)

Berton, Henri Montan (b. Paris, 17 Sept. 1767; d. Paris, 22 Apr. 1844). French composer. Violinist at Opéra from early age; début as composer with sacred drama at the Concert Spirituels. Most famous for his *Les Rigueurs du Cloître* (1790), the first rescue opera from which *Fidelio* took its example; and for *Montano et Stéphanie* (1797).

Berton, Pierre Montan (b. Maubert-Fontaines, Ardennes, 7 Jan. 1727; d. Paris, 14 May 1780). French bass, conductor, and composer, father of the above. Début Paris, O., 1744; conductor there from 1756 to his retirement in 1778; director in 1770, and in full charge from 1775 to 1778. He introduced most of Gluck's operas to Paris; he wrote ballet music for operas and several operas of his own.

Bertoni, Ferdinando Giuseppe (b. Salò, Lake Garda, 15 Aug. 1725; d. Desenzano, Lake Garda, 1 Dec. 1813). Italian composer. Best known for his *Quinto Fabio* (Milan 1778), which led to him being engaged for the King's Theatre, London. Here he wrote a long series of operas, mostly on classical subjects, which Burney noted 'would soothe and please by their grace and facility, but not disturb an audience by enthusiastic turbulence'.

Besanzoni, Gabriella (b. Rome, 20 Sept. 1890; d. Rome, 8 July 1962). Italian mezzo-soprano. Studied with Alessandro Maggi and Hilde Brizzi. Originally a light soprano, but found voice changing and became contralto. Début Viterbo 1911, Adalgisa. Appeared at all leading Italian opera houses including La Scala, where she sang Orfeo and Carmen under Toscanini. N.Y., Met., 1919–20; Chicago and South America. Well known for her Isabella and Cenerentola. (R)

Bettelstudent, Der (The Beggar Student). Operetta in 3 acts by Millöcker; text by Zell and Genée. Prod. Vienna, W., 6 Dec. 1882; N.Y. 19 Oct.

1883; London, Alhambra, 12 Apr. 1884. Also the title of an operetta by Winter (1785), based on Cervantes's story *La Cueva de Salamanca.*

Bettoni, Vincenzo (b. Melegnano, 1 July 1881; d. Milan, 4 Nov. 1954). Italian bass. Début 1902, Silva. Well established in Italy before the First World War. Milan, Sc., 1926–40, especially in buffo roles. Glyndebourne 1934, Don Alfonso; London, C.G., 1935, as Don Magnifico, Mustafà, Don Basilio, Colline, and Sam. Created Eziel in *Il Dibuk* (Rocca), Scala, 1934. (R)

Betz, Franz (b. Mainz, 19 Mar. 1835; d. Berlin, 11 Aug. 1900). German baritone. Studied Karlsruhe. Début Hanover 1856, Heinrich. Appeared as guest in Berlin 1859 with great success and engaged by Royal Opera there until 1897; created Hans Sachs, Munich 1868; Wotan in first complete *Ring* (Bayreuth) 1876, and the first Berlin Falstaff (Verdi); sang in Richter concerts in London.

Bevignani, Enrico (b. Naples, 29 Sept. 1841; d. Naples, 29 Aug. 1903). Italian conductor and composer. Studied with Albanese and Lillo. Went to London 1863 as *répétiteur* at H.M.'s, then at C.G. 1869–87 and 1890–6 as conductor; N.Y., Met., 1894–1900, and appearances in Moscow and St. Petersburg. Conducted first London *Aida* (1876), *Gioconda* (1883), *Amico Fritz* (1892), *Pagliacci* (1893), and Patti's last appearance at C.G. (1895).

Bianca und Giuseppe, oder die Franzosen vor Nizza. Opera in 4 acts by Kittl; text by Richard Wagner, after Heinrich König's novel. Prod. Prague 19 Feb. 1848. Wagner wrote the scenario in 1836 for himself, but did not use it; he revised it in 1842 for Reissiger, who did not use it either.

Bianchi, Bianca (orig. Bertha Schwarz) (b. nr. Heidelberg, 27 June 1855; d. Salzburg, Feb. 1947). German soprano. Studied under Pauline Viardot-Garcia; début Karlsruhe 1873, Barbarina (*Figaro*); London 1874, where she was admired as a light soprano of much charm—her Susanna and Aennchen were highly praised—but at a time dominated by Patti and other great singers she was overshadowed.

Bielefeld. Town in Westphalia, Germany. Opera is performed at the Stadttheater am Schillerplatz (cap. 900), built 1904.

Billington, Elizabeth (b. London, *c.* 1765; d. Venice, 25 Aug. 1818). English soprano. Daughter of Carl Weischel, first oboe at King's Theatre, and a popular singer who was a favourite pupil of J. C. Bach. She studied with Bach and James Billington, a double-bass player and singing teacher, whom she married. Début Dublin 1783, Polly (*Beggar's Opera*). C.G. from 1786. Heard by King of Naples, 1794, who procured her an engagement at the San Carlo where she appeared in Bianchi's *Iñes de Castro*, specially written for her. Successful appearances all over Italy and at the King's, Haymarket, with the Italian Company, where she was the first English Vitellia (*Clemenza di Tito*) (1806), greatly admired by the Prince of Wales, whose mistress she was said to have been. Mountedgecumbe likened her voice to a flute or flageolet.

Billy Budd. Opera in 4 acts by Britten; text by E. M. Forster and Eric Crozier, after Melville's unfinished novel (1891). Prod. London, C.G., 1 Dec. 1951, with Pears, Uppman, and Dalberg; N.Y., N.B.C. Television, 19 Oct. 1952. New 2-act version broadcast 13 Nov. 1960, prod. C. G. 9 Jan. 1964. The opera has no female roles, being set on board a late 18th-century man-o'-war, and tells of the hanging of the good young sailor Billy for the accidental killing of his tormentor Claggart; Captain Vere respects Budd, but is unable to save him. The subject has also been set by Ghedini (1948).

Bindernagel, Gertrud (b. Magdeburg, 11 Jan. 1894; d. Berlin, 3 Nov. 1932). German soprano. Especially successful in Wagner roles. Berlin Staatsoper 1919–27, and Städtische Oper. After singing Brünnhilde in *Siegfried* in Berlin she was shot by her husband as she left the theatre. (R)

Bing, Rudolf (b. Vienna, 9 Jan. 1902). Manager and impresario. Studied Vienna. Manager of Viennese concert agency from 1923. Then held appointments at Darmstadt and Berlin under Carl Ebert (q.v.) who called him to Glyndebourne as General Manager in 1936, a position he held for ten years. In 1946 became a naturalized British subject and helped to found the Edinburgh Festival; director 1947–9. General Manager of the Met., N.Y., 1950–72.

Birmingham. Town in Warwickshire, England. Despite the enterprise of Granville Bantock in putting on the English première of Gluck's *Iphigénie en Aulide*, the city was for long dependent on touring companies. A performance of Raybould's *The Sumida River* in 1916 was followed by the première of Messager's *Monsieur Beaucaire* in 1919 and then a series of productions at the Repertory Theatre from 1920, when Sir Barry Jackson mounted *Così fan tutte*, *The Immortal Hour*, *Don Pasquale*, *Il Matrimonio Segreto*, *Don Giovanni*, *The Boatswain's Mate*, and the première of *Fête Galante*. Local amateur companies have contributed—the Barfield Opera Company with a number of lesser-known 19th-century works as well as one new work, Margaret More's *The Mermaid* (1951); the Midland Music Makers with some enterprising productions, including *William Tell*, *Prince Igor*, *Les Huguenots*, *Les Troyens*, *Ivan the Terrible*, *Masaniello*, and *I Lombardi*.

Bis. See *Encore*.

Bishop, (Sir) Henry (b. London, 18 Nov. 1786; d. London, 30 Apr. 1855). English composer and conductor. His bent towards dramatic music revealed itself early, and at the age of 24 he was already engaged to compose and direct the music at C.G. He adapted a number of foreign operas—*Don Giovanni*, *Figaro*, *Barbiere*, and *Fidelio* among them—mercilessly rewriting portions and introducing music of his own, as was then fashionable. He became also director at the King's, and for Drury Lane composed his *Aladdin* (q.v.) in rivalry to Weber. In 1830 he became music director at Vauxhall. He wrote nearly 60 operatic pieces, 11 musical adaptations of Scott's novels, and 15 arrangements of other operas, as well as contributing music to plays, masques, pageants, ballets, and other men's operas. His music is at best pretty and pert, never original except, strangely, in the use of his song 'Home, Sweet Home' in *Clari, The Maid of Milan*, where its recurrence in different guises suggests, if not actually leitmotive, at least an early appearance of theme-song plugging. Knighted in 1842.

Bispham, David (b. Philadelphia, 5 Jan. 1857; d. New York, 2 Oct. 1921). American baritone. First appearance London in concert, 1890; following year stage début English Opera House as Longueville in *La Basoche* (Messager); D.L. 1892, Kurwenal; C.G. 1892–1902; N.Y., Met., 1896–1903. Great advocate of opera in English. Autobiography, *A Quaker Singer's Recollections* (1920). (R)

Bizet, Georges (b. Paris, 25 Oct. 1838; d. Bougival, nr. Paris, 3 June 1875). French composer. Teachers at the Conservatoire included Gounod. His earliest operatic essays stand in the first period of composition he later disavowed; of them perhaps *Le Docteur Miracle* (comp. 1856) and *Don Procopio* (comp. 1858–9, prod. 1906) are the most promising, containing passages of true originality as well as competent imitations of the best models (Donizetti and Rossini chief among them). *Ivan IV* (comp. 1862–3, prod. 1946) has languished, though parts of it are familiar from use in later works. The first important opera was *Les Pêcheurs de Perles* (1863), which while more widely derivative is also of greater originality and freedom, with some ravishing passages of the finest Bizet. *La Jolie Fille de Perth* (comp. 1866, prod. 1867), though still eclectic, shows an impressive advance, with increased dramatic command now joining a vein of refined lyricism. *La Coupe du Roi de Thule* (1868, surviving only in fragments) is said to advance still further, strikingly anticipating *Carmen*. Bizet completed his father-in-law Halévy's *Noé*, unpromisingly; and then a brief but intense concentration on *opéra-comique* with *Calendal* (comp. 1870), *Clarissa Harlowe* (comp. 1870–1), and *Griséldis* (comp. 1870–1) led to *Djamileh* (comp. 1871, prod. 1872). This failed chiefly because of Bizet's too original treatment of a poor libretto. A lost operetta and *Don Rodrigue* (comp. 1873), the surviving fragment of which does not impress, preceded his last and greatest work, *Carmen* (comp. 1873–4, prod. 1875). Here at last was the perfect libretto for him. He was at his fullest mastery; the characterization is superb, the progress of the drama magnificently portrayed in music of unprecedented strength and colour. *Carmen* is the greatest of all *opéras-comiques*.

Björling, Jussi (Johan) (b. Stora Tuna, 2 Feb. 1907; d. Stockholm 9 Sept. 1960). Swedish tenor. Taught by father and first sang in public when six. Member of Björling Male Quartet with father and two brothers. Studied Royal Opera School, Stockholm, with John Forsell and Tullio Voghiera. Début Stockholm 1930, Don Ottavio; sang there regularly till 1939. Vienna and Chicago 1937; London, C.G., 1939 and not again until 1960; member of Met., N.Y., 1938–60 (except during war years). Sang Italian, French, and Russian repertory, but (except for Mozart) not German. Had a warm and appealing voice, and sang with excellent taste. His brother **Gösta** (b. 1912) sang in Stockholm from 1940 until his early death in 1957. (R)

Björling, Sigurd (b. Stockholm, 2 Nov. 1907). Swedish baritone. Studied Stockholm Conservatory 1933–4 and Royal Opera School 1934–6 with Forsell. Début Stockholm 1935, Alfio. Encouraged to study Wagner roles by Leo Blech. London, C.G., 1951, Kurwenal, Amfortas, and Wotan; Bayreuth 1951; N.Y., Met., 1952–3. No relation to Jussi. (R)

Blacher, Boris (b. Newchang, China, 6 Jan. 1903). German composer. Despite great difficulties he pursued his studies rigorously, and since 1945 has become recognized as one of Germany's most important composers and teachers. His brilliant intellect has applied itself to the problem of original dramatic music in a dance drama *Fest im Süden*, some ballets, a scenic oratorio *Romeo und Julia* (after Shakespeare), a dramatic oratorio *Der Grossinquisitor* (after Dostoyevsky), and six operas—*Fürstin Tarakanova* (1945), the chamber opera *Die Flut* (1947), *Die Nachtschwalbe* (1948), *Preussisches Märchen* (1952), *Abstract Oper No. 1* (1953), *Rosamunde Floris* (1960). Librettist, with Einem (q.v.), of the latter's *Dantons Tod* and *Der Prozess*.

Blachut, Beno (b. Ostrava-Vićkova, 14 Apr. 1913). Czech tenor. Studied Prague 1935–9. Début Olomouc 1939. Prague National Theatre since 1941. Especially distinguished in works of Smetana, Dvořák, and Janáček. (R)

Blamont, François Colin de (b. Versailles, 22 Nov. 1690; d. Versailles, 14 Feb. 1760). French composer. In his capacity as court composer he produced various works upholding the traditions of French operatic style, reinforcing his views with a pamphlet during the Guerre des Bouffons (q.v.).

Blanc, Ernest (b. Sanary, 1 Nov. 1923). French baritone. In 1946 won scholarship to Toulon Conservatory where he studied for four years. Début Marseilles 1950, Tonio; Paris, O., since 1954. Admired both in Italian roles (Germont, Amonasro, and Rigoletto) and in German roles (Wolfram, Don Giovanni). Bayreuth 1958; American début, San Francisco 1958; Glyndebourne 1960, Riccardo and Don Giovanni; London, C.G., 1961, Rigoletto. (R)

Bland, Maria Theresa (b. Italy, 1769 (?); d. London, 15 Jan. 1838). English singer. Born of Italian-Jewish parents called Romanzi, under which name she first appeared in public, 1773. Member of D.L. Company 1786–1826, excelling in operas of Storace, Arnold, &c. Her son Charles was the first Oberon in Weber's opera at Covent Garden, 1826; and another son, James, was a successful bass-buffo.

Bleat. A vocal device used by Monteverdi whereby a single note is quickly reiterated with interruptions of the breath. From the sound, the Germans call it the *Bockstriller*, or goat's trill. Wagner demands it of the tailors in *Meistersinger*, Act 3, sc. 2.

Blech, Leo (b. Aachen, 21 Apr. 1871; d. Berlin, 25 Aug. 1958). German conductor and composer. Studied Berlin with Bargiel and Rudorff, then Humperdinck. Conductor, Aachen 1893–9; Deutsches Theater, Prague, 1899–1906; Berlin Royal Opera 1906–23 (Generalmusikdirektor from 1913). After a short absence in Vienna and elsewhere, returned to Berlin as joint Generalmusikdirektor with Erich Kleiber (q.v.) of the Staatsoper, his appointment being terminated in 1937 because of his Jewish descent. Riga 1937–41; Stockholm 1941–6, where his Wagner performances were greatly admired. Returned to Berlin as conductor of the Städtische Oper 1949. He celebrated his 80th birthday by conducting in Berlin his *Das war ich* (Dresden 1902) and *Versiegelt* (Hamburg 1908). (R)

Bliss, (Sir) Arthur (b. London, 2 Aug. 1891). English composer. From the dramatic nature of his music, it is curious that Bliss did not attempt an opera before *The Olympians* (q.v.) of 1949; the reason is possibly that his talents in this direction were absorbed by his brilliant ballet scores. J. B. Priestley provided him with an original and imaginative subject, but the opera did not make its promised impact despite some fine music.

Blitzstein, Marc (b. Philadelphia, 2 Mar. 1905; d. Martinique, 22 Jan. 1964). American composer. He studied with Siloti, Boulanger, and Schoenberg, eventually abandoning his early experimental style because of the belief that music should readily communicate a message to the widest number of people. Turning therefore to the stage, he has written a number of operas, among them *The Cradle Will Rock* (1937), *No for an Answer* (1940), and *Regina* (1949). He was also responsible for a version of Weill's *Threepenny Opera* (1954).

Bloch, Ernest (b. Geneva, 24 July 1880; d. Portland, U.S.A., 15 July 1959). American composer of Swiss birth, though his Jewish origins have had the largest emotional, and to a limited extent technical, influence on his style. His only opera is *Macbeth* (Paris 1910; revived Naples 1938 and Brussels 1958). It is the only Shakespeare opera to make successful use of leitmotiv; and is said to reveal dramatic gifts of a very high order.

Blockx, Jan (b. Antwerp, 25 Jan. 1851; d. Antwerp, 26 May 1912). Belgian composer. His eight operas written to French and Flemish texts were successful in their day, winning praise for their post-Wagnerian rather than pseudo-Wagnerian qualities; in style they are kindred to Charpentier and D'Albert. His *Herbergprinses* was given by Hammerstein at the Manhattan Opera; and a revival of *De Bruid der Zee* in Brussels in 1958 showed the genuinely operatic talents of its composer.

Blondchen (or **Blonde).** Constanze's maid (sop.) in Mozart's *Entführung aus dem Serail.*

Blow, John (b. Newark, Feb. 1648 or 1649; d. London, 1 Oct. 1708). English composer. His only work for the stage, and probably his best-known composition, is *Venus and Adonis* (*c.* 1685).

Bluebeard. A character in Perrault's *Contes de Ma Mère l'Oye* (*Mother Goose's Tales*, 1697) (perhaps deriving from Gilles de Rais) who attempted to kill his latest wife Fatima for unlocking the forbidden door behind which lay the bodies of his previously murdered wives. Grétry's *Raoul Barbe-Blue* (1789) was probably the first of the many Bluebeard operas, of which the better known are Offenbach's *Barbe-Bleue* (1866), Dukas's *Ariane et Barbe-Bleue* (1907), Bartók's *Duke Bluebeard's Castle* (1918) (q.v.), and Rezniček's *Ritter Blaubart* (1920). According to some versions of her legend, Mélisande was one of Bluebeard's escaped wives, hence her traumatic state at the start of Debussy's opera.

Boatswain's Mate, The. Opera in 1 act by Ethel Smyth; text by the composer, after W. W. Jacobs's story. Prod.

London, Shaftesbury, 28 Jan. 1916. The composer's most successful opera.

Bockelmann, Rudolf (b. Bodenteich, nr. Luneburg, 2 Apr. 1892; d. Dresden, 9 Oct. 1958). German bass-baritone. Educated Celle and Leipzig, studied singing with Oscar Lassner 1920–3. Début Leipzig 1923, Herald (*Lohengrin*); Hamburg 1926–32; Berlin, Staatsoper, 1932–45. Appeared regularly at Bayreuth 1928–42, and C.G. 1929–30 and 1934–8; Chicago Civic Opera 1930–1. An outstandingly fine Hans Sachs and Wotan. His Nazi sympathies prevented him from resuming his career after the war and except for a few appearances in Hamburg and the German provinces he devoted his time to teaching. A German Kammersänger. (R)

Bockstriller. See *Bleat*.

Bodanzky, Artur (b. Vienna, 16 Dec. 1877; d. New York, 23 Nov. 1939). Austrian conductor. Studied Vienna Conservatory. Violinist in Royal Opera Orchestra and from 1902 to 1904 Mahler's assistant at the Opera. After appointments in Prague and Mannheim, he conducted the first performances of *Parsifal* in England at C.G. in 1914, and the following year succeeded Alfred Hertz as chief German conductor at the Met., N.Y., which position he held till his death. He prepared new editions of *Oberon*, *Fidelio*, and *Boccaccio* for New York and Wagnerians were always annoyed by the notorious 'Bodanzky cuts' in *The Ring* and other operas.

Bohème, La. Opera in 4 acts by Puccini; text by Giacosa and Illica, after Henri Murger's novel *Scènes de la Vie de Bohème* (serially 1847–9). Prod. Turin, T.R., 1 Feb. 1896 under Toscanini, with Cesira-Ferrani, Gorga; Manchester 22 Apr. 1897; Los Angeles 14 Oct. 1897.

Act 1. In their chilly attic, two of the four Bohemians are trying to keep their fire alight: the painter Marcello (bar.) is prevented from burning a chair by the poet Rodolfo (ten.) who instead sacrifices his manuscript. Schaunard (bar.) appears with food and drink, having been paid for a music lesson. With Colline (bass), the philosopher, all except Rodolfo adjourn to the Café Momus. Mimì (sop.), a neighbour, comes in for a light for her candle, returning later for the key she has left behind and lost; as they look for it, he takes her cold hand and in answer Mimì tells him of herself and her life, and of her longing for warmth and spring. They join in a love duet before leaving to join the other Bohemians.

Act 2. At the Café Momus, Marcello is embarrassed by the arrival of his old flame Musetta (sop.) with a wealthy councillor Alcindoro (bass). She sings a waltz song of her attractions and is reunited to Marcello; the Bohemians escape in a hurry, leaving Alcindoro with the bill.

Act 3. Mimì appears shivering and ill at the Barrière de l'Enfer, and confides to Marcello how difficult life with Rodolfo has become; then hiding behind a tree she overhears his complaints about her. They meet and decide to part, while Marcello and Musetta have yet another quarrel; but realizing they cannot separate Rodolfo and Mimì, depart together, their love renewed.

Act 4. Back in their attic, Rodolfo and Marcello recall happy days with their lovers. Spirits are raised by the arrival of Schaunard and Colline laden with food and drink; but Musetta bursts in with Mimì, deathly sick. She and Rodolfo sing of their love, while Colline parts with his coat to provide medicine. But it is too late, and Rodolfo suddenly realizes what the others have already seen—that Mimì is dead.

Written at the same time as Leoncavallo's *La Bohème* (Venice, F., 6 May 1897), which deals with the same subject-matter, Puccini's opera was at first a comparative failure. Only after its third presentation (Palermo 1896) were its merits fully recognized.

Bohemian Girl, The. Opera in 3 acts by Balfe; text by Alfred Bunn based on a ballet-pantomime by Saint-Georges, and originally from Cervantes's *La Gitanella* (*c.* 1614). Prod. London, D.L., 27 Nov. 1843; N.Y. 25 Nov. 1844. Tells of the love of Thaddeus, a proscribed Polish nobleman, for

Arline, daughter of Count Arnheim, who was kidnapped by gipsies when a child and is falsely accused of stealing a medallion from a young nobleman. She is recognized by her father, Count Arnheim, Governor of Pressburg, and allowed to marry Thaddeus, despite his murky political past. The score includes 'I dreamt that I dwelt in marble halls', 'The heart bowed down', and 'When other lips'. It was continuously in the repertories of British touring companies until the 1930's, and was revived by Beecham at Covent Garden in 1951.

Böhm, Karl (b. Graz, 28 Aug. 1894). Austrian conductor. Originally studied law, then music at Graz Conservatory and Vienna. In 1917 coach at Graz, and then in 1918 second and 1920 first conductor. Recommended by Karl Muck to Walter who engaged him for Munich in 1921. Generalmusikdirektor, Darmstadt 1927–31; Hamburg 1931–4; Dresden 1934–42; Vienna 1942–4, and Generalmusikdirektor of rebuilt house 1954; resigned a year later following criticism of his long absences abroad. London début with Dresden Company at C.G. 1936; N.Y., Met., from 1957. Regularly at Salzburg and Italian theatres. Bayreuth since 1963. With Krauss, the leading Strauss conductor in the 1930's and 1940's, directing premières of *Daphne* and *Die schweigsame Frau*. Also distinguished in Mozart and the modern repertory, including *Wozzeck*. (R)

Böhme, Kurt (b. Dresden, 5 May 1908). Studied Dresden Conservatory with Kluge. Début Dresden 1930, Caspar; Dresden 1930–50; Munich since 1950. London, C.G., 1936, with Dresden Company, and since 1956. N.Y., Met., 1954–7. Has sung all over Europe and in South America. An outstanding Baron Ochs, and highly regarded for his Wagner interpretations. (R)

Bohnen, Michael (b. Cologne, 2 May 1887; Berlin, 26 Apr. 1965). German bass-baritone. Studied with Fritz Steinbach and Schulz-Dornburg. Début Düsseldorf 1910, Caspar; Wiesbaden 1912–13; Berlin, Hofoper, 1913–21; N.Y., Met., 1922–32; Berlin, Deutsches Opernhaus, 1933–45. Intendant of the Städtische Oper, Berlin, 1945–7. Also sang at Bayreuth in 1914 (Hunding and Daland); London, D.L., in the Beecham season that year as Ochs and Sarastro, and at Salzburg. His large voice of extensive range enabled him to cope with both bass and baritone roles. As a gifted and individual actor he was attracted by roles that lay outside the normal repertory. While a member of the Met. sang Francesco in Schillings's *Mona Lisa* and Jonny in Křenek's *Jonny spielt auf*. (R)

Boïeldieu, Adrien (b. Rouen, 16 Dec. 1775; d. Jarcy, 8 Oct. 1834). French composer. His first operas were written in his native Rouen; these and the first group he wrote on arrival in Paris show a fluent talent relying on the example, even the mannerisms, of more famous composers. He replied to Cherubini's accusation, after a performance of *Le Calife de Bagdad* (1800), 'Are you not ashamed of such undeserved success?' by offering himself as a pupil; and *Ma Tante Aurore* (1803) shows the older man's good influence. He then spent eight years in Russia, where he wrote a number of operas and ruined his health. Back in Paris he reasserted his popularity, clinching it with *Jean de Paris* (1812) and, above all, *La Dame Blanche* (1825), whose romantic and modernistic incidents set against a traditional popular background, its vintage *opéra-comique* musical idiom dramatically and emotionally heightened by chromatic harmony and expressive orchestration, proved instantly popular.

Boito, Arrigo (b. Padua, 24 Feb. 1842; d. Milan, 10 June 1918). Italian librettist and composer. Son of an Italian painter and Polish countess. Musical education at Milan under Mazzucato. Went to Paris with his friend Faccio (q.v.) having been granted 2,000 lire by the Ministry of Public Instruction, and there met Victor Hugo, Berlioz, Rossini, and Verdi. While in Paris, conceived the idea of composing an opera on Faust and another on Nero. Greatly impressed by the music he heard in

Germany. He returned to Milan and his *Mefistofele* was given at La Scala in 1868. It met with a poor reception, and was accused of being Wagnerian. Under the anagrammatic pen name of Tobia Gorrio he provided Ponchielli with his libretto for *La Gioconda*; and under his own name he helped Verdi refashion *Simone Boccanegra* and wrote the librettos of *Otello* and *Falstaff*, the finest in Italian opera. His *Nerone* was produced posthumously at La Scala under Toscanini in 1924. He also translated *Rienzi* and *Tristan* into Italian.

Bologna. Town in Emilia, Italy, whose operatic history goes back to 1610. One of its chief contributions to opera in Italy was its championship of Wagner's operas at the Teatro Comunale under Angelo Mariani between 1871 and 1877. In 1875 it also welcomed Boito's *Mefistofele* after the Scala fiasco. The Comunale dates from 1763 and its auditorium, which holds 1,350 people, was designed by Antonio Galli Bibiena.

Bolshoy Theatre. See *Moscow*.

Bonci, Alessandro (b. Cesena, 10 Feb. 1870; d. Viserba, 10 Aug. 1940). Italian tenor. Studied at the Rossini Conservatory, Pesaro. Début Parma 1896, Fenton. Engagements all over Italy, including Sc., followed. London, C.G., 1900; N.Y., Manhattan Opera, 1906. Appeared intermittently at C.G. until 1908, and in America until 1921. Continued to sing in Italy until 1935. Was a singer of taste and refinement, greatly admired by Lilli Lehmann. At his best in Bellini, Rossini, and Donizetti. (R)

Bondini, Pasquale (b. ? ; d. Bruneck, Tyrol, 30 Oct. 1789). Italian bass. Director of the Italian Opera in Prague 1781–8. *Figaro* was performed there with tremendous success, to Mozart's great happiness, in Dec. 1786, as a result of which Bondini requested his next opera, *Don Giovanni*, and produced it there, 29 Oct. 1787.

Boninsegna, Celestina (b. Reggio Emilia, 26 Feb. 1877; d. Milan, 14 Feb. 1947). Italian soprano. Without any formal vocal or musical study made her début when 15 as Norina. Then went to Pesaro Conservatory; second début, Bari 1897, in *Faust*. Her voice was a dramatic soprano of great power and range, and her *mezza voce* singing and phrasing were much admired. London, C.G., 1904–5, as Aida and Leonora (*Trovatore*). After retiring from the stage she taught; pupils include Margherita Grandi (q.v.) (R)

Bononcini, Giovanni (b. Modena, 18 July 1670; d. Vienna (?), 9 Aug. 1747). Italian composer. His first operatic ventures were in Rome, Vienna, and Milan: but in 1720 he arrived in London, where he was welcomed in high circles, receiving a salary from the Duke of Marlborough. Many of his operas were produced there before he returned to Vienna, where he died in obscurity. He was a skilful musician who suffered from comparison with Handel, and (it is said) from his own arrogant disposition, though his operas satisfied the increasingly sentimental taste of the day.

Bordeaux. Town in the Gironde, France. The present Grand Théâtre Municipal dates from 1780, when Bordeaux was one of the greatest ports in the world. Its beautiful auditorium (cap. 1,158) was designed by Victor Louis. In recent years the theatre has been under the direction of Vanni Marcoux (q.v.) and (since 1954) Roger Lalande. The first perf. of Bizet's *Ivan IV* was given there in Oct. 1951, and the first perf. in French of *Peter Grimes* in 1954.

Bordoni, Faustina (b. Venice, *c.* 1695; d. Venice, 4 Nov. 1781). Italian soprano. A brilliant début in 1716 in Pollarolo's *Ariodante* led to her becoming known as 'The New Siren'. After her wide successes in Italy, Handel brought her to London in 1726 where she delighted all with her impeccable technique, intelligence, and delightful presence—all except Cuzzoni, with whom she had a famous quarrel (see *Beggar's Opera*) and with whom she sharply divided London's popular favour. She returned to Venice, where she married Hasse.

Borgatti, Giuseppe (b. Cento, 17 Mar. 1871; d. Reno, Lago Maggiore, 18 Oct.

1950). Italian tenor. Studied Bologna. Début Castelfranco Veneto 1892, Faust. After singing Lohengrin and Walther, was invited by Toscanini to sing Siegfried at La Scala, where he became Italy's finest Heldentenor. He sang widely in Europe and South America but did not appear at C.G. or the N.Y. Met. (R)

Borghi-Mamo, Adelaide (b. Bologna, 9 Aug. 1829; d. Bologna, 28 Sept. 1901). Italian mezzo-soprano. On the advice of Pasta and Donzelli studied for the stage with Festa. Début Urbino 1843, in Mercadante's *I Giuramento.* Sang with great success all over Europe including Paris (1854–60) and London (1860). Created roles in operas by Halévy, David, Mercadante, &c. Married tenor Michele Mamo 1849. Her daughter **Erminia** (1855–1941) was born in Paris, one hour after her mother had sung Azucuna in a perf. of *Trovatore.* She studied with her mother and was chosen by Boito to sing Margherita and Elena in the revised *Mefistofele* at Bologna 1875.

Borgioli, Armando (b. Florence, 19 Mar. 1898; d. nr. Codogno, 20 Jan. 1945). Italian baritone. Début Milan 1925, Amonasro (*Aida*); London, C.G., 1927–39, and from 1931 to 1935 sang at the N.Y. Met. A famous Verdi baritone and Barnaba, Jack Rance, and Enrico. Was killed in an air attack on a train taking him from Milan to Modena. (R)

Borgioli, Dino (b. Florence, 15 Feb. 1891; d. Florence 12 Sept. 1960). Italian tenor. Studied with Eugenio Giachetti at Florence. Début Milan, T. de V., 1917. Engaged by Melba for her farewell tour of Australia. Début London, C.G., 1925 as Edgardo (Lucia). Regular visitor to C.G. until 1939, Glyndebourne, Salzburg, San Francisco, &c. Much admired as a Rossini and Mozart singer and for his elegance and good taste. In 1949 was appointed vocal director of the New London Opera Company (q.v.) and produced for them *La Bohème* and *Il Barbiere di Siviglia.* (R)

Bori, Lucrezia (orig. Lucrecia Borja y Gonzalez de Riancho) (b. Valencia, 24 Dec. 1887; d. New York, 14 May 1960). Spanish soprano. Educated in a convent, she did not begin her vocal training until she was 20 (Milan, under Vidal). Début Rome, C., 1908, Micaëla. Sang with Caruso in Paris as Manon 1910; first Italian Octavian, Milan 1911; American début at the N.Y. Met. as Manon Lescaut 1912. Her career was threatened in 1915 by a throat operation, but after further study she was able to return to the stage, Monte Carlo 1919. Reappeared at the Met. in 1921 and remained a member of the company until her retirement in 1936. Considered one of the greatest stylists of her day. Never sang in England. (R)

Boris Godunov. Opera in 4 acts, with a prologue, by Mussorgsky; text by the composer after Pushkin's drama *The Comedy of the Distress of the Muscovite State, of Tsar Boris, and of Grishka Otrepiev* (1826) and Karamzin's *History of the Russian Empire* (1829). Original version comp. 1868–9, rejected by St. Petersburg Opera 1870. Three scenes of composer's revision (1871–2) prod. St. Petersburg, charity perf., 17 Feb. 1873; whole opera 8 Feb. 1874, Melnikov as Boris. Banned after 25 performances, revived after composer's death in Rimsky-Korsakov's version, St. Petersburg 10 Dec. 1896; N.Y., Met., 19 Mar. 1913, with Didur, under Toscanini; London, D.L., 24 June 1913, with Chaliapin. Original version first performed abroad, London, S.W., 30 Sept. 1935. This had 7 scenes—4 from Pushkin, 2 devised by Mussorgsky from indications in the play, 1 developed from two separate scenes in it.

1. Boris (bass) has murdered the young Dmitri, heir to the throne, and is pretending to decline the crown himself. His agents incite the crowd to persuade him to 'relent'. 2. Though plagued by guilt, Boris goes to be crowned. 3. In his cell the old monk Pimen (bass) is concluding a history of Russia; with him is the novice Grigory (ten.), who resolves to avenge Dmitri. 4. Grigory, who claims to be Dmitri, with two other friars, Varlaam (bass), and Missail (ten.), reaches an inn on the Lithuanian border. Grigory is identified but escapes the pursuing

soldiers. 5. To Boris in his rooms word is brought by his councillor Shuisky (ten.) of the pretender in Lithuania. To reassure him on the death of Dmitri, Shuisky recounts the murder, which throws the guilt-racked Tsar into a state of hallucination. 6. Outside St. Basil's Cathedral in Moscow the people begin to believe in the right of the false Dmitri. A Simpleton (ten.) robbed of a groat asks Boris to repeat his murder on the robbers; Boris prevents his arrest, and asks for prayer, but the Simpleton refuses and falls to mending his shoes with a song for poor Russia. 7. In the Council Hall an edict against the pretender is being read when Boris breaks in distraught and collapses dead.

In his second version Mussorgsky made considerable additions and alterations, and arranged the scenes as follows.

Prologue: 1 and 2. Act 1: 3 and 4. Act 2: 5. Act 3 (recast): Scene 1—Dmitri's lover Marina sits in her father's Polish castle dreaming of when she will rule Russia, and Rangoni (bass) pleads the Catholic cause; Scene 2—Marina (mezzo) joins Dmitri in the gardens, and she persuades him not to give up his ambitions. Act 4: 7 and an extra scene in the Kromy Forest, in which the people are in revolt against Boris; the pretender passes *en route* for Moscow, leaving the Simpleton singing sadly for Russia as in the now discarded 6. The order of these last two scenes is frequently reversed in order to allow the protagonist the final curtain; the counter-argument holds the protagonist to be, in fact, the Russian people. A revival at C.G. 1958, with Christoff, used all these scenes, as did that at the Met. in 1957. Both reverted to the original orchestration.

Borkh, Inge (b. Mannheim, 26 May 1917). German soprano. Début Linz 1937, as actress. Two years later went to Italy to study singing with Muratti in Milan, and then at the Mozarteum, Salzburg. Début Lucerne 1940, Czipra (*Zigeunerbaron*). Engagements in Switzerland until 1952 when her performance of Magda Sorel caused a sensation and led to engagements in Germany (1952) and America (1953). English début Royal Festival Hall, London, with Stuttgart Opera, 1955, as Elektra; N.Y., Met., 1958; C.G. 1959, Salome. Renowned for her Lady Macbeth and Elektra. (R)

Borodin, Alexander (b. St. Petersburg, 12 Nov. 1833; d. St. Petersburg, 27 Feb. 1887). Borodin only finished one opera, a pastiche *The Bogatirs* (1867); material from *The Tsar's Bride* was used in other works; the solitary Act 4 of *Mlada* (1872) has languished; and his masterpiece, *Prince Igor* (1869–87), was completed by Rimsky-Korsakov and Glazunov and produced in 1890. If *Boris Godunov* is Russia's greatest operatic tragedy, *Igor* (perhaps even more than *A Life for the Tsar*) is her epic, filled with historical splendour, noble attitudes, lyrical outpourings, and the exhilarating clash of Russian patriotic feeling with the Oriental brilliance of the Polovtsians.

Boronat, Olimpia (b. Genoa, 1867; d. Warsaw, 1934). Italian soprano. Studied in Milan and made her début in Genoa or Naples in 1885. After appearances in Spain, Portugal, and South America, was invited to appear at St. Petersburg in 1891, where she became a great favourite. Married into the Polish aristocracy and abandoned the stage between 1893 and 1905. She then sang again in Russia, and in 1909, returned to sing in Italy after a long absence. She possessed a beautiful, limpid voice, a flawless technique, and was a consummate musician. Her great roles were Rosina, Violetta, Elvira in *I Puritani*, and Ophélie in *Hamplet*. After retiring from the stage she established a school of singing in Warsaw. (R)

Borosini, Francesco (b. Modena, *c.* 1690; d. ?). Italian tenor. Best known for his successful appearances in Handel's operas in London, beginning with *Tamerlano* in 1724.

Bortnyansky, Dmitri (b. Glukhov, Ukraine, 1751; d. St. Petersburg, 7 Oct. 1825). Russian composer. One of the first Russian opera composers, he studied in Italy, having his *Creonte* performed at Venice in 1776 and his

Quinto Fabio at Modena, both in 1778. Like others of his day—Fomin, Matinsky, Berezovsky—he was concerned to learn from the best Italian models rather than to found more than the very beginnings of an original Russian school.

Boschi, Giuseppe (b. Viterbo (?), ? ; d. ?). Italian bass, much admired for his Handel performances in London between 1710 and 1728.

Bosio, Angiolina (b. Turin, 22 Aug. 1830; d. St. Petersburg, 12 Apr. 1859). Italian soprano. Studied Milan with Cataneo; début Milan 1846 (*I Due Foscari*). Engagements in Europe and America followed. London, C.G., début 1852, Adina; first real success there Elvira in *Puritani* when she replaced the indisposed Grisi. The first C.G. Violetta and Gilda. A great favourite in Russia, where she fell suddenly ill in 1859 and died.

Boston. Town in Mass., U.S.A. First opera heard in Boston was *Love in a Village*, July 1769, given in a concert performance owing to the authorities having banned public stage performances in 1750. The first stage performance was *The Farmer* (a ballad opera) in July 1794. Opera in English was the rule up to the 1850's when touring companies began to visit the city. In 1855 Grisi and Mario sang in Boston for the first time, and in 1860 Patti sang the first Rosina of her career there. The Mapleson Company began to visit Boston in 1878 and Grau's French Company in 1879. During the 1880's and 1890's the Boston Ideal Opera Company, the Theodore Thomas American Company, and the Madison Square Company all gave seasons in Boston.

In November 1909 the Boston Opera Company, for which the Boston Opera House was specially built, began its short but spectacular career (516 perfs. of 51 operas) with *La Gioconda* (Nordica in title role). Under the management of Henry Russell, who took the company to Paris in 1914, Boston enjoyed five magnificent seasons during which the company included Bori, Garden, Destinn, Melis, Georgette Leblanc, Dalmores, Clément, Muratore, and Vanni Marcoux. Weingartner made his American début in 1912 conducting *Tristan*. The company collapsed through lack of funds in 1914. In 1915 and 1916 the Boston Grand Opera Company gave two seasons, with many of the singers of Russell's company. Then followed nine seasons organized by the Boston Opera Association, which brought the Chicago Opera each spring to Boston. Although the Metropolitan Opera first visited Boston in 1884, it was not until 1934 that it began to pay yearly visits (except 1943), sometimes at the Metropolitan Theatre, sometimes at the Boston Opera House. In 1958 the latter theatre was demolished.

Boston is the home of the New England Opera Theatre, founded by Boris Goldovsky, which gave the American première of *Les Troyens* in 1955. In 1959 the Little Opera House opened under the auspices of the Opera Group Inc., with Sarah Caldwell as artistic director.

Bouche fermée (Fr. = closed mouth). An instruction to vocalize without words and with the lips nearly shut, as in the Humming Chorus at the end of Act 2, scene 1, of *Madama Butterfly*.

Boué, Geori. See *Bourdin*.

Bouffes-Parisiens. Theatre in Paris (cap. 820) opened on 5 May 1855 with Offenbach's *Les Deux Aveugles*. Was the home of operetta and light opera by Offenbach, Hervé, Lecocq, Audran and Messager. Still a boulevard theatre with an operetta tradition.

Bouffons, Guerre des. The controversy that between 1752 and 1754 divided Paris into partisans of the Italian music introduced by visiting *buffi* in Pergolesi's *La Serva Padrona* and the native French music, as exemplified by Rameau (q.v.). Writers who contributed to it included Rousseau (*Lettre sur la Musique Française*) and Diderot, both on the Italian side.

Boughton, Rutland (b. Aylesbury, 23 Jan. 1878; d. London, 24 Jan. 1960). English composer. His brave and systematic attempt to establish an

English school of Wagnerian music drama was pursued with remarkable single-mindedness and energy; and though his 'Bayreuth' at Glastonbury did not, after many efforts, establish itself permanently, he at least saw *The Immortal Hour* win wide popularity in London in 1922. His music has tunefulness and imagination, though not on the Wagnerian scale he hoped, and his faith in his purpose never wavered in the face of prolonged neglect. Operas include *The Birth of Arthur*, *Alkestis* (1922), *The Queen of Cornwall* (1924), and *The Lily Maid* (1934). (R)

Bouhy, Jacques (Joseph André) (b. Pepinster, 18 June 1848; d. Paris, 29 Jan. 1929). Belgian baritone. Début Paris, O., 1871, Méphistophélès. Created Escamillo (1875). London, C.G., 1882. Director of N.Y. Conservatory 1885–9, and taught there 1904–7, then in Paris.

Boulevard Solitude. Opera in 7 scenes by Henze; text by the composer and Grete Weil. Prod. Hanover, Landestheater, 17 Feb. 1952; London, S.W., 25 June 1962. A modern setting of the Manon Lescaut story.

Bourdin, Roger (b. Paris, 14 June 1900). French baritone. Studied Paris Conservatory with Gresse and Isnardon. Début Paris, O.C., 1922, as Lescaut (Massenet). Member of O.C. and O. ever since, where he has created many roles. London, C.G., 1930, Pelléas; appearances in Italy, South America. Married to the soprano **Geori Boué** (b. 1918), who made her Paris début in 1942 as Thaïs. (R)

Bovy, Vina (b. Ghent, 22 May 1900). Belgian soprano. Studied Ghent. Début Ghent 1917, Gretel. After appearances in Brussels, Paris, South America, and Italy, was engaged in 1936 for the N.Y. Met., début as Violetta. Reappeared in the Belgian and French provinces after the war, and from 1947 until 1955 was director of the Royal Opera, Ghent. (R)

Boyce, William (b. London (?), *c.* 1710; d. London, 7 Feb. 1779). English composer, organist, and musical editor. He began activities as a stage composer in 1747 with a revival of his masque *Peleus and Thetis*, producing a number of works for Drury Lane up to 1760 in rivalry with Arne, with whom he worked under the shadow of Handel.

Braham (orig. Abraham), **John** (b. London, 20 Mar. 1774; d. London, 17 Feb. 1856). English tenor of Jewish parentage. Studied with Leoni; début when ten at C.G. in benefit for his teacher. After his voice had broken he was taken up by a rich benefactor and became a teacher of the piano. In 1794 began to sing again, and in 1796 was engaged at Drury Lane by Storace. Was then engaged by the Italian Opera, and from 1798 to 1800 appeared in Italy with great success. In 1801 sang at C.G. for the first time, and then at the Lyceum and King's Theatre. Was considered without rival on the Italian stage, and was a renowned Handel singer. He often, as was the custom of the time, composed his own music for certain works in which he appeared. Sang Max in *Freischütz* in English in 1824, and created the role of Huon in *Oberon* (1826), for which he made Weber write him a different principal aria. In the 1830's his voice became lower and he sang Don Giovanni and William Tell at Drury Lane. Toured America with little success 1840–2, and made his last appearance in a concert in 1852.

Braithwaite, Warwick (b. Dunedin, N.Z., 9 Jan. 1898; d. London, 18 Jan. 1971). N.Z. conductor. Studied R.A.M. 1916–19. Conductor of O'Mara Company 1919–22, and later on musical staff of B.N.O.C. After appointments with the B.B.C., joined S.W. and was, with Lawrance Collingwood, responsible for many important productions there (1933–40), including the first performance by the company of *Fledermaus*, *Mastersingers*, *Fidelio*, and *Don Carlos*. Conducted London, C.G., 1950–2; music director of the Welsh National Opera Company (q.v.) 1956–60; returned S.W. 1960. (R)

Brambilla. Famous Italian family of singers. **Marietta** (b. Cassano d'Adda, 6 June 1807; d. Milan, 6 Nov. 1875), contralto, created the roles of Maffeo

Orsini (*Lucrezia Borgia*) and Pierotto (*Linda di Chamounix*). **Teresa** (b. Cassano d'Adda, 23 Oct. 1813; d. Milan, 15 July 1895), soprano, created Gilda, and sang with success in Paris and St. Petersburg. In addition there were six other sisters who became singers, Emilia, Amelia, Erminia, Giuseppina, Laura, and Annetta. A niece of Teresa, **Teresina** (b. Cassano d'Adda, 15 Apr. 1845; d. Vercelli, 1 July 1921), soprano, was chosen by Ponchielli (whom she married in 1874) to sing Lucia in the new version of his *I Promessi Sposi*, which opened the Teatro dal Verme, Milan, 1872. Her roles included Aida, Gioconda, and Elsa. She retired from the stage 1889, and then taught at Geneva and Pesaro. A descendant of the family, **Arturo,** was head of the costume department at La Scala in recent years.

Brandt, Marianne (orig. Marie Bischoff) (b. Vienna, 12 Sept. 1842; d. Vienna, 9 July 1921). Austrian mezzo-soprano. Début Graz 1867, Rachel; London, C.G., 1872, Leonore (*Fidelio*). Ten years later sang Brangäne in the first English *Tristan* at D.L.; in the same year sang Kundry in the second Bayreuth *Parsifal*. N.Y., Met., 1886. After 1890 settled in Vienna and taught singing. (R)

Brangäne. Isolde's attendant (mezzo) in Wagner's *Tristan und Isolde*.

Brannigan, Owen (b. Annitsford, nr. Newcastle, 10 Mar. 1908). English bass. Studied G.S.M. Début Newcastle with S.W. 1943, Sarastro. S.W. 1944–9 and 1952–8. Created Swallow (*Peter Grimes*) 1945, Collatinus in *Rape of Lucretia*, 1946, Noye in *Noye's Fludde*, 1958, Bottom in *A Midsummer Night's Dream*, 1960. One of the best English buffo singers, possessing a voice of large size and excellent quality. (R)

Branzell, Karin (b. Stockholm, 24 Sept. 1891). Swedish mezzo-soprano. Educated Stockholm, studied with Thelma Hofer and Enrico Rosati. Début Stockholm 1912, Prince Sarvilaka in D'Albert's *Izeyl*; N.Y., Met., 1924, Fricka, and remained there as leading mezzo-soprano until 1944; London, C.G., 1935–8. One of the finest mezzos of the inter-war years. (R)

Bratislava (Pressburg, Pozsony). Town in Slovakia, Czechoslovakia. The National Theatre (cap. 900) was built soon after the First World War, and the company built up by Oskar Nedbal.

Braunschweig. See *Brunswick*.

Brazil. Opera in Brazil is chiefly given at the Teatro Municipal at Rio de Janeiro and at São Paolo, mainly by visiting companies. Apart from the works of Carlos Gomez, who was trained in Italy and whose *Lo Schiavo* and *Il Guaraney* have been performed in Europe, and of Villa Lobos, there is little or no Brazilian operatic tradition. A number of Brazilian artists, including Bidú Sayão and Carlos Walter, made considerable international careers.

Break. The point where the tone quality changes between different registers of the voice.

Brecht, Bertolt (b. Augsburg, 10 Feb. 1898; d. Berlin, 15 Aug. 1956). German dramatist. Wrote the version of *The Beggar's Opera* known as *Die Dreigroschenoper* (1928) for Weill, as well as providing librettos for his *Happy End* (1929), *Mahagonny* (1930), *Der Jasager* (1930), and for Wagner-Régeny's *Persische Episode* (*Der Darmwäscher*) (1940–50) and *The Trial of Lucullus* by Sessions (1947) and Dessau (1951).

Bregenz. Town in Austria. A summer open-air festival was inaugurated in 1956 in the specially constructed lakeside theatre (cap. 6,400). Artists from the Vienna State Opera take part in performances of Mozart operas and Austrian operettas, and Italians in works by 18th- and early 19th-century composers.

Brema, Marie (orig. Minny Fehrmann) (b. Liverpool, 28 Feb. 1856; d. Manchester, 22 Mar. 1925). English mezzo-soprano. Stage début London, Shaftesbury Theatre, 1891, Lola, in first English *Cavalleria Rusticana.* Established herself as a Wagnerian and sang Ortrud, Fricka, and Kundry at Bayreuth. Although a mezzo sang the *Götterdämmerung* Brünnhilde in Paris under Richter. Created Beatrice in Stanford's *Much Ado About Nothing,* C.G., 1901, and in 1910 organized an opera season of her own at the Savoy Theatre, singing Orfeo in English. After leaving the stage she was for many years director of the opera class at the R.M.C.M.

Bremen. Town in Saxony, Germany. The earliest *Faust* opera, I. Walter's *Doktor Faust,* had its first performance there in Dec. 1797. The former Staatstheater, scene of the première of Gurlitt's *Wozzeck* (1926), was destroyed during the Second World War. The new Theater am Goetheplatz (cap. 1,100) was opened 27 Aug. 1950. Heinz Wallberg was Generalmusikdirektor 1955–61.

Brent, Charlotte (b. ? ; d. London, 10 Apr. 1802). English soprano. Studied with Arne; début Dublin 1755. One of the most famous interpreters of Polly (*Beggar's Opera*) at C.G. and created the role of Mandane in Arne's *Artaxerxes* (1762). Specially renowned as a Handel singer.

Brescia. Town in Lombardy, Italy. Opera is given today at the Teatro Grande (cap. 1,070), opened 1893. In the following year the young Toscanini conducted *Manon*, *Puritani*, and *Traviata*, and it was there on 28 May 1904 that the revised *Madama Butterfly* scored its first success after the Scala fiasco three months earlier. Eva Turner sang her first Turandot in Italy there in 1926.

Bréval, Lucienne (orig. Bertha Schilling) (b. Männedorf, 4 Nov. 1869; d. Neuilly-sur-Seine, 15 Aug. 1935). Swiss, then French, soprano. Début Paris, O., 1892, Selika; London, C.G., 1899; N.Y., Met., 1901. Created Grisélidis (Massenet), Salammbô (Reyer), Ariane (Dukas), and Pénélope (Fauré). One of the greatest French singers of her day. (R)

Brindisi. From the Italian *far brindisi*, 'to drink one's health': a drinking song, as Alfredo's and Violetta's 'Libiamo' in *La Traviata*.

British Broadcasting Corporation. Opera came into the broadcasting programmes as early as 6 Jan. 1923 when 2LO relayed a B.N.O.C. performance of *Hansel and Gretel* from C.G.—this was the first broadcast from an opera house in Europe. Further B.N.O.C. broadcasts included *Figaro*, *Walküre*, and *Siegfried*. In Oct. 1923 the first studio opera was given, *Roméo et Juliette*. As well as broadcasts from C.G. and other theatres in the 1920's, the B.B.C. began an ambitious series of studio performances under Percy Pitt which lasted from 1926 to 1930 and included *Le Roi D'Ys*, *Pelléas*, and *Louise*, as well as the more popular works in the repertory. From 1929 to 1931 the Labour government subsidized C.G. through the B.B.C. and there were many broadcasts from that theatre. Studio opera, however, ceased until 1937, when a Music Productions Unit was formed with Stanford Robinson as its musical director. Between 1934 and 1939 the Corporation gave concert performances at the Queen's Hall of *Wozzeck*, *Lady Macbeth of Mtsensk*, and *Mathis der Maler*.

Since the war and with the establishment of the Third Programme more and more opera has been given on the B.B.C. Not only are there broadcasts from British opera houses, but also direct transmissions from the European summer festivals at Bayreuth, Salzburg, Munich, &c., and broadcasts of tapes made of studio performances in France, Germany, and Italy, often of works unfamiliar to the English listener. Studio opera in England has revived, and since 1946 there have been performances of *Tristan*, *Die Walküre*, *Les Troyens*, *La Jolie Fille de Perth*, *Elektra*, *Les Deux Journées*, all under Beecham, as well as numerous other works, familiar and unfamiliar, under Stanford Robinson, Nikolai Malko, Rudolf Kempe, Ernest Ansermet, &c. See *Radio Opera*.

British National Opera Company. Formed in 1922 by leading singers and musicians of the Beecham Company forced into liquidation in Dec. 1920. Its Board of Directors included Robert Radford, Percy Pitt, Walter Hyde, Aylmer Buesst, Agnes Nicholls, and Norman Allin. Pitt was the company's first Artistic Director, succeeded by Frederic Austin. The company was launched at Bradford in Feb. 1922, and in May of that year gave its first season at C.G. It gave performances of *The Ring*, *Parsifal*, *Tristan*, and other full-scale works, and included the leading British singers and conductors of the day in its ranks. In the spring of 1924 it was prevented from giving its annual season at C.G. as the directors of the Royal Opera wished to restore International Opera, and its subsequent London seasons were given at His Majesty's, where the first performance of *Hugh the Drover* was given that season. Other new works given by the company included Holst's *The Perfect Fool* (1923) and *At the Boar's Head* (1925).

Guest artists included Melba, Joseph Hislop, Dinh Gilly, and Edward Johnson who appeared with the company during its C.G. seasons. By 1928 the company was in serious financial straits. It owed some £5,000, but had, during its last working year, paid more than £17,000 in entertainment tax. The company was taken over as the Covent Garden English Company in 1929, but survived as such only three seasons.

Britten, Benjamin (b. Lowestoft, 22 Nov. 1913). English composer. Britten regards opera as 'the most fascinating of all musical forms', and his own contribution to it has been of outstanding importance.

His early operetta *Paul Bunyan* (1941) is withdrawn; *Peter Grimes* (1945), established him as an opera composer of the first importance. The hero is the first of Britten's 'outsider' figures, and the opera reveals the deep sympathy for victims of misunderstanding, hatred for the destruction of innocence, and attachment to his native Suffolk sea-coast that have always marked the composer's work. In 1945, just as the war was over, a delighted England fastened upon *Grimes* as token that a major operatic talent was at last working on these shores.

But, largely owing to the uneconomic conditions of grand opera, Britten now turned to chamber opera, forming the English Opera Group (q.v.) for the presentation of such works. *The Rape of Lucretia* (1946) was given at Glyndebourne, and shows more vividly than *Grimes* Britten's mastery of simple means to an expressive end: the use of the 12-piece orchestra is astonishingly resourceful and creative, while there is also a deepening of Britten's individual imagination.

From this tragedy, he turned to *Albert Herring* (1947), a comedy—though pathos is an important ingredient of the work. The transfer of a Maupassant story to a Suffolk setting rekindled Britten's ability to create, with simple musical strokes, local rural types vividly in operatic terms—this had already been shown in *Grimes*, and has remained an important element in Britten's art. *Herring* is faster and more intricate than *Lucretia*. Britten's natural ingenuity summons a wide range of musical devices to comic ends, but though the technique is still more assured, it is the widened range of expressive power (which this serves) that makes *Herring* so remarkable.

For his next two stage works Britten turned to unusual forms: to Gay's *Beggar's Opera* (1948) for a recomposition which is unfailingly fertile and apt; and to *Let's Make an Opera* (1949), the first part of which is a play rehearsing a cast of children and grown-ups, as well as the theatre audience, for participation in the second part, the opera *The Little Sweep*.

In 1951 Britten gave further evidence of his versatility with a realization of *Dido and Aeneas* (he profoundly admires Purcell). In 1951, too, appeared Britten's first large-scale opera since *Grimes*, *Billy Budd*. Since the action takes place on a man-o'-war, the cast was all-male: and this posed special problems of texture and variety which were, with characteristic mastery, turned to advantage in creating an original atmosphere. The scoring is fascinating, drawing especially richly on woodwind and brass; thematically the work is the most closely knit, and formally it is the most complex and subtle of any opera Britten had yet composed.

The opera that followed was again large scale—*Gloriana* (1953), written for the coronation of Queen Elizabeth II. It excited a good deal of non-musical hostility, largely on account of the libretto; this naturally drew the non-musicians' attention more closely than the music, which includes some splendid large-scale inventions that deserve better than mere burial.

In the chamber opera *The Turn of the Screw* (1954), the process of thematic integration is carried still further: the technique of using one principal theme which 'turns' in orchestral interludes is used as a metaphor of the drama, mirroring the inexorable turning of Henry James's screw.

Noyes Fludde (1958) was based on one of the Chester Miracle Plays, and is a marvel of composition with slender, even makeshift means turned to positive emotional advantage. Boys' bugle classes and school recorder groups are used in the orchestra, children's voices on the stage (the work should be given in church).

A Midsummer Night's Dream (1960) was written with both chamber and large-scale performance in mind. Aided by a well-chosen libretto (himself with Peter Pears), Britten has penetrated deep into the mystery of the play and into the world of sleep that has long been another of his fascinations. Fairies, nobles, and rustics are skilfully characterized, and the music is made a strong symbol of how, through the action of the dream, the lovers shed their tensions and find each other, to wake again to a greater happiness.

Britten has followed up some suggestions in *Noyes Fludde* and his experience of Japanese No plays with three so-called Church Parables, *Curlew River* (1964), *The Burning Fiery Furnace* (1966), and *The Prodigal Son* (1968). He has also successfully tackled the special problems of TV opera with *Owen Wingrave* (1971), a treatment of Henry James's story with a pacifist theme. (R)

Brno (Brünn). Town in Moravia, Czechoslovakia. The National Opera House (renamed the Janáček Opera House), founded in 1884 (cap. 1,195), was the scene of the first performance of most of Janáček's operas, and was the centre of the 1958 congress when all of these were given. Three of Martinů's operas have also had their premières there. The theatre was renovated in 1945–6. New opera house opened, Oct. 1965.

Brouwenstijn, Gré (b. Den Helder, 26 Aug. 1915). Dutch soprano. Studied Amsterdam Music Lyceum. Stage début Amsterdam, 1947, Tosca. Sang five seasons with the Nederlandsche Oper. London, C.G., Aida, 1951; has appeared regularly in London in Verdi operas. Bayreuth 1954–6, Elisabeth, Gutrune, Eva, Sieglinde; and Leonore in Wieland Wagner's Stuttgart *Fidelio*. South American début at the Colón, Buenos Aires, under Beecham, 1958; Glyndebourne 1959; Chicago 1959. One of the most musically intelligent of post-war sopranos, with a warmly vibrant voice. (R)

Brownlee, John (b. Geelong, 7 Jan. 1900; d. N.Y., 10 Jan. 1969). Austral. baritone. Studied first in Melbourne; heard by Melba who brought him to London. Début as Marcello in Acts 3 and 4 of *La Bohème* on the night of Melba's farewell, 8 June 1926. Then studied further with Dinh Gilly. Regular member of the Paris Opéra 1927–36, appearing also at C.G. Glyndebourne 1935, and sang Count Almaviva, Don Giovanni, and Don Alfonso there regularly until the war. He was a member of the N.Y. Met. 1937–57, and since 1957 has been head of the opera department at the Manhattan School of Music. A finely schooled singer, with a pleasing if not brilliant voice. (R)

Bruch, Max (b. Cologne, 6 Jan. 1838; d. Friedenau, nr. Berlin, 2 Oct. 1920). German composer and conductor. Bruch's reputation rests upon his concert works rather than upon his three operas, which were never more than moderate successes: they are an operetta, *Scherz, List und Rache* (Cologne 1858); *Die Loreley*, to a text by Giebel first written for Mendelssohn (Mannheim 1863); and *Hermione*, based on Shakespeare's *The Winter's Tale* (Berlin 1872).

Bruneau, Alfred (b. Paris, 3 Mar. 1857; d. Paris, 15 June 1934). French composer and critic. His early, and to conservative listeners sensational, opera *Le Rêve* was based on Zola, to whom he turned for many of his later stage works. Its success was followed up with the maturer *L'Attaque du Moulin* (1893); and then followed three with Zola as his enthusiastic librettist. *Messidor* (1897) suffered from the public opposition to Zola during the Dreyfus case; but *L'Ouragan* (1901) was a triumph, as was *L'Enfant-Roi* (1905), a lighter piece despite its serious thesis on the importance of children in marriage. Zola was by now dead, mourned by Bruneau in *Lazare*, but his subjects continued to occupy the composer. Without being stylistically influenced by Wagner, Bruneau benefited French opera by his use of Wagnerian principles; his music serves its texts faithfully and seriously despite a certain intrusive crudity in its realism. Bruneau was also a gifted critic.

Brünn. See *Brno*.

Brünnhilde. A Valkyrie (sop.), Wotan's favourite daughter, in Wagner's *Die Walküre*, *Siegfried*, and *Götterdämmerung*.

Brunswick (Ger. Braunschweig). Town in Saxony, Germany. The first performances of a large number of German operas by Kusser, Keiser, Schürmann, Hasse, and others were given in the last half of the 17th and first half of the 18th century. The former Landestheater was destroyed during the Second World War, and the present Staatstheater (cap. 1,370) was opened on 25 Dec. 1948 with *Don Giovanni*.

Bruscantini, Sesto (b. Porto Civitanova, 10 Dec. 1919). Italian baritone. Studied with Luigi Ricci in Rome. Début Milan, Sc., 1949, Geronimo. At Glyndebourne since 1951 he has established himself as a stylist in Mozart and Rossini, and has sung buffo roles all over Europe. Began singing Verdi dramatic roles in 1961. (R)

Brussels (Fr. Bruxelles). Capital of Belgium. One of the earliest Flemish operas was Benoît's *Isa*, produced at the Théâtre du Cirque in 1867. The principal home of opera in Brussels now is the Théâtre Royale de La Monnaie, named after an *atelier monetaire* which occupied the site in the 17th century. The present building (cap. 1,700) dates from 1856, but the first Monnaie was built in 1700. The theatre's most glorious period was between 1875 and 1889 under Lapissida, when the premières of Massenet's *Hérodiade* (1881) and Reyer's *Sigurd* (1884) and *Salammbô* (1890) were given; the company included Sylva, Vergnet, Devriès, Soulacroix, Devoyod Fursch-Madi(er), Calvé, Caron, and Melba, and the chief conductor was Joseph Dupont. For many years the theatre was under the direction of Corneil du Thorant, and from 1953 to 1959 the tenor Joseph Rogatschewsky was director, during which period the company included Rita Gorr, Huberte Vecray, Pierre Fleta, and Huc-Santana.

In 1959 M. Huismann became director. He dispensed with the permanent ensemble, and instead invited foreign companies to visit Brussels, and engaged French and Belgian artists for specific operas.

Bucharest (Rum. Bucureşti). Capital of Rumania. Opera was first given by an Italian company in 1787. The German Gregor Company played at Princess Ralu's theatre 'At the Red Fountain' in 1818; Kreibig's Company followed in 1828, the Fourreaux Company in 1831–2, the Müller Company (*en route* home from Russia) with 60 performances in 1833–4. Some of the latter company remained, including the conductor, Wachmann. Application was made for an Italian opera theatre in 1833, and the basis was also laid for a national theatre with the new Philharmonic Society, which gave the first performance in Rumanian—Boïeldieu's *Jean de Paris*. From this period date the beginnings of the movement for a Rumanian national culture. In 1835 the students responsible for *Jean de Paris* staged the first Rumanian opera, a vaudeville *The Triumph of Love*, and in 1838 the first libretto in Rumanian was published, Bellini's *Norma*. When the National Theatre was opened in 1853, the Rumanian company (with Wachmann as director) alternated with an Italian company, under Basilio Samsoni, that had established itself, with a state subsidy, in 1843. The Conservatoire was founded by the conductor and composer Alexandru Flechtenmacher in 1864. Gheorghe Stefanescu's appointment as director of the theatre in 1875 marked a major advance in its fortunes, and the prestige of the best Rumanian singers ensured a decree in the 1885–6 season insisting on operas in Rumanian only.

Rumanian artists were still lower paid than the Italians, and this resulted in the closure of the Rumanian company after a season and the emigration of its best artists. Stefanescu continued his efforts and gave 31 performances between 1889 and 1891; from 1897 to 1901 another company occupied the theatre, and Stefanescu renewed his work without much success in 1902. Efforts at a Rumanian National Opera persisted. In 1914–15 'Student Opera' gave 63 performances; in 1915 the tenor Stefanescu-Cerna organized a company at the Blanduzia Garden, the Gabrielescu Company was founded, and another company gave a season at the Leon Popescu Theatre; in 1916 the baritone Jean Atansiu founded a company. Then in 1919 the Rumanian Lyric Society was founded, opening with *Aida* in the National Theatre in 1920; in 1921 it was made a state institution, housed at the Lyric Theatre, and opened at its new home with *Lohengrin* under Enesco. In 1924, 11 of the best singers resigned in protest against the government's restrictive attitude; and in 1930 the company had to move to an unsuitable building and halve its singers' salaries. The earthquake of 1940 and the bombing of 1944 wrecked the old theatre, but the company managed to continue in a hall intended for a sports ground. The new Opera was opened in 1953 (cap. 1,100), and the repertory includes 30 operas and ballets. There is also a flourishing operetta theatre.

Büchner, Georg (b. Godelau, 17 Oct. 1813; d. Zürich, 19 Feb. 1837). German dramatist. Operas based on his works are Weismann's *Leonce und Lena* (1925), Schwaen's *Leonce und Lena* (1961), Berg's *Wozzeck* (1925), Gurlitt's *Wozzeck* (1926), Wagner-Régeny's *Der Günstling* (text by Caspar Neher on Büchner's version of Hugo's *Marie Tudor* (1935)), Einem's *Dantons Tod* (1947), and Pfister's *Wozzeck* (1950).

Buckman, Rosina (b. Blenheim, ?; d. London, 30 Dec. 1948). New Zealand soprano. Studied Birmingham and Midland School of Music. Début Australia 1911, with Melba Grand Opera Company. London, C.G., 1914; Beecham Company 1915–20. A famous Aida, Butterfly, and Isolde. Married the tenor Maurice d'Oisly. (R)

Budapest. Capital of Hungary. The first Metropolitan Opera Company was formed in the National Theatre (opened 1837), where opera performances were given twice weekly, between performances of plays. Ferenc Erkel, father of Hungarian opera, trained an orchestra of European fame, assembled the excellent soloists, and shaped the varied repertory. It was a fully mature company with a wide repertory that moved to the new opera house in 1884. This State Opera House, one of the most beautiful late Renaissance theatres in Europe, was designed by Miklós Ybl and opened on 27 Sept. 1884; it seats 1,476. Operas and ballets are given here, and the company also mounts performances on the open-air stages at the Zoo and at Margaret Island; chamber works are performed on the Odry stage. Between 1948 and 1955, the company formed a 'Rolling Opera' which toured towns, villages, and industrial settlements in a special train. Between 1911 and 1917 the Erkel Theatre (built 1911 by Márkas, Jakab, and Komor; cap. 2,508) worked under the name of the Folk Opera, and from

1917 as the City Theatre until 1953, when it was linked to the Opera as Budapest's second opera house. The Opera staff now numbers about 1,000, and in all some 600 performances are given annually to 1 m. people.

The company has worked under a distinguished line of resident conductors, including Erkel, Mahler, Nikisch, Sergio Failoni, and Otto Klemperer; while guests have included Strauss, Walter, Furtwängler, Kleiber, Schalk, Balling, Knappertsbusch, and Dobrowen. The greatest singers of their generations have visited the company, whose native artists have included Kálmán Pataky, Sándor Svéd and Mihály Székely.

Buenos Aires. Capital of Argentina. The first theatre of 'Opera and Comedies' was opened in Buenos Aires in 1757. In 1804 the theatre, later known as the Argentina, was built, and in 1813 a zarzuela was included in a programme there. In 1825 the first complete Italian opera was heard, Rossini's *Il Barbiere di Siviglia*, and two years later there was a season which included *Don Giovanni*, *Otello* (Rossini), *Tancredi*, and *La Vestale*. In May 1838 the Victoria Theatre was opened, and opera was given there in excerpts until 1849, when the first Verdi opera was heard in Buenos Aires, *Ernani*. In 1853 a French company from Montevideo visited the city and performed works by Auber and Thomas, and in 1854 two Italian companies and a French one gave opera during the season. In 1857 the first Colón Theatre (q.v.) was opened. In addition to the seasons at the Colón, opera has also been performed at the Teatro de la Opera (opened 1872 with *Il Trovatore*), the Coliseo, the Politeama, and the Doria. It was at the Teatro de la Opera between 1901 and 1906 that Toscanini conducted many memorable performances and established Wagner opera in Buenos Aires. The first Argentinian opera on a national theme was Berutti's *Pampa* (1897); his Inca opera, *Yupanky*, had its title role created by Caruso in 1899. Operas by the Argentinian-born Panizza and Castro are regularly performed in Buenos Aires.

Buesst, Aylmer (b. Melbourne, 28 Jan. 1883; d. St. Albans, 25 Jan. 1970). Australian conductor. Studied Melbourne, Brussels, and London; subsequently at Leipzig under Nikisch. After engagements at Breslau and Görlitz came to England; engaged by the Moody-Manners (1914–16) and Beecham Companies (1918–20). One of the founders of the B.N.O.C. Married May Blyth, a soprano of that company. Particularly admired for his Wagner interpretations, and author of an excellent analysis of *The Ring*. (R)

Buffo (It. = gust or puff). On the stage a *buffone* is a comic actor; in opera a *buffo* is a singer of comic roles—hence *basso buffo*. *Opera buffa* is another term for comic opera.

Bühne (Ger. = stage or theatre). Used for titles, in plural as theatre, e.g. Städtische Bühnen.

Bühnenfestspiel (Ger. = stage festival play). Wagner's term for *Der Ring des Nibelungen*.

Bühnenweihfestspiel (Ger. = stage consecration festival play). Wagner's term for *Parsifal*.

Bulgaria. Western art forms were introduced, mainly by foreign bandmasters, after Bulgaria obtained autonomy from Turkish rule in 1878. The first regular orchestra, founded 1880, was military. In 1890 the first dramatic and operatic company was founded in Sofia; in the following years a series of operas were performed and the first Bulgarian libretto, a translation of *Lucrezia Borgia*, was published. The first music school was established in 1904, and in 1908 the National Opera was founded. The first opera sung in Bulgarian was *Pagliacci* in 1909. A separate professional operetta group gave its first performance in 1917, and in 1944 a state operetta theatre was opened in Sofia. Opera companies were set up in the provinces, where school performances had been presented since the beginning of the century (the first recorded was at Kolarovgrad in 1906). At present there are large opera companies at Stara Zagora, Plovdiv, Ruse, Varna, and Vratsa.

Government-subsidized amateur companies with professional assistance exist at Burgas, Sliven, and Kolarovgrad, and about 30 other amateur groups with professional assistance give short seasons in their own towns and local villages. There is no sharp distinction between amateur and professional performers in the smaller companies.

The Czech bandleader Kaucki used Bulgarian themes for his opera *Karmen i Khina*, but the first opera by a Bulgarian composer was probably *Siromakinya* by Emanuel Manolov (1860–1902), a military conductor who had studied in Moscow. Other composers of opera and operetta were Panayot Pipkov (1871–1942), Hadji Georgiev (1874–1932), Petar Boyadjiev and Georgi Atanasov (1881–1931). The so-called 'Maestro' Atanasov (q.v.), a pupil of Mascagni, composed six operas and many operettas and is considered the founder of Bulgarian opera. Living Bulgarian operatic composers include Parashkev Hadjiev (b. 1912), Marin Goleminov (b. 1908), Viktor Raichev (b. 1922), Lyubomir Pipkov (b. 1904), Veselin Stoyanov (b. 1902), Georgi Zlatev-Cherkin (b. 1905), Pancho Vladigerov (b. 1899), Asen Karastoyanov (b. 1893), Yosif Tsankov (b. 1911), Zhivka Klinkova (b. 1924), Ilya Iliev (b. 1912), Jules Levi (b. 1930), Naydan Genov, Dimitr Vlchev, and Boris Leviev. The earlier Bulgarian operas, including those of Atanasov, employ national themes and rhythms, and this is still the tendency in modern theatre music, most of which is operetta or comic opera. See *Sofia*.

Bülow, Hans von (b. Dresden, 8 Jan. 1830; d. Cairo, 12 Feb. 1894). German conductor and pianist. After early musical training he went to Leipzig University to study law, and to Berlin where he wrote for *Die Abendpost* (defending Liszt and Wagner). The first performance of *Lohengrin* at Weimar under Liszt so overwhelmed him that he threw up the law and went to Zürich to study with Wagner. In 1851 he studied the piano under Liszt, whose daughter Cosima he married in 1857. In 1864 he became chief conductor at the Royal Opera, Munich, conducting there the first performances of *Tristan* (1865) and *Meistersinger* (1868) of which he also made piano scores. When Cosima deserted him for Wagner in 1869 he left Munich and toured Europe. In 1878 he was appointed conductor at the Court Theatre, Hanover, and in 1880 Court Music Director at Meiningen.

Bungert, August (b. Mülheim o/Ruhr, 14 Mar. 1845; d. Leutesdorf, 26 Oct. 1915). German composer. His Wagnerian ambitions, doomed to failure by his lack of Wagner's genius, included the intention to build a 'Bayreuth' on the Rhine for the performance of his Homeric tetralogy *Die homerische Welt*; this embraced *Odysseus Heimkehr* (Dresden 12 Dec. 1896), *Kirke* (Dresden 29 Jan. 1898), *Nausikaa* (Dresden 20 Mar. 1901), and *Odysseus Tod* (Dresden 30 Oct. 1903). Some contemporaries actually considered Bungert the equal of Wagner.

Bunn, Alfred (b. London, 8 Apr. 1806 or 1807; d. Boulogne, 20 Dec. 1860). English theatre manager and librettist. After being stage manager at D.L. and manager of the Theatre Royal, Birmingham, he became joint manager of D.L. and C.G. in 1833. Between 1833 and 1835 he was responsible for the London appearances of Malibran and Schröder-Devrient. In 1835 he paid Malibran £3,375 for 19 appearances at C.G. He provided bad librettos and translations for a number of operas. His cheeseparing measures of economy have become legendary, and artists often found themselves engaged to sing in both theatres on the same evening. It is recorded that during the 1834–5 season 'female dancers pattered from one house to the other six times during the evening, and underwent the operation of dressing and undressing no less than eight'. Autobiography, *The Stage* (1840).

Buona Figliuola, La (The Good Daughter). Opera in 3 acts by Piccinni; text by Goldoni, after Samuel Richardson's novel *Pamela, or Virtue Rewarded* (1740). Prod. Rome, Teatro delle Dame, 6 Feb. 1760; London, Hm., 25 Nov. 1766. It has enjoyed revivals in Italy since 1945. Piccinni's 18th opera and greatest success. The text had already been set by Dani (1756) and Perillo. Piccinni's less successful sequel, text by Goldoni, was *La Buona Figliuola Maritata*, prod. Bologna, 10 June 1761; a further sequel by Latilla, text by Bianchi, was *La Buona Figliuola supposta Vedova*, Venice, Carnival 1766.

Burgstaller, Alois (b. Holzkirchen, 27 Sept. 1871; d. Gmünd, 19 Apr. 1945). German tenor. Studied with Bellurth and Kniese. After singing small roles at Bayreuth, was heard there between 1896 and 1902 as Siegmund, Siegfried, Erik, and Parsifal. His singing of this latter role at the N.Y. Met. in 1903, before the copyright had expired, resulted in his banishment from Bayreuth. Remained at the Met. until 1909. (R)

Burgtheater (Theater bei der Hofburg). The predecessor in Vienna of the Opera House on the Ring, where all the important productions took place until 1869. It was the scene of the premières of Gluck's *Orfeo*, *Alceste*, and *Paride ed Elena*, of Mozart's *Entführung*, *Figaro*, *Così fan tutte*, of Cimarosa's *Il Matrimonio Segreto*, and of the first Viennese performances of *Lohengrin* and Cherubini's *Médée*. Now the State Theatre for spoken drama.

Burian, Karel (known more generally as Carl Burrian) (b. Rousinov, Rakovnik, 12 Jan. 1870; d. Senomaty, 25 Sept. 1924). Czech tenor. Studied Prague with Pivoda. Début Brno, National Theatre, 1891; London, C.G., 1904 and subsequently, as Tristan, Tannhäuser; N.Y., Met., 1906, remaining until 1913 and singing Siegfried, Tannhäuser, Lohengrin, and Herod in *Salome*, which role he had created in Dresden in 1905. Arnold Bax wrote that Burrian was a 'horrifying Herod, slobbering with lust and apparently almost decomposing before our eyes'. (R)

Burkhard, Paul (b. Zürich, 21 Aug. 1911). Swiss composer. Popular for his operettas, among them *Casanova in der Schweiz* (1943) and *Feuerwerk* (1950).

Burkhard, Willy (b. Évilard-sur-Bienne, 17 Apr. 1900; d. Zürich, 18 June 1955). Swiss composer. His single opera, *Die schwarze Spinne* (1948, rev. 1954), had a considerable success.

Burletta (Ital. = a little joke). A term describing a form between ballad opera and comic opera.

Busch, Fritz (b. Siegen, Westphalia, 13 Mar. 1890; d. London, 14 Sept. 1951). German conductor. Studied locally and then at Cologne under Steinbach. Appointed Riga 1909, Aachen 1912, Stuttgart 1918, where he became Generalmusikdirektor. Succeeded Reiner at Dresden 1922; under his leadership the Dresden Opera (q.v.) enjoyed one of its most glorious periods. His uncompromising attitude to Hitler caused him to leave Germany in 1933. He first went to Buenos Aires where he conducted 1933–6 and 1941–5, and also came to establish the Glyndebourne Opera (q.v.) with Carl Ebert in 1934, returning each year until the war, and again in 1950 and 1951. N.Y., Met., 1945–9, also appearances elsewhere in Europe and America. His Mozart was superb, and he was also an outstanding conductor of Wagner and Verdi. (R) His son, **Hans Busch**, is a producer, and head of the opera department at Indiana University.

Bush, Alan (b. London, 22 Dec. 1900). English composer. His sympathy with Communism has dictated his choice of operatic subjects. These include a children's operetta *The Press-Gang* (1946), *Wat Tyler* (1950), an operetta *The Spell* (1953), and *The Men of Blackmoor* (1955), all with librettos by the composer's wife Nancy. His works have succeeded in East Germany, and are also admired by many who cannot accept their dominantly political outlook.

Busoni, Ferruccio (b. Empoli, 1 Apr. 1866; d. Berlin, 27 July 1924). Italian composer and pianist. His four operas have won limited but enthusiastic appreciation in Germany though never in Italy, and are occasionally revived, *Arlecchino* (1917) with conspicuous success at Glyndebourne (1954). The others are *Die Brautwahl* (1912), *Turandot* (1917), and *Doktor Faust* (completed by Jarnach, prod. 1925), for which Busoni's great friend and champion E. J. Dent claimed nobility and beauty despite an austere intellectual vein. Revived Berlin 1955, with Fischer-Dieskau.

Büsser, Henri (Paul) (b. Toulouse, 16 Jan. 1872). French conductor and composer. Studied Paris Conservatoire with Widor and Gounod. Début Paris, O.C., 1902, conducting *Le Roi d'Ys*. Was responsible for revivals of *Iphigénie en Tauride*, *Orfeo*, *La Reine Fiaminette*. Also conducted at the Opéra, and from 1939 to 1941 was musical director of the Comique. His works include *Jane Grey* (1891), *Les Noces Corinthiennes* (1922), and *Le Carrosse du Saint-Sacrement* (1948).

Butt, Dame Clara (b. Southwick, Sussex, 1 Feb. 1873; d. North Stoke, 23 Jan. 1936). English contralto. Studied with Rootham at Bristol and at the R.C.M., London, and subsequently with Bouhy and Gerster. In 1892 sang Orfeo in a student performance at the Lyceum Theatre. Her whole career was devoted to the concert platform, but in 1920 she was persuaded by Beecham to sing Orfeo under his baton at C.G. (R)

Byron, George Gordon, Lord (b. London, 22 Jan. 1788; d. Missolonghi, 19 Apr. 1824). English poet. Operas based on his works are as follows. *The Bride of Abydos* (1813): Lebrun (1848); Poniatowski (1848). *The Corsair* (1813): Schumann (begun 1844, unfin.). *The Giaour* (1813): Natanael Berg (*Leila*, 1912). *Lara* (1814): Maillart (1864). *Parisina* (1815): Donizetti (1833); Keurvels (1890). *Manfred* (1817): Petrella (1872). *Don Juan*—Canto 2, the Haidée episode (1819): Fibich (*Hedy*, 1896). *Marino Faliero* (1820): Donizetti (1835); Holstein (publ. 1881). *Cain* (1821): Delvincourt (*Lucifer*, 1949); Lattuada (1957). *Heaven and Earth* (1821): Glière (1900). *The Two Foscari* (1821): Verdi (1844); Bogatirev (*c*. 1940).

C

Cabaletta (also *cabbaletta*, *cavaletta*. From It. *cavatinetta*, dim. of *cavatina*, which in turn dim. of *cavata* = extraction). The term has several meanings. It is usually applied to a short aria of simple, reiterated rhythm, with repeats. Rossini, whose operas have many, told Clara Novello that the first statement should be sung as written; thereafter the singer could embellish as he pleased. Anne's cabaletta in Stravinsky's *The Rake's Progress* is of this type, though deviations from the score would hardly be encouraged. In the 19th century the term grew to mean the final section only of an aria in several parts, usually quick and brilliant but now actually written down. It has also been used to describe the first section of an aria; this would on its reappearance be varied and often with triplets in the accompaniment (this has suggested a derivation from *cavallo*, a horse, from the galloping movement). See also *Cavatina*.

Caccini, Giulio (b. Rome, *c.* 1545; d. Florence, 10 Dec. 1618). Italian singer and lutenist to the Duke of Tuscany in Florence, but famous as one of the first opera composers. By 1589 he was a member of the Camerata (q.v.). Following Vincenzo Galilei, he wrote music giving increased importance to single voice; hence he has wrongly been called the inventor of monody. His recitatives sung to his own accompaniment led to dramatic scenas, and so towards opera. Some of Caccini's music was included in *Euridice* (1600) by his rival Peri, and he then also set Rinuccini's text complete. This was, if not the first performed, the first published opera. He also set the same writer's *Dafne* and contributed to *Il Rapimento di Cefalo*. His arias and choruses for this are in his collection *Le Nuove Musiche* (1602), which marked the new change in style from polyphony to monody. Other important collections appeared later. Caccini was also one of the first composers to use a figured bass.

Cadenza. Literally Italian for cadence, whence an elaborate flourish ornamenting a final cadence at any point in an aria. From a tonic chord in its second inversion, the singer took off in flights of his own fancy that displayed his vocal virtuosity. He would come to rest on the dominant, which was played by the accompaniment with its succeeding tonic. The ternary form of the da capo aria allowed three cadenzas, the last being reserved for the singer's most brilliant acrobatics. The instrumental cadenza grew from this operatic example.

Caffarelli (orig. Gaetano Majorano) (b. Bitonto, 12 Apr. 1710; d. Naples, 31 Jan. 1783). Italian male soprano. Discovered by Domenico Caffarelli, whose name he took. Studied with Porpora for five years, allegedly concentrating on studies and emerging, in Porpora's opinion, as 'the greatest singer in Europe'. Début Rome, T.V., 1724 (i.e. when 14). After triumphs in Venice, Milan, and Bologna, Caffarelli settled again in Naples. Spent six months in London during 1738, singing chiefly in Handel's operas, but was said then to have been in poor voice. From 1741 sang regularly at Naples, S.C., also travelling widely in Italy. Visited France 1753, giving private recitals to cheer the Dauphine during the last months of her pregnancy as well as appearing in concerts and opera in Paris. A highly quarrelsome man, who had once been under house arrest and once imprisoned for his behaviour to other singers, he challenged the poet Ballot de Sauvot to a duel over the merits of French and Italian music, managing to wound his adversary. Later sang in Lisbon, surviving the famous earthquake of 1 Nov. 1755. Retiring to Italy, he bought a dukedom and two palaces with the huge fortune he had amassed. One of the most famous of all the great castrati (Bartolo refers to him in the Lesson Scene of *Barbiere*).

Cahier, Mme Charles (orig. Sarah-Jane Layton Walker) (b. Nashville, Tenn., 6 Jan. 1870; d. Manhattan Beach, Cal., 15 Apr. 1951). American contralto. Début Nice 1904; leading contralto of the Vienna Opera 1907–11; joined the Metropolitan Opera 1912. Taught at the Curtis Institute. Also known as Mrs. Morris Black. (R)

Cairo. Capital of Egypt. The Opera House was opened in 1869. *Aida*, commissioned for the opening by the Khedive, was not finished until 1871, and performed there on Christmas Eve, with Arabian trumpeters, a Cairo military band, and 300 extras. In 1912 an open-air performance was given at the Pyramids. Opera is now given by visiting companies, mostly Italian.

Calaf. A Tartar prince (ten.), hero of Puccini's *Turandot*.

Calife de Bagdad, Le. Opera in 1 act by Boïeldieu; text by Saint-Just. Prod. Paris, O.C. 16 Sept. 1800; London, H.M.'s, 11 May 1809; New Orleans, 2 Mar. 1806.

Callas (orig. Kalogeropoulou), **Maria** (b. New York, 3 Dec. 1923). Greek soprano. Studied Athens with Elvira de Hidalgo. Début Athens 1938, Santuzza; Verona Arena 1947, Gioconda; Milan, Sc., 1951–8 and again 1960–2, where she sang in revivals of *Norma*, *Medea*, *Anna Bolena*, *Il Pirata*, *Poliuto*, &c.; London, C.G., 1952–3, 1957–9, 1964; Chicago 1954–6; N.Y., Met., 1957–8, 1965; Dallas 1958–9. Her range, technique, and style make her the first soprano since Lilli Lehmann to have sung both Isolde and Lucia, Brünnhilde and Violetta. Her highly individual voice and great dramatic and musical talent have been responsible for the revival of works by Rossini, Bellini, and Donizetti. Her vocal technique, which is less than perfect, coupled with her intelligent treatment of the text and her dramatic intensity, combine to make her the most controversial singer in contemporary opera. (R)

Calunnia, La. Don Basilio's (bass) aria in Act 1, scene 2, of Rossini's *Il Barbiere di Siviglia*. It describes gleefully the effective growth of slander from a little breeze to a gale that can blast a man's reputation.

Calvé, Emma (orig. Rose Calvet) (b. Décazeville, 15 Aug. 1858; d. Millau, 6 Jan. 1942). French soprano. Début Brussels, La M., 1882, Marguerite. After further study with Mathilde Marchesi, made London début, C.G., 1892; there regularly until 1904. N.Y., Met., from 1893. Created Suzel (*L'Amico Fritz*), Anita (*La Navarraise*), and title role in Massenet's *Sapho*. Retired from the opera stage 1910. Best remembered for her Carmen. Autobiography *Sous tous les ciels j'ai chanté* (Paris 1940). (R)

Calzabigi, Ranieri (b. Livorno, 23 Dec. 1714; d. Naples, July 1795). Italian writer. His librettos brought him into touch with Metastasio, an edition of whose works he published during a stay in Paris. Here he and his brother ran a lottery, with Casanova as partner and under the protection of Mme de Pompadour, before being expelled. He is famous as the author of three librettos for Gluck (q.v.) who owed the inspiration for many of his reforms to Calzabigi.

Cambiale di Matrimonio, La (The Bill of Marriage). Opera in 1 act by Rossini; text by Rossi founded on Camillo Federici's comedy (1790). Prod. Venice, Teatro San Moisè, 3 Nov. 1810; N.Y. 8 Nov. 1937; London, S.W., 23 Apr. 1954. Rossini's first opera to be performed. The duet 'Dunque io son' was later used in Act 1 of *Il Barbiere di Siviglia*.

Cambridge. English university town. The Cambridge University Musical Society has done well by English opera (especially if one considers Handel a native composer), above all in the period 1902–41 under E. J. Dent (q.v.), who was lecturer at King's from 1902, and Professor of Music there from 1926. During this latter period the following works were performed: Purcell's *King Arthur* (1928), Honegger's *King David* (1929), Purcell's *The Fairy Queen* (1931), Handel's *Samson*

(1932), *Susanna* (1935 and 1938), *The Choice of Hercules* (1935), Vaughan Williams's *The Poisoned Kiss* (1936), Handel's *Saul* (1937). and Purcell's *The Tempest*, (1938). Before these productions the most important event, which had a far-reaching effect on opera in English, was the 1911 production of *The Magic Flute*, in Dent's translation, with a cast that included Steuart Wilson and Clive Carey. This led to the long-overdue acceptance of Mozart's opera into the English repertory.

Productions in recent years have included Handel's *Solomon* (1948), Cavalieri's *La Rappresentazione di Anima e di Corpo* (1951), Monteverdi's *Orfeo* (1950), Tranchell's *The Mayor of Casterbridge* (1951), Handel's *Athalia*, and Vaughan Williams's *Pilgrim's Progress* (1954). In 1954 the Cambridge University Opera Group was formed, probably in the hope of staging works less academic than those chosen for the official university productions. It has performed Cimarosa's *Il Matrimonio Segreto* (1955), Stravinsky's *The Rake's Progress* and Vaughan Williams's *Sir John in Love* (1956), Honegger's *Jeanne au Bûcher* (1957), Orff's *Catulli Carmina* and Liebermann's *The School for Wives* (1958), *The Mayor of Casterbridge*, Berkeley's *A Dinner Engagement*, Bizet's *Don Procopio* (1959). It was from the group's efforts in 1956 that the New Opera Company (q.v.) sprang.

Camerata. The group of poets and musicians which met in a room (hence the title) of the houses of the Florentine nobles Giovanni de' Bardi and Jacopi Corsi about 1600; from their discussions and experiments was born the new art form of opera. The members included the composers Vincenzo Galilei (father of the astronomer), Peri (q.v.), Caccini (q.v.), Emilio de' Cavalieri, and the poet Rinuccini. Their aim was to restore the dramatic use of music as practised in ancient Greek drama. Accordingly they evolved a new monodic style known as the *stile rappresentativo* to replace the current polyphonic music. Peri's *Dafne*, described as a *dramma per musica* and now unfortunately lost, resulted and was the first opera.

Probably this work, certainly the other works that immediately followed, were extended recitatives, stressing carefully the meaning of the words, with slender accompaniment by lutes and harpsichord.

Cammarano, Salvatore (b. Naples, 19 Mar. 1801; d. Naples, 17 July 1852). Italian playwright and librettist. Provided Donizetti with libretti for *Lucia di Lammermoor*, *Belisario*, *L'Assedio di Calais*, *Pia de' Tolomei*, *Roberto d'Evereux*, *Maria di Rudenz*, and Verdi with *Alzira*, *La Battaglia di Legnano*, *Luisa Miller*, *Il Trovatore*. Also wrote libretti for Pacini and Mercadante.

Campana Sommersa, La (The Sunken Bell). Opera in 4 acts by Respighi; text by Guastalla based on Gerhard Hauptmann's *Die versunkene Glocke*. Prod. Hamburg, Municipal Theatre, 18 Nov. 1927; N.Y., Met., 24 Nov. 1928, with Rethberg.

Campanello di Notte, Il (The Night Bell). Also known as *Il Campanello dello Speziale*. Opera in 1 act by Donizetti; text by the composer based on a French vaudeville, *La Sonnette de Nuit*, by Brunswick, Troin, and Lhérie. Prod. Naples, Teatro Nuovo, 1 June 1836; London, Ly., 30 Nov. 1837; N.Y., Lyceum, 7 May 1917. Written in a week to save an impresario from bankruptcy. Still often performed.

Campanini, Cleofonte (b. Parma, 1 Sept. 1860; d. Chicago, 19 Dec. 1919). Italian conductor. Studied Parma Conservatory. Début Parma 1883, *Carmen*. Music staff N.Y., Met., 1883–4; N.Y., Ac. of M., 1888; Milan, Sc., 1903–6; London, C.G., 1904–12. Conducted premières of *Adriana Lecouvreur*, *Siberia*, and *Madama Butterfly*. Conducted first London *Madama Butterfly*, *Pelléas et Mélisande*, *La Fanciulla del West*, and *I Gioielli della Madonna*. Manhattan Opera 1906–9 (Artistic Director), Chicago 1910–19 (General Manager 1918–19). Married the soprano Eva Tetrazzini. One of the great opera conductors of this century.

Campanini, Italo (b. Parma, 30 June 1845; d. near there, 22 Nov. 1896).

Italian tenor, brother of above. Studied Parma Conservatory, and later with Lamperti in Milan. Début Odessa 1869 (Manrico). First Italian Lohengrin, Bologna, 1871. London début, D.L., 1872, Gennaro (*Lucrezia Borgia*); regularly there until 1881. N.Y., Ac. of M., 1873. Faust at opening of Met. 1883 and member of company 1891–4. Also impresario, and brought his brother Cleofonte to the Met., to conduct American première of *Otello*.

Campiello, Il. Opera in 3 acts by Wolf-Ferrari; text by Ghisalberti from Goldoni's comedy (1756). Prod. Milan, Sc., 12 Feb. 1936. The action includes a street fight between two mothers sung by tenors *en travesti* in the piazza from which the opera takes its name.

Camporese, Violante (b. Rome, 1785; d. Rome, 1839). Italian soprano. An aristocrat and married to a nobleman (Giustiniani), she did not begin her career until 1815. Studied Paris with Crescenti. After success at Milan, Sc., was engaged for the King's Theatre, London, in 1817, made début in title role of Cimarosa's *Penelope*. A fine Mozart singer; her roles included Donna Anna, Dorabella, and Sextus (*La Clemenza di Tito*). Sang principal soprano roles in first London performances of *La Gazza Ladra* and *Otello* (Rossini). Retired 1824.

Campra, André (b. Aix-en-Provence, 4 Dec. 1660; d. Versailles, 29 June 1744). French composer of Italian descent. Started career as a church musician and was director of music at Notre Dame, Paris, by the age of 34. Began writing operas in secret for fear of the Church's displeasure. In 1700 left Notre Dame, and wrote many stage works that won great popularity. The most successful was the first, *L'Europe Galante* (opera-ballet, 1697). His works satisfied the current French taste for variety and ingenuity while showing marked originality and progressiveness. His declared aim was to combine the best of the French and Italian schools.

Canada. See *Toronto*, *Vancouver*.

Caniglia, Maria (b. Naples, 5 May 1906). Italian soprano. Studied at Naples with Roche. Début Turin 1930, Chrysothemis. Swiftly became leading Italian lyric-dramatic soprano of the 1930's, singing at Milan, Sc., 1930–42 and since the war. London, C.G., 1937, 1939, and 1950, with Scala Company; N.Y., Met., 1938–9. Married Pino Donati 1939, director of Verona Arena and latterly of Teatro Comunale, Bologna. An admired Tosca and Adriana Lecouvreur. (R)

Canio. The leader (ten.) of the strolling players in Leoncavallo's *Pagliacci*.

Cantelli, Guido (b. Novara, 27 Apr. 1920; d. Paris (air-crash), 24 Nov. 1956). Italian conductor. Studied Milan Conservatory with Pedrollo and Ghedini. Début Novarra 1943. Conducted the Scala Orchestra in London 1950. Turned his attention to opera in 1956 when he conducted *Così fan tutte* at the Piccola Scala. The announcement of his appointment as music director of La Scala was made a few days before his death. (R)

Canterbury Pilgrims, The. (1) Opera in 3 acts by Stanford; text by G. A. A'Beckett after Chaucer's poem (unfin. 1400). Prod. London, D.L., 28 Apr. 1884.

(2) Opera in 4 acts by De Koven; text by Percy Mackaye after Chaucer. Prod. N.Y., Met., 8 Mar. 1917.

Cantilena. (It. = cradle song, sing-song). Orig. the part of a choral composition with the main tune, or a small piece for one voice. Now used to describe a smoothly flowing, melodious part, or to indicate that a passage should thus be performed.

Canzone. A word of Provençal origin (*canzo*) describing a certain style of lyrical poetry. It has had various musical meanings; in operatic usage it came, by the 18th century, to mean an actual song outside the dramatic situation, e.g. 'Voi che sapete' in *Le Nozze di Figaro*. The diminutive Canzonetta usually describes a short, simple song.

Capoul, Joseph-Amédée-Victor (b. Toulouse, 27 Feb. 1839; d. Pujaydran-du-Gers, 18 Feb. 1924). French tenor.

Studied Paris. Début O.C., 1861, Daniel in Adam's *Le Chalet*. London, D.L., 1871–5; C.G., 1877–9; N.Y., Ac. of M., 1871; Met. 1883–4. Created many roles in Paris, and was a fine Fra Diavolo and Roméo. Taught N.Y. 1892–9. Stage manager Paris, O., 1897.

Capriccio. Opera in 1 act by Richard Strauss; text by Clemens Krauss and the composer. Prod. Munich 28 Oct. 1942, with Ursuleac, Ranczak, Hann, Hotter, cond. Krauss; London, C.G., by Munich Opera Company, 22 Sept. 1953; N.Y., Juillard School, 2 Apr. 1954. A dramatized conversation piece on whether words or music are of greater importance in opera. The subject remains unresolved.

Capuana, Franco (b. Fano, 29 Sept. 1894; d. Naples, 10 Dec. 1969). Italian conductor. Studied Naples with De Nardis. Début Brescia 1919. Until 1929 conducted in most Italian provincial theatres. Naples, S.C., 1930–7; Milan, Sc. 1937–40, 1946–52 (from 1949 as musical director). Conducted first post-war opera at C.G., *La Traviata*, with San Carlo Company, 5 Sept. 1946; and performances by the resident company 1951–2. Specialist in the non-Italian repertory, notably Wagner and Strauss. (R)

Capuleti e i Montecchi, I (The Capulets and the Montagues). Opera in 4 parts by Bellini; text by Romani after Shakespeare's tragedy *Romeo and Juliet* (*c.* 1595–7). Prod. Venice, F., 11 Mar. 1830; with Giuditta Grisi, Caradori-Allan, London 20 July 1833; New Orleans, 4 Apr. 1847. Text originally set by Vaccai, whose last act was, until 1895, substituted for Bellini's in Italy. Bellini himself used parts of his unsuccessful *Zaira* (1829) in it. A somewhat free adaptation of Shakespeare with a happy ending.

Cardiff. Capital of Wales. See *Welsh National Opera Company*.

Cardillac. Opera in 3 acts by Hindemith; text by Ferdinand Lion, after E. T. A. Hoffmann's story *Das Fräulein von Scuderi* (1818). Prod. Dresden, 9 Sept. 1926, with Claire Born, Robert Burg. Concert performance in English, London, Q.H., 18 Dec. 1936. Revised version (new libretto by composer, score unchanged), Zürich 20 June 1952. Concerns a master jeweller who murders his customers rather than part with his creations.

Carelli, Emma (b. Naples, 12 May 1877; d. Montefiascone, 17 Aug. 1928). Italian soprano. Studied with her father, the composer Beniamino Carelli. Début Altamura 1895 in Mercadante's *Vestale*; Milan, Sc., 1899–1900, where she was the first Italian Tatiana. Married the impresario Walter Mocchi who managed the Rome Opera and the Colón, Buenos Aires, where Carelli regularly sang. She managed the Rome Opera herself 1912–26. Made her last appearance in 1914 as Iris. Her greatest role was Zazà. (R)

Carey, Clive (b. Hedingham, 30 May 1883; d. London, 30 Apr. 1968). British baritone and later teacher and producer. Studied R.C.M. and under Jean de Reszke. Papageno in the famous Cambridge *Magic Flute* 1911. Old Vic Opera Company 1920, sang in and produced *Figaro*, *Don Giovanni*, *Magic Flute*. Professor of Singing, Adelaide 1924–8. Toured U.S.A. and Canada as Macheath (*Beggar's Opera*). Opera producer at S.W. 1933; Adelaide Conservatory 1939, and Melbourne 1943–5. Director S.W. 1945–6. Professor of Singing and director of opera at R.C.M. 1946–53.

Carl Rosa Opera Company, Royal. English opera company founded by Karl August Nicolaus Rose, a German violinist from Hamburg who came to England in 1866. After the death of his wife, the soprano Euphrosyne Parepa, in 1874, Rosa (as he was now known) decided to devote his life to presenting opera in English. In Sept. 1875 the Carl Rosa Opera Company came into being with a performance of *Le Nozze di Figaro* at the Princess's Theatre, London. Rosa became associated with Augustus Harris, manager of Drury Lane, and a prosperous 5 years followed (1883–8). Harris then took over Covent Garden, and in 1889 Rosa died. The company became a touring organization, giving only occasional London seasons.

In 1893 Queen Victoria conferred the title 'Royal' on the company following a performance at Balmoral Castle. From 1900 until 1916 the company was under the management of Alfred van Norden; and from 1916 until 1923 Arthur Winckworth and Mrs. Carl Rosa (Rosa's second wife) were co-directors. After the First World War the company took over both the Harrison–Frewin and the Alan Turner companies. The former was under the management of H. B. Phillips, who in 1923 took over the direction of the Carl Rosa Company. At this time Phillips had two and sometimes three companies touring the provinces.

Phillips died in 1950 and his widow directed the company, with Arthur Hammond as music director, from then until 1957, when she was succeeded by H. Procter-Gregg. In 1953 the Arts Council made a grant of £20,000 to the company which was increased in stages to £61,000 for 1957–8. At the same time the Arts Council provided the funds for the purchase of the company from her. Internal differences between the board of directors and Procter-Gregg led to the latter's resignation in 1958 and to the withdrawal of the Arts Council's subsidy. At the end of 1958 most of its personnel were taken over by Sadler's Wells, when Norman Tucker and his associates launched their new scheme of opera and operetta in London coupled with a greater amount of touring of the provinces. The company made an unsuccessful attempt to stage a come-back in 1960.

The company gave the first performance in England of *Manon* (1885), *La Bohème* (1897), and *Andrea Chénier* (1903), and the premières of a number of British works, including Goring Thomas's *Esmeralda* (1883) and *Nadeshda* (1885), Stanford's *The Canterbury Pilgrims* (1884), and Lloyd's *John Socman* (1951).

Carmelites, The. See *Dialogues des Carmélites*.

Carmen. Opera in 4 acts by Bizet; text by Meilhac and Halévy, after Mérimée's *nouvelle* (1845). Prod. Paris, O.C., 3 Mar. 1875, with Galli-Marié, Chapuy, Lhérie, Bouhy; Vienna 23 Oct. 1875 (in German, with recitatives by Guiraud in place of spoken dialogue); London, H.M.'s, 22 June 1878, with Minne Hauk; N.Y., Ac. of M., 23 Oct. 1878, with Hauk and Campanini. Bizet's last and ultimately most successful opera; he died on the night of its 33rd performance.

Act 1. A bustling square in Seville in about 1820. A guard is being relieved; Micaela (sop.), a peasant, is seeking Don José (ten.), a corporal under the command of Capt. Zuniga (bass). Not finding him, she leaves. At noon the girls from the cigarette factory come out, among them the attractive gipsy Carmen (mezzo), who tries her charms on José and throws him a flower. When the girls go back to work Micaela returns with word from José's mother. A quarrel in the factory leads to Carmen's arrest, but the fascinated José lets her escape.

Act 2. Lillas Pastia's tavern, a smugglers' haunt. The bullfighter Escamillo (bar.) attracts Carmen with his Toreador Song. She is there to meet José on his release from prison; when he later wants to return to barracks she tries to prevent him. Zuniga appears and orders José away; they fight, and when the hidden smugglers seize Zuniga, José has to flee with Carmen to the mountains.

Act 3. The smugglers' cave. Carmen is taunting José and thinking of Escamillo. She learns from the cards of her impending death. Escamillo comes and fights with José; again the smugglers intervene, and as Escamillo goes it is obvious to all that José has lost Carmen to him. Micaela reappears, with news that José's mother is dying, and leads him away.

Act 4. Outside the Seville bullring. Carmen promises Escamillo her love if he wins. After the crowd has gone in, José appears, dishevelled. When she spurns him he stabs her, and gives himself up as the victorious Escamillo emerges triumphantly with the crowd.

Carmina Burana. Scenic cantata by Orff; Latin text based on poems in Latin, Old German, and Old French. Prod. Frankfurt 8 June 1937; San

Francisco, 3 Oct. 1958; London, Royal Festival Hall, 26 Jan. 1960.

Caro nome. Gilda's (sop.) aria in Act 1, scene 2, of Verdi's *Rigoletto*, expressing her love for the 'student' Gualtier Maldé, who is in fact the Duke of Mantua.

Caron (orig. Meuniez), **Rose** (b. Monserville, 17 Nov. 1857; d. Paris, 9 Apr. 1930). French soprano. Début Brussels 1884, Alice (*Robert le Diable*) where she created Brunehilde in Reyer's *Sigurd* (La M. 1884) and title role in his *Salammbô* (1890). Paris, O., 1885–7 and 1890–1902, where she was the first French Sieglinde and Desdemona. Professor of singing Paris Conservatoire from 1902. (R)

Carosio, Margherita (b. Genoa, 7 June 1908). Italian soprano. Début Novi Ligure 1924, Lucia. London, C.G., 1928, 1946, 1950. Milan, Sc., from 1929. Created the role of Egloge in Mascagni's *Nerone*, 1935. Originally a light soubrette, she developed into a lyric soprano and returned to London as Violetta in the San Carlo 1946 season. (R)

Carré (orig. Giraud), **Marguerite** (b. Cabourg, 16 Aug. 1880; d. Paris, 26 Dec. 1947). French soprano. Daughter of the theatre director of Nantes where she made her début as Mimì, 1899. Paris, O.C., 1902, whose director, Albert Carré, she subsequently married, divorced in 1924, and remarried in 1929. Created 15 roles at the Comique. Also the first Paris Cio-Cio-San, Snegurochka, and Salud (*La Vida Breve*), and an outstanding Louise, Manon, and Mélisande. (R)

Carré, Michel (b. Paris, 1819; d. Argenteuil, 27 June 1872). French librettist. Furnished most of the leading French composers of the second half of the 19th century with libretti, including Meyerbeer (*Dinorah*), Gounod (*Mireille*, *Faust*, *Roméo et Juliette*, and five more), Bizet (*Pêcheurs de Perles*), Thomas (*Hamlet*, *Mignon*), Offenbach (*Contes d'Hoffmann*). He was Albert Carré's uncle (see above).

Carron (orig. Cox), **Arthur** (b. Swindon, 12 Dec. 1900; d. Swindon, 10 May 1967). British tenor. Début London, Old Vic., 1929; subsequently leading tenor there and S.W. until 1935; C.G. 1931, 1939. N.Y., Met., 1935–46; also sang in Chicago, Cincinnati, Philadelphia, and South America. Returned to England, C.G., 1947–51. One of the best English dramatic tenors of the inter-war years.

Carte, Richard D'Oyly (b. London, 3 May 1844; d. London, 3 Apr. 1901). English impresario. He was the son of a music publisher and was originally destined for a musical career, but soon turned to the business side of music, first as manager of Patti, Mario, Gounod, and others, then as a theatre manager, introducing to England Lecocq's *Giroflé-Girofla* and Offenbach's *La Périchole* and *Whittington.* In 1875 he commissioned *Trial by Jury* from Gilbert and Sullivan, and its great success led to his forming a company to continue to present works by this remarkable combination at the Opéra-Comique in London. He then built his own theatre, the Savoy, which opened with *Patience* in 1881, where the Gilbert and Sullivan partnership flourished for ten uninterrupted years, to be resumed in 1893 with *Utopia Ltd.* and 1896 with *The Grand Duke.* In 1891 Carte made an attempt to establish English Grand Opera and built the English Opera House (now the Palace Theatre) in Cambridge Circus, which opened with Sullivan's *Ivanhoe.* The venture was not a success. Carte introduced electric lighting into the theatre and abolished charges for programmes and cloakrooms. His theatrical enterprises were continued by his widow until her death in 1913, and then by his sons, and now by his granddaughter Bridget. (See also *Sullivan.*)

Cartellone (It. = a large placard; hence a playbill). Has come to mean the list of operas to be performed during the season. The Cartellone does not include the names of artists appearing; they are listed under a separate heading, *L'elenco artistico.*

Carteri, Rosanna (b. Verona, 14 Dec. 1930). Italian soprano. Began vocal studies with Cusinati when 10. Winner of vocal contest organized by Radio Italiana 1948. Début Rome, Terme di Caracalla, 1949, Elsa. Milan, Sc., since 1951. San Francisco 1954. London, C.G., 1960. Created title role in Pizzetti's *Ifigenia* 1950, Flavia in Castro's *Proserpina e lo Straniero* 1952, and Natasha in first European performance of Prokofiev's *War and Peace*, Florence 1953. (R)

Caruso, Enrico (b. Naples, 25 Feb. 1873; d. Naples, 2 Aug. 1921). Italian tenor. Studied with Guglielmo Vergine and Vincenzo Lombardi. His début at the Teatro Nuovo, Naples, 16 Nov. 1894, in *L'Amico Francesco* (Morelli), led to engagements all over Italy. Created Maurizio (*Adriana Lecouvreur*) and Loris (*Fedora*). Appeared with Melba at Monte Carlo early in 1902. London, C.G., 1902, as Duke of Mantua, 1904–7, 1913–14. N.Y., Met., 1903–20, making more than 600 appearances in nearly 40 operas including Dick Johnson in the world première of *La Fanciulla del West* and the first Metropolitan performances of *Armide* and *La Forza del Destino*.

Caruso possessed one of the most beautiful tenor voices the world has ever known. In his young days it was mellow, sumptuous, of baritone-like quality in its lower register, and until 1906 he sang with almost reckless abandon and gaiety. During the next stage of his vocal career he perfected his art, and his phrasing and style became wellnigh impeccable. In 1908–9 he suffered a temporary vocal setback, and subsequently his voice darkened. But all who heard him sing at any stage in his career claim that no sound like it has been heard since. He was moreover a convincing actor, especially in such roles as Eleazar, Canio, and Vasco da Gama.

Caruso was perhaps the first true 'gramophone' tenor; he began recording in 1902 and made his last recordings in 1920. It is said that during his lifetime his royalties from records amounted to something between four and five hundred thousand pounds. From his many records perhaps his 'Una furtiva lagrima' (1904) and 'O Paradiso' (1910) represent operatic singing at its very greatest. His career came to an end on Christmas Eve 1920 when he was singing Eleazar in *La Juive* while suffering from acute pain which developed into bronchial pneumonia.

A film of his life, *The Great Caruso*, with Mario Lanza, was made in 1950; and among the many biographies of him are *Enrico Caruso, His Life and Death*, by his widow, Dorothy Caruso (1945), and *Caruso*, by T. R. Ybarra (1953). (R)

Carvalho, Léon (orig. Carvaille) (b. Port-Louis, France, 18 Jan. 1825; d. Paris, 29 Dec. 1897). French impresario. Studied in Paris (Conservatoire) and was for a time a singer at the Opéra-Comique where he met Marie Miolan (q.v.) whom he married in 1853. Director, T.L., 1856–8; then stage manager, O., and director, O.C., 1876–87. In the latter year the theatre was burned down and 131 people were killed; Carvalho was fined and imprisoned for negligence, but in 1891 after a successful appeal was reinstated in his former position.

Casanova de Stingalt, Giovanni Jacopo (b. Venice, 2 Apr. 1725; d. Dux, Bohemia, 4 June 1798). Italian adventurer. He was notorious for his amorous exploits, and these, his daring escape from the Piombi in Venice, and many other incidents are colourfully described in his 12 volumes of *Mémoires* (1791–8). They have inspired various operas. *Casanova*, in 3 acts, by Lortzing (text by composer on a French vaudeville *Casanova au Fort St-André*), was produced Leipzig 31 Dec. 1841. There are also works by Pulvermacher (1890), Różycki (Warsaw 3 May 1923), and Andreae (four 1-act operas, Dresden 17 June 1924). A friend of Mozart's librettist Da Ponte.

Casavola, Franco (b. Modugno, 13 July 1891; d. Bari, 7 July 1955). Italian composer. Early adherent of Italian futurism. Later turned to opera composition with greater general success; works include 1-act comic opera *Il Gobbo del Califfo* (1929), *Astuzie d'amore* (1936), and *Salammbô* (1948).

Casazza, Elvira (b. Ferrara, 15 Nov. 1887; Milan, Jan. 1965). Italian mezzo-soprano. Début San Remo 1910, Azucena. Milan, Sc., 1915–40; London, C.G., 1926, 1931. A favourite artist of Toscanini, famous for her Mistress Quickly. Created Debora in Pizzetti's *Debora e Jaele*. After 1948 taught singing, first at Pesaro, latterly in Rome. (R)

Casella, Alfredo (b. Turin, 25 July 1883; d. Rome, 5 Mar. 1947). Italian composer. Studied and worked at first in Paris; returned to Italy in 1915. He wrote three operas: *La Donna Serpente* (1932), a 1-act chamber opera *La Favola d'Orfeo*, and a 1-act mystery, *Il Deserto Tentato* (1937), which glorified the Abyssinian war.

Cassel. See *Kassel*.

Casta Diva. Norma's (sop.) aria with chorus in Act 1 of Bellini's *Norma*, praying to the Moon for peace between Gaul and Rome.

Castagna, Bruna (b. Bari, 15 Oct. 1908). Italian contralto. Début 1925 Mantua, Marina (*Boris Godunov*). Milan, Sc., 1925–8, 1932–4. N.Y., Hippodrome, 1934; Met. 1935–45, where her Adalgisa, Laura, and Verdi roles were much admired. Her sister **Maria Castagna** (sometimes known as Maria Falliani) was also active as a contralto in Italy in the 1920's and 1930's. (R)

Castellan, Jeanne Anaïs (b. Beaujeu, Rhône, 26 Oct. 1819; d. ?, ?). French soprano. Studied with Cinthie-Damoreau, Bordogni, and Nourrit at the Paris Conservatoire, where she gained first prize for singing 1836. Début Varese 1838. After appearances in Italy and Austria, engaged for a Philharmonic Concert in London 1844. H.M.'s 1845; C.G. 1848–52. Created Bertha (*Le Prophète*); first London Glicera (Gounod's *Sapho*), Cunegunda (Spohr's *Faust*) and Amazili (Spohr's *Jessonda*).

Castil-Blaze, François (b. Cavaillon, 1 Dec. 1784; d. Paris, 11 Dec. 1857). French writer on music and composer. His chief work is the 2-vol. *De l'Opéra en France*, which discusses the suitability of words for music and the components of opera, also attacking theatre managers, critics, and translators. He was himself a critic (of the *Journal des Débats*, 1822–32) and a distinguished translator; but he was guilty of needlessly adapting foreign works and upsetting their proportions, not least by inserting numbers of his own. His version of Weber's *Der Freischütz* as *Robin des Bois* (1824) excited the rage of his successor on the *Journal*, Berlioz. He also included parts of *Euryanthe* (which he later translated, 1831) in a pasticcio, *La Forêt de Sénart* (1826).

Castle Gardens. A place of popular entertainment in New York in the middle of the last century, and the scene of performances by visiting foreign opera companies after the destruction of the Park Theatre in 1848. It was here that Grisi and Mario made their American débuts in *Lucrezia Borgia* in 1854.

Castor et Pollux. Opera in prologue and 5 acts by Rameau; text by Pierre Joseph Bernard. Prod. Paris, O., 24 Oct. 1737, with Tribou and Chassé—rev. without prologue and new Act 1, 1754; Glasgow (amateur) 27 Apr. 1927; N.Y., Vassar College, 6 Mar. 1937. Rameau's most famous work.

Castrato (It. = castrated). A male soprano or contralto whose unbroken voice has been preserved by means of a surgical operation before puberty. Castrati were in great demand as leading singers in the 17th and 18th centuries, first in Italy, and then in the Italian opera houses throughout Europe. Although the range of the castrato was similar to that of the female soprano or contralto, the voice was stronger and more flexible, often voluptuous in tone, and capable of the utmost delicacy and technical brilliance.

One of the first castrati to play a prominent part in the history of opera was Giovanni Gualberto, who sang the title role in Monteverdi's *Orfeo* (1607).

Most of the composers of the 18th century wrote roles for castrati in their operas. They were often as vain as any female prima donna, but were tolerated for their artistry, which won them enormous popular following. Among the more famous castrati were Francesco Bernardi (Senesino, q.v.), Carlo

Broschi (Farinelli, q.v.), Vincenzo dal Prato, Gaetano Majorano (Caffarelli, q.v., or Cafferiello), Gaetano Guadagni (q.v.), and Giovanni Battista Velluti (q.v.). Gluck composed his *Orfeo* for Guadagni; Mozart wrote the part of Idamante (*Idomeneo*) for Dal Prato, and Rossini and Meyerbeer the leading role in *Aureliano in Palmira* and *Il Crociato in Egitto* for Velluti.

The modern breeches role or *travesti* part in opera is a continuation of the castrato tradition, as is the principal boy in the English pantomime.

Castrati continued to be heard in the Vatican Chapel and other Roman churches until the present century. Domenico Mustafà, a celebrated male soprano, was director of the Papal music until 1895, and was heard by Calvé when she was in Rome for the première of *L'Amico Fritz* (1891); Wagner wanted him to sing Klingsor at Bayreuth. Alessandro Moreschi (1858–1922) made ten records in 1902–3; on the labels he is described as 'Soprano della Cappella Sistina'.

Castro, Juan José (b. Avellareda, 7 Mar. 1895; d. Buenos Aires, 1968). Argentinian composer, conductor, pianist, and violinist. In 1951 won the Verdi prize offered by La Scala for his opera *Proserpina e lo Straniero* (1952). He also wrote the operas *La Zapatera Prodigiosa* (1949) and *Bodas de Sangre* (1956).

Catalani, Alfredo (b. Lucca, 19 June 1854; d. Milan, 7 Aug. 1893). Italian composer. Studied Paris and Milan. His first opera, *La Falce* (Milan 1875), text by Boito, was followed by *Elda* (1880), later revised as *Loreley*. His most popular work, *La Wally* (1892), is still performed in Italy. His works were championed by Toscanini, who named his daughter Wally. Other works include *Dejanice* (1883) and *Edmea* (1886).

Catalani, Angelica (b. Sinigaglia, 10 May 1780; d. Paris, 12 June 1849). Italian soprano. Educated at a convent in Rome, but forced by her parents' reduced circumstances to take up singing. Début Venice 1797, Lodoiska (Mayr); London 1806. The first London Susanna (*Figaro*) 1812. Manager of the Théâtre des Italiens, Paris, 1814–17. Retired from the operatic stage 1819 and founded a school near Florence. One of the highest-paid prima donnas, receiving as much as 200 guineas for singing *Rule Britannia* or *God Save the King*.

Catania. Town in Sicily. Bellini's birthplace: the Teatro Massimo Bellini (cap. 2,000) was opened in 1890 with a performance of *Norma*. The theatre was modernized 1948–52, and gives a spring and autumn season annually. In Nov. 1951 the 150th anniversary of the birth of Bellini was celebrated there with gala performances of *Norma*, *Il Pirata*, *I Puritani*, and *La Sonnambula*.

Catulli Carmina. Scenic cantata by Orff; Latin text based on the poems of Catullus. Prod. Leipzig 6 Nov. 1943; Cambridge, Arts Theatre, 4 Mar. 1958.

Cavalieri, Katharina (b. Währing, 19 Feb. 1760; d. Vienna, 30 June 1801). Austrian soprano. Studied with Salieri, who wrote several operas for her, and when barely 15 was engaged to sing at the Italian Opera in Vienna. Joined the German Opera founded by Emperor Joseph II 1776. Mozart composed Constanze (*Entführung*) and Mme Silberklang (*Schauspieldirektor*) for her, as well as Elvira's 'Mi tradì' in *Don Giovanni* for its Vienna première. He wrote that she was 'a singer of whom Germany might well be proud'.

Cavalieri, Lina (b. Viterbo, 25 Dec. 1874; d. Florence, 7 Feb. 1944). Italian soprano. Début Naples 1900, Mimì. N.Y., Met., 1906–8; other American appearances with Manhattan and Chicago companies; London, C.G., 1908; in 1911 sang Salome in Massenet's *Hérodiade* and Giulietta (*Hoffmann*) at the London Opera House. Married to tenor Lucien Muratore 1913–27. (R)

Cavalieri di Ekebù, I (The Knights of Ekebù). Opera in 4 acts by Zandonai; text by A. Rossato, after Lagerlöf's *Gösta Berling*. Prod. Milan, Sc., 7 Mar. 1925, cond. Toscanini.

Cavalleria Rusticana (Rustic Chivalry). Opera in 1 act by Pietro Mascagni; text by G. Menasci and G. Targioni-Tozzetti, after G. Verga's drama (1884) based on his story (1880). Winner of the contest for a 1-act opera organized by Sonzogno in 1889. Prod. Rome, C., 17 May 1890, with Bellincioni, Stagno, cond. Mugnone; Philadelphia 9 Sept. 1891; London, Shaftesbury Theatre, 19 Oct. 1891, with Musiani, Vignas, cond. Arditi.

After a short orchestral prelude, the voice of Turiddu (ten.) is heard serenading Lola. The curtain rises to disclose a small Sicilian village; it is early on Easter morning, and the villagers are preparing for Mass. The young peasant girl Santuzza (sop.) appears. She is sad and asks Lucia (con.) for news of her ex-lover Turiddu.

The village teamster Alfio (bar.), husband of Lola (mezzo), now enters; he sings about his life and his beautiful Lola. He tells Lucia that Turiddu has been seen near his house. After the 'Easter Hymn' the crowd in the square enters the church, but Santuzza remains behind with Lucia, and confesses to her that she has been betrayed by Turiddu.

Turiddu now arrives and is upbraided by Santuzza for his deceit; during the scene between the two former lovers, Lola makes her way across the square, likening her flower to Turiddu and making fun of Santuzza. The latter begs Turiddu to return to her, but he hurls her to the ground and joins Lola in church.

Alfio returns, looking for his wife, and the embittered Santuzza tells him that Turiddu and Lola are lovers. He swears vengeance.

The stage is now empty and the orchestra plays the most famous of all operatic intermezzi. The Easter Service is over, the villagers fill the square once again, and Turiddu invites them to join him in a toast to Lola. Alfio refuses to drink and challenges Turiddu to a duel. Turiddu says good-bye to his mother and rushes off to fight Alfio. A distant murmur is heard: several women rush on and one shrieks 'they have murdered neighbour Turiddu'; Santuzza collapses.

Cavalli, Pier Franceso (b. Crema, 14 Feb. 1602; d. Venice, 14 Jan. 1676). Italian composer (born Caletti-Bruni, took surname from patron). Began writing for the theatre in 1629, and continued to do so for 30 years, producing 42 operas of which 28 are extant. Egon Wellesz has suggested that Cavalli stands in the same relationship to Monteverdi as Strauss does to Wagner: 'Monteverdi is unquestionably the greater genius, but Cavalli is the more brilliant of the two.' But Cavalli was also one of the first opera composers to write his works in a dramatic style throughout, without self-contained numbers, and with short melodic phrases developed, thus perhaps offering a closer comparison with Wagner. Cavalli's first opera, and the first work thus described, was *Le Nozze di Teti e di Peleo* (1639). *L'Egisto* (1643) is for soloists only. His best-known and originally most successful work is *Giasone* (1649).

Cavaradossi. A painter (ten.), hero of Puccini's *Tosca*.

Cavatina (It., dim. of *cavata*—an 'extraction' of tone from an instrument). Originally a short song without the *da capo* of an aria. Barbarina's 'L'ho perduta' at the beginning of Act 4 of *Le Nozze di Figaro* is so described. Also used of a song-like air included as part of a long *scena* or accompanied recitative, and of a song-like piece of instrumental music, e.g. Raff's *Cavatina*. See also *Cabaletta*.

Cebotari, Maria (b. Kishinev, Bessarabia, 10 Feb. 1910; d. Vienna, 9 June 1949). Russian soprano. After singing in school and church choirs, joined a travelling company; then Moscow Arts Theatre. Studied Berlin with Oskar Daniel. Début Dresden 1931, Mimì; remained member of company until 1941; Berlin 1936–44; Vienna 1946–9. London, C.G., 1936 (with Dresden Company—Susanna, Zerlina, and Sophie); returned with Vienna Opera 1947 (Countess, Donna Anna, Salome). Created Aminta in Strauss's *Schweigsame Frau* (1935), Julia in Sutermeister's *Romeo und*

Julia (1940), Lucille in Einem's *Dantons Tod* (1947), and Iseut in Martin's *Le Vin Herbé* (1948). A fine artist, with a beautiful fresh voice and charming stage appearance. (R)

Cecilia. *Azione sacra* in 3 acts by Refice; text by E. Mucci. Prod. Rome, T.R., 15 Feb. 1934, with Muzio in title role; Buenos Aires, Colón, 1934, also with Muzio. Has been revived several times in Italy in recent years. Refice's most successful work for the theatre, based on the legend of Cecilia and Valerian, and of Cecilia's martyrdom.

Celeste Aida. Radamès's (ten.) aria praising Aida's beauty in Act 1 of Verdi's *Aida*.

Cenerentola, La; ossia La Bontà in Trionfo (Cinderella). Opera in 2 acts by Rossini; text by Jacopo Ferretti after Étienne's text for Steibelt's opera. Prod. Rome, Valle, 25 Jan. 1817, with Giorgi-Righetti; London, Hm., 8 Jan. 1820, with Teresa Belocchi; N.Y. 27 June 1826 by Garcia's company.

The plot follows the familiar fairy-story by Charles Perrault. Act 1. The house of Don Magnifico (bass), father of the ugly sisters Clorinda (sop.) and Tisbe (mezzo), and of Angelina, known as La Cenerentola (con.). The philosopher Alidoro (bass), tutor of the Prince, Don Ramiro (ten.), calls disguised; unlike her sisters, Cenerentola welcomes him. He announces that the Prince will wed the fairest guest at a forthcoming ball, which elates the Ugly Sisters. The Prince appears, having changed clothes with his valet Dandini (bass); he and Cenerentola fall in love. Against her father's wishes, Alidoro arranges for her to attend the ball in a fine dress. The scene changes to the palace, where Magnifico is now an over-enthusiastic cellar-master. Cenerentola enters the ballroom so sumptuously dressed that her relations, though curious, do not recognize her.

Act 2 begins with Dandini (still dressed as the Prince) in love with Cenerentola, who loves the real Prince. She gives the Prince a bracelet, one of a pair, and tells him to find her and claim her by its companion. The changes of dress meanwhile cause confusions and upsets with her relations.

Back at home the family is surprised at Cenerentola's resemblance to the lady at the ball. A storm roused by Alidoro causes the Prince's coach to break down outside. Entering, the Prince recognizes Cenerentola by her bracelet, and claims her; the family is forgiven for its past harshness.

Other operas on the story are by Laruette (1759), Isouard and Steibelt (same libretto, both 1810), Garcia (1826), Langer (1874), Rozkošny (*Popelka*, 1885), Massenet (1899), and Wolf-Ferrari (his first opera, 1900).

Censorship in opera. Like the legitimate theatre, opera has come into conflict with the censorship in various countries. In England, religious subjects were forbidden on the stage: Rossini's *Mosè* and Verdi's *Nabucco* appeared under different guises in Victorian times. *Samson et Dalila* was kept off the London stage until 1909; Massenet's *Hérodiade* appeared under the guise of *Salome* with the names of the characters changed, and Strauss's own *Salome* had to be altered for its Covent Garden première, 1910. In Italy and France political rather than moral censorship was responsible for the troubles attendant on the productions of *Nabucco*, *I Lombardi*, *Rigoletto*, *Un Ballo in Maschera*, and other works. Nazi Germany banned many operas for political and racial reasons, and there were similar bans in Italy and the U.S.S.R. Since the war the East German authorities have banned the original version of Dessau's *Lukullus* and Orff's *Antigone*; and the strict control over art in Communist countries suppresses many works.

Céphale et Procris, ou l'Amour Conjugal. Opera in 3 acts by Grétry; text by Jean François Marmontel. Prod. Versailles 30 Dec. 1773 and Paris, O., 2 May 1775. Other operas on the story are by Caccini (*Il Rapimento di Cefalo*, 1600), Hidalgo (*Celos aun del Ayre Matan*, the first Spanish opera, 1660), Elisabeth Laguerre (the first work by a woman at the Paris Opéra 1694), Araia (a very early Russian opera, 1694), and Gilliers (1711).

Cercar la nota (It. = to seek the note). The vocal habit of anticipating notes by scooping up to them.

Cerquetti, Anita (b. Montecosaro, nr. Macerata, 13 Apr. 1931). Italian soprano. Studied Perugia. Début Spoleto 1951, Aida. Chicago 1955; Milan, Sc., 1958. Quickly established herself as one of the finest Italian dramatic sopranos, her best roles being Norma, Abigaille, and Amelia. But after an operation in 1958 she quickly went into eclipse. (R)

Čert a Káča. See *Devil and Kate*.

Cesti, Pietro Antonio (b. Arezzo, 5 Aug. 1623; d. Florence, 14 Oct. 1669). Italian composer. Wrongly known as Marc'Antonio from a contraction of his later title of Marchese. Studied with Carissimi in Florence, having previously become a friar. His first operas, *Orontea* (1649) and *Cesare Amante* (1651), established him as a leading composer of the day. He was later released from his vows, and led a busy and adventurous life that included a period as *maestro di cappella* to the Archduke Ferdinand of Austria. His most famous work was *Il Pomo d'Oro* (q.v.). Cesti was, with Cavalli, the most important of the composers who followed up the original invention of the Camerata. His music is marked by lyricism and expressiveness, aided by an inventive use of dissonance.

Chabrier, Emmanuel (b. Ambert, Puy-de-Dôme, 18 Jan. 1841; d. Paris, 13 Sept. 1894). French composer. He studied music, but was prevented by his father from taking it up professionally. After 18 years in a Ministry, during which time he composed and made friends with artists, poets, and composers, he gave himself wholly up to composition on hearing *Tristan* at Munich. Before this he had written two operettas, *L'Étoile* (1877) and *Une Éducation Manquée* (1879). He worked on Wagner productions with Lamoureux, but his taste for Wagner was never reconciled to his own musical inclinations. *Gwendoline* (refused by the Paris Opéra as too Wagnerian, prod. Brussels 1886) and *Briséis* (unfinished at his death, one act prod. 1899) are for this reason less successful or typical than the comic opera *Le Roi Malgré Lui* (1887).

Chaliapin, Feodor (b. Kazan, 11 Feb. 1873; d. Paris, 12 Apr. 1938). Russian bass. Of a humble peasant family, he had little education, musical or otherwise. After an engagement in St. Petersburg he joined Mamontov's private company in Moscow, where his Ivan the Terrible, Melnik (Dargomizhsky's *Rusalka*), and Boris led to engagements at La Scala (1901 and 1904) and N.Y., Met. (1907). His realistic acting and robust vocalization were not to the liking of American audiences at that time. London début, D.L., 1913, in Sir Joseph Beecham's Russian season; sang in the first London *Boris Godunov*, *Khovanshchina*, *Ivan the Terrible*, and *Prince Igor*. C.G. 1926, 1928, 1929, and Ly. 1931. Returned to N.Y. 1922, remained at Met. until 1929. He made a film of *Don Quichotte*. Unrivalled as a singing actor. Autobiographical books *Pages from my Life* (1926) and *Man and Mask* (1932). (R)

Chamber Opera. Since opera was born from the meetings of the Florentine Camerata (q.v.) around 1600, chamber opera may be said to be the original form. It has now come to mean a work cast on a small scale, generally with a few singers and instrumentalists, consequently telling a simple story and lasting but a short time. Though strictly an intermezzo (q.v.), Pergolesi's *La Serva Padrona* ranks as a chamber opera, as do the pieces currently performed by the Intimate Opera Company (q.v.). A notable attempt at exploring the possibilities of the genre, for its own virtues as well as for reasons of economy, has been made by Benjamin Britten (see *English Opera Group*). His small orchestra has proved, in his hands more effectively than in those of most other composers, capable of the widest range of expressive effects, supporting chamber operas as different as the comedy *Albert Herring*, the classical tragedy *The Rape of Lucretia*, and *The Turn of the Screw*. Lennox Berkeley has also written two chamber operas for the Group, the comedy *A Dinner Engagement* and the biblical romance *Ruth*. See also *Intimate Opera*.

Champagne Aria. See *Finch' han dal vino*.

Chanson de la puce (The Song of the Flea). Méphistophélès's (bass or bar.) aria in the second part of Berlioz's *La Damnation de Faust*.

Charley. The co-author with John E. Barker of *The New Opera Glass* (Leipzig, 1877). This was written to provide 'English-American visitors with the plots of the popular operas of modern times'. Charley's classic mishandling of English—vows of love to him were 'lovely swears'—was perpetuated in further editions of which he was the sole author. A selection from Charley was published in London in 1951, edited by Robert Elkin.

Charlotte. Werther's lover (sop.) in Massenet's *Werther*.

Charlottenburg. See *Berlin*.

Charpentier, Gustave (b. Dienze, Meurthe, 25 June 1860; d. Paris, 18 Feb. 1956). French composer. Pupil of Massenet and winner of the Prix de Rome with his *scène lyrique*, *Didon*, 1887. His most famous work is the opera *Louise* (1900). The success of this, partly for its startling realism and liberal social views, partly for its musical simplicity, was as great as the failure of its sequel *Julien* (1913). Charpentier also founded, in 1902, a Conservatoire Populaire de Mimi Pinson, where working girls such as his Louise could act and sing and learn music and dancing.

Charpentier, Marc-Antoine (b. Paris, 1634; d. Paris, 24 Feb. 1704). French composer. Studied in Rome with Carissimi, and on his return to Paris collaborated with Molière at the Théâtre-Français. He wrote some 17 operas, which had a considerable success and won their composer high respect even at a time when Lully's influence was supreme. *Médée* (1693) was, through the poor poem, never the success it promised to become; it contains some strong and original music.

Chausson, Ernest (b. Paris, 21 Jan. 1855; d. Limay, 10 June 1899). French composer. First studied law, taking to music later and becoming a pupil of Franck. Never needing to earn his own living, he worked slowly, carefully, and diffidently at composition until his accidental death. He wrote three operas: *Les Caprices de Marianne*, *Hélène*, and (the only one performed) *Le Roi Arthus* (1903).

Che farò senza Euridice. Orfeo's (mezzo) lament at the loss of his wife Euridice in Act 3 (Act 4 in some versions) of Gluck's *Orfeo ed Euridice*.

Che gelida manina. Rodolfo's (ten.) aria to Mimì in Act 1 of Puccini's *La Bohème*, with which he makes his first approach to her. She replies with the equally famous *Mi chiamano Mimì*.

Ch'ella mi creda libero. Dick Johnson's (ten.) aria in Act 3 of Puccini's *La Fanciulla del West* in which he asks that Minnie should not be told that he is to be lynched, but that he has been set free.

Chemnitz (now known as Karl-Marx-Stadt). Town in Saxony, Germany. Former Opera-Louise opened 1909, destroyed during the 1939–45 war. New theatre (cap. 1,073) opened 1950.

Che puro ciel. Orfeo's (mezzo) aria as he gazes on the beauties of the Elysian Fields in Gluck's *Orfeo*.

Cherevichki. See *Vakula the Smith*.

Cherubini, Luigi (b. Florence, 14 Sept. 1760; d. Paris, 15 Mar. 1842). Italian composer of the French school. Studied in Italy, producing at first church music and then an opera *Quinto Fabio*, the first of some 30, in 1780. He visited London, and then settled in Paris, where he reformed his operatic style from Italian traditions to those of Gluck. His first great success there was the brilliant *Lodoïska*, followed by others including *Médée* (1797) and *Les Deux Journées* (*The Water Carrier*) (1800). On a visit to Vienna he met Beethoven, who admired his music, and saw the première of *Fidelio* (influenced by *Les Deux Journées*), as well as that of his own *Faniska*. Back in Paris, Napoleon's hostility caused a mental disturbance. He was, nevertheless, the director of the Conservatoire from 1821 until his death. His music, though by his own admission somewhat severe, has a distinct purity, brilliance, and originality. He is one of the principal originators of romantic opera.

Cherubino. Countess Almaviva's page (sop.) in Mozart's *Le Nozze di Figaro*.

Chest voice. The lowest of the three main registers of the voice, the others being the 'middle' and the 'head'. So called because the tone of the lower notes in the singer's range, when using this voice, almost seems to go from the larynx into the chest. This method of production gives the richest notes, and is essential for strength and carrying power in the lower register. Garcia considered that the chest voice predominated in men, and it is favoured especially by Italians.

Cheval de Bronze, Le (The Bronze Horse). Opera in 3 acts by Auber; text by Scribe. Prod. Paris, O.C., 23 Mar. 1835; London, C.G., 14 Dec. 1835; N.Y., Bowery T., 23 Oct. 1837.

Chicago. Town in Ill., U.S.A. The first opera given in Chicago was Bellini's *Sonnambula*, 29 July 1850. Two years later an Italian company gave a season of grand opera under the direction of Luigi Arditi, with Rosa de Vries as leading soprano. The first opera house in the city, the Crosby Opera House, was built in 1865, and destroyed by fire in 1871; and opera had no permanent home until 1889, when the Chicago Auditorium opened with *Roméo et Juliette*; from then until 1910 short seasons were given by visiting companies, including the Abbey and Grau, Damrosch, Savage, Mascagni, and Conried organizations.

In 1910 the Chicago Grand Opera Company was formed, consisting of elements of the recently disbanded Hammerstein Company, with Andreas Dippel as Artistic Director and Cleofonte Campanini as Music Director. Mary Garden, who sang Mélisande on the second evening (4 Nov. 1910), became the dominating figure of opera in Chicago. Not only did she sing there from 1910 to 1931, scoring special successes in the French repertory, but she was appointed General Director for the 1921–2 season, Campanini having died in 1919 and his successor Marinuzzi resigning after a year. Garden's sole season as Director, during which the world première of Prokofiev's *The Love of the Three Oranges* was given, resulted in a deficit of more than a million dollars.

From 1922 to 1930 the finances of the opera were guaranteed by Samuel Insull, who also became President of the organization; it was then known as the Chicago Civic Opera Company. On 4 Nov. 1929 the new Civic Opera House (cap. 3,593) was opened, with a performance of *Aida*, but in 1932 the company was one of the casualties of the depression.

From 1933 to 1946 there were various attempts to put opera on a more or less permanent basis, none of which proved very successful. Then came seven years during which the only opera in Chicago was given by visiting companies. Since 1954 the Chicago Lyric Theatre and its successor, the Lyric Opera of Chicago, under the chairmanship of Carol Fox, have given successful seasons with international artists including Callas, Nilsson Simionato, Tebaldi, Del Monaco, Di Stefano, and Gobbi. See *Ravinia*.

Chile. Regular opera seasons are given in the Teatro Municipal Santiago.

Chi mi frena? The sextet sung by Lucia, Alisa, Edgardo, Arturo, Enrico, and Raimondo in Act 2 of Donizetti's *Lucia di Lammermoor*.

Chisholm, Erik (b. Glasgow, 4 Jan. 1904; d. Cape Town, 7 Jan. 1965). Scottish conductor and composer. Studied with Tovey in Edinburgh. Conductor of Glasgow Grand Opera Society 1930–9, giving performances of *Benvenuto Cellini*, *Les Troyens*, *Idomeneo*, and *La Clemenzadi Tito*. 1945–65 Professor of Music at University of Cape Town, where he was responsible for the production of many little-known operas. His own operas are *Simoon*, *Dark Sonnet*, *Before Breakfast*, and *The Inland Woman*.

Chorus. From the Greek χορός, a festive dance or those who performed it. The Attic drama first consisted of tales told by a single actor in the intervals of the dance; later the function of the chorus was to join in and comment upon the drama from the place before and below the stage known as the ὀρχήστρα (orchestra). This function passed, with modifications, into opera. For some time the chorus took little part in the actual drama, but supported it in ensembles that served also as a musical contrast. Gluck first made the chorus a vital part of the drama. From then on crowds of courtiers, nobles, guests, priests, citizens, boyars, slaves, prisoners, and so on thronged opera, sometimes joining in the arias (a famous instance is Norma's 'Casta diva'), but more often acting as a static point of repose, commenting on the action, summing it up, joining in usually to provide a bustle of activity parallel to it, and abetting the soloists rather than furthering it on their own. With Wagner the chorus assumed a still more dramatic role. No chorus appears in *The Ring* until the Gibichungs' entry in *Götterdämmerung*, but the citizens of Nuremberg are intrinsic to the plot of *Die Meistersinger*. Britten, while using the chorus as the main dramatic force pitted against the hero in *Peter Grimes*, places his Male and Female Chorus as soloists in *The Rape of Lucretia* outside the action physically as well as dramatically. A still more definite reversion to Greek method occurs, for obvious reasons, in Stravinsky's *Oedipus Rex*. In general the chorus today is involved in opera more closely than ever before.

An opera chorus is normally divided into the conventional soprano, contralto, tenor, and bass (19th-century French choruses were usually simply S.T.B., though), with the numbers varying according to requirements. It is maintained on the permanent staff of an opera house under the direction of a chorus-master. Additional choruses of children are sometimes needed (e.g. for the Urchins' Chorus in Act 1 of *Carmen*), and certain schools specialize in their provision.

Christiania. See *Oslo*.

Christie, John (b. Glyndebourne, 14 Dec. 1882; d. Glyndebourne, 4 July 1962). English organ builder and operatic amateur. Educated at Eton, where he was for a time a master, and Cambridge. Married the soprano Audrey Mildmay (q.v.) 1931, and in 1934 founded the Glyndebourne Opera (q.v.) at his country seat in Sussex, for the artistic achievements of which he was awarded the C.H. in 1955.

Christoff, Boris (b. Sofia, 18 May 1918). Bulgarian bass. Joined the Gussla Choir, Sofia, as amateur, was heard by King Boris, and encouraged to take up singing professionally. Studied with Stracciari (Rome) and Buratti (Salzburg). Début Rome, Arg., 1946, Colline; Milan, Sc., since 1947. London, C.G., 1949–50 and 1958–63 as Boris and King Philip. San Francisco 1948–50; Chicago 1958–63. Though not large, his voice is firm and is used with great dramatic skill; he is outstanding as a singing actor. (R)

Christophe Colomb. Opera in 2 parts (27 scenes) by Milhaud; text by Claudel. Prod. Berlin, S.O., 5 May 1930, with German text by R. S. Hoffmann. Concert performances London, Queen's Hall, 16 Jan. 1937; N.Y., Carnegie Hall, 6 Nov. 1952. Claudel treats of Columbus's life in allegorical religious vein. The first opera on the subject was by Ottoboni—*Il Colombo, overo L'India Scoperta*, 1690, but lost; others are by Morlacchi (1828), Carnicer (1831; the first by a Spaniard), Franchetti (1892; celebrating the 400th anniversary of the discovery of America), Egk (1931 for broadcasting, revised 1941 for stage), and Vassilenko (1938).

Chrysothemis. Elektra's sister (sop.) in Strauss's *Elektra*.

Cibber, Mrs. Susanna (b. London, Feb. 1714; d. London, 30 Jan. 1766). English singer (mezzo?) and actress. Probably trained by her brother, Thomas Arne; début 1732. Sang and acted in many productions, including first performance of *Messiah* (Dublin 1742). Her singing of 'He was despised' moved Dr. Delaney to exclaim, 'Woman, for this thy sins be forgiven thee!' Her voice was not of outstanding power or beauty in an age of great voices, though described as 'sweet' and 'plaintive'. But Handel admired her singing greatly, and she sang many of his works until 1746, when she devoted herself entirely to the stage.

Cid, Le. Opera in 4 acts by Massenet; text by d'Ennery, Gallet, and Blau, after Corneille's drama (1637). Prod. Paris, O., 30 Nov. 1885, with Jean de Reszke; New Orleans 23 Feb. 1890. Other operas on the subject are by Farinelli (1797), Aiblinger (*Rodrigo und Zimene*, 1821), Pacini (1853), and Cornelius (1865).

Cielo e mar! Enzo's (ten.) aria praising the sky and sea in Act 2 of Ponchielli's *La Gioconda.*

Cigna (orig. Sens), **Gina** (b. Paris, 6 Mar. 1900). French-Italian soprano. Studied with Calvé, Darclée, Storchio, and Russ. Début Milan, Sc., 1927, as Ginette Sens (Freia). From 1933 a leading Italian dramatic soprano, possessing a repertory of over 70 operas, and being particularly famous for her Gioconda and Turandot. London, C.G., 1933, 1936, 1937, 1939. N.Y., Met., 1936–8; San Francisco and Chicago. Resumed singing after war, but seriously injured in motor accident in 1948, and had to give up stage career. Since then has been teaching in Canada and Italy. (R)

Cilea, Francesco (b. Palmi, 23 July 1866; d. Varazza, 20 Nov. 1950). Italian composer. When still a student at Naples produced his first opera, *Gina*, whose success led Sonzogno to commission the equally successful *La Tilda* (1892). His *L'Arlesiana* (1897) was less well received. From 1896 to 1904 Cilea taught at Florence; during this period he produced his most popular opera, *Adriana Lecouvreur* (1902). His last opera, *Gloria*, had a successful production in 1907. His music is conspicuous for its charm and ingenuity rather than its dramatic urgency.

Cimarosa, Domenico (b. nr. Naples, 17 Dec. 1749; d. Venice, 11 Jan. 1801). Italian composer. Wrote some 60 operas in all, the first while still a student at Naples. Until 1787, busy in Rome and Naples as Paisiello's great rival; then spent three years in St. Petersburg and a short period in Vienna. Here he wrote *Il Matrimonio Segreto*, whose success caused the Emperor to serve supper to the entire cast before having it repeated.

Back in Naples he was highly successful, but was then imprisoned for revolutionary sympathies. Released, he set out for St. Petersburg, dying in Venice *en route.* His comic operas are in the best *buffo* tradition, garrulous and gay, sparkling and witty; serious subjects brought out a more conventional vein in him.

Cincinnati. Town in Ohio, U.S.A. The musical tradition of Cincinnati is German, and the May Festival choral and orchestral rather than operatic. But there is an annual summer season of open-air opera at the Zoological Gardens (founded in 1920) which has been predominantly Italian, though in more recent years Wagner and Strauss works have come into the repertory. Regarded as 'the cradle of American opera singers'. Artists who made either their operatic débuts there, or first appearances in roles for which they later became famous, have included James Melton, Jan Peerce, and Dorothy Kirsten.

Cinderella. See *Cenerentola.*

Cinti. See *Damoreau, Laure Cinthie-.*

Cio-Cio-San. The Japanese name of Madama Butterfly, the heroine (sop.) of Puccini's opera.

Ciro in Babilonia (Cyrus in Babylon). Opera in 2 acts by Rossini; text by Aventi. Prod. Ferrara 14 Mar. 1812. Among some 20 other operas on Cyrus are those by Cavalli (*Il Ciro*, 1654), Caldara (1736), Hasse (*Il Ciro Riconosciuto*, 1751), and Agnesi (*Ciro in Armenia*, 1753; the most important work of one of the first women opera composers).

Cisneros (orig. Broadfoot), **Eleanora de** (b. New York, 1 Nov. 1878; d. New York, 3 Feb. 1934). American mezzo-soprano. Studied with Muzio-Celli and Jean de Reszke. Sang as Eleanor Broadfoot, N.Y., Met., 1899–1900; after further study, second début as De Cisneros, Turin 1902. London, C.G., 1904–6, appearing in first London *Adriana Lecouvreur* and *Andrea Chénier*. Manhattan Opera 1907–9; Melba Company (Australia) 1911. First Italian Countess in *Queen of Spades* (1906), and Klytemnestra (1909). Retired 1916. (R)

City Center of Music and Drama Inc., New York. The theatre (cap. 3,010) which houses the City Center Ballet and New York City Opera Company. The latter was founded in Feb. 1944, the late Mayor La Guardia and Newbold Morris, former president of the New York City Council, being the prime movers in its foundation. The aim was 'to present opera with the highest artistic standards, while maintaining the civic and democratic ideas of moderate prices, practical business planning and modern methods'.

László Halász was the music director from 1944 to 1951, when he was summarily dismissed on the grounds that his conduct was 'a threat to the prosperity and advancement of the City Center'. He was succeeded by Joseph Rosenstock, who resigned in 1956; next came Erich Leinsdorf, who lasted one season. Since 1957 the music director has been Julius Rudel.

The initial seasons of the company were short and the repertory popular; but gradually the length of the seasons was extended to six or eight weeks in both spring and autumn. Between 1949 and 1962 ten world premières were given, including William Grant Still's *The Troubled Island* (1949), David Tamkin's *The Dybbuk* (1951), Aaron Copland's *The Tender Land* (1954), and Carlyle Floyd's *Susannah* (1958); as well as the first American performances of Bartók's *Duke Bluebeard's Castle*, Einem's *Der Prozess*, Martin's *Der Sturm*, Walton's *Troilus and Cressida*, Orff's *Der Mond*, Strauss's *Die schweigsame Frau*, and revivals of *Cenerentola*, *The Love of the Three Oranges*, and *Wozzeck*. Since 1958 successful seasons entirely devoted to American opera have been given. The company has since 1965 been housed in the Lincoln Center.

Claque (Fr. = smack, clap). A group engaged by a performer to applaud him, demand encores, and do whatever else they can as apparently ordinary members of the audience to sway opinion in his favour.

Attempts by managements to suppress the claque have generally ended in failure, though at the Metropolitan, New York, Rudolf Bing circulated handbills threatening to abolish standing-room, the traditional post of the claque, if disorders continued, and succeeded in improving behaviour. But most singers have supported the claque. Even great artists have employed it: at Covent Garden in the 1890's Jean de Reszke was allowed *faveurs de claque*, free tickets to distribute among his admirers. Singers have also been known to employ an 'anti-claque' to attend performances by rivals. These may even clash: when a rival singer's fans tried to boo Maria Callas at La Scala, the claque responded so briskly that two people were sent to prison as a result of the ensuing brawl.

Claqueurs pride themselves on their artistic integrity and professional standards of behaviour. The Vienna Opera claque is not alone in applauding, free of charge, for his exceptional artistry a singer who had refused to employ it. Conversely, the claque at the Teatro Regio, Parma, once refunded a tenor his money and booed his subsequent performances (see *Audience*). Applause is carefully planned and executed: the leader (*capo di claque*) will attend rehearsals and consult the singer for special requirements, clearing these arrangements with the conductor. He will control matters firmly, posting his subordinates strategically and directing their entry like a conductor, and with a comparable sense of timing. They will usually consist of students and poor music-lovers who clap for their tickets alone; the leader is paid. Forty years ago a tariff was published in Italy—it included 'insistent applause, 15 lire; interruptions with "bene" or "bravo", 5 lire; a "bis", 50 lire; wild enthusiasm—a special sum to be arranged'. Nowadays the usual practice is for the leader to be paid a flat sum.

The most famous and powerful contemporary claque is at La Scala, organized by Carmelo Alabiso (a former Toscanini tenor of the 1920's) and Antonio Carrara. It is 30 strong (on important occasions, 40) and includes students, teachers, music-lovers (one, Nino Grassi, a veteran *claqueur* of 50 years' experience), and two barbers.

Clarkson, Stanley (b. Sydney, 23 Aug. 1905; d. London, 22 Jan. 1961). Australian bass. Educated Fort High School and Sydney Conservatory under Rex de Rego and Spencer Thomas. Début Sydney 1940, Sarastro. Came to London 1947. After further operatic and vocal coaching with Joan Cross, Arnold Matters, and Clive Carey, became leading bass at S.W. 1948. Sang Dikoy in the first performance in England of *Kaťa Kabanova* (1951), Friar Laurence in Sutermeister's *Romeo und Julia* (1954).

Clément, Edmond (b. Paris, 28 Mar. 1867; d. Nice, 24 Feb. 1928). French tenor. Début O.C. 1889, Vincent (*Mireille*); remained there as leading tenor until 1909. N.Y., Met., 1909–11; Boston 1911–13. Created leading roles in many French operas while at the Comique. One of the most elegant and stylish French singers of his day. (R)

Clemenza di Tito, La (The Clemency of Titus). Opera in 2 acts by Mozart; text by Metastasio, altered by Mazzolà. Prod. Prague 6 Sept. 1791; London, H.M.'s, 27 Mar. 1806 (the first Mozart opera in London, with a cast that included Billington and Braham); Tanglewood, U.S.A., 4 Aug. 1952. Mozart's last opera, in which he reverted to *opera seria*, was written and performed in 18 days for the coronation of Leopold II as King of Bohemia, three weeks before *Der Zauberflöte* and nine weeks before the composer's death. The plot concerns the unremitting clemency of a Roman emperor to conspirators against him. Metastasio's text was also set by some 20 other composers, including Gluck (1752).

Cleopatra. The heroine of some 20 operas. The first was by Mattheson (1704), who sang and played alternately in it. After one performance Handel's refusal to give up his seat at the cembalo led to his famous duel with Mattheson. Other operas are by Graun (*Cleopatra e Cesare*, 1742), Cimarosa (1789), Nasolini (*La Morte di Cleopatra*, 1791), Massé (*Une Nuit de Cléopâtre*, after Gautier, 1885), Morales (1891), Enna (1894), Massenet (1914), Hadley (1920), and Malipiero (*Antonio e Cleopatra*, after Shakespeare, 1938).

Cleva, Fausto (b. Trieste, 17 May 1902; d. Athens, 6 July 1971). Italian-American conductor. Assistant cond. N.Y., Met., 1920–1; chorus-master 1935–42; leading conductor of Italian wing from 1950. Also conducted in Chicago (artistic director 1944–6), San Francisco, Cincinnati Summer Opera, and elsewhere in America. (R)

Cloches de Corneville, Les (The Bells of Corneville). Opera in 3 acts by Planquette; text by Clairville and Gabet. Prod. Paris, Folies-Dramatiques, 19 Apr. 1877; N.Y. 22 Oct. 1877; London, Folly, 23 Feb. 1878. Planquette's most popular work; at the end of a run of 461 performances the manager served the last audience with 2,000 rolls and free beer.

Cluj (Ger. Klausenburg). Town in Rumania, principal town of Transylvania. The first season of the Rumanian Opera was given in 1920. The company prospered under the tenor D. P. Bayreuth, and has introduced a number of new Rumanian operas. There is also an opera house that gives performances in Hungarian.

Cluytens, André (b. Antwerp, 26 Mar. 1905; d. Paris, 5 June 1967). Belgian conductor. Studied Antwerp. Antwerp Opera 1927–32; Lyons from 1935; Paris, O. and O.C., since 1947;

Bayreuth (first French conductor there) 1955–8, 1965. Appears as guest Vienna and Italy. (R)

Coates, Albert (b. St. Petersburg, 23 Apr. 1882; d. Cape Town, 11 Dec. 1953). Anglo-Russian conductor and composer. Originally in commerce in St. Petersburg; began musical studies at Leipzig when 20. Appointed *répétiteur* at Leipzig by Nikisch with whom he studied 1904. Conducting appointments at Elberfeld, Dresden, and Mannheim followed. Chief conductor and artistic director of St. Petersburg Opera 1914–18. London, C.G., 1914 and 1919–24; also *The Ring* with B.N.O.C. 1929 (*Boris* with Chaliapin), 1935–8. In 1936 organized Coates–Rosing Opera Company. Operas include *Samuel Pepys* (Munich 1929) and *Pickwick* (London, C.G., 1936). (R)

Coates, Edith (b. Lincoln, 31 May 1908). English mezzo-soprano. Engaged for Old Vic Shakespeare Company 1924, but soon joined the opera company, first in the chorus, then in small solo parts, the first of which was Giovanna in *Rigoletto*. Leading mezzo-soprano S.W. 1931–46; C.G. 1937–9, 1947, 1963. Created Auntie (*Peter Grimes*), Mme Bardeau (*The Olympians*). The Countess in *The Queen of Spades* was one of her most striking roles. (R)

Coates, John (b. Girlington, nr. Bradford, 29 June 1865; d. Northwood 16 Aug. 1941). English tenor. Originally a baritone, and sang Valentine as an amateur with Carl Rosa without success; engaged by D'Oyly Carte Company 1894. Retired for a further period of study and emerged as tenor singing in light opera 1899–1900. London, C.G., 1901, Faust; created Claudio in Stanford's *Much Ado about Nothing* the same year. Later member of Moody–Manners and Beecham companies. One of the best British Tristans and Siegfrieds. (R)

Cobelli, Giuseppina (b. Salò, 1 Aug. 1898; d. Salò, 1 Sept. 1948). Italian soprano. Début Piacenza 1924, Gioconda. Great success as Sieglinde, Milan, Sc., in the following year led to yearly appearances there in Wagner (her Isolde was much admired) and modern Italian works. Created leading roles in Respighi's *La Fiamma* and Montemezzi's *La Notte di Zoraima*. (R)

Cocteau, Jean (b. Maisons-Laffitte, 5 July 1889; d. Paris, 12 Oct. 1963). French writer and librettist. Collaborated with Honegger in *Antigone* and Stravinsky in *Oedipus Rex*. Also furnished librettos for Milhaud (*Le Pauvre Matelot*), Poulenc (*La Voix Humaine*), and others. (R)

Coertse, Mimi (b. Durban, 1932). South African soprano. Began vocal studies South Africa 1949; continued in Vienna with Josef Witt and Maria Hittorff. Début Naples, S.C., 1955, Flower-maiden (*Parsifal*). Vienna Opera since 1956; London, C.G., 1956–8, Queen of Night, Olympia, Gilda; Glyndebourne, Zerbinetta. (R)

Colbran, Isabella (b. Madrid, 2 Feb. 1785; d. Bologna, 7 Oct. 1845). Spanish soprano. Studied in Madrid with Pareja and Italy with Marinelli and Crescenti. Début Paris 1801; Milan, Sc., 1807; engaged by Domenico Barbaia, whose mistress she became, to sing at Naples 1811; and also became the *favorita* of the King of Naples. She deserted both in 1815 to live with Rossini, whom she married in 1822. For her he wrote *Elisabetta, Regina d'Inghilterra*. She also created the leading soprano roles in his *Otello*, *Armida*, *La Donna del Lago*, *Mosè*, *Semiramide*, and *Maometto II*. She was considered the finest dramatic coloratura soprano in Europe from 1801 to 1822, though her voice began to weaken after 1815. She composed 4 vols. of songs.

Colla voce. (It. = with the voice). A direction to the instrumental part to follow the voice part carefully, usually in a passage where the rhythm is, or is likely to become, free. The phrase *colla parte* is also used.

Colline. The philosopher (bass) of the four Bohemians in Puccini's *La Bohème*.

Collingwood, Lawrance (b. London, 14 Mar. 1887). English conductor and composer. Choirboy at Westminster

Abbey, then went to Russia and became Albert Coates's assistant at St. Petersburg. Joined Old Vic in the 1920's; principal conductor S.W. 1931; music director S.W. 1940–6. His *Macbeth* had its first performance at S.W. in 1934; he also conducted there the first performance in England of *Tsar Saltan* (1933) and the original version of *Boris Godunov* (1935). (R)

Cologne (Ger., Köln). Town in Prussian Rhine, Germany. While not one of the most important operatic centres, Cologne has enjoyed a good Wagner and Verdi tradition under Otto Lohse, Eugen Szenkar, Fritz Zaun, Otto Ackermann, and recently Wolfgang Sawallisch. The theatre's greatest period was 1917–24 under Otto Klemperer; these years included the première of Korngold's *Die tote Stadt* (1920), and the first German performance of *Káťa Kabanova* (1922). The old opera house was destroyed by bombs in 1943; the newly built Grosses Haus (cap. 1,346) opened in Apr. 1957 with *Oberon*. Oscar Fritz Schuh was appointed Intendant in 1959, and Sawallisch Music Director in 1960. Both resigned at the end of the 1962–3 season. Istvan Kertesz was appointed Music Director.

Colón, Teatro, Buenos Aires. The leading opera house of South America which still enjoys the old-fashioned type of international season (May to Sept.) with French, German, and Italian operas sung in the original language by leading foreign artists. The first Colón was opened in Apr. 1857; the present building (cap. 2,500, with standing room for 1,000) dates from May 1908 with a season that included a new opera, Panizza's *Aurora*, commissioned by the Argentine government.

Coloratura. (Not, as commonly supposed, an Italian word, but derived from the German Koloratur.) Coloratura of itself means elaborate ornamentation of melody; thus a coloratura soprano is one who specializes in this type of music, formerly known as *canto figurato*, distinguished by light, quick, agile runs and leaps and sparkling *fioriture* (which is the correct Italian word for 'flowering' or ornamentation).

Colzani, Anselmo (b. Budrio, nr. Bologna, 23 Mar. 1918). Italian baritone Studied with Zambelli. Début Bologna 1947, Herald (*Lohengrin*). Milan, Sc., since 1953; San Francisco 1956; N.Y., Met., since 1960. Created title role in Milhaud's *David* at Sc., and has sung in many modern works, as well as in the classical Italian repertory. (R)

Com'è gentil. Ernesto's (ten.) aria in Act 3 of Donizetti's *Don Pasquale* which takes the form of a serenade.

Come scoglio. Fiordiligi's (sop.) famous aria in Act 1 of Mozart's *Così fan tutte*, declaring that she will remain 'as firm as a rock' against all temptations by her would-be seducer.

Come un bel dì di maggio. Chénier's (ten.) aria in Act 4 of Giordano's *Andrea Chénier*, sung while he awaits execution.

Comic Opera. See *Opéra-Comique*.

Comme autrefois. Leïla's (sop.) cavatina in Act 2 of Bizet's *Les Pêcheurs de Perles*.

Commedia dell' Arte. A dramatic genre of unknown origin that flourished in Italy from the 16th century and had a strong influence on literary drama and so on opera. The plots were simple love affairs—between master and servant, old and young alike—and their attendant difficulties. The chief characters were Pantaloon (often an elderly merchant), the swaggering Captain, the pedantic Doctor, and Inamorata; with Inamorata, her friend the Soubrette, and the Cantatrice and the Ballerina. Their servants were the foolish, agile Harlequin, the cunning, agile Brighella, and the cunning, cowardly Scapino (whence 'escapade'). Other characters include Scaramouche, Pulcinella, Mezzetino, and Pedrolino. Many operas, especially *opere buffe*, owe a direct debt to the *commedia dell'arte* in spirit, plot, even in the characters (whether under their original names or not), e.g. Rossini's *Barbiere*. Leoncavallo's *Pagliacci* is a famous instance of the clash of reality and illusion via the *commedia dell'arte*. The characters appear in other operas, e.g. Busoni's *Arlecchino*, Ethel Smyth's *Fantasio*, Strauss's *Ariadne auf Naxos*, and Mascagni's *Le Maschere*.

Commedia per musica. A term used in Italy in the 18th century for comic opera.

Como. Town in Lombardy, Italy. Opera is given in spring and autumn. The Teatro Sociale (cap. 1,000) was opened in 1813. After the Scala was destroyed in 1943 the Sociale offered the company hospitality for part of the 1943–4 season.

Competitions. From time to time competitions have been sponsored by various bodies for the composition of operas. Possibly the most famous was that (one of a series) organized by the publisher Edoardo Sonzogno for a 1-act opera in 1889; three prizes were awarded, one to Mascagni's *Cavalleria Rusticana*. In more recent years there have been two important competitions: one organized by the Arts Council of Great Britain in 1950 for the Festival of Britain, and the other organized by La Scala, Milan, for the 1951 Verdi celebrations. The former resulted in four operas being awarded prizes: Arthur Benjamin's *The Tale of Two Cities*, Alan Bush's *Wat Tyler*, Berthold Goldschmidt's *Beatrice Cenci*, and Karl Rankl's *Deirdre of the Sorrows*. So far only Benjamin's has been performed in Great Britain (and also in Metz). Bush's has been staged in Leipzig and Weimar, and has also been given by the B.B.C. The Italian competition resulted in a Scala production of Castro's *Proserpina e lo Straniero*, and one at the San Carlo, Naples, of Jacopo Napoli's *Mas' Aniello*.

Vocal competitions are more frequent: the Metropolitan Auditions of the Air have discovered Eleanor Steber and Leonard Warren; while in Europe, international vocal contests in Austria, Holland, Switzerland, and Italy have helped many subsequently famous singers at the start of their careers.

Comprimario (It. = with the principal). A secondary or small-part artist or singer. Examples of comprimario roles are Spoletta, Goro, and the whole host of duennas and confidantes.

Comte Ory, Le (Count Ory). Opera buffa in 2 acts by Rossini; text by Scribe and Lestre-Poirson. Prod. Paris, O., 20 Aug. 1828 with Cinthie-Damoreau, Nourrit, Levasseur; London, Hm., 28 Feb. 1829; N.Y. 22 Aug. 1831. Revived Florence Festival 1952 under Vittorio Gui, and Edinburgh Festival 1954 by the Glyndebourne Company, again under Gui. The first of Rossini's two French operas and his penultimate stage work; it contains much of the music of *Il Viaggio a Reims* with 12 additional numbers.

Act 1. The Count of Fourmoutiers has gone on a Crusade leaving his sister, the Countess Adèle (sop.), in the castle with her companion Ragonde (con.). Count Ory (ten.) is encamped at her gates disguised as a hermit and attended by Raimbaud (bass-bar.); here his expert advice on amorous matters has won him fame among the peasants. Ragonde decides to consult him about Adèle's melancholy, and Ory promptly asks to see her, alone. Ory's tutor (bass) now arrives in search of him, with the page Isolier (mezzo), who also loves the Countess, his cousin. The peasants' accounts of the wonderful hermit arouse the tutor's suspicion, and he leaves to get help. Isolier confides a plan to enter the castle disguised as a nun to Ory, who is impressed. The Countess now descends, and is advised by the 'hermit' to fall in love (though not with Isolier). He is about to follow her into the castle when he is unmasked by his tutor, returning with an escort. A messenger reports the impending return of the Crusaders.

Act 2. Inside the castle, the ladies are sewing. A storm breaks, and a party of nuns fleeing from the Count is admitted for shelter. The Countess receives the Mother Superior, the disguised Ory himself, who disturbs her with ardent protestations of gratitude. Left alone, the 'nuns' augment their simple meal with wine discovered by Raimbaud; they contain themselves with increasing difficulty on the

Countess's reappearances. Isolier brings news of the returning Crusaders, and on hearing of the nuns puts two and two together. Ory approaches, but in the darkness woos Isolier, who transmits these attentions, with interest, to the not unwilling Countess. The situation is just getting out of hand when a trumpet announces the Crusaders. Ory concedes defeat and escapes.

Connais-tu le pays? Mignon's (mezzo) aria in Act 1 of Thomas's *Mignon*, the famous 'Kennst du das Land' of Goethe's original, trying to answer Wilhelm's questions about her origins.

Conner, Nadine (b. Compton, Cal., 20 Feb. 1913). American soprano. Studied with Armando Fernandez and from 1939 with Albert Coates in Los Angeles. Début Los Angeles 1939, Marguerite. Has frequently appeared with San Francisco Opera. (R)

Conried (orig. Cohn), **Heinrich** (b. Bielitz, 13 Sept. 1848; d. Meran, 27 Apr. 1909). German operatic impresario and manager. Began career as an actor in Vienna; after holding managerial positions in a number of German cities went to America in 1888. Succeeded Maurice Grau (q.v.) as director of Metropolitan Opera, 1903, and also organized his own company. Resigned owing to ill health in 1908.

Consul, The. Opera in 3 acts by Gian-Carlo Menotti; text by composer. Prod. Philadelphia 1 Mar. 1950 with Neway, Powers, Lane, Marlo, MacNeil, Lishner, and McKinley, cond. Engel; London, Cambridge Theatre, 7 Feb. 1951 with virtually the same cast, cond. Schippers.

The action of the opera takes place in a nameless European country.

Act 1. John Sorel (bar.), fleeing the secret police, stumbles wounded into his shabby apartment. His wife Magda (sop.) dresses his wound and hides him as the police arrive to question her and her Mother (con.); they discover nothing. John tells his wife to go to the Consulate for visas. In the waiting-room of the Consulate the Secretary (mezzo) frustrates all attempts to see the Consul by giving out innumerable forms.

Act 2. A month later Magda is still waiting for her visa; her baby is dying. She has a nightmare in which she sees her husband bloodstained and bandaged. The window is broken by a stone—a signal that John has a message for her. The Mother discovers that the child has died. Back at the Consulate a magician hypnotizes the applicants and they dance. Magda arrives, unrecognized by the Secretary, and in a dramatic outburst condemns the inhumanity and red tape of the Consulate. Moved, the Secretary agrees to ask the Consul to see her. The door of his office opens and the Police Chief emerges. Magda faints.

Act 3. Magda is again at the Consulate. A friend arrives with news that John is on his way. Magda sends a note to prevent him returning and leaves. A few minutes later John arrives, followed by the Police Chief, who arrests him.

The last scene takes place in the apartment. Magda prepares to gas herself. She sees her husband and all the people at the Consulate; they urge her to join them on the journey to Death, whose frontiers are never barred.

Contes d'Hoffmann, Les (The Tales of Hoffmann). Opera in 3 acts by Offenbach; text by Barbier after the play by Barbier and Carré, founded in turn on stories by E. T. A. Hoffmann. Recitatives and part of scoring by Guiraud. Prod. Paris, O.C., 10 Feb. 1881 with Adèle Isaac, Talazac, Taskin; N.Y., Fifth Avenue, 16 Oct. 1882; London, Adelphi Theatre, 17 Apr. 1907.

Prologue. Luther's wine-cellar in Nuremberg. Councillor Lindorf (bar.), who assumes during the course of the opera Hoffmann's evil genius (Coppelius, Dapertutto, Dr. Miracle), bribes Andrès (ten.) to give up a letter from Stella the prima donna to Hoffmann (ten.) arranging a rendezvous. The students arrive and with them Hoffmann and his friend Nicklausse (mezzo). Hoffmann is persuaded to tell the story of his three loves. Each act of the opera is one of his 'tales'.

Act 1. Hoffmann's first love was Olympia the doll, invented by Spalanzani (bar.) and Dr. Coppelius (bass-bar.). Coppelius sells Hoffmann a pair of magic spectacles through which Olympia (sop.) appears human. At a party given by Spalanzani for his 'daughter's' coming-out, Hoffmann declares his love for Olympia, and dances with her. Coppelius, who has been swindled by Spalanzani, returns and smashes Olympia; Hoffmann discovers that his love is a doll.

Act 2. Hoffmann is in Venice, where he has met the beautiful courtesan Giulietta. She is in the power of Dapertutto (bass-bar.) the magician, who wishes to procure Hoffmann's reflection (in other words, his soul). Giulietta finds no difficulty in fascinating Hoffmann and carrying out Dapertutto's wish; and Hoffmann, bereft of his shadow, tries to obtain the key to Giulietta's room from Schlemil (bass) whom he kills in a duel, only to find Giulietta drifting away in a gondola with the dwarf Pitichinaccio.

Act 3. Hoffmann has now come back to Munich where he has fallen in love with the frail young singer Antonia (sop.), daughter of Councillor Crespel (bass). Antonia is consumptive and has been forbidden to sing, but Dr. Miracle (bass-bar.), by bringing her mother's picture to life, forces her to sing and thus brings about her death. For a third time Hoffmann has lost his love.

Epilogue. Back in Luther's tavern, the 'tales' are over. Hoffmann is drunk, and when Stella arrives it is Lindorf and not Hoffmann who leads her away.

Offenbach felt himself to be dying as he wrote *Hoffmann*, and urged haste on Carvalho, manager of the Opéra-Comique. But he died before it was ready; revision, orchestration, and the furnishing of recitatives were undertaken by Guiraud.

Contralto (It. = against the alto, i.e. contrasting with the high voice). The lowest category of female (or artificial male) voice. Several subdivisions exist within opera houses: the two commonest in general use (though seldom by composers in scores) are given below, with examples of roles and their approximate *tessitura*. In general distinction is more by character than by *tessitura*: thus the examples of the roles give a more useful indication of the different voices' quality than any attempted technical definition.

German: dramatischer Alt (Erda: f–f''); komischer Alt (Frau Reich in *Die lustige Weiber von Windsor*: f–f'').

Italian and French contralto roles are not generally further subdivided into categories, and have a similar *tessitura* to the German.

See also *Castrato*, *Mezzo-soprano*.

Contratenor. See *Countertenor*.

Converse, Frederick (b. Newton, Mass., 5 Jan. 1871; d. Westwood, Mass., 8 June 1940). American composer. He studied at Harvard, then in Munich. *The Pipe of Desire* was produced at Boston in 1906; in 1910 it became the first American opera performed at the Metropolitan, New York. His other operas are *The Sacrifice* (1911), *Beauty and the Beast*, *Sinbad the Sailor* (1913), and *The Immigrants* (1914).

Cook, Thomas Aynsley (b. London, July 1831 or 1836; d. Liverpool, 16 Feb. 1894). English bass. Originally boy soprano and trained by Hopkins at the City Temple; then studied with Staudigl (q.v.) in Germany. After singing in several German theatres made British début at Manchester 1856. Member of Lucy Escott's National English Opera Company and the Pyne-Harrison Company. Carl Rosa Company from 1874. Devilshoof (*The Bohemian Girl*) was probably his most famous role. See Goossens.

Cooke, Tom (b. Dublin, 1782; d. London, 26 Feb. 1848). Irish singer, composer, and instrumentalist. Sang in various stage works in Dublin and then London; principal tenor, D.L. 1815–35, and director from about 1821. Produced his own *Oberon* in the same year as Weber's, in either rivalry or parody. Adapted many foreign operas, with substitutions of his own, including *Abu Hassan*, *La Dame Blanche*, *La Muette de Portici*, and *La Juive*.

Cooper, Emil (b. Kherson, 20 Dec. 1877; d. New York, 16 Nov. 1960). Russian conductor. Studied Odessa, Vienna, Moscow. Début Odessa 1896; Kiev 1900; Zimmin Opera, Moscow, 1904, where he conducted the world première of *The Golden Cockerel*, which he also conducted in its London première at D.L. in 1914. Left Russia 1922, and after various engagements in Europe was engaged for the Chicago Opera 1929–31; N.Y., Met., 1944–50, where he introduced *Peter Grimes* and *Khovanshchina*. Also a distinguished Wagner conductor, directing the first Russian performances of *Meistersinger* and the *Ring*. (R)

Copenhagen. (Dan., Kjøbenhavn). Capital of Denmark. Foreign companies began visiting Copenhagen from the middle of the 18th century: Italian and French opera was given, and a German company was in residence at the Court Theatre from Dec. 1721 to Jan. 1723, during which time it gave the première of Keiser's *Ulysses* (1722) for Frederick IV's birthday. In 1749 Prince Christian's birth was celebrated with the première of Gluck's *La Contessa dei Numi*. One of the earliest operas produced at the Danish National Theatre was Scalabrini's *Love Rewarded* (1758). The first opera by a Danish composer was Walter's *Faithfulness Proved* (1774). Hartmann's *Balders Død* (1778) is interesting for its inclusion of an ensemble of Valkyries; his *Fiskerne* (1780) makes use of the Danish national anthem. The first grand opera in Danish was Naumann's *Orpheus og Euridice* (1786), but the outstanding 18th-century work was Kunzen's *Holger Danske* (1789) (see *Oberon*). The present Royal Theatre (cap. 1,300) dates from 1874. Singers who began their careers there include Peter Cornelius, Vilhelm Herold, Lauritz Melchior, and Else Brehms. During the German occupation Gershwin's *Porgy and Bess* surprisingly received its first performance outside America at the Royal Theatre (1943). Italian companies visited Copenhagen regularly during the inter-war years; and appearances were also made by the Stockholm Opera.

Copland, Aaron (b. New York, 14 Nov. 1900). American composer. Studied with Wittgenstein and Rubin Goldmark at the American Conservatory at Fontainebleau, and with Nadia Boulanger in Paris. His first opera was *The Second Hurricane* (1937), a 'play opera' for high schools. *The Tender Land* (1954) is a pastoral drama set in the mid-west during the depression years; its idiom is similar to that of *Appalachian Spring*, while the earlier opera uses Copland's more nervy, jazz-influenced manner. (R)

Coq d'Or, Le. See *Golden Cockerel, The.*

Corder, Frederick (b. London, 26 Jan. 1852; d. London, 21 Aug. 1932). English conductor, composer, and translator. Trained at R.A.M. and Cologne. *Nordissa* (1887) was performed by the Carl Rosa Company; but Corder is best remembered for his now rather quaint-sounding translations of *The Ring* and *Tristan*, in which he was assisted by his wife.

Cordon, Norman (b. Washington, 20 Jan. 1904 d. Chapel Hill 1 Mar. 1964). American bass. After appearing in N.Y. in a musical, studied with Gaetano de Luca at Nashville and Hadley Outland in Chicago. Début San Carlo Touring Company 1933, the King (*Aida*); Chicago 1933–4; N.Y., Met., 1936–46. One of the outstanding American basses of his day.

Corelli, Franco (b. Ancona, 8 Apr. 1923). Italian tenor. Studied Milan, Florence, Spoleto. Début Spoleto 1951, Don José; London, C.G., 1957, Cavaradossi; N.Y., Met., 1961, Manrico. Has sung regularly at Milan, Sc., since 1954, and has established himself as one of the leading Italian heroic tenors. Especially successful as Manrico, Dick Johnson, and Calaf. (R)

Corena, Fernando (b. Geneva, 22 Dec. 1916). Swiss-Italian bass. Originally intending to take holy orders, studied at Fribourg University. Began vocal career as amateur and won contest in Geneva; further encouraged by Vittorio Gui and studied in Milan with Enrico Romano. Début Trieste 1947, Varlaam. N.Y., Met., 1953, succeeding Salvatore Baccaloni as leading basso-buffo. Edinburgh Festival 1955, Falstaff; London, C.G., 1960, Bartolo (*Barbiere*). (R)

Corfu (Gr., Kerkyra). Capital of the Greek island of that name. Opera was first given there in 1771 (Galuppi's *Il Marchese Villano*), and regular seasons were established. Since the Second World War the opera house has been closed.

Cornelius, Peter (b. Mainz, 24 Dec. 1824; d. Mainz, 26 Oct. 1874). German composer and author. He took to music after an attempt at an acting career, and became a disciple of the 'New German School' and its prophets, Liszt and Wagner, with whom he was very friendly. Liszt produced *Der Barbier von Bagdad* at Weimar (1858), but owing to organized opposition it was withdrawn; as a result Liszt resigned as court conductor. After his association with Wagner in Vienna he composed *Der Cid* (Weimar 1865). His last opera, *Gunlöd* (prod. 1891), for which, as before, he wrote the text, was less successful. Cornelius's fame now rests upon the entertaining *Der Barbier*.

Cornelius, Peter (b. Labjerggaard, 4 Jan. 1865; d. Copenhagen, 25 Dec. 1934). Danish tenor. Studied in Copenhagen and Berlin. Début Copenhagen, as baritone, 1892, Escamillo; after further study, tenor début (again at Copenhagen) 1899, Steersman. Bayreuth 1906; London, C.G., 1907–14; chosen by Hans Richter to sing Siegfried in the English *Ring* performances of 1908 and 1909. (R)

Corno di Bassetto. See *Shaw, G. Bernard*.

Corregidor, Der. Opera in 4 acts by Wolf; text by Rosa Mayreder, after Alarcón's story *El Sombrero de Tres Picos* (1874). Prod. Mannheim 7 June 1896; London, R.A.M. (in English), 13 July 1934; N.Y., Carnegie Hall, 5 Jan. 1959 (concert perf.). Wolf's only completed opera, based on the same story as Falla's ballet.

Corsaro, Il (The Corsair). Opera in 4 acts by Verdi; text by Piave, after Byron's poem, *The Corsair* (1813). Prod. Trieste 25 Oct. 1848. Verdi's least successful opera, chiefly due to the poor libretto.

Corsi, Jacopo. See *Camerata*.

Corsica. The theatre at Ajaccio was inaugurated in 1835 with Rossini's *Cenerentola*. Opera was also given at Bastia as early as 1797.

Cortis, Antonio (b. Valencia, 12 Aug. 1891; d. Valencia, 2 Apr. 1952). Spanish tenor. Début 1915 as comprimario, then graduated to larger roles. International career began in Rome, 1920. Chicago 1924–32; London, C.G., 1931, Calaf. One of the best interpreters of Dick Johnson (*La Fanciulla del West*). Retired from the stage while still at the height of his powers in the mid-1930's. (R)

Così fan tutte (Women are like that). Opera in 2 acts by Mozart; text by Da Ponte (his third and last for Mozart) based on a supposedly true incident. Prod. Vienna, B., 26 Jan., 1790; London, Hm., 9 May 1811; N.Y., Met., 24 Mar. 1922.

Act 1, Scene 1. A café in Naples. Two officers, Ferrando (ten.) and Guglielmo (bar.), wager the cynical Don Alfonso (bar.) that their respective lovers Fiordiligi (sop.) and Dorabella (sop.) will be faithful in their absence.

Scene 2. Don Alfonso tells the ladies of their lovers' impending departure on active service. Tears surround the soldiers' farewell.

Scene 3 introduces the maid Despina (sop.). The officers return disguised as Albanians, and having unsuccessfully made love to each other's lady pretend to take poison. Despina, disguised as a doctor, magnetizes them to life, and they resume the attack.

Act 2 finds Guglielmo beginning to wear down his friend's lover Dorabella; Ferrando, more slowly, succeeds with Fiordiligi, and Despina (now a lawyer) prepares a double marriage contract. Word that the officers are returning sends the 'Albanians' packing, to return in their true guise pretending fury at their betrayal. Alfonso reveals the truth, thus allowing all to end happily.

The supposed immorality of the plot caused many adaptations in the 19th century.

Costa, Michael (Andrew Angus) (orig. Michele Andrea Agniello) (b. Naples, 4 Feb. 1808; d. Hove, Sussex, 29 Apr. 1884). Italian composer and conductor of Spanish descent. Studied at the Royal College, Naples. Settled in London and eventually became naturalized. Engaged as *maestro al piano* at the King's Theatre 1830; director and conductor there from 1833 to 1846, during which period he brought the orchestra and ensemble to a state of efficiency hitherto unknown in London. From 1846, conductor of the Philharmonic Society; 1847–69, music director of the newly opened Royal Italian Opera, Covent Garden; knighted 1867. In 1871 he was again appointed to Her Majesty's Opera, and continued there until 1879. His operas include *Il Delitto Punito, Il Sospetto Punito, Il Carcere d'Ildegonda, Malvina, Malek Adhel,* and *Don Carlos.*

Costanzi, Teatro. Opera house built by Domenico Costanzi in Rome and opened 27 Nov. 1880 with *Semiramide.* Designed by Achille Sfondrini, with a seating capacity of 2,200. Largely rebuilt and modern stage equipment installed 1926–7. Reopened as the Teatro Reale dell'Opera with Boito's *Nerone,* 28 Feb. 1928. It remained open throughout the Second World War, and in 1946 was renamed simply the Teatro dell'Opera. World premières there include Mascagni's *L'Amico Fritz* (1891), *Iris* (1898), and *Lodoletta* (1917); Puccini's *Tosca* (1900); Zandonai's *Giulietta e Romeo* (1922); Pizzetti's *Lo Straniero* (1930); Refice's *Cecilia* (1934); Alfano's *Il Dottor Antonio* (1949).

Cotogni, Antonio (b. Rome, 1 Aug. 1831; d. Rome, 15 Oct. 1918). Italian baritone. Studied with Achille Faldi; début Rome, Teatro Metastasio, 1852, Belcore (*L'Elisir d'Amore*). Milan, Sc., from 1860. London, C.G., 1867, Valentine (*Faust*); member of company until 1889, being the Enrico in *Lucia* on the night of Melba's début 1888. Had a repertory of more than 150 roles. Retired from the stage in 1894, and in 1902 became a professor of voice at Santa Cecilia, Rome. Famous singers who studied with him include Jean de Reszke and Battistini, and among his pupils in Rome were Lauri-Volpi, Gigli, and Stabile. (R)

Countertenor. A high male voice that uses naturally produced tone with a large degree of head resonance; not to be confused with male alto, castrato, or falsetto. Though covering the soprano or contralto range, it is essentially masculine in timbre—clean, penetrating, and flexible, with an almost instrumental purity. Popular from medieval times to about the 18th century, the high countertenor has been revived in recent times with great success by Alfred Deller and Russell Oberlin; the low countertenor, associated mostly with church music, seems now non-existent. Britten uses it to suggest a non-human quality for Oberon in his *Midsummer Night's Dream.*

Countess (Almaviva). The Count's wife (sop.) in Mozart's *Le Nozze di Figaro.*

Coup de glotte (Fr. = stroke of the glottis). A method of attacking a note whereby the false vocal chords (two membranes above the true vocal chords) are closed and then quickly opened to release the tone. It should not be an abrupt release from pressure, when a sharp cough or click results, but a start of pressure from stopped breath.

Covent Garden. The name of three theatres that have occupied roughly the same site in Bow Street, London, since 1732. The site of the theatre had been church land (in fact a convent garden, hence its name).

The first theatre was opened by John Rich on 7 Dec. 1732 with Congreve's *The Way of the World*; the first musical work heard there was *The Beggar's Opera.* The majority of events at Covent Garden during its first hundred years was of a dramatic rather than operatic nature, though Handel's *Atlanta, Alcina,* and *Berenice* all had their first performances there. The theatre was destroyed by fire on 19 Sept. 1808.

The second theatre opened a year later. In 1826 Kemble, the manager, invited Weber to compose a work for

Covent Garden; this was *Oberon*. In 1847 the theatre became the Royal Italian Opera, with a company which included a number of artists who had seceded from Her Majesty's Theatre with their music director Costa (q.v.). They began operations with Rossini's *Semiramide*. In 1851 Frederick Gye became the manager, a position he held until 1879. The second theatre was burnt down in 1856, and the present building opened on 15 May 1858 with Meyerbeer's *Les Huguenots*.

From 1858 until 1939, with the exception of an interruption during the First World War, opera was given every year during the London 'season', and virtually every artist of international repute has appeared there. All operas were sung in Italian until the days of Augustus Harris (manager 1888–96) who introduced opera in the original language, and Covent Garden became the Royal Opera in 1892.

Beecham first conducted there in 1910 but did not take part in a summer season until after the First World War. Bruno Walter was chief conductor 1924–31, and Beecham 1932–9.

The theatre was used as a dance hall 1940–5, but in 1946 it reopened as the home of a permanent company with a government subsidy, paid through the Arts Council. Karl Rankl was music director 1946–51; Rafael Kubelik from 1955 to 1958; Georg Solti from 1961 to 1971; and Colin Davis from 1971.

During the post-war period, seven native operas have received world premières, including Britten's *Billy Budd* (1951) and *Gloriana* (1953), Walton's *Troilus and Cressida* (1954), and Tippett's *The Midsummer Marriage* (1955) and *The Knot Garden* (1970). In addition, the staging of Berg's *Wozzeck* under Kleiber (1952), Janáček's *Jenůfa* (1956) and Berlioz's *Les Troyens* (1957), both under Kubelik, Verdi's *Don Carlos* under Giulini (1958), *Fidelio* (1961) under Klemperer, and *Tosca* (1964) with Callas and Gobbi, *Arabella* and *Moses and Aaron* (1965) with Solti were worthy of special note.

Covered tone. The tone-quality produced when the singer's voice is pitched in the soft palate. It is gentler, more veiled in timbre, than open tone (q.v.).

Crabbé, Armand (b. Brussels, 23 Apr. 1883; d. Brussels, 4 July 1947). Belgian baritone. Studied Brussels with Désiré Demest. Début Brussels, La M., 1904, Nightwatchman (*Meistersinger*); London, C.G., 1906–14. Returned after a long absence in 1937 as Gianni Schicchi. Also appeared in Chicago, Buenos Aires, and Milan, Sc. Much admired as Beckmesser, Figaro (Rossini), and Mârouf, which part was specially transposed for him by the composer, Rabaud (R)

Cracow. See *Poland*.

Credo in un Dio Crudel. Iago's (bar.) aria in Act 2 of Verdi's *Otello* in which he expounds his belief in a cruel god who has fashioned him in his likeness. This is Boito's own invention.

Crescendo (It. = growing). Increasing in loudness. It is now a basic part of music, but was once a controversial novelty. According to Burney, the first opera in which it is used seems to have been Terradellas's *Bellerofonte* (1747). This refutes the claim made by Mosca to have used it for the first time in his *I Pretendenti Delusi* (1811). The innovation was, and still is, often credited to Rossini, with whom it bordered on a mannerism. Perhaps his finest use of it is in *Barbiere* to suggest graphically the rising gale of slander in Don Basilio's 'La Calunnia'.

Crespin, Régine (b. Marseilles, 23 Mar. 1927). French soprano. Début Mulhouse, 1950, Elsa. Bayreuth 1958, Kundry; Glyndebourne 1959, Marschallin; London, C.G., since 1960, the Marschallin, Tosca, and Elsa. N.Y., Met., since 1962. Has established herself as one of the most sensitive and moving French singers of the day. One of the finest contemporary Marschallins. (R)

Crimi, Giulio (b. nr. Catania, 10 May 1885; d. Rome, 29 Oct. 1939). Italian tenor. Début Treviso, 1912, Hagenbach (*La Wally*); London, C.G., 1914, Avito in first London *L'Amore dei Tre Re*. N.Y., Met., 1918–22, created Luigi and Rinuccio in world premières of *Il Tabarro* and *Gianni Schicchi*;

Chicago 1916–18 and 1922–4. Returned to Italy and continued to sing in Milan and Rome until 1928. After his retirement taught: pupils include Gobbi. Was also creator of Paolo in Zandonai's *Francesca da Rimini* (Turin 1914). (R)

Critic, The, or An Opera Rehearsal. Opera in 2 acts by Stanford; text by Lewis Cairns James, after Sheridan's comedy (1779). Prod. London, Shaftesbury, 14 Jan. 1916.

Crociato in Egitto, Il (The Crusader in Egypt). Opera in 2 acts by Meyerbeer; text by Rossi. Prod. Venice, F., 7 Mar. 1824 with Velluti; London, Hm., 3 June 1825 with Velluti and Malibran—the first Meyerbeer opera given in London, and the last and most successful of the composer's Italian works.

Crooks, Richard (b. Trenton, 26 June 1900). American tenor. Studied with Frank La Forge and Sydney Bourne. Début Hamburg 1927, Cavaradossi; Philadelphia 1930; N.Y., Met., 1933–43; appearances also in Chicago, San Francisco, Cincinnati, &c. His best roles include Des Grieux (Massenet), Faust, Roméo, Wilhelm Meister, and Ottavio. (R)

Cross, Joan (b. London, 7 Sept. 1900). English soprano. Joined chorus of Old Vic 1924, soon graduated to small roles (First Lady, Cherubino) and then to leading ones. Principal soprano S.W. 1931–46; director of Opera Company 1943–5. C.G., 1931, 1934–5, 1947–54. One of the founder members of the English Opera Group 1945. Created Ellen Orford (*Peter Grimes*, 1945), Female Chorus (*Rape of Lucretia*, 1946), Lady Billows (*Albert Herring*, 1947), and Queen Elizabeth (*Gloriana*, 1953)—all by Britten. Since 1955 has devoted herself to teaching, especially at the National School of Opera (formerly the Opera School) which she founded with Anne Wood in 1948. Has also produced opera for Sadler's Wells and Covent Garden, as well as in Holland. One of the outstanding British operatic artists of the century.(R)

Crown Diamonds, The. See *Diamants de la Couronne*.

Crozier, Eric (b. London, 14 Nov. 1914). English writer and producer. With Benjamin Britten and John Piper, co-founder of the English Opera Group (1946). Librettist of Britten's *Albert Herring* and *Let's Make an Opera*, and (with E. M. Forster) *Billy Budd*; also of Berkeley's *Ruth*. Produced new English version of *The Bartered Bride* (made by Crozier and Joan Cross), S.W. 1943, and premières of *Peter Grimes*, S.W. 1945, and *The Rape of Lucretia*, Glyndebourne 1946; also U.S. première of *Grimes*, Tanglewood 1946.

Cruvelli (orig. Cruwell), **Jeanne** (b. Bielefeld, 12 Mar. 1826; d. Monte Carlo, 6 Nov. 1907). German soprano. Studied Paris with Permarini and Bordogni. Début Venice 1847, Elvira (*Ernani*). London, H.M.'s, 1848 (also Elvira), Paris, T.I., 1851; Paris, O., 1854 at a salary of 100,000 francs, where she created Hélène in Verdi's *Les Vêpres Siciliennes* (1855).

Cuba. See *Havana*.

Cuénod, Hugues (b. Coiseaux-sur-Bevey, 26 June 1902). Swiss tenor. Studied Lausanne, Basle, Vienna. After teaching at the Geneva Conservatory, began career as singer, first in concerts then in opera. Milan, Sc., 1951; Glyndebourne since 1954; London, C.G., 1954, 1956, 1958. Specializes in a number of selected roles including Sellem (*The Rake's Progress*), Basilio (*Figaro*), and the Astrologer (*Golden Cockerel*). (R)

Cui, César Antonovich (b. Vilna, 18 Jan. 1835; d. St. Petersburg, 26 Mar. 1918). Russian composer. With Balakirev founded the Russian nationalistic group of composers known as the 'Mighty Handful' (Borodin, Mussorgsky, and Rimsky-Korsakov were the others). Wrote six operas and completed Mussorgsky's *Sorochinsky Fair*.

Curtain Call. The bow made by singers and conductor (and on special occasions producer, designer, and even chorus-master) at the end of a scene or act of an opera. The applause of the audience generally regulates the number of bows taken by artists; but see also *Claque*. In Italy the main curtain calls occur during the course of the evening, the audience generally leaving the theatre immediately after the final curtain; in England, on the other hand, the greatest enthusiasm is reserved for the calls at the end of the evening. At the Metropolitan, Rudolf Bing has recently abolished solo curtain calls, though there have been recalcitrant prima donnas. In German opera houses solo calls are rare. At Bayreuth until after the war there were no curtain calls, the curtain being raised just once to display the final tableau; but in recent years singers, conductor, and Wieland Wagner have been called at the end of the performance.

Curtin, Phyllis (b. Clarksburg, West Va., 3 Dec. 1930). American soprano. Studied Wellesley College, Mass., New York, and with Boris Goldovsky at Boston and Tanglewood. New England Opera Theatre 1946. N.Y., C.C., since 1953; Met. 1961. Vienna 1960. Created Cathy in Floyd's *Wuthering Heights* and title role in same composer's *Susannah*; first N.Y. Cressida in Walton's *Troilus and Cressida*. Also successful as Salome, Mistress Ford, and in Mozart. (R)

Cycle. In opera, the name given to a group of works telling a more or less consecutive story, but for reasons of length separable and performable on different nights. The earliest recorded operatic cycle is Sartorio's pair *La Prosperità di Elio Seiano* and *La Caduta di Elio Seiano*, both in 3 acts with text by Niccolò Minato (prod. Venice 1667). The best-known cycle remains Wagner's *Ring*, upon which certain others were modelled, e.g. Bungert's now forgotten tetralogy *Die Homerische Welt*, based on the *Odyssey*, and Holbrooke's *The Cauldron of Annwyn*.

Cyrano de Bergerac. (1) Opera in 4 acts by Alfano; text by Henry Cain after Rostand's drama (1891). Prod. Rome, T.R., 22 Jan. 1936. (2) *Cyrano*. Opera in 4 acts by Damrosch; text by W. J. Henderson after Rostand. Prod. N.Y., Met., 27 Feb. 1913.

Czechoslovakia. See *Bratislava, Brno, Košice, Liberec, Olomouc, Opava, Ostrava, Plzeň, Prague, Ústi nad Labem.*

Czerwenka, Oscar (b. Linz, 5 July 1924). Austrian bass. Début Graz 1947, Hermit (*Freischütz*). Vienna, O., since 1951; Salzburg since 1953. Glyndebourne 1959, Ochs; N.Y., Met., 1959. Has a repertory of more than 75 roles. (R)

D

Da Capo Aria (da capo: It. = from the beginning). From about 1660 (e.g. Tenaglia's *Clearco*) to about the time of Mozart, arias were written in three sections, the third being a repeat of the first, after a contrasting middle section. An example is 'Non più di fiori' in *La Clemenza di Tito*.

Dafne. Opera in a prologue and 6 scenes by Peri; text by Ottavio Rinuccini. Prod. in Jacopo Corsi's house, probably during Carnival 1597. The first opera, music now lost. See also *Daphne*.

Daland. A Norwegian sea-captain (bass), father of Senta, in Wagner's *Der fliegende Holländer*.

Dalayrac, Nicolas (b. Muret, Laun-guedoc, 8 June 1753; d. Paris, 27 Nov. 1809). French composer. His *opéras-comiques*, almost 60 in number, were enormously popular for their naïve, sentimental tunefulness throughout the Revolution and the Empire. His characteristically romantic rescue subjects and his occasional musical originalities scarcely affected the essentially pretty, 'galant' atmosphere.

D'Albert, Eugen. See *Albert, Eugen D'*.

Dalibor. Opera in 3 acts by Smetana; German text by Joseph Wenzig, trans. into Czech by Ervin Spindler. Prod. Prague, Czech T., 16 May 1868; Chicago, Sokol Hall, 13 Apr. 1924; Edinburgh, King's, by Prague Nat. T.' 20 Aug. 1964. Dalibor is imprisoned for supposed revolutionary scheming; his lover Milada is fatally wounded leading a rescue party. In Czechoslovakia it is regarded as a rescue opera of a significance almost comparable to that of *Fidelio*.

Dalila. The Philistine temptress (mezzo) in Saint-Saëns's *Samson et Dalila*.

Dalis, Irene (b. San José, Cal., 8 Oct. 1929). American mezzo. Studied with Edyth Walker and Paul Althouse; then in Milan with Otto Mueller. Heard by Mödl at a student performance, who recommended her to the Oldenburg Staatstheater; début there 1953, Eboli. Engaged by Ebert for Städtische Oper, Berlin, 1954; N.Y., Met., from 1956; London, C.G., 1958; Bayreuth 1961. (R)

Dallas. Town in Texas, U.S.A. Since Nov. 1957 it has, under Lawrence Kelly (general manager) and Nicola Rescigno (music director), presented short but brilliant annual seasons with Callas, Berganza, Simoniato, Sutherland, Schwarzkopf, Bastianini, Taddei, Vickers, &c., and with Zeffirelli as chief producer, in works including *Alcina*, *Il Barbiere*, *Don Giovanni*, *L'Italiana in Algeri*, *Medea*, *La Traviata*. The operas are performed in the State Fair Music Hall (cap. 4,100).

Dallapiccola, Luigi (b. Pisino, 3 Feb. 1904). Italian composer. The leading dodecaphonist of his country, he has successfully reconciled the stringent formal demands of the technique to his native lyricism and love of the voice, not least in his operas. *Volo di Notte* (1940) is based on *Vol de Nuit* by the French author and aviator Antoine de St-Exupéry. His obsessive sympathy with prisoners finds moving expression in *Il Prigioniero* (q.v.) (1950).

Dalla Rizza, Gilda (b. Verona, 12 Oct. 1892). Italian soprano. Début Bologna 1910, Charlotte (*Werther*). Her singing of Minnie brought her to the notice of Puccini, who wrote Magda for her in *La Rondine*; this she created at Monte Carlo in 1917. The first Italian Lauretta and Angelica, she created these roles in London, C.G., 1920. Greatly admired by Toscanini who engaged her for La Scala from 1923. Created leading roles in *Anima Allegra* (Vittadini), *Giulietta e Romeo* (Zandonai), and *Il Piccolo Marat* (Mascagni). Retired 1939, but sang Angelica at Vicenza 1942 in the Puccini celebrations. Now teaches: pupils include Elena Rizzieri. (R)

Dalla sua pace. Ottavio's (ten.) aria in Act 1 of Mozart's *Don Giovanni*, declaring that upon Donna Anna's joy or sorrow his own depends.

Dal Monte, Toti (orig. Antonietta Meneghel) (b. Mogliano Veneto, 27 June 1893). Italian soprano. Piano studies interrupted by an injury, so studied voice with Barbara Marchisio. Début Milan, Sc., 1916, Biancafiore (*Francesca da Rimini*). After a further period of study with Pini-Corsi, and appearances in the Italian provinces, sang in Beethoven's 9th Symphony at Turin under Toscanini, who engaged her to sing Gilda at La Scala in 1922. After this she decided to concentrate on the *soprano leggiero* repertory. Sang regularly in Milan, Rome, and Naples; Chicago from 1924 to 1928; N.Y., Met., 1924–5; London, C.G., 1925. One of the last Italian 'divas' to delight audiences in old-fashioned Patti-like concerts. Her voice was small, pure, and inclined to whiteness; its agility was remarkable. In recent years she enjoyed a brief period on the straight stage, and now devotes her time to teaching. Her pupils include Gianna d'Angelo and Dolores Wilson. (R)

Dalmorès, Charles (orig. Henry Alphonse Boin) (b. Nancy, 31 Dec. 1871; d. Hollywood, 6 Dec. 1939). French tenor. Début Rouen 1899; Brussels, La M., 1900–6; London, C.G., 1904–5, 1909–11; N.Y., Manhattan Opera, 1906–10; subsequently with Chicago Opera. Famous for his Faust, Jean (*Le Jongleur de Notre Dame*), Julien, Pelléas, &c. Also appeared in Wagner roles later in his career. Devoted the latter part of his life to teaching. (R)

D'Alvarez, Marguerite. See *Alvarez, Marguerite D'*.

Dal Verme, Teatro. See *Milan*.

Dame Blanche, La (The White Lady). Opera in 3 acts by Boïeldieu; text by Eugène Scribe, after Scott's novels *The Monastery* (1820) and *Guy Mannering* (1815). Prod. Paris, O.C., 10 Dec. 1825; London, D.L., 9 Oct. 1826; N.Y., 24 Aug. 1827.

Damnation de Faust, La. *Légende dramatique* in 4 parts by Berlioz; text by composer and Almire Gandonnière, after Gérard de Nerval's French version (1828 and 1840) of Goethe's *Faust*. Completed 1846, incorporating *Huit Scènes de Faust* (1828). Concert performance Paris, O.C., 6 Dec. 1846 with Duflot-Maillard prod. Monte Carlo 18 Feb. 1893 with Jean de Reszke as Faust, Renaud as Méphistophélès; Liverpool 3 Feb. 1894, Carl Rosa Company; New Orleans 1894. There have been many subsequent attempts at staging the work.

D'amor sull' ali rosee. Leonora's (sop.) aria, in Act 4 of *Trovatore*, in which she sings of her love for Manrico as she stands beneath the tower in which he is imprisoned.

Damoreau, Laure Cinthie- (orig. Montalant) (b. Paris, 6 Feb. 1801; d. Chantilly, 25 Feb. 1863). French soprano. Before marriage to Damoreau, known as Mlle Cinti. Studied Paris. Début Paris, T.I., 1819, Cherubino. Paris, O., 1826–35, where she created leading soprano roles in Rossini's *L'Assedio di Corinto*, *Mosè*, *Comte Ory*, and *Guillaume Tell*, and was the first Isabelle (*Robert le Diable*) and Elvira (*Masaniello*). At the Opéra-Comique, 1834–43, she created leading roles in a number of Auber's works including *Le Domino Noir*. London, Hm., 1822 and 1832. Retired 1835 and was professor of singing at the Paris Conservatoire from then until 1856. She wrote a *Méthode de Chant*.

Damrosch, Leopold (b. Posen, 22 Oct. 1832; d. New York, 15 Feb. 1885). German opera conductor who occupied an important place in the musical life of New York. After the financially disastrous first season of Italian opera at the Metropolitan, 1883–4, Damrosch was called on to organize a German season there for 1884–5. Engaged a fine company of singers, and conducted every performance from 17 Nov. until 9 Feb. including the first American *Walküre*. He was succeeded on his death by his son **Walter** (b. Breslavia, 30 Jan. 1862; d. New York, 22 Dec. 1950), a pupil of Bülow. Between 1885 and 1891 he directed the American premières of

Rienzi, *Meistersinger*, *Tristan und Isolde*, *Rheingold*, *Siegfried*, *Götterdämmerung*, *Euryanthe*, *Queen of Sheba*, and *Barbier von Bagdad*. Formed his own opera company 1895, but returned to the Met. 1900–3. The rest of his life was spent in the concert and educational worlds. Composed five operas, *The Scarlet Letter* (1896), *Cyrano de Bergerac* (1913), *The Dove of Peace* (1912), *The Man Without a Country* (1937), and *The Opera Cloak* (1942).

Damrosch Opera Company. Formed and financed by Walter Damrosch in 1894, after successful concert performances at Carnegie Hall of *Walküre* and *Götterdämmerung*. Singers during first three seasons included Gadski, Sucher, Klafsky, Ternina, Brema, Alvary, Bispham, and Fischer. The first season resulted in a profit of more than $50,000, despite the heavy expenses of touring Wagner operas from coast to coast in America. In the spring of 1898 Melba intimated that she would like to join the company, and her manager, C. A. Ellis of Boston, became the company's business manager. The name of the organization was changed to the Damrosch–Ellis Company, and its ranks included Calvé and Lilli Lehmann. In 1900, owing to a mounting deficit, the company was disbanded.

Dance of the Apprentices. Dance in 3/4 time by the young Nuremberg apprentices and the maidens from Fürth in the final scene of Wagner's *Meistersinger*.

Dance of the Blessed Spirits. Dance in Act 2 of Gluck's *Orfeo ed Euridice*.

Dance of the Comedians. Dance in Act 3 of *The Bartered Bride* in which the clowns and dancers of the travelling circus are put through their paces.

Dance of the Hours. The entertainment put on by Alvise Badoero for his guests in Act 3 of *La Gioconda*, in which the eternal struggle between darkness and light is symbolized. Further popularized by Walt Disney in the film *Fantasia*.

Dance of the Seven Veils. Salome's dance before Herod in *Salome*.

Dance of the Sylphs. Part of Faust's dream in Berlioz's *La Damnation de Faust* as he sleeps on the banks of the Elbe.

Dance of the Tumblers. Dance of acrobats before the Tsar Berendey in Act 3 of Rimsky-Korsakov's *The Snow Maiden*.

Dances, Polovtsian. Dances in Act 2 of Borodin's *Prince Igor* with which the Khan Khonchak entertains Igor.

Danco, Suzanne (b. Brussels, 22 Jan. 1911). Belgian soprano. Studied in Prague with Fernando Carpi. Début Genoa 1941, Fiordiligi. Has sung extensively in Italy where she was the first Scala Ellen Orford (1947); Marie in *Wozzeck* at the Naples S.C. (1949). Edinburgh (with Glyndebourne O.) 1948, Fiordiligi; London, C.G., 1951, Mimì; Glyndebourne, Donna Elvira. (R)

Dandini. Prince Ramiro's valet (bar.) in Rossini's *La Cenerentola*.

Danon, Oskar (b. Sarajevo, 1913). Yugoslav conductor. Studied Prague. Musical Director, Belgrade Opera, 1944–59. Chicago, 1962; Edinburgh Festival, 1962. (R)

Dante Alighieri (b. Florence, May 1265; d. Ravenna, 14 Sept. 1321). Italian poet. Operas based on the Francesca da Rimini episode in his *Divina Commedia*, mostly with her name as their title, are by the following composers: Morlacchi (unfinished), Mercadante (1828), Generali (1829), Staffa (1831), Fournier-Gorre (1832), Borgatta (1837), Devasini (1841), Canetti (1843), Brancaccio (1844), Marcarini (1871), Götz (1877), Moscuzza (1877), Cagnoni (1878), Thomas (*Françoise de Rimini*, 1882), Napravnik (1902), Rachmaninov (1906), Mancinelli (1907), Emil Ábrányi (*Paolo e Francesca*, 1912), Zandonai (1914), and Henreid. Puccini's *Gianni Schicchi* is based on an episode in the *Divina Commedia*, which the hero mentions scathingly at the end. Operas on Dante himself are Philpot's *Dante and Beatrice* (1889), Godard's *Dante* (1890), Nouguès's *Dante*, and Foulds's concert opera *Vision of Dante*.

Dantons Tod (Danton's Death). Opera in 2 parts by Einem; text by the composer and Blacher after Büchner's drama (1835). Prod. Salzburg 6 Aug. 1947 with Cebotari, Patzak, Schoeffler; cond. Fricsay. Subsequently heard in Vienna, Hamburg, Berlin, and Brussels.

Daphne. In classical mythology the daughter of the Thessalian river-god Peneus: she narrowly escaped the pursuing Apollo by being changed into a laurel-tree. Some of the first operas were on her legend to Rinuccini's text —by Jacopo Corsi (undated and incomplete, two fragments extant), Peri (*Dafne*, 1597, q.v.), Caccini (lost, perhaps perf. 1600), Gagliano (*Dafne*, 1608), Schütz (*Dafne*, 1627, the first German opera, music lost). Other operas are by Alessandro Scarlatti (*Dafni*, 1700), Astorga (*Dafni*, 1709), Mulé (*Dafni*, 1928), and Strauss (*Daphne*, 1938).

Daphne. Opera in 1 act by Richard Strauss; text by Josef Gregor. Prod. Dresden 15 Oct. 1938 with Teschemacher, cond. Böhm (given in double bill with *Friedenstag*); Santa Fé, 31 Jul. 1964, with Sylvia Stahlman. Frequently performed in Germany.

Dapertutto. The evil sorcerer (bar.) in the Giulietta episode in Offenbach's *Contes d'Hoffmann*.

Da Ponte, Lorenzo. See *Ponte, Lorenzo da.*

Darclée, Hariclea (orig. Haricly Hartulary) (b. Bucharest, 1868 (?); d. Bucharest, 12 Jan. 1939). Rumanian soprano. Studied Bucharest, and Paris with Faure. Début Paris, O., 1888, Marguerite. Success dated from Feb. 1889, when she replaced Patti at the O. as Juliette. Milan, Sc., from 1890, where she created La Wally (1892). In Rome she created Iris and Tosca. Successful as Valentine, Elisabeth, Manon Lescaut, and in the *bel canto* operas of Bellini and Donizetti. Considered by the Italians to be vocally similar to Lilli Lehmann. Her vocal decline began in 1905, and though rich when she retired from the stage in 1918, she was forced to spend her declining years in the Verdi Home in Milan, and died penniless in Bucharest. (R)

Dargomizhsky, Alexander (b. Tula, 14 Feb. 1813; d. St. Petersburg, 17 Jan. 1869). Russian composer. His first opera was *Esmeralda*, based on Victor Hugo's *Notre-Dame de Paris* (comp. 1839, prod. 1847), a light work acknowledging the best French models. *Russalka* (1856) took further a few hints in *Esmeralda* of the composer's interest in melodic recitative. Its failure discouraged him for a time, until, impelled by the desire among Balakirev's disciples for a new Russian musical idiom, he completed his last opera *The Stone Guest* (posth. prod. 1872) in which the characters express themselves in 'mezzo-recitative'. This pays the closest attention, in short irregular phrases, to the inflection of Pushkin's words, with the orchestra in its turn subordinate to the voice. Though embodying a reform as radical as any of Wagner's, *The Stone Guest* remains only a historical curiosity through Dargomizhsky's failure to write music of sufficient quality to match his principles.

Darmstadt. Town in Hesse-Darmstadt, Germany. Opera is given in the Landestheater (cap. 550), opened in 1945.

Daudet, Alphonse (b. Nîmes, 13 May 1840; d. Paris, 16 Dec. 1897). French author. Operas on his works are as follows. *L'Arlésienne* (1872): Cilea (1897). *Sapho* (1884): Massenet (1897). *Tartarin sur les Alpes* (1885): Pessard (1888).

David. Opera in 5 acts by Milhaud; text by Lunel. Originally commissioned by the Koussevitsky Foundation. Prod. (concert version) Jerusalem 1 June 1954. First stage performance Milan, S.C., 2 Jan. 1955 with Colzani in title role, cond. Sanzogno; Hollywood Bowl 22 Sept. 1956.

David. Hans Sachs's apprentice (ten.) in Wagner's *Meistersinger*.

David, Félicien (b. Cadenet, 13 Apr. 1810; d. St-Germain-en-Laye, 29 Aug. 1876). French composer. His travels in the Near East not only inspired his own works, among which are the operas *La Perle du Brésil* (1851), *Herculanum* (1859), *Lalla Roukh* (1862), and *Le Saphir* (1865), but stimulated more distinguished contemporaries, such as Gounod, Bizet, and Delibes, in their Oriental operas. His delicate, tuneful music was greatly admired by Berlioz.

Davide, Giovanni (b. Naples, 15 Sept. 1790; d. St. Petersburg, 1864). Italian tenor. Son of Giacomo Davide, also a tenor. Studied with his father. Début Brescia 1810; Milan, Sc., 1814, where he created Narciso in Rossini's *Il Turco in Italia*. Subsequently Rossini wrote parts for him in *Otello*, *La Donna del Lago*, and other works. Appeared in London in 1818 and 1829. In the latter year his voice had begun to fade. He subsequently became manager of the opera house in St. Petersburg. He had a range of three octaves. Stendhal considered him the finest tenor of his generation.

Davies, Ben(jamin) (b. Pontardawe, nr. Swansea, 6 Jan. 1858; d. Bath, 28 Mar. 1943). Welsh tenor. Début Birmingham 1881, Thaddeus (*Bohemian Girl*). Sang with Carl Rosa and D'Oyly Carte's Royal English Opera, creating the title role in Sullivan's *Ivanhoe* (1891). Sang Faust at C.G. 1892, and the title role in Cowen's *Signa* there in 1894. (R)

Davies, Cecilia (b. London, *c.* 1750; d. there, 3 Jul. 1836). English sopr. Appeared at early age in Dublin, and in 1767 in London. Sang in Vienna, where with her sister Marianne taught Maria Theresa's daughters to sing and act. Appeared in Milan with great success in 1771, christened by the Italians 'L'Inglesina' and considered superior to any Italian singer except Gabrielli whom she 'even rivalled in neatness of execution' (Mount-Edgecumbe).

Davies, Tudor (b. Cymmer, S. Wales, 12 Nov. 1892; d. London, 2 Apr. 1958). Welsh tenor. Joined B.N.O.C. at its inception; C.G. début as Rodolfo on opening night of its first London season. Remained with the company several seasons, creating Hugh the Drover (1924) and leading roles in Holst's *At the Boar's Head* and Smyth's *Fête Galante*. Leading tenor Old Vic and S.W. 1931–41, and Carl Rosa 1941–6. Sang in first S.W. perf. of Benjamin's *The Devil Take Her*, *The Snow Maiden*, and *Don Carlos*. His voice, originally fresh and warm, was affected by singing roles (like Florestan and Manrico) that were too heavy for him. (R)

Davis, Colin (b. Weybridge, 25 Sept. 1927). English conductor. Studied clarinet R.C.M.; début R.F.H. as ballet cond., 1952, after engagements with Kalmar Orchestra and Chelsea Opera Group. After appointment with B.B.C. Scottish Orch., engaged at S.W 1959, music director 1961–5. C.G. début 1966; music director from 1971. Has appeared at Glyndebourne, N.Y. Met., and widely elsewhere. A gifted and lively musician, with a special feeling for Mozart, Berlioz, Britten, Stravinsky, and Tippett. (R)

De Angelis, Nazareno (b. Rome, 17 Nov. 1881; d. Rome, 14 Dec. 1962). Italian bass. Sang as boy in Sistine Chapel Choir. Début 1903, Acquila, Il Podestà (*Linda di Chamounix*). Sang in all leading Italian theatres until 1959, and with Chicago Opera 1910–11 and 1915–20. Considered one of the greatest Italian basses of his day and particularly renowned for his Mefistofele, Mosè, Oroveso, and his Wagner interpretations. (R)

De Begnis, Giuseppe (b. Lugo, Romagna, 1793; d. N.Y., Aug. 1849). Italian bass. Début Modena 1813 in Pavesi's *Ser Marcantonio*. Developed into leading buffo of his day, and as such engaged by Rossini in 1817 to create Magnifico in *La Cenerentola*. Sang London 1821–7—début as Geronio (*Il Turco in Italia*) with his wife Giuseppina as Fiorella. 1823–4 directed opera season at Bath, and 1834–7 in Dublin, where he had first sung in 1829.

De Begnis, Giuseppina Ronzi (b. Milan, 11 Jan. 1800; d. Florence, 7 June 1853). Italian soprano, wife of above. Studied with Garat. Début Genoa 1817. More successful in London and Naples than in Paris, though even there her Donna Anna was considered the finest ever heard, and the best until Sontag. Excelled, however, in light roles.

Debora e Jaele. Opera in 3 acts by Pizzetti; text by the composer, after Judges xvi. Prod. Milan, Sc., 16 Dec. 1922 with Tess, Cassazza, Pinza, cond. Toscanini. Often revived in Italy.

Debrecen. Town in north-eastern Hungary. The Csokonai Theatre (cap. 669) was built in 1865 by Skalnitzky. It has worked as a state theatre since 1949, acquiring in 1952 an opera company which also plays regularly in various provincial towns of the region.

Debussy, (Achille) Claude (b. St-Germain-en-Laye, 22 Aug. 1862; d. Paris, 25 Mar. 1918). French composer. Despite plans for operas on the subject of Tristram and Yseult and on *As You Like It*, as well as on works by Heine and by Poe (who deeply influenced him), Debussy's only opera is *Pelléas et Mélisande* (1902). This remains one of the most original operas in the history of music, where it occupies a pivotal place. Wagnerian in its use of the orchestra to carry most of the emotion (especially with the interludes later incorporated), it is also anti-Wagnerian in its reticence with a story of love, jealousy, and murder. Though based on Maeterlinck's deliberately vague Symbolist drama and making subtle use of the symbol of Mélisande's long golden hair and the theme of men's blindness, its clarity of declamation looks forward to a new directness in expression. *Pelléas* is a masterpiece inhabiting a unique and haunting world of its own creation, and its allusive twilight atmosphere continues to fascinate by reason of the inventiveness with which Debussy realizes the shadowy emotions in music. Maeterlinck violently opposed the opera and even threatened Debussy with assault when the role of Mélisande was taken away from his wife, Georgette Leblanc, and given to Mary Garden by Carré, director of the Opéra-Comique. He did not find it hard to arouse hostility; but *Pelléas* has long since been accepted as a masterpiece.

Decembrists, The. Opera in 4 acts by Shaporin; text by V. A. Rozhdestvensky, after the events of the December rising of 1825 in St. Petersburg. Prod. Moscow, Bolshoy, 23 June 1953.

Deems Taylor, Joseph. See *Taylor, Joseph Deems.*

De Falla, Manuel. See *Falla, Manuel de.*

Deh, vieni alla finistra. Don Giovanni's (bar.) serenade to Elvira's maid in Act 2 of Mozart's *Don Giovanni*, in which he sings to his own mandolin accompaniment (often played pizzicato on a violin).

Deh vieni, non tardar. Susanna's (sop.) aria in Act 4 of Mozart's *Figaro* in which she expresses her love for Figaro.

Deidamia. Opera in 3 acts by Handel; text by P. Rolli. Prod. London, Hm., 10 Jan. 1740. Handel's last opera; originally unsuccessful, being given for three nights only. Revived with success in London by the Handel Society in E. J. Dent's translation, 3 June 1955; in Hamburg, Munich, and elsewhere in Germany. First perf. in America, Univ. of Hartford, 25 Feb. 1959.

De Lara (orig. Cohen), **Isidore** (b. London, 9 Aug. 1858; d. Paris, 2 Sept. 1935). English composer. Trained Milan Conservatory where he studied composition under Mazzucato and singing under Lamperti, and in Paris under Lalo. Maurel suggested that he should change his cantata *The Light of Asia* into an opera, which was performed under its Italian title *La Luce dell'Asia* at C.G. 1892. His *Amy Robsart* was performed there the following year. Other operas that enjoyed a limited success were *Messaline* (1899) and *Naïl* (1912). His compositions owe a lot to Massenet and Saint-Saëns. He constantly campaigned for the establishment of a permanent British Opera.

Delibes, Léo (b. St-Germain-du-Val, 21 Feb. 1836; d. Paris, 16 Jan. 1891). French composer. A series of short operettas from 1857 was popular. His appointment to the Opéra as accompanist (1863) and second chorus-master (1865) turned his interest towards ballet, in which field he won fame with *Sylvia* and *Coppélia*. But opera drew him back, and he wrote three works for the Opéra-Comique—*Le Roi l'a dit* (1873), *Jean de Nivelle* (1880), and the famous *Lakmé* (1883). Succumbing to (or exploiting) the current vogue for 'the mysterious East', an *opéra comique* tradition refreshed by the Romantic poets' fascination, Delibes set his tale of the English lieutenant and the Indian girl Lakmé with a wealth of delightful mock-Oriental melody. It is chiefly for the charming colouring of the scoring that *Lakmé* and the ballets retain an appeal which led Tchaikovsky to rate Delibes above Brahms.

Delius, Frederick (b. Bradford, 29 Jan. 1862; d. Grez-sur-Loing, 10 June 1934). English composer. Delius's operas belong to the earlier part of his career. The most successful has been *A Village Romeo and Juliet* (1900–1, prod. 1907) (q.v.), whose high-spot is the beautiful interlude 'The Walk to the Paradise Garden'. *Irmelin* (1890–2) was first produced at Oxford in 1953 by Beecham, to whose enthusiasm is also due the English production, at C.G. in 1935, of *Koanga* (1895–7, prod. 1904). Delius's other operas are almost entirely known, if at all, through excerpts. They are *The Magic Fountain* (1893, unprod.), *Margot-la-Rouge* (1902, unprod.), from which the Idyll was salvaged, and *Fennimore and Gerda* (1908–10, prod. 1919).

Della Casa, Lisa (b. Burgdorf, nr. Berne, 2 Feb. 1919). Swiss soprano. Began vocal training when 15 in Zürich with Margarete Haeser, who has been her only teacher. Début Solothurn-Biel 1941, Butterfly; Zürich, Stadttheater, 1943–50; Salzburg 1947, Zdenka; Glyndebourne 1951, Countess (*Figaro*), and later that year Munich as Sophie and in her most famous role, Arabella, which she sang in London in 1953 and 1965; Vienna, S.O., 1952; N.Y., Met., since 1953. Outstanding in the Strauss repertory, having graduated from Sophie through Octavian to the Marschallin. She is able to spin out Strauss's soaring vocal line with controlled legato, and is also an admirable Mozart singer. (R)

Delle Sedie, Enrico (b. Leghorn, 17 June 1822; d. Paris, 28 Nov. 1907). Italian baritone. Début Pistoia 1851, Nabucco. Sang all over Europe with great success. First London Renato. Despite his great style, musicianship, and dramatic talents, his vocal limitations earned him the nickname of 'Il baritono senza voce'. Invited by Auber to accept a professorship at the Paris Conservatory. Publ. *L'Art Lyrique* (1874).

Delmas, Jean-François (b. Lyons, 14 Apr. 1861; d. Saint-Alban de Monthel, 29 Sept. 1933). French bass. Studied Paris Conservatoire with Bussine and Obin. Début Paris, O., 1886, St. Bris; between then and 1911 he sang and created more than 50 roles there including parts in *Salammbô* (Reyer), *Ariane et Barbe-Bleue*, *Thaïs*, and *Monna Vanna*. The first French Gurnemanz, and a distinguished Hans Sachs and Wotan. (R)

Del Monaco, Mario (b. Florence, 27 July 1915). Italian tenor. Sang (non-professionally) Teatro Beniamino Gigli, Mondaldo, at age of 13, in Massenet's *Narcisse*. When 20 invited by Serafin to compete for a place in the studio attached to the Teatro dell'Opera, Rome, and gained the place from 80 competitors. After six months decided to rely on personal study and gramophone records of the great singers of the past. Début Pesaro 1939, Turiddu. London. C. G., with San Carlo, 1946, returned 1962. San Francisco 1950; N.Y., Met., 1951–9, where he was exceedingly popular, Possesses a thrilling natural voice of enormous power and great dramatic intensity. (R)

Delna (orig. Ledan), **Maria** (b. Meudon, nr. Paris, 3 Apr. 1875; d. Paris, 23 July 1932). French contralto. Début Paris, O.C., 1892, Dido. After six years at the O.C. went to the Opéra where she was leading contralto, 1898–1901. Retired temporarily after her marriage in 1903, reappeared 1908, and continued to sing until her retirement. She was the first Paris Charlotte and Mistress Quickly. London, C.G., 1894; N.Y., Met., 1909–10. (R)

De los Angeles, Victoria. See *Los Angeles, Victoria de.*

De Luca, Giuseppe (b. Rome, 25 Dec. 1876; d. New York, 26 Aug. 1950). Italian baritone. Début Piacenza 1897, Valentine. Engaged Scala for 1903–4 and during his initial season created Sharpless, and Gleby in Giordano's *Siberia.* London, C.G., 1907, 1910, and a solitary appearance as Figaro (Rossini), 1935; N.Y., Met., 1915–35 and 1939–40. During his period in N.Y. made more than 800 appearances in 100 different operas, creating Paquiro in *Goyescas* (1917) and Gianni Schicchi (1918). In Nov. 1947 celebrated his golden jubilee as a singer in a special concert in N.Y.; spent the rest of his life as teacher at Juilliard School. His classic phrasing, effortless style, and immaculately produced voice marked him out as one of the finest exponents of *bel canto* of this century. When 70 could still sing Rigoletto and Sharpless. (R)

De Lucia, Fernando (b. Naples, 11 Oct. 1860 or 1 Sept. 1861; d. Naples, 21 Feb. 1925). Italian tenor. Début Naples 1885, Faust; London, D.L., 1887, C.G. 1892–6, 1900, where he was the first London Fritz, Canio, and Cavaradossi, and the first C.G. Turiddu. N.Y., Met., 1893–4. In Italy he created Fritz and *I Rantzau* (Mascagni). A highly accomplished singer and master of *bel canto*, renowned for his singing of Rossini, Bellini, and Verdi. (R)

De Lussan, Zélie (b. New York, 21 Dec. 1861; d. London, 18 Dec. 1949). American soprano. Trained by her mother; début in concert when 16. Stage début Boston 1886, Arline. Engaged by Augustus Harris for his first C.G. season, 1888, and sang Carmen. During her career appeared in this role over 1,000 times with nearly 60 Don Josés. Carl Rosa 1890–1910; N.Y., Met., 1894–5 and 1898–1900. A famous Zerlina, Mignon, Cherubino, and Nedda. (R)

Demeur (orig. Charton), **Anne** (b. Sanjon, nr. Saintes, 5 Mar. 1824; d. Paris, 30 Nov. 1892). French soprano. Début Bordeaux 1842, Lucia. London, D.L., 1846; St. James's T. 1849–50; H.M.'s 1852. The first London Eudoxie (*La Juive*), Angèle (*Le Domino Noir*), Countess (*Comte Ory*), Catherine (*Les Diamants de la Couronne*); sang also in first London performances of many other French works. Created Béatrice in Berlioz's *Béatrice et Bénédict* (1862) and Dido in *Les Troyens à Carthage* (1863). Sang at the Paris O. in the Berlioz festival 1870 with Christine Nilsson. In 1879 sang Cassandre in the first performance (in concert) of *La Prise de Troie.*

De' miei bollenti spiriti. Alfredo's (ten.) aria which opens Act 2 of *La Traviata* and in which he sings of his happiness with Violetta.

Demon, The. Opera in 3 acts by Anton Rubinstein; text by P. A. Viskovatov, after Lermontov's poem (1841). Prod. St. Petersburg 25 Jan. 1875; London, C.G., 21 June 1881, the first Russian opera in England, with Albani, Lassalle, and E. de Reszke; and when given in 1888, the first opera to be sung in Russian in London. San Francisco 17 Jan. 1922. Still performed in Russia where it was once very popular, probably more for its romantic ingredients than its musical interest.

Denhof Opera Company. Formed in 1910 by Ernst Denhof, a German-born musician living in Edinburgh, to give performances of *The Ring* in English in the provinces. The first series, under Balling, was followed in 1911 by appearances in Leeds, Manchester, and Glasgow, and in 1912 in Hull, Leeds, Liverpool, Manchester, and Glasgow. By this time the repertory had been enlarged to include *Elektra* (first performance in English), *Orfeo, Fliegende Holländer*, and *Meistersinger*. In 1913, *Pelléas, Rosenkavalier*, and *Zauberflöte* were added, but by then the company was making a heavy loss. After two weeks in Birmingham and one in Manchester the company had lost £4,000. Beecham, who was one of the conductors, took it over; and its personnel, which included Agnes Nicholls, Walter Hyde, Frederic Ranalow, Frederic Austin, and Robert Radford, soon became associated with Beecham's own opera company.

Denmark. See *Copenhagen.*

Dent, Edward J. (b. Ribston, 16 July 1876; d. London, 22 Aug. 1957). English scholar and teacher. His influence upon English operatic life, and its relationship to the European scene, is incalculable. His translations of Mozart's operas set a new standard: if idiosyncratic, their wit, fluency, and singability were unsurpassed in their day, and they quickly became standard. His productions of Mozart's operas to these texts at Cambridge from 1911 set in motion the reappraisal of Mozart's genius in England; he also arranged and produced several early English operas, especially those of Purcell, and apart from his reworking of *The Beggar's Opera* (q.v.) did some original composition. His study of *Mozart's Operas* (1913) is a masterpiece of knowledge and shrewd scholarship; other important books were *Alessandro Scarlatti* (1905), *The Foundations of English Opera* (1928), and *Ferruccio Busoni* (1935). He also contributed widely to journals of every description; while his immense store of learning was ever at the disposal of younger and less wise men.

Denzler, Robert (b. Zürich, 19 Mar. 1892). Swiss conductor. Pupil of Andreae at Zürich, further training at Bayreuth and Cologne. Music director, Zürich Opera, 1915–27 and 1934–47. During the latter period he directed world premières of *Lulu* (1937) and *Mathis der Maler* (1938). (R)

De Paolis, Alessio (b. Rome, 5 Apr. 1893; d. N.Y., 9 Mar. 1964). Italian tenor. Studied Rome, Santa Cecilia, with Di Pietro. Début Bologna 1919, Duke of Mantu. Sang Fenton on the opening night of Toscanini's new régime at La Scala 1921. After several seasons there and with other Italian theatres as leading lyric tenor, turned to character roles, and developed into one of the outstanding comprimario singers of the day. As such has sung at the Metropolitan since 1938. (R)

Depuis le jour. Louise's (sop.) aria in Act 3 of Charpentier's *Louise*, recalling the day when first she yielded to Julien.

De Reszke, Édouard (b. Warsaw, 22 Dec. 1853; d. Garnek, 25 May 1917). Polish bass, brother of Jean (see below). Studied Warsaw with Ciaffei and Italy with Steller and Coletti. Engaged by Escudier for Paris, and accepted by Verdi as the King in Paris première of *Aida* (1876), in which role he made his début under the composer's baton. London, C.G., 1880; Chicago 1891. With his brother Jean was a key member of the Paris, Met., and C.G. companies during the last decade of the century. Sang Méphistophélès in the 500th *Faust* at the Opéra (1887) with Jean in the title role; was a distinguished Saint-Bris, Frère Laurent, and Leporello. Later in his career he assumed with equal success Wagner roles, first in Italian, then in German, including Sachs, King Mark, and Hagen. Left the stage in 1903, and after an unsuccessful attempt to teach in London retired to his estate in Poland, where after the outbreak of war in 1914 he lived in extreme poverty and seclusion, first in the cellar of his house and then in a cave. His voice was of great volume and richness, and he was able to sing rapid passages with consummate ease. His great height and imposing stage presence, coupled with a powerful dramatic personality, made him one of the greatest basses in the history of opera. (R)

De Reszke, Jean (b. Warsaw, 14 Jan. 1850; d. Nice, 3 Apr. 1925). Polish tenor, brother of Édouard (above). Studied with Ciaffei and then Cotogni in Milan. Début as baritone (as Giovanni de Reschi) Turin 1874, Alfonso. London, D.L., same year in same role and as Don Giovanni and Valentine. Two years later sang in Paris, still as a baritone. His brother, convinced he was a tenor, suggested he study with Sbriglia, and after a period with that teacher he sang the title role in *Robert le Diable*, with little success. For the next five years only sang in concerts; but in 1884 was persuaded by Maurel and Massenet to sing John the Baptist in *Hérodiade* at its Paris première, which he did with great success. This led to Massenet completing his *Le Cid* with De Reszke in mind; sang in the world première the following year. In 1887 sang Radamès on the opening night in Augustus Harris's first Grand Opera season at D.L.; C.G. début 1888, Vasco da Gama. Returned to London nearly every year until 1900, as Roméo, Raoul, Faust, and later Lohengrin, Walther, Tristan, and Siegfried. N.Y., Met., 1891–1901, after which he sang only once more, Canio (his only appearance in the role), in Paris. A revival of *Orfeo* with him in the tenor role was suggested, and he even rehearsed for a revival of Reyer's *Sigurd*. Spent the rest of his life teaching, first in Paris and then in Nice. His many pupils included Edvina, Saltzman-Stevens, Sayão, Teyte, and Steuart Wilson. His voice was one of exceptional beauty, which he coloured with great skill. His musicianship and phrasing were considered impeccable, and his personal charm and dramatic ability made him one of the greatest tenors of all time. His sister **Joséphine de Reszke** (b. Warsaw, 4 June 1855; d. Warsaw, 22 Feb. 1891), soprano, sang at the Paris Opéra with great success, but retired at the height of her career to marry Baron Leopold de Kronenburg. Perhaps the best biographical study of the De Reszkes is C. Leiser's *Jean de Reszke and the Great Days of Opera* (N.Y., 1934).

D'Erlanger, (Baron) Frédéric (b. Paris, 29 May 1868; d. London, 23 Apr. 1943). English (naturalized) composer. Born of German and American parents, was brought up in Paris where he studied under Anselm Ehmant. His *Inès Mendo* was given at C.G. in 1897, when the composer's name appeared as Ferd. Regnal, and his *Tess* (based on Hardy's novel) in 1909, with Destinn, Zenatello, and Sammarco in the cast. A banker by profession, he gave much monetary support to C.G. and for many years was one of its directors.

Dermota, Anton (b. Kropa, 4 June 1910). Yugoslav tenor. Début Vienna 1936, Alfredo; has sung there and at Salzburg ever since. Sang with Vienna Company at C.G. in 1947 (Ottavio, Ferrando, and Narraboth). It is as a Mozart tenor that he is most renowned. (R)

Der Vogelfänger bin ich. Papageno's (bar.) aria introducing himself as the birdcatcher in Act 1, scene 1, of Mozart's *Der Zauberflöte*.

De Sabata, Victor (b. Trieste, 10 Apr. 1892; d. S. Margherita, 10 Dec. 1967). Ital. cond. and composer. After conducting in the concert hall he turned to opera, first at Monte Carlo, where he conducted the world première of *L'Enfant et les Sortilèges* (1925) and the first local performances of *Sadko*, *Rosenkavalier*, *Il Trittico*, and *Turandot*; then from 1929 to 1953 was at La Scala, first as conductor and then as musical and artistic director. Conducted *Tristan* at Bayreuth 1939, and appeared with the Scala Company at C.G. 1950, conducting an unforgettable *Otello* and *Falstaff*. His incandescent and exciting readings of Verdi and Wagner reminded many listeners of Toscanini's. His opera *Il Macigno* was produced at La Scala in 1917. (R)

Desdemona. Otello's wife (sop.) in Verdi's and Rossini's *Otello*.

Des Grieux. The hero (ten.) of Massenet's *Manon* and Puccini's *Manon Lescaut*.

Desormière, Roger (b. Vichy, 13 Sept. 1898; d. Paris, 25 Oct. 1963). French conductor. Studied Paris Conservatoire. Conducted with Diaghilev Ballet 1925–30; joined Opéra-Comique 1937. In 1938 conducted first performance there of Chabrier's *Une Éducation Manquée*, *L'Étoile*, and *Ariadne auf Naxos*, and important revivals of *L'Heure Espagnole*, *Le Médecin malgré Lui*, and *Pelléas*, which he conducted at C.G. in 1949. Music Director, O.C., 1944–6. Forced by ill health to retire 1950. (R)

Despina. Fiordiligi's and Dorabella's maid (sop.) in Mozart's *Così fan tutte*.

Dessau. Town in Anhalt, Germany. Noted for its strong Wagner traditions. *Die Meistersinger* was performed there soon after its Munich première in 1869, and Bayreuth artists have frequently appeared there, under Knappertbusch, Schmitz, Rother, &c. The opera house (cap. 1,245), opened in 1885, was rebuilt in 1938 and again in 1949.

Destinn, Emmy (orig. Ema Kittl) (b. Prague, 26 Feb. 1878; d. Budějovice, 28 Jan. 1930). Czech soprano. Studied Prague with Marie Loewe-Destinn, whose surname she adopted for professional purposes. Début Berlin 1898, Santuzza; London, C.G., 1904–14, 1919; N.Y., Met., 1908–16 and 1919–21. Chosen to sing Senta in first Bayreuth *Fliegende Holländer* (1901). The first Berlin Salome (1906); at C.G., the first Butterfly (1905), Tatiana (1906), Tess (1908), and Minnie (1911), which she had created at the world première in N.Y. (1910). Under the name of Ema Destinnová returned to London 1919 as Aida. Retired from stage in 1921. Her voice, of a highly individual timbre, was even in range and impeccably produced, added to which she was a remarkably fine actress, especially in tragic roles. (R)

Detroit. Town in Mich., U.S.A. Opera in Detroit dates back to the middle of the last century when seasons were given by the Pyne-Harrison and De Vries Companies, and by an Italian ensemble under Arditi. Then came visits from the Damrosch and Met. Companies. In 1928 the Detroit Civic Opera Company was formed by Thaddeus Wroński; in 1934 it became associated with the Detroit Symphony Orchestra and between then and the war gave performances of several works including *Tristan*, *La Rondine*, *Peter Ibbetson*, and *Il Dibuk* (Rocca).

Deutsche Oper am Rhein. See *Düsseldorf–Duisburg*.

Deutsches Opernhaus. See *Berlin*.

Deux Aveugles de Tolède, Les (The Two Blind Men of Toledo). Opera in 1 act by Méhul; text by Benoît Marsollier. Prod. Paris, O.C., 28 Jan. 1806.

Deux Journées, Les (The Two Days). Opera in 3 acts by Cherubini; text by Jean Nicolas Bouilly. Prod. Paris, T. Feydeau, 16 Jan. 1800; London, C.G., 14 Oct. 1801; New Orleans 12 Mar. 1811. Cherubini's most important work, also known as *The Water Carrier*. Armand falls into disfavour with Mazarin and arranges with the water-carrier Michele to escape from Paris in a barrel. He and his wife are caught, but Michele brings news of their pardon.

Devil and Daniel Webster, The. Opera in 1 act by Douglas Moore; text by composer, after Stephen Vincent Benét's story (1937). Prod. N.Y., Martin Beck Theatre, 18 May 1939. Jabez Stone is rescued from a pact selling his soul to the devil by Daniel Webster's brilliant defence before a jury of famous villains of history.

Devil and Kate, The (Čert a Káča). Opera in 3 acts by Dvořák; text by Adolf Wenig. Prod. Prague, Nat. T., 23 Nov. 1899; Oxford 22 Nov. 1932. Kate, a stout elderly maid, fails to secure a dancing partner at a country fair, so says she would dance with the devil himself, Marbuel, who now carries her off. Her garrulity oppresses even Hell, which gladly relinquishes her to a rescuer. Marbuel returns to earth to capture the domineering lady of the manor, but vanishes at the sight of Kate.

Devin du Village, Le (The Village Soothsayer). *Intermède* in 1 act by Jean-Jacques Rousseau; text by composer. Prod. Fontainebleau 18 Oct. 1752; public prod. Paris, O., 1 Mar. 1753; London, D.L., 21 Nov. 1766; N.Y., 21 Oct. 1790. One of the most successful and influential works of its age. Of its innumerable parodies, imitations, and adaptations, the most familiar is Mozart's *Bastien und Bastienne* (q.v.).

Diaghilev, Sergey Pavlovich (b. Novgorod, 19 Mar. 1872; d. Venice, 19 Aug. 1929). Russian impresario. Although renowned as founder of the Russian Ballet Company that bore his name, was also an important figure in opera, in Paris (1907–9), Paris and London (1913–14), and Paris and Monte Carlo (1922–4). In 1907 presented scenes from *Sadko*, *Tsar Saltan*, *Boris*, and *Russlan and Ludmilla* in concert form at the Paris Opéra, and in 1908 the first full stage performance outside Russia of *Boris*, with Chaliapin. In 1909 he gave *Ivan the Terrible* in Paris; in 1913, at the Théâtre des Champs-Élysées, the first performance outside Russia of *Khovanshchina*; and in June and July that year, the first Russian season at Drury Lane. In 1914, in association with Beecham, he gave seven Russian operas (*Boris*, *Ivan*, *Prince Igor*, *Golden Cockerel*, *Rossignol*, *May Night*, and *Khovanshchina*). In Paris was responsible for the first performance of Stravinsky's *Mavra* (1923) and *Oedipus Rex* (1927), and in Monte Carlo in 1923 prod. Gounod's *Le Médecin malgré Lui* (with recitatives by Satie), *La Colombe* (with recitatives by Poulenc), *Philémon et Baucis*, and Chabrier's *Une Éducation Manquée* (recitatives by Milhaud).

Dialect in opera. A number of attempts have been made since the 18th century to write operas in a local dialect; many more operas make occasional use of dialect words, phrases, even long passages. The most famous of these is Strauss's *Der Rosenkavalier*, in which use of the Viennese dialect spoken at court gave considerable offence. Some operas entirely in dialect are as follows. Bavarian: Orff's *Die Bernauerin* (Stuttgart 1947). Languedoc: Mondonville's *'pastouralo' Toulouzeno, Daphnis et Alcimadure* (Fontainebleau 1754); also given in concert performance at Montpellier, in the town's *patois*, 1758. Piedmontese: a version of Donizetti's *Lucia di Lammermoor* (Turin 1859). Plattdeutsch: Schoeck's *Vom Fischer un syner Fru* (Dresden 1930). Provençal: a version of Duni's *Les Deux Chasseurs et la Laitière* as *La Laytayro dé Naubernad* (publ. Toulouse 1783). Walloons: some operas by the Liège composer Jean-Noël Hamal, an *opera burless' es treuz act*, *Voègge di Chôfontaine* (Liège 1757), and *Li Ligeoi Egagy*, *Li Fiesse di Houte-si-Plou*, and *Les Ypoconte*; Ysaye's only opera *Piér li Houîeu* (Liège 1931).

Dialogues de Carmélites, Les (The Carmelites). Opera in 3 acts by Poulenc; text by Georges Bernanos adapted from Gertrude von le Fort's novel *Die letzte am Schafott* (1931) and a film scenario by the Rev. Fr. Bruckenberger and Philippe Agostini. Prod. Milan, Sc., 26 Jan. 1957; San Francisco 20 Sept. 1957; London, C.G., 18 Jan. 1958. The opera tells of the martyrdom of Carmelite nuns during the French revolution.

Diamants de la Couronne, Les (The Crown Diamonds). Opera in 3 acts by Auber; text by Eugène Scribe and Jules Vernoy de Saint-Georges. Prod. Paris, O.C., 6 Mar. 1841; New York 12 July 1843; London, Princess's, 2 May 1844. One of Auber's most successful works.

Dibdin, Charles (b. Southampton, Mar. 1745; d. London, 25 July 1814). English composer, singing actor, and musical factotum. After some successes in pieces of his own authorship and composition at Covent Garden, became famous for his long series of musical pieces and his popular sea-songs. His illegitimate son, **Charles,** followed in these footsteps, no less vigorously if without equal success.

Dich, teure Halle (known as 'Elisabeth's Greeting'). Aria opening Act 2 of *Tannhäuser*, in which Elisabeth (sop.) greets the Hall of Song in the Wartburg where the contest of song is to take place.

Dick Johnson. The cowboy hero (ten.) of Puccini's *La Fanciulla del West*.

Dickens, Charles (b. Landport, 7 Feb. 1812; d. Gadshill, 9 Jan. 1870). English writer. His solitary excursion as a librettist, made just before the first instalment of *The Pickwick Papers*, was for Hullah's *The Village Coquettes* (1836). Operas based on his novels are as follows. *The Pickwick Papers* (monthly, 1836–7): Charles Wood (1922); Albert Coates (1936). *Barnaby Rudge* (1841): Julian Edwards's *Dolly Varden* (early 20th century). *The*

Cricket on the Hearth (1846): Goldmark (1896); Zandonai (1905); Mackenzie (1914). *A Tale of Two Cities* (1889): Benjamin (1949–50, prod. 1957).

Dickie, Murray (b. Bishopton, 2 Apr. 1924). Scottish tenor. Studied Vienna with Pollmann, London with Dino Borgioli, and Milan with Guido Farinelli. Début London, Cambridge T., with New London Opera Company, 1947, Almaviva. C.G. 1948–52 when he created the Curé in *The Olympians* (1949); Glyndebourne from 1950; Vienna since 1952, where he has enjoyed considerable success as David, Pedrillo, Jacquino, and in other light tenor roles. (R) His elder brother, **William Dickie**, who studied with Pollmann, Ruffo, De Luca, and Bechi, sang in Glasgow before the war, and in Italy and London from 1946. (R)

Dido and Aeneas. Opera in a prologue and 3 acts by Purcell; text by Nahum Tate, after Book 4 of Virgil's *Aeneid* (unfin., 19 B.C.). Prod. Josias Priest's School for Young Gentlewomen, Dec. (?) 1689 or poss. summer 1690, outdoors; public prod. London, *c.* Feb. 1700 and 9 Feb. 1704, then not revived on stage until 20 Nov. 1895, by R.C.M. at Ly. for bicentenary of Purcell's death; N.Y., Hotel Plaza, 10 Feb. 1923.

Various versions of the opera survive, the one most generally accepted by scholars being the manuscript now in the Library of St. Michael's College, Tenbury. The libretto includes the text of an elaborate mythological Prologue, not in the Tenbury score; this was included in the original production, when an Epilogue by D'Urfey was spoken. It is not known whether Purcell set the Prologue: we know the opera only as an adaptation, 'A Mask in Four Musical Entertainments', made at the beginning of the 18th century. The libretto has a different arrangement of the acts, and most editions of the music follow this, as follows.

Act 1. Dido (sop.) cannot bring herself to declare her love for Aeneas (ten.). Belinda (sop.) and the court succeed in making her yield, and a chorus celebrates the triumph of love and beauty.

Act 2. Scene 1. The Witches assemble in their cave to plot the downfall of Dido and of Carthage. They agree to conjure up a storm so as to force the royal lovers, out hunting, to take shelter in the cave, where one of them, disguised as Mercury, will remind Aeneas of his duty to go on to Italy. In Scene 2, this happens. Dido and Aeneas are entertained with a masque of Diana and Actaeon: the storm drives Aeneas alone to the cave, where he is deceived by the false Mercury.

Act 3. At the harbour, Aeneas plans to leave, while the Witches exult in their success: they plan to sink his fleet and fire Carthage. When Dido appears she silences Aeneas's explanations, and in the famous lament 'When I am laid in earth' she takes her leave of life; Cupids mourn above her tomb.

Dido's betrayal has been treated operatically almost 60 times—more often than any other subject.

Didur, Adam (b. Sanok, 24 Dec. 1874; d. Katowice, 7 Jan. 1946). Polish bass. Début Rio 1894; London, C.G., 1905, Colline; N.Y., Met., 1908, Méphistophélès. Leading bass Met. 1908–32; first American Boris (1913). Appointed director Lwów Opera, Poland, 1939. Taught at Katowice; his pupils include Marian Nowakowski and Eugenia Zareska. (R)

Dies Bildnis ist bezaubernd schön. Tamino's (ten.) aria in Act 1 of *The Magic Flute* declaring his love for Pamina at first sight of her portrait.

Di Luna, Count. The villainous nobleman (bar.) in love with Leonora in Verdi's *Il Trovatore.*

Dimitri. The Pretender (ten.) in Mussorgsky's *Boris Godunov.*

Di Murska, Ilma (b. Zagreb, 1836; d. Munich, 14 Jan. 1889). Croatian soprano. Studied Vienna, and Paris with Mathilde Marchesi. Début Florence 1862; London, H.M.'s, 1865, Lucia; N.Y. 1873, Amina. First London Senta 1870, which she sang in Italian. Her voice had a compass of nearly three octaves, and she excelled in such roles as Constanze and the Queen of the Night, as well as in more dramatic parts.

D'Indy, Vincent (b. Paris, 27 Mar. 1851; d. Paris, 2 Dec. 1931). French composer. Apart from a number of projects and the unimportant 1-act *opéra-comique*, *Attendez-moi sous l'Orme* (1882), D'Indy's first opera was *Le Chant de la Cloche* (Brussels 1912, but first heard in concert form, Paris 1886), a so-called *légende dramatique* based on Schiller and heavily indebted to *Parsifal*, of 1882, which won recognition for the young composer's technical ability. He further expressed his love of Wagner, his ancestral feeling for the Cévennes, and his discipleship of Franck in his next and most important stage work, the *action musicale*, *Fervaal* (1897). *L'Étranger* (1903) continues in the same line while discovering a greater refinement of texture. Nevertheless, this work came to stand for values opposite to those recently expressed by Debussy's *Pelléas et Mélisande* (1902). *La Légende de St. Christophe*, a *drame sacré* (1920), continues to oppose the new values in an extraordinary, ambitious *mélange* of Wagner and medieval mysteries. His last stage work, *Le Rêve de Cinyras* (1927), is an unambitious operetta.

Dinner Engagement, A. Comic opera in 1 act by Lennox Berkeley; text by Paul Dehn. Prod. Aldeburgh 17 June 1954. The modern buffo plot concerns the attempts of a *nouveau-pauvre* couple to marry their daughter to a Prince—with ultimate success, though not through their schemes.

Dinorah, ou Le Pardon de Ploërmel. Opera in 3 acts by Meyerbeer; text by Barbier and Carré. Prod. Paris, O.C., 4 Apr. 1859, with Cabel and Faure; London, C.G., 26 July 1859 with Miolan-Carvalho; New Orleans, 4 Mar. 1861. A slight pastoral opera about the peasant girl Dinorah, a goatherd Hoël, and a hidden treasure. Now rarely performed; it includes the famous 'Shadow Song', a great coloratura soprano show-piece.

Dio, mi potevi scagliar. Otello's (ten.) monologue in Act 3 of Verdi's *Otello*, the equivalent of 'Had it pleased heaven to try me with affliction' in Act 4, scene 2, of Shakespeare's play.

Dippel, Andreas (b. Kassel, 30 Nov. 1866; d. Hollywood, 12 May 1932). German tenor and impresario. Début Bremen 1887; N.Y., Met., 1890; London, C.G., 1897. Joint manager of Met. with Gatti-Casazza 1908–10, and of Chicago Opera 1910–13. Had an enormous repertory of some 150 roles, and was always ready to step in for an indisposed colleague. In London and New York substituted for Jean de Reszke in Wagner roles on several occasions. (R)

Di Provenza. Germont's (bar.) aria in Act 2 of *La Traviata* in which he tries to persuade his son Alfredo to return to his home in Provence.

Di quella pira. Manrico's (ten.) aria in Act 3 of *Il Trovatore*, a rousing call to his followers to join him in saving his mother Azucena from being burnt alive. The famous high C which most tenors interpolate in the line 'O teco almeno, corro a morir' is not in Verdi's score.

Di Stefano, Giuseppe (b. Molta, 24 July 1921). Italian tenor. Studied Milan, with Montesanto; début 1946, Reggio Emilia, Des Grieux (Massenet). N.Y., Met., 1948, Duke of Mantua; London, C.G., 1961, Cavaradossi. In the early stages of his career he confined himself to lighter roles including Wilhelm Meister, Elvino, Fritz, and Nadir. His singing was notable for its unfailingly beautiful tone and the use of an exquisite pianissimo, the voice possessing a rich velvety sound. Since 1953–4 he has assumed heavier roles, adding Don José, Canio, Turiddu, Radamès, Alvaro, and Osaka in Mascagni's *Iris* to his repertory. (R)

Di tanti palpiti. Tancredi's (con.) love song in Act 1 of Rossini's *Tancredi*. It was possibly the most popular aria of its day, and was sung and whistled in the streets all over Europe. In Venice it was known as the *aria dei risi* (the Rice Aria) as Rossini is said to have composed it in four minutes one evening while waiting for the rice to cook.

Dite alla giovine. Part of the duet between Violetta (sop.) and Germont *père* (bar.) in Act 2 of Verdi's *La Traviata* in which she begs him to make her sacrifice known to his daughter.

Dittersdorf, Karl Ditters von (orig. Karl Ditters) (b. Vienna, 2 Nov. 1739; d. Neuhof, 24 Oct. 1799). Austrian composer. His 34 operas include a setting of Beaumarchais's *Marriage of Figaro*, probably preceding Mozart's, though the best known today is perhaps *Doktor und Apotheker* (1786), which has been successfully revived. His bright, blameless invention has not generally proved of enduring value.

Divinités du Styx. Alceste's (sop.) aria in Act 1 of Gluck's *Alceste* offering to die in place of her husband.

Djamileh. Opera in 1 act by Bizet; text by Louis Gallet after Alfred de Musset's poem *Namouna* (1832). Prod. Paris, O.C., 22 May 1872; Manchester 22 Sept. 1892; Boston Opera House, 24 Feb. 1913.

Haroun pensions off his old mistress once a month and is bought a new one in the market by his servant Splendiano. Djamileh, the current mistress, falls in love with Haroun, and bargains with Splendiano to be readmitted disguised: this ruse wins Haroun's heart.

Dobbs, Mattiwilda (b. Atlanta, 11 July 1925). American soprano. Studied with Naomi Maise and Willis James, and then Lotte Leonard in New York. Début Holland Festival 1952 in title role of Stravinsky's *Le Rossignol*. Appearances followed in Italy. Glyndebourne (1953), Zerbinetta; London, C.G. (1954), Queen of Shemakhan and Gilda, and later Olympia and Queen of Night. N.Y., Met., since 1957. One of the best present-day coloratura sopranos. (R)

Dobrowen, Issay (b. Nizhny-Novgorod, 27 Feb. 1894; d. Oslo, 9 Dec. 1953). Russian conductor. Studied Moscow with Taneyev and Vienna with Godowsky. Début Moscow, Bolshoy, 1919. In 1923 with Fritz Busch principal conductor at Dresden, and responsible there for the first German performance of *Boris*. Vienna, V.O., 1924–7; Royal Opera, Sofia, 1927–8; between then and 1936 rarely conducted opera, but from 1936 to 1939 was a frequent visitor at the Budapest Opera. In 1941 began association with Royal Opera, Stockholm, as conductor and producer. Was responsible for several operas in the Russian repertory at La Scala between 1948 and his death. Conducted *Boris Godunov* at C.G., 1952. (R)

Docteur Miracle, Le. (1) Operetta in 1 act by Bizet; text by Battu and Halévy. Prod. Paris, B.-P., 9 Apr. 1857; London, Park Lane Group, 8 Dec. 1957. (2) Operetta in 1 act by Lecocq, prod. Paris, B.-P., 8 Apr. 1857. Both works were entries in a competition opened by Offenbach in 1856, being awarded the 1st prize among 78 entrants, by a jury headed by Auber, Halery, Thomas, and Gounod.

Doctor Miracle. The evil doctor (bass) in the Antonia episode of Offenbach's *Les Contes d'Hoffmann*.

Dodon. The King (bass) in Rimsky-Korsakov's *The Golden Cockerel*.

Doktor Faust. Opera in 2 prologues, an interlude, and 3 scenes by Busoni (completed by Jarnach); text by composer after the Faust legend and Marlowe's treatment of it in *Dr. Faustus* (1589). Prod. Dresden 21 May 1925, cond. Busch; broadcast concert performance London, Q.H., 17 Mar. 1937; concert perf., N.Y., 1 Dec. 1964. Successfully revived Berlin 1955, with Fischer-Dieskau.

Domgraf-Fassbänder, Willi (b. Aachen, 19 Feb. 1897). German baritone. Studied Aachen, where his family had sent him to study church music; was heard by Erich Orthmann, conductor of the Aachen Opera, singing a solo part in a concert of church music and was immediately engaged for the local opera house, where he made his début in 1922. After engagement in Berlin, Düsseldorf, and Stuttgart, became first lyric baritone at Berlin Staatsoper, where he remained until the end of the war. English début Glyndebourne on opening night of the first season in 1934 as Figaro; reappeared there in 1935 and 1937 as Figaro, Guglielmo, and Papageno. After the war sang in Hanover, Vienna, Munich, and Nuremberg, where he is now *Oberspielleiter*. His daughter **Brigitte** is a leading mezzo at the Bavarian State Opera. (R)

Domino Noir, Le (The Black Domino). Opera in 3 acts by Auber; text by Scribe. Prod. Paris, O.C., 2 Dec. 1837 with Cinthie-Damoreau; London, C.G., 16 Feb. 1838; New Orleans Nov. 1839.

Don Alfonso. The philosopher (bar.) who engineers the plot of Mozart's *Così fan tutte*.

Don Bartolo. The old doctor (bass) in Mozart's *Le Nozze di Figaro*, and, as Rosina's guardian, in Rossini's *Il Barbiere di Siviglia*.

Don Basilio. The priest and music-master (ten.) in Mozart's *Le Nozze di Figaro* and (bass) in Paisiello's and Rossini's *Il Barbiere di Siviglia*.

Don Carlos. Opera in 5 acts by Verdi; text by Méry and Du Locle after Schiller's drama (1787). Prod. Paris, O., 11 Mar. 1867 with Sass, Guéymard, Morère, Faure, and Obin; London, C.G., 4 June 1867 with Lucca, Fricci, Naudin, Graziani, Petit; N.Y., Ac. of M., 12 Apr. 1877. The 5-act version composed for Paris was revised by Verdi and Ghislanzoni for La Scala in 1884, dispensing with the opening Fontainebleau scene; this was restored in the 1887 version.

Act 1. Don Carlos, Infante of Spain (ten.), has come to France disguised in the retinue of the Spanish Ambassador, to see Elisabeth de Valois (sop.) to whom he is betrothed, but whom he has never met. The couple meet in the forest near Fontainebleau and re-affirm in person their betrothal vows. Their happiness is short-lived, for the Spanish Ambassador informs her that as a condition of the signing of the peace treaty between France and Spain, King Philip II of Spain, Carlos's father, requests her hand in marriage.

Act 2. Carlos has sought refuge at the Monastery of San Yuste in an attempt to forget his sadness. There, according to rumour, his grandfather Charles V still lives on as one of the brethren. Rodrigo (bar.), tries to persuade him to join him in his crusade to help the people of Flanders, and the two men pledge their friendship.

The Princess Eboli (mezzo) awaits the Queen and sings a Moorish love-song. Elisabeth now enters and Rodrigo hands her a message from Carlos. She agrees to see Carlos, who again declares his love for her; but she reminds him of his duty to his father. Philip (bass), finding the Queen unattended, is furious, and dismisses her Lady-in-waiting. Rodrigo remains and tells the King of his hopes for Flanders. Philip warns him of the Grand Inquisitor and bids him watch Carlos and the Queen.

Act 3. Carlos comes to the Queen's Gardens by night to meet Elisabeth, but it is Eboli, who is in love with him, who comes masked to keep the assignation. When she reveals her identity Carlos cannot conceal his disappointment. She threatens to bring about his downfall. Rodrigo and Carlos renew their oath of friendship.

In the Square before the Cathedral preparations for an *auto-da-fé* are being made. Carlos, leading the Flemish deputies, pleads with Philip for clemency. Philip refuses this request and Carlos draws his sword against his father. Rodrigo disarms his friend.

Act 4. Philip, alone, laments his wife's coldness to him. The Grand Inquisitor (bass) tells Philip that he has the support of the Church if he should punish his son by death, but informs him that Rodrigo's championing of the cause of Flemish freedom is an even greater crime than Carlos's. Elisabeth rushes in asking Philip to help her recover her jewel-box which is missing—it is on his table, and when she opens it Carlos's portrait falls out. Philip accuses her of adultery. Eboli and Rodrigo enter and, after the two men have withdrawn, Eboli confesses that she has been Philip's mistress and curses her fatal gift of beauty.

Rodrigo comes to visit Carlos in prison, and tells him he is prepared to sacrifice his life for Carlos's. A servant of the Inquisition steals into the cell and shoots Rodrigo; as he dies he tells Carlos to meet Elisabeth on the morrow at San Yuste. Philip arrives to restore Carlos his sword, which his son refuses. A mob storms the prison and demands Carlos's release, but the Grand Inquisitor castigates them for daring to raise their hands against the Lord's anointed.

Act 5. Elisabeth, awaiting Carlos at San Yuste, sings of her former happiness. Carlos arrives and the lovers bid each other a last farewell. Philip enters with the Inquisitor and is about to hand over his son to the Inquisition when the tomb of Charles V opens, and the Emperor himself in the guise of a monk saves Carlos from the wrath of his father and the Inquisition.

Don Carlos di Vargas. Leonora's brother (bar.) in Verdi's *La Forza del Destino*.

Don Giovanni (orig. Il Dissoluto Punito, ossia Il Don Giovanni). *Dramma giocoso* in 2 acts by Mozart; text by Da Ponte, after the Don Juan legend and particularly after Bertati's play (1775). Prod. Prague, N., 29 Oct. 1787, with Luigi Bassi as Don Giovanni; London, Hm., 12 Apr. 1817, with Ambrogetti and Camporese in the cast; N.Y., Park, 23 May 1826, in Da Ponte's presence, with four members of the Garcia family, Manuel (senior and junior), Mme Garcia, and Maria, in the cast.

Act 1, Scene 1. Leporello (bar.) deplores being kept waiting in the dark outside the house where his master Don Giovanni (bar.) is engaged with a lady. Giovanni emerges with Donna Anna (sop.) trying to unmask him. Her father the Commendatore (bass) appears and is reluctantly killed by Giovanni, who escapes with Leporello. Anna returns with her lover Don Ottavio (ten.), and they swear vengeance on the unknown murderer. Scene 2. An argument between Giovanni and Leporello is interrupted by the arrival of a lady, who turns out to be Giovanni's former mistress Donna Elvira (sop.); he escapes while she is held in conversation by Leporello, who then recounts to her the list of Giovanni's conquests. Scene 3. A wedding is to be celebrated between the peasants Masetto (bar.) and Zerlina (sop.). Giovanni has Masetto removed by Leporello and makes advances to Zerlina; she has just succumbed when Elvira returns and rescues her. Anna and Ottavia return, and Giovanni swears friendship, but Elvira's presence complicates matters; she leaves, Giovanni following, with Anna having recognized him as her father's murderer. Ottavio declares that his peace of mind rests on hers. Leporello returns and recounts his actions to Giovanni, who tells him to prepare a party. Scene 4. In Giovanni's garden, Masetto jealously accuses Zerlina, who slyly submits to his wrath and regains his love. Giovanni returns and discovers Zerlina, then Masetto. Anna, Ottavio, and Elvira appear, masked, and are invited in. Scene 5. At the party, Giovanni renews his efforts with Zerlina and leaves with her; he blames her subsequent scream on Leporello, but the masqueraders reveal themselves and Giovanni has to escape.

Act 2, Scene 1. Giovanni patches up a quarrel with Leporello, and changes clothes with him so as to seduce Elvira's maid. Elvira appears on her balcony, still in love with Giovanni, and is lured away by Leporello. Giovanni sings his serenade, but Masetto and the villagers appear, armed and searching for him; thinking him Leporello, they disperse at his orders and he beats Masetto. Zerlina hears Masetto's wails and comes to comfort him. Scene 2. Leporello leads Elvira in, and they are found by Anna, Ottavio, Masetto, and Zerlina; Leporello is forced to reveal himself, but manages to escape. Ottavio declares his intention of avenging Anna's father. (In a scene now always cut, Leporello mistakes his way and is caught by Zerlina, who ties him up and threatens him with a razor. He is released by a peasant just as Zerlina returns with Elvira.) Elvira, alone, confesses that she still loves the monstrous Giovanni. Scene 3.

In the cemetery reached in flight, Giovanni tells Leporello of his latest exploits, but his laughter is interrupted by the threatening voice of the Commendatore's statue. Giovanni makes Leporello invite it to supper, and it accepts. Scene 4. In her house, Anna rejects Ottavio's offer of immediate marriage, but tries to console him. Scene 5. Giovanni is at supper, entertained by a band, when Elvira rushes in with a last plea for his repentance; as she leaves, she screams and the statue enters. It, too, fails to make Giovanni repent, and drags him off to Hell. The others assemble and point the moral.

Don José. The hero (ten.) of Bizet's *Carmen.*

Don Juan. Operas on the legend, first set down in about 1630 by Tirso de Molina, are by Melani (*L'Empio Punito*, 1669), Righini (*Il Convitato di Pietra*, 1777), Callegari (ditto, 1777), Tritto (ditto, 1783), Albertini (1784), Gazzaniga (*Il Convitato di Pietra*, 1787), Gardi (*Il Nuovo Convitato di Pietra*, 1787, in hurried imitation of Gazzaniga), Fabrizi (*Il Convitato di Pietra*, 1787), Reeve (1787), Mozart (1787), Federici (1794, concocted with Da Ponte, music also by Gazzaniga, Sarti, and Guglielmi), Dibdin (*Don Giovanni, or A Spectre on Horseback*, music by many hands, 1817), Carnicer (1818), Pacini (*Il Convitato di Pietra*, 1832), D'Orgeval (*Don Juan de Village*, 1863), Dargomizhsky (*The Stone Guest*, 1872), Manent (*El Convidado de Piedra*, a *zarzuela*, 1875), De Polignac (*Don Juan et Haidée*, 1877), Delibes (*Le Don Juan suisse*, 1880), Graener (*Don Juans letzte Abenteuer*, 1914), Lattuada (1929), and Haug (1930).

A variant of the legend, *Don Juan de Mañara*, showing ultimate repentance, is derived from Prosper Mérimée's story *Les Ames du Purgatoire* (1834), based on the notorious Miguel de Mañara, who died in 1679. Operas are by Alfano (*L'Ombra di Don Giovanni*, 1914, rev. as *Don Juan de Mañara*, 1941), Enna (1925), and Goossens (1937).

Don Magnifico. Cenerentola's father (bass) in Rossini's opera.

Don Ottavio. Donna Anna's lover (ten.) in Mozart's *Don Giovanni.*

Don Pasquale. Opera buffa in 3 acts by Donizetti; text by Ruffini and the composer after Anelli's *Ser Marc' Antonio* (1810). Prod. Paris, T.I., 3 Jan. 1843 with Grisi, Mario, Tamburini, Lablache; London, H.M.'s, 29 June 1843 with same cast but Fornasari replacing Tamburini; New Orleans, 7 Jan. 1845.

Act 1. Don Pasquale, an elderly bachelor (bass), awaits the arrival of his physician Malatesta (bar.) who describes to him in glowing terms his young sister, who he tells Pasquale is in love with him. In reality she is Norina (sop.), a gay young widow, who wishes to marry Pasquale's nephew Ernesto (ten.); but the marriage is opposed by Pasquale. The old man breaks the news of his impending wedding to Ernesto and tells him he must leave the house.

Malatesta coaches Norina in her role of the shy young girl from the convent.

Act 2. Ernesto sadly packs his bags ready to leave Rome and even Europe. Malatesta now arrives with the shy young bride and introduces her to Pasquale. A mock marriage ceremony takes place, during which Ernesto arrives. Malatesta explains the situation to him in a hurried aside. Norina, once the ceremony is over, becomes a little spitfire and Pasquale exclaims that he has been tricked.

Act 3. Pasquale's house has become peopled with servants; Norina has invested in an expensive wardrobe and indulged in other extravagances. She tells Pasquale that she is going to the theatre and when he tries to stop her she boxes his ears. On her way out she carefully drops a letter from Ernesto arranging a meeting that night in the garden. Pasquale sends for Malatesta, and while awaiting his arrival, the servants comment on the strange happenings in the household. Pasquale and Malatesta confer on the situation in one of the most famous buffo duets in Italian opera.

In the garden Ernesto serenades his beloved, and Norina joins him in a love duet. Pasquale traps the lovers, who with Malatesta explain the plot to the old man. Pasquale is by now only too pleased to agree to the marriage of the young couple.

Don Pedros Heimkehr (Don Pedro's Homecoming). Opera in 3 acts compiled by Erismann from neglected music of Mozart; text by Walterlin and Galusser from Da Ponte and Varesco. Prod. Zürich, Stadttheater, 19 Jan. 1952, cond. Reinshagen; N.Y., Lemonade Opera, 1 June 1953; London, King George's Hall, 19 Sept. 1956. The bulk of the music is drawn from *L'Oca del Cairo* and *Lo Sposo Deluso*, to which have been added about 19 other arias by Mozart dating from about 1783.

Don Quixote. The hero of Cervantes's novel of that name (in two parts, 1605 and 1615) who, his mind twisted by tales of chivalry, sets out as knight errant with his squire Sancho Panza. After many adventures he is brought home, and dies sane and repentant. The most important opera on the subject is by Massenet, prod. Monte Carlo 19 Feb. 1910; New Orleans 27 Jan. 1912; London, Opera House, 18 May 1912. Others are by Förtsch (1690), Eve (1700), Conti (1719), Feo (1726), Treu (1727), Caldara (1727), Ristori (1727), Boismortier (1743), Holzbauer (1756), Philidor (1762), Paisiello (1769), Piccinni (1770), Salieri (1771), Hubaček (1791), Tarchi (1791), Generali (1805), Miari (1810), Garcia (1827), Mendelssohn (1827), Mercadante (1829), Donizetti (1833), Mazzucato (1836), Macfarren (1846), Clapisson (1847), Hervé (1848), Boulanger (1869), Pessard (1874), Clay (1876), Ricci (1881), Roth (1888), Jaques-Dalcroze (1897), Rauchenecker (1897), Kienzl (1898), Heuberger (1910), Ábrányi (1917), Falla (1923), and Frazzi (1952).

Donalda, Pauline (orig. Lightstone) (b. Montreal, 5 Mar. 1883; d. Montreal, 22 Oct. 1970). Canadian soprano. Début Nice 1904, Manon; London, C.G., 1905, where she was sponsored by Melba, and thus sang there for several seasons, creating Concepción (*L'Heure Espagnole*). Also sang N.Y. and Paris. Married baritone Paul Seveilhac, and after his death the tenor Mischa Léon. After her retirement taught singing in Montreal; her pupils included the bass Joseph Rouleau. (R)

Donizetti, Gaetano (b. Bergamo, 29 Nov. 1797; d. Bergamo, 8 Apr. 1848). Italian composer. Studied Bergamo with Salari, Gonzales, and J. S. Mayr, and Bologna under Pilotti and Padre Mattei. His student works included three unproduced operas. Owing to parental opposition to a musical career he enlisted in the Austrian army, but still found time for composition. His first success was *Enrico di Borgogna*, text by his friend Merelli, which was produced at Venice, Teatro S. Lucia, in 1818. *Zoraide di Granata* (1822) was so successful that it procured him exemption from further military service. From then until 1830 operas (nearly 30 in number) streamed from his pen and were produced in Naples, Milan, Rome, Palermo, and Genoa. These were mostly a poor imitation of Rossini, and can be said to constitute Donizetti's first period. Spurred on by the success of Bellini, he concentrated all his efforts on *Anna Bolena* (1830), the success of which was helped by Romani's libretto and a brilliant cast of singers including Pasta and Rubini; this was long regarded as his masterpiece, and was the first of his operas to be accepted throughout Europe. *L'Elisir d'Amore* (1832) disclosed his light touch and feeling for comedy; *Lucrezia Borgia* (1833) and *Lucia di Lammermoor* (1835), his tragic masterpiece, cemented his international success. In 1839 his *Poliuto* was forbidden by the Naples censor, and Donizetti went to Paris, where the opera was produced in 1840 as *Les Martyrs*. In the same year in Paris his *Lucrezia Borgia* was withdrawn on the orders of Victor Hugo, who objected to Romani's adaptation of his tragedy. In Paris his *La Fille du Régiment* and *La Favorite* were produced in 1840, the former another light tuneful comedy, the latter a full-scale French grand opera. There were two more Paris operas, his comic masterpiece *Don Pasquale* and *Don Sebastiano*, which has been described as a 'funeral in five acts'. For Vienna he composed *Linda di Chamounix* (1842), which aroused such enthusiasm that the Emperor made him Court Composer and Master of the Imperial Chapel, and *Maria di Rohan* (1843). His last composition was *Caterina Cornaro* (Naples 1844). Three of his works were produced posthumously: *Rita* (comp. 1841, prod. Paris 1860), *Gabriella di Vergy* (comp. 1826, prod. Naples 1869), and *Il Duca d'Alba* (comp. 1840, prod. Rome 1882). Donizetti died at Bergamo in 1848, where a monument by Vincenzo Vela was erected to his memory in 1855.

Donizetti wrote for the great voices of his day, but while his operas are to be regarded mainly as display pieces for singers, one should not overlook his gifts for melody and for creating a sentimental atmosphere. It has often been said that his orchestration is commonplace and his power of characterization not particularly strong, but his best works contain pages that refute these accusations.

In addition to the titles mentioned above, Donizetti's 75 works for the stage include *Alfredo il Grande* (1823), *Emilia di Liverpool* (1824), *Elisabetta al Castello di Kenilworth* (1829), *Fausta* (1832), *Parisina* (1833), *Torquato Tasso* (1833), *Marino Faliero* (1835), *Il Campanello di Notte* or *Il Campanello dello Speziale* (1836), *La Betly* (1836), and *Roberto d'Evereux* (1837).

Donna Anna. Don Ottavio's lover (sop.) in Mozart's *Don Giovanni.*

Donna del Lago, La (The Lady of the Lake). Opera in 2 acts by Rossini; text by Tottola, after Walter Scott's poem (1810). Prod. Naples, S.C., 24 Sept. 1819, with Pisaroni, Colbran, and Davide; London, Hm., 18 Feb. 1823, with De Begnis, De Vestris, Curioni; N.Y. 26 Aug. 1829. Very popular during the first half of last century, after which it virtually vanished from the repertory until its revival at the Florence Festival 1958.

Donna Diana. Opera in 3 acts by Rezniček; text by composer, after Moreto's comedy *El Lindo Don Diego* (1654). Prod. Prague 16 Dec. 1894.

Donna Elvira. A lady (sop.) of Burgos deserted by Don Giovanni in Mozart's opera.

Donna non vidi mai. Des Grieux's (ten.) aria in Act 1 of *Manon Lescaut,* in which he gives voice to his feelings as he sets eyes on Manon for the first time.

Donzelli, Domenico (b. Bergamo, 2 Feb. 1790; d. Bologna, 31 Mar. 1873). Italian tenor. Studied Bergamo; début there 1808 as comprimario; Naples, Rome from 1816. London, Hm., 1829. Continued to sing in Italy and Vienna until 1841. Rossini wrote a role for him in *Torvaldo e Dorliska* (1815) and Mercadente one in *Elisa e Claudio.* Created Pollione at La Scala 1831, and was its first interpreter in London.

Dorabella. Fiordiligi's sister (sop.) in Mozart's *Così fan tutte.*

Dorn, Heinrich (b. Königsberg, 14 Nov. 1804; d. Berlin, 10 Jan. 1892). German conductor and composer, friend of many eminent musicians of his day and enemy of Wagner, whom ironically he anticipated by producing an opera *Die Nibelungen* in 1854. He was much admired as a conductor and teacher.

Dorset Garden Theatre. One of London's earliest homes for music and drama. Erected by the widow of Sir William Davenant on plans by Wren and opened 1671. Several of Purcell's works had first performances there, including *King Arthur* (1691) and *The Fairy Queen* (1692).

Dortmund. Town in North Rhine-Westphalia, Germany. Opera is given in the Städtische Bühnen (cap. 650), opened in 1950.

Dorus-Gras (orig. Steenkiste), **Julie** (b. Valenciennes, 7 Sept. 1805; d. Paris, 6 Feb. 1896). Belgian soprano. Studied Paris Conservatoire with Henri and Blangini, and subsequently Paer and Bordogni. Début Brussels 1825; Paris 1830 where she succeeded Cinthie-Damoreau London 1839 (concerts), 1847, D.L., Lucia, which she sang in English, although not knowing the language; 1849, C.G., when she sang two of the roles she had created, Alice

(*Robert le Diable*) and Marguerite de Valois. Also a famous Elvira (*Masaniello*), and sang that role in the performance of the opera in Brussels, Sept. 1830, which touched off the revolt of the Low Countries.

Dositheus. The leader (bass) of the Old Believers in Mussorgsky's *Khovanshchina*. In Russian, Dosifey.

Dostoyevsky, Feodor (b. Moscow, 30 Oct. 1821; d. St. Petersburg, 28 Jan. 1881). Russian novelist. Operas on his works are as follows. *The Gambler* (1866): Prokofiev (1929). *From the House of the Dead* (1861–2): Janáček (1930). *Crime and Punishment* (1866): Pedrollo (1926); Sutermeister (*Raskolnikoff*, 1948). *The Brothers Karamazov* (unfin. 1879–80): Jeremiáš (1928); Blacher (*Der Grossinquisitor*).

Dove sono. The Countess's (sop.) aria in Act 3 of *Figaro* mourning the loss of her husband's love.

Down in the Valley. Folk opera by Kurt Weill; text by Arnold Sundgaard. Prod. Bloomington 15 July 1948; Bristol 23 Oct. 1957.

D'Oyly Carte, Richard. See *Carte, Richard D'Oyly*.

Dramaturg. The member of the staff of a German opera house who combines the duties of adapter of librettos, editor of programmes, and press officer, sometimes also producer and even actor.

Drame lyrique. A contemporary French term for a serious opera.

Dramma giocoso. An Italian term, current chiefly in the late 18th century, for a comic opera which could include tragic episodes, such as *Don Giovanni*.

Dramma per musica. An Italian term, current in the 17th–18th centuries for a libretto destined for music; hence also the resulting opera, always serious.

Drei Pintos, Die (The Three Pintos). Opera begun by Weber, but abandoned in 1821 in favour of *Euryanthe*; text by Theodor Hell, after Seidel's story *Der Brautkampf* (1819). Completed and scored by Mahler and prod. Leipzig 20 Jan. 1888; London, John Lewis Theatre, 10 Apr. 1962.

Dreigroschenoper, Die (The Threepenny Opera). Opera in a prologue and 8 scenes by Weill; text a modern interpretation of *The Beggar's Opera* (q.v.), based on a translation by Hauptmann, with lyrics, drawn also from Kipling and Villon, by Brecht. Prod. Berlin, Theater am Schiffbauerdamm, 31 Aug. 1928 with Lotte Lenya; N.Y., Empire, 13 Apr. 1933; London, Royal Court, 9 Feb. 1956.

Dresden. Town in Saxony, E. Germany. In the 18th and early 19th centuries its operatic traditions were wholly Italian, and not until Weber came to reorganize the Opera did the emphasis shift to German music. The Royal Opera House was built from plans by Gottfried Semper between 1837 and 1841. In 1842 *Rienzi* had its première there, after the success of which Wagner was appointed music director. This was followed by the premières of *Der fliegende Holländer* in 1843 and *Tannhäuser* in 1845. Wagner had to leave Dresden as a result of his part in the 1849 revolution. In 1869 the opera house was destroyed by fire; rebuilt again on Semper's plans, it opened in 1878. Ernst von Schuch was chief conductor from 1882 and artistic director from 1889 until 1914. During his régime the company included Malten, Schuch-Proska, Sembrich, Schumann-Heink, Burian, Scheidemantel, and later Siems, Von der Osten, Nast, Perron, Plaschke; and the premières of Strauss's *Feuersnot*, *Salome*, *Elektra*, and *Rosenkavalier* were given. During the First World War D'Albert's *Toten Augen* and *Christelflein* had their premières, and Fritz Reiner was chief conductor. In 1918 the Royal Opera became the Staatsoper. In 1922 the Fritz Busch era began, during which *Doktor Faust*, *Cardillac*, and *Die Aegyptische Helena* had their premières and the German Verdi revival began. Busch left Dresden when the Nazis came to power, and was succeeded by Karl Böhm, who brought the company to London in 1936. During the Böhm régime, *Arabella*, *Die schweigsame Frau*, *Daphne*, and *Romeo* *und Julia* (Sutermeister) were among the works that enjoyed their premières. Dresden singers between the wars included Cebotari, Rethberg, Seinemeyer, Marta Fuchs, Höngen, Goltz, Ralf, Tauber, Lorenz, Pattiera, Schoeffler, Boehme, and Frick. The theatre was completely destroyed by bombing on 13 Feb. 1945. From July 1945 to 1948 the company was housed in the Town Hall where its musical director was Joseph Keilberth; in 1948 it moved into the rebuilt Schauspielhaus (cap. 1,131). Rufolf Kempe was music director 1950–3. He was succeeded by Konwitschny (1953–5); Lovro von Matacic (1955–8); Wilhelm Scheuling (1958–60); Otmar Suitner (1960–4); Kurt Sanderling (from 1964).

Drottningholm Castle Theatre, Sweden. Built in 1764–6 by Carl Frederick Adelcrantz. The theatre saw much activity between 1777 and 1792 under Gustavus Adolfus III. It was rarely used from 1800 till 1912, when it was restored, and occasional performances were given by the Stockholm Opera. Since 1948 regular summer seasons of opera with works by Cimarosa, Handel, Gluck, &c., are given in the manner of the 18th century, with the orchestra in powdered wigs and satin coats.

Drury Lane, Theatre Royal. Although primarily the home of drama and later of 'musicals', Drury Lane has been the scene of several important operatic seasons. In the 17th and 18th centuries Arne, Bishop, Lacey, and Tom Cooke were at one time or another connected with the theatre. In the 1830's Bunn gave performances of Italian opera in English with Malibran, and later attempted to establish English opera on a permanent basis. During this period the premières of several works by Balfe, Wallace, and Benedict were given. Between 1867 and 1877, Her Majesty's Opera (Mapleson's company) was housed at Drury Lane after the burning down of Her Majesty's Theatre in the Haymarket, and it was there that the first performance in England of a Wagner opera, *Der fliegende Holländer*, was given in 1870. In 1882 Richter and a German company gave a series of performances including the first in London of *Tristan* and *Meistersinger*, and from 1883 for a number of years Drury Lane was the scene of the London seasons of the Carl Rosa. In 1887 Augustus Harris started his Italian opera revival there, transferring the following year to Covent Garden; and in 1892 and 1893 he used Drury Lane for extra performances of German opera. From 1894 to 1913 there were some English seasons; in 1913 and 1914 Sir Joseph Beecham's Russian seasons had their home there (see Diaghilev). During the First World War Beecham's English Company gave some of their London seasons there; but it was not until 1958 that opera was heard there again, when S. A. Gorlinsky gave a two months' season of Italian opera, including *William Tell*, which had had its first English performance there in 1830.

Du bist der Lenz. Sieglinde's (sop.) rapturous outburst in Act 1 of *Die Walküre*, part of the Siegmund–Sieglinde love-duet.

Dublin. Capital of Eire. Opera was first heard there in 1711 when Handel's *Rinaldo* was given at the Smock Alley Theatre with Nicolini. Italian opera was given from time to time during the 18th century; in the 19th century the Theatre Royal was the scene of several outstanding seasons with artists who were heard regularly at the Italian Opera houses in London. In 1871 the Gaiety Theatre was opened, and was the home of the Dublin seasons given by the Blanche Cole, Carl Rosa, Mapleson, Augustus Harris, O'Mara, and other touring companies. Between 1908 and 1910 the short-lived Dublin Opera Company gave performances and John MacCormack was heard as Faust. From then until 1928 opera was again provided by touring companies, and from 1928 to 1938 the Irish Opera Society presented opera at the Gaiety Theatre. In 1941 the Dublin Grand Opera Society was formed, and has given two seasons each year. The orchestra is that of Radio Eireann, and the chorus is made up of locals; but soloists from England and the Continent are regularly engaged; and occasionally whole foreign ensembles from Paris, Hamburg, Munich, and elsewhere. In addition to the more popular works in the repertory, Dublin has heard in recent years *La Favorite, Don Carlos, Simone Boccanegra, La Gioconda, Pelléas et Mélisande*, and *Cecilia* (Refice).

Dubrovnik (It., Ragusa). Town in Dalmatia, Yugoslavia. Since the Second World War it has staged spectacular operatic performances in the open air.

Duca d'Alba, Il (The Duke of Alba). Opera in 4 acts by Donizetti; text by Scribe. Originally written for Paris, O., in 1840 but not produced: the libretto was later altered by Scribe and became the text of *Les Vêpres Siciliennes*. Donizetti's score was recovered at Bergamo in 1875 and completed by Matteo Salvi, prod. Rome 22 Mar. 1882 with Gayarré. Revived Spoleto 1959. N.Y., Town Hall, 20 Oct. 1959. Also opera by Pacini (1842).

Due Foscari, I. Opera in 3 acts by Verdi; text by Piave after Byron's drama *The Two Foscari* (1821). Prod. Rome, Arg., 3 Nov. 1844 with Barbieri-Nini; London, H.M.'s, 10 Apr. 1847, with Grosi, Mario, Ronconi; Boston, 10 May 1847. Though seldom heard now, it was the work which caused Donizetti to exclaim, 'This man is a genius!'

Due Litiganti, I (The Two Litigants). Correct title: *Fra Due Litiganti il Terzo Gode*. Opera in 3 acts by Sarti; text an altered version of Goldoni's *Le Nozze*. Prod. Milan, Sc., 14 Sept. 1782; London 6 Jan. 1784 (as *I Rivali Delusi*). In its day immensely popular, so that Mozart could not only use the aria 'Come un agnello' for a set of piano variations (K. 460), but quote it with certainty of recognition in Giovanni's supper scene as the wind band's second tune; whereupon Leporello exclaims, 'Evvivano *I Litiganti*!'

Duenna, The, or The Double Elopement. (1) Opera in 3 acts composed and compiled by Thomas Linley, sen. and jun.; text by Sheridan. Prod. London, C.G., 21 Nov. 1775; N.Y. 10 July 1786. One of the most successful English comic operas of the 18th century, surpassing even *The Beggar's Opera* on its first run (75 performances as against 63). Its revivals include productions in Calcutta (1915, in Bengali) and Bombay (1925, in Marathi). (2) Opera in 4 acts by Prokofiev (sometimes known as *Betrothal in a Monastery*); text by Prokofiev with verses by Mira Mendelson, after Sheridan. Prod. Leningrad, 3 Nov. 1946 (3) Opera in 3 acts by Roberto Gerhard; text by composer, after Sheridan. Concert perf., Wiesbaden, 1951.

Duet. A composition for two performers, with or without accompaniment, in which the interest is equally shared. The *duetto da camera* (chamber duet) for two voices was a popular form from the late 17th century; and from about the mid-18th century it became an important ingredient of opera, the love duet being its most familiar manifestation.

Dugazon (orig. Lefèvre), **Louise** (b. Berlin, 18 June 1755; d. Paris, 22 Sept. 1821). French mezzo, after Mme Favart the best-known *opéra comique* artist of her day. She created over 60 parts, inspired a volume of laudatory odes as well as a host of paintings, and caused the genres in which she excelled to be known as Dugazon roles (*see* Soprano).

Dukas, Paul (b. Paris, 1 Oct. 1865; d. Paris, 17 May 1935). French composer. Dukas's only opera, *Ariane et Barbe-Bleue* (q.v.), is also his most ambitious and remarkable work. The first important work to be influenced by *Pelléas*, it differs in its broader structural scheme, its scope for purely musical development, its more brilliant scoring, its direct emotional appeal. It was one of the first works to find more than Grand Guignol in the legend; but whereas Bartók treats it as a drama of questing man, Maeterlinck provided the theme that women prefer even the harshest marriage to lack of security. Dukas also helped Saint-Saëns to complete Guiraud's *Frédégonde* and edited several of Rameau's operas.

Duke Bluebeard's Castle (Hung., A Kékszakállú Herceg Vára). Opera in 1 act by Bartók; text by Béla Balázs. Prod. Budapest, 24 May 1918; N.Y., C.C., 2 Oct. 1952; London, Rudolf

Steiner Hall, 16 Jan. 1957. Bluebeard (bass) is not the Gilles de Rais monster of the *Ma Mère l'Oye* fairy-tale, but a sorrowing, idealistic man who takes Judith (sop.), his newest bride, home to his murky castle. She makes him unlock his secret doors one by one and when she has penetrated his innermost secret she takes her place, another failure, among the other wives behind the last door, leaving Bluebeard in his loneliness.

Duke of Mantua, The. The licentious duke (ten.) who pursues Gilda in Verdi's *Rigoletto*.

Dulcamara. The quack (bass) in Donizetti's *L'Elisir d'Amore*.

Dumas, Alexandre (sen.) (b. Villers-Cotterets, 24 July 1802; d. Dieppe, 5 Dec. 1870). French author. Operas on his works are as follows. *Henry III* (1829): Flotow (*La Duchesse de Guise*, 1840). *Charles VII chez ses Grands Vassaux* (1831): Donizetti (*Gemma di Vergy*, 1834): Cui (*The Saracen*, 1899). *Les Demoiselles de Saint-Cyr* (1843): Humperdinck (*Heirat wider Willen*, 1905). *Ascanio* (1843): Saint-Saëns (1890). *Les Trois Mousquetaires* (1844): Visetti (1871); De Lara (1921).

Dumas, Alexandre (jun.) (b. Paris, 28 July 1824; d. Paris, 27 Nov. 1895). French author. *La Dame aux Camélias* (1848) provided the libretto for Verdi's *La Traviata* (1853). Unsuccessful operas on his dramas are by Minchejmer and Salvayre.

Duni, Egidio Romoaldo (b. Matera, 9 Feb. 1709; d. Paris, 11 June 1775). Italian composer. After some travels, success in Italy with a French opera *Ninette la Cour* (1755) brought him to Paris, where he rapidly became one of the principal *opéra comique* composers of his day. His greatest successes were *Les Deux Chasseurs* (1763), *La Fée Urgèle* (1765), *La Clochette* (1766), and *Les Moissonneurs* (1768). He brought an Italian liveliness to the genre; and if shallow and unambitious, his music has point and a certain originality of orchestration.

Dunn, Geoffrey (b. London, 13 Dec. 1903). English tenor and producer. After early successes, especially as a character singer, has devoted himself to translating little-known foreign operas (among them Handel's *Serse*, Wolf's *Der Corregidor*, Rimsky-Korsakov's *Mozart and Salieri*, and Pizzetti's *Assassinio nella Cattedrale*).

Dunque io son. The duet between Rosina (mezzo) and Figaro (bar.) in Act 1, scene 2, of Rossini's *Il Barbiere di Siviglia* in which he spins a story about his cousin, a poor student, who is in love with a certain girl—and eventually is given an already written letter for the disguised Count Almaviva.

Duodrama. The name given, by Mozart among others, to works for two actors with musical accompaniment. Mozart refers with enthusiasm to the best-known work of the genre, by Jiří Benda, and himself contemplated writing one, *Semiramis*.

Duprez, Gilbert (b. Paris, 6 Dec. 1806; d. Passy, 23 Sept. 1896). French tenor. Studied Paris Conservatoire with Choron. Début Odéon 1825, Almaviva, with little success. Then went to Italy for further study and was chosen by Donizetti to create Edgardo at Naples 1835. Returned to Paris as tenor at the Opéra 1837–45, where he created the title role in *Benvenuto Cellini*, Fernando (*La Favorite*), Poliuto (*Les Martyrs*), and several other parts, as well as taking over several of Nourrit's parts in Meyerbeer and Halévy works. From 1842 to 1850 he was professor of singing at the Conservatoire and in 1853 founded his own school. His pupils included Battu and Albani. He composed eight operas and a quantity of other music, and wrote two books on singing.

Durch die Wälder. Max's (ten.) aria in Act 1 of Weber's *Der Freischütz* in which he tells how he once wandered joyfully through the countryside.

Dušek (orig. Hambacher), **Josepha** (b. Prague, 6 Mar. 1754; d. Prague, 8 Jan. 1824). Bohemian soprano, composer, pianist, and friend of Mozart, who wrote the concert aria 'Bella mia Fiamma' for her. She appeared at the King's Theatre in the 1808 season. Wife of František Dušek.

Düsseldorf-Duisburg. Two German industrial cities in North Rhine–Westphalia, Germany, which together house the Deutsche Oper am Rhein, one of the strongest German operatic ensembles. Alberto Erede was the Generalmusikdirector 1958–62, Hermann Juch the Intendant 1955–63; they were succeeded by Günther Wich and Grischa Barfuss in 1964. It has been the scene of the premières of Klebe's *Die Räuber* (1957) and the new version of Křenek's *Karl V* (1958). Before the formation of the Deutsche Oper am Rhein the Düsseldorf Company was under the direction of Hollreiser and then Szenkar. The Düsseldorf Opera House (cap. 1,400) was built in 1875 and rebuilt in 1956; the Duisburg Stadttheater (cap. 1,183) was built in 1912 and rebuilt in 1950.

Duval, Denise (b. Paris, 23 Oct. 1921). French soprano. Début Paris, O.C., 1947, Cio-Cio-San. Leading soprano Opéra and Opéra-Comique since. Created Thérèse (*Mamelles de Tirésias*), Blanche (*Carmélites*), Elle (*La Voix Humaine*). Also noted for her Concepción in *L'Heure Espagnole*, and Princesse in *Mârouf*. Has sung with success in Italy, U.S.A., and elsewhere. Edinburgh Festival 1960 in British première of *La Voix Humaine*; Glyndebourne 1962, Mélisande. Retired 1965 (R)

Dux, Claire (b. Witkowicz, 2 Aug. 1885; d. Chicago, 27 Nov. 1967). Polish soprano. Début Cologne 1906, Pamina. Berlin 1911–18; London, C.G., 1913, as first English Sophie (also sang Eva). The following year she sang Pamina under Beecham at D.L. From 1921 to 1923 sang at Chicago and, marrying a wealthy American, retired from the stage at the height of her powers. (R)

Dvořák, Antonín (b. nr. Prague, 8 Sept. 1841; d. Prague, 1 May 1904). Czech composer. Though some of them are popular in Czechoslovakia, Dvořák's ten operas have had difficulty in penetrating foreign repertories. Even in their own land, *Alfred* (1870, prod. 1938), *King and Collier* (1874), the historical *Vanda* (1876), and the romantic *Armida* (1904) have languished. But the sentimental humour of *The Jacobin* (1889) is appreciated, as are the folk charms of *The Pig-Headed Peasants* (1874, prod. 1881) and *The Peasant a Rogue* (1878). *The Devil and Kate* (1899) has had some success abroad, and *Dimitrij*, whose plot begins where *Boris Godunov* ends, has had a few performances. Dvořák's greatest success has always been the fairy-tale *Rusalka* (1901), which is as popular among Czech children as *Hänsel und Gretel* is among Germans. It is for occasional delights rather than for his individual style that he is remembered as an opera composer.

Dybbuk, The. A Yiddish drama (1916) by Sh. An-Sky based on the Hebrew belief that a living person can be possessed by the spirit of a dead person. The subject of two operas, (1) by Rocca; text by Simoni; prod. Milan, Sc., 24 Mar. 1934: (2) by David Tamkin; text by Alex Tamkin; prod. N.Y., C.C., 4 Oct. 1951. Projected, partly sketched opera by Gershwin, abandoned when he heard that the rights belonged to Rocca.

Dyck, Ernest van (b. Antwerp, 2 Apr. 1861; d. Berlaer-lès-Lierre, 31 Aug. 1923). Belgian tenor. Studied with Saint-Yves Bax. Début Paris, Théâtre Eden, 1887, in French première of *Lohengrin*. The following year, after a period of study with Mottl, sang Parsifal at Bayreuth, and continued to appear there in that role until 1912. London, C.G., from 1891, including the 1907 winter season when he acted as manager and artistic director of a German company; N.Y., Met., 1898–1902. As well as in Wagner's Heldentenor roles, he was famous as Werther and Des Grieux. Much admired by Bernard Shaw. (R)

E

Eadie, Noël (b. Paisley, 10 Dec. 1901; d. London, 11 Apr. 1950). Scottish soprano. Studied with Esta d'Argo. Début London, C.G., 1926, Woglinde. First major role, Queen of Night with B.N.O.C., Edinburgh 1928; Chicago Opera 1931–2; Glyndebourne 1935–6; S.W., C.R., C.G. (R)

Eames, Emma (b. Shanghai, 13 Aug. 1865; d. New York, 13 June 1952). American soprano. Studied Boston with Clara Munger, Paris with Marchesi. Début Paris, O., 1889, Juliette (chosen by Gounod), and during next two years created Colombe in Saint-Saëns's *Ascanio* and title role in De la Nux's *Zaïre*. Forced to leave Paris because of intrigues. C.G. début 1891, Marguerite, sang there until 1901 (not every season) where her success aroused Melba's jealousy. N.Y., Met., 1891–1909; Boston 1911–12. Retired when in her prime. Greatly admired as Aida, Desdemona, and Tosca, she also sang Elsa, Sieglinde, and Pamina. Autobiography, *Some Memoirs and Reflections* (1927). (R)

Easton, Florence (b. Middlesbrough, 25 Oct. 1884; d. New York, 13 Aug. 1955). English soprano. Studied R.C.M. London, Paris with Elliot Haslam. Début Moody-Manners Co. 1903, Shepherd (*Tannhäuser*). Joined Henry Savage Company, Baltimore, 1905; Berlin, Royal Opera, 1907–13; Hamburg 1914–16; N.Y., Met., 1917–29, 1935–6, during which time she created Lauretta (*Schicchi*) and Aelfrida in Deems Taylor's *The King's Henchman*. Sang Turandot at C.G. 1927, Brünnhilde and Isolde in 1932, and Tosca at S.W. 1934. One of the most versatile sopranos of the inter-war years, having a repertory of 150 roles in four languages, ranging from Brünnhilde to Carmen. She could learn a new score in 12 hours, and was always ready to step into any of her parts when a colleague fell ill. (R)

Ebers, John (b. London, 1785; d. London, *c.* 1830). English impresario. Originally a bookseller, became manager of the King's Theatre 1821–7; this venture ended in ruin. His company included De Begnis, Colbran, Camporese, Pasta, Vellutti, and Vestris. Among the operas he introduced to London were *La Gazza Ladra*, *Il Turco in Italia*, *La Donna del Lago*, *Il Crociato in Egitto*, and *La Vestale*. His memoirs, *Seven Years of the King's Theatre*, were published in 1828.

Ebert, Carl (b. Berlin 20 Feb. 1887). German producer and opera manager. Trained as an actor by Reinhardt and after engagements in Berlin and Frankfurt became general director of the State Theatre at Darmstadt 1927. In 1931 was appointed director general and producer of the Städtische Oper, Berlin, where his productions came as a revelation to critics and public. Refused to collaborate with the Nazis and left Germany in 1933; besides producing opera in Florence and Buenos Aires, founded, with Fritz Busch, the Glyndebourne Festival (q.v.). Organized Turkish National Theatre and Opera 1936–47; Director of opera department at University of Southern California 1948–56. Returned to Glyndebourne 1947–59, and to his former position in Berlin 1956–61. N.Y., Met., 1959–62. His productions of Verdi and Mozart have set a particularly high standard: his intensive rehearsals result in performances notable for their detail and fine ensemble. His son **Peter** has worked at Glyndebourne and elsewhere as producer.

Eboli. Ex-mistress (mezzo) of King Philip and Lady-in-waiting to Elisabeth, in Verdi's *Don Carlos*.

Edelmann, Otto (b. Vienna, 5 Feb. 1916). Austrian bass. Studied Vienna Academy with Lierhammer and

Graarud. Début Gera 1938, Figaro. Resumed his career, which was interrupted by the war, in 1947 by joining the Vienna Opera. Sings regularly in San Francisco and N.Y., Met., where his Baron Ochs is much admired. (R)

Edgar. Opera in 4 acts by Puccini; text by Ferdinando Fontana, after Alfred de Musset's verse drama *La Coupe et les Lèvres* (1832). Prod. Milan, Sc., 21 Apr. 1889, cond. Faccio; N.Y., Waldorf-Astoria, 12 Apr. 1956.

Edgar (ten.) is torn between his love of Fidelia (sop.) and his passion for Tigrana (mezzo). He yields to the latter, but tiring of it returns to Fidelia, who is stabbed by the jealous Tigrana.

Edgardo. Edgar of Ravenswood (ten.), lover of Lucy, in Donizetti's *Lucia di Lammermoor.*

Edinburgh. Capital of Scotland. Except for visits by touring companies Edinburgh has had little or no opera; it was, however, the birthplace of the Denhof Opera Company (q.v.). The annual Edinburgh Festival was started in 1947 by the Glyndebourne Society Limited, and not unnaturally the opera during the first five years was given by this company—*Figaro*, *Macbeth*, *Don Giovanni*, *Così fan tutte*, *Ballo in Maschera*, *Ariadne auf Naxos* (original version, under Beecham), and *Forza del Destino*. Subsequent seasons were as follows—1952: Hamburg State Opera, *Fidelio*, *Freischütz*, *Zauberflöte*, *Rosenkavalier*, *Mathis der Maler* (first stage performance in Britain), and *Meistersinger*; 1953–5: Glyndebourne, *Cenerentola*, *Idomeneo*, *The Rake's Progress*, *Comte Ory*, *Ariadne* (revised version), *Così fan tutte*, *Falstaff*, *Barbiere*, and *Forza del Destino*; 1956: Hamburg State Opera, *Zauberflöte*, *Oedipus Rex*, *Mavra*, *Barbier von Bagdad*, and *Salome*; 1957: Piccola Scala, *La Sonnambula* (with Callas), *Matrimonio Segreto*, *Turco in Italia*, and *Elisir d'Amore*; 1958: Stuttgart State Opera, *Euryanthe*, *Tristan und Isolde*, *Wildschütz* and *Entführung aus dem Serail*, and also a Spanish ensemble, *La Vida Breve* (with Los Angeles); 1959: Stockholm Opera (its first visit to Great Britain), *Walküre*, *Wozzeck*, *Ballo in Maschera*, *Rigoletto*, and *Aniara* (Blomdahl); 1962: Belgrade Opera, *The Gambler* and *The Love of the Three Oranges* (Prokofiev), *Prince Igor*, *Don Quixote* (Massenet), and *Khovanshchina*; 1963: San Carlo Opera, *Don Pasquale*, *Luisa Miller*, *Adriana Lecouvreur*; 1964: National Theatre of Prague, *Dalibor*, *Rusalka*, *Káťa Kabanová*, *From the House of the Dead*, Cikker's *Resurrection*; 1965: Holland Festival in *Le Pescatrici*, Bavarian State Opera in *Intermezzo*. Lord Harewood, artistic director from 1961 to 1965, succeeded by Peter Diamand. Operatic events since 1966 include productions of *Lulu* and *Wozzeck* (Stuttgart Opera, 1966); *Peter Grimes*, *Elegy for Young Lovers*, and *The Trojans* (Scottish Opera, 1968, 1970, and 1972); *Orfeo ed Euridice* (Haydn) and *I Capuletti ed i Montecchi* (Edinburgh Festival Opera 1967); *Maria Stuarda*, *I Sette Canzoni* (Malipiero), and *Il Prigioniero* (Florence Opera 1969); *The Fiery Angel* (Stuttgart Opera, 1970); and Reimann's *Melusine* (German Opera, W. Berlin, 1971).

Éducation Manquée, Une. Operetta in 1 act by Chabrier; text by Leterrier and Vanloo. Prod. Paris, Cercle de la Presse, 1 May 1879; Tanglewood, 3 Aug. 1953; London, St. Pancras Town Hall, 14 Mar. 1961.

Edvina, Louise (b. Montreal, *c.* 1880; d. London, 13 Nov. 1948). French-Canadian soprano. Studied Paris with Jean de Reszke; début London, C.G., 1908 as Marguerite, singing there regularly until 1914, and again in 1919, 1920, and 1924. She was the first London Louise, Maliella (*Gioielli della Madonna*), Fiora, Francesca da Rimini. Also appeared in Boston and N.Y. An elegant singer, especially of French roles. (R)

Edwin and Angelina, or The Banditti. Opera in 3 acts by Pelissier; text by E. H. Smith after Goldsmith's ballad (1764). Prod. N.Y., John Street Theatre, 19 Dec. 1796. The second American opera (see *Archers, The,* for the first), only once performed.

Egk, Werner (b. Auchsesheim, nr. Augsburg, 17 May 1901). German composer. His first opera was *Die Zaubergeige* (1935), successfully using numbers based on popular tunes. This was followed by *Peer Gynt* (1938), which became popular on receiving Hitler's blessing. Next came a revision of the broadcast opera of 1933, *Columbus* (1941), *Circe* (1948), *Irische Legende* (1954), *Der Revisor* (1957), and *Verlobung in San Domingo* (1963). Egk's dramatic flair and capacity for drawing on the most readily acceptable aspects of his seniors and predecessors, notably Stravinsky, has made him a popular composer in Germany.

Egypt. See *Cairo*.

È il sol dell' anima. The Duke's (ten.) aria declaring his love to Gilda in Act 1, scene 2, of Verdi's *Rigoletto*, leading to the love duet.

Einem, Gottfried von (b. Berne, 24 Jan. 1918). Austrian composer. Best known for his two operas *Dantons Tod* (1947), after Büchner, and *Der Prozess* (1953), after Kafka. His work is direct and theatrically effective, and draws on a wide range of influences. He has also written a third opera, *Aus dem Leben eines Taugenichts*.

Ein Mädchen oder Weibchen. Papageno's (bar.) aria in Act 2, scene 5 of Mozart's *Die Zauberflöte*, in which he sings of his longing for a wife. Beethoven wrote a set of variations on it for cello and piano.

Einsam in trüben Tagen. Elsa's (sop.) aria, known as 'Elsa's Dream', in Act 1 of Wagner's *Lohengrin*, in which she recounts her dream of a rescuing hero.

Ein Schwert verhiess mir der Vater. Siegmund's (ten.) narration in Act 1 of Wagner's *Die Walküre*.

Eire. See *Ireland*.

Eisenstein. A wealthy Viennese (ten.), husband of Rosalinde, in J. Strauss's *Die Fledermaus*.

Eleazar. The Jewish goldsmith (ten.) in Halévy's *La Juive*.

Elektra. Opera in 1 act by Strauss; text by Hugo von Hofmannsthal after Sophocles's play (411 or 410 B.C.). Prod. Dresden, 25 Jan. 1909 with Anny Krull, Siems, Schumann-Heink; N.Y., Manhattan O., 1 Feb. 1910 (in French), with Mariette Mazarin as Elektra; London, C.G., 19 Feb. 1910, with Edyth Walker, Rose, Mildenburg, cond. Beecham.

The opera is divided into seven stages. In the first the servants drawing water discuss the behaviour of Elektra; the fifth maid, who expresses love for her, is taken off on the overseer's instructions and beaten. Elektra (sop.) enters and mourns the death of her father Agamemnon, and swears that she and her brother Orest will avenge his murder. In the second stage Elektra tries to persuade her sister Chrysothemis (sop.) to join in plans for revenge; Chrysothemis, longing for love, refuses. The third section of the opera is a long scene between Elektra and her mother Klytemnestra (mezzo), who is tormented by dreams and asks for help. She is told that the nightmares will vanish when the gods are placated by the shedding of blood of someone near to her. Elektra then describes the coming death of Klytemnestra. A confidante comes and whispers some news to Klytemnestra, who returns to the palace with a triumphant look. In the fourth stage Chrysothemis reappears with news of Orest's death. Elektra says that now she must help in her task of killing Klytemnestra and Aegisth; Chrysothemis again refuses and rushes from the courtyard. In the fifth stage Elektra begins to dig for the buried axe that had killed Agamemnon, but is interrupted by the arrival of a stranger demanding to see Klytemnestra with news of Orest's death. Elektra reveals her name to the stranger; he replies that Orest is not dead. Servants come in and kiss his hand. Elektra asks who he is; he answers that all have recognized him except his own sister. Stage 6 is the recognition scene between sister and brother. Elektra will not allow him to embrace her; they plan to avenge their father's murder. In the final stage of the opera Elektra waits in the courtyard while Orest kills his mother. Aegisth now appears and Elektra joyfully lights his way into the palace, where he too is slain. After dancing in a demented manner Elektra collapses, dead, while Chrysothemis rushes to the door of the palace with the cry of 'Orest' on her lips.

Also operas by Lemoyne (1782), Häffner (1785), and Gnecchi (*Cassandra*, 1905), who sued Strauss for plagiarism.

Elenco Artistico. (It. = artistic catalogue). Properly the names of the actors or singers of a company. More recently the complete list of artists, including producers, designers, conductors, &c., engaged by an Italian opera house.

Elisabeth. The daughter (sop.) of the Landgrave in Wagner's *Tannhäuser*.

Elisabeth de Valois. The wife (sop.) of King Philip in Verdi's *Don Carlos*.

Elisabetta, Regina d'Inghilterra (Elizabeth, Queen of England). Opera in 2 acts by Rossini; text by Giovanni Schmidt. Prod. Naples, S.C., 4 Oct. 1815 with Colbran; London, 30 Apr. 1818 with Fodor. The overture and finale were taken from *Aureliano in Palmira*, and the former now replaces the lost overture to *Il Barbiere di Siviglia*. A special performance was recorded by the Italian Radio for the coronation of Queen Elizabeth II.

Elizabeth I was also the subject of operas by Pavesi (1810), Giacometti (1853), and Britten (*Gloriana*, 1953).

Elisir d'Amore, L' (The Love Potion). Opera in 2 acts by Donizetti; text by Romani, after Scribe's libretto *Le Philtre* (1831, for Auber). Prod. Milan, T. della Canobbiana, 12 May 1832; London, Ly., 10 Dec. 1836; N.Y., Park T., 18 June 1838.

Nemorino (ten.) acquires courage to approach Adina (sop.) through faith in an elixir provided, in exchange for his last coin, by the quack Dulcamara (bass). His confident behaviour so annoys her that she decides to marry his rival, the recruiting sergeant Belcore (bar.), without delay. In Act 2 Nemorino complains to Dulcamara, who recommends another bottle; Nemorino pays for this by signing on with Sgt. Belcore. News of the death of Nemorino's rich uncle makes him suddenly desirable to the village girls; Adina is now sad, but is quickly consoled by Nemorino. Dulcamara points triumphantly to the potency of his wares.

Elle a fui, la tourterelle. Antonia's (sop.) aria at the piano, in Act 3 of Offenbach's *Les Contes d'Hoffmann*.

Ellen Orford. The schoolmistress (sop.) who befriends Peter in Britten's *Peter Grimes*.

Elliott, Victoria (b. Gateshead, 7 Mar. 1922). English soprano. Début C.R. 1944. W.N.O.C., 1947–51; S.W., 1951–63. (R)

Elmendorff, Karl (b. Düsseldorf, 25 Jan. 1891; d. Taunus, 21 Oct. 1962). German conductor. Studied Cologne Hochschule für Musik. Engagements Düsseldorf, Wiesbaden, Munich, Mannheim, and Berlin. Distinguished Wagnerian who conducted at Bayreuth 1927–42; also directed Wagner performances at the Florence Festival. (R)

Elmo, Cloe (b. Lecce, 9 Apr. 1910; d. Ankara, 24 May 1962). Italian mezzo. Début Cagliari 1934, Santuzza, and quickly reached the Scala where she sang regularly from 1936 to 1943, and after the Second World War. N.Y., Met., 1947–9. (R)

Elsa. A noblewoman (sop.) of Brabant, heroine of Wagner's *Lohengrin*.

Elvino. A well-to-do young Swiss farmer (ten.), hero of Bellini's *La Sonnambula*.

Elvira. (1) A lady (sop.), of Burgos, deserted by Don Giovanni in Mozart's opera. (2) The Bey's about-to-be-discarded wife (sop.) in Rossini's *L'Italiana in Algeri* (3) Daughter of Gualtiero Valton, heroine (sop.) of Bellini's *I Puritani* (4) A Spanish noblewoman (sop.), heroine of Verdi's *Ernani*.

Emperor Jones, The. Opera in 2 acts by Louis Gruenberg; text by Kathleen de Jaffa, after Eugene O'Neill's drama (1921). Prod. N.Y., Met., 7 Jan. 1933. Given in Europe, Amsterdam (1934) and Rome (1952).

Encore (Fr. = again). The word shouted by members of a British audience when they want an artist or artists to repeat a number. On the Continent, including France, the shout of 'Bis' (= a second time) is heard; this has become more common in British opera houses since the war. The demand for encores has caused many artistic crises, especially in Italian opera houses under Toscanini, who refused to grant audience and artists repetitions of favourite pieces.

Enfant et les Sortilèges, L' (The Child and the Enchantments). *Fantaisie lyrique* in two parts by Ravel; text by Colette. Prod. Monte Carlo 21 Mar. 1925; San Francisco 19 Sept. 1930; Oxford 3 Dec. 1958. Toys, books, and furniture rebel against a bad child who has ill-used them; fleeing to the garden he finds the trees and animals equally hostile. They relent when he bandages the paw of a baby squirrel hurt in the rumpus. The child runs back to the comforting figure of his mother.

English Opera Group, The. A company founded by Britten, John Piper, and Eric Crozier in 1946 after the first performance at Glyndebourne of Britten's *The Rape of Lucretia*, 'to be devoted to the creation and performance of new operas . . . and to encourage poets and playwrights to tackle the writing of librettos in collaboration with composers'. Since its foundation the Group has been responsible for the foundation and artistic direction of the Aldeburgh Festival (q.v.), the formation of the Opera Studio, subsequently the Opera School and then the National School of Opera, under Joan Cross and Anne Wood, and the commissioning and/or production of new works by Britten (*Albert Herring*, *Beggar's Opera*, *Turn of the Screw*, *Noyes Fludde*, the three Church Parables), Berkeley (*Ruth*, *A Dinner Engagement*, and *Castaway*), Birtwistle (*Punch and Judy*), Williamson (*English Eccentrics*), Walton (*The Bear*), and Crosse (*Purgatory*, *The Grace of Todd*), as well as the revival of works by Purcell, Bickerstaffe, and Holst. Besides performing in England the Group has visited Holland, France, Germany, Italy, Scandinavia, and Canada. The management and financial responsibility of the Group were assumed by Covent Garden in 1961. In 1964 the Group was the first British opera company to visit the U.S.S.R.

Enna, August (b. Nakskov, 13 May 1860; d. Copenhagen, 3 Aug. 1939). Danish composer, several of whose operas, notably those on Hans Andersen subjects, have won European as well as local success.

Enrico. Henry Ashton (bar.), brother of Lucy, in Donizetti's *Lucia di Lammermoor*.

Enschede. Town in Overijssel, Holland. The Forum Opera Company was founded in 1955 as a continuation of the earlier Utrecht Opera and the chamber group 'Camerata'. It aims at giving young graduates intermediate experience between studentship and a full professional career. It tours the province of Overijssel and N. and E. Holland, giving about 165 performances a year.

Ensemble (Fr. = together). As a noun, used in English as well as French and German either for a group of performers or for their musical unanimity.

Ente autonomo (It. = autonomous being). The name given to the independent, self-governing corporations which control leading Italian opera houses (e.g. Milan, Sc., and Naples, S.C.), as opposed to the commercial impresario who is given a concession to manage short seasons in smaller provincial theatres. The Ente Autonomo idea was formulated during Toscanini's 1922–9 régime at La Scala.

Entführung aus dem Serail, Die (The Escape from the Seraglio). Opera in 3 acts by Mozart; text by Gottlob Stephanie, altered from Christoph Friedrich Bretzner's libretto for André's *Belmont und Constanze* (1781), which was adapted from one of various English and Italian plays and comic operas on the subject. Prod. Vienna,

B., 16 July 1782 with Cavalieri, Adamberger, Fischer, cond. Mozart; London, C.G., 24 Nov. 1827; N.Y., Brooklyn Athenaeum, 16 Feb. 1860.

Act 1. Belmonte (ten.) arrives at the Pasha's palace in Turkey seeking Constanze (sop.), who has been captured with her English maid Blonde (sop.) and with his servant Pedrillo (ten.). Despite the suspicions of the Pasha's servant Osmin (bass), who is in love with Blonde, Pedrillo gains admittance to the service of the Pasha (speaking part), who has been rejected by Constanze.

Act 2. Blonde repels Osmin and, with the great aria 'Martern aller Arten', Constanze declares that not even torture will make her accept the Pasha. Pedrillo makes Osmin drunk in order to facilitate their escape.

Act 3. The fleeing lovers are caught, but the Pasha magnanimously pardons and frees them.

Entr'acte (Fr. = between acts). A piece of orchestral music played between the acts or scenes of an opera.

Enzo. A Genoese noble (ten.), La Gioconda's lover in Ponchielli's *La Gioconda*.

Épine, Margherita de l' (b. ?; d. London, 9 Aug. 1746). Italian soprano who appeared at D.L. between 1704 and 1718. Said to have been the first Italian to sing publicly in England. In 1710 sang in *Almahide*, the first opera to be sung wholly in Italian in England, and subsequently in Handel's *Rinaldo* and *Il Pastor Fido*. Married Pepusch in 1718.

Era la notte. Iago's (bar.) aria in Act 2 of Verdi's *Otello*, in which he pretends to substantiate his accusations against Desdemona by saying that he once heard Cassio talking in his sleep about Desdemona and their love for one another.

Erb, Karl (b. Ravensburg, 13 July 1877; d. Ravensburg, 13 July 1958). German tenor. Joined Stuttgart Opera chorus 1907, and five months after sang solo role. After engagements in Lübeck and Stuttgart, joined Munich Opera in 1913 remaining there until 1925, and creating title role in *Palestrina*, 1917. London, C.G., 1927, Belmonte. A fine Mozart singer. Husband of Maria Ivogün. (R)

Erda. The Earth Goddess (con.) and mother, by Wotan, of the Valkyries in Wagner's *Ring*.

Erede, Alberto (b. Genoa, 8 Nov. 1909). Italian conductor. Studied Genoa, Milan, and Basle; then with Weingartner 1929–31, and Busch at Dresden. Début Turin 1935 conducting the *Ring*. Brought by Busch to Glyndebourne, where he conducted several performances before the war. He returned to England in 1946 to become music director of the New London Opera Company (q.v.). From 1950 to 1955 at the N.Y. Met., and from 1956 at the Deutsche Oper am Rhein, where he was the music director 1958–62. A fine trainer of young singers and a great believer in team work and ensemble. (R)

Erevan. See *Yerevan*.

Erhardt, Otto (b. Breslau, 18 Nov. 1888; d. Buenos Aires, Feb. 1971). German producer. Studied Berlin and Munich, and philosophy at Oxford. Staged the first performance in Germany of Monteverdi's *Orfeo* at Breslau in 1913. Held important posts at Aachen, Düsseldorf, Stuttgart, and Dresden, where he produced the first performance of *Die aegyptische Helena*. After the advent of Hitler, worked in Vienna and Salzburg; was Beecham's chief producer at C.G., 1934–6. Was chief producer at the Colón, Buenos Aires, 1939–56, and has returned to work from time to time in Europe since the war.

Eri tu. Renato's (bar.) aria in Act 3, scene 1 of Verdi's *Un Ballo in Maschera*, resolving to punish not his supposedly disloyal wife but his friend and king, Riccardo.

Erkel, Ferenc (b. Gyula, 7 Nov. 1810; d. Budapest, 15 June 1893). Hungarian composer. His efforts to establish a national Hungarian opera, which began with the successful *Bátori Mária* (1840), were followed up by *Hunyadi László* (1844), whose enthusiastic reception paralleled that of

Verdi's operas of revolt, and for similar reasons. His *Bánk Bán* (1844–52, prod. 1861) became a national symbol, and is traditionally given on the national holiday. These operas use recitatives and set numbers; his later works parallel Mussorgsky in style.

Erlanger, Frederic d' (Baron). See *D'Erlanger.*

Ernani. Opera in 4 acts by Verdi; text by Piave after Hugo's drama *Hernani* (1830). Prod. Venice, F., 9 Mar. 1844 with Löwe, Guasco; London, H.M., 8 Mar. 1845; N.Y., Park T., 15 Apr. 1847.

Ernani (ten.), in reality Don Juan de Aragon, outlawed by the King of Castile, has been leading the life of a bandit. He is in love with Elvira (sop.) who is about to marry her elderly kinsman, Don Ruy Gomez de Silva (bass), a grandee of Spain. She is also loved by Don Carlo, King of Castile and later the Emperor Charles V (bar.). Silva conceals Ernani in his castle and refuses to hand him over to Carlo, who takes Elvira as a hostage. Ernani gives Silva a hunting-horn, promising that when Silva shall sound it he will take his own life. Then they join together to rescue Elvira. Carlo is elected Emperor, and having ordered the deaths of those plotting against him, pardons them when appealed to by Elvira. He further agrees to the marriage between Ernani and Elvira. As the couple prepare for their marriage, the sound of the hunting-horn is heard. Silva appears and demands that Ernani fulfil his word. Ernani takes a dagger and stabbing himself dies in Elvira's arms.

Also operas by Gabussi (1834), Mazzucato (1844), and Laudamo (1849).

Ernani, involami. Elvira's (sop.) aria in Act 1 of *Ernani* in which she sings of Ernani and hopes that he will flee with her.

Ernesto. Norina's lover (ten.) in Donizetti's *Don Pasquale.*

Ernster, Deszoe (b. Pécs, 23 Nov. 1898). Hungarian bass. Début Düsseldorf 1925; America with Salzburg Opera Guild 1937; interned in concentration camp during war, but returned to America in 1946 and became leading bass at N.Y., Met., in German repertory. Sang Hagen at C.G., 1949 and 1954, and Banquo and Alfonso at Glyndebourne in 1952. Deutsche Oper am Rhein since 1959. (R)

Ero the Joker (Yug., Ero sonoga suijeta). Opera in 3 acts by Gotovać; text by M. Begović. Prod. Zagreb 2 Nov. 1935; London, Stoll, 28 Jan. 1955. One of the most popular Yugoslav operas. Micha, on the advice of his mother, tests the love of his future wife Jula, by pretending that he is Ero from the world beyond.

Ershov, Ivan (b. nr. Novocherkassk, 8 Nov. 1867; d. Leningrad, 21 Nov. 1943). Russian tenor, notable above all for his Wagner interpretations at the Maryinsky Theatre from 1895. (R)

Erwartung (Expectation). *Mimodrama* in 1 act by Schoenberg; text by Marie Pappenheim. Comp. 1909, prod. Prague 6 June 1924; London, S.W. (New Opera Co.), 4 Apr. 1960; Washington, D.C., 28 Dec. 1960 with Helga Pilarczyk. Schoenberg's first opera. It has one character, a woman who searches for her lover in a dark wood; she stumbles upon his dead body, and sings over it of the other woman who stole him and of the night in which she is abandoned.

Escamillo. The toreador (bar.) in Bizet's *Carmen.*

È scherzo od è follia. Quintet sung by Edgardo, Ulrica, Riccardo, Samuele, and Tommaso in Act 1, scene 2 of Verdi's *Un Ballo in Maschera.*

Essen. Town in North Rhine–Westphalia, Germany. Opera is given in the Städtische Bühnen (cap. 800), built in 1892, and rebuilt after the war in 1950.

Estonia. Two of the earliest Estonian operas were Lemba's *Armastus ja Surm* (Love and Death) (Tallin 1931) and *Elga* (Tallin 1934).

Esty, Alice (b. Lowell, Mass., 1864; d. Farnham, 1 Feb. 1935). American, later naturalized British, soprano. Studied Boston with Clara Smart. Début Albert Hall, London, 1891 in

Patti concert. Opera début Belfast, Micaëla. Member of C.R. and Moody-Manners Companies. First English Mimì, 1897. Had repertory of more than 50 roles, including Eva, Marguerite, Santuzza. (R)

Esultate! Otello's (ten.) opening lines in the first act of Verdi's opera, announcing victory over the Turks. One of the most effective and vocally most difficult opening lines for any tenor.

Etcheverry, Bertrand (b. Bordeaux, 29 Mar. 1900; d. Paris, 14 Nov. 1960). French bass-bar. Studied Paris. Début Paris, O., 1932, Ceprano (*Rigoletto*); O.C. from 1937 where he was considered the best Golaud of his generation. Created roles in a number of contemporary works including Hahn's *Le Marchand de Venise*. His most popular roles, apart from Golaud, were Boris, Méphistophélès, and St. Bris. (R)

Étoile du Nord, L' (The Star of the North). Opera in 3 acts by Meyerbeer; text by Scribe. Prod. Paris, O.C., 16 Feb. 1854—100th perf. on 1st anniversary; London, D.L., 26 Feb. 1855; New Orleans, 5 Mar. 1855. Tsar Peter loves the village girl Katherine. She substitutes herself for her brother in the Russian Army, and informs the Tsar of a conspiracy. Discuised as a carpenter, the Tsar woos Katherine and makes her his Tsarina. Meyerbeer included six numbers from his *Ein Feldlager in Schlesien* (1844). Constant Lambert adapted some of the ballet music for the ballet *Les Patineurs*.

Eugene Onegin. Opera in 3 acts by Tchaikovsky; text by Shilovsky and the composer after Pushkin's poem (1831). Prod. Moscow, 29 Mar. 1879 (student performance); professional première, Bolshoy, 23 Apr. 1881; London, Olympic Theatre, 17 Oct. 1892, with Eugene Oudin and Fanny Moody; N.Y., Met., 24 Mar. 1920, with De Luca and Muzio.

The opera takes place in St. Petersburg in the early 19th century.

Act 1. Tatiana (sop.), the young and impressionable daughter of Madame Larina (mezzo), falls in love with the Byronic Onegin (bar.), a friend of her sister Olga's fiancé, Lensky. Tatiana stays up all night writing an impassioned letter to Onegin telling him of her feelings. The following day he meets her in the garden and, lecturing her on maidenly reticence, urges her to forget him.

Act 2. Tatiana's birthday is being celebrated by a ball. Some of the elderly women gossip about Tatiana and Onegin who have been dancing together. Onegin, annoyed, dances with Olga (mezzo), who had promised the dance to Lensky (ten.). The latter remonstrates with his fiancée, who is so piqued that she offers a further dance to Onegin. Monsieur Triquet (ten.), the French tutor, sings a little song in French in praise of Tatiana. When the dancing is resumed Lensky quarrels with Onegin and challenges him to a duel. Early next morning the two men meet beside an old mill near a stream. Lensky is killed.

Act 3. Six years have passed and Onegin, who has been abroad, returns to St. Petersburg. A ball is in progress at the palace of Prince Gremin (bass) who has married Tatiana. Onegin is one of the guests, and when he meets Tatiana again he realizes that he loves her. He writes asking her to see him again. She agrees and he comes to her boudoir. He tells her he loves her and urges her to flee with him. At first Tatiana wavers, and then responds ardently; but after a few moments she reminds Onegin of her duty to her husband and sends him away for ever.

Euridice. Orpheus's wife (sop.) in Gluck's *Orfeo ed Euridice*.

Euripides (b. Salamis, 480 B.C.; d. Pella, 406 B.C.). Greek dramatist. Fragments of some 55 plays are extant. Operas based on these, or on their treatment of a legend, are as follows. *Alkestis*: Gluck (1767), Boughton (1922), Wellesz (1924). *The Bacchae*: Wellesz (1931), Ghedini (1948). *Hecuba*: Malipiero (1941), Martinon (1951). *Hippolytus*: Rameau (1733), Drysdale (unprod.), Senilov (1915), Bell (unprod.). *Iphigenia in Aulis*: D. Scarlatti (1713), Gluck (1774).

Iphigenia in Tauris: Campra and Desmarets (1704), D. Scarlatti (1713), Gluck (1779). *Medea*: Cherubini (1797), Engel (1935). *Orestes*: Křenek (*Leben des Orest*, 1930). *The Trojan Women*: Cecil Gray (unprod.).

Euryanthe. Opera in 3 acts by Weber; text by Helmine von Chézy, after a 13th-century French romance. Prod. Vienna, Kä., 25 Oct. 1823; London, C.G., 29 June 1833, with Schröder-Devrient; ? N.Y., Wallack's, 1863 (or Met., 23 Dec. 1887 with Lilli Lehmann). The plot turns on the virtue of Euryanthe, wife of Adolar, which is questioned by Lysiart but eventually established. Attempts at revision, in the effort to salvage some magnificent music, have been made by Moser (*Die sieben Raben*, 1917, a new story), Lauckner (1922), Honolka (1955, Edinburgh 1958), and Franz Manton (Philopera Circle 1962).

Eva. Pogner's daughter (sop.), heroine of Wagner's *Die Meistersinger von Nürnberg*.

Evangelimann, Der (The Evangelist). Opera in 2 acts by Kienzl; text by composer, after L. F. Meissner's story (1894). Prod. Berlin, O., 4 May 1895 with Marie Goetz and Wilhelm Grüning; London, C.G., 2 July 1897; Chicago, Gt. Northern T., 3 Nov. 1923. Mathis loves Martha. His brother Johannes, who also loves her, burns a monastery and has Mathis imprisoned for ten years for the crime. Martha commits suicide. Mathis becomes an evangelist; he receives Johannes's deathbed confession and is reconciled to him. One of the most successful German operas between Wagner and Strauss, it had 5,300 performances in its first 40 years.

Evans, Geraint (b. Pontypridd, S. Wales, 16 Feb. 1922). Welsh baritone. Studied Hamburg with Theo Hermann and Geneva with Fernando Carpi. Début London, C.G., 1948, Nightwatchman (*Meistersinger*), since when he has established himself as one of the leading British baritones of the day, singing Figaro, Papageno, Beckmesser, &c. Sang regularly at Glyndebourne 1949–61, Guglielmo (*Così*), Masetto, Leporello, Abbate (*Arlecchino*), and Falstaff. San Francisco since 1959; Milan, Sc., 1960; Vienna 1961; Salzburg 1962. His voice is a warm lyric baritone of considerable range; his diction is admirable and his stage presence engaging. Among the roles he has created in London are Mr. Flint (*Billy Budd*), Mountjoy (*Gloriana*), and Antenor (*Troilus and Cressida*). Awarded C.B.E., 1959. (R)

Evans, Nancy (b. Liverpool, 19 Mar. 1915). English mezzo. Studied with John Tobin, Maggie Teyte, Eva de Reusz. Début London 1938, Sullivan's *Rose of Persia*. Sang small roles C.G. 1939; joined E.O.G. 1946, alternating with Ferrier as Lucretia, creating Nancy (*Albert Herring*), and singing Polly (*Beggar's Opera*), Dido, and Lucinda Woodcock (*Love in a Village*). Glyndebourne 1957–60. (R)

Evirato (Ital. = unmanned). See *Castrato*.

F

Fabbri, Guerrina (b. Ferrara, 1868; d. Turin, 21 Feb. 1946). Italian contralto. A coloratura of the Supervia type renowned for her *Cenerentola* and *L'Italiana in Algeri*. Début Viadana 1885, La Cieca; London, D.L., Amneris on opening night of Augustus Harris's famous 1887 season. Heard again in London 1891 as Orfeo, Fidalma, and Cenerentola. (R)

Faccio, Franco (b. Verona, 8 Mar. 1840; d. Monza, 21 July 1891). Italian conductor. Studied Milan Conservatory. Until the 1870's was primarily a composer and teacher. His *I Profughi Fiamminghi* was performed at La Scala in 1863, his *Amleto* (libretto by Boito) at Genoa 1865. Appointed conductor at La Scala 1871, where he directed the first performances of *Aida* and *Otello*, as well as the first Italian performance of a Wagner opera—*Lohengrin*. Conducted London première of *Otello*, 1889. The first great modern Italian opera conductor.

Fafner. With Fasolt, one of the two giants (bass) in Wagner's *Das Rheingold*. He has turned into a dragon in *Siegfried*.

Failoni, Sergei (b. Verona, 18 Dec. 1890; d. Sopron, 25 July 1948). Italian conductor. Studied Verona and Milan. Début Milan, 1921, conducting Rameau's *Platée*. Held appointments at various Italian theatres, including La Scala, 1932–4, and was a well-known figure at the Verona Arena; but his most important work was at the Budapest State Opera (q.v.), where he was music director from 1928 to 1947. (R)

Fair at Sorochinsk. See *Sorochinsky Fair*.

Fairy Queen, The. 'Opera' in a prologue and 5 acts by Purcell; text an anonymous adaptation (by Elkanah Settle?) of Shakespeare's comedy *A Midsummer Night's Dream* (1595–6). Prod. London, Dorset Gardens, Apr. 1692; next stage production, Cambridge, 10 Feb. 1920; San Francisco, 30 Apr. 1932. The score was lost by Oct. 1700, when an advertisement offered 20 gns. for its recovery; it was found in 1901 by J. S. Shedlock in the library of the R.A.M. The first work staged by the Covent Garden Opera, after its formation in 1946. Not really an opera, but a succession of masques.

Falcon, Marie Cornélie (b. Paris, 28 Jan. 1814; d. Paris, 25 Feb. 1897). French soprano. Studied Paris Conservatory with Bordogni and Nourrit. Début Paris, O., 1832, Alice (*Robert le Diable*). Her career lasted only until 1838, when she lost her voice and had to retire. Created Mme Ankerstroem (*Gustavus III*), Rachel (*La Juive*), Valentine (*Huguenots*), and was a famous Donna Anna and Giulia (*Vestale*). Her name became synonymous with the dramatic soprano roles in which she was unapproachable, and the term *falcon* still survives to describe this type of voice.

Falla, Manuel de (b. Cadiz, 23 Nov. 1876; d. Alta Gracia, Argentina, 14 Nov. 1946). Spanish composer. *La Vida Breve* is an early work (1905) with a weak plot; yet already Falla's authentic voice is to be heard behind the different manners he adopts. Despite unevenness it is a work of genuine and affecting beauty. *El Retablo de Maese Pedro* (1923) handles an incident in *Don Quixote*. The forces are miniature, and there is a disciplined refinement and intensity in Falla's mature style that is more essentially Spanish than the surface colour of the earlier work. His *Atlantida*, which was completed posthumously by Ernst Halffter, was first heard in concert version in Barcelona 24 Oct. 1961 and on the stage at La Scala, Milan, 14 June 1962.

Falstaff. Opera in 3 acts by Verdi; text by Boito after Shakespeare's comedy *The Merry Wives of Windsor* (1600–1) and *Henry IV* (Pt. 1, 1597; Pt. 2, 1598). Prod. Milan, Sc., 9 Feb. 1893 with Maurel in the title role; London, C.G., 19 May 1894, with Pessina; N.Y., Met., 4 Feb. 1895 with Maurel.

Act 1. In the Garter Inn, Falstaff (bar.) having failed to get Bardolph (ten.) or Pistol (bass) to deliver love letters to Mistresses Page and Ford, dispatches them by a page boy, and lectures his followers on the subject of honour.

In Ford's garden Alice Ford (sop.) and Meg Page (mezzo) compare the letters they have received and resolve to trick Falstaff. They send Mistress Quickly (mezzo) to arrange for Falstaff to visit Alice that afternoon. Meanwhile Bardolph and Pistol tell the jealous Ford (bar.) that Falstaff has designs on his wife. Ford's troubles are further increased by the fact that his daughter Anne (sop.) is in love with Fenton (ten.), of whom he disapproves, and that she refuses to contemplate marriage with Dr. Caius (ten.). Ford decides to visit Falstaff in disguise.

Act 2. Back at the Garter Inn, Mistress Quickly tells Falstaff that Alice is awaiting him that very day between the hours of two and three, when her husband will be out. Left alone, Falstaff sings of his certain success with Alice. A Master Brook is now announced; it is Ford in disguise. He tells Falstaff that he is deeply in love with Alice Ford, and asks for his help in winning her. Falstaff tells him it will be easy, and reveals that he is in ıact shortly to meet her. When Falstaff goes to change into his best clothes, Ford rails against all women in the 'Jealousy Monologue'.

In a room in Ford's house, Alice, Meg, Anne, and Mistress Quickly prepare for Falstaff's arrival. When he arrives he declares his love to Alice, recalling the days of his youth when he was a slim young page to the Duke of Norfolk. Meg rushes in with the news of Ford's sudden return home, and Falstaff hides behind a screen. When Ford really does arrive with his companions, suspecting that Alice is entertaining a lover, Falstaff is bundled into a laundry basket. A wild search of the house ensues. Taking advantage of the chaos, Anne and Fenton hide together behind the screen, only to be discovered by Ford. The laundry basket is carried out of the room and its contents pitched into the river; Ford now joins in the general merriment at Falstaff's expense.

Act 3. Falstaff, miserably seated outside the Garter Inn, consoles himself with wine and soliloquizes on the cruelties of the world. Mistress Quickly arrives with another invitation for him to meet Alice, this time in Windsor Great Park at midnight, where he must come disguised as Herne the Hunter. As Quickly leaves, she overhears Ford and Caius plotting to announce the latter's marriage to Anne that very night.

It is shortly before midnight in Windsor Park. Fenton, disguised as Oberon, sings of his love for Anne. Falstaff enters; Alice joins him. They are interrupted by noises, and Falstaff hides. Anne, dressed as Titania, summons the 'fairies' and the rest of her followers who discover Falstaff and torment him. When the fun is at its height he recognizes Bardolph. Ford then leads forward Dr. Caius and a figure whom he thinks is Anne, while Alice presents another masked couple, so that a double betrothal can be celebrated. Caius and Ford find they have been tricked, for the supposed Anne is Bardolph in disguise. Ford then agrees to the marriage of Anne and Fenton, and Falstaff leads the company in the final fugue, 'Tutto nel mondo è burla'—'All the world 's a stage'.

Also operas by Dittersdorf (1796), Salieri (1798), Balfe (1838), Nicolai (1849), and Adam (1856).

Fancelli, Giuseppe (b. Florence, 24 Nov. 1837; d. Florence, 23 Dec. 1887). Italian tenor. Début Milan, Sc., 1866; London, C.G., same year as Alfredo. First Scala Radamès 1872. He possessed a vibrant and telling voice and, according to Klein, held a high C with an ease never surpassed by Tamagno or Caruso. But he could not read a note of music, and his dramatic gifts were very limited.

Fanciulla del West, La (The Girl of the Golden West). Opera in 3 acts by Puccini; text by Civinini and Zangarini, after Belasco's drama *The Girl of the Golden West* (1905). Prod. N.Y., Met., 10 Dec. 1910, with Destinn, Caruso, Amato, cond. Toscanini; London, C.G., 29 May 1911, with Destinn, Bassi, Ghilly, cond. Campanini; Rome, C., 12 June 1911.

The opera, set in California in the days of the Gold Rush, tells of the love of Minnie (sop.), owner of the Polka saloon, for Dick Johnson (ten.), who in reality is Ramerrez, a notorious bandit. The Sheriff, Jack Rance (bar.), is also in love with Minnie, and when he reveals to her that Johnson is a bandit, she sends the latter away. But when he is wounded, Minnie, who has relented, hides him in the loft of her cabin. Drops of blood from the ceiling reveal to Rance that Johnson is there. Rance and Minnie play poker: if she should win Rance must let Johnson go free; if she loses, she will marry Rance. By cheating she wins the game. But Johnson is captured and is condemned to be hanged. Minnie rides up on horseback and successfully pleads for Johnson's life. Together they set off to start a new life.

Fanget an! Walther's (ten.) trial song in Act 1 of Wagner's *Die Meistersinger*.

Faninal. A wealthy, newly ennobled merchant (bar.), Sophie's father, in Strauss's *Der Rosenkavalier*.

Farewell. The name commonly given to the last performance in public of a favourite artist. Some singers, especially sopranos, announced their farewell seasons years before they took their actual leave of the stage—Grisi is a notable example. Melba's Farewell, including her speech, at Covent Garden in 1926 was recorded by H.M.V. German provincial houses give 'Abschied' performances for a favourite singer when he or she leaves to take up an engagement in another theatre.

Farinelli (orig. Carlo Broschi) (b. Andria, 24 Jan. 1705; d. Bologna, 15 July 1782). Italian male soprano. Studied with Porpora; début 1722 in his teacher's *Eumene*. In 1727 he was defeated in a public exhibition of vocal skill by Bernacchi, who then consented to teach him further. He sang in Vienna and London, where he became a great favourite, women fainting from excitement at his performances. Became the star performer in Porpora's rival company to Handel's at Lincoln's Inn Fields. Sang in Madrid in 1737; his voice so cheered the melancholia of Philip V that he was offered 50,000 francs a year to remain in Madrid. This he did for 25 years, singing him the same four songs every night. He persuaded Philip's successor, Ferdinand VI, to establish an Italian opera in Madrid, and in 1750 received the Cross of Calatrava. On Charles III's accession he had to leave Spain for political reasons. When he was visited by Burney in Bologna in 1771 he no longer sang, but played the harpsichord and viola d'amore; he had a fine collection of pictures by Murillo and Ximenes.

Farrar, Geraldine (b. Melrose, Mass., 28 Feb. 1882; d. Ridgefield, 11 Mar. 1967). American soprano. At the age of ten appeared in a pageant, as Jenny Lind, when her voice attracted attention. Studied in Boston, N.Y., and Paris, then (on Nordica's advice) in Berlin with Graziani. Début there, Hofoper, 1901, Marguerite. Heard by Lilli Lehmann, whose pupil she then became. N.Y. début 1906, Juliette; remained a member of the Met. until her retirement in 1922, singing nearly 500 times in 29 roles. Created Amica (Mascagni) (Monte Carlo, 1905), the Goosegirl in *Königskinder* (1910), and Suor Angelica (1918). An outstanding Butterfly, Manon, and Zazà. She enjoyed great popularity, especially among young feminine opera-goers, who were nicknamed 'Gerry-flappers'. She made more than a dozen films, and in 1938 published her autobiography, *Such Sweet Compulsion*. (R)

Fasolt. With Fafner, one of the giants (bass), in Wagner's *Das Rheingold*.

Fassbänder, Zdenka (b. Tetschen, 12 Nov. 1880; d. Munich, 14 Mar. 1954). Bohemian soprano. Studied Prague with Sophie Loewe-Destinn; début

Karlsruhe 1899. Leading dramatic soprano Munich 1906–19; specially noted for her Strauss and Wagner. Sang Elektra and Isolde in London under Beecham, 1910 and 1913. Married Felix Mottl (q.v.).

Fauré, Gabriel (b. Pamiers, 12 May 1845; d. Paris, 4 Nov. 1924). French composer. *Prométhée* (1900) shows the influence of Wagner, though the treatment is essentially classical, portraying and suggesting, rather than conveying, emotion. Wagner's shadow still falls across *Pénélope* (1913), together with the heavier one of romantic convention—an opening spinning chorus, a final 'Gloire à Zeus'. But it is in this work that Fauré comes closest to exemplifying the true connexion between the French and the Greek genius—a spare, brilliant quality of thought rather than the Hellenistic languor on which the comparison generally rests.

Faure, Jean-Baptiste (b. Moulins, 15 Jan. 1830; d. Paris, 9 Nov. 1914). French baritone. Studied Paris Conservatoire. Début Paris, O.C., 1852 in *Galathée* (Massé). He went to the Opéra in 1861 where he remained leading baritone for 17 years, creating Nelusko (*L'Africaine*), Posa (*Don Carlos*), Hamlet, &c. Début C.G. 1860, Hoël (*Dinorah*), and sang there and at D.L. and H.M.'s frequently until 1877. Was an admired Don Giovanni and William Tell. From 1857 to 1860 taught singing at the Conservatoire. He wrote two books on singing, and was the subject of two portraits by Manet.

Faust. A wandering conjuror who lived in Germany about 1488–1541. The legend that he had sold his soul to the Devil in exchange for a fixed period of renewed youth inspired various writers, above all Goethe (q.v.), whose dramatic poem is the source for most operas on the subject. The best-known Faust operas not based on Goethe are by Spohr (1816) and Busoni (*Doktor Faust*, 1925).

Faust. Opera in 5 acts by Gounod; text by Barbier and Carré, after Goethe's poem (pt. 1, 1808; pt. 2, 1832). Prod. Paris, Th.L., 19 Mar. 1859—500 perfs. by 1887, 1,000 by 1894, 2,000 by 1934; London, H.M.'s, 11 June 1863 with Tietjens, Trebelli, Giuglini, Santley, Gassier—and in every C.G. season 1863–1911; Philadelphia, 18 Nov. 1863; inaugural opera at Met. 22 Oct. 1883 with Nilsson, Scalchi, Campanini, Del Puente, Novara. One of the most successful operas ever written, with translations in at least 25 languages.

Act 1. Faust (ten.) makes his bargain with Méphistophélès (bass), encouraged by a vision of Marguerite (sop.).

Act 2. Valentin (bar.), Marguerite's brother, enters a fair and encourages her lover Siebel (sop.) to protect her in his impending absence in the wars. Méphistophélès appears, and delights the crowd with a song and with magically causing wine to flow from the inn sign, then declaring that flowers touched by Siebel will wither. Valentin attacks him, but the sword breaks. Recognizing the Devil, all chase him off by reversing their swords to form crosses. Faust is gently rebuffed on approaching Marguerite as she leaves church.

Act 3. Siebel gathers flowers for Marguerite in her garden, but they wither; on dipping his hand in holy water all is well. Faust appears and apostrophizes her dwelling. Having sung an old ballad to herself at her spinning-wheel, Marguerite is tempted by a jewel-casket left by Méphistophélès, who now distracts her neighbour Martha's attention so as to leave Faust free with Marguerite.

Act 4. Scene 1, often omitted, shows Marguerite bemoaning her betrayal and desertion by Faust, uncomforted by Siebel. Scene 2 shows her at prayer in the cathedral, mocked by Méphistophélès. In scene 3 (originally scene 2) soldiers return singing of victory, Valentin among them; uneasy at Siebel's evasiveness, he rushes to Marguerite's cottage. Méphistophélès sings a mocking serenade, and in a duel fatally wounds Valentin, who dies cursing his sister.

Act 5. Scene 1, in the Hartz Mountains, is often omitted. Watching the Walpurgis Night, Faust is disturbed by a vision of Marguerite struck with an axe, and demands to be taken back to her. Scene 2 shows Marguerite in prison awaiting execution for the murder of her child. Faust appears calling her, and Méphistophélès cannot persuade them to flee. Marguerite's prayer for redemption is answered by angels, but Faust is dragged off by Méphistophélès.

Favart, Charles-Simon (b. Paris, 13 Nov. 1710; d. Belleville, 12 Mar. 1792). French librettist and impresario. Stage manager at O.C., then summoned to Brussels by Maurice de Saxe to organize a theatre for the troops in Flanders. Succeeded Monnet as director of the Opéra-Comique (q.v.) 1758, and held position until he retired in 1769. Provided more than 150 libretti for different composers, including Grétry, Philidor, and Gluck. The Opéra-Comique is called the Salle Favart after him.

Favart (orig. Duronceray), **Marie** (b. Avignon, 15 June 1727; d. Paris, 21 Apr. 1772). French soprano, wife of above. One of the favourite artists of the Comédie Italienne.

Favero, Mafalda (b. Ferrara, 6 Jan. 1905). Italian soprano. Studied Bologna with Alessandro Vezzani. Début Parma 1927, Lìu. Engaged by Toscanini for La Scala 1929, and sang there regularly until 1942 and again 1945–50, creating Gasparina (*Il Campiello*) and *La Dama Boba*. London, C.G., 1937 and 1939; San Francisco, N.Y., Met., 1938. A fine Mimì, Manon, Thaïs, Adriana Lecouvreur, and Zazà. (R)

Favola d'Orfeo, La (The Legend of Orpheus). *Favola in musica* in a prologue and 5 acts by Monteverdi; text by Alessandro Striggio. Prod. (privately) Mantua, Accademia degl' Invaghiti, Feb. 1607, and on 24 Feb. same year at the Court Theatre there with Giovanni Gualberto as Orfeo. Revived Paris 1904, concert version (arr. D'Indy), and first modern stage performance there Théâtre Réjane, 1911. N.Y., Met. (concert perf.), 14 Apr. 1912 with Fornia, Weil, and Witherspoon; first American stage performance Smith College, Northampton (in Malipiero's version), 14 May 1929 with Kullman. First English performance (D'Indy's version) London, Institut Français, 1924 (concert); stage, Oxford, 7 Dec. 1925, the University Opera Club's first production.

Favola per musica, or **Favola in musica.** (It. = fable for music.) A 17th-century term for an opera libretto of legendary or mythological nature.

Favorite, La (The Favourite). Opera in 4 acts by Donizetti; text by Royer, Vaëz, and Scribe. Prod. Paris, O., 2 Dec. 1840 with Rosine Stoltz and Duprez; New Orleans 9 Feb. 1843; London, D.L., 18 Oct. 1843. Originally planned to be called *L'Ange de Nisida*, and has variously been played as *Dalila*, *Leonora di Guzman*, and *Riccardo e Matilda*. The action takes place in Spain in 1340 and tells of the unhappy love of Fernando, a novice in the Monastery of St. James, for Leonora de Guzman, mistress of Alfonso XI, King of Castile.

Fear, Arthur (b. Blaina, 1902). Welsh baritone. Studied R.A.M. with Thomas Neux. Début B.N.O.C. 1927 as Sachs, but had previously been heard in student performances in same role and as Falstaff. Created Holofernes in Goossens's *Judith*, C.G., 1929, where he sang regularly until 1939. Sang Sachs in the first complete *Meistersinger* in English in America at Cincinnati. (R)

Federici, Vincenzo (b. Pesaro, 1764; d. Milan, 26 Sept. 1826). Italian composer. First opera, *L'Olimpiade*, Turin 1789; cond. Bianchi's *La Villanella Rapita*, London 1790, followed by his own *L'Usurpatore Innocente*. Connected with King's T. for ten years. Returned to Italy in 1802 and settled in Milan, where he wrote more operas for La Scala and taught at the Conservatory.

Fedora. Opera in 3 acts by Giordano; text by Colautti after Sardou's drama (1882). Prod. Milan, T.L., 17 Nov. 1898 with Bellincioni, Caruso; London, C.G., 5 Nov. 1906 with Giachetti and Zenatello; N.Y., Met., 5 Dec. 1906 with Cavalieri and Caruso. The story of the tragic love of Count Loris Ipanov, a Russian nihilist, for the Princess Fedora Romanov.

Fedra. Opera in 3 acts by Pizzetti; text by D'Annunzio. Prod. Milan, Sc., 20 Mar. 1915. Also title of one-act opera by Romano Romani, text by Alfredo Lenzoni: prod. Rome 3 Apr. 1915, with Raisa; London, C.G., 18 June 1931, with Ponselle.

Feen, Die (The Fairies). Opera in 3 acts by Wagner; text by composer after Gozzi's comedy *La Donna Serpente* (1762), first used in Himmel's *Die Sylphen* (1806), the first German Gozzi setting. Prod. Munich 29 June 1888. Wagner's first completed opera, written in 1833–4. Casella used the same text for his *La Donna Serpente* (1932).

Feinhals, Fritz (b. Cologne, 14 Dec. 1869; d. Munich, 30 Aug. 1940). German baritone. Studied Milan with Giovanini and Selva. Début Essen 1895, Silvio. Leading baritone Munich Opera 1898–1927; London, C.G., 1898 and 1907; N.Y., Met., 1908. A famous Sachs, Wotan, Telramund, Amfortas, and Kurwenal; but also heard often in Mozart and Verdi. (R)

Felsenstein, Walter (b. Vienna, 30 May 1901). Austrian producer. Studied Graz and Vienna. Originally an actor in Lübeck, Mannheim, &c. Subsequently opera producer in Cologne, Frankfurt, Munich, and Zürich. Producer and intendant of Berlin Komische Oper since 1947, where his productions of *The Cunning Little Vixen*, *Figaro*, *Contes d'Hoffmann*, *Zauberflöte*, *Carmen*, and *Otello* have won international acclaim.

Fenice, Teatro La. See *Venice*.

Fenton. Anne's (Nannetta's) lover (ten.) in Nicolai's *Die lustigen Weiber von Windsor* and Verdi's *Falstaff*.

Fenton (orig. Beswick), **Lavinia** (b. London, 1708; d. Greenwich, 24 Jan. 1760). English soprano. Originally an actress, she sang Polly Peachum at the first performance of *The Beggar's Opera* (1728). After singing the role more than 60 times she left the stage and became the mistress of the Duke of Bolton, whom she married in 1751.

Feo, Francesco (b. prob. Naples, 1691; d. Naples, 28 Jan. 1761). Italian composer of a large number of operas that were popular and respected in their day but have failed to keep a place in the repertory.

Fermata (It. = stop, pause). The term used for a pause on a held note or chord; the Italians use the word *corona*.

Fernand Cortez, ou La Conquête du Mexique. Opera in 3 acts by Spontini; text by Esmenard and De Jouy, after Alexis Piron's tragedy (1744). Prod. Paris, O., 28 Nov. 1809—about 250 perfs. by 1840; N.Y., Met., 6 Jan. 1888; never in London, chiefly through prod. of Bishop's unsuccessful opera on same subject, text by Planché (C.G. 1823). Revived Naples, S.C., 1951, with Tebaldi.

Ferne Klang, Der (The Distant Sound). Opera in 3 acts by Schreker; text by composer. Prod. Frankfurt 18 Aug. 1912; B.B.C. broadcast 3 Feb. 1957. Schreker's first opera.

Ferrando. An officer (ten.), Dorabella's lover, in Mozart's *Così fan tutte*.

Ferrani (orig. Zanazzio), **Cesira** (b. Turin, 8 May 1863; d. nr. Biella, 4 May 1943). Italian soprano. Studied with Antonietta Fricci. Début Turin 1887, Micaëla. Created Manon Lescaut (1893), Mimì (1896). Celebrated for her interpretations of Eva and Elsa, and chosen by Toscanini to create Mélisande in Italy (La Scala 1908). In Rome in 1909 *Pelléas* was hissed off the stage and Ferrani retired to Turin, where she founded a salon which became the centre of intellectual life there for many years. (R)

Ferrier, Kathleen (b. Higher Walton, 22 Apr. 1912; d. London, 8 Oct. 1953). English contralto. Studied with J. E. Hutchinson and Roy Henderson. Was established as a concert singer before her opera début in 1946 in Britten's *The Rape of Lucretia* in its world première at Glyndebourne. Sang Orfeo at Glyndebourne, 1947, and in Holland and at C.G. under Barbirolli in 1953. Her beautiful voice, warm stage presence, and deep sincerity made her one of the best-loved singers of her day. (R)

Fervaal. *Action dramatique* in a prologue and 3 acts by D'Indy; text by composer. Prod. Brussels, M., 12 Mar. 1897.

Festa teatrale (It. = theatrical festival). An 18th-century term for an opera, usually on a mythological or allegorical subject and spectacular in nature, e.g. Mozart's *Ascanio in Alba*, celebrating a festive occasion, e.g. a royal birthday or a great victory.

Festivals. The term derives from the Latin *festivitas* (= merriment), and was used at the time of the Renaissance to describe the celebrations with music that took place in the royal courts to mark special occasions, as, for example, the meeting at Bologna in 1515 between Francis I and Pope Leo X. In more modern times the word came to be applied to a grand musical occasion, in the first place dedicated to one composer, as, for example, the Handel Festival in England in 1862, the Haydn Festivals in Austria in 1808–11, and the Beethoven celebrations in Germany in 1845.

Summer festivals are very much a product of the post-1945 period, and are often highly commercialized affairs, arranged to attract the tourist from abroad. There are of course honourable exceptions to this, especially the now annual Bayreuth Festival (July–Aug.) which is the oldest of the European opera festivals, having started in 1876. Wiesbaden (May) began in 1900. The Munich Opera Festival (mid-Aug.–early Sept.) was begun in 1901; Salzburg (July–Aug.) was established in 1920; Zürich (June) in 1932; Florence (May–June) in 1933; Glyndebourne (May–Aug.) in 1934; Edinburgh (Aug.–Sept.) in 1947; Aldeburgh (June) in 1948; Aix-en-Provence (July) in 1948; Holland (June–July) in 1949; Spoleto (June–July) in 1958. (See also separate entries for above-named places.)

Fête Galante. *Dance-Dream* in 1 act by Ethel Smyth; text by Edward Shanks after Maurice Baring's story. Prod. Birmingham 4 June 1923.

Feuersnot (Fire-famine). *Singgedicht* in 1 act by Strauss; text by Ernst von Wolzogen after a Flemish legend, *The Quenched Fires of Audenarde*. Prod. Dresden 21 Nov. 1901, with Annie Krull, Scheidemantel, cond. Schuch; London, H.M.'s, 9 July 1910, with Maud Fay, cond. Beecham; Philadelphia 1 Dec. 1927. Kunrad is so enranged at his public humiliation by Diemut that he conjures the extinction of all fire; this is restored at the moment of his acceptance by the repentant Diemut. The opera pokes fun at the Munichers who rejected Richard I (Wagner), and then his disciple, Richard Strauss.

Fiamma, La (The Flame). Opera in 3 acts by Respighi; text by Guastalla. Prod. Rome, T.R., 23 Jan. 1934, with Cobelli, cond. Marinuzzi; Chicago Opera 2 Dec. 1935 with Raisa. A story of witchcraft in 7th-century Ravenna.

Fibich, Zdeněk (b. Šeboriče, 21 Dec. 1850; d. Prague, 15 Oct. 1900). Czech composer. It is for his seven operas that Fibich is chiefly remembered. *Bukovín* (1874) and *Blaník* (1881) are both early and uneven, but with *The Bride of Messina* (1884) Fibich's skill and imagination as an opera composer became fully apparent. *The Tempest* (1895) is said to be effective. Fibich's last three operas were written with Anežka Schulzová, the poetess for whom he abandoned his family. *Hedy* (1896) contains fine music, but his masterpiece is *Šárka* (1897), a powerful and musically gripping treatment of the popular Czech legend. *The Fall of Arkun* (1900) turns away from popular taste. Though less melodically gifted than either Smetana or Dvořák, Fibich had a considerable ability to think symphonically.

Fidelio, oder Die eheliche Liebe. Opera in 3 acts by Beethoven; text by Josef Sonnleithner, a German version of Bouilly's *Léonore, ou L'Amour Conjugal*, music by Gaveaux (1798) and then set, in an Italian version, by Paer (1804) and by Mayr (1805). Altered and reduced to two acts by Stefan von Breuning in 1806; given final form by

Georg Friedrich Treitschke in 1814. First version prod. Vienna, W., 20 Nov. 1805 with Anna Mildner; 2nd version, W., 29 March. 1806; 3rd version, Kä., 23 May 1814. London, H.M.'s, 18 May 1832 with Schroeder-Devrient; N.Y., Park, 9 Sept. 1839.

Act 1 (divided into 2 scenes by Mahler). Scene 1. Florestan (ten.), a Spanish nobleman, has been thrown into prison, whither his wife Leonore (sop.) has followed him disguised as a boy, Fidelio, in the hope of rescue. The kindly jailer Rocco (bass) employs 'Fidelio', with whom his daughter Marzelline (sop.) falls in love, to the annoyance of her lover Jacquino (ten.). The famous quartet expresses their reactions. Scene 2. The tyrannical governor Pizarro (bass-bar.) decides to kill Florestan to prevent his discovery at an impending inspection. Leonore persuades Rocco to allow the prisoners out for a moment; they emerge groping towards the sunlight. But Florestan is not among them.

Act 2. Scene 1. Florestan is chained in his dungeon, whither Rocco comes with Leonore to dig the prisoner's grave. Pizarro tries to kill Florestan, but is prevented by Leonore with a pistol. Far-off trumpets announce the arrival of the inspecting minister. Scene 2. The prisoners are all released; Pizarro is arrested, and Leonore herself unshackles Florestan.

The overture now played is entitled *Fidelio*; three other *Leonore* overtures exist, the third of which is often played before the final scene—but mistakenly, since it summarizes the opera.

Fidès. John of Leyden's mother (mezzo) in Meyerbeer's *Le Prophète*.

Fiery Angel, The. Opera in 5 acts by Prokofiev; text after Valery Bryusov's story (1908). Paris (concert 25 Nov. 1954, with Lucienne Marée, Xavier Depraz, cond. Charles Bruck; Venice, La F., 29 Sept. 1955, with Dorothy Dow Rolando Panerai, cond. Nino Sanzogno; London, S.W., 27 Jul. 1965, with Marie Collier; N.Y., C.C., 22 Sept. 1965.

Act 1. At an inn, Rupprecht (bass) meets Renata (sop.) in a state of possession in which she mistakes him for Heinrich, a former lover whom she associated with her guardian angel. He agrees to take her to Cologne to look for Heinrich (bar.), having fallen in love with her himself.

Act 2. In the first scene the couple try by magic to find Heinrich; in the second Rupprecht is equally disappointed by a visit to the magus Agrippa of Nettesheim.

Act 3. Renata has met and been repulsed by Heinrich; she urges Rupprecht to fight him. Rupprecht loses, but wins Renata.

Act 4. Renata threatens to leave Rupprecht, whose obsessive physical passion for her contrasts with memories of her 'guardian angel'. In a garden by the Rhine, Renata hurls a knife at Rupprecht, accusing him of being possessed by the Devil, as Faust and Mephistopheles enter. Rupprecht watches Mephistopheles angrily devour a slow-moving serving-boy and then resurrect him from a nearby rubbish dump. He joins the party.

Act 5. Rupprecht is in the suite of the Inquisitor who is investigating a story of diabolical possession in a convent. The source of the trouble is a new nun—Renata. Signs of possession appear; as the exorcism rite begins, hysteria seizes the community and the opera ends with the Inquisitor sentencing Renata to be burnt alive for having dealings with evil spirits.

Fiesco. Genoese nobleman (bass) in Verdi's *Simone Boccanegra*.

Figaro. The Barber of Seville (bar.) in Rossini's opera of that name, subsequently Count Almaviva's valet (bar.) in Mozart's *Le Nozze di Figaro*.

Figlia del Reggimento, La. See *Fille du Régiment, La*.

Figlia di Jorio, La (The Daughter of Jorio). Opera in 3 acts by Pizzetti; text, word-for-word setting of D'Annunzio's tragedy (1903). Prod. Naples, S.C., 4 Dec. 1954 with Petrella, Nicolai, Picchi, Guelfi, cond. Gavazzeni. One of Pizzetti's most successful operas.

Figner, Nikolay Nikolayevich. See *Mei-Figner*.

Filar il tuono (or **Filar la voce,** or

un filo di voce) and **Filer la voix** (or **Filer le son**) (Ital. and Fr. = to spin the voice, or tone). The instruction to hold a long, soft note without crescendo or diminuendo, e.g. Violetta's final A in 'Addio del passato'.

Filippeschi, Mario (b. Pisa, 7 June 1907). Italian tenor. Début Colorno 1937. After several seasons in the Italian provinces in lyric roles, began to assume heavier parts, and has sung all over Europe and South America as Arnold (*Guillaume Tell*), Arturo (*Puritani*), Pollione (*Norma*), Manrico and Radamès, in which roles he is looked on as the successor to Lauri-Volpi. Has also made several films. (R)

Fille de Madame Angot, La (Madame Angot's daughter). Operetta in 3 acts by Lecocq; text by Clairville, Siraudin, and Koning, after A. F. Eve Maillot's *vaudeville, Madame Angot ou La Poissarde Parvenue*, 1796. Prod. Brussels, Alcazar, 4 Dec. 1872; London, St. J.'s, 17 May 1873; N.Y. 25 Aug. 1873. Lecocq's most popular work, and one of the most successful post-Offenbach operettas.

Fille du Régiment, La (The Daughter of the Regiment). Opera in 2 acts by Donizetti; text by Vernoy de Saint-Georges and Bayard. Prod. Paris, O.C., 11 Feb. 1840 with Anna Thillon; New Orleans, 2 Mar. 1843; London, H.M.'s, 27 May 1847 with Jenny Lind. Marie, brought up in a regiment by the kindly Sulpice, loves Tonio, but when it is announced that she is a Countess's niece she has to leave. The Countess teaches Marie noble ways; French soldiers, Tonio among them, storm the castle, and Marie succeeds, with the soldiers' help, in getting her way and returning to Tonio.

This was Donizetti's first French opera, and one of his most successful works.

Film opera. Great difficulty has been experienced in overcoming the essential contradiction of media; namely, that opera requires the remoteness and formalization of the stage, with voice and personality projected to meet the audience, while the cinema destroys the barrier of the footlights and needs to vary its distances, from vast panorama to intimate close-up. Some operas have been shot as if on the stage, e.g. the Italian *Barber of Seville*; this merely stresses at second hand the artificiality that in the theatre is acceptable. Some have attempted to compromise by using the cinema's greater mobility of viewpoint without taking the action beyond the natural limits of the stage, e.g. Paul Czinner's *Don Giovanni* and *Der Rosenkavalier*. Some have removed from the theatre altogether, and made free use of distant landscape shots, panning shots, and close-ups, e.g. Stroyeva's Bolshoy *Boris Godunov*—one of the most successful film operas to date. The voices are usually added after the action has been photographed: this helps to overcome the disadvantage that a singer rarely looks attractive in close-up.

Filosofo di Campagna, Il (The Country Philosopher). Opera in 3 acts by Galuppi; text by Goldoni. Prod. Venice, S. Sam., 26 Oct. 1754; London 6 Jan. 1761; Boston, 26 Feb. 1960. Galuppi's most famous work, and the most successful comic opera of its day. Successfully revived by the Piccola Scala in recent years.

Finale. The last movement of a work. It was important in the days of aria and recitative as a strong climax to an act; from its start, the music became continuous, with arias, ensembles, and recitatives included in one design. The greatest examples are the finales to Acts 2 and 4 of Mozart's *Figaro*. With Wagner, it disappeared as no longer necessary, though Sullivan (among others) retained it, with distinction in Act 1 of *The Gondoliers*.

Finch' han del vino. Don Giovanni's aria in Act 1 of Mozart's *Don Giovanni*, in which he bids Leporello prepare for the party. (Sometimes called the 'Champagne Aria'.)

Finland. See *Helsinki*.

Finta Giardiniera, La (lit., The Feigned Gardener's Girl). Opera in 3 acts by Mozart; text by Calzabigi for Anfossi's opera (1774), altered by Coltellini. Prod. Munich 13 Jan. 1775; N.Y., Mayfair, 18 Jan. 1927; London,

Scala, 7 Jan. 1930. Other operas on the subject are by Piccinni (1770) and Anfossi (1774).

Finta Semplice, La (lit., The Feigned Simpleton). Opera in 3 acts by Mozart; text by Coltellini, after a libretto by Goldini first set by Perillo (1764). Prod. Salzburg 1 May 1769; London, Palace T., 12 Mar. 1956 in Paumgartner's version; Boston, 27 Jan. 1961.

Finto Stanislao, Il (The False Stanislaus). Opera in 2 acts by Gyrowetz; text by Romani. Prod. Milan, Sc., 5 Aug. 1818. Text set by Verdi in 1840 for his comic opera *Un Giorno di Regno* (q.v.).

Fioravanti, Valentino (b. Rome, 11 Sept. 1764; d. Capua, 16 June 1837). Italian composer. He wrote over 75 operas, though the last was called *Ogni eccesso è vizioso*. Fresh and easily written, they were popular in their day, but only *Le Cantatrici Villane* has stood the test of time. His son **Vincenzo** (b. Rome, 5 Apr. 1799; d. Naples, 28 Mar. 1877) had great popular success in Naples, but few of his operas found their way north. *Il Ritorno di Pulcinella dagli Studi di Padova* (1837) had a wider success, thanks to the adaptation by the singer Carlo Cambaggio, even finding its way to London and America.

Fiordiligi. Dorabella's sister (sop.) in Mozart's *Così fan tutte*.

Fioritura (It. = flowering). An ornamental figure, written or improvised, decorating the main line of the melody. Also known, less correctly, as coloratura.

Firenze. See *Florence*.

Fischer, Anton (b. Ried (bapt. 13) Jan. 1778; d. Vienna, 1 Dec. 1808). From 1800 he worked at the Theater auf der Wieden, where a number of his *Singspiele* were fairly successful.

Fischer, Emil (b. Brunswick, 13 June 1838; d. Hamburg, 11 Aug. 1914). German bass-baritone. Studied with his parents, both of whom were opera singers. Début Graz 1857 in title role of *Jean de Paris* (Boïeldieu). Engaged Pressburg, Stettin, Brunswick, Danzig, and Dresden. C.G. 1884 as Sachs. Broke his contract with Dresden the following year to join the Met. where he remained until 1891. The first American Sachs, Steffano (*Rienzi*), King Mark, Wotan (*Rheingold*), Wanderer, Lysiart, Hagen. He settled in New York and became a teacher, but sang some performances with the Damrosch Company in 1895 and 1897. In Mar. 1907 a Testimonial Performance which realized $10,000 was given in his honour at the Met., in which he sang Sachs in Act 3, scene 1, of *Meistersinger*.

Fischer, Ludwig (b. Mainz, 18 Aug. 1745; d. Berlin, 10 July 1825). German bass. Contemporary and great friend of Mozart. The original Osmin; sang with success in Munich, Vienna, Berlin, and Paris. Possessed a compass of two-and-a-half octaves, and was regarded as the greatest German bass of his day. Appeared in London as the Count in the first performance in England of *Figaro* in 1812, but his German method of singing was not liked, though the critic of the *Examiner* wrote: 'He however breathes in tune, and that is praise due to no other male performer at the theatre.'

Fischer, Res (b. Berlin, 8 Nov. 1896). German contralto. Studied Stuttgart. Début Basle 1928. Engagements followed at Frankfurt and Stuttgart, where she has been leading contralto since 1941. Created the title role in Orff's *Antigonae* at Salzburg in 1949, and has appeared as a guest artist all over Europe, including London (Klytemnestra with Stuttgart Opera, 1955). (R)

Fischer-Dieskau, Dietrich (b. Berlin, 28 May 1925). German baritone. Studied Berlin with Georg Walter and Weissenborn. Prisoner of war in Italy, but was able to begin his career in 1947. Stage début Berlin Städtische Oper 1948, Posa; here he has been leading baritone ever since. Bayreuth 1954–6, Wolfram, Herald (*Lohengrin*), Kothner, Amfortas; Salzburg since 1957. London, C. G., 1965, Mandryka. Roles include Dr. Faust (Busoni), the Count, Falstaff, Jochanaan, Mandryka (*Arabella*), Mathis der Maler,

Wozzeck, Onegin, Mittenhofer (*Elegy for Young Lovers*), Don Giovanni, Renato (*Ballo in Maschera*). One of the great singers of this century, and an equally thoughtful interpreter of *lieder* and opera. (R)

Fischietti, Domenico (b. Naples, *c.* 1720; d. Salzburg, 1810). Italian composer. He was active as an opera composer in Naples, Palermo, Venice, Prague, Dresden, and became Kapellmeister (in preference to Leopold Mozart) at Salzburg in 1772, continuing to visit Italy for productions of new operas. A reference by the younger Mozart indicates respect.

Fisher, Sylvia (b. Melbourne, 1910). Australian soprano. Studied Melbourne Conservatory with Adolf Spivakovsky. Début Melbourne 1932, Hermione in Lully's *Cadmus and Hermione*, while still a student. Stage début London, C.G., 1949, Leonore (*Fidelio*). The company's leading dramatic soprano until 1958, being especially successful as the Marschallin, Sieglinde, and the Kostelnička. Made guest appearances in Italy, 1952 and Chicago, 1959. E.O.G. since 1963. (R)

Fiume. See *Rijeka*.

Flagstad, Kirsten (b. Hamar, Norway, 12 July 1895; d. Oslo, 7 Dec. 1962). Norwegian soprano. Studied with her mother and Ellen Schytte-Jacobsen. Début Oslo 1913, Nuri (*Tiefland*). Until 1933 she appeared only in Scandinavia, in a vast repertory of opera and operetta, and was on the verge of retiring in 1933 when she was engaged to sing small roles at Bayreuth. In 1934 she sang Sieglinde there and an engagement for the Met. N.Y. followed where she made her début in 1935 in the same role. During her initial N.Y. season sang Brünnhilde and Kundry for the first time in her life, immediately establishing herself as the greatest Wagner soprano of the day. Appeared at C.G. in 1936 and 1937, and after the war did much to restore the Wagner repertory there, not only singing Isolde, Kundry, Sieglinde, and Brünnhilde in German, but learning the *Walküre* Brünnhilde in English. Sang Dido in English at the Mermaid Theatre (q.v.) in London. Retired in 1954, but continued to record. Director of the Norwegian National Opera 1959–60. Her voice was not sensuous in quality, but was of great power and radiance, and superbly projected. Her autobiography, edited by Louis Biancolli, was published in 1953. (R)

Fledermaus, Die (The Bat). Operetta in 3 acts by J. Strauss; text by Haffner and Genée after a French *spirituel vaudeville, Le Réveillon* (1872), by Meilhac and Halévy, based in its turn on Roderich Benedix's comedy *Das Gefängnis* (1851). Prod. Vienna, W., 5 Apr. 1874; N.Y., Stadt Theatre, 21 Nov. 1874; London, Alhambra, 18 Dec. 1876: later entered the repertories of the leading opera houses beginning in Vienna 1894 under Mahler. N.Y., Met., 1905 with Sembrich, Alten, Edyth Walker, Dippel; London, C.G., 1930 with Lehmann, Schumann, Olszewska, Wittrisch, cond. Walter.

Act 1. Rosalinde (sop.), the beautiful wife of Eisenstein, is being serenaded by her former admirer Alfred (ten.), an opera singer who threatens to return later that evening. She tells her maid Adele (sop.) that she can go and visit a sick aunt—in reality Adele wants to go to the masked ball that night given by Prince Orlofsky. Eisenstein (ten.) arrives home: his jail sentence for having insulted the tax collector has been increased. Falke (bar.) comes, ostensibly to conduct Eisenstein to prison, but while Rosalinde is out of the room he suggests to Eisenstein that he accompany him to Orlofsky's ball, and give himself up the next morning. Rosalinde has also been asked to the ball, but her husband knows nothing of that. Eisenstein departs with Falke, supposedly for jail. Soon Alfred returns and sups with Rosalinde. Frank, (bar.), the prison governor, arrives to take Eisenstein away, and Rosalinde has to pretend that Alfred is Herr von Eisenstein: he is led off to prison.

Act 2. Orlofsky (mezzo) welcomes the guests to his ball. Eisenstein thinks he recognizes Adele, for she is wearing one of his wife's gowns, but she eludes him. A Hungarian countess is announced (Rosalinde in disguise). Eisenstein fails to recognize his wife, and, already a little drunk, flirts with her outrageously, timing her heartbeats with a chiming watch. Rosalinde manages to gain possession of the watch; she sings a *csárdás* for the guests after a chorus in praise of champagne, the clock strikes six, and Eisenstein, calling for his hat and cloak, hurries off to prison.

Act 3. Frosch, the drunken jailer (speaking part), grumbles about the noisy prisoner in one of the cells (Alfred). Frank arrives back from the ball, also a little drunk, and is soon followed by Adele and her sister Ida. Adele asks the governor to help launch her as an actress and displays her talent for mimicry. Eisenstein now enters, and finding that his cell is already occupied by someone masquerading under his name, changes clothes with his lawyer Dr. Blind (ten.), in the hope of obtaining a confession from the supposed Eisenstein. Rosalinde arrives to try to get Alfred released. They both confess the events of the previous evening to the disguised Eisenstein, and when he reveals his identity, she produces the tell-tale watch. The rest of Orlofsky's guests now enter, and after a general reconciliation, they sing in praise of King Champagne.

Fleischer, Editha (b. Falkenstein, 5 Apr. 1898). German soprano. Studied Berlin with Lilli Lehmann; début Berlin 1919. Went to America with the German Opera Company in 1922, and joined the N.Y. Met. in 1926, remaining a member of the company until 1935. Sang Lisette in first Met. *La Rondine*, Yvonne in *Jonny spielt auf*, Aïthra in *Die aegyptische Helena*. Sang regularly at the Colón, Buenos Aires from 1933, and was appointed head of the opera school there. Since 1950 professor of singing at Vienna Academy. (R) Her brother **Hans Fleischer** was a well-known German *Spieltenor* at Leipzig 1926–38, and sang at C.G. 1933–6.

Fleta, Miguel (b. Albalate, 28 Dec. 1893; d. La Coruña, 30 May 1938). Spanish tenor. Studied Barcelona Conservatory. Début Trieste 1919, Paolo (*Francesca da Rimini*); N.Y., Met., 1923; Milan, Sc., 1923–6 where he created Calaf. Also the first Romeo in Zandonai's *Giulietta e Romeo* (Rome 1922). (R) His son **Pierre Fleta** (b. 1925) sings at La Monnaie, Brussels, and in France. (R)

Fliegende Holländer, Der (The Flying Dutchman). Opera in 3 acts by Wagner; text by composer after the old legend as told in Chapter 7 of Heine's *Aus den Memoiren des Herren von Schnabelewopski* (1831). First used as scenario for Dietsch's *Le Vaisseau Fantôme* (1842). Prod. Dresden 2 Jan. 1843 with Schroeder-Devrient as Senta, cond. Wagner; London, D.L., 23 July 1870 with Di Murska and Santley (first Wagner opera in London); Philadelphia, Ac. of M., 8 Nov. 1876, in Italian.

Act 1. The Dutchman (bar.) has been condemned, for his blasphemy, to sail his ship until redeemed by a faithful woman. This salvation he is allowed to attempt once every seven years. In one of these periods he is driven by storms to a Norwegian harbour. He moors beside Daland (bass), who, impressed by the Dutchman's wealth, offers him shelter.

Act 2. Daland's daughter Senta (sop.) sings to her friends, as they spin, the ballad of The Flying Dutchman. Her lover Erik (ten.) pleads his own cause, unsuccessfully. But when the Dutchman enters, she is confused by his declaration of love.

Act 3. The Dutchman overhears Erik being rejected again, and concludes that he too may be deserted by Senta. He sets sail; but Senta leaps to him from a cliff-top. Her faith redeems him, and together they are seen rising heavenwards.

Floquet, Étienne (b. Aix-en-Provence, 23 Nov. 1748; d. Paris, 10 May 1785). French composer. His first success was *L'Union d'Amour et des Arts* (1773), his greatest (the first successful French lyric comedy), *Le Seigneur Bienfaisant* (1780). Fétis admired the latter's freshness and originality.

Florence (It., Firenze). Town in Tuscany, Italy. Birthplace of opera in the 16th century when Peri's *Dafne* was performed there in 1597 as a result of the establishment of the Camerata (q.v.). In the 17th century the Teatro della Pergola was built (it still stands and is used for special performances) and it was there that the first performances in Italy of *Figaro* (1788), probably *Don Giovanni* (1792), and *Die Entführung aus dem Serail* (1935) took place; also the premières of Donizetti's *Parisina* and Verdi's *Macbeth.* It was there, too, that the first Italian performance of *Les Huguenots* was given under the title of *Gli anglicani* as well as *Le Prophète, Robert le Diable,* and *Dinorah.*

The Teatro Comunale was built, without a roof, in 1862, and covered over in 1883. Originally called the Teatro Politeama Fiorentino Vittorio Emmanuele, it was renamed the Comunale in 1932 when it was taken over by the Florentine authorities. It was rebuilt and modernized 1959–60, reopened 1961 (cap. 2,000). The Florence May Festival (Maggio Musicale, q.v.) was established in 1933.

Florestan. A Spanish nobleman, Leonore's husband (ten.) in Beethoven's *Fidelio.*

Flotow, Friedrich von (b. Teutendorf, 26 Apr. 1812; d. Darmstadt, 24 Jan. 1883). German composer. Almost all his work is operatic, though only *Martha* (1847) now survives. *Alessandro Stradella* first appeared, as a *pièce lyrique,* in 1837; rewritten and expanded into an opera in 1844, it had a wide success in Germany, though failing in England. His music has little dramatic force, but at its best a certain melodic charm and deftness.

Flower duet. Duet 'Scuoti quella fronda di ciliegio' sung by Butterfly (sop.) and Suzuki (mezzo) in Act 2 of Puccini's *Madama Butterfly* as they strew the house with flowers against Pinkerton's expected return.

Flower song. José's (ten.) aria 'La fleur que tu m'avais jetée' in Act 2 of Bizet's *Carmen,* telling Carmen how he has treasured the flower she threw him, and with it the hope of her love.

Floyd, Carlisle (b. Latta, South Carolina, 11 June 1926). American composer. Studied Syracuse University and privately with Firkušný. Came to the fore with his opera *Susannah* (prod. Florida 1955), which revealed a talent for the stage. This was followed by *Wuthering Heights* (1958) and *The Passion of Jonathan Wade* (1962).

Fodor-Mainvielle, Joséphine (b. Paris, 13 Oct. 1789; d. Saint-Genis, nr. Lyons, 14 Aug. 1870). French soprano. Daughter of the violinist Joseph Fodor, and wife of the actor Mainvielle whom she married in 1812. Début St. Petersburg 1810 in Fioravanti's *Le Cantatrici Villane.* London, King's Theatre, 1816–18, where she sang with great success in Mozart (Fiordiligi, Vitellia, Countess, Zerlina); the first London Rosina and Elisabetta in Rossini's *Elisabetta, Regina d'Inghilterra.* Appeared with success in Paris, Naples, and Vienna, where she sang 60 performances of Semiramide in the 1824–5 season. On 9 Dec. 1825, when she was singing this role for the first time in Paris, before an audience that included Rossini and Cherubini, she lost her voice at the beginning of the second scene; after a long delay she agreed to finish the opera, but collapsed at the end of the evening, her voice quite gone. She retired to Naples, attempting two come-backs at the San Carlo in 1828 and 1831, and then retired to Fontainebleau. She published her *Conseils et Réflexions sur l'Art de Chant* in 1857. Her daughter **Enrichetta** sang in Berlin 1846–9.

Foerster, J. B. (b. Dětenice, 30 Dec. 1859; d. Nový Vestec, 29 May 1951). Czech composer. His six operas show an increasing metaphysical interest. *Deborah* (1893) and *Eva* (1899) reflect real life. *Jessica* (1905) is based on *The Merchant of Venice,* which title it later took. With *The Invincibles* (1919), *The Heart* (1923), and *The Simpleton* (1936) the characters are increasingly identified with moral states; the expression is inward, personal, and symbolical, the drama spiritual.

Foli (Foley), A(llan) J(ames) (b. Cahir, Tipperary, 7 Aug. 1835; d. Southport, 20 Oct. 1899). Irish bass. Studied Naples. Début Catania 1862, Elmiro in Rossini's *Otello*. After appearances in other Italian cities, London début H.M.'s 1865, Saint-Bris. Sang more than 60 operas at C.G., H.M.'s, and D.L. Appeared in America with Mapleson's company, and in Russia and Austria. The Daland of the first Wagner performance in London, 1870. Possessed a powerful voice, ranging from E to f'.

Ford. A citizen of Windsor (bar.), Alice's husband in Verdi's *Falstaff*.

Formes, Karl (b. Mülheim, 7 Aug. 1815; d. San Francisco, 15 Dec. 1889). German bass. Son of a sexton; first sang in a benefit concert to raise funds for Cologne Cathedral. Stage début Cologne 1841, Sarastro; London, D.L., 1849; N.Y., 1857. His brother **Theodor** (b. 1826), a tenor, died insane in 1874.

Formichi, Cesare (b. Rome, 15 Apr. 1883; d. Rome, 21 July 1949). Italian baritone. Studied Rome with Lombardo. Début Milan, T.L., 1911; London, C.G., 1924; Chicago 1922–32. Admired for his Scarpia, Rigoletto, &c., and in Italy for his Wagner interpretations. In 1937 was responsible for the badly organized Italian performances during the Coronation season at C.G.; also acted as artistic director of the Vichy Casino. (R)

Forsell, John (Johan) (b. Stockholm, 6 Nov. 1868; d. Stockholm, 30 May 1941). Swedish baritone. Début Stockholm 1896, Figaro; sang there regularly until 1909 when he went to the N.Y. Met. for one season. Also appeared in London, Berlin, Vienna. One of the finest Don Giovannis of his generation; he sang this role at Salzburg under Schalk in 1930. Intendant of the Stockholm Opera 1923–39. Professor of singing at the Stockholm Conservatory: his pupils included Jussi Björling and Svanholm. (R)

Fortner, Wolfgang (b. Leipzig, 12 Oct. 1907). German composer. Interest in the German Youth Music Movement of the 1930's led to his first stage work, the school opera *Cress ertrinkt* (1931). *Die Witwe von Ephesus* (1951) is in one act with small orchestra. His two Lorca operas, *Bluthochzeit* (1957) and *In seinem Garten liebt Don Perlimplin Belisa* (1962), reconcile varying techniques—the basic musical one being serial.

Forza del Destino, La (The Force of Destiny). Opera in 4 acts by Verdi; text by Piave, after the drama *Don Alvaro, ó La Fuerza del Sino* (1835), by Angel de Saavedra Ramírez de Banquedano, Duke of Rivas. Prod. St. Petersburg, Court Theatre, 10 Nov. 1862, with Barbot, Tamberlik, Graziani; Rome, T. Apollo, 7 Feb. 1863 (as *Don Alvaro*); N.Y., Academy of Music, 24 Feb. 1865; London, H.M.'s, 22 June 1867, with Tietjens, Mongini, Santley.

Act 1. When Don Alvaro (ten.) is discovered eloping with Leonora (sop.) by her father, the Marquis of Calatrava (bass), he insists on shouldering the blame; he throws his pistol aside, but it goes off and kills the old man, who dies cursing his daughter.

Act 2. Scene 1. Disguised as a man, Leonora comes to an inn seeking Alvaro. She sees her brother Don Carlo (bar.), who has sworn to kill the lovers, and flees. Scene 2. Leonora begs sanctuary in a monastery; the Padre Guardiano (bass) allows her refuge in a mountain cave, and all pray that he who attempts to harm her may be cursed.

Act 3. Scene 1. Don Alvaro, fighting with the Spaniards against the Germans under an assumed name, thinks of Leonora, whom he believes dead. He saves the life of a man whom he does not recognize as Carlo; they swear eternal friendship. Scene 2. Alvaro, wounded, begs Carlo to destroy some letters; among them Carlo recognizes his sister's picture, and now swears to destroy Alvaro. Scene 3. Alvaro, recovered, is forced to a duel by Carlo, and wounds him. He seeks peace in a monastery.

Act 4. Scene 1. In five years Alvaro, now Father Raphael, has found peace. Carlo comes seeking vengeance, and so insults Alvaro as to bring him angrily out of the monastery to fight. Scene 2. In the mountains, Leonora prays for oblivion of the past. Alvaro mortally wounds Carlo, but no longer feeling himself a holy man he refuses to give absolution; the 'hermit' summoned proves to be Leonora, whom Carlo stabs. Dying, she begs Alvaro to turn to religion, and the Padre Guardiano commands him to seek forgiveness.

Forzano, Giovacchino (b. Borgo S. Lorenzo, 19 Nov. 1883; d. Rome, 28 Oct. 1970). Italian librettist and producer. Studied as singer, and appeared in baritone roles in the Italian provinces. Provided libretti for *Lodoletta, Il piccolo Marat, Gianni Schicchi, Suor Angelica, Sly, Il Re, Oedipus Rex* (Leoncavallo), *Palla di Mozzi* (Marinuzzi). Began producing operas in 1904 and was responsible for the staging of the world premières of *Turandot, Nerone* (Boito), *La Cena delle Beffe* (Giordano), and *I Cavalieri di Ekebù* (Zandonai). Has worked at C.G., Vienna State Opera, and in recent years Verona Arena, Rome, and Naples.

Foss, Lukas (b. Berlin, 15 Aug. 1922). American composer of German origin. His first opera, *The Jumping Frog of Calaveras County* (1950), gave evidence of a fertile and brilliant talent. His second opera, *Griffelkin*, was produced on TV in 1955.

Four Saints in Three Acts. 'An opera to be sung' in 4 [*sic*] acts by Virgil Thomson; text by Gertrude Stein. Concert perf. Ann Arbor 20 May 1933; prod. Hartford, Conn., by Society of Friends and Enemies of Modern Music, Avery Memorial Theatre, 8 Feb. 1934.

Fourestier, Louis (b. Montpellier, 31 May 1892). French conductor and composer. Studied locally and then Paris Conservatoire with Leroux, D'Indy, Dukas, and others. Opéra-Comique 1927–32; Opéra since 1938. Conducted N.Y. Met. 1946–8. (R)

Fra Diavolo. *Opéra-comique* in 3 acts by Auber; text by Scribe. Prod. Paris, O.C., 28 Jan. 1830; London, D.L., 1 Feb. 1831; N.Y. 17 Oct. 1831. Fra Diavolo is a bandit who involves a girl in one of his robberies. Later he is betrayed and shot, but absolves the girl of blame and reunites her to her lover. An alternative ending in which Fra Diavolo escapes is sometimes given.

Fra Gherardo. Opera in 3 acts by Pizzetti; text by composer after the Chronicles of Salimbene da Parma (13th century). Prod. Milan, Sc., 16 May 1928, cond. Toscanini; N.Y., Met., 21 Mar. 1929.

Françaix, Jean (b. Le Mans, 23 May 1912). French composer. His first opera was a chamber *opéra-comique, Le Diable Boiteux* (1937); this was followed by the musical comedy *L'Apostrophe* (1942) and then by the full-length (4-act) *La Main de Gloire* (1950).

France. See *Académie de Musique, Aix-en-Provence, Bordeaux, Lyons, Mulhouse, Paris, Strasbourg.*

Francesca da Rimini. Opera in 4 acts by Zandonai; text by Tito Ricordi after D'Annunzio's tragedy (1902). Prod. Turin, T.R., 19 Feb. 1914 with Linda Canetti and Giulio Crimi; London, C.G., 16 July 1914, with Edvina, Martinelli; N.Y., Met., 22 Dec. 1916, with Alda, Martinelli. Frequently performed in Italy. There are over 20 other operas on the legend.

Franchetti, Alberto (b. Turin, 18 Sept. 1860; d. Viareggio, 4 Aug. 1942). Italian composer. His private means allowed him prolonged and carefully selected training in Italy and Germany, and later helped to stage the nine operas that were its fruit under the best conditions. *Germania* (1902) reached England (C.G. 1907), though *La Figlia di Jorio* (1906) has been the most successful. Not only his wealth but also his fondness for spectacular tableaux won him the title of the Meyerbeer of modern Italy.

Franci, Benvenuto (b. Siena, 1 July 1891). Italian baritone. Studied Rome with Cotogni and Rosati. Début Rome, 1918, Giannetto in *Lodoletta*. Leading baritone Rome Opera 1928–49 and at La Scala from 1923 where he created Manuel in Boito's *Nerone*;

London, C.G., 1925, 1931, and 1946, where his Scarpia (opposite Jeritza), Rigoletto, and Gérard were greatly admired. Also famous for his William Tell, Macbeth, Barnaba, and Telramund. (R) His daughter **Marcella** had a short career as a soprano after the Second World War; his son **Carlo** is a conductor and composer.

Franck, César (b. Liège, 10 Dec. 1822; d. Paris, 8 Nov. 1890). French composer of Belgian origin. Even D'Indy allowed that Franck's operas were insignificant, less operatic than some of the sacred music. The early comic opera *Le Valet de Ferme* (1851–2) was never produced. *Hulda* (1882–5) was produced at Monte Carlo, 8 Mar. 1894. *Ghisèle* (1888–90) was finished by Bréville, Chausson, D'Indy, Coquard, and Rousseau, and produced at Monte Carlo, 6 Apr. 1896.

Franckenstein, Clemens von (b. Wiesentheid, 14 July 1875; d. Hechendorf, Pilsensee, Bavaria, 19 Aug. 1942). German composer, conductor, and Intendant. Studied Vienna with Bruckner; also Munich and Frankfurt. Conducted Moody-Manners Company 1902–7; then held posts in Wiesbaden and Munich. Director Munich Opera 1912–18, and then 1924–34, when it enjoyed great prestige. Composed four operas. His brother was for many years Austrian Ambassador to Great Britain; his wife, **Maria Nezadal,** a Czech soprano, sang in Munich, Vienna, and London.

Frankfurt-on-Main. Town in Hesse, Germany. Enjoyed a fine period of operatic performances between 1880 and 1933 under Weingartner, Rottenberg, Clemens Krauss, and Steinberg. During the Nazi régime Wetzelsberger and Konwitschny were its musical directors; and after the war, Bruno Vondenhoff, Solti, Matacic, and Dohnányi. The present Grosses Haus was opened in 1951 (cap. 1,430). Works that have received their premières at Frankfurt include Schoenberg's *Von heute auf morgen* (1930), Egk's *Die Zaubergeige* (1935), Orff's *Carmina Burana* (1937) and *Die Kluge* (1952).

Franklin, David (b. London, 17 May 1908). English bass. Sang first as an amateur; heard by John Christie in 1934, then by Fritz Busch, who sent him to Vienna to study with Jani Strasser. Début Glyndebourne 1936, Commendatore; regularly there until 1939. Leading bass at C.G. 1947–50; sang Mars in the première of Bliss's *Olympians*. Left the stage in 1951 to teach, lecture, and write: librettist of Phyllis Tate's *The Lodger*. He brought to all his roles a great intelligence and a fine sense of the theatre. (R)

Frantz, Ferdinand (b. Kassel, 8 Feb. 1906; d. Munich, 25 May 1959). German bass-baritone. Début Kassel 1927, Ortel (*Meistersinger*). Hamburg (1937–43); Munich 1943–59; N.Y., Met., 1949–51, 1953–4; London, C.G., 1953–4. Although originally a bass, singing Pogner, Gurnemanz, Landgrave, King Mark, &c., he could also sing baritone roles and became a distinguished Hans Sachs, Wotan, Kurwenal, and Pizarro. (R)

Franz, Paul (orig. François Gautier) (b. Paris, 30 Nov. 1876; d. Paris, 20 Apr. 1950). French tenor. Studied with Louis Delaquerrière. Début O. 1909, Lohengrin. Remained leading tenor there until 1938, singing in the first Paris *Parsifal* (1913), and in many other premières both in Paris and at Monte Carlo, as well as Aeneas in the 1922 revival of *Les Troyens* at the Opéra. London, C.G., 1910–14. Professor of singing at the Conservatoire from 1938. (R)

Frau ohne Schatten, Die (The Woman without a Shadow). Opera in 3 acts by Strauss; text by Hugo von Hofmannsthal, after his own story (1919). Prod. Vienna, O., 10 Oct. 1919, with Lehmann, Jeritza, Oestvig, Mayr; San Francisco, 18 Sept. 1959; London, S.W., Hamburg Opera, 2 May 1966. A complicated fantastic allegory on the theme of the importance to humanity of unselfishness.

Frazzi, Vito (b. San Secondo Parmense, 1 Aug. 1888). Italian composer. He has composed two ambitious operas, *Re Lear* (1939) and *Don Chisciotte* (1951), and edited early Italian operas.

Freia. The goddess of youth (sop.) in Wagner's *Das Rheingold.*

Freischütz, Der (The Freeshooter.) Opera in 3 acts by Weber; text by Friedrich Kind, after a tale in the *Gespensterbuch* (1811) of Johann Apel and Friedrich Laun. Prod. Berlin, Sch., 18 June 1821 (500 perfs. there by 1884); London, Ly., 22 July 1824; New York, 2 Mar. 1825.

Act 1. Max (ten.), in love with Agathe (sop.), is eager to win a shooting competition to decide the next head ranger, but loses in a trial. Kaspar (bass) has sold his soul to the evil spirit Samiel (speaker), and must bring another victim; Max agrees to get magic bullets from Samiel.

Act 2. Scene 1. Agathe, apprehensive though soothed by Aennchen (sop.), is interrupted by Max, who pretends he must fetch a stag he has shot in the haunted Wolf's Glen. Scene 2. Amid weird sights and sounds in the Glen, Kaspar forges seven bullets for Max—the last to go where Samiel wills, though Max does not know this.

Act 3. Scene 1. Preparing to marry Max, Agathe prays for protection; she has had bad dreams, but Aennchen again comforts her. Scene 2. Max amazes everyone at the shooting contest with his remarkable shots. The Prince orders Max to shoot a passing dove with the seventh; Agathe's voice is heard begging him not to. Max fires. Agathe falls, but it is Kaspar who now has to die instead. Max confesses his pact with Samiel, but eventually on the intercession of the Hermit (bass) is promised forgiveness.

Fremstad, Olive (orig. Olivia Rundquist) (b. Stockholm, 14 Mar. 1871; d. Irvington, N.Y., 21 Apr. 1951). Swedish, later American, soprano. Début Boston 1890 as Lady Saphir (Sullivan's *Patience*). 1893 studied Berlin with Lilli Lehmann; début Cologne 1895, Azucena. Engagements followed in Munich, Vienna, and Bayreuth; C.G. début 1902, and next year N.Y. Met. as Sieglinde. Leading soprano there until 1914. One of the great Isoldes and Brünnhildes of the century; at her farewell appearance in N.Y. 1914 was given 19 curtain calls and 21 minutes of applause. (R)

Freni, Mirella (b. Modena, 27 Feb. 1936). Italian soprano. Studied with Campogalliani. Début Modena 1955, Micaëla. After appearances in the Italian provinces and a season with the Netherlands Opera (1959–60), was engaged for Glyndebourne 1960, Zerlina; 1962, Susanna and Adina. London, C.G., since 1961, Nannetta, Zerlina, and Susanna; Milan, Sc., 1963, Mimì in the Karajan-Zeffirelli *Bohème*. Chicago, 1963, Marguerite. Repertory also includes Liù, Elvira in *Puritani*. One of the most musical Italian sopranos of recent years, with a charming soubrette personality. (R)

Frère Laurent. The holy man (bass) and friend of Romeo and Juliet in the operas by Gounod and Sutermeister.

Fretwell, Elizabeth (b. Melbourne, 1922). Australian soprano. Début Australian National Opera 1947, Senta. Came to Britain 1954; after singing Aida and Musetta with the Dublin Grand Opera, engaged as leading soprano at S.W. 1955, where her Violetta earned high praise. Created the part of Blanche in *The Moon and Sixpence* (Gardner); the first British Ariadne. (R)

Frezzolini, Erminia (b. Orvieto, 27 Mar. 1818; d. Paris, 5 Nov. 1884). Italian soprano. Studied with her father, Giuseppe Frezzolini, a well-known buffo and first Dulcamara, and later with Nencini, Ronconi, Manuel Garcia, and Tacchinardi. Début Florence 1838, Beatrice di Tenda. London 1842 and 1850. Created Viclinda (*Lombardi*) and the title role in Verdi's unsuccessful *Giovanna d'Arco* (1845); the first N.Y. Gilda. Retired in 1860.

Fricci (orig. Frietsche), **Antonietta** (b. Vienna, 8 Jan. 1840; d. Turin, 7 Sept. 1912). Austrian soprano. Studied Vienna with Marchesi and in Italy. Début Pisa 1858, Violetta; London, C.G., 1862, where she was the first London Eboli (1867). Sang at La Scala and elsewhere in Italy. Famous for her Norma, Lady Macbeth, and Lucrezia Borgia.

Frick, Gottlob (b. Olbronn, 28 July 1906). German bass. Studied Stuttgart Conservatory. Joined chorus Stuttgart Opera 1927. Engaged as soloist Coburg 1934, Königsberg, Freiburg, Dresden 1940–50, Berlin, Städtische Oper, 1950–3; Munich and Vienna since 1953. London, C.G., since 1950. N.Y., Met., 1962. As well as being a distinguished Wagnerian he sings Sarastro, Padre Guardiano, and Philip II. (R)

Fricka. Wotan's wife (sop.) in Wagner's *Ring*.

Fricsay, Ferenc (b. Budapest, 9 Aug. 1914; d. Basel, 20 Feb. 1963). Hungarian conductor. Studied with Kodály and Bartók. When 19 appointed conductor at Szeged. First conductor Budapest Opera 1939–45. International career dates from 1947 when he took over the première of Einem's *Dantons Tod* at Salzburg from Klemperer, who was indisposed. Director Berlin Städtische Oper 1951–2 (resigning after differences with the management); Munich State Opera 1956–8; returned to Berlin to conduct at the rebuilt Deutsches Opernhaus 1961. Has recorded several operas with the R.I.A.S. Orchestra of Berlin, which he trained into a fine instrument. Conducted premières of *Le Vin Herbé* and *Antigonae* at Salzburg. (R)

Friedenstag (Peace Day). Opera in 1 act by Strauss; text by Gregor after Calderón's drama *La Rendención de Breda* (1625). Prod. Munich 24 July 1938 with Ursuleac, Patzak, Hotter, cond. Krauss. This work, which deals with a beleaguered citadel during the Thirty Years War, and ends with a hymn to peace, enjoyed great popularity in Germany in the crisis years of 1938–9.

Froh. The God of Spring (ten.) in Wagner's *Das Rheingold*.

From the House of the Dead. See *House of the Dead, From the*.

Frunze. Town in the U.S.S.R., capital of Kirghizia. The Musical Drama Theatre has been an opera house since 1942, and has built up a small but international repertory that includes several Kirghiz operas.

Fuchs, Marta (b. Stuttgart, 1 Jan. 1898). German soprano, originally mezzo. Début Aachen 1928. Dresden Opera 1930–6; Berlin State Opera 1936–42; Stuttgart 1949–51. One of the best German dramatic sopranos of her day; was a distinguished Isolde, Brünnhilde, and Kundry, all of which she sang at Bayreuth. (R)

Fugère, Lucien (b. Paris, 22 July 1848; d. Paris, 15 Jan. 1935). French baritone. Début 1870 at the Café-Concert, Ba-ta-can, Paris. Engaged for the B.-P. in 1874, and in 1877 reached the Opéra-Comique, where he remained until 1910, singing more than 100 roles, of which more than 30 were world premières, including Le Père in *Louise*. He was also the first Paris Schaunard and Boniface (*Le Jongleur de Notre-Dame*) and a famous Papageno, Figaro, and Leporello. He sang the latter role at C.G., in 1897. He continued to sing until he was 80 when he celebrated his birthday in a performance of *La Basoche* at Le Touquet.(R)

Furmedge, Edith (b. London, 27 Mar. 1898; d. London, 9 Oct. 1956). English contralto. Studied with Dinh Gilly, whom she later married. First sang small Wagner roles at C.G. (1924) and then in the 1930's was heard as Erda, Fricka, Maddalena (*Rigoletto*). After her husband's death she continued to teach in the school he had founded. (R)

Fürsch-Madi(er), Emma (b. Bayonne, 1847; d. Warrenville, New Jersey, 20 Sept. 1894). French soprano. Studied Paris Conservatoire. Début Paris 1870; London, C.G., 1881, Valentine (*Huguenots*); New Orleans, with French Company, 1874; N.Y., Met., 1883–4 and 1893–4. A regular visitor to London until 1890; an excellent Donna Anna, Aida, and Lucrezia Borgia.

Furtwängler, Wilhelm (b. Berlin, 25 Jan. 1886; d. Baden-Baden, 30 Nov. 1954). German conductor. Studied Munich with Rheinberger and Schillings. After early engagements in Zürich, Strasbourg, and Lübeck, appointed to Mannheim in 1915 where he remained until 1920. There then followed a period devoted mostly to the concert hall, but from 1924 his Wagner performances in Berlin and Paris attracted great attention. He conducted at Bayreuth in 1931, 1936, 1937, 1943, and 1944; and the opening concert there after the war (1951) devoted to the Choral Symphony. C.G. début 1935, *Tristan*; returned in 1937 and 1938 to conduct the *Ring*. A regular visitor to Salzburg and Vienna; and his Wagner performances at La Scala and for the Italian Radio set a high standard. His position during the Nazi régime has been the subject of much controversy and he was refused permission to conduct in America. (R)

Fux, Johann Joseph (b. Hirtenfeld, 1660; d. Vienna, 14 Feb. 1741). Austrian composer. Though best known for his *Gradus ad Parnassum* and his sacred music, Fux wrote 19 operas, most of them sumptuously produced at the Austrian court where he was an honoured Kapellmeister.

G

Gabrieli, Adriana (b. Ferrara, *c.* 1755; d. Venice, ?). Italian soprano. Known as La Ferrarese, and Ferrarese del Bene after her marriage to Luigi del Bene in 1783. Début London 1783. Sang in Milan and Vienna, where she created role of Fiordiligi in *Così fan tutte* 1790—truly one of the *dame ferraresi*, as Da Ponte calls the two sisters in his libretto. In 1789 Mozart had composed for her the aria 'Al desio di chi t'adora' which she sang instead of Susanna's 'Deh vieni' in Act 4 of *Figaro*.

Gabrielli, Caterina (b. Rome, 12 Nov. 1730; d. Rome, 16 Feb. 1796). Italian soprano. Daughter of Prince Gabrielli's cook, and known as La Coghetta. Studied Rome with Francesco Garcia, and Naples with Porpora. Début probably Venice 1754 as Ermione in Galuppi's *Antigona* (appearances in Lucca and Naples in 1747 and 1750 have not been confirmed). Created a number of roles in Gluck's Italian operas 1755–60. London début 1775. According to Burney she possessed a remarkably flexible voice of a thrilling quality. Her personal beauty and capriciousness involved her in many intrigues with royalty and nobility all over Europe. Her sister **Francesca**, often confused with Adriana Gabrieli (above), was a poor singer, who accompanied Caterina as a *seconda donna* in many operas.

Gadski, Johanna (b. Anclam, 15 June 1872; d. Berlin, 22 Feb. 1932). German soprano. Début Berlin 1889, Agathe; N.Y. with Damrosch Company, 1895, Elsa; London, C.G., 1899, Elisabeth. Member of N.Y., Met., 1898–1904 and 1907–17 where she was specially noted for her Wagner interpretations. Left America when her husband was deported as an enemy alien, 1917; when she returned with a Wagnerian touring company 1929–31 she was past her prime. Also appeared at Bayreuth and Munich Festivals. (R)

Gagliano, Marco da (b. Gagliano, nr. Florence, *c.* 1575; d. Florence, 24 Feb. 1642). Italian composer, one of the fathers of opera. According to Peri, his *Dafne* (1607) was a finer setting of the words than any made before. The preface is important: written a century and a half before the preface to Gluck's *Alceste*, it shows the same determination to banish singers' abuses in favour of dramatic naturalness, and gives practical advice on performance. He collaborated with Peri on *Il Medoro* (1616), but the music of this and of two other opera-oratorios is lost. His last opera, *La Flora* (1628), survives. A severe self-critic, he printed only music he considered worthy of survival.

Gailhard, Pierre (b. Toulouse, 1 Aug. 1848; d. Paris, 12 Oct. 1918). French bass and manager. Studied Toulouse and Paris Conservatoires. Début Paris, O.C., 1867, Falstaff (Thomas); London, C.G. 1879 where his Méphistophélès was considered the best since Faure. Manager of the Paris Opéra with Ritt 1884–91, with Bertrand 1893–9, with Capoul 1900–5, and by himself 1905–8. Sang in the premières of several works by Offenbach, Auber, Thomas, &c., and was responsible for the French premières of most of Wagner's major works and the engagements in Paris of the De Reszkes, Renaud, Melba, &c. (R) His son **André** was a composer and a number of his works were produced in France.

Galeffi, Carlo (b. nr. Venice, 4 June 1882; d. Rome, 22 Sept. 1961). Italian baritone. Studied with Cotogni. Début Rome 1904, Enrico. N.Y., Met., 1910; Chicago 1919–21. Sang in leading opera houses of Europe, and was a great favourite in South America. Created Fanuel in Boito's *Nerone*, Manfredo in Montemezzi's *L'Amore dei Tre Re*, and the leading baritone roles in three Mascagni operas—*Amica*, *Parisina*, and *Isabeau*. He was also the first Italian Amfortas and European

Schicchi. Famed for his interpretations of Rigoletto, Nabucco, Boccanegra, and Tell. (R)

Galitsky, Prince. Igor's brother-in-law (bass), in Borodin's *Prince Igor*.

Galli, Caterina (b. ? *c.* 1727; d. London, 1804). Italian mezzo-soprano. Début London, 1743 in Galuppi's *Enrico*. A great favourite in London, performing leading roles in Handel's *Theodora*, *Jephtha*, and *Joshua*. Reappeared in the 1770's at the King's Theatre. Became companion of Martha Ray, the mistress of the Earl of Sandwich, and was with her when she was murdered outside Covent Garden in 1779. She became extremely poor, and when 70 was induced to reappear in oratorio at Covent Garden.

Galli, Filippo (b. Rome, 1783; d. Paris, 3 June 1853). Italian tenor, later bass. Début Bologna 1804, and for ten years one of the leading Italian tenors. A serious illness changed his voice to bass, and, encouraged by Paisiello, he became one of the greatest basses of the day. His first appearance as such was at Venice, 1812, in the première of *L'Inganno Felice* by Rossini, who also wrote Fernando in *La Gazza Ladra*, the title role in *Maometto II*, Mustafà, and other roles for him; also created Henry VIII in Donizetti's *Anna Bolena*. London, King's, from 1827. After 1840 his vocal powers declined and he became chorus master at Lisbon and Madrid; he taught at the Paris Conservatoire 1842–8; and from then until his death he lived in poverty. His brother **Vincenzo** (1798–1858) was a buffo bass and sang for many years at Milan, Sc., London, and Vienna.

Galli-Curci, Amelita (b. Milan, 18 Nov. 1882; d. La Jolla, Calif., 26 Nov. 1963). Italian soprano. Entirely self-taught as a singer. Début Trani 1906, Gilda; Chicago 1916; N.Y., Met., 1921–30. Renowned for her Gilda, Violetta, Elvira (*Puritani*), Dinorah, &c. She possessed a pure limpid voice of amazing agility, but never quite overcame a tendency to sing slightly sharp. A throat illness forced her to retire; after an operation in 1935 she attempted a come-back, singing Mimì in Chicago 1936, with but little success. She then finally retired. She never appeared in opera in England. (R)

Galli-Marié, Célestine (orig. Marié de l'Isle) (b. Paris, Nov. 1840; d. Vence, nr. Nice, 22 Sept. 1905). French mezzo. Studied with her father, Claude Marié de l'Isle. Début Strasbourg 1859. Engagements followed in France, Belgium, and Italy. Paris, O.C., 1862–85, where she created Mignon (1866) and Carmen (1875). Sang in London, H.M.'s, 1886 with a French company. In 1890 participated in a performance of *Carmen* at the O.C. with Melba, Jean de Reszke, and Lassalle to raise funds for a Bizet memorial.

Gallo, Fortune (b. Torremaggiore, 9 May 1878; d. New York, 27 Apr. 1970). Italian impresario. Established himself in America after 1895 as manager of several touring companies. In 1909 founded the San Carlo Touring Company (q.v.) and was a pioneer of the production of opera sound films.

Galuppi, Baldassare (b. Burano, nr. Venice, 18 Oct. 1706; d. Venice, 3 Jan. 1785). Italian composer. He wrote 100-odd operas, beginning (unsuccessfully) with one at the age of 16. His works began taking the stage in Venice, London (where in Burney's view he came to have more influence on English music than any other Italian), and St. Petersburg. He seems to have been the first composer to realize the significance of the finale (q.v.). His fame mainly rests on his comic operas, especially *Il Filosofo di Campagna* (1754). Dent declared that, while his melody was attractive but not strikingly original, 'he had a firmer grasp of harmony, rhythm and orchestration than most of his Italian contemporaries'.

Gambler, The. Opera in 4 acts by Prokofiev; text by composer, after Dostoyevsky's story (1866). Prod. Brussels, La M., 29 Apr. 1929 (projected Leningrad prod. cancelled because of Revolution); N.Y., 85th St. Playhouse, 4 Apr. 1957; Edinburgh (by Belgrade Co.), 30 Aug. 1962. Alexey is in the service of a General in the

German spa of Roulettenburg. In love with the coquettish Mlle Blanche and, having gambled away most of his money, in debt to a French Marquis, the General anxiously awaits the death of his rich grandmother. But she turns up, and proceeds to lose her fortune at the tables. The General's daughter Paulina, whom Alexey loves, is now faced with marrying the Marquis; to prevent this, Alexey tries to win some money and succeeds in breaking the bank. But when he presents her with the money, she hysterically flings it in his face.

Gand. See *Ghent*.

Garcia, Gustave (b. Milan, 1 Feb. 1837; d. London, 12 June 1925). Italian baritone and teacher. Son and pupil of Manuel II. Début London, H.M.'s, Don Giovanni. Sang at La Scala and elsewhere in Italy, and then taught in London from 1880. His son **Albert Garcia** (1875–1946) was a baritone and teacher at the R.C.M. and G.S.M. London.

Garcia, Manuel I (b. Seville, 22 Jan. 1775; d. Paris, 2 June 1832). Spanish tenor, composer, and teacher. Début Paris 1808 in Paer's *Griselda*. Went to Italy in 1811 where he created Norfolk in Rossini's *Elisabetta, Regina d'Inghilterra* (1815) and Almaviva (1816). Appeared in Paris, London, and New York, where he founded Italian opera in 1825. On 23 May 1826 gave U.S. première of *Don Giovanni* with Da Ponte in the audience. He then took his company to Mexico, where he was robbed by bandits of some £6,000 in gold. He wrote nearly 100 operas and was probably the greatest teacher of singing in his day. His pupils included his children Maria (Malibran), Pauline (Viardot), and Manuel II; also Méric-Lalande, Nourrit, and Géraldy.

Garcia, Manuel II (b. Madrid, 17 Mar. 1805; d. London, 1 July 1906). Spanish bass and teacher. Son of above, who was his teacher. Début N.Y., 1825, Figaro (*Il Barbiere*). From 1829 he devoted himself entirely to teaching. The first to undertake the scientific study of voice production and inventor of the laryngoscope. Published *Mémoires sur la Voix Humaine* (1840) and *Traité Complet de l'Art du Chant* (1847). Went to London 1848, where he was professor at R.A.M. until 1895. His pupils included Jenny Lind, Mathilde Marchesi, Santley, and Stockhausen.

Garcia, Maria Felicita. See *Malibran*.

Garcia, Pauline. See *Viardot*.

Garden, Mary (b. Aberdeen, 20 Feb. 1874; d. Aberdeen, 3 Jan. 1967). Scottish soprano. Went to America as a child, studied singing in Chicago. In 1895 sent by wealthy patroness to Paris where her teachers included Sbriglia (for a week), Bouhy, Marchesi, and Fugère. Befriended by Sybil Sanderson (q.v.) who recommended her to Carré at the O.C. in 1900. Caused a sensation by taking over the role of Louise from Rioton, its creator, halfway through a performance in April that year. Created Mélisande (1902), Leroux's *La Reine Fiammette*, Saint-Saëns's Hélène, Massenet's Chérubin and Sapho, and Erlanger's Aphrodite. N.Y., Manhattan Opera, 1907, Thaïs. Joined Chicago Opera 1910 and became its director 1919–20, running up an enormous deficit; continued to sing with the company until 1931. Her last operatic appearance was an outdoor Carmen at Cincinnati. Autobiography, *The Mary Garden Story*, 1951. (R)

Gardner, John (b. Manchester, 2 Mar. 1917). English composer. Gained experience on the music staff at C.G. (1946–53), when he not only coached singers and conducted but could be seen playing the broken-down piano in *Wozzeck*. His only opera is *The Moon and Sixpence* (1957).

Gardoni, Italo (b. Parma, 12 Mar. 1821; d. Paris, 26 Mar. 1882). Italian tenor. Studied with De Cesari. Début Viadana 1840, Roberto Devereux. After engagements in France, Italy, and Germany came to London in 1847 and created the tenor role in Verdi's *I Masnadieri*. Returned to London regularly until 1874.

Garrick, David (b. Hereford, 19 Feb. 1717; d. London, 20 Jan. 1797). English actor and playwright. His play *The Clandestine Marriage*, which he wrote in collaboration with Coleman, served as a subject to Cimarosa's *Il Matrimonio Segreto*. He supplied the libretto for Arne's *Cymon* and is the subject of operas by Somerville and Stoessel.

Gasparini, Francesco (b. Camaiore, 5 Mar. 1668; d. Rome, 22 Mar. 1727). Italian composer. Of his 65-odd operas, most of them written for Venice, one of the most successful was *Amleto* (1705). The first Hamlet opera, this was not based on Shakespeare's play and had a different plot.

Gassier, Édouard (b. France, 30 Aug. 1820; d. Havana, 18 Dec. 1872). French bass-bar. Studied Paris Conservatoire. Début Paris, O.C., 1845. After appearances in Italy engaged for the T.I., Paris, 1854, and the following year London, D.L. Sang regularly in London until 1870. The first London Méphistophélès, Page (*Merry Wives*), Melitone, Thoas (*Iphigénie en Tauride*). His wife **Josefa Gassier** (*née* Fernández) was a Spanish soprano who first sang in London 1846 under her maiden name.

Gassmann, Florian (b. Most, 3 May 1729; d. Vienna, 20 Jan. 1774). Czech composer. He wrote some 20 operas that won him respect, from Burney among others; the most successful were *L'Amore Artigiano* (1767) and *La Contessina* (1770).

Gatti-Casazza, Giulio (b. Udine, 3 Feb. 1869; d. Ferrara, 2 Sept. 1940). Italian impresario. After training as an engineer took his father's place as director of the Teatro Municipale, Ferrara, 1893. His success led to his appointment as director of La Scala in 1898, where with Toscanini he did much for the theatre's prestige, giving the first performances in Italy of *Boris Godunov* and *Pelléas et Mélisande*, and popularizing Wagner. Director of N.Y. Met. 1908–35, during which period he staged more than 5,000 performances of 177 works. He made the Met. internationally famous by the standard of his productions and the galaxy of stars he assembled. Married first the soprano Frances Alda and then the dancer Rosina Galli. Autobiography, *Memories of Opera* (1941).

Gaubert, Philippe (b. Cahors, 6 July 1879; d. Paris, 8 July 1941). French conductor and composer. Studied Paris Conservatoire. After various orchestral appointments became principal conductor at the Paris Opéra in 1920, a position he held until his death. Conducted *Alceste* and *Ariane et Barbe-Bleue* in London in 1937. His opera *Naïlla* was produced in Paris in 1927. (R)

Gavazzeni, Gianandrea (b. Bergamo, 25 July 1909). Italian conductor, critic, and composer. Studied Milan Conservatory. Until 1940 he was mostly engaged in composition, occasionally conducting performances of his own works. Since 1948 he has conducted regularly at La Scala. He has published books on Donizetti, Pizzetti, Wagner, and Mussorgsky. Glyndebourne 1965. (R)

Gay, John (b. Barnstaple, 16 Sept. 1685; d. London, 4 Dec. 1732). English poet, playwright, and theatre manager. Furnished libretti for Handel's *Acis and Galatea* and Pepusch's *The Beggar's Opera* and *Polly*. Obtained Davenant's letters patent which enabled him to build the first Covent Garden Theatre in 1732.

Gay, Maria (b. Barcelona, 13 June 1879; d. New York, 29 July 1943). Spanish mezzo-contralto. Voice discovered while in prison after being arrested for singing a revolutionary song. Originally self-taught, then studied with Adiny in Paris. Début Brussels, La M., 1902, Carmen; London, C.G., 1906, same role; N.Y., Met., 1908; Chicago 1913–27. Married Zenatello (q.v.) in 1913 with whom she set up a singing school in 1927. Her pupils included Nino Martini and Hilde Reggiani. She and her husband were responsible for the discovery of Lily Pons. (R)

Gayarré, Julián (b. Valle de Roncal, 9 Jan. 1844; d. Madrid, 2 Jan. 1890). Spanish tenor. Studied Madrid Conservatory. Début Padua 1868; London, C.G., 1877, where he created a furore as Fernando in *La Favorite*. Sang in London regularly until 1881 and again 1886–7. Sobin in first London performance of Glinka's *Life for the Tsar*. Created Enzo in *Gioconda* at La Scala, and Duca d'Alba (Donizetti).

Gazza Ladra, La (The Thievish Magpie). Opera in 2 acts by Rossini; text by Gherardini, after the comedy *La Pie Voleuse* (1815) by Baudouin d'Aubigny and Caigniez. Prod. Milan, Sc., 31 May 1817 with Belloc and Galli; London, Hm., 10 Mar. 1821 with Camporese; Philadelphia 14 Sept. 1829. Revived, Florence 1965.

A servant girl, condemned to death for stealing a spoon, is exonerated when it is found in the magpie's nest.

Gazzaniga, Giuseppe (b. Verona, Oct. 1743; d. Crema, 1 Feb. 1818). Italian composer. He wrote over 50 operas, most of them *drammi giocosi*, which were generally popular in his own day. His *Don Giovanni Tenorio* (1786) was among the most successful; both libretto and music were known by Da Ponte and Mozart before they wrote their own *Don Giovanni*.

Gedda, Nicolai (b. Stockholm, 11 July 1925). Swedish tenor of Russian parents. Studied Stockholm with Carl Martin Oehmann. Début Stockholm 1952 in *Le Postillon de Longjumeau*. His success was immediate and led to engagements in Paris and Aix-en-Provence. London, C.G., 1954; N.Y., Met., since 1957, where he created Anatol in Barber's *Vanessa*. This he also sang at Salzburg, where he had appeared in 1957 in Liebermann's *School for Wives*. A musicianly and aristocratic artist. (R)

Gencer, Leyla (b. Istanbul, 10 Oct. 1928). Turkish soprano. Studied Istanbul. Début Ankara 1950, Santuzza. Further study Italy with Arangi-Lombardi and Apollo Granforte. Italian career began Naples, S.C., 1953; Milan, Sc., since 1956, where created Mme Lidoine (*Carmélites*) 1957, and First Woman of Canterbury (*Murder in the Cathedral*) 1959. San Francisco 1956–8; Salzburg 1961; London, C.G., 1962, Elisabeth de Valois and Donna Anna; Glyndebourne 1962, Countess Almaviva. and 1955, Anna Bolena. Also sings Renata (*Fiery Angel*), Lida (*La Battaglia di Legnano*), Lucrezia (*I due Foscari*), and Norma. A highly dramatic singer and actress. (R)

Generalintendant (or **Intendant**) (Ger. = superintendent). The name given to the administrator of a German opera house—often but not necessarily the artistic or musical director.

Gennaro. The hero (ten.) in Donizetti's *Lucrezia Borgia*.

Genoa (It., Genova). Town in Liguria, Italy. First opera performed there, Ferrari's *Il Pastor Regio*, during the 1640's. Genoa did not possess an opera house worthy of so prosperous a town until King Charles Felix (Carlo Felice) urged the building of an opera house there in 1821. The architect was Carlo Barabino, and the beautiful T. Carlo Felice (cap. 2,500) was opened on 7 Apr. 1828 with Bellini's *Bianca e Fernando*. Between 1891 and 1894 the theatre was the scene of the young Toscanini's early triumphs. Wagner's operas have always enjoyed a great popularity there, and Strauss's works have also been given frequently. The theatre was destroyed during the Second World War, but has been partially rebuilt (cap. 1,500). Its present Sovrintendente is Sra. Lanfranco.

Genoveva. Opera in 4 acts by Schumann; text by Robert Reinick, altered by composer, after Tieck's tragedy, *Leben und Tod der heiligen Genoveva* (1799), and Hebbel's tragedy *Genoveva* (1843). Prod. Leipzig 25 June 1850; London, D.L., by R.C.M., 6 Dec. 1893. Revived Florence Festival 1951.

Siegfried departs for the war leaving his wife Genoveva in the care of Golo, who loves her. Because she resists, he tells Siegfried she is unfaithful; Siegfried learns of the treachery just in time to prevent Golo from carrying out his orders to kill Genoveva.

Schumann's only opera. Hebbel's tragedy was also set by Natanael Berg (1947).

Gentle Shepherd, The. A Scots ballad opera in 5 acts; text by Allan

Ramsay. Prod. Edinburgh, Taylor's Hall, 29 Jan. 1729; London, D.L., anglicized as *Patie and Peggie* by Theophilus Cibber, 20 Apr. 1730. Many other versions: that by Richard Tickell prod. D.L. 29 Oct. 1781; N.Y. 7 June 1786. It deals with the loves of two shepherds, the gentle Patie who loves Peggie and the rich Roger who loves Jenny. Originally a comedy without songs (1725), it was changed into a ballad opera after the success of *The Beggar's Opera* at Haddington in 1728, and quickly reached a similar standing in Scotland.

Gérard. A revolutionary leader (bar.) in Giordano's *Andrea Chénier*.

Gerl, Thaddeus (b. Straubing, 28 Oct. 1766; d. Bayreuth, 13 Apr. 1844). German bass and composer. Sang in the Salzburg Choir under Leopold Mozart. Joined Schikaneder's company in 1788 and was first bass at the Theater auf der Wieden, 1789–93. Mozart wrote the aria 'Per questa bella mano' for him. The first Sarastro (1791); his wife Franziska was the first Papagena. He collaborated with Schack (q.v.) in providing music for a number of operas performed in Vienna.

German, (Sir) Edward (b. Whitchurch, 17 Feb. 1862; d. London, 11 Nov. 1936). English composer. Hopes that he would prove Sullivan's successor in the field of light opera were encouraged by the success of *Merrie England* (1902), but his gift was much more slender. *Tom Jones* (1907), a long way after Fielding, and *Fallen Fairies* (1909), with text by Gilbert, were popular. His music had an open if rather simple charm, and was admirably written for the voice.

Germany. See *Aachen, Bayreuth, Berlin, Bielefeld, Braunschweig, Bremen, Chemnitz, Cologne, Darmstadt, Dessau, Detmold, Dortmund, Dresden, Düsseldorf, Duisburg, Essen, Frankfurt, Hagen, Halle, Hamburg, Hanover, Karlsruhe, Kassel, Kiel, Koblenz, Lübeck, Mainz, Mannheim, Munich, Münster, Nuremberg, Oldenburg, Regensburg, Rostock, Saarbrücken, Schwerin, Schwetzingen, Stuttgart, Ulm, Weimar, Wiesbaden, Wuppertal.*

Germont. Alfredo's father (bar.) in Verdi's *La Traviata*. Often referred to as Germont *père*.

Gershwin, George (b. New York, 26 Sept. 1898; d. Hollywood, 11 July 1937). American composer. His first opera *Blue Monday* (1923), later renamed *135th Street*, was a 1-act piece using jazz-type recitative to connect popular songs. It was unsuccessful. *Porgy and Bess* (1935) has come to be regarded as the American national opera. Though hybrid in that it mixes without reconciling jazz and 'serious' music, it triumphs by its melodic charm and exuberance, its brilliant colour, humour, and dramatic vitality, and not least by its power of touching characterization. And that Gershwin's command of two kinds of music was greater than is generally allowed is confirmed by enormous, enduring, popular commercial success and by the warmly expressed admiration of no less a judge than Schoenberg.

On 26 Dec. 1955 in Leningrad a travelling *Porgy* company became the first American theatrical group to perform in the Soviet Union.

Gerster, Etelka (b. Košice, 25 June 1855; d. Pontecchio, 20 Aug. 1920). Hungarian soprano. Studied Vienna with Marchesi. Heard by Verdi who recommended her to the Fenice, Venice, where she made her début as Gilda in 1876. Appearances followed in France, Germany, and Italy. London, H.M.'s, 1877 as Amina, singing there for the next three years, and C.G. 1890, when she was past her prime. She appeared in America 1878–87 where she almost rivalled Patti in popularity: a bitter dislike arose between the two singers. In 1896 she opened a school for singing in Berlin.

Gerster, Ottmar (b. Braunfels, 29 June 1897; d. Leipzig, 1 Sept. 1969). German composer. His *Enoch Arden* (1936), after Tennyson, used popular tunes in separate numbers as well as leitmotives; this with *Die Hexe von Passau* (1941) has been by far the most successful of his operas.

Gerusalemme. See *I Lombardi*.

Ghedini, Giorgio (b. Cuneo, 11 July 1892; d. Genoa, 25 Mar. 1965). Italian composer. The most popular of his seven operas have been *Re Hassan* (1939) and *Billy Budd* (1949).

Ghent (Fr., Gand). Town in E. Flanders, Belgium. First opera performances were in 1698, when Lully's *Thésée* was given by a company of 40, who were allowed free accommodation. Opera is now given regularly at the Royal Opera, opened Aug. 1840 as the Théâtre Lyrique, renamed Royal Opera, 1921. Until 1940 all performances were sung in French. During the German occupation, 1940–4, performances were sung in Flemish. Since 1947 the French and Italian repertory have been sung in French and German and other works in Flemish. A very large repertory and appearances by outstanding international artists have been two of the prominent features of the present régime. Constant Meillander was succeeded as Director in 1961 by Karel Locufier.

Ghislanzoni, Antonio (b. Lecco, 25 Nov. 1824; d. Caprino-Bergamasco, 16 July 1893). Italian writer. Originally a baritone, he took up writing and produced over 80 libretti, the most famous of which was *Aida* for Verdi.

Gianni Schicchi. Opera in 1 act by Puccini; text by Forzano, after an episode (perhaps based on fact) in Canto XXX of Dante's *Inferno* (*c.* 1307–21). The third of Puccini's *Trittico*: prod. N.Y., Met., 14 Dec. 1918, De Luca in title role; Rome, C., 11 Jan. 1919, with Galeffi; London, C.G., 18 June 1920, with Badini.

The relatives of the recently dead Buoso Donati try to alter in their own favour his will leaving his fortune to a monastery. Schicchi (bar.) is called in, and yields to pleas for help from his daughter Lauretta (sop.), in love with Buoso's nephew Rinuccio (ten.). He offers to impersonate the dead man, whose death is not yet public, and dictate a new will leaving money to the relatives; first he warns them of the serious penalties involved in the event of discovery. In bed, disguised as Buoso, he then leaves the most valuable properties to himself, later giving the house to the lovers.

Giannini, Dusolina (b. Philadelphia, 19 Dec. 1902). American soprano. Her father, **Ferruccio,** went to America from Italy in 1885 and made his début at Boston in 1891, singing later with the Mapleson Company, 1891–4, and making the first operatic records for Emile Berliner in 1896. He opened a small theatre in Philadelphia where Dusolina sang La Cieca in *La Gioconda* when only 11. Accepted as a pupil by Marcella Sembrich in 1918. Début Hamburg 1925, Aida. Appearances followed in Berlin, Vienna, London, C.G. (1928); Salzburg 1934–6 as Donna Anna and Alice Ford; N.Y., Met., 1935–42. Created Hester in her brother's opera *The Scarlet Letter*, Hamburg (1938). In recent years devoted her time to teaching. (R)

Giannini, Vittorio (b. Philadelphia, 19 Oct. 1903; d. N.Y., 28 Nov. 1966). American composer. Brother of above. Studied Milan and Juilliard School, N.Y. Operas include *Lucidia* (Munich 1934), *The Scarlet Letter* (Hamburg 1938), *The Taming of the Shrew* (Cincinnati 1953), *The Harvest* (Chicago 1961).

Giaurov, Nicolai (b. Velingrad, 13 Sept. 1929). Bulgarian bass. Studied Moscow. Début Sofia 1956, Don Basilio. Milan, Sc., since 1959; London, C.G., 1962; Vienna since 1962; Chicago 1964. Generally considered the finest bass of his kind since Pinza, especially impressive as Méphistophélès and in Verdi roles. (R)

Gigli, Beniamino (b. Recanati, 20 Mar. 1890; d. Rome, 30 Nov. 1957). Italian tenor. Studied Rome, Santa Cecilia, with Enrico Rosati. Won first prize in international contest at Parma, 1914 ('We have found THE tenor', wrote Bonci in his report). Début Rovigo 1914, Enzo (*Gioconda*). Milan, Sc., 1918, Faust in Boito celebrations under Toscanini. N.Y., Met., 1920–32 and 1938–9, where he was regarded as Caruso's successor. London, C.G., 1930–1, 1938–9, and 1946, in the latter year singing with his daughter Rina in *Bohème* and *Pagliacci* and appearing on the same evening as both Turiddu and Canio. Left America for Italy in 1932 in protest against salary cuts at the Met., and was outspoken in his criticism of the United States. At the end of the war was accused of having been a Fascist. His voice was one of the most beautiful of this century and his technique was as secure at 60 as it had been when he was a young man. He did not always display good taste, and his acting was generally rudimentary. Nemorino, the Duke of Mantua, Des Grieux, Cavaradossi, Lionel, and Chénier were among his best roles. (R)

Gilda. Rigoletto's daughter (sop.) in Verdi's opera.

Gilibert, Charles (b. Paris, 29 Nov. 1866; d. New York, 11 Oct. 1910). French baritone. Studied Paris Conservatoire. Début Paris, O.C., 1889; London, C.G., 1894–1909; N.Y., Met., 1900–3, and Manhattan Opera, 1906–10. First London Le Père (*Louise*) and Boniface (*Le Jongleur de Notre-Dame*). (R)

Gilly, Dinh (b. Algiers, 19 July 1877; d. London, 19 May 1940). French baritone. Studied Paris Conservatoire and with Cotogni. Début Paris, O., 1899, Priest in *Sigurd*; N.Y., Met., 1909–14, where he was heard by Kirkby Lunn who recommended him to C.G. Début there 1911, Amonasro; remained until 1914, reappeared 1919–24. First London Jack Rance and Athanael. Did not possess a great voice, but was an intelligent and musical singer. Settled in England and appeared at C.G. with the Beecham, Carl Rosa, and B.N.O. companies. Married Edith Furmedge and opened a singing school in London. Pupils included Brownlee and Noble. (R) **Renée Gilly,** his daughter, studied with him and made her début Paris, O.C., 1933 as Charlotte. Sang Carmen at C.G. 1937. (R)

Gioconda, La (lit., The Joyful Girl). Opera in 4 acts by Ponchielli; text by 'Tobia Gorrio' (anagram of Arrigo Boito), after Victor Hugo's drama *Angelo, Tyran de Padoue* (1835). Prod. Milan, Sc., 8 Apr. 1876 (two months after Cui's setting of the same subject was prod. in St. Petersburg), with Mariani, Gayarré; London, C.G., 31 May 1883, with Marie Durand, Marconi; N.Y., Met., 20 Dec. 1883, with Nilsson, Stagno.

Act 1. ('La Bocca dei Leoni'.) Disguised in the crowd at a Venetian festival is Enzo Grimaldo (ten.), a banished nobleman loved by the singer La Gioconda (sop.) and loving Laura (mezzo), wife of Alvise Badoero, an Inquisition leader (bass). Barnaba (bar.), an Inquisition spy, is repulsed by La Gioconda and denounces her blind mother La Cieca (con.) as a witch; Alvise has her arrested, but Laura obtains mercy for her, and is given a rosary in gratitude. Laura recognizes Enzo; but so does Barnaba, who promises to persuade Laura to come and see Enzo that night so that they can escape in his boat. He then denounces Laura's unfaithfulness in a letter, which La Gioconda is horrified to overhear being dictated.

Act 2. ('Il Rosario'.) Barnaba guides Laura to the meeting-place. La Gioconda appears and is only stopped from stabbing her rival by recognizing her, from the rosary, as her mother's helper. She persuades Laura to leave and warns Enzo of Alvise's approach. He sets fire to his boat and jumps into the sea.

Act 3. ('La Ca' d'Oro'.) Scene 1. Alvise accuses Laura of unfaithfulness, but the poison she is ordered to drink is changed for a sleeping-drug by La Gioconda. Scene 2. At a party the Dance of the Hours is performed. Barnaba bursts in with the blind woman, who has been praying for the dead. Alvise reveals the body of his wife; Enzo attacks him, but is hauled off to prison. La Gioconda offers herself to Barnaba if he will rescue Enzo.

Act 4. ('Il Canal Orfano'.) Laura is carried to the Giudecca. La Gioconda prepares to kill herself. Enzo appears, and is reunited to Laura as she awakes; they escape. Barnaba arrives to claim La Gioconda, but she stabs herself. Frustrated, he shouts at her that he has killed her mother.

Gioielli della Madonna, I (The Jewels of the Madonna). Opera in 3 acts by Wolf-Ferrari; text by Golisciani and Zangarini—German version *Der Schmuck der Madonna* by Hans Liebstöckl. Prod. Berlin, Kurfürstenoper,

23 Dec. 1911, with Ida Salden, Marak, Wiedemann; Chicago, Auditorium, 16 Jan. 1912, with Carolina White, Bassi, Sammarco; London, C.G., 30 May 1912, with Edvina, Martinelli, Sammarco.

Rafaele is willing even to steal the Madonna's jewels to prove his love for Maliella; but Gennaro wins her by this very deed. Remorsefully she confesses to the enraged Rafaele and rushes away to drown herself, while Gennaro returns the jewels to an image of the Madonna, and then stabs himself.

Owing to the subject being considered profane by the Church in Italy, the opera had to wait until 26 Dec. 1953 for a stage performance in that country, when it was given at Rome.

Giordani, Tommaso (b. Naples, *c.* 1730; d. Dublin, end of Feb. 1806). Italian composer. As member of a family strolling opera company he came to England, then to Ireland. He wrote many operas for London and Dublin, playing an active part in the musical life of both cities.

Giordano, Umberto (b. Foggia, 27 Aug. 1867; d. Milan, 12 Nov. 1948). Italian composer. His ten operas matched the current taste for violent *verismo* in post-Mascagni vein; but even in the most successful of them, *Andrea Chénier* (1896) and *Fedora* (1898), the final impression is of clever exploitation of the proven devices for theatrical and vocal effect rather than genuinely creative composition.

Giorgetta. Michele's wife (sop.) in Puccini's *Il Tabarro*.

Giorgi, Teresa. See *Belloc*.

Giorno di Regno, Un (King for a Day) (sometimes known as *Il finto Stanislao*). Opera in 2 acts by Verdi; text by Romani. Prod. Milan, Sc., 5 Sept. 1840; N.Y., Town Hall, 18 June 1960; London, St. Pancras Town Hall, 21 Mar. 1961. Verdi's second opera, and apart from *Falstaff* his only comic work. A failure, at first receiving only one performance. The plot concerns an imposture as the King of Poland so as to engineer a happy conclusion for the lovers.

Giovanna d'Arco (Joan of Arc). Opera in 4 acts by Verdi; text by Solera after Schiller's drama *Die Jungfrau von Orleans* (1801). Prod. Milan, Sc., 15 Feb. 1845 with Frezzolini in the title role. Initially successful, it soon fell into neglect, though an attempt was made to revive it in Paris for Patti in the 1870's. It was given in Naples and Paris during the Verdi celebration of 1951 with Tebaldi.

Giovanna de Guzman. See *Vêpres Siciliennes, Les*.

Giraldoni, Eugenio (b. Marseilles, 20 May 1871; d. Helsinki, 24 Oct. 1924). Italian baritone. Son of the baritone Leone Giraldoni and the soprano Carolina Ferni, a pupil of Pasta and a famous dramatic soprano. Studied with his mother. Début Barcelona 1891, Escamillo. N.Y., Met., 1904–5. Created Scarpia, Rome, 1900; a famous Gérard and Boris. (R)

Girl of the Golden West, The. See *Fanciulla del West, La*.

Giuditta. Opera in 3 acts by Lehár; text by Paul Knepler and Fritz Löhner. Prod. Vienna, S.O., 20 Jan. 1934 with Novotná and Richard Tauber. Lehár's only full-scale opera.

Giuglini, Antonio (b. Fano, 1827; d. Pesaro, 12 Oct. 1865). Italian tenor. Studied with Cellini. Début Fermo; London, H.M.'s, 1857, Fernando (*La Favorita*). Appeared there, D.L., and Ly. for the next seven years with great success. The first London Riccardo (*Ballo*), Rodolfo (*Luisa Miller*), and Arrigo (*Les Vêpres Siciliennes*). Showed signs of insanity in 1865 in St. Petersburg and when he returned to London in the spring of that year had to be confined to an asylum. Was taken back to Italy in the autumn and died shortly afterwards.

Giulietta. The courtesan (sop. or mezzo), one of Hoffmann's love Offenbach's *Les Contes d'Hoffmann*.

Giulietta e Romeo. See *Romeo and Juliet*.

Giulini, Carlo Maria (b. Barletta, 9 May 1914). Italian conductor. Studied Rome, Santa Cecilia. Music director of Radio Italiana 1946–51; Milan, Sc., 1951–6; London, C.G., 1958–67, where his direction of *Don Carlos* earned him the highest praise. Has conducted at the leading European Festivals including Edinburgh, Aix, Holland, and Florence. Has successfully collaborated with the producer Visconti (q.v.) and Callas in a number of productions at La Scala, including *Alceste* and *Traviata*. One of the most outstanding post-war Italian conductors. (R)

Giulio Cesare (Julius Caesar). (1) Opera in 3 acts by Handel; text by Nicola Francesco Haym. Prod. London, Hm., 20 Feb. 1724 with Senesino and Cuzzoni; Northampton, Mass., Smith College, 14 May 1927. Performed in Germany frequently since 1922. (2) Opera in 3 acts by Malipiero; text by the composer, after Shakespeare. Prod. Genoa, C.F., 8 Feb. 1936, with Inghilleri; N.Y., abridged concert version 13 Jan. 1937. Other operas on the subject are by Cavalli (1646), Sartorio (1677), Freschi (1682), Novi (1703), Keiser (1710), and Perez (1762).

Gizziello (orig. Gioacchino Conti) (b. Arpino, Naples, 28 Feb. 1714; d. Rome, 25 Oct. 1761). Italian male soprano. Studied with Gizzi from whom he took his stage name. Début Rome 1730; London 1736 in Handel's *Ariodante*; subsequently created leading roles in same composer's *Atalanta*, *Arminio*, *Giustino*, and *Berenice*. From 1743 to 1753 he was mostly in Lisbon, but managed to visit Naples in 1747 to take part in a celebrated performance of *Achille in Sciro* with Caffarelli. Retired 1753.

Glasgow. Town in Scotland. Apart from the usual visits by touring opera companies, there have been seasons by the Glasgow Grand Opera Society, formed in 1905, which has given Goldmark's *The Queen of Sheba* (1921), Ponchielli's *I Promessi Sposi* (1932), *Idomeneo* (1933), *Les Troyens* (1935), and *Béatrice et Bénédict* (1936). These last three were all British premières and were given under the direction of Erik Chisholm. Since 1945 the Society's productions have included *Mefistofele*, *Le Roi d'Ys*, *Nabucco*, and MacCunn's *Jeannie Deans*. The first season of Scottish Opera was given there in 1962 (*Madama Butterfly* and *Pelléas et Mélisande*). By 1971 the company had been able to mount a complete *Ring* cycle and *Les Troyens*.

Glastonbury. See *Boughton*.

Glinka, Mikhail Ivanovich (b. Novospasskove, Govt. of Smolensk, 1 June 1804; d. Berlin, 15 Feb. 1857). Russian composer. Though sketches exist for operas on Scott's *Rokeby*, Zhukovsky's *Marina Grove* (1834), and Kukolnik's *The Bigamist* (1855), Glinka completed only two operas, *A Life for the Tsar* (originally, and now renamed, *Ivan Susanin*) (1834–6) and *Ruslan and Ludmila* (1838–41); upon these his position as father of Russian music principally rests. 'The idea of contrasting the national music of Russia and Poland' was the spur that set him to work on *A Life for the Tsar*. In some ways reminiscent of French and Italian grand opera—Glinka was an assiduous absorber of influences—it is nevertheless Russian to the core, deep below the top dressing of local settings and folk melodies. It is the first Russian opera to give expression to a passionate sense of national unity. *Ruslan* is by contrast a brilliant fairy-tale, a riot of colourful episodes that gave Glinka rich opportunity to indulge his talent in this direction without taxing too severely his limited structural ability. Even the score's brightest gems show an extraordinary mixture of manners, in each of which Glinka distinguishes himself without properly unifying them into a cogent personal style—a sign of the inspired amateur that he was at heart.

Gloriana. Opera in 3 acts by Britten; text by William Plomer, after Lytton Strachey's study *Elizabeth and Essex* (1928). Commissioned by C.G. for the Coronation of Queen Elizabeth II, and produced at a Gala Performance in her presence, 8 June 1953, with Cross and Pears; Cincinnati 8 May 1955, with Borkh, Conley, and Krips.

Gluck, Alma (orig. Reba Fiersohn) (b. Bucharest, 11 May 1884; d. New

York, 27 Oct. 1938). American soprano of Rumanian birth. Studied N.Y. Début N.Y., Met., 1909, Sophie (*Werther*). After three seasons at the Met. and a further period of study with Sembrich she devoted herself to the concert platform. (R) Her daughter **Marcia Davenport** has written a *Life of Mozart* and an operatic novel *Of Lena Geyer* based on incidents in her mother's life.

Gluck, Christoph Willibald (b. Erasbach, 2 July 1714; d. Vienna, 15 Nov. 1787. German composer, (?) of Bohemian stock. Gluck is opera's second founder. His first opera, *Artaserse* (1741), had a Metastasio libretto, and to begin with he accepted the Metastasian conventions of the day—*da capo* arias, profusely ornamented, sung perhaps by castratos and linked in *recitativo secco*. Established in Vienna after a London visit, he gradually became dissatisfied with the tyranny of singer over composer which these artifices represented. The librettist Durazzo encouraged his restlessness, though their *L'Innocenza Giustificata* (1755) is as blameless as its title. In 1758 a Viennese vogue gave him the chance to set a number of French *opéras comiques*; if their strings of numbers linked by speech represented no formal advance, Gluck was now writing music for characters more vividly alive than the two-dimensional Metastasian gods and kings. In 1761 he set Gaspar Angiolini's *Don Juan*, a dramatic *ballet d'action* in place of the conventional *divertissement en danse*. Then in 1762 came *Orfeo ed Euridice*, in which Gluck, stimulated now by his librettist Calzabigi, stood forth as reformer: *recitativo accompagnato* made the music more fully continuous, and the singers' claims were set below the aim of a purer, more genuinely classical approach to drama in music. A few conventional operas followed; then in *Alceste* (1767) opera finally became music-drama, and in the famous preface Gluck declared his aims: to purge singers' abuses, to 'restrict music to its true office by means of expression and by following the situations of the story', and to strive always for perfect clarity and simplicity. *Alceste* triumphed. *Paride ed Elena* followed in 1770, and then Gluck turned to French opera. *Iphigénie en Aulide* (1773) was reluctantly accepted by the Paris Opéra, and its production in 1774, followed by new versions of earlier operas, touched off an artistic rivalry with Piccinni, to the city's delight. In *Armide* (1777) Gluck set out to be 'more of the poet and painter than the musician', and claimed to have discovered how to identify characters musically. *Iphigénie en Tauride* (1779) was an instant success, but *Écho et Narcisse* (1779) failed. Gluck returned to Vienna, where he composed little more.

It is the simplicity he sought that remains Gluck's greatest quality—a simplicity that can be barren but frequently reaches the sublime. His greatness was achieved with a bewildering lack of technical resources, but such is his mastery that this is almost always turned to positive, expressive account. Said Berlioz, 'La nudité ne convient qu'aux déesses.'

Glückliche Hand, Die (The Favoured Hand). *Drama mit Musik* in 1 act by Schoenberg; text by the composer. Prod. Vienna, V.O., 14 Oct. 1924; Philadelphia, Ac. of M., 11 Apr. 1930.

The subject is the artist's quest for happiness; this is undertaken by a man (bar.), who is the protagonist, though there are mimed parts for another man and a woman, and a chorus which comments at the start and finish.

Glyndebourne. The name of the house and estate of John Christie near Lewes, Sussex, in the grounds of which a festival opera house was built in 1934 for the purpose of giving model performances of opera in ideal surroundings. The inspiration behind the venture came from Christie's wife, the soprano Audrey Mildmay (q.v.). The first Glyndebourne Festival opened on 28 May 1934 with *Figaro*, followed the next evening by *Così fan tutte*. The conductor was Fritz Busch and the producer Carl Ebert, who between them set a standard in musical ensemble and production which far exceeded anything seen or heard in British opera at that time.

By 1939 the theatre had been enlarged, and the seating capacity was increased from 300 to 600; the present capacity is 800. The repertory then included *Figaro*, *Così*, *Entführung*, *Zauberflöte*, *Don Giovanni*, *Don Pasquale*, and Verdi's *Macbeth* (first perf. in England). Audrey Mildmay, Ina Souez, Luise Helletsgrüber, Irene Eisinger, Margherita Grandi, John Brownlee, Dino Borgioli, Willi Domgraf-Fassbänder, David Franklin, Roy Henderson, Mariano Stabile, Heddle Nash, and Francesco Valentino were among the regular artists. During the war years Glyndebourne became the home of evacuees. It reopened in 1946, when the English Opera Group produced *The Rape of Lucretia*; in 1947 the same organization gave *Albert Herring*, and Ebert returned to produce *Orfeo* with Ferrier. In 1948 and 1949 there were no opera performances, though Glyndebourne, which was under the general management of Rudolf Bing (q.v.), was responsible for the opera at the first five Edinburgh Festivals. Glyndebourne resumed its own annual summer festivals in 1950, when Busch returned to collaborate again with Ebert. Busch died in 1951, and his place as chief conductor was taken by Vittorio Gui, who has been responsible for the inclusion of several of Rossini's operas in the repertory. Ebert announced his retirement at the end of the 1959 Festival and was succeeded by Rennert. Additions to the repertory in the post-war period have included *La Cenerentola*, *L'Italiana in Algeri*, *Il Barbiere di Siviglia*, *Le Comte Ory*, *La Pittra del Paragone*, *Falstaff*, *Arlecchino*, *Il Segreto di Susanna*, *Ariadne auf Naxos*, *Idomeneo*, *Alceste*, *The Rake's Progress*, *Der Schauspieldirektor*, *Rosenkavalier*, *Fidelio*, *I Puritani*, *L'Elisir, d'Amore Elegy for Young Lovers* (Henze), *L'Incoronazione di Poppea*, *Pelléas et Mélisande*, *Capriccio*, and *Anna Bolena*; and at Edinburgh, *La Forza del Destino* and *Un Ballo in Maschera*. The post-war generation of Glyndebourne artists has included Oralia Dominguez, Sena Jurinac, Ilva Ligabue, Graziella Sciutti, Elsie Morison, Monica Sinclair; Sesto Bruscantini, Geraint Evans, Richard Lewis; the conductors John Pritchard (now music director), Paul Sacher, Raymond Leppard; and the designers Oliver Messel, Osbert Lancaster, John Piper, and Ita Maximovna.

Glynne, Howell (b. Swansea, 24 Jan. 1907; d. Toronto, 29 Nov. 1969). Welsh bass. Studied with Ben Davies and Reinhold v. Warlich. Joined Carl Rosa chorus, occasionally taking small roles; Sept. 1931 sang Sparafucile. Leading bass S.W. 1946–51 and again from 1956; C.G. 1951–6. Fiesco in the English première of *Simone Boccanegra*, and Mr. Crusty in *The School for Fathers* at S.W.; created Lavatte in Bliss's *The Olympians* at C.G. He had a rich voice and a penchant for buffo roles. (R)

Gobbi, Tito (b. Bassano del Grappa, 24 Oct. 1915). Italian baritone. Originally studied law, then turned to singing. Studied Rome with Crimi; début Rome 1938, Germont; London, C.G., since 1950; San Francisco 1948; Chicago since 1954. Has sung at all the leading Italian opera houses, and appears regularly in Vienna. Intelligence, musicianship, and acting ability, allied to a good if not powerful voice, make Gobbi one of the finest singing actors of his generation. A distinguished Verdi and Puccini interpreter (Rigoletto, Macbeth, Boccanegra, Posa, Iago, Falstaff, Scarpia, Rance, Michele); also a celebrated Wozzeck and Figaro. Has a repertory of nearly 100 operas, and has made 26 films. Début as producer, Chicago and C.G., 1965, *Simon Boccanegra*. (R)

Godard, Benjamin (b. Paris, 18 Aug. 1849; d. Cannes, 10 Jan. 1895). French composer. The most successful of his six operas was *La Vivandière* (1895), which reached England; but it is only the Berceuse from *Jocelyn* (1888) that has survived.

Goethe, Johann Wolfgang von (b. Frankfurt, 28 Aug. 1749; d. Weimar, 22 Mar. 1832). German poet. Operas based on his works are as follows. *Die Mitschuldigen* (1769): Riethmüller (1957). *Götz von Berlichingen* (1773): Goldmark (1902). *Erwin und Elmire* (1773): G. L. Vogler (1781); Bergt

(1840); Schoeck (1916). *Satyros* (1773): Borkovec (1938). *Clavigo* (1774): Ettinger (1926). *Die Leiden des jungen Werthers* (1774): R. Kreutzer (1792); Puccita (1804); Gentili (1862); Massenet (1882). *Stella* (1776): Deshayes (*Zélia*, 1791; *La Suite de Zélia*, 1792). *Claudine von Villa Bella* (1776): Kerpen (18th cent.); Beecke (18th cent.); J. R. Reichardt (1789); Eberwein (1815); Stolze (1831); Kienlen (19th cent.). *Scherz, List und Rache* (1780): P. C. Kayser (? 1786); Winter (1790); E. T. A. Hoffmann (1799); Bruch (1858); Wellesz (1928). *Jery und Bätely* (1780): Winter (1790); Schaum (1795); J. F. Reichardt (1801); Bierey (?1803;) K. Kreutzer (1810); Frey (*c.* 1810); Rietz (1825); A. Marx (1825); Bronsart (1873); Stiehl. *Egmont* (1787): Dell'Orefice (1878); Salvayre (1886); Meulemans (1960). *Faust* (Pt. 1, 1808; Pt. 2, 1832): I. Walter; Lickl (1815); Béancourt (1827); Berlioz (*Huit Scènes de Faust*, 1829; some used in *La Damnation de Faust*, 1846); Lindpainter (1831); Bertin (1831); Pellaert (1834); Rietz (1836); Lutz (*Faust and Marguerite*, 1855); Gounod (1859); Boito (*Mefistofele*, 1868); Lassen (1876); Zöllner (1887). *Wilhelm Meister* (1829): Thomas (*Mignon*, 1866). Lehár's *Frederica* (1928) is a quasi-biographical operetta on Goethe.

Goetz. See *Götz.*

Gogol, Nikolai Vassilievich (b. Sorochintsi, 31 Mar. 1809; d. Moscow, 3 Mar. 1852). Russian writer. Most Gogol operas are on the stories in *Evenings on a Farm near Dikenka* (1831–2). These are as follows. *Christmas Eve*: Tchaikovsky (*Vakula the Smith*, 1874; revised as *Cherevichki* (*The Slippers*) 1885: sometimes known in the West as *Les Caprices d'Oxane*); Soloviev (1880); Rimsky-Korsakov (1895); Afanasiev; Lissenko. *A Night in May*: Sokalsky (1867); Rimsky-Korsakov (1879); Lissenko (*The Drowned Woman*). *St. John's Eve*: Tikhotsky (?1912). *The Terrible Revenge*: Kochetov (1903). *Sorochinsky Fair* (1831–2): Mussorgsky (unfin., 1880). *The Portrait*: Rosenberg (1953). *Diary of a Madman*: Searle (1958). Others are as follows. *The Marriage* (1834, one act only); Jiránek; Martinů (1953). *The Nose* (1835): Shostakovich (1927–8). *Viy* (1835): Gorielov (1897); K. Moor (1903). *Taras Bulba* (1835): Afanasiev; Kashperov; Lissenko; Sokalsky (*The Siege of Dubno*); M. S. Rousseau (1919). *Revizor* (1836): Zádor (1935): Zanella (1940); Egk (1957).

Golaud. Mélisande's husband (bass-bar.), in Debussy's *Pelléas et Mélisande.*

Golden Cockerel, The. Opera in 3 acts by Rimsky-Korsakov; text by Byelsky, after Pushkin's poem (1834). Prod. Moscow, 7 Oct. 1909; London, D.L., 15 June 1914; N.Y., Met., 6 Mar. 1918. The 14th and last of the composer's operas. The censor refused to sanction performance during the composer's lifetime owing to the resemblance between King Dodon's Court and that of Tsar Nicolas II and the implied criticism of the inefficient conduct of the Russo-Japanese war. The composer wanted his singers to dance as well as sing, but this was found too exhausting and so for the Petrograd production Fokine devised the idea of having them in boxes, with the action mimed by ballet dancers. Despite protests from the composer's family this version introduced the work to Western Europe; but recent productions in New York and London have reverted to the original version.

The opera tells of the miraculous golden cockerel, given to the old King Dodon by the Astrologer, which crows at the sign of imminent danger. Dodon brings back the beautiful Queen of Shemakhan to his capital; when the Astrologer demands payment for the cockerel he is killed by Dodon, and the cockerel kills the King.

Goldmark, Carl (b. Keszthely, 18 May 1830; d. Vienna, 2 Jan. 1915). Austro-Hungarian composer. His first opera, *Die Königin von Saba* (1875), was also his most successful: colourful and tuneful, it was taken up all over Germany and also in England and America. Goldmark's later operas were *Merlin* (1886), *Das Heimchen am Herd*, after Dickens (1896), *Die Kriegsgefangene* (1899), *Götz von*

Berlichingen, after Goethe (1902), and *Ein Wintermärchen*, after Shakespeare (1908).

Goldoni, Carlo (b. Venice, 25 Feb. 1707; d. Paris, 6 Feb. 1793). Italian dramatist. His brilliant comedies were the basis for countless opera librettos of the day, and have not infrequently been used in modern times.

Goldovsky, Boris (b. Moscow, 7 June 1908). Russian, now naturalized American, opera producer and conductor. Studied Moscow, Berlin, and Budapest, and at the Curtis Institute, N.Y., with Reiner. Has held appointments in the opera departments of the Cleveland Institute of Music, the New England Conservatory, and the Berkshire Music Center (q.v.), where he was the organizer of the productions of *Peter Grimes*, *Albert Herring*, *La Clemenza di Tito*, &c. He acts as commentator for the weekly broadcasts during the season from the Metropolitan.

Goldschmidt, Berthold (b. Hamburg, 18 Jan. 1903). British composer and conductor of German birth. In 1926–7, asst. cond. Berlin State Opera; 1927–9, cond. Darmstadt Opera; 1931–3, artistic adviser Berlin Städtische Oper; 1947, cond. Glyndebourne Opera at Edinburgh. His operas are *Der gewaltige Hahnrei* (1932) and *Beatrice Cenci* (1951), a prize-winner in the Arts Council competition for the Festival of Britain, but not produced.

Goldschmied von Toledo, Der (The Goldsmith of Toledo). A *pasticcio*, made up of music by Offenbach, by Stern and Zamara; text by Zwerenz after Hoffmann's story *Das Fräulein von Scuderi* (1818). Prod. Mannheim 7 Feb. 1919; Edinburgh 16 Mar. 1922 by B.N.O.C., subsequently at C.G. Subject also used by Hindemith for *Cardillac*.

Goltz, Christel (b. Dortmund, 8 July 1912). German soprano. Studied with Ornelli-Leeb in Munich. Joined chorus of Furth Opera 1935; début there as Agathe. Dresden State Opera 1936–50; London, C.G., 1951; N.Y., Met., 1954. Sings regularly in Munich, Vienna, and Berlin. Created Orff's *Antigonae*, Dresden 1949, and Liebermann's *Penelope*, Salzburg 1954. Possesses a clear and brilliant voice, three octaves in range, and sings and enacts her roles with great intensity. A renowned Salome, Elektra, Marie (*Wozzeck*); has a repertory of more than 120 roles. (R)

Gomes, Carlos (b. Campinas, 11 July 1836; d. Belém, 16 Sept. 1896). Brazilian composer of Portuguese origin. For his first opera, *A Noite do Castelo* (1861), he was officially honoured; for his second, *Joana de Flandres* (1863), he won a scholarship to Italy. Several operas were produced there, and his style became Italianate, before a triumphant return to Brazil, where more works followed. *O Guarani* (1870) has been given with success in Italy and England; other successful operas include *Salvator Rosa* (1874), *Maria Tudor* (1879), and *O Escravo* (*The Slave*) (1889).

Good Friday Music (Karfreitagzauber). The music in Act 3, scene 1, of Wagner's *Parsifal* as Parsifal is anointed in preparation for his entry into the Grail castle.

Goossens, Eugène I (b. Bruges, 25 Feb. 1845; d. Liverpool, 30 Dec. 1906). English conductor of Belgian origin. Came to England in 1873; in 1882 joined Carl Rosa, with whom cond. first performance in English of *Tannhäuser* (1882). In 1892 cond. command performance *La Fille du Régiment* before Queen Victoria. His son **Eugène II** (b. Bordeaux, 28 Jan. 1867; d. London, 31 July 1958) worked under him in the Carl Rosa; then principal cond. in succession of Burns-Crotty, Arthur Rousbey, and Moody-Manners companies. Principal cond. Carl Rosa 1899–1915, maintaining high standards set by his father, and making many additions to the repertory. Joined Beecham's company at Birmingham 1917, and cond. in Beecham season at H.M.'s. Opened 1918 Beecham season at D.L. with *Ivan the Terrible*. Married Annie Cook, former contralto of Carl Rosa and daughter of basso buffo

T. Aynsley Cook; their five children included **Eugène III** (b. London, 26 May 1893; d. London, 13 June 1962), composer and conductor. Eugène III began conducting career assisting Beecham and his father, cond. some performances of B.N.O.C. and Carl Rosa; latterly he conducted little opera, though he directed his own *Judith* (1929) and *Don Juan de Mañara* (1937) at C.G. Both operas have librettos by Arnold Bennett. In them his operatic experience is evident in the dramatic presentation of librettos whose merits are primarily literary, though his own highly chromatic yet chaste style is itself not essentially operatic. (R)

Gorr, Rita (really Marguerite Geimaert) (b. Ghent, 18 Feb. 1926). Belgian mezzo-soprano. Début Antwerp 1949, Fricka; Strasbourg 1949–52. Won first prize at International Contest at Lausanne 1952, after which she was engaged at the Paris Opéra. London, C.G., since 1959; N.Y., Met., 1962. Has sung in Lisbon, Naples, Rome with success, and in 1958 sang Fricka at Bayreuth. Repertory includes Kundry, Dalila, Hérodiade, Charlotte, Octavian, and Orphée. (R)

Gossec, François Joseph (b. Vergnies, 17 Jan. 1734; d. Passy, 16 Feb. 1829). Netherlands composer. His innovations, which suggest he is a forerunner of Berlioz, are seldom evident in his 19 operas, all but one of which were prod. in Paris. He was less successful with his serious operas than with his comedies, which include *Les Pêcheurs* (1766) and the once popular *Toinon et Toinette* (1767). On the staff of the Paris Opéra 1780–5.

Göteborg (Gothenburg). Town in Sweden. The main operatic centre outside Stockholm. The Lyric Theatre was originally intended for drama and operetta, but after 1890 attention was increasingly given to opera. From 1918 a mixed repertory of drama, opera, and operetta was abandoned in favour of a Volksoper type of repertory. During the inter-war years many notable names were associated with the theatre, including Flagstad and Thorborg. The present director is Bernhard Sönnerstedt, whose interest in modern works is reflected in the repertory.

Gotovac, Jakov (b. Split, 11 Oct. 1895). Yugoslav conductor and composer. His best-known work is *Ero the Joker* (1935), a consciously folk-influenced, eclectic piece transferring with some success tried Italian methods to a local setting. Cond. Zagreb Opera from 1923, and visited England with the company in a repertory that included *Ero* in 1955.

Götterdämmerung. See *Ring des Nibelungen*.

Götz, Hermann (b. Königsberg, 7 Dec. 1840; d. Hottingen, 3 Dec. 1876). German composer. His *Der widerspänstigen Zähmung* (1874) (based on *The Taming of the Shrew*) became, as soon as Götz (with the help of Ernst Frank) managed to achieve a production, a European success, though not an enduring one. The music (much admired by G. B. Shaw) is tender, sincere, elegant, but scarcely robust enough for the comedy. *Francesca da Rimini*, finished by Ernst Frank and prod. posthumously 1877, was unsuccessful.

Gounod, Charles (b. Paris, 17 June 1818; d. Saint-Cloud, 18 Oct. 1893). French composer. He declared that 'the composer who would achieve a successful career must create it through writing operas'. His first, *Sapho* (1851), indicates his gifts in this direction; Adam suggested Gluck as the main influence. *La Nonne Sanglante* (1854) attempted the melodramatic, but Gounod recovered himself in the witty *Le Médecin Malgré Lui* (1858) and in *Philémon et Baucis* (1860); both have charm and certainty of touch. Meanwhile he had been at work on *Faust* (1859), his masterpiece. With it Gounod became the foremost French composer of his day, though it held the seeds of his decline: the grand manner so enraptured him that he never really escaped back to the style of which he was potentially a great master. The finest moments of *Faust* are not those of high drama, but the humbler delights in which the score abounds. *La Colombe* (1860) was a 2-act piece, prod. at Baden-Baden; Gounod's conquest of the Opéra was unhappily not clinched with *La Reine de Saba* (1862) or *Roméo et Juliette* (1867), which suffer from adherence to the musical conventions of the day. *Mireille* (1864) has a much simpler charm. Religious music claimed him almost completely until 1876, when he returned without conspicuous success to opera. *Cinq-Mars* (1877), *Polyeucte* (1878), and *Le Tribut de Zamora* (1881) represent the more sanctimonious, grandiose side of his nature that stifled what were undoubtedly original and appealing expressive gifts. *Mireille* and *Roméo* remain in the French repertory; the once ubiquitous *Faust* seems to have lost some of its former popularity.

Goyescas. Opera in 3 scenes by Granados, amplified and scored from piano pieces after Goya's paintings; text added by Fernando Periquet. Prod. N.Y., Met., 28 Jan. 1916—first Spanish opera in N.Y.; London, R.C.M., 11 July 1951. When he hears that Rosario has been invited to a ball by his rival, the toreador Paquiro, Fernando decides to go too. He is fatally wounded by Paquiro in a duel, and dies in Rosario's arms. The song 'The Lover and the Nightingale' occurs in scene 2.

Gozzi, Carlo (b. Venice, 13 Dec. 1720; d. Venice, 14 Apr. 1806). Italian playwright, whose comic *fiabe drammatiche*, many of them written in opposition to Goldoni, were a popular source for operas, especially in Germany since the beginning of the Romantic movement; some were translated by Schiller. Operas on his works include the following. *L'Amore delle Tre Melarance* (1761): Prokofiev (1919). *Il Corvo* (1761): A. J. Romberg (1788); J. P. E. Hartmann (1832). *Il Re Cervo* (1762): Henze (1956). *La Donna Serpente* (1762): Himmel (*Die Sylphen*, 1806); Wagner (*Die Feen*, 1888); Casella (1931). *Turandot* (1762): Blumenroeder (1810); Reissiger (1835); Hoven (1839); Løvenskjöld (1854); Bazzini (1867); Busoni (1917); Puccini (1924, unfin.). *I Pitocchi Fortunati* (1764): Benda (*Das tartarische Gesetz*, 1780).

Graener, Paul (b. Berlin, 11 Jan. 1872; d. Salzburg, 13 Nov. 1944). German composer. The best known of his eight operas are *Don Juans letzte Abenteuer* (1914), his first success, and *Friedemann Bach* (1931).

Graf, Herbert (b. Vienna, 10 Apr. 1904). Austrian, now American, producer. Son of famous Viennese critic Max Graf. Studied Vienna and held appointments in Münster, Breslau, and Frankfurt. Left Germany during Hitler régime and went to America where he staged opera in Philadelphia and was at the Met., N.Y., 1936–60. Director Zürich Opera 1960–3. Geneva, Grand Théâtre, from 1965. Produces regularly at Salzburg, La Scala, Verona, Holland Festival. Responsible for Handel's *Samson*, *Boris*, and *Parsifal* at C.G. 1958–9.

Gramophone. Opera and opera singers have played an important part in the history of the gramophone; indeed, it has been said with some truth that 'Caruso made the gramophone and the gramophone Caruso'. In the mid-1890's Gianni Bettini began to record the voices of singers in New York on cylinders, and he offered for sale items by Ancona, Saléza, Plançon, Van Dyck, and Van Rooy; it is also known that he possessed cylinders made by Arnoldson, Calvé, Melba, Nordica, Sembrich, Nicolini, Campanini, Tamagno, the De Reszkes, Lassalle, and Maurel. Meanwhile Emil Berliner had perfected his machine, which played a disk. In Europe, the Gramophone Company was established in 1898, and by 1902 its artists included Caruso, Chaliapin, Calvé, and Battistini. Various other companies quickly established themselves, and virtually every singer of note began to record. The first complete opera recording (with many cuts) was *Il Trovatore*, made sporadically between 1903 and 1906 and sung by sixteen different singers. There was also a virtually complete *Pagliacci* conducted by the composer. In Germany there was a *Fledermaus* in 1907, *Faust* (Destinn,

Jörn, Knüpfer) in 1908, *Carmen* (Destinn, Jörn), *Cavalleria* (Hempel), and *Pagliacci*. In France nine complete operas were recorded by the Pathé Company before 1914, including *Roméo et Juliette* (Gall, Affre, Journet), *Faust*, and *Carmen*.

Electrical recording replaced the acoustic techniques in the 1920's. Sizeable extracts from *Parsifal*, *The Ring*, and *Tristan* were recorded at Bayreuth in 1927, and excerpts from a live performance in Berlin of *Meistersinger* (Schorr, List, Schützendorf, Hutt, Blech) in 1928. In the same year complete recordings of operas by the company of La Scala, Milan, began in Europe with *Rigoletto*; the popular Verdi–Puccini repertory was nearly all recorded twice, once by H.M.V. and once by Columbia; in Paris, performances of *Carmen*, *Pelléas*, *Faust*, and *Manon* were quickly recorded. In the 1930's and even during the war years the Italian studios were able to record Gigli in complete performances of *Pagliacci*, *Cavalleria*, *Tosca*, *Bohème*, *Madama Butterfly*, *Andrea Chénier*, *Ballo in Maschera*, and *Aida*; and during the occupation of France there were complete recordings made of *Pelléas* and *La Damnation de Faust*. In America in 1947 Columbia signed a contract with the Met. Opera, and its first complete opera was *Hänsel und Gretel*.

The advent of long-playing recording opened up a whole new horizon, and since 1950 the operatic gramophone repertory has been widened to include complete recordings of many works that even ten years ago were only names in reference books. Not only have the popular works been recorded and re-recorded, but the old favourites of the last century by Rossini, Bellini, Donizetti, and unfamiliar Verdi works have all appeared; the Slavonic repertory (Czech and Russian) and some important modern works can now be heard in one's own home. If no composer has yet written an opera specially for the gramophone as he has for radio and television, contemporary operas by Britten, Menotti, Stravinsky, and others are also available. The coming of stereophonic sound has meant another bout of recording the standard repertory, as well as first recordings of *Das Rheingold*, *Siegfried*, and *Peter Grimes* by a Decca team under John Culshaw, which has evolved new and brilliantly successful 'production' techniques to create a realistic, non-theatrical image of the opera in the mind's eye and ear.

Along with all the benefits and pleasures of the gramophone there remains the danger that recorded opera may become a thing so artificial, so contrived, that the theatrical impulse vanishes from the finished product; one must also recognize the fact that gramophone records of great singers make for a celebrity-minded operatic public which has little time for performances by an ensemble without 'stars', and which expects its stars to shine as brightly in the opera house as they do on records.

Granados, Enrique (b. Lérida, 27 July 1867; d. at sea, 24 Mar. 1916). Spanish composer. *María del Carmen* (1898) was an immediate success on its Madrid production; this was followed by five works to texts by Apeles Mestre —*Petrarca*, *Picarol* (1901), *Follet* (1903), *Gaziel* (1906), and *Liliana* (1911)—before he revised some of his piano pieces based on Goya in 1914 to make his masterpiece, *Goyescas* (N.Y., Met., 1916). Though influenced to some extent by the late 19th-century European romantic tradition, Granados's music is Spanish not merely in its contours but in essence and technique.

Grand opera. In English, serious opera without spoken dialogue. In French, more precisely, *grand opéra* as opposed to *opéra comique* means a serious epic or historical work in four or five acts that uses the chorus actively and includes a ballet. This was the typical genre of the Paris Opéra in the 19th century.

Grandi, Margherita (b. Hobart, Tasmania, 10 Oct. 1899). Italian soprano, born of Italian and Irish parents, educated in France. Studied with Giannina Russ. Début Milan 1932, Aida. After engagements in the Italian opera houses, engaged for Lady

Macbeth, Glyndebourne 1939. Returned to England 1947 to sing Tosca, Cambridge Theatre. C.G. 1949–50; created Diana in Bliss's *Olympians*. One of the few modern singers of the 'grand style', whose Tosca and Lady Macbeth were sung and acted with a sweep and conviction rare today. (R)

Grane. Brünnhilde's horse in the *Ring*. Seldom seen on the stage since the war, but formerly ridden with effect into the flames by singers including Leider and Lawrence.

Grassini, Josephina (orig. Giuseppina) (b. Varese, 8 Apr. 1773; d. Milan, 3 Jan. 1850). Italian contralto. Studied Milan; début Parma 1789. Heard by Napoleon 1800, who took her to Paris. In London, 1804, she became Billington's rival. Not everyone admired her voice: according to Mount-Edgcumbe, 'No doubt the deaf would have been charmed by Grassini, and the blind must have been delighted with Mrs. Billington'. Sang in English première of Cimarosa's *Gli Orazi ed i Curiazi*. Continued to sing in public until 1829 and then turned to teaching; her pupils included Pasta, Giuditta, and Giulia Grisi. Biographies by Pougin (Paris, 1920) and Gavoty (Paris, 1947).

Grau, Maurice (b. Brno, 1849; d. Paris, 14 Mar. 1907). Czech impresario. Went to America when a child. Began management in 1872, organizing tours of Bernhardt, Offenbach, and the Kellogg Opera Company. Joined Abbey 1890 to give season at N.Y. Met., and from 1891 to 1897 directed Met. with Abbey and John B. Schoeffel; became sole manager of theatre 1897–1903. On death of Augustus Harris appointed managing director of C.G., London, a position he held until the end of the 1900 season.

Graun, Karl Heinrich (b. Wahrenbrück, nr. Dresden, 7 May 1704; d. Berlin, 8 Aug. 1759). German tenor and composer. Studied Dresden; début Brunswick 1725, where he produced several of his own Italian works and met the Crown Prince of Prussia, later Frederick the Great, who invited him to become court Kapellmeister in Berlin in 1740. There Graun produced more than 30 Italian works during the next 15 years.

Graupner, Christoph (b. Hartmannsdorf, 13 Jan. 1683; d. Darmstadt, 10 May 1760). German composer. Wrote eight operas for Hamburg and three for Darmstadt before he gave up the stage for church and chamber music. One of the most important German opera composers of Bach's time.

Graz. Town in Steiermark, Austria. Opera is performed at the Opernhaus (cap. 1,400), built 1899.

Graziani, Francesco (b. Fermo, 26 Apr. 1828; d. Fermo, 30 Jun. 1901). Italian baritone. Début Ascoli Piceno 1851. London, C.G., 1855 (début as Carlos in *Ernani*) until 1880. The first London Di Luna, Nelusko, Posa, and Amonasro. He possessed one of the most beautiful and mellow voices of the last century, but apparently little artistry, for he was constantly criticized for his unmusical and poor phrasing and his unpurposeful acting. His brother **Lodovico** (1820–85) was a dramatic tenor who created Alfredo in *Traviata*. Two other brothers, **Giuseppe** and **Vincenzo,** had brief careers as bass and baritone respectively.

Great Britain. See *Aldeburgh, Arts Council, Birmingham, British Broadcasting Corporation, British National Opera Company, Cambridge, Carl Rosa, Denhof Opera Company, Edinburgh, English Opera Group, Glasgow, Glyndebourne, Intimate Opera Company, London, Manchester, Oxford, Welsh National Opera Company.*

Greece. The first opera given in Greek seems to have been *Entführung* (Alexandria, 1889), though a Greek translation of *Cenerentola* was published at Patras in 1879. Samara's *Flora Mirabilis* (1886) was to an Italian text; the first Greek opera was Kalomiris's *O Protomastoras* (*The Master Builder*) (1916). The first operatic performances in Greece took place at the Teatro San Giacomo, Corfu, towards the middle of the 18th century. This was the period when the Ionian islands were occupied by the Venetians, and the performances were given by

Italian companies. Elsewhere in Greece opera was not heard until about 1840, when an Italian company performed in Athens and other towns. The first Greek company was formed in 1887 and after a year's preparation performed for the first time on 14 Mar. 1888 at the Boucoura Theatre, Athens, in the Greek comic opera, *The Parliamentary Candidate*, by Spyros Xinda. The leading tenor in this company, Jean Apostollou, enjoyed a considerable success in Italy before his early death in 1904. Special performances of opera for Maria Callas have been given at the ancient theatre of Epidaurus. See also *Athens* and *Lavranga*.

Gregor, Joseph (b. Cernăuti, 26 Oct. 1888; d. nr. Vienna, 12 Oct. 1961). Austrian librettist and writer. He wrote the librettos for Strauss's *Friedenstag*, *Daphne*, and *Die Liebe der Danae*. For many years he was the stage archivist of the Austrian National Library. He wrote books on Strauss and Clemens Krauss, and his correspondence with Strauss was published during the 1950's.

Greindl, Josef (b. Munich, 23 Dec. 1912). German bass. Studied Munich with Bender and Bahr-Mildenburg. Début Munich in a semi-professional performance of *Freischütz*, 1935, then Krefeld as Hunding, 1936. Berlin since 1942, first Staatsoper, then Städtische Oper. Bayreuth 1943, and leading bass there since 1951. Has also appeared in England, Italy, and North and South America. (R)

Gretel. Hänsel's sister (sop.) in Humperdinck's opera.

Grétry, André (b. Liège, prob. 10 or 11 Feb. 1741; d. Montmorency, nr. Paris, 24 Sept. 1813). French composer of Walloon descent. While studying in Rome his intermezzo *La Vendemmiatrice* (1765) was successful, but his aim was Paris and *opéra comique*. Encouraged by Voltaire, whom he had met in Geneva, he arrived there in 1767, where his works (especially *Le Tableau Parlant* of 1769) quickly found favour. Some 50 operas followed in 35 years, witness to Grétry's fertility and, within limits, to his versatility; for as well as comedies and fairy stories—of which *Zémire et Azor* (1771) is the best known—he attempted serious opera, as in *Richard Cœur de Lion* (1784), his finest work. The neatness with which Grétry as a theorist labelled the constituents of music was at once his strength and his weakness as a composer. That the theorist saw the composer's shortcomings is revealed in several comments; he knew himself to be a good melodist but to lack harmonic or contrapuntal art. He tried to relegate harmony to the position of 'the base of the statue'. His works are graceful, untroublesome, always effective, and in certain instances unexpectedly imaginative in the handling; but in most of his *opéras comiques* the harmonic poverty and the enervating tidiness of the conception tend to dominate for any but the most benevolent listener.

Grieg, Edvard (b. Bergen, 15 June 1843; d. Bergen, 4 Sept. 1907). Norwegian composer. Only three scenes of his sole attempt at opera, *Olav Trygvason* (1873), were completed; they survive as a cantata.

Grisélidis. Opera in a prologue and 3 acts by Massenet; text by Silvestre and Morand. Prod. Paris, O.C., 20 Nov. 1901 with Bréval, Fugère, cond. Messager; N.Y. 19 Jan. 1910 with Garden, Dalmorès.

Alain loves Grisélidis, wife of the Marquis. The Devil tries to persuade her of her husband's infidelity and to accept Alain. She resists, and he takes her child; this is eventually retrieved by the Marquis.

Grisi, Giuditta (b. Milan, 28 July 1805; d. Robecco, 1 May 1840). Italian mezzo-soprano. Niece of Grassini and cousin of Carlotta Grisi, the dancer. Studied Milan; début Vienna 1826. Bellini wrote Romeo for her in *I Capuletti ed i Montecchi* (1830). Appeared in London and Paris but was overshadowed by her sister Giulia.

Grisi, Giulia (b. Milan, 28 July 1811; d. Berlin, 29 Nov. 1869). Italian soprano. Sister of above, who was her first teacher. Début 1828, Milan, in Rossini's *Zelmira*. Created Juliet to her sister's Romeo in *I Capuletti ed i*

Montecchi, and then Adalgisa in *Norma*, La Scala. Dissatisfied with conditions in Milan and unable to obtain a release from La Scala, she fled Italy and went to Paris, where her aunt Grassini, her sister, and Rossini were at the Théâtre Italien; here she obtained an engagement. Sang regularly in Paris 1832–49, where she created Elvira in *Puritani* and Norina in *Don Pasquale*, the former with Rubini, the latter with Mario, whom she married. London début 1834. Except in 1842, sang in London every season until 1861, first at King's Theatre (later Her Majesty's Opera), then C.G. An attempted reappearance in 1866 at H.M.'s as Lucrezia Borgia was disastrous. Appeared in America 1854. Her voice was rich, beautiful, and flexible, and suitable for lyric and dramatic roles.

Griswold, Putnam (b. Minneapolis, 23 Dec. 1875; d. New York, 26 Feb. 1914). American bass-baritone. Studied London, R.C.M., and with Randegger. Début London, C.G., 1901; then followed further study with Bouhy in Paris and Emmerich in Berlin. After appearances in Germany he toured America with Savage Company as Gurnemanz. N.Y., Met., 1911–14. A famous Daland, Pogner, King Mark.

Grob-Prandl, Gertrud (b. Vienna, 11 Nov. 1917). Austrian soprano. Studied Vienna with Burrian. Début Vienna, V.O., 1938, Santuzza. After several years in Zürich engaged for Vienna, S.O., 1948 as dramatic soprano. London, C.G., 1951, Turandot. Appearances at all leading theatres in Europe and South America. Noted for her Brünnhilde, Isolde, and Ortrud. (R)

Grossmächtige Prinzessin. Zerbinetta's (sop.) recitative and aria in Strauss's *Ariadne auf Naxos*, in which she tries to convert Ariadne to her more fickle view of love. Technically one of the hardest coloratura arias in opera.

Gruhn, Nora. See *Grünebaum*.

Grümmer, Elisabeth (b. Diedenhofen, Alsace-Lorraine, 31 Mar. 1911). German soprano. Spent three years as professional actress at Aachen. Singing début there 1941, First Flowermaiden. After engagements at Duisburg and Prague went to Berlin Städtische Oper as leading lyric soprano 1946. London, C.G., 1951, Eva; Bayreuth since 1957; divides time equally between Vienna, Berlin, and Hamburg. Possesses a beautiful voice and aristocratic style which particularly suit her to Mozart and Strauss. (R)

Grünebaum, Hermann (b. Giessen, 2 Jan. 1872; d. Chipstead, Surrey, 5 Apr. 1954). German conductor and coach. Studied Frankfurt and Berlin. Début 1893 Coblenz. Chorus-master London, C.G., 1907–33; chief coach B.N.O.C. and in charge of Opera class, R.C.M., from 1924, where he conducted the première of Holst's *Sāvitri*. His daughter **Nora Gruhn** (b. 1908), soprano, sang at Cologne 1930–1, C.G. 1929–32, and S.W. 1932–6 and 1945–8. Lucinda in the first English performance of *The School for Fathers*.

Gruppetto (It. = little group). Its most common form is the alternation of a main note with two subsidiaries, immediately above and below. Beginning as one of the myriad ornaments of baroque composition, it has survived with particularly beautiful effect in Wagner.

Guadagni, Gaetano (b. Lodi, *c.* 1725; d. Padua, Nov. 1792). Italian male contralto, later soprano. Début Parma 1747. Went to London in 1748 as member of a burletta company. Heard by Handel who engaged him to sing in *Samson* and *Messiah*. After a further period of study under Gizziello in Lisbon, created title role in Gluck's *Orfeo* (1762) and *Telemaco* (1765). Returned to London 1769 and thought by Burney to have no equal on the operatic stage as an actor. Still singing in Italy in the 1780's.

Guarnieri, Antonio (b. Venice, 2 Jan. 1883; d. Milan, 25 Nov. 1952). Italian conductor. After playing the cello in the Martucci Quartet, turned to conducting at Siena 1904, quickly making his mark. Engaged on a seven-year contract for Vienna 1912, but quarrelled because of the conditions of work and quickly resigned. Followed Toscanini at La Scala 1929, and conducted there regularly until shortly before his death. Conducted the first performances in Italy of Bloch's *Macbeth* and Respighi's *Belfagor*. Highly regarded as a musician and technician by his colleagues and singers. (R) His son **Arrigo** (b. Lugo di Romagna, 22 May 1910) is one of the resident conductors of the Nederlandsche Oper.

Guarrera, Frank (b. Philadelphia, 3 Dec. 1923). American baritone. Studied Curtis Inst., N.Y. Début Boston 1949. Engaged by Toscanini to participate in Boito Commemoration at La Scala 1948. N.Y., Met., from 1948 in French and Italian repertory. (R)

Gudehus, Heinrich (b. Altenhagen, nr. Celle, 30 Mar. 1845; d. Dresden, 9 Oct. 1909). German tenor. Studied Brunswick with Malwina Schnorr von Carolsfeld and Berlin with Gustav Engel. Début Berlin 1871, Nadori in Spohr's *Jessonda*. After engagements in Lübeck, Freiburg, and Bremen, was leading tenor at Dresden 1880–90; Bayreuth 1882–9. First C.G. Tristan and Walther. First London Parsifal (concert version, R.A.H., 1884). N.Y., Met., 1890–1.

Güden, Hilde (b. Vienna, 15 Sept. 1917). Austrian soprano. Studied Vienna Conservatory with Mme Wetzelsberger. Début Zürich, 1939, Cherubino. After an engagement in Munich joined the Vienna S.O. 1946. London, C.G. (with Vienna Company), 1947; N.Y., Met., since 1950, in which year she was also made Austrian Kammersängerin. A versatile artist equally at home in Mozart and Lehár, Johann and Richard Strauss. Has sung in a number of modern works including Weill's *Mahagonny*, Britten's *Rape of Lucretia*, Blacher's *Romeo und Julia*, and Stravinsky's *Rake's Progress*. (R)

Guerre des Bouffons, La. See *Bouffons, Guerre des*.

Guglielmi, Pietro Alessandro (b. Massa di Carrara, 9 Dec. 1728; d. Rome, 18 Nov. 1804). Italian composer. Began career in Naples; composer to King's T. 1767–72, when he also introduced a version of Gluck's *Orfeo* to London. Back in Italy, he regained popularity with difficulty in the face of Cimarosa and Paisiello. He wrote some 100 operas, which Burney credited with 'some Neapolitan fire' marred by haste and lack of self-criticism. His son **Pietro Carlo Guglielmi** (b. ? Naples, *c.* 1763; d. Naples, 28 Feb. 1817), also a composer, also visited London (1808–10) before returning home. He wrote about 40 operas that were chiefly vehicles for singers and have not lasted.

Guglielmo. Fiordiligi's lover (bar.) in Mozart's *Così fan tutte*.

Guglielmo Ratcliff. Opera in 4 acts by Mascagni; text by Andrea Maffei after Heine's tragedy (1822). Prod. Milan, Sc., 16 Feb. 1895. A work of Mascagni's student days, though subsequently revised, with a libretto that was a literal translation of the Heine play. The work had little success. Also opera by Cui (1869).

Gui, Vittorio (b. Rome, 14 Sept. 1885). Italian conductor and composer. Studied Rome, Santa Cecilia, under Falchi. Début Rome, Teatro Adriano, 1907, *La Gioconda*. Milan, with Toscanini, 1923–5 and 1932–4; London, C.G., 1938–9 and 1952; Glyndebourne since 1952. Established the Florence Orchestra 1928, from which emerged the Florence May Festival in 1933. One of the finest Italian conductors of Gluck, Mozart, and Rossini, and responsible for revivals of several neglected operas in Italy, including *Comte Ory*, *Alceste*, and *Così fan tutte*. His own works include *Fata Malerba* (Turin 1927). (R)

Guillaume Tell (William Tell). Opera in 4 acts by Rossini; text by Étienne de Jouy and Florent Bis after Schiller's dramatic version (1804) of the well-known William Tell legend. Prod. Paris 3 Aug. 1829, with Cinti-Damoreau, Nourrit, Dabadie; London, D.L., 1 May 1830 (in an adapted version by Planché and Bishop), and H.M.'s 11 July 1839 (orig. version);

N.Y. 19 Sept. 1831. Although highly admired by Bellini and Wagner, the inordinate length of the opera (nearly six hours) prevents it from becoming a firm repertory favourite; but it does contain ensemble passages of the greatest dramatic power, especially in Act 2. Donizetti said of it: 'The first and last acts were written by Rossini; the second by God!' Also operas by Grétry (1791) and B. A. Weber (1795).

Guiraud, Ernest (b. New Orleans, 23 June 1837; d. Paris, 6 May 1892). French composer. He is less well known by his own operas—the last of which, *Frédégonde*, was completed after his death by Saint-Saëns—than for writing recitatives for Bizet's *Carmen* and finishing the orchestration of Offenbach's *Contes d'Hoffmann*.

Gulbranson (orig. Norgren), **Ellen** (b. Stockholm, 4 Mar. 1863; d. Oslo, 2 Jan. 1947). Swedish soprano. Studied Stockholm and Paris with Marchesi. Début Stockholm 1889, Amneris, Bayreuth 1896–1914, Kundry and Brünnhilde; London, C.G., 1900 and 1907–8. Greatly admired by Melba, who begged her to come and sing some of her Wagner repertory to her in private. (R)

Gunsbourg, Raoul (b. Bucharest, 25 Dec. 1859; d. Monte Carlo, 31 May 1955). Rumanian composer and impresario. After managing opera in Russia and Nice, became director of the Monte Carlo Opera in 1890, a position he held for more than 50 years. Under his régime Monte Carlo saw the premières of many important works including the stage version of *La Damnation de Faust* (1893) (his own adaptation), *Le Jongleur de Notre-Dame* (1902), *Don Quichotte* (1910), *Pénélope* (Fauré) (1913), *La Rondine* (1917), *L'Enfant et les Sortilèges* (1925), *Judith* (Honegger) (1926), *L'Aiglon* (Honegger–Ibert) (1937). His own operas included *Le Vieil Aigle* (Monte Carlo 1909, Chicago 1916) and *Ivan the Terrible* (Brussels 1910).

Gunther. Hagen's half-brother (bar.), King of the Gibichungs, in Wagner's *Götterdämmerung*.

Guntram. Opera in 3 acts by Strauss; text by the composer. Prod. Weimar, 10 May 1894, with Pauline de Ahna and Heinrich Zeller; cond. Strauss. Revived Berlin 1942 for composer's 78th birthday. Strauss's first opera. Set in 13th-century Germany, it tells of Guntram and Friehold, members of the Holy Society of Peace, to which they have vowed fidelity and obedience; and of Guntram's love for Freihild, daughter of Duke Robert.

Gura, Eugen (b. nr. Žatec, 8 Nov. 1842; d. Aufkirchen, 26 Aug. 1906). German bass-baritone. Studied Vienna and Munich. Début Munich 1865 in *Der Waffenschmied* (Lortzing). Appeared in Breslau, Leipzig, and Hamburg; and again in Munich 1883–95. Created Donner and Gunther, Bayreuth 1876; also heard there as Mark and Sachs. First London Mark and Sachs, D.L. 1882, when he also sang Lysiart in revival of *Euryanthe*. Published his memoirs, *Erinnerungen aus meinem Leben*, 1905.

Gura, Hermann (b. Breslau, 5 Apr. 1870; d. Bad Wiessee, 13 Sept. 1944). German baritone, son of above. Studied Munich. Début Weimar 1890. Later became a producer; director of the Berlin Komische Oper from 1911; was responsible for the first London production of *Rosenkavalier* and other works in the 1913 Beecham season at C.G., when he also sang Beckmesser. (R). His wife **Annie Gura-Hummel** (b. 1884), soprano, sang the Goose-girl in the first London production of *Königskinder* (1911). (R)

Gurlitt, Manfred (b. Berlin, 6 Sept. 1890). German composer and conductor. Studied with Humperdinck and Karl Muck. After various appointments, music director Bremen 1914–27. His works were banned by the Nazis, and he settled in Japan, where he organized opera performances. His nine operas include a setting of *Wozzeck* made at about the same time as Berg's, and independently successful on its production in 1926. He returned to Germany in 1953 to direct some of his works. (R)

Gurnemanz. The veteran Knight of the Grail (bass) in Wagner's *Parsifal*.

Gutheil-Schoder, Marie (b. Weimar, 10 Feb. 1874; d. Bad Ilmenau, 8 Oct. 1935). German soprano. Studied Weimar; début there 1891. Engaged by Mahler for Vienna 1900, remaining there until 1926. At first she was attacked by the Viennese critics as 'the singer without a voice', but later became a firm favourite as Carmen, Pamina, Elvira, Elektra, and Octavian. Only London appearance, C.G. 1913, Octavian. (R)

Guthrie, (Sir) Tyrone (b. Tunbridge Wells, 2 July 1900; d. Newbliss, 15 May 1971). British producer. Connected with Old Vic since 1933, became director of the Sadler's Wells Opera in 1941, and produced *Figaro*. When Joan Cross became Director of Opera, Guthrie remained director of the Vic-Wells organization, and continued his operatic work with productions of *Bohème* and *Traviata*. Other operas he produced for S.W. included a highly controversial *Carmen*, and *Barber of Seville*. At C.G. he was responsible for *Peter Grimes* (1946) and *Traviata* (1948), and at the Met., N.Y., for *Carmen* (1952) and *Traviata* (1957). Guthrie eschewed tradition and aimed at great naturalness in his productions; he handled crowd scenes with much success, but his approach to opera was not always dictated by the music.

Gutrune. Gunther's sister (sop.) in Wagner's *Götterdämmerung*.

Gwendoline. Opera in 2 acts by Chabrier; text by Catulle Mendès. Prod. Brussels, La M., 10 Apr. 1886. The Viking King Harald loves Gwendoline, daughter of his prisoner, the Saxon Armel, who pretends to consent to their marriage but arranges for her to kill Harald. She refuses, and commits suicide when Armel kills Harald.

Gye, Frederick (b. London, 1809; d. Dytchley, 4 Dec. 1878). English impresario. Manager of C.G. 1849–77. Joined by Mapleson for two seasons at C.G. 1869–70. Statue stands today by the gentlemen's cloak room at C.G. His son **Ernest** succeeded him, and married Albani.

Gyrowetz (Cz., Jirovec), **Adalbert** (b. Budějovice, 19 Feb. 1763; d. Vienna, 19 Mar. 1850). Bohemian composer. After successes in Vienna, Naples, and Paris, came to London. *Semiramide* was commissioned for the Pantheon, but the score was destroyed when the theatre burned down in 1792. Back in Vienna, he wrote more operas, among them the successful *Der Augenarzt* (1811) and *Hans Sachs*, the first treatment of the subject of Wagner's *Die Meistersinger*. His *Il finto Stanislao* (1818) was written to the Romani libretto later used by Verdi. In all, he wrote some 30 operas, *Singspiele* and melodramas that were very successful in their day. He was liked and admired by Mozart, Haydn, and Beethoven.

H

Hába, Alois (b. Vizovice, 21 June 1893). Czech composer, the principal advocate of microtonal music. *New Earth* (comp. 1935–6) is in the normal semi-tonal system, and remains unperformed. *The Mother* (1931) uses a quarter-tone scale; it was first produced in Munich in 1931. *Thy Kingdom Come* (1934) requires the singers to master sixth-tones. After 1948 his microtone class at Prague Conservatory was dissolved, though he has continued composing and teaching.

Habanera. A Spanish erotic song and dance imported from Africa via Havana (whence the name). The most familiar operatic example is Carmen's 'L'Amour est un oiseau rebelle' in Act 1 of Bizet's opera. Also the name of an opera by Laparra (1908).

Habich, Eduard (b. Kassel, 3 Sept. 1880; d. Berlin, 15 Mar. 1960). German baritone. Début Koblenz 1904; Berlin, S.O., 1910–30; London, C.G., 1924–36; N.Y., Met., 1935–7; Bayreuth's Alberich 1911–31, Klingsor 1912–27; also a famous Beckmesser and Faninal. (R)

Hadley, Henry (b. Somerville, 20 Dec. 1871; d. N.Y., 6 Sept. 1937). American composer. His operas are *Safié* (1909), *Azora* (1917), *Bianca* (1918), *Cleopatra's Night* (1920), *A Night in Old Paris* (1925), *The Garden of Allah*, and *Nancy Brown*.

Häfliger, Ernst (b. Davos, 6 July 1919). Swiss tenor. Studied Zürich, Vienna under Patzak, and Prague under Carpi. Début Salzburg 1949, Tiresias in Orff's *Antigone*. Berlin, Städtische Oper, since 1953; Glyndebourne 1956. Excels in Mozart and in modern music. (R)

Hageman, Richard (b. Leeuwarden, 9 July 1882; d. Beverly Hills, 6 Mar. 1966). Dutch, later naturalized American, composer and conductor. Studied Amsterdam and Brussels. After acting as coach for Netherlands Opera and accompanist to Mathilde Marchesi and Yvette Gilbert, engaged as conductor at N.Y., Met., 1912–21 and 1935–6. His *Caponsacchi* was produced at Freiburg 1932, and N.Y., Met., 4 Feb. 1937.

Hagen. Alberich's son (bass) and Gunther's half-brother in Wagner's *Götterdämmerung*.

Hagen. Town in North Rhine–Westphalia, Germany. Opera is given in the rebuilt Städtische Bühnen (cap. 940), opened 1949.

Hahn, Reynaldo (b. Caracas, 9 Aug. 1875; d. Paris, 28 Jan. 1947). French composer and conductor. Of his numerous operettas, the most successful were *Ciboulette* (1923) and *Mozart* (1925). As a conductor he specialized in Mozart. Director of Paris Opéra 1945–6.

Haitzinger, Anton (b. Wilfersdorf, Liechtenstein, 14 Mar. 1796; d. Vienna, 31 Dec. 1869). Austrian tenor. Studied Vienna. Début Vienna, W., 1821, Gianetto (*La Gazza Ladra*). Created Adolar (*Euryanthe*) which he sang in London, C.G., 1833, when he was also heard as Florestan, Tamino, and Max, all opposite Schröder-Devrient. Later established a singing school at Karlsruhe, and published a handbook on singing.

Halasz, László (b. Debrecen, 6 June 1905). Hungarian, later naturalized American, conductor and manager. Studied Budapest; began professional career as pianist. Held conducting appointments in Budapest (1929–30), Prague (1930–2), Vienna (1933–6), and Salzburg (1929–36). American début St. Louis 1936, *Tristan und Isolde*. Director St. Louis Grand Opera Association 1939–42; N.Y., City Center (q.v.), 1943–51, when he was dismissed after differences with the Board of directors. Subsequently conducted in Europe.

Halévy (orig. Lévy), **Fromental** (b. Paris, 27 May 1799; d. Nice, 17 Mar.

1862). French-Jewish composer. Studied Paris with Berton and Cherubini and won Prix de Rome (1819). First success with *Clari*, Malibran in the title role, at Théâtre Italien, 1829. His real fame dated from 1835 when his masterpiece *La Juive* was produced, followed the same year by the charming *L'Éclair*. Although he composed some 20 or more operas, most were handicapped by poor libretti and his own careless workmanship. He was overshadowed by Meyerbeer, whom he tried to imitate. He taught successfully at the Paris Conservatoire from 1827, and his pupils included Gounod, Massé, and Bizet, who married his daughter. His brother Léon was an author and dramatist, whose son **Ludovic** (1834–1908) collaborated with Meilhac in writing librettos for Offenbach, Bizet, and Delibes.

Halka (Helen). Opera in 2 (later 4) acts by Moniuszko; text by Włodzimierz Wolski, after K. W. Wójcicki's story *Góralka*. Prod. Wilno, 20 Dec. 1847 by amateurs. In revised form, Warsaw 1 Jan. 1858—1,000th performance in 1935; N.Y. June 1903; London, University College, 8 Feb. 1961. Still the most popular Polish opera. Halka loves Janusz, who loves Sophie. Janusz seduces Halka, but forsakes her; she kills herself while Janusz and Sophie are being married. Wallek-Walewski wrote a sequel called *Jontek's Revenge*. *Halka* has been translated into many languages, including Esperanto.

Halle. Town in Saxony, Germany. Birthplace of Handel. The Theater des Friedens was destroyed in 1945. The new Stadttheater (cap. 1,035), opened on 31 Mar. 1951, gives a yearly Handel Festival under the musical direction of Hans-Tanu Margraf. Recent revivals include *Deidamia*, *Radamisto*, *Rinaldo*, *Ezio*, *Ottone*, *Tamerlano*, *Admeto*, *Giulio Cesare*, *Poro*, and *Orlando*.

Hallé, Charles (orig. Carl Halle) (b. Hagen, 11 Apr. 1819; d. Manchester, 25 Oct. 1895). English pianist and conductor of German birth. Though best known for his foundation of the orchestra bearing his name, his work for opera included seasons conducting in Manchester 1854–5 and at H.M.'s 1860–1, and the first English concert performance of Berlioz's *Damnation de Faust*.

Hallström, Ivar (b. Stockholm, 5 June 1826; d. Stockholm, 11 Apr. 1901). Swedish composer. Best known for his operas, whose use of folk-song made him Sweden's national opera composer. The most popular were *The Enchanted Cat* (1869) and *The Bewitched One* (1874).

Hamburg. City-state in north Germany. Possesses the oldest-established permanent opera company in Germany, dating from 1678, in which year the Theater am Gänsemarkt was opened, with *Adam und Eva*, a *Singspiel* by Johann Theile. This building was pulled down in 1750, by when it had seen more than 280 operas produced, both Italian and German. From 1738 the operas were purely Italian, under the management of Mingotti, who in 1751 continued at the Reithaus. Hamburg has been the scene of the first performance of Handel's *Almira* (1705), of the first German *Otello* (1888), *Eugene Onegin* in the presence of the composer (1892), *Peter Grimes* (1947), and *A Midsummer Night's Dream* (1961). The Hamburg Stadttheater was built in 1874 with Pollini as artistic director; Mahler was music director 1891–7, Klemperer 1910–14, Pollak 1917–30, Böhm 1930–3, Jochum 1933–44, Grüber 1946–51, Ludwig since 1951. The Staatsoper was destroyed during an air-raid in 1943, but in 1945 the stage portion of the old opera house was refitted to accommodate stage, orchestra, and auditorium. In 1949 the auditorium was enlarged; and on 15 Oct. 1955 the new opera house, seating 1,649, built at the cost of 5½ million marks, was opened with a performance of *Die Zauberflöte*, produced by Rennert (q.v.). He was intendant from 1946 until 1956; Heinz Tietjen 1956–9; Liebermann 1959–72; Everding succeeded him in 1972. Since 1946 Hamburg has staged more than 40 contemporary operas, and in Feb. 1961, Liebermann was able to give a week of contemporary works: *Wozzeck*, *Lulu*,

Oedipus Rex, *Antigone* (Honegger), *Schule der Frauen*, *Prinz von Homburg*, *Aniara*, and *A Midsummer Night's Dream*.

The Hamburg Company has included during the last 100 years Jenny Lind, Lilli Lehmann, Lotte Lehmann, Schumann, Melchior, Bockelmann, Hotter, and Pilarczyk.

Hamlet. Opera by Thomas; text by Barbier and Carré, after Shakespeare's tragedy (1600–1). Prod. Paris, O., 9 Mar. 1868; Lon., C.G., 19 June 1869; N.Y., Ac. of M., 22 Mar. 1872. Also opera by Searle; text by composer after Shakespeare. Prod. Hamburg, 5 Mar. 1968; Lon., C.G., 18 Apr. 1969.

Hammerstein, Oscar (b. Stettin, 8 May 1846; d. N.Y., 1 Aug. 1919). German, later naturalized American, impresario. Went to America as an immigrant and made a fortune from inventing a cigar-making machine. Wrote plays and built a number of theatres. Turned to opera in 1906 when he built the Manhattan Opera House (q.v.) where he established a brilliant company and an interesting repertory which threatened to rival the Met. In 1908 he built the Philadelphia Opera House which he ran in association with his N.Y. Company. In 1910 the Met. purchased his interests and stipulated that he should not produce opera in the U.S. for ten years. He went to London and built the London Opera House (Stoll Theatre) in 1911, which could not stand up to the opposition of C.G. and collapsed after two seasons. In 1913 he built the Lexington Opera House in N.Y. and attempted to produce opera there, but was restrained legally by the Met. His grandson, **Oscar Hammerstein II** (b. 12 July 1895), is known for his work in American musicals.

Hammond, Joan (b. Christchurch, New Zealand, 24 May 1912). New Zealand soprano. Studied Sydney Conservatory, Vienna, and London with Dino Borgioli. Début as singer 1931; stage début Vienna 1939. Carl Rosa Co. 1942–5 and guest appearances C.G. 1948–51; S.W. 1951 and 1959 when she sang the title role in the first British stage performance of *Rusalka*. Has made guest appearances in opera in N.Y., Russia, and Spain. Awarded O.B.E. 1953. Retired 1965. (R)

Handel, George Frideric (b. Halle, 23 Feb. 1685; d. London, 14 Apr. 1759). German, later English, composer. Studied with Zachau, the Halle organist, becoming assistant organist himself in 1697. Leaving for Hamburg in 1703, he joined the opera house under Reinhard Keiser (q.v.); here his first operas, *Almira* and *Nero* (lost), were produced in 1705. Two more, *Florinda* and *Dafne*, were written before he left for Italy in 1706. These are modelled on Keiser's operas, not least in their mixture of styles. In Florence he wrote *Rodrigo* (*c.* 1707 or 1708, partly lost) and in Venice *Agrippina* (1709), which shows him struggling to assert his personality against the influence of Alessandro Scarlatti: the Italian style he absorbed on this journey coloured much of his later work. He returned to Germany in 1710 before journeying on to London.

Here he found Italian *opera seria* (q.v.), with all its stultifying conventions, the ruling social passion and the dominant force on music. *Rinaldo* (1711, at the Queen's, later King's, Theatre) typifies this pattern, which consists of a minimum of recitative and elaborate *da capo* arias (a few duets, hardly any trios or quartets) for singers' display that were usually either emotional, aphoristic, or metaphorical; it was the disconcerting convention that the singer should exit immediately after each one. *Rinaldo* was a success and swiftly led to *Il Pastor Fido* (1712), which drew on previous works; *Teseo* (1713), Handel's only 5-act opera; and *Silla* (1713). *Amadigi* (1715) is a more mature piece, developing the bolder orchestral effects, achieved by great variety of instrumental means, which increase in number as time goes by.

Five years elapsed, during which Handel became a director with Bononcini and Ariosti of the Royal Academy of Music (an operatic business venture that functioned 1720–8) and went to scour Italy for singers, before *Radamisto* (1720), in which his style is fully mature. The orchestration is richer, the invention more personal and confident, the forms treated with greater originality wherever convention permitted. It is a more striking opera than the three which followed: *Muzio Scevola* (1721), of which Handel wrote only Act 3; *Floridante* (1721), in which the music has to survive an unusually stilted libretto; and *Ottone* (1723), a still more conventional piece with a few striking numbers. *Flavio* (1725) also suffers from a stilted libretto. But by now Handel's ascendancy over his great London rival Bononcini was established, and he could command the services, if not predict the behaviour, of all the great singers of the day.

With *Giulio Cesare* (1724) the range of effects is widened and the conventions begin to be more richly vitalized. It has many thrilling orchestral effects, including a stage orchestra. But in total achievement it is perhaps excelled by *Tamerlano* (1724), which contains much great music, including a wealth of accompanied recitatives, that culminates in an elaborate death scene, linking seven movements of aria and recitative, that is one of the most powerful scenes in all Handel. *Rodelinda* (1725) maintains this level of invention. Both are remarkable for that rarity with Handel, an important tenor part.

The 1725–6 season was the one in which the engagement of Faustina Bordoni precipitated the notorious rivalry with Cuzzoni: partisanship led to rowdy scenes at the opera house, lampoons were published, Handel's rivalry with Bononcini was played up. In Feb. 1726 Handel became an English citizen. *Scipione*, which dates from this year, is comparatively dull; it was quickly followed by *Alessandro*, in which Bordoni made her début with Cuzzoni. *Admeto* (1727) sets a thoroughly conventional classical plot of the day, but the arias are extremely fine; much the same is true of *Riccardo Primo* (1727) (which anticipates Verdi's *Otello* by opening with a storm off the coast of Cyprus). Only *Siroe* (1728) and *Tolomeo* (1728) followed before the Academy collapsed.

Having set himself up again at the King's Theatre with Heidegger, Handel made a fresh recruiting trip to Italy and returned for *Lotario* (1729), which failed: it is distinguished chiefly for a typically Handelian matriarch figure. *Partenope* (1730), to an excellent comic libretto, strikes out in a new direction, though it contains a no less typically Handelian battle scene whose noisy orchestral symphony caused much public uneasiness. *Poro* (1731) is a striking work, but *Ezio* (1732), which is all solo *da capo* arias except for a chorus at the end, is more conventional. *Sosarme* (1732) contains another fine matriarch, as well as an excellent long finale and some good bass arias, but is musically uneven. *Orlando* (1733) is on an altogether higher level of invention —it is also notable for its striking scenic and structural effects: the hero's madness is portrayed in a scene of linked movements and symbolized by the first use in history of 5/8 time.

In the next year Handel and Heidegger gave up their partnership under pressure from the rival 'Opera of the Nobility' at Lincoln's Inn Fields, which had lured away the best singers; they vacated the King's Theatre to their rivals, and Handel moved to Lincoln's Inn Fields, having produced *Arianna* (1734), a decline from *Orlando*'s richness. But in 1735 the new season opened, this time at Covent Garden, with *Ariodante*, a spectacular if uneven opera that included a ballet (Handel had secured the services of the French dancer Marie Sallé). From about this time, too, simple use is made of a separate chorus; previously the final *coro* implied an ensemble of soloists. *Ariodante*'s immediate successor was *Alcina* (1735), a piece rich in scenic effects and distinguished by some of Handel's most passionate and touching arias. *Atalanta* (1736) is a lighter work (it ends with a display of fireworks), though a finely imagined one. Handel's serious decline in health is reflected in the poverty of *Arminio* (1737) and *Giustino*, which includes a consort of recorders (1737). *Berenice* (1737) is basically dull, apart from the overture (with its famous minuet) and one or two numbers. Its successor, *Faramondo* (1738), is a little broader in range. *Serse* (1738) has become celebrated through the *larghetto* 'Ombra mai fu', now inescapably known as 'Handel's Largo'; it is a light and entertaining opera, with a buffo servant who antedates Leporello. *Imeneo* (1740), called by Handel an operetta, is a little like his last opera *Deidamia* (1741), an ironic, almost anti-heroic comedy with touches of sentiment.

The revival of Handel's operas dates from Germany in the 1920's, and has gathered force in recent years, especially in England. The artificiality of *opera seria* has proved less of a stumbling-block than anticipated; perhaps its very formality and neatness offers something to a society lacking these qualities and failing to find them in the music of its own time. The dramatic force which the genre still holds is impressive, and producers who attempt 'special' presentation of works written by a composer with shrewd stage sense quickly discover their error. Difficulties remain, for few singers possess the elaborate technique of Handel's day, and the castrato parts must either be transposed or given to a woman or a countertenor.

However magnificently Handel filled *opera seria* form and however boldly he tried to transcend its cramping conventions, the attempt to establish it as a living art form was bound to fail; accordingly he turned his attention to oratorio. But inevitably most of his oratorios are intensely dramatic in conception: the scores contain stage directions, and though after 1732 he had no stage performances in view there is evidence that he 'visualized' his heroes and their actions while composing their music. It is not surprising, then, that when writing in a dramatic form liberated from *opera seria* conventions, he should have achieved greater dramatic range. Many problems attend the staging of these dramatic oratorios, not least the question of how to place the chorus, which now played a large part. Another major effect on Handel was his release from the domination of the *da capo* aria and the elimination of *castrati* and star singers. Thus the oratorio arias have richer accompaniments. Indeed, the whole dramatic structure becomes more organic. Religious scruples and mistrust of the theatre as a den of vice long kept these dramatic oratorios out of the theatre, and it was not until the German revival of interest in Handel's operas after the First World War, already mentioned, that the dramatic oratorios began appearing on the stage. Almost all have now done so in England, some (e.g. *Acis and Galatea*) repeatedly, staged by both professionals and enthusiastic amateurs.

Hann, George (b. Vienna, 30 Jan. 1897; d. Munich, 9 Dec. 1950). Austrian bass-baritone. Munich State Opera 1927–50. Also appeared Salzburg, Vienna. One of the best buffo artists in Germany, and especially remembered for his Kecal, Falstaff, Ochs, and Leporello, though he also sang dramatic roles—Gunther, Amfortas, Pizarro, and Sarastro. (R)

Hanover (Ger., Hannover). Town in Lower Saxony, Germany. The first opera given there was probably Cesti's *Orontia*, in 1649. The first opera house was inaugurated in 1689 with Steffani's *Enrico Leone*. The present opera house (Landestheater) was built in 1845, and rebuilt in 1950 (cap. 1,300). Operas that had their premières at Hanover include Stanford's *The Veiled Prophet*, Wolf-Ferrari's *Der Kuckuck in Theben* (*Gli Dei a Tebe*) (1943), and Henze's *Boulevard Solitude* (1952). Since the Second World War Franz Konwitschny, Johannes Schüler, and Günther Wich have been the theatre's chief conductors.

Hans Heiling. Opera in prologue and 3 acts by Marschner; text by Devrient. Prod. Berlin, O., 24 May 1833; Oxford 2 Dec. 1953. Hans, son of the Queen of the Spirits, takes human form and falls in love with Anna. When she learns who he is, she leaves him for Konrad, and he vanishes, vowing never to be seen again by mortals. Marschner's principal opera, and one of the most significant German romantic operas between Weber and Wagner.

Hänsel und Gretel. Opera in 3 acts by Humperdinck; text by Adelheid Wette (composer's sister), after the Grimm brothers' story in *Kinder- und*

Hausmärchen (1812–14). Prod. Weimar, 23 Dec. 1893; London, Daly's, 26 Dec. 1894; N.Y., Daly's, 8 Oct. 1895. Act 1. Gertrude (mezzo), wife of Peter (bar.), scolds her children Hänsel (mezzo) and Gretel (sop.) for playing instead of working and sends them into the woods to gather strawberries. Peter is alarmed on learning this, and follows them. Act 2. The children eat the strawberries they have gathered, and as darkness falls the Sandman (sop.) sends them to sleep and angels encircle them ('Dream Pantomime'). Act 3. Waking, the children see a gingerbread house, and nibble it. The Witch (mezzo) emerges, locks Hänsel in a cage and sets Gretel to do the housework. Gretel frees her brother with the Witch's wand. They trick the Witch into peering into the oven, and push her in. It explodes, and all the enchanted gingerbread children return to life as Peter and Gertrude arrive to share in the rejoicing. Humperdinck's most successful work, called by Strauss (who originally accepted the work for production) 'a masterpiece of the first rank'. Another opera on the story is by Reichardt (1772).

Hanslick, Eduard (b. Prague, 11 Sept. 1825; d. Baden, 6 Aug. 1904). Austrian critic. His first work on aesthetics, *Vom Musikalisch-Schönen* (1854), remains his most important book, though he published a dozen more and contributed thoughtful and forthright criticism to the Vienna press for many years. A conservative, his opposition to Liszt and especially to Wagner is famous, and resulted in his being pilloried as Beckmesser (originally named Hans Lick) in *Die Meistersinger*.

Hans Sachs. See *Sachs, Hans*.

Hardy, Thomas (b. Upper Bockhampton, 2 June 1840; d. Dorchester, 11 Jan. 1928). English poet and novelist. Operas on his works are as follows. *The Mayor of Casterbridge* (1886): Tranchell (1951). *Three Strangers* (1888): Bath; Gardiner (1936). *Tess of the D'Urbervilles* (1891): D'Erlanger (*Tess*, 1906). *The Queen of Cornwall* (1923): Boughton (1924).

Harewood, Earl of (George Henry Hubert Lascelles) (b. London, 7 Feb. 1923). English critic and administrator. Son of H.R.H. the Princess Royal, and first cousin of H.M. Queen Elizabeth II, Lord Harewood has inherited his great-great-grandparents' (Queen Victoria and Prince Albert) love for music, in particular for opera. He founded the magazine *Opera* in 1950; served on the Board of Directors at C.G. 1951–3; and was controller of opera planning there 1953–60. Produced revised edition of Kobbe's *Complete Opera Book*, 1953. He has championed the English Opera Group, the Opera School, and other native operatic enterprises. Director General of the Leeds Festival 1958; Director of Edinburgh Festival from 1961–5. Managing Director, S.W., from 1972.

Hargreaves, John (b. Colne, Lancs., 1914). English baritone. Studied R.A.M. with Sumner Austin. Début S.W. 1936, Valentine. Remained member of the Company until 1945, and leading baritone from 1952. His large repertory includes Guglielmo, Don Giovanni, Onegin, and Strickland in Gardner's *The Moon and Sixpence*, which he created. (R)

Harmonie der Welt, Die (The Harmony of the World). Opera in 5 scenes by Hindemith; text by composer. Prod. Munich, P., 11 Aug. 1957 with Josef Metternich as Kepler. Based on the life of the astronomer Kepler and his musical theories of planetary motion, the work is, like *Mathis der Maler* (q.v.), a study of the artist's or philosopher's relation to the political and social movements of his times. As with *Mathis*, a symphony has been drawn from the music.

Harris, (Sir) Augustus (b. Paris, 1852; d. Folkestone, 22 June 1896). English impresario. Son of stage-manager of C.G. Was Mapleson's assistant manager, and then in 1879 became lessee of D.L. Brought C.R. Company to London 1883 and managed their seasons until 1887, when he gave a trial season of Italian opera at D.L. with great success. He took C.G. for the following year, and in 1888–96 achieved great artistic and financial success with the help of a brilliant company that included Melba and the De Reszkes. He introduced opera in the original language to C.G., and did much to popularize Wagner.

Harrison, Julius (b. Stourport, 26 Mar. 1885; d. London, 5 Apr. 1963). English conductor. Studied Birmingham under Bantock. C.G. 1913 with Raymond Roze's Company. Sent by Grand Opera Syndicate to Paris the following year to help Nikisch and Weingartner prepare performances of *Parsifal*, *Tristan*, and *Meistersinger*. Conductor Beecham Co. and B.N.O.C. (R)

Harrison, William (b. London, 15 June 1813; d. London, 9 Nov. 1868). English tenor and impresario. Studied R.A.M. Début C.G. 1839 in Rooke's *Henrique*. After seasons at D.L., where he created leading tenor roles in *The Bohemian Girl*, *Maritana*, and other works, he established, in 1856, an English opera company in conjunction with the soprano Louisa Pyne. The company performed every autumn and winter at C.G. 1858–64, and gave the first performances of works by Balfe, Wallace, Benedict, and others.

Harshaw, Margaret (b. Narbeth, Penn., 12 May 1912). American soprano, orig. mezzo. Studied Philadelphia, Juilliard School, N.Y. Début N.Y. 1935. Won Met. Auditions of Air 1942. N.Y., Met., since 1942, first as mezzo. In 1950 discovered her voice was changing and after singing Senta in 1951 and the *Götterdämmerung* Brünnhilde in 1952 established herself as one of the leading Wagner sopranos of the day. London, C.G., 1953–6 and 1960, where she sang Brünnhilde in the 1954 *Ring* production; Glyndebourne 1955, as Donna Anna. (R)

Hart, Fritz (b. London, 11 Feb. 1874; d. Honolulu, 9 July 1949). English conductor and composer. In 1915 he became director of Melbourne Conservatory, where Melba taught and where many of his 22 operas were produced. A gifted writer, he provided most of his own librettos, favouring Celtic Twilight subjects; and his intense practical sense (he had appeared as an actor) helped to make his works theatrically effective.

Hartmann, Karl Amadeus (b. Munich, 2 Aug. 1905; d. Munich, 30 Nov. 1963). German composer. His chamber opera *Des Simplicius Simplicissimus Jugend* (1948) is popular in Germany.

Hartmann, Rudolf (b. Ingolstadt, 11 Oct. 1900). German producer and manager. Studied stage design, &c., Munich, and in Bamberg under Berg-Ehlert. Engaged as *Oberspielleiter* Altenberg 1924; Nuremberg 1928–34 and 1946–52; Berlin State Opera 1934–8 where he began his collaboration with Clemens Krauss and produced the première of *Die Zaubergeige*; Munich 1938–44, and 1953–67 Staatsintendant there. Staged premières of *Friedenstag* and *Capriccio* there and revivals of most of Strauss's major works as well as première of *Liebe der Danae*, Salzburg, 1952. London, C.G., *Elektra*, 1953, and new *Ring* production 1954. Hartmann has no special theories on production but inclines towards tradition.

Háry János (John Háry). Opera in prologue, 5 parts, and epilogue by Kodály; text by Paulini and Harsányi, after the poem by János Garay. Prod. Budapest 16 Oct. 1926. N.Y., Juilliard School, 18 Mar. 1960. János Háry is a famous liar in Hungarian folklore. The opera tells how Napoleon's wife competes with a peasant girl, Örzse, for his love; how he defeats Napoleon's avenging army single-handed; and how he returns home to Örzse.

Hasse, Johann (b. Bergedorf, 25 Mar. 1699; d. Venice, 16 Dec. 1783). German composer. After his first opera, *Antioco* (1721), was produced at Hamburg he went to Italy, where he quickly established his fame and popularity so firmly as to become known as *il caro Sassone* (though not actually a Saxon). In 1729 he married Faustina Bordoni, for whom he wrote several operas. He directed the Dresden opera from 1731, where his position was made difficult by rivalries and jealousies. After the siege of Dresden, in which most of his music was destroyed, he moved in 1760 to Vienna, where his conservative style made him an opponent of Gluck. His music was elegantly tailored to suit the conventions of the day, and especially to flatter singers' voices; it was too unadventurous and formal in style to outlast them. His greatest gift was as a melodist. Immensely prolific, he set all Metastasio's 70-odd librettos.

Hasselmans, Louis (b. Paris, 25 July 1878; d. San Juan, 27 Dec. 1947). French conductor. Studied Paris Conservatoire. Début with Lamoureux Orchestra; Paris, O.C., 1909–11; Montreal Opera 1911–13; Chicago 1918–20; N.Y., Met., 1921–36 where he conducted N.Y. premières of *L'Heure Espagnole* and *Habanera*.

Hauer, Josef (b. Wiener-Neustadt, 19 Mar. 1883; d. 27 Sept. 1959). Austrian composer. His theories of atonal music, which were respected by Schoenberg, found practical expression in two operas, *Salammbô* and *Die schwarze Spinne*.

Haug, Hans (b. Basel, 27 July 1900). Swiss composer and conductor. He has had considerable success in Switzerland as a comic-opera composer. His works in this genre include two Molière operas, *Tartuffe* (1937) and *Le Malade Immortel* (1946).

Hauk, Minnie (orig. Mignon Hauck) (b. N.Y., 16 Nov. 1851; d. Triebschen, 6 Feb. 1929). American soprano. Studied New Orleans and New York. Début Brooklyn 1866, Amina; London, C.G., 1868. Appeared with success in Paris, Brussels, Moscow, Berlin. The first American Juliette (which she sang the day before her sixteenth birthday), Carmen, and Manon; first London Carmen. Appeared for one season at N.Y., Met., 1890–1 and then organized her own opera company, but after a season's tour suddenly retired from the stage at the height of her powers and went to live with her husband in Wagner's villa at Triebschen. She lost her fortune during the First World War and was supported by funds raised by American opera-lovers. Autobiography, *Memories of a Singer* (1925).

Hauptstimme. Ger. = Principal voice or role.

Häusliche Krieg, Der. See *Verschworenen, Die.*

Havana. Capital of Cuba. First theatre opened there Oct. 1776 with Metastasio's *Dido Abbandonata*. The Teatro Taco, opened 1838 and modelled on the Teatro Real of Madrid and the Liceo of Barcelona, for many years was the home of visiting opera companies from Europe. It became the Teatro Nacional in Apr. 1915 and opened with *Aida*, conducted by Serafin. In 1920 Caruso appeared there for a special season with a company that included Barrientos, Besanzoni, Melis, Stracciari, and Mardones. He sang in ten performances and received the highest fee he was ever paid—$90,000.

Havana Italian Opera Company. A company organized by Francesco Marty, under the musical direction of Arditi with leading Italian and French singers. It appeared in N.Y. 1847–50.

Hawes, William (b. London, 21 June 1785; d. London, 18 Feb. 1846). English composer. From 1824 directed Lyceum, where he introduced Weber's *Freischütz*, with some airs of his own. Apart from his own operettas, he was responsible for adapting many operas for the English stage, among them *Così fan tutte* and *Don Giovanni*.

Haydn, Joseph (b. Rohrau, 31 Mar. 1732; d. Vienna, 31 May 1809). Austrian composer. Haydn's first five operas are lost, but 15 survive, largely neglected. There were also five puppet operas, of which only *Philemon und Baucis* (1773) is extant. Yet Haydn rated opera high in his interests, and used to say that if he had gone to Italy he might have become a first-rate opera composer. Weak librettos are partly to blame for dragging some fine music into obscurity. Though bound to convention, in his case a mixed one of *opera seria* and *opera buffa*, Haydn's operas give a steadily larger role to the music:

their mixture of comic and serious elements was one developed to perfection by Mozart. The beginnings are already discernible in *Lo Speziale* (1768). The later operas discard, or develop out of recognition, the *aria da capo*, and greater importance is allotted to ensembles. *Il Mondo della Luna* (1777) (frequently revived in a new edition by Robbins-Landon (1959)) has some subtle orchestral commentaries; and in *La Vera Costanza* (1779), still more in *L'Isola Disabitata* (1770), the music has a deliberately Gluckian indissolubility from the drama. With *La Fedeltà Premiata* (1780) Haydn began to lose interest in opera of a mixed nature; *Armide* (1784) is a wholly serious work. *L'Anima del Filosofo* (1791) was the only opera not limited by the needs of the Esterházy company. In it Haydn tried to develop *opera seria* along Gluck's lines: greater dramatic use is made of the chorus, for instance. But it shows, in Geiringer's words, 'that Haydn did not feel himself sufficiently at home in opera composition to free himself completely from the bondage of the prevailing taste and to create a musical drama'.

Hayes, Catherine (b. Limerick, 25 Oct. 1825; d. London, 11 Aug. 1861). Irish soprano. Studied Dublin with Sapio, Paris with Garcia, Milan with Ronconi. Début Marseilles 1845, Elvira (*Puritani*). After successful appearances in Italy and Austria, appeared at C.G. 1849 as Linda, Lucia, and other roles. Thackeray pays her tribute in his *Irish Sketch-book.*

Head voice. A method of tone production in the upper register, so called from the sensation experienced by the singer of the voice functioning at the top of the head. The tone is weaker but lighter and clearer.

Hedmont, Charles (actually Christian Emmanuel) (b. Maine, U.S.A., 24 Oct. 1857; d. London, 25 Apr. 1940). American tenor. Studied Leipzig. Début Berlin. After appearances in Leipzig, Bayreuth (David 1886), and U.S.A. was principal tenor Carl Rosa Company 1891–1909. Presented a season of opera in English at C.G. in the autumn of 1895 which included the first performance in English of *Walküre* with himself as Siegmund. Sang Loge in the English *Ring* at C.G. 1908 under Richter, and also acted as stage-manager.

Heger, Robert (b. Strasbourg, 19 Aug. 1886). German conductor and composer. Studied Strasbourg, Zürich, and Munich. Début Ulm 1909; held appointments in Barmen, Vienna, Nuremberg, Munich, Berlin (1933–50), and again Munich from 1950. London, C.G., 1925–35 and with Munich Company 1953, when he directed first London performance of *Capriccio*. Has composed four operas. (R)

Heidegger, John (orig. Johann Jakob) (b. *c.* 1659; d. London, 4 Sept. 1749). English impresario of Swiss birth. Manager King's Theatre, Haymarket, 1708–34; in partnership with Handel 1729–34. Wrote libretto for Handel's *Amadigi.*

Heine, Heinrich (orig. Harry) (b. Düsseldorf, 13 Dec. 1797; d. Paris, 17 Feb. 1856). German poet, playwright, and novelist. A close friend of Meyerbeer and music critic of the *Allgemeine Zeitung*, Augsburg, 1840–7. His *Almansor* (1823) was the basis of an opera planned by Debussy and later destroyed by the composer. Operas on his works are as follows. *William Ratcliff* (1823): Cui (1869); Mascagni (1895); Dopper (1909); Andreae (1914); Leroux (1906). *Der Schelm von Bergen* (1846): Atterberg (*Fanal*, 1934); Liebeswogen; Gerlach (1903). *Memoiren des Herrn von Schnabelewopski* (1831): Wagner (*Der fliegende Holländer*, 1843).

Heinefetter, Maria (b. Mainz, 16 Feb. 1816; d. Vienna, 23 Feb. 1857). German soprano. Sang with success in Vienna as Mme Stöckl-Heinefetter. London, C.G., with German company 1842, the first London Valentine in *Huguenots*. Died insane. She had five sisters. **Sabine** (b. Mainz, 19 Aug. 1809; d. Illemau, 18 Nov. 1872), soprano, was originally a harpist and was encouraged to take up singing by Spohr. Studied Paris with Tadolini, and sang at Théâtre des Italiens until

1842. Like Maria, she died insane. **Kathinka** (1820–58) sang in Paris and Brussels from 1840 onwards; and **Fatima, Eva,** and **Nanette** were also opera singers.

Heinrich. The King of Saxony (bass) in Wagner's *Lohengrin;* also known as Henry the Fowler.

Heldenbariton (Ger. = Heroic baritone). See *Baritone.*

Heldentenor (Ger. = Heroic tenor). See *Tenor.*

Heldy, Fanny (b. Liège, 1888). Belgian soprano. Studied Liège and Brussels. Début Brussels, La M., 1913; London, C.G., 1926; Paris, O. and O.C., 1917–39. Chosen by Toscanini to sing Louise and Mélisande at La Scala; created L'Aiglon (Monte Carlo 1937). Admired in these roles and as Manon, Thaïs, and Concepción. (R)

Helsinki (Swedish, Helsingfors). Capital of Finland. Opera was given from the beginning of the 19th century by touring German companies. Pacius's *Kung Carls Jakt* (King Charles's Hunt) (Helsinki 1852) is regarded as the first Finnish opera, though the composer was Ge man and the performance in Swedish. His last opera, *Lorelei*, was given at Helsinki in German (1887), while even Sibelius's only opera, *Jungfruburen* (Maiden's Bower), was given in Swedish (Helsinki 1896), a language still then common owing to the former Swedish colonization. The first opera to a Finnish text was O. Merikanto's *Pohjan Neito* (The Maid of Bothnia), composed 1898, open-air prod. Viipuri 1908. The most successful Finnish opera has been Madetoja's *Pohjalaisia* (The East Bothnians), prod. Helsinki 1924 and in Sweden, Denmark, and Germany. The first permanent Finnish company was founded in 1873, but had only a chequered career until 1911, when Edward Fazer and Aino Ackté started a company as a private enterprise which in 1914 became the Suomalainen Ooppera. Fazer was director 1911–38 (with Järnefelt as artistic director 1932–6 and Ackté 1938–9), and Oiva Soini 1939–52. In 1953 the management was entirely reorganized.

Heming, Percy (b. Bristol, 6 Sept. 1883; d. London, 11 Jan. 1956). English baritone. Studied London, R.A.M., with Frederick King, Dresden with Henschel. Début Beecham Co. 1915, Mercutio. Sang Marcello on the opening night of the B.N.O.C.'s first C.G. season and became one of its leading baritones; then joined the C.G. English Touring Company. S.W. 1933–5. Assistant artistic director C.G. 1937; artistic director C.G. English Company 1937–9; artistic adviser C.G. 1946–8. Sang a great variety of roles ranging from Bartolo to Amfortas, Kecal to Scarpia. Toured U.S.A. as Macheath. (R)

Hempel, Frieda (b. Leipzig, 26 June 1885; d. Berlin, 7 Oct. 1955). German soprano. Studied Berlin with Nicklass-Kempner. Début Schwerin: her success resulted in the Kaiser asking the Schwerin authorities to release her to sing in Berlin, where she made her début as Frau Fluth in 1905. London, C.G., 1907, Bastienne. N.Y., Met., 1912, Marguerite de Valois. The first Berlin and N.Y. Marschallin, a role she sang in London in 1913. Such was her amazing versatility that she could sing Eva and Euryanthe as well as Queen of Night, Rosina, and Oscar. After 1919 she devoted her time to the concert hall and was famed for her Jenny Lind recitals in costume. Autobiography, *Mein Leben dem Gesang* (1955). (R)

Henderson, Roy (b. Edinburgh, 4 July 1899). British baritone and teacher. Studied London, R.A.M. Début London, C.G., 1929, Donner. Glyndebourne 1934–9 as Count Almaviva, Guglielmo, Masetto, and Papageno. Teacher of Ferrier and many other singers. (R)

Henry VIII. Opera in 4 acts by Saint-Saëns; text by Détroyat and Silvestre. Prod. Paris, O., 5 Mar. 1883 with Lassalle; London, C.G., 14 July 1898 with Renaud. Concerns the love of the king for Anne Boleyn, whom he marries despite her love for Gomez, the Spanish Ambassador, and in the face of the Pope's disapproval.

Hensel, Heinrich (b. Neustadt, 29 Oct. 1874; d. Hamburg, 23 Feb. 1935). German tenor. Studied Vienna and Milan. Début Freiburg 1897; London, C.G., 1911, Loge; N.Y., Met., 1911, Lohengrin. First London Parsifal, a role he also sang at Bayreuth. (R)

Henze, Hans Werner (b. Gütersloh, 1 July 1926). German composer. His first opera was *Das Wundertheater* (1948, 1 act), after Cervantes; then followed the radio opera *Ein Landarzt* (1951) and *Boulevard Solitude* (1950–1, prod. 1952). The latter, a version of the Manon Lescaut story, was an instant success at its première; it makes much use of ballet, in which Henze has shown great interest, and is constructed in separate numbers, as is the radio opera which came next, *Das Ende einer Welt* (1953). This first reveals, in the form of a puncturing satire on snob arty society, Henze's consistent interest in the problem of the artist as man and his relationship and duty to his fellows. *König Hirsch* (1952–5, prod. 1956) is a very large-scale treatment of a Gozzi fable, concerning the conflicting claims on a king's duty, and aroused violent enthusiasm and antagonism. Henze's special gift for a somewhat fantastic vein of lyricism was first fully revealed here, and this was perhaps brought to flower by his growing love of Italy, where he has latterly lived. In emphasizing the poetic timelessness of the hero's predicament in his next opera, *Der Prinz von Homburg* (1960), he further showed his distaste for German military values; these are subdued in his operatic treatment of Kleist's ambivalent soldier-dreamer. The score reveals a new power in absorbing the various influences and manners to which Henze has been dangerously subject by virtue of his sheer skill at all forms of musical language, while the vein of fantasy is undiminished. *Elegy for Young Lovers* (Schwetzingen 1961, with Fischer-Dieskau; Glyndebourne 13 July 1961) concerns a great poet who devours those around him in order to nourish his art. *The Bassarids* (Salzburg, 26 Aug. 1966) is to a treatment of Euripides's *Bacchae* by W. H. Auden and Chester Kallmann.

Her Majesty's Theatre, Haymarket (for history before 1837, see *King's Theatre*). The King's Theatre was renamed Her Majesty's on the accession of Queen Victoria in 1837, during the management of Laporte (q.v.). Two years later, following on Laporte's refusal to re-engage Tamburini as a protest against the clique of singers known as *La Vieille Garde*, he was succeeded by Lumley (q.v.), whose management lasted until 1859; and he by Mapleson (q.v.) 1862–7 and 1877–87. From 1847, the year Covent Garden opened, both Lumley and Mapleson had to face the rivalry of a second Royal Italian Opera in London. Although the theatre was burned down in 1867 and rebuilt two years later, it did not become an opera house again until 1877, which was the last year in which Tietjens sang. During the Lumley and Mapleson managements the first performances in England of many operas were given. These included the later Donizetti works, most of the early and middle Verdi works down to *Vêpres Siciliennes*, and *Faust*, *Carmen*, and *Mefistofele*. The Carl Rosa Company's London sessions of 1879, 1880, and 1882 were given there, and in the latter year a German company under Seidl gave the first London performance of the *Ring*. In 1886 there took place a French season in which Galli-Marié sang her original role of Carmen, and the following year Patti made her only appearance in that house. The theatre was pulled down in 1891 and the present building opened in 1897 under the management of Beerbohm Tree. There in the early 1900's occasional performances were given by the R.C.M. student class. *The Wreckers* received its English première there under Beecham in 1909; the following year Beecham gave his season of *opéra comique* and in 1913 the London première of *Ariadne auf Naxos*. After the B.N.O.C. left C.G. in 1924 their London West End seasons were given there. The theatre has not housed opera for the last 30 years—unless one counts Bernstein's opera-ballet *West Side Story* and the 1962 Tyrone Guthrie productions of Gilbert and Sullivan.

Herbert, Victor (b. Dublin, 1 Feb. 1859; d. New York, 26 May 1924). Irish-American composer. Went to N.Y. in 1886, where his wife, Therese Herbert-Förster, sang in the German Opera at the Met.; he was a cellist in the orchestra. Remembered chiefly as the composer of a large number of tuneful and highly successful operettas, Herbert also wrote two operas, *Natoma* (1911) and the 1-act *Madeleine* (1914).

Hérodiade. Opera in 4 acts by Massenet; text by Paul Milliet and 'H. Grémont' (Georges Hartmann), after Flaubert's story (1877). Prod. Brussels, La M., 19 Dec. 1881, with Lassalle; New Orleans 13 Feb. 1892; London, C.G., 6 July 1904 (as *Salome*), with Calvé, Dalmorès, Renaud. The story is that of Salome, though it differs from Strauss's treatment in that John the Baptist admits his love for Salome, who stabs herself after the jealous Herod has had him killed.

Hérold, Ferdinand (b. Paris, 28 Jan. 1791; d. Paris, 19 Jan. 1833). French composer. After his operatic début in Naples he collaborated with Boïeldieu in an *opéra comique*, following it with several of his own which he found time to write while acting as accompanist at the Théâtre Italien 1820–7. *Marie* (1826) is the most enterprising, combining elements of Italian vocal writing and *Singspiel* within an essentially French framework. Ambitious and hardworking, he continued trying to improve his art, which reached its high point before his early death with *Zampa* (1831) and *Le Pré aux Clercs* (1832). *Zampa* has echoes of *Freischütz* in its technique of handling a romantic subject, and gives a larger role to the orchestra than was customary. The Germans have always preferred it to *Le Pré aux Clercs*, which is lighter and more traditional in manner, and has been the favourite of the French. Near his death Hérold remarked that he was going too soon: 'I was just beginning to understand the stage.'

Herold, Vilhelm Kristoffer (b. Hasle, 19 Mar. 1865; d. Copenhagen, 15 Dec. 1937). Danish tenor. Studied Copenhagen; début Copenhagen 1893, Faust; Chicago 1893; London, C.G., 1904, Lohengrin, when his voice was compared to J. de Reszke's. Member of Stockholm Opera 1901–3, 1907–9. Opera director at Royal Theatre, Copenhagen, 1922–4. Was Pedro in *Tiefland* at Oslo in 1913 in the performance in which Flagstad made her début as Nuri. (R)

Hertz, Alfred (b. Frankfurt, 15 July 1872; d. San Francisco, 17 Apr. 1942). German, later naturalized American, conductor. Studied Frankfurt; début Halle 1891. After appointments in Germany went to N.Y., Met., in 1902 where he was conductor of German opera until 1915. He conducted the first American performances of *Parsifal* in 1903, which so enraged Cosima Wagner that the doors of all German opera houses were henceforth closed to him. He conducted the world premières of *Königskinder*, *Cyrano de Bergerac* (Damrosch), and the American premières of *Rosenkavalier* and *Salome*. He appeared in London, C.G., in 1910.

Hervé (orig. Florimond Ronger) (b. Houdain, 30 June 1825; d. Paris, 4 Nov. 1892). French composer and theatre manager. Conductor Odéon 1848; Palais-Royal 1850; manager Folies-Nouvelles 1854–6; conductor Délassements-Comiques 1859–62. Composer of over 100 stage works, most of them operettas and *opéras bouffes* of widely varying merit. A number of them were written for London, where he was for some years conductor at the Empire.

Herzeleide. Kundry's (sop.) narration in Act 2 of *Parsifal* in which she tells Parsifal of his mother.

Heure Espagnole, L' (lit., The Spanish Hour). Opera in 1 act by Ravel; text by Franc-Nohain, after his own comedy. Prod. Paris, O.C., 19 May 1911 with Vix, Périer; London, C.G., 24 July 1919 with Donalda, Maguénat; Chicago 5 Jan. 1920, with Gall, Maguénat. The clockmaker Torquemada goes off to attend to the town clocks, leaving a customer, the muleteer Ramiro, in the shop to await his return. Concepción, who is accustomed to receive her lovers in her husband's absence, sets him carrying clocks about. Gonzalve, a poet, enters and serenades her protractedly. On the arrival of a second lover, Don Inigo Gomez, Ramiro is made to carry Gonzalve, hidden in a clock, up to the bedroom. The same happens to Don Inigo, while the first clock is brought down. Annoyed by their ineffectiveness, Concepción eventually admiringly orders Ramiro upstairs again—without a clock. Torquemada returns, finds the two lovers inside clocks 'examining' them, and effects a quick sale. The opera ends with a brilliant quintet.

Hidalgo, Elvira de (b. Aragón, 1882). Spanish soprano. Début Naples 1908, Rosina. Sang all over the world. The last of the Spanish *soprani d'agilità* which included Pacini, Galvany, Barrientos, Pareto. Taught in Athens, where she was the only teacher of Maria Callas (q.v.), and later at Ankara. (R)

Hiller (orig. Hüller), **Johann** (b. Wendisch-Ossig, 25 Dec. 1728; d. Leipzig, 16 June 1804). German composer. More than any other single man, the founder of the *Singspiel*, introducing into the pieces played by the Leipzig theatre company (not trained singers) separate *Lieder* which in his hands bore an added dramatic and characteristic force. He even included ensembles and something near the beginnings of the dramatic scene. The best known of his dozen *Singspiele* was *Die Jagd* (1770).

Hin und Zurück (There and Back). *Sketch mit Musik* in 1 act by Hindemith; text by Marcellus Schiffer, after an English revue sketch. Prod. (in same programme as works by Milhaud, Toch, and Weill) Baden-Baden 17 July 1927; Tanglewood, U.S.A., 1940; London, S.W., 14 Feb. 1958 by Opera da Camera of Buenos Aires. After the murder of his unfaithful wife by a husband, supernatural intervention reverses the plot: the wife comes back to life, the lover retreats, the husband puts away his revolver, and all ends as it began.

Hinckley, Allen C. (b. Gloucester, Mass., 11 Oct. 1877; d. N.Y., 28 Jan. 1954). American bass. Studied Philadelphia, N.Y. with Oscar Saenger, and Germany with Cosima and Siegfried Wagner. Début Hamburg 1903, Heinrich; London, C.G., 1904; N.Y., Met., 1908 as Hagen in Toscanini's first *Götterdämmerung;* Met. 1908–11, 1913–14. Sang Hunding, Hagen, and Heinrich in Bayreuth; appeared with Beecham Company. Head of Kansas City Conservatory for 25 years.

Hindemith, Paul (b. Hanau, 16 Nov. 1895; d. Frankfurt, 28 Dec. 1963). German composer. His first three (1-act) operas are now forgotten—they are *Mörder, Hoffnung der Frauen* (text by Kokoschka) (1921), a Burmese marionette play *Das Nusch-Nuschi* (1921), and *Sancta Susanna* (1922). *Cardillac* (1926, rev. 1952) treated a tragic subject with emotional intensity, while *Neues vom Tage* (1929) is a sharp satire on the Press. Determinedly modern, the latter includes an aria sung by the heroine in her bath praising the merits of electric heating over gas: this brought an injunction from the local gas company. *Mathis der Maler* (1938) is based on the life of the painter Matthias Grünewald, and aroused violent Nazi antagonism for its portrayal of peasants rebelling against authority, with the artist first siding with them and then withdrawing into his work. Even Furtwängler's vigorous advocacy could not prevent a ban on the scheduled Berlin première in 1934. *Die Harmonie der Welt* (1957) is based on the life of the astronomer Kepler, whose laws of planetary motion have a musical basis. Here Hindemith's thoughtfully evolved harmonic theories, which are founded on the harmonic series and its resulting tensions and relationships, are dramatically defended as being founded on natural laws rather than on the arbitrary rules which he sees as the weakness of atonality. But the central dramatic theme, as in *Mathis*, is the relationship of the artist or scientist to the social or political movements of his time, and of his private life to his work. Hindemith's last opera, after

Thornton Wilder, is a drama of different generations of a family simultaneously appearing, *Der lange Weinachtsmahl* (1961).

Hines, Jerome (b. Hollywood, 8 Nov. 1921). American bass. Studied Los Angeles. Début San Francisco 1941, Biterolf. After appearances with various small American companies, auditioned and engaged for N.Y., Met., 1947. A fine Boris, Grand Inquisitor, and Gurnemanz, which he sang at Bayreuth 1958. (R)

Hinrichs, Gustav (b. Ludwigslust, Mecklenburg, 10 Dec. 1850; d. Mountain Lakes, N.J., 26 Mar. 1942). German, later naturalized American, conductor. Conducted Philadelphia, N.Y., Met., and elsewhere and directed first American performances of *Cavalleria, Pagliacci,* and *Manon Lescaut.*

Hislop, Joseph (b. Edinburgh, 5 Apr. 1884). Scottish tenor and teacher. Studied Stockholm and Italy. Début Stockholm 1916, Faust. London, C.G., 1920–8; Chicago 1920. A fine Puccini and Verdi singer, who also specialized in French repertory (Faust, Roméo, Des Grieux). Taught in Stockholm and London; his pupils include Birgit Nilsson. Now adviser on singing to S.W. (R)

Hoengen, Elisabeth (b. Gevelsberg, Westphalia, 7 Dec. 1906). German mezzo-soprano. Studied Berlin with Hermann Weisenborn. Début Wuppertal 1933. After engagements at Düsseldorf (1935–40) and Dresden (1940–3) became leading singer at Vienna, S.O. London, C.G., 1947, with Vienna Company, and 1959–60; N.Y., Met., 1951–2. An impressive singing actress, particularly noted for her Lady Macbeth, Klytemnestra, Herodias, and Ortrud. (R)

Hoesslin, Franz von (b. Munich, 31 Dec. 1885; d. nr. Site, 28 Sept. 1946). German conductor. Studied Munich with Reger and Mottl. Début St. Gall 1908. Held appointments at Riga, Lübeck, Mannheim, Berlin, Dessau, Barmen-Elberfeld, and Breslau. Bayreuth 1927–8, 1934, 1938–40. Then followed his Jewish wife into exile in Switzerland. Killed in air-crash.

Hoffman, Grace (b. Cleveland, 14 Jan. 1925). American mezzo-soprano. Studied New York with Friedrich Schorr and Milan with Mario Basiola. Début Florence 1952, Priestess in *Aida.* Zürich 1953–5; Stuttgart since 1955. London, with Stuttgart Company 1955, C.G. 1959–60; N.Y., Met., 1958. Bayreuth since 1957, and guest appearances elsewhere in Europe. Equally at home in Verdi and Wagner; has sung successfully as Eboli, Brangaene, and Kundry. (R)

Hoffmann, E. T. A. (b. Königsberg, 24 Jan. 1776; d. Berlin, 25 June 1822). German novelist and composer. One of the most famous literary figures of the Romantic movement, Hoffmann was also a composer and conductor; he was music director at Bamberg from 1808, and conducted opera with the Sekonda Company at Leipzig and Dresden 1813–14. His own ten operas, warmly romantic in flavour, include *Die Maske* (1799), *Scherz, List und Rache* (1801), *Die lustigen Musikanten* (1805), *Aurora* (1811), and *Undine* (1816). He was also a music critic of perception and originality. Chief among a number of works based on his stories are Offenbach's *Contes d'Hoffmann* (1880), Busoni's *Die Brautwahl* (1910), Hindemith's *Cardillac* (1926), and Malipiero's *Capriccio di Callot* (1942).

Hofmann, Ludwig (b. Frankfurt, 14 Jan. 1895; d. Frankfurt, 28 Dec. 1963). German bass-baritone. Studied Frankfurt and Milan. Début Bamberg 1918. London, C.G., 1932, 1939, and 1955; N.Y., Met., 1932–8. Appeared regularly Bayreuth and Vienna in both Wagner bass and baritone roles and the Italian and French repertory. (R)

Hofmannsthal, Hugo von (b. Vienna, 1 Feb.1874; d. Rodaun, 15 July 1929). Austrian poet and dramatist. Operas of Strauss for which he wrote librettos are *Elektra* (1906–8), *Der Rosenkavalier* (1909–10), *Ariadne auf Naxos* (1st version, 1911–12; 2nd version, 1915–16); *Die Frau ohne Schatten* (1914–17), *Die ägyptische Helene* (1924–7; rev. 1933), and *Arabella* (1930–2). The collaboration is recorded in fascinating detail in their published correspondence. He also wrote the libretto for Wellesz's *Alkestis* (1924), and his play *Die Hochzeit der Sobeide* was the source of Cherepnin's opera (1933).

Hofoper (Ger. = Court Opera). Name given in pre-1918 days to the Court or Royal Opera houses in a number of German and Austrian cities, including Munich and Vienna.

Ho-jo-to-ho! Brünnhilde's war-cry in Act 2 of Wagner's *Die Walküre*.

Holbrooke, Josef (b. Croydon, 5 July 1878; d. London, 5 Aug. 1958). English composer. After conducting his own *Pierrot and Pierrette*, he devoted himself to a massive quasi-Wagnerian trilogy on Celtic legends, *The Cauldron of Anwen—The Children of Don*, *Dylan*, and *Bronwen*. He also wrote three slighter works, *The Enchanter*, *The Snob*, and *The Stranger*. Though inflated and now unfashionable, Holbrooke's music—of which the finest is said to be in the operas—is by no means devoid of imagination and lyricism, though these qualities are maimed by an almost total lack of self-criticism.

Holland. The first Dutch opera was Hacquart's *De Triomfeerende Min*, written as early as 1679 (to celebrate the Peace of Nijmegen); but, like most countries, Holland was for long dependent on visiting Italian, French, and German companies. The many short-lived Dutch national opera companies were shared between Amsterdam (q.v.) and The Hague. The Holland Festival was founded in 1947 under H. J. Reinink, with Peter Diamand as secretary and later as guiding artistic light. It is unique in being a nation-wide festival, centred on Amsterdam and The Hague, and it embraces music, drama, and the visual arts as well as other entertainments. Opera has always played an important part in it, and the programmes have shown a high regard for quality as well as great enterprise. Events have included: Ferrier in *Orfeo* under Monteux in 1949; *Oberon* in 1950; *Jenůfa* in 1951; *Oedipus Rex* and *The Nightingale* in 1952; *Lulu* (by the Essen Opera) in 1953; *From the House of the Dead* and (by La Scala) *Cenerentola* in 1954; *The Love of the Three Oranges* (by the Ljubljana Opera), Tomasi's *Sampiero Corso*, and *Peter Grimes* in 1956; *The Rake's Progress* in 1957; *Von Heute auf Morgen* with *Erwartung* in 1958; *Il Mondo della Luna* in 1959; *A Midsummer Night's Dream* in 1960; *Benvenuto Cellini* and *Cardillac* in 1961, *Il Ritorno d'Ulisse in Patria* and *Doktor Faust* in 1962; *M, de Pourceangnac*, *L'Infedelta Delusa* in 1963; and *Katerina Ismailova* and *Iphigénie en Tauride* in 1964. See also *Amsterdam*.

Holm, Richard (b. Stuttgart, 3 Aug. 1912). German tenor. Début Kiel 1936. After engagements in Nuremberg and Hamburg joined Munich State Opera in 1948. London, C.G., with Munich Co. 1953 and 1958–60. N.Y., Met., 1951 and from 1958. One of the most successful Davids of the day and also successful in Mozart roles and as Tom Rakewell and Loge. (R)

Holst, Gustav (b. Cheltenham, 21 Sept. 1874; d. London, 25 May 1934). English composer of Swedish origin. His first five operatic works are now forgotten: the first four are said to be pale Sullivan; and Holst afterwards dismissed the fifth, *Sita* (1899–1906), as 'good old Wagnerian bawling'. Its Sanskrit interest is pursued in *Sāvitri* (1916), a 1-act chamber opera (it can also be performed in the open); this achieves an extraordinarily strong atmosphere with very economic means. *The Perfect Fool* (1923) displays the essential Holstian dichotomy: an earthy, conversational musical manner is uncouthly set against one more ethereal and unreal. *At the Boar's Head* (1925), which collects all the Falstaff episodes from the Henry plays, is a brilliant, densely ingenious failure. *The Tale of the Wandering Scholar* (1934) returns with success to the comic style he originally sought. But rewarding as Holst's music is, the man whose ultimate home was the fastness of *Egdon Heath* could never be entirely himself in the richly human world of opera.

Holzbauer, Ignaz (b. Vienna, 17 Sept. 1711; d. Mannheim, 7 Apr. 1783). Austrian composer. His *Günther von Schwarzburg* (1776), the most celebrated of his operas, was admired by Mozart and is significant as the first effort at using a German subject in a German opera, with recitative as opposed to the spoken dialogue of Singspiel.

Home, Sweet Home. Originally an aria in Bishop's *Clari, or The Maid of Milan* (called by the composer a 'Sicilian Air'); also occurs in altered form in Donizetti's *Anna Bolena*, which resulted in Bishop's bringing an action for 'piracy and breach of copyright'. Used to be sung by Patti, Melba, and other prima donnas in the Lesson scene in *The Barber*, who often accompanied themselves on a piano wheeled on to the stage for the purpose.

Homer, Louise (orig. Louise Dilworth Beatty) (b. Pittsburgh, 28 Apr. 1871; d. Winter Park, Florida, 6 May 1947). American contralto. Studied Philadelphia and Boston, where she met the composer Sidney Homer whom she married. He took her to Paris where she studied with Fidèle König and Lhérie. Début Vichy 1898, Leonora (*La Favorite*); London, C.G., 1899, Lola; San Francisco 1900, Amneris. Leading contralto N.Y., Met., 1900–19. Sang Orfeo and Hate (*Armide*) in the famous Toscanini performances at the Met. Created the Witch in *Königskinder* (1910), and leading roles in *Manrù* (Paderewski), *Mona* (Parker), *Pipe of Desire* (Converse). Much admired in Wagner. Her husband wrote about her in *My Wife and I* (1939). (R)

Honegger, Arthur (b. Le Havre, 10 Mar. 1892; d. Paris, 27 Nov. 1955). French-born composer of Swiss parentage. His first dramatic work, *Le Roi David* (1921), established him as a composer of importance; already in it is present the extremely characteristic opposition of a delicate, simply framed style, often expressed almost archaically, to an aggressive, barbaric modernity associated with thick harmony and severe rhythms. This was followed by the opera *Antigone* (1927), the biblical opera *Judith* (1926), the melodrama *Amphion* (1931), the operetta *Les Aventures du Roi Pausole* (1930), and the stage oratorio *Cris du Monde* (1930–1) before his best-known work, the stage oratorio *Jeanne d'Arc au Bûcher* (1936). This is marked by the same unerringly apt use of means, sometimes very slender means, within a large framework as in *David*. Part melodrama (the main role is spoken), part oratorio, part opera, it is the most successful realization of Honegger's essential dualism. The attempts to fuse his opposing elements continue (as before, the special titles perhaps reflect what he felt as a special problem) in the opera *L'Aiglon* (1937, with Ibert), the 'spectacle', *Les Mille et Une Nuits* (1937), the operetta *Les Petites Cardinal* (1937), the dramatic legend *Nicolas de Flue* (1941), and the opera *Charles le Téméraire* (1944).

Hook, James (b. Norwich, ?3 June 1746; d. Boulogne, 1827). English composer of a large number of comic operas that were highly popular in their day.

Hopf, Hans (b. Nuremberg, 2 Aug. 1916). German tenor. Studied Munich with Paul Bender. Début 1936 with Bayerische Landesbühnen. After engagements at Augsburg, Dresden, and Berlin, joined Munich Opera 1949. London, C.G., 1951–3, 1963; N.Y., Met., 1952–5. Has participated in Bayreuth, Salzburg, and Munich Festivals; among his best roles are Max (*Freischütz*), Kaiser (*Frau ohne Schatten*), and Otello. (R)

Hopkins, Antony (b. London, 21 Mar. 1921). English composer. His operas include the facetious burlesque *Lady Rohesia* (1948), a miniature opera for the choristers of Canterbury Cathedral *The Man from Tuscany* (1951), and *Three's Company* (1953) for the Intimate Opera Company, which he directs. The latter two in particular show his fluent skill in matching the needs of the moment with music of charm and wit.

Horn, Charles Edward (b. London, 21 June 1786; d. Boston, Mass., 21 Oct. 1849). English singer and composer. Studied with his father Karl Friedrich Horn, and at Bath with Rauzzini. Début London, Ly., 1809. Participated in many English operatic ventures as singer and conductor. Responsible for bringing Balfe to London in 1823. Sang Kaspar in *Freischütz*, London, D.L., 1824. His voice was said to be poor but of extensive range, so that he could sing tenor as well as baritone parts. Of his 30 works for the stage, *Peveril of the Peak* (1826) was the most successful.

Hosenrolle. See *Travesti*.

Hotter, Hans (b. Offenbach-am-Main, 19 Jan. 1909). German bass-baritone. After a period as organist, choirmaster, and studying church music, he turned to opera. Studied with Matthaeus Roemer, a De Reszke pupil. Début Opava 1929, Speaker (*Zauberflöte*). After engagements in Prague, Breslau, and Hamburg (1934–8) he became a member of the Munich and Vienna Operas, and still divides his time between these two houses. London, C.G., 1947 with Vienna Company; regularly since then, especially in Wagner; N.Y., Met., 1950–4. Created the Kommandant (*Friedenstag*) and Olivier (*Capriccio*). Has established himself as the leading exponent of Wotan at post-war Bayreuth; and is also a distinguished Dutchman, Borromeo (*Palestrina*), and Grand Inquisitor. An intellectual singer in the best sense of the word, and highly endowed as an actor and musician. Responsible for the new production of *The Ring* at C.G. beginning in 1961. (R)

House of the Dead, From the (Cz., *Z Mrtvého Domu*). Opera in 3 acts by Janáček; text by composer, after Dostoyevsky's novel based on his prison reminiscences (1862). Prod. Brno 12 Apr. 1930; Edinburgh, by Prague Nat. T., 28 Aug. 1964. The 'plot' consists of barely connected scenes from prison life, each act with a long prisoner's narrative, lent some continuity by the initial arrival and final release of a political prisoner (in the novel, Dostoyevsky himself).

Hugh the Drover. Opera in 2 acts by Vaughan Williams; text by Harold Child. Prod. London, R.C.M., 4 July 1924; first professional performance H.M.'s, by B.N.O.C., 14 July 1924 with T. Davies, Mary Lewis; Washington, 21 Feb. 1928. Mary is engaged to John the Butcher, whom Hugh defeats in a boxing match for her hand. He is then accused of being a Napoleonic spy, but the arresting sergeant recognizes him and removes John instead. Hugh leaves with Mary.

Hughes, Arwel (b. Rhosllanerchrugog, 25 Aug. 1909). Welsh composer. *Menna* (1950–1) is one of the few indigenous Welsh operas on a national subject.

Hugo, Victor (b. Besançon, 26 Feb. 1802; d. Paris, 22 May 1885). French poet, novelist, and playwright. Operas on his works are as follows. *Hernani* (1830): Gabussi (1834); Mazzucato (1844); Verdi (1844). *Marian Delorme* (1831): Bottesini (1862); Pedrotti (1865); Ponchielli (1885). *Notre-Dame de Paris* (1831): L. Bertin (*Esmeralda*, adaptation by Hugo, 1836); Prévost (do., *c.* 1840); Mazzucato (do.); Bizet (do., 1859); W. Fry (1864); Pedrell (*Quasimodo*, 1875); G. Thomas (*Esmeralda*, 1883); F. Schmidt (*Notre-Dame*, 1914). *Le Roi s'amuse* (1832): Verdi (*Rigoletto*, 1851). *Lucrèce Borgia* (1833): Donizetti (1833). *Marie Tudor* (1833): Ferrari (1840); Pacini (1843); Kashperov (1859); Balfe (*The Armourer of Nantes*, 1836): Gomes (1879); Wagner-Régeny (*Der Günstling*, 1931–4). *Angelo* (1835): Mercadante (*Il Giuramento*, 1837); Ponchielli (*La Gioconda*, 1876); Cui (1876); Bruneau (1928). *Ruy Blas* (1838): Poniatowski (1843); Besanzoni (1843); W. Glover (1861); Chiaromonte (*Maria di Nemburgo*, 1862); Zenger (1868); Marchetti (1869). *Les Burgraves* (1843): Salvi (*I Burgravi*, 1845). *Torquemada* (1882); Rota (1943). *L'Homme Qui Rit* (1868): Enna (*Komedianten*, 1920); Pedrollo (1920). *La Légende des Siècles* (1859): Mancinelli (*Isora di Provenza*, 1884).

Huguenots, Les. Opera in 5 acts by Meyerbeer; text by Scribe and Deschamps. Prod. Paris, O., 29 Feb. 1836 with Falcon, Dorus-Gras, Nourrit, Levasseur; New Orleans, 29 Apr. 1839;

London, C.G., 20 June 1842. A lavish grand opera in the typical Meyerbeer manner, centring on the massacre of the Huguenots on St. Bartholomew's Day in Paris in Aug. 1572. In the days of the great singers of last century the work enjoyed enormous popularity in London, Paris, and N.Y. At the Met. in the 1890's the performances were called 'Les nuits de sept étoiles' when the cast included Nordica, Melba, Scalchi, Jean and Édouard de Reszke, Maurel, and Plançon. It was the work chosen to open the present C.G. building in 1858.

Hullah, John (b. Worcester, 27 June 1812; d. London, 21 Feb. 1884). English composer and manager. Studied London with Horsley and Crivelli. Wrote the music to Charles Dickens's *The Village Coquettes* (1836). His *The Barbers of Bassora* and *The Outpost* were produced at C.G. in 1837 and 1838. He subsequently turned to teaching and the training of teachers.

Hummel, Johan Nepomuk (b. Pozsony, 14 Nov. 1778; d. Weimar, 17 Oct. 1837). Hungarian composer and pianist. The best known of his four operas was *Mathilde von Guise* (1810). He also wrote a new finale to Auber's *Gustave III* in 1836.

Humming Chorus. The unseen chorus which ends the first scene of Act 2 of Puccini's *Madama Butterfly* as Butterfly, Suzuki, and the baby take up their stance at the *shosi* awaiting Pinkerton.

Humperdinck, Engelbert (b. Siegburg, 1 Sept. 1854; d. Neustrelitz, 27 Sept. 1921). German composer. He assisted Wagner in the preparation of *Parsifal* at Bayreuth 1880–1, even composing a few bars of it for a transformation. His own first opera, *Hänsel und Gretel* (1893), has remained his most successful. Its simple nursery tunes are used in a Wagnerian manner with unique charm and success, so that it has remained a work *sui generis*, unrepeatable even by Humperdinck. His other operas are *Die sieben Geislein* (1895), like *Hänsel* based on Grimm, *Dornröschen* (1902), *Königskinder* (1910), *Die Marketenderin* (1914), and *Gaudeamus* (1919).

Hunding. Husband (bass) of Sieglinde in Wagner's *Die Walküre*.

Hungary. The first flowering of Hungarian opera was in the 17th century, when opera halls built in various aristocrats' palaces saw performances that reached remarkably high standards. The most famous was at Eszterháza, where Haydn worked in a separate opera house. The first opera performances in Hungarian were given in the Buda Castle Theatre in 1795, and from 1821 there were regular performances at Kolozsvár (now Cluj, Rumania). The first surviving Hungarian opera was Ruzsicska's *Béla Futása* (*Bela's Flight*) (1822): the first comic opera was Bartay's *Csel* (*The Trick*) (1839). The first Metropolitan Opera Company was formed in the National Theatre at Budapest. From 1948 to 1955 this company also formed a 'Rolling Opera' which travelled on a special train giving performances in provincial towns, villages, and industrial settlements. See also *Budapest*, *Debrecen*, *Pécs*, and *Szeged*.

Hüni-Mihacsek, Felice (b. Pécs, 3 Apr. 1891). Hungarian soprano. Studied Vienna with Rose Papier. Début Vienna 1919; Munich State Opera 1926–45. One of the best Mozart singers of the inter-war years (Fiordiligi, Constanze, Queen of Night, Donna Anna), and also a distinguished Marschallin and Eva. (R)

Huon of Bordeaux. A knight (ten.), Duke of Guienne, hero of Weber's *Oberon*.

Hüsch, Gerhard (b. Hanover, 2 Feb. 1901). German baritone. Studied with Hans Emge. Début Osnabrück 1924. Engagements in Cologne (1927–30) and Berlin (1930–42), first at the Städtische Oper, then at the Staatsoper. London, C.G., 1930, Falke in Walter's famous *Fledermaus* production; subsequently heard as Papageno. Bayreuth 1930–1 when he sang an outstanding Wolfram in *Tannhäuser*. (R)

Hyde, Walter (b. Birmingham, 6 Feb. 1875; d. London, 11 Nov. 1951).

English tenor. Studied R.C.M. with Garcia and as a student appeared in *Euryanthe* and Stanford's *Much Ado About Nothing*. After singing in light musical plays was engaged by Pitt to sing Siegmund in the English *Ring* at C.G. under Richter. Appeared regularly at C.G. from 1908 to 1923, and was member of the Beecham Company and subsequently the B.N.O.C., of which he became a director. The first London Sali (*A Village Romeo and Juliet*) and the first English Parsifal. (R)

Hymn to the Sun. Aria sung by the Queen of Shemakhan (sop.) in Act 2 of Rimsky-Korsakov's *The Golden Cockerel*.

I

Iago. Otello's villainous lieutenant (bar.), in Verdi's and (ten.) in Rossini's *Otello*.

Iași (Jassy). Town in Rumania, capital of Moldavia. The Artists' Association of the Rumanian Opera was founded during the First World War. In 1956 the present company was formed, and gave five operas in its first season. In 1958 the National Theatre was modernized, and the company began touring towns and villages of Moldavia.

Ibert, Jacques (b. Paris, 15 Aug. 1890; d. Paris, 5 Feb. 1962). French composer. His numerous works include nine operas, of which the most successful has been *Angélique* (1927). Assistant director of Paris Opéra 1955–7.

Ibsen, Henrik (b. Skien, 20 Mar. 1828; d. Oslo, 23 May 1906). Norwegian playwright. Operas on his plays are as follows. *The Warriors at Helgeland* (1858): K. Moor (*Hjørdis*, 1905). *Peer Gynt* (1867): Ullmann; Heward (unfin., from 1922); Egk (1938). *The Feast at Solhaug* (1856): Stenhammer (1899).

Ich baue ganz auf deine Stärke. Belmonte's (ten.) aria in Act 3 of *Die Entführung aus dem Serail*, which he is instructed to sing by Pedrillo to conceal the placing of the ladders to the Seraglio windows. Often omitted in performance.

Idomeneo, Re di Creta. Opera in 3 acts by Mozart; text by G. B. Varesco, after Danchet's libretto for Campra's *Idoménée* (1712) and the ancient legend. Prod. Munich 29 Jan. 1781, with Anton Raaf; Glasgow 12 Mar. 1934; Tanglewood 4 Aug. 1947.

Act 1. Idomeneo, King of Crete (ten.), has sent home from Troy captives including Ilia (sop.), daughter of Priam. She and Idomeneo's son Idamante (sop. or ten.) are in love, though he has not declared himself: Elettra (sop.) also loves him. The impending return of Idomeneo is the sign for an amnesty of prisoners. But a sudden storm causes the King to vow to the sea god a sacrifice of the first living thing he meets on shore. This is his son. Horrified, he hurries away without speaking; a joyful chorus welcomes the warriors.

Act 2. The King tries to evade his vow by sending Idamante to escort Elettra home to Argos, much to the distress of Ilia. But a storm arises, followed by a monster who ravages the island. The people hold that some unknown sinner has offended the gods, and Idomeneo admits his guilt and is ready to die.

Act 3. Idamante and Ilia declare their love before he sets out to attack the monster. Elettra, mad with jealousy, interrupts, followed by the King, who is torn between anxiety for his son and guilt. He is forced, by the people's demand for a victim, to reveal the truth. The High Priest hesitates to make the sacrifice on hearing that the monster has been killed by Idamante, who nevertheless offers himself as a victim so as not to break his father's vow. But the voice of the god spares him, announcing that Idomeneo must abdicate. Idamante ascends the throne with Ilia at his side.

Other operas on the subject are by Campra (1712), Gazzaniga (1790), Paer (1794), Farinelli (1796), and Federici (1806).

I have attained the highest power. Boris's (bass) monologue in Act 2, scene 2, of *Boris Godunov*.

Il balen. Di Luna's (bar.) aria in Act 2, scene 2, of *Il Trovatore* in which he sings of the tempest raging within his heart. When first heard, speedily attained popularity throughout Europe and was whistled by all the errand boys and played on all the barrel organs.

Ilia. Daughter (sop.) of Priam in Mozart's *Idomeneo*.

Il lacerato spirito. Fiesco's (bass) aria in the prologue to *Simone Boccanegra*, in which he sings of his tortured soul.

Illica, Luigi (b. Piacenza, 9 May 1857; d. Piacenza, 16 Dec. 1919). Italian playwright and librettist. Wrote, or collaborated in, some 80 librettos, of which the most famous are (with Giacosa) for Puccini's *Manon Lescaut*, *La Bohème*, *Madama Butterfly*, and *Tosca*. Among his best-known librettos for other composers are those for Catalani's *La Wally*, Gnecchi's *Cassandra*, Franchetti's *Cristoforo Colombo*, Mascagni's *Iris*, and Giordano's *Andrea Chénier*. Though he lacked Giacosa's sensibility, 'he had plenty of imagination', in Puccini's words.

Il mio tesoro. Don Ottavio's (ten.) love song to Donna Anna in Act 2, scene 2, of Mozart's *Don Giovanni*.

Ilosvay, Maria von (b. Hungary, 8 May 1913). Hungarian mezzo-soprano. Studied Budapest and Vienna with Laura Hillgermann, Maria Budanovitz, and Mme Kaschowska. Won first prize in International Contest Vienna 1937, and engaged for the Salzburg Opera Guild to tour America and Europe under Erede. Member of Hamburg State Opera since 1940. Bayreuth 1953–8; London, C.G., 1954–9. A fine Fricka and Waltraute. (R)

Immortal Hour, The. Opera in 2 acts by Rutland Boughton; text by 'Fiona Macleod' (William Sharp). Prod. Glastonbury 26 Aug. 1914; N.Y. 6 Apr. 1926. The fairy Etain and the king Eochaidh are to be married. The fairy prince Midir enchants Etain, and she follows him to the Land of Heart's Desire. Dalua, the Shadow God, touches Eochaidh and he falls dead. The opera had an outstandingly successful season of 216 nights at the Regent T., London, from 13 Oct. 1922, when its simple melodious score and escapist world of 'Celtic Twilight' attracted a wide audience. An attempt at revival after the Second World War was unsuccessful; by then the work's whimsy and *naïveté* were outmoded.

Impresario (from It. *impresa* = undertaking). Organizer and/or manager of an opera company.

Impresario, The. See *Schauspieldirektor, Der*.

In alt. The term used to describe the notes in the octave immediately above the top line of the treble stave, running from g'' to f'''. The next octave, from g''' to f'''', is **in altissimo.**

Incledon, Charles (b. St. Keverne, Cornwall, 5 Feb. 1763; d. London, 18 Feb. 1826). English tenor. As choirboy at Exeter Cathedral studied under Langdon and Jackson. Went to sea where his fine tenor voice impressed Admiral Pigot. Engaged Southampton 1784, Bath 1785 where he was heard by Rauzzini, who gave him lessons. London, C.G., from 1790. His son, also Charles, appeared briefly in London in the 1820's and then taught in Vienna.

Incoronazione di Poppea, L' (The Coronation of Poppaea). Opera in prologue and 3 acts by Monteverdi; text by G. F. Busenello, after Tacitus. Prod. Venice, SS. G. e P., autumn 1642; Smith Coll., Northampton, Mass., 27 Apr. 1926; Oxford, Univ. Opera Club, 6 Dec. 1927; Glyndebourne (arr. Leppard), 29 June 1962. Poppaea replaces Nero's Empress and assumes the throne. The first opera on a historical (other than biblical) subject. Monteverdi's last opera.

Indes Galantes, Les. Opera-ballet in prologue and 3 *entrées* by Rameau; text by Louis Fuzelier. Prod. Paris, O., 23 Aug. 1735—fourth *entrée* added 10 Mar. 1736; N.Y., Town Hall, 1 Mar. 1961. In this form the work tells four tales of love in different parts of the world: the *entrées* are *Le Turc Généreux*, *Les Incas du Pérou*, *Les Fleurs*, *Feste Persane*, and *Les Sauvages*. Rameau's third opera and greatest success. Revived in a sumptuous production by Lehmann, Paris, O., 1952.

India. Though Western opera has not taken root in India, performances were sometimes staged during the British Raj. Scenes from *Don Giovanni* were given in 1833 and *Cenerentola* was given in 1834 at Calcutta, for instance;

Cavalleria Rusticana was given at Simla in 1901, Linley's *The Duenna* at Calcutta in 1915 and at Bombay in 1925. The so-called Opera House at Calcutta was really for drama and variety, though Pollard's Lilliputian Opera Company (probably more of a concert party group) performed there in 1896–9.

Native Indian opera is a genre outside the scope of this dictionary. One may, however, mention the work of Rabindranath Tagore, who attached greater importance to his music than to his poetry. His operas are based on the traditional music of India but he was not afraid to make use of Western folk music as well—the resulting style became known as Rabindra-Sangeet (Tagore Music). One of his operas, *Shyama*, has been recorded: it is a simple ballad opera on a tragic story.

In diesen heil'gen Hallen. Sarastro's (bass) aria in Act 2 of *Die Zauberflöte* in which he tells Pamina that no one thinks of violence within the sacred walls of the temple of Isis and Osiris.

Indy, d'. See *D'Indy*.

In fernem Land. Lohengrin's (ten.) narration in the last scene of *Lohengrin* in which he discloses his identity and tells of the Holy Grail. In German known as *Gralserzählung*.

Inghelbrecht, D.-E. (b. Paris, 17 Sept. 1880; d. Paris, 14 Feb. 1965). French conductor and composer. Director Ch.É. 1913; asst. cond. O.C. 1924; cond. O.C. 1932; cond. O. 1945. Author of *Comment on ne doit pas interpréter 'Carmen', 'Faust', et 'Pelléas'*. (R)

Inghilleri, Giovanni (b. Porto Empedocle, 9 Mar. 1894; d. Milan, 10 Dec. 1959). Italian baritone. Début Milan, Teatro Carcano, 1919, Valentine. Sang regularly in Rome and other Italian centres. London, C.G., 1928–30, 1935; Chicago 1929–30. His roles included Gérard (which he sang on the 50th anniversary of the première of *Chénier* under the composer's direction at La Scala), Scarpia, Amfortas, and Shaklovity in *Khovanshchina* which he continued to sing until 1953. (R)

In quelle trine morbide. Manon Lescaut's (sop.) aria in Act 2 of Puccini's opera in which she sings of the chill in the splendour among which she lives, and wishes she were back in the humble dwelling where she and Des Grieux were so happy.

In questa reggia. Turandot's (sop.) narration in Act 2, scene 2, of Puccini's opera.

Intendant (Ger. = superintendent). The administrator of a German opera house—not necessarily the artistic or musical director.

Interlude. A short piece of music played between parts of a larger work.

Intermezzo. (1) Originally a short musical entertainment appearing in the course of elaborate festivities. The earliest recorded was at Florence in 1539. Given between the acts of a play, the intermezzo gradually drew a large measure of interest to itself; and with the appearance of opera it continued its function. Its importance to the history of opera lay in its contrast of more realistic, popular entertainment with the remote Metastasian gods and heroes of *opera seria*. The comic characters admitted into *opera seria* had begun by the beginning of the 18th century to appear only in scenes near the end of the act, thus forming an almost separate plot—an intermezzo to the main events. The most famous intermezzo was Pergolesi's *La Serva Padrona*, which has survived the loss of its 'host' opera *Il Prigioniero Superbo*. If *opera seria* stood for the establishment of order and the importance of conformity, the intermezzo satisfied the complementary human wish not to conform, and so began encroaching on the larger entertainment, making it seem artificial and stilted. It is thus the beginning of *opera buffa* (q.v.).

(2) The word is used in the same sense as Interlude (q.v.); and also for a piece of music, often virtually a short tone-poem, denoting the passing of time, e.g. between scenes 1 and 2 of Mascagni's *Cavalleria Rusticana*, or describing or summarizing events taking place between two scenes, e.g. between Acts 3 and 4 of Puccini's *Manon Les-*

caut or 'The Walk to the Paradise Garden' between the 5th and 6th 'pictures' of Delius's *A Village Romeo and Juliet*.

Intermezzo. Opera in 2 acts by Strauss; text by composer. Prod. Dresden 4 Nov. 1924 with Lotte Lehmann and Joseph Correck, cond. Busch; N.Y., Lincoln Center, 11 Feb. 1963, with Phyllis Curtin, Donald Bell, cond. Scherman; Edinburgh, King's T., 9 Sep. 1965. Based on incidents in Strauss's own life when his happy marriage was threatened by his having received, by mistake, a passionate love-letter from an unknown female admirer. Strauss himself supervised the designing of the sets, which were made to look like his home at Garmisch, and the two leading singers were made up to look like Strauss and his wife.

Intervals. Not the musical term, but an integral part of the evening's proceedings in the opera house, and to some of the audience as important as the music. Interval behaviour at C.G. has changed since Victorian days when the ladies remained seated in their boxes, and held court to the gentlemen, all in their 'indispensable evening dress'. At the festivals at Bayreuth and Glyndebourne the long interval is occupied by taking a dinner, supper, or picnic, and walking in the open air. On opening nights of the season, especially in the Italian opera houses, the interval between the acts may last anything up to 45 minutes.

Intimate Opera Company. Founded in 1930 by Frederick Woodhouse, and since 1952 under the musical and artistic direction of Antony Hopkins assisted by Joseph Horovitz. This company has given performances all over Great Britain and has also toured the United States. Its repertory has included works by Purcell, Pergolesi, Storace, Carey, Arne, Dibdin, Offenbach, Mozart, as well as modern pieces by Hopkins, Horovitz, Geoffrey Bush, and Gerald Cockshott. Singers who have appeared with the company include Patricia Hughes, Ann Dowdall, Winifred Radford, Eric Shilling, Stephen Manton, Leyland White, and Frederick Woodhouse.

Intonation. The quality of singing or playing in tune.

Intrusive H. A common singer's fault found chiefly in long runs on one syllable: each new note is started with an unvocalized breath so that the effect is not 'a-a-a-' but 'ha-ha-ha-'. An accusation of this fault levelled against Steuart Wilson by a schoolmaster in a letter to the *Radio Times* in 1933 led to a libel action. Wilson won his case, in which a large number of musicians were called as witnesses, and was awarded £2,100 damages against the B.B.C. and the schoolmaster. He spent it on a production of Boughton's *The Lily Maid*.

Invano, Alvaro. The duet between Carlo (bar.) and Alvaro (ten.) in Act 4, scene 1, of *La Forza del Destino*, in which Alvaro, now Padre Raffaello, tries to dissuade Carlo from challenging him to a duel.

Inszenierung (Ger. = Production). Hence *Neuinszenierung* for a new production of an opera.

Iphigenia. In mythology, the daughter of Agamemnon and Clytemnestra. Agamemnon killed a hart in the sacred grove of Artemis, who then becalmed the Greek fleet waiting to sail from Aulis for Troy. Agamemnon decided to follow the priest Calchas's advice and sacrifice her, but Artemis carried her off to Tauris to be a priestess. There she was discovered years later by her wandering brother Orestes, and brought home again to Mycenae. The subject, in Euripides's treatment, of numerous operas, the first in 1632 by an unknown composer. Beside Gluck's two operas, there are at least 30 settings of *Iphigenia in Aulis* between 1632 and 1819; and more than 15 of *Iphigenia in Tauris* between 1704 and 1817.

Iphigénie en Aulide. Opera in 3 acts by Gluck; text by Roullet, after Racine's play from Euripides (prob. *c.* 407 B.C., unfin.). Prod. Paris, O., 19 Apr. 1774 with Sophie Arnould; Oxford 20 Nov. 1933; Philadelphia 22 Feb. 1935. There are over 30 other operas on the legend.

Iphigénie en Tauride. Opera in 4 acts by Gluck; text by Guillard, after

Euripides's play (*c.* 415–406 B.C.). Prod. Paris, O., 18 May 1779 with Levasseur; London, King's T., 7 Apr. 1796, with Giorgi-Banti; N.Y., Met., 25 Nov. 1916. There are over 15 other operas on the legend.

Ippolitov-Ivanov, Mikhail (b. Gachina, 19 Nov. 1859; d. Moscow, 28 Jan. 1935). Russian composer, author of seven operas between 1887 and 1934. From 1899 cond. Moscow Private Opera, where he did valuable and influential work.

Ireland. The first opera in Erse was O'Dwyer's *Eithne* (1910). Palmer's *Sruth na maoile* (*The Sea of Moyle*), text by T. O'Ceallaigh (T. O'Kelly) and founded on the Irish saga *The Children of Lir*, was first given in Dublin in 1923. The first Italian opera given in Ireland was Handel's *Rinaldo* (1711) performed in Dublin by Niccolini's troupe. In 1726 *Midas* (text by O'Hara), a famous parody on Italian *opera seria*, had its première in Dublin. See *Dublin*, *Wexford*.

Iris. Opera in 3 acts by Mascagni; text by Illica. Prod. Rome, C., 22 Nov. 1898 with Darclée, cond. Mascagni; revised and given at La Scala 19 Jan. 1899; Philadelphia 14 Oct. 1902 with Farnetti; London, C.G., 8 July 1919 with Sheridan. The opera, set in 19th-century Japan, tells of the vain attempt by Osaka (ten.) to win the love of the pure young Iris (sop.). He arranges with Kyoto (bar.), the keeper of a brothel, to have her abducted, and her blind father, thinking she has gone there voluntarily, curses her and flings mud at her. Iris drowns herself in a sewer.

Irische Legende. Opera in 5 scenes by Egk; text by the composer after W. B. Yeats's drama *The Countess Cathleen* (1892). Prod. Salzburg Festspielhaus, 17 Aug. 1955, with Borkh, Klose, Lorenz, Böhme, Frick, cond. Szell.

Irmelin. Opera in 3 acts by Delius; text by composer. Prod. Oxford 4 May 1953; cond. Beecham. The princess Irmelin waits for her ideal lover; Nils, a prince disguised as a swineherd, follows the silver stream that will lead him to his true love and meets Irmelin at its end.

Isabeau. Opera in 3 acts by Mascagni; text by Illica. Prod. Buenos Aires, Teatro Colón, 2 June 1911 with Maria Farnetti; Chicago 12 Nov. 1917 with Raisa. The opera is based on the legend of Lady Godiva.

Isabella. The heroine (mezzo) of Rossini's *L'Italiana in Algeri*.

Isolier. The Count's page (mezzo) in Rossini's *Le Comte Ory*.

Isolde. The Irish princess (sop.) in Wagner's *Tristan und Isolde*.

Isouard, Nicolo (b. Malta, 6 Dec. 1775; d. Paris, 23 Mar. 1818). Maltese composer, often known simply as Nicolo. During Boïeldieu's absence in Russia he won the public's favour, though only *Cendrillon* (1810) is in fact a worthy competitor to Boïeldieu's operas. His comic operas were generally escapist, a distraction from current events rather than a reflection or witty distortion.

Istanbul. See *Turkey*.

Italian Opera House, New York. The first theatre built specially for opera in N.Y. Erected on the instigation of Da Ponte, and opened on 18 Nov. 1833 with *La Gazza Ladra*. Destroyed by fire 1835.

Italiana in Algeri, L' (The Italian Girl in Algiers). Opera in 2 acts by Rossini; text by Anelli. Prod. Venice, Teatro San Benedetto, 22 May 1813; London, Hm., 26 Jan. 1819 with Belocchi and Garcia; N.Y. 5 Nov. 1832. Isabella, 'l'Italiana' of the title, has been sailing the seas in search of her lover Lindoro who is a slave of Mustaphà, Bey of Algiers. A storm drives Isabella's ship to the shores of Algiers, and she arrives at the court accompanied by her elderly admirer Taddeo, whom she passes off as her uncle. The Bey falls in love with her, and after many complications Lindoro and Isabella plan to enrol Mustaphà in the order of the 'Pappatacci'. The most important rule of the order is to eat and be silent, and be a model husband.

Isabella and Lindoro are able to sail away reunited, and the Bey returns to his neglected wife Elvira. Also an opera by L. Mosca (1808).

Italy. See *Bari, Bergamo, Bologna, Brescia, Catania, Florence, Genoa, Milan, Naples, Palermo, Parma, Rome, Siena, Spoleto, Turin, Venice, Verona.*

Ivan Susanin. See *Life for the Tsar, A.*

Ivan the Terrible. See *Maid of Pskov, The.*

Ivanhoe. Opera in 5 acts by Sullivan; text by Julian Sturgis, after Scott's novel (1819). Prod. for inauguration of short-lived Royal English Opera House (now Palace Theatre) in Cambridge Circus, 31 Jan. 1891. Sullivan's only grand opera, and perhaps the only grand opera ever to have a continuous run (160 perfs.). Other operas by Rossini (1826), Pacini (1832), Savi (1863), and Ciardi (1888).

Ivogün, Maria (orig. Ilse von Günther) (b. Budapest, 18 Nov. 1891). Hungarian soprano. Studied Vienna and engaged by Bruno Walter for Munich 1913. Created Ighino (*Palestrina*). London, C.G., 1924 and subsequently; Chicago 1925. Career came to a premature close through ill health but she continued to teach until 1958. Her pupils include Elisabeth Schwarzkopf and Rita Streich. Was considered one of the finest coloratura sopranos of the interwar period, and greatly admired as Constanze, Gilda, Zerbinetta, and Mistress Ford (Nicolai). (R)

Ivrogne Corrigé, L' (The Drunkard Reformed). Comic opera in 2 acts by Gluck; text by Louis Anseaume, after La Fontaine's fable (Book 3, No. 7) (1668). Prod. Vienna, B., Apr. 1760; Hartford, 26 Feb. 1945; Birmingham Sept. 1955. Mathurin, the drunkard of the title, is cured by being brought face to face, while drunk, with an 'infernal tribunal' that judges and sentences him—actually it is staged by his wife.

J

Jacobin, The (Cz., *Jakobín*). Opera in 3 acts by Dvořák; text by Marie Červinková-Riegrová. Prod. Prague, Cz., 12 Feb. 1889; London, St. George's Hall, 22 July 1947 by Workers' Music Assoc. The Jacobin returns from an exile caused by his political views and with the help of the musician Benda manages to regain his former position.

Jacquino. Rocco's young assistant jailer (ten.) in Beethoven's *Fidelio*.

Jadlowker, Hermann (b. Riga, 5 July 1877; d. Tel-Aviv, 13 May 1953). Latvian tenor. Studied Vienna. Début Cologne 1899; N.Y., Met., 1910–13 where he created the King's son (*Königskinder*). Greatly admired in Berlin where he sang until 1929; then taught first at Riga and from 1938 in Tel-Aviv. (R)

Janáček, Leoš (b. Hukvaldy, 3 July 1854; d. Ostrava, 12 Aug. 1928). Czech composer. Passionate humanist that he was, Janáček increasingly found opera to be the form in which he could most richly express his intense love of life and of people. His operas contain his greatest work, and it is chiefly upon them that his rapidly increasing European reputation rests. *Šárka* (1887; rev. 1888, 1918, prod. 1925) treats the Czech legend with skill and an occasional foretaste of his mature style, but in *The Beginning of a Romance* (1894) he reverted, in the attempt to compose a light folk comedy, to a pale imitation of Smetana. Then came *Jenůfa* (1894–1903); though produced at Brno in 1904 it was not until a visitor overhearing some of the music succeeded in obtaining a Prague performance that Janáček became suddenly a famous composer. *Jenůfa* is his lyrical masterpiece, a wise and tender setting in an idiom now fully mature. For the first time Janáček's lifelong interest in speech-rhythms is turned to wonderfully expressive use; the short phrases of Czech folk music and of his own abrupt Lachian dialect are at the root of a short-phrased melodic idiom that can be devastatingly trenchant and yet take flight in a curve of memorable beauty. In *Osud* (*Fate*) (1904, prod. 1958), some charming music is buried beneath a feeble libretto. *The Excursions of Mr. Brouček* (1920) caused Janáček some difficulty: the first act, *Mr. Brouček's Excursion to the Moon*, needed much revision before he was satisfied; *Mr. Brouček's Excursion to the XVth Century* followed. *Káťa Kabanová* (1921) is a dark-hued yet ineffably tender work amply expressive of sympathy for its touching, tragic heroine. *The Cunning Little Vixen* (1924) celebrates Janáček's boundless love of nature; the woodland scenes are enchanting tone-pictures, there is opportunity for rich comedy, and the final pages are perhaps the most rapturous affirmation of love for life that Janáček ever wrote. In *The Makropoulos Affair* (1926) the long legal wrangles of the first act seem to have daunted the composer, but the closing drama is affectingly set. With *From the House of the Dead* (1930), Janáček crystallized his idiom into its most intense, at times wildly eccentric, form. Yet though the work has no plot and little incident, the music presents a shatteringly powerful portrait of the prisoners as they go about their life. His love, never sentimental in its passionate declarations, is here extended to all men. At the head of the score he set the words, 'In every human being there is a divine spark.'

Jansen, Jacques (b. Paris, 22 Nov. 1913). French baritone. Studied with Panzéra. Début Paris, O.C., 1941, Pelléas; N.Y., Met., 1949 and London, C.G., 1949 in same role. Has appeared at Colón, Buenos Aires, and throughout Italy. His roles include Mârouf, Fragonard, and Valerien in Hahn's *Malvina*. (R)

Janssen, Herbert (b. Cologne, 22 Sept. 1895; d. N.Y., 3 Jun. 1965). German, then naturalized American, baritone. Studied Cologne and Berlin with Daniel. Début Berlin 1924; London, C.G., 1926, and every season until 1939; N.Y., Met., 1939–51. Greatly admired as Amfortas, Wolfram, Gunther, and Kurwenal, all of which he sang in Bayreuth, London, and New York. During the war years, when there was a shortage of dramatic baritones in America, he unwisely undertook Wotan and Sachs, which were too heavy for him. His Kothner in *Meistersinger* has rarely been bettered. (R)

Japan. Gluck's *Orfeo* was given a concert performance in Tokyo in 1935, and *Carmen* produced (in Japanese) in the same year. The enormous sale of European gramophone records has increased interest especially in Italian opera, and in recent years the Italian government has subsidized visits to Japan of companies that included Del Monaco, Gobbi, Tagliavini, and Gui. Companies currently flourishing in Japan are a Younger Operatic Group, the Nobuko Hara Research Group, and the Fujiwara Opera Company. The fashion for operas on Japanese subjects grew originally out of the French Romantics' fascination with the Orient. It was started by Saint-Saëns's first opera, *La Princesse Jaune* (1872), and has included such famous examples as *Madama Butterfly* and *Iris*; as recently as 1960 *Gracia Hokosawa*, by Vincenzo Cimatti, an Italian priest living in Japan, was performed in Tokyo.

Järnefelt, Armas (b. Viipori, 14 Aug. 1869; d. Stockholm, 23 June 1958). Swedish conductor and composer of Finnish birth. Director of opera Helsinki 1903–7; conductor Stockholm Opera 1907–32; conductor Helsinki Opera 1932–6. **Maikki Järnefelt** (b. Joensuu, 26 Aug. 1871; d. Turku, 4 July 1929), his wife, from 1893 to 1908 was a well-known soprano, a Marchesi pupil, especially admired in Wagner.

Jassy. See *Iași.*

Jeanne d'Arc au Bûcher (Joan of Arc at the Stake). *Oratorio dramatique* by Honegger; text by Claudel. Prod. Basle 12 May 1938, with Ida Rubinstein; San Francisco 15 Oct. 1954, with Dorothy Maguire; London, Stoll, 20 Oct. 1954, with Ingrid Bergman. Throughout, Joan remains tied to her stake, reliving the events that have led to her martyrdom.

Je crois entendre encore. Nadir's (ten.) aria in Act 1 of *Les Pêcheurs de Perles*, in which he sings of his love for Leila.

Jehin, Léon (b. Soa, 17 July 1853; d. Monte Carlo, 14 Feb. 1928). Belgian conductor. Studied Liège and Brussels. Conductor Brussels, La M., 1882–4; Paris, O., 1889–93; London, C.G., 1891–2 where he directed first London performances of *Philémon et Baucis* and *Le Rêve*. Subsequently at Monte Carlo Opera. Married the mezzo-soprano **Blanche Deschamps** who created La Mère in *Louise* and Margared in *Le Roi d'Ys* at the Opéra-Comique, and was the first Fricka at the Opéra.

Jeník. The hero (ten.) of Smetana's *The Bartered Bride.*

Jenůfa. Opera in 3 acts by Janáček; text by composer after Gabriela Preissová's drama (1890). Prod. Brno 21 Jan. 1904; N.Y., Met., 6 Dec. 1924 with Jeritza, Matzenauer, cond. Bodanzky; London, C.G., 10 Dec. 1956 with Shuard, Fisher, cond. Kubelik. Originally (and still in Czechoslovakia) known as *Její Pastorkyňa* (Her Foster-daughter).

Act 1. In the mill of Grandmother Buryjovka in the Moravian mountains lives the ne'er-do-well Števa Buryja (ten.); his stepbrother Laca Klemeň (ten.) is a farm-hand and their cousin Jenůfa (sop.) helps in the house. She is the stepdaughter of Grandmother Buryjovka's daughter-in-law who, from her position as sexton, is known as the Kostelnička (sop.). Jenůfa is expecting Števa's child, and anxiously awaits the result of a conscription ballot to know whether he will return and marry her. He returns, unrecruited but also drunk, and the Kostelnička forbids him to marry Jenůfa until he has proved his worth by a year's total abstinence.

When Števa, who is only physically attracted to Jenůfa, leaves, Laca offers her flowers and tries to kiss her; repelled, he slashes her face with a knife.

Act 2. Jenůfa has secretly had a son. The Kostelnička, tormented by the disgrace, sends for Števa to marry Jenůfa; but he denies responsibility, and says that he is engaged to the mayor's daughter Karolka (mezzo). Laca appears, penitent and willing to marry Jenůfa though shocked by hearing of the birth of Števa's child. The Kostelnička, hoping to help the marriage on, tells Laca that the child has died; she takes it and drowns it in a brook. When Jenůfa awakes, she is also told that the child has died.

Act 3. Jenůfa and Laca are about to be married, as are Števa and Karolka. As the ceremony begins, news comes that the body of a baby has been found under the ice. Jenůfa realizes the truth and reveals whose baby it is. To save her from being accused the Kostelnička steps forward and confesses her guilt. Comforted by Jenůfa's forgiveness, she is led away. Jenůfa now turns to Laca and gives him his freedom; but he is faithful, and as the curtain falls they pledge their love.

Jerger, Alfred (b. Brno, 9 June 1889). Austrian baritone. Studied Vienna. Passau 1913 as conductor; 1917 as singer; Munich 1919–21. Début Vienna 1921, and leading baritone there until 1953. Appeared regularly at Salzburg as Don Giovanni, Pizarro, Guglielmo, and Count Almaviva. Created Mandryka, Dresden 1933 and sang same role at C.G. 1934. In recent years has produced at the Vienna V.O. and taught at the Academy. (R)

Jeritza, Maria (orig. Mimi Jedlitzka) (b. Brno, 6 Oct. 1887). Czech soprano. Studied Brno and Olomouc, where she made her début as Elsa 1910. Engaged Vienna, V.O., 1912. Chosen by Strauss to create title role of *Ariadne auf Naxos*, Stuttgart 1912. Vienna Opera 1913–32, 1949–52; N.Y., Met., 1921–32, 1951; London, C.G., 1925–6. In Vienna created Marietta in *Die tote Stadt* and Die Kaiserin in *Frau ohne Schatten*. Was the first American Jenůfa and Turandot, and was renowned for her Thaïs, Maliella, Tosca, Carmen, Minnie, and Fedora. Her personal beauty, acting ability, and lovely voice combined to make her one of the most admired and sought-after artists of the inter-war years. Autobiography *Sunlight and Song* (1924). (R)

Jerum! Jerum! Hans Sachs's (bar.) cobbling song in Act 2 of *Die Meistersinger*.

Jérusalem. See *I. Lombardi*.

Jewels of the Madonna, The. See *Gioielli della Madonna, I*.

Joan of Arc (b. Domrémy, 6 Jan. 1412; d. Rouen, 30 May 1431). The French martyr who led an army against the English besieging Orléans, and was burned at the stake. Operas on her story are by R. Kreutzer (1790), Andreozzi (1793), Vaccai (1827), Pacini (1830), Balfe (1837), Verdi (1845), Mermet (1876), Tchaikovsky (1879), Rezniček (1886), Honegger (1938), and Dello Joio (1956).

Jobin, Raoul (b. Quebec, 8 Apr. 1906). Canadian tenor. Studied Quebec. Début Paris 1930, Tybalt. O. and O.C. until 1940 and then 1946–56; N.Y., Met., 1939–50. Sang widely in North and South America, especially in the French repertory, his Don José, Julien, Werther, Hoffmann, and Samson being much admired. Opened School for Singing, Montreal 1957. (R)

Jochanaan. John the Baptist (bar.) in Strauss's *Salome*.

Jochum, Eugen (b. Babenhausen, 1 Nov. 1902). German conductor. Studied Augsburg and Munich. After appearances in Kiel and Mannheim was appointed Generalmusikdirektor at Duisburg 1930. Same position at Hanover 1934–9. Since then has appeared regularly at Hamburg and Munich, and at Bayreuth in 1953. (R)

John Lewis Partnership Music Society. An amateur society, sponsored by the public-spirited John Lewis shops in London, which with the help of professional conductors, producers, and designers has produced a number of operas since 1947 of a remarkably high artistic standard, including the first stage performances in England of Dvořák's *Rusalka* (1950) and *The Peasant Rogue* (1963) and Sutermeister's *The Black Spider* (1954), the première of Hugo Cole's *The Tunnel* (specially commissioned by the John Lewis Partnership) (1960), and such rarities as Wolf-Ferrari's *Le Donne Curiose*, Puccini's *Le Villi*, Smetana's *The Kiss*, Boïeldieu's *La Dame Blanche*, Bizet's *Don Procopio*, Offenbach's *La Périchole*, and the Weber–Mahler *Die drei Pintos*.

Johnson, Edward (b. Guelph, Ontario, 22 Aug. 1878; d. Guelph, 20 Apr. 1959). Canadian tenor and manager. Studied N.Y. with Mme von Feilitsch and Florence with Vincenzo Lombardi. Début (as Edoardo di Giovanni) Padua 1912, Chénier. Engaged for La Scala 1913–14 where he created Parsifal in Italy. Between 1914 and 1919 he created in either Milan or Rome leading tenor roles in Montemezzi's *La Nave*, Pizzetti's *Fedra*, and Alfano's *L'Ombra di Don Giovanni*; he was also the first Italian Rinuccio and Luigi, and an admirable Siegfried and Tannhäuser. Chicago Opera 1919–21; N.Y., Met., 1922–34; sole appearance London, C.G. (with B.N.O.C., 1923), as Faust. At Met. created leading tenor roles in *The King's Henchman*, *Peter Ibbetson*, and *The Merry Mount*. Was also a distinguished Pelléas, Romeo, Avito, and Sadko. General manager of Metropolitan (q.v.) 1935–50, and after his retirement played an active part in the opera class in the Musical Faculty at Toronto University. (R)

Johnston, James (b. Belfast, *c.* 1900). Irish tenor. Début Dublin 1940, Duke of Mantua; London, S.W., 1945–50 and guest artist until 1957. C.G. 1950–8. Created Hector in Bliss's *Olympians* and was the first Gabriele Adorno in *Simone Boccanegra* at S.W. 1948. His lyric-dramatic voice admirably suited him for Canio, Radamès, Manrico, Calaf, and Don José. He sang Italian roles with a ringing tone and intensity rare among British singers. (R)

Jolie Fille de Perth, La (The Fair Maid of Perth). Opera in 4 acts by Bizet; text by St-Georges and Adenis, a long way after Scott's novel *The Fair Maid of Perth* (1832). Prod. Paris, T.L., 26 Dec. 1867; Manchester 4 May 1917.

Jommelli, Niccolò (b. Aversa, nr. Naples, 10 Sept. 1714; d. Naples, 25 Aug. 1774). Italian composer. His long list of operas, now rarely explored, includes few light works. He was remarkable for his interest in the use of expressive recitative and his dislike of the *da capo* aria unless it had dramatic point—in these respects anticipating Gluck. His orchestration shows considerable originality.

Jones, Parry (b. Blaina, Monmouthshire, 14 Feb. 1891; d. London, 26 Dec. 1963). Welsh tenor. Studied London, R.C.M., Italy with Colli, Dresden with Scheidemantel, and England with John Coates. After touring America and surviving the torpedoing of the *Lusitania* in 1915, he sang with the Beecham and D'Oyly Carte Companies. Leading tenor Carl Rosa 1919–22, and B.N.O.C. 1922–8. Appeared at C.G. in small roles during the pre-war international seasons, and also with the C.G. Touring Company. Sang in the first English performances of *Wozzeck*, *Mathis der Maler*, *Doktor Faust*, and other works given in concert versions by the B.B.C. From 1949 to 1953 again at C.G., notably as Shuisky and the Captain in *Wozzeck*. Taught singing, London, G.S.M. (R)

Jongleur de Notre-Dame, Le (Our Lady's Juggler). Opera in 3 acts by Massenet; text by Maurice Léna, from a story by Anatole France in *L'Étui de Nacre* (1892), and based on a medieval miracle play. Prod. Monte Carlo 18 Feb. 1902, with Adolphe Maréchal and Renaud; London, C.G., 15 June 1906; N.Y. 27 Nov. 1908, with Mary Garden in role of Jean, originally sung by a tenor. The opera takes place in the 14th century in the Abbey of Cluny and tells how the humble Jean makes the only offering he can by juggling before an image of the Virgin, which by a miracle stoops to wipe his brow.

Jonny spielt auf (Johnny strikes up). Opera in 2 parts (11 scenes) by Křenek; text by composer. Prod. Leipzig

10 Feb. 1927; N.Y., Met., 19 Jan. 1929 with Bohnen and Schorr. Originally caused a sensation as the first jazz opera. Jonny, a jazz-band leader, steals a violin from Daniello and becomes so immensely successful that his performance from the North Pole sets the world dancing the Charleston.

Jonson, Ben (b. London, *c.* 11 June 1572; d. London, 6 Aug. 1637). English poet and dramatist. Operas on his works are as follows. *Volpone* (1606): Gruenberg (1945); Demuth (1949); Antheil (1953); Coombs (1957); Zillig (1957); Zimmermann (1957); Burt (1960). *Epicœne* (1609): Salieri (*Angiolina*, 1800); Lothar (*Lord Spleen*, 1930); Strauss (*Die schweigsame Frau*, 1935).

Joseph. Opera in 3 acts by Méhul; text by Duval. Prod. Paris, O.C., 17 Feb. 1807; Philadelphia, 15 Oct. 1828; London, D.L., 7 Apr. 1841 (in concert form). Revised by Weingartner and given in his version, C.G., 1914.

Journet, Marcel (b. Grasse, France, 25 July 1867; d. Vittel, 7 Sept. 1933). French bass. Studied Paris Conservatoire. Début Brussels, La M., 1891; London, C.G., 1897–1907, 1927–8; N.Y., Met., 1900–8. After the First World War was engaged by Toscanini for La Scala where he sang Hans Sachs, Le Père (*Louise*), Golaud, Mefistofele, Escamillo, and the Wanderer. Created Simon Mago in Boito's *Nerone*. (R)

Juch, Emma (b. Vienna, 4 July 1863; d. New York, 6 Mar. 1939). American soprano. Her parents were both Austrian by birth, but had become naturalized Americans, and she was born while they were on a visit to Austria. Studied with her father and Murio-Celli. Début London, H.M.'s, 1881, Philine (*Mignon*); N.Y., Ac. of M., 1881, same role. Then joined the American Opera Company, subsequently the National Opera Company, which foundered in 1889 and was reorganized by her as the Juch Grand Opera Company, which toured the U.S., Canada, and Mexico until 1891 after which she withdrew from opera. A great champion of opera in English. Her pure diction was often quoted as a model. She possessed an enormous vocal range and sang the Queen of the Night and Senta with equal success. (R)

Judith. Biblical opera in 3 acts by Honegger; text by Morax, after *The Book of Judith* in the Apocrypha. Prod. Monte Carlo, 13 Feb. 1926. Also operas by Levi (1844), A. Peri (1860), Serov (1863), Silveri (1885), Falchi (1887), Righi, Rezniček (1923), and Goossens (1929).

Jugoslavija. See *Yugoslavia*.

Juilliard School, New York. One of America's leading musical academies, the Juilliard School has always favoured opera in English. The first opera it staged was *Hänsel and Gretel* in 1929, since when it has staged many works, including the American stage premières of Britten's *The Beggar's Opera* (1950) and Strauss's *Capriccio* (1954). Albert Stoessel was the school's musical director 1929–43, and after his death he was succeeded by Wilfred Pelletier and Edgar Schenkman. In 1947 William Schuman, president of the school, appointed Frederic Cohen head of the opera department which became the Juilliard Opera Theatre. Past students of the school who have become established in the world of opera include Frances Bible, Gloria Davy, Mack Harrell, Margaret Harshaw, Charles Kullman, Risë Stevens, Leontyne Price, and Thomas Stewart.

La Juive (The Jewess). Opera in 5 acts by Halévy; text by Scribe. Prod. Paris 23 Feb. 1835, with Falcon, Dorus-Gras, Nourrit, Levasseur; New Orleans 13 Feb. 1844; London, D.L., 29 July 1846. The opera, set in 15th-century Constance, tells of the persecution of the Jews in that city led by Cardinal Brogni, and how Rachel, the supposed daughter of Eleazar the goldsmith, refuses to betray her lover Leopold, prince of the Empire. She is condemned with her 'father' to death by being thrown into a cauldron of boiling water. As she goes to her death Eleazar reveals she is not his daughter but that of Cardinal Brogni. Famous interpreters of Eleazar have included Tamberlik, Caruso, and Martinelli; and of Rachel, Pauline Viardot, Raisa, and Ponselle.

Julien. Opera in a prologue and 4 acts by Charpentier; text by the composer. Prod. Paris, O.C., 4 June 1913 with Carré and Rousselière; N.Y., Met., 26 Feb. 1914 with Farrar and Caruso. Written as a sequel to *Louise*, but not successful, receiving only 20 performances in Paris. Never revived.

Juliette. Romeo's lover (sop.) in Gounod's *Roméo et Juliette*.

Julius Caesar. See *Giulio Cesare*.

Jullien, Louis (b. Sisteron, 23 Apr. 1812; d. Paris, 14 May 1860). French conductor. Conducted in London from 1840, where his flamboyant personality attracted much attention to his concerts, directed opera, and composed an unsuccessful opera *Pietro il Grande* (C.G. 1852, with Tamberlik), which he financed himself. Originator of the unsuccessful speculation at D.L. in 1847 when English operas were to be given with Berlioz as conductor and with Bishop superintending rehearsals.

Jumping Frog of Calaveras County, The. Opera in 2 scenes by Lukas Foss; text by Jean Karsavina, after the story by Mark Twain. Prod. Bloomington, Indiana, 18 May 1950.

Jurinac, Sena (Srebrenka) (b. Travnik, Yugoslavia, 24 Oct. 1921). Yugoslav soprano. Studied Zagreb with Maria Kostrencić. Début Zagreb 1942, Mimì. Member of Vienna State Opera since 1944; London, C.G., with Vienna Company 1947, Dorabella; 1959, Butterfly, Octavian; 1961 Leonore; Glyndebourne Festivals 1949–56; San Francisco 1959. One of the finest Mozart singers of the day—a beautiful Cherubino, Fiordiligi, Ilia, Donna Elvira, and Pamina. As her voice grew in size she assumed heavier roles—Donna Anna, the Countess. Considered by many people to be the finest Octavian of the century and the best Composer (*Ariadne auf Naxos*) since Lotte Lehmann. Since 1957 she has sung Elisabeth de Valois, Desdemona, and Butterfly with equal success. (R)

Juyol, Suzanne (b. Paris, 1 Jan. 1920). French soprano. Studied Paris Conservatoire. Début Paris, O., 1942, Margared (*Roi d'Ys*). As well as being noted for her interpretations of Arianne (Dukas), Margared (*Roi d'Ys*), Charlotte, and Tosca, she has made a name for herself as Isolde and Brünnhilde and has sung these roles in Berlin. (R)

K

Kabalevsky, Dmitri (b. St. Petersburg, 30 Dec. 1904). Russian composer. His fertile if unprofound talent and easy tunefulness have found expression in five operas: *The Craftsman of Clamecy* (1938), after Romain Rolland's *Colas Breugnon*, under which title the brilliant overture is known; *Before Moscow* (1942); *The Family of Taras* (*c.* 1944, rev. 1949); *Nikita Vershinin* (1954); and *Armoured Train 14–69* (1956).

Kalisch, Alfred (b. London, 13 Mar. 1863; d. London, 17 May 1933). English critic and librettist. Originally a barrister. Took up musical journalism in 1894. Translated *Salome, Elektra, Rosenkavalier, Ariadne auf Naxos*, and other works into English. Was a great champion of Strauss's operas, writing many pamphlets and articles and delivering lectures on them. Apart from Beecham, he probably did more than anyone else for Strauss in England.

Kalisch, Paul (b. Berlin, 6 Nov. 1855; d. St. Lorenz am Modensee, 27 Jan. 1946). German tenor. Originally an architect, his voice was discovered by Pollini who sent him to Milan to study with Lamperti. After five years in Italy and a period in Munich was engaged for the Berlin Opera 1884–7. N.Y., Met., 1888–92 where he sang Tannhäuser in the first American performance of the Paris version of the opera, Nureddin in the American première of *Der Barbier von Bagdad*, Pollione in the 1890 benefit performance for Lilli Lehmann, whom he had married in 1888, and Manrico when Lehmann sang her first role in Italian in 1891.

Kalter, Sabine (b. Jarosław, 28 Mar. 1890; d. London, 1 Sept. 1957). Hungarian mezzo-soprano. Début Vienna, V.O., 1911. Leading mezzo-soprano Hamburg 1915–35, where her Lady Macbeth and Wagner interpretations were greatly admired. Forced to leave Germany, she went to London where she sang at C.G. 1935–9 as Fricka, Ortrud, Brangaene, and Herodias. (R)

Kammersänger (Kammersängerin) (Ger. = Chamber singer). High honorary title given by the German and Austrian governments to distinguished singers. Originally the title was bestowed by the various courts.

Kapellmeister (Ger. = chapel master). Originally the choirmaster in a court chapel, but now generally used in Germany for a conductor.

Kapp, Julius (b. Steinbach, 1 Oct. 1883; d. Hinang bei Alstädten im Algau, 18 Mar. 1962). German musicologist. Connected with Berlin Staatsoper from 1921; first as editor of *Blätter der Staatsoper* and then as *Dramaturg*. Adapted many operas for the German stage, including *Les Huguenots, Les Troyens*, and *Guillaume Tell*. Has written books on Wagner, Meyerbeer, Berlioz, Weber, and Schreker; and several historical works on the Berlin Opera.

Kappel, Gertrude (b. Halle, 1 Sept. 1884; d. Munich, 3 Apr. 1971). German soprano. Studied Leipzig with Nikisch. Début Hanover 1903, Leonora (*Trovatore*); leading soprano Munich 1927–31; London, C.G., 1912–14, 1924–6; N.Y., Met., 1928–36. A famous Brünnhilde and Isolde, she also sang Elektra and the Marschallin with success. (R)

Karajan, Herbert von (b. Salzburg, 5 Apr. 1908). Austrian conductor. Studied Salzburg Mozarteum and Vienna Conservatory. Début Ulm 1928, conducting *Figaro*. Appointments Ulm 1928–33; Aachen 1934–8; Berlin State Opera 1938–45; Vienna State Opera as artistic director 1956–64. Milan, Sc., since 1948; Bayreuth 1951–2; artistic director Salzburg Festival 1958–60 and from 1964. Karajan possesses one of the most remarkable conducting talents of the day. His very personal, high-powered approach to classical composers has sharply divided opinion. His catholic taste is evident in his direction of such different works as *Lucia di Lammermoor* and *Il Trovatore* on the one hand, and the Mozart–Wagner–Strauss repertory on the other. Also a producer. (R)

Karfreitagzauber. See *Good Friday Music.*

Karl-Marx-Stadt. See *Chemnitz.*

Karlsruhe. Town in Baden-Württemberg, Germany. Opera performed in the rebuilt Grosses Haus (cap. 1,055). The first complete production of *Les Troyens* was given at Karlsruhe under Mottl in 1890.

Kaschmann (orig. Kašman), Giuseppe (b. Mali Losing, 14 July 1847; d. Rome 11 Feb. 1925. Italian baritone. Studied Rome. Début Zagreb 1869, and sang in inauguration of Zagreb Opera 2 Oct. 1870 (title-role in Zajc's *Mislav*); N.Y., Met., 1883 for inaugural season, and sang the first Enrico (*Lucia*) in that theatre. Returned in 1896 to sing Telramund in *Lohengrin* in German. In Italy was greatly admired in Wagner. With advancing years he turned to buffo roles, and was singing Pasquale and Bartolo when he was nearly 70. (R)

Kassel. Town in Hessen, Germany, which has enjoyed several periods of distinguished opera-giving, notably under Spohr (1822–57), Mahler (1883–5), Heger (1935–9), Paul Schmitz (1951–63), Dohnányi (1963–6), Gerd Albrecht (from 1966). The new Staatstheater (cap. 1,010) was opened in Sept. 1959 with the première of Wagner-Régeny's *Prometheus.*

Káťa (Katya) Kabanová. Opera in 3 acts by Janáček; text by composer, after Ostrovsky's tragedy *The Storm* (1859). Prod. Brno 23 Nov. 1921, with Veséla; London, S.W., 10 Apr. 1951, with Shuard; Cleveland, Karamu House, 26 Nov. 1957. Káťa is married to Tichon, whose mother hates her. She loves Boris, in spite of attempts to remain loyal to her husband, and meets him secretly outside her garden while her friend Varvara meets the teacher Kudrjaš. During a storm, Káťa confesses her guilt to her family and other sheltering passersby; she escapes from Tichon's arms, and saying good-bye to Boris, throws herself into the Volga.

Katerina Ismailova. See *Lady Macbeth of Mtsensk.*

Kaunas. See *Lithuania.*

Kecal. The marriage-broker (bass) in Smetana's *The Bartered Bride.*

Keilberth, Joseph (b. Karlsruhe, 19 Apr. 1908; d. Munich, 21 July 1968). German conductor. Studied Karlsruhe; joined local opera company as *répétiteur* 1925; soon conductor, and Generalmusikdirektor 1935–40. Held similar position Dresden State Opera 1945–50; Munich State Opera 1951–68; music director 1959–68. Conducted *Ring* and other works at Bayreuth 1952–6, and guest conductor at other European festivals, including Edinburgh. His readings of Strauss operas particularly admired. (R)

Keiser, Reinhardt (b. Teuchern, 9 Jan. 1674; d. Hamburg, 12 Sept. 1739). German composer. Succeeded Kusser as conductor and composer at Brunswick 1694, when his first operas began appearing on the stage. Moved to Hamburg 1696 or 1697, where he wrote four or five operas a year. Took over direction of the opera 1703, and after various visits (notably to Copenhagen and Ludwigsburg) settled there again 1724. In 1728 he became cathedral cantor, and shortly before his death saw the decline and close of the Hamburg Opera. His importance to German opera, both through his compositions and by his work in creating the highest standards at Hamburg, is enormous. Mattheson called him the first dramatic composer in the world, and for a time he assured the position of German opera. One of his violinists (later harpsichordist) at Hamburg was Handel, whose first opera *Almira* is modelled on Keiser's works, even to details in orchestration (Keiser loved showy arias with trumpets or horns). Handel several times borrowed from Keiser's works at later stages of his career.

Kellogg, Clara Louise (b. Summerville, S. Carolina, 12 July 1842; d. New Haven, Conn., 13 May 1916). American soprano and impresario. Début N.Y., Ac. of M., 1861, Gilda. Sang in London in 1867 and 1872, when she joined Pauline Lucca in management of Lucca-Kellogg Company. Organized English company in America 1874. Autobiography *Memoirs of an American Prima Donna* (1913).

Kelly, Michael (b. Dublin, 25 Dec. 1762; d. Margate, 9 Oct. 1826). Irish tenor and composer. Studied with Morland and Arne, and later with Rauzzini. Début Dublin 1779, Count in Piccinni's *La Buona Figliuola.* Went to Naples where he studied for a further period. After appearances throughout Italy went to Vienna where he was engaged at the Court Theatre and created Basilio and Curzio in Mozart's *Figaro* (1786). Appeared London, D.L., 1787; King's Theatre 1793, where besides being leading tenor was acting manager. Farewell appearance Dublin Oct. 1811, in *The Bard of Erin*, one of his many compositions. His two volumes of *Reminiscences* published in 1826 give an amusing and valuable picture of the opera stage of his day. Known in Italy as Signor Occhelli.

Kemble, Adelaide (b. London, 1814; d. Warsash House, Hants, 4 Aug. 1879). English soprano. Younger daughter of the actor Charles Kemble. After a short career as a concert singer, went to Italy where she studied with Pasta and made début at Venice as Norma 1839. After appearances throughout Italy she returned to England where she sang Norma in English at C.G. 1841. Leading member of the English Company at C.G. 1841–2, appearing with great success in *Figaro*, *Sonnambula*, *Semiramide*, and *Norma*. Retired 1843 upon her marriage to Edward John Sartoris. Accounts of her career are embodied in her sister's (Fanny Kemble's) *Records of a Girlhood.*

Kemp, Barbara (b. Cochem, Mosel, 12 Dec. 1881; d. Berlin, 17 Apr. 1959). German soprano. Studied Strasbourg; début there 1903. After engagements at Rostock and Breslau, became leading soprano at Berlin 1913–30. There she created the title role in *Mona Lisa* by her husband (Max von Schillings). N.Y., Met., 1922–4; Bayreuth (Senta and Kundry) 1914–27. Stage director in Berlin in the 1930's where she produced her husband's *Ingwelde* in 1938. (R)

Kempe, Rudolf b. Niederpoyritz, nr. Dresden, 14 June 1910). German conductor. Studied Dresden with Fritz Busch. First oboe Leipzig Gewandhaus Orchestra 1929–36. *Répétiteur* and junior conductor Leipzig Opera 1925–9, where he made his conducting début, 1935, *Wildschütz.* Chemnitz 1942–8; Weimar 1948–9; Generalmusikdirektor Dresden 1949–52; Munich 1952–4. London début, C.G., with Munich Company 1953, and has appeared there regularly since; N.Y., Met., 1954–6; Bayreuth since 1960, conducting new prod. of the *Ring.* Although Kempe first made a name for himself in Strauss and Wagner, he is one of the few German opera conductors whose readings of Puccini and Verdi command respect. He is a first-rate orchestral trainer, and procures the most beautiful playing from his instrumentalists; indeed his 'chamber-music' approach to the *Ring* and other works has been adversely criticized. (R)

Kern, Adele (b. Munich, 25 Nov. 1901). German soprano. Début Munich 1924; Vienna 1929–30; Munich 1937–43. London, C.G., 1931 and 1933. Appeared regularly at Salzburg 1927–35; at Berlin and in South America. One of the brilliant company of singers in the Clemens Krauss régimes in Vienna and Munich. Especially famous for her Sophie, Zerbinetta, and Mozart soubrette parts. (R)

Khovanshchina. Opera in 5 acts by Mussorgsky; text by composer and Stassov. Left unfinished, completed and orch. by Rimsky-Korsakov. Prod. (posth.) St. Petersburg, Kononov T., 21 Feb. 1886; Paris, Ch.É., 5 June 1913 in version altered by Stravinsky and Ravel; London, D.L., 1 July 1913 with Chaliapin; Philadelphia 18 Apr. 1928. The intensely complicated plot reflects the confusion of the period of

Russian history it describes, the end of the 17th century before the advent of Peter the Great. A revised version was made by Shostakovich.

Khrennikov, Tikhon (b. Elets, 10 June 1913). Russian composer. His opera *The Brothers* (1936) revived in 1939 with great success as *In the Storm*. *Frol Skobeyev* prod. Moscow in 1950, *The Mother* in 1957.

Kienzl, Wilhelm (b. Waizenkirchen, 17 Jan. 1857; d. Vienna, 3 Oct. 1941). Austrian composer. A confirmed Wagnerian, he showed in his operas that Wagner's principles could apply to music below that of the loftiest music drama. *Urvasi* (1886) attracted some attention; *Heilmar der Narr* was not produced until 1892 through staging difficulties; and then with *Der Evangelimann* (1895) Kienzl produced his greatest success. Seven less popular operas followed. He also edited Mozart's *La Clemenza di Tito* and published a study of Wagner, with whose family he had once lived at Bayreuth.

Kiepura, Jan (b. Sosnowiec, Poland, 16 May 1902; d. N.Y., 15 Aug. 1966). Polish tenor. Studied Warsaw. Début Lwów 1924, Faust. Guest appearances 1926–39 Vienna, Berlin, Milan, Paris, and Budapest. N.Y., Met., 1938–41; appearances elsewhere in U.S.A. Famous as interpreter of Don José, Des Grieux, Calaf, Cavaradossi, and Rodolfo. A strikingly handsome man, he made a considerable success in several films, into which he introduced operatic arias. Married the Hungarian soprano **Martha Eggerth** (b. 1912) with whom he sang both in America and Europe in performances of *The Merry Widow*. (R)

Kiev. Town in the U.S.S.R., capital of the Ukraine. Kiev's opera tradition goes back 100 years, and the present company at the Shevchenko Opera House enjoys a high reputation. Ukrainian singers are famous beyond the borders of the U.S.S.R., where their reputation stands higher than that of any other republic's artists.

Kindermann, August (b. Potsdam, 6 Feb. 1817; d. Munich, 6 Mar. 1891). German bass-baritone. Began career in chorus of Berlin Opera. Sang bass and baritone roles Leipzig 1839–46. Munich Opera 1846–91, where he celebrated his 25th anniversary in 1871 singing Figaro, and his 40th in 1886 as Stadinger in *Waffenschmied*. Titurel in the first performance of *Parsifal* at Bayreuth 1876. His elder daughter **Marie** enjoyed a career at Kassel; his younger daughter was **Hedwig Reicher-Kindermann** (q.v.).

King Arthur, or The British Worthy. 'A dramatick opera' in prologue, 5 acts, and epilogue by Purcell; text by Dryden. Prod. London, Dorset Gardens, summer 1691; N.Y. 28 Apr. 1800.

King Mark. Isolde's prospective husband (bass) in Wagner's *Tristan und Isolde*.

King Priam. Opera in 3 acts by Tippett; text by composer. Prod. Coventry Theatre 29 May 1962, with Collier, Veasey, Elkins, Lewis, Robinson, Godfrey, Dobson, Lanigan, cond. John Pritchard; Karlsruhe, 26 Jan. 1963. Tippett declares the subject of his opera to be 'the mysterious nature of human choice'.

Act 1. Priam (bass-bar.), supported by Hecuba (sop.), chooses the death of his baby son Paris, who (it is prophesied by the Old Man (bass)) will cause his father's death. But he is relieved to find, in the next scene, when out hunting, that the boy (sop.) has been spared; he and Hector (bar.) take him to Troy. Here Paris (ten.) and Hector quarrel; Paris fetches Helen (mezzo) from Sparta. In the last scene of the act, Hermes (ten.) arranges the Judgement of Paris; Aphrodite (i.e. Helen) is chosen.

Act 2. In the war that ensues, Achilles (ten.) is sulking in his tent; the Trojans drive the Greeks back and fire their ships, but are weakened by Hector and Paris quarrelling. Patroclus (bar.) puts on Achilles's armour, but is killed by Hector. The Trojans' rejoicing is interrupted by Achilles's war-cry.

Act 3. The women reflect upon their role in the war. News of Hector's death at the hands of Achilles is brought to Priam. He goes to beg his son's body, and rouses Achilles's pity. He then withdraws into himself, and is killed before the altar by Achilles's son.

King Roger. Opera in 3 acts by Szymanowski; text by Jarosław Iwaszkiewicz and composer. Prod. Warsaw 19 June 1926; Palermo 1949. The more successful of Szymanowski's two operas, it tells of the struggle between Christianity and Eastern paganism in medieval Sicily. Queen Roxane falls in love with a shepherd-prophet from India, denounced as a heretic. King Roger is finally converted, and the work closes with a bacchanal in a Greek temple.

King's Henchman, The. Opera in 3 acts by Deems Taylor; text by Edna St. Vincent Millay. Prod. N.Y., Met., 17 Feb. 1927 with Easton, Johnson, Tibbett.

Eadgar, King of England, sends Æthelwold to win the Princess Ælfrida for him; Æthelwold marries her, sending word that she is ugly, but when Eadgar comes to visit them and finds how beautiful she is, Æthelwold kills himself in remorse.

King's Theatre, Haymarket. Built by Vanbrugh to house the Lincoln's Inn Fields Theatre Company and opened on 9 Apr. 1705 as the Queen's Theatre with Greber's *Gli Amori d'Ergasto*, the first Italian opera to be heard in London. Opera alternated with the drama until the end of 1707, when the theatre became wholly devoted to opera. At first some works were sung in English, others in Italian, and some in a mixture of both tongues; but from 1710 onwards the theatre in the Haymarket was the exclusive home in London of Italian opera. The Queen's Theatre was renamed the King's in 1714 on the accession of George I, and became Her Majesty's in 1837 on the accession of Queen Victoria. Heidegger (q.v.) was the theatre's manager 1710–34 and in the years 1729–34 shared the management of the theatre with Handel. During the whole of this period more than 24 of Handel's operas, 7 of his *pasticcios*, and one or two of his secular choral works and oratorios all received their first performances there. From the time of Handel until the fire of 1789 the English premières of many long-forgotten operas by Bononcini, Tarchi, Cimarosa, and other Italians were given. The new King's Theatre, then the largest in England (cap. 3,300), was designed by a Polish architect, Michael Nowosielski, and opened on 16 Jan. 1793 with Paisiello's *Il Barbiere di Siviglia*. The company was under the management of Storace and Kelly. During the years 1793–1820 *Iphigénie en Tauride*, *La Clemenza di Tito*, *Così fan tutte*, *Die Zauberflöte*, *Figaro*, *Don Giovanni*, *Il Barbiere di Siviglia*, *L'Italiana in Algeri*, *La Cenerentola*, and *Tancredi* all received their English premières there. The singers included Giorgi-Banti, Teresa Bellochi, Mrs. Billington, Catalani, Joséphine Fodor-Mainvielle, Grassini, Mara; Ambrogetti, Graham, Garcia, Kelly, Levasseur, and Naldi. During the régime of Ebers (1821–7) more Rossini works, including *La Gazza Ladra*, *La Donna del Lago*, *Otello*, *Il Turco in Italia*, *L'Italiana in Algeri*, and Spontini's *La Vestale*, were produced, as well as the first Meyerbeer opera to be heard in England, *Il Crociato in Egitto*. New singers included Brambilla, Camporose, Colbran, Caradori, De Begnis, Pasta, and Velluti. Ebers was succeeded as manager by Laporte (q.v.) (1821–31 and 1833–41), during whose régime the theatre became Her Majesty's Royal Italian Opera House. (For the continuation of this history see *Her Majesty's*.)

Kipnis, Alexander (b. Zhitomir, 1 Feb. 1891). Russian bass. Studied Warsaw where he graduated as a conductor; then Berlin with Grenzebach. Although an enemy alien during the First World War, was allowed to continue his studies in Germany and made his début at Hamburg 1915; Wiesbaden 1916–18; Berlin 1918–25; Chicago Opera 1923–32 and after 1938; N.Y., Met., 1939–46. London, C.G., 1927, début as Marcel in the ill-fated revival of *Les Huguenots*; returned 1929–35, and was especially admired as Gurnemanz, Hagen, Mark, and Rocco. Bayreuth 1927–33; he also sang Sarastro at Glyndebourne and Salzburg. Forced by Hitler to leave Germany, he settled in America, and became an American citizen in 1934. Was considered one of the finest singers in German opera of his day, possessing a beautiful voice of great flexibility and colour. (R)

Kirchoff, Walter (b. Berlin, 17 Mar. 1879; d. Wiesbaden, 26 Mar. 1951). German tenor. Studied with Lilli Lehmann and in Milan. Début Berlin 1906, Faust; here he was leading tenor until 1920. London, C.G., 1913 and 1924; N.Y., Met., 1926–31. Renowned mostly as a Heldentenor, though he also sang Max in *Jonny spielt auf* and Pietro in *Boccaccio* in N.Y. (R)

Kirghizia. See *Frunze*.

Kirkby Lunn, Louise. See *Lunn*.

Kirsten, Dorothy (b. New Jersey, 6 July 1917). American soprano. Studied Juilliard School, N.Y. Hearing her in a radio programme, Grace Moore sponsored her further studies in Italy with Pescia and arranged for her début at the Chicago Opera in 1940 as Poussette in *Manon*. After three seasons in Chicago and other American cities, made N.Y. début at City Center as Violetta; was engaged for Met. from 1945, where her roles have included Louise, which she studied with Charpentier, Fiora (*L'Amore dei Tre Re*), Cio-Cio-San, Marguerite, and Manon Lescaut. Has appeared in a number of films, including *The Great Caruso*. (R)

Kiss, The (Cz., *Hubička*). Opera in 3 acts by Smetana; text by Eliška Krásnohorská, after the story (1871) by 'Karolina Světlá' (Johanna Mužáková). Prod. Prague, Cz., 7 Nov. 1876; Liverpool 8 Dec. 1938. Hanno, a young widower, is anxious to kiss his new bride Marinka before their marriage, but she is reluctant as it is said that this arouses the anger of a dead wife. After many complications, he succeeds.

Klafsky, Katharina (b. Sz. János, Moson, Hungary, 19 Sept. 1855; d. Hamburg, 22 Sept. 1896). Hungarian soprano. Joined chorus of Vienna Komische Oper 1874, and soon attracted attention. Introduced to Mathilde Marchesi who gave her free tuition. Leipzig 1876–86, where she was the first local Brangaene; London in 1882 with Neumann's company as Wellgunde and Waltraute (*Walküre*). Hamburg 1886–95. Returned to London 1892, making great impression as Leonore (*Fidelio*), Brünnhilde, Isolde, Elisabeth, Agathe, and Elsa. Several of the performances were conducted by her husband Otto Lohse (q.v.). America 1895–6 as principal soprano of the Damrosch Company. She was at the height of her powers at the time of her premature death.

Klausenburg. See *Cluj*.

Kleiber, Erich (b. Vienna, 5 Aug. 1890; d. Zürich, 27 Jan. 1956). Austrian, later Argentinian, conductor. Studied Prague. Darmstadt 1912–18; Wuppertal 1919–21; Mannheim 1922–3; Generalmusikdirektor Berlin State Opera 1923–33. Guest conductor at many leading opera houses 1933–56, notably Teatro Colón, Buenos Aires, 1937–49; C.G. 1938 and 1950–3; Amsterdam 1933–8 and 1949–50. Kleiber's directorship of the Berlin Opera was one of the most brilliant periods in the theatre's history, with the world premières of *Wozzeck* and *Christophe Colomb* and the introduction of *Jenůfa* and *Schwanda* into the repertory. He resigned his Berlin post in 1934 at the time of the *Mathis der Maler* controversy (see *Hindemith*) and did not return to Germany again until 1950. He was reappointed to his old position at the State Opera in 1954 but again resigned as a protest against political interference. His contribution to the development of the English Company at Covent Garden, 1950–3, cannot be overestimated. He was beloved by all orchestras with whom he worked; and his eloquent stick technique enabled him to indicate to each player every shade of expression. Biography by John Russell (1958). (R)

Klein, Herman (b. Norwich, 23 July 1856; d. London, 10 Mar. 1934). English critic and teacher. Studied singing with Manuel Garcia. Taught privately and at the G.S.M. Began writing criticism in 1875. Critic of *The Sunday Times* 1881–1901; during part of this period the paper was owned by Augustus Harris, and Klein acted as an unofficial adviser to him as far as the engagement of singers at C.G. was concerned. 1902–9 critic of the *N.Y. Herald*. His many publications include *The Reign of Patti* (1920); *The Art of Bel Canto* (1924); *Musicians and Mummers* (1925); *Great Women Singers of Our Time* (1931); and *The Golden Age of Opera* (1933).

Klein, Peter (b. Zündorf, 25 Jan. 1907). German tenor. Studied Cologne. Cologne Opera chorus 1930–1; then after a period at Düsseldorf, Kaiserslautern, and Zürich he joined the Hamburg Opera, where he sang with success as Shuisky, Mime, Pedrillo, &c., 1937–41. Since 1942 he has been a member of the Vienna Opera, and appears regularly at Salzburg, where his Basilio, Valzacchi, Captain in *Wozzeck*, and Monsieur Taupe in *Capriccio* have been praised. London début C.G. 1947 with Vienna Company; has returned regularly to sing Mime in *The Ring* until 1960. He sang two seasons in N.Y., 1949–51, as Mime, Jacquino, David, Basilio, and Valzacchi. (R)

Klemperer, Otto (b. Wrocław, 14 May 1885). German conductor. Studied Frankfurt and Berlin. Recommended by Mahler to the National Theatre, Prague, where he conducted 1907–10. Engagements followed at Hamburg 1910–14; Strasbourg 1914–17; Cologne 1917–24; Wiesbaden 1924–7; Berlin 1927–33, first at the Kroll Opera, and then at the State Opera. During his Berlin period he conducted the premières and first Berlin performances of many important works including *Cardillac*, *Neues vom Tage*, *Erwartung*, *Die glückliche Hand*, *Das Leben des Orest*, *From the House of the Dead*, and *Mavra*; as well as standard repertory works including *Luisa Miller*, *Il Trittico*, *Rosenkavalier*, *Tannhäuser*, and *Der fliegende Holländer*. Except for a period at the Budapest State Opera (1947–50) he has conducted little opera in recent years but made a belated Covent Garden début, conducting and producing *Fidelio* in 1961; returned to conduct and produce *The Magic Flute* 1962 and *Lohengrin* 1963. (R)

Klenau, Paul von (b. Copenhagen, 11 Feb. 1883; d. Copenhagen, 31 Aug. 1946). Danish composer and conductor. The most successful of his seven operas was *Gudrun auf Island* (1924). Worked at Freiburg Opera 1907; at Stuttgart Court Opera 1908–14.

Klingsor. The evil magician (bass) in Wagner's *Parsifal*.

Klose, Margarete (b. Berlin, 6 Aug. 1902; d. Berlin 14 Dec. 1965). German mezzo-soprano. Début Ulm 1927. Young Gipsy in *Countess Maritza*. Mannheim 1929–32; Berlin State Opera 1932–49, 1958–61, Städtische Oper 1949–58; Bayreuth Festivals 1936–42; London, C.G., 1935, 1937; Buenos Aires 1950. One of the finest German mezzo-sopranos of her day; especially distinguished in Wagner and Verdi. Her repertory also includes Orfeo, the Kostelnička, Carmen, and Klytemnestra. (R)

Kluge, Die (The Clever Girl). Opera in 6 scenes by Carl Orff; text by composer, after Grimm's story *Die Geschichte von dem König und der klugen Frau*. Prod. Frankfurt 20 Feb. 1943; Cleveland, Karamu House, 7 Dec. 1949; London, S.W., 27 July 1959.

Klytemnestra. Murderess of her husband Agamemnon, then wife (mezzo) of Aegisth in Strauss's *Elektra*.

Knappertsbusch, Hans (b. Elberfeld, 12 Mar. 1888; d. Munich, 25 Oct. 1965). German conductor. Studied Cologne with Steinbach and Lohse. Début Mulheim 1911; after engagements at Bochum, Elberfeld, Leipzig, and Dessau was appointed Generalmusikdirektor of the Munich Opera in 1922, a position he had to relinquish in 1936 owing to his hostility to the Nazis. Vienna State Opera 1936–50. From 1951 he conducted at Bayreuth; and he returned to Munich in 1954. He appeared as a guest conductor in Paris, Milan, Rome, and Zürich. Sole London appearance, C.G., 1937, *Salome.* Strauss and Wagner were Knappertsbusch's special study, and his *Parsifal* reading was generally considered the finest of this century. He was one of the few remaining Wagner conductors of the old school. (R)

Knoch, Ernst (b. Karlsruhe, 1 Aug. 1875; d. New York, 20 Mar. 1959). German conductor. Studied Karlsruhe and privately with Mottl, whose assistant he was at Karlsruhe 1898–1901. Strasbourg 1901–7; Essen 1907–9; Cologne 1909–12. Worked at Bayreuth 1904–7 and joined the Quinlan Company to give the first Australian performances of *Tristan* and other works 1912. Conducted various touring companies in America and settled in N.Y. as teacher in 1938.

Knote, Heinrich (b. Munich, 26 Nov. 1870; d. Garmisch, 12 Jan. 1953). German tenor. Studied Munich with Kirchner. Début Munich 1892; London, C.G., 1901; N.Y., Met., 1904. Appeared regularly in both London and N.Y. until 1914, and continued to sing in Germany until 1924. A famous Siegfried, Tristan, and Tannhäuser. In N.Y. was also heard as Assad in *The Queen of Sheba* and Manrico. An extremely handsome man, with a clear resonant voice and excellent diction. (R)

Knüpfer, Paul (b. Halle, 21 June 1866; d. Berlin, 4 Nov. 1920). German bass. Studied Sonderhausen where he made his début 1885. Leipzig 1887–98; Berlin 1898–1920; Bayreuth 1901–6; London, C.G., 1909–14, where he was the first London Barber of Bagdad, Baron Ochs, and Gurnemanz. (R) Married the soprano **Marie Egli** who appeared often at C.G. before the First World War. (R)

Koanga. Opera in prologue, 3 acts, and epilogue by Delius; text by C. F. Keary, after George Washington Cable's novel *The Grandissimes* (1880). Prod. Elberfeld 30 Mar. 1904; London, C.G., 23 Sept. 1935 with Slobodskaya, Brownlee, cond. Beecham. On a Mississippi plantation the mulatto Palmyra spurns the slave-driver Simon Perez and falls in love with Koanga, a prince of her own tribe. The planter Don José Martínez allows the wedding, during which Palmyra is abducted by Perez. Koanga quarrels with the planter and flees into the forest, where he and a voodoo priest invoke a plague on their enemies. But Palmyra is also afflicted. Koanga arrives in time to save her from Perez, whom he kills before being himself killed. Palmyra stabs herself with Koanga's spear.

Kobbé, Gustav (b. N.Y., 4 Mar. 1857; d. Long Island, 27 July 1918). American critic and writer. Studied Wiesbaden and N.Y. After editing *The Musical Review* served as critic on several N.Y. papers including *The World*, which sent him to Bayreuth in 1882 for the first performance of *Parsifal.* Wrote several books, including a two-volume study of Wagner (1890) and the famous *Complete Opera Book* (1919), revised by Lord Harewood 1954.

Koblenz. Town in Rhineland-Palatinate, Germany. Opera is performed at the Stadttheater (cap. 500), opened 1787 with *Die Entführung aus dem Serail*, and modernized in 1953.

Kodály, Zoltán (b. Kecskemét, 16 Dec. 1882; d. Budapest, 6 Mar. 1967). Hungarian composer. His three stage works (though actually in separate numbers with dialogue) are a vital contribution to Hungarian national opera. *Háry János* (1926), familiar from the orchestral suite, draws strongly on Magyar folk-lore. *The Spinning Room of the Székelys* (1932) is a 1-act *Singspiel* using Transylvanian material. *Czinka Panna* (1948) is an historical piece written to celebrate the centenary of the 1848 rising, and makes greater use of dialogue.

Köln. See *Cologne.*

Konetzni, Anny (b. Vienna, 12 Feb. 1902; d. Vienna, 6 Sept. 1968). Austrian sopr. First sang in chorus of Volksoper but dismissed for loss of voice. Joined Vienna Conservatory where studied with Erik Schmedes. Début Chemnitz as contralto 1927; Berlin State Opera

1931–5; Vienna State Opera 1935–54; London, C.G., 1935–9 and 1951; N.Y., Met., 1934–5. (R)

Konetzni, Hilde (b. Vienna, 21 Mar. 1905). Austrian soprano. Sister of above. Studied Vienna Conservatory and Prague with Ludmilla Prochaska-Neumann. Début Chemnitz, 1929, Sieglinde. Prague 1932–6; Vienna State Opera from 1936. London, C.G., 1938 when she made her début during a performance of *Rosenkavalier* replacing Lehmann who became ill half-way through first act; sang Chrysothemis, Sieglinde, Mařenka, Donna Elvira, and Elisabeth at C.G. 1938–9. Returned in 1947 with the Vienna Company as Leonore in *Fidelio,* and has appeared subsequently as Sieglinde (with her sister as Brünnhilde) and Gutrune. One of the most popular artists in Vienna, she still possesses a most beautiful voice and a strong sense of Wagner style. (R)

König Hirsch (The Stag King). Opera in 3 acts by Henze; text by Heinz von Cramer, after Gozzi's *fiaba, Re Cervo* (1762). Prod. Berlin, Städtische Oper, 23 Sept. 1956, with Pilarczyk, Fischer-Dieskau, cond. Scherchen. Revised and shortened version as *Re Cervo,* Kassel 1963; Santa Fé, 4 Aug. 1965.

Abandoned in the forest as a child by the Governor, the King has been cherished by wild beasts. Grown up, he returns to claim his throne and choose a bride, but the Governor's scheming contrives that he shall renounce the crown and return to the forest from what he now believes to be a world of lies. After various adventures he enters the body of a stag, while the Governor takes his shape and returns to the city to initiate a reign of terror. But, driven by human longings, the stag king returns to the city, the Governor is killed by his own assassins, and the King regains human form.

Königskinder (The Royal Children). Opera in 3 acts by Humperdinck; text by 'Ernst Rosmer' (Elsa Bernstein-Porges). Prod. N.Y., Met., 28 Dec. 1910, with Farrar, Jadlowker, Goritz; London, C.G., 27 Nov. 1911. Based on incidental music for the play of 1897. The story of the Goose-girl who falls in love with the King's son who comes to the woods disguised as a beggar. The Witch, with whom the Goose-girl lives, brings about the lovers' deaths.

Königin von Saba, Die (The Queen of Sheba). Opera in 4 acts by Goldmark; text by Salomon Mosenthal. Prod. Vienna, Court Opera, 10 Mar. 1875, with Materna; N.Y., Met., 2 Dec. 1885 with Lilli Lehmann; London, Kennington Theatre, 29 Aug. 1910. The opera tells of the love of Assad, King Solomon's favourite courtier, for the Queen of Sheba, and of his banishment by the King when he rejects his betrothed Sulamith.

Konwitschny, Franz (b. Fulnek, 14 Aug. 1901; d. Belgrade, 27 July 1962). German conductor. Studied Leipzig. Stuttgart 1926–33; Freiburg 1933–8; Frankfurt 1938–45; Hanover 1946–9; Dresden 1953–5. Chosen to succeed Kleiber, when the latter resigned, as Generalmusikdirektor of the rebuilt Berlin State Opera 1955. London, C.G., 1959, conducting *The Ring.* (R)

Kónya, Sándor (b. Sarkad, 23 Sept. 1923). Hungarian tenor. Studied Budapest and Hanover. Début Bielefeld 1951, Turiddu. After engagements in Darmstadt, Stuttgart, and Hamburg he joined the Berlin Städtische Oper in 1955. Bayreuth as Lohengrin 1958; Milan, Sc., since 1960; San Francisco since 1960; N.Y., Met., since 1962; London, C.G., 1963. (R)

Korngold, Erich (b. Brno, 29 May 1897; d. Hollywood, 29 Nov. 1957). Austrian composer. 'Operatic' début aged 11, when his pantomime *Der Schneemann* was given at the Vienna Court Opera. His first two (1-act) operas *Der Ring des Polykrates* and *Violanta* were produced at Munich when he was 19, but his greatest success was *Die tote Stadt* (1920). Lush and eclectic, his operas nevertheless had a wide appeal in their day. He later lived in America and worked chiefly as a film composer; one of his films,

Give Us This Night, included an original 1-act opera.

Košice. Town in Slovakia, Czechoslovakia. The theatre, which serves the whole of eastern Slovakia, gives regular opera seasons.

Koslovsky, Ivan (b. Marjanovka, 24 Mar. 1900). Russian tenor. Studied Kiev. Début Poltava 1920. Member of the Bolshoy Company since 1926; here his roles have included Lensky, Faust, and Lohengrin. (R)

Köth, Erika (b. Darmstadt, 15 Sept. 1927). German soprano. Sang with a jazz orchestra in order to earn enough for her musical training. Won first prize in competition organized by Hessische Radio 1947—sharing it with Christa Ludwig (q.v.). Début Kaiserslautern 1948, Adele; Karlsruhe 1950–3; Munich and Vienna since 1953. London, C.G., with Munich Company, 1953 as Fiakermilli (*Arabella*) and Italian singer (*Capriccio*). A very high coloratura, excelling as Zerbinetta. *Lucia di Lammermoor* was specially revived for her in Munich in 1957. (R)

Koussevitzky, Serge (b. Vishny Volochek, 26 July 1874; d. Boston, 4 June 1951). Russian conductor. Although primarily known as a symphonic conductor, he was one of the pioneers in introducing Russian opera to western Europe, conducting *Boris*, *Khovanshchina*, *Prince Igor*, and *The Queen of Spades* in Paris in 1921, and *The Snow Maiden* and other works in Barcelona the same year. He was responsible for the commissioning of Britten's *Peter Grimes* for the Berkshire Festival, although the première took place in London. (R)

Kraus, Ernst (b. Erlangen, 8 June 1863; d. Wörthsee, 6 Sept. 1941). German tenor. Studied Milan and Munich. Début Mannheim 1893, Tamino. Principal tenor Damrosch Company in U.S.A. 1894–5. Leading tenor Berlin 1896–1924, when he retired to teach. London, C.G., 1900, 1907, 1910, when he was the first London Herod. Also appeared at Bayreuth as Siegmund, Siegfried, Walther, and Erik. (R)

Kraus, Otakar (b. Prague, 10 Dec. 1909). Czech, later British, baritone. Studied Prague with Konrad Wallerstein, Milan with Fernando Carpi. Début Brno 1935, Amonasro; Bratislava 1936–9; then came to England. After war-time appearances in *Sorochinsky Fair* and with the Carl Rosa Opera, joined the English Opera Group in 1946, creating Tarquinius in *The Rape of Lucretia*, and also singing Lockit, and the Vicar in *Albert Herring*. Netherlands Opera 1950–1; C.G. since 1951. Created Nick Shadow in *The Rake's Progress*, Venice 1951, Diomede in *Troilus and Cressida* and King Fisher in *The Midsummer Marriage*, both at C.G. A fine Alberich, which he sang at Bayreuth 1960–2. Kraus is a first-rate singer-actor and a master of make-up. (R)

Krauss, Clemens (b. Vienna, 31 Mar. 1893; d. Mexico, 16 May 1954). Austrian conductor. Studied Vienna with Graedener and Heuberger. Début Brno 1913, *Zar und Zimmermann*. After seasons in Stettin and Graz he went to Vienna 1922–4 as assistant to Schalk. Director of the Frankfurt Opera 1924–9; Vienna 1929–35; Berlin 1935–7. Generalmusikdirektor at Munich 1937–42. Krauss's leading singers, including Adele Kern, Viorica Ursuleac (whom he married), were faithful to him, and Julius Patzak followed him from Vienna to Berlin and from Berlin to Munich. A close friend of Strauss, he conducted the premières of *Arabella* (Dresden 1933), *Friedenstag* (Munich 1938), *Capriccio*, for which he wrote the libretto (Munich 1942), and *Die Liebe der Danae* (Salzburg 1952). London, C.G., 1934 (*Arabella* and *Schwanda*); 1947 with the Vienna Opera (*Salome* and *Fidelio*); 1949 Stoll Theatre (*Falstaff* and *Tosca*), and C.G. again 1951–3, *Tristan*, *Fidelio*, and *Meistersinger*. Arrangements for a further period at C.G. were under discussion at the time of his sudden death. Biography, *Clemens Krauss in Munich*, by Oscar von Pander, 1955. (R)

Krauss, Felix von (b. Vienna, 3 Oct.

1870; d. Munich, 30 Oct. 1937). Austrian bass. Studied Vienna. Début Bayreuth 1899, Hagen, appearing there until 1909. London, C.G., 1907. Professor at Munich Conservatory 1908 and artistic director of Munich Opera. (R) His wife, the contralto **Adrienne von Krauss-Osborne** (1873–1951), sang at Leipzig, Munich, and Bayreuth 1902–9 (Erda, Waltraute).

Krauss, Gabrielle (b. Vienna, 24 Mar. 1842; d. Paris, 6 Jan. 1906). Austrian soprano. Studied Vienna Conservatory and with Marchesi. Début Vienna 1859, Mathilde (*William Tell*). Remained in Vienna until 1867, then sang in Italy and Russia. Paris, T.I., 1867–70; O., 1875, singing Rachel in *La Juive* at the opening performance of the present building (5 Jan.) and remaining there until 1888. Created a number of roles including Pauline in Gounod's *Polyeucte* and Katherine of Aragon in Saint-Saëns's *Henry VIII*. Her repertory further included Donna Anna, Valentine, Norma, Lucia, Gilda, Elsa, and Aida. Her acting powers were such that the French nicknamed her 'La Rachel Chantante'.

Křenek, Ernst (b. Vienna, 23 Aug. 1900). Austrian, later American, composer. His first opera, *Die Zwingburg*, was written at 22; *Der Sprung über den Schatten* (1924) incorporates jazz in an atonal idiom. Worked in the opera houses at Kassel and Wiesbaden 1925–7; his *Orpheus und Eurydike* appeared at Kassel in 1926, as did his most famous work, the jazz opera *Jonny spielt auf* (1927). He attempted to follow up this success with three political *Zeitopern*, then with a self-styled grand opera *Leben des Orest*; their style is more openly romantic in what has been called a neo-Schubertian manner. Settling in Vienna, he now adopted 12-note technique, putting it to use in his *Karl V* (1938), a huge musical drama that includes pantomime, film, and play. Banned by the Nazis in 1934, it was eventually produced in Prague in 1938. Křenek now moved to America, where he has made a reputation as a distinguished teacher. A brilliantly equipped musician, Křenek has ceaselessly striven in his four main periods to find some universally valid principle of contemporary composition and thus to achieve wide popular appeal without any sacrifice of artistic conscience. All his work, among which his operas hold perhaps the most distinguished place, is composed to this end.

Krenn, Fritz (b. Vienna, 11 Dec. 1897; d. Vienna, 13 July 1963). Austrian bass. Studied Vienna. Début Vienna, V.O., Alfio. Vienna, S.O., 1920–5; Wiesbaden 1924–7; Berlin 1927–38; Vienna since 1938. London, C.G., 1935; N.Y., Met., 1951. Has appeared as guest artist in Spain, France, Holland, and Buenos Aires. Sang in the premières of *Cardillac* and *Neues vom Tage*. A distinguished buffo singer. (R)

Krips, Josef (b. Vienna, 8 Apr. 1902). Austrian conductor. Studied Vienna with Weingartner. Vienna, V.O., 1921; Dortmund 1925–6; Karlsruhe 1926–33; Vienna State Opera 1933–8, when he was dismissed by the Nazis. He conducted the first opera performance in Vienna after the war in 1945, and under his direction the Vienna Opera was restored to its pre-war eminence in the years 1945–50. London début C.G. 1947 with Vienna Company (*Don Giovanni*, *Figaro*, and *Così fan tutte*). He played an important part in the resumption of the Salzburg Festival where he had first conducted in 1935. (R)

Kroll Oper. See *Berlin*.

Krombholc, Jaroslav (b. Prague, 30 Jan. 1918). Czech conductor. Studied Prague with Novák and Talich. Prague National Theatre 1940–4 and since 1945, where he is one of the leading conductors. London, C.G., 1959, *Boris Godunov*. (R)

Krusceniski (orig., Kruszelnicka), **Salomea** (b. Tarnopol, *c.* 1872; d. Mar. 1953). Polish soprano. Studied Milan. Début Trieste 1896. Sang Cio-Cio-San at Brescia 1904, when *Butterfly* had its first success after the Scala fiasco. Engaged for La Scala 1907 where she was the first Italian Elektra; and created the title role in Pizzetti's

Fedra. Other successful roles were Isolde, Brünnhilde, and Salome. (R)

Kubelik, Rafael (b. Bychory, 29 June 1914). Czech conductor and composer. Son of the famous violinist Jan Kubelik. Studied Prague. After a period with the Czech Philharmonic, appointed chief conductor National Theatre, Brno, 1939–41. Left Czechoslovakia 1948 when he went to Edinburgh to conduct *Don Giovanni*. S.W. 1954, *Káťa Kabanová*. Musical director C.G., London, 1955–8, where his successes included *Otello*, *Jenůfa* (first stage performance in England), and *The Trojans*. Although he encouraged native singers, his insistence on copious rehearsals led to a restricted repertory with unchanging casts. (R)

Kullman, Charles (b. New Haven, Conn., 13 Jan. 1903). American tenor of German parentage. Studied Juilliard School and the American Conservatory, Fontainebleau, with Salignac. Début American Opera Company 1929, Pinkerton; Berlin 1931–4; London, C.G., 1934–5 and 1938; N.Y., Met., 1935–62. Has appeared with all the leading American operatic companies, and in Salzburg, Florence, and Buenos Aires. Has a wide repertory including most of the standard French, German, and Italian roles. (R)

Kundry. The enchantress (sop.) who tries to seduce Parsifal in Wagner's opera.

Kunz, Erich (b. Vienna, 20 May 1909). Austrian bass-baritone. Studied Vienna with Lierhammer and Duhan. Début Opava 1933, Osmin. After engagements in Plauen and Breslau, came to Glyndebourne in 1935 and sang in the chorus. Vienna Opera since 1940. London, C.G., 1947 with Vienna Company as Leporello, Figaro, and Guglielmo, all of which parts he has sung with success at Salzburg and elsewhere in Europe. N.Y., Met., 1952–4; Bayreuth 1943–4 and 1951, as Beckmesser. In this role and as Papageno he has few equals today, though his sense of comedy sometimes overcomes his artistry. (R)

Kupper, Annelies (b. Glatz/Schlesien, 21 July 1906). German soprano. Studied Breslau where she made her début 1935. After seasons at Schwerin and Weimar joined Hamburg Opera 1940, remaining there until 1946, since when she has been leading soprano at Munich. London, C.G., 1953 as Chrysothemis, and then with Munich Company as Danae, which role she had created, at Strauss's request, at Salzburg in 1951. (R)

Kurt, Melanie (b. Vienna, 8 Jan. 1880; d. N.Y., 11 Mar. 1941). Austrian soprano. Studied Vienna under Leschetizky and appeared as a solo pianist 1897–1900, when she began to take singing lessons with Fannie Müller in Vienna. Début Lübeck 1902, Elisabeth. Leipzig 1902–3; then followed two years' further training with Lilli and Marie Lehmann. Brunswick 1905–8; Berlin 1908–12; London, C.G., 1910 as Sieglinde and Brünnhilde and 1914 Kundry; N.Y., Met., 1915–17 as Isolde, Kundry, Brünnhilde, Pamina, Leonore, Fricka (*Rheingold*), Iphigénie in the first Met. performance of *Iphigénie en Tauride* and other roles. When America entered the war her contract was cancelled. Taught Berlin, Vienna, and N.Y. from 1939. (R)

Kurwenal. Tristan's retainer (bar.) in Wagner's *Tristan und Isolde*.

Kurz, Selma (b. Bielitz, Silesia, 15 Nov. 1874; d. Vienna, 10 May 1933). Austrian soprano. Studied Vienna. Début Hamburg 1895 as mezzo, Mignon. Engaged by Mahler for Vienna 1899 where she sang until 1927, first as a lyric-dramatic soprano, e.g. Sieglinde, Elisabeth, and Eva, then as a coloratura, e.g. Lucia, Gilda, and Violetta. London, C.G., 1904–7. Her remarkable trill, as well as her success in certain roles, is said to have aroused Melba's jealousy, and she did not reappear until 1924. (R)

Kusche, Benno (b. Freiburg, 30 Jan. 1916). German bass-baritone. Coblenz 1938–9; Augsburg 1941–2; Munich since 1946. London, C.G., 1952 as Beckmesser; 1953 with Munich

Company as La Roche; Glyndebourne 1954, Leporello. One of the best character singers in post-war German opera. (R)

Kuznetsova, Maria (also known as Marie Kousnetzoff) (b. Odessa, 1880; d. Paris, 26 Apr. 1966). Russian. sopr. Début St. Petersburg 1905; London, C.G., 1909, Mimì, Marguerite; 1910, Manon; D.L. 1914 in the ballet *Josephslegende*; In Russia, before the Revolution, one of the most admired and versatile of artists, singing Elsa and Carmen as well as the Russian repertory. Chicago Opera 1915–17. Escaped from Russia 1920 disguised as a boy and hidden in a trunk in a Swedish ship; reappeared at C.G. that year. Later settled in Barcelona, where she acted as artistic adviser at the Liceo for the Russian operas. (R)

Kuybyshev (Samara). Town in the R.S.F.S.R., U.S.S.R. The first opera season was in 1931, and the town has since built up a repertory of Russian, French, and Italian operas. The company acquired a new building in 1938, which the Bolshoy took over in the wartime evacuation of Moscow in 1941—this period has had a lasting influence on the local company. It tours widely, visiting many towns without permanent companies such as Astrakhan, Ordzhonikidze, Yalta, and Rostov.

L

Labia, Fausta (b. Verona, 3 Apr. 1870; d. Rome, 6 Oct. 1935). Italian soprano. Début Verona 1893, *Robert le Diable*. Became a great favourite in Stockholm, but retired early in her career after her marriage to the tenor **Emilio Perea.** She established a school of singing in Rome, and her *L'Arte del respiro nella recitazione e nel canto* was published posthumously in 1936. Her daughter **Gianna Perea-Labia** (b. 1908) had an Italian career in the 1930's and 1940's.

Labia, Maria (b. Verona, 14 Feb. 1880; d. Malcesine del Garda, 11 Feb. 1953). Italian soprano, sister of the above. Début Stockholm 1906, Mimì. Berlin 1907, where she was the first Berlin Tosca, and Martha (*Tiefland*), and became a great favourite in other *verismo* roles. An actress of great emotional power, she was a celebrated Salome, Thaïs, Fedora, and Carmen. Appeared Manhattan Company 1908, Vienna, &c. From 1930 until her death taught, first at Warsaw, then Siena, and finally at her own villa on Lake Garda. (R)

Lablache, Luigi (b. Naples, 6 Dec. 1794; d. Naples, 23 Jan. 1858). Italian bass of French and Irish parentage. Studied Naples, where he made his début in 1812 in Fioravanti's *La Molinara*. Then followed a further period of study and a five-year engagement at Palermo. Milan, Sc., 1817, Dandini; Vienna 1824 (while here sang in Mozart's *Requiem* at Beethoven's funeral); London, H.M.'s, 1830, Geronimo (*Il Matrimonio Segreto*); Paris the same year; St. Petersburg 1852. Sang regularly in Paris and London until 1856, and was one of the few singers who remained loyal to Lumley and H.M.'s Theatre at the time of the opening of Covent Garden, though he went over to the latter house in 1854. He created Riccardo in *I Puritani*, and Don Pasquale, and was their first interpreter in London. Also first London Podestà (*Linda di Chamounix*), Karl von Moor (*I Masnadieri*), and Caliban (*La Tempesta*). Famous as Leporello, Bartolo, Pollione, and Baldassare. His voice had a compass of two octaves (E♭–e♭'). He was an enormous man—as Leporello he used to carry off Masetto under his arm. He was for a time Queen Victoria's singing teacher. His elder son, **Frederick,** also was a singer, and his daughter married the pianist Thalberg. His *Méthode de chant* did not add to his reputation.

La Calunnia. See *Calunnia, La*.

Lachner, Franz (b. Rain ober Lech, 2 Apr. 1803; d. Munich, 20 Jan. 1890). German conductor. Studied Vienna where he became conductor at the Kärntnerthor Theater 1826–34. From 1834 to 1836 he was at Mannheim and from 1836 until his death at Munich, becoming Generalmusikdirektor there in 1852. The real fame of the Munich Opera dates from his directorship. At first a great opponent of Wagner's music, he was persuaded to produce *Tannhäuser* in 1855 and *Lohengrin* in 1858. He was also a prolific composer and three of his four operas were produced at Munich. His younger brother **Ignaz** held appointments in Vienna, Stuttgart, Munich, Hamburg, Stockholm, and Frankfurt. A third brother **Vincenz** conducted in Vienna and at Mannheim (1836–73); and conducted a German company at C.G. in 1842 which gave the first performance in England of *Les Huguenots* and performances of *Iphigénie en Tauride*, *La Vestale*, and other works.

Lachnith, Ludwig (b. Prague, 7 July 1746; d. Paris, 3 Oct. 1820). Bohemian composer, notorious as an arranger ('dérangeur' according to some) of famous operas to suit them to public taste (he made *The Magic Flute* begin with the finale and included Don Giovanni's 'Finch' han dal vino' arranged as a duet). He wrote some operas of his own.

Là ci darem la mano. Duet in which Don Giovanni (bar.) woos Zerlina (sop.) in Act 1, scene 3, of Mozart's *Don Giovanni*; after hesitating, she succumbs.

Lacy, Michael (b. Bilbao, 19 July 1795; d. London, 20 Sept. 1867). Irish violinist. He was a skilful if unprincipled adapter of many famous operas for the London stage, among them a *pasticcio* jumbling Handel's *Israel in Egypt* and Rossini's *Mosè in Egitto*.

La donna è mobile. The Duke of Mantua's (ten.) aria in Act 3 of Verdi's *Rigoletto*, proclaiming his philosophy of fickleness. By its final appearance, sung in the distance, Rigoletto realizes that the body he has in a sack at his feet cannot be that of the Duke. One of the most famous of all arias, it was kept secret by Verdi until the day of the première.

Lady Macbeth of Mtsensk. Opera in 4 acts by Shostakovich; text by composer and A. Preis, after Leskov's story (1865). Prod. Moscow 22 Jan. 1934; Cleveland, Ohio, 31 Jan. 1935; London (concert version), Queen's Hall, 18 May 1936. The wife of a merchant takes one of his workmen as a lover. She gives her father-in-law rat-poison and, aided by her lover, strangles her husband. On their way to Siberia, the lover deserts her for one of the women convicts, and she kills her rival and herself. At first acclaimed as a model of Soviet realism, the opera was after two years suddently condemned by the authorities in the most violent terms. Latterly it has been revised and produced abroad; Moscow, Jan. 1963, as *Katerina Ismailova*.

Lakmé. Opera in 3 acts by Delibes; text by Gondinet and Gille, after the former's *Le Mariage de Loti*. Prod. Paris, O.C., 14 Apr. 1883, with Van Zandt and Talazac; London, Gaiety, 6 June 1885, with Van Zandt and Dupuy; Chicago, Grand O.H., 4 Oct. 1883. The opera set in mid-19th-century India, tells of the love of a British officer, Gerald, for Lakmé (daughter of the Brahmin priest Nilakantha) which ends in suicide. The opera contains the famous coloratura show-piece, the 'Bell Song'.

Lalo, Édouard (b. Lille, 27 Jan. 1823; d. Paris, 22 Apr. 1892). French composer of Spanish descent. Of his three operas—*Fiesque* (1866, unprod.), *Le Roi d'Ys* (1888), and *La Jacquerie* (unfinished, prod. 1895)—only the second has become at all known; it is still performed in Paris. The Aubade was made famous by Melba.

L'altra notte. Margherita's (sop.) aria in Act 3 of Boito's *Mefistofele* as she lies in prison and describes the drowning of her child.

La mamma morta. Madeleine de Coigny's (sop.) aria in Act 3 of Giordano's *Andrea Chénier* in which she tells Gérard of the terrible death of her mother when their house was burned by the revolutionary mob.

Lambert, Constant (b. London, 23 Aug. 1905; d. London, 21 Aug. 1951). English conductor, composer, and critic. Although primarily associated with the growth of ballet in Great Britain, in particular at S.W., Lambert had a great love of Italian opera, and conducted *Manon Lescaut* and *Turandot* at C.G. before the Second World War, as well as *The Fairy Queen* (for which he arranged the score) and *Turandot* (1946–7). (R)

Lamento. A plaintive aria common in early 17th-century opera, usually placed immediately before the tragic climax of the plot. The most famous is Monteverdi's 'Lamento d'Arianna', the only part of the opera to survive.

Lammers, Gerda (b. Berlin, 25 Sept. 1915). German soprano. Studied Berlin Hochschule with Lula Mysz-Gmeiner and Margret Schwedler-Lohmann. After 15 years as a concert and lieder singer made stage début Bayreuth 1955 as Ortlinde. Kassel since 1955, making début as Marie in *Wozzeck*, following it with Elektra. Also appeared there as Senta, Alceste, the Singer in *Cardillac*, Medea, Isolde, and Brünnhilde. When Goltz fell suddenly ill in 1957, Lammers made an unheralded London début at C.G. as Elektra, scoring one of the greatest individual triumphs in post-war London opera. Sang Dido in *Dido and Aeneas* at Ingestre Hall in 1958, and Kundry at C.G. in 1959. (R)

L'amour est un oiseau rebelle. Carmen's (mezzo) Habanera, in Bizet's opera.

Lamoureux, Charles (b. Bordeaux, 28 Sept. 1834; d. Paris, 21 Dec. 1899). French violinist and conductor. For many years a member of the Opéra orchestra; cond. O.C., 1876–7, O., 1877–9, resigning after a dispute about the tempo of an aria in *Don Giovanni*. A pioneer Wagnerian, he included long operatic excerpts in his famous series of concerts. He gave distinguished performances in Paris of *Lohengrin* and *Tristan*, and lived to see Wagner's cause triumphant.

Lampe, Johann Friedrich (b. Saxony, *c.* 1703; d. Edinburgh, 25 July 1751). German-English bassoonist and composer. From 1725 he was in London, where he played in the orchestra of the King's T., and composed many works for Hm. His collaboration with Henry Carey culminated in *The Dragon of Wantley* (1737), a burlesque much appreciated by Handel. His wife and Arne's were sisters, both accomplished singers, and Lampe toured with them successfully.

Lamperti, Francesco (b. Savona, 11 Mar. 1811; d. Como, 1 May 1892). Italian singing teacher. Educated Milan Conservatory. With Masini directed the Teatro Filodrammatico, Lodì, whither students came from all over Europe. Appointed professor of singing at Milan Conservatory 1850. His pupils included Albani, Campanini, Artôt, Cruvelli, Sembrich, Stolz, and Waldmann, and he was a friend of Pasta and Rubini. He based his teaching on the method of the old Italian school, and wrote several vocal studies and a treatise on singing. His son **Giovanni** (1839–1910) was also a teacher. His pupils included Bispham, Sembrich, Schumann-Heink, and Stagno. Writings include *The Technique of Bel Canto* (1905).

Lampugnani, Giovanni Battista (b. Milan, 1706; d. Milan, 1781). Italian composer. Succeeded Galuppi as composer at King's T. in 1743, where he produced two of his own operas; also shared the conducting at Hm. (with Gluck, among others). His works continued to be produced in London and in Milan, where he played the cembalo with Mozart in *Mitridate* in 1770. He wrote 29 operas.

Landgrave. Hermann, the Landgrave of Thuringia (bass), in Wagner's *Tannhäuser*.

Laparra, Raoul (b. Bordeaux, 13 May 1876; d. nr. Paris, 4 Apr. 1943). French composer. Studied with Gédalge, Massenet, and Fauré in Paris. He used Spanish and Basque themes and rhythms for his operas, of which *La Habanera* (1908) is the best known, having been performed in Paris, London, and New York.

Laporte (orig. Delaporte), **Pierre François** (b. 1799; d. nr. Paris, 1841). French actor and operatic manager. Manager of King's T., London, 1828–31 and 1833–41. His management included the first performances in London of *Il Pirata*, *La Sonnambula*, *Anna Bolena*, *Norma*, *I Capuleti e i Montecchi*, *I Puritani*, *Beatrice di Tenda*, *L'Elisir d'Amore*, and *Lucrezia Borgia*. Among the singers he brought to London for the first time were Rubini, Grisi, Nourrit, Tamburini, Persiani, Mario, Lablache, and Pauline Viardot.

Largo. The name by which the *larghetto* aria 'Ombra mai fù' from Handel's *Serse* has become known in countless arrangements.

Largo al factotum. Figaro's (bar.) aria introducing himself in all his versatility and popularity in Act 1, scene 1, of Rossini's *Il Barbiere di Siviglia*.

Larsén-Todsen, Nanny (b. Hagby, Sweden, 2 Aug. 1884). Swedish soprano. Studied Stockholm, Germany, and Italy. Début Stockholm 1906, Agathe (*Freischütz*). Leading lyric soprano Stockholm from 1907 to 1922, by which time she had become a dramatic soprano and begun to specialize in Wagner. Milan, Sc., 1923–4, Isolde; N.Y., Met., 1924–7, Brünnhilde, Isolde, Kundry, Fricka, Leonore (*Fidelio*), Rachel (*La Juive*), and La Gioconda; London, C.G., 1927 and 1930, Brünnhilde; Bayreuth 1927–8, 1930–1. Continued to sing until the 1930's, after which she taught in Stockholm. (R)

La Scala, Milan (rightly Teatro alla Scala). Built in 1778 by the architect Piermarini to replace the Royal Ducal Theatre that had been burned down two years previously, the theatre was named after Regina della Scala, wife of the Duke Barnabò Visconti of Milan, who had founded a church on the same site in the 14th century. It opened on 3 Aug. 1778 with Salieri's *Europa Riconosciuta*. Every great Italian composer has written for La Scala—Rossini, Donizetti, Bellini, Verdi, and Puccini—and it has been the scene of the first performances of *La Gazza Ladra*, *Lucrezia Borgia*, *Norma*, *Otello*, *Falstaff*, *Madama Butterfly*, and *Turandot*, as well as many more works, some of which survived no more than a season. The Scala's most glorious periods were those under Toscanini's direction, 1898–1903, 1906–8 and 1921–9. During the first period Toscanini brought Wagner into the Scala repertory and gave the first performances in Italy of *Salome*, *Louise*, and *Pelléas et Mélisande*; during the third there were the premières of *Debora e Jaele* (Pizzetti), *Nerone* (Boito), *Turandot*, *Belfagor* (Respighi), *La Cena delle Beffe* (Giordano), *I Cavalieri di Ekebù* (Zandonai), and some famous productions of *Falstaff*, *Boris Godunov*, *Rigoletto*, and *Lucia di Lammermoor*. The company at this period included Cobelli, Bruna Rasa, Dal Monte, Dalla Rizza, Raisa, Pampanini, Casazza, Supervia, Pertile, Merli, Trantoul, Badini, Galeffi, Journet, Pasero, and Stabile. The conductors who were associated with Toscanini at this time were Panizza, Guarnieri, Ghione, Gui, Santini, and Votto.

After Toscanini's departure from the Scala in 1929, owing to his quarrel with the Fascists, two rather mediocre seasons followed; then in the 1931–2 season De Sabata (q.v.) began his long association with the theatre, to be joined in the 1934–5 season by Marinuzzi (q.v.). Despite Mussolini's attempt to turn the Rome Opera into the premier theatre in Italy, the Scala continued to set a standard of performance that few other theatres could equal. The theatre was almost destroyed by bombs in Aug. 1943. By May 1946 it had been rebuilt (cap. 3,600) and today looks much as it always has with its six tiers, four of them boxes (146), all lined with red, the walls cream, gold, and maroon, and the beautiful 20-foot chandelier. The theatre reopened on 11 May 1946 with a concert conducted by Toscanini, who had subscribed 100,000 lire to its rebuilding. The soloists included the veterans Stabile, Nessi, and Pasero, and a young new-comer, Renata Tebaldi. The Sovrintendente of the theatre since 1946 has been Antonio Ghiringhelli.

De Sabata continued as musical and artistic director until forced to retire by ill health in 1954. Since then Gavazzeni, Sanzogno, and Votto have been the chief conductors each season. From 1952 to 1958 the presence of Callas in the Scala Company (she was called 'La Regina della Scala') led to the revivals of many long-neglected works, including *Anna Bolena*, *Il Pirata*, and *Médée*, and splendid productions by Luchino Visconti of *La Traviata*, *La Vestale*, and *La Sonnambula*.

In Dec. 1955 a chamber theatre, built within the large Scala building and called La Piccola Scala (cap. 600), was opened. On its stage *Il Matrimonio Segreto*, *Così fan tutte*, *La Buona Figliuola*, *Don Pasquale*, *Il Signor Bruschino*, *Il Campanello*, and works by modern composers are performed.

The Scala Company has paid several visits abroad since the war, including London, C.G., in 1950, Edinburgh in 1957, Moscow in 1964.

Lassalle, Jean (-Louis) (b. Lyons, 14 Dec. 1847; d. Paris, 7 Sept. 1909). French baritone. Studied Paris Conservatoire and privately with Novelli. Début Liège 1869 as St. Bris (*Huguenots*). After appearances in the French provinces, Holland, and Belgium, was engaged for the Paris Opéra (1872) where he made his début as William Tell. He succeeded Faure as principal baritone and remained there for more than 20 years, creating leading roles in Reyer's *Sigurd*, Saint-Saëns's *Henry VIII*, Paladilhe's *La Patrie*, and other works. He sang at C.G. 1879–81 and 1888–93. Was the first London Alim (*Le Roi de Lahore*), and the Demon in Rubinstein's opera of that name. Greatly admired as Hans Sachs in the De Reszke performances of *Meistersinger*, and was also heard as the Dutchman and Telramund. N.Y., Met., 1891–2, 1893–4, 1896–7. Retired 1901 and spent the rest of his life as a teacher. (R)

Last Rose of Summer, 'Tis the. An old Irish air, *The Groves of Blarney*, for which Thomas Moore wrote new words; in this form used as Lady Harriet's (sop.) song in Act 2 of Flotow's *Martha*.

Laszlò, Magda (b. Marosvásárhely, ?1919). Hungarian soprano. Studied Franz Liszt Academy of Budapest, and with Irene Stowaser. Budapest Opera 1943–6, singing Elisabeth (*Tannhäuser*), Maria Boccanegra, &c. Went to Italy, where she created the role of the Mother in Dallapiccola's *Il Prigioniero*, radio 1949 and Florence 1950. She sang the title roles in Gluck's *Alceste* (1953) and Monteverdi's *Poppea* (1962) at Glyndebourne, and in 1954 she created Cressida in Walton's *Troilus and Cressida* at C.G. Her wide repertory includes many modern roles. (R)

Lattuada, Felice (b. Milan, 5 Feb. 1882; d. Milan, 2 Nov. 1962). Italian composer. His operas, which are his most important works, include *Le Preziose Ridicole* (1929) and *Don Giovanni* (1929).

Latvia. Now part of U.S.S.R. Opera was first given in Latvia in 1782 (Monsigny's *La Belle Arsène*). The National Opera at Riga was inaugurated in 1919 with *Tannhäuser*. The first Lettish opera (discounting an amateurish work of 1890, Ozols's *Spoka Stunda*) was Kalniņš's *Banuta* (1920). Mediņš's *Uguns un Nakts* (*Fire and Night*) followed in 1921, his *Deevi un Cilveki* (*Gods and Men*), on an Egyptian subject, in 1922. Kalniņš has also written an historical opera, *Dzimtenes Atmoda* (*The Country's Awakening*) (1933) and a version of *Hamlet* (1936). See *Riga*.

Laubenthal, Rudolf (b. Düsseldorf, 10 Mar. 1886; d. Starnbergsee, Oct. 1971). German ten. Originally a doctor, turned to opera while in Berlin, studied with Lilli Lehmann. Début, Berlin, 1913. N.Y., Met., 1923–33 where he sang in the American premières of *Jenůfa* (Števa), *Die Aegyptische Helena* (Menelaos), *Schwanda* (Babinsky), as well as in other roles. In London he sang Wagner roles 1926–30. (R)

Laura. Alvise's wife (sop.) and Enzo's lover in Ponchielli's *La Gioconda*.

Lauretta. Schicchi's daughter (sop.) in Puccini's *Gianni Schicchi*.

Lauri-Volpi, Giacomo (b. Rome, 11 Dec. 1892). Italian tenor. Originally a lawyer, he turned to music and studied at the Accademia di Santa Cecilia, Rome, with Cotogni, and later with Enrico Rosati. Début (under name of Giacomo Rubini) Viterbo 1919, Arturo (*Puritani*); then under his own name, Rome 1920, Des Grieux (*Manon*) opposite Storchio. N.Y., Met., 1923–34, singing in 232 performances of 26 operas, including Calaf in the American première of *Turandot* and Rodolfo in the Met. première of *Luisa Miller*. London, C.G., 1925 (Chénier) and 1936 (Duke of Mantua, Radamès, and Cavaradossi). Chosen to sing Nerone (Boito) at the opening of the Teatro Reale dell'Opera, Rome, 1927 and Arnold in *William Tell* in the centenary performance of that opera at La Scala. His bright ringing tone, beautifully poised, with a superb legato and ringing top notes, made him one of the finest lyric-dramatic tenors of his day.

As late as 1959 he was still making occasional appearances in Italy. Writings include *Voci parallele* (1955). (R)

La vergine degli angeli. Leonora's (sop.) scene with chorus in Act 2, scene 2, of Verdi's *La Forza del Destino* in which she and the monks pray for her protection.

Lavranga, Denis (b. Argostoli, 17 Oct. 1864; d. Razata, 30 July 1941). Greek composer. After conducting opera in France and Italy he settled in Greece and in 1898 established the National Hellenic Opera, his life work. The company began with *La Bohème* in 1900, and in face of many difficulties managed to maintain itself, touring in Greece and in Egypt, Turkey, Rumania, and Russia. Lavranga's own operas were in the repertory, chief among them *Dido* (1909). His great contribution to the musical development of Greece culminated in the establishment in 1940 of the small but vigorous National Opera House. His own operas show a consciously national style grafted on to Italian methods.

Lawrence, Marjorie (b. Deans Marsh, Australia, 17 Feb. 1909). Australian soprano. Studied Melbourne and Paris with Cécile Gilly. Début Monte Carlo 1932, Elisabeth in *Tannhäuser*. Paris, O., 1933–8, where her roles included Alceste, Valentine in *Les Huguenots*, Salome, Brünnhilde, and Ortrud; N.Y., Met., 1935–41 where she shared the leading Wagner roles with Flagstad, and was also heard as Salome, Tosca, and Thaïs. At Mexico City in 1941 she was stricken with poliomyelitis during a performance of *Die Walküre*, but although she has never been able to walk unaided since then, she has appeared as Venus, Isolde, and Amneris in specially staged performances at the Met., Cincinnati, and Paris. She sang in a concert performance of Elektra in Chicago in 1947. Autobiography, *Interrupted Melody* (1949). (R)

Lawrence, Martin (b. London, 26 Sept. 1909). English bass. Studied privately. Début Carl Rosa Company 1945, Méphistophélès. New London Opera Company 1946–8, Don Pasquale, Colline, Bartolo, Leporello, Don Basilio, Pistol, and Sparafucile. Sang Devilshoof in Beecham's *Bohemian Girl* production at C.G. and has appeared in Budapest, Moscow, and Israel. (R)

Lazzari, Virgilio (b. Assisi, 20 Apr. 1887; d. Castel Gandolfo, 4 Oct. 1953). Italian, later naturalized American, bass. Studied Rome with Cotogni. Début Vitale Light Opera Company 1908 as L'Incognito in Suppé's *Boccaccio*. After appearances in Rome and South America he went to America, making his début in 1916 at St. Louis as Ramfis. Chicago Opera 1918–33; N.Y., Met., 1933–50. Salzburg Festivals 1934–9 as Leporello, Bartolo, and Pistol. London, C.G., 1939, Leporello. A fine singing actor with a repertory of some 55 operas. His most famous role was Archibaldo in *L'Amore dei Tre Re*. (R)

Lecocq, Charles (b. Paris, 3 June 1832; d. Paris, 24 Oct. 1918). French composer. After initial difficulties he became established as one of the most successful operetta composers of his day. His sole attempt at a more serious vein, *Plutus* (1886), was a failure, and he returned to the long series of works in which his gay, untroubled style repeatedly delighted the Paris public. Of his 50-odd pieces, *La Fille de Mme Angot* (1872) was the most successful, running initially for 500 nights.

Legend of Kleinzach, The. Hoffmann's (ten.) aria in the Prologue to Offenbach's *Les Contes d'Hoffmann*, telling the story of the dwarf at the court of Eisenach.

Legend of the Invisible City of Kitezh, The. Opera in 4 acts by Rimsky-Korsakov; text by Vladimir Belsky. Prod. St. Petersburg 20 Feb. 1907; London, C.G. (concert), 30 Mar. 1926; Ann Arbor, Mich. (concert), 21 May 1932. Prince Vsevolod marries Fevronia, whom he has met in a forest, but she is captured by Tartars. Two of them fight for her, while the drunken Grisha helps her to escape. She flees through a haunted forest and is led back to Kitezh by the spirit of the Prince.

Leghorn (It., Livorno). Town in Tuscany, Italy. Short seasons are given at the Teatro Goldoni.

Legend of Tsar Saltan, The. See *Tsar Saltan, The Legend of.*

Legros, Joseph (b. Monampteuil, nr. Laon, 7 Sept. 1730; d. La Rochelle, 20 Dec. 1793). French tenor and composer. Début Paris, O., 1764, where he continued to sing until 1783. Created four Gluck roles, Achilles (*Iphigénie en Aulide*), Admète (*Alceste*), Pylades (*Iphigénie en Tauride*), and the tenor Orphée, as well as roles in operas by Monsigny, Philidor, Piccinni, and Grétry.

Lehár, Franz (b. Komárom, 30 Apr. 1870; d. Ischl, 24 Oct. 1948). Hungarian composer. After some early operas he turned to operetta, where his greatest triumphs took place. *Die lustige Witwe* (*The Merry Widow*) (1905) is the most famous, but many others regularly appear in German operetta repertories. His appearance, after the deaths of the Strausses, Suppé, Zeller, and Millöcker, revived the apparently doomed tradition of operetta, and opened the way for Oscar Straus, Leo Fall, and Emmerich Kálmán. Though less sparkling than Johann Strauss's, his operettas have comparable melodic charm, and his gentle waltzes are probably the ancestors of the modern dance-music slow waltz. His lavish use of dance, dominated always by the waltz, almost created a form of ballet-operetta. After 1925 Lehár's popularity began to decline, but thanks in part to the championship of Richard Tauber he made a remarkable recovery with operettas centring on the principal singers, though the plots now tended o have unhappy endings. Of the latter, *Giuditta* (1934) has been the most successful. His chief works are *Die lustige Witwe*, *Der Graf von Luxembourg* (1909), *Gipsy Love* (1910), *Frasquita* (1922), *Paganini* (1925), *Frederica* (1928), and *Das Land des Lächelns* (*The Land of Smiles*) (1929). (R)

Lehmann, Lilli (b. Würzburg, 24 Nov. 1848; d. Berlin, 17 May 1929). German soprano. Her father August Lehmann was a singer; her mother, Marie Loewe, had been leading soprano at Kassel under Spohr, and was harpist in the Prague National Theatre's orchestra at the time of her daughter's birth. Taught singing by her mother. Début Prague 1865, 1st Boy in *Zauberflöte.* After appearances in Danzig and Leipzig was engaged as lyric and coloratura soprano in Berlin 1870–85. In the first Bayreuth *Ring* (1876), sang Woglinde, Helmwige, and Waldvogel. Début London, H.M.'s, 1880, Violetta and Philine; one of the Rhinemaidens in the first London *Ring*, 1882. She developed into a dramatic soprano and sang Isolde under Richter at C.G. 1884. American début 1885, N.Y., Met., as Carmen; between then and 1889 was heard in a variety of roles, including the first American Isolde and *Götterdämmerung* Brünnhilde. When she overstayed her leave from Berlin the Kaiser barred her from all German opera houses until 1891. In 1896 returned to Bayreuth as Brünnhilde, and in 1905 she sang in the Mozart Festival at Salzburg, where she became the artistic director. Returned to the Met. in 1898–9 and C.G. in 1899. She continued to sing in Europe and was heard as Isolde in Paris in 1903 and in Vienna in 1909. Her recital work continued until the 1920's. She sang 170 roles in 119 operas in German, French, and Italian. As a teacher she had uncompromisingly high ideals. Her pupils included Geraldine Farrar and Olive Fremstad. Her writings include *Meine Gesangkunst* (translated into English by Richard Aldrich as *How to Sing*), *Mein Weg* (her autobiography), and *Studie zu Fidelio.* (R) Her younger sister **Marie Lehmann** (1851–1931), although somewhat overshadowed by her sister, was a valued member of the Vienna Opera 1881–1902, and sang with Lilli in the first Bayreuth *Ring* as Wellgunde and Ortlinde. (R)

Lehmann, Lotte (b. Perleberg, 27 Feb. 1888). German, later naturalized American, soprano. Studied Berlin with various teachers and finally Mathilde Mallinger. Début Hamburg 1909, 3rd Boy in *Zauberflöte*. Vienna 1914–38, where she created the roles of the Composer in *Ariadne* and the Dyer's Wife in *Die Frau ohne Schatten*. The first Vienna Suor Angelica and Arabella; also created Christine in *Intermezzo* at Dresden. London, C.G., 1924–35 and 1938. The outstanding Marschallin of her day; also greatly admired as Sieglinde, Eva, Elsa, and Leonore. N.Y., Met., 1934–45, after which she continued to sing in concerts for another six years. Teaches at Santa Barbara. Her sincerity, musicianship, and beautiful voice endeared her to audiences the world over. Leaving Vienna at the time of the *Anschluss*, she did not return until the opening of the State Opera in Nov. 1955, when she was greeted by the public and old singers as if she were royalty. Returned to London in 1957 and 1959 to give master-classes at the Wigmore Hall. Her writings include her autobiography *Anfang und Aufstieg* (translated *On Wings of Song*), a novel *Orplid, Mein Land* (*Eternal Flight*), and poems. (R)

Lehmann, Maurice (b. Paris, 14 May 1895). French producer and manager. After a period in the straight theatre, became producer at the Porte St-Martin, where he staged Pierné's *Fragonard* (1934), and then at the Théâtre du Châtelet. After the liberation of France he was asked to reorganize the Opéra and Opéra-Comique, which he did with the assistance of Reynaldo Hahn and Albert Wolff. Between 1951 and 1955 he was responsible for productions of *Oberon*, *The Magic Flute*, *L'Aiglon*, *Antar*, and *Les Indes Galantes* at the Opéra.

Leider, Frida (b. Berlin, 18 Apr. 1888). German soprano. Studied in Berlin and Milan. Début Halle 1915, Venus. Rostock 1917–18; Königsberg 1918–19; Hamburg 1919–23; Berlin State Opera 1923–40; continued to sing there until 1940. London, C.G., 1924–38; Chicago Opera 1928–32; N.Y., Met., 1933–4; Bayreuth 1928–38. Her rich and often beautiful voice and great dramatic intensity combined to make her the outstanding Brünnhilde and Isolde of the inter-war years. She also appeared in London as the Marschallin, Armide, and Donna Anna, and in Berlin in several Verdi roles. Autobiography, *Das war mein Teil*, 1959. (R)

Leigh, Adèle (b. London, 15 June 1928). English soprano. Studied London with Maggie Teyte and at the Juilliard School, N.Y. Début London, C.G., 1948, Xenia in *Boris*. Remained member of the C.G. ensemble until 1956, graduating from small roles like Barbarina, and the Page in *Rigoletto*, to Pamina and Manon. Created the role of Bella in Tippett's *The Midsummer Marriage*. Has appeared in America and Europe, and returned to C.G. as Octavian in 1961. She has a pure soprano voice, a good sense of style, and a natural talent for the stage. Vienna Volksoper since 1963. (R)

Leigh, Walter (b. London, 22 June 1905; d. nr. Tobruk, 12 June 1942). English composer. With his melodic gift and expert craftsmanship he raised the standard of English light opera in *The Pride of the Regiment* (1932), a brilliantly parodistic piece, and *Jolly Roger* (1933), which originally ran for six months.

Leila. The Brahmin priestess (sop.) in Bizet's *Pêcheurs de Perles*,

Leinsdorf, Erich b. Vienna, 4 Feb. 1912). Austrian, now American, conductor. Studied Vienna. Went to Salzburg in 1934 as Walter's assistant; assisted Toscanini there 1935–7. Engaged at the Met., N.Y., for the 1937–8 season, making his début in Jan. 1938 conducting *Die Walküre*. Succeeded Bodanzky as chief conductor of the German repertory there 1939, remaining until 1943. He returned as Bing's 'Musical Consultant' and conductor 1958–62. Has also conducted the San Francisco Opera, and for a season was music and artistic director of the N.Y. City Center. (R)

Leipzig. Town in Saxony, E. Germany. Unlike other German towns, Leipzig has not enjoyed a particularly brilliant operatic history, though from the inauguration of the first opera house in 1693 until 1720, 100 operas were given. In the 18th century it was the home of the German *Singspiel*. Standfuss's *Der Teufel ist los* was given there in 1752. In 1833–1845 and 1849–50 Lortzing was a singer and conductor at Leipzig, and the premières of all his works were given there. Between 1876 and 1882, under the managership of Angelo Neumann (q.v.), Leipzig became the base of the Wagner company that gave the first *Ring* performances in London, Amsterdam, Brussels, Venice, and a number of other European cities. From 1878 to 1889 Artur Nikisch was the first conductor at Leipzig, and from 1886 to 1888 he was assisted by Mahler. The period 1923–33, when Gustav Brecher was the musical director, saw the premières of Křenek's *Jonny spielt auf* (1927) and *Leben des Orest* (1930) and of Weill's *Mahagonny* (1930). In 1938 the Opera gave a 12-week Wagner Festival (Leipzig was Wagner's birthplace) during which two complete cycles of the composer's works were given in chronological order, including *Die Hochzeit*, *Das Liebesverbot*, and *Die Feen*. The opera house was destroyed by bombs in Dec. 1943, but has been rebuilt on its old site and opened in Oct. 1960 (cap. 1,682), with Helmut Seidelmann (1901–61) as music director. The theatre's orchestra is that of the Leipzig Gewandhaus. Premières since the end of the war include Blacher's *Die Nachtschwalbe* (1948), Schoeck's *Die Laune des Verliebten* (1949), Bush's *Wat Tyler* (1953), and Burring's *Plautus in Nonnenkloster* (1959). Members of the ensembles since 1920 have included Margarete Bäumer, Irma Beilke, Hedwig Müller-Bütow, Rudolf Bockelmann, Frederick Dalberg, and August Seider.

Leise, leise. Agathe's (sop.) aria in Act 2 of Weber's *Der Freischütz* praying for protection for her lover Max.

Leitmotiv (Ger. = leading motive). A term invented by the Weber scholar F. W. Jähns to denote a short musical figure identifying a person, thing, or idea in music and above all in opera. The origins of this idea are hard to trace: there are certainly suggestions in Gluck and Mozart, and a more consistent use by Weber (e.g. Samiel's chords in *Der Freischütz*, and throughout *Euryanthe*). Not until Wagner are *Leitmotiv*'s powers fully used, most of all in *The Ring*. Here use of *Leitmotiv* increases in subtlety from simple tags in *Das Rheingold* to a dense, intricately expressive network of ideas working in the music of *Götterdämmerung*. The *Leitmotiv* became obsessional with Wagner's followers, as it never had with him. Wagner used the term *Hauptmotiv* in 1867, but this and others (e.g. *Gedächtnismotiv*) have given way to 'leitmotiv'.

Leitner, Ferdinand (b. Berlin, 4 Mar. 1912). German conductor. Studied Berlin with Schnabel and Karl Muck. Assistant to Busch at Glyndebourne 1935. Début as conductor Berlin 1943. Hamburg 1945–6; Munich 1946–7; musical director Stuttgart 1947–69; Zurich since 1969. Guest appearances all over Europe and South America. (R)

Lemmens-Sherrington, Helen (b. Preston, 4 Oct. 1834; d. Brussels, 9 May 1906). English soprano. Studied Rotterdam and Brussels. After singing in London in concerts she appeared at C.G. during the Royal English Opera season 1864–5 as Helvelyn and Rose in *Rose, or Love's Ransom*. From 1866 to 1868 she sang at the Royal Italian Opera, C.G., where her roles included Adalgisa, Donna Elvira, Élisabeth de Valois, Prascovia (*L'Étoile du Nord*), and Isabella (*Robert le Diable*). She was generally regarded as the leading English soprano of her day.

Lemnitz, Tiana (b. Metz, Lorraine, 26 Oct. 1897). German soprano. Studied Metz. Début Heilbronn 1921; Aachen 1922–9. Leading soprano Hanover 1929–33, and Berlin State Opera 1934–57, when she retired. C.G. 1936 and 1938. Sang leading roles in German, French, Italian, and Russian repertories, and her repertory ranged from Pamina to Sieglinde, Euridice to Aida, and Micaëla to Jenůfa. Her Octavian was considered one of the best of its day, and her Pamina, in which her exquisite *pianissimo* was employed to the full, was hailed as the finest since that of Claire Dux. (R)

Lemshev, Sergey (b. Staroe Knydzevo, 10 July 1902). Russian tenor. Studied Moscow, where he was first heard as Lensky in a student performance of *Eugene Onegin* in 1920. After engagements in the Russian provinces, including Tiflis (1926–31), he was engaged for the Bolshoy, Moscow, in 1932, where he has excelled in the lyric repertory. His best parts, besides Lensky, are the Duke of Mantua, Alfredo, and Roméo (Gounod). (R)

Leningrad. Town in U.S.S.R., formerly St. Petersburg (to 1914) and then Petrograd (1914–24), founded by Peter the Great in 1703. The first opera given there was Araia's *La Forza dell'Amore e dell'Odio* in Feb. 1736. Araia wrote several works for the Russian court including *Semiramide Riconosciuta*. He was succeeded by Manfredini (1759–66), Galuppi (1766–8), Traetta (1768–76), Paisiello (1776–83), Sarti (1784–6 and 1792–6), Cimarosa (1787–91), Martín y Soler (1788–94), and Cavos (1797–8). In the latter year Italian opera was prohibited by Paul I. Among the works written for Russia by these composers were Galuppi's *Ifigenia in Tauride* (1768), Paisiello's *Il Barbiere di Siviglia* (1782), *Gli Astrologi Immaginari* (1779), *La Serva Padrona* (1781), and Cimarosa's *Idalide* (1789). In 1783 the Teatr Bolshoy was opened; it was rebuilt in 1836, opening with Glinka's *A Life for the Tsar* on 27 Nov. 1836. Every new season here opened with this work, and before the end of the century it had been given nearly 700 times. An Italian opera company was established there in 1843, but moved to Moscow three years later. In 1850 the Teatr Tsirk, opposite the Bolshoy, was opened; it was destroyed by fire in 1859 and rebuilt as the Maryinsky Teatr in 1860. Napravnik (q.v.) was the chief conductor there 1863–1916. Premières at St. Petersburg after 1860 included *La Forza del Destino* (1862); Serov's *Judith* (1863); Dargomizhsky's *The Stone Guest* (1872); Rimsky-Korsakov's *The Maid of Pskov* (1873), *May Night* (1880), *Snow Maiden* (1882), *Christmas Eve* (1895), and *Kitezh* (1907); Tchaikovsky's *The Oprichnik* (1874), *Vakula the Smith* (1876), *The Maid of Orleans* (1881), *The Sorceress* (1887), *The Queen of Spades* (1890), and *Iolanthe* (1892); Rubinstein's *The Demon* (1875); Mussorgsky's *Boris Godunov* (second version, 1874), and *Khovanshchina* (1886); Napravnik's *Dubrovsky* (1895) and *Francesca da Rimini* (1902). In 1917 one of the first premières was Mussorgsky's *Sorochinsky Fair* in the version completed by Cui. The Maryinsky Teatr is now known as the Kirov Teatr.

Lensky. Onegin's friend (ten.) in Tchaikovsky's *Eugene Onegin*.

Leo, Leonardo (b. San Vito degli Schiavi, 5 Aug. 1694; d. Naples, 31 Oct. 1744). Italian composer. His long list of operas includes some of the finest examples of *opera buffa*, in which his sense of humour and high-spirited melodic invention find ample expression. His pupils included Jommelli, Pergolesi, and Piccinni.

Leoncavallo, Ruggiero (b. Naples, 8 Mar. 1858; d. Montecatini, 9 Aug. 1919). Italian composer. Leoncavallo's ambitions are shown in his early *Chatterton* (1896) and his scheme for a vast trilogy embracing the Renaissance in Italy; but his reputation rests on a single 2-act opera *Pagliacci* (1892), which at once made him famous. The subsequent failure of *I Medici* (1893) discouraged him from continuing the trilogy. *La Bohème* (1897) suffered from comparison with Puccini's work, with which it coincided. But the promise of *Pagliacci* proved false. Apart from *Zazà* (1900), which won some praise from so unlikely a judge as Fauré, little appeared to confirm Leoncavallo's own ambitions and his friends' hopes; certainly not *Der Roland von Berlin* (1904), commissioned in admiration for *I Medici* by Wilhelm II. He turned to a series of trivial operettas, gathering himself for one final effort at the end—*Edipo Re* (1920). Here he strove to confound his adversaries and recapture the grand manner of his youth. It is neither in this nor in the frivolities of his operettas that we find the best of him, but in the famous *Pagliacci*. Here his strong dramatic flair and direct melodic appeal, coupled with a certain originality of technique, find full expression.

Leoni, Franco (b. Milan, 24 Oct. 1864; d. London, 8 Feb. 1949). Italian composer. He became famous for his *L'Oracolo* (1905).

Leonora. (1) Heroine (sop.) of Verdi's *Il Trovatore.* (2) Heroine (sop.) of Verdi's *La Forza del Destino.* (3) The King's mistress (mezzo) in Donizetti's *La Favorita.*

Leonore. Heroine (sop.) of Beethoven's *Fidelio*; and the title of its original version.

Léonore, ou L'Amour Conjugal. Opera in 2 acts by Gaveaux; text by Jean Nicolas Bouilly. Prod. Paris, T. Feydeau, 19 Feb. 1798. Historically important as the first setting of the *Fidelio* story; others are by Paer (1804), Mayr (1805), and Beethoven (*Fidelio*, 1805), all based on Bouilly.

Leonore 40/45. Opera in 2 acts by Liebermann; text by Heinrich Strobel. Prod. Basel 26 Mar. 1952. The French and German libretto tells of the love of a German soldier for a French girl, who symbolizes European civilization, between 1940 and 1945.

L'Épine, Margherita de (b. ?; d. London 9 or 10 Aug. 1746). Italian or French-Italian soprano. Appeared in London from 1692 onwards at Lincoln's Inn Fields, D.L., and elsewhere. In 1710 sang in *Almahide* (q.v.) and in 1712 and 1713 in Handel's *Pastor Fido* and *Rinaldo*. Continued to appear until 1718 when she married Pepusch, to whom she is said to have brought a fortune of £10,000. Reputedly an ugly woman but a very fine musician.

Leporello. Don Giovanni's servant (bass) in Mozart's opera.

Lescaut. Manon's cousin (bar.) in Massenet's *Manon* and brother in Puccini's *Manon Lescaut.*

Let's Make an Opera. Children's opera in 2 parts by Britten; text by Eric Crozier. Prod. Aldeburgh 14 June 1949. In the first part the preparations for the opera are discussed by the children and grown-ups taking part and the audience is rehearsed for its part in four songs. The second part, *The Little Sweep*, tells of the rescue by a family of children of the sweep's boy Sammy, the audience providing comments with its songs.

Letter Duet. The duet 'Sull' aria' between the Countess and Susanna (sops.) in Act 3 of Mozart's *Figaro* in which the Countess dictates to Susanna the letter to be sent to the Count making the assignation that evening in the garden.

Letter Scene. The extended *scena* for Tatyana (sop.) in Tchaikovsky's *Eugene Onegin* in which she writes to Onegin declaring her love.

Levasseur, Nicolas (b. Bresles, Oise, 9 Mar. 1791; d. Paris, 7 Dec. 1871). French bass. Studied Paris. Début Paris, O., 1813, as Osman Pacha in Grétry's *La Caravane*. London, King's T., 1815–17 and again 1832 when he sang Bertram in the first London performance of *Robert le Diable*. In 1819–27 principal bass at the Théâtre des Italiens, Paris, and 1827–53 again at the Opéra. Created many roles in Paris, including Bertram, Marcel (*Huguenots*), Zacharie (*Le Prophète*). Retired from the stage in 1853 but continued to teach at the Conservatoire until 1870.

Levasseur, Rosalie (b. Valenciennes, 8 Oct. 1749; d. Neuwied, 6 May 1826). French soprano. Début Paris 1776. Sang L'Amour in première of *Orphée* under name of Mlle Rosalie. Her talents as a singer and actress were recognized by the Austrian Ambassador, whose mistress she became, and resuming her own name of Levasseur she succeeded Sophie Arnould as leading soprano at the Opéra, and created (the title roles in Gluck's *Armide* (1777) and *Iphigénie en Tauride* (1779) as well as in works by Philidor, Piccinni, and Sacchini.

Le Veau d'Or. The song in praise of gold, sung by Méphistophélès (bass) in Gounod's *Faust.*

Levi, Hermann (b. Giessen, 7 Nov. 1839; d. Munich, 13 May 1900). German conductor. Studied Mannheim with Lachner and at Leipzig. After appointments at Saarbrücken, Rotterdam, and Karlsruhe he became principal conductor at Munich (1872–96). He conducted the first performance of *Parsifal* at Bayreuth, being specially engaged by Wagner for the 'Christian feelings' he displayed, despite Wagner's anti-semitism. He revised the librettos of *Così fan tutte*, *Don Giovanni*, and *Figaro*; translated into German the text of *Les Troyens* and Chabrier's *Gwendoline*; and wrote *Gedanken aus Goethes Werken* (1901).

Lewis, Mary (b. Hot Springs, Ark., 7 Jan. 1900; d. New York, 31 Dec. 1941). American soprano. While appearing with the Ziegfield Follies she attracted the attention of Otto Kahn, director of the Met., who persuaded Gatti-Casazza to offer her a contract: this she refused as she felt she was not ready for it. She then studied with William Thorner and in 1923 made her début at the Vienna V.O. as Marguerite. After appearances in Monte Carlo, Paris, Berlin, and London (Mary in the première of *Hugh the Drover*, 1924), she was engaged for the Met. 1926–30. (R)

Lewis, Richard (b. Manchester, 10 May 1914). English tenor. Studied privately with T. W. Evans, R.M.C.M., and after the war R.A.M. with Norman Allin. Début Glyndebourne 1947, Male Chorus in *The Rape of Lucretia*; C.G. 1947, Grimes. Since then has sung regularly at Glyndebourne (Don Ottavio, Ferrando, Idomeneo, Admète, Bacchus, Tom Rakewell, Florestan), and on numerous occasions at C.G. (Simpleton in *Boris*, Tamino, Alfredo, Hoffmann, Don José, Troilus, Mark in *The Midsummer Marriage*, and Achilles in *King Priam*; these last three roles he created). San Francisco Opera since 1955, including Jason (*Médée*), Des Grieux, Jeník, and Pinkerton. An extremely versatile and intelligent artist. (R)

Liberec. Town in northern Bohemia, Czechoslovakia. The theatre's opera seasons serve the industrial region of which Liberec and Jablonec are the centres.

Libiamo, libiamo. *Brindisi*, or drinking song, sung by Alfred (ten.) and Violetta (sop.) in Act 1 of Verdi's *La Traviata*.

Libretto (It. = little book). The name generally given to the book of the words of an opera. Though the earliest were some 8½ in. in height, the diminutive was always used and the term has been current in English since about 1742. The first ever written was for Peri's *Dafne* at Florence in 1600; there have since been over 30,000. Early librettos usually began with an *argomento*, invaluable for its setting out of the events leading up to the action, and continued with cast-lists, dedications, and (until around the beginning of the 19th century) a *protesta* in which the poet affirmed that all words such as *numi*, *fati*, &c. referring to pagan religion did not reflect his own views, which were devoutly Catholic. Essentially, a good libretto is a play moulded to the needs of music drama. In the 17th and 18th centuries the established pattern of recitative, aria, and chorus made special demands upon the librettist and determined the course of the action: the battle about how much precedence music or words should have has been raging ever since, and found operatic expression in Strauss's *Capriccio*. The literary quality of a libretto is no less thorny a subject. While such manifest rubbish as Helmine von Chézy's book for *Euryanthe* can wreck an opera's chances despite its fine music, too great literary finesse can threaten the musical drama hardly less seriously. The vital element is dramatic potency; and, less tangibly, the quality of being able to fire a composer's imagination. Collaboration has not proved indispensable: Metastasio is the great example of a librettist, 27 of whose works did duty for 1,000 settings by 50 composers. At the other extreme, very fruitful results have come from the careful mutual planning of Quinault and Lully, Calzabigi and Gluck, Da Ponte and Mozart, Boito and Verdi, Gilbert and Sullivan,

Hofmannsthal and Strauss. Berlioz, Wagner, Charpentier, and Menotti are some of the most successful of those composers who have preferred to shape their own librettos.

The popularity of published librettos is as steady as ever, and many opera-lovers, if in lesser numbers outside Italy, still furnish themselves with copies both to study at home and to take to the performance. As candle-grease spots on the early specimens show, there is even an historical precedent for the intolerable habit of trying to read the libretto with a light during the opera. The translation of librettos became widespread during the development of national opera houses in the 19th century, and some works have been given in many different languages—*Lohengrin* in at least 22, *Rigoletto* in at least 21—and their librettos published. It is principally certain gramophone companies who now follow the enlightened practice of printing original and translation side by side, which was normal practice at Covent Garden in Victorian times. Then the libretto was still a natural part of a gentleman's equipment for the opera—palmy days when *Punch* imagined a young man saying:

A pound, dear father, is the sum,
That clears the opera wicket:
Two lemon gloves, one lemon ice,
Libretto, and your ticket.

Libuše. Opera in 3 acts by Smetana; text (original German) by J. Wenzig, translated into Czech by E. Spindler. Prod. Prague, for the inauguration of the Czech National Theatre, 11 June 1881. With *Dalibor*, Smetana's most important serious opera, frequently performed in Czechoslovakia. The opera tells of the rivalry of two brothers, Chrudos and Stahlav, for the love of Krasava. They are brought to trial before Libuše, Queen of Bohemia, who is insulted by Chrudos. The Queen abdicates in favour of a man who can rule with a rod of iron. The new king effects a reconciliation between the brothers. Also opera by Škroup (*Libušin Sňatek*, 1828—one of the first Czech operas).

Licette, Miriam (b. Chester, 9 Sept. 1892; d. Twyford, 11 Aug. 1969). English soprano. Studied Milan and Paris with Marchesi, Jean de Reszke, Sabbatini. Début Rome 1911, Cio-Cio-San. Beecham Coy. 1916–20; B.N.O.C. 1922–8. Also appeared in important roles during C.G. International seasons 1919–29 (Marguerite, Mimì, Euridice, Desdemona, Donna Elvira, Gutrune). Much admired as Mozart singer and for her Louise and Juliette. (R)

Liebe der Danae, Die (The Love of Danae). Opera in 3 acts by Strauss; text by Gregor. Prod. Salzburg 14 Aug. 1952 with Kupper, Gostic, Schoeffler, cond. Krauss. The work reached dress-rehearsal at Salzburg in 1944 (16 Aug. with Ursuleac, Taubmann, and Hotter, cond. Krauss), but then the theatres were closed by a Nazi edict. London, C.G., 16 Sept. 1953 with Kupper, Vandenburg, Frantz, cond. Kempe; Los Angeles, 10 Apr. 1964.

Liebermann, Rolf (b. Zürich, 14 Sept. 1910). Swiss composer. He followed up the success of *Leonore 40/45* (1952) with *Penelope* (1954) and *The School for Wives* (1955). His style extends from 12-note music to jazz, and though freely experimental is based on knowledge of practical effect. Intendant Hamburg Opera since 1959.

Liebestod (Ger. = love-death). The title used today for Isolde's death scene in Wagner's *Tristan und Isolde*, but used by Wagner of the mystic love duet in Act 2.

Liebesverbot, Das (The Ban on Love). Opera in 2 acts by Wagner; text by the composer, after Shakespeare's play *Measure for Measure* (1604–5). Prod. Magdeburg, 29 Mar. 1836; London Univ. Coll., 15 Feb. 1965. Wagner's first performed opera. Revived in Munich (1923), Berlin (1933), Leipzig (1938), and Dortmund (1957).

Liederspiel (Ger. = song play). A combination of play and opera in which music and spoken dialogue alternate. See also *Singspiel*.

Liège. Town in Belgium. The Grand Théâtre, whose architecture followed that of the Odéon in Paris, opened in

1820 with Grétry's *Zémire et Azor*. Until 1914 the theatre had a permanent company of French and Belgian singers and all operas were performed in French. During the inter-war years opera was given by visiting companies. Since 1945 the theatre has been under the direction of André d'Arkor (q.v.) who has raised it to the standard of the best French provincial theatres.

Life for the Tsar, A. Opera in 4 acts and epilogue by Glinka; text by Baron Georgy Fedorovich Rosen. Prod. St. Petersburg 9 Dec. 1836; London, C.G., 12 July 1887 with Albani, Sealchi, Gayarré; N.Y. (concert version) 14 Nov. 1871. The opera, also known as *Ivan Susanin*, is set in Russia and Poland during the winter of 1612. News arrives of the Poles' defeat, while Antonida thinks of her love for Sabinin. In the Polish camp soldiers vow to fight on, and decide to advance against the Russians on hearing that Romanov has been made Tsar. They compel Susanin, a Russian, to guide them, but he leads them on a false trail and is killed. The new Tsar comes to Moscow; he praises his supporters and laments the death of Susanin.

Lily of Killarney, The. Opera in 3 acts by Benedict; text by John Oxenford and Dion Boucicault, after the latter's drama *Colleen Bawn* (1860). Prod. London, C.G., 8 Feb. 1862 with Pyne and Santley; Philadelphia 20 Nov. 1867.

Lincoln's Inn Fields Theatre. The first theatre on the site was known as the Duke's Theatre 1661–73. The second theatre, 1695–1705, was the scene of the first public performance of *Dido and Aeneas* in 1700. The third theatre, built by Christopher Rich and opened by his son John Rich (q.v.) in 1714, was the scene of the first production of *The Beggar's Opera* (1728). It was the home of the Italian opera company set up in opposition to Handel, with Porpora as composer and Senesino as leading singer, 1733–4. Handel's last opera, *Deidamia*, was given there in 1741. It later became a barracks, then a warehouse, and its site is now occupied by the Royal College of Surgeons.

Lind, Jenny (orig. Johanna) (b. Stockholm, 6 Oct. 1820; d. Malvern, 2 Nov. 1887). Swedish soprano. Studied Stockholm. Début there 1838, Agathe. After three years went to Paris where she met with failure and suffered a temporary loss of voice. She then studied with Garcia and perfected her technique. Meyerbeer recommended her to the Berlin Opera where she made her début in 1844 as Norma, and then created the leading role in Meyerbeer's *Feldlager in Schlesien*. After successful appearances throughout Germany, Scandinavia, and Vienna—where her Norma gained her 30 curtain calls, and where after her Amina the Empress threw one of her own bouquets on to the stage (an unprecedented action)—she was engaged by Lumley for H.M.'s Theatre in 1847 as a rival attraction to the stars assembled at the newly opened C.G. In her first London season she created the role of Amelia in Verdi's London opera *I Masnadieri*. She continued to appear in opera for the next two seasons, making her final appearances on the operatic stage on 10 May 1849 as Alice in *Robert le Diable*. In 1852 she married Otto Goldschmidt, the founder of the Bach Choir. Thereafter she sang only in oratorio and concert. She became Professor of Singing at the R.C.M. in 1883, and devoted much of her time to charitable causes and other 'good works'. Her voice was remarkable for its purity, range (b to g^{II}), agility, breath control, and sympathetic quality. She was known as the Swedish Nightingale and has been the subject of nearly 20 books in English, German, and Swedish, of which H. E. Holland's and W. S. Rockstro's *Jenny Lind the Artist* (2 vols., London, 1891) and Joan Bulman's *Jenny Lind* (London, 1956) can be recommended. Rockstro also published a short study on her method with a selection of the cadenzas and other ornaments she used (1894).

Linda di Chamounix. Opera in 3 acts by Donizetti; text by Rossi. Prod. Vienna, Kä., 19 May 1842 with Tadolini, Brambilla, Mariani, Varesi; London, H.M.'s, 1 June 1843 with Persiani, Brambilla, Mario, Lablache; N.Y.,

P.O.H., 4 Jan. 1847. Linda loves Charles, a nobleman disguised as a painter. Believing herself deserted, she goes mad, but he restores her to sanity by returning and reminding her of their love with an old song.

Lindoro. (1) Isabella's lover (ten.) in Rossini's *L'Italiana in Algeri*. (2) The name assumed by Count Almaviva in Rossini's *Il Barbiere di Siviglia*.

Linley, Thomas, sen. (b. Badminton, 17 Jan. 1733; d. London, 19 Nov. 1795). English singing teacher and composer. He wrote, mostly for Drury Lane, a large number of stage works under various headings—opera, pantomime, ballad opera, musical entertainment, musical farce, &c. The best known was *The Duenna* (1775), a composition and compilation of music for his son-in-law Sheridan's play, done in collaboration with his eldest son **Thomas** (b. Bath, 5 May 1756; d. Grimsthorpe, 5 Aug. 1778). A friend of Mozart, Linley jun. showed precocious musical gifts; he was drowned in a boating accident, leaving little more than a 3-act opera *The Cady of Bagdad* (1776), an oratorio, and some songs. His sister **Elizabeth** (b. Bath, 5 Sept. 1754; d. Bristol, 28 June 1792), Sheridan's wife, was a gifted soprano, as to a lesser degree were her sisters **Mary** (1758–87) and **Maria** (1763–84). Their brother **Ozias** (1765–1831) was an organist, and **William** (1771–1835) brought out three pieces at Drury Lane which became known as *The Ring*, before taking up an official post in India.

Linz. Town in Upper Austria. Opera is performed in the Landestheater (cap. 800) built in 1958.

Lionel. The young farmer (ten.) in love with Lady Harriet in Flotow's *Martha*.

Lionel and Clarissa. Opera in 3 acts by Dibdin; text by Isaac Bickerstaffe. Prod. London, C.G., 25 Feb. 1768; Philadelphia 14 Dec. 1772.

Lipp, Wilma (b. Vienna, 26 Apr. 1925). Austrian soprano. Studied Vienna with Anna Bahr-Mildenburg and Alfred Jerger. Début Vienna 1943, Rosina. Vienna, S.O., since 1945, first in coloratura and soubrette roles, more recently in *lirico-spinto* parts. London, C.G., 1950, Gilda; San Francisco 1962. (R)

Lisbon (Port., Lisboa). Capital of Portugal. Opera was first heard there regularly in the 18th century. The Royal Opera di Tejo was opened on 31 Mar. 1755 with Pérez's *Alessandro nell'Indie*. Opera was given there, and at the Teatro d'Ajuda, until 1792, when a group of business men decided to erect an opera house which was a replica of the San Carlo in Naples. The Teatro San Carlos was designed by José da Costa and Silva, and opened on 30 June 1793 with Cimarosa's *La Ballerina Amante*. In Dec. 1794 the first opera to be sung in Portuguese there was heard, Moreira's *A Vingança da Cigana*. The oval-shaped auditorium (cap. 1,700) has 120 boxes arranged in 5 tiers with 12 boxes on each side; there are two balconies and a gallery. The history of the theatre has been that of a first-class Italian opera house outside Italy, with occasional excursions into the French and German repertories. All the great singers of the last two centuries have appeared there. The theatre is now known as the National Theatre of San Carlos, being under state control with Dr. José Duarte de Figueiredo as its artistic director.

Lisitsyan, Pavel (b. Vladikavkaz, 6 Nov. 1911). Russian baritone. Member of the Bolshoy, Moscow, since 1940. Début N.Y., Met., 1960, Amonasro. His repertory includes Onegin, Escamillo, Janusz (*Halka*), and parts in modern Soviet works. (R)

Lissenko, Nicolai Vitalevich (b. Grinsky, 22 Mar. 1842; d. Kiev, 6 Nov. 1912). Ukrainian composer. His operas and operettas, mostly based on Gogol, were highly popular in his native Ukraine, and were admired by Tchaikovsky and Rimsky-Korsakov. His refusal to allow the Ukrainian texts to be translated into Russian hindered the operas' wider acceptance.

List, Emanuel (b. Vienna, 22 Mar. 1890; d. Vienna, 21 June 1967). Austrian bass. After singing as boy chorister at Theater an der Wien, touring Europe in a vocal quartet and America in vaudeville, studied in N.Y. with Josiah Zuro. Début Vienna 1922, Méphistophélès. Berlin 1923–33; London, C.G., 1925, 1934–6; N.Y., Met., 1933–50. Also sang at Bayreuth and Salzburg. Possessing a rich deep bass, he was especially noted for his interpretations of Hunding, Hagen, Pogner, and King Mark, and was a distinguished Baron Ochs. (R)

Liszt, Franz (b. Raiding, 22 Oct. 1811; d. Bayreuth, 31 July 1886). Hungarian pianist and composer. His sole attempt at opera was *Don Sanche* (1824–5), [a 1-act operetta written with the help of his teacher Paer. It was produced in Paris in 1825 and after four performances forgotten. He became Kapellmeister at Weimar 1848, where he produced Wagner's *Lohengrin* (1850) and championed both this composer and Berlioz, resigning in 1859 after differences concerning the production of Cornelius's *Der Barbier von Bagdad*. His daughter **Cosima** married first Hans von Bülow, then Wagner (see *Wagner*, *Cosima*).

Lithuania. Now part of U.S.S.R. The opera house at Kaunas was opened in 1920 when Lithuania was still an independent country—this was the National Theatre (Lietuvos Valstybes Teatras). The first opera sung in Lithuanian was *La Traviata*, that year. Mainly instrumental in organizing the company were the singer Kipras Petrauskas (whose *Birute*, the first Lithuanian opera, was prod. 1921) and the composer Tallat-Kelpshi, who became the first conductor. The Kaunas opera became quite well known; Chaliapin and Kiepura sang there, and Malko and Coates were among its guest conductors. In 1933 Karnavičis's *Gražina* was prod. to celebrate the 15th anniversary of the Lithuanian State. After the Russians took over, the capital was transferred to Vilnius, and with it the opera company. In May 1959 Kaunas organized a new company, at present under the direction of the conductor, Iuozas Indra. A catholic repertory includes two Lithuanian operas, *The Drowned Woman* by Baumilas and the satirical *Frank Kruk* by Gorbulskis.

Little Sweep, The. See *Let's Make an Opera*.

Litvinne, Félia (orig. Françoise-Jeanne Schütz) (b. St. Petersburg, 11 Oct. 1860; d. Paris, 12 Oct. 1936). Franco-Russian soprano. Studied Paris with Barthe-Banderali and Pauline Viardot. Début Paris, T.I., 1883, replacing Fidès Devriès as Maria Boccanegra. Six months later official début as Elvira (*Ernani*) under name of Litvinova. Appeared in various European cities and in N.Y. with Mapleson Company 1885–6; N.Y., Met., 1896–7; London, C.G., from 1899. The first Isolde in Paris (1899); the Brünnhilde of the first complete *Ring* at La Monnaie, Brussels (1903), and in Paris at the Opéra (1911). Her last operatic performances were in 1916, after which she continued to appear in concerts until 1924. She taught in Paris and her pupils included Nina Koshetz, Marcelle Denya, and Germaine Lubin. Her performance of Gluck's *Alceste* is said to have set a standard still not surpassed in our day. Her voice was brilliant and flexible and her singing impassioned. (R)

Liù. The slave girl (sop.) in love with Calaf in Puccini's *Turandot*.

Ljubljana (Laibach). Town in Yugoslavia, capital of Slovenia. The first theatre performances with music were the sacred plays performed by German Jesuits in the 16th century. In 1652 an Italian opera company visited Ljubljana and further visits took place throughout the 18th century until the increasing domination of Austro-Hungary brought an influx of German opera and Italian influence faded. The first theatre in the town was built in 1765 and the first Slovene opera composed 1780. The theatre was burnt down in 1887 but a new theatre was built in 1892 and regular performances of Slovene operas were given. This is still the case, and many Slovene works have been performed since the war, but as they are seldom translated into Croatian they are never heard at other Yugoslav opera houses. The company has toured abroad and made several fine recordings since the war. Opera is given at the Slovensko Narodno Gledališče (Slovenian National Theatre).

Ljungberg, Göta (b. Sundsvall, 4 Oct. 1893; d. Lidingö, 28 June 1955). Swedish soprano. Studied Stockholm. Début Stockholm 1918, Elsa. London, C.G., 1924–9 where she created title role in Goossens's *Judith* (1929) and was praised as Salome and Sieglinde. N.Y., Met., 1932–5, creating Lady Marigold Sandys in Hanson's *Merry Mount* (1933), also Isolde and Brünnhilde. After retiring from the stage taught in N.Y. for several years. (R)

Lloyd, George (b. St. Ives, 28 June 1913). English composer. His three operas all have texts by his father, William Lloyd. The first, *Iernin* (1933–4), attracted the attention of Albert Coates, who conducted *The Serf* (1936–8) at C.G. *John Socman* followed in 1951.

Lloyd, Powell (b. London, 6 May 1900). English tenor. Studied London, Morley College, and G.S.M. First appeared in small roles with the Old Vic Shakespeare Company, then became leading character tenor there and at S.W. Also sang the Witch in *Hänsel und Gretel* and Bartolo in *The Barber*, originally a mezzo-soprano and a bass role. Since 1941 has produced and designed sets for S.W., Dublin, Welsh National Opera, &c. Has also designed sets for a number of operas.

Lodoïska. Opera in 3 acts by Cherubini; text by Fillette-Loraux. Prod. Paris, T. Feydeau, 18 July 1791, a fortnight before Rodolphe Kreutzer's opera on the same subject (Paris, C.-I., 1 Aug. 1791); N.Y. 4 Dec. 1826. Also operas by Storace (1794), Mayr (1796), Caruso (1798), and R. Kreutzer (1791).

Lodoletta. Opera in 3 acts by Mascagni; text by Forzano, after Ouida's novel *Two Little Wooden Shoes* (1874). Prod. Rome, C., 30 Apr. 1917 with Storchio and Gigli; N.Y., Met., 12 Jan. 1918 with Farrar and Caruso. Antonio gives Lodoletta a pair of new red shoes. After his death she falls in love with a painter, Flammen, and follows him from Holland to Paris. She is afraid to enter his house, where a party is in progress, and dies in the snow. Flammen finds her and laments that he has always loved her.

Loewenberg, Alfred (b. Berlin, 14 May 1902; d. London, 29 Dec. 1949). British musical historian of German birth. His *Annals of Opera: 1597–1940* (Cambridge, 1943; rev. ed. Zürich, 1954) is a monument of painstaking scholarship and research, containing details of some 4,000 opera performances in chronological order. Essential to any student of operatic history.

Loge. The fire god (ten.) in Wagner's *Das Rheingold.*

Logroscino, Nicola (b. Bitonto, 22 Oct. 1698; d. prob. Palermo, after 1765). Italian composer. After settling in Naples in about 1738 he became highly popular as a comic opera composer. Many of his later works were written in collaboration, some with Piccinni, who eventually captured his popularity.

Lohengrin. Opera in 3 acts by Wagner; text by the composer. Prod. Weimar, Court Theatre, 28 Aug. 1850, with Agthe, Fastlinger, Beck, von Milde, Hoder, cond. Liszt; N.Y., Stadt Theatre, 3 Apr. 1871; London, C.G., 8 May 1875 with Albani, D'Angeri, Nicolini, Maurel. The opera was originally intended for production at Dresden, but was rejected there in 1848 because of Wagner's revolutionary activities. It was through Liszt that it received its Weimar première (with an orchestra of 38!), when Wagner was in exile in Switzerland. He did not attend a performance of the opera until 1861 in Vienna.

Act 1. The banks of the River Scheldt near Antwerp in the early years of the 10th century. King Henry the Fowler (bass), who has been visiting Antwerp to raise an army, holds court. He asks Frederick of Telramund (bar.) why the kingdom of Brabant is torn by strife and dissension. Telramund accuses his ward Elsa (sop.)

of having murdered her young brother Gottfried in order to obtain the throne. Elsa is called upon to defend herself, and she describes a dream in which a knight in shining armour has come to defend her. The King's Herald (bar.) twice calls for a champion. She falls on her knees and prays, and a swan-drawn boat bearing a knight in shining armour arrives. The knight (Lohengrin, ten.) bids the swan farewell, and agrees to champion Elsa, offering her his hand in marriage on condition that she will never ask him his name or origin. Lohengrin defeats Telramund, generously sparing his life. Elsa joyfully embraces her hero, and the pair are carried off in triumph.

Act 2. In the courtyard of the castle in Antwerp, Telramund, who has been banned as a traitor by the King, and his wife Ortrud (sop.), an evil woman who exercises some kind of supernatural power over him, are brooding on the state of events. Elsa appears on a balcony and sings a song to the night breezes. She descends, and Ortrud, offering her friendship, begins to sow distrust of Lohengrin in her mind. Dawn breaks, and processions form for the marriage of Elsa and Lohengrin. On the steps of the Cathedral, Ortrud accuses Lohengrin of having defeated Telramund by evil means, and then Telramund repeats his wife's accusations. Elsa assures the knight that she trusts him; but the seeds of suspicion have taken root.

Act 3. A brilliant orchestral prelude and the celebrated Wedding March open the scene, which is set in Elsa's bridal chamber. The King blesses the couple, and then withdraws. A beautiful love-duet for Elsa and Lohengrin ensues, but Elsa's happiness and rapture give way to hysteria and she demands to know her husband's name. Telramund and four of his followers break into the room to attack Lohengrin, who immediately kills Telramund. He bids the nobles to bear the body to the King, and tells Elsa that he will reveal his secret to them all.

The scene changes to the banks of the Scheldt. The King and court assemble, and Lohengrin tells them that he has come from the Temple of the Holy Grail in Monsalvat; his father was Parsifal, and Lohengrin is his name. He bids Elsa a sad farewell, and then turns to greet the swan which has brought the boat for him. Ortrud rushes on and reveals that the swan is in reality Gottfried, Elsa's brother. Lohengrin falls on his knees and prays. The swan becomes Gottfried, and a white dove of the Grail flies down and draws the boat away. Elsa collapses.

Lohse, Otto (b. Dresden, 21 Sept. 1858; d. Baden-Baden, 5 May 1925). German conductor. Studied Dresden with Richter, and originally cellist in Dresden Court Orchestra. Début as conductor Riga 1889. Music director at Hamburg 1893–5, where he met Katharina Klafsky (q.v.) whom he married. Conducted Damrosch Company in U.S.A. 1895–7; London, D.L., 1894; C.G. 1901–4. Subsequently at Cologne (1904–11), Brussels (1911–12), and Leipzig (1912–23). His son **Georg Lohse** was for many years leading Heldentenor at the Chemnitz Opera.

Lola. Alfio's wife (mezzo) and Turiddu's lover in Mascagni's *Cavalleria Rusticana*.

Lombardi alla Prima Crociata, I (The Lombards at the First Crusade). Opera in 4 acts by Verdi; text by Solera. Prod. Milan, Sc., 11 Feb. 1843 with Frezzolini; London, H.M.'s, 12 May 1846 with Grisi and Mario; N.Y., P.O.H., 3 Mar. 1847—first Verdi opera in U.S.A. A second version in French under the title of *Jérusalem*, with text by Royer and Vaëz, was produced at the Paris O. on 26 Nov. 1847 and Milan, Sc., 26 Dec. 1850.

The opera tells of the rivalry of two brothers Arvino and Pagano for the love of Viclinda at the time of the first Crusade. Pagano, in an attempt to abduct Viclinda and kill his brother, in error murders his own father. He is exiled to the Holy Land, where he lives as a hermit. Giselda, daughter of Arvino, who has accompanied her father on the Crusade, is captured by Acciano, tyrant of Antioch; she falls in love with his son Oronte. The couple escape, but Oronte is mortally wounded and before he expires is baptized by the Hermit. The latter leads the attack on Jerusalem and he too is wounded. He reveals his identity to Arvino and dies forgiven in his brother's arms.

London. Capital of Great Britain. See *Covent Garden, Dorset Garden Theatre, Drury Lane, Her Majesty's Theatre, Lincoln's Inn Fields, London Opera House, Lyceum Theatre, Mermaid Theatre, Old Vic, Pantheon, Sadler's Wells.*

London (orig. Burnstein), **George** (b. Montreal, 30 May 1920). Canadian bass-baritone. Studied Los Angeles. Début as George Burnson, Hollywood Bowl 1942, Doctor in *La Traviata.* After appearing in musical comedy and touring in concerts, he auditioned in Brussels for Karl Böhm in 1949 and was engaged for the Vienna Opera where he made his début in Sept. that year as Amonasro. N.Y., Met., since 1951, where he has been especially admired as Boris, Don Giovanni, and Scarpia. Bayreuth since 1951 as Amfortas and Dutchman. He possesses a rich and sonorous bass-baritone voice, has an imposing stage presence, and is an intense actor. (R)

London Opera House. Built by Oscar Hammerstein (q.v.) in 1911 and opened on 13 Nov. that year with Nougès's *Quo Vadis?* It survived two seasons, during which Massenet's *Le Jongleur de Notre-Dame* and *Don Quichotte* and Holbrooke's *The Children of Don* were given their first London performances. It was closed on 13 July 1913 and (as the Stoll Theatre) became a variety theatre and cinema. During the First World War a short season of Russian, French, and Italian opera, including the English première of *The Queen of Spades,* was given there under the direction of Vladimir Rosing, and then no opera was heard there again until the summer of 1949 when a season of Italian opera was given by Jay Pomeroy's company. Further seasons were given by Italian touring companies between 1952 and 1957; and it was also the scene of *Porgy and Bess* (1951), the Zagreb Opera visit (1955), and Honegger's *Jeanne d'Arc au Bûcher*. Now pulled down.

London Philharmonic Orchestra. Founded by Beecham in 1932, it became the official C.G. orchestra for the international opera seasons from 1933 to 1939. Glyndebourne from 1964.

London Symphony Orchestra. Founded in 1904. Played for the German winter season at C.G. in 1906 and provided the bulk of the players for the C.G. orchestra from 1924 to 1931. It also provided many of the players for pre-war Glyndebourne. Played for the 1957 and 1958 seasons at the Stoll and D.L.

Long Thursday. The term given to the non-subscription nights at the Royal Italian Opera, C.G., in the 1850's and 1860's, when complete acts of operas were given in addition to the evening's advertised programme. The entertainment often lasted until well after midnight—hence the name. A typical Long Thursday might consist of *Norma* followed by the last act of *Lucia di Lammermoor*, with a ballet to round off the evening.

L'onore, ladri! The opening words of Falstaff's (bar.) monologue on honour, in Act 1, scene 1 of Verdi's opera.

Loreley, Die. Unfinished opera by Mendelssohn (1847); text by Emanuel von Giebel, after the old legend. Other operas on the subject are by Lachner (1846), Wallace (*Lurline*, 1860), Bruch (1863), Catalani (*Elda*, 1880—still given in Italy as *Loreley*), Mohr (1884), Pacius (1887), Sommer (1891), Albert Becker, and Emil Naumann.

Lorenz, Max (b. Düsseldorf, 10 May 1901). German tenor. Studied Berlin with Grenzebach. Début Dresden 1927, Walther von der Vogelweide (*Tannhäuser*). Berlin, S.O., 1933–7; Vienna State Opera since 1937. N.Y., Met., 1931–4 and 1947–50; London, C.G., 1934 and 1937; Bayreuth 1933–9 and 1952. One of the finest Wagner tenors of his day and considered by the Viennese the best Otello since Slezak. (R)

Lortzing, Albert (b. Berlin, 23 Oct. 1801; d. Berlin, 21 Jan. 1851). German actor, singer, librettist, and composer.

His connexion with the theatre began in childhood, and he produced his first opera, *Ali Pascha*, at the age of 23. In 1833 he and his wife were engaged as actors at Leipzig. He now turned to comedy, beginning with *Die beiden Schützen* (1837). It was this work that founded a reputation clinched with *Zar und Zimmermann* (1837). *Caramo* (1839), *Hans Sachs* (1840), and *Casanova* (1841) proved less enduring, but with *Der Wildschütz* (1842) Lortzing produced his greatest triumph. Meanwhile he was also acting as producer, singer, and conductor. With *Undine* (1845) he attempted romantic opera without conspicuous success, though the work is remarkable for its early use of leitmotiv. In 1846 he moved to Vienna, where *Der Waffenschmied* was given. *Zum Grossadmiral* (1847) was given at Leipzig. With *Regina* (prod. 1899) he attempted a grand opera on the topical subject of revolution, but the work was everywhere turned down as too liberal in its views. He lost his job, but was called to Leipzig to supervise his *Rolands Knappen* (1849), a great success. An appointment as conductor there fell through, and in 1850 he moved to Berlin as conductor of a small theatre. Here his family lived in great poverty in spite of the frequent performance of his works, and he died when about to be dismissed from even this humble post. His last work was *Die Opernprobe* (1851). His music has a simple charm that fits it well to the type of romantic comedy he preferred; though not a polished composer, and sometimes an over-sentimental one, his works represent the most agreeable type of German comic opera.

Los Angeles. Town in California, U.S.A. The first opera seasons in Los Angeles were given by various touring companies in the 1880's and 1890's, including the Abbott, Juch, and National Opera Companies. In 1897 the Del Conti Opera Company, which had been appearing in Mexico City, was brought to Los Angeles by L. E. Beyhmer and C. Modini, and gave the first performance in the United States of *La Bohème*. Beyhmer also brought the Metropolitan Opera from New York to the west coast for the first time in 1900. In 1911 the Lombardi (later the San Carlo) Company began its visits, and from 1914 until the end of the 1920's the Chicago Opera made 11 visits to Los Angeles. Among the many visiting companies during the 1920's were the Scotti Company and a Russian company with Chaliapin. In 1924 the Los Angeles Grand Opera Association was formed with Gateano Merola as general director, and worked in close contact with the San Francisco Opera. In 1925 Merola withdrew and formed a rival company, the California Grand Opera Association. Two years later Merola rejoined the Los Angeles Grand Opera Association, and seasons were given at the Shrine Auditorium until 1932. Since 1936 the San Francisco Opera has visited Los Angeles regularly at the close of the autumn San Francisco season. Opera has also been given from time to time in the Hollywood Bowl, a vast open-air arena, beginning with H. W. Parker's *Fairyland* in 1915. The Opera School of Los Angeles University gives interesting performances, and from 1946 to 1954 was under the direction of Carl Ebert.

Los Angeles, Victoria de (orig. Victoria Lopez) (b. Barcelona, 1 Nov. 1923). Spanish soprano. Studied Barcelona Conservatory, completing the six-year course in three, and gaining every prize. First public appearance while still a student, in Monteverdi's *Orfeo*. Début Barcelona, Teatro Liceo, Jan. 1945, Countess (*Figaro*). Gained first place in International Festival, Geneva, 1947. In 1949 invited by B.B.C. to sing Salud in Falla's *La Vida Breve*. London, C.G., 1950, Mimì; has frequently returned since. N.Y., Met., from 1951. Possesses a beautiful natural voice and a charming stage presence, and has become a moving interpreter of the roles she sings. (R)

Louise. *Roman musical* in 4 acts by Charpentier; text by composer. Prod. Paris, O.C., 2 Feb. 1900, with Rioton—950 performances by 1950; N.Y., Manhattan Opera, 3 Jan. 1908, with Mary Garden; London, C.G., 18 June 1909, with Edvina.

Act 1. Julien (ten.) has written to the parents (bar. and con.) of Louise (sop.) asking to marry her; he urges her to elope if permission is refused, but she is hesitant. The mother reproaches her for thinking of a worthless Bohemian and demands that he be rejected; she quarrels with her husband, who is more tolerant, and Louise has to promise not to see Julien.

Act 2. Scene 1. Louise and her mother go to work. Julien reappears and reiterates his pleas; still uncertain, Louise rushes into the shop. Scene 2 (sometimes omitted). The other seamstresses guess that Louise is in love. Julien serenades her, and she goes to him.

Act 3. Julien and Louise are living happily in a cottage; she recalls the day when first she yielded ('Depuis le jour'). A group of Bohemians appears and crowns Louise Queen of Montmartre; but Louise's mother comes with news that her father is dying. Only when she promises to return will Julien let her go.

Act 4. Louise has nursed her father back to health, but is not allowed to return to Julien. Father and daughter quarrel, and he throws her out, lamenting after she has gone that the lures of Paris have destroyed his home.

Love in a Village. Ballad and *pasticcio* opera in 3 acts partly composed and partly compiled by Arne and Bickerstaffe. Prod. London, C.G., 8 Dec. 1762; Charleston, 10 Feb. 1766. New edition by Arthur Oldham, Aldeburgh 1952.

Love of the Three Oranges, The. Opera in 4 acts by Prokofiev; text by composer, after Gozzi's comedy (1761). Prod. Chicago, 30 Dec. 1921 with Koshetz, cond. Prokofiev; Edinburgh (Belgrade Opera) Aug. 1962; London, S.W., May 1963. An opera is taking place in which a melancholy prince can only be cured by laughter. Every attempt is thwarted by Fata Morgana until she herself falls down and he laughs. He is now forced to find three oranges. He finds them in a kitchen and drags them with him into the desert. Each contains a princess. Two die of thirst; the third is revived by some of the stage-audience with a bucket of water. Eventually the prince and princess are united and the sorceress is confounded.

Lualdi, Adriano (b. Larino, 22 Mar. 1887; d. Milan, 8 Jan. 1971). Italian composer, conductor, and critic. In his operas (he wrote his own librettos), revived older Italian forms. They include an intermezzo *Il Cantico* (1915), a puppet intermezzo *Le Furie di Arlecchino* (1915), a dramatic *scena*, *La Morte di Rinaldo* (1920), and another puppet opera *Guerin Meschino* (1920). Other operas include *La Figlia del Re* (1922), *Il Diavolo del Campanile* (1925), and *La Granceola* (1930).

Lubin, Germaine (b. Paris, 1 Feb. 1890). French soprano. Originally studied medicine, then turned to music, studying in Paris with Martini, Isnardon, and Litvinne. In 1912 won three prizes for singing and joined O.C. same year; début Antonia (*Tales of Hoffmann*). Paris, O., 1914–44; London, C.G., 1937 as Alceste and Ariane, and 1939 as Isolde and Kundry. First French artist to sing Kundry and Isolde at Bayreuth. She possessed a beautiful voice and was an excellent actress. Her career was brought to a premature end after the war as a result of her collaboration with the Germans. (R)

Lucca, Pauline (b. Vienna, 25 Apr. 1841; d. Vienna, 28 Feb. 1908). Austrian soprano. Studied Vienna where she first sang in the chorus of the Court Opera. Début Olomouc 1859, Elvira in *Ernani*. Engaged Berlin 1861 on recommendation of Meyerbeer with whom she studied several roles. London, C.G., 1863 as Valentine and created there Selika. Her Marguerite, Cherubino, and Carmen were considered unsurpassed in their day. She sang in the United States 1872–4 and was leading soprano in Vienna 1874–89, when she retired. Her voice had a range of two and a half octaves (f'–c'''').

Lucia di Lammermoor. Opera in 3 acts by Donizetti; text by Cammarano, after Scott's novel *The Bride of Lammermoor* (1819). Prod. Naples,

S.C., 26 Sept. 1835 with Persiani and Duprez; London, H.M.'s, 5 Apr. 1838 with Persiani and Rubini; New Orleans 28 Dec. 1841 with Julia Calvé and Nourrit. Lord Henry Ashton wrongfully holds the estates of Edgar, Master of Ravenswood, between whose family and his own there has long been a deadly feud. In addition, Henry's political activities have placed him in a perilous position. To re-establish his family's position he has decided to marry his sister Lucy to Lord Arthur Bucklaw. Lucy herself is in love with Edgar.

Act 1. Scene 1. In a wood near the Ravenswood castle, Norman, captain of the guard (ten.), tells Henry (bar.) that he believes Lucy has secretly been meeting Edgar. Henry swears that he will prevent the union between the two lovers. Scene 2. Lucy (sop.), accompanied by her companion Alice (sop.), awaits Edgar (ten.) by the fountain. She sings of a young woman murdered long ago by one of the Ravenswoods, whose ghost she believes she has seen. Edgar arrives with the news that he has to leave for France. They vow eternal love and exchange rings.

Act 2. Scene 1. Henry tells Norman that he believes he can persuade Lucy to change her mind and marry Arthur by showing her a forged letter from Edgar, which will make her believe that he is in love with someone else. Lucy is summoned and Henry's plan works. Scene 2. The guests assemble in the great hall of the castle for the wedding. Looking pale and distraught, Lucy signs the contract. Edgar rushes in and confronts her (here occurs the famous sextet). Edgar curses her and the Ravenswood family.

(A scene in which Henry challenges Edgar to a duel while a storm rages occurs at this point; it has never been performed in any production in living memory, though it is included in the Decca recording.)

Act 3. Scene 1. The wedding celebrations continue, but are interrupted when Raimond the chaplain arrives with the news that Lucy has lost her reason and murdered her husband. Lucy herself appears, and in the most famous 'mad scene' in all opera goes through an imaginary wedding ceremony with Edgar. She begs that a tear should be shed when she dies, and accompanied by a flute, executes the most intricate and dazzling coloratura. Scene 2. Edgar, unaware of Lucy's fate, has come to the tomb of the Ravenswoods (the site chosen for the duel), anxious to join them, as he has nothing to live for. A sad procession wends its way from the castle. Edgar learns what has happened, and as a tolling bell announces Lucy's death he stabs himself.

Lucio Silla. *Dramma per musica* in 3 acts by Mozart; text by Gio. da Gamerra, altered by Metastasio. Prod. Milan, T.R.D., 26 Dec. 1772; first perf. in Germany, Dresden, 23 Sept. 1955. London, Camden T.H., 7 Mar. 1967; Baltimore, 19 Jan. 1968. Also operas by Anfossi (1774) and J. C. Bach (1777).

Lucrezia Borgia. Opera in prologue and 2 acts by Donizetti; text by Romani, after Victor Hugo's tragedy (1833). Prod. Milan, Sc., 26 Dec. 1833 with Lalande and Pedrazzi. London, H.M.'s, 6 June 1839 with Grisi and Mario; New Orleans, 27 Apr. 1844. Alfonso suspects Lucrezia of an affair with Gennaro; he is actually her son, though she alone knows it. When he is arrested she arranges his escape. She poisons some men who taunt her, only to find that she has also killed her son. When produced in Paris 1840, Hugo objected and the work was withdrawn. The libretto was rewritten, the title being changed to *La Rinegata* and the action transferred to Turkey.

Ludikar, Pavel (b. Prague, 3 Mar. 1882; d. Vienna, 19 Feb. 1970). Czech bass-baritone. Studied Prague. Début Prague, National Theatre, 1904, Sarastro. After appearances in Austria, Germany, and Italy, made American début with Boston Civic Opera 1913. N.Y., Met., 1926–32, singing the role of Figaro more than 110 times. In 1935 appointed manager of Prague National Theatre where he created the title role in Křenek's *Karl V* in 1938. (R)

Ludwig II of Bavaria (b. Nymphenburg, 25 Aug. 1845; d. Lake Starnberg, 13 Jun. 1886). Son of Maximilian II, he succeeded his father in 1864. He took little interest in affairs of state but devoted himself to the patronage of Wagner and his music. He gave Wagner a home in Munich; appointed Bülow court pianist at Wagner's request; allotted him a private summer residence, the Villa Pellet on Lake Starnberg; and made plans to build a festival theatre in Munich for the *Ring*, engaging the architect Semper for this purpose. He was instrumental in getting the Court Opera to give the premières of *Tristan* (1865), *Meistersinger* (1868), *Rheingold* (1869), and *Walküre* (1870). Wagner's autobiography *Mein Leben* was undertaken at Ludwig's request. They quarrelled after Ludwig found out about Cosima's affair with Wagner, though Ludwig continued to provide support. Finally he helped Wagner with money to build the Bayreuth Festspielhaus (he lent 200,000 marks) and the Villa Wahnfried.

Ludwig, Christa (b. Berlin, 16 Mar. 1928). German mezzo-soprano. Her parents, Eugenie Besalla and Anton Ludwig, were both singers at the Vienna Volksoper in the 1920's. Her father later became intendant at Aachen. She studied with her mother and Felice Hüni-Mihaček. Début Frankfurt 1946, Orlofsky. After engagements in Darmstadt, Hanover, and Hamburg she sang Cherubino at Salzburg in 1954 and was engaged for the Vienna State Opera in 1955. N.Y., Met., 1959–60. As Octavian, the Composer, and Eboli, she established herself as one of the leading mezzo-sopranos of the day; then in 1962 sang successfully as Leonore in *Fidelio*. (R)

Ludwig, Leopold (b. Witkowitz, 12 Jan. 1908). Austrian conductor. Studied Vienna. Held appointments at Opava (1931), Brno, Oldenburg (1936–9), Vienna (1939–43), Berlin (Städtische Opera 1943–50). Hamburg State Opera as Generalmusikdirektor since 1950. Has appeared as guest conductor all over Europe, including Edinburgh (1952 and 1956), Glyndebourne (1959), San Francisco (since 1959), and at the Colón. Hamburg State Opera as Generalmusikdirektor, 1950–71.

Lugo, Giuseppe (b. Verona, 1899). Italian tenor. Début Paris, O., 1930, Rodolfo. After singing as leading tenor at Brussels, La M., and Paris, O.-C., for a number of years, sang one performance of Cavaradossi at C.G. in 1936 which brought him to the attention of the Italian opera houses, where he enjoyed a brief but highly successful career, 1936–42, especially in Puccini roles, Faust (Boito) and Duke of Mantua. Possesses a rich and beautiful voice of the Gigli type. (R)

Luisa Miller. Opera in 3 acts by Verdi; text by Cammarano after Schiller's tragedy *Kabale und Liebe* (1784). Prod. Naples, S.C., 8 Dec. 1849 with Gavazzaniga; Philadelphia, 27 Oct. 1852; London, S.W., 3 June 1858 (and five days later at H.M.'s with Piccolomini). The opera, set in the Tyrol in the early 18th century, tells of the love of Luisa, daughter of an old soldier, Miller, for Rodolfo, son of Count Walter. Rodolfo is expected to marry Frederica, Duchess of Ostheim, and when he refuses is imprisoned by his father. He also arrests Luisa's father and then gets his follower Wurm to make Luisa write a letter to Rodolfo saying she is in love with someone else. When Rodolfo is released from prison he makes Luisa confess that she wrote the letter, and poisons both himself and Luisa. Before the poison takes effect, Luisa reveals to Rodolfo that Wurm forced her to write the letter, and Rodolfo kills him.

Lully, Jean-Baptiste (b. Florence, 28 Nov. 1632; d. Paris, 22 Mar. 1687). French composer of Italian origin. He early attracted the attention of Louis XIV, and entered his service, becoming master of music at court. From 1664 to 1671 he collaborated with Molière in opera-ballets, producing his first French opera, *Les Fêtes de l'Amour et de Bacchus*, in 1672. In the next 14 years he composed 20 operas to texts of every type by Quinault, establishing the tradition which was later to represent one side in the *guerre des bouffons* (q.v.)—the formal French overture, accompanied recitative strictly conforming to the rules of good declamation, conventionally planned arias: everything disciplined and elevated, as befitted the entertainment of the king. That this should result in a certain monotony of treatment was inevitable, but Lully's skill and sense of proportion are indisputable, and it is no small tribute that operas composed to so rigid a formula should have proved so durable once the frame that held them was broken.

Lulu. Unfinished opera in 3 acts by Berg; text by composer, after Wedekind's dramas *Erdgeist* (1895) and *Die Büchse der Pandora* (1901). Prod. Zürich 2 June 1937 with Nuri Hadzič; London, S.W., by Hamburg Opera, 3 Oct. 1962; Santa Fé, 7 Aug. 1963, with Joan Carroll. Lulu is a *femme fatale* who destroys all her lovers—though there is little love in any of the transactions, except from the Countess Geschwitz. Eventually she comes to London as a prostitute, and is killed by Jack the Ripper.

Lumley (orig. Levy), **Benjamin** (b. London, 1811; d. London, 17 Mar. 1875). English opera manager. A lawyer by profession, he was the legal adviser to Laporte (q.v.) whom he succeeded as manager of H.M.'s in 1841. He remained manager of the theatre until 1852, when he was forced to close owing to lack of public support after the opening of C.G. He reopened the theatre in 1856 and retired in 1859. From 1850 to 1851 he was also manager of the T.I., Paris. During his management of H.M.'s he gave the first performances in England of *Linda di Chamounix*, *La Favorite*, *Maria di Rohan*, *Don Pasquale*, *Ernani*, *I Due Foscari*, *Attila*, *I Lombardi*, *Nabucco*, *Luisa Miller*, *La Traviata*, *Il Trovatore*, and *I Masnadieri* (the latter commissioned by him from Verdi). He introduced several great singers to London, including Jenny Lind, Frezzolini, Cruvelli, Piccolomini, Tietjens, Staudigl, Giuglini, and Ronconi. His company further included Grisi, Mario, Persiani, Tamburini, and Lablache, and it was his quarrel with the first four that led to the establishment of the Royal Italian Opera at C.G. His *Reminiscences of the Opera*, published in 1864, gives a vivid, if one-sided, picture of London operatic life in the 1840's and 1850's.

Lunn, Louise Kirkby (b. Manchester, 8 Nov. 1873; d. London, 17 Feb. 1930). English mezzo-soprano. Studied Manchester and R.C.M. Début, while still a student, D.L. 1893 as Margaret in Schumann's *Genoveva*. Appeared in Stanford's *Shamus O'Brien* at Opéra-Comique, London, 1896; then sang small roles at C.G. that summer. Carl Rosa 1897–9; C.G. regularly 1901–14 and 1919–22. N.Y., Met., 1902–3, 1906–8. In 1904 she sang Kundry in the first performance in English of *Parsifal* at Boston. At C.G. she was a famous Fricka, Brangaene, Ortrud, Amneris, and Delilah. She sang in the first C.G. performances of *Hélène* and *Hérodiade* (Massenet), *Armide*, and *Eugene Onegin*. Her large rich voice, under perfect control, ranged from g to b♭♭''. (R)

Lussan, Zélie de. See *De Lussan*.

Lustigen Weiber von Windsor, Die (The Merry Wives of Windsor). Opera in 3 acts by Nicolai; text by Mosenthal, after Shakespeare's comedy (1600–1). Prod. Berlin, Court, 9 Mar. 1849; Philadelphia, 16 Mar. 1863; London, H.M.'s, 3 May 1864 (as *Falstaff*), with Tietjens, Santley. Nicolai's last and most important opera, at one time exceeding even Verdi's *Falstaff* in popularity on German stages.

Lustige Witwe, Die (The Merry Widow). Operetta in 3 acts by Lehár; text by Viktor Léon and Leo Stein, after Meilhac's comedy *L'Attaché*. Prod. Vienna, W., 30 Dec. 1905, with Mizzi Günther; London, Daly's, 8 June 1907, with Lily Elsie; N.Y., New Amsterdam T., 21 Oct. 1907. Lehár's most successful work. The gay, complicated plot deals with the attempts of Baron Mirko Zeta to obtain the Merry Widow Hanna Glawari's fortune for his impoverished country of Pontevedria by getting his young compatriot Danilo to marry her.

Lyceum Theatre, London. Built originally as a home for the drama, it housed the Drury Lane English Opera Company in 1809, when that theatre was burned down. It was later renamed the English Opera House, and was rebuilt as such in 1815. The scene of the English première of *Der Freischütz* in 1824. Rebuilt in 1834, it housed Italian companies in 1837, 1838, and 1841; became the Royal Italian Opera in 1856 and 1857 while C.G. was being rebuilt; housed the Carl Rosa in 1876 and 1877, and for some of its London seasons in the years between the wars; saw the English première of *Otello* by the company of La Scala in 1889; and was the scene of the Beecham Russian season of 1931. Now a dance hall.

Lyons (Fr., Lyon). Town in Rhône, France. Opera first performed in a theatre built by Soufflot 1754–6. Present Grand Théâtre (cap. 1,800) dates from 1831. Known as 'the cradle of *le Wagnérisme français*', having staged the first performances in French of *Meistersinger* and subsequently many performances of Wagner's operas. Since 1955 the theatre has been directed by Paul Camerlo.

Lysiart. The Count of Forest (bar.), villain of Weber's *Euryanthe.*

M

Maas, Joseph (b. Dartford, 30 Jan. 1847; d. London, 16 Jan. 1886). English tenor. Studied Rochester, where he was a chorister in the cathedral, and later in Milan. Début Kellogg English Opera Company, U.S.A., 1873. Carl Rosa 1878–81; London, H.M.'s, 1880; and C.G. 1883 as Lohengrin; D.L. 1885, where he was the first Des Grieux (Massenet) in London.

Maastricht. Town in Limburg, Holland. The Zuid-Nederlandse Opera, founded 1948, gives 70 performances a year in Limburg, N. Brabant, and Zeeland.

Macbeth. Opera in 4 acts by Verdi; text by Piave, after Shakespeare's tragedy (1605–6). Prod. Florence, Teatro della Pergola, 14 Mar. 1847 with Barbieri-Nini and Varesi, cond. Verdi; N.Y., Niblo's Garden, 24 Apr. 1850 with Bosio and Badiali; Glyndebourne, 21 May 1938 with Schwarz and Valentino, cond. Busch (productions had been announced in London for 1861 and 1870). When it was performed at St. Petersburg in 1855 it was given as *Sivardo, il Sassone* (*Siward the Saxon*). For the Paris première in 1865 a new version was made by Verdi for the French translation of Nuitter and Beaumont, which includes Lady Macbeth's 'La luce langue' in Act 2, the Act 3 final duet, the Chorus of the Exiles in Act 4, and the whole battle scene after Macbeth's last aria.

McCormack, (Count) John (b. Athlone, 14 June 1884; d. Dublin, 16 Sept. 1943). Irish tenor. Won gold medal for singing in 1904; then studied with Sabatini in Milan. Début Savona 1906 as Fritz; London, C.G., 1907 as Turiddu; N.Y., Manhattan Opera, 1909 as Alfredo. Sang with Boston, Philadelphia-Chicago, and Met. Opera Companies. Created Lieut. Paul Merrill in Victor Herbert's *Natoma* (1911). Gave up opera after 1913, being on his own admission a poor actor, and devoted rest of his life to concert work. Repertory of 21 roles, of which the most famous were Don Ottavio, Rodolfo, Elvino, Edgardo, and the Duke of Mantua. His exquisite phrasing, impeccable breath control, and pure, limpid voice made him one of the outstanding singers of his day. His autobiography *John McCormack: His Life Story* was published in 1919; and a biography, *I Hear You Calling Me*, was written by his widow (1949). Discography publ. by L. F. X. McDermott Roe (1956). (R)

MacCunn, Hamish (b. Greenock, 22 Mar. 1868; d. London, 2 Aug. 1916). Scottish composer. MacCunn's influences were basically Germanic; and his own talent, though considerable, was not profound enough to reconcile them with the Scottish musical cause so dear to his heart. The *rapprochement* is most successfully achieved in the opera *Jeanie Deans* (1894) and to a lesser extent in *Diarmid* (1897). Latterly he moved away from Scottish interests, and two later light operas are undistinctive. Conducted C.G. 1910 with Beecham Company and later with C.R.

MacFarren, George (b. London, 2 Mar. 1813; d. London, 31 Oct. 1887). English composer. Produced four successful operas in London. Later Professor of Music at Cambridge (1875) and then Principal, R.A.M. (1876). Knighted 1883. His wife **Natalia MacFarren** (b. Lübeck, 1827; d. Bakewell, Derbyshire, 9 Apr. 1916) was a contralto (she appeared in her husband's *Charles II* in 1849) and a gifted translator of operas and *Lieder*.

M'Guckin, Barton (b. Dublin, 28 July 1852; d. Stoke Poges, 17 Apr. 1913). Irish tenor. Studied Armagh, Dublin, and Milan. Appeared in concerts from 1874; stage début Birmingham with Carl Rosa 1880. Remained with C.R. until 1887, creating Phoebus in G. Thomas's *Esmeralda* (1883), Orso in Mackenzie's *Colomba* (1883), Waldemar in G. Thomas's *Nadeshda* (1885), Oscar in Corder's *Nordissa* (1887). The first Des Grieux (Massenet) in England (Liverpool). Appeared in U.S.A. 1887–8; rejoined C.R. 1889–96. (R)

Macintyre, Margaret (b. India, *c.* 1865; d. London, Apr. 1943). British soprano. Studied London with Garcia. Début C.G. 1888, Micaëla, and sang there until 1897. Her repertory included Donna Elvira, Senta, and Elisabeth. Created Rebecca in Sullivan's *Ivanhoe* at Royal English Opera (1891) and also appeared with success at La Scala (she was the first Sieglinde there), and in St. Petersburg and Moscow.

Ma dall' arido stelo divulsa. Amelia's (sop.) aria that opens Act 2 of Verdi's *Un Ballo in Maschera*, when she has come to a lonely spot to pick a herb to cure her love for Riccardo.

Madama Butterfly. Opera in 2 acts by Puccini; text by Giacosa and Illica, after David Belasco's drama (1900) on the story by John Luther Long, possibly based on a real event. Prod. Milan, Sc., 17 Feb. 1904, with Storchio, Zenatello, De Luca, when it was a fiasco. New version (three acts) prod. Brescia, Grande, 28 May 1904, with Krusceniski, cond. Toscanini; London, C.G., 10 July 1905 with Destinn, Caruso, Scotti; Washington, D.C., Belasco Theatre, 15 Oct. 1906, by Savage Company.

Act 1. Goro (ten.), the Japanese marriage broker, is showing Pinkerton (ten.), lieutenant of the U.S. Navy, the little house he has leased for him and his Japanese child-bride, Cio-Cio-San (Madama Butterfly). The American Consul Sharpless (bar.) comes to see Pinkerton who tells him jokingly that he is going to marry in Japanese fashion for 999 years; and he drinks to the day he will marry an American girl. Sharpless warns Pinkerton that Butterfly really loves him and has renounced her religion to marry him. Butterfly (sop.) and her friends appear and the wedding ceremony takes place. In the midst of the celebrations the Bonze, a Japanese priest and her uncle, arrives and denounces her for giving up her religion. Pinkerton comforts the weeping Butterfly, and the act ends with an extended love duet.

Act 2. Scene 1. Three years have passed, and the faithful Butterfly still awaits Pinkerton. She tries to convince her servant Suzuki (mezzo) in the famous aria 'Un bel dì vedremo' that he will return. Sharpless now comes to see Butterfly with a letter from Pinkerton telling him that he is indeed returning. She is so thrilled with the prospect of seeing Pinkerton again that Sharpless is unable to tell her that Pinkerton will be bringing his new American wife. Goro appears with Prince Yamadori, a wealthy suitor. Sharpless tries to persuade her to accept Yamadori's proposal. He asks Butterfly what she would do if Pinkerton was never to return. She replies that she would kill herself, and then brings in the child she has borne Pinkerton. The harbour cannon announces the arrival of a ship—it is Pinkerton's. Butterfly, with Suzuki, decks the house with flowers; she then puts on her wedding dress, and they watch for Pinkerton's arrival. Night falls.

Act 2. Scene 2. After an intermezzo, the curtain rises to show Suzuki and the baby asleep, with Butterfly still waiting. Suzuki awakens and persuades her to rest. Pinkerton now arrives, and when Suzuki sees the American woman with him she guesses the truth. He sings a farewell to the little dwelling he had loved so well, and thrusting some money into Sharpless's hand leaves him to resolve the situation as best he can. Butterfly enters, and seeing Suzuki in tears, and then Kate Pinkerton, realizes what has happened. Kate begs her to let them have the child, and Butterfly agrees on condition that Pinkerton comes to collect him. Butterfly bids him a tearful farewell and then stabs herself. As she falls dying to the floor, Pinkerton's voice is heard calling her name. He enters the house to fetch his son just as Butterfly expires.

Madame Sans-Gêne. Opera in 3 acts by Giordano; text by Simoni after the drama by Sardou and Moreau. Prod. N.Y., Met., 25 Jan. 1915, with Farrar, Martinelli, Amato, cond. Toscanini; Turin, 28 Feb. 1915. The story of Catherine Huebscher (the laundress, later Duchess of Danzig), Napoleon Bonaparte, and Lefebvre.

Madamina. Leporello's (bass) 'catalogue aria' in Act 1, scene 2, of Mozart's *Don Giovanni* enumerating Giovanni's conquests to Donna Elvira.

Maddalena. Sparafucile's sister (mezzo) in Verdi's *Rigoletto*.

Madeira (orig. Browning), **Jean** (b. Centralia, Ill., 14 Nov. 1924). American mezzo-soprano. Studied Juilliard School. Début Chautauqua as Jean Browning 1943. N.Y., Met., 1948. Sang Carmen, Puerto Ricco 1954, and in Vienna, Aix-en-Provence, Munich. London, C.G., 1955, Erda; Bayreuth same year; Salzburg 1956, Klytemnestra. Possesses a rich dark voice and is a compelling stage figure (R)

Madeleine de Coigny. Heroine (sop.) of Giordano's *Andrea Chénier*.

Madre, pietosa Vergine. Leonora's (sop.) prayer in Act 2, scene 2, of Verdi's *La Forza del Destino*.

Madrid. Capital of Spain. The first Spanish opera was Hidalgo's *Celos aun del Ayre Matan* (*Jealousy Even of the Air is Deadly*) (Madrid 1660). The first Italian opera house in Spain was the Teatro de los Canos de Peral, in Madrid, inaugurated in 1738 with Hasse's *Demetrio*. That year Corselli's *Alessandro nell'Indie* was written for the wedding of Charles IV of Naples (later King of Spain) and produced at the Palacio Real Buen Retiro. Opera here was controlled by Farinelli, whose cure of Philip IV's melancholy brought him honours including the managership of the court theatre, to which he invited many Italian artists. Farinelli's friend Conforton wrote his *Nitteti* especially for the Retiro, where it was produced for Ferdinand VI's birthday in 1756. The Teatro Real was inaugurated in 1850; the Teatro del Zarzuela in 1856; the Teatro Lirico in 1902 (with Chapí's *Circe*). See *Zarzuela*.

Madrigal Opera. A sequence of madrigals in dramatic form, one of the 16th-century forerunners of opera. The most famous example is Vecchi's *Amfiparnasso* (1594). Revived by Menotti in *The Unicorn, the Gorgon, and the Manticore*.

Mad Scene. A scene in which the heroine lost her reason, generally with tragic results, occurred in many Italian operas of the 19th century. The most famous is in Donizetti's *Lucia di Lammermoor*. Other mad scenes occur in the same composer's *Anna Bolena* and *Linda di Chamounix*, in Bellini's *I Puritani* and in Thomas's *Hamlet*. Madness or mental derangement of one sort or another is also depicted in Strauss's *Elektra*, Berg's *Wozzeck*, and Stravinsky's *The Rake's Progress*. The convention is satirized in Sullivan's *Ruddigore* (Mad Meg).

Maestro (It. = master). A courtesy title given to composers, conductors, and even impresarios in Italy. The *Maestro al cembalo* used to sit at the harpsichord and play the accompaniment to the recitatives. The *Maestro di cappella* was orig. the equivalent of the German Kapellmeister (q.v.) but today the term is used only with reference to religious music. The *Maestro sostituto* is a coach or répétiteur.

Maeterlinck, Maurice (b. Ghent, 29 Aug. 1862; d. Nice, 6 May 1949). Belgian writer. Operas on his works are as follows. *Ariane et Barbe-Bleue* (1901): Dukas (1907). *Alladine et Palomides* (1894): Chlubna (1925); E. Burian (1923); Burghauser (1944). *La Mort de Tintagiles* (1894): Nougès (1905); Collingwood. *Pelléas et Mélisande* (1892): Debussy (1902). *Monna Vanna* (1902): E. Ábrányi (1907); Février (1909). *Sœur Béatrice*: Rasse, Grechaninov, Marquez Puig. *Les Sept Princesses*: Nechayev. *L'Intruse*: Pannain (1940).

Magdalene. Eva's nurse (sop.) in Wagner's *Die Meistersinger*.

Magda Sorel. The heroine (sop.) of Menotti's *The Consul.*

Maggio Musicale Fiorentino. The annual May Festival in Florence was established in 1933, largely due to the initiative of Vittorio Gui (q.v.) who had, in 1928, founded the Florence Orchestra round which the festival was built. Originally planned as a biennial event, it became a yearly festival in 1938, and has continued as such ever since, apart from a wartime interruption, 1943–7. Opera performed in the Teatro Comunale, Teatro Pergola, and in the Boboli Gardens is the chief attraction of the festival. Verdi and Rossini are the composers who have contributed most to the festival's success, though it has also been the organizers' aim to include works by Bellini, Cherubini, Donizetti, and Spontini, and occasionally by contemporary Italian composers, as well as works by Mozart and Wagner generally performed by visiting companies from Germany and Austria.

Magic Flute, The. See *Zauberflöte.*

Mahagonny. See *Aufstieg und Fall der Stadt Mahagonny.*

Mahler, Gustav (b. Kalište, 7 July 1860; d. Vienna, 18 May 1911). Austrian composer and conductor. Studied Vienna. Début as conductor Summer Theatre, Bad Hall, 1880. Appointments followed at Ljubljana 1881; Olomouc 1882–3; Kassel 1884; Prague 1885 (where Seidl was first conductor and where Mahler gave notable performances of *The Ring*); Leipzig 1886–8 (under Nikisch); Budapest 1888–91 (as director—originally engaged for ten years, but he resigned after two owing to insuperable difficulties); Hamburg 1891–7; Vienna 1897–1907 (appointed conductor in May 1897, director July 1897, and artistic director Oct. 1897). Also conducted London, C.G., 1892, first *Ring* cycle at that theatre and other German works, and D.L.; N.Y., Met., 1907–10, including first American performances of *The Bartered Bride* and *The Queen of Spades.* It was during his ten years at the Vienna Opera that Mahler's true greatness as a conductor and director was revealed. He was an ardent perfectionist ('Tradition ist Schlamperei (slovenliness)' he said at the outset) and aimed always at the ideal performance. He built up an ensemble of singers who brought to the Vienna Opera some of its greatest glories; they included Gutheil-Schoder, Kurz, Mildenburg, Weidt, Mayr, Slezak, Schmedes, Winkelmann, Weidemann; his chief designer was Alfred Roller. Mahler's newly studied productions in Vienna included *The Ring, Figaro, Così, Entführung, Don Giovanni,* and *Zauberflöte* (these five for Mozart's 150th birthday celebrations), *Fidelio, Aida, Falstaff, Die lustigen Weiber, Louise, Der Corregidor, Taming of the Shrew* (Götz), *Iphigénie en Aulide.* He had many enemies during his period in Vienna—he was Jewish, dictatorial, and he spent lavishly on productions—yet he succeeded in wiping out the deficit which the Opera had accumulated, and raising the performances to a standard rarely if ever equalled anywhere in the world. His two early operas *Die Argonauten* and *Herzog Ernst von Schwaben* remain unpublished. He completed and scored Weber's *Die drei Pintos.*

Maid of Pskov, The (also known as Ivan the Terrible). Opera in 4 acts by Rimsky-Korsakov; text by composer, after Mey's drama (1860). Prod. St. Petersburg 13 Jan. 1873 (revised Moscow 1898, with new prologue); London, D.L., 8 July 1913, with Chaliapin. The Tsar terrorizes Novgorod; the inhabitants of Pskov unite against him and Olga and her lover Tucha are killed. She turns out to have been Tsar Ivan's daughter.

Maid of the Mill, The. *Pasticcio* in 3 acts arranged by Samuel Arnold; text by Bickerstaffe, after Richardson's 'series of familiar letters', *Pamela* (1740). Prod. London, C.G., 31 Jan. 1765; N.Y. 4 May 1769. The first English work since Purcell in which concerted music was used to accompany stage action, and the first of Arnold's many stage pieces. It drew upon music by 18 composers.

Maillart, Aimé (orig. Louis) (b. Montpellier, 24 Mar. 1817; d. Moulins, 26 May 1871). French composer. The best known of his six operas was *Les Dragons de Villars* (1856), often performed in Germany as *Das Glöckchen des Eremiten*.

Mainz. Town in the Rhineland-Palatinate, Germany. Opera is given in the new city theatre (cap. 1,100), opened 1951.

Maio, Giovanni Francesco di (b. Naples, 24 Mar. 1732; d. Naples, Nov. 1770). Italian composer. Known by his many operas as a typical representative of the Neopolitan school.

Maiorano, Gaetano. See *Caffarelli*.

Maître de Chapelle, Le. Opera in 2 parts by Paer; text by Sophie Gay, after Duval's comedy *Le Souper Imprévu* (1796). Prod. Paris, O.C., 29 Mar. 1821; London, C.G., 13 June 1845; N.Y. 25 June 1852. Paer's most successful work.

Makropoulos Affair, The. (Cz., Věc Makropulos). Opera in 3 acts by Janáček; text by composer, after Karel Čapek's drama. Prod. Brno 18 Dec. 1926; London, S.W., 12 Feb. 1964; San Francisco, 19 Nov. 1966. The famous singer Emilia Marty intervenes in a lawsuit concerning some events of 300 years previously and shows first-hand knowledge of the case. She proves to be the victim of a process, invented at that time, for prolonging life, and to be unable to die until she finds the formula. Others, convinced of the truth of her story, are eager to share the secret; but for her, life has grown to be an intolerable burden, every pleasure hopelessly staled. In the end the formula is burnt, and she dies.

Malatesta. Pasquale's friend (bar.) in Donizetti's *Don Pasquale*.

Malherbe, Charles (b. Paris, 21 Apr. 1853; d. Corneilles, 5 Oct. 1911). French musicologist and composer. Assistant archivist Paris, O., 1896; archivist 1898. Author of books on Wagner, Mozart, Auber, *opéra comique*, and the Salle Favart. Composer of several *opéras comiques*. Owner of a great collection of musical autographs, now in the Conservatoire.

Malheurs d'Orphée, Les. Opera in 3 acts by Milhaud; text by Armand Lunel. Prod. Brussels, La M., 7 May 1926; N.Y., T.H., 29 Jan. 1927; London, St. Pancras Town Hall, 8 Mar. 1960. Orpheus is a chemist with animals for clients. He takes his lover Eurydice to the mountains where, in spite of all he and his animals can do to help her, she dies.

Malibran (orig. Garcia), **Maria** (b. Paris, 24 Mar. 1808; d. Manchester, 23 Sept. 1836). Spanish mezzo-contralto. Daughter of Manuel Garcia (q.v.) with whom she studied. Appeared aged five at Naples in the child's role in Paer's *Agnese*. Début London, King's T., 1825, Rosina. During her first season sang Felicia in the London première of Meyerbeer's *Il Crociato in Egitto*. N.Y. 1825–7 with her father's opera company, singing in Mozart and Rossini works; while in N.Y. married François Eugène Malibran, from whom she was soon separated. Returned to Europe and enjoyed a series of unparalleled triumphs in Paris, London, Milan, Rome, Naples, and Bologna. In 1830 she formed an attachment with the Belgian violinist De Bériot whom she married in 1836. In London in 1833 and 1834 she sang at C.G. and D.L. in English (Amina, Leonore in *Fidelio*); D.L. 1836 creating title role in Balfe's *The Maid of Artois*. She was also a renowned Norma, in which character a statue of her by Geefs was erected in a mausoleum built by her husband in Laeken, Belgium. She died of serious injuries received when she was thrown from her horse in Apr. 1836. She concealed her injuries and insisted on singing at the Manchester Festival in Sept. that year. Her voice was that of a contralto with a soprano register added, but with an interval of dead notes in between, which she had learned to conceal with great skill. Its chief attraction seems to have lain in the unusual colour and extent of her voice, and in her excitable temperament. She has been the subject of several biographies and tributes, including Musset's famous *Stances* and

Pougin's *Marie Malibran: The Story of a Great Singer* (London, 1911). Also the heroine of Robert R. Bennett's 3-act opera, *Maria Malibran.*

Maliella. The heroine (sop.) in Wolf-Ferrari's *I Gioielli della Madonna.*

Malipiero, Gian Francesco (b. Venice, 18 Mar. 1882). Italian composer. His great knowledge and love of old music has found practical expression in editorial work on complete editions of Monteverdi and Vivaldi, and has also deeply influenced his composing style. Though contemporary in spirit and outlook he owes much in his technique to modal harmony, dislike of counterpoint or thematic development, and great rhythmic freedom following syllabic declamation. His long list of operas, many of which were first produced outside Italy, includes *Canossa* (1914), the trilogies *L'Orfeide* (1925) and *Il Mistero di Venezia* (1932), seven nocturnes *Torneo Notturno* (1931), *Giulio Cesare* (1936), *Antonio e Cleopatra* (1938), *Ecuba* (1941), *I Capricci di Callot* (1942), *La Vita è Sogno* (1943), six novels in one drama *L'Allegra Brigata* (1950), '*tre atti con sette donne*', *Mondi Celesti e Inferni* (1950), *Il Figliuol Prodigo* (1953), and *Venere Prigioniera* (1957).

Malipiero, Riccardo (b. Milan, 24 July 1914). Italian composer and critic, nephew of the preceding. He has written one opera in the 12-note system, of which he is a firm advocate, *Minnie la Candida* (1942), and an opera-buffa, *La Donna è Mobile* (1954).

Mallinger (orig. Lichtenegger), **Mathilde** (b. Zagreb, 17 Feb. 1847; d. Berlin, 19 Apr. 1920). Croatian soprano. Studied Zagreb, Prague, Vienna. Début Munich 1866, Norma. Created Eva (*Meistersinger*) 1868; Berlin Opera 1869–82, where in 1871 she became rival of Pauline Lucca (q.v.). Quarrels and intrigues resulted, culminating in a performance of *Figaro* (1872) in which they both appeared. Lucca was hissed on her entrance, as a result of which she broke her contract. Professor of singing Prague 1890–5, Berlin from 1895. Her pupils included Lotte Lehmann.

Malten (orig. Müller), **Therese** (b. Insterburg, 21 June 1855; d. Nauzschieren, Saxony, 2 Jan. 1930). German soprano. Studied Berlin with Engel. Début Dresden 1873, Pamina; leading soprano there for 30 years. Bayreuth 1882, Kundry (alternating with Materna and Brandt), and until 1894; also heard there as Isolde. London, D.L., 1882, Leonore, Elsa, Elisabeth, Eva.

Mamelles de Tirésias, Les. *Opéra-bouffe* in 2 acts by Poulenc; text by Guillaume Apollinaire. Prod. Paris, O.C., 3 June 1947, with Denise Duval; Brandeis Univ. 13 June 1953; Aldeburgh 16 June 1958, with Jennifer Vyvyan and Peter Pears. The surrealist plot deals with a husband and wife changing sexes; he produces 40,000 children before reverting to masculinity and advising his audience to proliferate.

Manchester. Town in Lancashire, England. The first theatre in Manchester was built in 1753 and in 1775 the first Theatre Royal was approved by Parliament. Opera was provided by touring companies and operatic excerpts in the 'Gentlemen's Concerts' until Hallé conducted a season of operas at the Theatre Royal in 1855, including *Fidelio*, *Don Giovanni*, *Der Freischütz*, *Robert le Diable*, *Les Huguenots*, *Lucrezia Borgia*, and *La Favorite*. He followed this with concert performances at the Free Trade Hall of *Fidelio*, *Die Zauberflöte*, and Gluck's *Armide*, *Iphigénie en Tauride*, which he also took to London, and *Orfeo ed Euridice*. The performances of *Iphigénie* and *Orfeo* were the first in English. Opera was also provided by the Rouseby and Carl Rosa companies. The latter began its existence in England with a performance in Manchester of *Maritana* on 1 Sept. 1873. After Hallé's death opera was again only provided by touring companies and by ambitious amateurs, though in 1897 Cowen conducted *Les Troyens à Carthage* after giving the first British performance at Liverpool earlier in the same year. Between 1916 and 1919 Thomas Beecham presented an ambitious series of opera seasons at the New Queen's Theatre, and it seemed as though Manchester would rival London as an operatic centre until Beecham's enforced withdrawal in 1920, when touring companies again took over. Since then amateur opera has flourished, and seasons have been given by C.G. and S.W., and Italian companies, at the Palace Theatre, Opera House, and occasionally at the Hippodrome, Free Trade Hall, and suburban theatres. The following operas have had their first performances in Manchester: Loder's *Raymond and Agnes* (1855), Nicholas Gatty's *Duke or Devil* (1909), Campbell's *Thais and Talmaae* (1921), Holst's *At the Boar's Head* (1925), and Walter Leigh's *Jolly Roger* (1933). Foreign works performed for the first time in Britain at Manchester theatres include Bizet's *Djamileh* (1892) and *La Jolie Fille de Perth* (1917), Gluck's *Le Cadi Dupé* (1893), and Puccini's *La Bohème* and *Le Villi* (both 1897).

Mancinelli, Luigi (b. Orvieto, 5 Feb. 1848; d. Rome, 2 Feb. 1921). Italian conductor and composer. Studied at Florence and led the cello section at the Teatro della Pergola, Florence, and Teatro Apollo, Rome, where in 1874 he was called on to fill the place of an absent conductor in *Aida*. After engagements in various Italian cities, conducted a concert in London in 1886 on the strength of which he was engaged by Harris as chief conductor at D.L., 1887, and C.G., 1888–1905, where he conducted the first performances in England of *Falstaff*, *Werther*, *Henri VIII* (Saint-Saëns), *Tosca*, *Much Ado About Nothing* (Stanford), as well as his own *Ero e Leandro* and many of the De Reszke Wagner performances in Italian. He was music director of the Theatre Royal, Madrid, 1888–95, and principal Italian conductor at the N.Y. Met. 1893–1903, directing the first Met. performances of *Werther*, *Falstaff*, *Samson et Dalila*, *Le Cid*, *Die Zauberflöte*, *La Bohème*, *Tosca*, and *Ernani*. As well as *Ero e Leandro*, his operas included *Isora di Provenza* and *Paolo e Francesca*.

Mancini, Francesco (b. Naples, 1679; d. Naples, 11 June 1739). Italian composer. His *Idaspe Fedele* was, with the anonymous *Almahide*, in 1710 the first opera to be sung in London wholly in Italian.

Mandryka. The rich landowner (bar.) who marries Arabella in Strauss's opera.

Manelli, Francesco (b. Tivoli, 1595; d. Parma, Sept. 1667). Italian composer and bass. In Feb. 1637 his *Andromeda* inaugurated the first public opera house in Italy, the Teatro San Cassiano in Venice. Manelli himself sang two parts on that occasion.

Manfredo. Fiora's husband (bar.) in Montemezzi's *L'Amore dei tre Re*.

Manhattan Opera Company. The company established by Oscar Hammerstein (q.v.) in 1906 at the Manhattan Opera House, West 34th Street, N.Y. Opened on 3 Dec. 1906 with *I Puritani*, with Bonci. The first season included the N.Y. débuts of Renaud and Bressler-Gianoli and appearances by Calvé and Melba. The 1907–8 season saw the American premières of *Thaïs*, *Louise*, and *Pelléas*, all with Mary Garden; the 1908–9 season included the N.Y. première of *Le Jongleur de Notre-Dame* and a revival of *Salome*; the 1909–10 season, the last, included the American premières of *Elektra* (in French), *Hérodiade*, *Sapho*, and *Grisélidis*. Other artists appearing with the company included Nordica, Tetrazzini, Schumann-Heink, Cavalieri, Zenatello, McCormack, Dalmorès. The company gave 463 performances of 49 operas during its four seasons; besides appearing in N.Y. it gave a weekly performance in Philadelphia, and also was seen in Baltimore.

Its success was so great as to threaten the Met., which finally offered Hammerstein $1,200,000 if he undertook to refrain from giving opera in N.Y. for ten years; he agreed to this proposal and signed a contract to that effect. He tried to break this in 1913 by building the Lexington Theatre, but was restrained by legal action from giving performances.

The Manhattan Opera House was used for the Chicago Opera's N.Y. seasons and other organizations. It was later sold to a Masonic order.

Manners, Charles (orig. Southcote Mansergh) (b. London, 27 Dec. 1857; d. Dublin, 3 May 1955). Irish bass and impresario. Studied Dublin and London and for a short time in Italy. Joined chorus of D'Oyly Carte Co. 1881; début Savoy Theatre, London, 1882, Private Willis (*Iolanthe*). Joined C.R. and then engaged C.G. 1890. Sang Gremin in English première of *Eugene Onegin* (1892). In 1897 he established the Moody-Manners Company (q.v.) with the soprano Fanny Moody, whom he had married in 1890. Appeared in U.S.A. 1893. Retired 1913.

Mannheim. Town in Baden-Württemberg, Germany. The Opera enjoyed a particularly prosperous period under the direction of V. Lachner 1837–72 and under August Nassermann 1895–1900. Music directors at Mannheim have included Weingartner (1889–91), Bodanzky (1909–15), Furtwängler (1915–20), Kleiber (1922–3), Elmendorff (1937–43). Among the works that had their premières at Mannheim are Wellesz's *Alkestis* (1923) and Orff's arrangement of Monteverdi's *Orfeo* (1925); while *Le Rossignol* and *Prince Igor* received their first German performances there, and in 1928 Verdi's *Nabucco* had its first German performance after many years of neglect. The National Theatre, built in 1779, was destroyed by bombs in 1943. The new National Theatre (cap. 1,200) was opened in Jan. 1957 with *Der Freischütz*. In 1963 Horst Stein was made Generalmusikdirektor.

Manon. Opera in 5 acts by Massenet; text by Meilhac and Gille, after Prévost's novel *Manon Lescaut* (1731). Prod. Paris, O.C., 19 Jan. 1884, with Marie Heilbronn and Talazac; Liverpool 17 Jan. 1885, with Marie Roze and M'Guckin; N.Y. Academy of Music 23 Dec. 1885, with Hauck and Giannini.

Act 1. In Amiens, Lescaut (bar.) awaits his cousin Manon (sop.) who is about to enter a convent. She arrives and sings of the sadness of giving up life and love. Des Grieux (ten.) is attracted to her, and persuades her to leave with him in a stolen coach for Paris.

Act 2. Lescaut is placated by evidence that Des Grieux intends to marry Manon. His companion de Brétigny (bar.) tries to persuade her to come away with him, insisting that Des Grieux's father will in any case break her romance. Manon takes a sentimental farewell of their life together in 'Adieu notre petite table'. Des Grieux returns from posting a letter to his father to find her in tears: he consoles her (the famous 'Rêve') but on answering the door is abducted by his father's men.

Act 3, scene 1. At a festival, Manon is gaily singing of her life of pleasure; but on hearing that Des Grieux is to enter the priesthood she rushes away to find him. Scene 2. Des Grieux is deaf to his father's plea not to reject life, but succumbs to Manon.

Act 4. With Manon, Des Grieux is gambling—so successfully that he is accused of cheating. The police arrive: Des Grieux is saved, but Manon is arrested as a prostitute.

Act 5. On the road to Le Havre, whence Manon is to be transported, Des Grieux bribes an officer and speaks to her. She is too ill to run away with him, and dies in his arms.

Ten years after *Manon*, Massenet wrote a one-act sequel, *Le Portrait de Manon* (1894). Other operas on the story are by Auber (1856), Kleinmichel (1887), and Puccini (see below).

Manon Lescaut. Opera in 4 acts by Puccini; text by Giacosa, Illica, Giulio Ricordi, Praga, and Oliva, after Prévost's novel (1731). Prod. Turin, T.R., 1 Feb. 1893, with Cesira Ferrani, Cremonini; London, C.G., 14 May 1894, with Olgina, Bedusche; Philadelphia, Grand Opera House, 29 Aug. 1894.

Act 1. Sitting outside an inn in Amiens, Des Grieux (ten.) is roused by the arrival of Manon (sop.) who is about to enter a convent. Géronte (bass) plans to abduct her, but it is Des Grieux who persuades her to fly to Paris with him—in Géronte's coach.

Act 2. Manon has deserted Des Grieux for Géronte, though with regrets at the exchange of love for wealth. Des Grieux's arrival sparks off bitter words that soon change to those of love. Géronte finds them, and leaves with a threat; and Manon's brother Lescaut (bar.) warns them that she is in danger from the police as an immoral woman. Delaying in order to collect her jewels, she is arrested.

Act 3. In Le Havre, where Manon is about to embark for exile, Des Grieux fails to bribe the guard but persuades the ship's captain to take him on the voyage.

Act 4. The lovers seek shelter in the desolate plain of New Orleans. Des Grieux leaves the weakened Manon to seek water, but on his return she dies in his arms.

Manon Lescaut was Puccini's third opera and first great success; at the première he took 50 curtain calls.

Manowarda, Josef von (b. Cracow, 3 July 1890; d. Berlin, 24 Dec. 1942). Austrian bass. Début Prague 1913; after engagements in Graz, Vienna V.O., and Wiesbaden was engaged Vienna, S.O., 1919–42. In his initial season in Vienna he created the role of the Geisterbote in Strauss's *Die Frau ohne Schatten*. He sang at Salzburg from 1922; at Bayreuth in 1931, 1934, and 1939; and at the Berlin State Opera 1934–42. His most famous roles were King Philip, Osmin, King Mark, and Gurnemanz. (R)

Manrico. A troubadour, hero (ten.) of Verdi's *Il Trovatore*.

Manru. Opera in 3 acts by Paderewski; text by Nossig, after Kraszewski's novel *The Cabin Behind the Wood* (1843). Prod. Dresden 29 May 1901; N.Y., Met., 14 Feb. 1902, with Sembrich. Against her mother's wishes, Ulana marries the gipsy Manru. She revives his love with a potion, but the gipsy girl Asa lures him back to his people. Ulana commits suicide and Manru, now chief of the tribe, is killed by Oros, the man he had deposed who himself loves Asa.

Mantelli, Eugenia (b. *c.* 1860; d. 9 Nov. 1926). Italian contralto. Début Lisbon 1883, Urbain. Joined N.Y., Met., 1894. The first N.Y. Dalila, and a famous Urbain, Amneris, and Ortrud. London, C.G., 1896, including Brünnhilde in a French *Walküre*. After leaving the Met. she sang in variety performances, then toured with her own company. In 1903 she joined Mascagni's company and subsequently toured with an English company. (R)

Mantua (It., Mantova). Town in Lombardy, Italy, where many early Italian operas, including Monteverdi's *Orfeo* and *Arianna*, were first produced. Opera is given today at the Teatro Sociale, built in 1822, which opened with Mercadante's *Alfonso ed Elisa*.

Man Without a Country, The. Opera in 2 acts by Damrosch; text by Guiterman, after Edward Everett Hale's story. Prod. N.Y., Met., 12 May 1937, with Traubel, Carron, cond. Damrosch. Subsequently prod. Chicago.

Mapleson, (Col.) James Henry (b. London, 4 May 1830; d. London, 14 Nov. 1901). English impresario, popularly known as 'The Colonel'. Studied London, R.A.M. Sang at Verona 1854 as Enrico Mariani. Began his career as impresario 1861 when he took the Lyceum after A. T. Smith, whose assistant he had been, abandoned Italian opera. Mapleson's first season included the English première of *Un Ballo in Maschera*. Managed H.M.'s, 1862–7; in 1868 he was at D.L.; in 1869 and 1870 he joined Gye at C.G. for the two famous 'coalition seasons' at that house; he was again at D.L. 1871–6, and in 1877 he reopened H.M.'s and continued to give seasons there until 1881. In 1885 and 1887 he gave his last seasons at C.G. and in 1887 and 1889 at H.M.'s. Promoted seasons at the Academy of Music, N.Y., 1878–96 and 1896–7, and he also took his company to other American cities.

Among the operas he produced for the first time in England were *Faust*, *Carmen*, *Ballo in Maschera*, *La Forza del Destino*, *Vêpres Siciliennes*, *Mefistofele*, and *Médée*. Singers he brought to London for the first time included Di Murska, Gerster, Nilsson, Scalchi,

Trebelli, Hauk, Nordica; Campanini, Fancelli, Ravelli, Jean de Reszke (as a baritone), Del Puente, and Pandolfini. The *Mapleson Memoirs* (London, 1888; reissued, 1966, ed. Rosenthal) give an amusing and highly coloured account of his operatic activities.

Mapleson, Lionel (b. London, 23 Oct. 1865; d. N.Y., 21 Dec. 1937). Violinist and librarian of the Met., N.Y. Son of Alfred Mapleson, music librarian and secretary to Queen Victoria, and nephew of J. H. Mapleson. He amassed an invaluable collection of operatic mementos (letters, autographs, programmes, Caruso caricatures, &c.), as well as the scores of all the operas given at the Met. since 1883, and the famous recordings on cylinders, made of a series of performances at the Met. early this century.

M'apparì. Italian translation of Lionel's (ten.) aria 'Ach, so fromm' in Act 3 of Flotow's *Martha*, in which he sings of his hopeless love for Martha.

Mara (orig. Schmeling), **Gertrud** (b. Kassel, 23 Feb. 1749; d. Reval, 20 Jan. 1833). German soprano. Studied London and Leipzig. Début Dresden; then in 1771 engaged by Frederick II for life at the Berlin Opera; she broke her Berlin engagement, however, in 1780 and sang in Paris and Vienna. London début 1786 in *Didone Abbandonata*. The following year scored great success as Cleopatra in Handel's *Giulio Cesare*. She sang at C.G. in 1790, earning special praise for her performance in Nasolini's *Andromaca*. Her voice ranged from g' to e''' and was of great beauty. She was an inferior actress.

Marais, Marin (b. Paris, 31 Mar. 1656; d. Paris, 15 Aug. 1728). French composer. Though most of his work is for viols, Marais produced several operas, of which the most successful (partly for its vivid representation of a storm) was *Alcyone* (1706).

Marcel (orig. Wasself), **Lucille** (b. New York, *c.* 1877; d. Vienna, 22 June 1921). American soprano. Studied N.Y., Berlin, and Paris with J. de Reszke. Début Vienna 1908 as Elektra in local première of that opera under Weingartner, whom she married in 1911. Also sang at Hamburg, Darmstadt, and Boston, where she sang title role in American première of *Djamileh* (1912). (R)

Marcellina. Rocco's daughter (sop.) in Beethoven's *Fidelio*.

Marcello. The bohemian painter (bar.) in Puccini's *La Bohème*.

Marchesi, Blanche (b. Paris, 4 Apr. 1863; d. London, 15 Dec. 1940). French soprano, daughter of Mathilde (below). Début Prague 1900, Brünnhilde. Sang with the Moody-Manners Company in England; later settled in London as a teacher. Her autobiography *A Singer's Pilgrimage* appeared in 1923. (R)

Marchesi de Castrone (orig. Graumann), **Mathilde** (b. Frankfurt a/M, 24 Mar. 1821; d. London, 17 Nov. 1913). German mezzo-soprano and teacher. Studied in Vienna with Nicolai and in Paris with Garcia, who was so impressed by her abilities that when an accident forced him to give up teaching he handed over all his pupils to her. Began career as a concert singer. Married Salvatore Marchesi (below) 1852. Professor of singing, Vienna, 1854–61 and 1869–78; Cologne Conservatory 1865–8. Set up own school in Paris 1861–5 and from 1881. Her pupils included Calvé, Di Murska, Eames, Gerster, Garden, Melba, and Sanderson. She wrote a method of singing and 24 books of exercises. Her memoirs *Marchesi and Music* appeared in 1897.

Marchesi, Salvatore, Cavaliere de Castrone, Marchese della Raiata (b. Palermo, 15 Jan. 1822; d. Paris, 20 Feb. 1908). Italian baritone and teacher. Studied Palermo and Milan with Lamperti and Fontana. Début N.Y., Carlos in *Ernani*. Returned to Europe to study with Garcia. Held various teaching posts in Vienna and Cologne. Translated into Italian the librettos of *La Vestale*, *Médée*, *Iphigénie*, *Lohengrin*, and *Tannhäuser*.

Marchisio, Barbara (b. Turin, 6 Dec. 1833; d. Mira, 19 Apr. 1919).

Italian contralto. Studied Turin. Début Vicenza 1856, Adalgisa. Sang all over Europe with success, including Paris (1860) and London, H.M.'s (1862). Her sister **Carlotta** (1835–72) often appeared with her and Rossini wrote his *Petite Messe Solennelle* for them. She later became a teacher and her pupils included Raisa and Dal Monte.

Marcoux, Vanni (orig. Jean Émile Diogène) (b. Turin, 12 June 1877; d. Paris, 22 Oct. 1962). French bass-baritone. Studied Paris. Début Bayonne 1889, Frère Laurent. After appearances in France and Belgium sang London, C.G., 1905–14, where he was the first English Arkel (*Pelléas*) (he returned to sing Golaud in 1937); Boston 1912; Chicago 1913–14 and 1926–32, where he was the first American Don Quichotte (Massenet), a role he had created at Monte Carlo 1910, and Colonno in Février's *Monna Vanna*, which he created in Paris 1909. He had a repertory of 240 roles. Taught at the Conservatoire 1938–43; director Grand Théâtre, Bordeaux, 1948–51. Made a few appearances in Paris, O.C., in the post-war years as Don Quichotte. (R)

Mařenka. The heroine (sop.) of Smetana's *The Bartered Bride*.

Maretzek, Max (b. Brno, 28 June 1821; d. New York, 14 May 1897). Czech, later American, composer, conductor, impresario. After playing the violin in various theatre orchestras, conducted in Germany and London. Engaged 1848 for Astor Place Opera House, N.Y., as conductor; later managed seasons there, the Ac. of M. and Niblo's Gardens. He presented a number of famous artists for the first time to the American public, including Patti (1859) and Hauk (1866), and introduced *Rigoletto*, *La Traviata*, *Il Trovatore*, *L'Africaine*, *Le Prophète*, *La Favorite*, *Linda di Chamounix*, *Don Pasquale*, and *Roméo et Juliette* to the American public. He was a picturesque and colourful figure, and his managerial career was full of trouble, with orchestra and chorus often on strike. He published two books of reminiscences: *Crotchets and Quavers, or Revelations of an Opera Manager in America* (1885), and *Sharps and Flats* (1870).

Marguerite. The heroine (sop.) of Gounod's *Faust*.

Marguerite de Valois. Henry IV's betrothed (sop.) in Meyerbeer's *Les Huguenots*.

Maria Antonia Walpurgis (b. Munich, 18 July 1724; d. Dresden, 23 Apr. 1780). German amateur composer, daughter of the Elector of Bavaria, later the Emperor Charles VII. Her most important works were two operas to her own librettos, *Il Trionfo della Fedeltà* (prod. 1754, after alterations and help by Metastasio and Hasse), and *Talestri, Regina delle Amazoni* (1760).

Maria di Rohan. Opera in 3 acts by Donizetti; text by Cammarano (orig. called *Il Conte di Chalais* and composed by Lillo 1839). Prod. Vienna, Kä., 5 June 1843; London, C.G., 8 May 1847, with Alboni and Ronconi; N.Y. 10 Dec. 1849. Revived Bergamo 1957.

Maria Egiziaca. Opera in 1 act (three episodes) by Respighi; text by C. Guastalla. Originally produced in concert form, N.Y., Carnegie Hall, 16 Mar. 1932. First stage production, Buenos Aires, Colón, 23 Jul. 1933 with Gilda dalla Rizza; London, Hyde Park Hotel, 11 Apr. 1937 (concert form).

Maria Golovin. Opera in 3 acts by Menotti; text by composer. Prod. Brussels, Pavilion Theatre, 20 Aug. 1958 with Franca Duval, cond. Peter Hermann Adler; N.Y., Martin Becket Theatre, 5 Nov. 1958.

Mariani, Angelo (b. Ravenna, 11 Oct. 1821; d. Genoa, 13 June 1873). Italian conductor and composer. Studied Ravenna, Rimini, and Bologna with Rossini. Début Messina 1844. Copenhagen 1847–8; Genoa, C.F., 1852–73, where he made the orchestra the best in Italy at that period. Conducted the Italian premières of *Lohengrin* and *Tannhäuser* and many important Verdi performances. The story of his friendship and subsequent breach with Verdi is admirably related in Frank Walker's *The Man Verdi.*

Marie. Wozzeck's mistress (sop.) in Berg's opera.

Marina. The Polish princess (mezzo) who marries the false Dimitri in Mussorgsky's *Boris Godunov.*

Marinuzzi, Gino (orig. Giuseppe) (b. Palermo, 24 Mar. 1882; d. Milan, 15 Aug. 1945). Italian conductor and composer. Studied Palermo. Début there. After engagements throughout Italy, including Palermo where he conducted the first performance there of *Tristan* in 1909, went to the Colón, Buenos Aires. Here he conducted the first local performance of *Parsifal,* 1913. Conducted the première of *La Rondine,* Monte Carlo, 1917. Succeeded Campanini at Chicago 1919–21. Chief conductor at Rome Opera 1928–34; at Sc. (with De Sabata) 1934–44. London, C.G., 1934. He wrote three operas, *Barberina* (Palermo 1903), *Jacquerie* (Buenos Aires 1918) and *Palla de' Mozzi* (Milan 1932). He was murdered by partisans in Milan in the uprising in Aug. 1945. His son **Gino Marinuzzi** (b. N.Y., 1920) is a composer; he also conducts occasionally at Rome. (R)

Mario, Giovanni (orig. Giovanni Matteo, Cavaliere di Candia) (b. Cagliari, 17 Oct. 1810; d. Rome, 11 Dec. 1883). Italian tenor. Eloped with a ballerina in 1836 to Paris, where he studied with Bordogni and Boncharde. Début Paris, O., 1838, Robert le Diable. Italian Opera in Paris 1840. Début London, H.M.'s, 1839, Gennaro (*Lucrezia Borgia*); sang there until 1846; C.G. 1847–67, returning to make farewell in 1871. With Grisi, whom he married in 1844, Tamburini, and Lablache, he sang in the première of *Don Pasquale* (1843). He was the first London Gennaro, Ernesto, Duke of Mantua, John of Leyden, and Roméo. Sang Don Giovanni as tenor, though otherwise an artistic singer. His voice was considered one of the most beautiful ever heard, and he sang with elegance and style. His handsome appearance and acting abilities made him the idol of Victorian opera-goers. After his retirement he soon became poverty-stricken, and a benefit concert was organized for him in London in 1880. His daughter, Mrs. Godfrey Pearce, and F. Hird wrote his biography, *The Romance of a Great Singer* (London, 1910).

Marionette Opera-Theatre. See *Puppet Opera.*

Maritana. Opera in 3 acts by Wallace; text by Edward Fitzball, after the drama *Don César de Bazan* by D'Ennery and Dumanoir. Prod. London, D.L., 15 Nov. 1845; Philadelphia 9 Nov. 1846.

Marlowe, Christopher (b. Canterbury, 6 Feb. 1564; d. Deptford, 30 May 1593). English poet and dramatist. Busoni's *Doktor Faust* (1925) is based on his *Dr. Faustus*; and he is the central figure of Mellers's *The Tragicall History of Christopher Marlowe* (comp. 1950–2).

Marmontel, Jean François (b. Bort, Limousin, 11 July 1723; d. Abloville, Eure, 31 Dec. 1799). French dramatist, librettist, and critic. He wrote librettos for Grétry and Rameau, and for Piccinni, with whom he sided against Gluck.

Mârouf, Savetier du Caire (Mârouf, Cobbler of Cairo). Opera in 4 acts by Rabaud; text by Népoty, after a story in Mardrus's French version of *The Arabian Nights.* Prod. Paris, O.C., 15 May 1914, with Jean Périer; N.Y., Met., 19 Dec. 1917, with De Luca. The cobbler Mârouf escapes his wife by going to sea. Shipwrecked, he is introduced by a friend to the Sultan as a wealthy merchant; he marries the Sultan's daughter and rifles his treasury, continually promising that his caravans will soon arrive. The princess loves him even when he confesses to her, and they flee. A magic ring provides them with a palace, and the pursuing Sultan forgives Mârouf on finding him surrounded by wealth. *Mârouf* was Rabaud's most successful opera.

Marquis de Brinvilliers, Le. Opera in 3 acts by Auber, Batton, Berton, Blangini, Boïeldieu, Carafa, Cherubini, Hérold, and Paer; text by Scribe and

Castil-Blaze. Prod. Paris, O.C., 31 Oct. 1831. The most famous of several collective works of the period.

Marriage, The. Unfinished opera by Mussorgsky; text after Gogol's comedy (1842). One act only completed in 1864; concert performance at Rimsky-Korsakov's house, 1906; stage performance with piano, St. Petersburg, Suvorin School, 1 Apr. 1909; first full prod., Petrograd 26 Oct. 1917, rev. Rimsky-Korsakov. Also opera in 1 act by Martinů, with text by the composer, after Gogol. N.B.C. Television Opera, 7 Feb. 1953; first stage performance, Hamburg 13 Mar. 1954.

Marriage of Figaro, The. See *Nozze di Figaro, Le.*

Marschallin (or **Feldmarschallin**). The Princess von Werdenberg (sop.) in Strauss's *Der Rosenkavalier*.

Marschner, Heinrich (b. Zittau, 16 Aug. 1795; d. Hanover, 14 Dec. 1861). German composer. After his early *Heinrich IV und Aubigné* (1820) had been produced by Weber at Dresden, he became joint Kapellmeister there (also with Morlacchi). Musikdirektor there 1824–6, but resigned on Weber's death and became Kapellmeister at Leipzig in the following year. Here he produced *Der Vampyr* (1828), a success there and in Britain, whither his thoughts turned with *Des Falkners Braut* (1832, ded. to William IV) and *Der Templer und die Jüdin* (1829), based on Scott. He moved to Hanover in 1831, where in 1833 he produced *Hans Heiling*, his masterpiece. Little else followed, though *Kaiser Adolf von Nassau* was produced in Dresden in 1845, Wagner conducting. Marschner is important in the history of German romantic opera. Though lacking Weber's imaginative penetration and lyrical gift, he possessed real dramatic feeling. His harmonic sense and gift for vivid orchestration were well adapted to express the supernatural side of Romanticism. In spite of his penchant for the macabre, he possessed an equally typical Romantic love of nature and peasant life that comes out in the comic episodes of his operas.

Marseilles (Fr., Marseille). Town in Provence, France. The first opera given there was Gautier's *Le Triomphe de la Paix* in Jan. 1685. The Grand Théâtre was opened in Oct. 1787 with Champein's *La Mélomanie*, and opera was given there regularly until it was destroyed by fire in 1919. The present theatre (cap. 2,300) dates from 1924.

Martern aller Arten. Constanze's (sop.) aria in Act 2 of Mozart's *Entführung*, in which she declares that neither torture nor death itself will make her yield to the Pasha. Written for Katharina Cavalieri, it holds up the action but is the finest number in the score.

Martha, oder Der Markt von Richmond. Opera in 4 acts by Flotow; text by W. Friedrich (Friedrich Wilhelm Riese), after Vernoy de Saint-Georges's ballet-pantomime *Lady Henriette ou La Servante de Greenwich*, to which Flotow had contributed some music. Prod. Vienna, Kä., 25 Nov. 1847, with Anna Kerr; London, D.L., 4 July 1849; N.Y., Niblo's Garden, 1 Nov. 1852, with Anna Bishop.

Act 1, scene 1. Lady Harriet (sop.), Maid of Honour to Queen Anne, is tired of court life and bored by her cousin, Lord Tristan de Mikelford (bass). She suggests that she, Tristan, and her maid Nancy (con.) should visit the Fair at Richmond in disguise. The two ladies go as the country girls Martha and Julia, Tristan as a farmer, John.

Act 1, scene 2. At the fair the Sheriff (bass) reads from a parchment that all contracts for the hiring of servants made at the fair are binding for at least a year. Lionel (ten.) and his foster-brother Plunkett (bass), two young farmers, offer to hire the girls; they accept as a joke, and find to their dismay that the contract is binding.

Act 2. Back in Plunkett's farm house the new servants are told to prepare the supper and try their hand at spinning. It is not long before Lionel has fallen in love with Martha and Plunkett with Nancy. Martha sings 'The Last Rose of Summer' for her master, and the four bid each other goodnight. The two men retire, and then a tap at the window is heard; it is Tristan with his carriage. The two girls escape.

Act 3. A royal hunt is in progress. Outside an inn Plunkett sings the praises of English Porter ale. Nancy is recognized by Plunkett as Julia. Lionel, sad at the loss of his love, enters. Lady Harriet, who now arrives on the scene, disclaims all knowledge of him, and when he upbraids her for treating him so cruelly and breaking the contract made at the fair she calls her attendants to arrest him.

Act 4. Lionel has a ring, bequeathed him when a child with instructions that he should send it to the Queen if ever in trouble. He is now freed, being none other than heir to the Earl of Derby. Lady Harriet, realizing that she truly loves Lionel, tries to make amends, but Lionel will have none of her; Plunkett and Nancy, now happy together, plan a reconciliation. A replica of Richmond Fair is set up in Lady Harriet's own garden. There once again Lionel sees Martha in her humble clothes, and is happily united to her.

Martin, Frank (b. Geneva, 15 Sept. 1890). Swiss composer. Apart from his dramatic oratorio *Le Vin Herbé* (1941), based on the Tristram legend, Martin's only opera is *Der Sturm* (1956), a word-for-word setting of *The Tempest* in Schlegel's translation. The poetry is sometimes allowed to stand unaccompanied, sometimes set in a *parlando* style resembling but not rivalling *Pelléas*. The music is most effective in Shakespeare's least poetic scenes.

Martin, Jean-Blaise (b. Paris, 24 Feb. 1768; d. Ronzières, 28 Oct. 1837). French baritone. Début Paris 1788, singing in various theatres there including the O.C. until 1823. Subsequently taught at the Conservatoire. His voice was of extraordinary range and gave the name to the type of French baritone known as Baritone Martin. See *Baritone*.

Martin, Riccardo (orig. Hugh Whitfield Martin) (b. Hopkinsville, Kentucky, 18 Nov. 1874; d. N.Y., 11 Aug. 1952). American tenor. Studied N.Y. and Paris with Escalais and Sbriglia, and Florence with Lombardi. Début Nantes 1904, Faust. New Orleans 1906; N.Y., Met., 1907–13; Boston 1916–17; Chicago 1920–2; London, C.G., 1910–11. A famous Puccini singer. At Met. created leading tenor roles in *The Pipe of Desire*, *Mona*, and *Cyrano de Bergerac*. (R)

Martín y Soler, Vicente (b. Valencia, 18 June 1754; d. St. Petersburg, 30 Jan. 1806). Spanish composer. After a successful début with an opera in Naples, he went to Vienna, where he found in Da Ponte his ideal librettist (the admiration was reciprocated). The best known of their first three operas was *Una Cosa Rara* (1786), quoted by Mozart (to whom Martín was reckoned a rival) in the Supper Scene of *Don Giovanni*. In St. Petersburg from 1788, he became Catherine II's court composer, writing operas to two of her librettos. He went to London in 1794, where he again collaborated with Da Ponte, though less successfully. He returned to Russia about 1798, and spent his last years as a singing teacher.

Martinelli, Giovanni (b. Montagnana, 22 Oct. 1885; d. N.Y., 2 Feb. 1969). Italian tenor. Voice discovered by army bandmaster while on military service. Studied Milan. Début Milan, T.D.V., 1910, Ernani. Heard by Puccini who engaged him for European première of *La Fanciulla del West* (Rome 1911). London, C.G., 1912–14, 1919, and 1937; N.Y., Met., 1913–46, during which time he sang in more than 50 operas, including the world première of *Madame Sans-Gêne*, the American premières of *Francesca da Rimini*, *La Campana Sommersa*, *Simone Boccanegra*, and *Goyescas*, and the first Met. performances of *Oberon* and *Gioielli della Madonna*. Late in his career he became a fine Otello and Eleazar, and in Chicago in 1939 he sang Tristan opposite Flagstad. His voice was sterling silver rather than golden, not very large in size but used with impeccable style and faultless technique. (R)

Martinů, Bohuslav (b. Polička, 8 Dec. 1890; d. Liestal, 29 Aug. 1959).

Czech composer. He wrote, in the course of his large output, a dozen operas: only the clever, economical *Comedy on the Bridge* (1951) has had a wide success, but *The Marriage*, originally written for N.B.C. Television, has been produced in several European theatres. Though infallibly skilful, the music even here lacks either dramatic directness or psychological penetration, making its effect more by deft musical underlining of an amusing situation.

Masaniello. See *Muette de Portici, La.*

Mascagni, Pietro (b. Leghorn, 7 Dec. 1863; d. Rome, 2 Aug. 1945). Italian composer and conductor. Studied Leghorn, and Milan Conservatory under Ponchielli. Unwilling to submit to the regular discipline of the Conservatory, he left to join a touring opera company as a conductor; he then settled in Cerignola as a piano teacher. In 1890 he won first prize in a competition sponsored by the publishers Sanzogno with his 1-act *Cavalleria Rusticana* (1890). This melodramatic *verismo* opera of love and hatred in Sicily speedily swept Europe and started the vogue for similar 1-act works. Despite the fact that Mascagni wrote more than a dozen other works, his fame rests solely on *Cavalleria. L'Amico Fritz* (1891) contains some charming pastoral passages, but is very slight musically; *Iris* (1898) has an unsavoury libretto but shows some originality in orchestration; *Le Maschere* (1901) had a brief and stormy career (see below); *Isabeau* (1911), based on the story of Lady Godiva, enjoyed a short-lived success; and *Il Piccolo Marat* (1921), which many musicians consider his best work, is very rarely played outside Italy. Mascagni was a not inconsiderable opera conductor and allowed himself to become the musical mouthpiece of Fascist Italy, composing his *Nerone* for La Scala with Mussolini in mind, and choral and orchestral works for various political occasions. As a result many Italian musicians, including Toscanini, broke off relations with him; and he spent the last few years of his life in comparative poverty and disgrace in a Rome hotel. (R)

Maschere, Le (The Masks). Opera in a prologue and 3 acts by Mascagni; text by Illica. Prod. simultaneously in six Italian cities, 17 Jan. 1901. In Milan (where it was conducted by Toscanini), Venice, Turin, and Verona it was hissed; in Genoa it was not allowed to be completed; only in Rome, where Mascagni conducted it, did it meet with any kind of favour. It is a *commedia dell'arte* opera, and has had a few revivals.

Mascherini, Enzo (b. Florence, 6 Aug. 1910). Italian baritone. Studied Florence and with Ruffo and Stracciari. Début Florence 1937, Germont. Sang at Sc. and other leading Italian opera houses, and in 1946 in Mexico. N.Y., C.C., 1946–7; Met. 1949–50; London, Stoll, 1953. Specially noted as a Verdi baritone; has sung Monforte at the Florence Festival and Macbeth at La Scala. (R)

Mascheroni, Edoardo (b. Milan, 4 Sept. 1852; d. Como, 4 Mar. 1941). Italian conductor and composer. Début Leghorn 1883; Rome, Teatro Apollo, 1885–92, where he conducted the first performance in Italy of *Fidelio*; Milan, Sc., 1892–5, where he conducted the premières of *La Wally* and, at Verdi's request, of *Falstaff*. He also directed the first Scala performances of *Tannhäuser*, *Fliegende Holländer*, and *Walküre*. He then conducted in Germany, Spain, and South America. His *Lorenza* (libretto by Illica) was produced in Rome in 1901, and his *La Perugina* (libretto again by Illica) at Naples in 1909.

Mascotte, La. Operetta in 3 acts by Audran; text by Duru and Chivot. Prod. Paris, B.-P., 28 Dec. 1880 (1,000 perfs. by 1885); N.Y., Abbey's Park Theatre, 5 May 1881; Brighton, 19 Sept. 1881. Audran's most popular work.

Masetto. The peasant (bar.) betrothed to Zerlina in Mozart's *Don Giovanni*.

Masini, Angelo (b. Terra del Sole, nr. Forlì, 28 Nov. 1844; d. Forlì, 28 Sept. 1926). Italian tenor. Début

Modena 1868, Pollione. After appearances in the Italian provinces, Spain, St. Petersburg, &c., was chosen by Verdi for the tenor role in the *Requiem*, which he sang in London, Paris, and Vienna under the composer's baton; also sang Radamès under Verdi in Paris. Engaged by Mapleson for London 1879, but owing to a misunderstanding never appeared, and was prevented by Mapleson from singing under any other management in London. Verdi offered to write an extended aria for him if he would create the role of Fenton in *Falstaff*—Masini refused.

Masini, Galliano (b. Leghorn, 1902). Italian tenor. Début 1924, Cavaradossi. Leading tenor Rome Opera 1930–50; also sang at La Scala, but with little success, though chosen by Mascagni to sing Turiddu in the 50th anniversary celebrations there of *Cavalleria Rusticana*. Sang with much success Chicago 1937–8, and N.Y., Met., 1938–9. Loris (*Fedora*), Cavaradossi, and Edgardo were among his best roles. (R)

Masnadieri, I (The Robbers). Opera in 4 acts by Verdi; text by Maffei, after Schiller's drama *Die Räuber* (1781). Prod. London, H.M.'s, 22 July 1847, with Jenny Lind, Gardoni, Lablache; N.Y. 31 May 1860. Given in Italy soon after its London première, and very occasionally since. Revived by Italian Radio for Verdi celebrations 1951.

Mason (orig. Barnes), **Edith** (b. St. Louis, 22 Mar. 1893). American soprano. Studied Paris with Clément, Bertram, Milan with Cottone and Vanzo, and N.Y. with Maurel. Début Boston 1912, Nedda. N.Y., Met., 1915–17 and 1935–6; Chicago 1921–42. Sang extensively in Europe, including Milan, Sc., and Salzburg under Toscanini, 1935. London, C.G., 1930. (R)

Massé, Victor (b. Lorient, 7 Mar. 1822; d. Paris, 5 July 1884). French composer. Early successes, notably with *Les Noces de Jeannette* (1853), roused hopes that he would equal Auber's talent; but though always charmingly tuneful, his later pieces did not prove enduring. His most ambitious work was *Paul et Virginie* (1876); here the short lyrical numbers were the most effective. Massé was chorus master at the Opéra 1860–76.

Massenet, Jules (b. Montaud, Loire, 12 May 1842; d. Paris, 13 Aug. 1912). French composer. Studied composition Paris Conservatoire with Ambroise Thomas. Won Prix de Rome 1863. On his return from Italy completed his 1-act *La Grand'-Tante* which was produced at the Paris O.C., 1867. However, it was not until the production of *Le Roi de Lahore* in 1877 that his position on the French opera scene was firmly established. Of his 27 operas *Hérodiade* (1881), *Manon* (1884), *Werther* (1892), *Thaïs* (1894), *Le Jongleur de Notre-Dame* (1902), and *Don Quichotte* (1910) have met the greatest popularity not only in France, but in Italy, in America, and, to some extent, in England, though there the 'discreet and semi-religious eroticism' (d'Indy) of his works has not found favour. In America the works had a special success during the Hammerstein régime in N.Y., and in Chicago in the 1920's, when Mary Garden proved an ideal interpreter of many of them. When sung and produced tastefully and sincerely, the natural charm of Massenet's melodies, and the unmistakable Gallic style, can make a considerable appeal. In an attempt to perpetuate this type of opera, Massenet continued to repeat his musical clichés in his later works, *Chérubin* (1905), *Ariane* (1906), *Thérèse* (1907), *Bacchus* (1909), *Roma* (1912), *Panurge* (1913), *Cléopâtre* (1914), and *Amadis* (1922), the last three produced posthumously. *La Navarraise* (1894) was written for C.G. None of these works enjoyed more than a *succès d'estime*. Massenet also orchestrated and completed Delibes's *Kassya*. From 1878 until his death he was professor of advanced composition at the Paris Conservatoire and among his pupils were Bruneau, Leroux, Pierné, Charpentier, and Rabaud.

Master Peter's Puppet Show. See *Retablo de Maese Pedro, El.*

Mastersingers. See *Meistersinger von Nürnberg*.

Matačić, Lovro von (b. Sušak, 14 Feb. 1899). Yugoslav conductor. Studied Vienna, and was a member of the Wiener Sängerknaben. Début Cologne 1919. After appointments in Ljubljana and Zagreb became director of Belgrade Opera 1938. Guest appearances in Germany (Munich, Stuttgart from 1954). Generalmusikdirektor Dresden 1956–8 and joint appointment Berlin with Konwitschny same period. La Scala and Vienna 1958, Chicago 1959. Succeeded Solti as Generalmusikdirektor at Frankfurt, 1961. (R)

Materna, Amalie (b. St. Georgen, 10 July 1844; d. Vienna, 18 Jan. 1918). Austrian soprano. Début as soubrette 1864. Sang at Karlstheater, Vienna, in operetta. Début, Hofoper, 1869, Selika, remaining there until 1897. First Bayreuth Brünnhilde 1876, and Kundry 1882. Sang under Wagner in concerts in London 1877. N.Y., Met., 1884–5, Elisabeth, Valentine, Rachel, and Brünnhilde in the first Met. *Walküre*. Joined Damrosch's Company (q.v.) 1894. Had few equals in Wagner roles. After her retirement taught in Vienna.

Mathis der Maler (Mathis the Painter). Opera in 7 scenes by Hindemith; text by composer, after Matthias Grünewald's life and his altar-piece at Colmar. Prod. Zürich 28 May 1938; London, Queen's Hall, 15 Mar. 1939 (concert performance); Edinburgh 29 Aug. 1952 with Ahlersmeyer; Boston University 17 Feb. 1956. In the Peasants' War of 1542 Grünewald leads the peasants against the Church. Losing faith in his cause, he escapes with Regina. He renounces the outside world in favour of his art. This portrayal of people rising against authority alarmed the Nazis, who despite protests by Furtwängler banned the scheduled 1934 première. Furtwängler was dismissed and Hindemith had to leave the country. A symphony drawing on music from the opera has become well known in the concert hall.

Matrimonio Segreto, Il (The Secret Marriage). Opera in 2 acts by Cimarosa; text by Bertati, after the comedy *The Clandestine Marriage* (1766) by Colman and Garrick. Prod. Vienna, Burgtheater, 7 Feb. 1792, when the whole work was encored at the request of Leopold II; London, King's T., 11 Jan. 1794; N.Y., Italian Opera House, 4 Jan. 1834. Cimarosa's most popular work and frequently revived. Chosen to inaugurate La Piccola Scala 26 Dec. 1955.

The opera tells of the attempts of Geronimo (bass), a wealthy citizen of Bologna, to marry off his daughter Elisetta (sop.) to an English 'Milord', Count Robinson (bass). The latter prefers Geronimo's other daughter Carolina (sop.) who is secretly married to Paolino (ten.), a young lawyer and business associate of Geronimo. Geronimo's sister Fidalma (mezzo), who rules the household, is herself in love with Paolino. Carolina and Paolino plan an elopement, and after a bedroom scene of mistaken identities, all ends happily with the Count agreeing to marry Elisetta.

Also opera by Graffigna (1883).

Mattei, Stanislao (b. Bologna, 10 Feb. 1750; d. Bologna, 12 May 1825). Italian composer. He was Martini's successor at San Francesco in Bologna, and later became famous as a teacher, his pupils including Rossini, Morlacchi, Donizetti, and Bertolotti.

Matters, Arnold (b. Adelaide, 11 Apr. 1903). Australian baritone. Studied Adelaide, then London. Début London, S.W., 1932, Valentine. S.W. until 1939, when he returned to Australia. S.W. 1947–53; C.G. 1935–9 and 1946–53. At C.G. created Pilgrim in Vaughan Williams's *Pilgrim's Progress* (1951) and Cecil in Britten's *Gloriana* (1953). (R)

Mattheson, Johann (b. Hamburg, 28 Sept. 1681; d. Hamburg, 17 Apr. 1764). German organist, harpsichordist, singer, and composer. From 1696 he sang female parts at Hamburg, producing his first operas there from 1699. As well as singing in these, he would step down and accompany them from the harpsichord. Here he met and befriended Handel, from whom he learnt much. His eight operas and other compositions are overshadowed by his writings on music, which are lively and thoughtful if egotistical and not a little truculent.

Matzenauer, Margarete (b. Temesvar, 1 June 1881; d. Van Nuys, Cal., 19 May 1963). Hungarian contralto, later soprano. Studied Graz and Berlin. Début Strasbourg 1901, Puck (*Oberon*). Munich 1904–11; N.Y., Met., 1911–30. Also Bayreuth, London, C.G., and Colón. Until 1914 she sang both contralto and soprano roles; after 1914 she sang mostly as a soprano. Specially distinguished in Wagner (Kundry, Brünnhilde, Isolde, Ortrud) and Verdi. Sang the Kostelnička in American première of *Jenůfa*, and Eboli in the first Met. *Don Carlos*. (R)

Maurel, Victor (b. Marseilles, 17 June 1848; d. New York, 22 Oct. 1923). French baritone. Studied Paris with Vauthrot and Duvernoy. Début Paris, Opéra, 1868, De Nevers (*Huguenots*), but made little impression and was only given small roles. After singing in St. Petersburg, Cairo, and Venice (where he once substituted for the tenor in *Linda di Chamounix*) appeared at La Scala 1870 in première of *Il Guarany*, and later created Iago (1887) and Falstaff (1893), both at Verdi's request. London, C.G., 1873–9, 1891–5, and 1904, where he was the first London Telramund (1875), Wolfram (1876), and the first C.G. Dutchman (1877); N.Y., Ac. of M., 1873, and Met., 1894–6 and 1898–9, where he was the first Falstaff. Paris, O., 1879–94. He did not possess an exceptional voice, but used it with consummate art and displayed extraordinary dramatic abilities (he appeared on the straight stage for a period early in the century). He also studied painting, and designed the sets for *Mireille* at the Met. (1919). For a short time he had an operatic studio in London, and from 1909 until his death he taught in N.Y. He wrote three books on singing, one on the staging of *Don Giovanni*, and an autobiography, *Dix Ans de Carrière* (1897), which was translated into German by Lilli Lehmann. (R)

Mavra. Opera in 1 act by Stravinsky; text by Kochno, after Pushkin's poem *The Little House at Kolomna*. Prod. Paris, O., 2 June 1922 (and previously in private at the Hôtel Continental) with Slobodskaya, cond. Fitelberg; Philadelphia 28 Dec. 1934; Edinburgh 21 Aug. 1956. Parasha replaces her mother's cook with her lover Vassily, who is disguised as a girl 'Mavra'. But 'Mavra' is found shaving and has to escape through the window.

Max. A huntsman (ten.), hero of Weber's *Der Freischütz*.

Maximowna, Ita (b. Pskov, 31 Oct. 1914). Russian designer. Studied Paris and Berlin. Her designs for *L'Incoronazione di Poppea* at Milan, Sc., *Fidelio* and *Don Giovanni* at Glyndebourne, and especially her work at Hamburg and Stuttgart in association with Günther Rennert, have established her as one of the leading designers of the post-war period.

May Night. Opera in 3 acts by Rimsky-Korsakov; text by composer, after Gogol's story. Prod. St. Petersburg, 21 Jan. 1880—also used to reopen the Maryinsky, renamed the Russian State Opera House, after the Revolution, Petrograd 12 Mar. 1917; London, D.L., 26 June 1914. A water-nymph, who was once a human being and has drowned herself, appears to Levko and helps him win the girl he loves.

Mayr, Richard (b. Henndorf, Austria, 18 Nov. 1877; d. Vienna, 1 Dec. 1935). Austrian bass-baritone. Studied medicine; then at 21, on the advice of Mahler, turned to music, studying at the Vienna Conservatory. Début Bayreuth 1902, Hagen. Vienna Opera 1902–35; London, C.G., 1924–31; N.Y., Met., 1927–30. Although particularly renowned for his Gurnemanz and other Wagner roles, it is as Baron Ochs, in which role he has never been equalled, that he will always be remembered. At Salzburg he appeared with no less success as Leporello, Figaro, and Sarastro. In Vienna he created, among other roles, that of Barak in *Frau ohne Schatten*. (R)

Mazeppa. Opera in 3 acts by Tchaikovsky; text by composer and V. P. Burenin after Pushkin's *Poltava*. Prod. Moscow, B., 15 Feb. 1884; Liverpool 6 Aug. 1888; Boston, O.H., 14 Dec. 1922. Revived Florence Festival 1954 (first performance in Italy) with Olivero, Radev, Poleri, Bastianini, Christoff. In the Ukraine in the 17th century, Mazeppa loves his godchild Maria, whom he marries against her parents' wishes. A plot against the Tsar is led by Mazeppa with the King of Sweden. Mazeppa, having caused the deaths of Maria's father and her lover Andrey, flees the country. Maria loses her reason. Other operas on the subject are by Maurer (1837), Wietinghoff (1859), Pedrotti (1861), Pourny (1872), Pedrell (1881), Grandval (1892), and Münchaymer.

Mazzinghi, Joseph (b. London, 25 Dec. 1765; d. Downside, 15 Jan. 1844). English composer of Corsican origin. From 1784 he was director of the King's T., for which he composed a number of popular operas.

Medea. In Greek legend, the sorceress who helps Jason to win the Golden Fleece, afterwards escaping with him. She prevented pursuit by casting the limbs of her brother behind her to delay the king, their father. Deserted by Jason, she killed his two children and poisoned his new wife; she then fled to Athens, where she married King Aegeus. Operas on her legend are by Cavalli (*Giasone* 1649), Gianettini (*Medea in Atene* 1675), Kusser (*Jason* 1692), M.-A. Charpentier (1693), Salomon (*Médée et Jason* 1713), Benda (1775), Vogel (*La Toison d'Or* 1786), Cherubini (1797), Mayr (*Medea in Corinto* 1813), Pacini (1843), Milhaud (1939), and others.

Médecin Malgré Lui, Le (lit., The doctor in spite of himself). Opera in 3 acts by Gounod; text a slight alteration of Molière's comedy (1666) by composer, Barbier and Carré. Prod. Paris, T.L., 15 Jan. 1858; London, C.G., 27 Feb. 1865; Cincinnati, 20 Mar. 1900. Gounod's first *opéra comique* and first wider success.

Médée (Medea). Opera in 3 acts by Cherubini; text by Hoffmann, after Corneille's tragedy (1635). Prod. Paris, Th. Feydeau, 13 Mar. 1797 with Julie Legrand. Popular in Germany, especially in version with recitatives by Lachner (Frankfurt 1855). London, H.M.'s (with recits. by Arditi), 6 June 1865 with Tietjens. Not performed in Italy until 30 Dec. 1909 at Milan, Sc., with Mazzoleni. N.Y., T.H., 8 Nov. 1955. Callas's performance of the title role at the 1953 Florence Festival gave the opera a new lease of life. In Germany it has also been revived with Borkh and Lammers.

Medium, The. Opera in 2 acts by Menotti; text by composer. Prod. Columbia Univ., 8 May 1946; London, Aldwych Theatre, 29 Apr. 1948. The Medium, Madame Flora (con.), helped by her daughter Monica (sop.) and the mute Toby, cheats her clients. During a seance she feels a hand on her throat and confesses to her clients that she is a fraud. They refuse to believe her, but she loses her nerve, beats Toby and turns him out of the house; she then turns to the whisky bottle. Toby, in love with Monica, returns to find her and hides in a closet. A noise awakens Madame Flora, and seeing the closet curtain move she shoots at it, killing Toby. 'I've killed the ghost!' she screams.

Mefistofele. Opera in a prologue, 4 acts, and an epilogue by Boito; text by composer. Prod. Milan, Sc., 5 Mar. 1868, but not a success. Revised and prod. Bologna 4 Oct. 1875 with Borghi-Mamo, Campanini, Nannetti. London, H.M.'s, 6 July 1880 with Nilsson, Campanini, Nannetti; Boston, 16 Nov. 1880.

Unlike Gounod in his *Faust*, Boito based his opera on both parts of Goethe's work; thus after Marguerite's death comes the scene of the Night of the Classical Sabbath introducing Helen of Troy.

Méhul, Étienne (b. Givet, nr. Mézières, 22 June 1763; d. Paris, 18 Oct. 1817). French composer. The son of a poor man, he was helped by a rich amateur to go to Paris. Arriving in time for the première of *Iphigénie en Tauride*, he won Gluck's friendship and advice. *Euphrosine* (1790) made his name and revealed a dramatic sincerity and forcefulness new to the world of *opéra comique*. Many operas followed quickly, the seriousness of purpose in the best of them—*Stratonice* (1792), *Ariodant* (1799), *Uthal* (1806)—emphasizing the new weightiness of the genre. There is in these an originality of technique (he had been reproached for lack of technique) that is absent from the more Italianate works of his lighter manner. By no means all his experiments were successful, but Méhul's strong dramatic sense and individual lyrical vein often triumphed. *Joseph* (1807) was admired by Beethoven. After the fall of Napoleon, who had championed him, Méhul's fortunes declined.

Mei-Figner, Medea (orig. Amedea Mei Zovaide) (b. Florence, 3 Apr. 1858; d. Paris, 8 July 1952). Italian soprano. Début Florence 1874, Azucena. In 1887 she began an association with the Russian tenor Nikolay Figner, whom she married two years later, appearing with him in London, C.G., and then St. Petersburg, where she became leading soprano. Noted for her Lisa in *The Queen of Spades* (which she prepared under Tchaikovsky), Tatiana, and Carmen. (R) Her husband **Nikolay Figner** (b. Kazan, 10 Feb. 1857; d. Kiev, 13 Dec. 1919) was leading tenor at St. Petersburg 1887–1903, and created Herman in *The Queen of Spades*. Was also a famous Lensky, Raoul, Otello, Canio, and Don José. According to Cheshikhin's *History of Russian Opera*, his first appearance as José opposite his wife's Carmen was greeted with a gigantic ovation. (R)

Mein Herr Marquis. Adele's (sop.) laughing song in Act 2 of Johann Strauss's *Die Fledermaus*, in which, disguised at Orlofsky's party, she flirts with her employer Eisenstein.

Meistersinger von Nürnberg, Die (The Mastersingers of Nuremberg). Opera in 3 acts by Wagner; text by composer. Prod. Munich 21 June 1868 with Mallinger, Betz, Nachbaur, cond. von Bülow; London, D.L., 30 May 1882, with Sucher, Gura, Winklemann, cond. Richter; N.Y., Met., 4 Jan. 1886 with Seidl-Kraus, Fischer, Stritt, cond. Seidl.

Act 1. In the Church of St. Katherine in 16th-century Nuremberg, Walther von Stolzing (ten.) tries to attract the attention of Eva (sop.) daughter of the goldsmith Veit Pogner, who is with her nurse Magdalene (sop.). He learns that Eva will be betrothed next day to the winner of a singing contest held by the Guild of Mastersingers. Magdalene's admirer, the apprentice David (ten.), explains the rules to Walther. The Mastersingers gradually enter, led by Pogner (bass) and Beckmesser (bass-bar.), the small-minded town clerk who himself hopes to win Eva's hand. Hans Sachs (bass-bar.) the cobbler finally arrives, and the baker Fritz Kothner (bass) calls the roll. Pogner addresses the masters and tells them of the contest. Walther is introduced as a candidate for the Guild; he is asked to tell of his background and training, and then invited to sing a trial song. Beckmesser is appointed marker, and enters a special box; Kothner reads the rules. Walther improvises a song about the spring and love, but soon Beckmesser's slate is full of the mistakes the knight has made. The meeting breaks up in disorder; only Sachs has seen something new and attractive in the song.

Act 2. It is Midsummer Eve, and the apprentices are closing Sachs's shop. The cobbler himself sits under the elder tree and reflects on the events in the church. Eva makes her way from her house opposite Sachs's shop and questions him about the trial. Sachs, a widower, is himself half in love with Eva, but realizes that he is too old for her. He teases her and she rushes home in tears. Seeing the situation, Sachs resolves to help the young couple, who have met and planned to elope. Sachs prevents this by opening his window and letting light stream across the roadway. Beckmesser now arrives to serenade Eva. When Beckmesser protests at Sachs's hammering, he is told that his shoes will not be ready unless work continues. Sachs suggests he act as a marker, hammering each time Beckmesser makes a mistake. Beckmesser agrees, seeing a figure in the window above—it is really Magdalene in Eva's clothes. The serenade and hammering wake the neighbours and apprentices. Beckmesser receives a drubbing, and in the tumult Sachs prevents Eva and Walther from running off, and takes the latter into his own house. The stage empties when the Night Watchman's horn sounds.

Act 3, scene 1. Sachs is musing over a large book. He does not hear the apologies proffered by David for his part in the riot. Left alone he soliloquizes on the madness of the world, and the love of Walther and Eva. Walther comes to tell Sachs of a wonderful dream. Sachs writes this down, for it is a prize song—only the final stanza is lacking. While Sachs and Walther change into their festal robes, the aching Beckmesser enters. He sees the song, and believing it Sachs's, hastily pockets it. Sachs now returns and allows Beckmesser to keep the song. Eva appears, pretending that her shoes hurt, but really hoping to see Walther. While Sachs is attending to her shoe, Walther enters, and the sight of Eva inspires him to his final stanza. David and Magdalene are summoned, David is made a journeyman; the song is christened. All depart for the festal meadow. Scene 2. On the banks of the River Pegnitz the apprentices and guildsmen assemble. The apprentices dance with some girls. They are interrupted by the entrance of the Masters, who take their places on the stand. Sachs is acclaimed, and thanks the people. Beckmesser rises and makes a fiasco of the song. When the crowd laughs he accuses Sachs of having written it. Sachs disclaims authorship, but summons Walther to show how the song should be sung. Walther wins the prize and Eva's hand, but when Pogner moves to invest him with the insignia of the guild, he brushes the chain aside, still smarting under his previous rejection. Sachs comes forward and persuades Walther to accept the honour, explaining the purpose of the Mastersingers in preserving the art of German song. Eva takes the wreath that she had placed on Walther's head and puts it on Sachs's amid the acclamations of the people.

Melani. A famous Italian family of eight brothers—three of them composers, the remainder singers (all but one, male sopranos)—who flourished in Italy, France, and Germany in the latter half of the 17th century.

Melba, (Dame) Nellie (orig. Helen Porter Mitchell) (b. Richmond, nr. Melbourne, 19 May 1861; d. Sydney, 23 Feb. 1931). Australian soprano. Studied Melbourne, Paris with Marchesi. Début Brussels, La M., 1887, Gilda. London, C.G., 1888, Lucia, successful but not triumphant; her great London triumphs began in 1889 as Juliette. Appeared regularly at C.G. until 1914 (missing only the 1909 season), and again 1919, 1922–4 (with B.N.O.C.), and 1926. N.Y., Met., 1893–7, 1898–9, 1900–1, 1904–5, and 1910–11. Also appeared with Damrosch's Company, Manhattan Company, and Chicago Opera in America; and at La Scala, St. Petersburg, Paris, and elsewhere in Europe. Bemberg wrote *Elaine* for her, and Saint-Saëns *Hélène*, both of which roles she created. At first a high coloratura famous for her Rosina, Lucia, Gilda, Violetta, &c., she later sang such lyric roles as Marguerite, Mimì, and Desdemona. She was also heard as Aida, Elsa, Nedda (of which she was the first London interpreter), and even the *Siegfried* Brünnhilde, which was her one great failure. Her voice, which retained its freshness and purity to the very end of her career, originally had a compass from b♭ to f''', and her technique and brilliant and easy ornamentations were a source of admiration and wonder. Her acting abilities were somewhat restricted, and many people found her interpretations cold. She was indeed the *prima donna assoluta*, and at C.G. she had for many years the final word in the engagements of other artists and the castings of the operas in which she sang. She gave her name to an ice-cream and a kind of toast. Her autobiography *Melodies and Memories* was published in 1925; and among books written about her are Colson's *Melba* (1931) and Agnes Murphy's *Melba* (1909), which contains a chapter on singing by Melba. A film was made of her life in 1953 with Patrice Munsel. (R)

Melchior, Lauritz (b. Copenhagen, 20 Mar. 1890). Danish, later American, tenor, orig. baritone. Studied Copenhagen. Début there 1913, Silvio, and continued to sing baritone roles for four years. Mme Charles Cahier, with whom he sang, suggested he should study tenor roles, which he did with Vilem Herold, making his second début in 1918 as Tannhäuser. Further study followed 1921–3 with Victor Beigel in London, Ernst Grenzebach in Berlin, Mildenburg in Munich, and Kittel in Bayreuth. London, C.G., 1924 as Siegmund, and 1926–39; Bayreuth 1924–31; N.Y., Met., 1926–50. His career as a Heldentenor has been unique: he sang Tristan over 200 times. His large, ringing voice never tired, and his singing was always exciting if sometimes lacking in musicianship. (R)

Mélisande. The heroine (sop.) of Debussy's *Pelléas et Mélisande*.

Mellon, Alfred (b. London, 7 Apr. 1820; d. London, 27 Mar. 1867). English conductor and composer. After playing in the orchestra at C.G. and elsewhere in London, became chief conductor for the Pyne-Harrison Company (q.v.). His *Victorine* was produced at C.G. in 1859.

Melnikov, Ivan (b. St. Petersburg, 4 Mar. 1832; d. St. Petersburg, 8 July 1906). Russian baritone. Studied with Lomakin and in Italy with Repetto. Début St. Petersburg 1867, Riccardo (*Puritani*). He created the title role in *Boris Godunov*, Don Juan in Dargomizhsky's *The Stone Guest*, Tokmakov in *Ivan the Terrible*, the title role in Rubinstein's *The Demon* and *Prince Igor*. He sang in all Tchaikovsky's operas except *Iolanta*, but Onegin was his least successful role and he relinquished it after five performances. He retired in 1890.

Melodrama. A dramatic composition in which actors recite to a musical commentary. Benda's duodramas (q.v.) were famous, and it is in Czechoslovakia that the form has flourished —Fibich wrote a trilogy *Hippodamia* (1890–1). Isolated scenes of melodrama occur frequently in opera, e.g. Rocco's and Fidelio's entry into the dungeon in *Fidelio* and the Wolf's Glen scene in *Der Freischütz*.

Mendelssohn(-Bartholdy), Felix (b. Hamburg, 3 Feb. 1809; d. Leipzig, 4 Nov. 1847). German composer. Mendelssohn attempted opera only three times—with *Die Hochzeit des Camachos* (1825), *Die Heimkehr aus der Fremde* (*Son and Stranger*) (1829), and the unfinished *Loreley* (1847).

Menotti, Gian Carlo (b. Cadegliano, 7 July 1911). American composer of Italian birth. His first opera was written at 11; the first to survive is the charming *Amelia Goes to the Ball* (1937), in which his light fertility of invention admirably serves the buffo plot. It is, indeed, in this vein that Menotti excels: *The Telephone* (1947) is a completely successful piece of modern buffo. Previously he had shown his wish to develop a more powerful dramatic vein in *The Old Maid and the Thief* (1939) and still more in *The Island God* (1942). In 1946 came a thriller, *The Medium*, which has often shared the bill with *The Telephone*; their double Broadway success in 1947 established Menotti as a 'serious' composer with a popular touch. *The Consul* (1950) showed Menotti at his most theatrically powerful, and though the work has been his greatest success, it was noticeable that the power and sincerity of the dramatic plea, which has a tragic relevance to the post-war European scene, was sharply at odds with the tepid sub-Puccini lyricism of the score. Experience gained in filming *The Medium* has stood Menotti in good stead in television, where *Amahl and the Night Visitors* (1951) is regularly shown at Christmas. *The Saint of Bleecker Street* (1954) marked a return to blood-and-thunder *verismo*; *The Unicorn, the Gorgon and the Manticore* (1956) was a satire, cast in madrigal opera form, on the vagaries of social fashion; and in *Maria Golovin* (1958) Menotti tackled the deeper theme of personal imprisonment—his hero is a blind man tormented by jealousy. In all his work Menotti has shown himself a brilliantly skilled man of the theatre, able to write librettos, produce, and conduct with complete versatility. Over his musical gifts there is controversy. The skill is unquestioned; but the lack of sustained musical imagination below a certain level of easy tunefulness has made even his many admirers increasingly restless. The comparison with Puccini is often heard: yet Puccini at his most vulgar always achieved his effect through music, whereas Menotti might often dispense with his music and not materially harm his theatrical creation. His latest works are a TV opera, *Labyrinth* (1963), which he considers a 20th-century morality, and *The Last Savage*, prod. Paris, O.C., 1963. In 1958 Menotti founded the Festival of Two Worlds in Spoleto, designed to give chances to young musicians.

Méphistophélès. The Devil (bass or bass-bar.) in Gounod's *Faust* and Berlioz's *Damnation de Faust*.

Mercadante, Saverio (b. Altamura, nr. Bari, 17 Sept. 1795; d. Naples, 17 Dec. 1870). Italian composer. After an early success with *L'Apoteosi d'Ercole* (1819) in Naples, he began composing operas at the rate of three or four a year. With *Il Giuramento* (1837) a change came over his style; from an easy acceptance of the current operatic coinage of the day, he now, under the influence of Meyerbeer, turned his thoughts towards reform. Various technical *tics* of the Rossini idiom were abolished, and greater attention was paid to dramatic force and richness of orchestration. There was in the 'reform operas' of this period a greater originality, but Mercadante was not profoundly gifted enough to avoid the pitfall of a stylistic jumble. Verdi was one composer who admired Mercadante's reforms; though their originator slipped back into his earlier ways with the works of his old age. Director Naples Conservatory 1840–70. Some 60 of his operas survive.

Mérimée, Prosper (b. Paris, 28 Sept. 1803; d. Cannes, 23 Sept. 1870). French author. Operas on his works are as follows. *Le Carrosse du Saint-Sacrament*: Offenbach (*La Périchole*, 1868); Berners (1923); Büsser (1948). *Carmen*: Bizet (1875). *Colomba*: Pacini (*La Fidanzata Corta*, 1842); Mackenzie (1883); Büsser (1921). *La Vénus d'Ille*: Schoeck (1922); Wetzler (*Die baskische Venus*, 1928). *Matteo Falcone*: Cui (1907). *La Dame de Pique*: Halévy (1850).

Merli, Francesco (b. Milan, 27 Jan. 1887). Italian tenor. Studied Milan. Début Milan, Sc., 1916, Alvaro in Spontini's *Fernando Cortez*. London, C.G., 1926–30, where he was the first Calaf; N.Y., Met., 1931–2. Sang regularly at Sc. and the Rome Opera, where in the mid-1930's he was a famous Otello, Dick Johnson, Samson, and Don José. (R)

Merlo, Marisa. See *Morel*.

Mermaid Theatre. The name given the theatre built by Bernard Miles in the back garden of his London home, which was inaugurated in 1951 by a performance of *Dido and Aeneas* with Flagstad. Subsequently rebuilt in the City of London at Puddle Dock.

Merola, Gaetano (b. Naples, 4 Jan. 1881; d. San Francisco, 30 Aug. 1953). Italian conductor and manager. Studied Naples Conservatory. Went to U.S.A. 1899 as assistant conductor at Met. Cond. Henry Savage and Hammerstein's Manhattan Company, of which he was also chorus master 1906–10, and London Opera House 1910–11. Toured U.S.A. with San Carlo Company, and then in 1923 became music director and manager of the San Francisco Company, remaining its director until his death. He raised the San Francisco Company to rank second only to the Met., bringing many famous artists to America for the first time. He collapsed and died while conducting an open-air concert with the San Francisco Symphony Orchestra. (See *San Francisco Opera*.)

Merrie England. Opera in 2 acts by German; text by Basil Hood. Prod. London, Savoy, 2 Apr. 1902.

Merrill, Robert (b. 4 June 1917). American baritone. Studied with his mother, Lillian Miller Merrill, a former concert singer, and later Samuel Margolis in N.Y. Début Trenton 1944, Amonasro. Won Met. Auditions of Air, 1945, and made début there 1945 as Germont. Sang Posa in *Don Carlos* on opening night of the Bing régime, Met. 1950, and was subsequently dismissed by Bing in Apr. 1951 when he failed to keep his engagements on the Met. tour through filming in Hollywood; reinstated the following season. Chosen by Toscanini to sing Germont and Renato in his broadcasts and recordings of *La Traviata* and *Un Ballo in Maschera*. (R)

Merriman, Nan (b. Pittsburg, 28 Apr. 1920). American mezzo-soprano. Studied Los Angeles with Alexia Bassian. Début Cincinnati 1942, La Cieca. Chosen by Toscanini for his broadcasts and recordings of *Orfeo* (title role), *Falstaff* (Meg), *Rigoletto* (Magdalena), *Otello* (Emilia). Sang Baba the Turk in the British première of *The Rake's Progress* and Laura in Dargomizhsky's *The Stone Guest*, Piccola Scala 1958. (R)

Merry Widow, The. See *Lustige Witwe, Die*.

Merry Wives of Windsor, The. See *Lustigen Weiber von Windsor, Die*.

Messa di voce (It. = placing of voice). The art of swelling and diminishing tone on a single note.

Messager, André (b. Montluçon, 30 Dec. 1853; d. Paris, 24 Feb. 1929). French conductor and composer. Studied Paris, where his teachers included Saint-Saëns. After occupying various organ and choirmaster posts, engaged as conductor at Paris, O.C., 1898–1908; where he conducted first performance of *Pelléas et Mélisande*, which is dedicated to him. From 1907 to 1915 he was director and principal conductor of the Opéra. He was artistic director of C.G. 1901–6, during which time he conducted the first performances there of Bunning's *Princess Osra*, Saint-Saëns's *Hélène*, Leoni's *L'Oracolo*, *Le Jongleur de Notre-Dame*, and *Armide*, as well as performances of French works.

As a composer he will be remembered for his light operas and operettas, which display a typical French elegance and lightness of touch. *La Basoche* (1890), *Madame Chrysanthème* (1893), *Véronique* (1898), *Fortunio* (1907), and *Monsieur Beaucaire* (1919) are probably the best known.

Metaphor aria. A term sometimes used for Metastasian arias in which the singer takes a metaphor, illustrated by the music, to demonstrate a situation. Perhaps the finest, though actually a parody of the Metastasian convention, is Fiordiligi's 'Come scoglio' (q.v.) in Mozart's *Così fan tutte*.

Metastasio (orig. Trapassi), **Pietro** (b. Rome, 3 Jan. 1698; d. Vienna, 12 Apr. 1782). Italian poet and librettist. He published his first work at 14, and for long enjoyed the protection of the singer Marianna Benti-Bulgarelli ('La Romanina'). From 1730 he lived in Vienna, where most of his dramas were written. Of his huge output, some texts were used as often as 60 or 70 times: *Artaserse* was set 40 times in a century, and Hasse set all Metastasio's librettos. The reason for his success lay in his skill in providing fluent, charming verse within a framework wholly approved by fashion: intricate plots and elaborate speeches served classical subjects in which the strictly maintained social structure was glorified—only the aristocracy could mingle with the gods, and neither group reveals any but the most detached, formalized human emotions. The rigidity of this convention, of which Metastasio was the greatest master though not the inventor, stressed the merits of conformity, and though the *intermezzi* (q.v.) began by providing an earthier, more human contrast, this soon told against Metastasian heroes, pointing fatally to their artificiality. It was against the abuses to which Metastasian opera lent itself—above all the halting dramatic progress, with the plot continually arrested to make way for demonstrations of vocal skill—that Gluck rebelled.

Metropolitan Opera Auditions of the Air. A series of weekly radio programmes instituted in 1936 by the A.B.C. Network in N.Y. to audition singers for the Met. Among those who have won contracts at the Met. as a result of these broadcasts (now discontinued) are Arthur Carron, Frank Guarrera, Margaret Harshaw, Raoul Jobin, Robert Merrill, Patrice Munsel, Risë Stevens, Regina Resnik, Eleanor Steber, and Leonard Warren.

Metropolitan Opera Guild. An organization founded in 1935 under the presidency of Mrs. Augustus Belmont, to help sell subscriptions for the Metropolitan Opera. This membership has increased from 2,000 to more than 50,000, and its activities now include performances for schools and other educational institutions; the publication of a weekly magazine during the season, *Opera News*, which prints articles and other features about the weekly Saturday afternoon broadcasts from the Met.; and the issuing of gramophone records. It also provides funds to finance at least one new production a season.

Metropolitan Opera House. New York's leading opera house stands on Broadway between 39th and 40th Streets. In the second half of last century opera was given at the Academy of Music, and a number of rich N.Y. business men, unable to get boxes there, decided to finance another opera house in N.Y. and subscribed $800,000 for this purpose. The Met. (cap. 3,615) opened on 22 Oct. 1883 with *Faust* under the management of Henry Abbey. This first season resulted in heavy losses, and the management was taken over by the stockholders who appointed Leopold Damrosch (q.v.) as artistic director. He died before the end of his first season and was succeeded by his son Walter Damrosch (q.v.), whose régime lasted until the end of the 1890–1 season. During this time all operas were sung in German, and the American premières of most of the later Wagner works were given.

Abbey returned to the management in 1892 and was joined by Maurice Grau (q.v.) and Edward Schoeffel until 1898. Grau was manager 1898–1903, and Heinrich Conried (q.v.) 1903–8. During the Grau régime the company included the De Reszkes, Eames, Lilli Lehmann, Nordica, Sembrich, Schumann-Heink, Ternina, Maurel, Plançon, and Van Dyck; and then Conried brought Caruso, Farrar, and Fremstad to the company, as well as Mahler and Mottl as conductors. He enraged Bayreuth by giving the American première of *Parsifal* some ten or more years before the copyright expired, and public opinion in New York by mounting *Salome*.

Conried was succeeded by Gatti-Casazza (q.v.), whose management lasted until 1935. The first seven of his seasons were distinguished by the presence of Toscanini as chief conductor, and the period included the world premières of *La Fanciulla del West*, Humperdinck's *Königskinder*, and Giordano's *Madame Sans-Gêne*, and the American premières of *The Queen of Spades*, *Boris Godunov*, *Le Donne Curiose*, *Der Rosenkavalier*, and *L'Amore dei Tre Re*. The company was strengthened by the débuts of Destinn, Alda, Tetrazzini, Bori, Hempel, Martinelli, Amato, and Renaud. Among Toscanini's colleagues as conductors were Hertz, Mahler, and Polacco.

After Toscanini there came a whole host of conductors, the most important of whom were Bodanzky, Moranzoni, Serafin, and Wolff. This period saw the débuts of Galli-Curci, De Luca, Ponselle, Gigli, Pinza, Lauri-Volpi, Muzio, Jeritza, Rethberg, Edward Johnson, Tibbett, Melchior, Grace Moore, Pons, and then, during the last three Gatti-Casazza seasons, Schipa, Leider, Olszewska, Lehmann, and Flagstad. As well as the Puccini *Trittico*, premières of a number of American works were given, and the first American performances of works by Strauss, Janáček, Křenek, Respighi, &c.

From 1935 to 1950 Edward Johnson (q.v.) was the company's general manager. He encouraged American artists, and his régime saw the emergence of Leonard Warren, Dorothy Kirsten, Jan Peerce, Richard Tucker, Helen Traubel, Blanche Thebom,

Patrice Munsel, Margaret Harshaw, &c. He also strengthened the conducting staff by engaging Beecham, Walter, Busch, Stiedry, Szell, and Reiner. This was the period too of great Wagner performances with Flagstad, Lawrence, Varnay, Traubel, Melchior, Svanholm, Schorr, Janssen, Berglund, Kipnis, and List.

After Johnson's retirement the general manager was Rudolf Bing (q.v.), who modernized stage techniques and brought in producers from the theatre, including Alfred Lunt, Margaret Webster, and Tyrone Guthrie. There have been more performances of opera in English, including successful excursions into the realms of operetta—*Fledermaus*, *La Périchole*, and *The Gipsy Baron*, as well as *The Rake's Progress*, *Wozzeck*, and Barber's *Vanessa*. The Italian repertory has fared particularly well with Callas, Tebaldi, Milanov, De los Angeles, Di Stefano, Del Monaco, Campora, Björling, Bergonzi, Siepi, Valletti, &c., and still more American artists have established themselves, including Dobbs Elias, Peters, Rankin, Resnik, Hines, Merrill, Tozzi, and Uppman. Bing was succeeded by Göran Gentele 1972, when Rafael Kubelik was appointed music director.

The new Metropolitan Opera House (cap. 3,800) in the Lincoln Center opened 16 Sept. 1966.

Mexico. The first Italian opera given in Mexico was Paisiello's *Il Barbiere di Siviglia* in 1806, though the Teatro Coliseo which was opened in 1773 presented various musical entertainments. In 1830 the company organized by Garcia visited Mexico, and from then dates the popularity of Italian opera there. Many operas were written by Mexican composers who included Paniagua (1821–82), Antonio (1825–76), and Morales (1838–1908). After the 1910 revolution foreign companies virtually ceased to visit Mexico, though some open-air performances were given of popular operas in bull-rings by, among others, Caruso, Ruffo, Stracciari, and Raisa before audiences of 25,000. During the 1930's opera was again in eclipse, though in 1932 the Palacio de las Bellas Artes was opened. In 1941 first steps were taken to establish a permanent company by Franz Steiner assisted by Karl Alwin and William Wymetal, all refugees from Vienna. The first opera was *Die Zauberflöte*, and the cast included both European and Mexican singers. During the war years conductors included Kleiber, Horenstein, Morel, and Beecham. Among the Mexican artists who have achieved international fame in the post-war period are Oralia Dominguez, Irma González, and Ernestina Garfias (Tina Garfi).

Meyer, Kerstin (b. Stockholm, 3 Apr. 1928). Swedish mezzo-soprano. Studied Stockholm. Début Stockholm 1952, Azucena. London, C.G., 1960 Dido (Berlioz); N.Y., Met., 1960–2. Vienna, Glyndebourne; Bayreuth since 1964. Her repertory includes Octavian, Carmen, Brangaene, and Italian roles. (R)

Meyerbeer, Giacomo (orig. Jakob Liebmann Beer) (b. Berlin, 5 Sept. 1791; d. Paris, 2 May 1864). German composer of Jewish parentage whose career was largely pursued in France, and who can claim to be one of the creators of French grand opera. He studied in Berlin, and was a child prodigy at the piano. He subsequently studied composition under the Abbé Vogler at Darmstadt, at which time his first two operas were written—*Jephthas Gelübde* (Munich 1812), and *Wirt und Gast, oder Aus Scherz, Ernst* (Stuttgart 1813). The first, more oratorio than opera, was a failure; the second, a comic work, was accepted for Vienna under the title of *Alimelek*, where it was a complete fiasco. In Vienna he pursued his career as a pianist; but, still hankering after the opera stage, he sought the advice of Salieri, who suggested that he should go to Italy to study the human voice. In Venice in 1815 he fell under the spell of Rossini's *Tancredi*, and immediately began to write Italian operas —*Romilda e Costanza* (Padua 1817), *Semiramide Riconosciuta* (Turin 1819), *Emma di Resburgo* (Venice 1819), *Margherita d'Anjou* (Milan 1820), *L'Esule di Granata* (Milan 1822), and *Il Crociato in Egitto* (Venice 1824)—all of which were immediately successful throughout Italy. He was entreated by Weber to give up Italian opera, but it was to France rather than to Germany that he turned. He was so attracted by Paris, where he went for the first performance of his *Crociato* in 1826, that he made his home there. The next few years were spent in assimilating French art, history, and character. His collaboration with Scribe began at this time, and the first result of their partnership was the highly successful *Robert le Diable* (Paris 1831), in which Meyerbeer's German technique, Italian melodies, and newly found French spirit, coupled with brilliant staging and singing, brought unprecedented success to the Paris Opéra. This was followed in 1836 by *Les Huguenots*, the grandest of all French grand operas, which despite its pomposity and musical weaknesses can still impress when properly staged and sung. In 1838 he began work on *L'Africaine*, which was put aside in favour of *Ein Feldlager in Schlesien*, written for Jenny Lind (Berlin 1844), and *Le Prophète* (Paris 1849). He was Generalmusikdirektor in Berlin 1842–9, where he conducted his own operas and those in which Lind sang. He was also responsible for the Berlin production of *Rienzi* (1847), and succeeded in getting the Berlin Opera to accept *Der fliegende Holländer*. Despite these services, and the influence that his French operas obviously had on Wagner's early style, Meyerbeer was bitterly attacked in *Das Judentum in der Musik*. *L'Étoile du Nord*, partly based on *Ein Feldlager*, was produced in Paris in 1854, *Le Pardon de Ploërmel* or *Dinorah* in 1859. Both these works, successful at the time, were, in essence, French *opéras comiques*, a genre in which the composer was not really happy. In 1863 he returned to Paris for rehearsals of *L'Africaine*, on which he had been working on and off for nearly 25 years. He was already in bad health, and he fell seriously ill on 23 Apr., dying ten days later. *L'Africaine* was finally produced in Apr. 1865. Despite its original length—more than six hours—and the protracted period spent on its composition, this is generally considered his finest work.

To assess Meyerbeer's place in operatic history is not easy. He was an assimilative composer rather than a creator or an innovator. At times more intent on writing music that would accompany stage spectacles, he could also, at moments of intense dramatic excitement, as in the Blessing of the Daggers in *Les Huguenots*, create music worthy of the situation. Fétis wrote, 'All that his works contain—characters, ideas, scenes, rhythm, modulation, instrumentation—all are his and his only.' Wagner himself admitted that he owed much to Meyerbeer's approach to the operatic stage, and the latter's treatment of dramatic spectacle in music is perhaps his great contribution to the development of opera.

Mezza voce (It. = half voice). The direction to sing at half power, with consequently muted expression.

Mezzo-soprano (It. = half-soprano). The middle category of female (or artificial male) voice. In Italy the mezzo-soprano differs from the soprano chiefly in that a few notes are missing at the top of the tessitura, and in that the voice has a darker quality. In Germany it is a more distinctly different voice, with a tessitura of about g–b♭''.

Micaëla. Don José's peasant sweetheart (sop.) in Bizet's *Carmen*.

Micheau, Janine (b. Toulouse, 17 Apr. 1914). French soprano. Studied Toulouse and Paris. Début Paris, O.C., 1933, La Plieuse (*Louise*); created, at the Comique, Zerbinetta and Anne Trulove. At the Opéra since 1936, where she has created Milhaud's *Médée* (1940) and Manuela in his *Bolivar* (1950). London, C.G., 1937, Micaëla; San Francisco 1938, Mélisande; Chicago 1956, Violetta and Micaëla. (R)

Michele. Giorgetta's husband (bar.) in Puccini's *Il Tabarro*.

Mi chiamano Mimì. Mimì's (sop.) aria in Act 1 of Puccini's *La Bohème* in which she describes herself.

Midsummer Marriage, The. Opera in 3 acts by Tippett; text by composer. Prod. London, C.G., 27 Jan. 1955, with Sutherland, Leigh, Dominguez,

Lewis, Lanigan, Kraus, cond. Pritchard. Tippett's first opera deals in a wealth of complex metaphor and cross-fertilizing ideas with a quest theme, and is consciously kin to *The Magic Flute*.

Midsummer Night's Dream, A. Opera in 3 acts by Britten; text by composer and Peter Pears after Shakespeare's comedy (*c.*1593–4). Prod. Aldeburgh 11 Jun. 1960, cond. Britten; San Francisco 10 Oct. 1961, cond. Varviso.

Mierzwiński, Władysław (b. Warsaw, 21 Oct. 1850; d. Paris, 15 July 1909). Polish tenor. Studied Warsaw and Paris. London, C.G., 1881–4; N.Y., Ac. of M., 1883. Had a large powerful voice with a range up to d'' which suited him to roles like Arnold, Raoul, John of Leyden, and Manrico.

Mignon. Opera in 3 acts by Thomas; text by Barbier and Carré, after Goethe's novel *Wilhelm Meisters Lehrjahre* (1795–6). Prod. Paris, O.C., 17 Nov. 1866, with Galli-Marié; London, D.L., 5 July 1870, with Christine Nilsson; New Orleans, 9 May 1871. Lothario, a wandering minstrel, is searching for his long-lost daughter. A band of gipsies arrive and try to make one of their number, Mignon, dance. She refuses and they start to beat her. She is rescued by Wilhelm Meister, who engages her as his servant and then falls in love with her. Later she is saved from a burning castle by Wilhelm who, with Lothario, nurses her back to health. Lothario, who had lost his memory when Mignon was first kidnapped, now remembers that he is Count Lothario, and recognizes Mignon as his long-lost daughter Sperata.

Mikhailov, Maxim (b. Koltsovka, Kazan, 1893). Russian bass. Studied Kazan. From 1924 to 1929 he was an archdeacon in the Russian Orthodox Church in Moscow; from 1929 to 1932 he made several concert tours, and since 1932 has been a leading singer at the Bolshoy. His roles include Susanin, Khonchak, and the Old Soldier in *The Decembrists*. (R)

Milan (It., Milano). Town in Lombardy, Italy. As well as at La Scala (q.v.) opera has been given at the Teatro della Cannobiana (cap. 2,000), the Teatro Carcano, the Teatro Lirico, and the Teatro Dal Verme, as well as at other smaller theatres. The Cannobiana was founded at the same time as La Scala and was built on land given free to the city by Maria Theresa. It opened in 1779 with a double bill comprising Salieri's *Fiera di Venezia* and *Il Talismano*. In 1807 it gave hospitality to La Scala and continued to be used for opera and ballet fairly regularly until the 1860's. The most famous première staged there was probably Donizetti's *L'Elisir d'Amore* in 1832. In 1894 it was demolished and replaced by the Teatro Lirico, which was built by Edoardo Sonzogno, the publisher. The theatre opened in 1894 with Samara's *La Martire*. In 1897 Caruso made his Milan début there in the première of Cilea's *L'Arlesiana*. The same composer's *Adriana Lecouvreur*, Giordano's *Fedora*, and Leoncavallo's *Zazà* also enjoyed their premières there, and it was also the scene of the first Italian performances of *Werther*, *Thaïs*, *Louise*, and *La Prise de Troie*. In 1938 the Lirico was destroyed and was rebuilt the following year. After the bombing of La Scala it served as the home of the Scala company for several seasons. It is now a cinema.

The Carcano was opened in Sept. 1803 with Federici's *Zaira*. It was the scene of the first Milan performances of Verdi's *La Battaglia di Legnano* in 1859, of the first concert of Wagner's music given in Milan under Faccio in 1883, and of the first Italian performance of *Manon* in 1893. The premières of Donizetti's *Anna Bolena* in 1830 and *La Sonnambula* the following year were also given there.

The Dal Verme was built in 1872 to replace the Politeama Ciniselli, which had been opened in 1864 in the square opposite the Palazzo Dal Verme. It opened with *Les Huguenots* but was primarily the home of drama, though the premières of Puccini's *Le Villi* (1884), Leoncavallo's *Pagliacci* (1892), and Zandonai's *Conchita* (1911) were all given there. It was also the scene of the famous Toscanini concerts during the First World War. It became a cinema in 1930.

Milanov (orig. Kunc), **Zinka** (b. Zagreb, 17 May 1906). Yugoslav soprano. Studied Zagreb and then three years with Ternina. Later with Kostrencić, Carpi in Prague, and Stueckgold in N.Y. Début Ljubljana 1927, Leonora (*Trovatore*). From 1928 to 1935 leading soprano Zagreb where she sang more than 350 performances, all in Croatian, including Sieglinde, the Marschallin, Rachel, and Minnie. Prague, German Theatre, 1936. Following year sang in Verdi *Requiem* at Salzburg under Toscanini. This led to her engagement at the Met., where she made her début in Dec. 1937 as Leonora. Except for a short break for the 1947–8 and 1949–50 seasons she has been leading dramatic soprano there ever since, and has also sung with the Chicago and San Francisco Operas, and at the Colón, Buenos Aires. London, C.G., 1956–7. In Verdi roles she had few equals in the 1940's, possessing one of the most exquisite soprano voices of the day, capable of beautiful *pianissimo* singing. (R)

Mildenburg, Anna von. See *Bahr-Mildenburg*.

Milder-Hauptmann, Pauline Anna (b. Constantinople, 13 Dec. 1785; d. Berlin, 29 May 1838). Austrian soprano. Came to the notice of Schikaneder, who urged her to study with Tomaselli and then Salieri. Début Vienna 1803 as Juno in Süssmayr's *Der Spiegel von Arkadien*. Created Leonore in *Fidelio* (1805). Went to Berlin 1812; was engaged there 1816–29, but left following a quarrel with Spontini. Greatly admired for her interpretation of Gluck's Iphigénie, Alceste, and Armide.

Mildmay, Audrey (b. Hurstmonceaux, 19 Dec. 1900; d. London, 31 May 1953). English soprano. Formerly member of Carl Rosa; toured U.S.A. with *Beggar's Opera*, then in 1931 married John Christie (q.v.) and inspired him to build an opera house at Glyndebourne and launch a festival there in 1934. She was heard as Susanna, Zerlina, and Norina. After the war she and Rudolf Bing conceived the idea of the Edinburgh Festival (q.v.). (R)

Milhaud, Darius (b. Aix-en-Provence, 4 Sept. 1892). French composer. Technically one of the best equipped of all 20th-century composers, and one willing and able to produce music in almost any style for any occasion, he invariably responds conscientiously to the individual demands of the work in hand. His shorter stage pieces, which include three children's operas, are remarkable for their certainty of touch, and at least once—in *Christophe Colomb* (1930)—he has managed to match himself impressively to a large theme. *Le Pauvre Matelot* (1927) is a simple little Cocteau *pièce noire* using slender resources to maximum effect, while *Christophe Colomb* musters an army of devices that includes cinema and a Greek chorus for the staging and *Leitmotiv* to assist the wholly un-Wagnerian music. His *Bolivar* (1943) enjoyed only a *succès d'estime* in Paris (1950), but *David*, written for the 3,000th anniversary of Israel where it was prod. in 1954, has subsequently been performed with success at La Scala and in Los Angeles.

Millöcker, Karl (b. Vienna, 29 May 1842; d. Baden, 31 Dec. 1899). Austrian composer and conductor. Studied Vienna, and held appointments at Graz and Vienna, where he was conductor and composer to the Theater an der Wien from 1869. He was a prolific composer of operettas, many still in the repertories of the German and Austrian opera houses. The best known of his works are *Der Bettelstudent* (1882), *Gasparone* (1884), and *Der arme Jonathan* (1890).

Milton, John (b. London, 9 Dec. 1608; d. London, 8 Nov. 1674). English poet. Operas on his works are as follows. *Paradise Lost* (1667): Lesueur (*Le Mort d'Adam*, 1809—also based on Klopstock and the Book of Genesis); Spontini (begun 1838, unfinished); Rubinstein (*c.* 1855). *Samson Agonistes* (1671): Handel (*Samson*, 1743). Spontini's *Milton* (1804) is based on the poet's life and provided material for *Das verlorene Paradies*; a projected *Miltons Tod* did not materialize.

Mime. The Nibelung dwarf (ten.), brother of Alberich, in Wagner's *Ring*.

Mimì. The seamstress (sop.), heroine of Puccini's *La Bohème*.

Minnie. The saloon proprietress (sop.), heroine of Puccini's *La Fanciulla del West*.

Mingotti, Regina (orig. Caterina Valentini) (b. Naples, 16 Feb. 1722; d. Neuburg-on-Danube, 1 Oct. 1808). Italian soprano. Studied with Porpora. Sang with great success in Galuppi's *Olimpiade* in Dresden and Naples, in both cities becoming the rival, and then the personal enemy, of Bordoni. Also appeared in Spain, France, and England, where she appeared between 1754 and 1763 in works by Jommelli, Hasse, &c. Her quarrels with Vaneschi, the manager of the Haymarket, rivalled the celebrated fights between Handel and Bononcini, or Bordoni and Cuzzoni. In the musical satire *Lethe* (1775) Kitty Clive gave a ridiculing imitation of her.

Miolan-Carvalho, Marie (b. Marseilles, 31 Dec. 1827; d. Puys, Seine-Inférieure, 10 July 1895). French soprano. Studied Paris Conservatoire under Duprez. Début Paris, O.C., 1849, Lucia, singing there until 1855; T.L. 1856–67, creating Marguerite (*Faust*), Juliette, and Mireille. London, C.G., 1859–64 and 1871–2, where she was the first London Dinorah. She also sang with success in Berlin and St. Petersburg. She married the impresario Léon Carvalho (q.v.).

Mira, o Norma. The duet between Norma (sop.) and Adalgisa (sop.) in Act 2 of *Norma*, in which Adalgisa pleads with Norma not to give up her children.

Mireille. Opera in 3 (orig. 5) acts by Gounod; text by Carré based on Mistral's poem *Mirèio* (1859). Prod. Paris, T.L., 19 Mar. 1864 with Miolan-Carvalho; London, H.M.'s, 5 July 1864, with Tietjens; Philadelphia, Ac. of M., 17 Nov. 1864 (2 acts only), in full at Chicago 13 Sept. 1880.

The opera takes place in Arles and tells of the love of Mireille for Vincent; this is opposed by Mireille's father Ramon, and complicated by a rival for Mireille's affections in the bull-tender Ourrias. The original 5-act version ended tragically with Mireille's death. The revised version ends with Vincent and Mireille happily united.

Mir ist so wunderbar! The canon quartet in Act 1 of *Fidelio* in which Leonore, Marcellina, Jacquino, and Rocco express their conflicting emotions.

Miserere. Properly the opening word of the 51st psalm (50th in the Vulgate). In opera the famous scene for Leonora (sop.), Manrico (ten.), and chorus in the last act of *Il Trovatore*.

Mitropoulos, Dimitri (b. Athens, 1 Mar. 1896; d. Milan, 2 Nov. 1960). Greek conductor and composer. Studied Athens, Brussels, Berlin (with Busoni). *Répétiteur* Berlin Opera, 1921–5. Conducted several opera performances in Athens, but did not conduct opera again until the 1950's when he directed concert performances of *Wozzeck* and *Elektra* with the New York Philharmonic. N.Y., Met., 1954–60, including première of *Vanessa*. Conducted *Wozzeck* at La Scala, and *Elektra* at Florence Festival. His opera *Sœur Béatrice* was produced at the Athens Conservatory (1920). (R)

Miura, Tamaki (b. Tokyo, 1884; d. Tokyo, 26 May 1946). Japanese soprano. Studied Tokyo and Germany. Début Tokyo, Santuzza. Sang Butterfly in London during First World War, and subsequently heard in the role in Boston, Chicago, and other American cities. Created Messager's *Madame Chrysanthème* in Chicago 1920; and sang Iris, Mimì, and other roles in Japan. (R)

Mlada. Opera in 4 acts by Rimsky-Korsakov; text by composer, based on text for earlier opera to be written with Borodin, Cui, and Mussorgsky. Prod. St. Petersburg 1 Nov. 1892.

Mocchi, Walter (b. Turin, 1870; d. Rio de Janeiro, July 1955). Italian impresario. His first operatic ventures were at Florence in 1906, followed a year later by a successful season at the T.L., Milan. He then took an Italian company to South America, and for many years was responsible for the great seasons in Buenos Aires at the Teatro Colón and Teatro Coliseo. Formed Società Teatrale Internazionale e Nazionale (S.T.I.N.), and controlled the seasons at the Costanzi in Rome, the Massimo in Palermo, the San Carlo in Naples, as well as Bari and Parma. From 1911 to 1926 the Constanzi, Rome, was under the artistic direction of his wife, the soprano Emma Carelli.

Mödl, Martha (b. Nuremberg, 22 Mar. 1912). German soprano, orig. mezzo-soprano. Studied Nuremberg. Début Remscheid 1942, Cherubino. Düsseldorf Opera 1945–9 as mezzo. Hamburg State Opera since 1949, also appearing regularly in Vienna. London, C.G., 1949–50, 1953. N.Y., Met., since 1956. Began to sing dramatic soprano roles 1950–1 and was engaged to sing Kundry, Bayreuth, 1951; since then as Isolde, Brünnhilde, Sieglinde, and Gutrune. Leonore in *Fidelio* at opening of Vienna State Opera. (R)

Moffo, Anna (b. Wayne, Penn., 27 June 1935). American soprano. Studied Curtis Inst., N.Y., and Rome. Début Italian TV as Cio-Cio-San 1956; stage début Spoleto, Norina. Chicago 1957; San Francisco 1960; N.Y., Met., since 1961; London, C.G., 1964. One of the most promising young sopranos of the day, and already a famous Violetta, Nannetta, and Amina. (R)

Mohaupt, Richard (b. Breslau, 14 Sept. 1904; d. Reichenau, Austria, 3 July 1957). German composer and conductor. Before being forced to leave Nazi Germany worked as opera conductor and had his *Die Wirtin von Pinsk* prod. at Dresden 1938. Works prod. in America included a children's opera *Boleslav der schamhafte*. After the war returned to Europe, where his *Bremer Stadtmusikanten* (Bonn 1949) and *Der grüne Kakadu* (prod. Hamburg posthumously 1958) were given.

Moïse. See *Mosè in Egitto*.

Molière (Jean-Baptiste Poquelin) (b. Paris, 15 Jan. 1622; d. Paris, 17 Feb. 1673). French playwright. Operas on his works are as follows. *Les Précieuses Ridicules* (1659): Zich (1926); Lattuada (1929). *L'École des Femmes* (1662): Liebermann (1955); Mortari (1959). *Le Mariage Forcé* (1664): F. Hart (1928). *La Princesse d'Élide* (1664): Galuppi (*Alcimena*, 1749); Laverne (*c.* 1706). *L'Amour Médecin* (1665): Poise (1880); Wolf-Ferrari (1913); Herbergis (1920). *Le Médecin Malgré Lui* (1666): Desaugiers (1792); Gounod (1857); Poise (1887); Kaufmann (1958). *Le Sicilien* (1666): K. H. David (1924). *Tartuffe* (1667): Haug (1937); Kosa (1952). *L'Avare* (1667): Burghauser (1950). *Amphitryon* (1668): Grétry (1788); Oboussier (1950). *Georges Dandin* (1668): Mathieu (1877); Ollone (1930). *M. de Pourceaugnac* (1669): Hasse (1727); Franchetti (1897). *Le Bourgeois Gentilhomme* (1670): Hasse (*Larinda e Vanesio*, 1726); Gargiulo (1947); see also Strauss, *Ariadne auf Naxos*. *Le Malade Imaginaire* (1673): Napoli (1939); Haug (*Le Malade Immortel*, 1946).

Molinari-Pradelli, Francesco (b. Bologna, 4 July 1911). Italian conductor. Studied Bologna and Rome with Molinari. Début as symphonic conductor 1938, then began to conduct at all the leading Italian opera houses. London, C.G., 1955, 1960; San Francisco since 1957; Vienna since 1959. (R)

Monaco. See *Monte Carlo*. Also Italian for Munich.

Mona Lisa. Opera in 2 acts by Schillings; text by Beatrice Dovsky. Prod. Stuttgart 26 Sept. 1915 with Hedy Iracema-Brügelmann, Forsell; N.Y., Met., 1 Mar. 1923 with Barbara Kemp.

Mon cœur s'ouvre à ta voix. Dalila's (mezzo) aria in Act 2 of Saint-Saëns's *Samson et Dalila*.

Mond, Der (The Moon). Opera in 3 acts by Orff; text by composer, after Grimm. Prod. Munich 5 Feb. 1939 with Patzak, cond. Krauss. N.Y., C.C., 16 Oct. 1956.

Mondo della Luna, Il (The World on the Moon). Opera in 3 acts by Haydn; text by Goldoni (first set by Galuppi 1750, also by Piccinni, Paisiello, and others). Prod. Esterháza 3 Aug.

1777. Revived, in incomplete form, London Opera Club, Scala T., 8 Nov. 1951. N.Y., Greenwich Mews Playhouse, 7 June 1949. Restored by Robbins Landon, performed Holland Festival 24 June 1959, cond. Giulini, and subsequently elsewhere.

Mongini, Pietro (b. Rome, 1830; d. Milan, 27 Apr. 1874). Italian tenor. Leading tenor London, H.M.'s, 1860's and 1870's. Succeeded Giuglini (q.v.) and also sang at C.G. 1869–70. Created Radamès at Cairo, and was a notable Manrico, Arnold (*William Tell*), and John of Leyden (*Le Prophète*).

Moniuszko, Stanisław (b. Ubiel, 5 May 1819; d. Warsaw, 4 June 1872). Polish composer, the most important figure in the development of Polish national opera. His first work, after some early operettas, was *Halka* (1848), which on its eventual production in Warsaw was joyfully welcomed as a representative national opera; it is still extremely popular in Poland. Standing half-way between the old tradition of separate numbers and the new music drama, *Halka* makes use of an idiom that is recognizably Polish (without drawing on folk music) as well as of most Romantic opera clichés. His later works were less successful, though *The Haunted Manor* (1865) is said to contain fine music. The failure of his last two works hastened his death.

Monna Vanna. Opera in 4 acts by Février; text by Maeterlinck. Prod. Paris, O., 10 Jan. 1909 with Bréval, Muratore, Marcoux; Boston, 5 Dec. 1913. Maeterlinck's play was also adapted for opera by Emil Abrányi.

Monnaie, Théâtre Royal de la. See *Brussels*.

Monostatos. Sarastro's black slave (ten.) in Mozart's *Die Zauberflöte*.

Monsigny, Pierre Alexandre (b. Fauquembergue, 17 Oct. 1729; d. Paris, 14 Jan. 1817). French composer. Encouraged by the success of *Les Aveux Indiscrets* (1759), he devoted himself to regular composition and already in *Le Cadi Dupé* (1761) showed considerable operatic mastery. He now continued to produce about an opera a year, generally simple pastoral comedies which gave scope to his melodic charm. His most important work was *Le Déserteur* (1769), which in its dramatic power and genuine pathos approaches grand opera. Here he also foreshadows later developments by making the final chorus provide the main theme of the overture. After *Le Déserteur* he composed no more, content to rest upon his laurels rather than take the risk of competing with Grétry.

Monte Carlo. Capital of Monaco. The small opera house (cap. 600) designed by Charles Garnier was opened in 1879 and enjoyed its greatest days under the management of Raoul Gunsbourg (q.v.) 1890–1954. The scene of many interesting premières (see *Gunsbourg*) and of famous performances by Patti, Melba, Caruso, and Chaliapin. The present director is Maurice Besnard, and the season usually lasts from Jan. to Apr., presenting popular works in the French, German, and Italian repertory sung by the leading artists of the day.

Montemezzi, Italo (b. Vigasio, 4 Aug. 1875; d. Verona, 15 May 1952). Italian composer. Studied Milan. A composer more akin to Boito than to his contemporaries of the *verismo* school. His works have enjoyed more success abroad than in his native Italy, though his first opera *Giovanni Gallurese* (1905) made so good an impression on its production in Turin that it was given 17 times in its first season. His masterpiece is undoubtedly *L'Amore dei Tre Re* (1913), founded on Sam Benelli's play. His other operas are *Hellera* (1909), *La Nave* (1918), *La Notte di Zoraima* (1931), and *L'Incantesimo* (1943).

Monterone. The nobleman (bass) who curses Rigoletto in Verdi's opera.

Monteux, Pierre (b. Paris, 4 Apr. 1875; d. Hancock, 1 Jul. 1964). French conductor. Studied Paris Conservatoire. Viola player at the Paris O.C.; cond. Paris, O., 1913–14; N.Y., Met., 1917–19, 1953–6, conducting American premières of *The Golden Cockerel*,

Mârouf, and *La Reine Fiammette*, and between 1953 and 1956 authoritative performances of *Manon*, *Faust*, *Orfeo*, *Hoffmann*, and *Samson et Dalila*. (R)

Monteverdi, Claudio (b. Cremona, ? May 1567; d. Venice, 29 Nov. 1643). Italian composer. His first opera was *La Favola d'Orfeo* (1607), which magnificently united the instrumental and vocal traditions of the day with the new dramatic recitative put forward by the Camerata (q.v.). A further group of operas composed for a festival at Mantua celebrating a ducal marriage included *Arianna* (1608), of which only the wonderful Lamento survives. Moving to Venice, he continued to write dramatic works, among them *Il Combattimento di Tancredi e Clorinda* (1624). Twelve operas for Parma and Mantua were lost in the sack of Mantua; this and the ensuing plague may have precipitated his admission to holy orders (1632). The opening in 1637 of the first public opera house, the San Cassiano in Venice, re-aroused his interest in opera. The rest of his life was largely taken up with a series of works—of which only two survive, *Il Ritorno d'Ulisse in Patria* (1641) and *L'Incoronazione di Poppea* (Venice, 1642)—in which he laid the foundations of Neapolitan opera. He inaugurated the *bel canto* and *buffo* styles, with *recitativo secco*; and this, with his dramatic vividness in reflecting moods and events in the orchestra, set up a model for generations of his successors. His convictions found a gifted advocate in the writings of his brother **Giulio Cesare Monteverdi** (b. Cremona, 31 Jan. 1573; d. ?).

Montecilli, Angelo Maria (b. Milan, *c.* 1710; d. Dresden, 1764). Italian male soprano. After appearances (notably in female roles) in Italy he came to London, where, Burney records, he made a powerful effect on English audiences.

Moody, Fanny (b. Redruth, Cornwall, 23 Nov. 1866; d. Dundrum, Ireland, 21 July 1945). English soprano. Studied privately. Début Liverpool 1887, Arline (*Bohemian Girl*), with C.R. Company. Leading soprano with C.R. until 1898, when with her husband Charles Manners (q.v.), whom she had married in 1890, she formed the Moody-Manners Company. She was the first Tatiana in England (1892) and created Rosalba in Pizzi's opera of that name (1902) and Militza in McAlpin's *The Cross and the Crescent* (1903).

Moody-Manners Company. Formed by the bass Charles Manners and his wife Fanny Moody (qq.v.) in 1898 and lasting until May 1916. At the height of touring opera's popularity in Great Britain there were two companies numbering 175 and 95 respectively. The singers included Florence Easton, Enid Cruickshank, Philip Bertram, Harry Brindle, Maria Gay, Zélie de Lussan, John Coates, Joseph O'Mara, Philip Brozel, and E. C. Hedmont. Richard Eckhold and Hamish McCunn were the chief conductors.

Moore, Douglas (b. Cutchogue, N.Y., 10 Aug. 1893; d. there 25 July 1969). American composer. *The Devil and Daniel Webster* (1938) and the folk opera *The Ballad of Baby Doe* (1956) have proved the most successful and are regularly performed in America.

Moore, Grace (b. Slabtown, Tenn., 5 Dec. 1901; d. Copenhagen (in air crash), 26 Jan. 1947). American soprano. Studied locally. After appearances in night clubs and musical comedy went to Europe for further study with Richard Berthélemy. Début Paris 1928. N.Y., Met., 1928, Mimì; sang there 1928–32, 1935–6, 1937–46; London, C.G., 1935. Also sang Paris, O.C., 1928, 1938, and 1946, when she appeared as Louise, having studied the role with Charpentier. Her most famous roles, apart from Mimì and Louise, were Manon, Tosca, and Fiora. She became known outside the opera house by her films (*One Night of Love*, *Love Me For Ever*, and *New Moon*). Her glamour and personality more than her voice and acting abilities made her a great favourite. (R)

Moore, Thomas (b. Dublin, 28 May 1779; d. Dublin, 28 Feb. 1852). Irish poet and musician. He was active as a poet and arranger of various songs which had an enormous popularity in their day, especially when sung by him. He wrote the libretto of a comic opera *The Gypsy Prince* (1801) for Michael Kelly, and in 1811 produced an opera of his own, *M.P., or The Blue Stocking*. His *Lalla Rookh* (1817) provided the book for operas by C. E. Horn (1818), Kashin (*The One-Day Reign of Nourmahal*), Spontini (*Nurmahal* 1822), F. David (1862), Rubinstein (*Feramors* 1863), and Stanford (*The Veiled Prophet* 1881). *The Light of the Harem* was set as an opera by A. G. Thomas in 1879.

Morel (orig. Merlo), **Marisa** (b. Turin, 13 Dec. 1914). Italian soprano and producer. Studied Turin. Début Milan, Sc., 1933, Musetta. After further appearances at Sc. and other Italian opera houses, and at the N.Y., Met., 1938–9, she formed her own company in 1941 for the production of Mozart operas and gave performances at Aix-en-Provence, Paris, Ch.-É., and elsewhere in Europe. Artists who participated in her productions included Suzanne Danco, Tatiana Menotti, Giulietta Simionato, Fernando Corena, Marcello Cortis, Petre Munteanu, Marko Rothmüller, and Heinz Rehfuss; and the conductors Ackermann, Ansermet, Böhm, and Krannhals.

Morena (orig. Meyer), **Berta** (b. Mannheim, 27 Jan. 1878; d. Rottach-Egern, 7 Oct. 1952). German soprano. Her great beauty attracted the painter Lenbach who persuaded her to study with Röhr-Brajnin. She was further encouraged by Ternina and made her début at Munich 1898 as Agathe, remaining a member of the Munich Opera until 1924. N.Y., Met., 1908–11 and 1924–5; London, C.G., 1914. A distinguished Brünnhilde and Isolde. (R)

Morgenlich leuchtend. The opening words of Walther von Stolzing's (ten.) Prize Song in Act 3 of *Meistersinger*.

Morison, Elsie (b. Ballarat, 1924). Australian soprano. Studied Melbourne and London, R.C.M., with Clive Carey. Début London, Albert Hall, 1948, *Acis and Galatea*. London, S.W., 1948–54, and C.G. since 1953. Sang Blanche in English première of *The Carmelites*, and Anne Trulove in *The Rake's Progress* for Glyndebourne, where she has also sung Zerlina and Marcellina (*Fidelio*). (R)

Morlacchi, Francesco (b. Perugia, 14 June 1784; d. Innsbruck, 28 Oct. 1841). Italian composer. Through fame won by early successes with operas in Italy he was appointed director to the Saxon Court at Dresden in 1811. Here his mastery of the Italian operatic style fashionable in court circles won him an immediate popularity that was only challenged when Weber was appointed Kapellmeister 1817. Their relationship was frigidly polite, but Morlacchi privately undermined Weber's activities and by long absences in Italy forced him to overwork. Weber wrote, in connexion with Morlacchi's *Barbiere di Siviglia*, that though not learned he had 'talent, ideas, and above all a fund of comic material'.

Moscow. Capital of Russia and the U.S.S.R. Moscow's first public theatre, the Petrovsky, was built by an Englishman, Maddox, in 1780. This housed the company which had been founded four years previously by Catherine the Great. Before that, opera had been performed in court and private theatres. At the Petrovsky, the first performance was given of works by the earliest Russian composers—Pashkevich, Sokolovsky, and others. The theatre was burnt down in 1805, and opera was given in private theatres again until the opening of the Bolshoy Petrovsky in 1825; this theatre saw the premières of Glinka's two operas. In 1853 the inside was burnt out; restored by Cavos, the theatre reopened in 1856. The auditorium seats a few less than C.G. (cap. 2,000), but its stage is half as wide again.

After the 1917 revolution the theatre was reorganized, and reopened on 8 Apr. 1918 with an act of *Russlan* and an act of *Sadko*. It also took over the nearby Filial Theatre. This was a private opera house until the Revolution, being used in turn by the Russian Opera Company (founded in the 1880's by Sava Mamontov), by the impresario Solodovnikov, and from 1904 to 1917 by the Zimin Opera (an experimental co-operative enterprise which lasted until 1924). Mamontov had been responsible for wooing the public away from the official Bolshoy style and for attracting numbers of outstanding artists—it was here that Chaliapin scored his greatest Moscow success. In 1960 the Filial underwent reconstruction. In Nov. 1964 the Bolshoy made its first visit outside Russia, to Milan, Sc. Opera is also given at the Stanislavsky Opera Theatre.

Bolshoy singers of recent years include Smolenskaya, Vishnevskaya, Lemshev, Kozlovsky, Nelep, Ivanov, Petrov, Reizen, and Pirogov.

See also *Russia*.

Mosè in Egitto (Moses in Egypt). *Azione tragica-sacra* in 3 acts by Rossini; text by Tottola. Prod. Naples, S.C., 5 Mar. 1818 with Colbran, Benedetti (the famous Prayer, 'Dal tuo stellato soglio', was added for its 1819 revival); London, H.M.'s, 23 Apr. 1822 as *Pietro l'Eremita* with Camporese, Ronza de Begnis, Zucchelli; N.Y., Masonic Hall, 22 Dec. 1832. A second version in 4 acts, text by Balocchi and Étienne de Jouy, prod. under title of *Moïse* at Paris, O., 26 Mar. 1827; London, C.G., 20 Apr. 1850 as *Zora* with Castellan, Vera, Tamberlik, Tamburini; N.Y., Ac. of M., 7 May 1860. Revivals this century include a diplomatically embarrassing one at the Florence Festival of 1935 when Hitler, as Mussolini's guest, had to watch the Egyptians drowning in the Red Sea and the Hebrews escaping.

Moses und Aron. Opera in 2 acts (the 3rd uncompleted) by Schoenberg; text by composer. Concert perf., Hamburg (N.W.D.R.), 12 Mar. 1954. Prod. Zürich 6 June 1957, with H. H. Fiedler, Helmut Melchert, cond. Rosbaud; London, C.G., 28 Jun. 1965, cond. Solti.

Act 1. (1) Moses is called by God from the Burning Bush. (2) He meets his brother Aaron in the waste land, and they discuss the problem of communicating God's message, Moses doubting the possibility of truth taking accurate form in imagery that the people may understand, Aaron doubting the possibility of anyone worshipping 'what you dare not even conceive'. (3) The people await Moses and Aaron, and the message they bear, with mixed emotions. (4) The people are puzzled by the impalpability of the new God they are told to worship, and mistrustful. Aaron performs miracles to convince the people of God's power. They prepare to flee from Egypt, Moses promising spiritual comfort, Aaron material sustenance.

Interlude: the people ask anxiously what has happened to Moses, now long absent on Sinai.

Act 2. (1) Aaron and the 70 elders wait for Moses' return, Aaron promising that idea and form will appear together. (2) After 40 days the people's impatience breaks out and they demand a tangible god again. At the priests' (and his own) urging, Aaron makes them the Golden Calf. (3) An orgy ensues round the Golden Calf, with the sacrifice of four virgins precipitating scenes of utter abandon and destruction. (4) Moses is discerned returning with the tables of the law. He destroys the inarticulate image of the Calf. (5) He bitterly reproaches Aaron, who defends his action as necessary for the humble people whom he loves and feels he understands well, who can never grasp more than a partial image. The tables, he suggests, are themselves but part of the idea. Moses, appalled, shatters the tables, and resolves to be released from his mission. Aaron proposes himself as mouthpiece, and moves away with the people after the pillar of fire and smoke—God's image, he feels. Left alone, Moses despairingly addresses his 'Inconceivable God, inexpressible, many-sided idea', and sinks to the ground mourning, 'O word, thou word that I lack.'

The 3rd act, which has been staged, shows Moses triumphing over an Aaron held prisoner; Moses insists that 'to serve the divine idea is the purpose of the freedom for which this folk has been chosen'. Images govern the idea instead of expressing it, he points out, and Aaron's gifts, despiritualized, have been turned not to leading the people but to hurling them back into the waste land. Aaron is freed, but falls dead. Moses concludes, 'But even in the waste land you shall be victorious and achieve the goal: unity with God.'

Mother, The (Cz., *Matka*). Opera in 10 scenes by Alois Hába; text by composer. Prod. Munich 17 May 1931. The first quarter-tone opera. Rev. Florence, 5 Jun. 1964. Also title of operas by Stanley Hollier (after Hans Andersen) (1954) and Khrennikov (after Gorky) (1956).

Mother of Us All, The. Opera in 3 acts by Virgil Thomson; text by Gertrude Stein. Prod. New York 7 May 1947.

Motif, motive. See *Leitmotiv*.

Mottl, Felix (b. Unter-Sankt-Veit, 24 Aug. 1856; d. Munich, 2 July 1911). Austrian conductor and composer. Studied Vienna, where his teachers included Bruckner. One of Wagner's assistants at the first Bayreuth Festival, 1876, and subsequently conducted there 1888–1902. At Karlsruhe, 1881–1903, he raised the standard of performance to considerable heights, and gave there the first complete performance of *Les Troyens* (on two consecutive nights, Dec. 1890) as well as a revised version of Cornelius's *Der Barbier von Bagdad* (1884). London, C.G., 1898–1900; N.Y. 1903–4; Munich 1903–11 (director from 1907). Composed three operas and edited the vocal scores of all Wagner's works. Married soprano Zdenka Fassbänder (q.v.).

Mount-Edgcumbe, Earl of (Richard Edgcumbe) (b. Plymouth, 13 Sept. 1764; d. Richmond, 26 Sept. 1839). English writer and composer. His *Reminiscences*, published anonymously in 1825, and containing an account of Italian opera in London from 1773, is an amusing and valuable source-book. His *Zenobia* was produced at the King's Theatre in 1800.

Mozart, Wolfgang Amadeus (b. Salzburg, 27 Jan. 1756; d. Vienna, 5 Dec. 1791). Austrian composer. It was, by and large, into his piano concertos and operas that Mozart poured his most intense and personal music. If in the concertos we sense him, through the medium of his favoured instrument, in a special relation to his art, it is to the operas that we turn for his vivid, tender reflection of the world's aspirations and follies. Goethe's comparison of Mozart to Shakespeare is not merely one of stature: they both belong to the category of artists whose sensibilities, ungoverned by reforming zeal, are at the disposal of everything mankind has to show. We may further compare Mozart to Chaucer, the unobtrusive figure in the crowd cherishing every detail of the busy scene.

Mozart was born into an age still dominated by Italian opera. Leaving aside two early stage pieces, the sacred play *Die Schuldigkeit des ersten Gebotes* and the Latin comedy *Apollo et Hyacinthus*, his first opera is *La Finta Semplice* (1769). It is a stock Goldoni *opera buffa*, fluently imitating the best models. *Bastien und Bastienne* (1768) does use a German text, but is scarcely more advanced in its agreeable reflection of the Rousseau-inspired village comedy. *Mitridate, Rè di Ponto* (1770) is an *opera seria* of not much more scope, though it was successful enough to draw a commission for the serenata *Ascanio in Alba* (1771). In *Lucio Silla* (1772) there are traces of a maturer Mozart beginning to show themselves intermittently, and *La Finta Giardiniera* (1775), again to a routine *buffo* plot, is charming in places and interesting for the first signs of Mozart's symphonic approach to opera. Yet the festival play *Il Rè Pastore* (1775) is once more a string of arias. With the unfinished *Zaide* (1779) there is a clear step forward. 'I prefer German opera, even though it means more trouble for us', he wrote a few years afterwards; and there is in this *Singspiel* the seed of much that was to flower so richly not only in *Die Entführung*, whose plot it anticipates, but in *Die Zauberflöte*. Turning back to *opera seria*, Mozart now produced his first great stage masterpiece, *Idomeneo* (1781). 'There is a monumental strength and a white heat of passion that we find in this early work of Mozart's and shall not find again', wrote Dent. *Opera seria* in form, it already possesses that most typically Mozartian quality, the power to transcend old forms without breaking them; for though the conventions are observed and influences (principally of Gluck) are present, *Idomeneo* looks directly forward across the later operas to Wagnerian music drama itself. *Die Entführung aus dem Serail* (1782) is a much simpler construction, a musical play with set numbers that charmingly illuminate the situations. *L'Oca del Cairo* and *Lo Sposo Deluso* (both 1783, unfin.) are unimportant; *Der Schauspieldirektor* (1786), though slight, entertainingly guys the opera world.

With *Le Nozze di Figaro* (1786) we enter upon the four late masterpieces. Mozart does not set the spinning intrigues of Beaumarchais's *folle journée* as social satire, but responds to the brilliantly contrasted figures with music of a new compassion and perception. The opera is an enormous advance on its predecessors: moving at a heightened pace, it none the less explores situation and character more fully, and whether in the beautiful set arias or in the great symphonic finales, this riotous harlequinade never loses contact with each of the human beings it creates. With *Don Giovanni*, musically and dramatically a less perfect structure, the range expands still further. Revolving round the possessed central figure are characters familiar to every age, and the music's supernatural power of simultaneously facing tragedy and comedy severs almost the last connexions, still present in *Figaro*, with set types. This vastly increased world of experience and understanding was next brought to bear upon an anecdote with, for title, the tavern catch-phrase *Così fan tutte* (1790). Yet Mozart cannot help bringing the six participants into our affections by giving them complete musical characters; and in so doing he transforms a practical joke into a ruefully humorous comment on our human failings. *Così* is insincerity and cynicism raised to the level of great art, qualities that roused the gravest Victorian misgivings and produced various bowdlerizations. The last masterpiece was also Mozart's strangest and most inspiring work—*Die Zauberflöte* (1791). To some it is but a muddled pantomime, redeemed (as the unsuccessful *opera seria*, *La Clemenza di Tito* (1791) was to a lesser extent) by some ravishing musical numbers. But for any who look further, Mozart's feeling for the brotherhood of many-sided man, and his lifelong care for truth in human behaviour, are now turned to spiritual ends. The absurd, contradictory fantasy mysteriously becomes a vessel for Mozart's innermost religious longings. He is the playful Papageno, but also the hero Tamino, whose quest transforms itself from simple amorous adventure to a journey, through rigorous self-chastening, towards an absolute truth.

Operas on him are by Riotte (*Mozarts Zauberflöte*, 1820), Lortzing (1832), Rimsky-Korsakov (see below), and Reynaldo Hahn (1925).

Mozart and Salieri. Opera in 2 acts by Rimsky-Korsakov; text a setting of Pushkin's dramatic poem. Prod. Moscow 7 Dec. 1898, with Chaliapin and Erslov; London, Albert Hall, 11 Oct. 1927; Forest Park, Pa., 6 Aug. 1933. The subject is the rivalry between the two composers and includes the unfounded story that Salieri had poisoned Mozart.

Much Ado About Nothing. Opera in 4 acts by Stanford; text by Sturgis, based on Shakespeare's comedy (1598–9). Prod. London, C.G., 30 May 1901, with Adams, Brema, Hyde, Bispham, Plançon. Performed in Leipzig 1902 and revived London, R.C.M., 1935.

Muck, Karl (b. Darmstadt, 22 Oct. 1859; d. Stuttgart, 3 Mar. 1940). German conductor. Studied Leipzig and began career as professional pianist. Chorus master, Zürich; subsequently conductor there and at Salzburg, Graz, and Brno. Engaged by Neumann for Prague 1886. Cond. Neumann's Wagner Company in first performances of *The Ring* in Moscow and St. Petersburg 1889. Berlin Opera 1892–1912 (Generalmusikdirektor from 1908). During period in Berlin he conducted 1,071 performances of 103 operas, of which 35 were novelties. London, C.G., 1899; Bayreuth 1901–

30, where he was generally considered the greatest conductor of *Parsifal* of his generation. (R)

Mudie, Michael (b. Manchester, 3 Dec. 1914; d. Brussels, 27 Apr. 1962). English conductor. Studied London, R.C.M. Conductor Carl Rosa 1935–9; S.W., 1946–53, when ill health forced him to retire from active music-making. He conducted the first performance in England of *Simone Boccanegra*, and was regarded as one of the most promising opera conductors of his day, especially in the Italian repertory. (R)

Muette de Portici, La (The Dumb Girl of Portici). Opera in 5 acts by Auber; text by Scribe and Delavigne. Prod. Paris, O., 29 Feb. 1828, with Damoreau and Nourrit; London, D.L. (as *Masaniello*, under which title it is generally known), 4 May 1829; N.Y. 15 Mar. 1831. Fanella, Masaniello's dumb sister, is imprisoned by Alfonso. Masaniello captures Naples and wins the crown, but he loses his mind after being poisoned, and Alfonso puts down the revolt. Masaniello is killed and Fanella commits suicide by leaping from her window into the crater of Vesuvius. The opera, based on historical happenings in Naples, 1647, when the people rose against their Spanish oppressors, was the signal for the Belgian revolt after a performance in Brussels on 25 Aug. 1830.

Mugnone, Leopoldo (b. Naples, 29 Sept. 1858; d. Naples, 22 Dec. 1941). Italian conductor and composer. Studied Naples, and began career by writing a comic opera, *Il Dottore Bartolo Salsapariglia*, prod. when he was 12. When 16 he directed a season of comic opera at La Fenice, Venice. Cond. the premières of *Cavalleria Rusticana* (1890) and *Tosca* (1900). La Scala from 1891. London, C.G., 1905, 1906, 1919, and 1924, where he conducted the first London performances of *Adriana Lecouvreur*, *Fedora*, and *Iris*. Beecham considered him the best Italian opera conductor of his period.

Mulè, Giuseppe (b. Termini Imerese, 28 June 1885; d. Rome, 10 Sept. 1951). Italian composer. Studied Palermo. Director Santa Cecilia from 1926. His six operas include two on classical subjects (which specially appealed to him) for which he drew on Sicilian folk-song, *Dafni* (1928) and *Taormina* (1938).

Mulhouse (Ger., Mülhausen). Town in Haut-Rhin, France. After more than a century of average provincial opera under both French and German direction, Mulhouse has, since 1946, become one of the best operatic centres in France. From 1946 to 1948 Roger Lalande was the theatre's director, and staged there the first production in France of Britten's *Rape of Lucretia*, as well as the première of Büsser's *Roxane*. Lalande was succeeded by Pierre Deloger from the Opéra-Comique, and under his administration there have been several premières including Paul Bastide's *Jeanne d'Arc*, Tomasi's *L'Atlantide*, and Michel-Maurice Lévy's *Moïse*, as well as the first performances in French of *Boris* and *The Consul*, and the first local performances of *Così fan tutte*, *Angélique*, *La Vida Breve*, *L'Aiglon*, and *Le Roi Malgré Lui*. Among singers who made their débuts at Mulhouse are Lily Pons and Fanély Révoil.

Müller, Maria (b. Theresienstadt, 29 Jan. 1898; d. Bayreuth, 13 Mar. 1958). Austrian soprano. Studied Vienna with Schmedes and N.Y. with Altglass. Début Linz 1919, Elsa. After engagements in Prague and Munich, N.Y., Met., 1925, remaining until end of 1934–5 season. In N.Y. the first Dorota (*Schwanda*), Mariola (*Fra Gherardo*), and Maria (*Simone Boccanegra*). Berlin (State and Städtische Operas) 1926–43, 1950–2; London, C.G., 1934 and 1937; Bayreuth 1930–9; Salzburg 1931–4. In addition to her Wagner roles, in which she was greatly admired, she sang with success as Jenůfa, Iphigénie, and Reiza. Her voice was warm and vibrant, and her acting abilities above the average. (R)

Müller, Wenzel (b. Trnava, 26 Sept. 1767; d. Baden, 3 Aug. 1835). Austrian composer and conductor. He was conductor at the Brno theatre by the age of 16, at the Theater in der Leopoldstadt in Vienna by 19, where apart from a period (1803–13) as director of the Prague Opera, he remained all his life. His operas are slight, though they were popular in their day and drew the attention of other composers. Schikaneder used several ideas in *Kaspar der Fagottist, oder die Zauberzither* (1791) for *The Magic Flute*. Müller's greatest successes were *Das Neusonntagskind* (1793) and *Die Schwestern von Prag* (1794), from which came the song 'Ich bin der Schneider Kakadu' used as the theme of some variations for piano trio by Beethoven (Op. 121a).

Mullings, Frank (b. Walsall, 10 Mar. 1881; d. Manchester, 19 May 1953). English tenor. Studied Birmingham. Début Coventry 1907, Faust. Denhof Company 1913; Beecham Company 1916–21; B.N.O.C. 1922–6. Created Hadyar in *Naïl* (De Lara) and Apollo in *Alkestis* (Boughton). The first Parsifal in English, and a distinguished Tristan, Siegfried, and Tannhäuser. His greatest role was Otello, for which his imposing stature and acting ability, coupled with a robust voice, ideally suited him. (R)

Munich (Ger., München). Town in Bavaria, Germany. The first recorded opera performance was in Aug. 1653, when Maccioni's dramatic cantata *L'Arpe Festante* was performed there. The Residenztheater, a model of rococo art designed by Cuvilliès, was opened in 1753 with Ferrandini's *Catone in Utica*, and among the works that received their first performances there were Mozart's *La Finta Giardiniera* (1775) and *Idomeneo* (1781). The Hof und Nationaltheater, built to plans by Karl von Fischer, was opened in 1818 (burned 1823; rebuilt 1825; bombed 1943). The fame of the Munich Opera dates from 1852 when Lachner (q.v.) became Generalmusikdirektor. The Ludwig–Wagner relationship led to the premières of *Tristan, Meistersinger, Rheingold*, and *Walküre* being given at Munich. Hans von Bülow was musical director 1867–9; Franz Wüller 1869–71; Hermann Levi 1872–96; Mottl 1903–11; Bruno Walter 1911–22; Knappertsbusch 1922–34; Clemens Krauss 1937–44; Ferdinand Leitner 1944–6; Georg Solti 1946–52; Rudolf Kempe 1952–4; Ferenc Fricsay 1955–9; Keilberth 1959–68; Sawallisch from 1971. Munich's Strauss tradition dates from 1919, when performances of his works became a feature of the season and annual summer festivals, under Knappertsbusch, Karl Böhm, Krauss, and the composer himself; *Friedenstag* and *Capriccio* both received their premières there (Strauss himself had been a Kapellmeister there in 1886–9 and 1894–8).

Munich's third opera house, the Prinzregententheater (cap. 1,122), was built as a festival theatre by Ernst von Possart on the same model as Bayreuth. It was intended originally only for Wagner, and opened on 28 Aug. 1901 with *Meistersinger*. From 1945 to 1963 it was the permanent home of the Bavarian State Opera. The destroyed Nationaltheater has been rebuilt and was opened in 1963; the Residenz has been rebuilt on modern lines, but Cuvilliès's rococo auditorium of the old Residenz has been reconstructed in the Alte Residenz and reopened in June 1958.

Operas that have had their premières in Munich in this century apart from the Strauss operas mentioned above include Pfitzner's *Palestrina*, Coates's *Samuel Pepys*, Orff's *Der Mond*, and Hindemith's *Die Harmonie der Welt*. The Munich Company has included at one time or another virtually every great German opera singer of the day.

Munsel, Patrice (b. Spokane, Washington, 14 May 1925). American soprano. Studied N.Y. with William Herman and Renato Bellini. Won Met. Auditions of Air 1943, début there (youngest singer ever to appear there) 1943, Filine in *Mignon* under Beecham. Has sung there regularly since, mostly in coloratura repertory, and as Adele, Despina, and Zerlina. European début Copenhagen 1948, Rosina. Took part of Melba in film of that name (1953). (R)

Münster. Town in North Rhine–Westphalia, Germany. Opera is given in the new city theatre (cap. 950) opened in 1956.

Muratore, Lucien (b. Marseilles, 29 Aug. 1878; d. Paris, 16 July 1954). French tenor. Studied Marseilles as horn-player. Began career on straight stage and appeared opposite Réjane and Sarah Bernhardt. Studied voice Paris Conservatoire. Début Paris, O.C., 1902, Le Roi in Hahn's *La Carmélite*. Paris, O., 1905–11; Boston 1913; Chicago 1913–22; never at C.G. Created more than 30 roles including Thésée in *Ariane*, title role in *Bacchus*, Lentulus in *Roma*, all by Massenet, Prinzivalle in Février's *Monna Vanna*, Edmond in Missa's *Miguette*. For seven years was mayor of Biot. In 1943 he settled in Paris and was manager of the O.C. at time of liberation. He was famous as a teacher and his pupils include Kenneth Neate. He was an impressive actor and a skilful vocalist. (R)

Murska, Ilma di. See *Di Murska*.

Musetta. Marcello's lover (sop.) in Puccini's and Leoncavallo's *La Bohème*.

Music drama. The name given to works in which the musical and dramatic elements are (or are intended to be) entirely unified, with every other consideration (such as opportunities for display by singers) subjugated to this end. The term first came into general use with Wagner: he realized in his later works the ideal to which German opera had been groping since Spohr and Weber, who preached it as an ideal and partly realized it in *Euryanthe*. See also *Dramma per musica*.

Mussorgsky, Modest (b. Karevo, 21 Mar. 1839; d. St. Petersburg, 28 Mar. 1881). Russian composer. Mussorgsky only completed one opera, his masterpiece *Boris Godunov*. His three earliest projects were *Han d'Islande* (1856), after Victor Hugo; *Oedipus in Athens* (1858–61), of which there survives only a choral scene, later to be incorporated in *Salammbô*, *Mlada*, and *Sorochinsky Fair*, and some other choruses; and *St. John's Eve* (1858), after Gogol. *Salammbô* (1863–6), after Flaubert, is also unfinished, and remains interesting chiefly for its lyrical elements and for a tough realism which hints at *Boris*. The latter quality is developed in the first and only completed act of *The Marriage* (1909), after Gogol, a lively comedy of manners that further exercised Mussorgsky's gift for realistically inflected musical speech and characterization, for the first time by way of *Leitmotiv*.

Mussorgsky was by now growing interested in an opera on Pushkin's *Boris Godunov*: the original version was completed by 1870. Here the lyrical and realistic elements are fully developed and balanced. Though *Boris* has antecedents in Romantic opera, in Meyerbeer, and more immediately in Dargomizhsky's (q.v.) *Stone Guest*, it is a unique and original product of them. The personal tragedy of Tsar Boris is played out against a living backcloth of the Russian people—there is not only intense individual characterization but a feeling for corporate emotions in boyars, foreign nobles, and peasants that gives the opera much of its Russian quality and extraordinary violence of impact. The subject suited Mussorgsky's talents ideally—his acute dramatic flair, his gift for reflecting broad and subtle detail in music, his humane and national sympathies. When he revised the opera in 1871–2 he softened his portrait of Boris and generally heightened the romantic elements, sacrificing thereby some of the work's grim strength.

While negotiating the production of *Boris* in 1870, Mussorgsky began a new opera, *Bobil*: one scene was later inserted in *Khovanshchina*. He also collaborated with Rimsky-Korsakov, Borodin, and Cui in a projected opera-ballet, *Mlada* (1872), using parts of the *Oedipus* music and *Night on the Bare Mountain*. He began planning another historical opera, *Khovanshchina* (1872–80). This is less dramatic or sharply characterized than *Boris*, but it contains moving and powerful scenes.

Work on *Khovanshchina* was interrupted by yet another project destined to remain unrealized, the comedy *Sorochinsky Fair* (1874–80), after Gogol. This draws heavily on Ukrainian folk-music. For the last project, *Pugachevshchina* (1877), he had begun noting down Kirghiz, Transcaucasian, and other tunes.

Mustafà. The Bey of Algiers (bass) in Rossini's *L'Italiana in Algeri*.

Muzio, Claudia (b. Pavia, 7 Feb. 1889; d. Rome, 24 May 1936). Italian soprano. Her father was stage manager at C.G. and Met. for many years. Studied Turin with Casaloni, and Milan with Viviani. Début Messina 1910, Gilda. London, C.G., 1914; N.Y., Met., 1916–22 and 1933–4 (created Giorgetta, *Tabarro*, 1918, and was first American Tatiana and first Met. Loreley and Madeleine de Coigny); Chicago 1922–31. Great favourite at Buenos Aires, Colón, and Rome Opera. Besides Giorgetta, created Baronessa di Carini (Mulè), Melenis (Zandonai), and Cecilia (Refice). Her greatest roles were Violetta, Desdemona, and Madeleine de Coigny. She possessed a beautiful voice and a moving warmth of personality. (R)

N

Nabucodonosor—more commonly, **Nabucco** (Nebuchadnezzar). Opera in 4 acts by Verdi; text by Solera. Prod. Milan, Sc., 9 Mar. 1842 with Strepponi, Ronconi; London, H.M.'s, as *Nino*, 3 Mar. 1846; N.Y., Astor Opera House, 4 Apr. 1848. The opera tells of the Babylonian captivity of the Hebrews and of Nabucco's madness, recovery, and subsequent conversion to the faith of Jehovah, despite the opposition of his daughter Abigaille. Also opera by Ariosti (1706).

Nachbaur, Franz (b. Weiler Giessen, Württemberg, 25 Mar. 1835; d. Munich, 21 Mar. 1902). German tenor. Studied Stuttgart with Pischek and Milan with Lamperti. After appearances in Mannheim, Prague, Darmstadt, and Vienna, joined Munich Opera 1866, remaining there until 1890. Created Walther and Froh. London, D.L., 1882, where he sang Adolar in a revival of *Euryanthe*.

Nacht in Venedig, Eine (A Night in Venice). Operetta in 3 acts by Johann Strauss II; text by 'F. Zell' (Camillo Walzel) and Genée. Prod. Berlin, Friedrich-Wilhelm Städtisches Theater, 3 Oct. 1883 for opening of theatre; N.Y. 8 Dec. 1889; London, Cambridge T., 25 May 1944.

Nadir. A fisherman (ten.), Zurga's friend and rival for Leïla's love in Bizet's *The Pearl Fishers*.

Nannetta. Ford's daughter (sop.) and Fenton's lover in Verdi's *Falstaff*.

Nantier-Didiée, Constance (b. Saint-Denis, 16 Nov. 1831; d. Madrid, 4 Dec. 1867). French mezzo-soprano. Studied Paris with Duprez. Début Turin, Giunia in Mercadante's *La Vestale*; London, C.G., 1853–4 (Ly. 1856–7), where she was the first London Maddalena (*Rigoletto*) and Ascanio (*Benvenuto Cellini*) and the first C.G. Ulrica and Siebel (Gounod wrote 'Si le bonheur a souri' especially for her). Also sang regularly in Paris, St. Petersburg (where she created Preziosilla), and Madrid.

Naples (It., Napoli). Town in Campania, Italy. The first opera performed here was Cirillo's *L'Orontea, Regina d'Egitto* on 3 Apr. 1654 at the Teatro di San Bartolomeo. By the end of the century Naples had supplanted Venice as the centre of opera in Italy, and the Neapolitans had built two more theatres, the Teatro dei Fiorentini and the Teatro Nuovo. There Alessandro Scarlatti and his contemporaries Stradella and Rossi flourished. By the middle of the 18th century *opera buffa* had developed under Pergolesi and Jommelli, and then Galuppi and Paisiello. See also *San Carlo*.

Napoli, Jacopo (b. Naples, 26 Aug. 1911). Italian composer. Studied Cons. S. Pietro, Naples, where he eventually became director. His comic operas, which use Neapolitan songs, include *Il Malato Immaginario* (1939), *Miseria e Nobiltà* (1945), and *Un Curioso Accidente* (1950), and have enjoyed a limited success. His *Masaniello* (1953) was awarded one of the prizes in La Scala's Verdi competition.

Napravnik, Eduard (b. Býšt, 24 Aug. 1839; d. Petrograd, 23 Nov. 1916). Russian conductor and composer of Czech birth. After some early composing and criticism he went to St. Petersburg to direct a private orchestra. He became Lyadov's assistant at the imperial theatres, rising to second conductor in 1867 and succeeding Lyadov as principal conductor in 1869. A brilliant musician and administrator, he raised the standard at the Imperial Opera, paying particular attention to the skill and welfare of the orchestra, which became famous. He conducted over 4,000 performances during his career there, many of them first performances, e.g. *The Stone Guest*, *Boris Godunov*, *The Maid of Pskov*, and three of Tchaikovsky's operas, *The Oprichnik*, *Vakula the Smith*, and *The Maid of Orleans* (which was dedicated to Napravnik). His own operas show considerable technical fluency unaccompanied by any striking individuality.

Nash, Heddle (b. London, 1896; d. London, 14 Aug. 1961). English tenor. Studied London and Milan with Giuseppe Borghatti. Début Milan 1924, Almaviva. London, Old Vic and S.W., from 1925; B.N.O.C.; C.G. 1929–39 and 1947–8; Glyndebourne 1934–8; Carl Rosa during war years; New Opera Company 1957–8. A cultured Mozart singer, his Ottavio being compared to McCormack's, and an incomparable David in *Meistersinger*. Created Dr. Manette in Benjamin's *Tale of Two Cities*. His lyrical voice had great natural charm. (R) His son **John Heddle Nash** (b. London, 30 March 1928) is a baritone and has sung with the S.W. and C.R. Companies. (R)

National Broadcasting Company Television Opera (N.B.C.). Formed in N.Y. 1949–50 with Samuel Chotzinoff as producer and Peter Herman Adler as music and artistic director. Has given performance of many operas, including the first in the U.S.A. of *Billy Budd*, *War and Peace*, and *Dialogues des Carmélites*. It commissioned Menotti's *Amahl and the Night Visitors* and Hollingsworth's *La Grande Bretèche*, and gave the world première of Martinů's *The Marriage*. It was also responsible for the controversial Auden–Kallmann version of *The Magic Flute* in the Mozart bicentenary year. In 1956 the N.B.C. Opera Company toured 47 American cities, and in 1957–8 55 cities, with *Figaro*, *Traviata*, and *Butterfly*.

Naudin, Emilio (b. Parma, 23 Oct. 1823; d. Bologna, 5 May 1890). Italian tenor of French parentage. Studied Milan. Début Cremona 1843 in Pacini's *Saffo*. London, D.L., 1858 and subsequently H.M.'s and C.G. where he sang regularly 1863–72, where he was the first London Don Carlos. A famous Vasco da Gama (which he had created in Paris 1865), Fra Diavolo, and Masaniello. Sang Lohengrin in the English provinces and Tannhäuser in Moscow (1877).

Navarraise, La (The Girl from Navarre). Opera in 2 acts by Massenet; text by J. Claretie and H. Cain, after the former's story *La Cigarette*. Prod. London, C.G., 20 June 1894 with Calvé, Alvarez, Gilibert, Plançon; Paris, O.C., 3 Oct. 1895 with Calvé, Jérome, Mondaud, Belhomme; N.Y., Met., 11 Dec. 1895 with Calvé, Lubert, Castelmary, Plançon. Revived Paris 1913, 1922, and 1928. Massenet's third opera of 1894 (*Thaïs* and *Le Portrait de Manon* being the other two), and his only contribution to *verismo*.

Navarrini, Francesco (b. Citadella, 1855; d. Milan, 23 Feb. 1923). Italian bass. Studied Milan. Début Treviso 1878, Alfonso (*Lucrezia Borgia*). Sang in most Italian opera houses. London, D.L., 1887; C.G. 1888; St. Petersburg, Moscow, &c. Created Lodovico (*Otello*) and other roles, and had a repertory that included leading bass roles in Wagner and French and Italian opera. His exceptional height (6 ft. 6 in.) and fine voice combined to make him one of the most imposing bass singers of his day. (R)

Nedda. Canio's wife (sop.) in Leoncavallo's *Pagliacci*.

Neher, Caspar (b. Augsburg, 11 Apr. 1897; d. Vienna, 30 June 1962). German designer and librettist. Studied Munich with Pasetti and Vienna with Roller. Designer at the Kroll Oper, Berlin, in Klemperer régime 1924–8, then Städtische Oper with Ebert 1931–3, designing *Macbeth*, *Ballo in Maschera*, and other works. Wrote and designed *Die Bürgschaft* (Weill). Neher's designs for *Macbeth* have also been seen in England (Glyndebourne) and N.Y., Met., and his *Wozzeck* at C.G., Salzburg, Vienna, and N.Y. Also provided the libretti for Einem's *Agamemnon* and Wagner-Régeny's *Der Günstling*, *Die Bürger von Calais*, and *Johanna Balk*.

Neidlinger, Gustav (b. Mainz, 21 Mar. 1912). German bass-baritone. Studied Frankfurt. Début Mainz

1931. Hamburg 1936–50; Stuttgart since 1950; Bayreuth since 1952. London, R.F.H., with Stuttgart Company, 1955; C.G. 1963, Telramund, 1965, Alberich. One the best of contemporary German character baritones, a fine Pizarro, Alberich, and Lysiart. (R)

Nelusko. The slave (bar.) in Meyerbeer's *L'Africaine.*

Nemeth, Maria (b. Körmend, 13 Mar. 1899; d. Vienna, 28 Dec. 1967). Hungarian sopr. Studied Budapest with Georg Anthes, Naples with De Lucia. Début Budapest 1923, Amelia. Vienna State Opera 1925–42; London, C.G., 1931. One of the best Turandots, Toscas, Donna Annas of the inter-war years. Her dramatic soprano voice of great flexibility and range also suited her to Constanze and the Queen of the Night. (R)

Nemico della patria. Gérard's monologue in Act 3 of Giordano's *Andrea Chénier.*

Nemorino. The peasant hero (ten.) of Donizetti's *L'Elisir d'Amore.*

Neri, Giulio (b. Siena, 1909; d. Rome, 21 Apr. 1958). Italian bass. Studied Rome. Début Rome 1938, where he became leading bass. London, C.G., 1953. His enormous repertory included bass roles in Wagner and Verdi. He was a famous Mefistofele and Basilio. (R)

Nerone (Nero). Opera in 4 acts by Boito; text by the composer. Music left unfinished at time of Boito's death and completed by Tommasini and Toscanini. Prod. Milan, Sc., 1 May 1924 with Raisa, Pertile, Galeffi, Journet, and Pinza; cond. Toscanini. Also opera in 3 acts by Mascagni; text by Targioni-Tozzetti, after Pietro Cossa's comedy (1872). Prod. Milan, Sc., 16 Jan. 1935, with Bruna Rasa, Carosio, Pertile, Granforte; cond. Mascagni.

Boito's opera is the work of a sincere and fine musician, and forcefully contrasts the dying pagan world with Christianity; Mascagni's work, on the other hand, has made little impression. He had started work on it originally in 1891 but had laid it aside when he heard from Verdi that Boito was working on the same subject. He offered it to various Italian opera houses within ten weeks of the production of Boito's work, and it was only much later, after years of negotiation with La Scala, and, it is said, with Mussolini's intervention, that the work was finally accepted.

There are about 10 other operas on Nero.

Nessi, Giuseppe (b. Bergamo, 25 Sept. 1887; d. Milan, 16 Dec. 1961). Italian tenor. Début Saluzzo 1910, Alfredo, but on Serafin's advice became a character tenor. La Scala's leading comprimario tenor 1921–59. London, C.G., 1927–37 and again with La Scala Co. 1950. Created Pang, Donna Pasqua (*Il Campiello*), and many roles in modern Italian works. An inimitable Bardolfo (which he sang at Salzburg under Toscanini), Goro, Spoletta, and Missail (*Boris*). (R)

Nessler, Victor (b. Baldenheim, 28 Jan. 1841; d. Strasbourg, 28 May 1890). German composer and conductor. The success of his early *Fleurette* decided him to devote himself entirely to music. After producing several more operas, he became chorus master at Leipzig in 1870. Nine years later he took over the conductorship of the Caroltheater and produced his first wider success, *Der Rattenfänger von Hameln.* A still greater triumph followed in 1884, *Der Trompeter von Säckingen.* None of his later works won a comparable success; its sentimental harmonies and catchy melodies illustrating a popular legend made *Der Trompeter* enormously fashionable.

Nessun dorma. Calaf's (ten.) aria in Act 3, scene 1, of Puccini's *Turandot,* sung while Pekin is searched all night to find someone who can tell Turandot Calaf's name.

Neues Deutsches Theater. See *Prague.*

Neues vom Tage (News of the Day). Opera in 3 parts by Hindemith; text by Schiffer. Prod. Berlin, Kroll, 8 June 1929, the last of Hindemith's operas to be produced in Germany until after the Hitler régime. It was revised by Hindemith and heard in Naples 1954, and again in Germany (Cologne) 1956; Santa Fé, New Mexico, 12 Aug. 1961.

Neumann, Angelo (b. Vienna, 18 Aug. 1838; d. Prague, 20 Dec. 1910). Austrian tenor and impresario. Studied with Stilke-Sessi. Début 1859. Vienna Opera 1862–76. Director of Leipzig Opera 1876–82; Bremen Opera 1882–5; Prague, Landestheater, 1885–1910. Formed a touring company based on Leipzig to take Wagner's operas, including *The Ring*, to London, Paris, Rome, St. Petersburg, &c. He wrote a volume of reminiscences, *Erinnerungen an R. Wagner* (1907).

Nevada (orig. Wixom), **Emma** (b. Alpha, California, 7 Jan. 1859; d. Liverpool, 20 June 1940). American soprano. Studied Vienna with Marchesi. Début London, H.M.'s, 1880 as Amina, taking name of Nevada from the city near which she was born. Sang widely in Europe and N.Y., Ac. of M., 1884–5. An especially fine Bellini singer, her medallion being placed alongside those of Pasta and Malibran on the composer's statue in Catania.

Nevada, Mignon (b. Paris, 14 Aug. 1886). English soprano, daughter of above, with whom she studied. Début Rome 1908, Rosina. London, C.G., 1910 in Beecham season. Sang elsewhere in Europe including Sc. and Paris, O.C.

New Opera Company, London. Originally a part-amateur and part-professional group founded in Cambridge, this company has, since 1960, become part of the S.W. organization and given short annual seasons devoted to modern opera. Works given by the company since 1957 include Benjamin's *A Tale of Two Cities*, Egk's *Der Revisor*, Dallapiccola's *Il Prigioniero*, Schoenberg's *Erwartung*, Henze's *Boulevard Solitude*, all first English stage performances, and Prokofiev's *Love of the Three Oranges*.

New Opera Company, New York. A short-lived organization that was founded by Mrs. Lytle Hull in 1941 with Fritz Busch as its musical director. Performances of *Così fan tutte* and *Macbeth* based on the Glyndebourne productions of the 1930's were given, as well as *The Queen of Spades*, *La Vie Parisienne*, *Sorochinsky Fair*, and *Die Fledermaus*. Singers who began their careers with the company include Regina Resnik, Jess Walters, Martha Lipton, Winifrid Heidt, and Virginia MacWatters. The conductors, in addition to Busch, were Antal Dorati, Herman Adler, Emil Cooper, Erich Korngold, and Fritz Stiedry.

New Orleans. Town in Louisiana, U.S.A. Operas given at the French Opera House, built 1859, destroyed 1919, which replaced the earlier T. St. Pierre, T. St. Philippe, and T. d'Orléans, included the American premières of many important works, among them *Hérodiade*, *Samson et Dalila*, *Benvenuto Cellini*, *Siberia*, *Amica*, *Le Chemineau*, *Don Quichotte*. Earlier New Orleans had been the scene of the American premières of *L'Elisir d'Amore*, *La Favorite*, *La Juive*, *Le Prophète*, and *La Vestale*. The New Orleans French Opera Troupe, with singers mostly recruited in Paris, toured the U.S.A. at intervals from 1900 to 1919. After the destruction of the French Opera House there was no resident opera until 1943 when the New Orleans Opera House Association came into being. In the following year Walter Herbert became its musical director, and by Oct. 1950 100 performances had been given of popular repertory works, with international artists in the leading roles. Renato Cellini was music and artistic director 1954–64 founding the Experimental Opera Theatre of America. The American débuts of Vinay, Menkes, Krenn, and others took place in New Orleans, and Kirsten, Conley, Hines, London, and Simoneau were all heard there before they became internationally famous.

New Theatre, New York. Opened 1909 and primarily a straight theatre, but used occasionally by opera companies. Renamed the Century Theatre, and used for opera 1913–14, and by a resident company giving opera in English in the early 1920's. Also used for the New York season of Gallo's San Carlo Company. Demolished *c.* 1930.

New York. Town in U.S.A. During the first half of the 18th century ballad operas were heard in N.Y. In 1752 the first theatre built for musical entertainment was opened, and in 1767 the John Street Theatre was opened. There in Mar. 1794 was performed Hewitt's *Tammanny, or the Indian Chief*, one of the earliest of American operas. In 1796 Carr's *The Archers, or Mountaineers of Switzerland* was given there; this is the first American opera of which parts of the music are extant. In 1798 the Park Theatre (q.v.) was opened and it was there that the first Italian opera in New York was heard, Rossini's *Il Barbiere di Siviglia*, given by Garcia's company in 1828. Other theatres in New York in which opera was heard in the last century included the Academy of Music (q.v.), Astor Place Opera House, the Broadway Theatre, Castle Gardens (q.v.), Italian Opera House (q.v.), New Theatre (q.v.), Palmo's Opera House (q.v.), Park Theatre (q.v.), Niblo's Gardens (q.v.), Richmond Hill Theatre, Stadt Theatre. See also *After Dinner Opera Company, City Center, Damrosch Opera Company, Juilliard School, Manhattan Opera Company, Metropolitan Opera House*.

New York City Opera. See *City Center.*

Neway, Patricia (b. Brooklyn, 30 Sept. 1919). American soprano. Début Chautauqua Summer Opera 1946, Fiordiligi. Female Chorus in *The Rape of Lucretia* on its N.Y. production (1948–9), created Magda Sorel in *The Consul* (1950), Leah in Tammkin's *The Dybbuk* (N.Y. 1951); also sang Marie in *Wozzeck* there. Iphigénie at Aix Festival 1952; Tosca, and Katiusha in Alfano's *Risurrezione*, which was revived for her at Paris, O.C. (R)

Newman, Ernest (orig. William Roberts) b. Liverpool, 30 Nov. 1868; d. Tadworth, 6 July 1959). English critic. While still in commerce studied music and philosophy, writing *Gluck and the Opera* (1895) and *A Study of Wagner* (1899). On staff of Midland Institute of Music, Birmingham 1903–5; critic *Manchester Guardian* 1905–19; *Observer* 1919–20; *The Sunday Times* 1920–58. Newman's great love was opera and Wagner in particular. His *Wagner as Man and Artist, Wagner Nights, Fact and Fiction about Richard Wagner*, and above all the four-volume *Life of Richard Wagner* form the most authoritative and valuable collection of works on this composer. Newman also translated most of Wagner's operas, and his versions of *Tannhäuser* and *Meistersinger* have been used at post-war C.G.

Niblo's Gardens. These gardens, between Broadway and Princes Street, New York, included the Sans Souci Theatre. It opened in July 1827, and was the scene of various opera seasons including those by Shireff's English Company (1838), the New Orleans French Company (1840), the Havana Italian Company (1848 and 1850)—the company included Steffanoni, Bosio, Marini, &c., and had Sontag as its prima donna (1854). The Gardens were closed in 1895.

Nicholls, Agnes (Lady (Hamilton) Harty) (b. Cheltenham, 14 July 1877; d. London, 21 Sept. 1959). English soprano. Studied London, R.C.M., with Visetti. Début London, Ly., 1895, Dido. London, C.G., 1901–8, and subsequently with the Denhof, Beecham, and B.N.O.C. Companies. Sang Sieglinde and *Siegfried* Brünnhilde in the English *Ring* under Richter 1908, and was also a famous Donna Elvira. (R)

Nicklausse. Hoffmann's friend (mezzo), in Offenbach's *Les Contes d'Hoffmann.*

Nicolai, Otto (b. Königsberg, 9 June 1810; d. Berlin, 11 May 1849). German composer and conductor. Running away from an unhappy home, he was helped in his studies in Rome by friends and by 1837 had become Kapellmeister and singing master at the Kärntnertor in Vienna, returning to Rome the following year. He later became Kapellmeister at the Court in Vienna, and in Berlin. His long list of operas culminated in his greatest success, *Die lustigen Weiber von Windsor* (1849), which, despite Verdi's greater

Falstaff, has with good reason retained its position in Germany as one of the most popular of comic operas.

Nicolini (orig. Nicolas), **Ernest** (b. Saint-Malo, 23 Feb. 1834; d. Pau, 19 Jan. 1898). French tenor. Studied Paris Conservatoire. Début Paris, O.C., 1857 in Halévy's *Mousquetaires de la Reine*. Sang in Italy as Nicolini. London, C.G., 1866 and again from 1872 to 1884, where he was the first London Lohengrin, Pery (Gomes's *Il Guarany*), and Radamès. He appeared frequently opposite Patti, whom he married in 1886.

Nicolino (real name Nicolò Grimaldi) (b. Naples, Apr. 1673; d. Naples, 1 Jan. 1732). Italian male contralto. After making his name in Italy, he came to London in 1708, where his success was enormous—in *The Spectator* Addison went so far as to call him 'the greatest performer in dramatic music that is now living, or that ever appeared upon a stage'. Praised equally for his acting and his singing. Handel's original Rinaldo and Amadigi.

Nielsen, Carl (b. Nørre Lyndelse, 9 June 1865; d. Copenhagen, 2 Oct. 1931). Danish composer. Nielsen's reputation rests chiefly upon his symphonic music, though his two operas have won praise. *Saul and David* (1902) is an imposing work of his first maturity, and was initially controversial; *Maskarade* (1906) is a comedy that won for itself a position comparable to *Halka* or *The Bartered Bride* as a national opera. It lacks the latter's deftness of touch, but contains some fine lyrical music.

Niemann, Albert (b. Erxleben, Magdeburg, 15 Jan. 1831; d. Berlin, 13 Jan. 1917). German tenor. Début Dessau 1849 in chorus and small roles. Trained by Schneider, Nusch, and later Duprez in Paris. After engagements in Stuttgart, Königsberg, Stettin, and Hanover, became a member of the Berlin Opera 1866–88. Sang Tannhäuser at the Paris première 1861; Siegmund at Bayreuth 1876. London, H.M.'s, 1882 where he was the first London Siegmund. N.Y., Met., 1886–8, as the first American Tristan, Siegfried (*Götterdämmerung*), and Cortez in Spontini's *Fernando Cortez*. A biography by Sternfeld appeared in 1904; in 1924 his correspondence with Wagner was published.

Nietzsche, Friedrich (b. Röcken, 15 Oct. 1844; d. Weimar, 25 Aug. 1900). German philosopher and poet. An amateur composer, his interest in music expressed itself chiefly in his writings on Wagner. At first an ardent Wagnerian, he later turned sharply against all German music, and not only declared that all music should be 'Mediterraneanized' but attacked Wagner in three pamphlets. At Bayreuth this was regarded as symptomatic of his approaching insanity.

Nightingale, The. Opera in 3 acts by Stravinsky; text by composer and Mitusov, after Hans Andersen. Prod. Paris, O., 26 May 1914, cond. Monteux; London, D.L., 18 June 1914, cond. Cooper; N.Y., Met., 6 Mar. 1926, cond. Serafin.

Act 1. The famous nightingale, whose song thrills all, sings to a poor fisherman. The imperial court arrives in search of the bird, who agrees to sing for the Emperor.

Act 2. The nightingale refuses any reward save the pleasure of seeing tears of emotion in the Imperial eyes. A mechanical nightingale arrives from the Emperor of Japan, but a comparison is prevented by the real bird's disappearance. The mechanical bird is installed at the royal bedside.

Act 3. Death sits by the Emperor's bed, but promises to return the crown when the nightingale returns and sings. This it does, and the Emperor's strength returns.

Nikisch, Artur (b. Lébényi Szant-Miklós, 12 Oct. 1855; d. Leipzig, 23 Jan. 1922). Hungarian conductor. Studied Vienna. Originally a violinist, played in the orchestra when Wagner conducted Beethoven's Ninth Symphony at the laying of Bayreuth's foundation stone. 1874–7, violinist of Vienna Opera Orchestra. 1877, engaged as chorus master Leipzig by Neumann and conducted his first opera there Feb. 1878. First conductor there

1879–89. Director Budapest Opera 1893–5; from 1895 till his death, mostly a concert conductor with a few guest appearances in leading opera houses of Europe, including London, C.G., 1907 (*Holländer*, *Freischütz*, and *Tristan*), London Opera House 1912 (Holbrooke's *Children of Don*), C.G. again 1913–14 when his incandescent readings of *The Ring* aroused great enthusiasm. His pupils included Albert Coates. (R)

Nilsson, Birgit (b. Karup, 17 May 1918). Swedish soprano. Studied Stockholm with Joseph Hislop. Début Stockholm 1946, Agathe. Royal Opera, Stockholm, since then, where she gradually built up a large repertory of Wagner and Verdi roles. Glyndebourne 1951 as Elettra (*Idomeneo*); but her international career dates from 1954–5 when she sang Brünnhilde and Salome at Munich. Since then she has established herself as the leading Wagner soprano of the day, singing at Bayreuth, Vienna, London, Chicago, and N.Y. She created a sensation at Sc. as Turandot in 1958. Ernest Newman, writing about her C.G. début as Brünnhilde in 1957, said he considered himself lucky to have lived long enough to hear so promising a young Brünnhilde. (R)

Nilsson, Christine (b. Sjöabol, nr. Vexiö, 20 Aug. 1843; d. Stockholm, 22 Nov. 1921). Swedish soprano. Studied Stockholm and Paris, where her teachers included Delle Sedie. Début Paris, T.L., 1864, Violetta. London, H.M.'s, 1867, and subsequently C.G. and D.L. until 1881; the first London Ophélie in *Hamlet* (which she had created in Paris in 1868), Margherita, and Elena in *Mefistofele*. N.Y., Ac. of M., 1870–4, where she was the first N.Y. Mignon, in which role she was considered incomparable. Sang Marguerite on opening night of Met., N.Y., 1883. Her voice was sweet and brilliant and encompassed two and half octaves from g to d‴; she possessed great personal charm and beauty.

Nissen, Hans Hermann (b. nr. Danzig, 20 May 1893). German bass-baritone. Studied Berlin with Raatz-Brockmann. Début Berlin, Volksoper, 1924. Munich State Opera since 1924. London, C.G., 1928; Chicago 1930–2; N.Y., Met., 1938–9. Sang as guest artist in Vienna, Berlin, and elsewhere in Europe. An outstandingly fine Wotan and Hans Sachs of the inter-war years. (R)

Niun mi tema. The opening words of Otello's (ten.) death scene in Act 4 of *Otello*.

No! pazzo son! guardate. Des Grieux's (ten.) aria in Act 3 of Puccini's *Manon Lescaut*, beseeching the ship's captain to allow him to accompany Manon on her journey into exile.

Noble, Dennis (b. Bristol, 25 Sept. 1899; d. Spain, 14 Mar. 1966). English baritone. Educated as chorister Bristol Cathedral. After First World War sang in Prologue to silent film of *The Prisoner of Zenda* in London heard by Pitt who invited him to audition for C.G. Début there 1924, Marullo (*Rigoletto*). Sang there regularly until 1938 and again 1947; also with B.N.O.C. and C.R. Companies; Cleveland, U.S.A., 1935–6. Created Sam Weller in Coates's *Pickwick*, Achior in *Judith*, and Don José in *Don Juan de Mañara*, both by Goossens. (R)

Nobles seigneurs, salut! Urbain the Page's song in Act 1 of *Les Huguenots*. Originally a soprano role, this part was later sung by a mezzo-soprano.

Non mi dir. Donna Anna's (sop.) aria in the last act of *Don Giovanni* in which she bids Ottavio to speak no more about his hopes of marrying her so soon after her father's death.

Non più andrai. Figaro's (bar.) aria in Act 1 of Mozart's *The Marriage of Figaro*, describing to the reluctant Cherubino his impending transformation from civilian to military life. It is also one of three numbers played by Don Giovanni's private band at supper in the penultimate scene of *Don Giovanni*, in recognition of the tune's popularity.

Non so più. Cherubino's (sop.) aria in Act 1 of Mozart's *The Marriage of Figaro*, declaring his bewilderment at the novel excitement of desire he feels burgeoning within him.

Noni, Alda (b. Trieste, 30 Apr. 1916). Italian soprano. Studied Trieste and Vienna. Début Ljubljana 1937, Rosina. Vienna State Opera 1942–6; London, Cambridge Theatre, 1946, Norina opposite Stabile, in first performance in London of opera in Italian after 1945. Glyndebourne 1949–53. Originally a high coloratura, she was chosen by Strauss for Zerbinetta in the special 80th birthday *Ariadne* performance in Vienna in 1943. She became one of the best Italian soubrettes of the day. (R)

Nordica, Lillian (orig. Lillian Norton) (b. Farmington, Maine, 12 May 1857; d. Batavia, Java, 10 May 1914). American soprano. Studied Boston and Milan. Début Milan 1879, Donna Elvira. After appearances in Germany and Russia, during which time she was heard as Marguerite and Ophélie (roles which she had studied with their composers), made American début N.Y., Ac. of M., with Mapleson's Company 1883. London, C.G., 1887–93; N.Y., Met., 1891–1910 (intermittently); Bayreuth (first American artist engaged there) 1894 as Elsa; then became famous as Brünnhilde and Isolde, which she sang in London and N.Y. Such was her vocal training that she was able to sing Brünnhilde one night and Violetta the next. Her singing was beautiful in both dramatic and florid roles. (R)

Nordmo-Løvberg, Aase (b. Malselv, 10 June 1923). Norwegian soprano. Studied Oslo. Début Oslo 1948 (in concert). Stockholm Opera since 1953; Vienna, S.O., since 1958; N.Y., Met., 1959; Edinburgh Festival 1959; London, C.G., 1959. Already distinguished for her Elisabeth, Sieglinde, Eva, and Elsa, she also sings in the Italian repertory. Was compared to Flagstad, who welcomed her as her successor. (R)

Norena, Eidé (orig. Kaja Hansen Eidé) (b. Horten, Norway, 26 Apr. 1884; d. Switzerland, 19 Nov. 1968). Norwegian sopr. Studied Oslo, Weimar, London, Paris. Début Oslo 1907, Amour (*Orphée*). Engaged by Toscanini for Milan, Sc. (début Gilda 1924). London, C.G., 1924–5, 1930–1, 1934, and 1937; Chicago 1926–8; N.Y., Met., 1933–8. She possessed a beautiful and perfectly trained soprano voice, and sang with impeccable taste. Her great roles were Desdemona, Gilda, Violetta, Juliette, and the three soprano parts in *Hoffmann*. (R)

Norina. The young widow (sop.) in Donizetti's *Don Pasquale*.

Norma. Opera in 2 acts by Bellini; text by Romani after Soumet's tragedy (1831). Prod. Milan, Sc., 26 Dec. 1831, with Pasta, Grisi, Donzelli; London, King's, 20 June 1833, with Pasta; New Orleans, 1 Apr. 1836.

The action takes place in Gaul, in about 50 B.C. Act 1. Led by their High Priest Oroveso (bass) the Druids come to the Sacred Grove to beg the Gods to rouse the people to war against their Roman occupiers. After their departure the Roman proconsul Pollione (ten.) tells his centurion Flavio (ten.) that he no longer loves the high priestess Norma, Oroveso's daughter, but has fallen in love with another young priestess, Adalgisa. The Druids assemble, and Norma (sop.) prays for peace in the celebrated 'Casta Diva'. The Druids depart and Pollione persuades Adalgisa (sop.) to flee with him to Rome.

In her dwelling Norma reveals to her confidante Clotilda (sop.) that Pollione is going to desert her and her two children for another woman whose identity she does not know. Adalgisa confesses to Norma that she too has broken her sacred vows and has fallen in love with a Roman. Remembering her own behaviour Norma is about to absolve Adalgisa from her vows when Pollione enters; she now realizes who her rival is. Adalgisa, however, loves Norma dearly, and turns reluctantly from Pollione.

Act 2. Norma in despair plans to kill her children, but cannot bring herself to raise her hand against them. She will confess her misdoings, however, and asks Adalgisa to look after the children. Adalgisa tells Norma that she will renounce Pollione and urge him to return to Norma.

Once again Oroveso and the Druids gather; they plan to rise against the Romans. Clotilda tells Norma that Pollione refuses to return to her, and, aroused to fury, she urges the people to wage war on their conquerers. There is a disturbance: a Roman has been captured breaking into the holy temple. It is Pollione. Norma promises him his freedom if he will renounce Adalgisa and return to her. When he refuses, Norma addresses the Druids and confesses her guilt. Moved by her action, Pollione asks to die with her, and together they mount the funeral pyre.

Norway. See *Oslo*.

Nothung! Nothung! Siegfried's (ten.) forging song in Act 1 of *Siegfried*. (Nothung—'Needful'—is the name of the sword.)

Nougès, Jean (b. Bordeaux, 25 Apr. 1875; d. Paris, 28 Aug. 1932). French composer. His early operas were produced at Bordeaux, but he made his name with *Quo Vadis?*, Nice 1909. It quickly became so well known that it was chosen for the opening of the London Opera House on 13 Nov. 1911. The shallow nature of *Quo Vadis?* may have contributed to the failure of this venture. None of his later operas approached its popularity.

Nourrit, Adolphe (b. Paris, 3 Mar. 1802; d. Naples, 8 Mar. 1839). French tenor. Studied Paris with Garcia. Début Paris 1821, Pylade (*Iphigénie en Tauride*). He succeeded his father, **Louis** (1780–1831), as leading tenor at the Opéra and remained there until 1837 when Dupréz's (q.v.) engagement so upset him that he left for Italy. He created Robert (*Robert le Diable*), Masaniello, Raoul, Éléazar, Ory, Arnold (*Tell*), and many other parts. Although well received when he sang in Naples and elsewhere in Italy, he came to suffer from severe melancholia and killed himself by throwing himself from his hotel window. There are a number of biographies of him in French.

Novák, Vítězslav (b. Kamenice o/ Lipa, 5 Dec. 1870; d. Skuteč, 18 July 1949). Czech composer. His affinity with the German romantics was later supplemented in his music by a passionate love of his native country; deliberately avoiding the example of Smetana and Dvořák, he invites comparison, in his exploration of the essential springs of human behaviour and his boundless love of nature, with Janáček. But where Janáček's inflexible devotion to truth led him to mistrust too much tampering with the raw material, Novák was ready to mould and polish his material. After the comic *The Imp of Zvíkov* (1915) his characteristic irony softened. *Karlštejn* (1916) is a patriotic gesture, *The Lantern* (1923) one of sympathy to his oppressed countrymen. *The Grandfather's Heritage* (1926) marks a return to local Slovak scenery.

Novello, Clara (b. London, 10 June 1818; d. Rome, 12 Mar. 1908). English soprano. Studied London, Paris, and Milan. After several years on concert platform made stage début Padua 1841 in *Semiramide*. Sang widely in Italy. London, D.L., 1843.

Novi Sad (Neusatz). Town in Vojvodina, Yugoslavia. Early centre of Hungarian opera, whose conductor introduced opera to Belgrade 1829. Serbian National Theatre founded 1864. Private company founded in Belgrade in 1900 settled here 1911. Company re-formed after 1945.

Novosibirsk. Town in W. Siberia, U.S.S.R. The theatre was founded in 1945, and in the ensuing 15 years produced 75 operas and ballets, with which it tours all the large towns of Siberia. The company has also made a good impression in Moscow.

Novotná, Jarmila (b. Prague, 23 Sept. 1907). Czech soprano. Studied Prague with Destinn; début Prague 1926, Violetta. After further studies in Milan joined Berlin Opera 1928. Vienna 1933–8; Salzburg 1935–7; N.Y., Met., 1939–53. One of the most aristocratic artists of her day, remembered for her Octavian and Donna Elvira. Also sang Pamina, Violetta, Eurydice, Manon, and the Czech repertory. Created title role in Lehár's *Giuditta*. (R)

Nozze di Figaro, Le (The Marriage of Figaro). Opera in 4 acts by Mozart; text by Da Ponte, after Beaumarchais's comedy *La Folle Journée, ou Le Mariage de Figaro* (1778). Prod. Vienna, B., 1 May 1786, with Benucci, Storace, Mandini, Kelly; London, Hm., 18 June 1812, with Naldi and Catalani; N.Y. 10 May 1824 (arr. Bishop).

Act 1. Figaro (bar.) is to marry Susanna (sop.), and is preparing the rooms allotted to them by the Count (bar.), whose roving eye has lit upon Susanna. Figaro is in further difficulties, having signed a contract promising to marry Marcellina (con.) if he cannot repay some money borrowed from her. She and Bartolo (bass) consider how he may be trapped, and there is naturally great tension between her and Susanna. The page Cherubino (sop.) is about to be banished for flirting; he sings about his susceptible nature, and hurriedly hides when the Count enters in search of Susanna. The arrival of the priest Basilio (ten.) sends the Count also into hiding, but they are both discovered. Cherubino is ordered off to the army.

Act 2. The Countess laments the loss of her husband's love, and Figaro and Susanna plan to re-arouse it by means of jealousy and ridicule. Cherubino enters with a love song for the Countess, but has to hide in a neighbouring room when the Count enters. He emerges when the Count goes in search of tools to break the door, and escapes through the window while Susanna takes his place. She baffles the Count by blithely emerging; but the gardener has seen Cherubino's escape and disaster is only averted by Figaro's claiming that it was he who jumped from the window.

Act 3. The Count tries to win Susanna by threatening to make Figaro marry Marcellina, and she pretends to yield. But Marcellina and Bartolo turn out to be Figaro's parents. The Countess, still mourning the loss of love, arranges a rendezvous between the Count and Susanna in which she will take Susanna's place. The marriage formalities of Figaro and Susanna are attended to.

Act 4. In the garden, Susanna and the Countess appear in each other's clothes. Figaro, believing that Susanna is to yield to the Count, jealously hears a serenade actually meant for him. Cherubino has an appointment with Barbarina (sop.), but tries to kiss 'Susanna'. He is routed by the Count, who makes approaches to his own wife, as he then discovers to his horror and remorse. She forgive him, and all ends well.

Nuitter (orig. Truinet), **Charles Louis Étienne** (b. Paris, 24 Apr. 1828; d. Paris, 24 Feb. 1899). French librettist and writer on music. Collaborated (especially with Beaumont) in librettos, also translating numerous works for the Théâtre-Lyrique and elsewhere. Archivist at Opéra from 1865. Also published several valuable books on opera, notably *Les Origines de l'Opéra Français*.

Nuremberg (Ger., Nürnberg). Town in Bavaria, Germany. *Seelewig*, generally regarded as the first extant German opera, was performed privately at Nuremberg in 1644. The present opera house (cap. 1,456) was opened in 1905; damaged during Second World War; reopened 1945. Robert Heger, Fritz Stiedry, and Rudolf Hartmann spent important years of their career here. Erich Riede was music director 1956–64, Hans Gierster from 1964.

O

O Carlo, ascolta. Posa's (bar.) death aria in the last act of Verdi's *Don Carlos*.

O cieli azzurri. The introduction to Aida's (sop.) aria in Act 3 of *Aida*. Sometimes known as the Nile Aria.

O du mein holder Abendstern. Wolfram's (bar.) song to the evening star in Act 3 of *Tannhäuser*.

O Isis und Osiris. Sarastro's (bass) prayer to the Egyptian gods in Act 2 of Mozart's *Die Zauberflöte*.

O luce di quest'anima. Linda's (sop.) aria in Act 1 of *Linda di Chamounix* in which she sings of her love for Arthur.

O Mimì, tu più non torni. The duet between Rodolfo (ten.) and Marcello (bar.) in Act 4 of Puccini's *La Bohème*.

O mio babbino caro. Lauretta's (sop.) appeal to her father to allow her to marry Rinuccio in *Gianni Schicchi*.

O mio Fernando. Leonora's (mezzo) aria in Act 3 of *La Favorite* in which she sings of her love for Fernando.

O namenlose Freude. The duet of reunion for Leonore (sop.) and Florestan (ten.) in Act 2, scene 1, of *Fidelio*.

O paradiso. Vasco da Gama's (ten.) apostrophe to the island of Madagascar in Act 4 of *L'Africaine*.

O patria mia. Aida's Nile Aria. See *O cieli azzurri*.

O soave fanciulla. The opening words of the love duet for Rodolfo (ten.) and Mimì (sop.) in Act 1 of *La Bohème*.

Ô souverain! ô juge! Rodrigo's (ten.) prayer in Act 2 of Massenet's *Le Cid*.

O terra, addio. The closing duet between Radamès (ten.) and Aida (sop.) in Act 4 of Verdi's *Aida* in which they bid farewell to life on earth.

O tu che in seno agli angeli. Alvaro's (ten.) aria in the first scene of Act 3 of *La Forza del Destino* which he sings on the battlefield, remembering Leonora, whom he believes dead.

O welche Lust. The prisoners' chorus in Act 1 of Beethoven's *Fidelio*, praising the sun and freedom as they stagger from their cells for exercise.

Obbligato (It. = obligatory). The term for an instrumental part in a vocal work essential but subordinate to the voice, e.g. the bassoon obbligato in Neris's aria in Act 2 of Cherubini's *Médée*.

Ober, Margaret Arndt- (b. Berlin, 15 Apr. 1885; d. Bad Sachs, 17 Mar. 1971). German mezzo-sopr. Studied Berlin. Début Frankfurt 1906. Berlin 1906–44; N.Y., Met., 1913–17, first Octavian, and Eglantine in Toscanini's revival of *Euryanthe* (1914). Interned in America during First World War and in 1919 resumed her career in Berlin with great success. First Berlin Kostelnička under Kleiber. (R)

Oberspielleiter (Ger. = senior producer). The name given to the chief resident producer of an opera company. He might sometimes also be the Generalintendant.

Oberon. Opera in 3 acts by Weber; text by Planché, after Sotheby's translation (1798) of Wieland's *Oberon* (1780) which is in turn based on a 13th-century French *chanson de geste*, *Huon de Bordeaux*. Prod. London, C.G., 12 Apr. 1826, with Braham, Paton, and Cawse, cond. Weber; Leipzig 23 Dec. 1826; N.Y., 9 Oct. 1828. Oberon's vow not to meet Titania again until a faithful pair of lovers can be found is made the pretext for involving Sir Huon and Reiza in a series of extravagant adventures. Their fidelity proved, and having (with some aid from Oberon's magic horn) survived all ordeals, they are transported triumphantly back to Charlemagne's court;

Oberon returns to his queen. Other operas on the subject are by Kunzen (*Holger Danske*, 1789—the principal 18th-century Danish opera) and Wranitzky (1789—very successful until replaced by Weber's work).

Oberto, Conte di San Bonifacio. Opera in 2 acts by Verdi; text by Piazza, revised by Merelli and Solera. Prod. Milan, Sc., 17 Nov. 1839 with Strepponi; Chicago, Oct. 1903 (concert form). Revived Busseto July 1939; Milan, Sc., 1951 for Verdi Celebrations. Verdi's first opera. The libretto was set to music two years later by Graffigna and prod. as *I Bonifazi ed i Salinguerra* at Venice in 1842.

Oca del Cairo, L' (The Goose of Cairo). Opera in 2 acts by Mozart; text by Varesco. Comp. 1783, unfinished. Prod. Paris, F.-P., 6 June 1867; London, D.L., 12 May 1870.

Ocean, thou mighty monster. Reiza's (sop.) aria in Act 2, scene 3 of Weber's *Oberon* first saluting the ocean and then hailing the boat she believes to be coming to her rescue.

Ochs von Lerchenau, Baron. The Marschallin's boorish cousin (bass) in Strauss's *Der Rosenkavalier*.

Octavian. Count Rofrano (sop. or mezzo), the hero and Rose Cavalier Strauss's *Der Rosenkavalier*.

Oedipus Rex (King Oedipus). Opera-oratorio in 2 acts by Stravinsky; text by Cocteau, after Sophocles's tragedy (*c.* 435–425 B.C.), trans. into Latin by Daniélou. Prod. Paris, Th. S.B., 30 May 1927, as oratorio; first stage prod. Vienna 23 Feb. 1928; Boston 24 Feb. 1928 (concert) and N.Y. 21 Apr. 1931 (stage); London, Queen's Hall, 12 Feb. 1936 (concert) and Edinburgh (by Hamburg Company) 21 Aug. 1956.

Oestvig, Karl (b. Oslo, 17 May 1889; d. Oslo, July 1968). Norwegian tenor. Studied Cologne under Steinbach and Walter. Début Stuttgart 1914; Vienna State Opera 1919–27, where he created the Kaiser in *Frau ohne Schatten*. Sang in leading German theatres, and was a distinguished Lohengrin, Parsifal, and Walther. Married soprano Maria Rajdl. (R)

Offenbach, Jacques (orig. Jakob Eberst) (b. Cologne, 20 June 1819; d. Paris, 4 Oct. 1880). German, later French, composer. Went to Paris when still young, and soon became conductor at the Théâtre Français. In 1855 became manager of Théâtre des Champs-Élysées, where his early pieces were produced, then took the Théâtre Comte and renamed it the Bouffes-Parisiens. Here he produced the long series of operettas which soon found their way into the Opéra-Comique and then the Opéra itself. His one opera was an attempt at the romantic genre which, though in this respect unconvincing, has remained popular for its tunefulness—*Les Contes d'Hoffmann*. But it is no less upon the deliciously frivolous musical comedies that entertained Paris for so many years that his true reputation rests. The impeccable *boulevardier* manner and exhilarating high spirits conceal the skill that went into their making, distracting attention, too, from the lack of a lyrical gift such as Johann Strauss possessed at his best. There is, moreover, a recurrent cynicism and fatalism well concealed behind the Second Empire merriment that led Mauriac to write of *La Grande Duchesse de Gérolstein*, 'The laughter I hear in Offenbach's music is that of the Empress Charlotte, gone mad.'

Ohms, Elisabeth (b. Arnhem, 17 May 1888). Dutch soprano. Originally a violinist, later studied singing in Amsterdam and Frankfurt. Début Mainz, 1921. Munich State Opera 1926–36; particularly successful in Wagner operas. London, C.G., 1928–9, 1935; N.Y., Met., 1930–2. Chosen by Toscanini to sing Fidelio and Kundry at Sc. 1927–9. Married the painter and designer Leo Pasetti. (R)

Olczewska, Maria (orig. Marie Berchtenbreitner) (b. Augsburg, 12 Aug. 1892; d. Klagenfurt, 17 May 1969). German mezzo-sopr. Originally operetta singer; heard at Hamburg by Nikisch, who engaged her for Leipzig 1920–3; Vienna State Opera 1923–36. London, C.G., 1924–32 as leading mezzo in Wagner and also Amneris, Orlofsky, Carmen; Chicago Opera 1928–32; N.Y., Met., 1933–5. Professor Vienna

Conservatory since 1947. Possessed a rich and beautiful voice and was a fine actress. Married (later divorced) Emil Schipper (q.v.). (R)

Oldenburg. Town in Lower Saxony, Germany. Opera is given in the Staatstheater (cap. 950), built in 1893.

Old Vic, The (properly The Royal Victoria Hall). The theatre in the Waterloo Road in south London, birth-place of the English opera company which later had its home at Sadler's Wells (q.v.). Built originally in 1818 by Joseph Glossop, an English impresario, who, as Giuseppe Glossop, was the impresario of the Scala, Milan, and the San Carlo, Naples, where he married one of the singers. Their son Augustus Glossop Harris was the father of Augustus Harris, manager of C.G. 1888–96, thus providing a generally unknown link between four famous opera houses. The Royal Coburg Theatre, as the Royal Victoria Hall was previously known, opened in 1818; it was renamed the Royal Victoria Hall in 1833. In 1880 its lease was acquired by the social reformer Emma Cons (q.v.) and it was rechristened the Royal Victoria Coffee Hall. Opera was first heard there in the form of excerpts in costume. Emma Cons was succeeded in 1898 by her niece Lilian Baylis (q.v.) who developed the theatre's opera along with its Shakespearian repertory, opera being given on two nights a week and on alternate Saturday matinées. Even works like *Tristan und Isolde* were heard, with the score drastically reduced by Charles Corri, the theatre's excellent music director. After the First World War Lilian Baylis decided that *Figaro* should be newly produced and invited the soprano Muriel Gough to undertake the task; she demurred, and suggested instead Clive Carey, who accepted and urged Lilian Baylis to accept a new translation by Edward J. Dent. This was the beginning of the Dent–Carey Mozart revival in England, and of the move towards sensible and singable translations. By 1931, when S.W. was opened, the repertory included *La Forza del Destino*, *Aida*, *Otello*, *Samson et Dalila*, *Tannhäuser*, and *Lohengrin*. The singers at that time included Joan Cross, Edith Coates, Winifred Kennard, Rose Morris, Constance Willis, Sumner Austin, Arthur Cox, Tudor Davies, Henry Brindle, Powell Lloyd, Booth Hitchin, and Henry Wendon. Lawrance Collingwood became one of the conductors, and there were also evenings of ballet under the direction of Ninette de Valois and conducted by Constant Lambert. No opera was given at the Old Vic after 1935.

Olitzka, Rosa (b. Berlin, 6 Sept. 1873; d. Chicago, 29 Sept. 1949). German contralto. Studied Berlin with Désirée Artôt and Julius Hey. Début Brno 1892; London, C.G., 1894; N.Y., Met., 1895–1901; Chicago 1910–11 and later taught there. A distinguished Wagner singer. (R) Her nephew **Walter Olitzki** (1903–49) sang in Germany and later at the N.Y. Met. 1939–47.

Olivero, Magda (b. Saluzzo, 1914). Italian soprano. Début Turin 1933, Lauretta (*Schicchi*). Distinguished as much for her acting as for her singing as Adriana Lecouvreur, Liù, Violetta, Suor Angelica, and Minnie. Married 1941, returned to stage in the 1950–1 season as Adriana, having promised Cilea that she would do so. London, Stoll, 1952, Mimì. (R)

Olomouc (Olmütz). Town in Moravia, Czechoslovakia. The opera house (cap. 750) is the largest and most important in Moravia after that of Brno, and gives regular seasons.

Olympia. The Doll (sop.), Hoffmann's first love in Offenbach's *Les Contes d'Hoffmann*.

Olympians, The. Opera in 3 acts by Bliss; text by J. B. Priestley. Prod. London, C.G., 29 Sept. 1949, with Grandi, Coates, Johnston, Glynne, Franklin, cond. Rankl. The story concerns the adventures of the Olympian gods, now reduced to a group of travelling players but restored to their former glory for one night of each year.

O'Mara, Joseph (b. Limerick, 16 July 1866; d. ?, 5 Aug. 1927). Irish tenor. Studied Milan. Début London, Royal English Opera House, 1891 in title-role of Sullivan's *Ivanhoe*. Sang at C.G. and D.L. during Harris's management, then became leading tenor Moody–Manners Company and finally formed his own company, the O'Mara Company. Sang often in Wagner operas. Retired 1926. (R)

Ombra mai fù. Serse's (male sop.) aria in Act 1 of Handel's *Serse*, apostrophizing the tree that gives him shade. Though marked *larghetto*, it has become irrevocably known as Handel's *Largo*.

Oncina, Juan (b. Barcelona, 15 Apr. 1925). Spanish tenor. Studied Barcelona with Capsir. Début Barcelona, 1946, Des Grieux (Massenet). Sang widely in Italy 1946–52, establishing himself as a leading exponent of Rossini, Donizetti, &c. Glyndebourne 1952–61, especially successful as Ramiro, Lindoro, Almaviva, and Ory. His voice is inclined to whiteness; he is a charming and witty artist. (R) Husband of the soprano **Tatiana Menotti.** (R)

Onegin, Sigrid (b. Stockholm, 1 June 1891; d. Magliaso, 16 June 1943). Swedish contralto. Daughter of a German father and a French mother, and married first to a Russian pianist and composer named Eugene Onegin. Studied Frankfurt, Munich, and Milan. Début Stuttgart 1912, Carmen, where she created Dryade in *Ariadne auf Naxos*; London début same role 1913, as Lilli Hoffmann-Onegin. Munich 1919–22; Berlin 1926–33; N.Y., Met., 1922–4; London, C.G., 1927. Possessed a voice of great power and range, and was famous as Lady Macbeth, Eboli, Orfeo, Fricka, and Brangäne. The last great interpreter of Fidès in *Le Prophète*. (R)

Opava (Troppau). Town in Moravia, Czechoslovakia. Formerly the scene of regular German seasons. Hotter made his début here in 1929. The Zdeněk Nejedlý Theatre, renovated in 1948, has only lately achieved professional maturity.

Open-air Opera. During the summer, *al fresco* performances of opera are regularly to be seen and heard, with varying degrees of success, in Italy, France, Germany, Austria, Yugoslavia, and America. One of the earliest open-air performances chronicled was given at Regensburg by Schikaneder's company in July 1788, of Hartmann's *Balders Død*. The present-day fashion for such entertainments dates from 1913 when the Roman amphitheatre at Verona began its new life as a vast open-air opera house with a performance of *Aida*—the originator of the idea was the tenor Zenatello (q.v.). The other most famous open-air opera in Italy is at the Terme di Caracalla, Rome, where performances were first given in 1937. In France similar use has been made of ancient arenas and theatres in Orange, Arles, &c., and an excellent and comfortable open-air theatre, surely the best, has been built for the opera performances at the Aix-en-Provence Festival. In Germany open-air opera has been given in Augsburg at the Rote Tor, and in Munich at Schloss Nymphenburg; Wagner performances were given in pre-1939 days at Sopot. At Bregenz in Austria opera and operetta are given on a specially constructed stage on the lake; while in America at Cincinnati an annual opera season with artists from the Met. and elsewhere is given in the gardens of the Cincinnati Zoo, where singers have occasionally to compete with the animals—just as at Augsburg and elsewhere railway trains and aeroplanes offer competition to the tenor's top notes. Several successful opera seasons were given by a company based on the Chicago Opera at Ravinia Park 1910–31. The English climate has not been conducive to open-air opera, though there have been university performances and an attempt was made in pre-war days at Scarborough. The London County Council have sponsored occasional performances in the London parks.

Opera (It. = work—an abbreviation for *opera in musica*). A drama to be sung with instrumental accompaniment by one or more singers in costume; recitative or spoken dialogue may separate set musical numbers.

Opera buffa (It. = comic opera). A

term for the Italian comic opera that developed, from the short comic scenes that ended the acts in *opera seria*, via the intermezzo (q.v.), into a form in its own right. The chief contrast with *opera seria* is the use of a comic subject deploying characters drawn from everyday life. Love intrigues, scheming servants, and the ancient cuckold joke were its stock in trade, simple, tuneful airs its medium.

Opéra comique. 'Comic opera' is a mistranslation of this vague but generally accepted term. The French themselves understand different things by it according to the date of its use. In all the genre's variants there are not more than two or three constants—chief among them light-heartedness, taking the form of some comment on accepted moral standards and temporal fashions. It thus tends to be a more ephemeral and local art than tragic opera, which concerns itself more with the eternal verities. The two gradually drew closer together until the only marked difference was *opéra comique*'s retention of spoken dialogue. Despite *Fidelio* and *Médée*, technically *opéras comiques*, simplicity of subject and lightness of treatment prevailed.

Opéra-Comique, Paris. Paris's second opera house, originally the home for French musical pieces with spoken dialogue. In 1715 an agreement between the *comédiens* and the director of the Académie Royale de Musique resulted in the setting up of the Institution known as the Opéra-Comique. Its success was so great that the Académie had it closed in 1745, but it was reopened seven years later by Monet at Saint-Germain. In 1762 it joined the Comédie-Italienne and had its home in the rue Mauconseil, and in 1783 moved to the rue Favart, where it was known first as the Comédie-Italienne, then the Théâtre de la rue Favart, and finally as the Opéra-Comique; it is sometimes colloquially called the Salle Favart. In 1791 a rival company was established at the rue Feydeau. This ended in ruin and both houses were closed in 1801; the companies then amalgamated. During the early days of the new régime, works by Dalayrac, Méhul, Auber, and Boïeldieu were produced. In 1840 the theatre saw the première of *La Fille du Régiment*, and in 1866 of *Mignon*. After the closing of the Théâtre-Lyrique (q.v.) and the assumption by Carvalho of the Comique's management, the theatre entered a successful period with the premières of *Hoffmann*, *Lakmé*, and *Manon*. In 1887 the building was destroyed by fire, and the company carried on at the Théâtre Sarah Bernhardt until the opening of the present building (cap. 1,750) on 7 Dec. 1898, with Albert Carré as manager. During his régime *Louise*, *Pelléas et Mélisande*, *Ariane et Barbe-Bleue*, and *L'Heure Espagnole* were produced. After Carré the directors were Gheusi and Isola (1914–18), Carré and Isola (1919–25), Masson and Ricou (1925–31), Masson (1931–2), Gheusi (1932–6), 1936–9 joint administration with that of the Opéra under Rouché assisted by Mariotte, Busser (1939–40), Max d'Ollonne (1941–4), Muratore (1944), Désormière, Jamin, Musy Rousseau (1944—after the Liberation), Wolff (1945–6), Malherbe (1946–8), Bondeville (1948–51), Beydts (1952–3), Agostini (1953–9), Lamy (1959–62). A. M. Julien was appointed joint Administrator of both the Opéra and the Opéra-Comique in 1959. He was succeeded by Georges Auric in 1962 and René Nicoly, 1969–71. Theatre closed in April 1972 due to reopen as 'Opera Studio de Paris' January 1973.

Opéra de Paris. See *Académie*, &c.

Opera seria (It. = serious opera). The principal operatic form of the 17th and early 18th centuries which rose to such a high degree of formality and complexity as to prompt a reaction in *opera buffa*. Elaborate arias, designed to give singers the utmost opportunity for display, were set in a framework of pageantry: mythological subjects prevailed, with emotions formalized and the existing moral, religious, and social order celebrated in the close relationship of gods and nobles.

Opera Workshop. The term used in

the U.S.A. for operatic study and preparation groups. It does not apply to the major activities of opera departments in the universities and academies, though the phrase is used to describe more elementary work in their opera departments. Some opera workshops resemble a local operatic society, and engage professional directors to prepare annual productions on a grand scale. Three out of every five performances of opera in the U.S.A. are sung by students, and many premières and first American performances of contemporary works have been given by these groups in recent years. In the 1957–8 season 228 workshops were listed in *Opera News*, ranging from Indiana University, which stages an annual *Parsifal*, and the Music Academy of the West, where Lotte Lehmann staged three *Rosenkavaliers*, to Louisiana State University, where *Fidelio* and Monteverdi's *Orfeo* were staged, and the University of Minnesota, which staged *Dido and Aeneas*, *The Magic Flute*, and *The Telephone*.

Operetta, opérette (It., Fr. = little opera). A term used for a play with an overture, songs, interludes, and dances.

Opernball, Der (The Opera Ball). Operetta in 3 acts by Heuberger; text by Léon and Waldeberg, after the farce *Les Dominos Roses* by Delacour and Hennequin. Prod. Vienna, W., 5 Jan. 1898; N.Y. 24 May 1909. Heuberger's most successful work.

Ora e per sempre addio. Otello's (ten.) farewell to his past glories in Act 2 of *Otello*.

Orchestra pit. The space before and below the stage which contains the opera orchestra. The covered pit at Bayreuth (Wagner's 'mystic gulf') allows an exceptionally faithful balance without any visual distraction to the audience. Most German opera houses are now built with pits in sections of variable height to assist the balance of different operas.

Orest. Elektra's brother (bass-bar.) in Strauss's *Elektra*.

Orfeo ed Euridice. *Azione teatrale per musica* in 3 acts by Gluck; text by Calzabigi, after the classical legend. Prod. Vienna, B., 5 Oct. 1762, with Guadagni; London, King's, 7 Apr. 1770; N.Y., Winter Garden, 25 May 1863. French version, translated by Moline and with the title role transposed for tenor, prod. Paris 2 Aug. 1774. The title role has also been sung by baritones. Revised by Berlioz and prod. Paris 1859, with Viardot. See also *Orpheus*.

Orff, Carl (b. Munich, 10 July 1895). German composer. After his studies in Munich he began his career as a *répétiteur* and then conductor at Mannheim and Darmstadt. In 1920 he resumed his studies with Kaminski and in 1926 began his career as a composer with his first realization of Monteverdi's *Orfeo* (a second followed in 1931 and a third in 1941). Orff has tried to free opera from what he considers the exaggerations that had accrued to it by the beginning of the present century; this he does by returning to elementary rhythm and popular folk-song. He eschews counterpoint or thematic development and regards opera, as Wagner did, as a *Gesamtkunstwerk*. In *Carmina Burana* (1937), *Catulli Carmina* (1943), and *Trionfi dell'Afrodite* (1953) he uses Latin texts, and unashamedly appeals to the most primitive levels of emotion in his musical settings of them. *Der Mond* (1939) is a Bavarian fairy-tale and contains some of the composer's more lyrical music, as does *Die Kluge* (1943), his most successful work. *Die Bernauerin* (1947) is a Bavarian folk play with music, and *Antigonae* (1949) is an austere setting of the Sophocles tragedy in Hölderlin's translation. Later works are *Oedipus der Tyrann* (1959) and *Ludus de Nato Infante Mirificus* (1960).

Orgeni, Aglaia (orig. Görger St. Jorgen) (b. Roma Szombat, 17 Dec. 1841; d. Vienna, 15 Mar. 1926). Hungarian soprano. Studied Baden-Baden with Pauline Viardot. Début Berlin 1865, Amina. London, C.G., 1866, Violetta. Sang extensively in Europe and was greatly admired for her elegant style. Taught at Dresden 1886–1914, where she became the first woman Royal Professor in 1908; and in Vienna from 1914. Her pupils included Erika Wedekind and Edyth Walker.

Orlofsky. The Russian Prince (con.) in Johann Strauss's *Die Fledermaus.*

Oroveso. The High Priest of the Druids (bass) in Bellini's *Norma.*

Orphée aux Enfers (Orpheus in the Underworld). *Opéra-Féerie* in 4 acts by Offenbach; text by Crémieux and Halévy, possibly from a German scenario by Cramer. Prod. Paris, B.-P. (2 acts), 21 Oct. 1858; N.Y. Mar. 1861; London, Hm., 26 Dec. 1865, adapted by Planché as *Orpheus in the Haymarket.* See also *Orpheus.*

Orpheus. In Greek mythology, the famous poet and singer who could charm wild animals with the beauty of his music. When his wife Eurydice died he followed her to Hades and won her back by his art with the condition that he should not look at her until he reached the world again. At the very last moment his loving anxiety overcame him, and turning, he saw her snatched back to Hades. His grief turned him against women, and he was torn to pieces by maenads in Thrace. The fragments of his body were collected by the Muses and buried at the foot of Olympus. The legend came to have deep religious significance, but it is principally the story of Eurydice's rescue that has drawn opera composers from the very first. Operas on the subject are as follows. Peri (*Euridice,* 1600, the first opera to survive); Caccini (*Euridice,* 1602); Ferrari (1607); Monteverdi (*La Favola d'Orfeo,* 1607); Belli (*Il Pianto d'Orfeo,* 1616); Landi (*La Morte d'Orfeo,* 1619); Ferrari (1637); Rossi (1647); J. J. Loewe (*Orpheus aus Thracien,* 1659); Sartorio (1672); R. Goodson (before 1698); Keiser (1698); Graun (1752); Gluck (1762); Guglielmi (1770); J. C. Bach (1770); Bertoni (1776); Asplmayr (1780); Naumann (1786); Tozzi (1789); Benda (1789); Paer (1791); Lamberti (1791); Haydn (1794); Cannabich (1800); Offenbach (*Orphée aux Enfers,* 1858); Malipiero (*L'Orfeide,* trilogy, 1918–22); Křenek (1926); Milhaud (*Les Malheurs d'Orphée,* 1926); Casella (*La Favola d'Orfeo,* 1932).

Ortrud. Telramund's wife (mezzo) in Wagner's *Lohengrin.*

Osborn-Hannah, Jane (b. Wilmington, Ohio, 8 July 1873; d. New York, 13 Aug. 1943). American soprano. Studied with Marchesi, Sucher, and Sbriglia. Début Leipzig 1904; London, C.G., 1908, Eva; N.Y., Met., 1910, Elisabeth. Sang also with the Chicago Opera and retired in 1914. A famous Wagner singer.

Oscar. The page (sop.) to King Gustavus (or Riccardo) in Verdi's *Un Ballo in Maschera.*

Osetia, Northern. District of the Caucasus, U.S.S.R.; part of Russia since 1774. The first Osetian operas are *Kosta* and *Spring Song* by the contemporary composer Khristofor Pliyev, the first based on a national hero-poet, the second on the clash of old ways with new in Osetian villages. More Osetian operas are being written, and an opera company has been formed. It visited Moscow in 1960.

Osijek (Esseq). Town in Croatia, Yugoslavia. Opera since early 19th century. Present company formed, 1907; regular opera and operetta since 1910.

Oslo (Kristiania). Capital of Norway. Though opera had been given in Norway in the 18th century, national opera was slow to establish itself. The first Norwegian opera was Thrane's *Fjeldeventyret* (*Mountain Adventures*), printed in 1824, concert performance 1827, prod. 1840. There were occasional opera performances at the Christiania Theatre; and at the National Theatre from 1899, though the first native work to appear there was Aspestrand's *Die Seemansbraut* in 1907 (orig. prod. Gotha, 1894). Grieg's unfinished *Olaf Trygvason* was given there in 1908, the year after his death. The Norwegian State Opera House was inaugurated with *Carmen* in 1900. Plans for a Norwegian National Opera, centred in Oslo but touring Stavanger, Bergen, and Trondheim, were completed in 1958;

this, known as Den Norske Oper and with Kirsten Flagstad as intendant, began with *Tiefland* in 1959. Flagstad resigned owing to ill health in 1960, and was succeeded by Odd Grunor-Hegge, conductor of the Oslo Philharmonic. *Opéra comique* was given at the Casino 1918–21. Norwegian singers who have won international fame include Flagstad, Graarud, Nordmo-Løvberg, and Norena.

Osmin. The steward (bass) in charge of the Seraglio in Mozart's *Entführung*.

Osten, Eva Plaschke von der (b. Heligoland, 19 Aug. 1881; d. Dresden, 5 May 1936). German soprano. Studied Dresden. Début Dresden 1902. Leading soprano Dresden 1902–30. Created Octavian 1911. C.G. 1913–14, first London Octavian and Kundry. U.S.A. 1923–4 with German Opera Co. Among her best roles were also Tosca and Tatiana. (R) She married the bass baritone **Friedrich Plaschke** (1875–1951), for many years a leading artist at Dresden. Stage director for *Arabella* première (1934). (R)

Ostrava (Ostrau). Town in northern Moravia, Czechoslovakia. The Zdeněk Nejedlý State Theatre (cap. 944) was reconstructed in 1945. It concentrates on French and Italian opera.

O'Sullivan, John (b. Cork, 1878; d. Paris, 28 Apr. 1955). Irish tenor. Studied Paris. Début Geneva 1912. After engagements in the French provinces was heard at the Paris, O., 1914–22 and 1929–30; appeared in Italy where he sang at Sc. as Raoul, in which role he made his C.G. début, 1927; Chicago 1919–20. His excellent top notes made him an especially fine interpreter of Arnold, Manrico, and Raoul. (R)

Otello. Opera in 4 acts by Verdi; text by Boito, based on Shakespeare's tragedy (1604–5). Prod. Milan, Sc., 5 Feb. 1887, with Pantaleoni, Tamagno, Maurel, cond. Faccio; N.Y., Ac. of M., 16 Apr. 1888, with Eva Tetrazzini, Marconi, Galassi, cond. Campanini; London, Lyceum, 5 July 1889, with Cataneo, Tamagno, Maurel, cond. Faccio. Famous Otellos have included Zenatello, Slezak, Zanelli, Martinelli, Vinay, and Del Monaco.

The opera follows Shakespeare's story closely, apart from the loss of his Act 1 and the addition of Iago's 'Credo'.

Act 1. Otello (ten.) arrives during a storm in Cyprus after his victory over the Turks. Iago (bar.) jealous because Cassio (ten.) has been chosen as lieutenant in his place, begins his scheme to get Cassio disgraced by making the latter drunk and provoking him to fight a duel with Montano (bass). Otello comes out from the castle and deprives Cassio of his rank. The crowd disperses and Otello is left alone with his wife Desdemona (sop.). The act ends with an extended love duet.

Act 2. Iago, determined to bring about Otello's downfall, expounds his philosophy in the famous 'Credo'. He advises Cassio to ask Desdemona to intervene with her husband on his (Cassio's) behalf and then proceeds to inflame Otello's jealous nature by drawing his attention to Cassio and Desdemona. Desdemona's handkerchief is picked up by Emilia (mezzo), Iago's wife. Iago snatches it and when alone with Otello relates to him how he heard Cassio talking in his sleep and mentioning Desdemona's name. He further goes on to tell Otello that he has seen Desdemona's handkerchief, Otello's first gift to her, in Cassio's hand. Otello swears to be avenged and is joined by Iago in the 'Oath Duet'.

Act 3. Otello questions Desdemona about her relationship with Cassio. She swears she is innocent, but is unable to produce the handkerchief. Iago now tells Otello to conceal himself, and asks Cassio about his love affair with Bianca; but Otello thinks Cassio's answers refer to Desdemona, and when Iago furtively shows Otello the handkerchief, the latter is beside himself. A trumpet announces the arrival of Lodovico (bass), the Venetian ambassador. Before going to welcome him, Otello appoints Iago captain. Lodovico announces that Otello has been recalled to Venice, and that Cassio has been appointed governor in his place. Otello insults Desdemona in public and strikes her. As the company withdraws, Otello falls to the ground in a swoon. As the crowd outside acclaims him as the Lion of Venice, Iago points at the prostrate Otello with the words 'Ecco il Leone!'

Act 4. Desdemona is preparing for sleep. She sings the touching Willow Song and bids Emilia farewell. After an 'Ave Maria' she goes to bed. Otello enters by a secret door and extinguishes the candle. He bends over and kisses the sleeping Desdemona three times. She awakens. He tries to make her confess her guilt. When she refuses he stifles her. Knocking at the door is heard: Emilia rushes in crying that Cassio has killed Roderigo. She hears Desdemona's dying gasps and screams for help. Cassio, Iago, and Lodovico enter. Emilia reveals her husband's infamy. Iago rushes from the room and Otello, surrendering his sword to Lodovico, bids Desdemona a last farewell, and stabs himself with a dagger.

Otello, ossia il Moro di Venezia. Opera in 3 acts by Rossini; text by Marchese Francesco Berio di Salsa after Shakespeare's tragedy (1604–5). Prod. Naples, Teatro del Fondo, 4 Dec. 1816, with Colbran, Davide; London, King's, 16 May 1822, with Camporese and Curioni; N.Y., Park Theatre, 7 Feb. 1826, with Garcia and Malibran. The plot follows Shakespeare fairly closely.

Otto, Lisa (b. Dresden, 14 Nov. 1919). German soprano. Studied Dresden. Début Beuthen 1941, Sophie; after engagements at Nuremberg, Dresden, and Berlin State Opera, joined the Städtische Oper, Berlin, 1952, where she sings regularly. Salzburg since 1953. Glyndebourne 1957. One of the best of contemporary German soubrettes. (R)

Overture. From the Italian *overtura*, opening, the word normally used for the instrumental prelude to an opera or play; later a concert work unconnected with the stage. The brief instrumental introduction of the earliest operas became formalized by Lully, who established the French overture as beginning with a slow introduction, continuing with a fugal passage, and ending with a dance; the Italian overture, introduced early in the 18th century by A. Scarlatti, differed chiefly in opening with a quick section. Not until Gluck did the overture have thematic connexion with the following drama; some of his overtures lead directly into the opera, which they have already foreshadowed. Mozart continued the principle, using in his *Don Giovanni* and *Magic Flute* overtures some elements that recur later in the opera; while in that to *Così fan tutte* he uses a motto theme to represent the words of the title. Beethoven took this principle of thematic anticipation further in the three 'Leonore' overtures he wrote for *Fidelio*; and it reached its climax in Weber, who (taking his cue from Spohr's *Faust*) made his later overtures virtually synopses of the ensuing opera while adhering to the sonata form principle. In Italy the overture was still designed chiefly to hush talkers and admit late-comers, only incidentally attempting to compose the audience's mind for the opera, so that the same overture often did duty for tragic and comic operas indiscriminately, e.g. Rossini's overture to *Aureliano in Palmira*, which was re-used for the tragedy *Elisabetta, Regina d'Inghilterra* and the comedy *Il Barbiere di Siviglia*. Wagner, though he came to prefer the term 'prelude', pursued Weber's methods at first; later he composed still more subtle introductions to his dramas, preparing the audience thematically and psychologically for what was to come. The *verismo* composers on the whole preferred the brief introduction that had latterly become Verdi's habit, while Strauss sometimes even raised the curtain directly on the drama. Light composers have generally remained faithful to the potpourri style of overture that assembles the opera's best tunes.

Oxford. Town in Oxfordshire, England. Except for Sir Hugh Allen's productions of *Fidelio* and *Der Freischütz* shortly before the First World War, there was no opera at Oxford sponsored by the University. The Oxford University Opera Club came into being as a result of the 1925 performance of

Monteverdi's *Orfeo*. For this, J. A. Westrup made a complete transcription of the 1615 edition of the score in the Bodleian Library. In 1927 *L'Incoronazione di Poppea* had its first stage performance in England. From 1928 to 1933 Sumner Austin was musical adviser. During this period productions included *The Bartered Bride*, *May Night*, and *The Devil and Kate* (first in England). In 1930, 1931, and 1932, Hans Strohbach, one of Germany's leading producers, came to Oxford to supervise the productions. Between 1933 and 1939 the productions included *Iphigénie en Aulide*, *Castor and Pollux*, and *Master Peter's Puppet Show*. There were no performances during the war years, but since 1947 the annual productions have included *Idomeneo*, *Iphigénie en Tauride*, *Les Troyens*, Wellesz's *Incognita* (première), *Hans Heiling* (first in England), *Macbeth*, *Ernani*, *The Fair Maid of Perth*, *The Secret*, *Oedipus Rex*, *L'Enfant et les Sortilèges*, *Khovanshchina*, *Russlan and Ludmilla*, and *Mitridate Eupatore*. Artists who have started at Oxford include the singers John Kentish, David Galliver, Doreen Murray, Thomas Hemsley, and Heather Harper; the conductors Trevor Harvey and Robert Irving; the producer Anthony Besch; and the administrators Basil Douglas and Robert Ponsonby.

P

Pace, pace, mio Dio. Leonora's (sop.) aria in the last scene of Verdi's *La Forza del Destino* in which she prays for peace of soul.

Pacchierotti, Gasparo (b. Fabriano (bapt. 21 May) 1740; d. Padua, 28 Oct. 1821). Italian male soprano. Began singing secondary parts at Venice, Vienna, and Milan before age of 16; successful in principal roles from 1769. His fame spread quickly through Italy and heralded him on his arrival in London in 1778, where he triumphed. After a long and brilliant career, he retired to Padua in 1792, reappearing only for the benefit of Napoleon in 1796.

Pacini, Giovanni (b. Catania, 17 Feb. 1796; d. Pescia, 6 Dec. 1867). Italian composer. From the age of 17 he produced 73 operas at the principal Italian houses, nearly all of them contentedly in the Rossini vein. Swiftly written, often with particular performers in mind, they pleased audiences of the day with their melodic charm, but their lack of stronger qualities made them ephemeral. *Saffo* (1840) attempted to break away from the Rossini manner, and though in this unsuccessful, it remains his best work. After the failure of his *Carlo di Borgogna* (1834) he opened a school of music in Viareggio, to which he later added a theatre. For his numerous pupils he wrote some theoretical treatises.

Padilla (y Ramos), **Mariano** (b. Murcia, 1842; d. Auteuil, nr. Paris, 23 Nov. 1906). Spanish baritone. Studied Florence. London, H.M.'s, 1881, Hoël (*Dinorah*). Also sang at C.G. and was heard as Don Giovanni in Prague in the centenary performance of Mozart's opera. Married soprano **Désirée Artôt** (q.v.) in Warsaw 1869 shortly after she had jilted Tchaikovsky. Their daughter was **Lola Artôt de Padilla** (q.v.).

Padmâvatî. *Opéra-ballet* in 2 acts by Roussel; text by Louis Laloy, after an event in 13th-century Indian history. Prod. Paris, O., 1 June 1923, cond. Gaubert. The Mogul sultan Alaouddin proposes an alliance with Ratansen, King of Tchitor. He is well received, but demands Ratan-sen's wife Padmâvatî as a condition; to this Ratan-sen reluctantly consents. A Brahmin who later asks for her to be handed over is torn to pieces, and the crowd riots. Alaouddin defeats Ratansen in battle, but rather than have the sin of betraying her rest on her husband's conscience, Padmâvatî stabs him. She therefore has to die on his funeral pyre.

Padre Guardiano. The abbot (bass) in Verdi's *La Forza del Destino*.

Paer, Ferdinando (b. Parma, 1 June 1771; d. Paris, 3 May 1839). Italian composer. He became *maestro di cappella* in Venice at 20, moving to Dresden in 1803. In 1806 he went to Paris as Napoleon's *maître de chapelle*, succeeding Spontini at the Italian Opera in 1812—his most successful opera was called *Le Maître de Chapelle* (1831). A composer of modest but genuine gifts, he succeeded best when writing fluently in the Italian idiom that came naturally to him. He managed to match his style more successfully to German requirements than to French; in both, his limited range and lack of emotional depth told against him. Nevertheless, he was to some extent admired by Beethoven, whose music bears some trace of Paer's influence.

Pagliacci (Clowns). Opera in 2 acts by Leoncavallo; text by composer. Prod. Milan, T. d. V., 21 May 1892, with Stehle, Giraud, Maurel, Ancona, cond. Toscanini; London, C.G., 19 May 1893, with Melba, De Lucia, Ancona, cond. Bevignani; N.Y., Grand Opera House, 15 June 1893, with Kört-Kronold, Montigriffo, Campanari.

The opera is based on an incident that occurred in Montalto in Calabria when an actor murdered his wife after a performance. The presiding judge at the murder trial was Leoncavallo's father.

The Prologue, sung by Tonio (bar.), tells the audience that the play is a real story with real people. The villagers of Montalto welcome the touring troupe of players—Canio (ten.), his wife Nedda (sop.), Tonio (bar.), and Beppe (ten.). Canio, Beppe, and some of the villagers go to the inn. Tonio makes advances to Nedda who, repelled by his ugliness and deformity, lashes him with a whip. Left alone, she is joined by her lover Silvio (bar.). Tonio, overhearing them, hastens to inform Canio, who arrives in time only to hear the lovers plan a further meeting. Canio raises a dagger to Nedda but is restrained by Beppe who reminds him that the play is soon to begin. Canio sings of his tragic plight, having to play the clown while his heart is breaking, in 'Vesti la giubba'.

The villagers assemble for the play. Harlequin (Beppe) serenades Colombine (Nedda). Taddeo (Tonio) enters and tries to make love to Colombine, who drives him away. The love scene between Colombine and Harlequin is interrupted by Pagliaccio (Canio). The situation is so like the reality that Canio forgets himself. He demands the name of Nedda's lover, and when she refuses he stabs her. When Silvio, who is in the audience, rushes to help her, Canio stabs him too. He drops the dagger and Tonio tells the audience that 'La commedia è finita' ('The comedy is ended').

This final announcement has often been made by Canio, a tradition thought to originate with Caruso. But both the original score and the composer's widow affirm that the words were intended to be sung (not spoken) by Tonio.

Pagliughi, Lina (b. New York, 1910). Italian soprano. Heard in a concert by Tetrazzini, whose pupil she became. Subsequently studied in Milan with Bavagnoli. Début Milan, Nazionale, Gilda, 1928. London, C.G., 1938, Gilda. Sang all over Italy and was greatly admired for her singing of Bellini, Donizetti, and Rossini. Possessed a pure, limpid voice, and an excellent technique. The latter part of her career was devoted to recording, and singing for the Italian radio until the late 1950's. (R)

Paisiello, Giovanni (b. Taranto, 8 May 1740; d. Naples, 5 June 1816). Italian composer. After copious successes in Italy during adolescence, he went to St. Petersburg at the invitation of Catherine the Great, composing there his *Barbiere di Siviglia* (1782). This became so popular in Italy as to prejudice the public against the more famous setting by Rossini that was to oust Paisiello's work. In Italy again after 1784, Paisiello became *maestro di cappella* at Naples. He sided with Napoleon in the disturbances of 1799, and, out of favour at the restoration, went to Paris. He returned to Naples, but the Bourbons did not forgive his previous actions and he died in comparative poverty. His 100-odd operas are distinguished for their ease and accomplishment more than for their profundity or wit. Some of his works have been revived in recent years at the Teatro di Corte, Naples, Piccola Scala, and elsewhere.

Palermo. Town in Sicily. Opera was first heard there in 1658 when the Teatro dello Spasimo was opened with a version of Cavalli's *Serse*. From 1693 to 1726 operas (including works by Alessandro Scarlatti, born in Palermo) were performed at the Teatro di Santa Cecilia. In 1726 a second opera house was built, the Teatro Santa Lucia, at first devoted to comic opera; in 1809 it was reconstructed and named the Real Teatro Carolina. There Donizetti conducted 1825–6 and from 1829 to 1830 Balfe sang there as leading baritone. In 1860, when Sicily was united with Italy, the theatre was renamed the Real Teatro Bellini. The theatre was still in private hands, and the local authorities decided to build a municipal opera house, the Teatro Politeama Garibaldi, which was opened in June 1874 with Bellini's *I Capuleti e i Montecchi*; it became the city's chief opera house until May 1897, when the Teatro Massimo (cap. 2,500) opened with *Falstaff*, conducted by Mugnone. The stage of the Massimo was, after the Paris Opéra, the largest in Europe until the reopening of the Vienna Opera. It became an *Ente Autonomo* in 1935. Leoncavallo's *La Bohème*, rechristened *Mimi Pinson*, had its first performance there in the composer's revised version in 1913, but otherwise there have been few premières there this century. Yet since the war the repertories have been among the most interesting and adventurous of any Italian opera house.

Palestrina. *Musikalische Legende* in 3 acts by Pfitzner; text by composer. Prod. Munich, N., 12 June 1917 with Karl Erb in the title role; cond. Walter. Never performed in Great Britain or America.

The opera tells how Palestrina saved the art of contrapuntal music for the Church in the 16th century through his *Missa Papae Marcelli*. The second act, which depicts the Council of Trent, introduces the excellently drawn character of Cardinal Borromeo. Julius Patzak has been the greatest recent interpreter of the title role in recent years. Also opera by Sachs (1886).

Pallavicino, Carlo (b. Brescia or Salò, *c.* 1630; d. Dresden, 26 Jan. 1688). Italian composer. Worked as Kapellmeister in Dresden at different periods, though most of his operas were produced at Venice. He was regarded as an ingenious and able composer.

Palmo's Opera House, N.Y. A theatre situated in Chambers Street, west of Broadway, which was built by Ferdinand Palmo, a New York restaurateur of Italian birth. It opened in Feb. 1844 with the N.Y. première of *I Puritani*. In July that year Cinti-Damoreau appeared there in a number of operas. In 1848 it was renamed Burton's Chamber Street Theatre and no more opera was heard there. Many of Palmo's former patrons, however, joined together and raised a subscription which resulted in the building of the Astor Place Opera House which opened 1847 with *Ernani*. In 1859 it was converted into the Mercantile Library.

Pamina. The Queen of the Night's daughter (sop.), heroine of Mozart's *Die Zauberflöte*.

Pampanini, Rosetta (b. Milan, 2 Sept. 1900). Italian soprano. Studied with Emma Molaioli. Début Rome 1920, Micaëla. After four further years of study, second début at Biella as Mimì; there she came to the notice of Toscanini, who engaged her for Butterfly at Sc. Sang there regularly until 1937. London, C.G., 1928, 1929, 1933; Chicago 1931–2. Sang Mimì in a special performance of *Bohème* under Mascagni outside Puccini's villa at Torre del Lago 1930. Other famous roles were Desdemona, Iris, and Liù. She retired in 1942 and has since taught. Pupils include Amy Shuard and Victoria Elliott. (R)

Panerai, Rolando (b. Campi Bisenzio, 17 Oct. 1924). Italian baritone. Studied Florence with Frazzi, Milan with Armani and Giulia Tess. Début Naples 1948, Mosè. One of the leading Italian baritones of the day. Appeared at Barcelona and Lisbon, as well as in Italy and at the Aix and Salzburg Festivals (esp. as Figaro and Guglielmo). London, C.G., 1960, Figaro (Rossini). (R)

Panizza, Ettore (b. Buenos Aires, 12 Aug. 1875; d. there, 27 Nov. 1967). Argentinian conductor of Italian descent. Studied Milan. Début 1890. London, C.G., 1907–14, 1924; Milan, Sc., as Toscanini's assistant, 1921–9, and then 1930–32, 1946–8; N.Y., Met., 1934–42; B.A. Colón 1921–67. In London he directed the first performances of Franchetti's *Germania*, Erlanger's *Tess*, Zandonai's *Conchita*, and *Francesca da Rimini*. He conducted the first Scala performances of the *Trittico*, *Khovanshchina* (first in Italy), *Sly* (Wolf-Ferrari), *Tsar Saltan* (first in Italy), *La Vedova Scaltra*. His own operas, including *Aurora* (1908) and *Bisanzio* (1939), had some success in South America.

Pannain, Guido (b. Naples, 17 Nov. 1891). Italian musicologist and composer. As well as a number of valuable studies, notably on Mercadante, he has composed three operas.

Pantheon. A building in Oxford Street, London, opened in Jan. 1772 and used mostly for concerts and appearances by such singers as Aguiari and Giorgi-Banti. After the destruction of the King's T. in 1789 it was adapted as a theatre and used to house Italian opera 1791–2. In 1812 it became the home of a company composed of singers from the King's who had quarrelled with the management; and in 1813 there was a short-lived attempt to establish an English opera company there.

Pantomime (Gr. παντόμιμος = imitation of everything). A dramatic entertainment in which the artists express themselves in dumb show. The old intermezzos often included a pantomime part (e.g. the mute servant Vespone in Pergolesi's *La Serva Padrona*) since most of the singers were needed for the main opera.

Papageno and **Papagena.** The bird-catcher, Tamino's attendant (bar.), and his lover (sop.) in Mozart's *Die Zauberflöte*.

Parable Aria. See *Metaphor Aria*.

Pardon de Ploërmel, Le. See *Dinorah*.

Parepa-Rosa, Euphrosyne (b. Edinburgh, 7 May 1836; d. London, 21 Jan. 1874). Scottish soprano. Daughter of the soprano Elizabeth Seguin (q.v.) and Demetrius Parepa, Baron de Boyescu, a Wallachian boyard. Début, when 16, Malta; London, Ly., 1857, Elvira (*Puritani*). Appeared at both C.G. and H.M.; then, after a tour of America with Carl Rosa (whom she married in 1867), became principal soprano of her husband's company. Her voice was powerful and of pleasing quality with an extensive range. After her death her husband founded the Parepa-Rosa scholarship at the R.A.M., London.

Pareto, Graziella (b. Barcelona, 6 Mar. 1888). Spanish soprano. Début Madrid 1908. After appearances throughout Italy was engaged for C.G. 1920, where she sang Leïla, Norina, and Violetta. Chicago 1923–5, Salzburg 1931. Considered by Beecham to be the finest coloratura soprano of the period after the First World War. (R)

Pari siamo. The opening words of Rigoletto's (bar.) great monologue in Act 1, scene 2, of Verdi's opera.

Paride ed Elena (Paris and Helen). Opera in 5 acts by Gluck; text by Calzabigi. Prod. Vienna, B., 3 Nov. 1770; N.Y., Town Hall, 15 Jan. 1954 (concert performance), by American Opera Society.

Parigi, o cara. The opening words of the duet in Act 3 of Verdi's *La Traviata* in which Alfredo (ten.) suggests to the dying Violetta (sop.) that they resume their life together far from the bustle of Paris.

Paris. Capital of France. The first opera given in Paris was an unknown work at the Palais Royal in Feb. or Mar. 1645, referred to in a letter written by the singer Atto Melani to Prince Matthias de' Medici. The first known Italian opera performed in Paris was Sacrati's *La Finta Pazza* given at the Salle du Petit Bourbon in Dec. 1645. The first French work was Dassoucy's *Andromède* given at the Petit Bourbon in Feb. 1650, which is regarded as the forerunner of French opera. Between 1660 and 1800 opera was performed in Paris in some 22 different theatres including the Académie de Musique (the Opéra) and the Opéra-Comique (q.v.). Other theatres in which opera was given in Paris during this period included the Colisée, the Théâtre de Monsieur, and the Odéon. Between 1800 and the period just after the First World War the number of theatres in which opera was performed increased to about 30 and included the Théâtre Italien (q.v.), the Bouffes-Parisiens (q.v.), the scene of the production of many of Offenbach's works, the Théâtre Lyrique (q.v.), the Trianon-Lyrique, the Gaîté Parisienne, the Théâtre Lyrique de la Renaissance, for which Messager wrote *Madame Chrysanthème* as the opening piece, the Marigny, the Eden, the Théâtre du Châtelet, where Strauss's *Salome* had its first Paris performance, and the Théâtre des Champs-Élysées (q.v.). In more recent times there has been little or no opera except at the two national theatres; since 1957 there has been an annual summer festival covering all the arts under the general title of the Théâtre des Nations, and opera performances have been given by leading ensembles from all over the world including the Berlin Komische Oper, the Berlin Städtische Oper, Glyndebourne, the Leipzig Opera, the Belgrade Opera, the Frankfurt Opera, and S.W.

In addition to the theatres mentioned above, opera has also been given in Paris in many other theatres including the Athénée-Musical, Lyrique-Dramatique, Nouveau-Théâtre, Moncey, Théâtre du Château d'Eau, Fantaisies-Parisiennes, Théâtre-Lyrique de la Gaîté, Théâtre de la Demoiselle Montausier, Opéra Populaire, Théâtre des Arts, Théâtre du Vaudeville Ghesui.

See also separate entries under *Académie de Musique et de Danse, Bouffes-Parisiens, Opéra-Comique, Théâtre des Champs-Élysées, Théâtre-Italien, and Théâtre-Lyrique.*

Park Theatre, New York. Three theatres of this name have occupied a site in Park Row, near Ann Street, N.Y. The first opened in Jan. 1798; the second (opened 1825) was the scene of the first Italian opera season in the U.S.A. given by Manuel Garcia's company. Like its predecessor it was destroyed by fire in 1848. A third theatre was likewise burnt down.

Parlando (It. = speaking). A direction to let the tone of the voice approximate to speech.

Parma. Town in Emilia, Italy. Its musical tradition dates back to the 15th century. In 1618 on the orders of Ranuccio Farnese a theatre, designed by Aleotti of Argenta, holding 3,000, was built. Here magnificent performances were given of works by various composers, including Monteverdi. Several other theatres were erected, and later under the Bourbons the finest singers and composers of the day made frequent visits. Between 1791 and 1809 several of Paer's operas received their premières in Parma, including his *Agnese*. During the reign of Marie-Louise the present Teatro Regio came into being (cap. 1,300), opening in May 1829 with Bellini's *Zaira*. Verdi, who was born near by, became identified with Parma; and between 1843 and 1951, the year of the Verdi celebrations, 1,382 performances were given of all his works, with the exception of *Il Finto Stanislao* and *Il Corsaro*. *Les Vêpres Siciliennes* received its first performance in Italy at Parma in 1855 under the title of *Giovanna di Guzman*. Parma was also the birthplace of Toscanini, who played the cello in the orchestra of the Regio while a student. Campanini (q.v.) conducted there often and was responsible for organizing the 1914 competition which discovered Gigli and Merli. It was at Parma, too, that Tebaldi studied and began her career. The audience of the Regio has the reputation of being the most difficult in Italy to please (see *Audience, Claque*).

Parmeggiani, Ettore (b. Rimini, 15 Aug. 1895; d. Milan, Jan. 1960). Italian tenor. Début Milan, T.d.V., 1922, Cavaradossi. Notable in Wagner roles during inter-war years, including Siegmund, Lohengrin, Parsifal, all of which he sang at Sc., where in recent years organized and led claque.

Parmi veder le lagrime. The Duke of Mantua's (ten.) aria in Act 2 of Verdi's *Rigoletto*, in which he regrets the loss of his lover Gilda.

Parody. It was common in the 18th and 19th centuries for parodies of the most popular operas of the day to be staged, generally contemporaneously with the original. In the case of *Der Freischütz*, for instance, an anonymous German parody entitled *Samiel, oder die Wunderpille* was produced in 1824, and even translated into Danish and Swedish. The same year saw an English parody, ostensibly by one Septimus Globus, Esq., '*Der Freischütz*, a new muse-sick-all and see-nick performance from the new German uproar. By the celebrated Funny-bear.'

This was also given at Edinburgh. Many other composers were paid these elaborate backhanded compliments. The last one seems to be Wagner. *Tannhäuser* was given a number of parodies, including a French one (1861) entitled *Ya-Mein-Herr, Cacophonie de l'Avenir, en 3 actes entr'acte mêlée de chants, de harpes et de chiens savants*. One of the last parodies of all is probably *Tristanderl und Süssholde* (1865), produced in Munich before *Tristan und Isolde* itself.

Parr, Gladys (b. Bury, Lancs., 3 Jan. 1892). English contralto. Studied R.A.M., London. Has sung with Carl Rosa, B.N.O.C., S.W., and at C.G. where she was heard during International seasons in the 1920's as Magdalene in *Meistersinger*. Has sung with the English Opera Group since its inception and created Miss Pike (*Albert Herring*) and Mrs. Noah (*Noyes Fludde*). Her performances have always been marked by clear diction and dramatic ability. (R)

Parsifal. *Bühnenweihfestspiel* (sacred festival drama) in 3 acts by Wagner; text by the composer. Prod. Bayreuth 26 July 1882, with Materna, Winkelmann, Reichmann, Scaria, cond. Hermann Levi; N.Y., Met., 24 Dec. 1903 (infringing the Bayreuth copyright, which did not expire until 31 Dec. 1913) with Ternina, Burgstaller, Van Rooy, Blass, cond. Hertz; London, C.G., 2 Feb. 1914, with Eva von der Osten, Hensel, Bender, Knüpfer, cond. Bodanzky.

The Bayreuth copyright was also broken before 1914 by performances in English in Boston and elsewhere in the U.S.A. 1904–5, in Amsterdam 1905, and in Zürich in 1903; the work was also given in Buenos Aires and Rio in 1913.

Act 1. In a forest near a lake at Monsalvat in the kingdom of the Grail, Gurnemanz (bass) and his two Esquires arouse themselves from sleep and offer up their morning prayers. They are interrupted by the wild entry of Kundry (sop.) who comes with balsam for the suffering Amfortas (bar.), who is carried in on a litter on his way to bathe his wounds. Gurnemanz relates to his Esquires how Amfortas, son of Titurel, who had entered the magic garden of the magician Klingsor armed with the Sacred Spear, had been seduced by Kundry and wounded by Klingsor, who had seized the Sacred Spear. The wound will only heal at the touch of the Spear, now in Klingsor's possession, and the only person who can gain possession of it is a 'Pure Fool made wise through pity'. Cries are now heard, and an unknown youth (Parsifal, ten.) is dragged in having killed a swan. In reply to Gurnemanz's questions it is clear that this youth may be the 'Pure Fool', and he is taken back to the castle to witness the unveiling of the Grail by Amfortas. Having failed to understand the ceremony, he is driven from the hall by the angry Gurnemanz.

Act 2. Klingsor (bar.) summons Kundry and instructs her to seduce Parsifal, whom they have both recognized as the only possible redeemer of Amfortas and Kundry. In Klingsor's magic garden the Flower Maidens tempt Parsifal, but he remains indifferent. Kundry calls him by his name and recalls for him memories of his childhood and his mother. As she kisses him on the lips all is revealed to him: 'Amfortas! the wound!' he cries. Realizing the nature of Amfortas's temptation, he becomes 'wise through pity'; while Kundry changes from temptress to suppliant as she recognizes that her one chance of salvation is now at Parsifal's hands. Klingsor hurls the Sacred Spear at him, but it remains suspended in mid-air over his head. He seizes the Spear and as he makes the sign of the cross Klingsor's domain falls in ruins.

Act 3. Many years have passed. Gurnemanz, now grown old, is a hermit, and the repentant Kundry comes to draw water for him. A knight in black armour approaches; it is Parsifal. He is recognized by Kundry but not by Gurnemanz, who chides him for coming armed on to holy ground on Good Friday. The knight kneels in prayer. Gurnemanz recognizes first the Sacred Spear, then Parsifal. After Kundry has bathed the knight's feet and dried them with her hair, Gurnemanz anoints Parsifal as the new King of the Holy Grail. His first task is to baptize Kundry. The three make their way to the Hall of the Grail where the funeral of Titurel is about to take place. The knights call on Amfortas to unveil the Grail, but he is unable to do so. He tears open his tunic and uncovering his wound asks the knights to kill him. Parsifal enters the hall and, touching the wound with the Spear, heals it. As the knights pay homage to their new King, Parsifal raises the Grail aloft; a white dove hovers over his head, and Kundry falls lifeless.

Pasero, Tancredi (b. Turin, 11 Jan. 1893). Italian bass. Studied with Pessina. Début Vicenza 1917, Rodolfo (*Sonnambula*). N.Y., Met., 1929–33; London, C.G., 1931. Leading bass at Milan, Sc., 1926–52. Sang regularly in all the leading Italian opera houses, South America, Spain, and Portugal. Possessed a large, resonant voice: at home in Italian, French, German and Russian repertory. Notable roles include Boris, Mefistofele, Gurnemanz, and Verdi bass parts. (R)

Pasta (orig. Negri), **Giuditta** (b. Saronno, nr. Milan, 9 Apr. 1798; d. Blevio, nr. Lake Como, 1 Apr. 1865). Italian soprano. One of the almost legendary figures among opera singers, the creator of Norma, Adina, and Anna Bolena. Studied Milan; début Brescia, 1815; London, 1817 but with little success. After period of study with Scappa, made second début 1819 with more success. Her real fame dates from the 1821 season in Paris, where her splendid soprano voice, ranging from a to d''', her gifts for dramatic interpretation, and the poignancy of her singing, created a sensation. Even at the height of her powers, however, her voice was not equal throughout its range, and on off-nights she received adverse criticism. Reappeared London 1824 as Desdemona (Rossini), and continued to appear regularly in London, Paris, and St. Petersburg until 1837. In 1840 she reappeared at St. Petersburg, being offered 200,000 francs; and in 1850 she unwisely returned to London with little or no voice left. Maria Ferranti Giulini's *Giuditta Pasta e i suoi tempi* (Milan 1935) is the most recent study of this singer. Chorley in his *Thirty Years' Musical Recollections* gives some vivid descriptions of Pasta's London performances.

Pasticcio (It. = pie). A play with airs, ensembles, dances, and other movements assembled from one or a number of composers; these were grouped together, not according to their original intention, to provide the audience with the maximum number of its favourite tunes in the briefest space of time. Particularly popular in the 18th century: a vintage example is *Thomyris* (D.L. 1707), for which Pepusch wrote recitatives, and adapted and arranged airs by Bononcini, Scarlatti, Steffani, Gasparini, and Albinoni.

Pastor Fido, Il (The Faithful Shepherd). Opera in 3 acts by Handel; text by Rossi, after Guarini's pastoral play (1585). Prod. London, Hm., 22 Nov. 1712; N.Y., T.H., 2 Nov. 1952. Also opera by Salieri (1789).

Pastorale. A stage piece on a legendary or pastoral subject. Originally without music, they spread through Europe from Italy; it was in France that they were first set to music and found a place as early forms of opera. *La Pastorale en Musique* (1659) and *Pomone* (1671) by Perrin and Cambay are regarded as the earliest French operas. The slender plots of pastorales allowed ample scope for the ballet and spectacle always beloved of the French.

Paton, Mary Ann (b. Edinburgh, Oct. 1802; d. Chapelthorpe, 21 July 1864). Scottish soprano. After singing in concerts made stage début London, Hm., 1822, Susanna. C.G. same year; created Reiza (*Oberon*) there 1826 and was highly praised by Weber. Sang C.G., D.L., and King's T. until 1844. Visited U.S. 1834 and subsequently with her husband, the tenor Joseph Wood. Her voice, ranging from a to d''' or e''', was notable for its purity, brilliance, and sweetness. Her personal beauty was much admired and there are numerous portraits of her by Lawrence, Newton, and others.

Patter song. A comic song in which the greatest number of words, delivered rapidly in conversational style, are fitted into the shortest space of time, with the music generally merely supporting their inflexion. From Haydn and Mozart to Sullivan the patter song has had a firm place in comic opera.

Patti, Adelina (b. Madrid, 10 Feb. 1843; d. Craig-y-Nos Castle, Wales, 27 Sept. 1919). Italian soprano. Her parents, Salvatore Patti and Caterina Barilli, were both singers, who took their daughter to N.Y. when very young, where she made her first public appearance in concert in 1850. Studied singing with her brother-in-law Strakosch, and piano with her sister Carlotta. Stage début N.Y. 1859 as Lucia, under the stage name of the 'Little Florinda'. London, C.G., 1861 as Amina, from which her fame dates. Hailed as Grisi's successor, she sang Zerlina in Grisi's last *Don Giovanni* in London. She appeared regularly London, Paris, and occasionally in Italy and America. Twenty-five consecutive seasons at C.G., where she sang some 30 roles in works by Rossini, Bellini, Donizetti, Verdi, Gounod, and Meyerbeer. The first London Aida and Juliette. The most highly paid singer of her day (200 guineas a performance at C.G., $5,000 in America), she had a clause in her contract excusing her from rehearsal and stipulating the size in which her name was to appear on posters. She was essentially a coloratura soprano, though she sang many lyric roles including Marguerite and Leonora (*Trovatore*) and even dramatic ones like Aida. Her voice ranged from c to f''' and was amazingly even and flexible. She was unrivalled for beauty and purity of tone, though her interpretations were said to lack temperament and she possessed only an average musical intelligence. She was married three times, her second husband being the tenor Nicolini (q.v.). Biography, Herman Klein's *The Reign of Patti* (1920). (R) Her sister **Carlotta Patti** (1835–89) confined her singing career to the concert platform.

Patzak, Julius (b. Vienna, 9 Apr. 1898). Austrian tenor. Studied originally to become a conductor with Franz Schmidt. Turned to singing 1926. Début Reichenberg 1926, Radamès. Munich State Opera 1928–45; Vienna 1945–60. London, C.G., 1938 as Tamino, and several post-war appearances, notably as Florestan, which, with Palestrina, is considered his greatest role. His voice has never been outstanding, but his style, intelligence, musicianship, superb enunciation, and complete identification with the role he is singing combine to make him one of the great singers of the day. (R)

Pauly, Rosa (orig. Rose Pollak) (b. Eperjes, 15 Mar. 1894). Hungarian soprano. Studied Vienna with Rosa Papier. Début Hamburg 1918, Aida; Cologne 1922–7; Berlin 1927–31; Vienna 1931–8; N.Y., Met., 1938–40; London, C.G., 1938. Also appeared Chicago, San Francisco, Buenos Aires, &c. The most famous Elektra of her day, and also a successful Marie (*Wozzeck*), Salome, and Aegyptische Helena. In recent years has been living in Israel. (R)

Pears, Peter (b. Farnham, 22 June 1910). English tenor. Studied R.C.M., London, and later with Elena Gerhardt. After singing with B.B.C. Chorus and Singers, and being a member of the Glyndebourne Chorus (1938), made stage début London, Strand Theatre, 1942, Hoffmann; S.W. 1943–6; E.O.G. since 1946; C.G. guest appearances since 1947. At S.W. sang in Italian repertory, Tamino, Vašek, and created title role in *Peter Grimes* (1945), since when he has been particularly associated with Britten's music, creating Male Chorus (*Lucretia*), Albert Herring, Vere (*Budd*), Essex (*Gloriana*), Quint (*Turn of the Screw*), Flute (*A Midsummer Night's Dream*), the Madwoman in *Curlew River*. An exceptionally intelligent and musical artist. (R)

Pease, James (b. Indianapolis, 9 Jan. 1916; d. N.Y., 26 Apr. 1967). American bass-baritone. Studied Philadelphia. Début Philadelphia 1941, Méphistophélès. N.Y., C.C., 1946–53; Hamburg State Opera 1953–8; London, C.G., 1955–60, Wotan, Sachs, Baron Ochs: Zürich Opera 1960–2. Balstrode and the Vicar in the American premières of *Peter Grimes* and *Albert Herring*. (R)

Pêcheurs de Perles, Les (The Pearl-fishers). Opera in 3 acts by Bizet; text by Cormon and Carré. Prod. Paris, T.-L., 30 Sept. 1863; London, C.G., as *Leila*, 22 Apr. 1887; Philadelphia 23 Aug. 1893. Zurga (bar.) is chosen chief by his tribe of fishermen in ancient Ceylon. His friend Nadir (ten.) returns, and after long estrangement caused by falling in love with the same priestess they are reconciled. A new priestess, Leïla (sop.), appears to offer her prayer and she and Nadir recognize each other. She is under a vow of chastity, with death as penalty. In a ruined temple she tells the high priest Nourabad (bass) how she risked death to save a fugitive and was given a gold chain. Later he finds Nadir and Leïla embracing, and denounces her to the people and to the enraged Zurga. She pleads for Nadir, and having failed, charges Zurga to give her mother her chain, which Zurga recognizes as one he had long ago given to a child who saved his life. He helps the lovers to escape by firing the village, but is himself killed.

Pécs. Town in Baranya, Hungary. The National Theatre (cap. 793) was built in 1895 by Steinhardt and Láng. Only since 1959 has it had an opera company, and now gives regular opera performances as well as operetta and drama.

Pederzini, Gianna (b. Vò di Avio, 10 Feb. 1906). Italian mezzo-soprano. Studied with Fernando de Lucia. Début Messina 1925, Preziosilla. Milan, Sc., 1930–42; Rome 1930–52. One of the outstanding mezzos of the inter-war years. Her roles included Carmen, Mignon, and the Rossini heroines. London, C.G., 1931; B.A., Colón, 1937–9, 1946–7. In more recent years has sung the title role in Menotti's *The Medium*, the Countess in *The Queen of Spades*, Mistress Quickly, for which her highly developed dramatic talents suit her admirably. Created the Prioress in *Dialogues des Carmélites*, Scala, 1957. (R)

Pedrell, Felipe (b. Tortosa, 19 Feb. 1841; d. Barcelona, 19 Aug. 1922). Spanish composer. Pedrell's position as the father of Spanish music-drama rests on his foundation of a Spanish national style; this took its inspiration from folk music and from the major achievements of centuries of great artistic development. His most serious studies were folk music and Victoria. The first operas he produced caused him, wrongly, to be regarded as a Spanish Wagnerian. There is a note of studiousness in his operas which, though they contain much fine music, prevents their wide acceptance. They include *El Comte Arnau* (1921) (intended for open-air performance) and a trilogy comprising *Los Pirineos* (1894), *La Celestina* (1903), and *Raimundo Lulio*. It is for his influence, directly on his pupils, among whom Falla is the most important, and indirectly in spurring Spanish musical self-confidence, that Pedrell is most significant.

Pedrillo. Belmonte's servant (ten.), in Mozart's *Die Entführung aus dem Serail*.

Peerce, Jan (orig. Jacob Pincus Perlemuth) (b. New York, 3 June 1904). American tenor. Began musical career as a violinist in dance bands, &c., and sometimes sang vocal refrains. This led to an engagement at Radio City Music Hall 1933–9. Opera début Cincinnati 1939, Duke of Mantua. Leading tenor N.Y., Met., since 1941. Chosen by Toscanini for his broadcast performances of *Bohème, Fidelio, Traviata*, and *Ballo in Maschera*, which were also recorded. Has sung with most American opera organizations as well as in Russia, Germany, and Holland Festival. (R)

Pelléas et Mélisande. *Drame lyrique* in 5 acts, 12 *tableaux*, by Debussy; text a slight alteration of Maeterlinck's tragedy (1892). Prod. Paris, O.C., 30 Apr. 1902, with Mary Garden; N.Y., Manhattan O.H., 19 Feb. 1908, with Garden; London, C.G., 21 May 1909, with Rose Féart.

Act 1. Scene 1. Golaud (bar.), grandson of King Arkel of Allemonde (bass), takes home a mysterious girl, Mélisande (sop.), he has found weeping in the forest. Scene 2. Geneviève (mezzo), mother of the half-brothers Pelléas (ten.) and Golaud, reads Arkel a letter from Golaud to Pelléas describing his meeting and marriage with Mélisande. Arkel accepts this marriage. Pelléas comes to tell of a summons he has had from a sick friend, but Arkel reminds him that he should stay with his own sick father, who lies upstairs. Scene 3. Mélisande and Geneviève are joined by Pelléas in the castle gardens and watch a ship departing.

Act 2. Scene 1. Playing with her wedding ring, Mélisande loses it down a well; Pelléas advises her to tell Golaud the truth. Scene 2. Golaud, thrown from his horse at the moment the ring fell, is being tended by Mélisande. He notices the ring's absence, and tells her to go and search in the grotto by the seashore, where she says she lost it. Scene 3. Pelléas and Mélisande explore the grotto. Frightened by three sleeping beggars, they abandon their pretended search.

Act 3. Scene 1. Mélisande drops her long hair from her window, and it is fondled by Pelléas. They are surprised by Golaud. Scene 2. Golaud shows Pelléas the stagnant castle vaults. Scene 3. Golaud warns Pelléas to let Mélisande alone. Scene 4. Golaud questions little Yniold (sop.), son of his former marriage, about Pelléas and Mélisande, and holds him up to the window to tell what he sees: they are sitting together.

Act 4. Scene 1. Pelléas plans to leave, on his father's advice. Golaud enters and in jealous fury seizes Mélisande's hair and hurls her to and fro. Scene 2. In the park, Yniold is trying to lift a large stone. Pelléas comes to say good-bye to Mélisande, but they declare their love as the castle gates shut. Golaud appears and strikes down Pelléas; Mélisande flees, pursued by Golaud.

Act 5. Arkel, Golaud, and the Physician wait by Mélisande's bed, where she is dying, having given birth to a child. Golaud, repentant but still jealous, questions her about her love for Pelléas—was it a 'forbidden' love? The castle servants enter, and fall on their knees as Mélisande dies without answering Golaud. Arkel leads Golaud out, saying it is now the turn of Mélisande's daughter.

Penelope. Opera semi-seria in 2 parts by Liebermann; text by Heinrich Strobel. Prod. Salzburg, Festspielhaus, 17 Aug. 1954, with Goltz, Schock, Böhme; cond. Szell. A modern adaptation of the Ulysses and Penelope legend based on an actual incident of the Second World War. Other operas on the Penelope legend include works by Cimarosa, Fauré, Galuppi, Piccinni, and Jommelli.

Pepusch, John Christopher (b. Berlin, 1667; d. London, 20 July 1752). English composer of German birth. He arrived in London in 1700 and joined the orchestra of D.L., also making some arrangements of operas. His best-known work is his arrangement of *The Beggar's Opera* (1728), though he also composed music for a number of masques while music director at Lincoln's Inn Fields Theatre.

Perfect Fool, The. Comic opera in 1 act by Holst; text by the composer. Prod. London, C.G., 14 May 1923 by B.N.O.C.; Wichita, 20 Mar. 1962. The opera, which parodies opera conventions and the music of Wagner and Verdi, enjoyed much success originally, but has been rarely performed since the 1920's.

Pergola, Teatro della. See *Florence.*

Pergolesi, Giovanni Battista (b. Jesi, 4 Jan. 1710; d. Pozzuoli, 16 Mar. 1736). Italian composer. His first opera, *Salustia* (1731), performed in Naples with an unnamed intermezzo of his, seems to have failed, but *Lo Frate 'nnamorato* succeeded there in 1732. *Il Prigionier Superbo* (1733) is now forgotten except for its association with the most famous of all intermezzos, *La Serva Padrona.* The same pattern was repeated with *Adriano in Siria* (1734) and its intermezzo *La Contadina Astuta. L'Olimpiade* (1735) was a failure, but the *opera buffa, Flaminio* (1735) was a considerable success. It is clear, in fact, that Pergolesi's talent lay in comic opera. His *opere serie* do contain some expressive music between frigid stretches; but in the intermezzos and *opere buffe* there is a charmingly natural wit and freshness of utterance.

Peri, Jacopo (b. Rome, 20 Aug. 1561; d. Florence, 12 Aug. 1633). Italian composer. He was a prominent member of the Camerata (q.v.), and his *Dafne* (1597) is reckoned as the first opera. A skilled singer, he played the part of Apollo himself at the first performance, later taking that of Orpheus in his *Euridice* (1600), the first opera to survive. This work it was that proved the validity of the new art form and showed some of the possibilities later to be fulfilled by greater artists. None of his subsequent works matched the success of *Euridice*, but he has his place in history as a founding father with his great rival Caccini. Nicknamed 'Il Zazzerino' from his abundant hair.

Périchole, La. *Opéra bouffe* in 3 acts by Offenbach; text by Meilhac and Halévy after Mérimée's *Le Carrosse du Saint Sacrement*. Prod. Paris, Théâtre des Variétés, 6 Oct. 1868; N.Y., Grand Opera House, 4 Jan. 1869; London, Princess's T., 27 June 1870. La Périchole and her lover Piquillo are street singers in Peru. The opera tells how La Périchole became the favourite of the Viceroy, and of her adventures before being reunited with Piquillo.

Périer, Jean (b. Paris, 2 Feb. 1869; d. Paris, 6 Nov. 1954). French baritone. Studied Paris Conservatoire. Début Paris, O.C., 1892, Monostatos, where he created many roles including Pelléas, Landry in Messager's *Fortunio*, Ramiro in *L'Heure Espagnole*, and Mârouf; was the first Sharpless in France. (R)

Perlea, Jonel (b. Ograda, 13 Dec. 1900; d. New York, 29 July 1970). Rumanian conductor. Studied Munich with Graener, and Leipzig with Lohse. Début Bucharest 1923. After appointments in Leipzig and Rostock, returned to Bucharest Opera 1926, where he was music director 1934–44. Gave first performances in Bucharest of many works, including *Rosenkavalier*, *Meistersinger*, *Falstaff* (all in Rumanian). Appeared Sc. and other Italian opera houses from 1946; N.Y., Met., 1949–50; Aix Festival 1958. (R)

Pernet, André (b. Rambervillers, 6 Jan. 1894; d. Paris, 23 June 1966). French bass. Studied Paris with Gresse. Début Nice 1921. Leading bass, Paris, O., 1928, and then O.C., 1931, where he was much admired as Boris, Don Quichotte, Méphistophélès, and Don Giovanni. Created leading roles in a number of contemporary operas including Milhaud's *Maximilien*, Hahn's *Marchand de Venise*, and Enesco's *Œdipe*. (R)

Per pietà. Fiordiligi's (sop.) aria with horn *obbligato* in Act 2, scene 2, of Mozart's *Così fan tutte*, her resistance weakening to the advances of her sister's disguised lover.

Persephone. See *Proserpine*.

Persiani (orig. Tacchinardi), **Fanny** (b. Rome, 4 Oct. 1812; d. Paris, 3 May 1867). Italian soprano. Her father was the tenor Nicola Tacchinardi, who was also her teacher. Married the composer Giuseppe Persiani 1830; début Leghorn 1832 in Fournier's *Francesca da Rimini*. Donizetti wrote Lucia for her, which she created in 1835. London, H.M.'s, 1838 as Amina, and sang there until 1846. Then from 1847 to 1849 at C.G., which theatre she helped establish as the Royal Italian Opera, her husband putting up much of the money. A great favourite in Paris 1837–48. Her voice, although thin and often not true to pitch, was of great range (b to f'''); her singing was brilliant and clear, and she was capable of the most dazzling displays of ornamentation.

Pertile, Aureliano (b. Montagnana, 9 Nov. 1885; d. Milan, 11 Jan. 1952). Italian tenor. Studied with Orefice. Début Vicenza 1911, Lionel (*Martha*). A further period of study followed in Milan with Bavagnoli. N.Y., Met., 1921–2; Milan, Sc., leading tenor 1921–37; London, C.G., 1927–31. At Sc. was Toscanini's favourite tenor; created the title roles in Boito's and Mascagni's *Nerone* and Wolf-Ferrari's

Sly. His last years were spent as professor of singing at the Milan Conservatory. His voice was not one of intrinsic beauty, but the great intensity of his singing and acting, his integrity, and his intelligence made him one of the most respected artists of the 1920's and 1930's. (R)

Peter Grimes. Opera in 3 acts by Britten; text by Montagu Slater, after Crabbe's poem *The Borough* (1810), especially Letter XXII. Prod. London, S.W., 7 June 1945, with Cross, Pears, cond. Goodall; Tanglewood 6 Aug. 1946, cond. Bernstein.

In a little fishing village in Suffolk, Peter Grimes (ten.) has lost an apprentice at sea in suspicious circumstances. He is acquitted at the inquest, but warned not to take another apprentice. Ellen Orford (sop.), the schoolmistress, alone stands by him, and helps him to get another boy. Later she discovers that the boy has been ill treated and she quarrels with Peter. He takes the boy to his hut on the cliff top, but they have been overheard, and popular feeling rises to such a pitch that the entire village sets out after him. Peter and his apprentice hear the mob coming, and as they descend by another route the boy falls to his death down the cliff. Three days later Grimes turns up in the village at dawn, exhausted. Balstrode (bar.) a retired sea captain, advises him that the only way to escape the village now is to sail his boat out to sea and sink in it. This Peter does as the village comes to life for another, ordinary day.

Peter Grimes has been the most successful of all modern British operas, and its appearance immediately after the war was exciting not only as a revelation of Britten's full talent but as a sign of new growth in English opera.

Peter Ibbetson. Opera in 3 acts by Deems Taylor; text by the composer and Constance Collier, after the latter's play founded on Du Maurier's novel. Prod. N.Y., Met., 7 Feb. 1931, with Bori, Johnson, Tibbett; cond. Serafin. One of the most successful American operas before Menotti. The story concerns Peter's childhood love for Mimsey Serraskier, now grown up and married. The death of her husband coincides with Peter's being imprisoned in Newgate for the justifiable murder of his uncle. Eventually the lovers are reunited.

Peters, Roberta (b. New York, 4 May 1930). American soprano. Studied N.Y. with William Hermann. Début N.Y., Met., 1950, Zerlina; since then has established herself as one of the leading American coloratura sopranos. London, C.G., 1951, Arline in Beecham's *Bohemian Girl* revival and 1961; Salzburg, 1963. (R)

Petrassi, Goffredo (b. Zagarolo, 16 July 1904). Italian composer. His operas form a comparatively small part of his output, though *Morte dell'Aria* (1950) has won some success. It is based on the incident early in this century when a would-be bird-man leapt to his death from the Eiffel Tower (a grim little piece of film has recorded the affair). Though obviously touched by this Icarus theme, Petrassi has not managed to gear his reflective style to its dramatic demands.

Petrella, Clara (b. Milan, 28 Mar. 1919). Studied Milan with her sister Micalla Petrella. Début Alessandria 1939, Liù; after appearing in the Italian provinces, engaged Sc. 1947, where she has sung regularly since, creating leading roles in Pizzetti's *Cagliostro* and *La Figlia di Jorio*. Has scored great success as Maliella in the first stage performance in Italy of *I Gioielli della Madonna* (Rome 1954). Chosen to sing Manon Lescaut for the 25th anniversary of the Rome Opera House. One of the best singing actresses in Italy, she has been called the 'Duse of Singers'. (R)

Petri, Mario (b. Perugia, 22 Jan. 1922). Italian bass-baritone. Début Milan, Sc., 1948, Creonte (*Oedipus Rex*). Has sung regularly all over Italy. Notable roles include Bluebeard, Don Giovanni, the Doctor in *Wozzeck*, and buffo parts in Rossini operas. Glyndebourne 1951 as Don Giovanni. (R)

Petrograd. See *Leningrad*.

Petrov, Ivan (b. Irkutsk, 23 Feb. 1920). Russian bass. Début Bolshoy, 1943, and has sung as a guest artist throughout Europe. Roles include Don Basilio, Ruslan, Boris. (R)

Petrov, Ossip (b. Elizavetgrad, 15 Nov. 1807; d. St. Petersburg, 14 Mar. 1878). Russian bass. Heard singing at a market fair at Kursk in 1830 by director of St. Petersburg Opera who immediately engaged him; début as Sarastro. Created Ivan Susanin, Russlan, the Miller in *Russalka*, Leporello in *The Stone Guest*, Ivan in *The Maid of Pskov*, and Varlaam, as well as roles in operas by Tchaikovsky, Serov, and Rubinstein. Voice ranged from B♭ to g♯.

Pfitzner, Hans (b. Moscow, 5 May 1869; d. Salzburg, 22 May 1949). German composer. Studied Frankfurt with his father who was director of the Opera. Cond. Mainz (1894–6), Berlin (1903–6), Strasbourg (1908–16); director of Strasbourg Opera 1910–16. A great admirer of Wagner and Schopenhauer, he expressed dislike for modernistic tendencies in music and became a fervent nationalist. His works have enjoyed little if any success outside Germany; even there the general public has not been unanimous in its acceptance of his operas, though *Palestrina* (1917) has become a regular feature of the Munich Summer Festivals, and is also heard once or twice a year in Vienna. His other works are *Der arme Heinrich* (1895), *Die Rose vom Liebesgarten* (1901), *Christelflein* (1906, rev. 1917), and *Das Herz* (1931). He espoused the Nazi cause and was found poverty-stricken after the war in a Home for the Aged in Munich by the president of the Vienna Philharmonic Orchestra, who took him to Vienna where he was supported by the orchestra.

Philadelphia. Town in Pennsylvania, U.S.A. Has supported opera in various guises since the 18th century. The first Italian opera, Mayr's *Che Originali*, was given there in 1829. The first American 'grand opera', Fry's *Leonora*, was given in Philadelphia in June 1845. It was also the scene of the premières of Herbert's *Natoma*, Menotti's *Amelia Goes to the Ball* and *The Consul*, Deems Taylor's *Ramuntcho*, as well as many American premières, including *Norma*, *Faust*, *Der fliegende Holländer*, *Cavalleria Rusticana*, *Ariadne auf Naxos*, and *Wozzeck*. The various companies that have functioned in Philadelphia include a Philadelphia company which gave opera in English under Gustav Hinrichs 1895–6, under Damrosch 1896–7, and Damrosch and Ellis 1897–9. The Metropolitan Opera has appeared regularly in Philadelphia 1899–1961 (except for the 1934 season), giving regular performances at the Ac. of M. From 1910 to 1915 the Philadelphia-Chicago served both those cities; from 1908 to 1911 Hammerstein gave seasons at the Philadelphia Opera House, which he built; from 1923 to 1930 the Philadelphia Civic Opera gave performances with Alexander Smallens as music director; from 1926 to 1932 the Philadelphia Grand Opera Company was in existence; and from 1927 to 1930 the Pennsylvania Grand Opera Company. The Philadelphia La Scala Opera Company (recently renamed the Philadelphia Grand Opera Co.), musical director Giuseppe Bamboscheck, and the Philadelphia Civic Grand Opera Company (now called the Philadelphia Lyric Opera) both give a dozen or so operas each during the course of the season.

Philidor, François André (b. Dreux, 7 Sept. 1726; d. London, 24 Aug. 1795). French composer, the most famous of a large family of musicians. His proficiency as a chess-player—he toured as a master and published a study of the game—was one facet of a gift for calculation that made him the first truly learned composer of *opéras comiques*. His works have a weight, originality, and dramatic cogency new to the form. His 35 operas were tremendously popular even in a Paris revelling in Gluck and Grétry; he was the first composer ever to be accorded a curtain call there.

Philip II. The King of Spain (bass) in Verdi's *Don Carlos*.

Piave, Francesco Maria (b. Murano, 18 May 1810; d. Milan, 5 Mar. 1876).

Italian librettist. Close friend of Verdi for whom he provided the librettos of *Ernani*, *La Forza del Destino*, *Macbeth*, *Simone Boccanegra*, *Rigoletto*, *Traviata*, *Il Corsaro*, *Stiffelio*, *Aroldo*, and *I due Foscari*. Also wrote librettos for Balfe, Mercadante, Ricci, and others.

Piccaver, Alfred (b. Long Sutton, 15 Feb. 1884; d. Vienna, 23 Sept. 1958). English tenor. Studied N.Y. Début Prague 1907, Roméo; then studied Milan and Prague. Leading tenor Vienna 1910–37, where he sang in the first performances in Austria of *La Fanciulla del West* and *Il Tabarro*: Chicago 1923–5; London, C.G., 1924. Possessed a large velvety voice which he used with skill; noted for the smoothness of his legato and expansive phrasing. From 1937 until 1955 lived in London, taking a few pupils, and returned to Vienna for the reopening of the State Opera in 1955 as an honoured guest, remaining there as a teacher until his death. (R)

Piccinni, Niccolò (b. Bari, 16 Jan. 1728; d. Passy, 7 May 1800). Italian composer. He made his début in 1754 with *Le Donne Dispettose*, quickly following up this success with a series of operas that culminated in *La Cecchina, ossia La Buona Figliuola* (1760), by far the most popular *opera buffa* of its day (and frequently revived in Italy). *L'Olimpiade* (1768) followed up this triumph. Rivalry with Anfossi upset him, but he continued composing diligently, and then in 1776 set out for Paris. His first French opera, *Roland* (1778), was not finished when there broke out the famous Gluck–Piccinni feud, fostered not by the composers but by their supporters. Paris was soon ranged in two camps. An enterprising director arranged for them each to compose an *Iphigénie en Tauride*, but Piccinni's (1781), though containing many beauties, could not rival Gluck's. After Gluck's departure in 1779 a new rival arose in Sacchini, and though *Didon* (1783) proved Piccinni's best French opera, his star was on the wane. At the Revolution in 1789 he returned to Naples, where he became involved in political trouble. He was fêted on his return to Paris in 1798, but never regained his old position. Though no innovator, and certainly no real rival to Gluck, Piccinni's best work has great distinction and dignity. It has been well said that his art was of a kind which adapts itself to its age; Gluck's is the art to which the age has, in time, to adapt itself.

Piccola Scala, La. See *La Scala*.

Piccolo Marat, Il. Opera in 3 acts by Mascagni; text by Forzano and Targioni-Tozzetti. Prod. Rome, C., 2 May 1921 with Lazaro in title role, Gilda Dalla Rizza, Franci. Prod. in several countries outside Italy, and revived in Italy from time to time. One of Mascagni's more successful works. An opera about the fanatics who terrorized Paris after the assassination of the revolutionary Jean-Paul Marat by Charlotte Corday.

Piccolomini, Marietta (b. Siena, 15 Mar. 1834; d. Florence, 23 Dec. 1899). Italian soprano. Studied Florence. Début Florence, Teatro Pergola, 1852, Lucrezia Borgia; London, H.M.'s 1856, Violetta in English première of *Traviata*; was the first interpreter of Luisa Miller in London 1858, and Arline in the Italian version of *The Bohemian Girl*. U.S.A. 1858. Married the Marchese Gaetani della Fargia in 1860 and retired from the stage, apart from one appearance at Lumley's benefit at D.L. 1863. Admired more for her beauty and histrionic abilities than for her voice, which aroused much adverse criticism.

Pierné, Gabriel (b. Metz, 16 Aug. 1863; d. Ploujean, 17 July 1937). French composer. His long list of works includes eight operas, of which the most successful have been *La Coupe Enchantée* (1895) and *On ne badine pas avec l'amour* (1910).

Pietra del Paragone, La (The Touchstone). Opera in 2 acts by Rossini; text by Romanelli. Prod. Milan, Sc., 26 Sept. 1812 (Rossini's first opera for Sc.), with Marcolini and Galli; Hartford, Hartt Coll. of Music, 4 May 1955; London, St. Pancras Town Hall, 19 Mar. 1963. The wealthy Count Asdrubale puts to the test three young widows who want to marry him. Disguising himself, he produces a document declaring the Count bankrupt. Only Clarice remains loyal. She then in turn tests the Count, disguising herself as her twin brother and threatening to remove Clarice. All ends happily.

Pilarczyk, Helga (b. nr. Brunswick, 12 Mar. 1925). German soprano. Studied Hamburg and Hanover. Début Brunswick 1951 (mezzo-sop.), Irmentraud, *Der Waffenschmied*. Hamburg Opera since 1954, where she has specialized in modern roles—the Woman in *Erwartung*, Marie in *Wozzeck*, Lulu, &c.—as well as in Verdi and Strauss. Glyndebourne 1958; London, C.G., 1958; Holland Festival, &c. One of the most intelligent and intensely dramatic artists of the day. (R)

Pilgrims' Chorus. The chorus of pilgrims on their march to and from Rome in Acts 1 and 3 of Wagner's *Tannhäuser*.

Pilgrim's Progress, The. Morality in 4 acts by Vaughan Williams; text by composer, after Bunyan's allegory (Pt. 1, 1674–9; Pt. 2, 1684). Prod. London, C.G., 26 Apr. 1951. Pilgrim's journey towards the Heavenly City is shown in a series of scenes depicting his most famous encounters, one of which, that with the Shepherds of the Delectable Mountains, Vaughan Williams had set as a 1-act 'pastoral episode' in 1922 and later incorporated into the main work.

Pimen. A monk (bass) in Mussorgsky's *Boris Godunov*.

Pini-Corsi, Antonio (b. Zara, June 1858; d. Milan, 22 Apr. 1918). Italian baritone. Début Cremona 1878, Dandini. Chosen by Verdi to create Ford in *Falstaff* at Sc. 1893. London, C.G., 1894–6, 1902–3; N.Y., Met., 1909–14 where he sang in the first performances of *La Fanciulla del West* (Happy), *Königskinder* (Inn-keeper), and other works, and in the American premières of *Le Donne Curiose*, *L'Amore Medico*, and *Germania*. His Bartolo, Pasquale, Leporello, &c. were considered the finest of his day. (R) His brother **Gaetano** was a tenor noted for his Mime in *Siegfried*. (R)

Pinkerton. The American naval lieutenant (ten.) in Puccini's *Madama Butterfly*.

Pinza, Ezio (orig. Fortunio) (b. Rome, 18 May 1892; d. Stamford, Conn., 9 May 1957). Italian bass. Studied Bologna. Début Soncino 1914, Oroveso, then six years of military service; real début Rome 1921, King Mark; Milan, Sc., 1921–4; N.Y., Met., 1926–48; London, C.G., 1930–9. Generally regarded as the greatest Italian bass of the inter-war years, possessing a beautiful, noble, basso-cantante voice, an imposing stage presence, and great dramatic ability. Chosen by Bruno Walter to sing Don Giovanni and Figaro at Salzburg 1934–7; was the first Met. Fiesco (*Boccanegra*), Gaudenzio (*Signor Bruschino*), and Chervek (*Sorochinsky Fair*). Appeared in every major opera house in the world, and had a repertory of more than 95 roles; sang Don Giovanni more then 200 times, and sang more than 750 times in 50 operas during his engagement with the Met. In 1949 appeared in *South Pacific* and then in *Fanny*, and made a number of films. (R) His daughter **Claudia** (sop.) had a brief career in the 1940's.

Pipe of Desire, The. Opera in 1 act by Converse; text by George Edward Burton. Prod. Boston 31 Jan. 1906—the first American opera to be prod. at the Met., 18 Mar. 1910. The Elf King's pipe, which has magic powers, is selfishly used by Iolan and brings disaster to himself and to his lover Naoia. The King pipes, and they die.

Piper, John (b. 13 Dec. 1903). English painter. One of the founder members of the English Opera Group in 1947 (with Benjamin Britten and Eric Crozier). Some of his designs for the Group, for Glyndebourne, C.G., and S.W., have been among the best to be seen in England since the war. His sets for Britten's operas—*The Rape of Lucretia*, *Albert Herring*, *Billy Budd*, *Gloriana*, *The Turn of the Screw*, and *A Midsummer Night's Dream*—have been particularly distinguished. Those for *The Magic Flute* at C.G., *Don Giovanni* at Glyndebourne, and *The Pearl-fishers* at S.W. were less so.

Pique Dame. See *Queen of Spades*.

Pirata, Il (The Pirate). Opera in 2 acts by Bellini; text by Romani. Prod. Milan, Sc., 27 Oct. 1827 with Méric-Lalande, Rubini, Tamburini; London, H.M.'s, 17 Apr. 1830, same cast—first Bellini opera in London; N.Y. 5 Dec. 1832. Imogene, married against her will in a useless attempt to save her father's life, is deserted by her lover, accused of adultery by her husband (who is killed by the man she loves, who is then condemned to death), and then loses her reason. The opera has been successfully revived for Callas.

Pirogov, Alexander (b. Ryazan, 5 June 1899; d. 27 June 1964). Russian bass. Début 1919. Leading singer at the Bolshoy since 1924 where his roles include Méphistophélès, Boris, Ivan the Terrible (*Maid of Pskov*) and Pestel (*The Decembrists*). (R)

Pisaroni, Benedetta Rosamunda (b. Piacenza, 6 Feb. 1793; d. Piacenza, 6 Aug. 1872). Italian soprano, later contralto. A serious illness affected her high notes, and after a brilliant career as a soprano she developed her lower register with such success that she became known as the first Italian contralto She was so conscious of the facial disfiguration she had suffered as a result of smallpox that she always warned intending impresarios by sending them her picture. A fine actress as well as a fine singer (excelling in Rossini), she retired when, in the early 1830's, she found her popularity waning.

Pitt, Percy (b. London, 4 Jan. 1870; d. London, 23 Nov. 1932). English conductor. Studied Leipzig and Munich. Apptd. music adviser and assistant conductor C.G., 1902; music director Grand Opera Syndicate 1907–24; collaborated with Richter in the production of the English *Ring* (1908–9); Beecham Opera Company 1915–18. Artistic director B.N.O.C. 1920–4, after which he devoted most of his time to the B.B.C. Conducted the first C.G. performances of *Bastien und Bastienne*, *L'Enfant Prodigue*, *Ivanhoe*, *Joseph*, *L'Heure Espagnole*, *Thérèse*, *Khovanshchina*, *The Goldsmith of Toledo*, and *Fête Galante*. (R)

Pizarro. The evil prison governor (bar.) in Beethoven's *Fidelio*.

Pizzetti, Ildebrando (b. Parma, 20 Sept. 1880; d. Rome, 13 Feb. 1968). Italian composer. After studying at Reggio Emilia and Parma he began to show an interest in the theatre, and his early attempts at opera included *Sabina* (1897), *Giulietta e Romeo* (1899), and *Il Cid* (1902) which he entered for the Sonzogno competition for 1-act operas. Between 1903 and 1907 he started work on a number of opera projects and abandoned them—*Sardanapalo* (Byron), *Mazeppa* (Pushkin), *Aeneas* (Virgil) were all begun. In 1905 came under the influence of D'Annunzio and composed some incidental music for his tragedy *La Nave*. Soon afterwards began work on the same author's *Fedra*, based on the Greek tragedy, which was produced at La Scala in 1915. The libretto is too wordy and the music not as free and expressive as in his later works. Thenceforth provided his own librettos for all his operas except *Ifigenia* (1950), for which collaborated with A. Perrini, *La Figlia di Jorio* (1954), for which adapted D'Annunzio's play, *L'Assassinio nella Cattedrale* (1958), for which Alberto Castelli adapted T. S. Eliot, and *Il Calzare d'Argento* (1961), for which Riccardo Bacchelli wrote text. *Debora e Jaele* (1922), is generally regarded as the best example of his conception of music drama. *Lo Straniero* (1930) and *Fra Gherardo* (1928) are both conceived in the same spirit. In his later works Pizzetti exhibits a tendency to the *arioso* type of opera—*Orsèolo* (1935), *L'Oro* (1938–42, but not produced until 1947), *Vanna Lupa* (1949), *Ifigenia* (his radio opera—1950), *Cagliostro* (1953), and *La Figlia di Jorio* and *L'Assassinio nella Cattedrale* mentioned above. These last two works have already enjoyed success outside Italy. He announced that he was closing his career with *Clittenestra* (1965).

Plaichinger, Thila (b. Vienna, 13 Mar. 1868; d. Vienna, 17 Mar. 1939). Austrian soprano. Studied Vienna. Début Hamburg 1893; after engagements at Strasbourg and Munich was leading soprano at Berlin 1901–14; London, C.G., 1904 as Isolde, Venus, and Ortrud, 1910 as Elektra, of which role she was the first interpreter in Berlin. She sang small roles at Bayreuth in 1897. After leaving the stage she taught in Berlin and Vienna. (R)

Planché, James Robinson (b. London, 27 Feb. 1796; d. London, 29 May 1880). English theatrical writer. He translated many operas for the English stage, including works by Rossini, Auber, Marschner, Bellini (*Norma*), Hérold, Offenbach, and Mozart (*Magic Flute* and *Marriage of Figaro*). It was his version of Weber's *Der Freischütz* (1821) that led Kemble to engage him as the librettist for *Oberon*. He thus became the last of the series of poor librettists that Weber had to suffer; his dedication of *Oberon* to Weber as 'the fragile threads upon which a great composer has ventured to thread his valuable pearls' is perhaps a more accurate self-judgement than was really intended. Wrote his *Recollections*.

Plançon, Pol (b. Fumay, Ardennes, 12 July 1854; d. Paris, 11 Aug. 1914). French bass. Studied Paris with Duprez and Sbriglia. Début Lyons 1877, St. Bris; Paris 1880, Opéra from 1883 to 1893; London, C.G., 1891–1904; N.Y., Met., 1893–1908. He created Don Gormas in *Le Cid*, Francis I in Saint-Saëns's *Ascanio* in Paris; Garrido in *La Navarraise*, Francis in *Much Ado About Nothing* (Stanford), and the King in *Princess Osra* (Bunning) at C.G. He was the most admired Méphistophélès of his day, and was also at home in the German and Italian repertory. His voice was a true bass of enormous range, smooth and even, and extremely flexible. His runs and trills were said to be the envy of many a soprano. (R)

Planquette, Robert (b. Paris, 31 July 1848; d. Paris, 28 Jan. 1903). French composer. After a modest beginning supplying *chansonnettes* to singers in Paris *cafés-chantants*, he turned to comic opera, producing his greatest success, *Les Cloches de Corneville*, in 1877. His popularity spread so quickly that by 1882 he was turning down an offer of £12,000 for the copyright of the score of *Rip van Winkle*, an adaptation of *Les Cloches*. This was first performed at the Comedy in London with a success which he followed up in a series of operettas. These found instant acceptance at a time when Parisian manners dominated the European operetta. Though a fluent, unprofound composer, he was also a scrupulous one, and he had a sharper ear for character and situation than most of his rivals.

Plzeň (Pilsen). Town in western Bohemia, Czechoslovakia. The theatre (cap. 1,000) is used for both opera and drama.

Pogner. The goldsmith, Eva's father (bass), in Wagner's *Die Meistersinger*.

Poisoned Kiss, The. Romantic extravaganza in 3 acts by Vaughan Williams; text by Evelyn Sharp, after Richard Garnett's story *The Poison Maid* in the collection *The Twilight of the Gods* (1888). Prod. Cambridge 12 May 1936; N.Y., Juilliard School, 21 Apr. 1937. The fantastic plot turns on the rivalry of a sorcerer and an empress; his daughter Tormentilla has been brought up on poisons so that when she meets the empress's son Amaryllus she will kill him with her kiss. In the end the sincerity of their love defeats the plot.

Polacco, Giorgio (b. Venice, 12 Apr. 1875; d. New York, 30 Apr. 1960). Italian conductor. Studied St. Petersburg, Venice, and Milan. Début London, Shaftesbury T., 1893, replacing an indisposed Arditi in a performance of *Orfeo*. After engagements throughout Italy, and appearances in Brussels, Lisbon, Warsaw, &c., he conducted the Italian première of *L'Attaque du Moulin* (Milan 1898) and the première of *Zazà* (Milan 1900). Engaged seven seasons at Rio, where he conducted local premières of *Bohème*, *Chénier*, *Tosca*, and *Boris*. Toured U.S. 1911 with the English production of *La*

Fanciulla. N.Y., Met., 1912–17, during which period he conducted 342 performances. From 1918 to 1930 Chicago Opera, becoming chief conductor there in 1921, directing many memorable performances of French opera with Mary Garden, as well as the Italian and German repertory. London, C.G., 1913–14 and 1930. Forced by ill health to retire at the height of his powers.

Poland. Opera was first given in Poland in 1613, when Prince Stanisław Lubomirski invited an Italian company to perform at his residence at Wiśnicz. In 1625, Prince Władysław Zygmunt of Poland visited the Grand Duchess of Tuscany, and in his honour was given the first performance of Francesca Caccini's *La Liberazione di Ruggiero dall'Isola d'Alcina* (the first opera by a woman). It may have been heard in Poland soon after; certainly a Polish translation by S. S. Jagodyński was published in Cracow in 1628. The Prince was crowned Władysław IV in 1632, and founded an Italian opera company with Cattaneo as prima donna; it included a few young Poles. Various operas, probably adaptations, were performed and published. At the end of 1637, the Mantuan architect Bartolomeo Bolzoni built a provisional wooden theatre in Warsaw (cap. 1,000); this was replaced when, for his wedding celebrations, Władysław decided to build a permanent theatre in the royal castle. But on his death in 1648, the fortunes of the opera declined.

Frederick Augustus, Elector of Saxony, was crowned Augustus II of Poland in 1697, and though he did almost nothing for his new country's art, he did bring in his retinue an ensemble directed by J. C. Schmidt and Jacek Różycki; and in 1699 he asked the French actor Costantini to form a troupe in Paris. This left Paris with 60 members in 1700, and stayed 5 days in Warsaw. Various other troupes visited Warsaw during Augustus's reign. In 1724–5 the Opera Theatre was built.

Augustus III was crowned in 1733, and at once revealed his enthusiasm for opera. He provided heavy subsidies, and bi-weekly performances were given with an orchestra of now over 100. Many Metastasian operas were given, with distinguished visitors that included Bordoni and Mingotti. But these were all aristocratic entertainments, chiefly Saxon, or French and Italian.

The first growth of Polish national opera dates from the second half of the 18th century and the reign (1764–95) of Poland's last king, the enlightened and intelligent Stanisław August Poniatowski, who summoned artists of every kind to Warsaw and vigorously encouraged the arts throughout the country. In 1765 the first public theatre in Warsaw was opened, with Tomatis as director (until 1767). A new theatre opened in the Radziwiłł Palace in 1773, and in 1776–7 *opera seria* was given here with famous Italian singers (accompanied by a trebling of the prices). The first Polish opera was Kamieński's *Nędza Uszczęśliwiona* (*Misery Made Happy*) (Warsaw, 1778): the music consisted of 11 airs and 2 duets. The Teatr Narodowy (National Theatre) was established in a new building in 1779 with Audinot's *Il Bottaio* (sung in Polish). Operas by Sacchini and Duni followed; then in 1779 came three new Polish operas, Kamieński's *Zośka* (*Sophia*) and *Prostota Cnotliwa* (*Virtuous Simplicity*) and a work by the royal Kapellmeister, Gaetano. Despite the three partitions of Poland at the end of the 18th century, Polish texts began superseding foreign ones, thanks largely to 'the father of the Polish theatre', Wojciech Bogusławski, an actor, producer, and singer who directed the National Theatre and translated many librettos; he also wrote the original text for Stefani's *Krakowiacy i Górale* (*The Cracovians and the Highlanders*)—the first long work based entirely on peasant life and customs. After Bogusławski, the most important figure in the early 19th century was Ksawery Elsner (who taught Chopin, and tried to persuade him to write operas). While Bogusławski offered a series of translated works, Elsner wrote a series of Polish operas, including *Mieszkańcy Wyspy Kamkatal* (*The People of Kamkatal*); this was given in 1807 before Napoleon, who followed with a French translation. In 1810 the composer Karol Kurpiński and the poet Jan Niemcewicz were appointed to the opera by the Tsar.

The events of 1812 brought Polish opera to a temporary halt, though works by Elsner, Kurpiński, Dalayrac, Mozart, and Rossini were being given by 1814. Kurpiński became director of the opera in 1823, and introduced a predominantly French and Italian repertory. In 1843 Giovanni Quattrini was summoned to direct the new Grand Theatre. *Halka* (*Helen*), first performed at Wilno in 1848, reached Warsaw in 1858; it became accepted as Poland's first great national opera, and its composer, Moniuszko, introduced many other Polish works during his 39-year tenure of office as director of the Warsaw opera. In 1865, after a period of inactivity following the 1863 insurrection against Tsar Alexander II, he gave his *Straszny Dwór* (*The Haunted Manor*). Cesare Trombini became director in 1876, introducing *Lohengrin* in 1879; famous Polish singers included Alexander Myszuga (Filippi). Composers included Żeleński, Różycki, and Szymanowski.

After the First World War there followed a period of intense activity in Warsaw, Cracow, Poznań, and Katowice; and many famous singers came as guests. In taste, however, it was a reactionary period, and in the 1930's many of the best artists left for Paris where the Society of Young Polish Musicians was formed under Szymanowski. The theatres fell on difficult times, and with the Second World War were closed. In 1939 the Opera was burnt down, and in 1944 bombs destroyed all but the fine Corazzi façade; rebuilt and reopened Nov. 1965.

After the liberation, a company was formed and opera began again in Warsaw (where all the theatres were destroyed) in the Roma Hall, an ex-cinema re-fitted in 1953 (cap. 1,000). Despite makeshift accommodation, opera quickly re-established itself: between 1949 and 1953 the annual number of performances increased from 700 to over 2,000. A new opera house on the site of the old was planned in 1950 and was due to open in 1964; while outside the capital there are nine companies, including those at Bytom, Wrocław, Łódz, Gdańsk, and Poznań (where, it is conceded even in Warsaw, the best opera is to be heard). There are also 10 operetta theatres, and an organization named Artos that takes concert opera to outlying towns. *Halka* and other Polish Romantic works remain popular; so do the Italian repertory and 19th-century Russian works. But other operas are also heard: in 1958 Britten's *Beggar's Opera* was given in Łódz, and the Gdańsk company brought *Peter Grimes* to the Warsaw Festival as well as a new Polish work, Szeligowski's *Krakatuk*. Opera continues to flourish despite considerable economic and other difficulties in Warsaw, and is extremely popular: a catholic repertory is supplemented by a cycle known as 'Opera Viva' designed to include representative works of all periods. The rebuilt National Theatre opened in Nov. 1965.

Poliuto. Opera in 3 acts by Donizetti; text by Cammarano, after Corneille's tragedy *Polyeucte* (1640). Written for the French tenor Nourrit for production in Naples but not passed by censor. New 4-act version with French libretto by Scribe prod. Paris, O., 10 Apr. 1840 as *Les Martyrs* with Duprez and Dorus-Gras. Retranslated into Italian as *I Martiri* by Bassi, prod. Lisbon, 15 Feb. 1843; London, C.G., 20 Apr. 1852 with Tamberlik and Julienne; New Orleans, 24 Mar. 1846. After Donizetti's death performed in Italy in original 3-act version, Naples, S.C., 30 Nov. 1848. Revived Milan, Sc., 1960, with Corelli and Callas.

Pollak, Anna (b. Manchester, 1 May 1915). English mezzo-soprano of Austrian origin. Studied Holland and Manchester, and began career on straight stage. Studied with Joan Cross who engaged her for S.W. in 1945. Début London, Princes Theatre with S.W. Opera, 1945, Dorabella; and remained member of Company until 1961. Created Lady Nelson (*Nelson*), Mrs. Strickland (*Moon and Sixpence*). E.O.G. since 1946, creating Bianca in *Rape of Lucretia* and the title role in

Berkeley's *Ruth*. Has appeared Holland Festival, Glyndebourne, and C.G. One of the most reliable and versatile artists of the S.W. Company.

Pollak, Eugen (b. Prague, 3 May 1879; d. Prague, 14 June 1933). Czech conductor. Studied Prague where he began career as chorus master at the Landestheater. Bremen 1905–10 as first Kapellmeister; Leipzig 1910–12; Frankfurt 1912–17; Hamburg 1917–32. London, C.G., 1914; Chicago 1931–2. Conducted première of *Die tote Stadt* at Hamburg 1920. Was greatly admired for his readings of Wagner, Strauss, and D'Albert. Collapsed and died while conducting a performance of *Fidelio*. (R)

Pollione. The Roman proconsul (ten.), in love with Adalgisa but loved by Norma, in Bellini's *Norma*.

Polly. Ballad opera in 3 acts by Gay, with music arranged by Pepusch and Arnold. Prod. London, Little Hm., 19 June 1777; N.Y., Cherry Lane, 10 Oct. 1925. The preface to the libretto is dated 1729, but owing to the intervention of the Lord Chamberlain (possibly at the instigation of Walpole, who had been lampooned in the previous *Beggar's Opera*), the piece was not then performed.

Pomo d'Oro, Il (The Golden Apple). *Festa teatrale* in 5 acts, with prologue, by Cesti; text by Sbarra; designs by Ludovico Burnacini. Prod. Vienna, Carn., 1667. Composed for the wedding of Leopold I and the Infanta Margherita (12 Dec. 1666), this was perhaps the most elaborate opera production ever staged: the cost of the décor alone was estimated at 100,000 Reichstaler. The music for Act 5 is lost; the rest has been published in a modern edition. The work has never been revived. The same season saw Cesti's *Le Disgrazie d'Amore*, for which Leopold himself wrote the prologue.

Ponchielli, Amilcare (b. Paderno, 31 Aug. 1834; d. Milan, 16 Jan. 1886). Italian composer. Studied Milan 1843–54. Two years later his first opera, *I Promessi Sposi*, was produced at Cremona. Of his nine operas only *La Gioconda* survives, and it requires a fine performance to satisfy present-day audiences, for musically it is full of old-fashioned clichés and is crudely scored. He married the singer Teresa Brambilla (q.v.).

Poniatowski, Józef (Prince of Monte Rotondo) (b. Rome, 20 Feb. 1816; d. Chislehurst, Kent, 3 July 1873). Polish-Italian singer and composer. Great-nephew of Stanisław August, King of Poland 1764–95. Studied Florence. Début Florence where he sang title role in his *Giovanni di Procida* (1839). His 13 operas written for France, Italy, and London include *Gelmina* (C.G. 1872), composed specially for Patti.

Pons, Lily (orig. Alice Joséphine Pons) (b. Cannes, 16 Apr. 1904). French soprano. Studied in Paris with Alberto di Gorostiaga. Début Mulhouse 1928, Lakmé. After appearances in the French provinces was heard by Maria Gay and Zenatello, who recommended her to Gatti-Casazza at the Met., N.Y. Début there 3 Jan. 1931, Lucia, and sang until 1959. London, C.G., 1935, Rosina. During a period of comparative paucity of coloratura sopranos, Pons achieved a considerable success. Her voice, while limited in colour, is flexible and appealing in quality, and her personal charm and vivacity are considerable. She also made a number of films. (R)

Ponselle (orig. Ponzillo), **Rosa** (b. Merifen, Conn., 22 Jan. 1897). American soprano. Born of immigrant Neapolitan parents, she first sang in public when in her early teens, first in local cinemas, and then in vaudeville with her sister Carmella. Studied N.Y. with William Thorner, then with Romani. Heard by Caruso, who suggested that Gatti-Casazza engage her to sing Leonora in *La Forza del Destino*, in which role she made her N.Y. début at the Met. 15 Nov. 1918. Sang Met. 1918–37; London, C.G., 1929–31; Florence, Maggio Musicale, 1933. Her rich dramatic soprano voice, perfectly covered and even in scale throughout its range, of a dark exciting quality, made her one of the greatest singers of the century. For her the Met. revived *La Vestale*, *Norma*, *La Gioconda*, and other works. She sang her first Violetta at C.G. 1930. In 1935 she sang Carmen, which was not an unequivocal success; and two years later she retired, while still at the height of her powers. She now lives and teaches in Baltimore. Some records made a few years ago still show the opulence of her voice. (R) Her sister **Carmella Ponselle** (b. 7 June 1892) appeared at the N.Y. Met. 1925–35, and sang Amneris, Azucena, Santuzza, &c.

Ponte, Lorenzo da (orig. Emanuele Conegliano) (b. Ceneda, 10 Mar. 1749; d. New York, 17 Aug. 1838). Italian poet and librettist. He first studied for the priesthood, but later settled in Vienna as court poet to Joseph II. He is famous for the three librettos he wrote for Mozart—*Le Nozze di Figaro*, *Don Giovanni*, and *Così fan tutte*. He left the city on the emperor's death in 1790, being out of favour with Leopold II. From 1793 he worked in London at D.L., but had to leave England secretly and reached America in 1805. From 1826 to 1837 he held a chair in Italian at Columbia University, also occupying himself with his entertaining, Casanova-esque autobiography. In 1825 he and Manuel Garcia were among the first to give Italian opera in the U.S.A., and in 1833 he was responsible for the establishment of the Italian Opera House in New York.

Ponticello (It. = little bridge). The term used by the *bel-cantists* for the join between the chest and head registers.

Porgi amor. The Countess's (sop.) aria in Act 2 of Mozart's *Marriage of Figaro*, lamenting that she has lost her husband's love.

Porgy and Bess. Opera in 3 acts by Gershwin; text by Du Bose Heyward and Ira Gershwin, after the drama *Porgy* by Du Bose and Dorothy Heyward. Prod. Boston 30 Sept. 1935 with Anne Brown, Todd Duncan; London, Stoll, 9 Oct. 1953, with Leontyne Price, William Warfield.

Act 1. The scene is Catfish Row, in Charleston, South Carolina. The Row comes to life at dawn; street-vendors are heard, and against a crap game, Serena (sop.) sings 'Summertime'. The cripple Porgy's (bar.) sweetheart Bess (sop.) has left him for Crown (bass), who now kills one of the gamblers in a quarrel. Porgy comforts Bess and takes her to live with him, despite the offer of Sportin' Life (ten.) to take her to New York. The murdered man's widow, Serena, mourns his death.

Act 2. During a picnic on Kittiwah Island, Crown appears from hiding and begs Bess to stay with him. She returns a few days later, sick and delirious, and Porgy nurses her back to health. A storm blows up; Crown reappears to claim Bess, and goes to help a capsized boat.

Act 3. Crown returns for Bess, but is killed by Porgy, who is arrested and imprisoned on suspicion for five days. Meanwhile Bess has been tempted away to New York with Sportin' Life, and the opera ends with Porgy setting out to look for Bess again.

Porpora, Nicola (b. Naples, 17 Aug. 1686; d. Naples, 3 Mar. 1768). Italian composer. His earliest operas were produced in Naples, where he established a school of singing that became famous—his pupils included Farinelli and Caffarelli. His busy life as composer and singing teacher took him all over Italy, Germany, and Austria (where Haydn accompanied his lessons), and to England, where he was eventually overwhelmed by the popularity of his rival Handel. As the greatest teacher of the day, his 50-odd operas are naturally superbly written for the voice; though not as extreme in his vocal demands or as stilted theatrically as others, his operas lacked the dramatic force of Handel's.

Portamento (It. = carrying). The smooth carrying of the voice from one note to another.

Portugal. See *Lisbon*.

Postillon de Longjumeau, Le. Opera in 3 acts by Adam; text by de Leuven and Brunswick. Prod. Paris, O.C., 13 Oct. 1836; London,

St. James's T., 13 Mar. 1837; N.Y., Park T., 30 Mar. 1840. Adam's most popular opera outside France. A centenary performance was given at Longjumeau in May 1936. Chapelou, the postilion of the title, possesses a fine voice, and is engaged by De Courcy, the manager of the royal amusements, to sing at Fontainebleau. Under the name of St-Phar he becomes a great singer, and promises marriage to the rich Madame de Latour. She is no other than Madeleine, whom he had previously married when he was a postilion and she the hostess of a village inn. All ends happily.

Pougin, Arthur (b. Châteauroux, 6 Aug. 1834; d. Paris, 8 Aug. 1921). French writer and critic. Published biographies of Rossini, Bellini, Meyerbeer, Verdi, Auber, and others, as well as of singers including Dugazon, Malibran, Favart, and Grassini.

Poulenc, Francis (b. Paris, 7 Jan. 1899; d. 30 Jan. 1963). French composer. The greater part of Poulenc's music has not been written for the theatre. After *Le Gendarme Incompris*, a *comédie-bouffe* (1920), there was nothing for the opera house until the brilliant satire *Les Mamelles de Tirésias* (1944). He showed himself in an entirely new light with *Dialogues des Carmélites* (1957), a deeply felt religious opera. Musically subdued, with vocal writing reminiscent of *Pelléas*, it has had some public success. *La Voix Humaine* (1958), with text by Cocteau, is a 45-minute monologue for a soprano.

Pourquoi me réveiller? Werther's (ten.) aria in Act 3 of Massenet's opera, in which the poet sings a song of tragic love from the verses of Ossian which in happier days he had translated with Charlotte.

Poveri fiori. Adriana Lecouvreur's (sop.) aria from Act 4 of Cilea's opera, which she sings as she looks at the faded bunch of violets (now poisoned by her rival the Princesse de Bouillon) that she had given Maurizio.

Poznań (Posen). See *Poland*.

Praetorius, Emil (b. Mainz, 27 June 1883). German scenic designer. Has designed sets for many notable productions in leading German opera houses, including Bayreuth's *Ring* (1933–42) and Munich's *Liebe der Danae* (1942). He designed C.G.'s *Der fliegende Holländer* (1957).

Prague (Cz., Praha). Capital of Czechoslovakia, previously the capital of Bohemia. Italian opera was first heard there as early as 1627; the first new opera produced there was Draghi's *La Patienza di Socrate* (1680). From 1724 performances were given on the Italian model by the Denzio, Lapis, Mingotti, Bustelli, and Bondini companies. In 1784 Count Nostic erected a beautiful theatre (Ständetheater) which was the home of Italian opera until 1807 (there the first performances of Mozart's *Don Giovanni* and *La Clemenza di Tito* were given), after which date it became the home of German opera, the first German opera in the new German Opera House being Rösler's *Elisene, Prinzessin von Bulgarien*. Spohr's *Faust* received its première there in 1816. Weber was musical director 1813–17, and was the first to conduct opera from a music stand facing the orchestra and singers, as is the custom today. He built up a large repertory and ensemble. Czech national opera was slow to develop. Škroup incorporated folk-tunes and even the national anthem (which he had composed) into his opera *Dráteník* (*The Tinker*—first opera to Czech words, 1826). In 1848 Kittl's *Bianca und Giuseppe*, for which Wagner wrote the libretto, was produced. In 1850 a movement was started to build a National Theatre, and on 18 Nov. 1862 the Královské Zemské České Prozatimní Divadlo, or Provisional Theatre, was opened (cap. 900). Its methods and resources were primitive—most of the singers were amateurs, the repertory was haphazard, the orchestra numbered 18 players who also worked in cafés, the ballet had only ten female dancers and no men. The first original Czech opera heard there was Skuherský's *Vladimír, Bohův Zvolenec* on 27 Sept. 1863. From 1866 to 1874 Smetana was director of the opera, and during this period six of his operas, including *The Bartered Bride, Dalibor*,

The Two Widows, and *The Secret*, were produced there, and so were the first stage works of Fibich and Dvořák: these three men are the founding fathers of Czech opera. In June 1881 the National Theatre was opened with the première of Smetana's *Libuše*, only to be burnt down two months later. By 1883 it had been rebuilt (cap. 1,598) and reopened on 18 Nov. with *Libuše*. Further works by Smetana, Fibich, and Dvořák were given, and then works by Karl Weiss, Karel Kovařovic, and Otakar Ostrčil (all pupils of Fibich). Modern Czech operas by Novák, Karel, Foerster, and Janáček next entered the repertory. The chief conductors have been Adolf Čech (1883–1900), Karel Kovářovic (1900–20), Otakar Ostrčil (1920–35), Václav Talich (1935–44 and 1947–8), Otakar Jeremiáš (1945–7 and 1948–51), Zdeněk Chalabala (from 1951).

The German Theatre occupied a new building in 1887 (cap. 1,554) and under Angelo Neumann (1885–1910) with Seidl, Mahler, and Klemperer as conductors, then under Zemlinsky, Steinberg, Szell, and Rankl, it was considered one of the finest German opera houses outside Germany; one of the last premières there before the war was Křenek's *Karl V*. In 1948, as the Smetana Theatre, it became the second building of the National Opera, the third being the Tyl Theatre (Nostic's Theatre, built 1783) which seats 1,129. The little theatre known as D34 was founded by Emil Burian in 1934, and has housed chamber opera as well as plays and ballets. There is also an Army Opera which performs in its own theatre in Prague, though giving most of its performances in parts of the country where opera is little known. The amateur group of the Ministry of Transport has also won respect. Prague has two theatres devoted to operetta.

Prandelli, Giacinto (b. Lumezzane, nr. Brescia, 1916). Italian tenor. Studied Rome and Brescia. Début Bergamo 1942, Rodolfo. Chosen by Toscanini to participate in the reopening concert season at Sc. 1946; and then by De Sabata to sing Loris on the fiftieth anniversary of Giordano's *Fedora* (1948). Created Peter Grimes in Italy the previous year. London, C.G., 1950 with Scala Co. and Stoll T. 1958; N.Y., Met., 1951–5. Has a repertory of more than 50 operas. His voice, while not of enormous dimensions, is used with refinement and intelligence. (R)

Pré aux Clercs, Le. Opera in 3 acts by Hérold; text by Planard. Prod. Paris, O.C., 15 Dec. 1832; London, Adelphi, 9 Sept. 1833; N.Y. 3 July 1843. The opera is based on Mérimée's *Chronique du Règne de Charles IX*, and tells how Marguerite de Valois brought about the marriage between Isabelle de Béarn and the young Baron de Mergy.

Prelude (from Lat. *praeludium* = something played before another work). There is no clear distinction between prelude and overture, though in general the former may be shorter and may also run directly into the opera which it introduces.

Prendi, l'anel ti dono. Elvino's (ten.) aria in the opening scene of Bellini's *La Sonnambula* as he places the ring on Amina's finger.

Preobrazhenskaya, Sofya (b. St. Petersburg, 27 Sept. 1904). Russian mezzo-soprano. Member of the Kirov Company since 1928. Roles include Martha (*Khovanshchina*), Joan of Arc, the Countess (*Queen of Spades*), Azucena. (R)

Près des remparts de Séville. The Seguidilla in Act 1 of Bizet's *Carmen*, sung by Carmen (mezzo) as she tempts Don José to release her and accompany her to Lillas Pastia's inn.

Pressburg. See *Bratislava*.

Previtali, Fernando (b. Adria, 16 Feb. 1907). Italian conductor. Studied Turin. Assisted Gui in organizing the Florence Orchestra and Festival 1928–36. Director Radio Italiana Orchestra since 1936, and responsible for many fine radio opera performances, including the Verdi cycle of 1951. Milan, Sc., 1942–3, 1946–8. Conducted the premières of many modern works, including Ghedini's *Re Hassan* (Venice 1939) and the same composer's *Le*

Baccanti (Sc. 1948), Dallapiccola's *Volo di Notte* (Florence 1940), as well as revivals of Busoni's *Turandot* and *Doktor Faust*. (R)

Prévost (d'Exiles), **Antoine-François, Abbé** (b. Hesdin, 1 Apr. 1697; d. Chantilly, 23 Nov. 1763). French writer. His *L'Histoire du Chevalier Des Grieux et de Manon Lescaut* (1731), vol. 7 of his *Mémoires d'un Homme de Qualité*, was the source of the following operas: Auber (1856); Kleinmichel (*Das Schloss de l'Orme*, 1883); Massenet (1884; a sequel, *Le Portrait de Manon*, appeared in 1894); Puccini (1893); Henze (*Boulevard Solitude*, 1952).

Preziosilla. The gipsy-girl (mezzo) in Verdi's *La Forza del Destino*.

Price, Leontyne (b. Laurel, Mississippi, 10 Feb. 1927). American soprano. Studied Juilliard School where she sang Mistress Ford in a student performance of *Falstaff*. Chosen by Virgil Thomson to sing in a revival of *Four Saints in Three Acts* in N.Y. and Paris; and then from 1952 to 1954 sang Bess in *Porgy and Bess*. San Francisco 1957 (Madame Lidoine in American première of *Carmélites*), 1958–9; Chicago 1959, Thaïs and Liù; Vienna since 1958, Pamina and Aida; London, C.G., 1958–9, Aida; Salzburg 1960, Donna Anna; N.Y., Met., since 1960; Milan, Sc., since 1962. Considered by many the finest contemporary Aida. Married to baritone William Warfield. (R)

Prigioniero, Il (The Prisoner). Opera in prologue and 1 act by Dallapiccola; text by composer, after Villiers de l'Isle-Adam's *La Torture par Espérance* (1883) and Charles Coster's *La Légende d'Ulenspiegel*. Prod. Florence, T.C., 20 May 1950 with Scipio Colombo, cond. Scherchen; London, S.W., 27 July 1959; N.Y., Juilliard School, 15 Mar. 1951. The prisoner's jailer speaks kindly to him as 'brother'. Finding his cell door open, the prisoner escapes, past monks who seem not to notice him, into the garden—where he is enfolded in the arms of the Grand Inquisitor, his jailer. The worst torture has been hope.

Prima Donna. Opera in 1 act by Benjamin; text by Cedric Cliffe. Prod. London, Fortune Theatre, 23 Feb. 1949; Philadelphia, 5 Dec. 1955. A witty little opera set in 18th-century Venice. It includes a comic duet between rival prima donnas 'La Filomela' and Olimpia, who try to outdo one another in a scene from *Ariadne Desolata*, much in the manner of *Le Cantatrici Villani*.

Prima donna (It. = first lady). The name given to the leading female singer in an opera, or the principal soprano of an opera company.

Prince Igor. Opera in a prologue and 4 acts by Borodin; text by the composer after a sketch by Stasov. Music completed by Rimsky-Korsakov and Glazunov. Prod. St. Petersburg 4 Nov. 1890; London, D.L., 8 June 1914, with Kuznetsov, Andreyev, Chaliapin; N.Y., Met., 30 Dec. 1915 with Alda, Amato, Didur. The opera tells of the capture of Prince Igor (bar.), with his son Vladimir (ten.), by the Polovtsians led by Khan Konchak (bass), who entertains his captive like a royal guest, treating him to a display of oriental dances. He offers to let Igor go free if he promises not to fight the Polovtsians again. Igor refuses, but manages to escape and rejoin his wife Yaroslavna (sop.). Igor's son Vladimir remains behind in the Polovtsian camp, having fallen in love with the Khan's daughter Konchakovna (mezzo) whom he is allowed to marry.

Prinzregententheater. See *Munich*.

Prise de Troie, La. See *Troyens, Les*.

Pritchard, John (b. London, 5 Feb. 1921). English conductor. Glyndebourne as *répétiteur*, 1947, where he became chorus master. Schooled by Fritz Busch, who gave him *Don Giovanni* and some performances of *Figaro* to conduct in 1951. Since then has conducted at Glyndebourne regularly, Mozart, Rossini, *Ariadne auf Naxos*, *Capriccio*, and the English première of Henze's *Elegy for Young Lovers*. C.G. since 1952, when he opened the season with a new production of *Un Ballo in Maschera*, and has directed the premières of *Gloriana*, *Midsummer Mar-*

riage and *King Priam*, and revivals of *The Trojans* and *Wozzeck* as well as works in the French, German, Italian, and Russian repertory. Vienna State Opera 1952–3, 1964–5; Ingestre 1958–9; Salzburg, 1966; N.Y., Met., 1971. (R)

Probe (Ger. = trial, rehearsal). Thus *Beleuchtungsprobe* (lighting rehearsal), *Hauptprobe* (main rehearsal), *Generalprobe* (final (dress) rehearsal). For *Rheingold* some German opera houses call a *Schwimmprobe* for the Rhinemaidens. See also *Sitzprobe*.

Procter-Gregg, Humphrey (b. Kirby Lonsdale, Westmorland, 31 July 1895). English producer, translator, and administrator. Studied Cambridge and London, R.C.M., with Stanford. Responsible for several productions at the College Opera School. Stage manager and designer for B.N.O.C., Carl Rosa, C.G. Touring Companies 1922–33, and responsible for many B.B.C. studio operas 1941–5, often providing new translations, including *Prince Igor*, *Dalibor*, *Falstaff*, *Manon Lescaut*, *Louise*. Director C.R. 1957–8, and Touring Opera 1958. Director of the London Opera Centre 1963–4.

Prodaná Nevěsta. See *Bartered Bride*.

Producer (in America, General Stage Director; in Germany, *Spielleiter*; in Italy, *Regista*; in France (and often Germany and elsewhere), *Régisseur*). The term is a comparatively modern one and did not appear on programmes regularly until after the First World War. When opera was in its infancy the ballet master probably instructed the chorus in its movements; and the stereotyped gestures of certain Italian singers, recalling the old conventions of mime, may derive from this. With the development of *opera buffa* in the 18th century, the principal basso buffo often took over the stage direction—a habit that survived throughout the last century (as with Tagliafico at C.G.) and can even today be found in small companies. Mozart was one of the first musical stage directors who not only rehearsed his operas from the pit, but controlled his singers' acting; he was followed by Weber and Spohr in Germany and in Italy by Verdi, who generally supervised every detail of production. But it was Wagner who recognized fully the importance of staging in his conception of the *Gesamtkunstwerk*, or 'unified work of art'; and not only the modern singing-actor but nearly every development in stage technique and production stems from him. The principles he laid down for Bayreuth, which were carried on by his widow and son, came to be generally accepted by conductors, producers, and singers in Germany. In Vienna it was Mahler who demonstrated the virtues of a musician as producer; in Italy it was Toscanini. Soon men of the theatre began to find their way into the opera house. The Munich Hofoper intendant early this century, Ernst von Possart, was a considerable actor. Max Reinhardt was summoned by Strauss a week before the première of *Der Rosenkavalier* to help with Act 3, and subsequently produced many operas. Carl Ebert, originally one of Germany's finest actors, came to opera through Fritz Busch. Günther Rennert and Walter Felsenstein began their careers in straight theatre. John Gielgud, Peter Brook, Tyrone Guthrie, and Sam Wanamaker have all produced opera in England. Italy's film revival after the war gave us Visconti and Zeffirelli, masters of elaborate veristic opera production. Ballet has, once more, contributed a fine producer in Margherita Wallmann. Mention should also be made of Russia, where the reforms of Constantin Stanislavsky (1863–1938) touched opera as they did everything else on the stage.

Prohaska, Jaro (b. Vienna, 24 Jan. 1891; d. Munich, 28 Sept. 1965). Austrian bass-baritone. Studied Vienna. Début Lübeck 1922; Nuremberg 1925–31; Berlin State Opera 1931–52; Bayreuth 1933–44. A notable Wotan, Sachs, Amfortas, and Dutchman between the wars. (R)

Prokofiev, Sergey Sergeyevich (b. Sontsovka, Ekaterinoslav, 23 Apr. 1891; d. Moscow, 5 Mar. 1953). Russian composer. Prokofiev wrote his first opera at the age of nine (*The Giant*), at least three others during adolescence, and seven mature works that are fully characteristic of him. The conception of the first to survive, *The Gambler* (1929), is both comedy and study of obsession: it first revealed Prokofiev's full lyricism and his fascination with abnormal states of mind. *The Love of the Three Oranges* (1921) represents a change of course; the treatment is basically anti-romantic, and Gozzi's fantastic comedy provides the composer with the opportunity for some pungent and wittily grotesque music. *The Fiery Angel* (1922–5, prod. 1955) is a very different matter. Here the fantastic strain in Prokofiev is turned to horrific purposes. Based on Bryusov's novel of possession and sorcery, the opera has its grotesque elements, but is an openly romantic, expressionistic work of violent dramatic power. Prokofiev thought it his best opera. But Soviet critics condemned these last two works for their qualities of parody and expressionism, and welcomed the returning prodigal with a chorus of only slightly reserved praise for *Semyon Kotko* (1940). Back in Russia after two decades of exile, Prokofiev quite sincerely hastened to prove himself a true Soviet citizen with this opera, based on *I, Son of the Working Class*, Katayev's novel of the closing stages of the Revolution in the Ukraine. Less successful when consciously attempting the broad gestures required to express bluff, optimistic Communist emotions, the work also finds room for some lyrical love music and some vividly colourful ensembles of true operatic mastery. 'Socialist realism' is abandoned in *The Duenna* (1940–1, prod. 1946; based on Sheridan, and known also as *Betrothal in the Monastery*). The simplicity here is not artificial, and the composer responds unaffectedly to the subject with some of his most charmingly accomplished music. *War and Peace* (1941–2; prod. 1946) could hardly avoid a return to the spacious manner; it is made with an expertness that may have quickly become Prokofiev's second nature in the face of political pressure, but was not his true one. *The Story of a Real Man* (1948) was written in a tone of apology after the notorious Zhdanov tribunal had condemned leading Soviet composers for 'formalism' and other supposed vices, but failed to please even the authorities for whom it was designed. That a large part of his interest lay in opera is beyond question; and this will become more widely appreciated as *The Love of the Three Oranges*, *The Fiery Angel*, and *The Duenna* gradually conquer the international repertory.

Prompter (in France and Germany *Souffleur*, in Italy *Maestro suggeritore*). Unlike in the straight theatre, where the prompter only intervenes when the actor forgets his words or cue, the prompter in the opera house helps the performers by giving them the opening words of every phrase a few seconds in advance. In Italian opera houses the prompter also relays the conductor's beat, which he sees reflected in a kind of driving mirror, to the singers on the stage. In Strauss's *Capriccio* we meet one of these characters in the person of Monsieur Taupe. Extra prompters are sometimes concealed on the stage. In the last act of *Tristan und Isolde* there is sometimes one lying under Tristan's couch. The **Prompter's box** is a little cupboard-like compartment wherein the prompter is seated, placed generally in the middle of the footlights and covered over on three sides so that he is invisible to the audience. Some producers make use of the prompter's box in their productions. Figaros have been known to place a foot on it to sing 'Aprite un po' quegl'occhi', and Papagenos and Papagenas to sit on it for their duet. Some temperamental Italian singers have been known to hiss rude remarks at the prompter for having failed to give them a cue in a loud enough voice, and the ensuing aria has even become a duet.

Prophète, Le. Opera in 5 acts by Meyerbeer; text by Scribe. Prod. Paris, O., 16 Apr. 1849, with Viardot, Castellan, Roger; London, C.G., 24 July 1849, with Viardot, Hayes, Mario; New Orleans 1 Apr. 1850. The opera is based on a historical episode during the Anabaptist rising in Holland in the 16th century; the real John of Leyden was Jan Neuckelszoon, born in 1509, who had himself crowned in Münster in 1535, when the city became the scene of orgy and cruelty. The plot describes the love of John of Leyden for Bertha, whom Count Oberthal, ruler of Dordrecht, desires for himself. The opera ends with the palace of Münster being set on fire and the powder magazine blowing up, killing the Anabaptists who have turned against John, who is now joined in death in the blazing palace by his mother Fidès. Famous interpreters of the title role have included Jean de Reszke, Caruso, and Martinelli.

Proserpine (Greek, Persephone). In Latin and Greek mythology the daughter of Jupiter (Zeus) and Ceres (Demeter) who was carried off by Pluto (Hades) to become his wife and rule over the shades. Ceres, goddess of agriculture, did not allow the earth to produce until Mercury (Hermes) had rescued Proserpine. Even after her rescue she was bound to return to the underworld for a third of the year—she thus represents the seed-corn, hidden in the ground and bursting forth to nourish men and animals. Operas on her legend are as follows. Monteverdi (1630); Ferrari (1641); Colonna (1645); Lully (1680); Sacrati (1696); Paisiello (1803); Winter (1804); Saint-Saëns (1887); Bianchi (1938).

Prospectus. The name given to the booklet issued by the managements of the large opera houses—especially C.G., and H.M.'s in the Gye–Mapleson era, and still issued by the Met.—announcing the coming season's plans. The C.G. prospectuses of the 1850's, 1860's, &c., generally contained promises of new works and artists, many of which never appeared. The managements themselves indulged in self-eulogy, and the 'nobility and gentry' were invited to take up subscriptions for the season. The German theatres issue their seasonal prospectus (*Spielplan*) well in advance, the Italian houses their *Indiscrezioni* rather nearer the beginning of each season.

Prova (It. = trial, rehearsal). The *prova generale* is the dress rehearsal to which members of the public and often critics are admitted. Both terms are currently used in many opera houses. (See also *Probe.*)

Puccini, Giacomo (b. Lucca, 22 Dec. 1858; d. Brussels, 29 Nov. 1924). Italian composer. Puccini's four immediate paternal ancestors were opera composers, and he received his first instruction at Lucca, where the family had always lived. His name won him a subsidy to study at Milan, where at the suggestion of his teacher, Ponchielli, he wrote his first opera, the 1-act *Le Villi* (1883). Rejected by a prize committee, the work was recommended by Boito and produced at Milan in 1884. Though it is a 'number' opera, bound by many conventions and influences, something of the later skill in handling ensembles and the orchestra already appears. This was one of the few operas by his juniors to win the admiration of the aged Verdi. *Edgar* (1889) was a notorious failure, largely because of its libretto; yet it contains some impressive strokes and certainly shows the composer's dramatic growth.

With *Manon Lescaut* (1893) we reach the first work of his mastery. Some elements—the choral scenes, for instance—are already fully mature; some are still developing; but the unevenness and certain failures of characterization are less noticeable than the fresh impulse and generous invention of the music.

In *La Bohème* (1896) the apprenticeship is complete. Puccini's voice is fully his own, though it is used to describe a foreign city, Paris. The characterization is more certain, deeper, lighter; there is a richer attention to detail and the melody of dialogue. Above all, perhaps, there is a deceptive casualness of method and raciness of incident that, concealing the immaculate craftsmanship, ideally mirror the gay, shiftless existence of the Bohemians.

Tosca (1900), based on Sardou's morbid thriller, has a darker intensity of feeling and a more powerful dramatic flow. The characters are more strongly, even violently, depicted, and dense use of *Leitmotiv* in a widened and tenser harmonic idiom provides the method for Puccini's clash of lurid personality and situation.

With *Madama Butterfly* (1904), Puccini turned to a play by David Belasco (a kind of American Sardou) and back to what was now established, as Mosco Carner has shown, as the typical Puccini heroine—the 'little girl' whose love involves tragic guilt that must be expiated. But the lessons of *Tosca* had been learnt: the *Leitmotive* (some based on genuine Japanese tunes) are more fluently and expressively used; the musical idiom is subtler in its penetration of a small, precious, remote world hemmed with conventions.

In *La Fanciulla del West* (1910), Puccini tackled exoticism of the geographically opposite sort in a superficially similar manner but showed his concern to modernize his idiom. Belasco's jumble of a plot—Wagnerian redemption in a mining camp—concerned the composer less than its strange and striking situations; the lack of lyrical scenes and the blankness of the characters—which partly account for the work's neglect—are largely compensated for by the vitality of the action, the expansive musical vision of the Californian setting, and the brilliant craftsmanship.

Resemblances to Verdi's opera caused *La Rondine* (1917) to be dubbed 'the poor man's *Traviata*'; Puccini was unhappy about this operetta from the start, and certainly his invention flagged—though not his accomplishment, as is shown in the crowd scenes. Harmonically it continues the *Fanciulla* advance and even foreshadows *Turandot*.

Il Trittico (1918) follows the unusual but successful plan of contrasting in one evening a lurid thriller, *Il Tabarro*, a sentimental tragedy, *Suor Angelica*, and a comedy, *Gianni Schicchi*. These 1-act pieces gain from the contrast, but each is successful in its own right. *Tabarro* is a dark, evocative work, compact but rich in atmosphere, harmonically tense and economical in structure, perceptively relating the weary lives of the characters to the river on which they live and toil. *Angelica* is a gentle work, largely low-pitched in tension and, despite a sympathetic evocation of the cloister's quiet, not escaping the charge of dramatic flatness. *Schicchi* is the most brilliant of farces, racy and bitingly witty, deftly scored—creating its own atmosphere as surely as its companion works.

Turandot (1926), begun in 1921, was to remain unfinished: it has been suggested that the task of showing fulfilled love was beyond Puccini. Yet here he was able to give rein, in an unusually sympathetic operatic framework and with long-mastered technique, to elements that form the basis of his style—the passionately heroic (Calaf), the 'little girl' pathetic (Liù), the comic-grotesque (the Masks), and the exotic (the Chinese setting). There is, moreover, a structural mastery that places *Turandot* at the peak of Puccini's achievement; while a plot both plainer and crueller than that of *Tosca* grows from fairy-tale thriller to tragedy and love story in one. Puccini has had no successor, and he was, in truth, plainly a more limited artist than his great predecessor, Verdi. Though he was at pains to modernize his style he is instinctively a 'late' artist.

Puppet opera. The popularity of puppet theatres throughout history, and the virtuosity of the puppeteers in some countries (notably Czechoslovakia), has led their managers to attempt opera from time to time. The first première given by puppets was probably of Ziani's *Damira Placata* (Venice 1680). Haydn wrote several puppet operas for Esterháza, one of which, *Philemon und Baucis*, has been given in London. In our own century the Teatro dei Piccoli in Rome has staged opera performances with singers behind the stage. Falla's *El Retablo de Maese Pedro* requires a puppet theatre which performs to live singers; the puppets are eventually attacked by Don Quixote, who becomes confused about their reality. At the first performance all, including Quixote, were puppets. The Salzburg Marionettentheater has given opera performances, and the Hogarth Puppets have staged *El Retablo* (Ingestre 1957).

Purcell, Henry (b. London, *c.* 1659; d. London, 21 Nov. 1695). English composer. It is clear from the one work of Purcell which may properly be classed as an opera, *Dido and Aeneas*, that the fashion of the day which deflected his dramatic powers into extravagant stage spectacles (such as the Dryden–Davenant version of *The Tempest*) deprived England of its greatest operatic composer. Purcell himself regretted the inferior position of music among the stage effects, especially in the light of Italian and French opera. *Dido* itself is a great operatic masterpiece—one of such dramatic potency and such depth of human understanding as to make its uniqueness a tragedy.

Puritani, I (rightly, *I Puritani di Scozia*—The Puritans of Scotland). Opera in 3 acts by Bellini; text by Pepoli, after the play *Têtes rondes et Cavaliers* by Ancelot and Saintine, in its turn derived from Scott's novel *Old Mortality* (1816). Prod. Paris, T.I., 25 Jan. 1835, with Grisi, Rubini, Tamburini, Lablache; London, King's T., 21 May 1835, with same cast; Philadelphia, 22 July 1943. Has enjoyed revivals for Carosio, Callas, and Joan Sutherland during the last quarter of a century.

The opera is set in Plymouth at the time of the civil war. Queen Henrietta, widow of Charles I, is held prisoner in a fortress whose warden is the Puritan Lord Walton. His daughter Elvira is in love with Lord Arthur Talbot, a Cavalier, and permission for the two to wed has been given. Arthur helps Henrietta to escape by dressing her in Elvira's bridal veil. Elvira, thinking she has been betrayed, loses her reason, which is restored when Arthur is reunited with her. Arthur is pardoned by the victorious Cromwell.

Pushkin, Alexander (b. Moscow, 26 May 1799; d. Moscow, 29 Jan. 1837). Russian poet. Operas on his works are as follows. *Russlan and Ludmilla* (1817–20): Glinka (1842). *The Captive in the Caucasus* (1820–1): Cui (1883). *The Fountain of Bakchisserai* (1823): Ilyinsky; Mechura (*Marie Potocka*, 1871). *The Gypsies* (1824): Rachmaninov (*Aleko*, 1893); Leoncavallo (1912). *Boris Godunov* (1825): Mussorgsky (1874). *Eugene Onegin* (1828): Tchaikovsky (1879). *Poltava* (1829): Tchaikovsky (*Mazeppa*, 1884). *The Miserly Knight* (1830): Rachmaninov (1906). *The Little House at Kolomna* (1830): Stravinsky (*Mavra*, 1922). *A Feast in Time of Plague*: Cui (1901); Lourié (*c.* 1925). *The Stone Guest* (1830): Dargomizhsky (1872). *Mozart and Salieri* (1830): Rimsky-Korsakov (1898). *The Tale of Tsar Saltan* (1831): Rimsky-Korsakov (1900). *Rusalka* (1832): Dargomizhsky (1856). *The Tale of the Fisherman and the Fish* (1833): Polovinkin (*c.* 1934). *The Queen of Spades* (1834): Tchaikovsky (1890). *The Golden Cockerel* (1834): Rimsky-Korsakov (1909).

Pyne, Louisa (b. ?, 27 Aug. 1832; d. London, 20 Mar. 1904). English soprano. Studied with George Smart. Début Boulogne 1849, Amina; appeared Princess's Theatre, D.L., Hm., and C.G. Toured U.S.A. 1854–6. C . her return to England joined Harrison (q.v.) in formation of the Pyne–Harrison Opera Company, giving seasons at the Ly., D.L., and C.G. 1858–64, during which time she created leading roles in *Satanella*, *Lurline*, *Bianca*, *Lily of Killarney*, *Armourer of Nantes*, *Blanche de Nevers*, &c. Said to have possessed a soprano voice of beautiful quality and great flexibility.

Q

Quadri, Argeo (b. Como, 23 Feb. 1911). Italian conductor. Has conducted in all the leading Italian opera houses. London, C.G., 1956; Vienna, V.O., since 1957, where he has conducted very many performances of *Nabucco* and *William Tell*. Directed Verdi commemoration performances of *La Traviata* at Busseto 1951, and Puccini performances at Viareggio of *La Fanciulla del West* and *Madama Butterfly*. (R)

Quand'ero paggio. Falstaff's (bar.) arietta in Act 2 of Verdi's *Falstaff* in which he recalls the days when he was a slender young page to the Duke of Norfolk.

Quando le sere al placido. Rodolfo's (ten.) aria in Act 2 of Verdi's *Luisa Miller*, in which he recalls his love for Luisa.

Quanto è bella! Nemorino's (ten.) aria in the opening scene of Donizetti's *L'Elisir d'Amore*, which he sings as he looks on the beautiful young Adina.

Quatro Rusteghi, I (The Four Curmudgeons). Opera in 3 acts by Wolf-Ferrari; text by Pizzolato, after Goldoni's comedy. Prod. in German as *Die vier Grobiane*, Munich 19 Mar. 1906; London, S.W., as *The School for Fathers*, 7 June 1946; N.Y., C.C., as *The Four Ruffians*, 18 Oct. 1951. The opera tells of the efforts of four boorish husbands to keep their womenfolk in order, and of the women's stratagems to allow Lunardo's daughter Lucieta to see Filipeto, son of Maurizio, before their wedding, despite the opposition of the men. The Intermezzo is one of the composer's most delightful little pieces.

Queen of the Night, The. Sarastro's evil adversary (sop.), Pamina's mother, in Mozart's *Die Zauberflöte*.

Queen of Shemakhan, The. The queen (sop.) in Rimsky-Korsakov's *The Golden Cockerel*.

Queen of Spades, The. Opera in 3 acts by Tchaikovsky; text by Modest Tchaikovsky, after Pushkin's novel (1834). Prod. St. Petersburg 19 Dec. 1890, with Figner; N.Y., Met., 5 Mar. 1910, with Destinn, Meitschek, Slezak, cond. Mahler; London, London Opera House, 29 May 1915, with Nikitina, Krassavina, Rosing, cond. Gourevitch.

The opera tells of the love of Herman, a young officer, for Lisa, granddaughter of the old Countess, once a gambler known as the Queen of Spades, who is said to possess the secret of winning at cards. Herman goes to the Countess's bedroom at night to obtain the secret from her so as to win enough money to marry, but frightens her to death. Her ghost appears to him and reveals the secret: 'Three, seven, ace.' As Herman becomes obsessed with winning, Lisa drowns herself. He wins on the first two stakes he makes—3 and 7. He then stakes all on the third card, which he thinks will be the ace, but which is the Queen of Spades; at the same time the Countess's ghost appears, and Herman, losing his reason, kills himself.

Questa o quella. The Duke of Mantua's (ten.) aria in the opening scene of Verdi's *Rigoletto* in which he declares that all women attract him.

Quickly, Mistress. A lady of Windsor (mezzo) who decoys Falstaff to his two disastrous rendezvous in Verdi's *Falstaff*.

Qui la voce. The opening words of Elvira's (sop.) Mad Scene in Bellini's *I Puritani*.

Quodlibet (Lat. = what you please). A kind of musical game of the 16th, 17th, and early 18th centuries involving extempore juxtaposition of different melodies. The three dances in the Act 1 finale in *Don Giovanni* form a quodlibet. In the 19th-century German theatre it came to mean the confections made of the favourite pieces of many composers which were interpolated in plays at the Theater an der Wien, rather in the same way that Arne and Arnold put together *Love in a Village* and *The Maid of the Mill*.

R

Rabaud, Henri (b. Paris, 10 Nov. 1873; d. Paris, 11 Sept. 1949). French composer. Studied with Massenet. The most successful of his eight operas has been *Mârouf, Savetier du Caire* (1914). He also wrote the score for *Le Miracle des Loups* (1924), the first film to be shown at the Opéra, where he was conductor 1908–14, and director 1914–18.

Rabelais, François (b. Chinon, *c.* 1494; d. ?Paris, *c.* 1553). French writer. Operas on his works are as follows. Monsigny (*L'Ile Sonnante* 1767); Grétry (*Panurge dans l'Ile des Lanternes* 1785); Planquette (1895); Terrasse (1911); Massenet (1913); Mariotte (1935).

Rachel, quand du Seigneur. Éléazar's (ten.) aria in Act 4 of Halévy's *La Juive*, in which the Jewish goldsmith sings of his conflicting emotions, torn as he is between letting Rachel die at the hands of the Christians or saving her life by telling Cardinal Brogni that she is in fact the latter's daughter.

Rachmaninov, Sergey (b. Onega Oneg, 1 Apr. 1873; d. Beverly Hills, 28 Mar. 1943). Russian composer and pianist. His three operas have not survived, though *Aleko* (1893) won good opinions at its production and was revived for Chaliapin. Like *Aleko, The Miserly Knight* (1906) is based on Pushkin. For *Francesca da Rimini* (1906) Rachmaninov was provided with a poor libretto by Tchaikovsky's brother Modest that effectively stifled the work at birth; certain sections are said to show a real operatic sense that might have been developed had these early experiences not deflected the composer's interests elsewhere. Apart from an incompleted setting of Maeterlinck's *Monna Vanna* (1906), Rachmaninov never returned to opera.

Racine, Jean (b. La Ferté-Milon, 21 Dec. 1639; d. Paris, 21 Apr. 1699). French poet and dramatist. Operas on his works are as follows. *Andromaque* (1667): Grétry (1780); Rossini (*Ermione*, 1814). *Bérénice* (1670): Magnard (1911). *Bajazet* (1672): Hervé (*Les Turcs*, a parody of Racine, 1869). *Mithridate* (1673): Mozart (1770). *Iphigénie en Aulide* (1675): Graun (1748); Gluck (1774). *Phèdre* (1677): Lemoyne (1786). *Esther* (1689): Handel (1732). *Athalie* (1691): Handel (1720); Poissl (1814).

Radamès. The leader of the Egyptian army (ten.), hero of Verdi's *Aida*.

Radford, Robert (b. Nottingham, 13 May 1874; d. London, 3 Mar. 1933). English bass. Studied London, R.A.M., with Randegger. Début London, C.G., 1904, Commendatore. Sang Hagen and Hunding in English *Ring* under Richter, and subsequently became leading member of the Beecham and B.N.O.C. companies; a founder and director of the latter. First Boris in English, greatly admired in Wagner and Mozart. (R) His daughter **Winifred Radford** sang at Glyndebourne. (R)

Radio opera. In the early days of the century an aria from *Carmen* sung by Mariette Mazarin was broadcast from the Manhattan Opera, and in 1910 parts of *Cavalleria Rusticana* (Destinn, Riccardo Martin) and *Pagliacci* (Caruso, Amato) were broadcast from the Met. The first European broadcast of a complete opera was *Hänsel und Gretel* (C.G., 6 Jan. 1923). Two years later a New York station began weekly opera broadcasts, and on 7 Sept. the first regular American opera performance was relayed (*Aida* at the Met.). The first transatlantic opera broadcast was from Dresden to America (*Fidelio*, 16 Mar. 1930). The first opera written for broadcasting was Cadman's *The Willow Tree* (3 Oct. 1933), though a première had already been given—Skilton's *Sun Bride* (17 Apr. 1930). Since the Second World War opera broadcasts have become a regular part of every station's programmes. Not only are listeners enabled to hear performances from opera houses(sometimes recorded and broadcast later), but works otherwise rarely or never performed can be presented with comparative economy. German and Italian stations have a carefully planned calendar—in Italy, a summer-autumn programme designed to link the opera-house seasons; in Germany, a programme lasting the whole year round. Most companies from time to time commission new works—e.g. Henze's *Elegy for Young Lovers* was commissioned by the Süddeutsche Rundfunk, Stuttgart. See also *Television Opera, British Broadcasting Corporation.*

Ragusa. See *Dubrovnik.*

Raimondi, Gianni (b. Bologna, 1925). Italian tenor. Début Bologna, 1948, Duke of Mantua. London, Stoll T., 1953; Milan, Sc., since 1955, S.F. 1957–8; Vienna, S.O., 1963; N.Y., Met., 1965. Specially successful in Donizetti and early Verdi roles. (R)

Rainforth, Elizabeth (b. ?, 23 Nov. 1814; d. Bristol, 22 Sept. 1877). English soprano. Studied London. Début London, St. James's, 1836, Mandane (*Artaxerxes*). C.G. 1838–43, then D.L., where she created Arline (*Bohemian Girl*), 1843.

Raisa, Rosa (orig. Rose Burstein) (b. Białystok, 23 May 1893; d. Los Angeles, 28 Sept. 1963). Polish soprano. Fled from Poland during a pogrom, found her way to Naples. Studied there with Eva Tetrazzini and Marchisio. Début Parma 1913, Leonora (*Oberto*); Chicago 1913–37, where she sang in the American premières of *Isabeau*, *La Nave*, and *La Fiamma*; London, C.G., 1914 and 1933; Milan, Sc., 1923–6, where she was the first Asteria (*Nerone*) and Turandot. A thrilling singer and actress, she was greatly admired as Norma, Tosca, and Maliella. She married the baritone **Giacomo Rimini** and together they set up a school of singing in Chicago. (R)

Rake's Progress, The. Opera in 3 acts and epilogue by Stravinsky; text by W. H. Auden and Chester Kallman, after Hogarth's eight engravings (1735). Prod. Venice, F., 11 Sept 1951, with Schwarzkopf, Tourel, Rounseville, Kraus, cond. Stravinsky; N.Y., Met., 14 Feb. 1953, with Gueden, Thebom, Conley, Harrell, cond. Reiner; Edinburgh (by Glyndebourne Opera) 25 Aug. 1953, with Morison, Merriman, Lewis, Hines, cond. Wallenstein. Tom Rakewell (ten.) leaves Anne Trulove (sop.) to go to London when Nick Shadow (bar.) appears with news of sudden wealth. His physical pleasures palling, Tom is easily tempted by Shadow, now his servant, first to marry the fantastic bearded lady Baba the Turk (mezzo) and then to place his trust in a fake machine for turning stones into bread. He goes bankrupt, and all his effects are sold. The year and a day stipulated by Shadow for their association being at an end, Shadow reveals himself as the Devil and claims Tom's soul. But Shadow suggests a gamble for Tom's soul, and Tom wins; Nick sinks into the ground, but makes Tom mad. The final scene finds Tom in Bedlam, believing himself Adonis; Anne now takes her last leave of him. In the Epilogue the characters point the moral: 'For idle hearts and hands and minds the Devil finds a work to do.'

Ralf, Torsten (b. Malmö, 2 Jan. 1901; d. Stockholm, 27 Apr. 1954). Swedish tenor. Studied Stockholm and Berlin. Début Stettin 1930, Cavaradossi. Frankfurt 1933–5; Dresden 1935–44, where he created Apollo in Strauss's *Daphne*; London, C.G., 1935–9 and 1948; N.Y., Met., 1945–8. Especially successful as Parsifal, Lohengrin, and Walther, and also in Verdi repertory (Radamès and Otello). (R) His elder brother **Oscar Ralf** (b. 1881) was leading tenor of the Stockholm Opera 1918–30, where he sang Wagner and Verdi, and was heard as Tristan in Paris. He translated more than 40 operas into Swedish. (R)

Rameau, Jean-Philippe (b. Dijon, prob. 25 Sept. 1683; d. Paris, 12 Sept. 1764). French composer. Not until he was in his forties did Rameau achieve any success as a composer; even then his first opera *Hippolyte et Aricie* (1733) met with a hostile reception that offset the enthusiasm of his supporters, among them Campra. The public responded more quickly than musicians, and in quick succession popular triumphs followed for *Les Indes Galantes* (1735), *Castor et Pollux* (1737), and *Dardanus* (1737). Thereafter Rameau's success was assured, though he remained a controversial figure. He it was who came to represent the French tradition in the *Guerre des Bouffons*—an ironic situation for a composer whose first works had been accused of Italianism. This element remains present in his operas, but the chief influence was Lully's. His development of Lully's recitative was his most notable contribution to that tradition: far greater flexibility of treatment, with devices carefully catalogued and labelled as befitted a great theorist, allowed increased subtlety of characterization. French classical opera remained formal and ornate in his hands, but he brought to it a new power, vividness, and physical excitement; and if the forms often recall those of Lully, the treatment has a modernity that looks far forward beyond Rameau's own day.

Ramfis. The High Priest (bass) in Verdi's *Aida*.

Ranalow, Frederick (b. Dublin, 7 Nov. 1873; d. London, 8 Dec. 1953). Irish baritone. Studied London, R.A.M., with Randegger. Leading baritone Beecham Company, where his Figaro, Papageno, and Sachs were highly regarded. In 1922–3 he sang Macheath in the long run of *The Beggar's Opera* at the Lyric, Hammersmith, more than 1,500 times. (R)

Rance, Jack. The Sheriff (bar.) in Puccini's *La Fanciulla del West*.

Randegger, Alberto (b. Trieste, 13 Apr. 1832; d. London, 18 Dec. 1911). Italian, later British, conductor, composer, and teacher. After holding appointments in Brescia and Venice, became professor of singing, R.A.M., 1868. Cond. C.R. 1879–85; D.L. and C.G. 1887–98. His comic opera *The Rival Beauties* was produced at Leeds in 1864.

Rankin, Nell (b. Montgomery, Alabama, 3 Jan. 1926). American mezzo-soprano. Studied locally, then N.Y. with Branzell. Début Zürich 1949, Ortrud. N.Y., Met., since 1951; London, C.G., 1953. (R)

Rankl, Karl (b. Gaaden, 1 Oct. 1898; d. St. Gilgen, 6 Sept. 1968). Austrian, later British, conductor and composer. Studied Vienna with Schoenberg and Webern. Vienna, V.O., 1921. After appointments in Reichenberg and Königsberg, became Klemperer's assistant at the Kroll Opera, Berlin, 1928–31; Graz 1932–7; Prague 1937–9, where conducted première of Křenek's *Karl V*. Appointed music director of new English Company at C.G., London, 1946, a position he held until 1951; his work in building up the new opera company was invaluable, though his conducting of Wagner and Verdi did not meet with general approval. At his best in Strauss. Music director, Elizabethan Opera Trust, Australia, 1958–60. His opera *Deirdre of the Sorrows* was one of Festival of Britain prizewinning works 1951, but has never been produced. (R)

Rape of Lucretia, The. Opera in 2 acts by Britten; text by Ronald Duncan, based on André Obey's play *Le Viol de Lucrèce* (1931), in turn based on Shakespeare's poem *The Rape of Lucrece* (1594) and on Livy. Prod. Glyndebourne 12 July 1946, with Cross, Ferrier, Pears, Kraus, cond. Ansermet; Chicago 1 June 1947, with Resnik, Kibler, Kane, Rogier, cond. Breisach. With a male (ten.) and female (sop.) Chorus commenting and eventually drawing a Christian moral, the opera relates the story of the proud, self-destroying Tarquinius (bar.). He rides from the camp where news has come of the Roman wives' infidelity to make an attempt on the virtue of the sole exception, Lucretia (mezzo), wife of Collatinus (bass). Claiming hospitality, he later enters her room and rapes her. Unable to bear the burden of her shame, she kills herself next day in the presence of her urgently summoned husband. This was the first of Britten's chamber operas.

Rappresentazione (It. = representation). A species of acted oratorio, forerunner of opera. See below.

Rappresentazione di Anima e di Corpo, La (The Representation of the Soul and the Body). Stage oratorio by Emilio de' Cavalieri; text by Agostino Manni. Prod. Rome, S. Filippo Neri, Feb. 1600. The characters represent not only man's soul and body, but various human attributes.

Rasa, Lina Bruna (b. nr. Padua, 24 Sept. 1907). Italian soprano. Studied Milan. Début Genoa 1925, Elena (*Mefistofele*). Created Doll Tearsheet in Wolf-Ferrari's *Sly* and Atte in Mascagni's *Nerone* at Sc. Became Mascagni's favourite interpreter of Santuzza, and recorded the role under him for *Cavalleria Rusticana*'s 50th anniversary. Also sang Tosca and Isabeau with success. (R)

Rasi, Francesco (b. Arezzo, ?; d. ?). Italian 16th–17th-century singer and composer. He was associated with the Camerata (q.v.), singing in some of the first operas (including Peri's *Euridice*, 1600), and composing an opera *Ati e Cibele* (1617, unperformed) in the new style.

Rataplan. An onomatopoeic word for the sound of a drum. Used for the name of solos and ensembles in operas by Donizetti (*Fille du Régiment*), Meyerbeer (*Huguenots*), Verdi (*Forza del Destino*); also a trio in *Cox and Box*. Also a *Singspiel* by Pillwitz (1830).

Rauzzini, Matteo (b. Camerino, 1754; d. Dublin, 1791). Italian singer, composer, and teacher. Début Munich 1771. Composed three operas; followed his brother Venanzio to England, then settled in Dublin as a teacher.

Rauzzini, Venanzio (b. Camerino, 19 Dec. 1746; d. Bath, 8 Apr. 1810). Italian male soprano, composer, and teacher. Brother of the above. Début Rome, Teatro della Valle, 1765. Sang in Munich, Dresden, Vienna, and in Milan, where he appeared in the première of *Lucio Silla* by Mozart, who also wrote 'Exsultate, jubilate' for him. Went to London 1774 and remained in Britain for the rest of his life. Five of his operas were produced in London, five in Munich. Best remembered as a teacher, his pupils including Braham, Storace, Incledon, Mara, and Mrs. Billington. Buried in Bath Abbey.

Ravel, Maurice (b. Ciboure, 7 Mar. 1875; d. Paris, 28 Dec. 1937). French composer. His two operas are unique contributions to the art. *L'Heure Espagnole* (1907) and *L'Enfant et les Sortilèges* (1925) are both masterpieces in miniature, calling for elaborate resources but focusing them shrewdly on two themes especially suited to the composer—the first a cynical, farcical romp with ample local colour, the other a touching story of innocence rediscovered that finds room for a rich array of amusing characterization in the furniture and animals that harry the child. Ravel is known to have contemplated at least three more serious subjects—*The Sunken Bell* (he was working on this as late as 1914), *Jeanne d'Arc*, and *Don Quixote*.

Ravinia. A suburb of Chicago where an annual summer opera festival was given in a semi-outdoor pavilion in a park from 1910 to 1931. The first festival consisted of seven performances of *Cavalleria Rusticana*; in subsequent years scenes and acts from operas were given, but gradually the season was lengthened until in the 1920's it lasted up to ten weeks. The company included Bori, Pareto, Raisa, Rethberg, Lauri-Volpi, Schipa, and Martinelli.

Re Cervo. See König Hirsch.

Recitative. The name given to the declamatory portions of opera, in which the plot is generally advanced, as opposed to the more static or reflective lyrical settings. In *recitativo secco* the notes and rhythm follow the verbal accentuation, with only the slenderest accompaniment, usually on a harpsichord, perhaps with a cello; in *recitativo stromentato* or *accompagnato* (probably introduced by Rovettino in 1663) the accompaniment is fuller and musically more organized. The distinction between recitative and aria is clear-cut in 17th- and 18th-century opera, especially in *opera seria*. But Mozart already foreshadows, in the range and expressiveness of some of his recitative, the eventual breakdown of the convention—a great example is the recitative to Elvira's 'Mi tradì' in *Don Giovanni*.

Recondita armonia. Cavaradossi's (ten.) aria in Act 1 of Puccini's *Tosca*, in which he contrasts the dark beauty of his beloved Tosca with the fair beauty of the Countess Attavanti, the model for his painting of the Magdalen.

Redlich, Hans (b. Vienna, 11 Feb. 1903). Austrian, later British, conductor and musicologist. Asst. cond. Charlottenburg, Berlin, 1924–5; cond. Municipal T., Mainz, 1925–9. Settled in England in 1939. Well known for his work on Monteverdi, and his book on Berg.

Reeves, Sims (orig. John) (b. Shooters Hill, Kent, 26 Sept. 1818; d. Worthing, 25 Oct. 1900). English tenor. Taught by father. Début as baritone, Newcastle 1838, in *Guy Mannering*. Studied further in London with Cooke, Paris with Bordogni, Milan with Mazzucato. Milan, Sc., 1846 as Edgardo; London, D.L., 1847, same role. Created Lyonnel in Balfe's *Maid of Honour* (1848); H.M.'s from 1848, where he sang Faust in English and other roles. The latter part of his career was devoted to oratorio.

Reggio Emilia. Town in Emilia-Romagna, Italy. Opera is given at the Teatro Municipale (cap. 1,600), opened in 1857 with Achille Peri's *Vittore Pisani*. The beautiful auditorium designed by Costa has 106 boxes.

Regina. Musical play by Blitzstein; text by the composer, after L. Hellmann's play *The Little Foxes*. Prod. Boston 11 Oct. 1949. Staged on Broadway as a 'musical' and subsequently prod. N.Y., C.C., 1953.

Régisseur. The French and German term for the producer (q.v.) of an opera. In German opera houses the word *Regie* corresponds to 'production'.

Regnava nel silenzio. Lucia's (sop.) aria in Act 1, scene 2, of Donizetti's *Lucia di Lammermoor*, in which she recounts to Alisa the legend of the fountain.

Reichardt, Johann Friedrich (b. Königsberg, 25 Nov. 1752; d. Giebichenstein, 26 June 1814). German composer. As Kapellmeister to Frederick the Great from 1776 he introduced various reforms that won him an unpopularity which, in some part due to his vanity, dogged him all his life. His music shows more intelligence and liberal-mindedness than talent; but he found a vigorous champion in Mendelssohn, and has his place in the history of German opera for the originality of his *Singspiele*.

Reicher-Kindermann, Hedwig (b. Munich, 15 July 1853; d. Trieste, 2 June 1883). German soprano. Daughter of the baritone August Kindermann (q.v.), with whom she studied. Début Munich 1870. After appearances in Karlsruhe and Berlin, engaged for Bayreuth where she sang Erda and Grimgerde in the first *Ring* 1876. Joined Neumann's company in Leipzig in 1880. London, H.M.'s, 1882, where she sang Fricka in the first London *Ring* and Brünnhilde in the second.

Reichmann, Theodor (b. Rostock, 15 Mar. 1849; d. Marbach, Bodensee, 22 May 1903). German baritone. Studied Berlin, Prague, and Milan with Lamperti. Début Magdeburg 1869. After engagements in Berlin, Strasbourg, Hamburg, and Munich, joined Vienna Opera in 1882, remaining there until 1889, returning from 1893 to 1902. Created Amfortas, Bayreuth 1882, and also sang Sachs and Wolfram there. London, C.G., 1884 and 1892, in Wagner; and N.Y., Met., 1889–91, where in addition to the German repertory he sang French and Italian.

Reine de Saba, La (The Queen of Sheba). Opera in 4 acts by Gounod; text by Barbier and Carré. Prod. Paris, O., 28 Feb. 1862; Manchester 10 Mar. 1880; New Orleans, 12 Jan. 1889.

Reiner, Fritz (b. Budapest, 19 Dec. 1888; d. N.Y., 15 Nov. 1963). Hungarian, later American, conductor.

Studied Budapest. Chorusmaster Budapest Opera 1909. After engagements in Ljubljana and Budapest appointed first cond. at Dresden 1914–21. From 1922 to 1935 mostly conducted concerts in U.S.A., returning to opera again in 1963 at San Francisco. London, C.G., 1936–7; N.Y., Met., 1949–53. (R)

Reinhardt, Delia (b. Elberfeld, 27 Apr. 1892). German soprano. Studied Frankfurt. Début Wrocław 1913. Munich 1917–24; Berlin 1924–32; London, C.G., 1924–9; N.Y., Met., 1922–4. Often sang Octavian in the Lehmann – Schumann – Mayr – Bruno Walter *Rosenkavalier* performances; also a famous Eva, Elsa, Desdemona, and Pamina. (R)

Reining, Maria (b. Vienna, 7 Aug. 1905). Austrian soprano. Vienna State Opera 1931–3 and 1937–55; London, C.G., 1938; Chicago 1938; N.Y., C.C., 1949. Chosen by Toscanini to sing Eva at Salzburg (1937); was heard there regularly until 1949, being especially successful as Arabella and the Marschallin. (R)

Reiss, Albert (b. Berlin, 22 Feb. 1870; d. Nice, 19 June 1940). German tenor. Originally an actor, he was discovered by Pollini who engaged him for Königsberg, where he made his début in 1897 as Ivanov (*Zar und Zimmermann*). After engagements in Poznań, Wiesbaden, and Munich, engaged for N.Y., Met., 1901, remaining there until 1920. London, C.G., 1902–5, 1924–9. One of the finest of Mimes, Davids, and Valzacchis. In New York he created many small roles including Nick in *La Fanciulla del West*. (R)

Reissiger, Karl (b. Belzig, 31 Jan. 1798; d. Dresden, 7 Nov. 1859). German composer and conductor. His early *Didone Abbandonata* (1823–4) was Italian in spirit, and though he succeeded both Marschner and Weber at the Opera and German Opera in Dresden, he continued writing Italian as well as German works. Many of these were once highly successful.

Reizen, Mark (b. Zaitsevo, 3 July 1895). Russian bass. Studied Kharkov. Début there 1921; Leningrad 1925–30; Moscow, B., since 1930. Guest appearances throughout Europe. Roles include Boris, Dosifey (*Khovanshchina*), Gremin (*Onegin*). (R)

Renard. *Histoire burlesque chantée et jouée* in 2 parts by Stravinsky; text by composer, after Russian folk-tales, translated into French by C. F. Ramuz. Prod. Paris, O., 3 June 1922; N.Y. 2 Dec. 1923. The fox persuades the cock down from his perch by preaching to him; but the cat and the goat rescue him. Renewing his efforts, the fox again lures the cock into his reach, and he is rescued again, just in time, by the others suggesting that Mrs. Fox is being unfaithful.

Renato. Amelia's husband (bar.) in Verdi's *Un Ballo in Maschera*.

Renaud, Maurice (b. Bordeaux, 24 July 1861; d. Paris, 16 Oct. 1933). French baritone. Studied Paris and Brussels. Début Brussels, La M., 1883, remaining there until 1890; Paris, O. and O.C., 1890–1902; London, C.G., 1897–1904, and London Opera House 1911; New Orleans 1893; N.Y., Manhattan Opera, 1906–10; Met., 1911–12. Created Gunther in Reyer's *Sigurd* and Hamilcar in same composer's *Salammbô* in Brussels; in Paris was the Opéra's first Telramund, Alberich, Beckmesser, Chorèbe, and Méphistophélès (Berlioz); in London the first Henry VIII (Saint-Saëns), Hares (*Messaline*), Herod (*Hérodiade*); in America the first High Priest (*Samson et Dalila*), Athanael. Although his voice was remarkable for neither range nor volume, it was of excellent quality and used with great skill. This, with his remarkable dramatic abilities and masterful make-up and costuming, made Renaud one of the most distinguished French singers of his day. (R)

Rennert, Günther (b. Essen, 1 Apr. 1911). German producer and intendant. Studied Germany and Argentina. Began producing for the cinema 1933; 1935–9 at Wuppertal, Frankfurt (where he came under the influence of Felsenstein), and Mainz; Königsberg 1939–42; Berlin 1942–4; Munich 1945, where he produced the *Fidelio* with which the Staatsoper resumed its post-war activities in 1945; Intendant, Hamburg 1946–56, since when he has been guest producer at Stuttgart, Hamburg, Milan, Glyndebourne (artistic counsellor since 1960), &c. London, C.G., 1952 (*Ballo*) and 1954 (*Hoffmann*). N.Y., Met., since 1960. A cosmopolitan with wide tastes, Rennert's productions are marked by humanity and deep understanding. His crowd movements and lighting are impressive, and in general he may be regarded as the finest producer in Western Germany. During his time as Intendant the Hamburg opera became the leading ensemble in Germany.

Re Pastore, Il (The Shepherd King). *Dramma per musica* in 2 acts by Mozart; text by Metastasio. Prod. Salzburg 23 Apr. 1775; London, St. Pancras Town Hall, 8 Nov. 1954. Metastasio's story of the royal shepherd was first set by Bonno in 1751; it was also used by Gluck (1775), and at least ten other composers.

Répétiteur (Fr. = rehearser). The member of the opera house's music staff who coaches the singers in their roles. In German theatres he is called *solo répétiteur*; in Italy, *maestro collaboratore*; in England, coach (when the French word is not used).

Répétition (Fr. = repetition, i.e. rehearsal). The *répétition générale* is the final dress rehearsal, usually attended by the critics and other guests.

Rescue opera. A popular type of opera that flourished from 1790 (Berton's *Les Rigueurs du Cloître*) until about 1820, in which the rescue of a hero or heroine by his or her partner was the theme. The French Revolution gave rise to a number of incidents on which rescue operas were based, among them Cherubini's *Les Deux Journées* (1800), Dalayrac's *Léhéman* (1800), and Beethoven's *Fidelio* (1805; the third setting in seven years of Bouilly's libretto). Dallapiccola's *Il Prigioniero* gives a sinister twist to rescue opera.

Residenztheater. See *Munich*.

Resnik, Regina (b. New York, 30 Aug. 1922). American mezzo-soprano (formerly sop.). Studied N.Y. with Rosalie Miller. Début N.Y., New Opera Co., 1942, Lady Macbeth; after appearances in Mexico and N.Y., C.C., joined Met. 1944; London, C.G., from 1957. As a soprano at the Met. she created Delilah in Rogers's *The Warrior*, and was the first N.Y. Ellen Orford; Female Chorus in American première of *Rape of Lucretia*, and appeared at Bayreuth as Sieglinde; as a mezzo-soprano created the Baroness in *Vanessa* and has appeared with success as Carmen, Amneris, Mistress Quickly, and Herodias. Her rich voice is allied to a good dramatic sense and vivid stage personality. (R)

Respighi, Ottorino (b. Bologna, 9 July 1879; d. Rome, 18 Apr. 1936). Italian composer. While a violist in the St. Petersburg opera orchestra, he studied composition with Rimsky-Korsakov; later worked in Berlin with Bruch. His first two operas, the comic *Re Enzo* (1905) and *Semirâma* (1910), made his name and led to his appointment to the Conservatory in Rome, where he settled. Of the seven operas which followed, *Belfagor* (1923), *Maria Egiziaca* (1932), and *La Fiamma* (1934) have had the greatest success. In them his sumptuously scored, sensuous music perhaps makes its richest effect; dramatic tension never came naturally to him. Keenly interested in the music of his early predecessors (he has reworked Monteverdi's *Orfeo*), Respighi reverted in his last opera, *Lucrezia* (1937), to a principle of dramatic recitative echoing the 17th century.

Reszke, de. See *De Reszke*.

Retablo de Maese Pedro, El. Opera in 1 act by Falla; text by composer after Cervantes's novel *Don Quixote*, part 2, chapter 26. Prod. Seville 23 Mar. 1923; Clifton 14 Oct. 1924; N.Y. 29 Dec. 1925.

Rethberg (orig. Sättler), **Elisabeth** (b. Schwarzenburg, 22 Sept. 1894). German, later American, soprano. Studied Dresden. Début Dresden 1915, Arsena (*Zigeunerbaron*); N.Y., Met., 1922–42; London, C.G., 1926,

1934–9. Also appeared in Salzburg, Milan, and elsewhere in Europe. Created title role in Strauss's *Aegyptische Helena* (1928), and sang Rautendelein in the American première of Respighi's *La Campana Sommersa*. Equally at home in the Italian and German repertory, she was generally considered the finest Aida of her day and was famous as Desdemona, Amelia, Sieglinde, Elsa, and Elisabeth. She possessed a lyric-dramatic soprano voice of great beauty. (R)

Reutter, Hermann (b. Stuttgart, 17 June 1900). German composer. His eight operas are based on ambitious themes (e.g. Faust, Don Juan, Odysseus), and are marked by his own distinguished literary texts and a feeling for the human voice which he developed in acting as accompanist to a number of eminent German singers, among them Karl Erb. *Dr. Johannes Faust* (1936) has been his greatest success.

Reyer, Ernest (orig., Louis Étienne Rey) (b. Marseilles, 1 Dec. 1823; d. Le Lavandou, 15 Jan. 1909). French composer. His early *opéra comique*, *Maître Wolfram*, was praised by both Berlioz and Halévy; his greatest successes, however, were *Sigurd* (prod. 1883, after long delays) and *Salammbô* (1901). As a critic he was active (he covered the Cairo première of *Aida*), defending Wagner and Berlioz with vigour and wit, as well as speaking up for younger French composers.

Reykjavik. Capital of Iceland. Opera is performed in the National Theatre (opened 1950, cap. 600). It is sung in Icelandic and the season lasts from Sept. to June. Visiting companies have come from China, Finland, Denmark, and Sweden. Formerly many artists had also to be imported; the first all-Icelandic production was *Tosca* in 1957.

Rezia (or Reiza). Haroun al Raschid's daughter (sop.), heroine of Weber's *Oberon*.

Rezniček, Emil Nicolaus von (b. Vienna, 4 May 1860; d. Berlin, 2 Aug. 1945). Austrian composer and conductor. He held many conducting posts, including Mannheim 1896–9, Warsaw 1907–8, Berlin Komische Oper 1909–11. Of his operas the best known are *Donna Diana* (1894) and *Till Eulenspiegel* (1902); comic subjects found the quickest response in him.

Rheingold, Das. See *Ring der Nibelungen.*

Ricci, Luigi (b. Naples, 8 July 1805; d. Prague, 21 Dec. 1859). Italian composer. Highly successful opera composer, best known for *Crispino e la Comare* (1850), written with his brother **Federico** (b. Naples, 22 Oct. 1809; d. Conegliano, 10 Dec. 1877).

Rich, John (b. London, *c.* 1682; d. London, 1761?). English producer and manager. As manager of Lincoln's Inn Fields Theatre, introduced *The Beggar's Opera* to London, which proved so successful that he decided to build another theatre—the first Covent Garden Theatre—in 1732.

Richard Cœur de Lion. Opera in 3 acts by Grétry; text by Sedaine. Prod. Paris, C.I., 21 Oct. 1784; London, C.G., 16 Oct. 1786; Boston 23 Jan. 1797.

Richter, Hans (b. Györ, 4 Apr. 1843; d. Bayreuth, 5 Dec. 1916). Austro-Hungarian conductor. Studied Vienna, where he was choirboy in the Court Chapel. Horn-player Kärntnerthor Theater 1862–6. Worked with Wagner at Triebschen 1866–7, making fair copy of *Meistersinger* score. Wagner recommended him to Bülow as chorus master for Munich. Cond. Munich 1868–9; prepared and conducted Belgian première of *Lohengrin* 1870; Budapest 1871–5; Vienna 1875–1900 (music director 1893–1900); Bayreuth 1876–1912, where he conducted the first *Ring*; London, D.L., 1882, conducting first performances in England of *Tristan* and *Meistersinger*; C.G. 1884, where he was instrumental in bringing Lilli Lehmann to London, and C.G. 1903–10, where, after his production of *The Ring* in English, his attempts to found a permanent English national opera in association with Percy Pitt (q.v.) were thwarted by the implacable attitude of the Grand Opera Syndicate.

H.M.'s 1880. Was regarded in his day as the authoritative interpreter of Wagner and the German classics. (R)

Ricordi. Italian (orig. Spanish) family firm of music publishers, founded in 1808 by **Giovanni Ricordi** (1785–1853). The firm scored its first success with the publication of Mosca's *I Pretendenti Delusi*, and has handled the works of Rossini, Bellini, Donizetti, Verdi, Boito, Catalani, Puccini, Zandonai, Montemezzi, Pizzetti, Respighi, Menotti, and Poulenc.

Giulio Ricordi (1840–1912) exercised a notable force on Italian opera. Himself a minor composer (his single opera, *La Secchia Rapita*, was to a text by Renato Simoni, later *Turandot*'s librettist), he combined a shrewd musical judgement in his choice of composers with ruthless business acumen in furthering their and the firm's interests. Though, it is true, he attacked Toscanini and rejected the works of Bizet, Leoncavallo, and Mascagni, he championed Verdi with a fervour that was based on personal friendship and belief in Verdi's supremely Italian genius (Wagner was an enemy so vile that Ricordi even continued the attacks after acquiring the composer's operas with Lucca's stock in 1887). Ricordi quickly recognized Puccini as the 'Crown Prince' to Verdi, and helped him incalculably in his early career. Librettos were bought in case Puccini might use them, and Ricordi came near to sharp practice when he and Illica persuaded Franchetti, who had the rights to *Tosca*, that this was a poor subject and thus won it for Puccini. 'Don Giulio' became for Puccini 'the only person who inspires me with trust, and to whom I can confide what is going through my mind'. He was the first to advertise operas with illustrated posters (starting with *La Bohème*), and these were later used for the early editions of the vocal scores.

His son **Tito** (1865–1933) was impulsive and dictatorial; as *Tosca*'s producer he showed the importance of good acting and realistic scenery in *verismo* opera, but his treatment of Puccini was less tolerant than his father's, and their relations deteriorated. Puccini even contemplated a London publisher for one projected opera. When Tito left the firm in 1919, Puccini patched up their quarrel. The firm retains many of Verdi's and Puccini's original scores, and controversy over discrepancies between these and the published versions even reached the Italian Senate in 1961.

Riders to the Sea. Opera in 1 act by Vaughan Williams; text, J. M. Synge's tragedy (1904). Prod. London, R.C.M., 30 Nov. 1937; Cleveland, 26 Feb. 1950. The setting is the west coast of Ireland, where Maurya loses all her sons to the sea, finding peace only in her final defeat. Also set by Rabaud (1924).

Rienzi (orig. *Cola Rienzi, der letzte der Tribunen*). Opera in 5 acts by Wagner; text by the composer, after Mary Russell Mitford's drama (1828) and Bulwer Lytton's novel (1835). Prod. Dresden, Hofoper, 20 Oct. 1842, with Schröder-Devrient, Wüst, Tichatschek, Dettmer, Wächter; N.Y., Ac. of M., 4 Mar. 1878, with Pappenheim and Charles Adams; London, H.M.'s, 27 Jan. 1879, with Crossmond, Vanzini, Maas, cond. Carl Rosa. The opera tells of the struggle between the Orsinis and Colonnas in 14th-century Rome, and ends spectacularly with the Capitol in flames and Rienzi, his sister Irene, and her lover Adriano perishing.

Riga. Capital of Latvia. Opera was first given at the new Vittinghoff Theatre in 1782 (Monsigny's *La Belle Arsène*); the National Opera was inaugurated in 1919 with *Tannhäuser*. Dorn's *Der Schöffe von Paris* was first introduced there in 1838. Wagner went to Riga to conduct at the opera in 1837, and returned during the period of his wife Minna's second desertion in 1838 for another engagement (at Dorn's instigation) and to write *Rienzi*. But the director, Holtei, arranged for Dorn to supersede Wagner, who fled the city secretly to escape his creditors. Regular seasons of opera are still given, and include Latvian operas. See *Latvia*.

Righini, Vincenzo (b. Bologna, 22 Jan. 1756; d. Bologna, 19 Aug. 1812).

Italian composer. His early operas included one on the Don Juan subject (1777; ten years before Mozart's). Many other works were well received in Germany and Austria, where he held conducting posts. He married the singer **Henrietta Kneisel,** and made a reputation as a singing teacher.

Rigoletto. Opera in 3 acts by Verdi; text by Piave, after Hugo's drama *Le Roi s'amuse* (1832). Originally called *La Maledizione*. Prod. Venice, F., 11 Mar. 1851, with Brambilla, Mirate, Varesi; London, C.G., 14 May 1853, with Bosio, Mario, Ronconi; N.Y., Ac. of M., 19 Feb. 1855, with Maretzek, Bolcioni, Barili.

The opera takes place in 16th-century Mantua. Act 1. At a ball, the licentious Duke (ten.) tells one of his courtiers, Borsa (ten.), that he is attracted by a young girl he has often seen in church. The hunchback jester Rigoletto (bar.) taunts the courtiers, and when Monterone (bass) enters and denounces the Duke for seducing his daughter, Rigoletto 'receives him in audience'. Monterone curses them both. Shaken, the hunchback is on his way home when the assassin Sparafucile (bass) offers his professional services. He is greeted by his daughter Gilda (sop.), and warns her not to go out. The Duke, disguised as a student, manages to slip into the house and bribe Giovanna (mezzo), Gilda's nurse. When Rigoletto departs the Duke declares his love to Gilda, giving a false name. He leaves, and Gilda muses on her lover's name. Rigoletto is tricked by the courtiers into helping them abduct his own daughter, whom they believe his mistress; he now fears that Monterone's curse is working.

Act 2. The courtiers tell the Duke of the abduction of Rigoletto's supposed mistress to the palace. The Duke rushes to her room. Rigoletto enters and inveighs against the courtiers. Gilda rushes in dishevelled, and in tears tells her father that she has been 'betrayed' by the Duke. On his way to execution, Monterone laments the failure of his curse on the Duke. Rigoletto vows to kill the Duke, despite Gilda's protests.

Act 3. In Sparafucile's wayside inn, the Duke woos the assassin's sister Maddalena (mezzo). Rigoletto and Gilda watch from outside. Rigoletto approaches Sparafucile. But Maddalena, charmed by the Duke, persuades Sparafucile to spare his life, to kill any other man who may arrive, and hand over that body to Rigoletto in a sack. Gilda, now disguised as a man, overhears this conversation and resolves to sacrifice herself. She knocks at the door, and is stabbed by Sparafucile. At midnight Rigoletto returns and is handed the sack; but, as he gloats over it, the Duke's voice is heard singing in the distance. Rigoletto tears open the sack to find his dying daugher. He takes a last farewell of her and collapses over her body.

Rijeka (Fiume). Town in Croatia, Yugoslavia. First theatre built 1765, closed by government, 1797. Zajc took over direction, 1895. Present theatre built 1885. Company re-formed, 1946.

Rimsky-Korsakov, Nikolay (b. Tikhvin, 18 Mar. 1844; d. St. Petersburg, 21 June 1908). Russian composer. With two exceptions, all Rimsky-Korsakov's operas are on Russian themes; mythology attracted him especially, as did fantastic subjects. Only *The Maid of Pskov* (1873) and *The Tsar's Bride* (1899) treat conventional human emotions. His gift for harmonic and orchestral colour, coupled with his love of legend and fairy-tale, drew him more to the type of opera of which *May Night* (1880) was the first—an old folk-tale involving supernatural elements, played out in a colourful setting. Thus he delighted in ballets or set numbers that could release his imagination and unshackle his virtuoso technique from story-telling or delineation of character. In *The Snow Maiden* (1882), fairy and human worlds impinge; but the heroine's dilemma is made touching more by Rimsky-Korsakov's demonstration that these are hopelessly irreconcilable than by anything beyond the very simplest characterization of the Maiden. *Christmas Eve* (1895) reveals this weakness the more vividly when compared with

Tchaikovsky's setting (*Vakula the Smith*, 1874). This and *Mlada* (1892) were regarded as studies for *Sadko* (1898), in which he wholly responds to the excitement and colour of the story; his already spectacular technique was now affected by a slight Wagner influence (*The Ring* had had its St. Petersburg première in 1888–9) and a wish to strengthen his feeling for Russia's past by use of a special type of bardic declamation. But the next work, *Mozart and Salieri* (1898), was a neo-classical opera (the first ever), based on the rumour that Mozart had been poisoned by his rival. *Kashchey the Immortal* (1902) is a fairy-tale with dark undercurrents, musically presaging *The Firebird* of Rimsky-Korsakov's pupil Stravinsky, it has been suggested. This has a high craftsmanship and an appeal to both intellect and ear which in *The Invisible City of Kitezh* (1907) are augmented by a warm human feeling and a touching quality of lyricism. *Tsar Saltan* (1900) and *The Golden Cockerel* (1909) combine the old fantastic elements with a sharp vein of satire; that much is left obscure is of little importance in a setting where no problems except those of virtuosity engage the composer and where the listener's delight is never touched by deeper reflections.

Rinaldo. Opera in 3 acts by Handel; text by Rossi, after a sketch by Aaron Hill from Tasso's first epic (1562). Prod. London, Hm., 24 Feb. 1711, the first of Handel's operas for England.

Ring der Nibelungen, Der (The Ring of the Nibelungs). A stage-festival play for three days and a preliminary evening (*Ein Bühnenfestspiel für drei Tage und einen Vorabend*)—sometimes called a tetralogy—by Wagner; text by the composer, based on the Nibelung Saga. Prod. Bayreuth, Festspielhaus, 13, 14, 16, 17 Aug. 1876, with Materna, Schefsky, Grün, Vogl, Niemann, Unger, Betz, Hill, Schlosser, cond. Richter. The separate operas were produced as follows:

Das Rheingold (The Rhine Gold). Prologue in 1 act to the trilogy *Der Ring der Nibelungen*. Prod. Munich, 22 Sept. 1869, with August Kindermann, Nachbau, Vogl, Fischer, Schlosser, Sophie Stehle; cond. Wüllner; London, H.M.'s, 5 May 1882, with Scaria, Vogl, Schelper, Schlosser, Reicher-Kindermann, Wiegand, cond. Seidl; N.Y., Met., 4 Jan. 1889, with Fischer, Grienauer, Mittelhauser, Alvary, Sedlmayer, Moran-Olden, cond. Seidl.

Die Walküre (The Valkyrie). Music-drama in 3 acts. Prod. Munich, Hofoper, 26 June 1870, with Stehle, Teresa Vogl, Kaufmann, Vogl, Kindermann, Bausewein, cond. Wüllner; N.Y., Ac. of M., 2 Apr. 1877, with Pappenheim, Canissa, Listner, Bischoff, Preusser, Blum, cond. Neuendorf; London, H.M.'s, 6 May 1882, with Vogl, Sachse-Hofmeir, Reicher-Kindermann, Niemann, Scaria, Wiegand, cond. Seidl.

Siegfried. Music-drama in 3 acts. Prod. Bayreuth, Festspielhaus, 16 Aug. 1876, with Materna, Unger, Betz, Schlosser, cond. Richter; London, H.M.'s, 7 May 1882, with Teresa Vogl, Vogl, Scaria, Schlosser, cond. Seidl; N.Y., Met., 9 Nov. 1887, with Lehmann, Alvary, Fischer, Ferenczy, cond. Seidl.

Götterdämmerung (The Twilight of the Gods). Music-drama in 3 acts. Prod. Bayreuth, Festspielhaus, 17 Aug. 1876, with Materna, Weckerlin, Jaïde, Unger, Gura, Siehr, cond. Richter; London, H.M.'s, 9 May 1882, with Therese Vogl, Schreiber, Reicher-Kindermann, Vogl, Wiegand, Biberti, cond. Seidl; N.Y., Met., 25 Jan. 1888, with Lehmann, Seidl-Krauss, Niemann, Robinson, Fischer, cond. Seidl.

The *Ring* is an allegory, and tells of the struggle for power between the Nibelung dwarfs, the Giants, and the Gods.

In *Rheingold*, the Nibelung dwarf Alberich (bass-bar.) renounces love so that he may steal the Rhinegold, guarded by the Rhine-maidens, and by forging himself a ring from it become master of the world. Wotan (bass-bar.), ruler of the gods, has engaged the giants Fasolt and Fafner (basses) to build Valhalla for the gods; unable to pay for it he has promised them Freia (sop.), goddess of youth. Loge (ten.), the fire god, persuades Wotan to accompany him to Nibelheim where by a trick Wotan obtains the ring and the Rhinegold from Alberich; he intends paying the giants with the gold and keeping the Ring himself. Alberich curses his misfortune. The giants see the Ring on Wotan's finger and demand it as well as a magic helmet, the Tarnhelm. Wotan at first refuses, and the giants prepare to drag Freia away. Wotan's wife Fricka (mezzo) urges her husband to give the giants the ring. Erda (con.), the earth goddess, warns Wotan of the consequences of retaining the ring. He adds it to the gold, whereupon Fasolt and Fafner quarrel. Fafner kills Fasolt and takes away the gold, the Tarnhelm, and the ring. The gods, watched cynically by Loge, enter Valhalla as the curtain falls.

[In order to defend Valhalla, Wotan begets with Erda nine warrior daughter Valkyries, who bear the bodies of dead heroes to Valhalla, where they are revived and help defend the castle. But in order to restore the ring to the Rhine-maidens and rid the gods of the curse, Wotan has to beget human children. He descends to earth and begets Siegmund and Sieglinde, hoping that the former will one day kill Fafner and restore the ring to the Rhine-maidens. The pair are separated, Sieglinde being married to Hunding (bass) and Siegmund driven to lead a wandering life of hardship.]

In *Walküre* Siegmund (ten.) is forced to shelter in Hunding's hut. He and Sieglinde(sop.) feel a mysterious attraction. Sieglinde shows him the sword Nothung that Wotan had left embedded in the trunk of the tree growing in Hunding's hut to be withdrawn by a hero. He pulls the sword out and rushes off with Sieglinde. Fricka, the guardian of marriage vows, commands Wotan to side with Hunding in the latter's coming combat with Siegmund. But Brünnhilde (sop.), Wotan's favourite Valkyrie, disobeys and sides with Siegmund. Wotan intervenes and Siegmund is killed, the sword Nothung being shattered by Wotan's spear. Brünnhilde gathers the fragments and entrusts them to Sieglinde, who will soon bear Siegmund's child—the hero Siegfried. Brünnhilde is punished by being put to sleep on a fire-girt rock, through which one day a hero will penetrate and claim her. The curtain falls on the magic fire.

[Sieglinde has died giving birth to Siegfried. The boy has been brought up by the dwarf Mime, brother of Alberich. Mime's cave is in the forest close to the cave where Fafner, who by means of the Tarnhelm has changed himself into a dragon, guards the treasure. Mime hopes to weld the fragments together so that Siegfried can kill Fafner.]

In *Siegfried* Wotan, disguised as a Wanderer, visits Mime (ten.) and prophesies that the sword will be forged by a hero. Mime recognizes Siegfried (ten.) as this hero and plans to kill him when it is done. Siegfried successfully forges the sword Nothung, and with Mime sets out to seek Fafner. After Siegfried has aroused and killed Fafner (bass), he burns his finger in the dragon's blood. Sucking it, he finds he can understand the language of the birds, one of which (sop.) warns him of Mime's treachery and then tells him of the sleeping Brünnhilde. Siegfried kills Mime, and with the ring and Tarnhelm follows the bird to the Valkyrie's rock. The Wanderer tries to bar his path, but Siegfried shatters his spear with Nothung and making his way through the fire awakens Brünnhilde and claims her as his bride.

In *Götterdämmerung* the Three Norns (con., mezzo, sop.) prophesy the end of the gods. Siegfried gives Brünnhilde the ring, and leaving her goes to seek adventure. He comes to the Hall of the Gibichungs where Alberich's son Hagen (bass) lives with his half-brother Gunther (bar.) and his half-sister Gutrune (sop.). Hagen plans Siegfried's death, and by giving him a drug to make him forget Brünnhilde, arranges for him to marry Gutrune, and to fetch Brünnhilde as Gunther's bride; thus Hagen will have the ring. To Brünnhilde comes her sister Waltraute (mezzo), who urges her to return the Ring to the Rhine-maidens. Brünnhilde refuses. Siegfried, wearing the Tarnhelm and in the guise of Gunther, penetrates the fire again, and overcoming Brünnhilde, tears the ring from her finger and takes her back, an unwilling bride for Gunther. Hagen summons the Gibichungs for the double wedding ceremony. Gunther leads on Brünnhilde, unrecognized by the drugged Siegfried. Seeing the ring on Siegfried's finger, she accuses him of treachery. With Gunther and Hagen she plans Siegfried's death.

Siegfried is resting on the banks of the Rhine, and the Rhine-maidens plead with him to return the ring. Hagen, Gunther, and the huntsmen now arrive. Siegfried is asked to relate his adventures. Hagen gives him a second drug to restore his memory, and he speaks of his love for Brünnhilde. Hagen spears him in the back. Siegfried's body is carried back to the Gibichung Hall, and in a quarrel over the ring Gunther is killed by Hagen. When the latter approaches the dead Siegfried to remove the ring, Siegfried's hand rises in the air. Brünnhilde orders a funeral pyre to be built for Siegfried, and taking the ring from his finger places it on her own. On her horse, Grane, she plunges into the flames. The hall collapses, the Rhine overflows, and as Hagen tries to snatch the ring from Brünnhilde, he is dragged below the waters by the Rhine-maidens. Valhalla rises in flames, and as the kingdom of the gods is destroyed, a new era of love dawns.

Rio de Janeiro. See *Brazil*.

Risurrezione (Resurrection). Opera in 4 acts by Alfano; text by Cesare Hanau, after Tolstoy's novel *Resurrection* (1900). Prod. Turin, V.E., 30 Nov. 1904, with Malgiulo, Mieli, Scandiani; Chicago, 31 Dec. 1925, with Garden, Ansseau, Baklanoff; revived Paris, O.C., 1954, with Neway, Jobin, Roux.

Rita. Opera in 1 act by Donizetti; text by Vaëz. Prod. Paris, O.C., 7 May 1860; Naples, 18 May 1876; N.Y., Hunter College, 14 May 1957. A charming trifle about Rita, proprietress of a Swiss inn, her husband Beppe and her admirer Gasparo.

Ritorna vincitor. Aida's (sop.) aria in Act 1 of Verdi's *Aida*, in which she sings of her conflicting emotions: she has joined in the Egyptian cries bidding Radamès to return victorious, only to realize that he is leading the army against her own father and kinsfolk.

Ritorno d'Ulisse in Patria, Il (The Return of Ulysses to his Country). Opera in prologue and 5 acts by Monteverdi; text by Badoaro. Prod. Venice, S. Cass., Feb. 1641; London, St. Pancras T.H., 16 Mar. 1965. Revived in concert form, Brussels 1925; Florence Festival and Milan, Sc., 1942 in an arrangement by Dallapiccola, which he revived and shortened for the 1962 Holland Festival.

Rizzieri, Elena (b. Rovigo, 6 Oct. 1922). Italian soprano. Studied Venice with Gilda dalla Rizza. Début Venice, La Fenice, 1946, Marguerite (*Faust*). Has sung all over Italy including Sc., Germany, Spain, and Portugal. Glyndebourne 1955–6, Susanna and Despina. Created Caterina in Pizzetti's *Vanna Lupa*. (R)

Robert le Diable (Robert the Devil). Opera in 5 acts by Meyerbeer; text by Scribe. Prod. Paris, O., 21 Nov. 1831, with Cinti-Damoreau, Dorus-Gras, Nourrit, Levasseur, and Taglioni dancing; London, D.L., 20 Feb. 1832; N.Y., Park T., 7 Apr. 1834. In 13th-century Palermo, Robert, Duke of Normandy, the son of a mortal and a devil, falls in love with the princess Isabella. Disguised and under the name of Bertram, the devil tries to gain Robert's soul; he prevents Robert from winning Isabella in a tournament, and Robert is then willing to use diabolical means. At a midnight orgy with ghostly nuns, Robert acquires a magic branch with which he gains access to Isabella; but she persuades him to break it. Robert denounces his father the devil, and he is married to Isabella.

Roberto d'Evereux, Conte di Essex. Opera in 3 acts by Donizetti; text by Cammarano, after F. Ancelot's tragedy *Élisabeth d'Angleterre*. Prod. Naples, S.C., 2 Oct. 1837 with Ronzi de Begnis; London 24 June 1841 with Grisi, Rubini, Tamburini; N.Y., Astor Place O.H., 15 Jan. 1849.

Robertson, James (b. Liverpool, 17 June 1912). English conductor.

Studied Cambridge, Leipzig, and London, R.C.M. Glyndebourne, music staff, 1937–9; Carl Rosa, chorus master and conductor, 1938–9; music director, S.W. 1946–54, when he conducted the English premières of *The School for Fathers* (*Quattro Rusteghi*) and Sutermeister's *Romeo and Juliet*, as well as the S.W. premières of *Werther* and *Don Pasquale*. (R)

Robin, Mado (b. nr. Tours, 29 Dec. 1918; d. Paris, 10 Dec. 1960). French soprano. Discovered by Ruffo, who sent her to study with Giuseppe Podestà. Won first prize in the 'Concours des soprani', Paris, O., 1937; but owing to the war did not make stage début until 1945, when she sang Gilda. Appeared in Brussels, Liège, French provinces, San Francisco. Her voice was extremely flexible and she is said to have been able to reach the highest note ever emitted by a singer—c''''. Her most famous roles were Lucia and Lakmé. (R)

Robin Hood. Opera in 3 acts by Macfarren; text by Oxenford. Prod. London, H.M.'s, 11 Oct. 1860, with Lemens-Sherrington, S. Reeves, Santley. The earliest celebrations of the hero seem to date from 16th-century May Day feasts. Among many early masques and ballad operas on the subject are works by Watts, Mendez, and Shield. Also operas by Baumgartner (1786), Dietrich (1879), Holmes, and De Koven (1890).

Rocca, Lodovico (b. Turin, 29 Nov. 1895). Italian composer. His two most famous works are *Il Dibuk* (1934) and *Monte Ivnor* (1939), which have established him as a composer in the *verismo* tradition.

Rocco. The jailer (bass) in Beethoven's *Fidelio*, Marzelline's father and Leonore's employer.

Rode, Wilhelm (b. Hanover, 17 Feb. 1887; d. Munich, 2 Sept. 1959). German bass-baritone. Début Erfurt 1908 Herald (*Lohengrin*). After engagements in Mannheim, Wrocław, and Stuttgart, joined Munich Opera in 1922, where he remained until 1934, also appearing in Vienna, Salzburg, and Dresden. London, C.G., 1928. Intendant Deutsches Opernhaus, Berlin, 1934–44 continuing to sing Sachs, Wotan, Dutchman, &c. Considered by some critics to be the finest Heldenbariton between the wars. (R)

Rodelinda. Opera in 3 acts by Handel; text by Salvi, altered by Haym. Prod. London, Hm., 13 Feb. 1725; Northampton, Mass., Smith College, 9 May 1931. Also set by Perti (1710) and Graun (1741).

Rodolfo. The poet (ten.), one of the bohemians, hero of Puccini's *La Bohème*.

Rodrigo. The Marquis of Posa (bar.) in Verdi's *Don Carlos*.

Rodziński, Artur (b. Split, Yugoslavia, 2 Jan. 1892; d. Boston, 27 Nov. 1958). Polish conductor. Studied Vienna with Schalk. Début Lwów 1920. Although most of his life was spent in the concert halls of the U.S.A. he conducted the American première of *Lady Macbeth of Mtsensk* (1935) and performances of Wagner and Strauss in Cleveland and Chicago. In Florence he conducted the première of Prokofiev's *War and Peace*, and also appeared at Milan, Sc., Rome, and Naples. He emerged after the war as a prominent opera conductor in Europe. (R)

Roger, Gustave (b. Paris, 17 Dec. 1815; d. Paris, 12 Sept. 1879). French tenor. Studied Paris. Début Paris, O.C., 1838, Georges in Halévy's *L'Éclair*. Paris, O., 1849–59, where he created John of Leyden in *Le Prophète* and other roles; London, C.G., 1847. In 1859 injured in hunting mishap and had right arm amputated. Continued on the stage for two more years with an artificial arm, but had to retire 1862. Became a teacher: professor, Paris Conservatoire, from 1868 till his death.

Roi David, Le (King David). *Psaume dramatique* in 2 parts by Honegger; text by René Morax. Prod. Mézières, T. du Jorat, 11 June 1921; N.Y. 26 Oct. 1925; London, R.A.H., 17 Mar. 1927. Honegger's first dramatic work.

Roi de Lahore, Le (The King of Lahore). Opera in 5 acts by Massenet;

text by Gallet. Prod. Paris, O., 27 Apr. 1877 with Joséphine de Reszke, Lassalle; London, C.G., 28 June 1879; New Orleans Dec. 1883. King Alim and his minister Scindia love Sita. Scindia kills Alim, who is allowed by a god to return as a beggar. Sita kills herself so as to join him in Paradise.

Roi d'Ys, Le (The King of Ys). Opera in 3 acts by Lalo; text by Blau. Prod. Paris, O.C., 7 May 1888; New Orleans 23 Jan. 1890; London, C.G., 17 July 1901. Mylio is to be married to Rozenn, but her sister Margared loves him too. On the wedding night Margared jealously lets the sea in on the town. She kills herself in remorse; the town is saved by its patron saint.

Roi l'a dit, Le (lit., The King has commanded it). Opera in 3 acts by Delibes; text by Gondinet. Prod. Paris, O.C., 24 May 1873; London, Prince of Wales's, 13 Dec. 1894. Having claimed to possess a son, the Marquis de Montecontour is compelled to produce a peasant boy pretender, who promptly embarrasses the Marquis by taking advantage of the situation. He is got rid of and marries his girl, while the Marquis is consoled for the loss of his 'son' with a dukedom.

Roi Malgré lui, Le (lit., The King in spite of himself). Opera in 3 acts by Chabrier; text by De Najac and Burani. Prod. Paris, O.C., 18 May 1887. Revived 1929 in revised version by Albert Carré.

Roller, Alfred (b. Vienna, 10 Feb. 1864; d. Vienna, 21 June 1935). Austrian designer and artist. Worked with Mahler in Vienna, where his designs for Wagner, Mozart, and Beethoven operas were greatly admired. He also designed the scenery and costumes for the première of *Rosenkavalier* (Dresden 1911) and for many of the productions at Salzburg.

Romani, Felice (b. Genoa, 31 Jan. 1788; d. Moneglia, 28 Jan. 1865). Italian librettist. Originally a lawyer, he turned to literature and provided more than 100 libretti for Mayr, Vaccai, Rossini, Donizetti, Bellini, and others. Among the well-known operas for which he wrote texts are *Norma, Il Pirata, La Sonnambula, L'Elisir d'Amore, Lucrezia Borgia, Il Turco in Italia.*

Romani, Pietro (b. Rome, 29 May 1791; d. Florence, 6 Jan. 1877). Italian composer. Wrote two operas, but better known for his aria 'Manca un foglio', which replaced 'A un dottor' in *Il Barbiere di Siviglia* in 1816 and is still found in some vocal scores.

Rome (It., Roma). Capital of Italy. The first operas in Rome were private entertainments in the palaces of the nobility, outstanding amongst whom were the Barberini. In their Palace of the Four Fountains a series of extravagant spectacles was presented between 1634 and 1656. Various private theatres were built in the latter part of the 17th century, one of which, the Teatro Capranica (189 private boxes), was opened to the public in 1695. It was the home of serious opera 1711–47; of comic opera from 1744; it finally closed in 1881. The first public opera house in Rome was the Teatro Tordinona, which opened in 1671 with Stradella's *Lesbo e Ceffea.* Pulled down in 1697, it was rebuilt in 1733, destroyed by fire 1787, and rebuilt in 1795 as the Teatro Apollo (22 rows of seats in the stalls, 174 boxes). The Teatro delle Dame (cap. 900) (opened 1717) and the Teatro Argentina (q.v.) (186 boxes) (opened 1732) were the leading opera houses of Rome during the 18th and early 19th centuries; and the Argentina, Apollo, and Valle until the opening of the Costanzi (q.v.) (cap. 2,260) in 1880. Rome enjoyed premières of operas by Jommelli, Gluck (*Antigono*), Piccinni (incl. *La Buona Figliuola*), Sacchini, Paisiello, Cimarosa (incl. *L'Italiana in Londra*), Rossini (incl. *Torvaldo e Dorliska, Il Barbiere di Siviglia, La Cenerentola, Matilde di Shabran*), Donizetti (*Torquato Tasso* and *Duca d'Alba*), Verdi (*I Due Foscari, La Battaglia di Legnano, Il Trovatore*), Mascagni (*Cavalleria Rusticana, L'Amico Fritz, Iris, Lodoletta, Il Piccolo Marat*), Puccini (*Tosca*). (See also *Costanzi.*)

Roméo et Juliette. Opera in 5 acts by Gounod; text by Barbier and Carré, after Shakespeare's tragedy (1594–5). Prod. Paris, T.L., 27 Apr. 1867, with Carvallo, Michot. London, C.G., 11 July 1867, with Patti, Mario; N.Y., 15 Nov. 1867, with Hauk.

Romer, Emma (b. ?, 1814; d. Margate, 11 Apr. 1868). English soprano. Studied with George Smart. Début London, C.G., 1830, Clara (*The Duenna*). Continued to appear at C.G. until 1848, and at D.L. and the English Opera House. In 1852 took over the Surrey Theatre, where she produced opera in English with a strong company of native singers. Her most famous role was Amina.

Romerzählung. Tannhäuser's (ten.) long narration of his pilgrimage to Rome in the last act of Wagner's opera.

Ronald (orig. Russell), **Landon (Sir)** (b. London, 7 June 1873; d. London, 14 Aug. 1938). English conductor and composer. Studied R.C.M. Engaged by Mancinelli as *maestro al piano* at C.G., 1891, subsequently touring with Augustus Harris's company, and conducting some performances at D.L. Toured as Melba's accompanist, and played for Patti when she recorded in 1905. (R)

Ronconi, Giorgio (b. Milan, 6 Aug. 1810; d. Madrid, 8 Jan. 1890). Italian baritone. Son of the tenor **Domenico Ronconi** (1772–1839), studied with his father. Début Pavia 1831; Sc. 1842, where he created title role in *Nabucco*; London, H.M.'s, 1842; C.G. 1847–66, where he sang principal roles in the English premières of *Poliuto*, *Rigoletto*, and other works, and was greatly admired as the Doge in *I Due Foscari*, Figaro (Rossini), and Iago in Rossini's *Otello*. According to Chorley he possessed 'such wonderful dramatic powers that one virtually forgot his vocal limitations, a compass of barely more than one octave, inferior in quality, weak, and habitually out of tune'. He married the soprano **Elguerra Giannoni,** who failed on virtually every opera stage of Europe. His brother **Sebastiano Ronconi** (1814–1900) was also a baritone and sang with success in Vienna, Spain, Portugal, and elsewhere.

Rondine, La (The Swallow). Opera in 3 acts by Puccini; text by Adami, translated from a German libretto by A. M. Willner and H. Reichert. Prod. Monte Carlo, 27 Mar. 1917, with Dalla Rizza, Ferraris, Schipa, Huberdeau, cond. Marinuzzi; N.Y., 10 Mar. 1928, with Bori, Fleischer, Gigli, Ludikar, cond. Bellezza; London, Fulham T.H., 9 Dec. 1965. Intended as an operetta for Vienna, the work was kept from production by the war, and the composer decided to set the libretto rather differently. The opera tells of the love of Magda, mistress of the wealthy Parisian, Rambaldo, for Ruggero, a young man of aristocratic family. Her moral scruples overcome her, and she renounces him. The action of the opera takes place in Paris and Nice during the Second Empire.

Ronzi, Giuseppina. See *De Begnis*.

Rooy, Anton van (b. Rotterdam, 1 Jan. 1870; d. Munich, 28 Nov. 1932). Dutch bass-baritone. Studied Frankfurt with Stockhausen. Début Bayreuth, 1897, Wotan; London, C.G., 1898–1913; N.Y., Met., 1898–1908. Amfortas in N.Y. première of *Parsifal* in 1903, which resulted in his being banned from Bayreuth. An extremely serious and sensitive artist, he was considered the finest Sachs, Kurwenal, and Wotan of the first decade of this century. (R)

Rosa, Carl (orig. Karl Rose) (b. Hamburg, 22 Mar. 1842; d. Paris, 30 Apr. 1889). German conductor and impresario. After touring Europe and America as a solo violinist, he met the soprano **Euphrosyne Parepa** (q.v.) whom he married and with whom he set up the Carl Rosa Opera Co. (q.v.).

Rosalinde. Eisenstein's wife (sop.), heroine of J. Strauss's *Die Fledermaus*.

Rosbaud, Hans (b. Graz, 22 July 1895; d. Lugano, 30 Dec. 1962). Austrian conductor. Studied Frankfurt. Held appointments before the war in Frankfurt, Mainz, Münster, and Strasbourg. Chief conductor of the Aix-en-Provence Festival 1947–59. Directed memorable performances of Schoenberg's *Erwartung* and *Von Heute auf Morgen* at the 1958 Holland Festival; conducted both radio and stage premières of *Moses und Aron*. Renowned for his understanding and able performance of modern music. (R)

Rosenkavalier, Der (The Knight of the Rose). Opera in 3 acts by Richard Strauss; text by Hugo von Hofmannsthal. Prod. Dresden, Hofoper, 26 Jan. 1911, with Siems, Von der Osten, Nast, Perron, cond. Schuch; London, C.G., 29 Jan. 1913, with Siems, Von der Osten, Dux, Knüpfer, cond. Beecham; N.Y., Met., 9 Dec. 1913, with Hempel, Ober, Case, Goritz, cond. Hertz.

The opera takes place in Vienna in the time of Maria Theresa.

Act 1. The Princess von Werdenberg (sop.) (the Feldmarschallin, or Field-Marshal's wife) and the young Count Octavian (mezzo) have passed the night together. They are interrupted in the morning, and thinking that it is her husband, the Marschallin tells Octavian to hide; he emerges a few moments later dressed as a serving-girl, 'Mariandel'. But it is the Marschallin's kinsman, the boorish Baron Ochs von Lerchenau (bass), with news of his coming marriage to Sophie von Faninal; he asks her to send a young nobleman with the traditional silver rose to his betrothed and then flirts with the Princess's 'maid'. The Princess produces a picture of Octavian, proposing him as the Baron's Rose Cavalier. The daily *levée* now takes place, during which 'Mariandel' escapes, an Italian tenor sings a song, and Ochs discusses his marriage settlement with the Princess's lawyer—all this while the Princess is having her hair dressed. When she looks at herself in the mirror she sees that she is an old woman: she dismisses the company, and reflects on her fleeting youth, trying to tell Octavian (who has returned undisguised) of her feelings. He cannot understand her and formally takes his leave. She sends her little negro servant after him with the silver rose, and once more sadly scans her face in the tell-tale mirror.

Act 2. In the Faninal household, excitement mounts as Sophie (sop.) and her duenna (sop.) await the arrival of the Rose Cavalier. Octavian enters, dressed in silver, and presents the rose to Sophie. The young couple are quickly attracted to one another. Faninal (bar.) ushers in his prospective son-in-law, Ochs, whose manner repels Sophie. Left with Octavian, Sophie is easily persuaded not to marry Ochs. They are surprised by Valzacchi (ten.) and Annina (mezzo), a pair of Italian intriguers who summon the Baron. Octavian lightly wounds the Baron, who makes an enormous fuss. Annina enters with a letter from 'Mariandel' inviting the delighted Baron to a rendezvous at an inn near Vienna.

Act 3. 'Mariandel', with the two intriguers, prepares the scene for supper with Baron Ochs. When the Baron tries to make love to 'Mariandel', he is interrupted by sinister faces at the window and the entrance of a woman claiming to be his wife surrounded by several screaming children. The noise brings the police, and the Baron has to pretend that 'Mariandel' is Sophie von Faninal. A few moments later Sophie and her father arrive, followed by the Marschallin, who quickly sums up the situation. She reminds the Baron of his rank and position, placates Faninal, and gives up Octavian to Sophie.

Rosenstock, Joseph (b. Cracow, 27 Jan. 1895). Polish conductor. Studied Cracow and Vienna with Schreker. Darmstadt 1922–5, Wiesbaden 1925–7. Invited to succeed Bodanzky at the Met. 1929, but after a few performances resigned. Mannheim 1930–3; music director Jewish Kulturbund, Berlin, 1933–6, after which he left Germany; N.Y., C.C., 1948–55; Cologne 1958–9. Returned to the Met. 1960. (R)

Rosina. Bartolo's ward (mezzo) in Rossini's and (sop.) in Paisiello's *Il Barbiere di Siviglia*.

Rosing, Vladimir (b. St. Petersburg, 23 Jan. 1890; d. Los Angeles, 24 Nov. 1963). Russian tenor. Teachers included Jean de Reszke and Sbriglia. Début St. Petersburg 1912, Lensky.

Directed and participated in season at London Opera House, 1915, in which he sang Herman in the English première of *The Queen of Spades*. In 1936, in collaboration with Albert Coates, he organized the British Music-Drama Opera Company, which survived for only one season, at C.G. In recent years he has been responsible for some productions at the C.C., N.Y., and at the Lyric Opera of Chicago. (R)

Rossi-Lemeni, Nicola (b. Istanbul, 6 Nov. 1920). Italian bass. Born of an Italian father and Russian mother (Xenia Lemeni Macadon, teacher of singing at Odessa). Début Venice 1946, Varlaam; Milan, Sc., since 1947; San Francisco 1951–3; N.Y., Met., 1953–4; London, C.G., 1952. Although noted for his interpretations of the Russian repertory (especially Boris), and Méphistophélès (Gounod and Boito), he has been extremely successful in such diverse roles as Gruenberg's Emperor Jones and Bloch's Macbeth. His imposing stage presence and dramatic abilities compensate for some vocal inequalities. Married to the soprano **Virginia Zeani** q.v. (R)

Rossignol, Le. See *Nightingale, The.*

Rossini, Gioacchino (b. Pesaro, 29 Feb. 1792; d. Paris, 13 Nov. 1868). Italian composer. Rossini's parents were both musicians, his father a town trumpeter, his mother a singer of *seconda donna* parts. By the age of 15, he had learnt the violin and harpsichord and had often sung in public. In 1806 he entered the Bologna Conservatory, and during his student years wrote an opera, *Demetrio e Polibio* (staged 1812). His first professional works for the stage were *La Cambiale di Matrimonio* (1810), *L'Equivoco Stravagante* (1811), and *L'Inganno Felice* (1812)—all *buffo* operas—and *Ciro in Babilonia* (1812), his first serious work, which like the comic *La Scala di Seta* (1812) was a failure. However, *La Pietra del Paragone* (1812), written for the soprano Marcolini who had procured him its commission for La Scala, was a success. It was in the finale of this work that the public first heard the famous Rossini *crescendo*; they had already learnt to enjoy the pace and verve of his tunes. Four works for Venice followed between Nov. 1812 and May 1813: *L'Occasione fa il Ladro, Il Signor Bruschino, Tancredi*, and *L'Italiana in Algeri. Tancredi* first made his name known outside Italy, and contains the warmest love music he ever wrote: in it there is a new approach to the handling of the orchestra, especially the use of woodwind to add expressiveness to the vocal line. *L'Italiana,* dashed off in just over three weeks, was Rossini's first great success in the field of *opera buffa*, and remains one of the best examples. A failure now came with *Aureliano in Palmira* (1813): the overture and part of the first chorus survive in *Il Barbiere di Siviglia. Il Turco in Italia* (1814) at first suffered from comparison with *L'Italiana*; and after these two failures Rossini returned from Milan to Venice, where he suffered a third failure with *Sigismondo* (1814)—some of its music is also to be found in *Il Barbiere*. Rossini was now engaged by Barbaia as music director of both the Naples Opera houses, the Teatro San Carlo and the Teatro del Pondo. For the former he wrote *Elisabetta, Regina d'Inghilterra,* in which for the first time recitatives were accompanied by strings and ornaments written out in full. Elisabetta was sung by Isabella Colbran, who was to become Rossini's wife. Several more operas were now written for Naples, including *Otello* (1816)—the tragic ending of which so distressed the public that a happy ending had to be provided for Rome; *Armida* (1817), another work of considerable musical power; *Mosè in Egitto* (1818), revived for Paris nine years later as *Moïse*; *La Donna del Lago* (1819); and *Maometto II* (1820), revised for Paris as *Le Siège de Corinthe*. During Rossini's Naples engagement his commissions included *Il Barbiere di Siviglia* (1816), which, after a stormy première at which the supporters of Paisiello's *Barbiere* were out in force, came to be accepted as one of the great masterpieces of comic opera. Other commissions included *La Cenerentola* (1817), which again made use of the coloratura contralto (or mezzo-soprano) which Rossini had first used in *L'Italiana*; *La Gazza*

Ladra (1817); *Bianca e Faliero* (1819); *Mathilde di Shabran* (1821); and *Semiramide* (1823), one of Rossini's longest and most ambitious works. He was now approaching his 31st birthday; he was the most popular and prolific composer of his day, having in the 10 years since *Tancredi* composed some 25 operas. Stendhal declared, 'The glory of the man is only limited by the limits of civilization itself; and he is not yet 32.'

Semiramide closed Rossini's Italian period, and after visits to Vienna (where he met Beethoven) and London, where he conducted and sang in concerts with his wife, he settled in Paris as director of the Théâtre Italien for 18 months. There his *Il Viaggio a Reims*, a stage cantata with a ballet, was produced in 1825. Written for the extravagant coronation of Charles X, it lasted three hours and was written for 15 voices—at the première these included Pasta, Cinti, Levasseur, Graziani, Donzelli, and Bordoni. He retained Paer at the theatre as *maestro al cembalo*, engaged the young Hérold as chorus master, and introduced Meyerbeer to Paris with *Il Crociato in Egitto*. He was then appointed Composer to the King and Inspector General of Singing for all royal institutions. This opened the doors of the Opéra to him, and after revising *Maometto II* and *Mosè in Egitto*, he produced his *Le Comte Ory* (1823) and *Guillaume Tell* (1829). *Tell* was his crowning achievement in opera, with which (according to Hanslick) 'a new era for opera began, and not only in France'. It was to have been the first of five works for the Opéra in ten years; but the 1830 revolution dethroned Charles and the new government set aside the contract, allowing (after much litigation) only an annuity that was attached. *Tell* was Rossini's last stage work, though he lived for another 39 years, composing two religious works and a host of trifles (the so-called *péchés de vieillesse*). He died on Friday, 13 Nov. 1868, and was buried near Cherubini, Chopin, and Bellini. In 1887 his body was handed over to the city of Florence for reburial, when there was a procession of more than 6,000 mourners, four military bands, and a chorus of 300 which sang the Prayer from *Mosè* to such effect that the crowd in front of the Church of Santa Croce cheered until it was encored.

Rostand, Edmond (b. Marseilles, 1 Apr. 1868; d. Paris, 2 Dec. 1918). French playwright. Operas on his works are as follows. *Les Romanesques* (1894): F. Hart (1918). *La Princesse Lointaine* (1895): Montemezzi (?); Witkowski (1934). *Cyrano de Bergerac* (1897): Damrosch (1913); Alfano (1936). *L'Aiglon* (1900): Honegger and Ibert (1937).

Roswaenge (orig. Rosenving-Hansen), **Helge** (b. Copenhagen, 29 Aug. 1897). Danish tenor. Début Neustrelitz 1921, Don José. After engagements in Altenburg, Basle, Cologne, joined Berlin State Opera 1924, remaining there until 1945; returned there 1949; Vienna since 1936; London, C.G., 1938; Bayreuth 1934–6, Parsifal; Salzburg 1933–9, where he was an admired Huon, Tamino, and Florestan. Generally considered in his prime one of the finest lyric-dramatic tenors in central Europe. He still appears with great success as Calaf, Radamès, Manrico, &c. (R)

Rota, Nino (b. Milan, 3 Dec. 1911). Italian composer. The most successful of his operas, which reflect a somewhat French wit and lyricism, has been *Il Cappello di Paglia di Firenze*, based on Labiche's comedy.

Rothenberger, Anneliese (b. Mannheim, 19 June 1924). German soprano. Début Coblenz 1948. Hamburg Opera since 1949. Vienna since 1956. Has appeared at N.Y., Met., Glyndebourne, Salzburg, &c. A charming and versatile artist, she has sung in many modern works, and is an outstanding Sophie, Zdenka, and Adele. (R)

Rothmüller, Marko (b. Trnjani, 31 Dec. 1908). Yugoslav baritone. Studied Zagreb and Vienna (composition with Berg and singing with Steiner). Début Hamburg 1932, Ottokar (*Freischütz*); Zürich 1935–47; London, C.G., 1939 and 1948–55; New London Opera Co. 1947–8; Edinburgh and Glyndebourne Festivals 1949–52, being especially successful as Macbeth; N.Y., C.C., 1948–52; Met. 1959–60; also appeared Vienna, Berlin, &c. Wozzeck (which he sang in the C.G. production under Kleiber 1951), Rigoletto, and Scarpia are his chief roles; in them his fine singing and musical characterization are at their best. (R)

Rousseau, Jean-Jacques (b. Geneva, 28 June 1712; d. Ermenonville, 2 July 1778). Swiss philosopher, composer, and writer on music. He produced his first opera, *Les Muses Galantes*, in 1742, when it was declared highly uneven by Rameau; but his most important composition was *Le Devin du Village* (to his own text), produced with great success in 1752. Siding with the Italians in the *Guerre des Bouffons* (q.v.), he then published his important *Lettre sur la Musique Française* (1753) expounding his musical beliefs: briefly, he takes a strong stand for melody as a form of heightened speech. His other writings on music include a dictionary. His *Pygmalion* (1775) uses orchestral interludes between speeches, and he left parts of an opera on *Daphnis et Chloé*. His influence was greater than his example, for he never acquired anything like complete technical security; *Le Devin du Village* stands entirely by its melodic charm.

Roussel, Albert (b. Tourcoing, 5 Apr. 1869; d. Royan, 23 Aug. 1937). French composer. Roussel's major stage work, the opera-ballet *Padmâvatî* (1923), is based on an Indian legend. He found in Oriental music the means for liberating and developing his own idiom—there ensued a greater flexibility and muscularity of melody, an increased harmonic palette, a subtler rhythmic sense.

Roze, Marie (orig. Hippolyte Ponsin) (b. Paris, 2 Mar. 1846; d. Paris, 21 June 1926). French soprano. Studied Paris Conservatoire. Début Paris, O.C., 1865 in Hérold's *Marie*. London, D.L., 1872; H.M.'s, 1873–81; and also appeared with Carl Rosa. Much admired as Marguerite, Carmen, and Manon, of which she was the first interpreter in London. She married Mapleson's son; their son **Raymond Roze** (1875–1920) organized a season of opera in English at C.G., 1913, in which his *Joan of Arc* was produced.

Rubato (It. = robbed). The art (sometimes the abuse) of hurrying or slowing the pace in varying degrees for expressive effect.

Rubini, Giovanni (b. Romano, nr. Bergamo, 7 Apr. 1794; d. Romano, 2 Mar. 1854). Italian tenor. Studied Bergamo. Début Pavia 1814. After 11 years of increasing success in Italy, went to Paris 1825, where his appearances in Rossini's *Cenerentola*, *Otello*, and *La Donna del Lago* caused a sensation. His successes were repeated in London, and at St. Petersburg, where he received the equivalent of £20,000 a season. The tenor roles in *Il Pirata*, *La Sonnambula*, and *I Puritani* and in Donizetti's *Anna Bolena* were composed for him. His voice was sweet, yet capable of organ-like power and volume, and extended from e to b' with an extension in falsetto register to f' and g'. He was the first great singer to make extensive use of the musical sob. He thoroughly identified himself with his roles—though Wagner, who heard him as Don Ottavio in Paris in 1840, thought differently. A portrait by Manet hangs in the Kröller-Müller Museum near Otterloo.

Rubinstein, Anton (b. Vekhvotinets, 28 Nov. 1830; d. Peterhof, 20 Nov. 1894). Russian pianist and composer. His 20 operas embrace local legends, Oriental subjects (*Feramors*, 1863), heroic opera (*The Maccabees*, 1875, and *Nero*, 1879), Russian pieces (*The Merchant Kalashnikov*, 1880), and religious opera-oratorio (*Moses*, 1887, and *Christus*, 1888). The most important was *The Demon* (1875), which in its Frenchified manner supported Rubinstein's contention that Russian composers must imitate Western models; its lurid, romantic story ensured temporary popularity.

Rudel, Julius (b. Vienna, 6 Mar. 1921). Austrian, later naturalized

American, conductor. Studied Vienna, and New York, Mannes School of Music. After conducting small operatic groups in New York, joined the City Center as a *répétiteur* in 1943. Music and artistic director New York City Opera since 1957, where he has been responsible for a progressive policy and several seasons devoted to contemporary American opera.

Ruffo, Titta (orig. Ruffo Cafiero Titta) (b. Pisa, 9 June 1877; d. Florence, 6 July 1953). Italian baritone. Studied Rome with Persichini, and Milan with Cassini. Début Rome 1898, Herald (*Lohengrin*). London, C.G., 1903; Chicago 1912–14; N.Y., Met., 1922–29. Possessed one of the largest and at the same time most beautiful baritone voices of his day. Superb in Verdi roles. De Luca considered him 'not a voice, but a miracle', and recorded that he could still sing $a\flat'$ in 1951. Also famed for his Scarpia, Tonio, and Hamlet. (R)

Rumania. The first operatic performances were given at Sibiu in 1722 by an Italian company; other companies toured, giving performances in Italian to the aristocracy. One such played at Bucharest in 1787; and a German company visited Iaşi in 1795. Rumania's long struggle for a national opera took place almost exclusively in Bucharest (q.v.). Early Rumanian operas included the operetta *Babu Hîrca* by Flechtenmacher; Skibinski's *Vorful cu Dor* (*Summit of Desire*), with a German text by 'Carmen Sylva' (Queen Elisabeth of Rumania), given by Italians in 1879; a comic opera, Caudella's and Otremba's *Oltenca* (1880); and Caudella's principal work, *Petru Rareţ* (1900). Important works of the period following the foundation of the State Opera in 1920 include Dragoi's *The Woe* (Bucharest 1928), Negrea's *A Boyard's Sin* (Cluj 1934), and Constantinescu's *A Stormy Night* (Bucharest 1935). As well as in Bucharest (q.v.), there are opera houses in Cluj (q.v.), Constanţa, Galaţi, Iaşi (q.v.), Oradea, Oraşul Stalin, and Timişoara (q.v.).

Rusalka. Opera in 3 acts by Dvořák; text by Kvapil. Prod. Prague, Nat. T., 31 Mar. 1901; Chicago, 10 Nov. 1935; London, Peter Jones T., 9 May 1950, by John Lewis Partnership; S.W., 18 Feb. 1959, with Joan Hammond. A watersprite becomes human so as to marry a prince, but when he deserts her she returns to her pool; following her remorsefully, he dies in her arms. Also opera in 4 acts by Dargomizhsky; text by composer, after Pushkin's dramatic poem (1832). Prod. St. Petersburg 16 May 1856; Seattle 23 Dec. 1921; London, Ly., 18 May 1931.

Russ, Giannina (b. Lodi, 27 Mar. 1873; d. Milan, 28 Feb. 1951). Italian soprano. Début Bologna 1903, Mimì. Milan, Sc., 1905 and later; London, C.G., 1904; N.Y., Manhattan O., 1906. A notable Verdi soprano and famous Norma of her day, whose voice and style were often reminiscent of Rethberg. (R)

Russell, Henry (b. London, 14 Nov. 1871; d. London, 11 Oct. 1937). English impresario and teacher. Son of the singer and composer of the same name. His novel method of vocal teaching attracted the attention of Melba, who sent him some of her best pupils. He organized the 1904 autumn season at C.G., bringing most of the Naples San Carlo Co.; and the following summer presented a season at the new Waldorf Theatre (now the Strand), London, with a company that included Bonci, De Lucia, Ancona, and Pini-Corsi. He took this company to Boston, where in 1909 he organized the Boston Opera Co., of which he was the general manager until 1914; he took the Boston Company to Paris in 1914. His brother was better known as Landon Ronald (q.v.). Memoirs, *The Passing Show* (1926).

Russia. The first Italian opera troupe arrived in Russia in 1731, during the reign of the Empress Anna Ivanovna, to perform comic intermezzos; the first *opera seria* was Araia's *La Forza dell'Amore e dell'Odio* in 1736. The Empress Elizabeth Petrovna's love of Italy encouraged opera to develop further: inevitably it acquired Russian roots, and this period saw the appearance of the first opera with a Russian text and the first sung in Russian by Russians, Araia's *Cephalus and Procris* (1755). Before his deposition by his Empress, Catherine the Great, Peter III had sent for Galuppi and Tartini, and this invitation, renewed by Catherine, inaugurated a century-long dynasty of Italian composers in Russia. Their dates are approximately: Araia 1735–59 and from 1762; Manfredini 1759–66; Galuppi 1765–8; Traetta 1768–76; Paisiello 1776–83; Sarti 1784–6 and 1792–6; Cimarosa 1787–91; Martín y Soler (a Spaniard) 1788–94; Cavos 1798–1840. In 1764 the first French *opéra comique* was staged in Russia, and the fashion remained until the events of 1812 made French influences no longer tolerable. The first English opera to join what was now an international repertory was Dibdin's *The Padlock* in 1771. Russian composers who studied opera in Italy included Fomin, Matinsky, Bortyansky, and Berezovsky, whose *Demofoonte* (Leghorn 1773) was the first opera by a Russian. Catherine, believing in opera's function as social commentary as vigorously as any present-day Russian ruler, provided librettos of political satire (*The False Hero Kosometovich*, 1789—attacking Gustav III of Sweden) and propaganda (*The Early Government of Oleg*, 1790). A fashion for German fairy opera was followed by the arrival of Catterino Cavos, who as well as founding a Russian school of singing composed fairy operas and operas based on Russian mythology. After 1812 heroic national subjects naturally became more popular; and the appearance of *Der Freischütz* in Russia in 1824 gave a strong lead to the only other Russian composer of significance, Verstovsky. His *Pan Tvardovsky* (1828), *Vadim* (1832), and above all *Askold's Tomb* (1835) made copious use of the nationalistic elements that had ensured *Freischütz*'s popularity, transferring them to Russian folklore. All these diverse strains served to prepare the way for the acknowledged Father of Russian Opera, Glinka (q.v.). Russian opera was now ready for the appearance of major composers, and by reference to such figures as Tchaikovsky, Mussorgsky, Dargomizhsky, Rimsky-Korsakov, Prokofiev, and Shostakovich its history may now best be traced.

Some 40 opera houses exist today in what is now the U.S.S.R., more than half of them representing the various national cultures the Union embraces. Among the most important outside Moscow (q.v.) and Leningrad (q.v.) are the following: Alma-Ata (Kazakhstan); Ashkhabad (Turkmenistan); Baku (q.v.) (Azerbaijan); Frunze (q.v.) (Kirghizia); Kaunas (q.v.) (Lithuania); Kiev (q.v.); Kuybyshev (q.v.); Minsk (Byelorussia); Riga (q.v.) (Latvia); Sverdlovsk (q.v.); Tallin (q.v.) (Estonia); Tashkent (Uzbekistan), where a traditional form of melodrama still flourishes alongside a semi-westernized form of opera based on local oriental melodies; Tbilisi (Georgia); and Yerevan (q.v.) (Armenia). A troupe of Buryats from Lake Baikal (Mongolia) visited Moscow in 1960 and gave *Prince Igor* in Mongolian; companies from Dagestan and Northern Osetia (q.v.) have also visited the capital.

Russlan and Ludmilla. Opera in 5 acts by Glinka; text by Shirkov and Bakhturin, after Pushkin's poem (1820). Prod. St. Petersburg, 9 Dec. 1842; London, Ly., 4 June 1931; N.Y., T.H., 26 Dec. 1942 (concert). Ludmilla disappears from a feast for her three suitors; her father promises her to the one who finds her. Russlan learns that she has been stolen by the dwarf Chernomor; another suitor, Farlaf, is advised by the witch Naina to follow Russlan and then capture Ludmilla. Russlan is saved from the fate of the suitor Ratmir, imprisoned after succumbing to the sirens' song, by his friend Finn, a magician. Russlan reaches Chernomor's house, and, cutting off the dwarf's magic beard, rescues Ludmilla, now flung into a deep sleep. Later she is roused by Finn, and united to Russlan.

Ruth. Opera in 1 act by Berkeley; text by Eric Crozier, after the Book of Ruth. Prod. London, Scala, 2 Oct. 1956, with Pollak, Pears.

Rysanek, Leonie (b. Vienna, 14 Nov. 1926). Austrian soprano. Studied Vienna with Jerger and later with the baritone Rudolf Grossmann, whom she married. Début Innsbruck 1949, Agathe. Sang Saarbrücken 1950–2; Munich since 1952; Vienna since 1954; London, C.G., 1953–5, 1959, and 1963; San Francisco since 1957; N.Y., Met., since 1959. Sang Sieglinde in the first post-war Bayreuth Festival, and later heard there as Elsa and Senta. Her rich voice with its strong upper register makes her an excellent Kaiserin (*Frau ohne Schatten*), Aegyptische Helena, and Danae; and has also been admired in Verdi roles. (R) Her sister **Lotte Rysanek** (b. 1928) is a lyric soprano in Vienna.

S

Sabata, Victor de. See *De Sabata.*

Sacchini, Antonio (b. Florence, 14 June 1730; d. Paris, 6 Oct. 1786). Italian composer. After early successes in Italy, he came to London and there produced 17 operas whose skill in vocal writing won him great popularity. He became even more popular in Paris, where he later settled, though the failure of his masterpiece, *Œdipe à Colone* (1785), to be chosen for Fontainebleau, owing to political pressure, broke his heart and hastened his death. Later it was to have 583 performances in 57 years at the Opéra. Burney called him a 'graceful, elegant and judicious composer', and the fluency of his music, coupled with his ability to match it to local taste and individual singers, won him a success in his day that for lack of more solid or personal gifts has not proved enduring.

Sachs, Hans. The philosopher-cobbler (bass-bar.) in Wagner's *Die Meistersinger.*

Sacra rappresentazione. See *Rappresentazione.*

Sadko. Opera in 7 scenes by Rimsky-Korsakov; text by composer and Belsky. Prod. Moscow 7 Jan. 1898 with David in title role; N.Y., Met., 25 Jan. 1930 with Edward Johnson; London, Ly., 9 June 1931. The wanderings of the minstrel Sadko bring him to Volkhova, Princess of the Sea, who promises him that his net will be filled with golden fish. He wagers a crowd that he can catch the golden fish; succeeds; and then sets sail with some companions. Becalmed, they throw gold overboard to pacify the Sea-King; but his daughter, the Princess, tells Sadko that one of the company must be sacrificed. Sadko is set adrift on a raft and sinks to the sea bed, where his song wins him Volkhova's hand. At the wedding, Sadko's singing so excites the sea that many ships sink; this brings down the anger of St. Nicholas, who orders Sadko back to land. On the shore of Lake Ilmen, Sadko bids farewell to Volkhova, who is transformed into the river that bears her name.

Sadler's Wells. Theatre in north London, home of Sadler's Wells Opera. Originally a place of entertainment in the grounds of one Sadler, who in 1683 discovered in his garden a well whose waters were drunk for medicinal purposes. In 1765 the first theatre was built and saw musical performances by Braham, the Dibdins, and others. It later became a music hall before falling into disuse. In Mar. 1925 a move was set on foot to turn the old theatre into an Old Vic for north London and some £70,000 was raised during the next five years. The theatre (cap. 1,650) was opened under the management of Lilian Baylis (q.v.) on 6 Jan. 1931. At first opera and ballet alternated with Shakespeare; in 1934, however, Sadler's Wells became the exclusive home of the opera and ballet companies. Between then and 1939 the repertory was enlarged and included the English premières of *The Snow Maiden*, *Tsar Saltan*, the original *Boris*, the first performance in English of *Don Carlos*, productions of *Valkyrie*, *Mastersingers*, *The Devil Take Her* (Benjamin), *The Boatswain's Mate* (Smyth), *Eugene Onegin*, and *Travelling Companion* (Stanford). Singers included Joan Cross, Edith Coates, Janet Hamilton-Smith, Ruth Naylor, Arthur Cox (Carron), Sumner Austin, Redvers Llewellyn, Powell Lloyd, Arnold Matters, Henry Wendon, and John Wright; conductors were Warwick Braithwaite and Lawrance Collingwood; and producers Clive Carey, Sumner Austin, and J. B. Gordon. Guest appearances were made by many distinguished British artists, including Noel Eadie, Florence Easton, Florence Austral, Miriam Licette, Heddle

Nash; Beecham, Barbirolli, Coates; and the German producer Strohbach. The 1939–40 season took place at Rosebery Avenue, but then the company concentrated on touring, though short seasons were given at the New Theatre in London by a reduced company under the direction of Tyrone Guthrie. Later the company was built up again and Joan Cross assumed its direction. By the end of the war there had been several new productions including a successful *Bartered Bride* and *Così fan tutte*, and artists new to the public had included Elisabeth Abercrombie, Victoria Sladen, Owen Brannigan, and Peter Pears. On 7 June 1945 the company returned to its home in north London with the première of *Peter Grimes*. Joan Cross then resigned to work with the English Opera Group and at the Opera School, and Clive Carey took charge for the 1946–7 seasons. In 1948 Norman Tucker (q.v.) began his association with the theatre. James Robertson was music director 1946–54, Alexander Gibson 1957–9, Colin Davis 1961–5. The post-war period has included the premières of Hopkins's *Lady Rohesia*, Berkeley's *Nelson*, Gardner's *The Moon and Sixpence*, and Bennett's *Mines of Sulphur*, the British premières of *I Quatro Rusteghi* (*The School for Fathers*), *Simone Boccanegra*, *Káťa Kabanova*, *Romeo and Juliet* (Sutermeister), *Rusalka* (Dvořák), *The Cunning Little Vixen* and *The Makropoulos Affair* (Janáček), and *Mahagonny*, and first productions at Sadler's Wells of *Schwanda*, *The Consul*, *Martha*, *Don Pasquale*, *The Flying Dutchman*, *The Merry Widow*, *Duke Bluebeard's Castle*, *Cenerentola*, *Oedipus Rex*, *Ariadne auf Naxos*, *Idomeneo*, *Love of Three Oranges*, *Girl of Golden West*, *Der Freischütz*, and *L'Enfant et les Sortilèges*. Many of the singers have been heard at C.G. and elsewhere; they include Victoria Elliott, Anna Pollak, Amy Shuard; Charles Craig, James Johnston, Howell Glynne, David Ward, and Owen Brannigan. The producers have included Denis Arundell, Basil Coleman, George Devine, Powell Lloyd, and Tyrone Guthrie, with Glen Byam Shaw as director of productions since 1962. In 1958 the theatre was threatened with a financial crisis, averted by amazing public and press response. Elements of the Carl Rosa Touring Company were taken over by Sadler's Wells, which is now responsible for most of the provincial touring opera in Great Britain, there now being two full companies available.

Not the least encouraging aspect of the spontaneous public warmth towards S.W. in the 1958 crisis was the sign that a stable opera company providing sound repertory performances week in week out can claim the loyalty of a public normally regarded as only intermittently opera-loving. Whereas C.G.'s function since the war has mainly been to house larger works and provide for international seasons, S.W. has concentrated on developing a stable opera company formed almost exclusively of British singers, singing in English, and on building up a large, well-balanced repertory in which modern works feature alongside established favourites. S.W. can now cast from strength, with several singers available for each role. The theatre has also been used by visiting companies during the spring and summer, and has been the London home of the Welsh National Opera Company, the New Opera Company, and companies from Italy and South America.

In the summer of 1961 the new plans for a National Theatre included a proposed move from Sadler's Wells to the projected South Bank site: these plans were eventually abandoned and the company moved to the Coliseum Theatre in Aug. 1968. Norman Tucker resigned in 1966 and was succeeded by Stephen Arlen (1966–72). Lord Harewood was appointed in April 1972. Charles Mackerras has been music director since 1970. At the Coliseum the company has introduced a number of productions of an adventurous theatrical nature, such as Berlioz's *Damnation de Faust*, and added to its superb *Meistersinger* several stages of a highly successful *Ring* in English.

Sainete. A kind of Spanish comic opera with scenes from low life.

Saint of Bleecker Street, The. Opera in 3 acts by Menotti; text by composer. Prod. N.Y., Broadway Theatre, 27 Dec. 1954; Milan, Sc., 8 May 1955; London, B.B.C. Television, 4 Oct. 1956.

St. Petersburg. See *Leningrad*.

Saint-Saëns, Camille (b. Paris, 9 Oct. 1835; d. Algiers, 16 Dec. 1921). French composer. In his long list of works there figure 12 operas, of which *Samson et Dalila* (1877) is the only outstanding example. Here Saint-Saëns's unfailing craftsmanship and fluency are supplemented by a genuine sense of characterization for the two principals and, if not a very potent dramatic flair, the ability to create a unique and consistent emotional world. It was, no doubt, these qualities which led Liszt to secure it for production at Weimar. His last three operas were written for Monte Carlo.

Salammbô. Opera in 5 acts by Reyer; text by Camille du Locle, after Flaubert's novel. Prod. Brussels, La M., 10 Feb. 1890, with Rose Caron, Renaud. New Orleans, 25 Jan. 1900; N.Y., Met., 20 Mar. 1901, with Bréval, Saléza, Salignac, Journet. Matho has stolen a sacred veil from the shrine of the Carthaginian goddess Tamit. He is condemned to die at the hands of Salammbô, who has fallen in love with him. She kills herself in his place, and Matho stabs himself. Also operas by Massa (1886), Fornaris, and Hauer; project (*c.* 1860) by Mussorgsky.

Salce, salce. Desdemona's (sop.) Willow Song in the last act of Verdi's *Otello*. (R)

Saléza, Albert (b. Bruges, Basses-Pyrénées, 28 Oct. 1867; d. Paris, 26 Nov. 1916). French tenor. Studied Paris Conservatoire. Début Paris, O.C., 1888, Mylio (*Le Roi d'Ys*). Sang with great success in Paris, Brussels, where he created Matho (*Salammbô*); Monte Carlo; Nice, where he was Aeneas in *La Prise de Troie*; London, C.G., 1898–1902; N.Y., Met., 1899–1901. His Roméo and Faust were compared with Jean de Reske's; also a fine Don José and Otello. (R)

Salieri, Antonio (b. Legnano, 18 Aug. 1750; d Vienna, 7 May 1825). Italian composer. His operas, some 40 in number, are entirely forgotten, and he himself is remembered chiefly for his hindrance of Mozart's career (though the allegation of poisoning now survives only in Rimsky-Korsakov's opera *Mozart and Salieri*). But he was admired by Gluck, Haydn, Beethoven, Schubert, and Liszt (the last three were his pupils), and his music was widely performed, finding enthusiastic audiences in Italy and also in Paris and Vienna, where he settled. His most ambitious and original opera was *Tarare* (1787), to a text by Beaumarchais, who contributed a lively preface on the principles of opera.

Salignac, Thomas (b. Générac, Gard, 19 Mar. 1867; d. Paris, 1945). French tenor. Studied Marseilles and Paris. Début Paris, O.C., 1893. N.Y., Met., 1896–1903; London, C.G., 1897–99, 1901–4. From 1905 to 1913 he was again at the O.C., creating numerous roles in French operas by Laparra, Milhaud, and Massenet. Created title role in *Mârouf*, Brussels 1918. He was director of the Nice Opéra 1914, and of a French *opéra comique* company that toured Canada and the U.S.A. 1926. Professor of singing Fontainebleau 1923, of elecution Paris Conservatoire 1924. Founded the periodical *Lyrica* 1922; organized the Congrès du Chant 1925, and singing competitions in 1933 and 1937. (R)

Salmhofer, Franz (b. Vienna, 22 Jan. 1900). Austrian conductor and composer. A descendant of Schubert on his mother's side, he studied in Vienna with Schreker and Schmidt. Cond. Vienna, B., 1929–39; S.O. 1945; director V.O. from 1955. His *Dame im Traum* (1935), *Ivan Tarassenko* (1938, revised 1946), and *Das Werbekleid* (1943) have enjoyed success in Vienna.

Salome. Opera in 1 act by Richard Strauss; text, Oscar Wilde's tragedy (1893) in the German translation of Hedwig Lachmann. Prod. Dresden, Court, 9 Dec. 1905, with Wittich, Burrian, Perron, cond. Schuch; N.Y., Met.,

22 Jan. 1907, with Fremstad, Burrian, Van Rooy, cond. Hertz; London, C.G., 8 Dec. 1910, with Ackté, E. Krauss, Whitehill, cond. Beecham. During a banquet Jochanaan (John the Baptist) (bar.) proclaims—from the cistern where he is imprisoned—the coming of the Messiah. He is brought out for Salome (sop.) to see, and repels her fascinated advances; he urges her not to follow the ways of her mother Herodias (mezzo.). He is taken back to the cistern. Herod (ten.) asks Salome to dance; she agrees on condition that he will grant her a wish. After her Dance of the Seven Veils she demands the head of Jochanaan, which Herod is forced to have brought to her. She fondles and kisses it until the revolted Herod orders his soldiers to crush her with their shields.

Saltzmann-Stevens, Minnie (b. Bloomington, Ill., 17 Mar. 1874; d. Milan, 25 Jan. 1950). American soprano. Studied Paris with J. de Reszke. Début London, C.G., 1909 Brünnhilde in English *Ring*, and heard in other Wagner roles 1910–13; Bayreuth 1911–13, Sieglinde and Kundry; also appeared in Berlin and Frankfurt and finally Chicago. Her highly promising career came to a premature end during the First World War through illness. (R)

Salut, demeure. Faust's (ten.) apostrophe to Marguerite's home in Act 2 of Gounod's *Faust*.

Salzburg. Town in Austria. Birthplace of Mozart and venue of an annual summer festival. The first Mozart festivals were held between 1877 and 1910 and included concerts and operas under Richter, Mottl, Mahler, Strauss, Muck, and Schalk. In 1917 the Salzburg Festspielhausgemeinde was formed with Hofmannsthal, Reinhardt, Schalk, and Strauss as artistic directors. In 1921 several operas were performed in the Landestheater. In 1926 the old riding school was converted into a theatre, and the following year the Festspielhaus was opened. Clemens Krauss, Strauss, and Bruno Walter were the principal conductors and the singers included the best of the Vienna and Munich Opera ensembles and several guest artists. Mozart and Strauss filled most of the repertory, with an occasional *Fidelio* and a work by Gluck or Weber. Toscanini conducted *Falstaff*, *Fidelio*, *Meistersinger*, and *Zauberflöte* between 1935 and 1937. After the *Anschluss* Toscanini and Walter were replaced by Furtwängler, Karl Böhm, and Gui. Strauss's *Liebe der Danae* was planned for 1944 but was only given a public dress rehearsal, waiting until 1952 for its Salzburg production. The Festival was resumed in 1946 and has included premières of *Dantons Tod* (Einem, 1947), *Antigonae* (Orff 1949), *Romeo und Julia* (Blacher 1950), *Der Prozess* (Einem, 1953), *Penelope* (Liebermann 1954), *Irische Legende* (Egk 1955), *Julietta* (Erbse 1959), and the European premières of *The School for Wives* (1957) and *Vanessa* (1958). Herbert von Karajan was artistic director of the festival, 1957–60 and from 1964. In 1960 the new Festspielhaus, which had cost almost three and a half million pounds to build, was opened. It adjoins the old Festspielhaus, and seats 2,160. The stage, the largest in the world, is 135 feet wide, 120 feet high, and 70 feet deep, and in order to accommodate it, a large part of the 160-foot-high Möchsberg, in the rear of the theatre, had to be blasted out to a depth of 50 feet. The architect was Clemens Holzmeister. An Easter Festival, under the musical and artistic direction of Herbert von Karajan, was inaugurated in 1966, since when there have been outstanding productions of the *Ring*, *Fidelio*, and *Tristan und Isolde*.

Sammarco, Mario (b. Palermo, 13 Dec. 1868; d. Milan, 24 Jan. 1930). Italian baritone. Studied Palermo and Milan. Début Palermo 1888, Valentine. Scala and other Italian houses from 1896; London, C.G., 1904, Scarpia, and then regularly until 1914, and in 1919; N.Y., Manhattan, 1908–10; Philadelphia–Chicago 1911–12. Created Gérard, Cascart (*Zazà*), Worms (*Germania*) in Italy, Alvardo in Herbert's *Natoma* and Don Fulgenzio in Parelli's *The Lovers' Quarrel* in Philadelphia; and was the first C.G. Alec (*Tess*), Conte Gil (*Segreto di*

Susanna), Raffaele (*Gioielli della Madonna*), and Zamor in Camussi's *Dubarry*. He had a voice of great beauty and evenness, covering a range of two octaves. (R)

Samson et Dalila. Opera in 3 acts by Saint-Saëns; text by Lemaire. Prod. Weimar (in German) 2 Dec. 1877, with Müller and Ferenczy; N.Y., 25 Mar. 1892 (concert performance); London, C.G., 25 Sept. 1893 (concert version), 26 Apr. 1909, with Kirkby Lunn and Fontaine. First performance in France did not take place until 3 Mar. 1890 at Rouen, Paris seven months later. The opera tells the biblical story of the betrayal of the Hebrew hero Samson to the Philistines by the temptress Delilah. Also operas by Graupner (1709) and Tuczek (1804).

San Carlo, Naples, Teatro di. Built in 270 days to replace the old St. Bartholomew Theatre, the San Carlo was opened on 4 Nov. 1737 with Sarro's *Achille in Sciro*. The first building was enlarged in 1777 and again in 1812 and was destroyed by fire in Feb. 1816; it was the scene of the production of many works by the Neapolitan school of composers—Pergolesi, Piccinni, Paisiello, Scarlatti, Cimarosa, Jommelli, and Spontini. It was also a 'singers' theatre', where vocal gymnastics and rivalry between the artists were the rule rather than the exception. The behaviour of its audience is said to have been the worst in Italy—as the noise on the stage rose so did that in the auditorium. In 1810 Domenico Barbaia (q.v.) became the theatre's manager and soon after commissioned Rossini to write for the San Carlo and invited him to become music director of the smaller Teatro del Fondo. The operas Rossini wrote for Naples included *Elisabetta Regina d'Inghilterra*, *Mosè*, *Otello*, *Armida*, *La Donna del Lago*, and *Maometto II*. Barbaia also discovered and encouraged Bellini and Donizetti: the former's *Bianca e Fernando* was staged in 1826 and the latter's *Lucia di Lammermoor* in 1835. Verdi's relations with the San Carlo were not of the happiest, with the failures there of his *Oberto* and *Alzira*, and censorship troubles which resulted in *La Traviata* being given as *Violetta*, *Rigoletto* as *Clara di Pert* and later *Lionello*, and *Les Vêpres Siciliennes* as *Batilde di Turenna* and *Giovanna di Sicilia*. His *Attila* and *Luisa Miller* received successful premières there.

The present theatre (cap. 3,500) was designed by Nicolini and built in 1816 in six months. It underwent extensive alterations in 1844. In 1929 the stage was modernized and a new foyer added. An air-raid in 1943 caused some destruction in the theatre but not enough to interrupt opera. The theatre came under the management of the British forces during the Allied occupation, and became the most popular opera house among the Allied troops, so much so that the San Carlo Company was invited to give the first opera performances at Covent Garden after the war in the autumn of 1946. Since then the theatre, under the direction of Pasquale di Costanzo, has pursued an adventurous artistic policy and enjoys a reputation in Italy second to that of La Scala. Modern works that have been produced at the San Carlo in recent years include Honegger's *Judith*, Hindemith's *Neues vom Tage*, Berg's *Wozzeck*, Henze's *Boulevard Solitude*, Prokofiev's *Duenna*, and Bloch's *Macbeth*.

Performances of chamber operas are given in the Teatro della Corte, in the adjoining Royal Palace; and summer open-air performances are given at the Arena Flegrea.

San Carlo (Touring) Company, U.S.A. A company founded in 1909 (disbanded 1955) by the impresario Fortune Gallo which gave popular-priced opera throughout America. There were seasons in New York and Chicago as well as in smaller cities. Its repertory was a popular one. Many of its singers later became famous, including Jean Madeira, Dorothy Kirsten, Eugene Conley, and the conductor Rescigno. In addition many famous singers have appeared with the ensemble as guest artists.

Sanderson, Sybil (b. Sacramento, 7 Dec. 1865; d. Paris, 15 May 1903). American soprano. Studied Paris Conservatoire with Marchesi and Sbriglia Début The Hague 1888, Manon (as Ada Palmer). Charmed by her voice, Massenet wrote *Esclarmonde* and *Thaïs* for her; and Saint-Saëns composed *Phryné* for her. Neither in London (C.G. 1891) nor N.Y. (Met. 1894–5 and 1901–2) did she repeat her Paris successes. Her voice ranged from g to g'''. Her personal beauty and dramatic talent were not the least of her attractions.

San Francisco. Town in California, U.S.A. Opera was first given in 1852 —*La Sonnambula* by a travelling troupe. The present San Francisco Opera Company is generally considered the second in the U.S.A. after the Met. Founded in 1923 by Gaetano Merola, who continued as director until his death in 1953. He was succeeded by the present director, Kurt Herbert Adler. Performances were originally given in the Civic Auditorium, but in 1932 the company found a permanent home in the War Memorial Opera House (cap. 3,252) which opened on 15 Oct. that year with *Tosca* (Muzio, D. Borgioli, Gandolfi). During the Merola régime a mostly popular repertory was given with the emphasis on the Italian works sung by leading singers, often from the Met., including Muzio, Bori, Pons, Rethberg, Gigli, Lauri-Volpi, Martinelli, and Pinza. German operas enjoyed a better showing in the 1930's with Flagstad, Melchior, Schorr, List, and others. Several artists went to the Met. after successful San Francisco débuts, including Mafalda Favero, Jarmila Novotná, Baccaloni, Svanholm, Tebaldi, Del Monaco, Borkh, and Rysanek. Other singers—Jurinac, Schwarzkopf, Taddei, Geraint Evans, Richard Lewis—have sung in San Francisco but never at the Met. In recent years San Francisco has staged the American premières of *Jeanne d'Arc au Bucher*, *Frau ohne Schatten*, *Dialogues des Carmélites*, *Troilus and Cressida*, and *A Midsummer Night's Dream*. After the San Francisco season the company performs at the Shrine Auditorium in Los Angeles. A history of the Company by Arthur J. Bloomfield was published in 1961.

Santini, Gabriele (b. Perugia, 20 Jan. 1886; d. Rome, 13 Nov. 1964). Italian conductor. Début 1906. Assistant to Toscanini at Sc., Milan, 1925–9; Rome, Opera, 1929–32, and since 1944 where he was music director until 1962. Has also conducted in Buenos Aires, Chicago, and London. (R)

Santley, Charles (Sir) (b. Liverpool, 28 Feb. 1834; d. London, 22 Sept. 1922). English baritone. Studied Milan with Nava, London with Garcia. Début Pavia 1857, Dr. Grenvil (*Traviata*); London, C.G., 1859, Hoël (*Dinorah*) in Pyne-Harrison English season; joined Mapleson's company 1862; first English Valentine 1863, pleasing Gounod so much that he composed 'Even bravest heart' for the following year's revival. Sang title role in *Der fliegende Holländer* in first London production of any Wagner opera. Joined company of Gaiety Theatre 1870, when heard in *Zampa*, *Zar und Zimmermann*, *Fra Diavolo*; Carl Rosa 1875–6. Also sang in America, Milan, Sc., and Barcelona. Knighted 1907; farewell at C.G. 23 May 1911 in Dibdin's *The Waterman*. Though not gifted with a beautiful voice, he sang with great expression and was especially effective in dramatic roles. Autobiography, *Reminiscences of My Life* (1909). (R)

Sanzogno, Nino (b. Venice, 13 Apr. 1911). Italian conductor and composer. Studied with Malipiero and Scherchen. Has conducted at Milan, Sc., since 1941, where he has been associated with modern works including *Arlecchino*, *Oedipus Rex*, *Le Pauvre Matelot*, *The Consul*, *David*, *Troilus and Cressida*, *The Fiery Angel*, and *Dialogues des Carmélites*. He also has a great affection for Scarlatti, Cherubini, Piccinni, Paisiello, Cimarosa, and Donizetti, and has conducted their works at La Piccola Scala. He conducted the opening performance there in 1955, and appeared with the company at Edinburgh in 1957. Appointed permanent conductor at Sc., 1962. (R)

São Paulo. See *Brazil*.

Sarajevo. Town in Bosnia–Hercegovina, Yugoslavia. Occasional performances after Austrian annexation of Bosnia 1878. First theatre with opera and operetta, 1921 (see *Split*). Company formed 1930; theatre opened in Banja Luka. Opera reorganized 1946.

Sarastro. The priest of Isis (bass) in Mozart's *Die Zauberflöte*.

Sardou, Victorien (b. Paris, 7 Sept. 1831; d. Paris, 8 Nov. 1908). French playwright. His works provided librettos for many composers, including Bizet (*Grisélidis* 1870–1, unperf.), Giordano (*Fedora* 1898; *Madame Sans-Gêne* 1915), and, best known of all, Puccini (*Tosca* 1900).

Sargent, Malcolm (Sir) (b. Stamford, 29 Apr. 1895; d. London, 3 Oct. 1967). English conductor. Although primarily a concert conductor, Sargent worked with the B.N.O.C., directing the first performances of *Hugh the Drover* and *At the Boar's Head* in 1924. D'Oyly Carte Company 1926–8, 1951; C.G. 1936, *Louise*; première of *Troilus and Cressida*, C.G., 1954. (R)

Sarti, Giuseppe (b. Faenza, bapt. 1 Dec. 1729; d. Berlin, 28 July 1802). Italian composer. His fame spread so early that at 24 he was invited to Denmark as director of opera. He did not finally return to Italy for over 20 years, and then after a brilliant nine years he left for St. Petersburg. Here collaborated in one of the earliest Russian operas, *The Early Reign of Oleg* (1790), to text by the Empress Catherine II who had appointed him. Founded a school of singing in the Ukraine, and later became head of St. Petersburg Conservatory. Died *en route* for Italy after 18 years in Russia. Sarti's operas are forgotten now, apart from the single air 'Come un agnello' from *Fra Due Litiganti*, which Mozart made Don Giovanni's private band play. Some 75 in number, they are well written for voices and have a certain stage flair.

Sass (orig. Saxe), **Marie** (b. Ghent, 26 Jan. 1838; d. Auteuil, nr. Paris, 8 Nov. 1907). Belgian soprano. Studied Paris; début Paris, T.-L., 1859; Paris, O., from 1860, where she was the Elisabeth in the disastrous Paris première of *Tannhäuser* (1861). Created Selika in *L'Africaine* and Élisabeth de Valois in *Don Carlos*. Married the bass Castelmary 1864; separated 1867. Died in great poverty.

Satie, Erik (b. Honfleur, 17 May 1866; d. Paris, 1 July 1925). French composer. His stage works include a puppet operetta *Geneviève de Brabant* (1899) and two operettas, *Pousse-l'Amour* (1905) and *Le Piège de Méduse* (1913).

Sauguet, Henri (b. Bordeaux, 18 May 1901). French composer. The most substantial of his five operas is a 4-act setting of *La Chartreuse de Parme* (1939), for which he composed music more substantial than that in his usual smart metropolitan style and tackled a large subject with the devotion it demands. His dextrous and eminently civilized *Les Caprices de Marianne* was prod. Aix-en-Provence 1954.

Savage, Henry (b. New Durham, 21 Mar. 1859; d. Boston, 29 Nov. 1927). American impresario. Originally a dealer in real estate, he was forced to take over the Castle Square Theatre, Boston, when a lessee failed in 1897. He proved a successful manager, and in 1900 collaborated with Grau in forming the English Grand Opera Company. In 1904–5 he presented *Parsifal* in English throughout the U.S.A., and in 1906–7 and 1911 he made similar tours with Puccini's *Madama Butterfly* and *La Fanciulla del West*.

Sāvitri. Opera in 1 act by Holst; text by composer, after an episode in the *Mahabharata*. Prod. London, Wellington Hall, 5 Dec. 1916; Chicago 23 Jan. 1934. Sāvitri (sop.) uses love and cunning to outwit Death (bass) who has come for her husband, the wood-cutter Satyavan (ten.).

Sawallisch, Wolfgang (b. Munich, 26 Aug. 1923). German conductor. Début Augsburg 1947, remaining there until 1953, progressing from *répétiteur* to first Kapellmeister. Generalmusikdirektor Aachen 1953–7; Wiesbaden 1957–9; Cologne 1959–63. Bayreuth 1957–61, where he cond. new productions of *Tristan* (1957), *Holländer* (1959), and *Tannhäuser* (1961). In 1971 he became Generalmusikdirektor of the Bavarian State Opera, Munich. (R)

Sayão, Bidu (orig. Baldwin de Oliveira) (b. Rio de Janeiro, 11 May 1902). Brazilian soprano. Studied Nice with Jean de Reszke. Début Rome, Costanzi, 1926, Rosina. After engagements in Paris, Milan, Naples, and Buenos Aires she went to the Met., N.Y., 1937–51, where her best roles included Manon, Juliette, Mélisande, Mimì, and Zerlina. Farewell performances Rio 1958. Married the baritone **Giuseppe Danise** (1883–1963). (R)

Sbriglia, Giovanni (b. Naples, 23 June 1832; d. Paris, 20 Feb. 1916). Italian tenor and teacher. Début Naples, S.C., 1853; N.Y. 1860, with Patti. Settled in Paris in 1875 as teacher. Pupils include the De Reszkes, Nordica, Plançon, and Sybil Sanderson.

Scala, Teatro alla. See *La Scala*.

Scala di Seta, La (The Silken Ladder). Opera in 1 act by Rossini; text by Rossi, after Planard's libretto. Prod. Venice, S. Moise, 9 May 1812. London, S.W., 26 Apr. 1954 by Teatro dell'Opera Comica, Rome. Previously set by Gaveaux 1808. The silken ladder of the title is used nightly by Dorvil to rejoin his wife Giulia, whom he has secretly married, but who is living in the house of her father Dormont.

Scalchi, Sofia (b. Turin, 29 Nov. 1850; d. Rome, 22 Aug. 1922). Italian mezzo-soprano. Début Mantua 1866, Ulrica. London, C.G., 1868, Azucena, regularly until 1890. N.Y., Met., 1883 (Siebel at opening of theatre) and 1891–6, where she was the first American Mistress Quickly, La Cieca, and Emilia. Although she spent more than 20 years at C.G., she created no important roles there; heard as Amneris, Arsace, Urbaine, &c. Her voice was of great volume and ranged from f to b♭'', with an amazing command of coloratura that enabled her to sing soprano cadenzas. It was very uneven, however: she was said to have four registers.

Scaria, Emil (b. Graz, 18 Sept. 1838; d. Blasewitz, nr. Dresden, 22 July 1886). Austrian bass. Studied Graz, Vienna, and London with Garcia. Début Pest 1860, St. Bris (*Huguenots*). Leipzig 1863–5; Dresden 1865–72; Vienna 1872–86. Created Gurnemanz (1882) and was also a notable Wotan, of which he was the first interpreter in London at H.M.'s 1882. He died insane.

Scarlatti, Alessandro (b. Palermo, 2 May 1660; d. Naples, 24 Oct. 1725). Italian composer. His first opera, *Gli Equivoci nel Sembiante*, produced at Rome when he was 19, won him the patronage of Queen Christina of Sweden and the encouragement to follow up his success. From 1702 he composed several operas for Ferdinando de' Medici in Florence; but he was dropped by the prince in the year in which he wrote his finest work, *Mitridate Eupatore* (1707). He was now at the height of his fame in Naples, where the major part of his career was spent; a brief period in Rome working for a now no less admiring audience followed before his final return to Naples in 1722 or 1723.

This is the bare outline of the career of one of the great figures of operatic history. Compelled as he was by the conditions of his age to please a long list of princes and bishops, his feat in establishing himself as a father of classicism in music is considerable. Needing a ready mould for music, he firmly established the *da capo* aria and the so-called Italian overture; he also made rich use of accompanied recitative for powerful dramatic effects and established the *secco* recitative conventions. His best work was for Ferdinando de' Medici: *Mitridate Eupatore* is a great classical document. The poetic dignity found here was never quite matched again, but Scarlatti's mastery subsequently allowed a loosening of the *da capo* aria's strictness. His style became less rigidly contrapuntal, more enterprisingly harmonic. Towards the end of Scarlatti's life, Rome caught the passion for opera so wholeheartedly as to overcome ecclesiastical objections and provide an audience capable of appreciating the master in its midst. Scarlatti had now rallied all his powers, and the works of this last period show both brilliance and emotional depth expressed with a complete technical resource. Only one of his 70-odd surviving operas (the total was 115) is wholly comic, *Il Trionfo dell' Onore* (1718); and even this succeeds chiefly in the scenes where Scarlatti was guying what he understood best—heroic figures in tragic predicaments. He has inevitably been more revered by musicologists than by music-lovers, for whom opportunities of seeing his operas are very rare; he has also been reproached with categorizing forms too firmly and so playing into the hands of singers and their embellishments. His best work shows a dignity of invention as well as a logical mastery of musical means that justify his lofty reputation. His son **Domenico** (b. Naples, 26 Oct. 1685; d. Madrid, 23 July 1757) is remembered now as a great keyboard composer, though he began his career in opera. In 1709, after various travels and studies, Domenico became composer to Queen Maria Casimira of Poland's court in Rome, for which he wrote seven operas.

Scarpia. The corrupt police chief (bar.) in Puccini's *Tosca*.

Scena (from Gr. σκηνή = stage). A solo operatic movement of primarily dramatic purpose, less lyrical or formally composed than an aria, to which it may nevertheless approximate in some of its greatest examples, e.g. Leonore's 'Abscheulicher' in Beethoven's *Fidelio*.

Schack (orig. Žak), **Benedikt** (b. Mirovice, 1758; d. Munich, 11 Dec. 1826). Bohemian-German tenor and composer. Début Schikaneder's company, in Paisiello's *La Frascatana* (1786); first Tamino (30 Sept. 1791, when his wife sang one of the Three Ladies and he himself played the eponymous flute); first to sing Don Ottavio and Almaviva in German (5 Nov. and 28 Dec. 1792); said to be one of the singers of the unfinished Requiem to Mozart on his death-bed. He also wrote five operas.

Schalk, Franz (b. Vienna, 27 May 1863; d. Edlach, 2 Sept. 1931). Austrian conductor. Studied with Bruckner. Début Liberec 1888; Graz 1889–95; Prague 1895–8; Berlin 1899–1900; Vienna from 1900, where he succeeded Gregor as director in 1918, and shared first conductorship with Strauss 1919–24, when differences arose between them and Strauss resigned, leaving Schalk in control until his death. One of the founders of the Salzburg Festival. London, C.G., 1898, 1907, and 1911, when he conducted the English première of *Königskinder* and three highly successful *Ring* cycles. N.Y., Met., 1898–9. (R)

Schauspieldirektor, Der (The Impresario). *Komödie mit Musik* in 1 act by Mozart; text by Gottlieb Stephanie, jun. Prod. Vienna, Schönbrunn Palace, 7 Feb. 1786; London, St. James's, 30 May 1857; N.Y. 9 Nov. 1870. The plot describes the rivalry of two prima donnas after the same part.

Scheff, Fritzi (orig. Anna Yager) (b. Vienna, 30 Aug. 1879; d. New York, 8 Apr. 1954). Austrian soprano. Daughter of the sop. Hortense, with whom she studied and whose name she eventually took, having first appeared in public as Fritzi Yager. Further study Frankfurt; début there, Juliette, 1897. Munich 1898–1900; London, C.G., 1900–3, where her Zerlina, Musetta, and Nedda were much admired, and N.Y., Met., 1900–3, where she was heard as Elsa and Asa in Paderewski's *Manru*, earning the nickname of the 'Little Devil of the Opera' from the composer. Turned to operetta and musical comedy, starring on Broadway in *Boccaccio*, *Giroflé-Girofla*, *Mlle Modiste*, then in straight plays, notably *Arsenic and Old Lace*. (R)

Scheidemantel, Karl (b. Weimar, 21 Jan. 1859; d. Weimar, 26 June 1923). German baritone. Studied with Borchers and Stockhausen. Début Weimar 1878, Wolfram, and sang there until 1886; Dresden 1886–1911; Bayreuth 1886–92 as Amfortas, Sachs, Wolfram; London, C.G., 1884 as

Kurwenal and Rucello in Stanford's *Savonarola*, 1899 as Sachs. In Dresden created Urok in Paderewski's *Manru*, Kunrad in *Guntram*, and Faninal. 1911–20 taught in Weimar; from 1920 to 1922 director, Dresden Landesoper. Produced a new text for *Così fan tutte* 1909 under the title of *Dame Kobold*, and his translation of *Don Giovanni* (1914) won the prize of the Deutscher Bühnenverein. Two books on singing, *Stimmbildung* (1907) and *Gesangbildung* (1913). (R)

Scherchen, Hermann (b. Berlin, 21 Jun. 1891; d. Florence, 12 Jun. 1966). German conductor. Originally viola player in Berlin Philharmonic, he made his conducting début in 1911, collaborating with Schoenberg. Although primarily a symphonic conductor he has made a number of appearances in the opera house, generally conducting contemporary works, of which he is a great champion: premières of Dallapiccola's *Il Prigioniero*, Florence 1950; Dessau's *Das Verhör des Lukullus*, Berlin 1951; Henze's *König Hirsch*, Berlin 1956; performances of *Von Heute auf Morgen*, *Salome*, Prokofiev's *The Gambler* at Naples, and *Mavra*, *Hin und Zurück* and Blacher's *Abstracte Oper No. 1* in Berlin. Adapted Webern's second cantata for the stage, and conducted its première in Naples 1958 as *Il Cuore*. (R)

Scherman, Thomas (b. New York, 12 Feb. 1917). American conductor. Studied Columbia University, and conducting with Carl Bamberger and Max Rudolph. Début Mexico National Opera 1947; in same year organized New York Little Orchestra Society, which has given many important concert performances of opera including *Ariadne auf Naxos*, *L'Enfant et les Sortilèges*, *Goyescas*, and *Iphigénie en Tauride*. (R)

Schikaneder, Emanuel (orig., Johann Schikeneder) (b. Straubing, 1 Sept. 1751; d. Vienna, 21 Sept. 1812). German theatre manager, singer, actor, and playwright. After an early life as a wandering musician he became manager of the Kärntnertor Theatre in Vienna, where he also made appearances. He took over the theatre at Regensburg briefly before returning to manage a small Viennese theatre in the suburb of Wieden. It was for this that Mozart set Schikaneder's libretto *Die Zauberflöte*; the success of the opera, with Schikaneder as Papageno at the première (30 Sept. 1791), made the fortunes of the venture. In 1800 he partnered a merchant in opening the Theater an der Wien, near the Theater auf der Wieden, and continued as manager until 1806. Composers who set his librettos, apart from himself, included Schack (the first Tamino), Süssmayr, Paisiello, Seyfried, and Winter; *Vestas Feuer* (1805), intended for and begun by Beethoven, was set by Weigl.

Schiller, Friedrich von (b. Marbach, 10 Nov. 1759; d. Weimar, 9 May 1805). German poet and playwright. Operas on his works are as follows. *Die Räuber* (1782): Mercadante (1836); Verdi (*I Masnadieri* 1847); Zajc (*Amelia* 1860); Klebe (1957). *Fiesco* (1783): Lalo (1866, unperf.). *Kabale und Liebe* (1783): Verdi (*Luisa Miller* 1849). *Don Carlos* (1784–7): M. Costa (1844); Verdi (1867). *Taucher* (1797–8): J. F. Reichardt (1811). *Die Bürgschaft* (1798): Schubert (1816, unfin.); Lachner (1828); G. Hellmesberger (1851, unperf.). *Wallenstein* (1798–9): Adelburg (?); Denza (1876); Weinberger (1937). *Das Lied von der Glocke* (1799): D'Indy (1912). *Die Jungfrau von Orleans* (Joan of Arc) (1801): Vaccai (1827); Balfe (1837); Vesque von Püttlingen (1840); Verdi (1845); Tchaikovsky (1881); Rezniček (1886). *Die Braut von Messina* (1803): Vaccai (1839); Fibich (1884). *Wilhelm Tell* (1804): Carr (*The Archers*, 1796); Rossini (1829).

Schillings, Max von (b. Düren, 19 Apr. 1868; d. Berlin, 24 July 1933). German composer, conductor, and manager. Studied Bonn and Munich where he came under the influence of Strauss. Assistant stage director, Bayreuth 1892, and chorus master there 1902. Stuttgart 1908–18, first as assistant to Intendant, then conductor, and from 1911 Generalmusikdirektor, being ennobled by the King of

Württemberg when the new Stuttgart Opera opened 1912; Intendant, Berlin 1919–25. U.S.A. 1924 and 1931 with German Opera Company. Married the soprano **Barbara Kemp** (q.v.) 1923, who had created the title role in his *Mona Lisa* (1915), the only one of his four operas to achieve any success. (R)

Schipa, Tito (b. Lecce, 2 Jan. 1888; d. N.Y., 16 Dec. 1965). Italian tenor. Began career as composer studying singing later with Piccoli in Milan. Début Vercelli 1911, Alfredo; after appearances in the Italian provinces, engaged Rome 1914 and Buenos Aires. Milan, Sc., 1915, and in same year chosen by Toscanini for his season at Dal Verme, Milan, singing Alfredo and Fenton. Created Ruggero in Puccini's *La Rondine*, Monte Carlo, 1917. Chicago Opera 1920–32 and subsequently; N.Y., Met., 1932–5 and 1940–1; San Francisco from 1924. Continued to appear at La Scala, Rome, &c., until 1950, and later in the Italian provinces. Never appeared in opera in England. He possessed a magnificent vocal technique and impeccable taste and style. His voice, which was not large, commanded a wide range of tone colour; his phrasing was aristocratic, his enunciation model. Gigli said of him, 'When Schipa sang we all had to bow down to his greatness.' His memoirs were published in 1962. (R)

Schipper, Emil (b. Vienna, 1882; d. Vienna, 20 July 1957). Austrian bass-baritone. Studied Vienna. Début Prague 1904, Telramund. Munich 1916–22, creating Borromeo (*Palestrina*); Vienna 1922–40; London, C.G., 1924–8; Chicago 1928–9. Also appeared at Salzburg and Munich Festivals and in South America. Excelled in Wagner and Strauss. (R)

Schippers, Thomas (b. Kalamazoo, 9 Mar. 1930). American conductor. Studied Curtis Institute, Philadelphia, and with Olga Samaroff. Début N.Y. 1948 with Lemonade Company. Conducted première of *The Consul* (1950) and has become associated with Menotti, also conducting his *Amahl and the Night Visitors*, *The Saint of Bleecker Street*, and at the Festival of Two Worlds, Spoleto. N.Y., Met., since 1955. (R)

Schira, Francesco (b. Malta, 21 Aug. 1809; d. London, 15 Oct. 1883). Italian composer and conductor. After early successes with operas in Milan and Lisbon, became music director at the Princess's in London. Succeeded Benedict at D.L. 1844–7; cond. C.G. 1848; D.L. 1852. The good reception given his operas in London was far exceeded by the success of *Selvaggia* in Venice (1875).

Schlusnus, Heinrich (b. Braubach, 6 Aug. 1888; d. Frankfurt, 18 June 1952). German baritone. Studied Frankfurt and Berlin. Début Hamburg 1915, Herald (*Lohengrin*), Nuremberg 1915–16; Berlin State Opera 1917–51; Chicago 1927–8; Bayreuth 1933. In Germany he established himself as the leading Verdi baritone in the years between the wars. (R)

Schmedes, Erik (b. Gjentofte, nr. Copenhagen, 27 Aug. 1866; d. Vienna, 23 Mar. 1931). Danish tenor, formerly baritone. Studied in Paris with Artôt. Début Wiesbaden 1891, Herald (*Lohengrin*). Dresden as baritone 1894–7, then further study with Iffert. Début as tenor Vienna 1898, Siegfried. Vienna 1898–1924; Bayreuth 1899–1902, Parsifal and Siegfried. N.Y., Met., 1908–9. One of the great singers of the Mahler period in Vienna; an admired Florestan and Palestrina. (R)

Schmidt-Isserstedt, Hans (b. Berlin, 5 May 1900). German conductor. Studied with Schreker. After appointments in Barmen-Elberfeld, Rostock, and Darmstadt, engaged Hamburg 1935 as first Kapellmeister. Berlin, Deutsches Opernhaus, 1943. Glyndebourne 1958; London, C.G., 1962. (R)

Schnorr von Carolsfeld, Ludwig (b. Munich, 2 July 1836; d. Dresden, 21 July 1865). German tenor, son of the painter Julius Schnorr von Carolsfeld. Studied Dresden, Leipzig, and Karlsruhe with Eduard Devrient, where he made his début 1858. After engagements at Wiesbaden, Frankfurt, Maiz, and Düsseldorf, became leading tenor at Dresden 1860–5. Wagner, who had heard him sing Lohengrin, insisted on his creating Tristan, Munich 1865. Died shortly afterwards of rheumatic fever and heart failure.

Schnorr von Carolsfeld (orig. Garrigues), **Malvina** (b. Copenhagen, 7 Dec. 1832; d. Karlsruhe, 8 Feb. 1904). Danish soprano. Wife of above. Created Isolde opposite her husband. After his death sang in Hamburg and Karlsruhe, then taught.

Schoeck, Othmar (b. Brunnen, 1 Sept. 1886; d. Zürich, 8 Mar. 1957). Swiss composer. His sensitivity to poetry and love of the human voice led him to express himself most fully in song and in opera. Some early stage works included a comic opera *Don Ranudo* (1919), and this period culminated in *Venus* (1919). Turning away from his first romantic manner, he purged and refashioned his style to suit what he felt to be modern requirements; his success is shown in *Penthesilea* (1927), regarded as the peak of his achievement. Two later operas, *Massimilla Doni* (1937) and *Das Schloss Dürande* (1943), have also won wide respect.

Schoeffler, Paul (b. Dresden, 15 Sept. 1897). German, later Austrian, baritone. Studied Dresden with Staegemann, Berlin with Grenzebach, Milan with Sammarco. Début Dresden 1925, Herald (*Lohengrin*), remaining there until 1937; Vienna since 1937. London, C.G., 1934–9 and 1949–53; N.Y., Met., 1949–53 and 1954–6. Has also appeared at Bayreuth, Salzburg, and in Italy. Starting his career as a lyric baritone, he graduated into the Wagner repertory, coming to be regarded as an outstanding post-war Hans Sachs. Among the roles he created were Danton in Einem's *Dantons Tod* and Jupiter in *Liebe der Danae*. Also appeared in the first Salzburg performance of *Capriccio* as La Roche. (R)

Schoenberg, Arnold (b. Vienna, 13 Sept. 1874; d. Los Angeles, 13 July 1951). Austrian composer. Schoenberg's four operas cover the major part of his creative life. *Erwartung* (1909, prod. 1924) was one of the first works in which tonality was definitely abandoned; *Von Heute auf Morgen* (1930) was the first 12-note opera; *Moses und Aron* (two acts finished 1932, resumed 1951; prod. 1957) was left unfinished by the composer, though the extant two acts have proved complete enough to be capable of providing an overwhelming experience in performance. In making use of only one character, a woman, for *Erwartung*, Schoenberg is able to follow with extraordinary depth of penetration the nightmare journey of her mind; there is no characterization (no thematic development), but a full world of the woman's crazing mind is explored. *Die glückliche Hand* (1913, prod. 1924) again uses one character, with mimed parts and a chorus; it concerns the quest for truth of the artist, whose *glückliche Hand* is his individual, specially favoured touch. *Von Heute auf Morgen* belies the suspicion that 12-note comic opera is a contradiction in terms: it is a brilliantly observed comedy of a witty and determined woman keeping hold of her husband—satirical, farcical, yet underpinned with deep understanding and optimism. *Moses und Aron* did not reach the stage until 1957. Schoenberg's largest opera, it is also his fullest expression of the quest theme that absorbed him so deeply. It concerns communication between God and Man, and the distortion suffered by pure truth (received by Moses) when it undergoes exposition (by Aaron) in terms comprehensible to Man. Schoenberg's religious nature and his artist's concern over communication were profoundly touched by this theme, and the opera has by its emotional power done much to overcome prejudices against the composer.

Schöne, Lotte (orig. Charlotte Bodenstein) (b. Vienna, 15 Dec. 1891). Austrian soprano. Studied Vienna. Début Vienna, V.O., 1912, a Bridesmaid in *Freischütz*, and sang there until 1925; Berlin 1925–33. Sang regularly at Salzburg 1922–34, where her best roles included Zerlina, Despina, and

Blondchen. London, C.G., 1927, where she was the first London Liù. Settled in Paris 1933, becoming a French citizen and appearing as guest at O. and O.C. where she sang Mélisande in 1933. (R)

School for Fathers. See *Quatro Rusteghi, I.*

Schorr, Friedrich (b. Nagyvárad, 2 Sept. 1888; d. Farmington, Conn., 14 Aug. 1953). Hungarian, later American, bass-baritone. Studied Vienna, and after singing small roles with the Chicago Opera 1912, made official début at Graz as Wotan, same year. Graz 1914–16; Prague 1916–18; Cologne 1918–23; Berlin 1923–31; N.Y., German Grand Opera Co., 1923; N.Y., Met., 1924–43; London, C.G., 1924–33; Bayreuth 1925–33. Guest appearances at many other leading operatic centres. Considered by many the greatest Wotan of the 1920's and 1930's, and also an outstanding Sachs and Dutchman. In N.Y. sang Daniello in the American première of *Jonny spielt auf* and the title role in *Schwanda.* In his prime his voice was opulent, noble, and dramatic, capable of ravishing beauty in *mezza-voce* passages. (R)

Schramm, Friedrich (b. Frankfurt, 26 Jan. 1900). German producer. Studied law. Stage director, Darmstadt 1921; Breslau 1923; Duisburg 1924; Düsseldorf 1926; Basle 1934 and 1939–50 and again from 1962; Prague 1937. Generalintendant, Wiesbaden 1951–62. Produced the first post-war Wagner performances and *Fidelio*, C.G., 1947–51. His father **Hermann Schramm** (1878–1951) was a well-known German *Spieltenor* who sang David at Bayreuth.

Schreker, Franz (b. Monaco, 23 Mar. 1878; d. Berlin, 21 Mar. 1934). Austrian composer. His first serious opera, *Der ferne Klang* (1912), made a powerful impression on his own generation; Schoenberg quoted passages in his *Harmonielehre*, and Berg, who made the piano score, was influenced by its use of set symphonic forms in *Wozzeck.* Three operas followed swiftly—*Das Spielwerk und die Prinzessin* (1920), *Die Gezeichneten* (1918), which at last won Schreker a wider success, and *Der Schatzgräber* (1920)—establishing Schreker as an *avant-garde* leader. But this position was challenged by the reaction against late romanticism that followed the war, and his later operas were decreasingly well received. His position as director of the Berlin Hochschule (1920–32) was taken from him by the Nazis, and the ensuing sharp decline in his fortunes hastened his death. His best work has real power, and—despite influences as diverse as Wagner and Debussy, Puccini and Strauss—an original if limited and claustrophobic world of its own.

Schröder-Devrient, Wilhelmine (b. Hamburg, 6 Dec. 1804; d. Coburg, 26 Jan. 1860). German soprano. Studied singing with her father, the baritone Friedrich Schröder, who was the first to sing Don Giovanni in German, and drama with her mother Antoinette Sophie Bürger, sometimes known as the German Siddons. Début Vienna 1821, Pamina; the following year sang Agathe under Weber in Vienna, and in 1823 sang Leonore in *Fidelio* in the famous Vienna revival in the presence of Beethoven. Dresden 1823–47, where she married the actor Karl Devrient (divorced 1828). Appeared with success in Paris 1830–2 and London 1832, 1833, and 1837, causing a sensation as Leonore, Donna Anna, and Euryanthe. Was heard by Wagner, and acted as an inspiration to him in his determination to write music drama. Created Adriano (*Rienzi*), Senta, and Venus. She was also famous for her interpretations in Bellini and Gluck, and made her last appearance in the title role of *Iphigénie en Aulide* in 1847. Her voice was extensive in range, but faulty training often resulted in imperfect singing, as well as in the loss of her top notes early in her career. Yet such was her dramatic genius, her artistry, and the sheer force of her personality, that her interpretations are assured of a place in operatic history. She earned for herself the title of 'The Queen of Tears'. Biography by C. Hagemann (Berlin 1904).

She is mentioned many times in Wagner's *Mein Leben*, and his *Über Schauspiel und Sänger* is dedicated to her memory.

Schubert, Franz (b. Vienna, 31 Jan. 1797; d. Vienna, 19 Nov. 1828). Austrian composer. Opera was, with oratorio, almost the only form in which Schubert's genius found itself ill at ease. Nevertheless, he returned again and again to the stage: the list of his works includes five operettas and ten operas (of which six were unfinished and one has disappeared). The charm of many of the numbers does not make any of these stageworthy, with the exception of *Die Verschworenen* (1823) which reappears occasionally. Later renamed *Der häusliche Krieg*, this makes lively use of the Lysistrata theme, though even here Schubert's natural vein of lyricism, essentially intimate, does not survive the public demands of dramatic effect. There are operettas on his life by Suppé (1864) and Berté (*Das Dreimäderlhaus*, 1916, trans. *Lilac Time*, London 22 Dec. 1922).

Schuch, Ernst von (b. Graz, 23 Nov. 1846; d. Dresden, 10 May 1914). Austrian conductor. Studied Graz and Vienna. Début Breslau 1867. After engagements in Würzburg, Graz, and Basle, went to Dresden in 1872, becoming court conductor in 1873, and remaining there until 1914. Ennobled by the Emperor of Austria 1877. Generalmusikdirektor Dresden Opera from 1882, raising it to great heights. Conducted the first performances of *Feuersnot*, *Salome*, *Elektra*, and *Rosenkavalier*, and memorable performances of *The Ring* and other Wagner operas. Was instrumental in introducing Puccini into the repertory there. He married the soprano **Clementine Proska** (orig. Procházka) (1850–1932) who became the leading coloratura soprano at Dresden 1873–1904. She was a Marchesi pupil and sang Agathe and Eva in London at C.G. 1884. Their daughter **Liesel von Schuch** (b. 1891) was a coloratura soprano.

Schuh, Oscar Fritz (b. Munich, 1904). German producer. After holding positions in Gera, Hamburg, and elsewhere, was appointed Oberspielleiter of the Vienna Opera, where his productions of Mozart operas and *Wozzeck* were famous. For several years he was director of the Berlin Kurfürstendamm Theater, from which position he resigned in 1959 to become Generalintendant of the Cologne Opera, remaining there until 1962.

Schüler, Johannes (b. Vietz/Neumark, 21 June 1894; d. Berlin, 3 Oct. 1966). German conductor. Studied Berlin. Début Gleiwitz 1920. Held appointments at Königsberg, Oldenburg, Halle, Essen; Berlin, S.O., 1936–49. Generalmusikdirektor, Hanover 1949–60, where he built up a very large repertory including *Wozzeck*, *Mathis der Maler*, *Volo di Notte*, *Jenůfa*, and *From the House of the Dead*. (R)

Schumann, Elisabeth (b. Merseburg, 13 June 1885; d. New York, 23 Apr. 1952). German soprano. Studied Berlin, Dresden, Hamburg. Début Hamburg 1909, Shepherd (*Tannhäuser*). N.Y., Met., 1914–15; Vienna 1919–37; London, C.G., 1924–31. Sang regularly at Salzburg and Munich Festivals. Left Austria after the *Anschluss* and settled in U.S.A., teaching singing at the Curtis Institute. She possessed a voice of pure silvery clarity. Her Sophie has probably never been equalled, and in Mozart soubrette roles (Susanna, Zerlina, Blondchen) and as Adele she was incomparable. (R)

Schumann, Robert (b. Zwickau, 8 June 1810; d. Endenich, 29 July 1856). German composer. Schumann's one opera, *Genoveva* (1850), reveals little but his inability to think in dramatic terms; there is no real characterization, and the effects are invariably muffled, in part through the composer's scorn of all he thought cheap in Italian opera.

Schumann-Heink (orig. Rössler), **Ernestine** (b. Lieben, 15 June 1861; d. Hollywood, 17 Nov. 1936). Czech, later American, contralto. Studied Graz and Dresden, where she made her début 1878, Azucena. Hamburg 1883–98; engaged on a ten-year contract Berlin 1898, but purchased her release in order to sing regularly in America. Chicago 1898; N.Y., Met., 1899–1903, then most seasons until 1932; London, C.G. 1892 (Erda, Fricka, Waltraute in first C.G. *Ring*), 1897–1900; Bayreuth 1896–1906. Created Klytemnestra in *Elektra*. Repertory of 150 roles. Her voice, which was of great power, opulence, and agility (it ranged from d^{I} to b^{II}), was allied to a dramatic temperament which made her one of the great singers of her time. (R)

Schützendorf, Gustav (b. Cologne, 1883; d. Berlin, 27 Apr. 1937). German baritone. Studied Cologne and Milan. Début Düsseldorf 1905, Don Giovanni. Munich, Berlin, and Leipzig; then N.Y., Met., 1922–35. He was a successful Alberich, Beckmesser, and Faninal. (R)

Schützendorf, Leo (b. Cologne, 7 May 1886; d. Berlin, 18 Dec. 1931). German baritone, brother of above. Studied Cologne. After engagements in Düsseldorf, Vienna, and Wiesbaden, joined Berlin, S.O., 1920, remaining there until 1929, where he created Wozzeck. Appeared in *Bettelstudent* with Alpar and Pattiera without obtaining leave from the S.O. and was accordingly dismissed. This led to a persecution mania and a breakdown resulting in his death in 1931. (R) He had two other brothers: **Guido Schützendorf** (b. 22 Apr. 1880), another baritone, singing mostly in the German provinces and with a German touring company in U.S.A. and teaching in Germany; and **Alfons Schützendorf** (1882–1946), a bass.

Schwanda the Bagpiper (Cz., *Švanda Dudák*). Opera in 2 acts by Weinberger; text by Miloš Kareš and Max Brod, after the folk tale by Tyl. Prod. Prague, Cz., 27 Apr. 1927; N.Y., Met., 7 Nov. 1931, with Müller, Laubenthal, Schorr, cond. Bodanzky; London, C.G., 11 May 1934, with Ursuleac, Kullmann, Schoeffler, cond. Krauss. Babinsky persuades Schwanda to try to win Queen Ice-Heart by means of his piping. Finding Schwanda is already married, she orders his execution, but he is saved by his music and by Babinsky. A rash promise lands him in Hell, whence he is again rescued by Babinsky, who cheats the Devil at cards. Very successful; the subject has also been set by Hřímalý (1896), Weis (1905), and Bendl (1906).

Schwarzkopf, Elisabeth (b. Jarocin, nr. Poznań, 9 Dec. 1915). German soprano. Studied Berlin with Lula Mysz-Gmeiner and Ivogün. Début Berlin, Städtische Oper, 1938, Flower-maiden. Remained in Berlin until 1942, first singing small roles, then graduating to Musetta, Susanna, and Zerbinetta, in which part she made her Vienna début 1942. Sang coloratura roles there until 1947, when she became a lyric soprano. London, C.G., 1947, Donna Elvira; 1948–51, member of permanent company singing in English; returned 1959 as Marschallin. Salzburg since 1947; Milan, Sc., since 1948; San Francisco since 1955; Chicago 1959. Created Anne Trulove (*Rake's Progress*) 1951. Awarded the Lilli Lehmann medal by Mozart Society of Salzburg, and the Italian *Orfeo d'Oro*. (R)

Schweigsame Frau, Die (The Silent Woman). Opera in 3 acts by Strauss; text by Stefan Zweig, after Ben Jonson's drama *Epicœne* (1609). Prod. Dresden 24 June 1935, with Cebotari, Sack, Plaschke, cond. Böhm; N.Y., C.C., 7 Oct. 1958, with Joan Carroll, Regina Safarty, Herbert Beattie, cond. Peter Hermann Adler; London, C.G., 20 Nov. 1961, with Barbara Holt, Elizabeth Vaughan, David Ward, cond. Kempe.

Schwetzingen. Town in Baden-Württemberg, Germany. Since 1956 scene of annual festival in the exquisite rococo theatre of the Castle. Scene of the première of Egk's *Der Revisor* (1958), Henze's *Elegy for Young Lovers* (1961), Fortner's *Don Perlimplin* (1962).

Scintille, diamant. Dappertutto's (bar.) aria in Act 2 of Offenbach's *Contes d'Hoffmann*.

Sciutti, Graziella (b. Turin, 17 Apr. 1932). Italian soprano. Studied Rome. Début Aix-en-Provence 1951, Lucy (*The Telephone*); here she has often sung as Susanna, Zerlina, and also created Marianne in Sauguet's *Les Caprices de Marianne*. Glyndebourne 1954–9; London, C.G., 1956–62; Milan, Sc., since 1956, especially at the Piccola Scala where she has proved a delightful Despina, Norina, Cecchina (*La Buona Figliuola*), &c. Her vivacity and pointed phrasing and diction make her an outstanding soubrette. (R)

Scott, Walter (b. Edinburgh, 15 Aug. 1771; d. Abbotsford, 21 Sept. 1832). Scottish novelist. Operas on his works are as follows. *Marmion* (1808): Mackenzie (1891). *The Lady of the Lake* (1810): Rossini (1819); Vesque von Püttlingen (1829). *Waverley* (1804–14): Holstein (1852). *Guy Mannering* (1815): Boïeldieu (*La Dame Blanche*, 1825). *The Black Dwarf* (1816): C. E. Horn (*The Man of the Moor*, 1817). *Old Mortality* (1816): Bellini (*I Puritani*, 1835). *Rob Roy* (1817): Flotow (1836); De Koven (1894). *The Heart of Midlothian* (1818): Carafa (*La Prison d'Edimbourg*, 1833); Ricci (*La Prigione d'Edimburgo*, 1838); MacCunn (*Jeanie Deans*, 1894). *The Bride of Lammermoor* (1819): Mazzucato (1834); Donizetti (1835); Mackenzie (*Ravenswood*, 1890). *Ivanhoe* (1819): Marschner (*Der Templer und die Jüdin*, 1829); Nicolai (*Il Templario*, 1840); Sullivan (1891). *Kenilworth* (1821): Donizetti (1829); Schira (*c.* 1848); Weyse (1836, libretto by Hans Andersen). *Peveril of the Peak* (1823): C. E. Horn (1826). *Quentin Durward* (1823): Gevaert (1858); Maclean (1920). *The Talisman* (1825): Balfe (1874). *The Fair Maid of Perth* (1828): Bizet (1867).

Scotti, Antonio (b. Naples, 25 Jan. 1866; d. Naples, 26 Feb. 1936). Italian baritone. Studied Naples. Début Malta 1889, Amonasro. After nine seasons in Italy, Spain, and South America, engaged for Scala 1898, as Hans Sachs. London, C.G., 1899, Don Giovanni, singing there regularly until 1910 and 1913–14. N.Y., Met., 1899–1933. First London Scarpia and Sharpless; a fine Falstaff and Iago. First N.Y. Scarpia and many others. Though not large, his voice was of great beauty, and used with rare artistry. His acting was outstanding. (R)

Scottish Opera. See *Edinburgh* and *Glasgow*.

Scotto, Renata (b. Savona, 24 Feb. 1934). Italian soprano. Studied Milan with Ghirardini and Llopart. Début Milan, Teatro Nazionale, 1953. Violetta. Scala since 1953. London, Stoll, 1957, Mimì, Adina, Violetta, Donna Elvira; Edinburgh 1957, Amina (*Sonnambula*), successfully replacing Callas at final performance; London, C.G., since 1962; N.Y., Met., 1965. One of the most outstanding of the younger Italian sopranos. (R)

Scribe, Eugène (b. Paris, 25 Dec. 1791; d. Paris, 21 Feb. 1861). French librettist. His enormous productivity of librettos—his complete works comprise 76 volumes—led to references to the 'Scribe factory'; but his brilliant sense of the stage is confirmed by the frequency with which the best composers of the age turned to him. The list, with the numbers of librettos used, is as follows. Adam (7), Auber (38), Audran (1), Bellini (1, *Sonnambula*), Boïeldieu (4, incl. *La Dame Blanche*), Cherubini (1), Cilea (1, *Adriana Lecouvreur*), Clapisson (6), Donizetti (5, incl. *Elisir d'Amore* and *Favorite*), Gatzambide (1), Gomis (1), Gounod (1), Grisar (1), Halévy (6, incl. *La Juive*), Hérold (2), Kastner (1), Kovařović (1), Lavranga (1), Macfarren (1), Meyerbeer (5, incl. *L'Africaine*, *Les Huguenots*, and *Le Prophète*), Moniuszko (1), Offenbach (2), Rossi (1), Rossini (2, incl. *Le Comte Ory*), Setaccioli (1), Södermann (1), Suppé (1), Verdi (2, *Vêpres Siciliennes* and *Ballo in Maschera*), Zandonai (1), and Zimmermann (1).

Sebastian, George (b. Budapest, 17 Aug. 1903). Hungarian conductor. Studied Budapest with Kodály and Munich with Bruno Walter, where he worked as a coach. Leipzig 1924–7; Berlin, Städtische Opera, 1927–31; San Francisco 1944–7; chief conductor Paris, O., since 1947, especially in the German repertory. (R)

Secret, The (Cz., *Tajemství*). Opera in 3 acts by Smetana; text by Eliska Krásnohorská. Prod. Prague, Cz., 18 Sept. 1878; Oxford 7 Dec. 1956. The plot concerns the separation through pride and poverty of two lovers, and their eventual reuniting by means of an underground passage.

Sedie, Enrico delle. See *Delle Sedie*.

Seefried, Irmgard (b. Köngetried, 9 Oct. 1919). German soprano of Austrian parentage. Studied Augsburg and Munich. Début Aachen 1939, Priestess (*Aida*), remaining there until 1943; Vienna since 1943. Chosen by Strauss to sing the Composer (*Ariadne*) in his 80th birthday celebrations. London, C.G., with Vienna Company 1947; N.Y., Met., 1953. Appeared regularly at Salzburg as Pamina, Susanna, and Zerlina. She now spends more time on the concert platform, and has only added two roles to her repertory since 1953—Blanche (*Dialogues des Carmélites*) and Cleopatra (*Giulio Cesare*). Gifted with a warm and beautiful voice and an engaging personality. (R)

Segreto di Susanna, Il (Susanna's Secret). Opera in 1 act by Wolf-Ferrari; text by Enrico Golisciani. Prod. Munich (as *Susannas Geheimnis*) 4 Dec. 1909; N.Y., Met., (by Philadelphia-Chicago Co.), 14 Mar. 1911; London, C.G., 11 July 1911. A slight but charming curtain-raiser about a jealous husband, Count Gil (bar.), who, smelling tobacco in the house, suspects his pretty wife Susanna (sop.) of secretly entertaining a lover. Susanna's secret is that she herself smokes.

Seguin, Arthur (b. London, 7 Apr. 1809; d. New York, 9 Dec. 1852). English bass. Sang in English opera at C.G. and D.L. and in Italian opera at the King's T. between 1831 and 1838. N.Y. 1838, where he became popular and formed his own company, the Seguin Troupe. Probably the only opera singer to be elected a chief by one of the Indian tribes, being given a name meaning 'the man with the deep mellow voice'. The career of his wife **Ann** (orig. Childe) (b. London, 1814; d. New York, Aug. 1888) coincided with his own. His sister **Elizabeth** (b. London, 1815; d. London, 1870) was a soprano, and the mother of Euphrosyne Parepa (q.v.).

Seidl, Anton (b. Pest, 7 May 1850; d. New York, 28 Mar. 1898). Hungarian conductor. Studied Leipzig. Engaged as chorus master, Vienna 1872, by Richter, who introduced him to Wagner. Remained with Wagner till 1876, helping him prepare the score of the *Ring*. Wagner recommended him to Neumann at Leipzig, where he became first conductor 1879–82; then conducted Neumann's Wagner Company on its great tour of Europe 1883. Bremen 1883–5, where he married the soprano Auguste Krauss. N.Y., Met., 1885–9, conducting first American performances of *Meistersinger*, *Tristan*, *Rheingold*, *Siegfried*, *Götterdämmerung*. London, H.M.'s, 1882, first English *Ring*; C.G., 1897. Bayreuth, 1897, *Parsifal*. Died suddenly at the height of his career.

Seidl-Krauss, Auguste (b. Vienna, 28 Aug. 1853; d. Kingston, N.Y., 17 July 1939). Austrian soprano. Wife of above. Member of Leipzig Opera and Neumann's Company. Married Seidl, Bremen, 1883; he took her to N.Y. where she sang Sieglinde in the first Met. *Walküre* and was the first American Eva, Woodbird, Gutrune.

Seinemeyer, Meta (b. Berlin, 5 Sept. 1895; d. Dresden, 19 July 1929). German soprano. Studied Berlin. Début there 1918. N.Y. with German Company 1923, Eva; Dresden 1925–9; London, C.G., 1929, Sieglinde and Eva. Established herself as one of the finest lyric-dramatic sopranos, especially in Verdi, in her few seasons at Dresden. (R)

Selika. The African queen (sop.) in Meyerbeer's *L'Africaine*.

Sembrich, Marcella (orig. Prakseda Marcellina Kochańská) (b. Wiśniewczyk, 15 Feb. 1858; d. New York, 11 Jan. 1935). Polish soprano. Took her mother's maiden name. Began career as a child pianist and violinist. Sang to Liszt, who urged her to study voice, which she did with Rokitansky and Lamperti. Début Athens 1877, Elvira (*Puritani*). Dresden 1878–80; London, C.G., 1880–4 and 1895, scoring great success as Lucia, Marguerite de Valois, Amina. N.Y., Met., 1883–4 and 1898–1909, where she was heard in more than 30 roles, of which Violetta was her favourite. Her voice, which ranged from c' to f''', was of great beauty and brilliance, and her technique was superb. From 1924 taught at the Curtis Institute, Philadelphia, and at the Juilliard School, N.Y. (R)

Semele. Masque, or musical drama, by Handel; text a version of Congreve's drama (1710), orig. libretto for John Eccles about 1707. Prod. London, C.G., 10 Feb. 1744, with Elisabeth Duparc. First stage production Cambridge 1925; Evanston, U.S.A., 30 Jan. 1959. Semele is taken by Jupiter as his lover, but the jealous Juno persuades her to seek immortality by asking Jupiter to appear in his full divine majesty. She is destroyed in the blaze of glory, leaving only the promise of a son, Bacchus, to console mankind. Eccles's opera was first perf., Oxford, 1964.

Semiramide. Opera in 2 acts by Rossini; text by Rossi, after Voltaire's tragedy *Sémiramis* (1748). Prod. Venice, F., 3 Feb. 1823, with Colbran; London, Hm., 15 July 1824, with Pasta; New Orleans 1 May 1837. Semiramis, Queen of Babylon, and her lover Assur murder the king. She later falls in love with a young man who turns out to be her son Arsace. She receives a mortal blow Assur intends for Arsace, who then kills Assur and becomes king. The list of some 40 operas on her legend includes works by Destouches (1718), Porpora (1724), Caldara (1725), Vinci (1729), Porpora (1729), Vivaldi (1732), Hasse (1747), Gluck (1748), Galuppi (1749), K. H. Graun (1754), Sacchini (1762), Sarti (1768), Paisiello (1773), Salieri (1784), Borghi (1791), Cimarosa (1799), Meyerbeer (1819), Manuel Garcia (1828), and Respighi (1910).

Sempre libera. The *cabaletta* to Violetta's (sop.) aria 'Ah! fors' è lui' in Act 1 of Verdi's *La Traviata.*

Senesino (orig. Francesco Bernardi) (b. Siena, whence his stage name, *c.* 1680; d. Siena, *c.* 1750). Italian male mezzo-soprano. Studied with Bernacchi at Bologna. Believed to have sung at Genoa *c.* 1709 and Naples *c.* 1715, though Angus Heriot in his book on *castrati* (1956) says his name first appears in a cast list at Venice 1714 in Pollarolo the elder's *Semiramide.* Dresden 1719: here he was heard by Handel who engaged him for London, where he made his début in Nov. 1720 in Bononcini's *Astarto*, remaining with Handel's company until 1728. Re-engaged by Handel 1730, but broke with him in 1733 and went over to Porpora's rival company at Lincoln's Inn Fields, remaining there until 1737. Returned to Italy and engaged Naples, S.C., 1738–9. Created leading roles in Handel's *Ottone, Flavio, Giulio Cesare, Tamerlano, Rodelinda, Scipione, Alessandro, Admeto, Riccardo, Siroe, Tolomeo, Poro, Ezio, Sosarme*, and *Orlando.* Senesino's voice was a mezzo-soprano, or according to some a contralto, of great beauty, and was considered by many people superior to Farinelli's in quality. A contemporary critic describes it as 'clear, penetrating, and flexible, with faultless intonation and a perfect shake'.

Andrea Martini (1761–1819) and Giusto Ferdinando Tenducci (q.v.) were also known as Senesino.

Senta. Daland's daughter (sop.), the heroine of Wagner's *Der fliegende Holländer.*

Senta's Ballad. The 'Legend of the Flying Dutchman' sung by Senta (sop.) to her friends in Act 2 of Wagner's opera.

Serafin, Tullio (b. Rottanova di Cavarzere, 8 Dec. 1878; d. Rome, 2 Feb. 1968). Italian conductor. Studied Milan, played violin in Scala Orchestra. Début Ferrara 1900. Turin 1903; Milan, Sc., 1909, 1919, 1939–40, 1946–7; London, C.G., 1907, 1931, 1959, 1960; N.Y., Met., 1924–34; C.C. 1952; Rome 1934–43, chief conductor and artistic director; Chicago 1956–8. Reappointed Rome Opera, 1962. At the Met. conducted world premières of *The Emperor Jones, The King's Henchman, Merry Mount*, and *Peter Ibbetson*, as well as the American premières of *La Cena delle Beffe, Turandot, La Vida Breve*, and *Sorochinsky Fair.* At the Scala he directed the premières of Montemezzi's *La Nave* and the first stage performance in Italy of *Peter Grimes*. During his Rome directorship he conducted many premières and revivals of old works. Under German occupation of Rome he gave a season of contemporary opera including *Wozzeck* and Dallapiccola's *Volo di Notte*. Has championed many young artists, and did much to help Ponselle and then Callas in their formative years, launching the latter as a dramatic coloratura. Coached Joan Sutherland for her C.G. Lucia. (R) His wife **Elena Rakowska** sang soprano roles at Sc. and the Met.

Seraglio, The. See *Entführung*.

Serenade (It. *serenata* = evening song, from *sera* = evening). By origin, a song sung under his lady's window by a lover, with or without instrumental accompaniment, which might in opera be provided by himself (as in Don Giovanni's 'Deh, vieni') or by a hired band. The term was soon applied to any instrumental piece of a light nature.

Serov, Alexander Nikolayevich (b. St. Petersburg, 23 Jan. 1820; d. St. Petersburg, 1 Feb. 1871). Russian composer and critic. He resisted the budding Russian nationalism of his day in articles and in his first, highly Wagnerian, opera *Judith* (1863). Its great success was followed up in *Rogneda* (1881). *The Power of Evil* (begun 1867) was at Serov's request finished by Soloviev (prod. 1871); *Christmas Eve Revels* remained unfinished.

Serpette, Henri (b. Nantes, 4 Nov. 1846; d. Paris, 3 Nov. 1904). French composer. Failing to realize his early ambitions as a serious composer, he took to writing operettas for the B.-P., where from 1874 he produced at regular intervals light pieces whose charm of manner won them great popularity.

Serse (Xerxes). Opera in 3 acts by Handel; text from a libretto by Minato, written for Caralli in 1654 and revised for Bononcini in 1694. Prod. London, Hm., 15 Apr. 1738; Northampton, Mass., 12 May 1928. Though set in ancient Persia, it includes some London street songs. Handel's only opera containing a purely comic character, it includes the famous *larghetto* aria 'Ombra mai fù', which was satirical by intent but is now invariably taken seriously as 'Handel's Largo'. Other operas by Caralli (1654), Förtsch (1689), and Bononcini (1694).

Serva Padrona, La (The Maid Mistress). Intermezzo in 2 parts to the opera *Il Prigionier Superbo* by Pergolesi; text by Federico. Prod. Naples, S.B., 28 Aug. 1733; London, Hm., 27 Mar. 1750; Baltimore, 13 June 1790. This most popular of all intermezzos tells how the servant girl Serpina lures her master Uberto into marrying her.

Se vuol ballare. Figaro's (bar.) aria in Act 1 of Mozart's *Le Nozze di Figaro* in which he threatens to pit his wits against those of the Count.

Shacklock, Constance (b. Sherwood, Nottingham, 16 Apr. 1913). English mezzo-soprano. Studied London, R.A.M., with Frederic Austin. Début London, C.G., 1947, Mercedes (*Carmen*). Member of company until end of 1955–6 season, singing leading roles in German, French, and Italian repertory. Admired by Kleiber, who invited her to Berlin to sing Brangäne, one of her best roles; also a successful Octavian and Amneris. Has appeared in Holland, Russia, and Australia. (R)

Shakespeare, William (b. Stratford-on-Avon, bapt. 26 Apr. 1564; d. Stratford-on-Avon, 23 Apr. 1616). English poet and dramatist. Operas on his works are as follows (the dates of the first seasons are those suggested by Sir Edmund Chambers):

Henry VI, pts. 2 and 3 (1590–1): None.

Henry VI, Pt. 1 (1591–2) None.

Richard III (1592–3): Canepá (1879); Salvayre (1883).

The Comedy of Errors (1592–3): Storace (*Gli Equivoci*, 1786); Lorenz (*c.* 1890) Krejči (*The Tumult at Ephesus*, 1946).

Titus Andronicus (1593–4): None.

The Taming of the Shrew (1593–4):

Braham and others (1828); Goetz (1874); Samara (1895); Maclean (*Petruccio*, 1895); Clapp (? 1948 N.Y.); Silver (1922); Bossi (*Volpino il Calderaio*, 1925); Persico (1931); Karel (comp. 1942–3, unfin.) Giannini (1953); Shebalin (1957).

Two Gentlemen of Verona (1594–5): None.

Love's Labour's Lost (1594–5): Folprecht (1926); A. Beecham (pub. 1936).

Romeo and Juliet (1594–5): Benda (1776); Schwanenberger (1776); Marescalchi (1789); Rumling (1790); Dalayrac (1792); Steibelt (1793); Zingarelli (1796); B. Porta (1806); P. G. Guglielmi (1810); Vaccai (1825); Bellini (*I Capuletti ed i Montecchi*, 1830); Morales (1863); Marchetti (1865); Gounod (1867); Mercadal (1873); H. R. Shelley (publ. 1901); D'Ivry (*Les Amants de Vérone*, 1878); Campo (1909); Barkworth (1916); Zandonai (1922); Sutermeister (1940); Malipiero (1950); Blacher (1950); Gaujac (1955).

Richard II (1595–6): None.

A Midsummer Night's Dream (1595–6): Purcell (*The Fairy Queen*, 1692); Leveridge (*Pyramus and Thisbe*, masque, 1716); Lampe (*Pyramus and Thisbe*, 1745); J. C. Smith (*The Fairies*, 1755); E. W. Wolf (*Die Zauberirrungen*, 1785); Manusardi (1842); Suppé (1844); Mancinelli (comp. 1917); Vreuls (1925); Arundell (20th cent.); Doubrava (1945); Delannoy (*Puck*, 1949); Orff (1952) [?]; Britten (1960).

The Merchant of Venice (1596): Pinsuti (1873); Taubmann (*Porzia*, 1916); Deffès (*Jessica*, 1898); Foerster (*Jessika*, 1905); Alpaerts (*Shylock*, 1913); Radó (*Shylock*, comp. 1913–14); A. Beecham (1922); Laufer (publ. 1929); Brumagne (?); Hahn (1935); Castel-nuovo-Tedesco (1961).

King John (1596–7): None.

Henry IV, Pts. 1 and 2 (1597–8): Mercadante (*La Gioventù di Enrico V*, 1834); Holst (*At the Boar's Head*, 1925).

Much Ado About Nothing (1598–9): Berlioz (*Béatrice et Bénédict*, 1862); A. Doppler (1896); Puget (1899); Podestà (*Ero*, 1900); Stanford (1901); Mojsisovics (*c.* 1930); Hahn (1936); Heinrich (1956).

Henry V (1598–9): None.

Julius Caesar (1599–1600): Segfried (1811); Roblez (late 19th cent.); Malipiero (1936); Klebe (1959).

As You Like It (1599–1600): Veracini (*Roselinda*, 1744); F. Wickham (*Rosalind*, 1938).

Twelfth Night (1599–1600): Steinkühler (*Cäsario*, 1848); Rintel (1872); Taubert (*Cesario*, 1874); Weis (*Viola*, 1892); Hart (*Malvolio*, 1913); Smetana (*Viola*, unfin., prod. 1924); Farina (1929); Kusterer (1932); Holenia (*Viola*, 1934); De Filippi (*Malvolio*, 1937); Gibbs (comp. 1947).

Hamlet (1600–1): Caruso (1789) (doubtful); Mercadante (1822); Mareczek (1840); Buzzolla (1847); Stadtfeld (1857); Moroni (1860); Faccio (1865); Thomas (1868); Hignard (1888); Heward (comp. 1916, unfin.); Kalniņš (1936); Zafred (1961); Kagen (1962); Machavariani (1964).

The Merry Wives of Windsor (1600–1): Papavoine (*Le Vieux Coquet*, 1761); Philidor (*Herne le Chasseur*, comp. 1773); Ritter (1794); Dittersdorf (1796); Salieri (*Falstaff*, 1799); Balfe (*Falstaff*, 1838); Nicolai (1849); Adam (*Falstaff*, 1856); Verdi (*Falstaff*, 1893); Vaughan Williams (*Sir John in Love*, 1929).

Troilus and Cressida (1601–2): Zillig (1951).

All's Well That Ends Well (1602–3); Audran (*Gillette de Narbonne*, 1882); Castelnuovo-Tedesco (comp. 1958).

Measure for Measure (1604–5): Wagner (*Das Liebesverbot*, 1836).

Othello (1604–5): Rossini (1816); Verdi (1887); Machavariani (? 1963).

King Lear (1605–6): Séméladis (1854); Gobatti (1881); Reynaud (1888); Cagnoni (late 19th cent.); Cottrau (1913); Ghislanzoni (1937); Frazzi (1939).

Macbeth (1605–6): Asplmayr (1777); Chélard (1827); Verdi (1847); Taubert (1857); Lauro Rossi (*Biorn*, 1877); E. Bloch (1910); Gatty (?); Collingwood (1934).

Antony and Cleopatra (1606–7): Kaffka (1779) (possible); Frendenberg (1882); Sayn-Witt-genstein-Berleburg (1883); ? Morales (1891); Yuferov (publ. 1900); Malipiero (1938).

Coriolanus (1607–8): Baeyens (1940); Sulek (1958).

Timon of Athens (1607–8): Leopold I, Holy Roman Emperor (1696) (probable).

Pericles (1608–9): Cottrau (comp. *c.* 1915).

Cymbeline (1609–10): R. Kreutzer (*Imogène*, 1796); Sobolewski (*Imogene*, 1833); Missa (*Dinah*, 1894); Eggen (1951).

A Winter's Tale (1610–11): Barbieri (*Perdita*, 1865); Bruch (*Hermione*, 1872); Nešvera (*Perdita*, 1897); Bereny (1898); Goldmark (1908).

The Tempest (1611–12); Locke, Humfrey, and others (1674); Purcell (1695); J. C. Smith (1756); Asplmayr (1781); Rolle (1784); Fabrizi (1788); Winter (1793); W. Müller (1798); Fleischmann (*Die Geisterinsel*, 1798); Reichardt (*Die Geisterinsel*, 1798); Zumsteeg (*Die Geisterinsel*, 1798); Haack (*Die Geisterinsel*, 1798); Ritter (1799); Caruso (1799); Hensel (1799); Kunzen (?); Emmert (1806); Riotte (1833); Rung (prob., 1847) [vice Kunz?] Raymond (comp. *c.* 1840); Kunz (1847); Halévy (1850); Napravnik (1860); Frank (1887); Urspruch (1888); Fibich (1895); Farwell (*Caliban*, masque, 1916); Hale (publ. 1917); Gatty (1920); Lattuada (1922); Sutermeister (*Die Zauberinsel*, 1942); Atterberg (1948); Martin (1956).

Henry VIII (1612–13): None.

Two Noble Kinsmen (1612–13): None.

Also: Logar (*Four Scenes from Shakespeare*) and Zelinka (*Evening with Shakespeare*, 1955). Opera *Shakespeare* by Serpette (1899). In Thomas's *Songe d'une Nuit d'Été*, Shakespeare, Queen Elizabeth, and Falstaff appear.

Shaporin, Yury (b. Glukov, 8 Nov. 1889; d. Moscow, 9 Dec. 1966). Russian composer. His sole opera, *The Decembrists* (1953), is based on the revolutionary incident of 1825 and has won approval in Russia for its heroic sentiments and 'optimistic' musical style.

Sharpless. The U.S. Consul (bar.) in Puccini's *Madama Butterfly*.

Shaw, George Bernard (b. Dublin, 26 July 1856; d. London, 2 Nov. 1950). Irish author and critic. He wrote music criticism for *The Hornet* under Vandeleur Lee's name (1876–7), *The Star* as 'Corno di Bassetto' (1889–90), and under his own name for *The World* between 1890 and 1894. His criticisms, which gave a personal, vivid, and invigorating picture of the London operatic scene, were republished in 1932, 1937, and 1961. His *The Perfect Wagnerite*, a socialist interpretation of *The Ring*, appeared in 1899. His play *Arms and the Man* became an operetta (Oscar Straus, *The Chocolate Soldier*) against his will; *Pygmalion* was made into a musical (Loewe, *My Fair Lady*) after his death.

Shaw, Mary (orig. Postans—also known as Mrs. Alfred Shaw) (b. Lea, Kent, 1814; d. Hadleigh Hall, Suffolk, 9 Sept. 1876). English contralto. Studied London, R.A.M. After several years of concert and oratorio work, début at Milan, Sc., 1839 in Verdi's *Oberto*; London, C.G. and D.L., from 1842, being especially successful as Arsace, Fidalma, and Malcolm Graeme (*Donna del Lago*). Her career came to a premature close when her husband's serious illness caused her to have a breakdown, and to lose her voice.

Shepherds of the Delectable Mountains, The. See *Pilgrim's Progress*.

Sheridan, Margaret (b. Castlebar, 15 Oct. 1889; d. Dublin, 16 Apr. 1958). Irish soprano. Studied London, R.A.M., and Milan. Début Rome 1918, Mimì. London, C.G., 1919, 1925–30; Milan, Sc., 1921–4. Sang the role of Olimpia in Respighi's *Belfagor* at Sc.; first London Iris (Mascagni). Chosen by Toscanini to sing in *La Wally* at Sc. 1922. (R)

Sheridan, Richard Brinsley (b. Dublin, 30 Oct. 1751; d. London, 7 July 1816). English dramatist. Operas on his works are as follows. *St. Patrick's Day* (1775): S. Hughes (1947). *The Duenna* (1775): Linley, sen. and jun., songs, &c., for original production, 1775; Bertoni (*La Governante*, 1779); Prokofiev (1946); Gerhard (comp. 1948, concert perf. 1951).

School for Scandal (1777): Klenau (1926). *The Critic* (1779): Stanford (1916).

Sherrington, Helen. See *Lemmens-Sherrington.*

Shield, William (b. Whickham, 5 Mar. 1748; d. Brightling, 25 Jan. 1829). English composer. Originally a violinist, played in orchestra at Italian Opera, London, 1772; principal viola 1773–91. Composer to C.G. 1778–91 and 1792–7. Wrote more than 50 light operas, including *The Flitch of Bacon* and *Robin Hood.*

Shostakovich, Dmitri (b. St. Petersburg, 25 Sept. 1906). Russian composer. His first opera, *The Nose* (1930), after Gogol, gave scope to his satirical abilities—in this case at the expense of the old Russian régime. Its experimental eccentricities were one of the causes of the reaction by the Party that led to the formulation of 'Socialist realism' as an artistic principle in 1932. This was the year in which *Lady Macbeth of Mtsensk* (begun 1930) was finished; in 1934 it became the first opera to be produced under the new rules in which the goal was 'the complete musical expression of the ideas and passions motivating Soviet heroes' (Stalin). Its first success was followed by an equally violent reaction, and it was denounced in a famous *Pravda* article. Shostakovich's deep sympathy for his heroine, Katerina Ismailova (the title of the revised version, 1959), is expressed in contrast to brilliant, but shallow, alienating satire for the other characters. *Moscow, Cheremushki* (1959) (the name of a new building estate) is a local-joke operetta on the housing question.

Shuard, Amy (b. London, 19 July 1924). English soprano. Studied London, T.C.M. Début Johannesburg 1949, Aida. London, S.W., 1949–55; C.G. since 1954. Has established herself as one of the leading British dramatic sopranos of the day. Sang title roles in first English stage performances of *Káťa Kabanova* and *Jenůfa*; has also been an impressive Aida, Amelia, Santuzza, Lady Macbeth, Elektra, and Magda (*The Consul*). In 1958 acclaimed as the finest Turandot since her teacher Eva Turner; first English-born C.G. Brünnhilde, 1964; Elektra, 1965; Bayreuth, 1965. Subsequently invited to Vienna, Buenos Aires, San Francisco, and Milan. (R)

Shuisky. A scheming boyar (ten.) in Mussorgsky's *Boris Godunov.*

Sicily. See *Catania, Palermo.*

Siege of Rhodes, The. Opera by Locke and others; text by W. D'Avenant. Prod. London, Rutland House, Sept. 1656. According to the preface of *The Fairy-Queen* (1695), 'That Sir William D'Avenant's *The Siege of Rhodes* was the first Opera we ever had in England, no Man can deny; and is indeed a perfect Opera . . . .' The music has been lost.

Siegfried. See *Ring der Nibelungen.* Also the young hero (ten.) in Wagner's *Siegfried* and *Götterdämmerung.*

Sieglinde. Hunding's wife and Siegmund's sister, later lover (sop.), in Wagner's *Die Walküre.*

Siegmund. Sieglinde's brother and lover (ten.) in Wagner's *Die Walküre.*

Siems, Margarethe (b. Wrocław, 30 Dec. 1879; d. Dresden, 13 Apr. 1952). German soprano. Studied with Orgeni, a pupil of Viardot and Marchesi. Début Prague 1902. Dresden 1908–22; London, C.G., 1913; D.L. 1914. Created Chrysothemis (*Elektra*), Marschallin (*Rosenkavalier*), Zerbinetta (*Ariadne*). First London Marschallin, in which role Strauss considered her ideal. Her voice could also cope with the coloratura roles of Bellini and Donizetti, and she also sang Aida, Amelia, Venus, and even Isolde. Took up a teaching appointment in Berlin 1920, and taught in Dresden and Wrocław until 1940. (R)

Siena. Town in Tuscany, Italy. Here in the 1930's Count Guido Chigi-Saracini founded the Accademia Chigiana, where every Sept. the Settimana Chigiana is held. Performances are given at the Teatro dei Rozzi and Teatro dei Rinnovati; this latter dates from 1753, and was adapted by Bibiena from the ancient hall of the Grand Council of the republic. Operas revived have included Vivaldi's *L'Olimpiade*, Scarlatti's *Il Trionfo dell'Onore*, Galuppi's *Il Filosofo di Campagna*, and works by Cimarosa, Cherubini, Sacchini, and Donizetti.

Siepi, Cesare (b. Milan, 10 Feb. 1923). Italian bass. Self-taught. Début Schio, nr. Venice, 1941, Sparafucile. Career interrupted by war, when he became an active anti-Fascist and had to take refuge in Switzerland. Resumed career Venice 1945. Milan, Sc., since 1946; London, C.G., 1950, 1962; N.Y., Met., since 1950; Salzburg 1953–8. In N.Y. he has sung Boris and the Verdi bass roles with considerable success. (R)

Siface (orig., Giovanni Francesco Grossi) (b. Uzzanese Chiesina, 12 Feb. 1653; d. nr. Ferrara, 29 May 1697.) Italian male soprano. He acquired his stage name from the part of Syphax in Cavalli's *Scipione Africano*, in which he excelled at Venice in 1678. His admirers during his English visit (from 1679) included Pepys, Evelyn, Burney, and Purcell, whose pretty harpsichord piece 'Sefauchi's Farewell' laments his departure for Italy. He was murdered while travelling between Bologna and Ferrara.

Si, fui soldato. Chénier's (ten.) defence of his actions in the revolutionary tribunal in Act 3 of Giordano's *Andrea Chénier*.

Signor, ascolta. Liù's (sop.) plea to Calaf in Act 1 of Puccini's *Turandot*.

Signor Bruschino, Il; ossia Il Figlio per Azzardo. Opera in 1 act by Rossini; text by Foppa, after a French comedy by de Chazet and Ourry. Prod. Venice, S. Moisè, late Jan. 1813; N.Y., Met., 9 Dec. 1932, with De Luca and Pinza; Orpington, Kentish Opera Group, 14 July 1960. Occasionally revived in Italy.

Sigurd. Opera in 5 acts by Reyer; text by Du Locle and Blau. Prod. Brussels, La M., 7 Jan. 1884 with Rose Caron; London, C.G., 15 July 1884 with Albani; New Orleans 24 Dec. 1891. The libretto is based on the Nibelung legend.

Si j'étais roi (If I were King). Opera in 3 acts by Adam; text by d'Ennery and Brésil. Prod. Paris, T.L., 4 Sept. 1852; N.Y. 29 Nov. 1881; Newcastle 20 Feb. 1893.

Silva. Don Ruy Gomez de Silva, a Spanish grandee and Ernani's rival (bass) in Verdi's *Ernani*.

Silveri, Paolo (b. Ofena, nr. Aquila, 28 Dec. 1913). Italian baritone. Studied Florence and Rome, Accademia di Santa Cecilia. Début Rome, as bass, 1939; from 1944 baritone (first role, Germont). London, C.G., 1946 with Naples Company, 1947–9 as member of permanent company; 1950 with Scala Company; N.Y., Met., 1950–3. Tenor début Dublin 1959, Otello. Reverted to baritone roles again 1960. As a baritone enjoyed a short but brilliant career, especially in Verdi and Puccini roles. (R)

Silvio. A villager, Nedda's lover (bar.), in Leoncavallo's *Pagliacci*.

Simionato, Giulietta (b. Forlì, 15 Dec. 1910). Italian mezzo. Studied Rovigo. Won first prize, Bel Canto Competition, Florence, 1933, and during next five years sang small roles in Florence, Padua, Milan. Sc. regularly since 1939–40; Edinburgh Festival 1947, Cherubino; C.G. 1953, Adalgisa, Amneris, Azucena; Chicago since 1954; N.Y., Met., since 1949. As well as singing the usual mezzo repertory, has made a great success in Rossini roles and as Jane Seymour in Donizetti's *Anna Bolena* and Romeo in Bellini's *I Capuleti e i Montecchi*. Her voice is a coloratura mezzo of great agility, with a warm characteristic timbre in its lower reaches; and she has a charming stage presence. In 1962 she sang the soprano role of Valentine in the Scala revival of *Les Huguenots*. (R)

Simon Boccanegra. Opera in a prologue and 3 acts by Verdi; text by Piave, based on the drama by António García Gutiérrez. Prod. Venice, F., 12 Mar. 1857 with Giraldoni in title role—libretto revised Boito, prod. Milan, Sc., 24 Mar. 1881, with D'Angeri, Maurel, Tamagno, and E. de Reszke, cond. Faccio; N.Y., Met., 28 Jan. 1932, with Rethberg, Tibbett, Martinelli, Pinza, cond. Serafin; London, S.W., 27 Oct. 1948, with Gartside, Matters, Johnston, Glynne, cond. Mudie.

The action of the opera takes place in and near Genoa in the 14th century.

Prologue. Paolo (bar.) proposes to Pietro (bass) that the plebeian Simon Boccanegra should be elected Doge of Venice. Boccanegra (bar.) accepts, hoping now to marry Maria, daughter of the patrician Fiesco, by whom he has had a child. Boccanegra asks Fiesco for friendship, but admits that Maria's child has vanished. Fiesco tells him that only the sight of his granddaughter will bring peace between them. Boccanegra enters Fiesco's dwelling to find Maria dead. The crowd acclaim him Doge.

Act 1. Twenty-five years have passed. Boccanegra's child has been brought up by Fiesco under the name of Amelia Grimaldi (sop.); neither of them knows her true identity. Her lover is a young patrician, Gabriele Adorno (ten.), whom she proposes marrying since she knows that Boccanegra is on his way to urge her to marry Paolo. Gabriele is undeterred by learning from Fiesco that she is not really a Grimaldi. When Boccanegra arrives, she shows him a locket with her mother's portrait. Father and daughter are reunited. Boccanegra now tells Paolo to give up Amelia, and Paolo plans to abduct her.

The Doge's Council is interrupted by a crowd of rioters, who drag Gabriele and Fiesco into the chamber. Gabriele has killed a man who was trying to abduct Amelia, accuses Boccanegra, and tries to stab him. Amelia intervenes, and hints that Paolo is guilty. The Doge suspects Paolo and makes him curse the criminal.

Act 2. Gabriele and Fiesco are summoned from prison by Paolo, who tries to enlist Fiesco's help in poisoning Boccanegra by offering him freedom, but is refused. He then tells Gabriele that Amelia has become Boccanegra's mistress and wins his support; when Amelia appears he bitterly reproaches her. Amelia pleads with her father for Gabriele's freedom. Left alone, Boccanegra drinks from a jug poisoned by Paolo, and falls asleep: Gabriele enters from hiding to stab the Doge, who is saved by Amelia. Gabriele learns that she is the Doge's daughter and offers his service.

Act 3. The revolt against the Doge is crushed. Fiesco and Paolo are led in, and Paolo reveals to Fiesco that he has given Boccanegra a slow lethal poison. Paolo is led away to execution. Fiesco reveals his true identity, and Boccanegra tells him that they can be reconciled since Amelia is his daughter and Fiesco's lost grandchild. He dies proclaiming Gabriele his successor.

Simoneau, Léopold (b. Montreal, *c.* 1920). Canadian tenor. Studied N.Y. with Paul Althouse. Début Montreal 1943, Basilio (*Figaro*). Paris, O., and London, C.G. 1947–9; Aix-en-Provence 1950; Glyndebourne 1951 and subsequently; London, R.F.H., with Vienna Company, 1954; Chicago 1954. Outstanding in Mozart, as Wilhelm Meister in *Mignon*, and as Nadir; also excels in French roles. (R)

Sinclair, Monica (b. Somerset, 1926). English mezzo. Studied London, R.A.M. and R.C.M. Début C.R. 1948, Suzuki. London, C.G., since 1949; Glyndebourne since 1954. Successful in Handel Opera Society's productions, in Lully's *Armide* in France, and *Alcina* in Venice. A most intelligent and musical singer. (R)

Singher, Martial (b. Oloron-Sainte-Marie, 14 Aug. 1904). French baritone. Studied Paris Conservatoire. Début Amsterdam 1930, Pylade (*Iphigénie en Tauride*). Paris, O., 1930–9; London, C.G., 1937; N.Y., Met., 1943–59. Equally at home in French, German, and Italian repertory, he has been praised in N.Y. for his Mercutio, Amfortas, Figaro, and the four roles in *Hoffmann.* (R)

Singspiel (Ger. = song-play). A German form of vernacular opera, corresponding to *opéra comique* and ballad opera, and usually comic, which included spoken dialogue. The term first appeared in the late 17th century. It covered a wide variety of works mostly now forgotten: the operas of Hiller and Reichardt are typical of the genre. Mozart's *Entführung* is an outstanding example, and the *Singspiel* reached its apotheosis in *The Magic Flute* and *Fidelio*.

Sì, pel ciel marmoreo giuro! The vengeance duet between Otello (ten.) and Iago (bar.) in Act 2 of Verdi's *Otello*.

Sì può? The prologue to Leoncavallo's *Pagliacci* in which the singer, generally Tonio (bar.), asks the audience to listen to his exposition of the situation.

Sir John in Love. Opera in 4 acts by Vaughan Williams; text selected by composer from Shakespeare's comedy *The Merry Wives of Windsor* (1600–1). Prod. London, R.C.M., 21 Mar. 1929; N.Y., Univ. of Columbia, 20 Jan. 1949.

Sitzprobe (Ger. = sitting rehearsal). The term for the first complete rehearsal of an opera, when soloists and chorus join with the orchestra, generally in the auditorium, with the singers sitting either in the stalls or on chairs on the stage. The term has been adopted in English opera houses.

Sladen, Victoria (b. London, 24 May 1910). English soprano. Studied London and Berlin with Grenzebach. Début London, Strand T., 1942, Giulietta (*Hoffmann*). S.W. 1943–50; C.G. 1947–8, 1950–2. (R)

Slezak, Leo (b. Krásná Hora, 18 Aug. 1873; d. Tegernsee, 1 June 1946). Austrian tenor. Studied with Adolf Robinson, and J. de Reszke in Paris 1908–9. Sang as a youth in chorus of Brno Opera, début there 1896, Lohengrin. Berlin 1898–9; Vienna 1901–26; London, C.G., 1900, 1909; N.Y., Met., 1909–13, where he sang in the American première of *The Queen of Spades*. A man of imposing physique with a voice to match. His Otello, Raoul (*Huguenots*), Radamès, and Lohengrin were much admired. Possessed a large and rather undisciplined sense of humour: he once so convulsed the chorus at the Met. during *Aida* that they were fined by the management (Slezak paid the fine). After leaving the stage he appeared in several films, and wrote a number of books including *Song of Motley: Being the Reminiscences of a Hungry Tenor*. (R) His son **Walter Slezak** has appeared in several American films and in *Fledermaus*, N.Y., Met. (R)

Slobodskaya, Oda (b. Vilno, 28 Nov. 1895; d. London, 30 July 1970). Russian sopr. Studied St. Petersburg. Début there, Maryinsky, 1918, Lisa (*Queen of Spades*). Remained in Russia until 1922, then to Paris. London, Ly., 1931; C.G. 1932, 1935; Savoy 1941. Also sang with success at Milan, Sc., and Buenos Aires, Colón. In London sang in first stage performance of Delius's *Koanga* and Dargomizhsky's *Russalka*, and title role in first broadcast performance of *The Queen of Spades*. Operetta career as Odali Careno, Coliseum and Palladium 1930–2. (R)

Sly. Opera in 3 acts by Wolf-Ferrari; text by Forzano, developed from an idea in the Induction of Shakespeare's comedy *The Taming of the Shrew* (1593–4). Prod. Milan, Sc., 29 Dec. 1927, with Pertile, cond. Toscanini; London, B.B.C., 11 Dec. 1954, with Howard Vandenburg, cond. Kempe.

Smallens, Alexander (b. St. Petersburg, 1 Jan. 1889). Russian, later American, conductor. Studied N.Y. and Paris. Boston 1911–14, Chicago 1919–22, Philadelphia 1924–31. Cond. premières of *The Love of the Three Oranges* and *Porgy and Bess*, and American premières of *Feuersnot*, *Ariadne auf Naxos*, *Hin und Zurück*, and *The Invisible City of Kitezh*.

Smareglia, Antonio (b. Pola, 5 May 1854; d. Grado, 15 Apr. 1929). Italian composer. His operas, which show a strong Wagner influence, were admired in Germany even by Brahms and Hanslick. The most successful of them was *Nozze Istriane* (1895); this and other works have been revived at Trieste in recent years.

Smart, Sir George (b. London, 10 May 1776; d. London, 23 Feb. 1867).

English conductor and teacher. Although primarily a concert conductor, he was closely connected with C.G. in the 1820's, and accompanied Kemble to Germany to engage Weber as the theatre's music director and to commission *Oberon*. He was much sought after as a teacher, and Sontag and Lind studied with him in London. Weber died in his house.

Smetana, Bedřich (b. Litomyšl, 2 Mar. 1824; d. Prague, 12 May 1884). Czech composer. His life coincided with the resurgence of Czech nationalism after the relaxation of the Austrian tyranny, and he became and has remained the outstanding musical spokesman for his country. The reawakening of artistic interests after the Austrian defeats by Italy in 1859 led to the establishment of a Provisional Theatre in 1862; Smetana started work on his first patriotic opera, *The Brandenburgers in Bohemia* (1862–3), produced there in 1866. Its success was eclipsed by *The Bartered Bride* (1866), which as well as remaining a national symbol for the Czechs has become Smetana's best-known opera throughout the world. *The Bartered Bride*, with its cheerful folk pleasures and vividly painted rustic types, was succeeded by the loftily heroic *Dalibor* (1868). The works typify two kinds of national feeling, but there were many who felt that with *Dalibor*'s massive style and thematic transformations, too much of Wagner had possessed Smetana. *Libuše* (1872, prod. 1881) is a 'solemn festival tableau'; in the marriage of the foundress of Prague to a wise peasant it attempts to combine the different appeals of its predecessors. *The Two Widows* (1874) is a complete contrast—a delightful and successful attempt at transferring a French drawing-room comedy to a Czech milieu. *The Kiss* (1876) and *The Secret* (1878) are both dramas of Czech life with music of great charm and sympathy overcoming somewhat strained librettos. *The Devil's Wall* (1882) suffers from a muddled libretto, and was finished despite Smetana's sufferings from aural and mental ill health; its music has won high praise. He worked on *Viola*, a version of Shakespeare's *Twelfth Night*, from 1874 to 1884 without finishing more than 365 bars. All his previous operas feature in Czech repertories.

Smyth, Ethel (Dame) (b. London, 23 Apr. 1858; d. Woking, 9 May 1944). English composer. Her output includes six operas—*Fantasio* (1898), *Der Wald* (1901), *The Wreckers* (1906), *The Boatswain's Mate* (1916), *Fête Galante* (1923), and *Entente Cordiale* (1925). Brought up in days when Germany reigned musically supreme, she studied in Leipzig and had the first three of her operas produced in Germany. In her music, her own breezy Englishry blows through a late German romantic scene: for all the local colour of their setting, and the use of English ballads, the structure and much of the music of *The Wreckers*, and still more those of *The Boatswain's Mate*, reveal this. Her entertaining series of memoirs conveys considerable relish for the long struggle against suspicion of a woman who composed, and did so not with a Chaminade-like wilt but with a robust professionalism that took men's breath away.

Snow Maiden, The. Opera in prologue and 4 acts by Rimsky-Korsakov; text by composer, after Ostrovsky's drama (1873) on a folk-tale. Prod. St. Petersburg 10 Feb. 1882; N.Y., Met., 23 Jan. 1922; London, S.W., 12 Apr. 1933. The Snow Maiden (sop.), who is safe from the sun only as long as she renounces love, begins the life of a mortal with two villagers. Mizgir (ten.), a merchant, deserts his lover for her; when she returns his love the sun destroys her, and Mizgir kills himself.

Sobinov, Leonid (b. Yaroslav, 7 June 1872; d. Riga, 14 Oct. 1934). Russian tenor. Studied Moscow; début there 1894. Sang with great success in St. Petersburg, where his Lensky was thought to eclipse that of Figner (q.v.). He excelled in such different roles as Roméo, Lohengrin, Orfeo, and Werther. (R)

Söderström, Elisabeth (b. Stockholm, 7 May 1927). Swedish soprano. Studied Stockholm. Début Drottningholm, 1947. Salzburg 1955; Glyndebourne since 1957; N.Y., Met., 1959–60. Repertory includes leading roles in Puccini, Strauss (sings all three soprano roles in *Rosenkavalier*), and modern roles such as Marie (*Wozzeck*), the Governess (*The Turn of the Screw*), and Elisabeth (*Elegy for Young Lovers*. (R)

Sofia. Capital of Bulgaria. The history of opera in Sofia follows the general development in Bulgaria. The National Opera (founded 1908) maintains a large ensemble and an orchestra independent of the Philharmonic and Radio Orchestras. Opera or ballet is presented every evening, with three performances on Sundays. Operetta was performed by a professional ensemble for the first time in 1917 at the Odeon Theatre and later at the Korona, Renesans, and Svoboden Theatres. In 1922 a Co-operative Operetta Theatre was founded, and in 1944 the State Operetta Theatre 'Stefan Makedonski' was established with its own soloists, chorus, ballet, and orchestra of 70. See *Bulgaria*.

Sola, perduta, abbandonata. Manon Lescaut's (sop.) final aria leading to her death scene in Act 4 of Puccini's *Manon Lescaut*.

Soldiers' Chorus. The gay chorus sung in Act 4, scene 3, of Gounod's *Faust* to the words 'Gloire immortelle de nos dieux'.

Solenne in quest' ora. The duet in Act 3, scene 2, of Verdi's *La Forza del Destino* between Alvaro (ten.) and Carlo (bar.) in which they swear eternal friendship.

Solti, Georg (b. Budapest, 21 Oct. 1912). Hungarian conductor. Studied Budapest with Dohnányi and Kodály. Conductor Budapest 1933–9. Worked with Toscanini, Salzburg, 1937–8. In Switzerland during war years. Music director, Munich State Opera, 1947–52 and Frankfurt 1952–61. San Francisco 1953; Chicago 1956–7. Edinburgh, with Hamburg Opera, 1952; Glyndebourne 1954; London, C.G., 1959: music director 1961–71. Built up the Royal Opera to a high musical and artistic level. One of the best Verdi, Wagner, and Strauss conductors of the day; also specializes in modern scores. (R)

Son lo spirito che nega. Mefistofeles's (bass) aria in Act 1 of Boito's *Mefistofele*.

Sonnambula, La (The Sleepwalker). Opera in 2 acts by Bellini; text by Romani. Prod. Milan, Teatro Carcano, 6 Mar. 1831, with Pasta and Rubini; London, King's, 28 July 1831, same singers; N.Y., Park T., 13 Nov. 1835.

In a quiet little Swiss village, early in the 19th century, Amina (sop.) foster-daughter of Teresa (mezzo), owner of the mill, is to become betrothed to Elvino (ten.), a young farmer. Lisa (sop.), the proprietress of the local inn and herself in love with Elvino, gladly entertains the handsome Count Rodolfo (bass), the lord of the castle recently returned to the village. Amina, unknown to her lover and friends, is a sleepwalker, and she enters the Count's bedroom by night and is discovered asleep in his room. The distraught Elvino is now ready to marry Lisa, but the Count tries to prevent this by explaining sleepwalking. The villagers scoff; but at that moment Amina is seen walking in her sleep along the edge of the roof (in some prods., the insecure bridge over the mill stream, which collapses once she is safely across). Elvino gives her the ring he had taken back after she was discovered in the Count's bedroom, and Amina awakens to find Elvino ready to marry her.

Sontag, Henriette (orig. Gertrud Walburga S., later Countess Rossi) (b. Coblenz, 3 Jan. 1806; d. Mexico City, 17 June 1854). German soprano. Daughter of a comedian and actress, she made her first public appearances at Darmstadt aged six. Studied Prague Conservatory. Début when 15 as Princess in Boïeldieu's *Jean de Paris*. Vienna from 1822. In 1823 heard in *La Donna del Lago* by Weber, who immediately offered her title role in *Euryanthe*. Berlin 1825, Paris 1826, London 1828. Her marriage to Count Rossi interrupted her stage career.

Returned to stage after the political unrest of 1848 had impaired their fortunes. Died of cholera caught in Mexico, 1854. Her voice, which she used with exquisite taste and charm, was a clear, bright soprano reaching e'''. Her execution was said to have been unsurpassed by any singer of her time—some thought she even excelled Catalani. Her most famous roles were Donna Anna, Susanna, Rosina, Semiramide, and Amina. She created Miranda in Halévy's *La Tempesta* at H.M.'s (1850). Biographies include those by Théophile Gautier (*L'Ambassadrice, Biographie de la comtesse Rossi*, Paris, 1850) and E. Pirchan (*Henriette Sontag*, Vienna, 1946).

Sonzogno, Edoardo (b. Milan, 21 Apr. 1836; d. Milan, 14 Mar. 1920). Italian publisher. His firm was founded end of 18th century by G. B. Sonzogno. He began to publish French and Italian music in 1874. Established a series of competitions for new works in 1883, the second contest of 1888 being won by Mascagni's *Cavalleria Rusticana*. Opened the Teatro Lirico Internazionale in Milan, 1894.

Soot, Fritz (b. Neunkirchen, 20 Aug. 1878; d. Berlin, 9 Jun. 1965). German tenor. Began career as actor at Karlsruhe and Vienna, B. Début as singer, Dresden, 1908, Tonio in *Fille du Régiment*. Dresden 1908–18; Stuttgart 1918–21; Berlin since 1921. Kammersänger 1912. London, C.G., 1924–5, Wagner roles. Famous in Berlin as Otello, Canio, and Palestrina. Was still singing character roles in the 1950's.(R)

Sophie. Faninal's daughter (sop.), the heroine of Strauss's *Der Rosenkavalier*.

Sophocles (b. Colonus, 495 B.C.; d. ?, 406 B.C.). Greek dramatist. Operas on his plays are as follows. *Elektra*: Lemoyne (1782); Haeffner (1787); Champein; R. Strauss (1909). *Oedipus* trilogy: Mereaux (1791); Desaugier (1779); Enesco (1936). *King Oedipus*: Leoncavallo (1920); Stravinsky (1927). *Oedipus at Colonus*: Sacchini (1786); Zingarelli (1802); Radoux-Rogier. *Antigone*: Honegger (1927); Pallantios (1942); Orff (1949).

Soprano (from It. *sopra* = above). The highest category of female (or artificial male) voice. Many subdivisions exist within opera houses: the commonest in general use (though seldom by composers in scores) are given below, with examples of roles and their approximate *tessitura*. These divisions often overlap, and do not correspond exactly from country to country. In general, distinction is more by character than by *tessitura*, especially in France: thus, the examples of the roles give a more useful indication of the different voices' quality than any attempted technical definition.

German: dramatischer Sopran (Brünnhilde: g–c'''); lyrischer Sopran (Arabella: b♭–c♯'''); hoher Sopran or Koloratur Sopran (Zerbinetta, Queen of the Night: g–f'''); Soubrette (Blonde, Aennchen: b♭–c''').

Italian: soprano drammatico (Tosca: g–c'''); soprano lirico (Countess, Mimì: b♭–c♯'''); soprano lirico spinto (Butterfly, Desdemona: a–c♯'''); soprano leggiero (Norina, Despina: g–f''').

French: soprano dramatique (Valentine, Alceste: g–c'''); soprano lyrique (Lakmé: b♭–c♯'''); soubrette (Zerline in *Fra Diavolo*: b♭–c'''); soprano demi-caractère (Manon, Cassandre: a–c♯'''); Dugazon (q.v.), divided as jeune Dugazon (Bérénice in Thomas's *Psyché*), première Dugazon (Djelma in Auber's *Le Premier Jour de Bonheur*), forte première Dugazon (La Comtesse in Thomas's *Raymond*), and mère Dugazon (Ellen in *Lakmé*); Falcon (q.v.) (Alice in *Robert le Diable*: b♭–c♯''').

See also *Castrato*, *Mezzo-soprano*.

Sorochinsky Fair. Opera (unfinished) by Mussorgsky; text after Gogol's story. Mussorgsky completed only the prelude, the market scene and part of the sequel, most of Act 2, a vision scene adapted from *A Night on the Bare Mountain*, an instrumental *hopak*, and two songs. The first editors were Lyadov (1904) and Karatygin (1912). A version from these editions, with Rimsky-Korsakov's version of *Night on the Bare Mountain*, prod. Moscow, Free T., 21 Oct. 1913. Then and subsequently, other hands contributed to the text and music. Version by Cui prod. St. Petersburg, T. of Musical Drama, 26 Oct. 1917. Version by Cherepnin prod. Monte Carlo, 17 Mar. 1923; N.Y., Met., 29 Nov. 1930; London, Fortune T., 17 Feb. 1934. These were published; version by Shebalin also published, 1933.

Sosarme, Re di Media. Opera in 3 acts by Handel; text an altered version of Noris's *Alfonso Primo*. Prod. London, Hm., 15 Feb. 1732.

Sotto voce (It. = below the voice). A direction to sing softly or 'aside'.

Soubrette (Fr. from Old Fr. *soubret* = cunning or shrewd). Used in opera for such roles as Serpina, Despina, Susanna, &c.—the cunning servant girl; then, more generally, to designate a light soprano comedienne, such as Marzelline (*Fidelio*), Adele (*Fledermaus*). In Italian opera the term *servetta* is used. See *Soprano*.

Souffleur. See *Prompter*.

South Africa. The first operas heard in Cape Town were the more popular British operas by Dibdin, Storace, &c. in the early years of the 19th century. The first serious opera was an amateur production of *Der Freischütz* (1831). In the 1870's touring companies began to visit South Africa and seasons were given at Johannesburg and elsewhere, among them the C.R., Moody-Manners, and Quinlan Companies. An annual opera season in Johannesburg grew out of the 'Music Fortnight' established in 1926, and visiting artists from Europe augmented local talent. In the Cape Town University, Erik Chisholm has given a number of outstanding opera performances, and in 1956 the Eoan Group, composed entirely of coloured singers, gave an opera season.

Sovrintendente (It. = superintendent). The administrator of an Italian opera house—not necessarily the artistic or music director.

Spain. See *Barcelona, Madrid*.

Spalato. See *Split*.

Spani, Hina (orig. Higinia Tuñon) (b. Puán, 15 Feb. 1896; d. Buenos Aires, Jul. 1969). Argentinian sopr. Studied Buenos Aires, Milan. Début Milan, Sc., 1915, Anna (Catalani's *Loreley*). Sang regularly in Italy until 1934; Buenos Aires, C., 1915–40. Created title role in first stage performance of Respighi's *Maria Egiziaca* (Colón 1934), as well as in a number of South American works. Her 70 roles ranged from Ottavia in Monteverdi's *L'Incoronazione di Poppea* to Verdi's Lady Macbeth. One of the finest lyric-dramatic sopranos of the inter-war period. (R)

Sparafucile. The professional assassin (bass) in Verdi's *Rigoletto*.

Spieloper (Ger. = opera-play). A type of 19th-century light opera, resembling *Singspiel* (q.v.), with a comic subject and spoken dialogue.

Spielplan (Ger. = performance plan). The published prospectus of the season's repertory. See *Prospectus*. Also a monthly publication giving programmes in all German opera houses.

Spieltenor (Ger. = acting tenor). A light tenor in a German company who plays such character roles as Mime, David, and Pedrillo. See *Tenor*.

Spinning Chorus. The chorus sung by Senta's friends in the opening of Act 2 of Wagner's *Der fliegende Holländer*.

Spirto gentil. Fernando's (ten.) aria in the last act of Donizetti's *La Favorite* in which he sings of his love for Leonora.

Split (It., Spalato). Town in Dalmatia, Yugoslavia. First theatre built in 17th century. Italians twice disbanded company, 1859 built theatre for their visiting companies. First local opera, 1921, foundation of National Dalmatian Theatre, but administration moved to Sarajevo. Post-war company gives indoor performances and summer festival performances in Diocletian's palace.

Spohr, Louis (b. Brunswick, 5 Apr. 1784; d. Kassel, 22 Oct. 1859). German composer and violinist. His first stage work, *Die Prüfung*, was an operetta which received a concert performance (1806) during his leadership of the ducal band at Gotha; its successor, *Alruna*, was rehearsed at Weimar in 1808, when it won Goethe's admiration, but was not performed. The first production he achieved was for *Der Zweikampf mit der Geliebten* (1811), followed in 1816 by *Faust*.

This was a landmark in Romantic opera; indeed, it is often claimed as the first true representative of the genre. The overture's use of leading themes from the opera was but one of many devices approved by Weber, whose review of it contains a remarkable formulation of the aims of German opera. But its popularity was at the time exceeded by *Zemire und Azor* (1819), given at Frankfurt during Spohr's two years (1817–19) as conductor of the opera. He planned an opera on *Der Freischütz*, abandoning this idea on hearing that the subject was being set by Weber, who later recommended him for Hofkapellmeister at Kassel. Here he remained for the rest of his life. The immensely successful *Jessonda* was produced in 1823; others which followed were *Der Berggeist* (1825), *Pietro von Albano* (1827), and *Der Alchymist* (1830). He also contributed to *Der Matrose* (1839), written in collaboration with Hauptmann, Grenzebach, and Baldewein. In 1842 he became the first musician of importance to uphold Wagner, when he produced *Der fliegende Holländer* at Kassel only five months after the Dresden première—a surprising gesture for one of conservative tastes. He later staged *Tannhäuser*, but was frustrated by the Elector in his attempts to follow this with *Lohengrin*. The last of his own operas was *Die Kreuzfahrer* (1845). His famous *Autobiography* gives a lively if prejudiced account of the European scene, musical and otherwise.

Spoleto. Town in Umbria, Italy. Menotti established the Festival of Two Worlds here in 1958. Performances are given in the Teatro Nuovo (cap. 1,000) and the 17th-century Teatro Caio Melisso.

Spoletta. The police agent (ten.) in Puccini's *Tosca*.

Spontini, Gasparo (b. Maiolati, 14 Nov. 1774; d. Maiolati, 24 Jan. 1851). Italian composer. After early local teaching, he studied in Naples, where his music quickly brought a commission from a visiting German opera director. The successful outcome, *Li Puntigli delle Donne*, was immediately followed up by five more works. When the Neapolitan court removed to Palermo before the advancing French, Spontini took on Cimarosa's post with it and in 1800 produced three deftly Neapolitan operas. Shortly afterwards he left Italy for Paris, where he was disappointed to find his light style unsuited to the special demands of *opéra comique*; but with the carefully composed *Milton* (1804), he won a success that carried his name into Germany and Austria. One of *Milton*'s librettists was Étienne de Jouy, who, understanding better than the composer himself where his gifts lay, provided for *La Vestale* (1807) a text that fully released Spontini's talent and thus led to his recognition as one of the leading opera composers of the day. The Empress Josephine's patronage carried him through all opposition; and after the constant rewriting that was to become his habit, *La Vestale* triumphed in 1807. For *Fernand Cortez* (1809) the librettist was again Jouy, the patron now Napoleon (who felt that the subject might influence opinion favourably in the Spanish War); a more polished work, its success was perhaps even greater. In 1810 Spontini took over the Italian opera, and at the Odéon formed a distinguished and enterprising ensemble before his dismissal in 1812; his restoration in 1814 was brief and again controversial, for his undoubted gifts were allied to a somewhat overbearing personality. A few minor pieces followed before what Spontini considered his masterpiece—*Olympie* (1819). Though carefully composed over a long period, it was in its first form coldly received in 1819, but assiduous revisions brought the work success in Paris as well as in Berlin, whither Spontini was now summoned. Frederick William III of Prussia, much impressed by the composer's work, engaged him for the

Berlin Court Opera, where he worked in uneasy harness with the intendant, Brühl. His temper and pomposity quickly caused difficulties, and when the imposing spectacle of *Olympie* was succeeded in a few weeks by the thrilling new experience of Weber's *Der Freischütz*, Berlin was divided, the court siding with Spontini's grandiose Italianate works, Brühl and the public with the new German Romantic opera. Spontini's star was setting: personal relationships were strained, and his painstaking method of composition prevented him from producing as much as was required of him. *Alcidor* (1825) hardened the public division of opinion, and he could not rally his scattering admirers even by a conscientious attempt at a German opera, *Agnes von Hohenstaufen* (1829). The sympathies of the new king who succeeded in 1840 lay elsewhere, but it was Spontini himself who hastened his own downfall; though fairly, even generously treated, he felt obliged to leave, and despite occasional visits to Germany (on one of which he conducted at Dresden a *Vestale* prepared by Wagner) he remained chiefly in Paris before returning to his native village.

Sprechgesang (Ger. = speech-song). A term used initially by Schoenberg and Berg for a form of musical declamation in which the notes are indicated before the voice immediately falls or rises in a manner somewhere between true speech and true song.

Stabile, Mariano (b. Palermo, 12 May 1888; d. Milan, 11 Jan. 1968). Italian baritone. Studied Rome, Santa Cecilia, with Cotogni. Début Palermo 1911, Marcello (*Bohème*). Milan, Sc., from 1922, when he sang Falstaff in the opening performance of Toscanini's third and greatest Scala régime; London, C.G., 1926–31; Glyndebourne 1936–9 and 1948 (Edinburgh); Cambridge and Stoll Theatres 1946–8; Chicago 1924–5; Salzburg 1935–9. Created title role in Respighi's *Belfagor*, and the Barber in the first Italian performance of *Die schweigsame Frau*. His repertory of some 60 parts also included Hamlet, Don Giovanni, Don Alfonso, Figaro (Mozart and Rossini), Malatesta (*Don Pasquale*), Iago, and Scarpia. As Falstaff, which role he was still singing with great success in 1961, he has not been surpassed in our day. His voice was never exceptional, but his style, elegance, phrasing, musicality—in short, his qualities as a singing actor—combined to make his performances unforgettable. (R)

Staatsoper (Ger. = state opera).

Städtische Oper (Ger. = city opera).

Stage design. Although the masques and other forms of elaborate entertainment which were the forerunners of opera often required elaborate scenery (Angelo Poliziano's *Orfeo* produced at Mantua in 1472 had scenery painted by Raphael), the first operas do not appear to have had it, and not until the spectacular performances staged in Cardinal Barberini's palace in Rome (*c.* 1630–50), and the establishment of the court theatres shortly after, did stage spectacles become the fashion.

It was in these court theatres, with their tiers of boxes, that the stage became separated from the audience by means of the proscenium frame. This, together with the two-dimensional flat scenery, was an entirely new concept. The perspective painting which characterized much Renaissance art was seized upon by the theatre designers, and splendid two-dimensional scenery characterized the magnificent baroque productions of opera. Cesti's *Pomo d'Oro*, performed in Vienna in 1668 for the marriage of the Emperor Leopold I to Margaret of Spain, had 23 different sets, designed by Lodovico Burnacini (1636–1707), who worked for the Imperial Court in Vienna.

The Bibiena family, descended from Giovanni Maria Galli (1619–65), a native of Bibiena in Tuscany, produced several generations of theatrical architects. Giuseppe Galli-Bibiena (1696–1757) worked almost entirely in Vienna; Ferdinando (1657–1743) and the two brothers Bernardino and Fabrizio Galliari were the designers at the old Ducal Theatre in Milan, and can be said to have set the pattern for Italian stage scenery. The Galliari brothers were also the first scene painters at La Scala, and they were followed by Pietro Gonzaga, whose daring use of colour and contrasts in light and shade in the Canaletto manner, in the days of rather poor stage lighting, brought, according to his contemporaries, 'the sun on to the stage'. Alessandro Sanquirico, whose settings for Rossini and Bellini at La Scala are still quoted as models of their kind, Carlo Ferrario, who was Verdi's favourite designer, and Antonio Rovescalli continued to paint splendid and sumptuous settings for La Scala and other Italian houses. Without stage towers, scenery had to be moved on and off the stage by means of grooves; it was not until the large reconstructions of 1919–21 that La Scala had a stage tower, being previously limited to 6–7 productions a season. More recently Alessandro and Nicola Benois, Giorgio De Chirico, Gianni Ratto, Salvatore Fiume, and Piero Zuffi, and the producers Franco Zeffirelli and Luchino Visconti, who like to design their own settings, can be cited as the best of this century's Italian stage designers.

In Germany and elsewhere in central Europe, Italian models were long copied, and designers even imported, though Karl Friedrich Schinkel's famous *Zauberflöte* designs (1816) and those of Karl von Gropius for *Der Freischütz* (1821) (both in Berlin), Eugen Quaglio's splendid scenery for Mozart and Wagner in Munich in the middle of last century, and Johann Kautsky's Wagner settings in Vienna (1860–90) deserve mention.

With the advent of Alfred Roller (1854–1935) in Vienna during the Mahler régime, Leo Pasetti in Munich in the 1920's and early 1930's, Adolf Mahnke and Hans Strobach in Dresden during the same period, and Caspar Neher at various German houses from the late 1920's, German opera scenery developed an individual style. This has resulted in the three-dimensional scenery of today; and the symbolic treatment of stage settings in which the subtle use of stage levels, and especially of lighting, has also replaced the old-fashioned two-dimensional scenery. These modern trends were greatly influenced by the writings and designs of the Englishman Edward Gordon Craig and the Swiss Adolphe Appia (q.v.) early this century. Present-day Bayreuth (q.v.), where sets and lighting are designed by the producers Wieland and Wolfgang Wagner, are the logical development of this type of scenery. Throughout Germany in the post-war period there are a number of scenic designers who, if not completely adopting the Bayreuth style, are clearly influenced by the methods of the Wagner brothers; these include Helmut Jürgens, Alfred Siercke, Ita Maximovna, Teo Otto, and Hein Heckroth.

With the increase in operatic activity in Great Britain, much of the scenery at Covent Garden and Sadler's Wells in the period since the end of the Second World War has been the work of native designers including Oliver Messel, John Piper, Leslie Hurry, Osbert Lancaster, and Malcolm Pride. Lancaster and Messel have also contributed greatly to post-war Glyndebourne. Covent Garden has also made great use of the French designer Georges Wakhevitch (who is in great demand in Italy and Austria), and even employed Salvador Dali to design a highly controversial *Salome* (1949). In the early 1960's the work of Visconti and Zeffirelli became increasingly familiar at Covent Garden.

In the United States, scenery was generally copied from European models until the mid-1930's, when the arrival in the U.S.A. of a number of refugees from the opera houses of Hitler's Germany, including Herbert Graf and Leopold Sachse, brought a fresh breath of life. Graf engaged Donald Oenslager, a Broadway artist, to design sets for *Tristan* in Philadelphia, and later *Salome*, *Otello*, and *Die Entführung aus dem Serail* at the Metropolitan. Influenced by Appia and by Robert Edmond Jones, a disciple of Max Reinhardt, Oenslager brought the ideas of a theatre to the opera stage. Harry Horner was another straight theatre designer to come to opera; he has worked for the San Francisco Opera and the Metropolitan. Eugen

Berman, a neo-Baroque designer, has been responsible for some fine work at the Metropolitan and the City Center, and was invited to design *Così fan tutte* for the Piccola Scala in Milan. Rolf Gérard's many designs for the Metropolitan also deserve mention.

Attempts have been made in most operatic countries in the use of slide-projections on to the cyclorama (sky-cloth) in order to dispense with heavy scenery and canvases; and the elaborate slide-projection technique of the Czech 'Magic Lantern' was tried for Nono's *Intolleranza* at Venice in 1961. So far these remain experiments.

Stagione (It. = season). The *stagione lirica* is the opera season at any Italian theatre.

Stanford, Charles (b. Dublin, 30 Sept. 1852; d. London, 29 Mar. 1924). Irish composer. Stanford's passionate interest in establishing English opera expressed itself in ten completed works, which have suffered neglect despite some vigorous championship. Still more than for *The Critic* (1916), high claims have been made for *Shamus O'Brien* (1896) and *The Travelling Companion* (1925).

Stasov, Vladimir Vassilievich (b. St. Petersburg, 14 Jan. 1824; d. St. Petersburg, 23 Oct. 1906). Russian critic. His influence on the development of Russian national opera was enormous, and his opinion was valued by all his contemporaries. He wrote valuable studies of Glinka, Mussorgsky, Borodin, Cui, and Rimsky-Korsakov.

Staudigl, Joseph (b. Wöllesdorf, 14 Apr. 1807; d. Döbling, 28 Mar. 1861). Austrian bass. After studying medicine, joined chorus of Vienna Kä.; then sang secondary roles. Established himself when he replaced a sick colleague as Pietro (*Masaniello*). Theater an der Wien 1845–8; Vienna Opera 1848–54; London, C.G., with German Company, 1842, when he sang Marcel n English première of *Les Huguenots*. Oroveso in first English performance of *Norma* 1843; H.M.'s 1847, where he sang Bertram in *Robert le Diable* at Jenny Lind's English début. His son **Josef** (1850–1916) was a baritone who became principal baritone at the Met., N.Y., 1884–6, where he was the first American Pogner. He subsequently appeared at Bayreuth, Berlin, and Hamburg.

Steber, Eleanor (b. Wheeling, 17 July 1916). American soprano. Studied Boston, and N.Y. with Althouse. Won Met. Auditions of the Air 1940, making début there same year as Sophie. Member of Met. ever since, where she has graduated from Sophie to the Marschallin; created title role, *Vanessa*, 1958. Glyndebourne (Edinburgh) 1947; Bayreuth 1953. Highly regarded in Mozart, Verdi, and Puccini, and as Marie (*Wozzeck*). (R)

Steffani, Agostino (b. Castelfranco, 25 July 1654; d. Frankfurt, 12 Feb. 1728). Italian composer and diplomat. His early career was spent in Germany, where he held appointments and had operas produced at Munich and Hanover. From 1696 he was successful as a diplomat, winning high honours for his services. He continued writing operas, which were universally admired in their day and won respect for their composer's contrapuntal skill.

Stehle, Sophie (b. Hohenzollern-Sigmaringen, 15 May 1838; d. nr. Hanover, 4 Oct. 1921). German soprano. Début Munich 1860, where she created Fricka (*Rheingold*) 1869, and Brünnhilde (*Walküre*) 1870.

Steinberg, William (orig. Hans Wilhelm S.) (b. Cologne, 1 Aug. 1899). German, later American, conductor. Studied Cologne. Cologne 1920, as Klemperer's assistant; Prague 1925–9; Generalmusikdirektor Frankfurt 1929–33, where cond. première of Schoenberg's *Von Heute auf Morgen* (1930); then removed by the Nazis. 1933–6 music director of Jewish Culture League, Germany. San Francisco 1944–8; N.Y., Met., 1965. His Wagner, Strauss, and Verdi performances are highly regarded. (R)

Stella, Antonietta (b. Perugia, 15 Mar. 1929). Italian soprano. Studied Perugia. Début Spoleto 1950, Leonora (*Trovatore*). Swiftly took her place as a leading Italian soprano. Milan, Sc., since 1953; London, C.G., 1955; N.Y., Met., 1956–60. (R)

Stendhal (orig. Henri Beyle) (b. Grenoble, 23 Jan. 1783; d. Paris, 23 Mar. 1842). French writer. His musical biographies include essays on Mozart, Haydn, and Metastasio, though his best-known work is the entertaining *Life of Rossini* (1824). His novel *La Chartreuse de Parme* (1839) was set as an opera by Sauguet (1939).

Stephens, Catherine (b. London, 18 Sept. 1794; d. London, 22 Feb. 1882). English soprano. Studied London. Début Pantheon 1812, small roles. C.G. 1813, as Mandane in Arne's *Artaxerxes*, singing there regularly until 1822; then at D.L. Polly, Donna Anna, and the Countess Almaviva were her best roles. Married the Earl of Essex 1838.

Stevens, Risë (b. New York, 11 June 1913). American mezzo. Studied N.Y., Juilliard School, with Anna Schoen-René, and Gutheil-Schoder in Vienna. Début Prague (Mignon) 1936; N.Y., Met., since 1938; Glyndebourne 1939 and 1956. A highly personable singer, she has scored her greatest successes as Octavian, Carmen, Dalila, Orlofsky, and Laura (*Gioconda*). Has also appeared in several films. General manager Met. Nat. Touring Co., 1964. (R)

Stich-Randall, Teresa (b. West Hartford, Conn., 24 Dec. 1927). American soprano. Studied Hartford School of Music. Sang Aida when 15. Appeared in première of Virgil Thomson's *The Mother of Us All* and first American *Macbeth* (Bloch). Sang Priestess in *Aida* and Nannetta in *Falstaff* under Toscanini for N.B.C. Won Lausanne singing contest 1951; and after a year at Basle, joined Vienna State Opera 1952. Aix-en-Provence since 1953; Chicago 1955; N.Y., Met. 1961. One of the most refined Mozart sopranos of the day. (R)

Stiedry, Fritz (b. Vienna, 11 Oct. 1883; d. Zurich, 8 Aug. 1968). Austrian, later American, conductor. Studied Vienna. Recommended by Mahler to Schuch, who engaged him for Dresden, 1907–8. First conductor Berlin 1914, remaining there until 1923; Vienna, V.O., 1924–5; Berlin, Städtische Oper, 1928–33, succeeding Walter as chief conductor 1929, and collaborating with Ebert in the famous *Macbeth* and *Boccanegra* productions of that period; also conducted the première of Weill's *Die Bürgschaft*. Forced to leave Germany by the Nazis, he conducted in Russia 1933–7; N.Y., New Opera Company, 1941; Chicago 1945–6; Met. 1946–58, where he was the principal Wagner conductor and also conducted important Verdi revivals. Glyndebourne 1947, *Orfeo*; London, C.G., 1953–4 preparing and conducting the new *Ring*, and *Fidelio*. (R)

Stierhorn (Ger. = bull horn). A medieval war-horn required by Wagner off-stage in *Walküre* (Act 2) and *Götterdämmerung* (Acts 2 and 3); played by trombonists.

Stiffelio. Opera in 3 acts by Verdi; text by Piave, after the play by Souvestre and Bourgeois. Prod. Trieste 16 Nov. 1850. Unsuccessful. Rev. as *Aroldo* (4 acts) and prod. Rimini, T. Nuovo (inauguration), 16 Aug. 1857; N.Y. 4 May 1863.

Stignani, Ebe (b. Naples, 10 July 1904). Italian mezzo. Studied Naples. Début Naples, S.C., 1925, Amneris. Milan, Sc., 1925–56, where her Eboli, Adalgisa, Laura (*Gioconda*), Azucena, and Leonora (*Favorite*) set a standard. London, C.G., 1937, 1939, 1952, 1955, 1957; San Francisco 1938, 1948. Her rich voice ranges from f to c‴ and can compass dramatic soprano roles. Her acting is nearly all in the voice, though she moves with dignity on the stage. (R)

Stile rappresentativo (It. = representative style). The term used by the first opera composers for their new effort to represent dramatic speech in music.

Still, William Grant (b. Woodville, 11 May 1895). American composer. His four operas have met with success in U.S.A., his *Troubled Island* being given by the N.Y. City Opera in 1949.

Stockholm. Capital of Sweden. Opera was first given during the reign of Queen Christina (1644–54). In the mid-18th century permanent French and Italian companies were established, and German companies paid visits. Queen Lovisa Ulrika built a theatre at Drottningholm (1754; burnt down 1762; reopened 1766); this still preserves stage machinery, a curtain, and some 30 18th-century stage sets used in the present annual summer seasons. On his accession in 1771, Gustav III dismissed the resident French troupe at the Stockholm Opera and set about the creation of a Swedish opera. The old Bollhus (Ball House) was put in order and opened in 1773 with *Thetis och Pelée*, based on a text by the king and set to music by Uttini (the former chief Drottningholm composer). This was later parodied in *Petis och Thelée* (1779) by Stenborg, who also wrote the first Swedish historical opera, *Konung Gustav Adolfs Jakt* (1777). But also in 1773 the Swedish opera had given Gluck's *Orpheus et Euridice* before the Paris première—a prized scoop. It was Gluck who formed the model for the busy operatic activity Gustav stimulated in the succeeding years. The crowning achievement was Naumann's *Gustav Vasa* (1786) based on a text by the king. In 1782 Gustav has opened the first Royal Opera House (pulled down in 1890 to make way for the present building); various other opera houses of the day were headed by the Munkbroteater, directed by Stenborg. This was bought by Gustav IV Adolf in 1799 and combined with the Arsenalsteater that had been set up in the Makalös Palace (founded 1793, burnt down 1825). Gustav's assassination in his own opera house (see Scribe's *Gustavus III ou Le Bal Masqué*, set by Verdi) meant the eclipse of the arts for some 20 years. The various 19th-century composers who attempted opera are now forgotten, even in Sweden, though the works of Rangström were noted as possessing an individuality lacking in those of, for instance, Stenhammar and Hallén. Swedish opera owes its renaissance largely to Rosenberg, whose example has been successfully followed by Blomdahl and Bäck. But foreign opera continued to flourish in the 19th century: a succession of able directors guided the opera house's destinies, and Swedish singers, among them Jenny Lind and Christine Nilsson, began to take their places on the international scene. The present Royal Opera House (cap. 1,264) was opened in 1898 with parts of Berwald's *Estrella de Soria*. Hallén's *Waldmarsskatten* (1899) was the first opera specially written for the new building. A fine Wagner tradition now developed, and famous Swedish Wagner singers have included Larsén-Todsen, Wettergren, Thorborg, Svanholm, Berglund, Sigurd Björling, and Birgit Nilsson. John Forsell was director 1924–39. Harald André 1939–49; Berglund 1949–54; Svanholm 1954–63. During the Hitler régime in Germany and the war, the Opera benefited from the presence of Leo Blech and Issay Dobrowen. In 1959 the company visited the Edinburgh Festival with a repertory that included Blomdahl's *Aniara* and an interesting 'historical' version of *Un Ballo in Maschera*; they brought these to London in the C.G. season, 1960.

Stoltz, Rosine (orig. Victoire Noël) (b. Paris, 13 Feb. 1815; d. Paris, 28 July 1903). French mezzo. Studied Paris. First sang in public, Brussels 1832 as Mlle Ternaux, then as Mlle Héloïse Stoltz, Lille 1833. Her fame dates from her Rachel in *La Juive*, Brussels 1836 (where she married Lescuyer, the theatre's manager), opposite Nourrit, who recommended her to the Paris O. Début here in same role in 1837, remaining for ten years. Created Leonora (*La Favorite*) and Zaida in Donizetti's *Don Sebastiano*. She formed a liaison with the Paris Opéra's manager Leon Pillet, and through him influenced the engagements of new singers, causing great hostility; after a series of attacks in the Press she resigned from the Opéra in 1847. She answered some of the attacks made on her in three pamphlets, and then became the mistress of the Brazilian Emperor Don Pedro, who invited her to make four tours of Brazil, 1850–9, at the salary of 400,000 fr.

a season. Her last appearances were in 1860 at Lyons. She married several times, becoming a Baroness, Countess of Kestchendorf, and Princess of Bassano. Biographies include Gustav Bord's *Rosine Stoltz de l'Académie Royale de Musique* (1909).

Stolz, Teresa (orig. Terezie Stolzová) (b. Kosteletz, 2 June 1834; d. Milan, 23 Aug. 1902). Czech soprano. Studied Prague, Trieste, and Milan with Lamperti. Début Tiflis. Italian début Bologna 1864, Mathilde (*Tell*), conducted by Verdi's friend Mariani, whose mistress she became. La Scala from 1865, and in 1866 joined the close Verdi–Mariani family circle. Elisabeth de Valois in the revised *Don Carlos* at La Scala 1868, the first Italian Leonora (*Forza*) and Aida, and creator of the soprano role in the Verdi *Requiem*. She broke with Mariani in 1871, and after the death of Verdi's wife Giuseppina, she became Verdi's inseparable companion. Her voice was described as 'vigorous, flexible, dramatic, limpid, clear, brilliant' ranging from g to $c\sharp'''$. See Frank Walker's *The Man Verdi* for a discussion of her relationship with the Verdis.

Stolze, Gerhard (b. Dessau, 1 Oct. 1926). German tenor. Studied Dresden. Début Dresden 1949. Bayreuth since 1951, Vienna since 1957. London, C.G., 1960. An outstanding Mime, David, Herod, and character tenor. Also specializes in contemporary works. (R)

Stone Guest, The. Opera in 3 acts by Dargomizhsky; text, Pushkin's drama (1830). Prod. St. Petersburg 28 Feb. 1872; Florence 14 Apr. 1954. Based on the Don Juan legend. Orchestration by Rimsky-Korsakov; overture by Cui. Famous for the natural setting of word-rhythms, and thus highly influential.

Storace, Ann (orig. Nancy) (b. London, 1766; d. London, 24 Aug. 1817). English soprano of Italian descent. Début in her teacher Rauzzini's *Le Ali d'Amore* (1776); further studies in Venice and appearances in Italy. From 1784 soprano at Imperial Theatre, Vienna; first Susanna in *Figaro* 1786. Continued a successful career in England from 1788. Toured with Braham and bore him a son. Her greatest triumphs were in comic opera, where her liveliness and acting abilities could compensate for a harsh tone. Her brother **Stephen** (b. London, 4 Jan. 1763; d. London, 19 Mar. 1796) joined her in Vienna and became friendly with Mozart. His numerous operas were successful in their day for their astute use of popular airs and their skilful provision for effective parts for his sister, Michael Kelly, and other singers.

Storchio, Rosina (b. Mantua, 19 May 1876; d. Milan, 25 July 1945). Italian soprano. Studied Milan. Début Milan, T.d.V., 1892, Micaëla; Scala from 1895. Chicago 1920–1; N.Y., Manhattan, 1921. Created Zazà (under Toscanini), Butterfly, Lodoletta (Mascagni), Stefana (Giordano's *Siberia*), Musetta (Leoncavallo's *Bohème*). Considered by Toscanini one of the finest lyric sopranos of her day. (R)

Stracciari, Riccardo (b. Casalecchio, nr. Bologna, 26 June 1875; d. Rome, 10 Oct. 1955). Italian baritone. Studied Bologna. Début Bologna, Marcello, 1898. Milan, Sc., from 1904 to 1905; London, C.G., 1905; N.Y., Met., 1906–8; Chicago 1918–19; San Francisco 1925. Continued to sing in Italy until 1942. Considered the finest Figaro (Rossini) in the 1920's and 1930's, and sang the role more than 900 times. Also admired in Verdi. (R)

Strada del Pò, Anna (b. ?; d. ?). Italian 18th-century soprano. The most loyal of Handel's London singers (1729–38). Thanks largely to his patient help, she triumphed over the disadvantages of succeeding Cuzzoni and Bordoni, and of an appearance that led to the nickname 'Pig'.

Stradella, Alessandro (b. Montefestino, 1642; d. Genoa, 28 Feb. 1682). Italian composer. His career is overlaid with mystery and fiction (see Flotow's opera *Alessandro Stradella* (1844)); but his operas give evidence of a serious, original talent that may have had some influence on Purcell and certainly did on the Neapolitans headed by Alessandro Scarlatti.

Strakosch, Maurice (b. Židlochovice, 1825; d. Paris, 9 Oct. 1887). Czech impresario. Studied Vienna and toured Europe and America as pianist. Brother-in-law of Patti and manager of her concerts. Undertook first opera season, N.Y. 1857; Chicago 1859; Paris 1873–4; Rome, Ap., with his brother Max, 1884–5. Often 'stood in' for Patti at rehearsals. Autobiography, *Souvenirs d'un Impresario* (1887). His brother **Ferdinando** was at various times director of the opera houses of Rome, Florence, Barcelona, and Trieste.

Straniera, La (The Foreigner). Opera in 2 acts by Bellini; text by Romani. Prod. Milan, Sc., 14 Feb. 1829, with Méric-Lalande, Rubini, Tamburini; London, King's T., 23 June 1832; N.Y. 10 Dec. 1834. Still occasionally revived in Italy.

Strasbourg. Town in Bas-Rhin, France. Opera is given at the Théâtre Municipal (cap. 1,190), orig. built 1821 and rebuilt after its destruction in the Franco-Prussian war in 1870. Between 1900 and 1918 the theatre's directors included Otto Lohse, Hans Pfitzner and Paul Bastide, and from 1915–17 Klemperer was music director there. The first performances in France of many important works have taken place at Strasbourg, including *Béatrice et Bénédict, Don Procopio, Peter Grimes, Duke Bluebeard's Castle, The Queen of Spades, Mathis der Maler, Wozzeck, The Love of the Three Oranges*, and *Il Prigioniero*.

Strauss, Johann (II) (b. Vienna, 25 Oct. 1825; d. Vienna, 3 June 1899). Austrian composer. Son of Johann Strauss I, famous composer of waltzes, marches, &c., and a conductor. Johann II began his musical career in a similar manner. His first operetta, *Indigo und Dit Vierzig Räuber* was produced at the Theater an der Wien in 1871. From his dozen or more operettas, the bubbling *Die Fledermaus* (Vienna 1874), the almost equally successful *Der Zigeunerbaron* (Vienna 1885), and *Eine Nacht in Venedig* (Berlin 1883) are regularly performed, not only in theatres entirely devoted to operetta but also in the world's leading opera houses. The operettas are notable for their fine melody, piquant charm, and first-rate orchestration.

Strauss, Richard (b. Munich, 11 June 1864; d. Garmisch-Partenkirchen, 8 Sept. 1949). German composer and conductor. His father, Franz Strauss, was a leading horn player at the Munich Opera, and is said to have modified the original version of Siegfried's horn call into a more playable shape at Wagner's request. The younger Strauss's reputation as a composer and conductor was made in the concert hall, and several of his most celebrated tone-poems had been written by the time of his first appearances as an opera conductor (he directed *Tannhäuser* at Bayreuth in 1894) and his first opera, *Guntram* (1894). There is a Wagnerian connexion between the two events in that *Guntram* concerns redemption by love. In 1898 he became conductor of the Royal Opera House in Berlin. *Feuersnot* appeared at Dresden in 1900: it is a rich score whose sumptuous love music has made the closing scene (the first of many successful closing scenes) fairly familiar in the concert hall.

Salome followed in 1905, bringing with it the most violent storm of controversy Strauss had yet encountered in a hectic career. Wilde's drama remains to this day a horrifying study in necrophily which Strauss did nothing to modify. The role of the orchestra here reaches a new importance: there is more than flippancy in Strauss's fabled exhortation, 'Louder! louder! I can still hear the singers.' It is a score designed for physical shock in every way; its loudness, its harmonic violence, the garishness of the orchestration, the morbid sweetness of the melody all intensify the sensual horror of the story to stifling-point.

Elektra, which followed in 1909, was the first product of Strauss's long and active collaboration with Hugo von Hofmannsthal. Though even more brutal in its emotional onslaught than *Salome*, there is ampler scope for the development not only of character but of genuine tragedy as distinct from neurotic horror. Over the whole score looms the figure of the murdered Agamemnon, his name pronounced by the orchestra in one of the principal *Leitmotive*, and except in the questionable dance finale the invention is even stronger and more precise in characterization than with *Salome*.

After *Elektra*, Strauss (having resigned from Berlin in 1910) turned his back on these extremes of violence with what remains the warmest comedy of modern times, *Der Rosenkavalier* (1911). The period Viennese setting, the comic licentiousness of Baron Ochs, the ardent love scenes, the lively ensembles, above all the bitter-sweet ending with the radiance of young love given an added dimension by the Marschallin's renunciation of Octavian to Sophie—these elements in the story tapped Strauss's richest humanity, and the score, long, elaborate, and densely lush as it is, remains simple and direct in its appeal to the heart.

Ariadne auf Naxos (1912) began life as a one-act opera to be played after Hofmannsthal's shortened German version of Molière's *Le Bourgeois Gentilhomme*, for which Strauss furnished incidental music. But the problems of assembling a cast of actors and singers on the same evening soon persuaded the authors to make their second, and better-known, version (1916), in which the events preparatory to the performance of *Ariadne* become a separate operatic Prologue. This new form brings forward one of Strauss's most moving characters, the young Composer whose ideals are affronted by the insult to music of telescoping comedy and tragedy at the master of the house's orders. There is later a brilliant coloratura aria for the comedienne Zerbinetta and a prolongedly radiant conclusion for Ariadne's ascension in the arms of Bacchus.

Die Frau ohne Schatten (1919) was the work by which Hofmannsthal set most store. It was intended as a complex psychological allegory, a kind of modern *Magic Flute*; but Strauss's talent was planted too firmly on theatrical boards to allow him to follow his librettist's flights of intellectual fancy. Despite many beautiful passages and ambitious ideas, the work is an elaborate failure.

The autobiographical interest that had marked Strauss's work both in the concert hall (*Ein Heldenleben*, *Sinfonia Domestica*) and intermittently in the theatre (*Feuersnot*) became the spur for a complete opera with *Intermezzo* (1924); this was based on a real-life domestic incident.

Strauss's language was by now established, and remained more or less constant for the rest of his life: inspiration waxed—notably in his very last years, with a group of concert works including his moving requiem for the bombed Munich Opera, *Metamorphosen*—and also waned, but there was little further development. Admirers have readily been found for the later operas, which are regularly revived in Germany and occasionally elsewhere, but it is upon *Salome*, *Elektra*, *Rosenkavalier*, and *Ariadne* that his reputation really rests. *Die aegyptische Helena* (1928) was a serious piece, *Arabella* (1933) another Viennese comedy. The latter was also his last collaboration with Hofmannsthal, who had died in 1929. *Die schweigsame Frau* (1935), with Stefan Zweig after Jonson's *Epicœne*, includes some of the old but less expert handling of love and comic misunderstanding, with an especially touching prolonged curtain to the second act. The Nazis prevented any further collaboration with Zweig, and Strauss now turned to Josef Gregor, with whom he wrote three operas, *Friedenstag* (1938), *Daphne* (1938), and (on a libretto partly sketched by Hofmannsthal) *Die Liebe der Danae* (comp. 1938–40, prod. 1952).

His last opera, *Capriccio* (1942), on an idea of his own developed by Clemens Krauss, is a dramatization of the old argument whether words or music should take priority in opera. The question had long occupied Strauss. In *Salome* and *Elektra* the decision is clearly for the music. The Prologue to the second version of *Ariadne* is closer to heightened conversation, with the music keeping pace; and *Intermezzo* reserves its musical outbursts chiefly for the interludes. None of the subsequent works resolves the question; nor indeed can *Capriccio*. It is a ripe, benign work, but it ends on a note of irresolution: the Countess who represents opera cannot choose between her two suitors, the poet Olivier and the composer Flamand. (R)

Stravinsky, Igor (b. Oranienbaum 17 Jun. 1882; d. N.Y., 6 Apr. 1971). Russian, then French, then American composer. His first opera, *The Nightingale*, both covers and concludes the period of his early spectacular, lavishly composed stage works. The first act was written in Russia in 1909; the last two were completed in Switzerland in 1914. In between came the three great early ballets, *The Firebird*, *Petrushka*, and *The Rite of Spring*. Stravinsky was the first to recognize the perils of returning to a half-finished work after such experiences, and agreed only under pressure to do so. The change of idiom is theoretically justified by the contrast between the scenes in the forest with the child who loves the nightingale's song and the later ornate luxury of the Chinese court; but the stylistic and technical development is sharp, and despite great beauties the opera as a whole cannot manage the impossible task of bestriding two separate worlds.

Most of Stravinsky's later stage works reflect a doubt about traditional opera and place the singers in a special position with regard to the action. *Les Noces* (1914–17; finally prod. 1923), a ballet with songs and choruses, was the first result, and the composer's ambiguous feelings towards the stage were further revealed in his next dramatic work. This was *Renard*, described as 'Une histoire burlesque chantée et jouée', which gave the action to dancers and placed the singers (all male) in the orchestra. Written in 1916–17, it was not performed until 1922, in the same programme as the more conventionally operatic *Mavra* (1922). Based on a Pushkin story, this is a careful reaction against Wagner's 'inflated arrogance' in the form of a modern *opera buffa* 'because of a natural sympathy I have always felt for the melodic language, the vocal style, and conventions of the old Russo-Italian opera'. There is no recitative, but a succession of arias and ensembles with simple accompaniment figures, reminiscent of classical *opera buffa*.

Oedipus Rex (1927) again places the singers on the stage, but in the interest of preserving the impersonal and universal sense of tragedy that led to the choice of a dead language, Latin, for the libretto, all are masked: the chorus is confined to one position and the soloists are allowed only formal entries and restricted gestures and movements. A speaker using the audience's language introduces each of the six episodes which make up the 'opera-oratorio'. Despite the wide variety of influences, the music has a powerful artistic unity, and a precise expression and conviction of purpose.

Two ballets, *Apollon Musagète* and *Le Baiser de la Fée*, followed before Stravinsky resumed his highly individual relationship with the stage in *Persephone* (1934); this is a 'melodrama' for reciter, tenor, chorus, dancers, and orchestra, nearer to sung ballet than danced opera. Two more ballets, *Jeu de Cartes* and *Orpheus*, separate this from Stravinsky's next opera, *The Rake's Progress* (1951) (a later opera on the rebirth of the world after atomic or cosmic disaster, with Dylan Thomas, was forestalled by the poet's death). Here the influences, again diverse, are consciously exposed, and help to set the old Hogarth moral tale in a fantastic framework. Yet the enigmatic shifts of emotional emphasis do create a curiously sympathetic figure of the puppet hero, and the final scene among the twitching lunatics of Bedlam drew from Stravinsky some of the most humanly compassionate music he had ever written. *The Flood* (1962), a setting of part of the York miracle play, is a slighter work in Stravinsky's neo-Webern manner. (R)

Streich, Rita (b. Barnaul, 18 Dec. 1920). German soprano, born of Russian and German parents. Studied Augsburg, Berlin with Maria Ivogün and Erna Berger, and with Domgraf-Fassbänder. Début Aussig 1943. Berlin State Opera 1946–50, Städtische

Oper since 1950; Vienna since 1953; London, with Vienna Co., 1954; San Francisco 1957; Glyndebourne 1958. Excels in Mozart and Strauss (Queen of the Night, Constanze, Zerbinetta, and Sophie). (R)

Strepponi, Giuseppina (b. Lodi, 8 Sept. 1815; d. Busseto, 14 Nov. 1897). Italian soprano. Her father Feliciano (1767–1832) was a composer and conductor. Studied Milan. Début Trieste 1835, Matilde di Shabran. After engagements in Vienna, Rome, Florence, &c., appeared Milan, Sc., where she helped to get Verdi's first opera, *Oberto*, produced; and created Abigaille in *Nabucco* (1842). Seven years later she left the stage to live with Verdi, whom she married in 1859. For a portrait of her sympathetic character, see Frank Walker's *The Man Verdi.*

Stretta (It. = tightening or squeezing). The passage at the end of an act, ensemble, aria, in which the tempo is accelerated to make a climax.

Stride la vampa. Azucena's (mezzo) narrative in Act 2, scene 1 of Verdi's *Il Trovatore.*

Stuttgart. Town in Baden-Würtemberg, Germany. Opera was first performed there in the Neues Lusthaus in the closing years of the 16th century. From 1753 to 1771 Jommelli was Kapellmeister to the Duke of Württemberg. Between 1812 and 1815 the Lusthaus underwent structural alterations and became the Hoftheater. It was destroyed by fire in 1902. The present theatre (cap. 1,400) was opened in 1912, during which year the première of *Ariadne auf Naxos* was given. During the 1920's the company included Ranczak, Teschemacher, Domgraf-Fassbänder, Weill, and Fritz Windgassen; and during the decade before the war Cunitz, Eipperle, and Suthaus. The theatre was closed for the 1944–5 season, but after the war the ensemble was quickly built up. In Dec. 1946 the first performance in Germany of *Mathis der Maler* was given, followed six months later by the première of Orff's *Die Bernauerin.* In 1947 Leitner was appointed Generalmusikdirektor, and in recent years both Wieland Wagner and Günther Rennert have spent much time there. The post-war company has included Eipperle, Res Fischer, Grace Hoffman, Mödl, Wissmann, Neidlinger, Traxel, and Windgassen; while Borkh, Rysanek, Varnay, London, Frick, and Schmitt-Walter appear there regularly. The repertory, a very large and catholic one, includes many modern works as well as all Wagner's operas (except *Die Feen* and *Das Liebesverbot*), and nearly all Strauss's and Mozart's operas. Francis Burt's *Volpone* had its première there in 1960. The company has visited Paris, London, and Edinburgh in recent years.

Subotica (Szabadka). Town in Vojvodina, Yugoslavia, on the Hungarian border. Centre of the Hungarian theatre with performances in Croatian and Hungarian. Theatre over 100 years old; company founded, 1945.

Sucher (orig. Hasselbeck), **Rosa** (b. Velburg, Bavaria, 23 Feb. 1849; d. Eschweiler, nr. Aachen, 16 Apr. 1927). German soprano. Studied Munich. Début Trier. Sang in Danzig, Berlin, and Leipzig, where she married the conductor Josef Sucher, 1877, after which their careers in Germany coincided. London, D.L., 1882, where she was the first London Isolde and Eva, also singing Euryanthe, Elsa, Senta, and Elisabeth; C.G., 1892, Brünnhilde and Isolde; Bayreuth 1886–94; N.Y., Met., 1895, with Damrosch Co. Farewell performance, Berlin 1903, Sieglinde. Lived in Vienna from 1908 and taught singing. Autobiography, *Aus meinem Leben* (1914).

Suchoň, Eugen (b. Pezinok, 25 Sept. 1908). Slovak composer. His opera *Krútňava* (*The Whirlpool*) is one of the most highly regarded modern native operas in Czechoslovakia; it is an attempt to follow Janáček's example in speech patterns.

Suicidio! La Gioconda's (sop.) dramatic monologue in the last act of Ponchielli's *La Gioconda* in which she contemplates suicide.

Sullivan, Arthur (b. London, 13 May 1842; d. London, 22 Nov. 1900). English composer. His first stage works were to librettos by F. C. Burnand, a one-act farce, *Cox and Box* (1867), and the two-act *Contrabandista* (1867). The first collaboration with W. S. Gilbert came in 1871 with *Thespis*, most of which is lost. In 1875 the impresario Richard D'Oyly Carte persuaded them to work together again on a piece to precede Offenbach's *La Périchole*: the result was the successful *Trial by Jury*, unique in their output as being the only operetta without spoken dialogue. In the same year Sullivan collaborated with B. C. Stevenson on *The Zoo*. It had a few performances, but Sullivan soon decided to join forces with Carte and Gilbert, and a theatre was taken.

Their first production was *The Sorcerer* (1877), which ran for 175 nights. This was followed by the immensely successful *H.M.S. Pinafore* (1878) and *The Pirates of Penzance* (1880), which established the pattern of what have become known as the Savoy Operas, from the theatre to which Carte transferred in 1881. Selecting venue and target carefully, Gilbert contrives successions of ingeniously whimsical or paradoxical situations in verse whose wit and brilliance of invention has rarely been matched: the chief reproaches against him are a certain mawkishness and his notoriously cruel handling of the middle-aged spinsters who recur as a fixation in most of the operettas. Sullivan brought to these admirable librettos many apt qualities. Above all, his quick melodic ear responded to the lilt and patter of Gilbert's rhythms, and gave them new and often unexpected expressive twists: an outstanding example is the treatment of 'Fair Moon' in *H.M.S. Pinafore*. Harmonically he was less original, and occasionally matches Gilbert's sentimentality too well; but his melodic brilliance extends to a contrapuntal ingenuity that enabled him to combine tunes of different character with satisfying musical and dramatic effect. The essence of his success as an operetta composer, however, was almost more in his vivid sense of parody and the sure instinct with which he seized and both guyed and used his models. Sometimes the parody is direct: more often he fastens on a composer (e.g. Handel) or form (e.g. madrigal) and absorbs as much of it as is needed to start his own invention running. His technical learning and wide knowledge of music stood him in good stead here.

Patience (1881) turns these devastating gifts on the current cult of the aesthetic, and in particular upon Oscar Wilde: the quality of the invention is proved by the work's continuing popularity long after the target has vanished. *Iolanthe* (1882) is a skilful mixture of fairy-tale and satire on the peerage; but in *Princess Ida* (1884), 'a respectful perversion of Tennyson's *Princess*', the combination of satire (on women's rights) and never-never-land court romp is less happily managed by Gilbert. Sullivan, however, provided for it some of his most ambitious and original operetta music, by which the piece has amply justified its revivals. A return to formula came with *The Mikado* (1885), which was pure never-never-land, spiced as ever with topical allusions, though it took its impulse from the Victorian cult of *japonaiserie*. It was at once a brilliant success, running for 672 nights, and has remained the most popular of the series. *Ruddigore* followed in 1887, a comedy on country life with ghostly goings-on that reach their climax in one of Sullivan's finest extended scenes, the so-called 'Ghosts' High Noon'. *The Yeomen of the Guard* (1888) was an attempt to break out into a more genuinely operatic manner; though it remains a vintage Gilbert and Sullivan operetta, it includes some of Sullivan's best numbers and successfully creates a pervading sense of grimness in the dominating presence of the Tower of London. *The Gondoliers* (1889) reverts, brilliantly, to the former type of success, and is further notable for the skilfully handled long introductions and finales without spoken dialogue.

During its run, Sullivan quarrelled with Gilbert and, having already failed in his much-cherished attempt to write a successful grand opera, *Ivanhoe* (1891), collaborated with Sidney Grundy in the operetta *Haddon Hall* (1892). Reconciliation with Gilbert followed, and the 13th Gilbert and

Sullivan operetta ensued, *Utopia Limited* (1893)—a satire which fails partly through trying to fire at too many targets in Victorian England at once. Together the partners remodelled Sullivan's old *Contrabandista* as *The Chieftain* (1895), and then produced a new piece, *The Grand Duke* (1896), their last.

Sullivan went on to write *The Beauty Stone* (1898) to a text by Pinero and Comyns Carr; and with *The Rose of Persia* (1899) it was hoped he had found his new Gilbert in Basil Hood. They began work on *The Emerald Isle*; after Sullivan's death in 1900 it was completed by Edward German (1901).

Suor Angelica. Opera in 1 act by Puccini; text by Forzano: part 2 of *Il Trittico*. Prod. N.Y., Met., 14 Dec. 1918, with Farrar; Rome, C., 11 Jan. 1919; London, C.G., 18 June 1920, with Dalla Rizza. Sister Angelica (sop.) has taken the veil in expiation of a love affair that has produced a child. News comes to her from her aunt (con.) of its death. Praying for forgiveness she commits suicide, but this second sin is forgiven when the Virgin and Child appear to her in a vision. Before the première Puccini played the opera through at the Convent of Vicopelago, a community that included his eldest sister, and the nuns all wept in sympathy for Angelica.

Supervia, Conchita (b. Barcelona, 8 Dec. 1895; d. London, 30 Mar. 1936). Spanish mezzo. Studied Barcelona. Début Buenos Aires 1910, Breton's *Los Amantes de Teruel.* Rome 1911, Octavian in Rome première of *Rosenkavalier*; Chicago 1915–16 and 1932–3; London, C.G., 1934–5. Supervia's fame as a Rossini singer (Isabella, Angelina, Rosina) dates from Turin 1925, when she sang in *L'Italiana in Algeri* under Gui. She sang the Rossini roles in their original keys in Italy, Paris, and London. Her Carmen was a controversial interpretation, but about her Rossini heroines there were no divided opinions. Her attractive stage personality, mischievous charm, and the characteristic Spanish timbre of her voice made her a highly individual and likeable singer. (R)

Suppé, Franz von (b. Split, 18 Apr. 1819; d. Vienna, 21 May 1895). Austrian composer of Belgian descent, born in Dalmatia of an Italianized family. From the moment of his appointment as conductor at the Josephstadt Theater in Vienna (1841), he began producing a long series of highly successful operettas, farces, and musical comedies that swiftly, if impermanently, conquered Europe. His music has an easily enjoyed, racy charm.

Susanna. Figaro's bride (sop.) in Mozart's *Le Nozze di Figaro*, and wife (sop.) of Count Gil in Wolf-Ferrari's *Il Segreto di Susanna.*

Süssmayr, Franz Xaver (b. Schwanenstadt, 1766; d. Vienna, 16 Sept. 1803). Austrian composer. Best known for his work in completing Mozart's *Requiem*, Süssmayr also produced over a dozen operas that held the stage in their day.

Sutermeister, Heinrich (b. Feuerthalen, 12 Aug. 1910). Swiss composer. Claiming Italian opera (especially Verdi's last works) and Orff as influences, he has deliberately set himself to write simple, melodic, modern operas without sacrificing character or quality. *Romeo und Julia* (1940) has won wide acceptance. Other works which recur frequently in German repertories are *Die Zauberinsel* (1942), *Raskolnikoff* (1948), *Die schwarze Spinne* (1936, rev. 1949), and *Titus Feuerfuchs* (1958).

Suthaus, Ludwig (b. Cologne, 12 Dec. 1906; d. Berlin, 9 Sept. 1971). German tenor. Studied Cologne. Début Aachen 1928, Walther. Stuttgart 1933–8; Berlin, S.O., 1941–9; Berlin, Städtische Oper, 1950–67; Vienna 1948–71; London, C.G., 1952–3; San Francisco 1953; Bayreuth 1943 and subsequently. A powerful Tristan and Siegmund. (R)

Sutherland, Joan (b. Sydney, 7 Nov. 1926). Australian soprano. Studied Sydney, and London, R.C.M., with Clive Carey. Début Sydney, Judith (Goossens). London, C.G., 1952, First Lady (*Magic Flute*). Created Jennifer in Tippett's *Midsummer Marriage* 1955, and the New Prioress in first English *Carmelites*. Her Gilda and Israelite Woman in Handel's *Samson* prepared the way for her highly successful Lucia (1959), which established her as one of the leading dramatic coloraturas of the day, and led to appearances in Italy, France, Austria, and U.S.A. Also scored great success as Alcina and Rodelinda for Handel Opera Society. Visited Australia with her own company, 1965. (R)

Suzel. A farmer's daughter (sop.), heroine of Mascagni's *L'Amico Fritz*.

Suzuki. Cio-Cio-San's faithful servant (mezzo) in Puccini's *Madama Butterfly*.

Svanholm, Set (b. Vasteras, 2 Sept. 1904; d. nr. Stockholm, 4 Oct. 1964). Swedish tenor, formerly baritone. Studied Stockholm with Forsell. Début Stockholm 1930, Silvio (*Pagliacci*). Sang baritone roles for a few years and then renewed his studies. Second début 1936, Radamès. First Wagner roles 1937, Lohengrin and Siegmund. Salzburg 1938; Bayreuth 1942; N.Y., Met., 1946–56; London, C.G., 1948–57. Intendant Stockholm Opera 1956–63. The leading Tristan and Siegfried during the first decade after the Second World War. In Sweden he has also sung in the Italian repertory, notably Otello and Radamès; created Peter Grimes there. His musicianship, intelligence, and dramatic intensity compensated for rather a dry tone and small stature. (R)

Sved, Alexander (b. Budapest, 28 May 1906). Hungarian baritone. Studied Budapest, and Italy with Sammarco and Ruffo. Début Budapest 1928, Di Luna. Vienna 1936–9; London, C.G., 1936; N.Y., Met., 1940–50. Also sang in Italy, where his Rigoletto, Tell, Boccanegra, and Macbeth were much admired. (R)

Sverdlovsk (Ekaterinburg). Town in R.S.F.S.R., U.S.S.R. An opera house was built by wealthy merchants in 1912, but the opening seasons were short and unpractically managed. After the October Revolution (1917) the authorities began building up the company and the town became the cultural centre of the Urals. The company tours Siberia and the Ukraine, and has made a good impression on its Moscow visits.

Swarthout, Gladys (b. Deepwater, Missouri, 25 Dec. 1904; d. Florence, 7 July 1969). American mezzo. Studied Chicago, and with Mugnone. Début Chicago 1924, Shepherd (*Tosca*). N.Y., Met., 1929–45, where her Carmen and Mignon were praised. (R)

Sweden. See *Drottningholm, Gothenburg, Stockholm.*

Szeged. Town in Csongrád, Hungary. The National Theatre was built in 1883 by the Viennese architects Fellner and Hellmer; it seats 980. Only since coming under state management in 1945 has it performed opera, and now also gives guest performances in other towns of the Tisza region.

Székely, Mihály (b. Jászberény, 8 May 1901; d. Budapest, 22 Mar. 1963). Hungarian bass. Début Budapest, 1923, Ferrando (*Trovatore*). N.Y., Met., 1946–50; Glyndebourne 1957–62. An outstanding 'dark-voiced' bass, especially successful in Wagner and as Bluebeard (Bartók), which he sang in Paris and at the Holland Festival as well as in Budapest. (R)

Switzerland. See *Zürich.*

Széll, Georg (b. Budapest, 7 June 1897; d. Cleveland, 30 July 1970). Hungarian, later American, conductor. Studied Vienna, Leipzig. After appearing as child prodigy pianist, persuaded by Strauss to take up conducting. Strasbourg 1917. After appearances in Prague, Darmstadt & Düsseldorf, 1st Kapellmeister, Berlin, S.O., 1924–9; Generalmusikdirektor, Prague, German Opera, 1929–37; N.Y., Met., 1942–6, when his conducting of Wagner and Strauss was highly praised. Salzburg since 1949, where he has conducted the world premières of Liebermann's *Penelope* (1954) and *School for Wives*, and Egk's *Irische Legende* (1955). (R)

Szenkar, Eugen (b. Budapest, 9 Apr. 1891). Hungarian conductor. Studied

Budapest. Prague, Landestheater, 1911–12; Altenburg 1916–20; Frankfurt 1920–3; Berlin, Volksoper, 1923–4; Generalmusikdirektor, Cologne, 1924–33. Returned to Germany 1950; Mannheim 1950–1; Generalmusikdirektor, Düsseldorf, 1952–6. (R)

Szymanowski, Karol (b. Timoshovka, 6 Oct. 1882; d. Lausanne, 29 Mar. 1937). Polish composer. His two operas *Hagith* (1922) and *King Roger* (1926) are representative works of an exceptionally gifted modern Romantic.

T

Tabarro, Il (The Cloak). Opera in 1 act by Puccini; text by Adami, after Didier Gold's tragedy *La Houppelande* (1910). Prod. as Part 1 of *Il Trittico*, N.Y., Met., 14 Dec. 1918, with Muzio, Crimi, Montesanto; Rome, C., 11 Jan. 1919; London, C.G., 18 June 1920, with Dalla Rizza, Burke, Gilly. The Seine bargee Michele (bar.) suspects his wife Giorgetta (sop.) of unfaithfulness, but tries to win her back by reminding her of how she used to shelter under his cloak. She has arranged a meeting with her lover, the barge-hand Luigi (ten.), who mistakes Michele's lighting of his pipe for the signal that the coast is clear. Michele kills him and covers the body with his cloak. When Giorgetta appears, Michele tells her to come under the cloak again; then he reveals Luigi's body and flings her down on top of her dead lover.

Tacchinardi, Niccolò (b. Leghorn, 3 Sept. 1772; d. Florence, 14 Mar. 1859). Italian tenor. Début 1804 Leghorn and Pisa. Sang at celebrations of Napoleon's coronation as King of Italy. His early interest in sculpture led to a friendship with Canova, whose bust of him records his extreme physical ugliness. Despite this, he triumphed even as Don Giovanni (transposed for tenor) through sheer vocal artistry, Paris 1811. Retired 1831, and became a distinguished teacher, his pupils including his daughter Fanny (Tacchinardi) Persiani (q.v.) and Frezzolini.

Tacea la notte placida. Leonora's (sop.) romantic soliloquy in Act 1, scene 2 of Verdi's *Il Trovatore*, leading into the *cabaletta* 'Di tale amor'.

Taddei, Giuseppe (b. Genoa, 26 June 1916). Italian baritone. Début Rome 1936; London, Cambridge T., 1947; San Francisco 1957; Salzburg 1948. One of the leading dramatic and character baritones of the post-war period, being especially gifted in Verdi roles, as Scarpia, and in buffo parts. (R)

Tagliabue, Carlo (b. Como, 13 Jan. 1898). Italian baritone. Début Lodi 1922, Amonasro. Milan, Sc., 1930–55; London, C.G., 1938, 1946; Stoll T. 1953; N.Y., Met., 1937–9. Has sung at most of the world's leading theatres; a fine Verdi baritone, also admired as a Wagnerian in Italy. Created Basilio in Respighi's *La Fiamma*. (R)

Tagliafico, Joseph (b. Toulon, 1 Jan. 1821; d. Nice, 27 Jan. 1900). French bass-baritone of Italian descent. Studied Paris with Piermarini and Lablache. Début Paris 1844; London, C.G., on opening night of first Royal Italian Opera Season as Oroe (*Semiramide*), singing there every season until 1876; 1877–82 stage manager. Also sang regularly in Russia, France, and U.S.A., and was music critic of *Le Ménestrel*, in which he wrote under the name of 'De Retz'. Appeared in the first performances in England of many operas, including *Le Prophète*, *Benvenuto Cellini*, *Il Trovatore* (as Ferrando), *Rigoletto* (as Sparafucile), *Roméo et Juliette*, &c. He married the soprano **Cotti**, who as **Mme Tagliafico** sang both at C.G. and H.M.'s.

Tagliavini, Ferruccio (b. Reggio Emilia, 14 Aug. 1913). Italian tenor. Studied Parma. Won the Concorso Nazionale Italiano 1938, gaining a scholarship to Florence where he studied under Amadeo Bassi. Début Florence 1939, Rodolfo. Established himself as the leading Italian lyric tenor during the war years. Buenos Aires, Colón, 1946–7; N.Y., Met., 1946–54; London, C.G., 1950 with Scala Co., 1955–6; Stoll 1953; D.L. 1958. At his best Tagliavini has had few contemporary equals as a *bel canto* singer; he was the outstanding post-war Nemorino and Elvino. Other roles in which he has excelled are the Duke of Mantua, Fritz (Mascagni), Edgardo, Werther, and Cavaradossi. He is married to the soprano (now mezzo) Pia Tassinari (q.v.). (R)

Tajo, Italo (b. Pinerolo, 25 Apr. 1915). Italian bass. Studied Turin. Début Turin 1935, Fafner. Edinburgh, with Glyndebourne Co., 1947, Figaro and Banquo; London, Cambridge T., 1947–8; C.G. 1950 (Scala Co.); San Francisco from 1948; N.Y., Met., 1948–50. In the immediate post-war period was in much demand in Mozart and Donizetti buffo roles, especially as Dulcamara, Leporello, and Figaro (Mozart); also successful as Méphistophélès, Philip, and Boris. (R)

Tale of Tsar Saltan, The. See *Tsar Saltan.*

Tale of Two Cities, A. Opera in prologue and 3 acts by Benjamin; text by Cedric Cliffe, after Dickens's novel (1859). Prod. London, S.W. (New Opera Co.), 23 July 1957, with Heather Harper, Ruth Packer, John Cameron, John Kentish, Heddle Nash, cond. Leon Lovett; Metz, 19 Oct. 1957; San Francisco, State College, 2 Apr. 1960.

Tales of Hoffmann, The. See *Contes d'Hoffmann, Les.*

Talich, Václav (b. Kroměříž, 28 May 1883; d. Beroun, 16 Mar. 1961). Czech conductor. After appointments in Odessa and Tiflis as a violinist and in Prague and Ljubljana as conductor, became conductor, Plzeň Opera 1912–15. From 1935 took over administration of National Opera, Prague, where he initiated important reforms. Discharged after disagreements 1945; restored 1947; removed from this post and others 1948. (R)

Tamagno, Francesco (b. Turin, 28 Dec. 1850; d. Varese, 31 Aug. 1905). Italian tenor. Studied Turin with Pedrotti. Member of the chorus at Turin, T.R., 1870. Début 1873, replacing Mongini in second tenor role in Donizetti's *Poliuto*, when his trumpet-like tone drew admiration. His fame dates from his Riccardo (*Ballo*), Palermo 1874. Scala from 1877, where he created Azael in Ponchielli's *Il Figliuol Prodigo*; and the title role in Verdi's *Otello*, being chosen by the composer. London, Ly., 1889, in first London *Otello*; C.G. 1895, 1901; Chicago 1889–90; N.Y., Met., 1891, 1894–5. Retired 1902. Judged the greatest *tenore di forza* of his day; his voice was virile and of seemingly limitless power, and it is said that the extraordinary facility of his upper range was such that he found it easier to sing certain pieces a semitone or a tone higher. (R)

Tamberlik, Enrico (b. Rome, 16 Mar. 1820; d. Paris, 13 Mar. 1889). Italian tenor. Studied Rome and Naples. Début Naples 1841 in *I Capuletti ed i Montecchi*. London, C.G., 1850, *Masaniello*; regularly until 1864; again in 1870; H.M.'s 1877. N.Y., Ac. of M., 1873–4. Also appeared in Paris, St. Petersburg, and Madrid. Created Alvaro in *La Forza del Destino*. First English Manrico (*Trovatore*) and Benvenuto Cellini, and a famous Otello (Rossini), John of Leyden, and Florestan. His strong, rich voice extended to a powerful c'': he sang with taste, and was a singularly handsome man and a good actor.

Tamburini, Antonio (b. Faenza, 28 Mar. 1800; d. Nice, 9 Nov. 1876). Italian baritone. Studied from age of ten. Sang in chorus at Faenza when 12. Début Cento 1818. From 1824 to 1832 appeared in all the important Italian theatres. London from 1832; Paris the same year, where his phenomenal technique earned him the name of 'Le Rubini des basse-tailles'. In Paris he sang Riccardo in the world première of *I Puritani* and Malatesta in *Don Pasquale*; in Milan, Valdeberg in Bellini's *La Straniera*. Among the many roles he created for England were Riccardo, Alfonso (*Lucrezia Borgia*), the Earl of Nottingham (*Roberto Devereux*), Enrico (*Lucia*), Malatesta, Faone in *Sapho* (first Gounod opera in London). Also a famous Don Giovanni. One of the *vieille garde* which sparked off the 'Tamburini row' leading to the establishment of a second Italian opera house in London in 1847 at Covent Garden. He married the soprano Marietta Goja, and their daughter married the tenor Italo Gardoni. Last public appearance 1859. His voice was full and round, encompassing two octaves.

Tamino. A Japanese [*sic*] prince (ten.), the hero of Mozart's *Die Zauberflöte.*

Tancredi. *Melodramma eroico* in 2 acts by Rossini; text by Rossi, after Tasso's poem *Gerusalemme Liberata* (1575) and Voltaire's *Tancrède* (1760). Prod. Venice, F., 6 Feb. 1813; London, 4 May 1820, with Belocchi; N.Y. 31 Dec. 1825. Rossini's first world success and first opera to be translated. Revived Florence 1952 with Simionato.

Tanglewood. See *Berkshire Festival.*

Tannhäuser und der Sängerkrieg auf Wartburg. *Handlung* in 3 acts by Wagner; text by the composer. Prod. Dresden 19 Oct. 1845 with Johanna Wagner, Schröder-Devrient, Tichatschek, cond. Wagner; N.Y., Stadt T., 4 Apr. 1859; London, C.G., 6 May 1876, with Albani, D'Angeri, Carpi, Maurel, cond. Vianesi. Revision, known as Paris version, Paris, O., 13 Mar. 1861 (withdrawn by Wagner after three performances), with Saxe, Tedesco, Niemann; N.Y., Met., 30 Jan. 1889, with Bettaque, Lilli Lehmann, Kalisch, cond. Seidl; London, C.G., 27 May 1896, with Eames, Adini, Alvarez, Ancona, cond. Mancinelli.

Act 1. In the Venusberg, Tannhäuser (ten.) sings in praise of the pleasures offered him by Venus (mezzo-sop.). But he longs to return to the world, and when he names the Virgin, the Venusberg disappears and he finds himself in the valley of the Wartburg where a young shepherd (sop.) is singing. A group of pilgrims pass on their way to Rome, and then horns herald the Landgrave Hermann (bass), Wolfram (bar.) (Tannhäuser's close friend), and other knights. They welcome Tannhäuser after his year's absence, and he decides to return with them on hearing how sad Elisabeth, the Landgrave's niece, has been since his departure.

Act 2. Elisabeth (sop.), happy at Tannhäuser's return, greets the Hall of Song in the Wartburg Castle. Tannhäuser will not tell her where he has been. The knights and guests enter for the contest of song. The Landgrave announces the theme as love. Wolfram sings of a pure selfless love. Tannhäuser follows with an outburst in praise of Venus. The knights threaten Tannhäuser, but Elisabeth intervenes. Tannhäuser promises atonement; he is banished to seek absolution from the Pope and joins the pilgrims.

Act 3. Several months later Elisabeth is praying in the valley of the Wartburg that Tannhäuser may be forgiven. When she sadly returns home, Wolfram prays to the evening star to guide and protect her. Tannhäuser staggers in, distraught at the Pope's refusal of absolution: he can now only return to Venus. A funeral procession approaches: Elisabeth has died of a broken heart. Tannhäuser sinks beside her bier, and he too dies. Pilgrims arrive from Rome bearing the Pope's staff, which has sprouted leaves in token that God has forgiven Tannhäuser.

Tarare. Opera in prologue and 5 acts by Salieri; text by Beaumarchais. Prod. Paris, O., 8 June 1787; London, Ly., 15 Aug. 1825. Salieri's most important work, even more successful in Da Ponte's Italian version *Axur, Re d'Ormus* (Vienna, B., 8 Jan. 1788, wedding of Archduke Francis II). Beaumarchais's preface 'To Opera subscribers who want to like opera' is a lively and interesting defence of the librettist's position.

Tárogató. A conical-bored clarinet associated to the point of national symbolism with the Hungarians. Sometimes used for the second of the shepherd's tunes in Act 3 of *Tristan und Isolde* where Wagner specifies a *Holztrompete* (wooden trumpet). Mahler's introduction of a tárogató at Budapest was followed at Bayreuth by Richter.

Taskin, (Émile-)Alexandre (b. Paris, 8 Mar. 1853; d. Paris, 5 Oct. 1897). French baritone. Studied Paris. Début 1875 Amiens; from

1879 to 1894 one of the finest artists in the Opéra-Comique company. When the O.C. caught fire on 25 May 1887, during a performance of *Mignon,* he saved many lives through his calmness and bravery, and was decorated by the government.

Tassinari, Pia (b. Faenza, 15 Sept. 1909). Italian mezzo-soprano, formerly soprano. Studied Bologna with Vezzani. Début Casale Monferrato 1929, Mimì. Milan, Sc., 1931–7, 1945–6; Rome, O., 1933–43 and 1951–2; N.Y., Met., 1947–8. In the 1930's was considered one of the leading lyric sopranos in Italy. More recently she has confined her darkening voice to mezzo roles, including Carmen, and Charlotte (*Werther*). She met her husband, the tenor Tagliavini (q.v.), during the war, and often sang with him in *Tosca, Bohème, Faust, Werther, L'Amico Fritz,* and *Manon.* (R)

Tasso, Torquato (b. Sorrento, 11 Mar. 1544; d. Rome, 23 Apr. 1595). Italian poet. Operas on his masterpiece *Gerusalemme Liberata* (1575) (generally under this title or as *Armida*) are as follows. Monteverdi (*Il Combattimento di Tancredi e Clorinda* 1624); M. A. Rossi (*Erminia sul Giordano* 1633); Lully (1686); Pallavicino (1687); Moratelli (*Erminia de' Boschi* 1687; *Erminia al Campo* 1688); Campra (*Tancrède* 1702; parodies, *Pierrot Tancrède* and *Arlequin Tancrède* 1729); Handel (*Rinaldo* 1711); Philip of Orléans (1711); Schürmann (1722); Traetta (1761); Jommelli (1770); Anfossi (1770); Sacchini (1772); Gluck (1777; parodies, *L'Opéra de Province* 1777, and *Mme Terrible* 1778); Winter (1780); Haydn (1784); Zingarelli (1786); Häffner (*Renaud* 1801); Righini (two 2-act operas, 1803); Zingarelli (1803); Persuis (1812; parody, *Jérusalème Déshabillée* 1812); Rossini (*Tancredi* 1813, *Armida* 1817); Dvořák (1904). Earliest work based on Tasso, Lasamino's madrigal opera *Novellette* (1594), after *Aminta.* Tasso's erratic career is the subject of Donizetti's *Torquato Tasso* (1833).

Tatyana. The heroine (sop.) of Tchaikovsky's *Eugene Onegin.*

Tauber, Richard (orig. Ernst Seiffert) (b. Linz, 16 May 1892; d. London, 8 Jan. 1948). Austrian, later naturalized British, tenor. Studied Freiburg i. B. Début Chemnitz (where his father was Intendant) 1913, Tamino. Dresden 1913–25; Vienna 1926–38, with periods of absence in operetta in Germany and England. London, C.G., 1938–9 and 1947 with Vienna Opera. Also sang at Salzburg and Munich festivals. As a Mozart tenor he was unequalled between the wars, and could still sing an impeccable Ottavio in 1947, when he made his last appearance as a guest with his old Vienna colleagues at C.G. He was the first German Calaf, and was also admired as Jeník, Rodolfo, &c. His voice had a highly individual timbre, sweet in quality and immaculately managed, though much singing in operetta tended in later years to vulgarize his art. (R)

Taylor, Deems (b. N.Y., 22 Dec. 1885; d. there, 3 July 1966). American composer. *The King's Henchman* (1927) led to Met. commission for *Peter Ibbetson* (1931), also successful. *Ramuntcho* (comp. 1937) was prod. Philadelphia, 1942.

Tchaikovsky, Petr Ilyich (b. Kamsko-Votinsk, 7 May 1840; d. St. Petersburg, 6 Nov. 1893). Russian composer. Tchaikovsky declared that to refrain from writing operas was a heroism he did not possess, and from his earliest days the stage—above all, Italian opera—fascinated him. He had no thought of reforms, admiring simplicity, clarity, and colour as the outstanding operatic virtues—which he admitted he had neglected in *The Voyevode* (1869). After *Undine* (1869, unprod.; music re-used in second symphony and as Odette's Adagio in *Swan Lake*) he refashioned some of the *Voyevode* music for *The Oprichnik* (1874); it is a 'number' opera, described by Gerald Abraham as Meyerbeer thoroughly translated into Russian. *Vakula the Smith* (1876; rev. as *Cherevichki* (The Little Shoes (1887), once known in Europe as *Oxana's Caprice*) was the first to please its composer; despite his grumblings about its excess of detail and thick scoring, he felt it 'almost my best opera'. Much use is made of Russian and Ukrainian folk tunes, but they are worked with consummate skill and an entirely individual lyrical feeling. There followed his masterpiece, *Eugene Onegin* (1879). At first doubtful about the possibilities of Pushkin's 'novel in verse', he became enraptured by Tatiana and quickly sketched a synopsis and composed the Letter Scene. This instinctive sympathy places her rather than Onegin in the centre of the stage; it is she who has the subtlest and most perceptive dramatic music. Turning from Russian subjects, Tchaikovsky set an adaptation of Schiller's *The Maid of Orleans* (1881); but the remote characters failed to stir him—and 'where the heart is not touched there can't be any music', he said. Only Joan of Arc herself approaches reality, and that principally in her Act 2 farewell and 'recognition'. The shadow of Meyerbeer and the Opéra falls across much of the rest, dimming Tchaikovsky's own personality. With *Mazeppa* (1884) he returned to a completely Russian milieu, with the typical all-patient heroine in Maria and fascinating Byron-cum-Dostoyevsky villain in Mazeppa. Yet though a divided character himself, he failed to respond illuminatingly to Mazeppa's ambivalence, and it is for its sideshows that *Mazeppa* is striking. *The Sorceress* (1887) again moved away into crude melodrama, its crowded action and wooden figures allowing still less opportunity for characterization or lyrical interludes. The further Tchaikovsky strayed from home ground, the more his lack of true dramatic skill was exposed. But *The Queen of Spades* (1890) came to absorb him, and in this hysterical melodrama, with its chances for representing extreme emotional tensions and for 18th-century pastiche, he found an unlikely but satisfactory stimulus. The 1-act *Iolanthe* (1892) is unsure by comparison, despite some typical inspirations.

Tebaldi, Renata (b. Pesaro, 1 Feb. 1922). Italian soprano. Studied Parma with Carmen Melis. Début Rovigo 1944, Elena (*Mefistofele*). Chosen by Toscanini for reopening of Scala 1946. Milan, Sc., 1949–54 and 1959. London, C.G., with Scala Co., 1950 and 1955. San Francisco 1950; Chicago since 1955; N.Y., Met., since 1954. One of the outstanding contemporary sopranos, she possesses a voice whose exquisite quality conceals great reserves of power; even when singing at extreme dynamics her voice retains its characteristic glowing beauty. Especially impressive in Verdi and Puccini and as Madeleine de Coigny and Adriana Lecouvreur. (R)

Telemann, Georg Philipp (b. Magdeburg, 14 Mar. 1681; d. Hamburg, 25 June 1767). German composer. He wrote some 40 operas, of which perhaps half a dozen were successful. *Pimpinone* (1725) has received several modern revivals.

Telephone, The. Opera in 1 act by Menotti; text by composer. Prod. N.Y., Heckscher T., 18 Feb. 1947; London, Aldwych T., 29 Apr. 1948. Ben's proposals of marriage are repeatedly frustrated by Lucy's devotion to her telephone; eventually he leaves and successfully makes contact by ringing her from a call-box.

Television opera. The first telecast of opera took place, after experiments, in Britain in 1937 (*Venus and Adonis*); America followed in 1941 (*Pagliacci*). The first opera written for television was Menotti's *Amahl and the Night Visitors* (N.B.C. 1951). The first colour transmission of opera was of *Carmen* (N.B.C. 1953).

The problems are obviously comparable to those of film opera. In transmissions from a theatre (e.g. Glyndebourne's *Comte Ory*) no special production can be attempted. Studio productions give a choice of techniques. In Italy it is customary to pre-record, with the singers miming at the transmission. The Germans go further and substitute possibly more personable actors. Britain, hampered by Union restrictions, prefers live transmission, and even the Germans have been swayed by such successes as the B.B.C. *Salome* (which included only one pre-filmed excerpt, for the Dance). The B.B.C.'s 1957 *Madama Butterfly* compromised with the actors miming to a live performance from another studio. Most television studios now produce opera, despite the problems in reducing an essentially theatrical, communal entertainment to a miniature, private presentation in two dimensions. Operas specially commissioned by the B.B.C. include Benjamin's *Mañana*, Bliss's *Tobias and the Angel*, and Britten's *Owen Wingrave*.

Telramund. Friedrich von Telramund (bar.), a Count of Brabant in Wagner's *Lohengrin*.

Templeton, John (b. Riccarton, 30 July 1802; d. New Hampton, 2 July 1886). Scottish tenor. London début, D.L., 1831; first English Raimbaut (*Robert le Diable*) 1832; first English Don Ottavio 1833, at short notice. Became 'Malibran's tenor', singing beside her in *Sonnambula*, D.L., 1833, and often subsequently; a wooden actor, till Malibran coached him. Took principal tenor roles in first performances in English of *Cheval de Bronze* (1836), *Zampa* (1836), *Siege of Corinth* (1836), *Magic Flute* (1838), *La Favorite* (1843), and many others.

Tender Land, The. Opera in 2 acts by Copland; text by Horace Everett. Prod. N.Y., City Opera, 1 Apr. 1954; Cambridge, Arts, 26 Feb. 1962. A harvester falls in love with the daughter of a Midwest farm. When he fails to keep a promise to elope with her, she goes out into the world alone.

Tenducci, Giusto Ferdinando (b. Siena, *c.* 1736; d. ?, after 1800). Italian male soprano. After successes in London, attracted attention in Dublin first by his singing in some adaptations of his own and still more by eloping with a councillor's daughter. Sang (with Mrs. Billington) in his own version of Gluck's *Orfeo*, then in London in the original. Mozart wrote a song for him. He published various compositions and a treatise on singing.

Tenor (It. *tenore* = holding: in early times the voice which held the plainsong). The highest category of natural male voice. Many subdivisions exist within opera houses: the commonest in general use (though seldom by composers in scores) are given below, with examples of roles snd their approximate *tessitura*. These divisions often overlap, and do not correspond exactly from country to country. In general, distinction is more by character than by *tessitura*, especially in France: thus, the examples of the roles give a more useful indication of the different voices' quality than any attempted technical definition.

German: Heldentenor (Huon, Bacchus: c–c''); Wagnerheldentenor (Siegfried: c–b♭'); lyrischer Tenor (Max: c–c''); Spieltenor (Pedrillo, David: c–♭'); hoher Tenor (Brighella, *Rosenkavalier* tenor: c–c'').

Italian: tenore (Radamès: c–c''); tenore spinto (Rodolfo: c–c''); tenore di forza (Otello: c–c''); tenore di grazia (Nemorino: c–d''); tenor-buffo (Dickson in *La Dame Blanche*: c–b♭').

French: ténor (José: c–c''); ténor-bouffe (Paris in *La Belle Hélène*: c–c''); Trial (q.v.): (Pelléas: c–a').

See also *Castrato*, *Countertenor*.

Tenuto (It. = held). A direction to hold notes for their full value, or very slightly longer. Consistently taken by singers as an invitation to hold them, especially if high ones, for as long as they please.

Ternina, Milka (b. Vesisce, 19 Dec. 1863; d. Zagreb, 18 May 1941). Croatian soprano. Studied Zagreb and Vienna. While a student at Zagreb, début as Amelia 1882. Leipzig 1883–4; Graz 1884–6; Bremen 1886–9; Munich 1890–99; N.Y., with German Opera Co., 1896; Met. 1899–1904; Bayreuth 1899; London 1898–1906, where she was the first London Tosca. In N.Y. created Kundry in the 'pirate' production of *Parsifal* and was accordingly banned from Bayreuth; also the first N.Y. Tosca. Considered the greatest Isolde of her day and the finest Leonore (*Fidelio*) since Tietjens. She possessed a perfect vocal method, a beautiful voice, and great dramatic temperament. Was forced by paralysis to retire at the height of her powers. (R)

Teschemacher, Marguerite (b. Cologne, 3 Mar. 1903; d. Tegernsee,

19 May 1959). German soprano. Début Cologne 1924, Micaëla; Mannheim 1928–30; Stuttgart 1930–5; Dresden 1935–46, where she created the title role in Strauss's *Daphne*, Miranda in Sutermeister's *Zauberinsel*, and sang the Countess in the first Dresden *Capriccio*; Düsseldorf 1948–52; London, C.G., 1931 and 1936. Admired as Jenůfa and Minnie (*La Fanciulla*). (R)

Tess, Giulia (b. Milan, 10 Feb. 1889). Italian soprano, formerly mezzo-soprano. Début Venice 1909, Mignon. After a successful career as a mezzo, she was advised by Battistini to become a soprano, and was engaged by Toscanini for La Scala 1922 where she created Jaele in Pizzetti's *Debora e Jaele*. Was a famous Salome and Elektra and also a fine interpreter of lighter roles in operas by Wolf-Ferrari. In 1940 she began teaching at the opera school in Florence, and since 1946 has taught at La Scala. In recent years she has produced operas at La Scala and other Italian theatres.

Tessitura (It. = texture). A term indicating the approximate average range of a piece of music in relation to the voice for which it is written. Thus we say that Zerbinetta's aria in *Ariadne auf Naxos* has a particularly high tessitura.

Tetrazzini, Eva (b. Milan, Mar. 1862; d. Salsomaggiore, 27 Oct. 1938). Italian soprano. Studied Florence. Début Florence 1882, Marguerite. N.Y., Ac. of M., 1888, first American Desdemona; London, C.G., 1890. Married the conductor Campanini. Sister of Luisa (below).

Tetrazzini, Luisa (b. Florence, 29 June 1871; d. Milan, 28 Apr. 1940). Italian soprano. Studied Florence and with her sister. Début Florence 1890, Inez (*L'Africaine*). After nearly 15 years of appearances in Italy and South America, made first real success with a company from Mexico at San Francisco 1904. London, C.G., 1907, creating sensation as Violetta and Lucia; and regularly 1908–12; N.Y., Manhattan Co., 1908–10; Met. 1911–12. She had an amazingly brilliant voice above the stave, and a phenomenal coloratura technique; her singing of staccato passages and ornamentation was likewise greatly admired. She barely attempted to act. Wrote *My Life of Song* (1921) and *How to Sing* (1925). (R)

Teyte (orig. Tate), **Maggie (Dame)** (b. Wolverhampton 17 Apr. 1888). English soprano. Studied London, R.C.M., and Paris with J. de Reszke. Début Monte Carlo 1907, in Offenbach's *Myriame et Daphné*. Paris, O.C., 1907–11, where she created Glycère in Hillemacher's *Circe*, and in 1908 sang her first Mélisande. London, C.G., 1910, 1914, 1922–3, 1930, 1936–8; Chicago 1911–14; Boston 1915–17. Created the Princess in Holst's *The Perfect Fool*. An outstanding Mélisande (which she studied with Debussy), Butterfly, Cherubino, and Hänsel. After the war reappeared as Mélisande in N.Y., and sang Belinda to Flagstad's Dido at the Mermaid Theatre, London 1951. Autobiography, *Star on the Door*. (R)

Thaïs. Opera in 3 acts by Massenet; text by Louis Gallet, after Anatole France's novel (1890). Prod. Paris, O., 16 Mar. 1894, with Sybil Sanderson, Delmas, Alvarez; N.Y., Manhattan O., 25 Nov. 1907, with Garden, Renaud, Dalmores; London, C.G., 18 July 1911, with Edvina, Gilly, Darmel. Set in 4th-century Egypt, the opera tells how the monk Athanaël converts the courtesan Thaïs, who becomes a nun, but loses his own soul in the process.

Thalberg, Zaré (orig. Ethel Western) (b. Derbyshire, 16 Apr. 1858; d. London, 1915). English soprano. Not the daughter of the Austrian pianist, but a pupil who took his name. Studied Paris, Milan. Début London, C.G., 1875, Zerlina, singing there five seasons and scoring a success as Susanna, Adina, &c. Lost her voice in 1881, and as Ethel Western acted in Shakespeare in Edwin Booth's company, retiring in the 1890's.

Theater an der Wien. Successor to the Theater auf der Wieden. Built by Schikaneder (q.v.) with funds provided by the merchant Zitterbarth, opened

13 June 1801 (cap. 1232) with Teyber's *Alexander* (text by Schikaneder). Scene of the premières of *Fidelio* (1805), *Der Waffenschmied* (1846), *Die Fledermaus* (1874), and other operettas by Strauss, Millöcker, and Lehár. Under the management of Barbaia (1821–2) saw the Viennese premières of many Rossini works. Scene of Jenny Lind's Vienna triumphs (1846–7) in *Norma, Sonnambula, Huguenots, Freischütz,* and *Ein Feldlager in Schlesien.* The international fame of *The Bartered Bride* dates from its first performance in German at this theatre in 1893; and in October 1897 *La Bohème,* the first Puccini opera in Vienna, was produced there. From 6 Oct. 1945 to 1954 it became the home of the Vienna State Opera while the Opera House was being rebuilt. Purchased by the city of Vienna in 1961, it was entirely renovated and reopened a year later on 30 May 1962 with *Die Zauberflöte.*

Theater auf der Wieden. Built in 1787 by Schikaneder in one of the courts of the Freihaus, and granted royal privilege by the Emperor, hence sometimes known as the Kaiserlich-königliches privilegiertes Theater auf der Wieden; was the scene of the first production of *Die Zauberflöte.* It closed on 12 June 1801.

Théâtre des Champs-Élysées. Paris Theatre (cap. 2,000) opened in 1913 with a series of special performances of *Benvenuto Cellini* and *Der Freischütz* conducted by Weingartner. It was the scene of Diaghilev's 1913 season and other Russian opera seasons in the 1920's and 1930's, of a Mozart season in 1924, and of a visit by the Bayreuth ensemble in 1929. From Nov. 1936 to Feb. 1937 it offered house-room to the Opéra while the latter's home was being redecorated, and has staged occasional seasons by visiting foreign companies in the post-war period.

Théâtre-Italien or **Théâtre des Italiens.** Italian companies performed in Paris as far back as 1570, during the reign of Charles IX. The Théâtre Ventadour, the home of the Opéra-Comique 1829–32, housed an Italian company headed by Rubini, Lablache, &c. in 1828; and from 1841 to 1871 was the centre of Italian opera in Paris, opening on 2 Oct. 1841 with *Semiramide.* During autumn and winter each year there appeared a strong company which included such singers as Grisi, Perisani, Mario, Lablache, and Tamburini—in fact the company that performed each spring and summer in London. Indeed from 1850 to 1852 Lumley (q.v.) directed both Her Majesty's Opera in London and the Théâtre des Italiens in Paris. The most famous première at the Italiens was probably *Don Pasquale* in 1843 with Grisi, Mario, Lablache, and Tamburini. After 1871 a number of attempts were made to restart Italian opera at the Ventadour (*Aida,* 1876) and then, after the theatre had been sold to the Bank of France in 1879, performances were staged at other theatres. Patti gave a series of performances at the Théâtre des Nations in 1881, and in Nov. 1883, in the same auditorium, the Théâtre-Italien began a series of performances with the French première of *Simone Boccanegra* with Maurel in the title role, E. de Reszke as Fiesco, and conducted by Faccio. The project failed after a few months.

Théâtre-Lyrique. Operatic enterprise in Paris, inaugurated 21 Sept. 1852, as successor to the Opéra-National. which had opened on 15 Nov. 1847 with Maillart's *Gastibelza.* Carvalho (q.v.) was director 1856–60 and 1862–8, during which periods the theatre enjoyed its greatest artistic triumphs, with the premières of Gounod's *Le Médecin malgré lui* (1858), *Faust* (1859), *Philémon et Baucis* (1860), *Mireille* (1864), and *Roméo et Juliette* (1867), Bizet's *Les Pêcheurs de Perles* (1863) and *La Jolie Fille de Perth* (1867), and Berlioz's *Les Troyens à Carthage* (1863). The theatre had been rebuilt between 1860 and 1862 and reopened in that year with a special *Hymne à la Musique* composed by Gounod and sung by an ensemble that included Miolan-Carvalho, Viardot, Faure.

Carvalho was succeeded by Pasdeloup, whose management lasted until 1870. In 1874 the theatre was again rebuilt (cap. 1,243) and was renamed the Théâtre des Nations, and between 1887 and 1898 it was the home of the Opéra-Comique. The following year it became the Théâtre Sarah-Bernhardt, by which name it is still known. Like the Champs-Élysées it has been used for occasional seasons by visiting foreign companies.

Thebom, Blanche (b. Monessen, Pa., 19 Sept. 1918). American mezzo of Swedish parents. Studied with Matzenauer and Edyth Walker. Début N.Y., Met., 1944, Fricka. London, C.G., 1957–8, Dido in *Les Troyens*. (R)

Thill, Georges (b. Paris, 14 Dec. 1897). French tenor. Studied Paris, and Naples with De Lucia. Début Paris, O., 1924, Nicias (*Thaïs*); London, C.G., 1928, 1937; N.Y., Met., 1931–2. Also sang in Italy and South America. Remained leading tenor of Paris O. until after the war. Successful as Roméo, Don José, Julien (*Louise*), as well as in other French and German roles. (R)

Thoma. See *Vogl*.

Thomas, Ambroise (b. Metz, 5 Aug. 1811; d. Paris, 12 Feb. 1896). French composer. In 1837 his works began appearing at the Opéra-Comique, and in 1841 he achieved the Opéra with his *Comte de Carmagnola*. Competition with Auber, Halévy, Meyerbeer, and Donizetti drove him back to the O.C., where his list of successes was headed by *Mignon* (1866). This was in turn followed by the success at the Opéra of *Hamlet* (prod. 1868, title role altered from tenor to baritone for Faure). Professor at Conservatoire from 1852; director from 1871, which office left him time for only one more work for the Opéra, *Françoise de Rimini* (1882).

Thomas and Sally. Opera in 2 acts by Arne; text by Isaac Bickerstaffe. Prod. London, C.G., 28 Nov. 1760; Philadelphia 14 Nov. 1766.

Thomas, Arthur Goring (b. Ratton Park, 20 Nov. 1850; d. London, 20 Mar. 1892). English composer. *The Light of the Harem* (1879) brought a Carl Rosa commission that led to his best-known work, *Esmeralda* (1883), after Hugo's *Notre-Dame de Paris*. In 1885 its success was followed, but not equalled, by *Nadeshda*. A comic opera *The Golden Web* was prod. in 1893. Thomas was one of the few English composers of his day with a real, if limited, operatic talent.

Thomson, Virgil (b. Kansas City, 25 Nov. 1896). American composer and critic. Studied initially with Nadia Boulanger; a later stay in Paris from 1925 to 1932 brought friendship with Satie and Gertrude Stein, both of whom influenced his work. *Four Saints in Three Acts* (1928) and *The Mother of Us All* (1947), both to texts by Stein, show the more diatonic, elliptical, and detached side of his talent, though there is ample charm as well as sophistication. Chief music critic, *N.Y. Herald-Tribune*, 1940–54, where he made a name as one of the liveliest and most penetrating and thoughtful of modern critics.

Thomyris, Queen of Scythia. Opera in 3 acts arr. from Scarlatti, Bononcini, Steffani, Gasparini, and Albinoni by Pepusch; text by Peter Motteux. Prod. London, D.L., 1 Apr. 1707. First true example of a London *pasticcio*, very popular in its day.

Thorborg, Kerstin (b. Venjan, 19 May 1896; d. Dalarna, 15 Apr. 1970). Swedish mezzo. Studied Stockholm; début there 1924, Ortrud. Stockholm Opera 1924–30; Nuremberg 1930–1; Prague 1932–3; Berlin 1933–5; Vienna 1935–8; Salzburg 1935–7; London, C.G., 1936–9; N.Y., Met., 1936–50. Considered by Newman the greatest Wagner mezzo he had seen or heard.

Thornton, Edna (b. Bradford, *c.* 1880; d. Worthing, 15 Jul. 1964). English contralto. London, C.G., 1905–10 and 1919–23. Leading member of Quinlan, Beecham, and B.N.O. Companies, and admired specially in Wagner. Chosen by Richter as Erda and Waltraute in English *Ring* (1908–9). Also a distinguished Amneris and Dalila. Sang in première of *The Perfect Fool*. (R)

Tibbett, Lawrence (b. Bakersfield, Cal., 16 Nov. 1896; d. New York, 15 July 1960). American baritone.

Studied N.Y. with Frank la Forge. Début N.Y., Met., 1923 as Monk (*Boris*). Fame dates from his Ford in *Falstaff* revival, 1925. Remained at Met. until 1950; London, C.G., 1937, and guest appearances in Paris, Vienna, and Prague. In N.Y. created baritone roles in *Peter Ibbetson*, *The King's Henchman*, *The Emperor Jones*, *Merry Mount*, *In a Pasha's Garden*, and *Caponsacchi*; as well as in the first Met. performances of *Simone Boccanegra* (title role), *Peter Grimes* (Balstrode), *Khovanshchina* (Ivan Khovansky). At C.G. created title role in Goossens's *Don Juan de Mañara*. Excelled as Scarpia and Iago. A vivid and exciting actor, he made a number of films, including *The Rogue Song* and *The New Moon*, starring with Grace Moore in the latter. (R)

Tichatschek (orig. Tichaček), **Joseph** (b. Ober-Weckelsdorf, 11 July 1807; d. Dresden, 18 Jan. 1886). Bohemian tenor. Abandoned medicine for singing, studied Vienna. Joined chorus of Kä., 1830; then chorus inspector; began singing small roles. Graz and Vienna again, principal tenor. Dresden 1837–70, where he was befriended and coached by Schröder-Devrient. Created Rienzi (1842) and Tannhäuser (1845), and was highly regarded by Wagner. London, D.L., 1841 as Adolar and Robert le Diable.

Tiefland (Lowland). Opera in prologue and 3 acts by D'Albert; text by Rudolf Lothar, after the Catalan play *Terra Baixa* by Angel Guimerá. Prod. Prague, German T., 15 Nov. 1903; N.Y., Met. (revised version), 23 Nov. 1908 with Destinn, Schmedes, Feinhals, cond. Hertz; London, C.G., 5 Oct. 1910, cond. Beecham. A German *verismo* opera of passion and murder. It tells of the betrayal of Martha by her employer Sebastiano, a rich landowner who gives her to the shepherd Pedro on condition that he leaves the mountains for the lowlands. She eventually confesses her past to Pedro, and when Sebastiano tries to take her back, Pedro strangles him and returns to the hills with Martha.

Tietjen, Heinz (b. Tangier, 24 June 1881; d. 30 Nov. 1967). German conductor and producer, born of German father and English mother. Trier, as cond. and prod., 1904–7, as Intendant 1907–22. Intendant Saarbrucken 1919–22. Breslau 1922–4; Berlin, Städtische Oper, 1925–30; General-intendant, Berlin, Preussisches Staatstheater, 1927–45; artistic director, Bayreuth, 1931–44, where conducted *The Ring*, *Meistersinger*, and *Lohengrin*. Intendant, Berlin, Städtische Oper, 1948–54; Hamburg 1954–9. London, C.G., prod. *Der fliegende Holländer* (1950), *Parsifal*, and *Meistersinger* (1951). Wagner productions traditional but never old-fashioned. In 1958 he combined with Wieland Wagner in a production of *Lohengrin* at Hamburg, Wagner producing, Tietjen conducting; returned Bayreuth to conduct 1959. (R)

Tietjens, Therese (b. Hamburg, 17 July 1831; d. London, 3 Oct. 1877). German soprano of Hungarian parents, and possibly Dutch origin. Studied Hamburg and Vienna. Début Hamburg 1849, Lucrezia Borgia; Frankfurt 1850–6; Vienna 1856–9; London, H.M.'s, 1858, Valentine (*Huguenots*). Regularly in London (H.M.'s, D.L., C.G.) until 1877, making her home there. N.Y., Ac. of M., 1874, 1876. First London Medea, Elena (*Vêpres Siciliennes*), Amelia (*Ballo*), Leonora (*Forza*), Marguerite (*Faust*), Mireille. In her day unsurpassed as Norma, Donna Anna, Lucrezia Borgia, and Agathe. Could also sing Semiramide, Fidès (*Le Prophète*), and Ortrud, her only Wagner role. Her voice, which extended from c^{I} to d^{III}, was powerful, rich, and pure, and of great flexibility. In the first period of her English career she was tall and elegant on the stage; later she became extremely stout. She collapsed on stage during her last performance, as Lucrezia Borgia (H.M.'s 1877), a few months before her death.

Timişoara (Temesvar). Town in Banat, Rumania. Opera house founded 1947; gave over 2,000 performances in first ten years.

Tippett, (Sir) Michael (b. London, 2 Jan. 1905). His deep humanity, richly stocked mind, and fascination with elaborate concepts and proliferating literary and other allusions are nowhere more evident than in *The Midsummer Marriage* (1955); here is some of his warmest and most exhilarating music. *King Priam* (1962), a tragedy of the Trojan War, concerns 'the mysterious nature of human choice'; much sparer of idiom. With *The Knot Garden* (1970), he has returned to the theme that has pervaded so much of his music, the necessity for reconciliation of the dark and light sides of human nature before there can be true growth and peace; in his first opera, this was required before the marriage could take place, while here a marriage is in difficulties. The music is richer than that of *King Priam*, without sacrificing directness. (R)

Toch, Ernst (b. Vienna, 7 Dec. 1887; d. Los Angeles, 7 Dec. 1964). Austrian, now American composer. His works include four operas composed between 1925 and 1930, of which *Die Prinzessin auf der Erbse* (1927) has won popularity.

Tofts, Catherine (b. ?; d. Venice, 1756). English soprano. The first singer of English birth to sing in Italian opera in England (1705), when she was heard in *Arsinoe*, *Camilla*, *Rosamond*, *Thomyris*, and *Love's Triumph*. Her salary of £500 was higher than any other paid in the Italian company of that time. Cibber wrote that 'the beauty of her fine proportioned figure and the exquisitely sweet, silver tone of her voice, with that peculiar rapid swiftness of her throat, were perfections not to be imitated by art or labour'.

Tonio. The clown (bar.) in Leoncavallo's *Pagliacci*.

Töpper, Hertha (b. Graz, 19 Apr. 1924). Austrian mezzo-soprano. Studied Graz. Début there 1945, Ulrica; Munich since 1952; London, C.G., 1953, with Munich O., as Clairon in first London *Capriccio*; 1958, Octavian; Bayreuth 1951–2, 1960; N.Y., Met., 1962. An elegant and musicianly singer, admired in Mozart, Wagner, and Strauss. (R)

Toreador's Song. Escamillo's (bar.) rousing account of the thrills of the bull ring in Act 2 of Bizet's *Carmen*.

Toronto. Toronto, like other Canadian cities, relied for its opera on visiting opera companies until 1946 when the Royal Conservatory Opera School was established by Dr. Arnold Walter, with Nicholas Goldschmidt as musical director. The first opera festival was organized in 1950 and the following year the administration of the festival was taken over by the Opera Festival Association of Toronto—later called the Opera Festival Company of Toronto. Since 1959 the company has been known as the Canadian Opera Company, with Herman Geiger-Torel, who had been stage director from 1948, as its general director. In 1958 the company began a programme of expansion with extensive tours which by 1963 covered 17,000 miles and included eighty communities. It has produced an impressive number of operas of various styles and periods, including *Der Rosenkavalier*, *Die Walküre*, *The Consul*, and *Die lustigen Weiber von Windsor*. Since 1961 the company has presented operas annually in the O'Keefe Centre. In 1964 the MacMillan theatre in the new Edward Johnson Building of the University of Toronto, designed primarily for the Opera School, was formally opened with a series of events including a presentation of Benjamin Britten's *Albert Herring*. Conductors include Ernesto Barbini, Ettore Mazzoleni, Mario Bernardi, Walter Susskind. Leading singers have included many Canadians who have become internationally prominent: Leopold Simoneau, Jon Vickers, Lois Marshall, Teresa Stratas, and Jan Rubes. Since 1948 the Canadian Broadcasting Corporation has played an active role in promoting opera on radio under the leadership of Dr. Geoffrey Waddington, and since its beginning, CBC-Television has given a place to opera in its programme planning: each year operas, produced in Toronto, are seen over the nationwide network.

Tosca. Opera in 3 acts by Puccini; text by Giacosa and Illica, after Sardou's drama *La Tosca* (1887). Prod. Rome, C., 14 Jan. 1900, with Darclée, De Marchi, Giraldoni, cond. Mugnone; London, C.G., 12 July 1900 with Ternina, De Lucia, Scotti, cond. Mancinelli; N.Y., Met., 4 Feb. 1901 with Ternina, Cremonini, Scotti, cond. Mancinelli.

The action of the opera takes place in Rome in June 1800.

Act 1. Into the Church of Sant'Andrea staggers Cesare Angelotti (bass), former consul of the Roman republic, now escaped from prison. Finding the key to the Attavanti chapel, hidden by his sister, he conceals himself. Cavaradossi (ten.), working on a picture of Mary Magdalene, which he has modelled on the Marchesa Attavanti, compares the face with a miniature of his lover, the singer Floria Tosca. He discovers Angelotti and promises help. Tosca (sop.) enters, her suspicions that Cavaradossi has been meeting another woman strengthened by recognition of the Attavanti's features in the portrait. Cavaradossi calms her and arranges a rendezvous. Angelotti emerges; but a cannon-shot announces that his escape is known and Cavaradossi offers to hide him. They leave. The Sacristan (bass) bustles in announcing that Bonaparte has been defeated and that a Te Deum will be sung. The dreaded chief of police, Scarpia (bar.), and his henchman Spoletta (ten.) appear, having traced Angelotti to the church. Tosca returns, and the fascinated Scarpia decides to use her to trap Angelotti. He suggests that Cavaradossi and the Marchesa were interrupted while making love; and as Tosca storms out of the church, sends Spoletta to follow her. The church has now filled, and a Te Deum has begun. Scarpia realizes that he can now destroy Cavaradossi and possess Tosca.

Act 2. In his room in the Farnese Palace, Scarpia awaits news of Angelotti. Spoletta returns, unable to find Angelotti, but having arrested Cavaradossi. The strains of a cantata and the voice of Tosca rise from a room below; Scarpia sends for her. As Cavaradossi is taken off for questioning, Tosca appears. Unable to stand her lover's torture, she reveals Angelotti's hiding-place. A guard runs in with news of Napoleon's defeat, and Cavaradossi rages against all tyranny. Scarpia orders his execution. Left alone with Tosca, Scarpia bargains Cavaradossi's life against her love. Tosca agrees, and Spoletta is told to arrange a mock execution 'as in the case of Palmieri'. Scarpia writes out a safe conduct for Tosca and her lover, and as he turns to embrace her, she stabs him. Having placed candles by his head and a crucifix on his breast, she steals from the room.

Act 3. On the battlements of the Castle of Sant'Angelo, Cavaradossi is interrupted in writing his farewell message to Tosca by her arrival with the safe conduct. She tells him of Scarpia's death, and explains about the mock execution. Cavaradossi stands ready: a volley of shots rings out and he falls. When the soldiers have gone, she tells her lover to get up. He does not move. Scarpia has tricked her: the bullets were real, 'as in the case of Palmieri'. Spoletta and his men come to arrest her, but with the cry of 'Scarpia, we will meet before God!', she jumps to her death from the battlements.

Toscanini, Arturo (b. Parma, 25 Mar. 1867; d. New York, 16 Jan. 1957). Italian conductor. Studied Parma Conservatory, and began career as cellist. On the second night of an Italian opera season in Rio de Janeiro (25 Jan. 1886) he was called on by members of the company to replace the regular conductor, against whom the public had demonstrated, and directed *Aida* (from memory) with great success. Back in Italy, he was engaged to conduct Catalani's *Edmea* at Turin. In 1892 he conducted the première of *Pagliacci* at the Dal Verme in Milan, and in 1896 that of *La Bohème* in Turin, where during the same season he introduced *Götterdämmerung* to Italy. He was summoned to La Scala in 1898 as principal conductor, and remained there until 1902, when he left after demonstrations against him for refusing to allow Zenatello an encore in *Un Ballo in Maschera*. He returned to La Scala in 1906–8 and 1921–9 (for details of premières, &c., during these periods, see *La Scala*).

From 1908 to 1915 Toscanini conducted at the other great centre of his influence, the Metropolitan Opera, New York, whither he went with Gatti-Casazza (q.v.). Here he gave the world première of *La Fanciulla del West*, and the first performances in America of *Boris Godunov* and *L'Amore dei Tre Re*. After he left the Scala in 1929, owing to the growing tension between himself and the Fascists, his only other operatic appearances were at Bayreuth (1930–1) and Salzburg (1934–7), where his performances of *Falstaff* and *Fidelio* became legendary. Between 1944 and 1954, however, he gave concert performances of a number of operas for the N.B.C. in New York, all of which were recorded and issued commercially. He also conducted the opening concert at the restored La Scala in May 1946.

Toscanini's main love was always Italian opera. He had, at his special request, played the cello in the première of *Otello*, and later won Verdi's friendship and admiration; he championed Puccini; he remained all his life faithful to lesser Italian works, even naming his daughter Wally after the heroine of Catalani's opera (which he especially admired). Yet he also introduced Italians to operas from the German repertory, and revived, among other neglected works, Gluck's *Orpheus*. His genius rested perhaps above all on his uncanny ability to identify himself with the composer's intentions and his intense personal magnetism in persuading players and singers to share that vision. Verdi and Puccini both paid tribute to his insight into their music. A certain tyranny went with this. Though acutely humble about his art, he was an autocrat in the opera house, ruling singers, management, and audience despotically in the service of music. Especially in his later days, he sometimes dominated singers too ruthlessly; but his refusal of encores, his intolerance of personal vanities, and his celebrated fits of temper were based on a love of music that at times seemed almost too intense for him to bear.

Biographies include *Toscanini* by Howard Taubman (1951) and *The Magic Baton* by Filippo Sacchi (1957); his work, with special reference to his many records, is studied in *Toscanini and the Art of Orchestral Performance* by Robert C. Marsh (1956). (R)

Tosi, Piero Francesco (b. Bologna, 1647; d. Faenza, Apr. 1732). Italian castrato and singing teacher. Studied with his father and sang with success in Italy and Germany. Settled in London 1692 where he sang and taught. His *Opinioni de' cantori antichi e moderni o sieno osservazioni sopra il canto figurato* was published in 1723 and in English in 1732. It was also translated into French and German, and reprinted in Italy in 1904 and in London in 1906. His theories on voice training are still highly regarded by teachers of *bel canto*.

Tote Stadt, Die (The Dead City). Opera in 3 acts by Korngold; text by Paul Schott, after G.-R.-C. Rodenbach's novel *Bruges-la-Morte* (1892). Prod. Hamburg 4 Dec. 1920, with Anne Munchow; N.Y., Met., 19 Nov. 1921, with Jeritza. Korngold's greatest success. Revived in Munich 1956.

Tourel, Jennie (b. Montreal, 26 June 1910). French-Canadian mezzo of Russian parentage. Studied Paris with Anna El-Tour, an anagram of whose name she adopted. Début Paris, O.C., 1933, Carmen, remaining there until 1940. N.Y., Met., 1937, Mignon, and 1943–7. Admired as Mignon, Charlotte, Djamileh, Adalgisa, and Rosina (original key). Created Baba the Turk (*Rake's Progress* 1951). Her voice ranges from g^{I} to c^{III}, and she possesses an excellent technique. (R)

Touring Company. An opera company without a permanent home, giving performances in a different theatre every week or fortnight. In Great Britain the Carl Rosa, Moody-Manners, Beecham, and B.N.O.C. have been the foremost touring companies; in America, the San Carlo Co. Provincial tours are also made by C.G. and S.W. in England, by the Met. in America. Germany and Italy, with their more numerous and widely dispersed centres, can afford to avoid this operatic hazard.

Toye, Geoffrey (b. Winchester, 17 Feb. 1889; d. London, 11 June 1942). English conductor and composer. Studied London, R.C.M. Governor of S.W. 1931; managed the opera company there until 1934; managing director, C.G., 1934–6, resigning after differences with Beecham and other members of the board following the engagement of Grace Moore (1935) and other moves to popularize opera.

Tozzi, Giorgio (b. Chicago, 8 Jan. 1923). American bass-baritone of Italian origin. Studied Chicago with Lovardi and Rimini. Début N.Y., Ziegfield T., 1949, Tarquinius (*Rape of Lucretia*). Then went to London for the musical *Tough at the Top*. After further study in Milan appeared in Italy, including Milan, Sc., 1954. N.Y., Met., since 1955, where he created the Doctor in *Vanessa* (1958) and has been most successful as Figaro, Sarastro, Gremin, and Sachs. (R)

Traetta, Tommaso (b. Bitonto, 30 Mar. 1727; d. Venice, 6 Apr. 1779). Italian composer. His first opera, *Farnace* (1751), brought commissions for six more operas, and his fame quickly spread. As well as producing a long series of operas throughout Italy, he wrote two works for Vienna. He succeeded Galuppi as Catherine II's court musician from 1768 until 1775, when he was able to endure the Russian climate no more. He then visited London without displacing Sacchini from favour. Highly praised by good judges in their day for their dramatic flair, and notable as an influence on early Gluck, Traetta's works are now forgotten.

Tragédie lyrique. A type of 17th-century French opera on a serious, but not necessarily tragic, theme.

Transposition. The term for the notation or performance of a piece of music in a key different from its original. Opera singers, particularly those of ripening years, may often require an aria to be transposed down, usually to accommodate their top notes (a typical example is Manrico's 'Di quella pira'), even during a complete performance when it may make nonsense of the composer's key structure.

Traubel, Helen (b. St. Louis, 20 June 1899). American soprano. Studied St. Louis and sang in concerts from 1925 to 1934. Engaged N.Y., Met., to create Mary in Damrosch's *The Man Without A Country* (1934) at the composer's request. Real success dates from 1939, when she sang Sieglinde. When Flagstad left the Met. in 1941, Traubel became the leading Wagner soprano, remaining there until 1953, when she and Bing disagreed over her night-club appearances. She sang in Buenos Aires, Rio, and Mexico. American critics compared her with Nordica. She has written detective stories, including *The Ptomaine Canary* and *The Metropolitan Opera Murders*. (R)

Traubmann, Sophie (b. N.Y., 12 May 1867; d. N.Y., 16 Aug. 1951). American soprano. Studied N.Y. with Fursch-Madi, and Paris with Viardot and Marchesi. She was also coached for Wagner roles by Cosima Wagner. Début N.Y., Ac. of M., Venus; Met., 1888–1902, where she was the first American Woglinde, and Margiana (*Barbier von Bagdad*). London, C.G., 1892.

Traurigkeit ward mir zum Lose. Constanze's (sop.) aria in Act 2 of Mozart's *Entführung aus dem Serail*, bewailing her imprisonment.

Travelling Companion, The. Opera in 4 acts by Stanford; text by Henry Newbolt, after Hans Andersen's fairy-tale. Prod. Liverpool 30 Apr. 1925.

Travesti (Fr. past part. of *travestir* = to disguise). Term used to describe such roles as Cherubino, Octavian, Orlofsky, Siebel, &c., which although sung by women are male characters. The English term is 'breeches-part', from the German *Hosenrolle*.

Traviata, La (lit., The Wayward One). Opera in 3 acts by Verdi; text by Piave, after the drama *La Dame aux Camélias* (1852) by Dumas *fils*, after his novel (1848) based on his own experiences. Prod. Venice, F., 6 Mar. 1853, with Salvini-Donatelli; London, H.M.'s, 24 May 1856, with Piccolomini; N.Y., Ac. of M., 3 Dec. 1856, with La Grange.

Act 1. At one of her parties the courtesan Violetta (sop.) is introduced to Alfredo Germont (ten.) who has long admired her from afar. As the guests go in to supper she almost faints, but recovers and makes light of it. Alfredo returns to declare his love. She tells him she is unworthy, but promises to meet him next day. Left alone, Violetta finds that at last her heart has been touched—then, laughing, she exclaims that she can only live a life of pleasure.

Act 2. Alfredo and Violetta have been living together near Paris. When Alfredo learns that Violetta has sold her jewels to meet expenses, he leaves for Paris to raise money. His father, Giorgio Germont (bar.), comes to ask Violetta to give up his son, as his daughter's engagement is threatened by the association. Reluctantly she agrees, and asks Germont to embrace her as a daughter. She writes a farewell note. Alfredo returns from Paris, having heard that his father is on the way. Violetta asks him to declare his love again, and rushes from the room. A few moments later a messenger brings Violetta's letter to Alfredo. His father attempts to comfort him, but he hurries off to Paris to find Violetta.

In Flora's (mezzo) house in Paris a party is in progress. Violetta arrives with the Baron Douphol (bar.). Alfredo appears and he begins to win at cards from the Baron. When the guests go in to supper, Violetta returns to ask Alfredo to leave, assuring him that she loves the Baron. Alfredo calls back the guests, and throws his winnings at her to pay for her past favours. Giorgio Germont arrives to denounce him for insulting Violetta in public, and the Baron threatens him with vengeance.

Act 3. Violetta is dying of consumption. She re-reads a letter from Germont saying that he has told all to Alfredo, who is coming to beg her forgiveness. Alfredo arrives to take her away from Paris to recover her health. She tries to dress, but the effort is too much for her. Alfredo sends for the doctor, who arrives followed by Germont. It is too late, and Violetta dies in her lover's arms.

Trebelli (orig. Gillebert, of which Trebelli is almost the reverse), **Zélia** (b. Paris, 1838; d. Étretat, 18 Aug. 1892). French mezzo. Studied with Wartel. Début Madrid 1859, Rosina; appearances followed in Germany where she was compared with Alboni. London, H.M.'s, 1862, as Maffeo Orsini (*Lucrezia Borgia*); C.G. 1868–71, 1881–2, 1888. Much admired in *travesti* roles. First Met. Carmen, 1884. She married the tenor Bettini: their daughter Antoinette sang first under her own name, then as **Antonia Dolores.**

Treptow, Günther (b. Berlin, 22 Oct. 1907). German tenor. Début Berlin, Deutsches Opernhaus, 1936. Steersman (*Der fliegende Hollander*); Berlin, Städtische Oper, 1936–42, 1945–50; S.O. since 1955; Vienna 1947–55; Bayreuth, 1951–2; N.Y., Met., 1950–1; London, C.G., 1953. One of the few true Heldentenors of the post-war period, admired as Siegmund, Siegfried, and Tristan; also sings Florestan and Otello. (R)

Trial. The term, derived from Antoine Trial (1736–95), traditionally applied at the Paris O.C. to a tenor of dramatic rather than vocal excellence specializing in comedy—e.g. Le Petit Vieillard (Arithmetic) in Ravel's *L'Enfant et les Sortilèges*. See *Tenor*.

Trieste. Free city at the head of the Adriatic, originally Italian, then French, Austrian, and again Italian. First opera given there, *Serpilla e Bacocco*, Teatro di S. Pietro, 1730. In 1801 the Teatro Nuovo (renamed Grande, 1819) was opened with Mayr's *Ginevra di Scozia*. During the next 50 years performances were given of most Rossini, Bellini, and Donizetti operas, with leading Italian singers. On 26 Oct. 1848 Verdi's *Il Corsaro* was given its première, and on 16 Nov. 1850 *Stiffelio*—both failures. In 1861 the theatre was taken over by the city and renamed the Comunale. First Italian *Mignon* there, 1870. The Teatro Politeama Rossetti opened 1878. During the last 20 years of the century, Wagner's operas enjoyed a great success. In 1936 the theatre became an

Ente Autonomo and was renamed the Teatro Comunale Giuseppe Verdi, with Giuseppe Antonicelli as Sovrintendente; the new régime began with *Otello*. Antonicelli remained director until 1945, and was reappointed in 1951. Open-air performances during the summer are given at the Castello San Giusto.

Trionfo d'Afrodite. *Concerto scenico* by Carl Orff; text by composer, after Catullus, Sappho, and Euripides. Part 2 of the 'Trionfi' triptych (the other two parts being *Carmina Burana* and *Catulli Carmina*, qq.v.). Prod. Milan, Sc., 13 Feb. 1953, with Schwarzkopf, Gedda, cond. Karajan.

Tristan und Isolde. Opera in 3 acts by Wagner; text by composer, after the old Cornish legend. Prod. Munich, Court, 10 June 1865, with Malvina and Ludwig Schnorr von Carolsfeld, cond. Bülow; London, D.L., 20 June 1882, with Sucher, Winkelmann, cond. Richter; N.Y., Met., 1 Dec. 1886, with Lilli Lehmann, Nieman, cond. Seidl.

Act 1. Tristan (ten.) is taking Isolde (sop.) to be King Mark's bride. He refuses through his squire Kurwenal (bar.) to see her on the ship. She describes to Brangäne how he was wounded in winning her from her betrothed, but healed by her (she will not admit love). She orders Brangäne to prepare poison for her and Tristan, but Brangäne substitutes a love potion. They drink it and become aware of their love.

Act 2. Isolde takes advantage of her husband Mark's absence hunting with Melot (ten.) to meet Tristan. In a great love duet they sing of their passion and how it can only flourish in night. Melot causes them to be surprised, but the king is too grief-stricken to show anger at Tristan's betrayal. Isolde answers Tristan that she will follow wherever he goes; he is attacked by Melot and allows himself to be wounded.

Act 3. In Tristan's castle in Brittany, Kurwenal tries to cheer his sick master, who thinks only of Isolde. The repeated sad strain of a shepherd's pipe tells that Isolde, sent for by Kurwenal, is not in sight. When the shepherd's joyful tune announces her ship, Tristan excitedly tears off his bandages, and dies in her arms. A second ship brings Mark and Melot, and Kurwenal dies killing Melot, unaware that they come to pardon Tristan. In her Liebestod, Isolde sings of the love which she can only now fulfil in the deeper night of death at Tristan's side.

Trittico. See *Tabarro*, *Suor Angelica*, and *Gianni Schicchi*.

Troilus and Cressida. Opera in 3 acts by Walton; text by Christopher Hassall, after Chaucer's poem (*c.* 1385). Prod. London, C.G., 3 Dec. 1954, with László, Lewis, Pears, Kraus, cond. Sargent; San Francisco, 7 Oct. 1955, with Kirsten, Lewis, McChesney, Weede, cond. Leinsdorf.

Trompeter von Säckingen, Der (The Trumpeter of Säckingen). Opera in 4 acts by Nessler; text by Rudolf Bunge, after von Scheffel's poem (1854). Prod. Leipzig, 4 May 1884; N.Y., 23 Nov. 1887; London, D.L., 8 July 1892. In the period after the Thirty Years War, the trumpeter Werner loves Maria, betrothed to a nobleman, Damian. When Werner proves his courage, and Damian his cowardice, and when Werner also proves to be of noble birth, Maria's parents give their blessing.

Troppau. See *Opava*.

Troutbeck, John (b. Blencowe, 12 Nov. 1832; d. London, 11 Oct. 1899). English translator. His English translations of opera include *Così fan tutte*, *Entführung*, Gluck's two *Iphigenias* and *Orfeo*, Götz's *Taming of the Shrew*, and *Der fliegende Holländer*.

Trovatore, Il (The Troubadour). Opera in 4 acts by Verdi; text by Cammarano, after the drama *El Trovador* by Gutiérrez. Prod. Rome, Apollo, 19 Jan. 1853, with Penco, Goggi, Baucardé, Guicciardi; N.Y., Ac. of M., 2 May 1855, with Steffanone, Vestvali, Brignoli, Amodeo; London, C.G., 10 May 1855, with Ney, Viardot, Tamberlik, Graziani.

The notoriously confused action takes place in Spain at the beginning of the 15th century during the civil war caused by the rebellion of the Count of Urgel against the King of Aragon. The leader of the King's army is the Count Di Luna.

Act 1, scene 1. Ferrando (bass), an old retainer of Di Luna, tells the soldiers how many years previously the Count's young brother had been kidnapped by a gipsy whose mother had been burned as a witch by the Count's father. It was believed that the stolen child was burned by the gipsy.

Scene 2. In the palace garden that night Leonora (sop.), lady-in-waiting to the Queen of Aragon, tells her companion Inez (sop.) of her love for the troubador Manrico, who nightly serenades her, and who is the leader of the rebel army. Di Luna (bar.), himself in love with Leonora, enters the garden. Leonora, hearing the voice of Manrico (ten.), rushes out, but mistakes Di Luna for her lover. Manrico now enters, and the two men prepare to fight.

Act 2, scene 1. Several months later in the gipsy camp, Manrico, who was wounded by Di Luna, is being nursed by Azucena (mezzo), whom he believes to be his mother. She relates how her mother had been burned at the stake, and how in her madness she had thrown the wrong child into the flames (she had in fact killed her own child, and Manrico is Di Luna's brother, though no one but Azucena knows this). A messenger brings news that Leonora, believing her lover dead, is to enter a convent. Manrico hurries off to prevent this.

Scene 2. Di Luna and his followers assemble outside the Jerusalem Convent to abduct Leonora. They are thwarted by Manrico, who takes Leonora to the castle of Castellor.

Act 3, scene 1. A military encampment. Di Luna and his men are besieging Castellor. Azucena is found lingering near the camp. Ferrando recognizes her; she says she is Manrico's mother. Di Luna condemns her to be burned.

Scene 2. Preparations are being made in the castle for Manrico's marriage to Leonora. Learning from his retainer Ruiz (ten.) that Azucena is to die, Manrico hurries off to rescue her.

Act 4, scene 1. Manrico has been captured trying to rescue Azucena. Leonora comes to the palace hoping to see him and prays that her love will ease his suffering. Monks chant a Miserere and Manrico sings of his longing for death. Leonora pleads with Di Luna for Manrico's life. He agrees to spare Manrico on condition that Leonora gives herself to him. She consents. Di Luna goes to order Manrico's release, and Leonora drinks poison from a ring.

Scene 2. Manrico tries to comfort Azucena, reminding her of their home in the mountains. Leonora arrives to tell Manrico that he is free. When he learns the price of his freedom he curses her. But already the poison is working, and Di Luna enters to see Leonora die in her lover's arms. He orders Manrico's execution—and as Manrico dies, Azucena tells him triumphantly that he has killed his own brother. 'Mother, you are avenged!' she cries as the curtain falls.

Troyens, Les (The Trojans). Opera in 5 acts by Berlioz; text by composer after Virgil's *Aeneid* (*c.* 27–19 B.C.). Composed 1856–8. To achieve a performance, Berlioz was obliged in 1863 to divide the work into 2 parts: Acts 1 and 2 into *La Prise de Troie* (The Capture of Troy) (3 acts), prod. Karlsruhe, 6 Dec. 1890; Acts 3, 4, and 5 into *Les Troyens à Carthage* (The Trojans at Carthage) (5 acts, with added prologue), prod. Paris, T.L., 4 Nov. 1863, with Charton-Demeur. The complete work was first prod. Karlsruhe, 6–7 Dec. 1890, cond. Mottl; Glasgow, 18–19 Mar. 1935, cond. Chisholm; Boston, 27 Mar. 1955, cond. Goldovsky.

In the following synopsis, the original arrangement is preserved, with the act divisions of the second version given in brackets.

Act 1 (*Troy*, 1). The Greeks have abandoned their camp, leaving behind the wooden horse. The forebodings of Cassandra (sop. or mezzo), daughter of Priam (bass), are disbelieved even by her lover Choroebus (bar.). (*Troy*, 2) The celebrations of peace are interrupted by Aeneas (ten.), who brings news that the priest Laocöon, who mistrusted the horse, has been devoured by serpents: the horse is thereupon dragged into the city to propitiate Athene.

Act 2 (*Troy*, 3). Hector's ghost (bass) tells Aeneas to flee from Troy and found a new city in Italy. The priest Pantheus (bass) describes the burning of Troy by Greeks who have hidden in the horse. In the Temple of Vesta, Cassandra tells the women of Choroebus's death and Aeneas's escape. As the Greeks rush in, the women stab themselves.

Act 3 (*Carthage*, 1). At Carthage, festivities are in progress. Queen Dido (sop. or mezzo) states her intention of remaining single in devotion to her dead husband: her sister Anna (con.) tries to shake this resolve. The poet Iopas (ten.) reports the arrival by sea of strangers. Aeneas's son Ascanius (sop.) successfully begs Dido for hospitality. When her minister Narbal (bass) brings news of invasion, Aeneas, hitherto disguised, steps forward and offers help. (*Carthage*, 2) In a symphonic interlude (Royal Hunt and Storm), Dido and Aeneas are driven into a cave where they make love.

Act 4 (*Carthage*, 3). Aeneas is fêted in Dido's gardens. Narbal's apprehensions over Aeneas's impending conflict between love and duty are seen to be justified as Dido allows her firm resolve to weaken. Mercury exhorts Aeneas to voyage on to Italy.

Act 5 (*Carthage*, 4). The ghosts of Trojan heroes add their exhortations to depart, and Aeneas, now deaf to Dido's pleas, sets sail. (*Carthage*, 5) On hearing this, Dido, distraught with grief, decides to die; prophesying the glory of Rome, she kills herself on Aeneas's sword.

Tsar Saltan, The Tale of. Opera in prologue and 4 acts by Rimsky-Korsakov; text by Belsky, after Pushkin's poem (1832). Prod. Moscow 3 Nov. 1900; London, S.W., 11 Oct. 1933; N.Y., St. James T., 27 Dec. 1937.

Tsar Saltan marries Militrissa, whose sisters, by telling the Tsar that she has produced a monster, cause her and her son Prince Guidon to be thrown into the sea in a cask. Washed up on an island, Guidon rescues a swan fleeing from a hawk; it turns out to be a disguised princess. Turned by her into a bee, he goes to find the Tsar; when the sisters try to dissuade the Tsar from visiting the island, the Prince stings them mercilessly. Back on the island, Guidon frees the princess from her enchantment, and when the Tsar arrives she restores his wife to him.

Tsar's Bride, The. Opera in 3 acts by Rimsky-Korsakov; text from L. A. Mey's drama (1849), additional scene by I. F. Tumenev. Prod. Moscow 3 Nov. 1899; Seattle 6 Jan. 1922; London, Ly., 19 May 1931. Martha, selected by Tsar Ivan as his bride, is loved by Lykov, whom she loves, and Gryaznoy, who tries to win her with a love potion. Gryaznoy's mistress substitutes poison, and Martha goes mad on learning as she lies dying in the Kremlin that the Tsar has had Lykov beheaded for the crime. Gryaznoy kills his mistress.

Tucker, Norman (b. Wembley, 24 Apr. 1910). English theatre director. Studied London, R.C.M. Joint director S.W., with James Robertson and Michael Mudie, Jan. 1948–June 1953; with Robertson, June 1953–June 1954; sole director 1954–66. Translated *Simone Boccanegra*, *Káťa Kabanova*, *Werther*, *Romeo and Juliet* (Sutermeister), *Luisa Miller* (with Tom Hammond), and the *Don Carlos* (including some drastic rearrangement) used by the company. (See also *Sadler's Wells*.)

Tucker, Richard (b. New York, 28 Aug. 1914). American tenor. Studied N.Y. with Althouse. Début N.Y., Met., 1945, Enzo (*Gioconda*), and leading tenor there ever since in Italian and French repertory, and as Alfred (*Fledermaus*) and Lensky. London, C.G., 1958, Cavaradossi. Verona Arena 1947, Enzo in performance of *La Gioconda* in which Callas made her Italian début. Chosen by Toscanini to sing Radamès in the N.B.C. performance 1949. (R)

Turandot. Opera in 3 acts by Puccini,

completed by Alfano; text by Adami and Simoni, after Gozzi's drama (1762), possibly after *The Arabian Nights*. Prod. Milan, Sc., 25 Apr. 1926, with Raisa, Zamboni, Fleta, cond. Toscanini; N.Y., Met., 16 Nov. 1926, with Jeritza, Garrison, Lauri-Volpi, cond. Serafin; London, C.G., 7 June 1927, with Scacciati, Schoene, Merli, cond. Bellezza.

Act 1. Princess Turandot of Pekin (sop.) will marry the solver of three riddles. In the crowd listening to the death sentence pronounced on a prince who has failed is the aged deposed King Timur (bass) with his son Prince Calaf (ten.) and slave girl Liù (sop.). Calaf condemns the princess's cruelty but is moved by her beauty to attempt the riddles. Liù fails to dissuade him.

Act 2. In the palace, the three masks Ping, the Chancellor (bar.), Pang, the Purveyor (ten.), and Pong, the Cook (ten.), long for true love to put an end to Turandot's bloodshed. Outside the palace, Turandot explains that she is taking revenge for her ancestor's murder on all who seek her love. Calaf answers the riddles, but agrees to release Turandot from the vow if she can discover his name by morning.

Act 3. The palace gardens are searched for information; Liù is tortured but refuses to reveal the Prince's name and stabs herself in order not to speak. Turandot is stirred by Liù's willingness to sacrifice herself. Calaf kisses Turandot and reveals his name, thus putting himself in her power. But in the pavilion of the palace she tells the Emperor that she has learned the Prince's name—it is love.

Other operas on the subject by Blumenroeder (1810), Reissiger (1835), Vesque von Püttlingen (1838), Jensen (*Die Erbin von Montfort*, 1864–5, adapted after his death to a *Turandot* libretto by his daughter), Bazzini (1867), Rehbaum (1888), Busoni (1917).

Turco in Italia, Il (The Turk in Italy). Opera in 2 Acts by Rossini; text by Romani. Prod. Milan, Sc., 14 Aug. 1814; London, H.M.'s, 19 May 1821, with De Begnis; N.Y. 14 Mar. 1826. Revived Rome in 1950 with Callas and Stabile, since when it has been performed widely in Italy and elsewhere. The opera is artificial to a degree, with the poet Prosdocimo manipulating the intrigue between Donna Fiorilla, the dissatisfied wife of Don Geronio, and Selim Damelec of Erzerum, the eponymous Turk. Censured in London in 1822 for immorality.

Turiddu. A young soldier (ten.), hero of Mascagni's *Cavalleria Rusticana*.

Turin (It., Torino). Town in Piedmont, Italy. The first opera performed there was *Zalizura* (Sigismondo d'India), 1662, in the Court Theatre of the Royal Ducal Palace. In 1741 the Teatro Regio was opened, in 1753 the Teatro Carignano. From 1880, with the première of Catalani's *La Wally*, Turin's operatic life took on a new guise. Toscanini's first important Italian engagements were at Turin in 1886 and 1889–91 and 1895–8; *Manon Lescaut* and *La Bohème* had their world premières in Turin in 1893 and 1896, and Zandonai's *Francesca da Rimini* in 1914, Alfano's *Risurrezione* in 1904. The Rossini revival under Gui began in Turin in 1925, and the first performances in Italy of *Ariadne auf Naxos*, *L'Heure Espagnole*, *The Golden Cockerel*, *L'Éducation Manquée* have taken place there. The Regio was destroyed by fire in 1936. Opera is now given at the Teatro Lirico (formerly the Teatro Vittorio Emmanuele II), the Carignano (cap. 1,000), the Alfieri, and the Teatro Nuovo (cap. 1,500), where the Ente Autonomo of the Teatro Regio functions. Plans to rebuild the Regio were finally announced in 1963.

Turkey. The first operas in Turkey were given by a visiting Italian company in 1797. From the 1840's to the 1870's Italian opera was given in the T. Naum in Istanbul. In 1859 the Sultan Abdul Mecit built an opera house (cap. 300) in the Dolmabahce Palace and appointed Giovanni Donizetti (the composer's brother) as director; this was burnt down in 1863. Another opera house was opened by the Sultan Abdul Hamit in the Yildiz Palace; it closed in 1908. The father of Turkish opera was an Armenian, Dikran Cuhatsyan (1840–98), whose compositions set an example to his successors. A second important figure was Adnan Saygun, whose *Özsoy*, on a Turko-Persian legend, was commissioned by Kemal Ataturk for the Shah's visit in 1934, and whose *Kerem* inaugurated the new Ankara Opera in 1948.

Turn of the Screw, The. Opera in prologue and 2 acts by Britten; text by Myfanwy Piper, after Henry James's story (1898). Prod. Venice 14 Sept. 1954; London 6 Oct. 1954, by English Opera Group with Pears, Vyvyan, Cross, Mandikian, Hemmings, Dyer, cond. Britten; N.Y., College of Music (Kaufmann Concert Hall), 19 Mar. 1958. The Governess (sop.) sent to look after two children in a country house run only by an old housekeeper Mrs. Grose (sop.) comes to realize that they are visited by the evil ghosts of two former servants; more, that the children cherish the relationship. In fighting this she has first to convince the housekeeper, and having persuaded her to take the girl away battles with the ghost who haunts the boy and wins—only to find him dead in her arms. The 'screw' of the title is represented by a theme that 'turns' through 15 variations, interludes between the 8 scenes of each act.

Turner, Eva (Dame) (b. Oldham, 10 Mar. 1892). English soprano. Studied London, R.A.M. Joined chorus Carl Rosa 1916; début Page, *Tannhäuser*, soon after. Sang with company until 1924, studying with Richard Broad and developing into a fine dramatic soprano. Auditioned by Panizza in London 1924, who sent her to Milan to sing for Toscanini. Scala début 1924, Freia. Established herself as leading dramatic soprano and considered by Alfano as the ideal Turandot. London, C.G., 1928–30, 1933, 1935–9, 1947–8. Also Chicago, Buenos Aires, Lisbon, &c. Taught voice, Univ. of Oklahoma, 1950–9; London, A.R.M., since 1959. Her voice, of enormous proportions in its prime, ranged from g to d''' and was admirably suited to the dramatic soprano roles in Verdi and Wagner. (R)

Tutte le feste. The opening words of Gilda's (sop.) account to her father of her betrayal by the Duke in Act 2 of Verdi's *Rigoletto*.

U

Udite, udite, o rustici. Dulcamara's (bass) aria in Act 1 of Donizetti's *L'Elisir d'Amore*, in which he advertises his quack's wares.

Uhde, Hermann (b. Bremen, 20 July 1914; d. Copenhagen, 24 Oct. 1965). German bass-baritone. Studied Bremen. Début Bremen 1936, Titurel (*Parsifal*). Freiburg 1938–40; Munich 1940–2; The Hague, German Opera, 1942–3; Hanover 1947; Hamburg 1949–50; Munich since 1951; Bayreuth 1951–7, 1960; London, C.G., 1953 with Munich Company as Mandryka, and 1954–60; N.Y., Met., 1955–61. Created Creon in Orff's *Antigonae*, Salzburg 1949, and Elis in Wagner-Régeny's *Das Bergwerk zu Falun* 1961. An outstanding Gunther and Dutchman. (R)

Ulrica. The fortune-teller (mezzo) in Verdi's *Ballo in Maschera*.

Un bel dì vedremo. Butterfly's (sop.) aria in Act 2 of Puccini's *Madama Butterfly*, in which she sings of Pinkerton's hoped-for return.

Un dì all'azzurro spazio. Andrea Chénier's (ten.) aria in Act 1 of Giordano's opera, in which the poet denounces the selfishness of those in authority. Sometimes known as the 'Improvviso'.

Un dì felice. The opening words of

the love duet between Violetta (sop.) and Alfredo (ten.) in Act 1 of Verdi's *La Traviata*.

Un' aura amorosa. Ferrando's (ten.) aria in Act 1, scene 3, of Mozart's *Così fan tutte*, in which he sentimentally describes Dorabella's love.

Una Cosa Rara. Opera in 2 acts by Martín y Soler; text by Da Ponte, after Luis Velez de Guevara's story *La Luna della Sierra*. Prod. Vienna, B., 17 Nov. 1786; London 10 Jan. 1789. One of the great successes of its day, it drew the Viennese public away from *Figaro*, causing Mozart to quote a piece from the Act 1 finale in the Supper Scene of *Don Giovanni* with Leporello's comment, 'Bravi! *Cosa Rara!*' Martín's use in the opera of a mandoline had a clear influence on Mozart in writing Don Giovanni's Serenade. The opera contains one of the first Viennese waltzes. Adapted by Stephen Storace as *The Siege of Belgrade* 1791. Sequel, music by Schack, text by Schikaneder, *Der Fall ist noch weit seltener!*, prod. Vienna, W., 10 May 1790.

Una donna di quindici anni. Despina's (sop.) aria in Act 2, scene 1, of Mozart's *Così fan tutte*, describing the wiles of love to her mistresses.

Una furtiva lagrima. Nemorino's (ten.) aria in Act 2 of Donizetti's *L'Elisir d'Amore*, in which he sees by a tear in Adina's eye that she loves him.

Una voce poco fa. Rosina's (mezzo, often transposed to sop.) aria in Act 1, scene 2, of Rossini's *Il Barbiere di Siviglia*, recalling the serenading voice of Almaviva that has awakened her love.

Undine. Opera in 4 acts by Lortzing; text by composer, after La Motte Fouqué's story (1811). Prod. Magdeburg 21 Apr. 1845; N.Y. 9 Oct. 1856. Hugo marries the water-nymph Undine, but when he deserts her for Berthalda, she lures him to death beneath the water. Lortzing's first serious opera and first major success. Also operas by E. T. A. Hoffmann (1816), Mori (1865), and Sporck (1877).

Unger, Caroline (b. Vienna, 28 Oct. 1803; d. Florence, 23 Mar. 1877). Austrian contralto. Studied Milan with D. Ronconi and Vienna with Aloysia Lang and J. M. Vogl. Début Vienna 1821, Dorabella. Engaged by Barbaia for Italy, where she created leading roles in Donizetti's *Parisina, Belisario, Maria di Rudenz*, Bellini's *La Straniera*, and works by Mercadante and Pacini. Sang at T.-I., Paris, 1833, when Rossini said of her that she possessed 'the ardour of the south, the energy of the north, brazen lungs, a silver voice, and golden talent'.

Unger, Georg (b. Leipzig, 6 Mar. 1837; d. Leipzig, 2 Feb. 1887). German tenor. Début Leipzig 1867. Heard at Mannheim by Richter, who recommended him to Wagner—created Siegfried, Bayreuth 1876. London, R.A.H., in Wagner series 1877. Remained at Leipzig until 1881. The first Wagnerheldentenor.

United States of America. The first American opera libretto was printed in 1797, *The Disappointment* by Andrew Barton; the music consisted of popular airs. Hewitt's *Tammany* (1794) is lost, and the first American opera with some surviving music is Carr's *The Archers* (1796); Pellesier's *Edwin and Angelina* dates from the same year. Davies's *Forest Rose* (1825) was a successful opera on an American subject, but the first publicly performed opera by a native American was Fry's *Leonora* (1845). *A Trip to Chinatown* (1890) uses local songs again, but begins to presage the American musical comedy. See *Berkshire Festival, Boston, Chicago, Cincinnati, Dallas, Damrosch Opera Company, Detroit, New Orleans, New York, Philadelphia, San Francisco.*

Uppman, Theodor (b. San José, 12 Jan. 1920). American baritone. Studied Curtis Institute with Steuart Wilson, Univ. of California with Ebert. Début Stanford Univ. 1946, Papageno. London, C.G., 1951–2, created title role in Britten's *Billy Budd*. N.Y., Met. since 1956. (R)

Urban, Joseph (b. Vienna, 26 May 1872; d. New York, 10 July 1933).

Austrian architect and stage designer. Designed sets for many of the Met.'s most successful productions in the inter-war years, as well as for the Boston Opera, Vienna, and C.G.

Urlus, Jacques (b. Hergenrath, nr. Aix-la-Chapelle, 6 Jan. 1867; d. Noordwijk 6 June 1935). Dutch tenor. Studied Amsterdam. Début Amsterdam 1894 Canio. Leipzig 1900–15; London, C.G., 1910, 1914, and 1924; Bayreuth 1911–12; Boston 1912; N.Y., Met., 1913–17. One of the leading Heldentenors of his day, much admired as Tristan and Parsifal. (R)

Ursuleac, Viorica (b. Cernăuţi, 26 Mar. 1899). Rumanian soprano. Studied Vienna and Berlin with Lilli Lehmann. Début Vienna, V.O., 1924; Frankfurt 1927–30; Vienna 1930–4; Berlin 1933–45; London, C.G., 1934. Salzburg Festivals 1930–4 and 1942. Created Arabella, Maria in Strauss's *Friedenstag*, and the Countess in *Capriccio*. Considered by Strauss as his ideal soprano; also successful as Senta, Sieglinde, and (in Germany and Austria) in Verdi. Wife of Clemens Krauss. (R)

U.S.A. See *United States of America.*

Ústí nad Labem (Aussig). Town in Bohemia, Czechoslovakia. The theatre (cap. 900) was modernized in 1947 and serves the large surrounding industrial region. The company performs regularly in Karlovy Vary, Mariánzké Lázně, and the Most district; it has a special interest in contemporary music.

U.S.S.R. See *Russia.*

V

Va, pensiero, sull' ali dorate. The chorus in Act 3 of Verdi's *Nabucco*, in which the Hebrew captives by the banks of the Euphrates sing of their lost fatherland.

Vaccai, Nicola (b. Tolentino, 15 Mar. 1790; d. Pesaro, 5 Aug. 1848). Italian composer and singer. Studied under Paisiello, bringing out his first opera *I Solitari di Scozia* in 1815. After two failures in Venice, he became a singing teacher. After the success of his *Giulietta e Romeo* (1825) in Milan, went to Paris as teacher and London as composer. From 1836 back in Italy, where he wrote operas and a cantata on Malibran's death. The penultimate scene of *Giulietta* was often substituted for the last scene of Bellini's *I Capuleti e i Montecchi.*

Vakula the Smith. Opera in 4 acts by Tchaikovsky; text by Polonsky, after Gogol's story *Christmas Eve* (1832). Prod. St. Petersburg 6 Dec. 1876. Revised in 1885 as *Cherevichki* (The Little Shoes—also known in western Europe as *Oxana's Caprice*), prod. Moscow, 31 Jan. 1887; N.Y. 26 May 1922.

Valdengo, Giuseppe (b. Turin, 24 May 1914). Italian baritone. Studied Turin. Début Parma 1936, Figaro (Rossini). Milan, Sc., 1939; N.Y., C.C., 1946–8; Met. 1946–54; Glyndebourne 1955. Chosen by Toscanini to sing Iago and Amonasro for N.B.C., 1947 and 1949, and coached by him for Falstaff 1950. (R)

Valentine. (1) Marguerite's brother (bar.) in Gounod's *Faust.* (2) St. Bris's daughter (sop.) in Meyerbeer's *Les Huguenots.*

Valentino, Francesco (orig. Francis Valentine Dinhaupt) (b. New York, 6 Jan. 1907). American baritone. Studied Milan. Début Parma 1927, Germont. Milan, Sc., 1937–40; Glyndebourne 1938–9 and 1947, as Macbeth. N.Y., Met., since 1940. Has sung most leading baritone roles in the French and Italian repertory. (R)

Valleria (orig. Schoening), **Alwina** (b. Baltimore, 12 Oct. 1848; d. Nice, 17 Feb. 1925). American soprano. Studied London with Arditi. Début St. Petersburg 1871, Linda di Chamounix. London, D.L., 1873, Martha; 1877–8; and C.G. 1879–82. The first London Micaëla and the first to sing Elisabeth (*Tannhäuser*) in English in London. Created title roles in Mackenzie's *Colomba* (1883), and Goring Thomas's *Nadeshda* (1885). N.Y., Ac. of M., 1879.

Valletti, Cesare (b. Rome, 18 Dec. 1922). Italian tenor. Studied privately. Début Bari 1947, Alfredo. London, C.G., 1950, with Scala Company as Fenton; 1958 as Alfredo; Milan, Sc., since 1950; N.Y., Met., 1953–62. Admired in Rossini, Wolf-Ferrari, Donizetti, and Mozart roles. (R)

Vallin, Ninon (orig. Eugénie Vallin-Pardo) (b. Montalieu-Vercien, 9 Sept. 1886; d. Lyons, 22 Nov. 1961). French soprano. Studied Lyons and Paris with Mme Héglon. Began career as concert singer singing in Débussy's *La Demoiselle Élue* and *Le Martyre de Saint Sébastien*. Heard by Carré, who engaged her for the O.C. 1912, début as Micaëla. Created there several roles in operas by D'Erlanger and Leroux, and sang the title role in Respighi's *Maria Egiziaca* in its Paris première. Sang with success in Milan, Sc., and Buenos Aires, Colón. The leading Louise, Manon, and Charlotte of her day. (R)

Valzacchi. An Italian intriguer (ten.), crony of Annina, in Strauss's *Der Rosenkavalier*.

Vampyr, Der. Opera in 2 acts by Marschner; text by Wohlbrück. Prod. Leipzig, 29 Mar. 1828; London, Ly., 25 Aug. 1289. The first of Marschner's important operas. Lord Ruthven, to avoid destruction by spirits, must sacrifice a girl every year; his vampire disguise is exposed and he is killed by lightning.

Van. For names with this prefix, see following word.

Vancouver. In 1951 Nicholas Goldschmidt brought opera to Vancouver when he included a course in opera as part of the University of British Columbia's Summer School of Arts. Under his guidance the opera programme developed rapidly, and in 1955 Menotti's *The Consul* was produced. In 1963 the notable success of the University Workshop and of its annual productions, and the need for trained singers, prompted the university authorities to include opera in the regular curriculum of the department of music. The first Vancouver International Festival in 1958 included a production of *Don Giovanni* with Joan Sutherland and the Canadian singers George London and Leopold Simoneau. Succeeding festivals also included operas, and their popularity led to the formation in 1960 of the Vancouver Opera Association with Irving Guttman as director. It gave four performances in its first season and twenty-one in its fourth. The operas have included *La Traviata*, *Les Contes d'Hoffmann*, *The Barber of Seville*, *La Bohème*, and *Norma*. The Association has been able to rely less each year on imported singers for leading roles, which are now given mainly to Canadians.

Varaždin. Town in Slovenia, Yugoslavia. Has a long musical tradition: fine theatre built in 1876. Company formed 1915; now performs mostly operetta.

Varesi, Felice (b. Calais, 1813; d. Milan, 13 Mar. 1889). French-Italian baritone. Début Varese 1834. Created title roles in Verdi's *Macbeth* and *Rigoletto* and was also the first Germont, a part he thought unworthy of him. London, H.M.'s, 1864. His daughter **Elena Varesi** (d. 1920) sang at D.L. in 1873 and 1875. She sang Zerlina opposite Giovanni di Reschi's (Jean de Reszke's) Don Giovanni.

Varlaam. The drunken monk (bass) in Mussorgsky's *Boris Godunov*.

Varnay, Astrid (b. Stockholm, 25 Apr. 1918). American soprano of Austrian and Hungarian parentage. Her father was Alexander Varnay, the Austrian singer and stage manager of the first opera company founded in Oslo, her mother a coloratura soprano, Maria Yavor. She studied with her mother and Herman Weigert, whom she married in 1944. Début N.Y., Met., 1941, Sieglinde, substituting at a few hours' notice for Lotte Lehmann. Remained at Met. until end of 1956 season, establishing herself as leading Wagner–Strauss soprano, but also singing occasionally in Verdi operas and creating Telea in Menotti's *The Island God*. London, C.G., 1948–9, 1951, 1958–9; Bayreuth since 1951; Florence Festival 1951, as Lady Macbeth. Despite a less than perfect vocal technique, her intense, passionate singing and acting made her the finest Wagnerian dramatic soprano between Flagstad's retirement and the emergence of Birgit Nilsson. (R)

Vasco da Gama. The hero (ten.) of Meyerbeer's *L'Africaine*.

Vašek. The shy son (ten.) of Micha in Smetana's *The Bartered Bride*.

Vaudeville (Fr., poss. from *Vaux de Vire*, the songs sung in the valleys (*vaux*) near Vire at the start of the 15th century by Olivier Basselin. Alternatively, from *voix de ville*; catches sung about town in the 16th century were already known as vaudevilles). Around 1700 street tunes began appearing on the stage, and by *Le Mariage de Figaro* (finished 1778) Beaumarchais was concluding with a *vaudeville final* in which each character sang a verse. The love of vaudevilles prompted operatic parody and even helped to create *opéra comique*. The most celebrated operatic example is the finale to Mozart's *Entführung*. Having come down in the world again, the true vaudeville may now be found only in Paris cafés or little theatre revues.

Vaughan Williams, Ralph (b. Down Ampney, 12 Oct. 1872; d. London, 26 Aug. 1958). English composer. Though not by temperament an opera composer, Vaughan Williams turned to the form six times, and E. J. Dent once even suggested that these works would outlast the symphonies. *Hugh the Drover* (1924), a ballad opera, finds the composer still flushed with excitement at the newly rediscovered English folk music. In the Falstaff opera *Sir John in Love* (1929), the folk influence is now absorbed, but the work remains above all earthily English even in its abounding lyricism. *Riders to the Sea* (1937), a word-for-word setting of Synge's tragedy, seems to have caught the composer up in a unique manner; it is one of his masterpieces. *The Poisoned Kiss* (1936) turns to musical comedy, but suffers from a facetious libretto that has buried with it some of the composer's most delightful and satirical dramatic music. *The Pilgrim's Progress* (1951), with its robust faith and love of simple allegory, was the work closest to V.W.'s Anglican heart—too close, perhaps, for the pastoral-modal meanderings and square English diatonics seem to act as personal reminders of the vision rather than as public evocations. It includes the 1-act *The Shepherds of The Delectable Mountains* of 1922.

Veau d'or, Le. Méphistophélès's (bass) mocking song to the crowd in Act 2 of Gounod's *Faust*.

Vecchi, Orazio (b. Modena, bapt. 6 Dec. 1550; d. Modena, 19 Feb. 1605). Italian composer. His operatic importance is due to *L'Amfiparnaso*, a 'comedia harmonica' prod. at Modena in 1594. This attempt to set the *commedia dell' arte* figures to music was not meant to be staged, and so can at most rank only as a 'pre-opera'; it has, however, been staged in modern times.

Vedrai, carino. Zerlina's (sop.) aria in Act 2, scene 1, of Mozart's *Don Giovanni*, in which she comforts Masetto after his beating from Giovanni.

Velluti, Giovanni Battista (b. Montolmo, 28 Jan. 1780; d. Bruson, Feb. 1861). Italian male soprano, the last great example. Despite tremendous early successes, he was unfavourably received in London in 1825 in Meyerbeer's *Il Crociato in Egitto* (his first opera given in London), where an audience unused to castrati (the last having sung at the King's in 1800) was fascinated and shocked. His voice was sweet and full, smoothly produced if of no great emotional range.

Veneziani, Vittorio (b. Ferrara, 25 May 1878; d. Ferrara, 14 Jan. 1958). Italian composer and chorus master. Studied Bologna with Martucci. Chorus master at Venice, Turin, and Bologna. Engaged for Sc. by Toscanini 1921, remaining there until 1938 when the racial laws compelled him to leave the country. Returned to Sc. 1945, remaining there until his retirement in 1954. He trained the Scala chorus into the most magnificent ensemble of its day. (R)

Venice (It., Venezia). Town in Italy. The first public opera house in the world, the Teatro San Cassiano, was opened in Venice in 1637 with a performance of Mannelli's *Andromeda*. It continued to function until 1800. In 1639 a second theatre was opened, the Teatro SS. Giovanni e Paolo, where Monteverdi's *L'Incoronazione di Poppea* had its première in 1642. In 1640 the Teatro San Moisè opened and gave opera regularly until 1818; in this theatre five Rossini operas had their premières—among them *La Cambiale del Matrimonio* (his first), *La Scala di Seta*, and *Il Signor Bruschino*. By 1678 Venice's tenth opera house was opened, the Teatro S. Giovanni Crisostomo, and after various vicissitudes, reopened as the Teatro Malibran, 1835. Venice's most famous opera house, La Fenice, designed by G. Selva, was opened on 16 May 1792 with Paisiello's *I Giuochi d'Agrigento*. It was the scene of the premières of Rossini's *Tancredi*, *L'Italiana in Algeri*, *Sigismondo*, and *Semiramide*, Bellini's *I Capuletti ed i Montecchi* and *Beatrice di Tenda*, and Donizetti's *Belisario*. The first Fenice was destroyed by fire in Dec. 1836, and a second theatre was built on the same site to the ground plan of the original architect in less than a year, opening on 26 Dec. 1837. This was the theatre which staged the premières of Verdi's *Ernani*, *Attila*, *Rigoletto*, *Traviata*, and *Simone Boccanegra*.

The theatre was restored in 1854 and in 1938, when it was opened as an Ente Autonomo. In recent years the season has lasted about two months, with a few late spring performances, and such opera as the Venice Festival may offer. Thus it staged the world premières of *The Rake's Progress* (1951), *The Turn of the Screw* (1954), and *Intolleranza* (1961). The auditorium seats 1,500, and with its dazzling chandelier, its 96 boxes, and blue, cream, and gold decorations is considered by many the most beautiful opera house in the world.

Venus. The goddess of love (sop.) in Wagner's *Tannhäuser*. See also below.

Venus and Adonis. Opera in prologue and 3 acts by Blow; text by unknown author. Prod. London *c.* 1684, when Venus was sung by Mary Davies, mistress of Charles II, and Cupid by Lady Mary Tudor, their daughter; Cambridge, Mass., 11 Mar. 1941.

Vêpres Siciliennes, Les (The Sicilian Vespers; in Italy, *I Vespri Siciliani*). Opera in 5 acts by Verdi; text by Scribe and Duveyrier. Prod. Paris, O., 13 June 1855, with Cruvelli and Guéymard; London, D.L., 27 July 1859, with Tietjens; N.Y. 7 Nov. 1859.

Specially commissioned for the Great Exhibition in Paris of 1855, it tells of the occupation of Sicily by the French during the 13th century, and the efforts of the Sicilians to remove them. The climax of the work is the slaughter of the unarmed French by Sicilian patriots, the signal for which is given by the ringing of the vesper bell to signal the wedding of the Duchess Elena, sister of Frederick of Austria and a Sicilian patriot, to Arrigo, son of Guy de Monfort, the French governor of the island.

Verdi, Giuseppe (b. Le Roncole, 10 Oct. 1813; d. Milan, 27 Jan. 1901). Italian composer. Born of humble parents, Verdi owed his first musical education to the local organist and his first advancement to Antonio Barezzi, a wealthy Busseto music-lover. He studied under Ferdinando Provesi, music director of the Busseto church, music school, and Philharmonic Society, deputizing for his teacher and conducting some of his own music. Barezzi soon arranged for him to go to Milan, where he failed the entrance exam. to the Conservatory; returning to Busseto he assumed, amid fierce controversy, the post of *maestro di musica* and settled down as the husband of Barezzi's daughter Margherita.

In this year, 1836, Verdi completed his first opera, *Rocester*; this is lost, but some of its music may have been incorporated into *Oberto, Conte di San Bonifacio* (1839), which already shows typical Verdian traits. This was staged partly through the good offices of the young soprano who took the lead, Giuseppina Strepponi. Verdi was promptly offered a contract for three more operas by the Scala's manager, Merelli; but the death of his wife and two children, as well as the failure of *Un Giorno di Regno* (1840), so seriously depressed him that he tried to cancel the contract. *Un Giorno di Regno* (subtitled *Il Finto Stanislao*) was Verdi's only comic opera before *Falstaff*, of which it contains certain curious foretastes such as the duet for the soprano/tenor lovers over a male trio.

Merelli, ever sympathetic, tempted Verdi to resume work with the libretto for *Nabucodonosor* (usually abbreviated as *Nabucco*) (1842); and the result was his first masterpiece. Though modest in harmonic and rhythmic invention, the work has an exuberance and warmth in its tunes, a firm dramatic structure, and a deep sense of humanity (it contains three strikingly mature pieces of characterization) that still keep it on the stage. *Nabucco* triumphed; and as with a number of the operas which followed, the theme of an oppressed people was taken as symbolic by Italians suffering under Austrian domination.

Neither *I Lombardi alla Prima Crociata* (1843) nor *Ernani* (1844), though originally successes, measures up to *Nabucco*. *I Lombardi* is something of an anthology of operatic clichés, given life by Verdi's greater experience in handling accompaniments and the scoring: there is a 'Jerusalem' chorus that rivals *Nabucco*'s famous 'Va pensiero'. *Ernani* is still more vigorous in patriotic expression, and is notable for the splendidly drawn figure of the vengeful Da Silva.

All the leading theatres were now demanding Verdi's services, and opera followed opera in quick, even hasty, succession. *I Due Foscari* (1844) contains more than a foretaste of *Traviata*, *Rigoletto*, and *Simone Boccanegra*; it is also notable for Verdi's first use of leading motives, and for winning Donizetti's opinion, 'This man is a genius'. It is a finer work than either *Giovanna d'Arco* (1845) (which had a short career despite Patti's appearances), *Alzira* (1845), or even *Attila* (1846), though the latter's robustness won it success at the time. Verdi later referred to this period as his 'years in the galleys', but they were years that established his popularity.

Macbeth (1847, rev. for Paris 1865) reaffirms Verdi's genius. It was the first-fruit of his lifelong admiration for Shakespeare, and its occasional weaknesses are flecks on the surface of a conception that is nobler and more intense than anything of his that had gone before. In dramatic force and characterization it overshadows *I Masnadieri* (1847, in London with Jenny Lind), which is notable for a beautiful prelude and the soprano/baritone Tomb Scene in Act 2, presaging much in *Forza*, as well as for some original scoring and the now familiar melodic verve: a certain dark forcefulness is *Macbeth*'s chief legacy, though *I Masnadieri* makes its own bequests to the Requiem, *Trovatore* and *Traviata*. *Il Corsaro* (1848) has little distinction; *La Battaglia di Legnano* (1849) survives occasionally by virtue of its vivid music of love and action—it contains another superb piece of characterization, in the brief but dominating appearance of Barbarossa. The same year saw *Luisa Miller*, a much finer work which exploits the darker side of Verdi's genius: the last act introduces a new, flowing style that is markedly an advance on the first two acts' more conventional manner. *Stiffelio* (1850) has been regarded as something of a relapse, chiefly through the baffling situations, for Verdi's first audience, of the almost Ibsenesque libretto: a good revival might well show otherwise.

Meanwhile, in Paris, Verdi had again met Giuseppina Strepponi. They became companions and eventually (1859) man and wife. Her influence was wholly good: the mellowing and relaxation which came over his art, and the fulfilment of all the promise hitherto glimpsed on the whole intermittently, was undoubtedly hastened by her presence. In 1851 came the first work of complete genius, *Rigoletto*. The characterization is bolder, subtler, and (especially as regards Rigoletto) extraordinarily original; and the remaining conventional elements are masterfully harnessed to the dramatic scheme. The famous quartet is still an outstanding example of the great opera composer's ability to express contrasting emotions in a single piece of music.

After *Rigoletto, Il Trovatore* (1853) is really a regression to the simple accompaniments and superbly vehement or pathetic tunes of *Nabucco*. In a sense it is the last early Verdi opera, though it comes in the centre of his middle period. This is crowned by *La Traviata* (1853). At first a notorious fiasco, it has long since been accepted as a great masterpiece. The old blunt divisions are smoothed into a more flexible language that ideally matches the subject; while the tunes achieve new subtlety in expressing complex and finely shaded states of mind. Reliance on the conventional forms of Italian opera was increasingly cramping Verdi's style: *Traviata* represents a liberation, and by it he achieves new heights as a composer.

Verdi returned to Paris in 1853 for *Les Vêpres Siciliennes*, written to a Scribe libretto. This was produced in 1855; it is a lengthy, uncharacteristic piece which has never achieved more than occasional revival. Back in Busseto, he revised *Stiffelio* (whose music he had already used to a knightly libretto, *Guglielmo von Wellingrode*, to satisfy the Roman censors) as *Aroldo*; this had a new fourth act. He also opened negotiations for what he hoped would be *King Lear*, a project that haunted him all his life. During another visit to Paris he began work on *Simone Boccanegra*, which was produced at Venice in 1857—unsuccessfully, largely owing to complexity of plot: a rescue operation by Verdi and Boito in 1881 presented the work's very fine episodes in a better light. It is a dark, imposing work, unequal but highly regarded for its particular atmosphere and for its noblest passages.

The beginning of 1859 saw *Un Ballo in Maschera* (q.v. for summary of its many censorship disputes). There are traces of Verdi's knowledge of Meyerbeer, but unlike *Les Vêpres Siciliennes*, *Ballo* absorbs them, enlarging thereby the Verdian vocabulary rather than straining it. It is also a more deftly contrapuntal work, and one which shows greater skill in developing themes.

Verdi's name had long been associated with the Risorgimento as an artist of revolt—his operas were read as political gestures for liberty, and his very name was used as an acrostic slogan: 'Viva VERDI' meant 'Viva Vittorio Emanuele, Re D'Italia'. In 1859 Napoleon III drove the Austrians out of Lombardy; Verdi represented Busseto at the assembly in Parma and then, pressed by Cavour, became a member of the new Italian Parliament. During his Parliamentary career (1861–5) he found time for only one opera, *La Forza del Destino* (1862). Written for St. Petersburg, this is again Verdi in dark mood. It is, moreover, implausible dramatically and disjointed musically: the contemporary cult of the *Schicksalstragödie*, or Fate Tragedy, was unsuited to Verdi. Individual scenes and arias are fine enough to retain much admiration for the work; while hints of the great comic opera that lay within Verdi are underlined in the characterization of the Friar Melitone.

Macbeth was revised in 1864–5 and presented in Paris, where Verdi agreed to write *Don Carlos* (1867). Once again the demands of French 'Grand' opera are felt, but this is an incomparably greater work than *Vêpres*. It is a long opera, grand and subtle, filled with highly original strokes of character and carrying forward its action largely in the duets which express clashes and developments of relationship. Verdi wrote no more majestic opera.

Aida (1871), commissioned for the opening of the Italian Theatre, Cairo, is purely Italian and embodies grandeur rather than majesty. The spectacular elements are part of the plot and so of the music, but Verdi was master enough now to place them firmly as the background against which his characters unfold their tragedy. Indeed, it is out of the contrast of public pomp and private emotion that *Aida* is composed: it was a design that matched the composer's gifts splendidly and drew some of his finest music.

But *Otello* (1887) excels even *Aida*. For this, the influence of Boito, who gave up his own composition to write librettos for Verdi, is largely responsible. Despite recurrent differences, he understood Verdi well, and as a composer himself, not only as a man of literary ability, he provided an ideal libretto. The fusion of aria and recitative into a single expressive language, varying its tension but hardly its nature, is complete. Melody is still supreme, but it is melody infinitely adaptable to situation and character, capable of running on in narration or bearing the weight of powerful expression, as the swift-moving drama demands. It is an opera abounding in sudden phrases whose curve illuminates what once needed an aria.

Falstaff (1893) is a fruit of the same collaboration in Verdi's beloved Shakespeare. It is swift-paced and genial, but also sharp: Verdi's ingenuity and his canny knowledge of human nature seemed actually heightened in his old age, and there is nothing of an old man's gentleness in his amused and affectionate jabs at his hero. Jealousy, tragic in *Otello*, becomes an object of laughter in *Falstaff*, and human fallibility is the source of wit, not regret. The score flashes with brilliance, yet there is a lyricism and sense of fantasy which give it a peculiar grace. All Verdi's skills are present, refined and sharpened, and all his delight in humanity. For the Verdi-lover it is an extraordinarily moving moment when, at the end of the opera, this comedy that ends the whole great series of operas, Falstaff turns to us in the audience and in the last fugal chorus reminds us that all the world's a stage.

Verismo (It. = realism). The term describing the realistic or naturalistic school of Italian opera as typified by Mascagni, Leoncavallo, Giordano, Puccini, and Zandonai.

Verona. Town in Veneto, Italy. The famous Roman Arena, seating some 25,000, has been the scene of spectacular open-air opera performances every summer since 1913 (with the exception of 1915–18 and 1940–5). The first season was devoted to eight performances of *Aida* and was conducted by Serafin. Operas that have been performed there are mostly of the spectacular variety.

Véronique. Operetta in 3 acts by Messager; text by Van Loo and Duval. Prod. Paris, B.-P., 10 Dec. 1898; London, Coronet T., 5 May 1903; N.Y., Broadway T., 30 Oct. 1905.

Verschworenen, Die (*The Conspirators*). Opera in 1 act by Schubert; text by Castelli, on the idea of Aristophanes' comedy *Lysistrata* (411 B.C.). Prod. Frankfurt 29 Aug. 1861; N.Y. 16 June 1877; London, R.C.M., 20 June 1956. The Crusaders' wives stage the time-honoured Aristophanic strike until their husbands forswear war. A touchy political censor insisted that the title be changed to *Der häusliche Krieg* (War in the Home).

Verstovsky, Alexis Nikolayevich (b. Gvt. of Tambov, 1 Mar. 1799; d. Moscow, 17 Nov. 1862). Russian composer. Began writing vaudevilles even before his appointment as inspector of the Imperial Opera in Moscow in 1824. His first opera, *Pan Tvardovsky*, inspired by the example of *Freischütz*, was a success in 1828; and of those that followed, *Askold's Tomb* (1835) rivalled even *A Life for the Tsar* in favour. This, avowedly trying 'to put into European form the character of Russian national music', slavishly copies some of *Freischütz*'s most famous scenes; but Martin Cooper has suggested that 'this ill-assorted romantic hotch-potch formed a kind of operatic bran-tub into which Russian composers were to fish, and to find many lucky dips, for the next half-century'.

Vespri Siciliani, I. See *Vêpres Siciliennes, Les*.

Vestale, La (The Vestal Virgin). Opera in 3 acts by Spontini; text by Étienne de Jouy. Prod. Paris, O., 16 Dec. 1807; London, King's, 2 Dec. 1826; New Orleans, 17 Feb. 1828. The opera tells of the love of the Roman captain Licinio for Giulia, who becomes a Vestal Virgin while her lover is in Gaul. He breaks into the temple to win her back, and she allows the holy fire to become extinguished. She is condemned to death, but as she is being led to execution a flash of lightning rekindles the fire, and she is spared from death and reunited with Licinio. The opera is revived from time to time for dramatic sopranos such as Ponselle or Callas.

Vesti la giubba. Canio's (ten.) aria closing Act 1 of Leoncavallo's *Pagliacci*, bewailing his duty to put on his motley and to clown though his heart be breaking.

Vestris (orig. Bartolozzi), **Lucia Elizabeth** (b. London, 3 Jan. or 2 Mar. 1787; d. London, 8 Aug. 1856). English contralto. The wife of Auguste Armand Vestris, *maître de ballet* of the King's Theatre, she studied singing with Corri, and made her début on the occasion of her husband's benefit in July 1815 as Proserpina in Winter's *Il Ratto di Proserpina*. She sang with success at the Italian Opera in Paris and regularly at the King's T. 1821–5. The first London Pippo in *La Gazza Ladra*, Malcolm Graeme in *La Donna del Lago*, Edoardo in *Matilde di Shabran*, and Emma in *Zelmira*. She created Fatima in Weber's *Oberon* at C.G. 1826. Subsequently she managed the Olympic, C.G., and Lyceum Theatres, and appeared in English versions of *Norma*, *Figaro*, &c. She was even known to have sung the title role in *Don Giovanni* and Macheath in *The Beggar's Opera*.

Viaggio a Reims, Il (The Journey to Rheims). Opera in 2 acts by Rossini; text by Balochi. Prod. Paris, T.-I., for coronation of Charles X, 19 June 1825—a resounding failure despite a cast that included Pasta, Cinti-Damoreau, Levasseur, Donzelli, surviving only three nights. Most of the music reused for *Le Comte Ory* in 1828; revived, without most of the *Ory* additions, Paris, T.-I., 26 Oct. 1848, as *Andremo a Parigi*.

Vianesi, Auguste (b. Legnano, 2 Nov. 1837; d. New York, 11 Nov. 1908). Italian, later French, conductor and composer. Studied Italy and then went to Paris in 1857 with a letter of introduction from Pasta to Rossini. London, D.L., 1858–9. Conducted regularly Moscow and St. Petersburg, and in 1887 became principal conductor at the Paris O. C.G. 1870–80, where he conducted the first performances in London of *Lohengrin* and *Tannhäuser*, as well as the French and Italian repertory. Conducted opening night of the first season at the N.Y. Met. and again 1891–2.

Viardot-Garcia, Pauline (b. Paris, 18 July 1821; d. Paris, 18 May 1910). French mezzo-soprano of Spanish birth. Daughter of Manuel Garcia and younger sister of Malibran. Studied voice with her parents and piano with various teachers including Liszt. Début Brussels 1837; London 1839, as Desdemona (Rossini). Real success dates from her Paris début at the Théâtre-Italien in 1839. This was under the management of Louis Viardot, whom she married in 1841. Created Fidès in *Le Prophète* at Meyerbeer's request and sang the role more than 200 times. London, C.G., 1848–51, 1854–5. It was largely owing to her efforts that *Les Huguenots* was produced at C.G. in 1848, when she sang Valentine. The first London Azucena and a greatly admired Donna Anna and Rachel. In 1859 she sang the title role in Gluck's *Orfeo* in the famous Paris revival in Berlioz's arrangement, and in 1861 she sang the title role in *Alceste*. Her last opera appearances were in 1863, after which she settled first in Baden-Baden, then in Paris, where she composed, wrote poetry and plays, and painted. She was for many years the constant companion of Turgenev, and a close friend of Schumann. She sang Dalila privately to Saint-Saëns and a select audience. Her pupils included

Désirée Artôt, Orgeni, and Marianne Brandt. Her own voice extended from c^1 to $f^{'''}$. Turgenev's *Lettres à Madame Viardot* were published in Paris in 1907, and Louise Héritte Viardot wrote about her mother Pauline in *Memories and Adventures* (1913).

Vibrato (It. = vibrated). A fluctuation of pitch and intensity in the voice, admirable when used judiciously to keep the note 'alive', but often abused; in the latter case, the word 'wobble' has almost become a technical term. Used as a direction by some composers in the Romantic period.

Vickers, Jon (b. Prince Albert, 29 Oct. 1926). Canadian tenor. Studied Toronto. Début Stratford Festival 1956, Don José. London, C.G., since 1957; Bayreuth 1958; Vienna 1959; San Francisco 1959; N.Y., Met., 1959. One of the finest Wagner and Verdi tenors to emerge since the war. (R)

Vida Breve, La (Brief Life). Opera in 2 acts by Falla; text by Carlos Fernández Shaw. Prod. (in French) Nice, 1 Apr. 1913 with Lilliane Grenville; N.Y., Met., 6 Mar. 1926 with Bori; Edinburgh 9 Sept. 1958 with Victoria de los Angeles. Salud loves Paco, who is secretly about to marry another. At the wedding she curses him, but is overcome by her love and dies brokenhearted at his feet. Awarded a prize in 1905, but not then produced.

Vienna (Ger., Wien). Capital of Austria. The first operas heard in Vienna were given during the reign of Ferdinand III—Bonacossi's *Ariadna Abbandonata* (1641) and Cavalli's *Egisto* (1643). During the reign of Leopold I (1658–1705), opera became firmly established as a court entertainment. The Emperor, himself a poet and a composer, contributed some of the music for the splendid production of Cesti's *Il Pomo d'Oro* (1666 or 1667), written for his marriage to the Infanta Margherita. To house the elaborate production the architect Burnacini designed a theatre in the main square of the Imperial Palace, the Hofburg, which was the predecessor of the Burgtheater. In Joseph I's reign (1705–11), Giuseppe Galli-Bibbiena was appointed chief theatre architect; he built two theatres, where the splendid productions of the court composer, Johann Josef Fux, were staged. Charles VI continued the royal patronage of opera, and increased the Court Orchestra from 107 to 134 musicians, but insisted that the production of opera should remain a royal monopoly, despite the demand for a theatre for the ordinary people. This resulted in the building of the Theater am Kärntnerthor in 1708.

The reign of Maria Theresa (1740–80) saw the erection of the Theater bei der Hofburg, which opened on 14 May 1748 with Gluck's *Semiramide Riconosciuta*. In 1754 Gluck was appointed court Kapellmeister, and between then and 1770 ten of his operas received their first performances in Vienna, including *Orfeo*, *Alceste*, and *Paride ed Elena*. After Gluck's departure for Paris the Burgtheater gradually yielded its position of Court Opera to the Theater am Kärntnerthor; the former, however, staged the premières of *Die Entführung aus dem Serail*, *Figaro*, *Così fan tutte*, and Cimarosa's *Il Matrimonio Segreto*. But Emanuel Schikaneder challenged the monopoly of the court theatres by producing *Die Zauberflöte*, for which he wrote the libretto, at his own Theater auf der Wieden in 1791. Meanwhile Salieri had been appointed court conductor, and opera after opera by him was produced at the Kärntnerthor. In 1801 Schikaneder moved to the new Theater an der Wien, where he produced *Fidelio* in 1805.

After the Napoleonic wars Rossini became the most popular composer in Vienna; and in 1821 an Italian, Barbaia (q.v.), was appointed manager of the Kärntnerthor and the Theater an der Wien. During his régime he produced the première of *Euryanthe* and introduced the subscription system for opera to Vienna. Between 1823 and 1842 only three now long-forgotten operas enjoyed Vienna premières; but in 1842 Donizetti was appointed court composer and conductor, and wrote *Linda di Chamounix* and *Maria di Rohan* for the Kärntnerthor. Except for Lortzing's *Der Waffenschmied* (1846) and Flotow's *Martha* (1847) there were no important Vienna premières during the next 30 years or so. The Vienna audiences, however, made the acquaintance of Verdi and Wagner, the latter conducting the local première of *Lohengrin* in 1861, which he was hearing himself for the first time in a theatre.

It had been decided in 1857 to rebuild the centre of Vienna, and part of the plans included the building of a new opera house, Die Oper am Ring, which was designed by Eduard von der Nüll and August Siccard von Siccardsburg, and which cost £600,000. Its seating capacity was 2,260, and it opened on 25 May 1869 with *Don Giovanni.* The first director was J. F. von Herbeck (1870–5), who mounted Goldmark's *Die Königin von Saba* and introduced Götz's *Der Widerspänstigen Zähmung*, Schumann's *Genoveva*, and *Aida* to Vienna. He was succeeded by Franz Jauner (1875–80), who brought Richter to Vienna as music director, staged *The Ring* and *Samson et Dalila*, and assembled a company that included Materna, Wilt, Papier, Reichmann, and Scaria. William Jahn, who followed Jauner, was himself a conductor. He retained Richter, however, and from 1880 to 1896 they both directed the destinies of the theatre; the ensemble included Materna, Winkelmann, Reichmann, Scaria (the four creators of Kundry, Parsifal, Amfortas, and Gurnemanz at Bayreuth in 1881), Toni Schläger, Lola Beeth, Ernest van Dyck, and Marie Renard (the last two, superb Massenet interpreters who had created Werther and Charlotte (1892)).

From 1897 to 1907, the Opera enjoyed its greatest triumphs under the direction of Gustav Mahler (q.v.). He was succeeded by Weingartner (1907–11) and Hans Gregor (1911–18). The famous Mahler singers, including Gutheil-Schoder, Mildenburg, Kurz, Weidt, Kittel, Schmedes, Slezak, Maikl, Demuth, and Mayr, continued as members of the ensemble. Weingartner's régime was generally undistinguished; Gregor's was more successful, and included the first Viennese performances of *Rosenkavalier*, *Pelléas*, *La Fanciulla del West*, *Parsifal*, works by Korngold and Pfitzner, and the engagements of Jeritza, Lotte Lehmann, and Piccaver.

In 1918 the Hofoper became the Staatsoper, and the music and artistic director was Franz Schalk, who held the position until 1929, for four of these years (1920–4) in association with Strauss. There were few world premières, but many first Vienna performances, including *Die Frau ohne Schatten*, the Puccini *Trittico*, *Turandot*, and *Boris*. Luise Helletsgruber, Felice Hüni-Mihacsek, Maria Rajdl, Elisabeth Schumann, Alfred Jerger, Emil Schipper, and Josef von Manowarda joined the company. Schalk was succeeded by Clemens Krauss (1929–34), Weingartner (1934–6), and Bruno Walter (1936–8). Angerer, Németh, Anday, Novotná, Kern, Ursuleac, Rünger, the Konetzni sisters, Olszewska, Wildbrunn, Kappel, Schwarz, Dermota, Kiepura, Tauber, Voelker, Schorr, Rode, and the conductors Karl Alwin and Josef Krips joined the company during these years. When the *Anschluss* came in 1938, many of the leading artists left Austria, including Walter, Lehmann, Schumann, Tauber, Piccaver, Schorr, Kipnis, and List.

After a period of artistic and administrative chaos, Karl Böhm was appointed director in 1943 and attempted to rebuild the ensemble. He began with a Strauss cycle, and produced *Capriccio*, the composer himself being present for his eightieth birthday. On 30 June 1944 Böhm conducted *Götterdämmerung*, the last performance in the old house; in Sept. 1944 the house remained closed on the orders of Goering; and on 12 Mar. 1945, seven years to the day after Hitler had entered Vienna, the Opera House was destroyed by bombs.

Opera began again on 1 May 1945 at the Volksoper with *Figaro* conducted by Krips. In June Franz Salmhofer was appointed director, and in October the old Theater an der Wien was reopened with *Fidelio*. For the next ten years the company played in two houses. With Böhm, Krips, and Krauss as its chief conductors, and an ensemble that included Gueden, H. Konetzni, Jurinac, Reining, Schwarzkopf, Lipp, Seefried, Welitsch, Dermota, Lorenz, Hotter, Kunz, Klein, Patzak, Schoeffler, and Weber, it quickly regained its pre-1938 prestige and made guest appearances all over Europe. In 1954 Böhm was again appointed director to prepare for the reopening of the rebuilt opera house (cap. 2,200), which opened on 5 Nov. 1955 with *Fidelio*. Böhm resigned after much public criticism in 1956 and was succeeded as artistic and music director by Karajan (q.v.), who resigned in 1964. The tendency in recent years has been for opera in the original language, with a strong Italian roster of singers and the exchange of productions between Vienna and La Scala, Milan. In 1955 the Volksoper (cap. 1,695) resumed its independence under the directorship of Salmhofer, and although its repertory is mostly made up of classical operetta, it also stages a number of operas each season, including *Guillaume Tell*, *Nabucco*, *Hoffmann*, and *Manon*. (See also *Theater auf der Wieden*, *Theater an der Wien*.)

Vieuille, Félix (b. Saugeon, 15 Oct. 1872; d. Saugeon, 28 Feb. 1953). French bass. Studied Paris Conservatoire. Début Aix-les-Bains 1897, Leporello. Leading bass, Paris, O.C., 1898–1928, where he created Arkel (*Pelléas*), Barbe-Bleue (*Ariane et Barbe-Bleue*), Sultan (*Mârouf*), Eumée (*Pénélope*), and many other parts. N.Y., Manhattan O., 1908–9. (R) His son **Jean Vieuille** was bass-baritone at the O.C. 1928–58. (R)

Viglione-Borghese, Domenico (b. Mondovì 13 July 1877; d. Milan, 26 Oct. 1957). Italian baritone. Studied Milan with Cotogni. Début Lodi, Herald (*Lohengrin*). Gave up career for commerce and while in San Francisco was recommended by Caruso to Tetrazzini, opposite whom he sang as Rigoletto, Enrico, Figaro, &c. Second Italian début Parma 1906, Amonasro. Established himself as the finest interpreter of Rance (*La Fanciulla*)—Puccini called him 'Il principe degli sceriffi'. Had repertory of more than 70 roles. Continued to sing until shortly before the Second World War. (R)

Village Romeo and Juliet, A. Opera in prologue and 3 acts by Delius; text by composer, after the story by Gottfried Keller. Prod. (in German), Berlin, K.O., 21 Feb. 1907; London, C.G., 22 Feb. 1910, cond. Beecham. The theme is the love of the children of two quarrelling farmers, which ends in their death together in a barge on the river. The intermezzo before the final scene, *The Walk to the Paradise Garden*, is well known in the concert hall.

Villi, Le. Opera in 1 act by Puccini; text by Fontana, after a popular folk legend (and perhaps suggested by Adam's ballet *Giselle*). Prod. Milan, T.d.V., 31 May 1884; Manchester 24 Sept. 1897; N.Y., Met., 17 Dec. 1908, with Alda, Bonci, Amato, cond. Toscanini. Puccini's first opera. Robert, betrothed to Anna, goes to seek his fortune. Plunging into vice, he forgets Anna, who dies brokenhearted. When Robert returns to find Anna, he is confronted by her ghost, and witches dance round him until he drops dead at their feet.

Vilnius. See *Lithuania*.

Vinay, Ramón (b. Chillan, 31 Aug. 1914). Chilean tenor, orig. baritone. Studied Mexico. Début Mexico 1938, Di Luna; tenor début 1943, Don José. N.Y., C.C., 1945–6, 1948; Met. 1946–61; London, C.G., 1950, Otello with Scala Co., and in Wagner 1953–60. Bayreuth 1952–7. Coached as Otello by Toscanini, with whom he sang and recorded the role. His voice has always retained its dark baritone-like colour; his acting is filled with pathos and nobility, and reaches a standard rare among operatic artists. In 1962 he resumed baritone roles, singing Telramund at Bayreuth and Iago, Falstaff, and Scarpia. (R)

Vinci, Leonardo (b. Strongoli, 1690; d. Naples, 27 May 1730). Italian composer. The success of his first opera, *Lo Cecato Fauzo* (Neapolitan dialect), was followed by similar pieces; later he turned to opera seria. Prompted by

Farinelli's gifts, Vinci differentiated even more sharply the central section of the aria, and so elaborated the contrasts between sections as to influence the development of sonata form. He was the most vigorous of Scarlatti's successors.

Violetta. The Lady of the Camelias (sop.), heroine of Verdi's *La Traviata.*

Vi ravviso. Count Rodolpho's (bass) aria in Act 1 of Bellini's *La Sonnambula* in which he greets the village he last saw as a young man.

Visconti, Luchino (b. Milan, 2 Nov. 1906). Italian producer and designer. Originally a film and theatre producer, turned to opera in 1954 after seeing Callas's *Norma.* Worked with Callas at La Scala, producing for her *La Vestale, La Sonnambula, La Traviata, Anna Bolena,* and *Iphigenia en Tauride.* Designed and produced C.G.'s *Don Carlos,* and Spoleto's *Macbeth* and *Duca d'Alba.* He accepts all grand opera's conventions and seizes on opera's dramatic spirit, re-creating it in visual terms to match the music. His colours, lighting, and groupings all make for the most satisfying of stage pictures. There is an opera on his eponymous ancestor by Amadei (1869).

Vishnevskaya, Galina (b. Leningrad, 25 Oct. 1926). Russian soprano. Début Leningrad, 1950, Polenka (Strelnikov's *Kholopka*). Member of Bolshoy Theatre since 1952. New York, Met., 1961–2, Aida and Butterfly; London, C.G., 1962, Aida. Other roles include Leonore (*Fidelio*), Tatyana, Marguerite. Married to the cellist Rostropovich. (R)

Vision fugitive. Herod's (bar.) aria in Act 2 of Massenet's *Hérodiade,* in which he sings of the vision of Salome that haunts him day and night.

Vissi d'arte. Tosca's (sop.) aria in Act 2 of Puccini's opera, lamenting the unjustness of her fate.

Vivaldi, Antonio (b. Venice, *c.* 1675; d. Vienna, [buried 28] July 1741). Italian composer. Though esteemed principally as an instrumental composer, especially for his violin music, Vivaldi also wrote some 44 operas. Many of these were hastily assembled in a few days for a production which Vivaldi himself would organize and supervise down to the last detail. Some show the vivid illustrative gift that is familiar to concert-goers from *The Seasons* and other violin concertos—for instance, the storm in *La Fida Ninfa* (1732) is paralleled in the *Tempesta di Mare* violin concerto (Op. 8, No. 5). But as the eminent Vivaldi scholar Marc Pincherle admits, 'there is probably more waste material in the operas, which the unlucky composer had to do . . . in haste and confusion'. A few arias, some bold strokes of characterization, a number of striking instrumental pictorial effects—these continue to impress the curious who investigate Vivaldi's operas. The works satisfied the elaborate and restricting conventions of Venetian opera, with its demand for mythological or historical plots deployed against elaborate scenic effects; and it is the passing of the culture this genre so intricately reflects that has proved fatal to Vivaldi's operas.

Voce di donna. La Cieca's (con.) prayer in Act 1 of Ponchielli's *La Gioconda.*

Voelker, Franz (b. Neu-Ilsenberg, 31 Mar. 1899; d. Darmstadt, 5 Dec. 1965). German tenor. Studied Offenbach a/M. Début Frankfurt 1926, Florestan. Frankfurt 1926–31; Vienna 1931–5; Berlin 1935–45; Munich 1945–9. London, C.G., 1934, 1937; Bayreuth 1933–43. One of the best Siegmunds and Lohengrins of inter-war years. Later a successful Otello and Canio. (R)

Vogl, Heinrich (b. Munich, 15 Jan. 1845; d. Munich, 21 Apr. 1900). German tenor. Studied Munich with Lachner. Début Munich 1865, Max (*Freischütz*). Succeeded Schnorr von Carolsfeld as leading Tristan. Created Loge and Siegmund. Bayreuth 1876–97, Loge, Siegmund, Parsifal, Tristan. London, H.M.'s, 1882, first London Loge and Siegfried. He also composed an opera, *Der Fremdling,* prod. Munich 1899, in which he sang the leading role. He married the soprano **Therese Thoma** (b. Tutzing, 12 Nov. 1845; d. Munich, 29 Sept. 1921) who for some years was the only Isolde in Germany. She created Sieglinde, and was the first London Brünnhilde (1882).

Vogler, Georg Joseph (called Abt, or Abbé, Vogler) (b. Würzburg, 15 June 1749; d. Darmstadt, 6 May 1814). German pianist, organist, composer, and teacher. His nine operas were generally unsuccessful (*La Kermesse* (1783) did not even complete its première), with the exception of the last of them, *Samori*. Weber, who became his pupil, prepared the vocal score before the première in Vienna in 1804.

Voi, che sapete. The canzonetta written and sung by Cherubino (sop.) to the Countess in Act 2 of Mozart's *Figaro*.

Voi lo sapete, O mamma. Santuzza's (sop.) account to Mamma Lucia of her betrayal by Turiddu in Mascagni's *Cavalleria Rusticana*.

Voix Humaine, La. Tragédie lyrique in one act by Poulenc; text by Cocteau. Prod. Paris, O.C., 6 Feb. 1959 with Denise Duval, cond. Prêtre. N.Y., Carnegie Hall, 23 Feb. 1960 with Duval, cond. Prêtre; Edinburgh Festival 30 Aug. 1960 with Duval, cond. Pritchard. This is almost a 45-minute 'concerto' for soprano voice and orchestra—a one-sided telephone conversation between a jilted young woman and her lover.

Volo di Notte (Night Flight). Opera in 1 act by Dallapiccola; text by composer, after St-Exupéry's novel *Vol de Nuit* (1931). Prod. Florence, P., 18 May 1940; Glasgow, Scottish Opera, 29 May 1963. Successfully given in many European theatres since the war.

Voltaire (orig. François Marie Arouet) (b. Paris, 24 Nov. 1694; d. Paris, 30 May 1778). French writer. Operas on his works are as follows. *Samson* (1732): Rameau, with Voltaire as librettist, unperformed. *Zaïre* (1732): Bellini (1829); La Nux (1890). *Alzire* (1736): Zingarelli (1794); Verdi (1845). *Mahomet* (1742): Rossini (1820). *Mérope* (1743): Graun (1756, lib. by Frederick II). *Zadig* (1748): Dupérier (1938). *Sémiramis* (1748): Bianchi (*La Vendetta di Nino*, 1790); Catel (1802); Rossini (1823). *L'Orphelin de la Chine* (1755): Winter (*Tamerlan*, 1802). *Candide* (1756): Knipper (comp. 1926–7); Bernstein (modern version, 1958). *Tancrède* (1760): Rossini (1813). *Ce qui plaît aux dames* (1764): Duni (*La Fée Urgèle*, 1765). *Olympie* (1764): Spontini (1819). *Charlot* (1767); Stuntz (*Heinrich IV zu Givry*, 1820). *L'Ingénu* (1767): Grétry (*Le Huron*, 1768). *La Bégueule* (1772): Monsigny (*La Belle Arsène*, 1773).

Von Heute auf Morgen (From Day to Day). Opera in 1 act by Schoenberg; text by 'Max Blonda' (the composer's wife). Prod. Frankfurt 1 Feb. 1930, cond. Steinberg. Schoenberg's only comic opera (the first 12-note opera, for long the only 12-note comic opera). It describes the wiles of a witty and determined woman in keeping her husband. Successfully revived Holland Festival, 1958 cond. Rosbaud.

Von. For names with this prefix, see following word.

Vorspiel (Ger. = prelude, q.v.).

Votto, Antonino (b. Piacenza, 30 Oct. 1896). Italian conductor. Studied Naples. Originally *répétiteur* at La Scala under Toscanini, then asst. cond. there 1925–9; regular cond. there since 1948. London, C.G., 1924–5, 1933; Chicago 1960–1. (R)

Vroons, Frans (b. Amsterdam, 28 Apr. 1911). Dutch tenor. Studied Amsterdam and Paris. Leading tenor Netherlands Opera since 1945 and assistant director since 1956. London, C.G., 1948–50. Don José, Hoffmann, and Grimes are among his best roles. (R)

Vyvyan, Jennifer (b. Broadstairs, 13 Mar. 1925). English soprano. Studied R.A.M., and with Roy Henderson. Glyndebourne Chorus; Jenny Diver in E.O.G.'s prod. of *The Beggar's Opera* (1947). Studied in Switzerland with Fernando Carpi 1950. London, S.W., 1952, Donna Anna, and Constanze; C.G., 1953, where she created Penelope Rich in Britten's *Gloriana*; Glyndebourne 1954, Electra (*Idomeneo*). Created role of Governess in Britten's *Turn of the Screw* (1954) and Tytania in *A Midsummer Night's Dream* (1960). (R)

W

Wach' auf. The chorus sung in Hans Sachs's honour in Act 3, scene 2 of Wagner's *Meistersinger*, to words by the historical Hans Sachs hailing Luther and the Reformation.

Wachtel, Theodor (b. Hamburg, 10 Mar. 1823; d. Frankfurt a/M, 14 Nov. 1893). German tenor. Studied with Mme Grandjean. Début Schwerin. Berlin 1865–8; London, C.G., 1862, 1864–5, 1870, and H.M.'s 1879. The first London Vasco da Gama and Alessandro Stradella. Particularly admired as Arnold and Manrico. One of his most famous roles in Germany was the postilion in Adam's *Le Postillon de Longjumeau*, which he sang more than 1,000 times: for this not only his chest high C but also his professional use of the whip (he had started life as a stable boy) particularly suited him. His son **Theodor** (1841–71) was also a tenor.

Wächter, Eberhard (b. Vienna, 8 July 1929). Austrian baritone. Studied Vienna. Début Vienna, V., 1953, Silvio. Vienna, S.O., since 1954. London, C.G., 1956, Count 1959, Amfortas and Renato; Bayreuth since 1958. One of the most striking baritones of recent years. (R)

Waffenschmied, Der (The Armourer). Opera in 3 acts by Lortzing; text by composer, after Ziegler's comedy *Liebhaber und Nebenbuhler in einer Person* (1790). Prod. Vienna, W., 31 May 1846; Milwaukee, 7 Dec. 1853. The subject was first set by Weigl, *Il Rivale di se stesso* (1808).

Wagner, Cosima (b. Bellaggio, 25 Dec. 1837; d. Bayreuth, 1 Apr. 1930). Daughter of Liszt; married first Hans von Bülow (1857) and then Wagner (1870) with whom she worked to establish Bayreuth. After Wagner's death she maintained an autocratic rule over Bayreuth until her own death.

Wagner, Johanna (b. Seelze, nr. Hanover, 13 Oct. 1826; d. Würzburg, 16 Oct. 1894). German soprano. Adopted niece of Richard Wagner, who procured her engagement at Dresden when she was 17; début as Agathe. Created Elisabeth in *Tannhäuser*, 1845. Studied with Viardot in Paris 1846–8; Berlin 1850–62, after which she lost her singing voice but followed a successful career on the straight stage. Her voice returned in the 1870's and she sang the alto part in the perf. of the Choral Symphony at Bayreuth in 1872, and Schwertleite and 1st Norn in the first Bayreuth *Ring*, 1876. Engaged for C.G., 1852, but prevented from appearing through a law-suit brought by Lumley. H.M.'s 1856, scoring great success as Tancredi, Lucrezia Borgia, and Romeo (Bellini). Taught at Munich 1882–4. Her son Hans Jackmann wrote *Wagner and his first Elisabeth* (1926); according to him, Brünnhilde was written for her.

Wagner, Richard (b. Leipzig, 22 May 1813; d. Venice, 13 Feb. 1883). German composer. Wagner's early musical studies were casual and frequently disrupted. His first important influences were the music of Beethoven and the singing of Wilhelmine Schröder-Devrient, but his serious training as a composer dates from 1828; in 1831 he enrolled as a music student at Leipzig University. Various works date from this period, including the symphony in C. In 1833 he became chorus master at Würzburg, where his theatrical experience was founded and where he began work on *Die Feen* (prod. 1888). He moved to Magdeburg as conductor in 1834, and here his next opera, *Das Liebesverbot*, was unsuccessfully given in 1836. In this year he married Minna Planer, who arranged his transfer to Königsberg. He remained for a year before moving to Riga. *Rienzi* was written at Riga, whence Wagner, in debt not for the first time, fled to London. Going on to Paris, he completed *Rienzi*, began work on the libretto of *Der fliegende Holländer*, and became acquainted with the stories of Lohengrin and Tannhäuser. He moved to Dresden in 1842 for the production there of *Rienzi.* The same year he visited Berlin to investigate chances of a production of *Holländer*, which took place in 1843.

Die Feen and *Das Liebesverbot* have seldom been revived. They seem to show little of Wagner's mature genius, though their nature clearly marks him as a committed composer of German opera in the Weber–Marschner succession. *Rienzi* is more ambitious in a Meyerbeer manner; but even *Der fliegende Holländer*, the first of his operas to stay in the repertory, retains many Weberian touches alongside passages that indicate an altogether larger mind. It is also notable for the introduction of an important Romantic *idée fixe* that came to possess Wagner, Redemption through Love.

Tannhäuser was completed in the spring of 1845 (when Wagner began work on an unfinished opera, *Die Sarazenin*, and on the text of *Meistersinger*), and performed with some success that Oct. It marks an advance over *Holländer*: the characterization is hardly subtler, but there is a major increase in the continuity of thought over a larger time-span. There are also more imposing effects, finer choruses and arias, richer orchestration, and a consistency of imagination that makes such lapses from it as the hymn-tune religiosity of the pilgrims seem secondary. A later revision (1861) for the Paris production commanded by the Emperor Napoleon extended the opening Bacchanale and the subsequent scene for Venus and Tannhäuser —very much in the light of *Tristan*, then behind Wagner.

1848 found Wagner in the middle of revolutionary activities; in the following year a warrant was out for his arrest, and he fled to Zürich. But banishment increased his fame, which Liszt and others were busy fanning; meanwhile he occupied his time chiefly with prose works. In 1850 Liszt celebrated Goethe's anniversary with the première of *Lohengrin* at Weimar. Less evenly inspired than *Tannhäuser*, it rises at its best to far greater heights. If much of Act 1 is beneath *Tannhäuser*, the conception of Ortrud and Telramund and the opening of Act 2 are considerably superior, while the Grail music of the opening can rank with Wagner's finest ideas. *Lohengrin* is still, however, a singer's work, and this exercises on its design an influence which it was part of Wagner's life work to shake off from opera.

This manner survived as far as sketches for *Siegfrieds Tod*, the first stage in the long, complex planning of *Der Ring des Nibelungen*, upon which Wagner was now engaged. This was commissioned from Weimar in 1851, when Wagner announced his wish to write a prefatory work, *Der junge Siegfried*; but later that year he was thinking in terms of three dramas with a 3-act *Vorspiel*. This was too much for Liszt's resources at Weimar, but Wagner went ahead to outline and write much of the text for *Der Ring* as we now know it in 1852.

In 1853 Liszt produced *Holländer* at Weimar and there was a successful Wagner Festival in Zürich; his growing fame also led to an invitation to London, where Queen Victoria and the Prince Consort defied *The Times* by admiring selections from *Lohengrin* and *Tannhäuser*. Back in Zürich, he worked on *Siegfried* and gave some thought to *Tristan*, moving in 1857 to a quieter house provided by his friends, the Wesendonck family. Wagner's entanglement with Frau Wesendonck is celebrated in five songs to her poems, influenced by the current work on *Tristan*. It is not possible to summarize his many marital and financial difficulties; the tide of his affairs reached its lowest ebb in Paris in 1861, where *Tannhäuser* was forced off the stage, and in the two years that followed.

Finally rescue came from King Ludwig II of Bavaria, a fervent admirer of Wagner and soon to be his greatest benefactor. Meanwhile the unhappy marriage to Minna had disintegrated. She died in 1860, but Wagner had already taken up with Liszt's daughter (and Hans von Bülow's wife) Cosima.

Tristan und Isolde was produced in Munich in 1865, and poorly received. Its stature now, a century later, is unquestioned. Music was never the same again after this pressing of chromaticism to and beyond the limits of tonality; while the brief but intense history of German Romanticism here reaches its most fervent climax. Wagner's Schopenhauerian studies influence its pessimistic philosophy, and musical continuity is achieved to a pitch that led the opera to be called one long love-duet. The orchestra assumes new prominence and eloquence, in part due to the development of *Leitmotiv* (q.v.) into a fully expressive language. There is in the treatment of the hero and heroine not so much straightforward characterization as the discovery of an infinite number of psychological undertones in their situation. Wagner here reveals himself as a poet of the subconscious.

Exiled for political reasons from Munich, Wagner found his way to Triebschen, near Lucerne. In his six years here, he completed *Meistersinger*, *Siegfried*, and most of *Götterdämmerung*. In 1870 he and Cosima were married. Ludwig had lost faith in Wagner personally over Cosima, but remained loyal to him as an artist.

In 1868 *Die Meistersinger von Nürnberg* was produced in Munich. Wagner here celebrates the virtues of a bourgeois normality to which his whole life ran counter. There is personal malice in the portrait of the town-clerk Beckmesser, enemy of the new and strange in art (a celebrated tilt at the anti-Wagnerian critic Hanslick); but the central figure is neither he nor the lovers Walther and Eva, but the wise cobbler-poet Hans Sachs. The score is less neurotically intense, no less rich than that of *Tristan*, and the discursive method Wagner had perfected proves adaptable to this new purpose. There are more set pieces than in *Tristan*, but they scarcely halt the action. And in the provincial town, its guilds and its quarrels, Wagner finds his most comforting vein of poetry. *Meistersinger* is an opera that persuades the listener of the goodness not of gods or heroes or ideals, but simple man.

Das Rheingold followed at Munich in 1869; but Ludwig was entitled to this and the whole cycle. A long-cherished plan for a festival theatre was now realized through his generosity. In 1871 the Wagners settled near Bayreuth (q.v.) for the purpose; and in the following April the foundation stone was laid. Liszt, visiting Bayreuth, was excited by the sketches of *Parsifal*. Wagner moved to a new house, 'Wahnfried', provided by the king, and elaborate preparations for the festival culminated in the opening of the theatre in 1876 with the complete *Der Ring des Nibelungen*—which thus also became the first artistic enterprise of a united Germany.

The fact that the composition of *Der Ring* was spread over more than 20 years colours it surprisingly little, so constant was Wagner's vision. His *Leitmotiv* system advances markedly from simple tags in *Rheingold* to a dense, expressive network of allusions in *Götterdämmerung* that speaks directly to the sensibilities. It is a unified work of art (the last successful attempt at a great dramatic cycle), a cosmic drama of vast ambition and hardly less achievement. Like so much that is concerned with Wagner, it is too huge, too subtle and rich in its statements and implications, to be summarized. Yet it is in a sense a summary of many disparate strands in the German experience, a residue of mythic and national feeling that also has a vast amount for the rest of the world. Such a scheme as that of *Der Ring* demands a versatility of invention of which Wagner was now fully master. He genuinely achieves his aim of 'unending melody'; yet it is the weaving of small fragments of *Leitmotiv* into an elaborate pattern that characterizes the score. The harmony, less advanced than *Tristan's*, has a fluidity that never loses its sense of expressive direction. This, he believed, was the road to the future; but it was more truly the end of a road.

Wagner had now achieved much of the impossible he set out to do. He was at last comfortably provided for, famous, and in control of a theatre built as temple for his art. The sacred nature of Bayreuth was further emphasized by the provision that *Parsifal* should never be staged elsewhere.

Certainly it is in the ritual atmosphere which Bayreuth still retains that *Parsifal* continues to make its best effect. The work is described as a 'stage dedication festival play', and its religious atmosphere has caused distress among both sincere Christians who deplored Wagner's own habits and beliefs and non-believers who are stifled by its heavily perfumed odour of sanctity. Wagner, it is true, conceived Montsalvat in terms closer to the theatre he knew than the organized religious life he did not. But the work nevertheless enshrines an extraordinary complex of sexual and spiritual truths, not least in the concept of Kundry as an ambiguous Virgin–Venus figure, temptress and redemptress together. *Parsifal* (1882) is even further advanced harmonically than *Tristan*, taking its musical language well into Schoenbergian territory.

In the autumn of 1882, Wagner and his family left for Venice. Here he died the following February. His body was taken to Bayreuth and buried in the garden of Wahnfried. Cosima survived him, an autocrat in her husband's artistic kingdom, until 1930, when she was laid beside him.

Wagner, Siegfried (b. Triebschen, nr. Lucerne, 6 June 1869; d. Bayreuth, 4 Aug. 1930). German composer and conductor. Son of Richard Wagner and Cosima von Bülow. Studied with Humperdinck and Kniese. Conducted at Bayreuth and elsewhere in Germany from 1896. Artistic director, Bayreuth 1908–30, producer from 1901. Twelve of his 15 operas were staged, *Der Bärenhäuter* (1899), *Der Kobold* (Hamburg 1904), and *Der Schmied von Marienburg* (Rostock 1923) being the most successful. He married Winifred Williams (b. England, 1894). (R)

Wagner, Wieland (b. Bayreuth, 5 Jan. 1917; d. Munich, 17 Oct. 1966). German producer and designer. Son of above, grandson of Richard. After working on stage staff at pre-war Bayreuth and designing the scenery for 1939 *Parsifal* assumed with his brother **Wolfgang** (b. Bayreuth, 30 Aug. 1919) the artistic and business administration of post-war Bayreuth. Together they completely revolutionized the style of Wagner productions (see *Bayreuth*). Wieland also produced regularly at Hamburg and Stuttgart, and other German cities. His productions of *Fidelio*, *Carmen*, *Orphée*, and *Aida* have aroused as much controversy as those of his grandfather's operas.

Wagner-Régeny, Rudolf (b. Szász-Régen, 28 Aug. 1903; d. Berlin, Sept. 1969). Hungarian, later German, composer. His operas include *Der Günstling* (Dresden 1935), *Die Bürger von Calais* (Berlin 1939), and *Johanna Balk* (Vienna 1941), all with librettos by Neher; *Prometheus*, Kassel 1959; *Das Bergwerk zu Falun*, Salzburg 1961.

Wagner Tuba. An instrument invented by Wagner to bridge the gap between the horns, which he regarded as lyrical and romantic, and the trombones, which he regarded as solemn, dignified, and heroic. The tone is brusquer than that of either instrument, with a certain dark masculinity that admirably suits the music of Hunding in *The Ring*. The quartet used in *The Ring* consists of two tenors in B♭ and two basses in F. They are played by the 5th–8th horns.

Wagner-Vereniging. See *Amsterdam*.

Wahn! Wahn! Hans Sachs's (bar.) monologue at the beginning of Act 3 of Wagner's *Meistersinger* in which he muses on the follies of the world.

Walker, Edyth (b. Hopewell, N.Y., 27 Mar. 1867; d. New York, 19 Feb. 1950). American mezzo-soprano. Studied Dresden with Orgeni. Début Berlin 1894, Fidès. Vienna 1895–1903 (where she also studied with Marianne Brandt); N.Y., Met., 1903–6; Hamburg 1906–12; Munich 1912–17; London, C.G., 1900, 1908, 1910 (when she was the first London Elektra); Bayreuth 1908, as Kundry and Ortrud. Also much admired as Isolde. On her retirement she taught at the American Conservatory at Fontainebleau 1933–6, and then in N.Y. (R)

Walküre, Die. See *Ring der Nibelungen, Der.*

Wallace, Ian (b. London, 10 July 1919). English bass. Début London, Cambridge T., 1946, Schaunard (*Bohème*). New London Opera Co. 1946–9; Glyndebourne since 1948; also at S.W. and with the E.O.G. and the London Opera Society; Parma and Venice. S.W. 1960, Don Magnifico. Has established himself as one of the leading English buffo singers; his most successful roles are Bartolo and Don Magnifico. (R)

Wallace, Vincent (b. Waterford, 11 Mar. 1812; d. Château de Haget, nr. Vieuzos, 12 Oct. 1865). Irish composer. In his adventurous life he found time to compose a number of popular operas, of which *Maritana* (1845) has proved the most enduring. In their day *Lurline* (1860) and *The Amber Witch* (1861) gave evidence of a skilful if unprofound dramatic talent. His other three completed operas were unsuccessful.

Wallerstein, Lothar (b. Prague, 6 Nov. 1882; d. New Orleans, 18 Nov. 1949). Czech, later American, conductor and producer. *Répétiteur* Dresden 1909; cond. and prod. Poznań 1910–14. Chief prod. Breslau 1918–22. Duisberg 1922–4; Frankfurt 1924–6; Vienna 1927–38, where he produced 65 operas including *Wozzeck*; Salzburg Festivals 1926–37. Guest producer at Milan, Sc., and Buenos Aires, Colón. Founded Opera School in The Hague 1939; joined N.Y., Met., 1941, remaining there until 1946 when he returned to Europe. Edited versions of *Idomeneo*, *Don Carlos*, and other operas.

Wallmann, Margherita (b. Vienna, 22 Jun. 1904). Austrian producer. Began career as ballet dancer at the Vienna Opera, but forced by an accident to give up dancing. Invited by Bruno Walter to produce *Orfeo*, Salzburg 1936. Has produced opera at the world's leading opera houses, and in recent years has established herself in Italy (especially at La Scala), where she staged the world premières of Milhaud's *David*, Poulenc's *Dialogues des Carmélites*, Pizzetti's *Assassinio nella Cattedrale*, as well as revivals of *Norma*, *Médée*, and *Alceste*. London, C.G., *Aida* 1957, *Carmélites* 1958; Paris 1958, *Ballo in Maschera*; Chicago 1959, *Carmen*.

Wally, La. Opera in 4 acts by Catalani; text by Illica, after Wilhelmine von Hillern's novel *Die Geyer-Wally* (1875, dram. 1880). Prod. Milan, Sc., 20 Jan. 1892, with Darclée; N.Y., Met., 6 Jan. 1909, with Destinn; Manchester 27 Mar. 1919. Catalani's last and best opera describes how La Wally is drawn still closer to her lover Hagenbach when her suitor Gellner tries to kill him; the lovers perish in an avalanche. Toscanini so esteemed the opera that he named his daughter after the heroine.

Walter (orig. Schlesinger), **Bruno** (b. Berlin, 15 Sept. 1876; d. Los Angeles, 17 Feb. 1962). German, later American, conductor. Studied Berlin. *Répétiteur* Cologne 1893–4; conductor, Hamburg 1894–6; Wrocław 1896–7; Bratislava 1897–8; Riga 1899–1900; Berlin 1900–1; Vienna 1901–12 (first as Mahler's assistant); Munich 1913–22 as Generalmusikdirektor; Berlin, Städtische O., 1925–9; Vienna, Generalmusikdirektor, 1936–8; Salzburg 1922–37; London, C.G., 1910 (*The Wreckers*) and 1924–31 (Wagner, Strauss, and Mozart); N.Y., Met., 1941–6, 1951, 1955–7, 1958–9. Also in Milan, Florence, Chicago. One of the great opera conductors of this century, his readings are characterized by a warmly humane lyrical approach. Autobiography, *Theme and Variations* (1946). (R)

Walters, Jess (b. New York, *c.* 1912). American baritone. Début N.Y., New Opera Co., 1941, Macbeth. After appearances with various American companies, including New Orleans and the City Center, engaged London, C.G., 1947 and from 1948 to 1959 as leading baritone. Netherlands Opera 1960–4.

Walther von Stolzing. A Franconian knight (ten.), hero of Wagner's *Die Meistersinger von Nürnberg*.

Walton, William (Sir) (b. Oldham, 29 Mar. 1902). English composer. His opera, *Troilus and Cressida* (1954), is in his mature late-romantic manner; this was followed by the 1-act *The Bear* (1967).

Waltz, Gustavus (b. ?; d. ? London, *c.* 1753). German bass singer and cook. He is said to have served Handel in both capacities, appearing, for instance, as Polypheme in *Acis and Galatea* in 1732. Handel's celebrated comment that Gluck knew 'no more of contrapunta than my cook Waltz' has some of its sting drawn if we remember that Waltz must have been a fine musician,

Wanderer, The. The guise in which Wotan (bass-bar.) appears in Wagner's *Siegfried.*

Ward, David (b. Dumbarton, 3 July 1922). Scottish bass. Studied London, R.C.M., with Clive Carey, and with Hotter. Joined Sadler's Wells chorus 1952; Count Walter in *Luisa Miller*, 1953. S.W. 1952–9; C.G. since 1960; Bayreuth 1960–2; N.Y., Met., 1963. One of the finest contemporary British basses, especially in Wagner bass and bass-bar. roles. (R)

Warren (orig. Vaarenov), **Leonard** (b. New York, 21 Apr. 1911; d. New York, on stage of Met., during perf. of *La Forza del Destino* 4 Mar. 1960). American baritone. Studied N.Y. and in Milan. Won N.Y. Met. Auditions of Air 1938. Début N.Y., Met., 1939, Paolo (*Boccanegra*). One of the leading baritones in Italian opera, being especially admired in Verdi. Also sang with success in Buenos Aires, Colón, Rio, Mexico, and throughout the U.S.A. Milan, Sc., 1953; tour of U.S.S.R. 1958. (R)

Warsaw (Pol., Warszawa). See *Poland.*

Weber, Carl Maria von (b. Eutin, 18 Nov. 1786; d. London, 5 June 1826). German composer. His work for the establishment of a German national opera is crucial. His first opera was a childish essay, later destroyed. In 1800 came *Das Waldmädchen*, later reworked as *Silvana* (1810). The interest in romantic subjects continued with *Peter Schmoll* (1803) and with *Der Beherrscher der Geister* (1805), of which only three numbers and the brilliant overture survive. *Abu Hassan* (1811) is a cheerful little operetta, *Preziosa* (1821) really a play with music. In 1816 Weber had written in a review of Hoffmann's *Undine* of 'the type of opera all Germans want; a self-contained work of art in which all elements, contributed by the arts in co-operation, disappear and re-emerge to create a new world'. This theory of what Wagner was to call a *Gesamtkunstwerk* was first put into practice in *Der Freischütz* (1821), which became a symbol of German operatic aspirations. It represents a new world of German romanticism and artistic independence. Weber's own musical personality simultaneously attains a power and individuality previously only intermittently realized. For *Euryanthe* (1825) Weber unwisely accepted an eccentric blue-stocking, Helmine von Chézy, as librettist, with the result that the work's beauties and its ambitious musical scheme are tethered to an unworthy text. Nevertheless, not until *Lohengrin* (1848) was *Euryanthe* overtaken; and it remains a monument to what Weber might have done had not ill health and ill luck dogged him. *Oberon* (1826) was written to an English libretto, for Covent Garden, where Weber conducted the première. It is an opera of many incidental beauties. *Die drei Pintos*, left unfinished in 1821, was completed and scored by Mahler.

Weber, Ludwig (b. Vienna, 29 July 1899). Austrian bass. Studied Vienna. Début Vienna, V.O., 1920. Barmen-Elberfeld 1925–7; Düsseldorf 1927–30; Cologne 1930–3; Munich 1933–45; Vienna since 1945. London, C.G., 1936–9, 1947, 1950–1; Bayreuth 1951–60. One of the finest Wagner basses of the century; Hagen and Gurnemanz are perhaps his greatest roles, and his Daland and Rocco (*Fidelio*) have rarely been equalled in our day. (R)

Webster, (Sir) David (b. Dundee, 3 July 1903; d. London, 11 May 1971). English manager. After serving as chairman to the Liverpool Philharmonic Society, was appointed general administrator, C.G., 1945–70. Knighted 1960.

Weidt, Lucie (b. Opava, 1879; d. Vienna, 31 July 1940). Austrian soprano. Studied Vienna with Rosa Papier. Début Leipzig 1900; Vienna 1903–26; N.Y., Met., 1910–11. Created the Nurse in *Die Frau ohne Schatten* and was the first Vienna Lisa, Marschallin and Kundry, and the first Kundry at Milan, Sc. One of the famous members of Mahler's Vienna ensemble. After her retirement she taught in Vienna. (R)

Weigl, Joseph (b. Kismarton, 28 Mar. 1766; d. Vienna, 3 Feb. 1846). Austrian composer. His long list of successful operas bears witness to a composer of great talent and charm, whose 'tender, graceful and pleasing melodies' (Reichardt) delighted musicians and princes alike. The best known was perhaps *Die Schweizerfamilie* (1809).

Weill, Hermann (b. Karlsruhe, 29 May 1877; d. Blue Mountain Lake, N.Y., 6 July 1949). German baritone. Studied Frankfurt with Dippel. Début Freiburg 1901, Wolfram. N.Y., Met., 1911–17; London, C.G., 1913; Bayreuth 1909–12. A much-admired Sachs and Kurwenal. Had a repertory of more than 100 roles. (R)

Weill, Kurt (b. Dessau, 2 Mar. 1900; d. New York, 3 Apr. 1950). German composer. His stage works range from grand opera to musical comedy, and have exercised a strong influence on the contemporary scene. His interest in artistic topicality was early signified (and largely misunderstood) in *Die Dreigroschenoper* (1928), which transposed *The Beggar's Opera* of 1728 to a Berlin of two centuries later. With Bertolt Brecht as librettist, Weill widened his range and effect in the moral and political operas *Mahagonny* (1930), *Der Jasager* (1930), and *Die Bürgschaft* (1932). In them we find the fullest expression of his style—popular and up-to-the-minute but uncompromising, basically romantic, pointing with brilliant and wounding musical symbols the message of the text, direct in appeal but bearing a deeply felt political message. Forced out of Hitler's Germany, he settled in America in 1935, where he wrote some musical comedy and light opera —*Street Scene* (1949) and *Down in the Valley* (1948) have been especially successful, though the earlier pieces are regaining acceptance. The works of many contemporary opera composers reflect Weill's influence.

Weimar. Town in Thuringia, Germany. It enjoyed a particularly distinguished operatic period between 1847 and 1858 when Liszt was chief Kapellmeister and Bülow one of the conductors. It was the scene of the premières of *Lohengrin* (1850), Schubert's *Alfonso und Estrella* (1854), and *Der Barbier von Bagdad* (1858), as well as the second performances of Berlioz's *Benvenuto Cellini* and Schumann's *Genoveva*. Liszt was succeeded by Eduard Lassen, who produced the première of *Samson et Dalila* (1877) and gave the first performances following the Munich première of *Tristan* (1874) and the first prod. in Germany of *Mignon* (1868). In 1893 *Hänsel und Gretel* received its première at Weimar and in the same year *Werther* its first performance in Germany. At this time the first conductor was Richard Strauss, whose *Guntram* had its première there in 1894. The present Deutsches National theater, formerly Hoftheater (cap. 2,000), was opened in 1907.

Weinberger, Jaromír (b. Prague, 8 Jan. 1896; d. St. Petersburg, Fla., 8 Aug. 1967). Czech composer. *Schwanda the Bagpiper* (1927) has been the only 20th-century Czech opera to follow the Smetana tradition with success. It is a tuneful, clever, but somewhat meretricious work which aimed with success at a low common denominator of current European taste.

Weingartner, Felix (b. Zara, 2 June 1863; d. Winterthur, 7 May 1942). Austrian conductor and composer. Studied Graz, Leipzig, and (with Liszt) Weimar. At Weimar his first opera, *Sakuntala*, was produced in 1884. Kapellmeister, Königsberg 1884–5; Danzig 1885–7; Hamburg 1887–9; Mannheim 1889–91; Berlin 1891–8; Vienna (succeeding Mahler) 1908–10; Hamburg 1912–14; Darmstadt 1914; Vienna, V.O., 1919–24, and S.O. 1935–6; Boston 1912–13; London,

C.G., 1939. Wrote seven other operas, and edited versions of *Oberon*, *Der fliegende Holländer*, and Méhul's *Joseph*. One of the great conductors of his day, still invoked as an exemplar to his successors. (R)

Weiss, W. H. (b. Liverpool, 2 Apr. 1820; d. London, 24 Oct. 1867). English bass. Studied with George Smart and Balfe. Début Dublin 1842, Oroveso; London, Prince's T., 1842, Count Rodolfo. Appeared with Pyne-Harrison and other English companies, singing in premières of many English works. His wife **Georgina Weiss** (1826–80) was a soprano who often sang with her husband—début D.L. 1847.

Welche Wonne, welche Lust. Blonde's (sop.) aria in Act 2 of Mozart's *Entführung* in which she delightedly receives the news of Belmonte's plan for escape.

Welitsch (Velichkova), **Ljuba** (b. Borisovo, 10 July 1913). Bulgarian soprano. Studied Vienna with Lierhammer. Début Sofia 1936. Graz 1937–40; Hamburg 1941–3; Munich 1943–6; Vienna 1946–58; London, C.G., 1947 with Vienna Co. 1948–52; Glyndebourne 1948–9; N.Y., Met., 1948–52. Welitsch's most famous role was Salome, which she first sang in a special performance under Strauss in Vienna in June 1944; she sang the part in English in the notorious Dali–Brook prod. at C.G. 1949. A highly temperamental and dramatic singer, her Tosca, Aida, Musetta, Donna Anna, and Amelia were all strikingly individual performances not easily forgotten. (R)

Wellesz, Egon (b. Vienna, 21 Oct. 1885). Austrian composer and musicologist. Five of Wellesz's operas were written in the years between 1918 and 1931, clearly a direct creative result of researches into baroque opera he pursued during the war. This, coupled with his interest in expressing not his own destiny but 'those things which betoken the link between the material and the spiritual world', drew him to myths in modern interpretations that would stress their continuing validity. Musically the influences are as varied as baroque opera, Schoenberg (his teacher), and medieval music, as well as an interest in integrating chorus and ballet with the drama—all unified by a scholarly and compassionate mind. *Incognita* (1951) dates from his years as Reader in Byzantine Music at Oxford, where the work was produced in 1951; it is a less adventurous or consistent achievement. He has published a collection of *Essays on Opera*.

Welsh National Opera. Launched in Apr. 1946 in Cardiff, chiefly by W. H. Smith. By 1954 the company had a repertory of 13 works, including Arwel Hughes's *Menna*, which was sung in Welsh that year at the National Eisteddfod. Works by Verdi (*I Lombardi*, *Nabucco*, *Vêpres Siciliennes*) and Boito (*Mefistofele*), which used the excellent amateur chorus, as well as the more popular repertory pieces, have been given by the company. London seasons were given at S.W. 1955–7, 1961–2. Charles Groves was music director 1961–3; Bryan Balkwill 1963–7; James Lockhart from 1968.

Werther. Opera in 4 acts by Massenet; text by Blau, Millet, and Hartmann, after Goethe's novel *Die Leiden des jungen Werthers* (1774). Prod. Vienna, O., 16 Feb. 1892, with Van Dyck; Chicago 29 Mar. 1894; London, C.G., 11 June 1894, with J. de Reszke. Werther loves Charlotte, who returns his love although betrothed to his friend Albert. He leaves her, returning to find Charlotte married. She urges him to leave her again, but on hearing that he has asked Albert for his pistols, rushes through a snowstorm to him to find that he has shot himself. For the 1902 St. Petersburg performance the title role was rewritten as baritone for Battistini.

Westrup, (Sir) J. A. (b. London, 26 July 1904). English musicologist. One of the founder members of the Oxford University Opera Club, for which he has prepared various editions (*Orfeo* 1925; *L'Incoronazione di Poppea* 1927) and, since his appointment as Professor of Music in 1947, conducted the productions. His literary works include translations for the O.U.O.C. and valuable studies of Handel and Purcell. He was knighted in 1960.

Wettergren (orig. Palson), **Gertrud** (b. Eslöv, 17 Feb. 1897). Swedish contralto. Studied Stockholm. Début Stockholm 1922, Cherubino. Stockholm, Royal O., 1922–52; N.Y., Met., 1935–8; London, C.G., 1936, 1939. One of the outstanding Swedish singers of the inter-war years. Much admired in Verdi and Wagner, and as Carmen. (R)

Wexford. Town in Eire. An autumn festival has taken place here since 1951. The moving spirit is Dr. T. J. Walsh. Opera is performed in the picturesque little Theatre Royal, and since the festival's inception works produced have included *La Cenerentola*, *La Gazza Ladra*, *L'Italiana in Algeri*, *La Fille du Régiment*, *Aroldo*, *I Due Foscari*, *La Sonnambula*, *Anna Bolena*, and *Ernani*, all with good Italian artists.

When I am laid in earth. Dido's (sop.) lament at the end of Purcell's *Dido and Aeneas*.

Whitehill, Clarence (b. Marengo, Iowa, 5 Nov. 1871; d. New York, 19 Dec. 1932). American baritone. Studied Chicago, and Paris with Giraudet and Sbriglia. Début Brussels, La M., 1899, Frère Laurent. Paris, O.C., 1900 (first American male singer to appear there); returned to U.S.A. 1900, and sang with Savage Co.; then, after a further period of study at Frankfurt with Stockhausen and with Cosima Wagner at Bayreuth, sang Wolfram at Bayreuth 1904, and Amfortas and Gunther 1908–9. Cologne 1903–8; N.Y., Met., 1909–10 and 1914–32; Chicago 1911–15; London, C.G., 1905–10 (Wotan in the famous English *Ring*); B.N.O.C. 1922. One of the best interpreters of Sachs, Wotan, and Amfortas. He was the first Met. Father in *Louise*, and a famous Golaud. (R)

Widdop, Walter (b. Norland, nr. Halifax, 19 Apr. 1892; d. London, 6 Sept. 1949). English tenor. Début B.N.O.C. 1923, Radamès; London, C.G., 1923, 1928–33, 1935, 1937–8. Also sang in Barcelona, Amsterdam, and Germany. A fine Siegmund and Tristan (he sang the latter opposite Flagstad). He sang Lohengrin's Farewell at the R.A.H., London, the night before he died. (R)

Wiesbaden. Town in Hesse, Germany. The present opera house (cap. 1,325) was opened in 1894. It was the scene of the première of Křenek's triple bill, *Schwergewicht*, *Der Diktator*, and *Das geheime Königreich*, in 1928. From 1952 to 1962, under the Intendantship of Friedrich Schramm and with Wolfgang Sawallisch and Heinz Walberg as music directors, it established itself as one of the leading German houses. The annual Wiesbaden Festival takes place from May to June.

Wildschütz, Der (The Poacher). Opera in 3 acts by Lortzing; text by composer, after Kotzebue's comedy *Der Rehbock*. Prod. Leipzig 31 Dec. 1842; Brooklyn, Mar. 1856; London, D.L., 3 July 1895.

William Tell. See *Guillaume Tell*.

Willow Song. See *Salce, salce*.

Wilno (Vilna). See *Poland*.

Wilson, (Sir) Steuart (b. Clifton, 21 July 1889; d. Petersfield, 18 Dec. 1966). English tenor and administrator. Studied with Jean de Reszke and George Henschel. Sang Tamino in *The Magic Flute*, Cambridge, in 1910. Sang in occasional performances with B.N.O.C., Old Vic, at Glastonbury, and at Clifton and Bristol in the opera festivals organized by Napier Miles. Deputy general administrator, C.G., 1949–55. (R)

Wilt (orig. Liebenthaler), **Marie** (b. Vienna, 30 Jan. 1833; d. Vienna, 24 Sept. 1891). Austrian soprano. Début Graz 1865, Donna Anna. Vienna 1867–77; London, C.G., as Norma (under the name Maria Vilda), 1866–7, 1874–5; Leipzig 1878, as Brünnhilde. Sang Donna Elvira in Vienna on the opening night of the Vienna Opera 1869; was the first Aida there 1874; created Sulamith in *Die Königin von Saba* (1875); and sang Donna Anna there in the centenary performances of *Don Giovanni* 1884. Hanslick said 'she delighted the ear, but had not a vestige of dramatic talent or education'.

Windgassen, Wolfgang (b. Annemasse, 26 June 1914). German tenor. Studied with his father, Fritz Windgassen, leading tenor Stuttgart Opera, 1923–44. His mother was a soprano, sister of Eva von der Osten. Studied further with Maria Ranzow and Alfons Fischer. Début Pforzheim 1941, Alvaro (*Forza*). Stuttgart since 1945; Bayreuth since 1951; Vienna since 1953; London, C.G., since 1954; N.Y., Met., 1956–7. Sang Parsifal at the first post-war Bayreuth and soon established himself as the leading European Heldentenor, singing Tristan, Siegfried, &c., all over Europe. A lightweight Wagnerian, he nevertheless sings with feeling and musicianship. (R)

Winkelmann, Hermann (b. Brunswick, 8 Mar. 1849; d. Vienna, 18 Jan. 1912). German tenor. Studied Hanover. Début Sonderhausen 1875. After engagements at Altenburg, Darmstadt, and Hamburg, where he created the title role in Rubenstein's *Nero*, sang Lohengrin and Tannhäuser in Vienna with such success that Richter recommended him to Wagner: created Parsifal, Bayreuth 1882, singing the role there until 1888. London, D.L., 1882, as Lohengrin and Tannhäuser, and was the first London Walther and Tristan. U.S.A. 1884, in Wagner Festival concerts. Vienna 1883–1906, first Vienna Tristan and Otello. His admirers formed themselves into the 'Hermann League', and performances were often disturbed by vociferous outbursts of applause. (R)

Witte, Erich (b. Bremen, 19 Mar. 1911). German tenor and producer. Début Bremen 1934. Wiesbaden 1937–8; N.Y., Met., 1938–9; Berlin, S.O., since 1945; London, C.G., 1954–9; Bayreuth 1943 and 1952–5. Originally a *Spieltenor*, later became a dramatic tenor singing Otello, Florestan, &c. His Loge has been much admired in Bayreuth and London, and his Peter Grimes in Germany. Prod. *Meistersinger* at C.G. and sang Walther. Apptd. Oberspielleiter Frankfurt a/M, 1961. (R)

Wittich, Marie (b. Giessen, 27 May 1868; d. Dresden, 4 Aug. 1931). German soprano. Studied Würzburg. After engagements in Basle, Düsseldorf, and Schwerin, engaged Dresden 1889–1914, where she created Salome in 1905. London, C.G., 1905–6; Bayreuth 1901–10, Sieglinde, Kundry, and Isolde.

Wittrisch, Marcel (b. Antwerp, 1 Oct. 1901; d. Stuttgart, 2 June 1955). German tenor. Début Halle 1925, Konrad (*Hans Heiling*). Brunswick 1927–9; Berlin 1929–43; Stuttgart 1950–5; London, C.G., 1931, as Tamino and Eisenstein; Bayreuth 1937, Lohengrin. Also famous in Lehár. (R)

Wolf, Hugo (b. Windischgraz, 13 Mar. 1860; d. Vienna, 22 Feb. 1903). Austrian composer. His only completed opera, *Der Corregidor* (1895), a setting of Alarcón's *The Three-Cornered Hat*, has great charm but little dramatic force, being in effect hardly more than a Wolf *Lieder* cycle in costume. Another opera, *Manuel Venegas*, was unfinished.

Wolf-Ferrari, Ermanno (b. Venice, 12 Jan. 1876; d. Venice, 21 Jan. 1948). Italian composer of German-Italian parentage. Original intention to be a painter changed by a visit to Bayreuth. Studied Munich with Rheinberger. His first opera, *La Cenerentola*, was prod. Venice 1901. His first success was with *Le Donne Curiose* (Munich 1903); this was followed in 1906 by *I Quatro Rusteghi*. Both these were based on Goldoni, as were also *Gli Amanti Sposi* (Venice 1925), *La Vedova Scaltra* (Rome 1931), and *Il Campiello* (Milan 1936). It was in these comic operas that Wolf-Ferrari excelled, with his elegant style, light touch, and skilful use of the orchestra. He wrote kindly for the voice in these and in the trifle *Il Segreto di Susanna* (Munich 1909), *L'Amore Medico*, after Molière (Dresden 1915), and *La Dama Boba*, set on a comedy by Lope de Vega (Milan 1939). He made one successful incursion into *verismo*, *I Gioielli della Madonna* (Berlin 1911); but his nearest attempt at music drama, *Sly* (Milan 1927), was less successful. Made an edition of *Idomeneo* (Munich 1931).

Wolff, Albert (b. Paris, 19 Jan. 1884; d. there, Feb. 1970). French cond. composer. Studied Paris Conservatoire. Chorus master, Paris, O.C., 1908, cond. from 1911. Cond. premières of Laparra's *La Jota*, *Angélique*, *Julien*, *Madame Bovary*, *Les Mamelles de Tirésias*. Music director, O.C., 1921–4, theatre director 1945–6. N.Y., Met., 1919–21, where his opera *L'Oiseau Bleu* was produced 1919; London, C.G., 1937, *Pelléas*. Also conducted French repertory for several seasons at Buenos Aires, Colón. (R)

Wolff, Fritz (b. Munich, 28 Oct. 1894; d. Munich, 18 Jan. 1957). German tenor. Début Bayreuth 1925, Loge. Bayreuth 1925–41; Berlin 1930–43; London, C.G., 1929–33, 1937–8; Cleveland 1934–5. A much admired Lohengrin, Loge, Parsifal, and Walther. From 1946 until his death he taught in Munich. (R)

Wolfram. A minstrel knight (bar.) and friend of Tannhäuser, in Wagner's opera.

Wood, Henry J. (Sir) (b. London, 3 Mar. 1869; d. Hitchin, Herts., 19 Aug. 1944). English conductor. Studied London, R.A.M., with Prout and Garcia. First conducted with the Arthur Rouseby Opera Co. 1889; helped Sullivan prepare *Ivanhoe* 1890; C.R. 1891: Burns-Crotty Co. 1892; London, Olympic T., Lago's 1892 season, when he conducted the English première of *Eugene Onegin*. Music adviser for the Mottl–Wagner concerts, 1894; conducted Stanford's *Shamus O'Brien* 1896, after which he devoted his life to concert work. (R)

Wotan. The ruler of the gods (bass-bar.) in Wagner's *Ring der Nibelungen*.

Wotan's Farewell. The title commonly given to the closing scene of Wagner's *Die Walküre* in which Wotan (bass-bar.) takes his leave of Brünnhilde as she lies encircled by fire on her rock.

Wozzeck. Opera in 3 acts by Berg; text by composer, after Büchner's play (1836). Prod. Berlin, S.O., 14 Dec. 1925, with Leo Schützendorf, Sigrid Johannsen, cond. Kleiber; Philadelphia 19 Mar. 1931, with Ivan Ivantzoff, Anne Roselle, cond. Stokowsky; London, C.G., 22 Jan. 1952, with Rothmüller, Goltz, cond. Kleiber.

The opera unfolds in a number of short scenes in set musical forms: each sentence of this synopsis relates to a scene.

Act 1. Wozzeck (bar.), an ordinary soldier, is lectured by the Captain (ten.) who despises him. Gathering sticks with his friend Andres (ten.), Wozzeck is alarmed by strange sounds and visions. Wozzeck's mistress Marie (sop.) flirts from her window with a passing Drum Major. Wozzeck is examined by a half-crazed doctor (bass) who is using him for experiments. The Drum Major (ten.) seduces Marie.

Act 2. Wozzeck becomes suspicious of Marie. The Captain taunts him with suggestions of her infidelity and Wozzeck accuses her. He finds her dancing with the Drum Major. The Drum Major boasts of his success, and when Wozzeck refuses to drink with him, beats him.

Act 3. The repentant Marie is reading the Bible. As they walk by a pond, the distraught Wozzeck stabs her. Later, drinking in a tavern, he is seen to have blood on his hands, and rushes away. Wading into the pond to find the knife, he drowns. Their child is playing with his hobby-horse, and does not understand when the other children tell him that his mother is dead.

Wranitzky, Paul (b. Nová Říše, 30 Dec. 1756; d. Vienna, 28 Sept. 1808). Austrian composer of Moravian origin. He was much admired by Haydn, and of his numerous works (including eight operas), the best known was *Oberon*, with a libretto by Giesecke from the Wieland poem later used for Weber's work. His brother **Anton** (b. 13 June 1761; d. 6 Aug. 1820) was also a composer, and had two daughters who became singers—**Anna Katharina** (married name Kraus) (1801–51) and **Karoline** (married name Seidler) (1794–1872), who was the first Agathe in *Der Freischütz*.

Wreckers, The. Opera in 3 acts by Ethel Smyth; text by 'H. B. Laforestier'

(Harry Brewster). Prod. Leipzig 11 Nov. 1906; London, H.M.'s, 22 June 1909, cond. Beecham (a concert perf. at Queen's Hall in 1908 was conducted by Nikisch). The scene is a Cornish community that lives by wrecking. When Pasco's wife Thirzen, in love with Mark, lights a bonfire, she is accused of warning ships off the coast and condemned to die with Mark.

Wüllner, Franz (b. Münster, 28 Jan. 1832; d. Braunfels, 7 Sept. 1902). German conductor and composer. His first wholly operatic appointment, at the Munich Court Theatre as Bülow's successor in 1869, brought him face to face with the difficulties surrounding the production of *Das Rheingold*. His successful handling of this and of *Die Walküre* led to his appointment as court Kapellmeister in chief in 1870. Dresden 1877; deprived of his post 1882. Prepared a new version of Weber's *Oberon*.

Wuppertal. Town in North Rhine-Westphalia, Germany. Opera is given in the new opera house (cap. 870) opened 1956 with *Mathis der Maler*. The company is one of the most progressive in Germany and maintains a high standard, its productions of Monteverdi operas being specially notable.

X

Xerxes. See *Serse*.

Y

Yaroslavna. Prince Igor's wife (sop.) in Borodin's opera.

Yeats, W. B. (b. Dublin, 13 June 1865; d. Menton, 28 Jan. 1939). Irish poet and dramatist. Operas on his works are as follows. *The Countess Kathleen* (1892): Egk (Irische Legende, 1954). *The Land of Heart's Desire* (1894): F. Hart (1914). *The Shadowy Waters* (1900): Kalomiris (1951); Swain (unfin.). *The Only Jealousy of Emer* (1919): Harrison (1949).

Yerevan. Capital of Armenia, U.S.S.R. The opera house (cap. 1,300) was begun in 1930 and finished in 1939; it was opened with *Almast*, by Spendaryan, after whom it is named. The company tours in the U.S.S.R. with a repertory of 39 works, including nine Armenian operas.

Young, Cecilia (b. London, prob. 1711; d. London, 6 Oct. 1789). English soprano. Made a mark as early as 1730 at D.L., and by 1735 was in Handel's company. Married Arne in 1737, and sang in his works in Dublin, but separated from him about 1755. Ill health dogged her, but Burney could find that, at her best, 'her voice, shape and singing were superior to those of any female singer in the country'. The Arnes' separation was caused by their quarrel over the apprenticeship of **Polly Young** (b. London, *c.* 1749; d. London, 20 Sept. 1799), who sang at King's and C.G., and in Italy with her husband Barthélemon in his works.

Yugoslavia. The development of opera in Yugoslavia has been influenced from three directions—the negative influence of the Turkish occupation in eastern Yugoslavia and the positive influence of Italy and Austria-Hungary in the west. The close proximity of Italy facilitated the introduction of opera in the 17th century and in 1629 the first Yugoslav opera, *Atalanta*, by Palmotić, was performed in Dubrovnik. Italian opera companies also visited Slovenia from the middle of the 17th century. There was, however, a strong German influence dating from the religious spectacles of the Jesuits, and by the end of the 18th century Italian influence in the interior of Yugoslavia had been completely replaced by the influence of Austria-Hungary. Palace and garrison theatres sprang up in Slovenia, Croatia, and in the Vojvodina as far east as Zemun, on the frontier a few miles from Belgrade. In the 19th century German theatres appeared in the larger towns, but Slav theatres had constant trouble with the authorities. A Slovene opera (*Belin*, by Župan) was composed in 1780, but it was not until the second half of the 19th century that a school of Yugoslav opera could be discerned. The first popular Croatian opera was *Ljubav i Zloba* (Love and Malice), by Lisinski (1846), followed by many successes by the same composer and by Ivan Zajc, whose *Nikola Šubić Zrinski* (1876) is still often performed. When Serbia became independent, the Prince organized theatrical performances in Belgrade under Šlezinger (1829). In 1864 a Serbian National Theatre was formed in Novi Sad and in 1882 the Belgrade National Theatre was founded. The Austrian occupation of

Bosnia brought opera to Sarajevo and Banja Luka, but regular performances did not take place until 1921. A Macedonian Opera was founded in Skoplje in 1947, but so far no company has been formed in the Republic of Montenegro.

After the romantic period of Lisinski (1819–54), Zajc (1832–1914), and Bersa (1873–1934), Serbo-Croatian composition followed traditional folk music, ranging from skilful adaptations by Lhotka (b. 1883) and Devčić (b. 1914) to uninspired arrangements of national songs. Opera composers of the folklore school include Gotovać (b. 1895), Baranović (b. 1894), Hristić (1885–1958), Nastašijević (b. 1902), Konjović (b. 1883), Dobronić (1878–1955), Binički (1872–1942), Brkanović (b. 1906), and in some works Papandopulo (b. 1906). Slovene composers have looked more towards Vienna; and Švara (b. 1902), Bravničar (b. 1897), and Kogoj (1895–1956) followed modern trends. The younger Serbo-Croatian composers, such as Bjelinski (b. 1909), Rajičić (b. 1910), Lhotka-Kalinski (b. 1913), Šulek (b. 1914), and Savin (b. 1915), have also broken away from the traditional idiom. See *Belgrade, Dubrovnik, Ljubljana, Novi Sad, Osijek, Rijeka, Sarajevo, Split, Subotica, Varaždin, Zagreb.*

Z

Zaccaria. The High Priest of Israel (bass) in Verdi's *Nabucco.*

Zagreb (Agram). Town in Croatia, Yugoslavia. The first centre of operatic life was at the palace of Count Amadea, who introduced a German company in 1797. For 37 years opera was performed there. In 1834 the first public theatre was built and was in use until 1895. It is interesting to note that a theatre journal was already in circulation in 1815. From 1841 regular visits of German companies were organized by the German Opera and Dramatic Society, but performances in Croatian began about the same time, and in 1846 Lisinski's *Ljubav i Zloba* (Love and Malice) was given its first performance (by amateurs). In 1861 official blessing was given to a policy of fostering Croatian opera, and the period of German domination thus ended. When Zajc, one of the first composers to write in the Croat language, returned from Vienna in 1870 he reorganized the Zagreb Opera and Operetta Theatres, the latter having been founded in 1863. At the end of the 19th century the Croatian theatre encountered difficulties from the Magyar Government, which closed the theatre in 1889. Performances continued in the open air in summer and in 1895 the present theatre, by Hellmer and Fellner, was opened, with the first Croatian national opera, Zajc's *Nikola Šubić Zrinski*, only to close again in 1902. It reopened in 1909 and has maintained regular performances except during the two wars. The company has toured abroad and made several recordings, but has been weakened by the loss to foreign companies of singers and conductors such as Sena Jurinac, Zinka Milanov, Vladimir Ruždjak, Nada Puttar, Josip Gostić, Rudolf Francl, Marijana Radev, Tomislav Neralić, Dragica Martinis, Berislav Klobučar, and Mladen Bašić. Opera is given at the National Theatre, operetta at the Comedy Theatre.

Zaïde. Opera in 2 acts left unfinished by Mozart; text by Schachtner. Prod. Frankfurt 27 Jan. 1866, when the dialogue was rewritten and completed by Gollmick and an overture and finale added by Anton André. London, Toynbee Hall, 10 Jan. 1953; Tanglewood, U.S.A., 8 Aug. 1955. The plot is similar to that of *Die Entführung.*

Zampa. Opera in 3 acts by Hérold; text by Mélesville. Prod. Paris, O.C., 3 May 1831; London, Hm., 19 Apr. 1833; Boston, 26 Jul. 1833.

Zandonai, Riccardo (b. Sacco, 28 May 1883; d. Pesaro, 5 June 1944). Italian composer. Basically an operatic composer, he was early spotted by Ricordi as a successor to Puccini in the Italian *verismo* school. *Il Grillo del Focolare* (1908) was well received, but his wider fame dated from *Conchita* (1911) and still more from *Francesca da Rimini* (1914). Of the six works that followed, the most popular have been *Giulietta e Romeo* (1922) and especially *I Cavalieri di Ekebù* (1925).

Zandt, Marie van (b. New York, 8 Oct. 1861; d. Cannes, 31 Dec. 1919). American soprano. Studied with her mother, the soprano Jennie van Zandt, and in Milan with Lamperti. Début Turin 1879, Zerlina; Paris, O.C., 1880–5, where she created Lakmé, which was specially written for her by Delibes. N.Y., Met., 1891–2 and 1896; London, H.M.'s, 1880; Gaiety T. 1885 (Lakmé); C.G. 1889. Her success as Lakmé caused jealousy among her French colleagues at the O.C., who accused her (falsely) of appearing on the stage drunk.

Zanelli (orig. Morales), **Renato** (b. Valparaiso, Chile, 1 Apr. 1892; d. Santiago, 25 Mar. 1935). Chilean tenor, orig. baritone. Studied Chile. Début Santiago 1916, Valentine. N.Y., Met., 1919–23 in Italian repertory as baritone. Went to Italy and after further study made tenor début Naples

1924, Raoul; London, C.G., 1928, 1930 as Otello. Established himself as leading Wagner tenor in Italy singing, Tristan and Siegmund with great success. Created Pizzetti's Lo Straniero, Rome 1933. Career cut short by ill health in 1933. One of the great Otellos of the century. (R)

Zanten, Cornelia van (b. Dordrecht, 2 Aug. 1855; d. The Hague, 10 Jan. 1946). Dutch soprano. Studied Cologne, and Milan with Lamperti, who developed her contralto voice into a coloratura soprano. Début Turin, *La Favorite*. U.S.A. 1886–7, with Theodore Thomas's National Opera Co. Sang in *The Ring* in Russia and then joined Nederlandsche Oper. Taught in Amsterdam and Berlin, her pupils including Julia Culp and Urlus.

Zar und Zimmermann (Tsar and Carpenter). Opera in 3 acts by Lortzing; text by composer, after the play by Mélesville, Merle, and De Boirie (1818). Prod. Leipzig 22 Dec. 1837; N.Y. 9 Dec. 1851; London, Gaiety T., 15 Apr. 1871. Peter I disguises himself as a carpenter, Peter Mikhailov; an envoy negotiating a treaty mistakes another carpenter, Peter Ivanov, for the Tsar, but in the end all is straightened out.

Zareska, Eugenia (b. Rava Ruska, 9 Nov. 1922). Ukrainian, later British, mezzo-soprano. Studied Lwów Conservatory and Milan. Début Milan, Sc., 1941, Dorabella. London, Cambridge T., 1947, Rosina; C.G. 1948–9, 1952–3, 1957–8; Glyndebourne 1948. Has appeared at Aix and Florence Festivals, and in 1949 sang the Gräfin Geschwitz in Berg's *Lulu* at the Venice Festival. (R)

Zarzuela. A type of Spanish *opera buffa*, generally in 1 act, concerned with and sometimes satirizing almost anything from fashion, politics, or literature to bull-fighting itself. For the scene to be foreign is rare, though a satire on English life is not unknown. The music is always colourful and straightforward, the dialogue lively and often improvised, with repartee running between stage and audience. The most familiar zarzuela composers are Bretón, Caballero, Chapí, Chueca, Guerrero, Guridi, Luna, Moreno Torroba, Serrano, Usanizaga, and Vives. There are a few surviving examples from as early as the 17th century.

Zauberflöte, Die (The Magic Flute). Opera in 2 acts by Mozart; text by Schikaneder, after the story *Lulu* in Wieland's collection of Oriental fairy-tales *Dschinnistan* (1786). Prod. Vienna, W., 30 Sept. 1791, with Josefa Weber, Nanina Gottlieb, Schack, Shickaneder; London, Hm., 6 June 1811; N.Y., P., 17 Apr. 1833.

Act 1. (1) Tamino (ten.) is saved from a serpent by three attendants of the Queen of the Night, but having fainted believes his rescuer to be the bird-catcher Papageno (bar.). For not admitting the truth, Papageno is punished by the attendants, who produce a picture of Pamina with which Tamino falls in love. Her mother, the Queen of the Night (sop.), appears to tell Tamino of Pamina's capture by Sarastro. For their rescue mission, Tamino is provided with a magic flute, Papageno with magic bells. (2) Pamina (sop.) is guarded in Sarastro's palace by the evil Moor, Monostatos (ten.), who flees, mistaking Papageno for the Devil. (3) Tamino learns that Sarastro is a wise priest, and that it is the Queen who is evil. Papageno and Pamina are caught trying to escape by Monostatos and his slaves, but the magic bells set the capturers dancing helplessly. Tamino and Pamina meet and fall in love; they are made ready for initiation ordeals.

Act 2. (1) Sarastro (bass) obtains the consent of the priests for Tamino to undergo initiation to their brotherhood. (2) In the vaults, Tamino and Papageno are under a vow of silence which the latter finds intolerable. Tamino refuses to flee when urged by the Queen's attendants. (3) Monostatos tries to kiss Pamina, who is told by the Queen to kill Sarastro; she asks mercy for her mother and is told by Sarastro that in a holy place there is no hatred. (4) Papageno is provided with a feast, and Tamino resists the temptation to speak to a hurt and bewildered Pamina, who thereupon longs for death. (5) Sarastro reassures the lovers. Papageno wishes for a wife, and an old woman (sop.) who had previously brought him water presents herself. As Papageno reluctantly accepts, she turns into a beautiful girl, but disappears immediately. (6) Pamina's suicide is forestalled by three boys. (7) The lovers pass together through fire and water, protected by the flute. (8) The dejected Papageno tries to hang himself but on the boys' advice he uses the magic bells to bring his girl Papagena back. (9) The Queen, her attendants, and Monostatos make a last attempt to destroy Sarastro and rescue Pamina, but flee before the noise of thunder. (10) Tamino and Pamina are united, and all join in praise of Isis and Osiris.

There is an opera *Mozarts Zauberflöte* by Riotte (1820).

Zauberoper (Ger. = magic opera). A form of opera popular in Vienna in the late 18th and early 19th centuries in which a fairy story was told with sumptuous scenic effects, ribald comedy, and music by a distinguished composer. It is this last qualification that separates it from its marginal survival, the English Christmas pantomime. Among the earliest and last examples were settings of the Oberon story by Wranitzky (1789) and Weber (1826). The greatest example—though it entirely transcends the form—is Mozart's *Magic Flute*.

Zazà. Opera in 4 acts by Leoncavallo; text by composer, after the play by Simon and Berton. Prod. Milan, T.L., 10 Nov. 1900, with Storchio, Garbin, Sammarco, cond. Toscanini; San Francisco 27 Nov. 1903; London, Coronet T., 30 Apr. 1909. Apart from *Pagliacci*, Leoncavallo's most successful opera; often revived in Italy when a fine singing actress (like Favero) can be found to undertake the title role. The opera tells of the Parisian music-hall singer Zazà's affair with Milio Dufresne, a married man about town, and her return to her lover Cascart.

Zeani, Virginia (b. Bucharest, 1928). Rumanian soprano. Studied Bucharest, and Milan with Lydia Lipkowska. Début Bologna 1948, Marguerite; London, Stoll, 1953, Violetta; 1957, Lucia. Milan, Sc., since 1956. Has been successful in Bellini and Donizetti roles. Married to bass Rossi-Lemeni. (R)

Zdenka. Arabella's sister (sop.) in Strauss's *Arabella.*

Zeffirelli (orig. Corsi), **Franco** (b. Florence, 12 Feb. 1923). Italian producer and designer. After working for the straight stage and films, Zeffirelli turned to opera in 1948. He produced and designed several works for Sc., Milan, notably *Il Turco in Italia*, *Cenerentola*, and *Don Pasquale*. He gave new life to Italian romantic opera with his production of *Lucia di Lammermoor* at C.G. in 1959, and later that year turned his attention to *verismo* with his *Cavalleria Rusticana* and *Pagliacci*. His production of Verdi's *Falstaff* was thought by some to be too fussy and un-Shakespearian. He has also produced opera in the U.S.A., notably at Dallas, San Francisco, and Chicago.

Zeffiretti lusinghieri. Ilia's (sop.) aria in Act 3, scene 1, of Mozart's *Idomeneo.*

Zeller, Karl (b. St. Peter-in-der-Au, 19 July 1842; d. Baden, nr. Vienna, 17 Aug. 1898). Austrian composer. Of his many successful operettas, the best known is *Der Vogelhändler* (prod. 1891).

Zémire et Azor. *Comédie-ballet* in 4 acts by Grétry; text by Marmontel, after La Chaussée's comedy *Amour par Amour* (1742). Prod. Fontainebleau (court) 9 Nov. 1771; London, D.L., 5 Dec. 1776; N.Y. 1 June 1787. Revived by Beecham, Bath Festival, 1955. This version of the *Beauty and the Beast* fairy-tale was also set by Baumgarten (1776), Tozzi (1792), Spohr (1819), and Garcia (1827); sequel by Umlauf, *Der Ring der Liebe* (1786).

Zemlinsky, Alexander von (b. Vienna, 4 Oct. 1872; d. Larchmont, N.Y., 16 Mar. 1942). Austrian, later American, conductor and composer.

Studied Vienna. Conductor Vienna, V.O., 1906, Court O. 1908; Mannheim 1909–11; Prague, Deutsche Oper, 1911–27; Berlin 1927–32; Vienna 1933–8. His six operas were all produced with moderate success in Germany and Austria. He was the teacher of Schoenberg, who married his sister. Other pupils were Bodanzky and Korngold.

Zenatello, Giovanni (b. Verona, 22 Feb. 1876; d. New York, 11 Feb. 1949). Italian tenor, formerly baritone. Studied Verona. Début Naples 1898. Tenor début Naples, T. Mercadante, 1899, Canio, having sung Silvio at previous performance. Milan, Sc., 1903–7, creating Pinkerton and the leading tenor roles in *Siberia*, *Figlia di Jorio*, *Gloria*, and *Germania*. London, C.G., 1905–6, 1908–9, 1926, where he was the first London Loris (*Fedora*), the first C.G. Chénier, and a much-admired Otello, a role he sang more than 300 times; N.Y., Manhattan O., 1907; Boston 1909–14; Chicago 1912–13. Instrumental in launching the Verona Arena project (q.v.). Married mezzo-soprano Maria Gay (1913). Retired 1930 and devoted the rest of his life to teaching. Pupils include Lily Pons and Nino Martini. (R)

Zeno, Apostolo (b. Venice, 11 Dec. 1668; d. Venice, 11 Nov. 1750). Italian librettist. Establishing the tradition later accepted by Metastasio, he wrote librettos that were used by a large number of composers, including Araia, Ariosti, Bononcini, Cherubini, Ciampi, Duni, Fux, Galuppi, Guglielmi, Handel, Hasse, Pergolesi, Porpora, Sacchini, Scarlatti, Traetta, Vivaldi, and Zingarelli.

Zerbinetta. The leader of the Harlequinade (sop.) in Strauss's *Ariadne auf Naxos*.

Zerlina. The peasant girl (sop.) betrothed to Masetto in Mozart's *Don Giovanni*.

Zigeunerbaron, Der (The Gipsy Baron). Operetta in 3 acts by Johann Strauss; text by Schnitzer, altered from a libretto by Jókai on his story *Saffi*. Prod. Vienna, W., 24 Oct. 1885; N.Y. 15 Feb. 1886; London (amateur performance), Rudolf Steiner T., 12 Feb. 1935. Like *Fledermaus*, in the repertory of many German opera companies, and often sung by casts of the best singers available. The complicated plot tells of Sandor Barinkay who comes to claim his ancestral lands only to find them overrun by gipsies. He falls in love with one of them, Saffi, who turns out to be a princess.

Zimmermann, Erich (b. Meissen, 29 Nov. 1892; d. Berlin, 24 Feb. 1968). German ten. Studied Dresden. Début there 1918. Munich 1925–31; Vienna 1931–4; Berlin, S.O., 1935–44; Bayreuth 1925–44. London, C.G., 1934, 1937–9, 1950. One of the outstanding Mimes and Davids of the inter-war years. (R)

Zingarelli, Niccolò Antonio (b. Naples, 4 Apr. 1752; d. Torre del Greco, 5 May 1837). Italian composer. His first opera was produced while he was still a student, and shortly afterwards his *Montesuma* (1781) is said to have been commended by Haydn. His greatest triumphs were in Milan, where he turned out popular works for the Scala at incredible speed. Returning to Milan after an unsuccessful venture in Paris, he concentrated on comic opera, which spread his fame to Germany, before a church appointment turned his attention to sacred music. In Rome from 1804, where he produced further operas, among them the popular *Berenice* (1811), his last opera. His resistance to Napoleon caused him to be arrested and taken to Paris, where the Emperor, an admirer of his music, released him and granted him a pension. Zingarelli's finest operas, chief among which is *Giulietta e Romeo* (1796), won wide praise in their day, though they are never revived now.

Zítek, Vilém (b. Prague, 9 Sept. 1890; d. Prague, 16 Aug. 1956). Czech bass. Studied Prague. Début Prague 1912. Established himself as leading Czech bass in the inter-war years. Sang widely in Italy, especially in Wagner. His most famous roles were Benes in *Dalibor*, Kecal, and Vokník in *Rusalka*. (R)

Zukunftmusik (Ger. = music of the future). The term coined by Wagner for his music, much used in the polemics that surrounded it.

Zumpe, Hermann (b. Taubenheim, 9 Apr. 1850; d. Munich, 4 Sept. 1903). German conductor and composer. Studied Leipzig. Helped Wagner to prepare first *Ring*, Bayreuth 1873–6. Appointments in Salzburg, Würzburg, Magdeburg, Frankfurt, Hamburg (1884–6), Stuttgart (1891–5), Schwerin (1897), and Munich (1900–3), where he conducted the first Wagner performances at the newly opened Prinzregententheater. London, C.G., 1898. He composed a number of operas and operettas.

Zürich. Town in Switzerland. Opera is given at the Stadttheater, first opened in 1833. The present theatre (cap. 1,200) dates from 1891. It was at Zürich that the first legitimate stage performance of *Parsifal* outside Bayreuth was given in 1913 (Swiss copyright having then expired, though this was hotly disputed by Cosima Wagner). Hans Zimmermann directed the theatre 1937–56, establishing the June Festival and staging the premières of *Lulu, Mathis der Maler*, and *Jeanne d'Arc au Bûcher*, During Zimmermann's régime Strauss and Wagner performances reached a very high standard with productions by Rudolf Hartmann, Karl Schmid-Bloss, and Oskar Wälterlin, under the musical direction of Ackermann, Knappertsbusch, Furtwängler, and with outstanding singers. The permanent Zürich company during this period included Lisa della Casa, Else Cavelti, Ira Malaniuk, Andreas Boehm, Franz Lechleitner, and Heinz Rehfuss. In 1955 Hans Rosbaud was appointed music director, and in 1956 Zimmermann was succeeded by Karl Heinz Krahl. Rosbaud resigned in 1958, and Herbert Graf succeeded Krahl in 1959, resigning in 1962.

PRINTED IN GREAT BRITAIN
AT THE UNIVERSITY PRESS, OXFORD
BY VIVIAN RIDLER
PRINTER TO THE UNIVERSITY